Let's Go®

the world's bestselling budget travel series

SPAIN & PORTUGAL

Including Morocco

completely updated & revised for

2002

D0092337

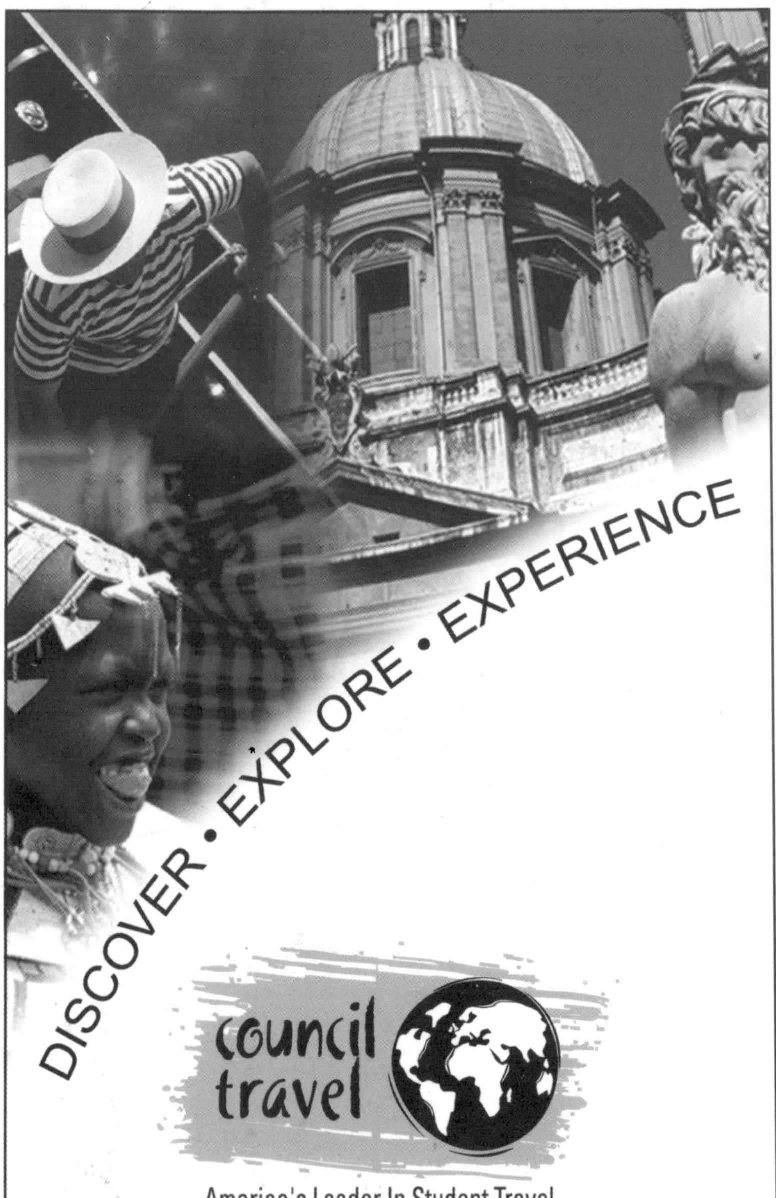
DISCOVER • EXPLORE • EXPERIENCE
council travel
America's Leader In Student Travel
CALL 1-800-2COUNCIL
CLICK www.counciltravel.com
VISIT one of our 75 retail locations

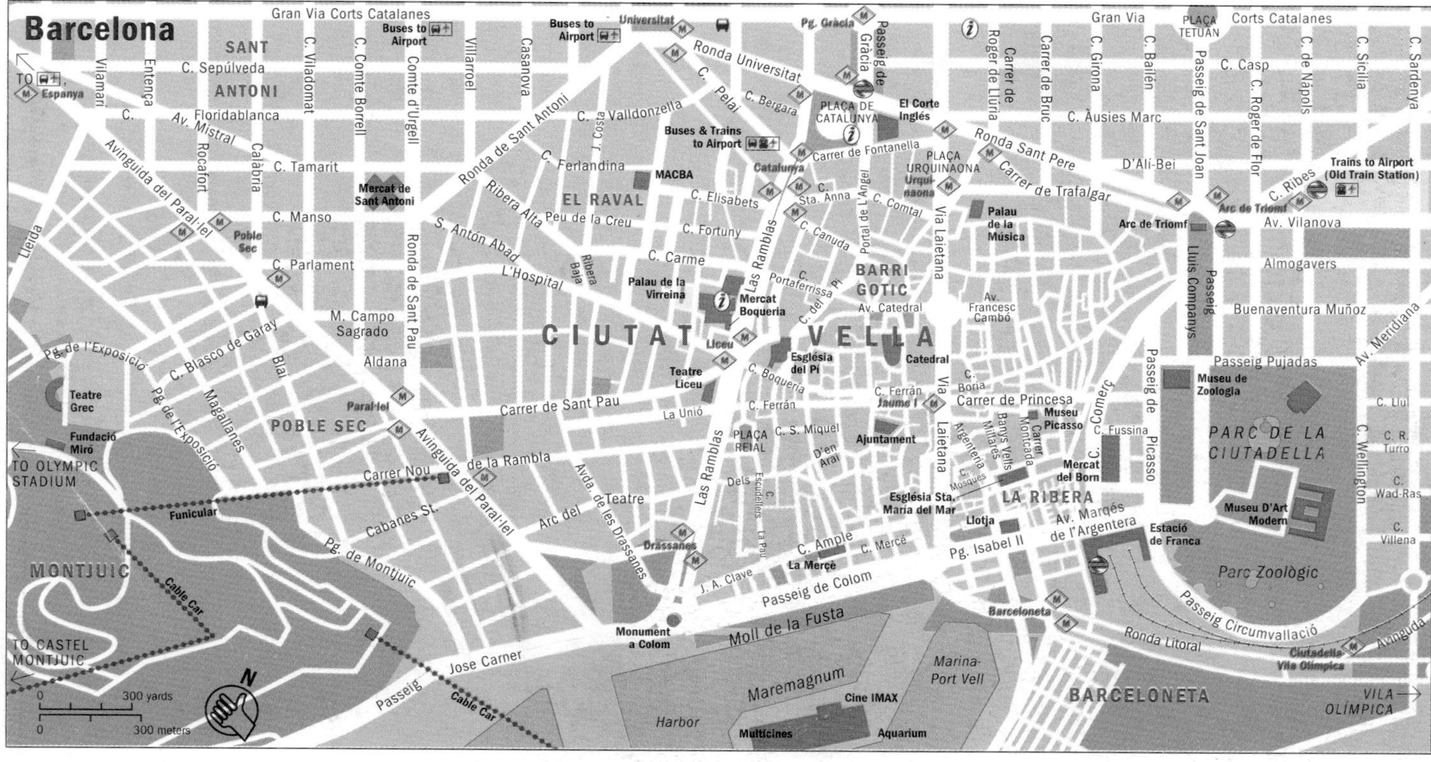

Barcelona
Gran Via Corts Catalanes
Buses to Airport
Universitat
Pg. Gràcia
Gran Via
PLAÇA TETUAN
Corts Catalanes
SANT ANTONI
C. Sepúlveda
TO Espanya
Vilamarí
Entença
C. Viladomat
C. Comte Borrell
Comte d'Urgell
Villarroel
Casanova
Ronda Universitat
C. Pelai
C. Bergara
Passeig de Gràcia
PLAÇA DE CATALUNYA
El Corte Inglés
Carrer de Roger de Llúria
Carrer de Bruc
C. Girona
C. Bailén
Passeig de Sant Joan
C. Casp
C. Roger de Flor
C. de Nápols
C. Sicilia
C. Sardenya
C. Floridablanca
Av. Mistral
C. Àusies Marc
Ronda de Sant Antoni
C. Valldonzella
J. Costa
Buses & Trains to Airport
Carrer de Fontanella
PLAÇA URQUINAONA
Urquinaona
Ronda Sant Pere
Carrer de Trafalgar
D'Alí-Bei
C. Ribes
Trains to Airport (Old Train Station)
Avinguida del Paral·lel
Rocafort
Calàbria
C. Tamarit
C. Ferlandina
MACBA
Catalunya
Mercat de Sant Antoni
EL RAVAL
C. Elisabets
C. Sta. Anna
C. Comtal
Arc de Triomf
Av. Vilanova
Ribera Alta
Peu de la Creu
C. Manso
Poble Sec
C. Fortuny
C. Canuda
Portal de L'Angel
Via Laietana
Palau de la Música
Lleida
S. Antón Abad
Ronda de Sant Pau
C. Carme
Las Ramblas
Passeig Lluis Companys
Almogavers
C. Parlament
L'Hospital
Ribera Baja
Palau de la Virreina
C. Portaferrissa
BARRI GOTIC
Av. Catedral
Av. Francesc Cambó
Buenaventura Muñoz
Mercat Boqueria
C. del Pi
M. Campo Sagrado
CIUTAT VELLA
Liceu
Av. Meridiana
Pg. de l'Exposició
C. Blasco de Garay
Blai
Aldana
Església del Pi
Catedral
Passeig Pujadas
Teatre Liceu
C. Boqueria
Museu de Zoologia
Teatre Grec
Magallanes
C. Ferrán
C. Boria
Carrer de Princesa
Jaume I
Paral·lel
Carrer de Sant Pau
La Unió
C. Ferrán
Museu Picasso
C. Llul
POBLE SEC
PLAÇA REIAL
C. S. Miquel
Ajuntament
Argenteria
Banys Vells
Millares
Carrer Montcada
C. Comerç
C. Fussina
Passeig de Picasso
PARC DE LA CIUTADELLA
C. R. Turro
Fundació Miró
D'en Arai
C. Wellington
TO OLYMPIC STADIUM
Carrer Nou
de la Rambla
Avda. de les Drassanes
Dels
C. Escudellers
C. Mosques
Mercat del Born
C. Wad-Ras
Funicular
Teatre
Arc del
Església Sta. Maria del Mar
LA RIBERA
Museu D'Art Modern
Cabanes St.
Llotja
Av. Marqués de l'Argentera
Estació de Franca
C. Villena
Drassanes
C. Ample
C. Mercè
La Pau
Pg. Isabel II
MONTJUIC
Pg. de Montjuïc
La Mercè
Parc Zoològic
J. A. Clave
Passeig de Colom
Cable Car
Barceloneta
Passeig Circumvallació
Monument a Colom
Moll de la Fusta
Ronda Litoral
Avinguda
TO CASTEL MONTJUIC
Jose Carner
Marina-Port Vell
Ciutadella-Vila Olímpica
N
0
300 yards
0
300 meters
Passeig
Cable Car
Maremagnum
Cine IMAX
BARCELONETA
VILA OLÍMPICA
Harbor
Multicines
Aquarium

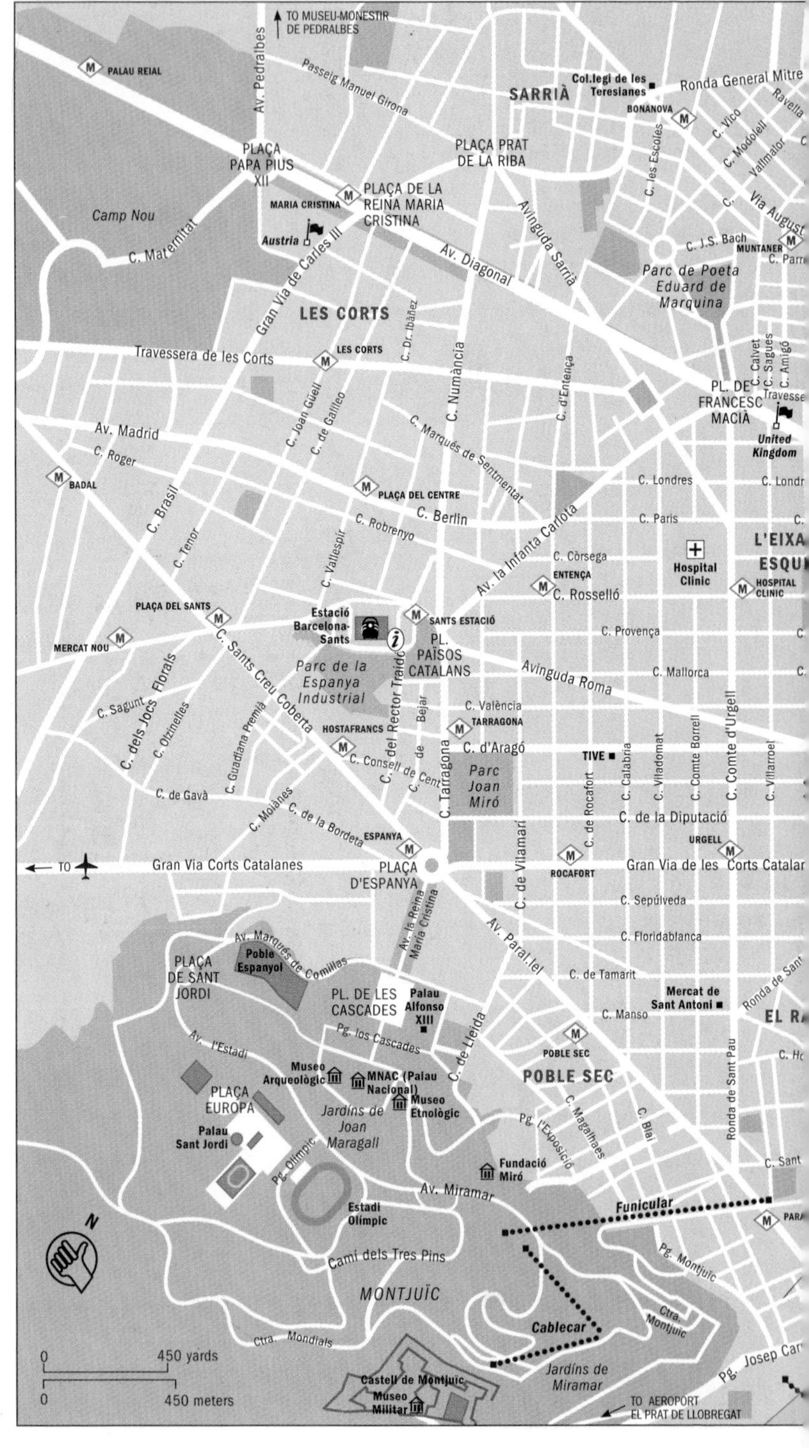
TO MUSEU-MONESTIR DE PEDRALBES
PALAU REIAL
Av. Pedralbes
Passeig Manuel Girona
SARRIÀ
Col.legi de les Teresianes
Ronda General Mitre
BONANOVA
PLAÇA PAPA PIUS XII
PLAÇA PRAT DE LA RIBA
PLAÇA DE LA REINA MARIA CRISTINA
MARIA CRISTINA
Camp Nou
C. Maremitat
Austria
Gran Via de Carles III
Av. Diagonal
Avinguda Sarrià
C. les Escoles
C. Vico
C. Modolell
Vallmajor
Via Augusta
C. J.S. Bach
MUNTANER
Parc de Poeta Eduard de Marquina
LES CORTS
C. Dr. Ibáñez
Travessera de les Corts
LES CORTS
C. Numància
C. d'Entença
C. Calvet
C. Sagues
C. Amigó
PL. DE FRANCESC MACIÀ
United Kingdom
Av. Madrid
C. Roger
BADAL
C. Joan Güell
C. de Galileo
C. Marquès de Sentmenat
PLAÇA DEL CENTRE
C. Berlin
C. Londres
C. Paris
C. Brasil
C. Tenor
C. Robrenyo
C. Vallespir
Av. la Infanta Carlota
C. Còrsega
ENTENÇA
C. Rosselló
Hospital Clínic
L'EIXA
HOSPITAL CLINIC
PLAÇA DEL SANTS
MERCAT NOU
Estació Barcelona-Sants
SANTS ESTACIÓ
PL. PAÏSOS CATALANS
C. Provença
C. Sants Creu Coberta
Parc de la Espanya Industrial
C. del Rector Triadó
Avinguda Roma
C. Mallorca
C. dels Jocs Florals
C. Sagunt
C. Olzinelles
C. Guadiana Premià
C. València
TARRAGONA
HOSTAFRANCS
C. Consell de Cent
C. Bejar
C. d'Aragó
TIVE
C. Tarragona
Parc Joan Miró
C. de Rocafort
C. Calabria
C. Viladomat
C. Comte Borrell
C. Comte d'Urgell
C. Villarroel
C. de Gavà
C. Moianès
C. de la Bordeta
ESPANYA
C. de la Diputació
URGELL
TO
Gran Via Corts Catalanes
PLAÇA D'ESPANYA
C. de Vilamarí
ROCAFORT
Gran Via de les Corts Catalanes
C. Sepúlveda
C. Floridablanca
Av. Marquès de Comillas
Av. la Reina Maria Cristina
Av. Paral.lel
PLAÇA DE SANT JORDI
Poble Espanyol
C. de Tamarit
PL. DE LES CASCADES
Palau Alfonso XIII
Mercat de Sant Antoni
C. Manso
Ronda de Sant Pau
EL RA
Av. l'Estadi
Pg. los Cascades
C. de Lleida
POBLE SEC
Museo Arqueològic
MNAC (Palau Nacional)
POBLE SEC
PLAÇA EUROPA
Museo Etnològic
Jardins de Joan Maragall
C. Magalhaes
C. Blai
Palau Sant Jordi
Pg. Olímpic
Pg. l'Exposició
Fundació Miró
Av. Miramar
Funicular
Estadi Olímpic
N
Camí dels Tres Pins
Pg. Montjuïc
MONTJUÏC
Cablecar
Ctra. Montjuïc
Ctra. Mondials
0 450 yards
0 450 meters
Castell de Montjuïc
Museo Militar
Jardins de Miramar
TO AEROPORT EL PRAT DE LLOBREGAT
Pg. Josep Car

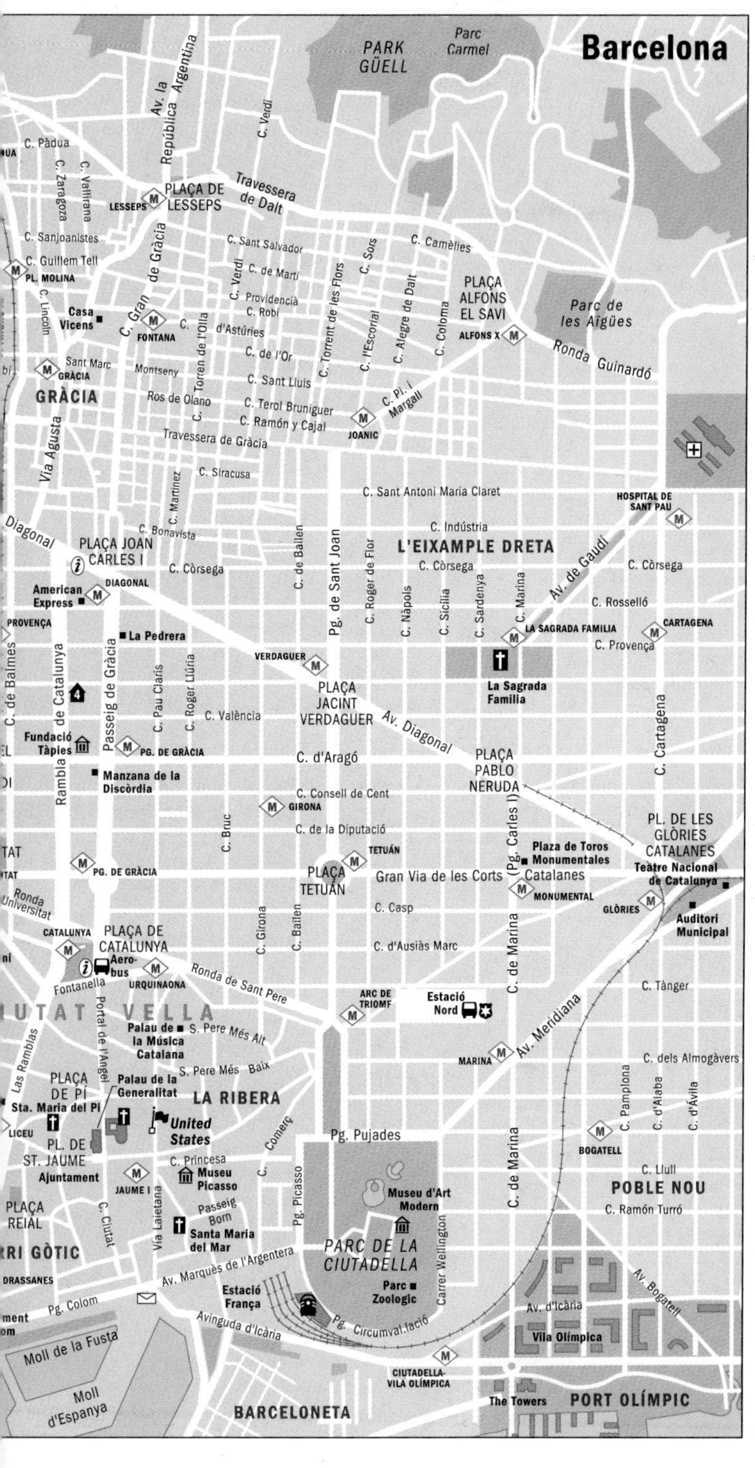
Barcelona
PARK GÜELL
Parc Carmel
PLAÇA DE LESSEPS
Travessera de Dalt
GRÀCIA
Casa Vicens
PLAÇA ALFONS EL SAVI
Parc de les Aïgües
Ronda Guinardó
Travessera de Gràcia
C. Sant Antoni Maria Claret
HOSPITAL DE SANT PAU
L'EIXAMPLE DRETA
PLAÇA JOAN CARLES I
American Express
La Pedrera
La Sagrada Familia
PLAÇA JACINT VERDAGUER
Av. Diagonal
Fundació Tàpies
Manzana de la Discòrdia
PLAÇA PABLO NERUDA
PL. DE LES GLÒRIES CATALANES
Plaza de Toros Monumentales
Teatre Nacional de Catalunya
Auditori Municipal
PLAÇA TETUAN
Gran Via de les Corts Catalanes
PLAÇA DE CATALUNYA
Aero-bus
Ronda de Sant Pere
Estació Nord
Av. Meridiana
Palau de la Música Catalana
PLAÇA DE PI
Palau de la Generalitat
LA RIBERA
Sta. Maria del Pi
United States
PL. DE ST. JAUME
Ajuntament
Museu Picasso
Museu d'Art Modern
PLAÇA REIAL
Santa Maria del Mar
PARC DE LA CIUTADELLA
Parc Zoologic
POBLE NOU
Estació França
Vila Olímpica
Moll de la Fusta
Moll d'Espanya
BARCELONETA
The Towers
PORT OLÍMPIC

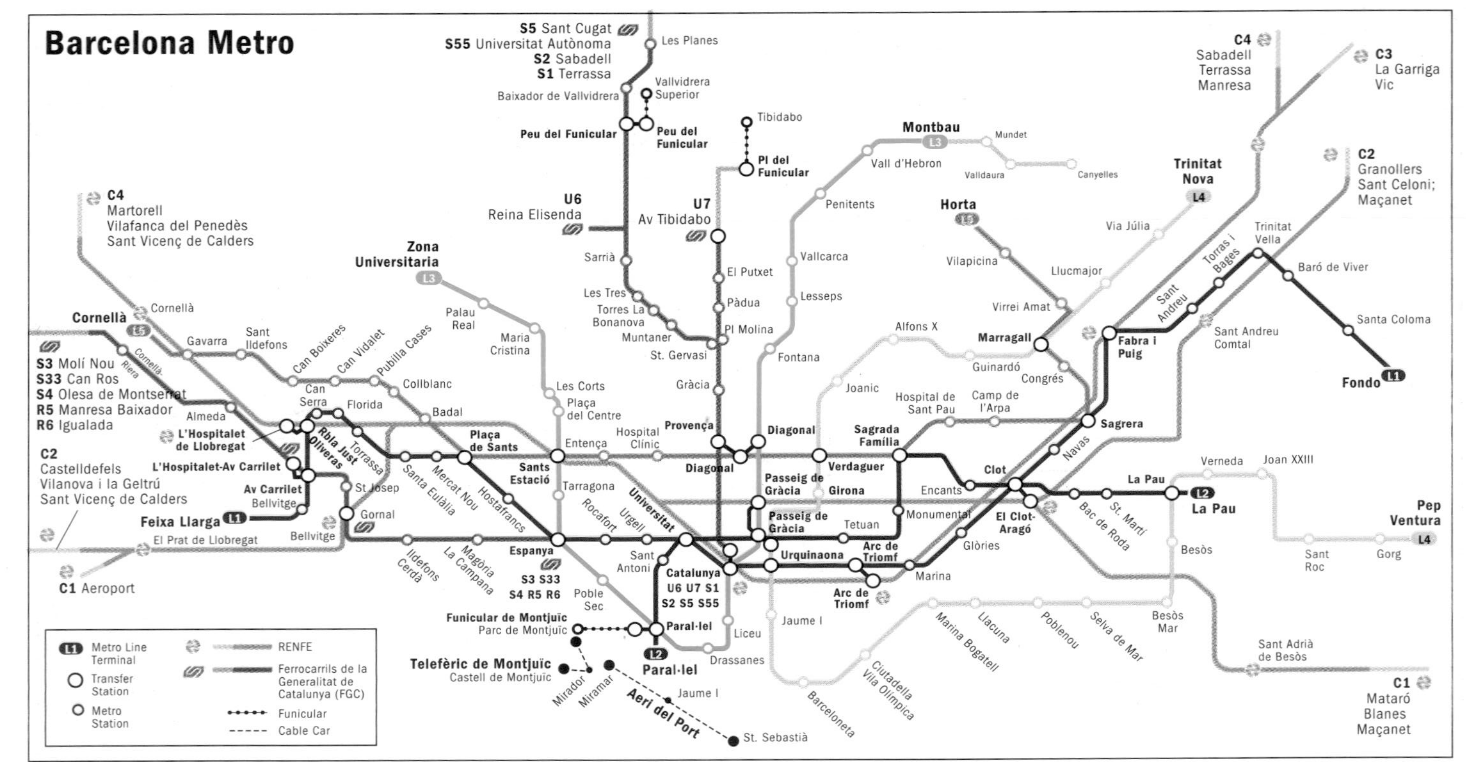
Barcelona Metro
S5 Sant Cugat
S55 Universitat Autònoma
S2 Sabadell
S1 Terrassa
Les Planes
Vallvidrera Superior
Baixador de Vallvidrera
Peu del Funicular
Peu del Funicular
Tibidabo
Pl del Funicular
Montbau
Mundet
Valldaura
Canyelles
Vall d'Hebron
Penitents
Vallcarca
Lesseps
Fontana
U6
Reina Elisenda
U7
Av Tibidabo
Sarrià
El Putxet
Pàdua
Pl Molina
Les Tres Torres
La Bonanova
Muntaner
St. Gervasi
Gràcia
Provença
Diagonal
Diagonal
Zona Universitaria
Palau Real
Maria Cristina
Les Corts
Plaça del Centre
Entença
Hospital Clínic
Horta
Vilapicina
Virrei Amat
Llucmajor
Via Júlia
Trinitat Nova
Marragall
Guinardó
Congrés
Alfons X
Joanic
Hospital de Sant Pau
Camp de l'Arpa
Sagrada Família
Verdaguer
Girona
Passeig de Gràcia
Passeig de Gràcia
Tetuan
Urquinaona
Arc de Triomf
Arc de Triomf
Monumental
Encants
Clot
El Clot-Aragó
Glòries
Marina
Sagrera
Navas
Fabra i Puig
Sant Andreu
Torras i Bages
Trinitat Vella
Baró de Viver
Santa Coloma
Fondo
Sant Andreu Comtal
C4
Sabadell
Terrassa
Manresa
C3
La Garriga
Vic
C2
Granollers
Sant Celoni;
Maçanet
La Pau
La Pau
Verneda
Joan XXIII
Sant Roc
Gorg
Pep Ventura
Besòs
Besòs Mar
St. Martí
Bac de Roda
Selva de Mar
Poblenou
Llacuna
Marina Bogatell
Ciutadella Vila Olímpica
Barceloneta
Jaume I
Liceu
Drassanes
Sant Adrià de Besòs
C1
Mataró
Blanes
Maçanet
C4
Martorell
Vilafanca del Penedès
Sant Vicenç de Calders
Cornellà
Cornellà
Cornellà-Riera
Gavarra
Sant Ildefons
Can Boixeres
Can Vidalet
Pubilla Cases
Collblanc
Badal
Can Serra
Florida
Almeda
S3 Molí Nou
S33 Can Ros
S4 Olesa de Montserrat
R5 Manresa Baixador
R6 Igualada
L'Hospitalet de Llobregat
Rbla Just Oliveras
Torrassa
Santa Eulàlia
Mercat Nou
Plaça de Sants
Hostafrancs
Sants Estació
Tarragona
Rocafort
Urgell
Universitat
Sant Antoni
Catalunya
U6 U7 S1
S2 S5 S55
Espanya
S3 S33
S4 R5 R6
Poble Sec
Paral·lel
Paral·lel
C2
Castelldefels
Vilanova i la Geltrú
Sant Vicenç de Calders
L'Hospitalet-Av Carrilet
Av Carrilet
Bellvitge
St Josep
Gornal
Feixa Llarga
Bellvitge
El Prat de Llobregat
Ildefons Cerdà
Magòria
La Campana
C1 Aeroport
Funicular de Montjuïc
Parc de Montjuïc
Telefèric de Montjuïc
Castell de Montjuïc
Mirador
Miramar
Aeri del Port
Jaume I
St. Sebastià
Metro Line Terminal
Transfer Station
Metro Station
RENFE
Ferrocarrils de la Generalitat de Catalunya (FGC)
Funicular
Cable Car

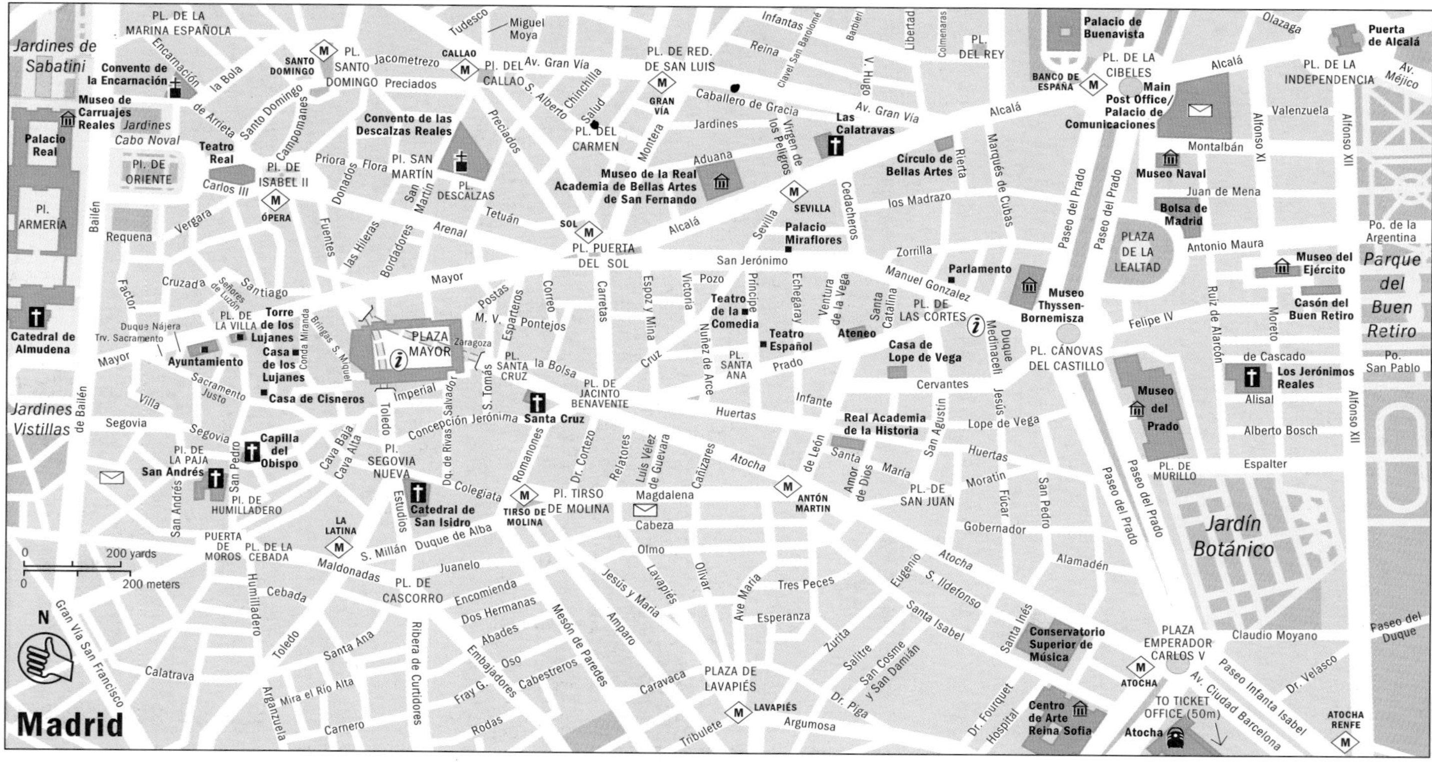
Madrid
N
0
200 yards
0
200 meters
Palacio Real
Pl. Armería
Catedral de Almudena
Jardines de Sabatini
Jardines Vistillas
Museo de Carruajes Reales
Jardines Cabo Noval
Pl. de Oriente
Convento de la Encarnación
Pl. de la Marina Española
Encarnación
la Bola
Santo Domingo
Teatro Real
Carlos III
Pl. de Isabel II
Ópera
Santo Domingo
Pl. Santo Domingo
Campomanes
de Arrieta
Vergara
Requena
Bailén
de Bailén
Factor
Mayor
Trv. Sacramento
Duque Nájera
Cruzada
Ayuntamiento
Pl. de la Villa
Señores de Luzón
Torre de los Lujanes
Casa de los Lujanes
Casa de Cisneros
Santiago
Conde Miranda
Bringas
S. Miguel
Sacramento
Justo
Villa
Segovia
Segovia
Pl. de la Paja
San Andrés
San Andrés
Capilla del Obispo
San Pedro
Pl. de Humilladero
Puerta de Moros
Pl. de la Cebada
Cebada
Humilladero
Gran Vía San Francisco
Calatrava
Toledo
Mira el Río Alta
Arganzuela
Carnero
Santa Ana
Maldonadas
La Latina
S. Millán
Cava Baja
Cava Alta
Pl. Segovia Nueva
Toledo
Plaza Mayor
Zaragoza
Imperial
Estudios
Catedral de San Isidro
Colegiata
Duque de Alba
Juanelo
Pl. de Cascorro
Ribera de Curtidores
Rodas
Fray G.
Embajadores
Oso
Cabestreros
Abades
Dos Hermanas
Encomienda
Mesón de Paredes
Dq. de Rivas
Salvador
Concepción Jerónima
S. Tomás
Pl. Santa Cruz
Santa Cruz
Esparteros
Postas
M. V.
Pontejos
la Bolsa
Tirso de Molina
Pl. Tirso de Molina
Romanones
Dr. Cortezo
Relatores
Luis Vélez de Guevara
Magdalena
Cabeza
Olmo
Lavapiés
Jesús y María
Amparo
Caravaca
Plaza de Lavapiés
Lavapiés
Tribulete
Argumosa
Mayor
Arenal
Bordadores
Las Hileras
Donados
Fuentes
Priora
Flora
San Martín
Pl. San Martín
Convento de las Descalzas Reales
Pl. Descalzas
Tetuán
Jacometrezo
Preciados
Preciados
Callao
Pl. del Callao
Tudesco
Miguel Moya
Av. Gran Vía
S. Alberto
Chinchilla
Salud
Pl. del Carmen
Sol
Pl. Puerta del Sol
Museo de la Real Academia de Bellas Artes de San Fernando
Montera
Gran Vía
Pl. de Red. de San Luis
Caballero de Gracia
Jardines
Aduana
Alcalá
Correo
Carretas
Espoz y Mina
Victoria
Pozo
Cruz
Pl. de Jacinto Benavente
Nuñez de Arce
Teatro de la Comedia
Príncipe
Pl. Santa Ana
Huertas
Cañizares
Atocha
Antón Martín
Olivar
Ave María
Esperanza
Tres Peces
Zurita
Salitre
San Cosme y San Damián
Dr. Piga
Santa Isabel
S. Ildefonso
Eugenio
Atocha
Santa Inés
Hospital
Dr. Fourquet
Centro de Arte Reina Sofía
Conservatorio Superior de Música
Atocha
To ticket office (50m)
Atocha
Plaza Emperador Carlos V
Av. Ciudad Barcelona
Paseo Infanta Isabel
Dr. Velasco
Atocha Renfe
Claudio Moyano
Paseo del Prado
Paseo del Prado
Pl. de Murillo
Jardín Botánico
Espalter
Alberto Bosch
Alisal
Alfonso XII
Paseo del Duque
Po. San Pablo
Parque del Buen Retiro
Po. de la Argentina
Los Jerónimos Reales
de Cascado
Moreto
Casón del Buen Retiro
Museo del Ejército
Ruiz de Alarcón
Felipe IV
Museo del Prado
Pl. Cánovas del Castillo
Museo Thyssen-Bornemisza
Plaza de la Lealtad
Antonio Maura
Bolsa de Madrid
Juan de Mena
Museo Naval
Montalbán
Alfonso XI
Alfonso XII
Valenzuela
Pl. de la Independencia
Puerta de Alcalá
Av. Méjico
Olazaga
Alcalá
Main Post Office/ Palacio de Comunicaciones
Pl. de la Cibeles
Palacio de Buenavista
Banco de España
Pl. del Rey
Colmenares
Libertad
Barbieri
V. Hugo
Infantas
Clavel San Bartolomé
Reina
Av. Gran Vía
Las Calatravas
Marqués de Cubas
Rierta
Círculo de Bellas Artes
los Madrazo
Zorrilla
Cedacheros
Sevilla
Sevilla
Palacio Miraflores
Virgen de los Peligros
Alcalá
San Jerónimo
Echegaray
Teatro Español
Prado
Ventura de la Vega
Ateneo
Santa Catalina
Manuel Gonzalez
Pl. de las Cortes
Parlamento
Duque Medinaceli
Casa de Lope de Vega
Cervantes
Jesús
Lope de Vega
Infante
Real Academia de la Historia
San Agustín
Huertas
Moratín
Pl. de San Juan
Fúcar
San Pedro
Gobernador
Alamadén
Santa María
Amor de Dios
de León

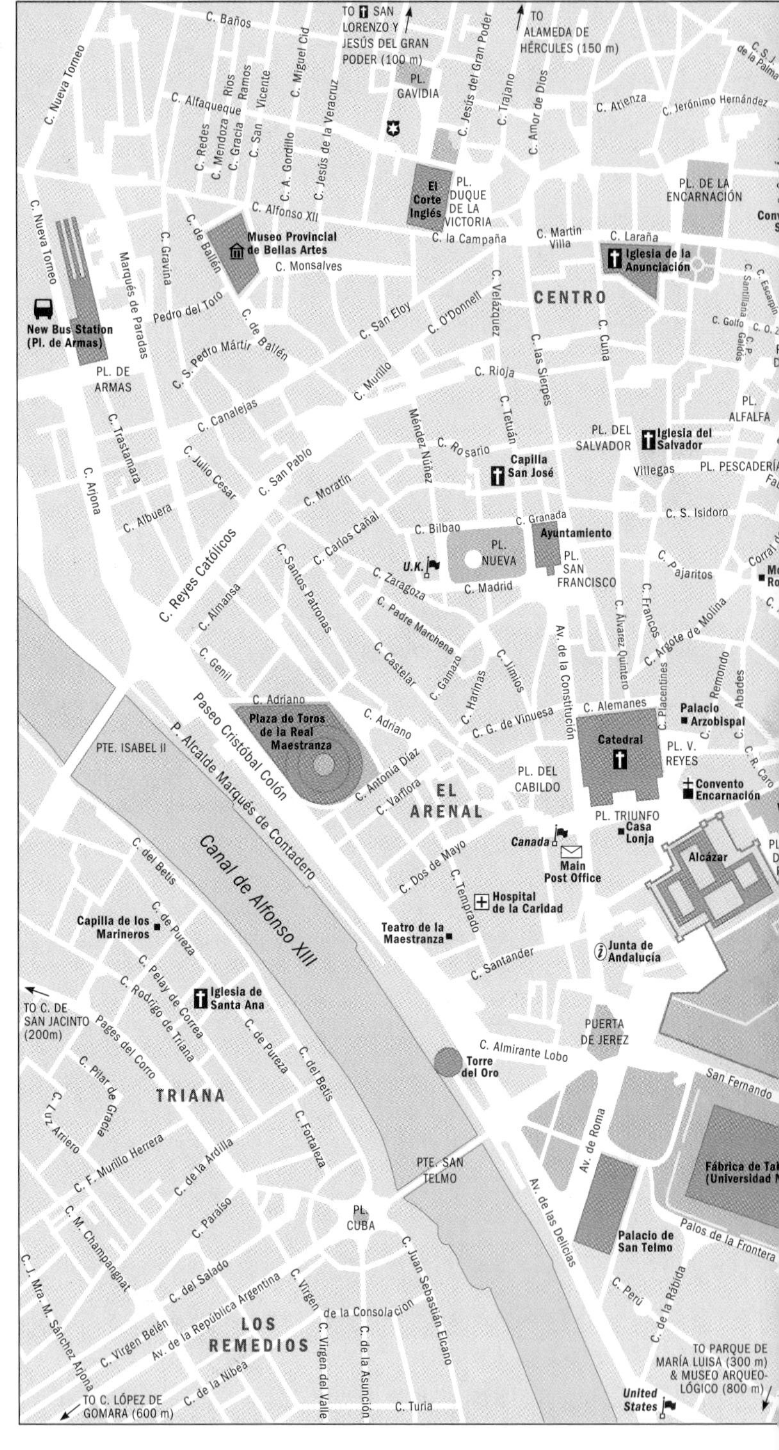

TO SAN LORENZO Y JESÚS DEL GRAN PODER (100 m)
TO ALAMEDA DE HÉRCULES (150 m)
C. Baños
C. Nueva Torneo
C. Alfaqueque
C. Redes
C. Mendoza Ríos
C. Gracia Ramos
C. San Vicente
C. Miguel Cid
C. A. Gordillo
C. Jesús de la Veracruz
PL. GAVIDIA
C. Jesús del Gran Poder
C. Trajano
C. Amor de Dios
C. Atienza
C. Jerónimo Hernández
C. S. J. de la Palma
PL. DE LA ENCARNACIÓN
El Corte Inglés
PL. DUQUE DE LA VICTORIA
C. Alfonso XII
C. de Ballén
Museo Provincial de Bellas Artes
C. Monsalves
C. la Campaña
C. Martín Villa
C. Laraña
Iglesia de la Anunciación
C. Gravina
Marqués de Paradas
New Bus Station (Pl. de Armas)
Pedro del Toro
C. de Ballén
C. S. Pedro Mártir
C. San Eloy
C. O'Donnell
C. Velázquez
CENTRO
C. Cuna
C. las Sierpes
C. Rioja
C. Murillo
C. Sanatillana
C. Golfo
C. P. Galdós
PL. DE ARMAS
C. Canalejas
C. Trastamara
C. Julio César
C. San Pablo
Méndez Núñez
C. Rosario
C. Tetuán
Capilla San José
PL. DEL SALVADOR
Iglesia del Salvador
Villegas
PL. ALFALFA
PL. PESCADERÍA
C. Arjona
C. Albuera
C. Moratín
C. Carlos Cañal
C. Bilbao
C. Granada
Ayuntamiento
PL. NUEVA
U.K.
PL. SAN FRANCISCO
C. S. Isidoro
C. Pajaritos
C. Reyes Católicos
C. Almansa
C. Santos Patronas
C. Zaragoza
C. Madrid
C. Padre Marchena
C. Álvarez Quintero
C. Francos
C. Argote de Molina
C. Genil
C. Castelar
C. Gamazo
C. Harinas
C. Jimios
Av. de la Constitución
C. Placentines
C. Remondo
C. Abades
C. Adriano
Plaza de Toros de la Real Maestranza
C. Adriano
C. G. de Vinuesa
C. Alemanes
Palacio Arzobispal
PTE. ISABEL II
P. Alcalde Marqués de Contadero
Paseo Cristóbal Colón
C. Antonia Díaz
C. Varflora
EL ARENAL
PL. DEL CABILDO
Catedral
PL. V. REYES
C. R. Caro
Convento Encarnación
PL. TRIUNFO
Casa Lonja
Canada
Main Post Office
Alcázar
Canal de Alfonso XIII
C. del Betis
C. Dos de Mayo
C. Temprado
Hospital de la Caridad
Capilla de los Marineros
C. de Pureza
Teatro de la Maestranza
Junta de Andalucía
C. Santander
C. Pelay de Correa
TO C. DE SAN JACINTO (200m)
Iglesia de Santa Ana
C. Rodrigo de Triana
Pages del Corro
C. de Pureza
C. del Betis
PUERTA DE JEREZ
C. Almirante Lobo
Torre del Oro
C. Pilar de Gracia
TRIANA
San Fernando
C. Luz Arriero
C. Fortaleza
C. F. Murillo Herrera
C. de la Ardilla
PTE. SAN TELMO
Av. de Roma
Fábrica de Tabacos (Universidad)
C. M. Champangnat
C. Paraíso
PL. CUBA
Av. de las Delicias
Palacio de San Telmo
Palos de la Frontera
C. J. Mra. M. Sánchez Arjona
C. del Salado
C. Virgen de la Consolación
C. Juan Sebastián Elcano
C. Perú
C. de la Rábida
C. Virgen Belén
Av. de la República Argentina
LOS REMEDIOS
C. Virgen del Valle
C. de la Asunción
TO PARQUE DE MARÍA LUISA (300 m) & MUSEO ARQUEOLÓGICO (800 m)
C. de la Nibea
TO C. LÓPEZ DE GOMARA (600 m)
C. Turia
United States

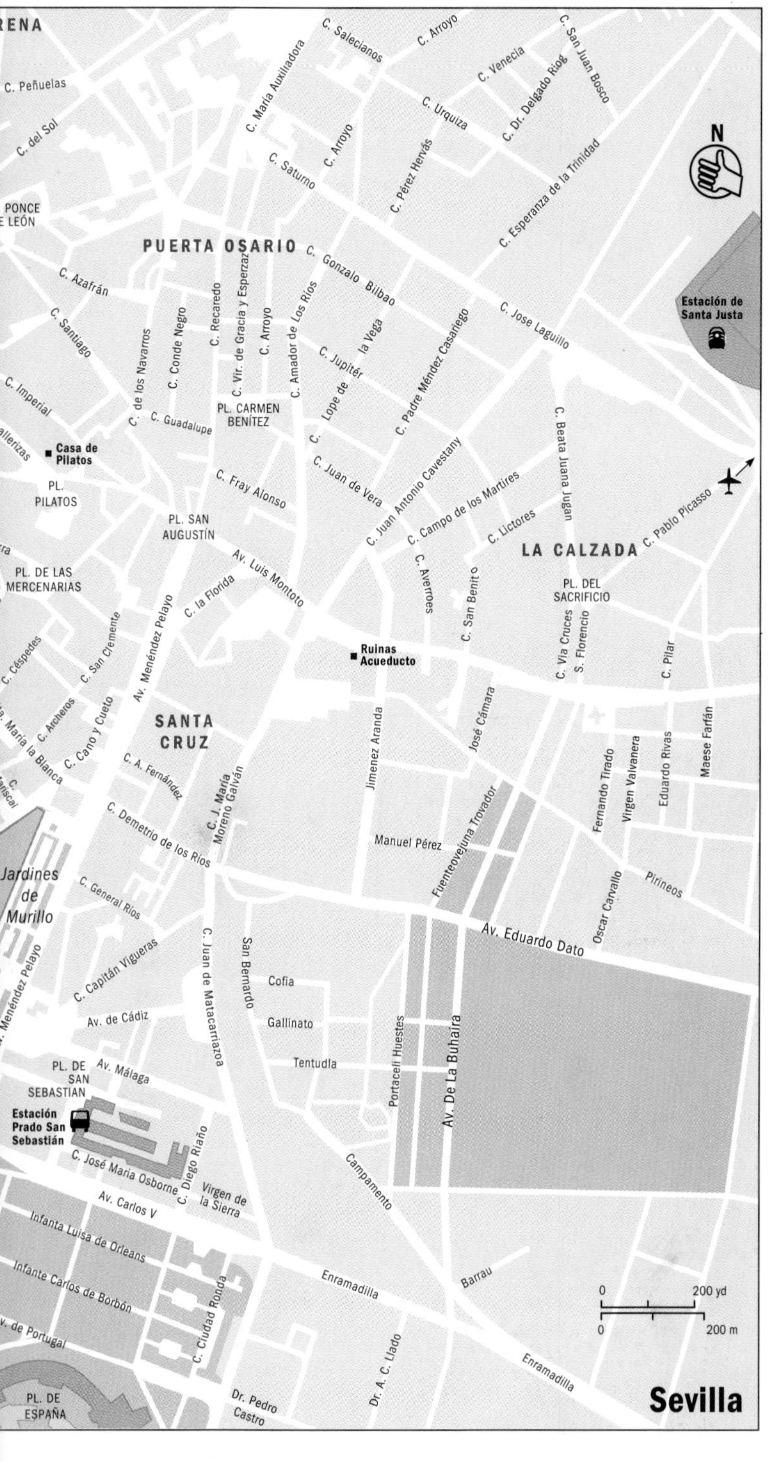

RENA
C. Peñuelas
C. del Sol
PONCE
LEÓN
PUERTA OSARIO
C. Azafrán
C. Santiago
C. Imperial
Casa de Pilatos
PL. PILATOS
PL. DE LAS MERCENARIAS
C. Céspedes
C. San Clemente
C. Archeros
C. Cano y Cueto
Sta. María la Blanca
Jardines de Murillo
Av. Menéndez Pelayo
C. de los Navarros
C. Conde Negro
C. Recaredo
C. Vir. de Gracia y Esperanza
C. Arroyo
C. Amador de Los Ríos
C. Guadalupe
PL. CARMEN BENÍTEZ
C. Fray Alonso
PL. SAN AUGUSTÍN
Av. Luis Montoto
C. la Florida
SANTA CRUZ
C. A. Fernández
C. J. María Moreno Galván
C. Demetrio de los Ríos
C. General Ríos
C. Capitán Vigueras
Av. de Cádiz
Av. Málaga
PL. DE SAN SEBASTIAN
Estación Prado San Sebastián
C. José María Osborne
C. Diego Riaño
Virgen de la Sierra
Av. Carlos V
Infanta Luisa de Orleans
Infante Carlos de Borbón
Av. de Portugal
PL. DE ESPAÑA
C. Ciudad Ronda
Dr. Pedro Castro
Dr. A. C. Llado
Enramadilla
Barrau
Campamento
C. Juan de Matacarriazo
San Bernardo
Cofia
Gallinato
Tentudla
Portaceli Huestes
Av. De La Buhaira
Av. Eduardo Dato
Manuel Pérez
Fuenteovejuna Trovador
Jimenez Aranda
José Cámara
Ruinas Acueducto
C. Averroes
C. San Benito
C. Juan Antonio Cavestany
C. Campo de los Martires
C. Lictores
C. Juan de Vera
C. Lope de la Vega
C. Jupitér
C. Padre Méndez Casariego
C. Gonzalo Bilbao
C. José Laguillo
C. Saturno
C. Arroyo
C. María Auxiliadora
C. Salecianos
C. Pérez Hervás
C. Urquiza
C. Venecia
C. Dr. Delgado Riog
C. San Juan Bosco
C. Esperanza de la Trinidad
N
Estación de Santa Justa
C. Beata Juana Jugan
C. Pablo Picasso
LA CALZADA
PL. DEL SACRIFICIO
C. Via Cruces
S. Florencio
C. Pilar
Fernando Tirado
Virgen Valvanera
Eduardo Rivas
Maese Farfán
Oscar Carvallo
Pirineos
0
200 yd
0
200 m
Sevilla

Madrid Metro

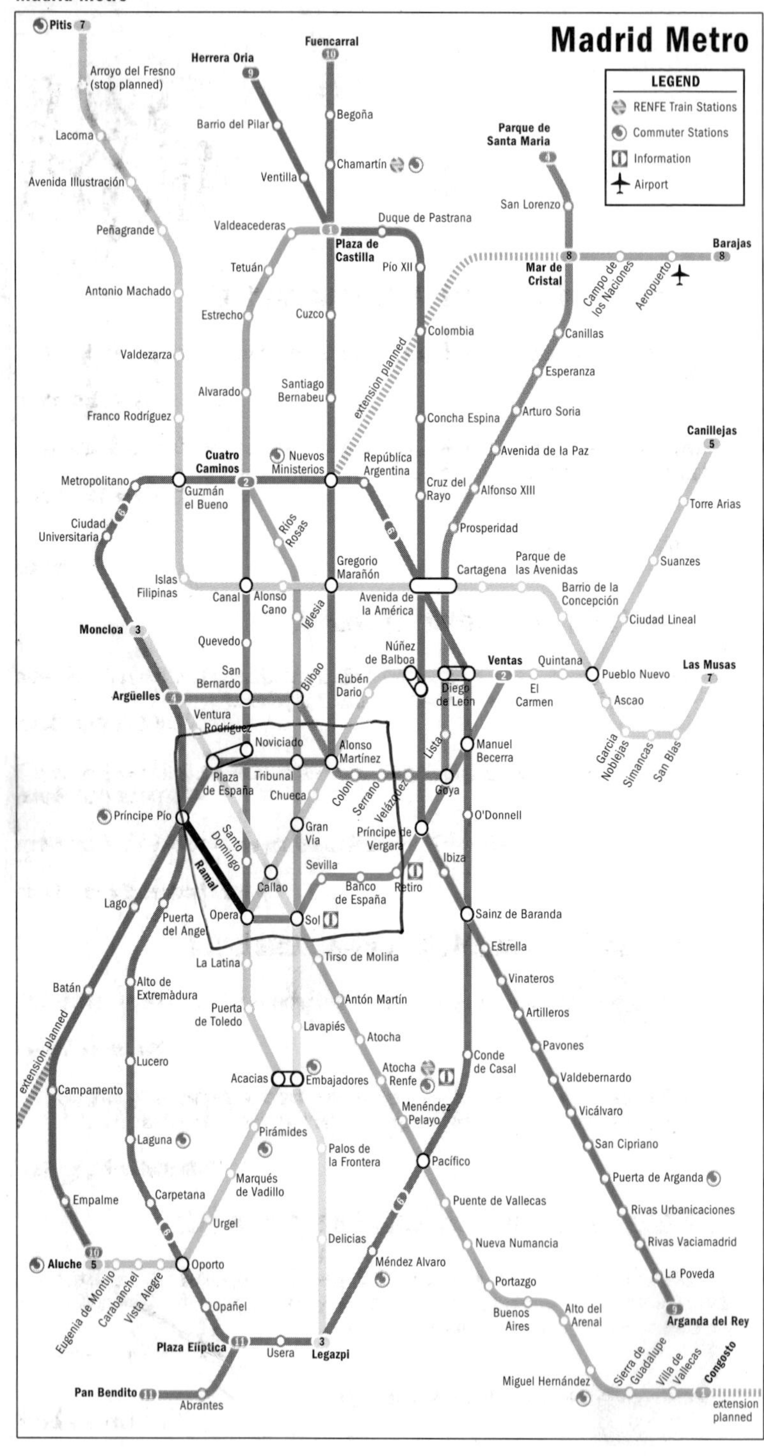

Let's Go writers travel on your budget.

"Guides that penetrate the veneer of the holiday brochures and mine the grit of real life."

—*The Economist*

"The writers seem to have experienced every rooster-packed bus and lunar-surfaced mattress about which they write."

—*The New York Times*

"All the dirt, dirt cheap."

—*People*

Great for independent travelers.

"The guides are aimed not only at young budget travelers but at the independent traveler; a sort of streetwise cookbook for traveling alone."

—*The New York Times*

"A guide should tell you what to expect from a destination. Here *Let's Go* shines."

—*The Chicago Tribune*

"An indispensible resource, *Let's Go*'s practical information can be used by every traveler."

—*The Chattanooga Free Press*

Let's Go is completely revised each year.

"A publishing phenomenon...the only major guidebook series updated annually. *Let's Go* is the big kahuna."

—*The Boston Globe*

"Unbeatable: good sight-seeing advice; up-to-date info on restaurants, hotels, and inns; a commitment to money-saving travel; and a wry style that brightens nearly every page."

—*The Washington Post*

All the important information you need.

"*Let's Go* authors provide a comedic element while still providing concise information and thorough coverage of the country. Anything you need to know about budget traveling is detailed in this book."

—*The Chicago Sun-Times*

"*Let's Go* guidebooks take night life seriously."

—*The Chicago Tribune*

Let's Go Publications

Let's Go: Alaska & the Pacific Northwest 2002
Let's Go: Amsterdam 2002 **New Title!**
Let's Go: Australia 2002
Let's Go: Austria & Switzerland 2002
Let's Go: Barcelona 2002 **New Title!**
Let's Go: Boston 2002
Let's Go: Britain & Ireland 2002
Let's Go: California 2002
Let's Go: Central America 2002
Let's Go: China 2002
Let's Go: Eastern Europe 2002
Let's Go: Egypt 2002 **New Title!**
Let's Go: Europe 2002
Let's Go: France 2002
Let's Go: Germany 2002
Let's Go: Greece 2002
Let's Go: India & Nepal 2002
Let's Go: Ireland 2002
Let's Go: Israel 2002
Let's Go: Italy 2002
Let's Go: London 2002
Let's Go: Mexico 2002
Let's Go: Middle East 2002
Let's Go: New York City 2002
Let's Go: New Zealand 2002
Let's Go: Paris 2002
Let's Go: Peru, Ecuador & Bolivia 2002
Let's Go: Rome 2002
Let's Go: San Francisco 2002
Let's Go: South Africa with Southern Africa 2002
Let's Go: Southeast Asia 2002
Let's Go: Southwest USA 2002 **New Title!**
Let's Go: Spain & Portugal 2002
Let's Go: Turkey 2002
Let's Go: USA 2002
Let's Go: Washington, D.C. 2002
Let's Go: Western Europe 2002

Let's Go *Map Guides*

Amsterdam
Berlin
Boston
Chicago
Dublin
Florence
Hong Kong
London
Los Angeles
Madrid
New Orleans
New York City
Paris
Prague
Rome
San Francisco
Seattle
Sydney
Venice
Washington, D.C.

SPAIN & PORTUGAL

INCLUDING MOROCCO

2002

George B.R. de Brigard editor

M. Sofia Vélez associate editor

Sarah C. Jessop associate editor

researcher writers

Nicholas Grossman

Melissa L. Gibson

Marla Kaplan

Aaron Litvin

Rianna Stefanakis

Heidi Wasson

Christian Westra

Katherine Douglas managing editor

Andrea R. Quintana map editor

St. Martin's Press New York

HELPING LET'S GO If you want to share your discoveries, suggestions, or corrections, please drop us a line. We read every piece of correspondence, whether a postcard, a 10-page email, or a coconut. Please note that mail received after May 2002 may be too late for the 2003 book, but will be kept for future editions. **Address mail to:**

Let's Go: Spain & Portugal
67 Mount Auburn Street
Cambridge, MA 02138
USA

Visit Let's Go at **http://www.letsgo.com,** or send email to:

feedback@letsgo.com
Subject: "Let's Go: Spain & Portugal"

In addition to the invaluable travel advice our readers share with us, many are kind enough to offer their services as researchers or editors. Unfortunately, our charter enables us to employ only currently enrolled Harvard students.

Maps by David Lindroth copyright © 2002, 2001, 2000, 1999, 1998, 1997, 1996, 1995, 1994, 1993, 1992, 1991, 1990, 1989, 1988 by St. Martin's Press.

Distributed outside the USA and Canada by Macmillan.

Let's Go: Spain & Portugal Copyright © 2002 by Let's Go, Inc. All rights reserved. Printed in the United States of America. No part of this book may be used or reproduced in any manner whatsoever without written permission except in the case of brief quotations embodied in critical articles or reviews. Let's Go is available for purchase in bulk by institutions and authorized resellers. For information, address St. Martin's Press, 175 Fifth Avenue, New York, NY 10010, USA.

ISBN: 0-312-27059-3

First edition
10 9 8 7 6 5 4 3 2 1

Let's Go: Spain & Portugal is written by Let's Go Publications, 67 Mount Auburn Street, Cambridge, MA 02138, USA.

Let's Go® and the thumb logo are trademarks of Let's Go, Inc.
Printed in the USA on recycled paper with biodegradable soy ink.

ADVERTISING DISCLAIMER All advertisements appearing in Let's Go publications are sold by an independent agency not affiliated with the editorial production of the guides. Advertisers are never given preferential treatment, and the guides are researched, written, and published independent of advertising. Advertisements do not imply endorsement of products or services by Let's Go, and Let's Go does not vouch for the accuracy of information provided in advertisements.

If you are interested in purchasing advertising space in a Let's Go publication, contact: Let's Go Advertising Sales, 67 Mount Auburn St., Cambridge, MA 02138, USA.

HOW TO USE THIS BOOK

Welcome to Let's Go: SPAM (Spain, Portugal, and Morocco) 2002! This space-age, all-beef, 100% free-range, stain-proof, peanut-free, indestructible, water-resistant Super Guide was handcrafted in remote mountain villages for your fun and enjoyment. Please help SPAM 2002 live a long, full life by feeding it only veterinarian-recommended foods and taking it on frequent walks. Remember, chocolate is bad for SPAM's stomach, and, if you leave it in the car, be sure to roll down all the windows an inch. SPAM 2002 should not be used indoors without proper ventilation and should never be used around an open flame. With proper watering, SPAM 2002 should last you, wherever in Spain, Portugal or Morocco you may go, for a full 12 months until SPAM 2003, that bastard child, is let loose on an innocent public.

ORGANIZATION OF THIS BOOK

THIN CANDY SHELL. The first chapter—**Discover Spain, Portugal, and Morocco**—provides you with an overview of travel in the three countries, including **Suggested Itineraries** that give you an idea of what you shouldn't miss and how long it will take to see it. The **Essentials** section outlines the practical information you will need to prepare for and execute your trip. Each country has its own **Life and Times** chapter with a general introduction to the county's history, art, culture, and food, as well as a brief country-specific Essentials section.

DARK CHOCOLATE CENTER. Coverage of **Spain** spirals out counter-clockwise from Madrid. After sandwiching in Spain's islands, coverage of **Portugal** runs south-to-north. **Morocco** is the kaboose. The **black tabs** in the margins will help you to navigate between chapters quickly and without stress. Each chapter begins with a regional intro, and each town or city is broken down into several sections: **Orientation and Practical Information, Accommodations, Food, Sights, Entertainment,** and **Nightlife**. For smaller towns, categories occasionally get thrown together.

APPENDIX. The appendix contains useful **conversions,** a **phrasebook** of handy phrases, and a **glossary** of foreign and technical (e.g. architectural) words.

A FEW NOTES ABOUT LET'S GO FORMAT

RANKING ESTABLISHMENTS. In each section (accommodations, food, etc.), we list establishments in order from best to worst. Our absolute favorites are so denoted by the highest honor given out by *Let' s Go*, the *Let's Go* thumbs-up (☒).

PHONE CODES AND TELEPHONE NUMBERS. The **phone code** for each city or town appears opposite the name of that region, city, or town, and is denoted by the ☎ icon. **Phone numbers** in text are also preceded by the ☎ icon. The first phone number in a listing includes the phone code; the second will not repeat it.

GRAYBOXES AND IKONBOXES. Grayboxes at times provide wonderful cultural insight, at times simply crude humor. In any case, they're usually amusing, so enjoy. **Whiteboxes,** on the other hand, provide important practical information, such as warnings (**!**), border crossing information (☒), etc.

Have a good time y'all. We did.

A NOTE TO OUR READERS The information for this book was gathered by *Let's Go* researchers from May through August of 2001. Each listing is based on one researcher's opinion, formed during his or her visit at a particular time. Those traveling at other times may have different experiences since prices, dates, hours, and conditions are always subject to change. You are urged to check the facts presented in this book beforehand to avoid inconvenience and surprises.

STUDENT TRAVEL

Over 2 million served every year.

STA TRAVEL

We appreciate your BUSINESS

1 Student ticket
1 flexible itinerary
1 Rail Pass
1 Language Program
1 Low-cost Hotel
1 Adventure tour
1 ISIC card
1 experienced, friendly Travel Advisor
300 Offices Worldwide

TOTAL trip of a lifetime
CASH Still in your Pocket
CHANGE your world

THANK YOU COME AGAIN!

World's largest student travel organization

We've Been There.

CSt 1017560-40 #05 22'01 REG0001

800.777.0112
www.statravel.com

STA TRAVEL

CONTENTS

RESEARCHER-WRITERS

Melissa L. Gibson *Castilla y León, Cantabria, Asturias, Galicia*

If you have a problem, if no one else can help, and if you can find them, maybe you can hire the A-Team. Us? We find Melissa. Swooping in from the 'real world,' Melissa took the Northern coast like a red-haired storm, lashing every daytrip into submission. Bringing her back-office experience to the frontlines, she returned copy so perfect, it said 'Just Add Water.' Dodging pork and shellfish, our super-senior dreamed of days immersed in literature and nights sunk in *flan*.

Nicholas Grossman *Morocco*

Sending back one minty present after another, Nick grabbed Morocco by the camel scruff and wouldn't let go. Overcoming his cold feet off the Straight of Gibraltar, this one-man office made sure his copy wasn't a dirham-a-dozen. He delved so deeply into the depths of the South that we were worried he would never come up for air. That is, until he surfaced with the pearls of the Sahara and the disks to prove it.

Marla Kaplan *Murcia, Valencia, Islas Baleares*

Hell-bent on perfection, Marla skipped to Spain in search of something more lasting than perfect tan lines and a moped license. With rapid-fire ease, this dynamo furnished the office with the facts, ma'am, just the facts. True to form, our Girl Friday attacked the Balearics as if it were the weekend all month long but never forgot to stop and smell the oranges.

Aaron Litvin *Portugal*

What can we say? Aaron came to team SPAM knowing more than God about Portugal. Leaving the countryside in his dust, our favorite Sprocket hit the nights with a determination that was almost threatening. Never letting an inconvenient bus schedule get in his way, Aaron left us wondering if our lives will ever be the same? Indeed, Aaron's work was a pleasure to behold.

Rianna Stefanakis *Madrid, Islas Canarias*

With a penchant for gray-haired Spanish men and a dash of *la vida loca*, Ri tore through copy so fast it left us gasping for air. As our correspondent for culture, she has no equal, marshalling prose as fun-loving and free-floating as *La Marcha* in Madrid. By the time Rianna reached the Canaries, the girl was golden, and it showed in her writing.

Heidi T. Wasson *Pyrenees, País Vasco, Extremadura*

Armed with a five-speed rental and an eye for the mountains, Heidi plunged into our longest itinerary. From the chilly slopes of Andorra to the frying pan of Spain, nothing could corrupt her schedules as she punched through copy like Mohammed Ali. Floating like a butterfly, with Spain spinning in her wake, she still managed to teach us all how to lean back and say Arghh.

Christian Westra *Algarve, Andalucía*

From summiting Moorish castles to plumbing the Swedish influence, Christian tackled Andalucía with a style that inspired love and devotion back on the home front. Never too busy to provide our readers with the skinny on a new town or city, Mr. Westra reminded us by the end of the summer of the adage: *in vino veritas*.

Barcelona 2002:

Emily Gann, Tom Malone, and Meredith Petrin brought us the city on a platter, aided by the nimble fingers of Sarah Kenney, Ed., and Monica Sullivan, Asst. Ed.

ACKNOWLEDGMENTS

The Let's Go 2002 series is dedicated to the memory of Haley Surti

SPAM THANKS: Kate, of course, our stellar team of RWs, Andrea for Barça maps; Team France for entertainment; Anne Chisholm for her support; Sarah Kenney for Catalan screaming; Ankur for Toscanini's; Abi B., Michelle Y., and Kate N. for last minute proofing; Alex L. and Marla K. for entering changes; Nick G. for the bottle of sand; and Elmo.

GEORGE: I would like to thank Kate, for her months of guidance; Sofía and Sarah, for their hard work and skill; the other editors whose camaraderie proved vital as the summer wore on; and, most of all, my roommates and my parents. To N. S. L. V. de G. and St. G

SOFÍA THANKS: George for his computer savvy and Sarah J. for her kindness; Emily G. for the B. Republic dream and Leo's, Sarah E. for wise advice; Sarah R. for the Owl; 10 DeWolfe #31 & Caleb & Natalie for providing me with a home when I was homeless and David H. for securing me with housing; Naz for "oats...they're *so* good;" Kim, Tene, Avi, Ankur, Fish; Mama, Carlo, and Andrés for being my family. But most of all, this book is dedicated with much love and reverence to the one man who showed me what being a true Spaniard is all about: Pepe Martínez. *Pepe, siempre tendré un ancla en mi bote desde donde estaré mirando una estrella.*

SARAH THANKS: George for blue cotton button downs and an internal OED; Sofía for caffeinated whole milk mochas. Team SAF for enthusiasm, refuge, and speedy comp. The 4th floor for vibe and Alyssa for Bolivian blanket. Miss Eno for the love and Megan for the blueberries. Kieran for Mongolian phone calls and warm words. The girl from Ipanema for her smooth swaying gait. Mom, Dad, and Catherine for their patience and their love.

Editor
George B. R. de Brigard
Associate Editors
M. Sofía Vélez, Sarah C. Jessop
Managing Editor
Katharine Douglas
Map Editor
Andrea R. Quintana

Publishing Director
Sarah P. Rotman
Editor-in-Chief
Ankur N. Ghosh
Production Manager
Jen Taylor
Cartography Manager
Dan Bames
Design & Photo Manager
Vanessa Bertozzi
Editorial Managers
Amélie Cherlin, Naz F. Firoz, Matthew Gibson, Sharmi Surianarain, Brian R. Walsh
Financial Manager
Rebecca L. Schoff
Marketing & Publicity Managers
Brady R. Dewar, Katharine Douglas, Marly Ohlsson
New Media Manager
Kevin H. Yip
Online Manager
Alex Lloyd
Personnel Manager
Nathaniel Popper
Production Associates
Steven Aponte, Chris Clayton, Caleb S. Epps, Eduardo Montoya, Melissa Rudolph
Some Design
Melissa Rudolph
Office Coordinators
Efrat Kussell, Peter Richards

Director of Advertising Sales
Adam M. Grant
Senior Advertising Associates
Ariel Shwayder, Kennedy Thorwarth
Advertising Associate
Jennie Timoney
Advertising Artwork Editor
Peter Henderson

President
Cindy L. Rodriguez
General Manager
Robert B. Rombauer
Assistant General Manager
Anne E. Chisholm

ASTURIAS AND CANTABRIA
pp. 430-454
Oviedo
Santander
ASTURIAS
CANTABRIA
Santiago de Compostela
GALICIA
pp. 455-474
León
Burgos
Viana do Castelo
Bragança
Valladolid
DOURO AND MINHO
pp. 633-653
TRÁS-OS-MONTES
pp. 653-659
CASTILLA Y LEÓN
pp. 144-180
Porto
Salamanca
Aveiro
THE THREE BEIRAS
pp. 620-633
MADRID
pp. 78-129
Coimbra
PORTUGAL
RIBATEJO AND
ESTREMADURA
pp. 601-619
Toledo
Castelo Branco
CASTILLA-
LA MANCHA
LISBON
pp. 542-575
EXTREMADURA
pp. 181-193
Mérida
Lisbon
Badajoz
Setúbal
ALENTEJO
pp. 592-600
Évora
Beja
Córdoba
ANDALUCÍA
pp. 194-277
Sevilla
Lagos
Faro
ALGARVE
pp. 576-591
Málaga
ATLANTIC
OCEAN
Gibraltar
Algeciras
ISLAS CANARIAS
pp. 501-526
Tangier
MOROCCO
pp. 660-733
TO
RABAT

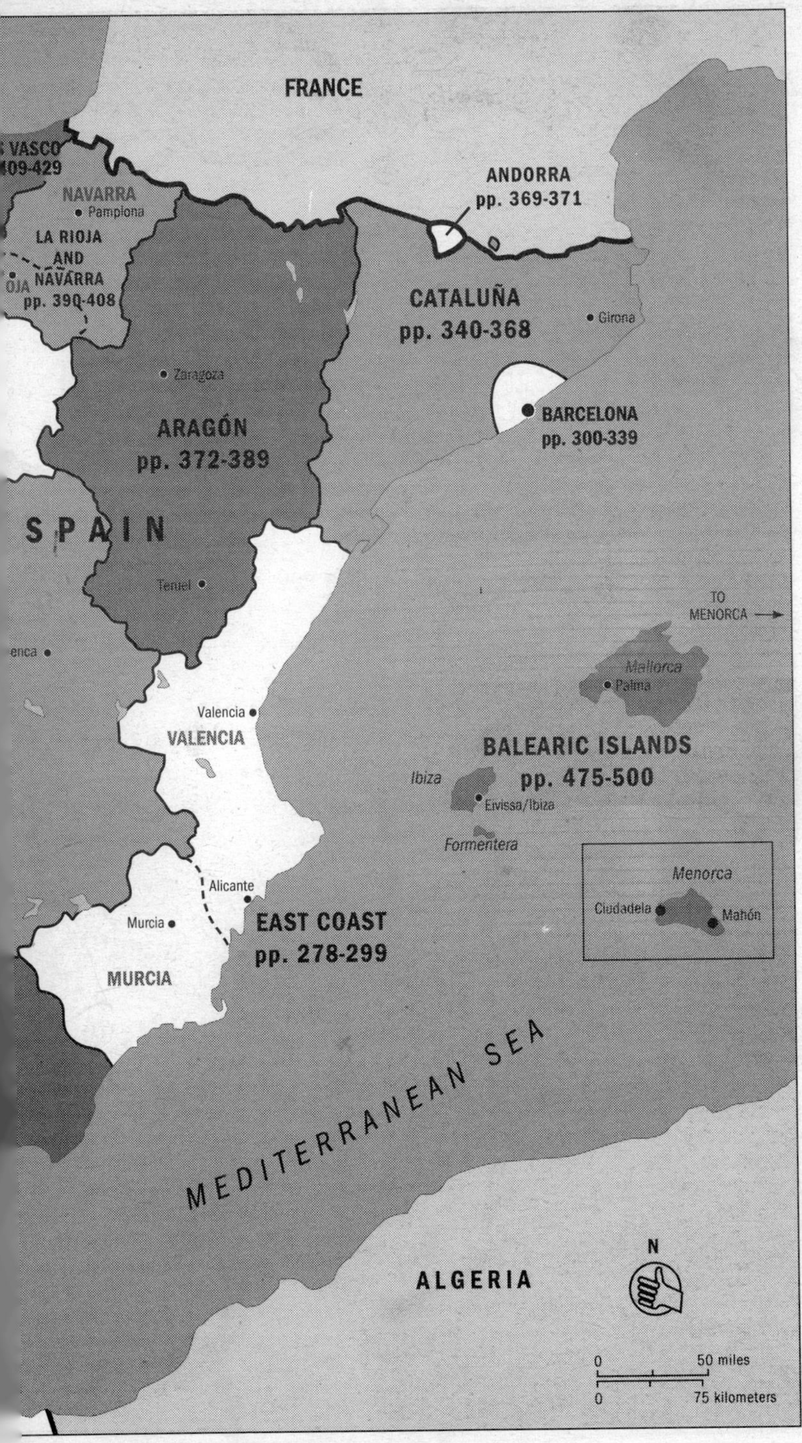

FRANCE
VASCO
409-429
NAVARRA
Pamplona
LA RIOJA
AND
NAVARRA
pp. 390-408
ANDORRA
pp. 369-371
CATALUÑA
pp. 340-368
Girona
Zaragoza
BARCELONA
pp. 300-339
ARAGÓN
pp. 372-389
SPAIN
Teruel
TO
MENORCA
Mallorca
Palma
Valencia
VALENCIA
BALEARIC ISLANDS
pp. 475-500
Ibiza
Eivissa/Ibiza
Formentera
Menorca
Ciudadela
Mahón
Alicante
Murcia
EAST COAST
pp. 278-299
MURCIA
MEDITERRANEAN SEA
ALGERIA
N
0
50 miles
0
75 kilometers

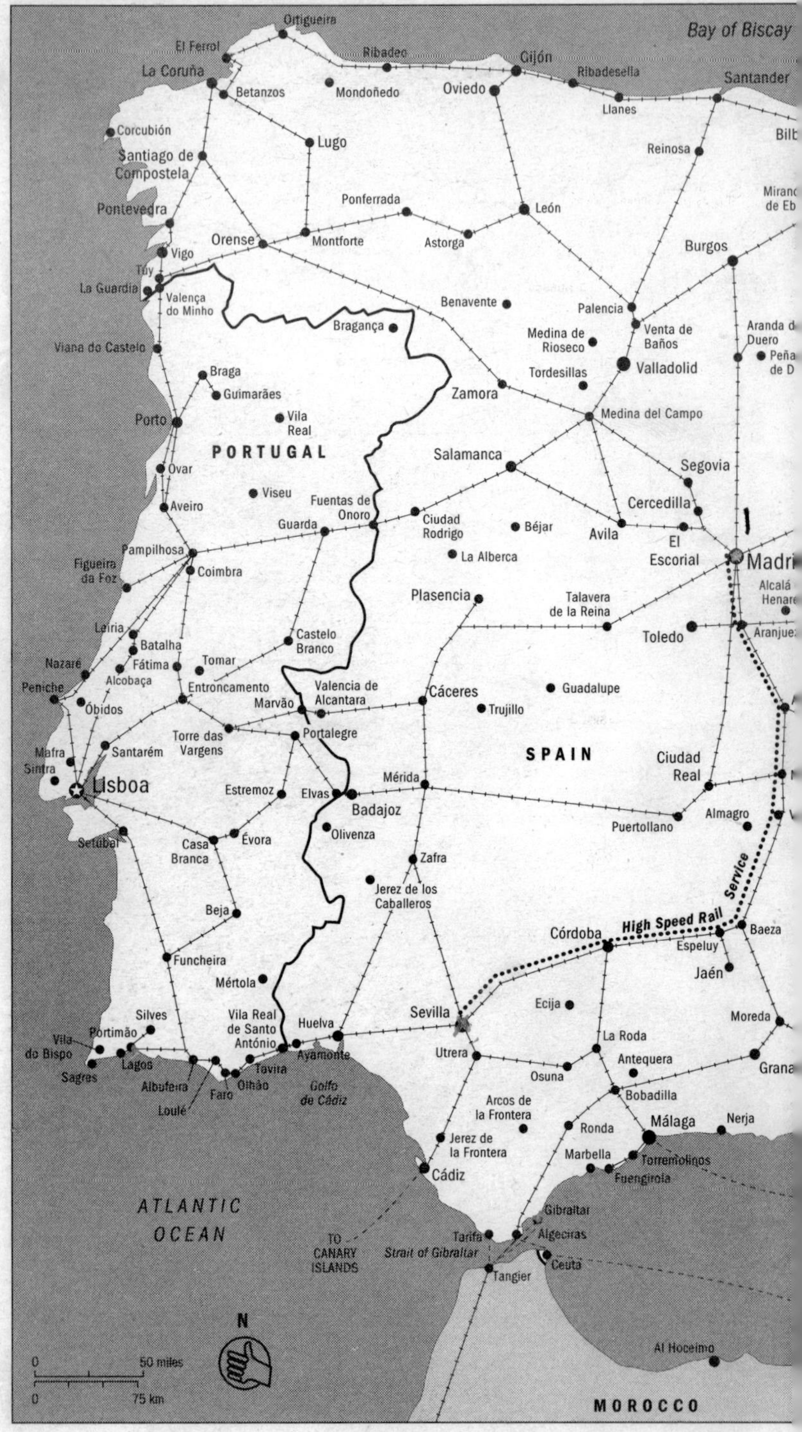
Bay of Biscay
Ortigueira
El Ferrol
La Coruña
Betanzos
Ribadeo
Mondoñedo
Gijón
Oviedo
Ribadesella
Llanes
Santander
Corcubión
Lugo
Santiago de Compostela
Reinosa
Pontevedra
Ponferrada
León
Orense
Montforte
Astorga
Vigo
Tuy
La Guardia
Valença do Minho
Burgos
Benavente
Palencia
Bragança
Venta de Baños
Medina de Rioseco
Aranda de Duero
Viana do Castelo
Valladolid
Tordesillas
Braga
Guimarães
Zamora
Medina del Campo
Porto
Vila Real
PORTUGAL
Salamanca
Segovia
Ovar
Viseu
Aveiro
Fuentas de Onoro
Cercedilla
Guarda
Ciudad Rodrigo
Béjar
Avila
El Escorial
Pampilhosa
Figueira da Foz
Coimbra
La Alberca
Plasencia
Talavera de la Reina
Leiria
Batalha
Castelo Branco
Toledo
Nazaré
Fátima
Tomar
Alcobaça
Peniche
Entroncamento
Valencia de Alcantara
Cáceres
Guadalupe
Óbidos
Marvão
Trujillo
Torre das Vargens
Portalegre
Mafra
Santarém
SPAIN
Ciudad Real
Sintra
Lisboa
Mérida
Estremoz
Elvas
Badajoz
Almagro
Puertollano
Setúbal
Casa Branca
Évora
Olivenza
Zafra
Jerez de los Caballeros
Service
Beja
High Speed Rail
Córdoba
Baeza
Espeluy
Funcheira
Jaén
Mértola
Ecija
Silves
Vila Real de Santo António
Huelva
Sevilla
Moreda
Vila do Bispo
Portimão
La Roda
Sagres
Lagos
Ayamonte
Utrera
Antequera
Albufeira
Tavira
Olhão
Faro
Osuna
Golfo de Cádiz
Loulé
Bobadilla
Arcos de la Frontera
Málaga
Nerja
Ronda
Jerez de la Frontera
Marbella
Torremolinos
Cádiz
Fuengirola
ATLANTIC OCEAN
Gibraltar
Algeciras
Tarifa
TO CANARY ISLANDS
Strait of Gibraltar
Ceuta
Tangier
N
Al Hoceima
0
50 miles
0
75 km
MOROCCO

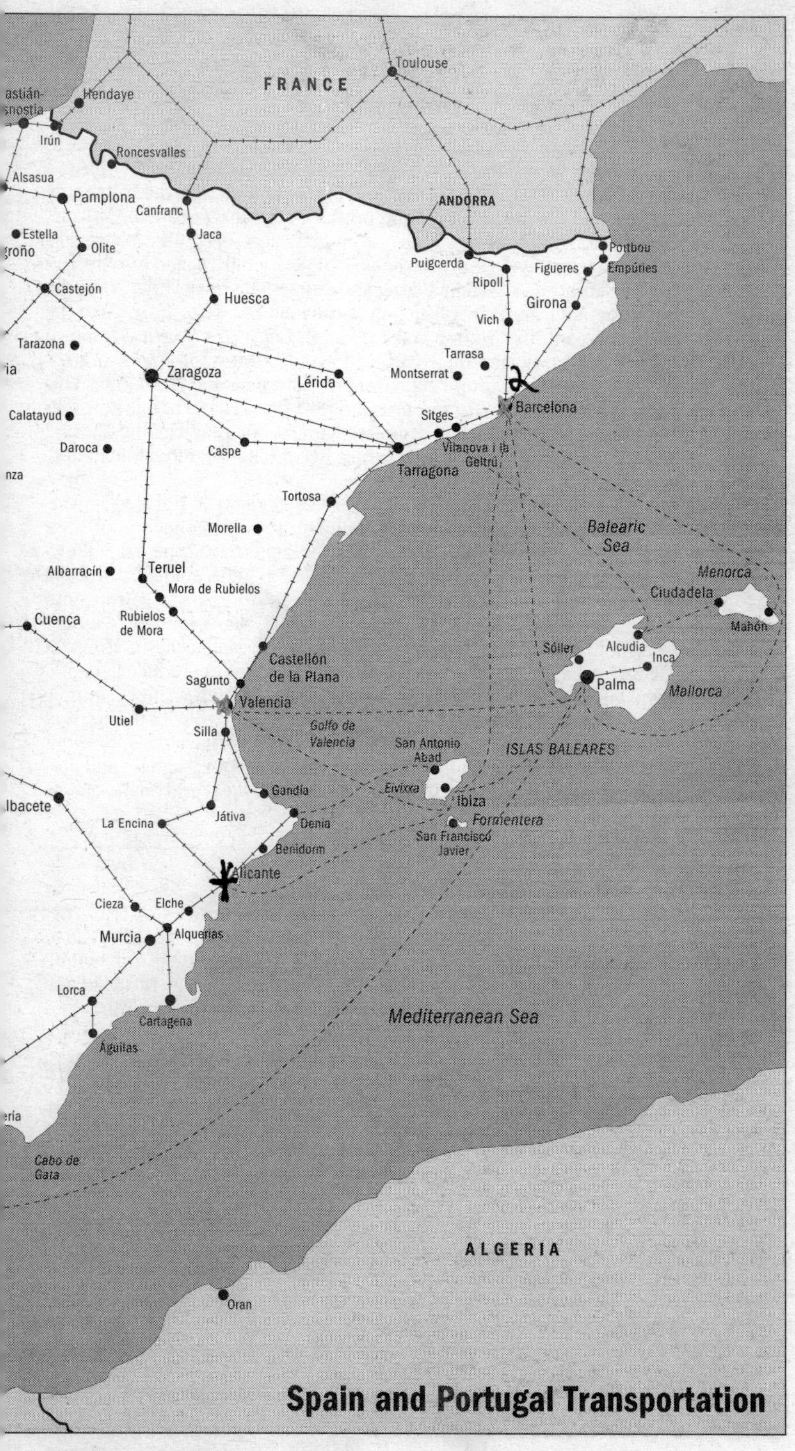

Spain and Portugal Transportation

ABOUT LET'S GO

FORTY-TWO YEARS OF WISDOM

For over four decades, travelers crisscrossing the continents have relied on *Let's Go* for inside information on the hippest backstreet cafes, the most pristine secluded beaches, and the best routes from border to border. *Let's Go: Europe*, now in its 42nd edition and translated into seven languages, reigns as the world's bestselling international travel guide. In the last 20 years, our rugged researchers have stretched the frontiers of backpacking and expanded our coverage into the Americas, Australia, Asia, and Africa (including the new *Let's Go: Egypt* and the more comprehensive, multi-country jaunt through *Let's Go: South Africa & Southern Africa*). Our new-and-improved City Guide series continues to grow with new guides to perennial European favorites Amsterdam and Barcelona. This year we are also unveiling *Let's Go: Southwest USA*, the flagship of our new outdoor Adventure Guide series, which is complete with special roadtripping tips and itineraries, more coverage of adventure activities like hiking and mountain biking, and first-person accounts of life on the road.

It all started in 1960 when a handful of well-traveled students at Harvard University handed out a 20-page mimeographed pamphlet offering a collection of their tips on budget travel to passengers on student charter flights to Europe. The following year, in response to the instant popularity of the first volume, students traveling to Europe researched the first full-fledged edition of *Let's Go: Europe.* Throughout the 60s and 70s, our guides reflected the times—in 1969, for example, we taught you how to get from Paris to Prague on "no dollars a day" by singing in the street. In the 90s we focused in on the world's most exciting urban areas to produce in-depth, fold-out map guides, now with 20 titles (from Hong Kong to Chicago) and counting. Our new guides bring the total number of titles to 57, each infused with the spirit of adventure and voice of opinion that travelers around the world have come to count on. But some things never change: our guides are still researched, written, and produced entirely by students who know first-hand how to see the world on the cheap.

HOW WE DO IT

Each guide is completely revised and thoroughly updated every year by a well-traveled set of nearly 300 students. Every spring, we recruit over 200 researchers and 90 editors to overhaul every book. After several months of training, researcher-writers hit the road for seven weeks of exploration, from Anchorage to Adelaide, Estonia to El Salvador, Iceland to Indonesia. Hired for their rare combination of budget travel sense, writing ability, stamina, and courage, these adventurous travelers know that train strikes, stolen luggage, food poisoning, and marriage proposals are all part of a day's work. Back at our offices, editors work from spring to fall, massaging copy written on Himalayan bus rides into witty, informative prose. A student staff of typesetters, cartographers, publicists, and managers keeps our lively team together. In September, the collected efforts of the summer are delivered to our printer, who turns them into books in record time, so that you have the most up-to-date information available for your vacation. Even as you read this, work on next year's editions is well underway.

WHY WE DO IT

We don't think of budget travel as the last recourse of the destitute; we believe that it's the only way to travel. Our books will ease your anxieties and answer your questions about the basics—so you can get off the beaten track and explore. Once you learn the ropes, we encourage you to put *Let's Go* down and strike out on your own. You know as well as we that the best discoveries are often those you make yourself. When you find something worth sharing, please drop us a line. We're Let's Go Publications, 67 Mount Auburn St., Cambridge, MA 02138, USA (feedback@letsgo.com). For more info, visit our website, www.letsgo.com.

DISCOVER SPAIN, PORTUGAL, AND MOROCCO

SPAIN

Spain is the ground zero of budget traveling. Inexpensive and politically stable, it is a country offering equally generous portions of art, architecture, beaches, and nightlife. The people have an unbeatable lifestyle that they are eager to share, and the regional diversity assures something for everyone. Art lovers flock to northern Spain to see trend-setting Barcelona vamp on the international scene, the coastline that inspired Dalí, and Bilbao's shining Guggenheim museum. Adventure-seekers trek through the dizzying Pyrenees, and architectural enthusiasts explore the Baroque cathedrals of northwestern Spain, the Modernist conjurings of Antoni Gaudí, and the Arab intricacies of Andalucía, Spain's southernmost region. Flamenco, bullfighting and *tapas*, Spain's most familiar cultural expressions, also hail from the south, while to the north, Madrid, Barcelona and Ibiza do enough insane, all-night partying to make up for every early-to-bed grandmother the world over. Spain is the perfect destination for first-time travelers, for seasoned adventurers, for families with children, or for college students in search of fast, easy fun. Once you're in Spain, you'll wonder why you never came before.

PORTUGAL

Sandwiched between Spain and the Atlantic Ocean, Portugal is the forgotten country of Western Europe. Most people know that it colonized Brazil, invented sugary-sweet port wine, and hosted Expo '98 (which, incidentally, was a disaster). Today there is much more to discover in Portugal as it becomes one of Europe's newest hotspots. Lisbon, the capital and largest city, has the country's most impressive imperial monuments, while the southern Algarve boasts spectacular beaches and wild nightlife. Northern Coimbra crackles with the energy of a university town, and Porto surpasses Lisbon in sophisticated elegance. Portugal's small interior towns retain a timeless feel, with medieval castles overlooking rushing rivers and peaceful town squares. Perhaps the most unique region of the country is its wild northern hinterlands, where some villages have not changed in nearly a millennium; the land in Trás-Os-Montes is among the most pristine in all of Europe.

MOROCCO

Morocco is an experience that goes beyond the common expectations of hustlers, drugs, snake charmers, and magic carpets. It is, above all, a land of beautiful extremes, characterized by both the snow-capped peaks of the Atlas mountains and the hot sun on Saharan dunes, by Europeanized coastal cities and isolated desert towns, by the sheer insanity of Marrakesh's Djemâa el-Fna and the peaceful seclusion of Essaouira's beaches. European backpackers come to Morocco lured by exotic fantasies, by "expat" legends, but in place of alienation they find themselves face to face with the real Morocco in medinas (large outdoor markets where you can buy everything from a camel saddle to fresh orange juice), excursions (treks across desert dunes or up North Africa's highest peak), and the wealth of architectural history (towering mosques, crumbling kasbahs, and Roman ruins).

COUNTRY FACTS

SPAIN	PORTUGAL	MOROCCO
Population: 39,371,000	**Population:** 9,964,000	**Population:** 27,225,463
Size: 504,784 sq. km	**Size:** 92,389 sq. km	**Size:** 458,730 sq. km
Capital: Madrid	**Capital:** Lisbon	**Capital:** Rabat
Currency: peseta (ptas)	**Currency:** escudo ($)	**Currency:** dirham (dh)

...AND FIGURES

Pork consumed annually per capita in Spain: 67kg (147 lb.)

Coastline per capita of Portugal: 1.8km

Mint tea consumed per capita in Morocco: 413.8 gallons

Ratio of yearly tourists to actual residents of Spain: 9 to 8

Amount of cork produced by Portugal annually: Enough to keep the entire population afloat–with each person wearing a 40lb. backpack.

Hours slept per capita each night in Madrid: 4.2

WHEN TO GO

Summer is **high season** (*temporada alta*) for coastal and interior regions in Spain, Portugal, and Morocco; winter is high season for ski resorts and the Canary Islands. In many parts of Spain and Portugal, high season extends back to **Semana Santa** (Holy Week; March 24-30 in 2002) and includes festival days. Tourism on the Iberian Peninsula reaches its height in August: the coastal regions overflow while inland cities empty out, leaving closed offices, restaurants, and lodgings.

Traveling in the **off-season** (*temporada baja*) has many advantages, most noticeably the lighter crowds and lower prices. Many hostels cut their prices by 30% or more, and reservations are seldom necessary. While major cities and university towns may burst with vitality during these months, many smaller seaside spots are left ghost towns, and tourist offices and sights cut their hours nearly everywhere. During **Ramadan** in Morocco (Nov. 6-Dec. 1), there is little activity outside the sacred realm. For a temperature table, see **Climate,** p. 733. For a chart of festivals in Spain, see p. 75, in Portugal p. 540, and in Morocco p. 673.

WHAT TO DO

There are as many ways to see Spain, Portugal, and Morocco as there are places to go. One can canvas the region in search of every baroque chapel, spend weeks trekking on some of Europe's best trails, or skip from metropolis to metropolis indulging cosmopolitan fantasies.

IT'S IN THE BLOOD

Spain, Portugal, and Morocco are *alive.* Two millennia of invading cultures have washed across these countries; the result is a vibrant, if confused, culture of varying arts and customs. The region bursts at the seams. You can see it in Madrid's famous flea market, **El Rastro** (p. 122), in the happy chaos of Fez's outdoor medina (p. 689), in the sidewalk cafés of downtown Lisbon (p. 541), and above all in Spain's spectacular festivals. During **Carnaval** in Cádiz (p. 230), Valencia's **Las Fallas** (p. 277), Sevilla's **Feria de Abril** (p. 193), and Pamplona's infamous **San Fermines** (p. 398), there is no denying the Spaniards' overwhelming cultural exuberance.

Still, like all passions, it's not entirely manic. Iberia's poignant expressions of heartbreak are often as blood-quickening as its celebrations. The ritually tragic expressions inherent in *flamenco* and *fado* bring tears to the eyes of even the most macho of bullfighters, who in turn create their own tragedies of life-and-death on the bullring sand. Actual tragedy on a larger scale has scarred Spain for a good part of this century—Picasso's powerfully cryptic **Guernica** (p. 112) and the propagandistic **Valley of the Fallen** (p. 126) give travelers a taste of the pain of fascism. All of this inherited emotional activity demands a break now and then. There is able opportunity for peace and quiet as well: the thin-aired reverence of **Montserrat** (p. 334), the calm to be found in a rowboat in the **Retiro** (p. 108) or on a surreal bench in **Parc Güell** (p. 323). Reverence, too, can be found in the likes of Portugal's **Trás-os-Montes** wilderness (p. 652).

ARCHITECTURE

From traditionally conservative to unconventionally decadent, the buildings and monuments of Iberia form a collage of architectural styles. The remains of ancient civilizations are everywhere—from the Celtiberian tower of **O Castro de Baroña** (p. 461) and the ruins of the Roman Augusta Emerita at **Mérida** (p. 186) to the Torre D'en Gaumés Talayotic settlement in **Menorca** (p. 485). Hundreds of years of Moorish occupation have left a powerful mark on Granada's spectacular **Alhambra** (p. 260), **Córdoba's Mezquita** (p. 224), and **Sintra's Castelo dos Mouros** (p. 568), among others, and the Catholic church has poured immense amounts of money into the construction of some of the world's most ornate religious complexes, ranging from the pastiche of the **Convento de Cristo** (p. 618) to the imposing **El Escorial** (p. 124), from which the Inquisition was conducted. Spain's magnificent cathedrals can be Gothic, Plateresque, built on top of mosques, or just plain bizarre, as with Gaudí's magnificent, still-unfinished **Sagrada Familia** in Barcelona (p. 321), a brilliant climax of the Modernista style. The quest for truly modern architecture will continue into the next millennium; the most recent manifestations include Santiago Calatrava's sensational bridges in Sevilla and Mérida, Lisbon's expansive **Park of Nations** (p. 560), Bilbao's shining **Guggenheim Museum** (p. 421) and Valencia's huge **Ciudad de las Artes y las Ciencias** (p. 282).

NATURE

Iberia's best-kept secret is its national parks and mountain chains, which range from green wildlife reserves to soaring, snowy peaks. Dozens of popular climbs explore tiny Andorra's glacial valleys, rolling forests, and wild meadows (p. 370.) In northern Spain, the **Parque Nacional de Ordesa** (p. 385) offers well-maintained trails along jagged rock faces, rushing rivers, and thundering waterfalls, and the **Parc Nacional d'Agüestortes** (p. 334) hides 50 ice-cold mountain lakes in its 24,700 acres of rugged peaks and valleys. Northern Portugal's **Parque Natural de Montesinho** (p. 654) is probably the most isolated, untouched land in all of Europe; the villages nestled within the park borders have hardly changed since the 8th century. Farther south, greenery-starved *madrileños* hike through the **Sierra de Guadarrama** (p. 126) and nature-lovers are drawn to Andalucía's huge **Parque Nacional Coto de Doñana** (p. 227), which protects nearly 60,000 acres of land for threatened wildlife. **Las Alpujarras** (p. 269), the southern slopes of the Sierra Nevada, are perfect for hiking among Spain's famous *pueblos blancos* (white towns), while trails in Mallorca (p. 476) and the Canary Islands (p. 500) offer a unique opportunity to take in mountain peaks and ocean horizons at the same time. In Morocco, ambitious explorers can trek to the top of the **Djebal Toubkal,** North Africa's highest peak (p. 724) or travel to the desert dunes near **Erfoud** (p. 732) or **M'Hamid** (p. 729).

BEACHES

It would be a shame to spend your *entire* time in Spain, Portugal and Morocco beach-hopping, but if you were to insist, there's enough tempting coastline to support even the most determined offensive against your tan lines. Marc Chagall deemed the red-cliffed, rocky shores of **Tossa de Mar** (p. 343) "Blue Paradise." **San Sebastián's** (p. 409) calm, voluptuous Playa de la Concha has been an elite vacation destination for decades. The beaches of **Galicia** (p. 454) curve around miles of crystal-green, misty inlets, one of which has inspired a pagan cult, the "Ninth Wave.'" On the **Balearic and Canary Islands,** bronzed, glistening bodies occupy every inch of coastline, and southern Spain's infamous **Costa del Sol** (p. 241) brings tourists to its scorched Mediterranean bays by the plane-load. The eastern **Costa Blanca** (p. 291) mixes small-town charm with ocean expanses, and the looming cliffs and turquoise waters of Portugal's southern **Algarve** adorn hundreds of postcards. In Morocco, windsurfers and beach-lovers seeking to escape the inland desert flock to the ex-pirate cove **Essaouira** (p. 712).

NIGHTLIFE

Nightlife in Spain, Portugal, and Morocco can be relaxing—sipping a cold beer in a local bar or people-watching in the town square. But who really wants that? Just setting foot outdoors is likely to lead to events of unabashed hedonism that you'll never be the same again. **Madrid** (p. 114) has earned international renown as the world's sexiest cities—come on, people don't look that good so they can strut their stuff on the way to work. **Barcelona** (p. 299) lays claim the world's only mall complex made of discos (complete with escalators), as well as its own outdoor disco theme park, the Poble Espanol. Residents of **Sevilla** (p. 193) pack discos floating in the Guadalquivir River to drink and dance the night away, and only on **Ibiza** (p. 492), the jetset's favorite party island, do clubs *open* at 4pm to catch crowds still going from the night before. Student-packed **Salamanca** (p. 152) is a crazed, international game of "find-your-fling," and **Lagos,** Portugal (p. 575), has more bars per square meter than any town in the world.

LET'S GO PICKS

BEST PLACE TO GET SKEWERED: Pamplona (S), on the horns of a stampeding bull (p. 398), or if you prefer, get trampled in **Ciutadella** (S), under the hooves of a wild horse (p. 489).

BEST UNFINISHED BUILDING: La Sagrada Familia, Gaudí's masterpiece in Barcelona (S). 118 years under construction, and counting (p. 321).

BEST PLACE TO HAVE SEX WITH A DJ FROM NEW JERSEY: Ibiza (S), where everybody comes to party all day, all night, and all day (p. 492).

BEST PLACE TO BE RIPPED OFF: Tangier (M), where "friends" are a *dirham*-a-dozen (p. 674).

BEST 5AM FOOD: *Churros con chocolate* (S), hands down. Hangovers have never felt this good.

BEST PLACE TO GET HIGH: Chefchaouen (M, p. 680) birthplace of much *hashish,* or gazing at the **Purple Isles** (M), once home to Jimi Hendrix (p. 715).

BEST MESSY FESTIVAL: La Tomatina, in tiny Buñol (S). For two hours every August, the entire town has a massive, juicy tomato war. No joke.

BEST PLACE TO TAN IN YOUR BIRTHDAY SUIT: The southern edge of **Formentera,** the Balearics' semi-deserted island paradise (p. 499).

BEST RELIGIOUS MONUMENT MADE OF DEAD PEOPLE: 5000 unwitting skeletons went into the making of the macabre **Capella de Ossos (Chapel of Bones)** in Évora (P, p. 591).

BEST TOILET: The velvet-covered baby seat in Aranjuez's **Palacio Real** (S). Even potty-training is easy for royalty (p. 127).

BEST PLACE TO PICK UP A HOTTIE BACKPACKER: Lagos (P), playground of too many tanned Kiwi and Australian 20-somethings to count (p. 575).

BEST FRESH-SQUEEZED ORANGE JUICE: Marrakesh (M), in the medina, for a mere 20 cents a pop (p. 689).

SUGGESTED ITINERARIES

SPAIN, PORTUGAL, AND MOROCCO (5 WEEKS) Start the party off in **Madrid** (4 days, 4 nights, p. 77), with daytrips to the reserved palace of **El Escorial** (p. 124) and the medieval streets of **Toledo** (p. 129). Visit the ancient center of **Salamanca** (1 day, p. 152) and hop the border into **Portugal,** heading up to the unpretentious **Porto** (2 days, p. 632). Continue down to the vibrant university town of **Coimbra** (2 days, p. 619). Immerse yourself in the sights, sounds, and cafés of **Lisbon** (2 days, 3 nights, p. 541) with a daytrip to the town of **Sintra** (1 day, p. 568). To the south lie the beaches and cliffs of the Algarve; stop in **Lagos** (2 days, p. 575) to dance the night away. Catch your shut-eye on the 7hr. bus from Lagos to **Sevilla** (2 days, p. 193) and prepare for a romantic stroll along the Guadalquivir River. Delve deeper into Iberia's Arab roots and take a ferry from **Algeciras** to **Tangier, Morocco,** escaping immediately to the beaches of **Asilah** (1 day, p. 698). Move inland to the imperial cities of **Fez** (2 days, p. 689) and **Marrakesh** (2 days, p. 715) with their enchanting medinas. Stop by the coastal capital **Rabat** (1 day), and then swing back through Algeciras and Sevilla to **Córdoba, Spain** (2 days, p. 214), with its gargantuan Mezquita, and **Granada** (2 days, p. 260), home to the world-famous Alhambra. Head up the Mediterranean Coast to **Valencia** (1 day, p. 277), where the food—*paella* and oranges—rivals the new planetarium as Valencia's top attraction. Onwards to **Barcelona** (4 days, p. 299), one of Europe's most vibrant cities full of Modernista architecture and fierce nightlife. During the summer, sun on the beaches in **Tossa de Mar** (1 day, p. 343), or visit the monastery in **Montserrat** (1 day, p. 334). In the winter, a better bet is skiing in **Puigcerdà** (1 day, p. 361). Visit Spain's second most popular museum, the Theatre-Museu Dalí in **Figueres** (1 day, p. 354) before heading on to **San Sebastián** (2 days, p. 409) and **Bilbao** (1 day, p. 417), home to the Guggenheim Museum.

BEST OF SPAIN, PORTUGAL, AND MOROCCO

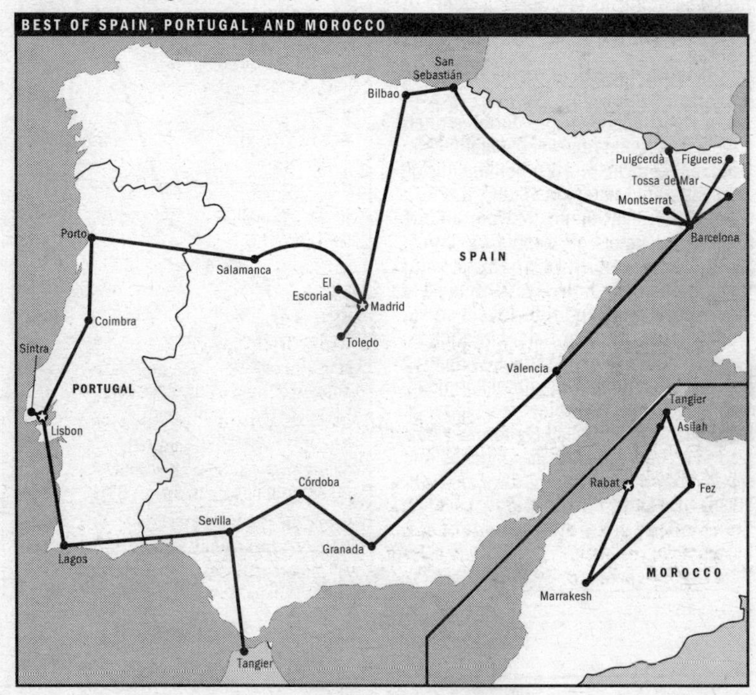

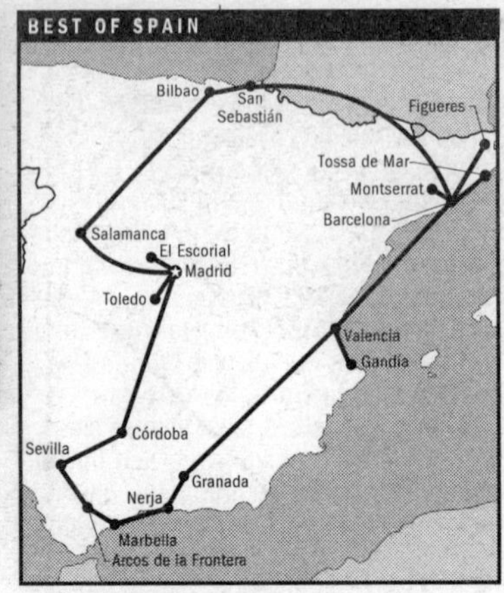

THE BEST OF SPAIN (3 WEEKS) Begin *la marcha* in **Madrid** (4 days, 4 nights, p. 77), with daytrips to **El Escorial** (p. 124) and **Toledo** (p. 129). Then speed out to **Córdoba** (2 days, p. 214), and on to **Sevilla** (2 days, p. 193). Board the bus to the peaceful *pueblo blanco* of **Arcos de la Frontera** (1 day, p. 228) where you'll inevitably swear like a native. Next, make your way south to the tanning fields of Spain's Costa del Sol. Layover in **Marbella** (1 day, p. 246) for raging nightlife and celebrity-watching. Idyllic beaches and relaxation await in **Nerja** (1 day, p. 248). Head inland to the cobblestoned streets and world-renowned Alhambra in **Granada** (2 days, p. 260) before cruising the coast up to **Valencia** (1 day, p. 277). Display your tight tummy as you tan and frolic in the waters off **Gandía** (1 day, p. 294). Venture north to Spain's costal jewel, **Barcelona** (2 days, p. 299), a pleasure for art and nightlife lovers alike. Worthwhile daytrips in Cataluña abound: partake of **Tossa de Mar's** beaches (1 day, p. 343), admire breathtaking mountain views from **Montserrat** (1 day, p. 334), or say Hello Dalí in **Figueres** (1 day, p. 354). Grab a bus to the beaches and *tapas* of **San Sebastián** (2 days, p. 409). Finally, it's on to **Bilbao** (1 day, p. 417), home of the incredible Guggenheim museum.

THE BEST OF ANDALUCÍA (2 WEEKS) Whisk away from Madrid on the high-speed AVE train to **Córdoba** (2 days, p. 214) to tour the Mezquita mosque-turned-cathedral. Hop back on the AVE to **Sevilla** (3 days, p. 193) to inspect the three towers dedicated to gold, silver, and God. A quick trip down to Costa del Luz yields the soft-sanded stretches of **Cádiz's** beaches (2 days, p. 230). Move into the heart of Andalucía and the classic *pueblo blanco* **Arcos de la Frontera** (1 day, p. 228). Party in the Costa del Sol resort town of **Marbella** (1 day, p. 246) before rejuvenating on the beaches of **Nerja** (2 days, p. 248). Continue inland to **Granada** (2 days, p. 260), where the Alhambra and Albacín are sights for sore eyes. Mountain air awaits hiking from town to town in the **Alpujarras** (1 day, p. 269). Ride the rails back to Madrid.

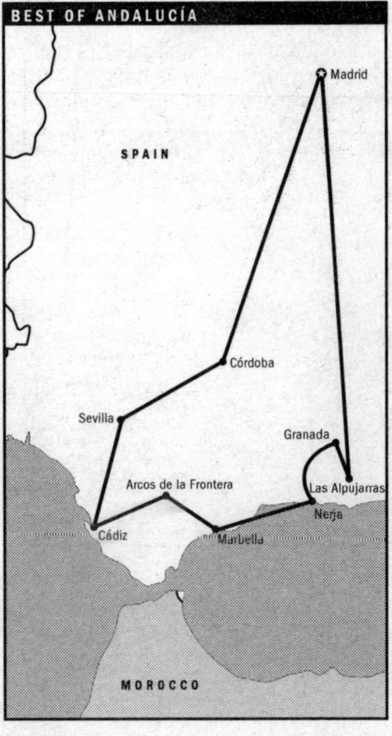

THE BEST OF PORTUGAL (2 WEEKS)

Begin in the busy capital **Lisbon** (2 days, 3 nights, see p. 541) and daytrip to fairy tale **Sintra** (1 day, see p. 568) Head down to the infamous beach-and-bar town **Lagos** (2-3 days, see p. 575) and spend an afternoon in **Sagres,** once considered the end of the world. Check out the creepy bone chapel in **Évora** (1 day, see p. 591) and the mysterious convent in **Tomar** (1 day, see p. 616). Slam shut those dusty books in the university town of **Coimbra** (3 days, see p. 619) and take in the youthful fun. Finish in **Porto** (2 days, see p. 632), home of–you guessed it–sweet port wine.

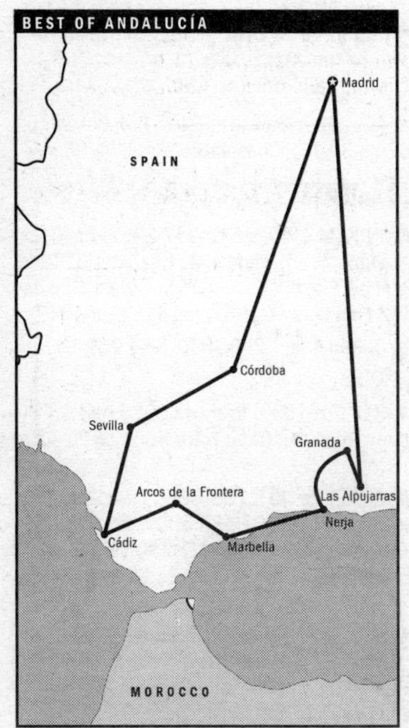

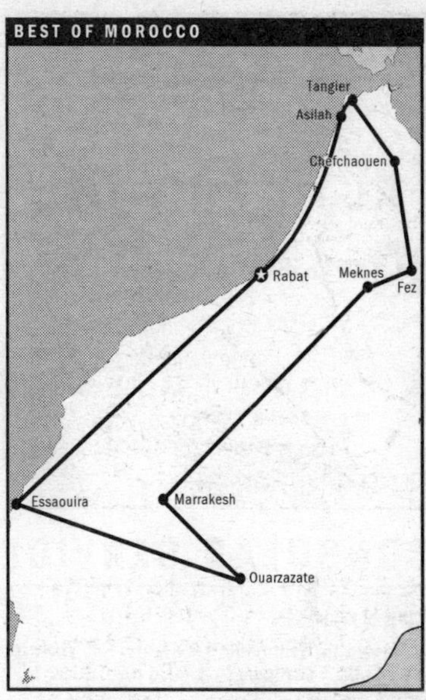

THE BEST OF MOROCCO (2 WEEKS)

From Spain, hop on a ferry from Spanish **Algeciras** to **Tangier.** Once on land, move directly to **Asilah** (1 day, p. 698). Decamp to the enchanting stoned medina of **Chefchaoun** (1 day, see p. 680) for sweet-smelling relaxation. Experience the dazzling imperial cities of **Fez** (2 days, see p. 689), **Meknes** (2 days, see p. 682), and **Marrakesh** (2 days, seen p. 715). Mounted on a camel, probe deeper into the desserts south of **Ouarzazate** (1 day, see p. 726). Back track through Marrakesh to beaches of **Essaouira** (2 days, see p. 712) before heading up the coast to the capital **Rabat** (1 day, see p. 701) on your way back to Tangier.

ESSENTIALS

ESSENTIALS

FACTS FOR THE TRAVELER

PASSPORT (P. 10). Required for all citizens of United Kingdom, Canada, Australia, New Zealand, South Africa, Ireland and the United States.
Visa (p. 11). Required in addition to a passport for South Africans going to Spain, Portugal, and Morocco, and for Australians going to Portugal.
Work Permit (p. 11). Required for all foreigners planning to work in Spain, Portugal, and Morocco.
Driving Permit (p. 43). Required for all those planning to drive in Spain, Portugal, and Morocco.

CONSULAR SERVICES AT HOME

SPANISH

Australia: Embassy: 15 Arkana St., **Yarralumla,** ACT 2600. Mailing address: P.O. Box 9076, Deakin, ACT 2600 (☎2 62 73 35 55; fax 2 62 73 39 18). **Consulates:** Level 24, St. Martin's Tower, 31 Market St., **Sydney,** NSW 2000 (☎2 92 61 24 33; fax 2 92 83 16 95); 540 Elizabeth St., 4th fl., Melbourne, VIC 3000 (☎3 93 47 19 66; fax 3 93 47 73 30).

Canada: Embassy: 74 Stanley Ave., **Ottawa,** ON K1M 1P4 (☎613-747-2252; fax 613-744-1224). **Consulates:** 1 Westmount Sq., Suite 1456, **Montreal,** Quebec H3Z 2P9 (☎514-935-5235; fax 514-935-4655); Simcoe Place, 200 Front St., West Oficina 2401, P.O. Box 15, **Toronto,** Ontario M5V 3K2 (☎416-977-1661; fax 416-593-4949).

Ireland: Embassy: 17a Merlyn Park, Ballsbridge, **Dublin** 4 (☎1 269 1640; fax 1 269 1854).

New Zealand: Refer to Embassy in Australia.

South Africa: Embassy: 169 Pine St., Arcadia, P.O. Box 1633, **Pretoria** 0083 (☎12 344 3875; fax 12 343 4891). **Consulate:** 37 Shortmarket St., **Cape Town** 8001 (☎21 422 415; fax 21 422 328).

UK: Embassy: 39 Chesham Pl., **London** SW1X 8SB (☎207 235 5555; fax 207 235 9905). **Consulates:** 20 Draycott Pl., **London** SW3 2RZ (☎207 589 8989; fax 207 581 7888); Suite 1A, Brook House, 70, Spring Gardens, **Manchester** M2 2BQ (☎161 236 1262; fax 161 228 7467); 63 N. Castle St., **Edinburgh** EH2 3LJ (☎131 220 1843; fax 131 226 4568.

US: Embassy: 2375 Pennsylvania Ave. NW, **Washington, D.C.** 20037 (☎202-452-0100; fax 202-833-5670). **Consulates:** 150 E. 58th St., 30th fl., **New York,** NY 10155 (☎212-355-4080; fax 212-644-3751); **others** in Boston, Chicago, Houston, Los Angeles, Miami, New Orleans, San Juan (PR), San Francisco, and Washington, D.C.

PORTUGUESE

Australia: Embassy: 23 Culgoa Circuit, **O'Malley,** ACT 2606; mailing address P.O. Box 9092, Deakin, ACT 2600 (☎62 90 17 33; fax 62 90 19 57; embport@dynamite.com.au) **Consulate:** Level 9 #30, Clarence St., **Sydney,** NSW 2000; mailing address P.O. Box 3309 (☎92 62 59 91; fax 92 62 59 91; info@consulportugalsydney.org.au)

Canada: Embassy: 645 Island Park Dr., **Ottawa,** ON K1Y OB8 (☎613 729-0883; fax 613 729-4236). **Consulates:** 2020 University, Suite 1725, **Montréal,** QU H3A 2A5 (☎514-499-0621 or 499-0359; fax 514-499-0366); 438 University Ave., Suite 1400, **Toronto,** ON M5G 2K8 (☎416-217-0966 or 217-0971; fax 217-0973); 700 W. Pender St., Suite 904, **Vancouver,** BC V6C 1G8 (☎604-688-6514; fax 604-685-7042).

New Zealand: Embassy: Refer to Embassy in Australia. **Consulates:** 33 Garfield St., Painell, P.O. Box 105 N2 **Auckland** 5 (☎9 308 1454; fax 9 308 9061); 21 Marion St., **Wellington** 1; mailing address P.O. Box 1024 (☎4 385 9639; fax 4 382 6659).

South Africa: Embassy: 599 Leyds St., Mucklenuk, **Pretoria;** mail: 002, P.O. Box 27102. (☎12 341 2340; fax 12 341 3975; portemb@sadis.co.ca) **Consulates:** Barclays Sq., 296 Walker St., Sunnyside, **Pretoria**, (☎12 341 5522; fax 12 341 5690); Portuguese House, 1st Floor, Ernest Oppenheimer Road, 2198, Room Bruma., **Johannesburg** (☎11 293 8206; fax 11 333 9009; olga@cardoso@cgjoa.eagaccp.pt) 321006 Main Tower, Standard Bank Centre, Hertzog Boulevard, **Capetown,** 8001. mail: P.O. Box 314, 8000; W. St., 16th fl., P.O. Box 315, **Durban** (☎31 305 7511; fax 31 304 6036).

UK: Embassy: 11 Belgrave Sq., **London** SW1X 8PP (☎20 7235 5331; fax 20 7245 1287 or 20 235 0739; portembassy-london@dialin.net. **Consulate:** Silver City House, 2&3rd floor, 62 Brompton Rd., **London** SW3 1BJ (☎20 7581 8722; fax 20 7581 3085).

US: Embassy: 2125 Kalorama Rd. NW, **Washington, D.C.** 20008 (☎202-328-8610; fax: 462-3726 or 518-3694; www.portugal.emb.org) **Consulates:** 630 5th Ave., 8th fl., Suite 801, **New York,** NY 10111 (☎212-246-4580 or 246-4582; fax 459-0190); **others** in Boston, Chicago, Coral Gables (FL), Houston, Honolulu, Los Angeles, Newark, New Bedford (MA), New Orleans, Philadelphia, Providence, San Francisco, San Juan (PR), Waterbury (CT), and Washington, D.C.

MOROCCAN

Australia: Embassy: 11 West St., Suite #2, **North Sydney,** NSW 2060 (☎2 99 22 49 99; fax 2 99 23 10 53; maroc@magna.com.au).

Canada: Embassy: 38 Range Rd., **Ottawa,** ON K1N 8J4 (☎613-236-7391 or 236-7392; fax 236-6164). **Consulate:** 1010 Sherbrooke West St., Suite 1510, **Montreal,** QU H3A 2R7 (☎514-288-8750; fax 288-4859).

South Africa: Embassy: 799 Shoeman St., **Pretoria** (☎12 343 0230; fax 12 343 0613).

UK: Embassy: 49 Queens Gate Gardens, **London** SW7 5NE (☎20 7581 5001; fax 20 7225 3862).

US: Embassy: 1601 21st St. NW, **Washington, D.C.** 20009 (☎202-462-7979; fax 265-0161). **Consulates:** 10 East 40th. St., 23th fl., **New York,** NY 10016 (☎212-213-9644; fax 779-7441); 1821 Jefferson Place NW, **Washington, D.C.** 20036 (☎202-462-7979; fax 452-0106).

TOURIST OFFICES

SPANISH

Spain's official tourist board operates an extensive website at www.tourspain.es. It also has offices in Canada, the United Kingdom, and the United States.

Canada: Tourist Office of Spain, 2 Bloor Street West, Suite 3402, **Toronto**, ON M4W 3E2 (☎416-961-3131; fax 961-1992).

United Kingdom: Spanish National Tourist Office, 22-23 Manchester Square, **London** W1M 5AP (☎171 486 8077; fax 486 8034; info.londres@tourspain.es).

United States: Tourist Office of Spain, 666 Fifth Avenue, 35th fl., **New York**, NY 10103 (☎212-265-8822; fax 265-8864). Additional offices in **Chicago**, IL (☎312-642-1992), **Beverly Hills**, CA (☎323-658-7188), and **Miami**, FL (☎305-358-1992).

PORTUGUESE

The official Portuguese tourism website is located at www.portugalinsite.pt. There are also offices in Canada, the United Kingdom, and the United States.

Canada: Portuguese Trade and Tourism Commission, 60 Bloor St. West, Suite 1005, **Toronto**, ON M4W 3B8 (☎416 921-7376; fax 921-1353; iceptor@idirect.com).

United Kingdom: Portuguese Trade and Tourism Office, 22-25A Sackville Street, 2nd-4th Floor, **London** W1X 2LY (☎20 7474 1441; fax 20 7494 1441; iceplond@aol.com).

United States: Portuguese National Tourist Office, 590 Fifth Ave., 4th fl., **New York**, NY 10036 (☎212 354-4403; fax 764-6137; www.portugal.org). Additional office in Washington D.C. (☎202 331-8222).

MOROCCAN

The official website for tourism in Morocco is www.tourism-in-morocco.com. There are also tourist offices located in Australia, Canada, and the US.

Australia: Moroccan National Tourist Office, 2/11 West St., **North Sydney** NSW 2060 (☎2 9922 4999; fax 2 9923 1053; maroc@magna.com.au).

Canada: Moroccan National Tourist Office, Place Montreal Trust, Suite 2450, 1800, Ave. McGill College, **Montreal** QC H3A 3J6 (☎514-842-8111; fax 842-5316).

United States: Moroccan National Tourist Office, 20 East 46th St., Suite 1201, **New York** NY 10017 (☎212-557-2520; fax 949-8148). Additional office in **Lake Buena Vista,** FL (☎407-827-5337).

DOCUMENTS AND FORMALITIES

PASSPORTS

REQUIREMENTS. Citizens of Australia, Canada, Ireland, New Zealand, South Africa, the UK, and US need passports to enter Spain, Portugal, and Morocco and to re-enter their own countries. For citizens of some countries, neither Spain, Portugal, nor Morocco allows entrance if the passport expires in under six months. Returning home with an expired passport is illegal, and may result in a fine.

PHOTOCOPIES. Be sure to photocopy the page of your passport with your photo, passport number, and other identifying information, as well as any visas, travel insurance policies, plane tickets, or traveler's check serial numbers. Carry one set of copies in a safe place, apart from the originals, and leave another set at home. Consulates also recommend that you carry an expired passport or an official copy of your birth certificate in a part of your baggage separate from other documents.

LOST PASSPORTS. If you lose your passport, immediately notify the local police and the nearest embassy or consulate of your home government. To expedite its replacement, you will need to know all information previously recorded and show ID and proof of citizenship. In some cases, a replacement may take weeks to process, and it may be valid only for a limited time. Any visas stamped in your old passport will be irretrievably lost. In an emergency, ask for immediate temporary traveling papers that will permit you to re-enter your home country. Your passport is a public document belonging to your nation's government. You may have to surrender it to a foreign government official, but if you don't get it back in a reasonable amount of time, inform the nearest consulate of your home country.

NEW PASSPORT. File any new passport or renewal applications well in advance of your departure date. Most passport offices offer rush services for a steep fee. Citizens living abroad who need a passport or renewal should contact the nearest consular service of their home country.

Australia: Info ☎13 12 32; www.dfat.gov.au/passports. Apply for passport at post office, passport office (Adelaide, Brisbane, Canberra, Darwin, Hobart, Melbourne, Perth, or Sydney), or overseas diplomatic mission. AUS$128 (32-page) or AUS$192 (64-page); valid for 10 years. Children AUS$64 (32-page) or AUS$96 (64-page); valid for 5 years.

Canada: Canadian Passport Office, Department of Foreign Affairs and International Trade, Ottawa, ON K1A OG3 (☎613-994-3500 or 800-567-6868; www.dfait-maeci.gc.ca/passport). Applications available at passport offices, Canadian missions, and post offices. Passports CDN$60; valid for 5 years (non-renewable).

ONE EUROPE. The idea of European unity has come a long way since 1958, when the European Economic Community (EEC) was created in order to promote solidarity and cooperation between its six founding states. Since then, the EEC has become the European Union (EU), with political, legal, and economic institutions spanning 15 member states: Austria, Belgium, Denmark, Finland, France, Germany, Greece, Ireland, Italy, Luxembourg, the Netherlands, Portugal, Spain, Sweden, and the UK.

What does this have to do with the average non-EU tourist? In 1999 the EU established **freedom of movement** across 14 European countries–the entire EU minus Denmark, Ireland, and the UK, but plus Iceland and Norway. This means that border controls between participating countries have been abolished, and visa policies harmonized. While you're still required to carry a passport (or government-issued ID card for EU citizens) when crossing an internal border, once you've been admitted into one country, you're free to travel to all participating states. Britain and Ireland have also formed a **common travel area,** abolishing passport controls between the UK and the Republic of Ireland. This means that the only times you'll see a border guard within the EU are traveling between the British Isles and the Continent and in and out of Denmark.

For more important consequences of the EU for travelers, see The Euro (p. 14) and **European Customs** and EU customs regulations (p. 12).

Ireland: Pick up an application at a *Garda* station or post office, or request one from a passport office. Then apply by mail to the Department of Foreign Affairs, Passport Office, Molesworth St., Dublin 2 (☎1 671 1633; fax 1 671 1092; www.irlgov.ie/iveagh), or the Passport Office, Irish Life Building, 1A South Mall, Cork (☎ (021) 27 25 25). Passports IR£45; valid for 10 years. Under 18 or over 65 IR£10; valid for 3 years.

New Zealand: Send applications to the Passport Office, Department of International Affairs, P.O. Box 10526, Wellington, New Zealand (☎0800 22 50 50 or 4 474 8100; fax 4 474 8010; www.passports.govt.nz; passports@dia.govt.nz). Standard processing time is 10 working days. Passports NZ$80; valid for 10 years. Children NZ$40; valid for 5 years. 3 day "urgent service" NZ$160; children NZ $120.

South Africa: Department of Home Affairs. Passports issued only in Pretoria, but all applications must still be submitted or forwarded to the nearest South African consulate. Processing time is 3 months or more. Passports around SAR80; valid for 10 years. Under 16 around SAR60; valid for 5 years. For more information, check out www.usaembassy.southafrica.net/VisaForms/Passport/Passport2000.html.

United Kingdom: Info ☎870 521 0410; www.open.gov.uk/ukpass/ukpass.htm. Get an application from a passport office, main post office, travel agent, or online (for UK residents only) at www.ukpa.gov.uk/forms/f_app_pack.htm. Then apply by mail or in person at a passport office. Passports UK£28; valid for 10 years. Under 15 UK£14.80; valid for 5 years. The process takes about 4 weeks; faster service (by personal visit to the offices listed above) costs an additional £12.

United States: Info ☎202-647-0518; www.travel.state.gov/passport_services.html. Apply at any federal or state courthouse, authorized post office, or US Passport Agency (in most major cities); see the "US Government, State Department" section of the telephone book or a post office for addresses. Processing takes 3-4 weeks. New passports US$60; valid for 10 years. Under 18 US$40; valid for 5 years. Passports may be renewed by mail or in person for US$40. Add US$35 for 3-day expedited service.

VISAS

As of August 2000, citizens of South Africa need a visa—a stamp, sticker, or insert in your passport specifying the purpose of your travel and the permitted duration of your stay—in addition to a valid passport for entrance to Spain, Portugal, or Morocco; citizens of Australia need a visa to enter Portugal but not Morocco or Spain; and citizens of Canada, Ireland, the UK, the US, and New Zealand do not need visas to enter Spain, Portugal or Morocco. Visas vary in cost based on the length of stay and can only be obtained with extensive documentation on your planned activity in the country. Applications are available at the nearest consulate or embassy for the country to which you are traveling. In some cases they can also be filed in the foreign country (Morocco even requires that some applications be filed within Morocco itself), but generally speaking visa applications must be filed in your home country. US citizens can take advantage of the **Center for International Business and Travel** (**CIBT**; ☎800-925-2428), which secures visas for travel to almost all countries for a variable service charge.

Double-check on entrance requirements at the nearest embassy or consulate of Spain, Portugal or Morocco for up-to-date info before departure. US citizens can also consult www.pueblo.gsa.gov/cic_text/travel/foreign/foreignentryreqs.html.

IDENTIFICATION

When you travel, always carry two or more forms of identification on your person, including at least one photo ID; a passport combined with a driver's license or birth certificate is usually adequate. Many establishments, especially banks, may require several IDs in order to cash traveler's checks. Never carry all your forms of ID together; split them up in case of theft or loss.

For more information on all the forms of identification listed below, contact the organization that provides the service, the **International Student Travel Confederation (ISTC),** Herengracht 479, 1017 BS Amsterdam, Netherlands (☎31 20 421 28 00; fax 31 20 421 28 10; www.istc.org).

TEACHER & STUDENT IDENTIFICATION. The **International Student Identity Card (ISIC),** the most widely accepted form of student ID, provides discounts on sights, accommodations, food, and transport. The ISIC is preferable to an institution-specific card (such as a university ID) because it is more likely to be recognized (and honored) abroad. All cardholders have access to a 24hr. emergency helpline for medical, legal, and financial emergencies (in North America call ☎877-370-ISIC, elsewhere call US collect 1 715-345-0505), and US cardholders are also eligible for insurance benefits (see **Insurance,** p. 23).

The card is valid from September of one year to December of the following year and costs US$22. Applicants must be degree-seeking students of a secondary or post-secondary school and must be of at least 12 years of age. Because of the proliferation of fake ISICs, some services (particularly airlines) require additional proof of student identity, such as a school ID or a letter attesting to your student status, signed by your registrar and stamped with your school seal. The **International Teacher Identity Card (ITIC)** offers the same insurance coverage as well as similar but limited discounts. The fee is AUS$13, UK£5, or US$22.

YOUTH IDENTIFICATION. The International Student Travel Confederation also issues a discount card to travelers who are 25 years old or under, but are not students. This one-year **International Youth Travel Card** (**IYTC;** formerly the **GO 25** Card) offers many of the same benefits as the ISIC. Most organizations that sell the ISIC also sell the IYTC (US$22).

CUSTOMS

Upon entering Spain, Portugal, or Morocco, you must declare certain items from abroad and pay a duty on the value of those articles that exceeds the allowance established by the country's customs service. Note that goods and gifts purchased at **duty-free** shops abroad are not exempt from duty or sales tax at your point of return and thus must be declared as well; "duty-free" merely means that you need not pay a tax in the country of purchase. Duty-free allowances were abolished for travel between EU member states on July 1, 1999, but still exist for those arriving from outside the EU. Upon returning home, you must similarly declare all articles acquired abroad and pay a duty on the value of articles in excess of your home country's allowance. In order to expedite your return, make a list of any valuables brought from home and register them with customs before traveling abroad. Also be sure to keep receipts for all goods acquired abroad. Spain and Morocco both have value-added taxes which can be redeemed upon leaving the country. See the **Essentials** sections for **Spain** (see p. 55) and **Morocco** (see p. 668) for more info.

CUSTOMS IN THE EU. As well as freedom of movement of people within the EU (see p. 11), travelers can also take advantage of the freedom of movement of goods. This means that there are no customs controls at internal EU borders (i.e., you can take the blue customs channel at the airport), and travelers are free to transport whatever legal substances they like as long as it is for their own personal (non-commercial) use—up to 800 cigarettes, 10L of spirits, 90L of wine (60L of sparkling wine), and 110L of beer. You should also be aware that **duty-free** was abolished on June 30, 1999, for travel between EU member states; however, travelers between the EU and the rest of the world still get a duty-free allowance when passing through customs.

ESSENTIALS

FURTHER RESOURCES

Australia: Australian Customs National Information Line (in Australia ☎1 30 03 63, from elsewhere call 2 6275 6666; www.customs.gov.au).

Canada: Canadian Customs, 2265 St. Laurent Blvd., Ottawa, ON K1G 4K3 (☎800-461-9999 (24hr.) or 613-993-0534; www.revcan.ca).

Ireland: Customs Information Office, Irish Life Centre, Lower Abbey St., Dublin 1 (☎1 878 8811; fax 1 878 0836; www.revenue.ie/customs.htm).

New Zealand: New Zealand Customhouse, 17-21 Whitmore St., Box 2218, Wellington (☎4 473 6099; fax 4 473 7370; www.customs.govt.nz).

South Africa: Commissioner for Customs and Excise, Privat Bag X47, Pretoria 0001 (☎12 314 9911; fax 12 328 6478; www.gov.za).

United Kingdom: Her Majesty's Customs and Excise, Passenger Enquiry Team, Wayfarer House, Great South West Road, Feltham, Middlesex TW14 8NP (☎20 8910 3744; fax 20 8910 3933; www.hmce.gov.uk).

United States: US Customs Service, 1330 Pennsylvania Ave. NW, Washington, D.C. 20229 (☎202-354-1000; fax 202-354-1010; www.customs.gov).

MONEY

CURRENCY AND EXCHANGE

CURRENCY (£)

AUS$ = 99.2PTAS	SPANISH PTA= AUS$0.01
CDN$ = 126.0PTAS	SPANISH PTA= CDN$0.0079
IR£ = 211.3PTAS	SPANISH PTA= IR£0.0047
NZ$ = 79.0PTAS	SPANISH PTA= NZ$0.013
ZAR = 23.5PTAS	SPANISH PTA= ZAR0.043
US$ = 194.1PTAS	SPANISH PTA= US$0.0052
UK£ = 271.6PTAS	SPANISH PTA= UK£0.0037
EUR€ = 166.4PTAS	SPANISH PTA= EUR€0.0060

As a general rule, it's cheaper to convert money in Spain, Portugal, or Morocco than at home. However, you should bring enough foreign currency to last for the first 24 to 72 hours of a trip to avoid being penniless should you arrive after bank hours or on a holiday. Travelers from the US can get foreign currency from the comfort of home: **International Currency Express** (☎888-278-6628) delivers foreign currency or traveler's checks second-day (US$12) at competitive exchange rates.

When changing money abroad, try to go only to banks or change bureaus that have at most a 5% margin between their buy and sell prices. Since you lose money with every transaction, **convert large sums** (unless the currency is depreciating rapidly), **but no more than you'll need.**

THE EURO. Since 1999, the official currency of 11 members of the European Union—Austria, Belgium, Finland, France, Germany, Greece, Ireland, Italy, Luxembourg, the Netherlands, Portugal, and Spain—has been the **euro.** But you shouldn't throw out your francs, pesetas, and Deutschmarks just yet; actual euro banknotes and coins won't be available until January 1, 2002, and the old national currencies will remain legal tender for six months after that (through July 1, 2002).

While you might not be able to pay for a coffee and get your change in euros yet, the currency has some important—and positive—consequences for travelers hitting more than one euro-zone country. For one thing, money-changers across the euro-zone are obliged to exchange money at the official, fixed rate (see below), and at no commission (though they may still charge a small service fee). So now you can change your guilders into escudos and your escudos into lire without losing fistfuls of money on every transaction. Second, euro-denominated travelers cheques allow you to pay for goods and services across the euro-zone, again at the official rate and commission-free. The exchange rate between euro-zone currencies was permanently fixed on January 1, 1999 at 1 EUR = 40.3399 BEF (Belgian francs) = 1.95583 DEM (German marks) = 166.386 ESP (Spanish pesetas) = 6.55957 FRF (French francs) = 0.787564 IEP (Irish pounds) = 1936.27 ITL (Italian lire) = 200.482 PTE (Portuguese escudos). For more info, see www.europa.eu.int.

If you use traveler's checks or bills, carry some in small denominations (the equivalent of US$50 or less) for times when you are forced to exchange money at disadvantageous rates, but bring a range of denominations since charges may be levied per check cashed. Store your money in a variety of forms; ideally, you will at any given time be carrying some cash, some traveler's checks, and an ATM and/or credit card. All travelers should also consider carrying some US dollars (or French francs in Morocco, about US$50 worth), which are often preferred by local tellers. Throwing around dollars for preferential treatment may be offensive, especially in Morocco, and it can attract thieves. It may also mark you as a foreigner and invite locals to jack up prices.

See the individual **Essentials** sections for **Spain** (see p. 55), **Portugal** (see p. 526) and **Morocco** (see p. 668) for currency exchange charts including local currency and US dollars, Canadian dollars, British pounds, Irish pounds, Australian dollars, New Zealand dollars, South African Rand, and European Union Euros.

TRAVELER'S CHECKS

Traveler's checks (**American Express** and **Visa** are the most recognized) are one of the safest and least troublesome means of carrying funds. Several agencies and banks sell them for a small commission. Each agency provides refunds if your checks are lost or stolen, and many provide additional services, such as toll-free refund hotlines abroad, emergency message services, and stolen credit card assistance.

While traveling, keep check receipts and a record of which checks you've cashed separate from the checks themselves. Also leave a list of check numbers with someone at home. Never countersign checks until you're ready to cash them, and always bring your passport (or a copy) with you to cash them. If your checks are lost or stolen, immediately contact a refund center to be reimbursed; they may require a police report verifying the loss or theft. Ask about toll-free refund hotlines and the location of refund centers (there are more in Spain than in Portugal, or Morocco) when purchasing checks, and always carry emergency cash.

Money From Home In Minutes.

If you're stuck for cash on your travels, don't panic. Millions of people trust Western Union to transfer money in minutes to over 185 countries and over 95,000 locations worldwide. Our record of safety and reliability is second to none. You can even send money by phone without leaving home by using a credit card. For more information, call Western Union: USA 1-800-325-6000, Canada 1-800-235-0000.

www.westernunion.com

WESTERN UNION | MONEY TRANSFER

The fastest way to send money worldwide.

©2001 Western Union Holdings, Inc. All Rights Reserved.

American Express: Call 800 251 902 in Australia; in New Zealand ☎0800 441 068; in the UK ☎0800 521 313; in the US and Canada ☎800-221-7282. Elsewhere call US collect ☎801 964-6665; www.aexp.com. From Spain call toll-free ☎900 994-426; from Portugal toll-free ☎800 844-080; and from Morocco ☎441 273 35 71 00. Traveler's checks are available at no commission at AmEx offices, 2.5% at banks, and commission-free at AAA offices (see p. 28). *Cheques for Two* can be signed by either of 2 people traveling together.

Citicorp: In the US and Canada call ☎800-645-6556; from Spain call ☎900 97 44 30; from Portugal call ☎800 844 140; and from Morocco and anywhere else call US collect ☎813-623-1709. Traveler's checks available at 1-2% commission. Call 24hr.

Thomas Cook MasterCard: In the US and Canada call ☎800-223-7373; in the UK call ☎800 62 21 01; elsewhere call UK collect ☎1733 31 89 50. Checks available in 13 currencies at 2% commission. There are no Thomas Cook offices in Spain; banks accept their checks but will charge commission. In Portugal, Marcus & Harting will cash checks commission-free in Faro, Lisbon, and the Algarve. In Morocco, Credit de Maroc will cash commission-free.

Visa: In the US call ☎800-227-6811; in the UK call ☎800 89 50 78; elsewhere call UK collect ☎20 7937 8091. Call for the location of their nearest office.

ESSENTIALS

CREDIT CARDS

Where they are accepted, credit cards often offer superior exchange rates—up to 5% better than the retail rate used by banks and other currency exchange establishments. Credit cards may also offer services such as insurance or emergency help, and are sometimes required to reserve hotel rooms or rental cars. **MasterCard** and **Visa** are the most welcomed; **American Express** cards work at some ATMs and at AmEx offices and major airports.

Credit cards are also useful for **cash advances,** which allow you to instantly withdraw pesetas, escudos, or dirhams from associated banks and ATMs throughout the country you are traveling in. However, transaction fees for all credit card advances (up to US$10 per advance, plus 2-3% extra on foreign transactions after conversion) tend to make credit cards a more costly way of withdrawing cash than ATMs or traveler's checks. In an emergency, however, the transaction fee may prove worth the cost. To be eligible for an advance, you'll need to get a **Personal Identification Number (PIN)** from your credit card company (see **Cash (ATM) Cards,** below). Be sure to check with your credit card company before you leave home, though; some companies have started to charge a foreign transaction fee.

CREDIT CARD COMPANIES. Visa (US ☎800-336-8472) and **MasterCard** (US ☎800-307-7309) are issued in cooperation with banks and other organizations. **American Express** (US ☎800-843-2273) has an annual fee of up to US$55. AmEx cardholders may cash personal checks at AmEx offices abroad, access an emergency medical and legal assistance hotline (24hr.; in North America call ☎800-554-2639, elsewhere call US collect 202-554-2639), and enjoy American Express Travel Service benefits. The **Discover Card** (in US call ☎800-347-2683, elsewhere call US 801-902-3100) offers small cashback bonuses on most purchases. These services are convenient, but beware that AmEx and Discover are only accepted about 20-40% of the time in Spain and Portugal, and even less in Morocco.

CASH (ATM) CARDS

Cash cards—popularly called ATM cards—are widespread in Spain, Portugal, and Morocco. Depending on the system that your home bank uses, you can most likely access your personal bank account from abroad. ATMs get the same wholesale exchange rate as credit cards, but there is often a limit on the amount of money you can withdraw per day (around US$500), and unfortunately computer networks sometimes fail. There is also typically a surcharge of US$1-5 per withdrawal. Be sure to memorize your PIN code in numeric form since machines elsewhere often don't have letters on their keys. Also, if your PIN is longer than four digits, ask your bank whether you need a new number.

The two major international money networks are **Cirrus** (US ☎800-424-7787) and **PLUS** (US ☎800-843-7587). To locate ATMs around the world, call the above numbers, or consult www.visa.com/pd/atm or www.mastercard.com/atm.

Visa TravelMoney is a system allowing you to access money from any Visa ATM, widespread throughout Spain, Portugal, and Morocco. For local customer assistance in Spain, call ☎900-9-51125 and for Portugal, call ☎800-8-11-426. There is no number for local customer assistance in Morocco. You deposit an amount before you travel (plus a small administration fee), and you can withdraw up to that sum. In the US, call ☎877-394-3347 to activate a card; from Spain ☎900 95 11 25; from Portugal ☎0800 81 14 26, and from Morocco and anywhere else call collect ☎410 581-9091. **Road Cash** (US ☎877-762-3227; www.roadcash.com) issues cards in the US with a minimum US$300 deposit.

GETTING MONEY FROM HOME

AMERICAN EXPRESS. Cardholders can withdraw cash from their checking accounts at any of AmEx's major offices and many representative offices (up to US$1000 every 21 days; no service charge, no interest). AmEx "Express Cash" withdrawals from any ATM are automatically debited from the cardholder's checking account or line of credit. Green card holders may withdraw up to US$1000 in any seven-day period (2% transaction fee; minimum US$2.50, maximum US$20). To enroll in Express Cash, cardmembers may call ☎800-227-4669 in the US. Elsewhere call the US collect ☎336-668-5041 or call the following national numbers directly: in Spain, ☎900 99 44 26; in Portugal ☎800 84 40 80; and in Morocco ☎441 273 57 16 00.

WESTERN UNION. Travelers from the US, Canada, and the UK can wire money abroad through Western Union's international money transfer services. In the US, call ☎800-325-6000; in Canada, ☎800-235-0000; in the UK, ☎800 833 833. To wire money within the US using a credit card, call ☎800 CALL-CASH (225-5227). The rates for sending cash are generally US$10-11 cheaper than with a credit card, and the money is usually available at the place you're sending it to within an hour. To locate the nearest Western Union location, consult www.westernunion.com.

FEDERAL EXPRESS. Some people choose to send money abroad in cash via FedEx to avoid transmission fees and taxes. While FedEx is reasonably reliable, note that this method is illegal. In the US and Canada, FedEx can be reached by calling 800-463-3339; in the UK, 0800 12 38 00; in Ireland, 800 535 800; in Australia, 13 26 10; in New Zealand, 0800 733 339; and in South Africa, 011 923 8000.

US STATE DEPARTMENT (US CITIZENS ONLY). In dire emergencies only, the US State Department will forward money within hours to the nearest consular office, which will then disburse it according to instructions for a US$15 fee. Contact the Overseas Citizens Service, American Citizens Services, Consular Affairs, Room 4811, US Department of State, Washington, D.C. 20520 (☎202-647-5225; nights, Sundays, and holidays ☎647-4000; http://travel.state.gov).

COSTS

The cost of your trip will vary considerably, depending on where you go, how you travel, and where you stay. The single biggest cost of your trip will probably be your round-trip **airfare** to Spain, Portugal or Morocco. Before you go, spend some time calculating a reasonable per-day **budget** that will meet your needs. To give you a general idea, a bare-bones day (camping or sleeping in cheap hostels, buying food at supermarkets) in Spain would cost about US$35, in Portugal about US$25, and in Morocco about US$18. A slightly more comfortable day (sleeping in nicer hostels, eating one or two meals a day in restaurants, going out at night) would run US$50 in Spain, US$40 in Portugal, and US$30 in Morocco. Also, don't forget to factor in emergency reserve funds (at least US$200) when planning how much money you'll need.

STAYING ON BUDGET. Considering that saving just a few dollars a day over the course of your trip might pay for days or weeks of additional travel, the art of penny-pinching is well worth learning. Learn to take advantage of freebies: for example, **museums** will typically be free once a week or once a month, and cities often host free open-air concerts or **cultural events** (especially in the summer). Bring a sleepsack (see p. 24) to save on sheet charges in hostels, and do your **laundry** in the sink (unless you're explicitly prohibited from doing so). You can split **accommodations** costs (in hotels and some hostels) with trustworthy fellow travelers; multi-bed rooms almost always work out cheaper per person than singles. You can also buy food in **supermarkets** instead of eating out; you'd be surprised how tasty (and cheap) varied sandwiches can be.

TIPPING, BARGAINING AND TAXES

See the individual **Essentials** sections for **Spain** (see p. 55), **Portugal** (see p. 526), and **Morocco** (see p. 668) for specifics on tipping, bargaining and taxes in each country.

SAFETY AND SECURITY

PERSONAL SAFETY

The following section is intended as a general guide; refer to the **Essentials** sections of **Spain** (p.67), **Portugal** (p.539) and **Morocco** (p.662) for more detailed info.

EXPLORING. To avoid unwanted attention, try to blend in as much as possible. Respecting local customs (in many cases, dressing more conservatively) may placate would-be hecklers. Familiarize yourself with your surroundings before setting out, and carry yourself with confidence; if you must check a map on the street, duck into a shop. If you are traveling alone, be sure someone at home knows your itinerary, and **never admit that you're traveling alone.**

SELF DEFENSE. There is no sure-fire way to avoid all the threatening situations you might encounter when you travel, but a good self-defense course will give you ways to react to unwanted advances. **Impact, Prepare, and Model Mugging** can refer you to local self-defense courses in the US (☎800-345-5425) and Vancouver (☎604-878-3838). Workshops (2-3hr.) start at US$50; full courses run US$350-500.

TRANSPORTATION. If you are using a **car,** learn local driving signals and wear a seatbelt. Children under 40 lbs. should ride only in a specially designed carseat, available for a small fee from most car rental agencies. Study route maps before you hit the road, and if you plan on spending a lot of time on the road, you may want to bring spare parts. If your car breaks down, wait for the police to assist you. For long drives in desolate areas, invest in a cellular phone and a roadside assistance program (see p. 42). Be sure to park your vehicle in a garage or well-traveled area, and use a steering wheel locking device in larger cities. **Sleeping in your car** is one of the most dangerous (and often illegal) ways to get your rest. For info on the perils of **hitchhiking,** see p. 45.

FINANCIAL SECURITY

PROTECTING YOUR VALUABLES. Spain and parts of Portugal are quite heavily touristed; along with that naturally comes a thriving pickpocket trade. Morocco is notorious for the prevalence of theft, even from hostel rooms and other supposedly secure places. But there are a few steps you can take to minimize the financial risk associated with traveling. First, **bring as little with you as possible.** Leave expensive watches, jewelry, cameras, and electronic equipment (like your Discman) at home; chances are you'd break them, lose them, or get sick of lugging them around anyway. Second, buy a few combination **padlocks** to secure your belongings either in your pack—which you should **never leave unattended**—or in a hostel or train station locker. Third, **carry as little cash as possible;** instead carry traveler's checks and ATM

TRAVEL ADVISORIES. The following government offices provide travel information and advisories by telephone, by fax, or via the web:

Australian Department of Foreign Affairs and Trade: ☎2 6261 1111; www.dfat.gov.au.

Canadian Department of Foreign Affairs and International Trade (DFAIT): In Canada call ☎800-267-8316 in Canada, elsewhere call +1 613-944-4000; www.dfait-maeci.gc.ca. Call for their free booklet, *Bon Voyage...But.*

New Zealand Ministry of Foreign Affairs: ☎04 494 8500; fax 494 8506; www.mft.govt.nz/trav.html.

United Kingdom Foreign and Commonwealth Office: ☎020 7008 0232; fax 7008 0155; www.fco.gov.uk.

US Department of State: ☎202-647-5225, automatic faxback 202-647-3000; http://travel.state.gov. For *A Safe Trip Abroad,* call ☎202-512-1800.

or credit cards, keeping them in a money belt—not a "fanny pack"—along with your passport and ID cards. Fourth, **keep a small cash reserve separate from your primary stash.** This should be about US$50 (or the equivalent in French francs in Morocco) sewn into or stored in the depths of your pack, along with your traveler's check numbers and important photocopies. Be particularly careful on **buses** and **trains;** horror stories abound about determined thieves who wait for travelers to fall asleep. Carry your backpack in front of you where you can see it. Use good judgment in selecting a train compartment: never stay in an empty one, and use a lock to secure your pack to the luggage rack. Try to sleep on top bunks with your luggage stored above you (if not in bed with you), and keep important documents and other valuables on your person.

CON ARTISTS AND PICKPOCKETS. Among the more colorful aspects of large cities are **con artists.** They often work in groups, and children are among the most effective. They possess an innumerable range of ruses. Beware of certain classics: nice young men (or several) wanting to introduce themselves to the beautiful foreign lady, sob stories that require money, rolls of bills "found" on the street, or mustard spilled (or saliva spit) onto your shoulder to distract you while your bag is snatched. Don't ever hand over your passport to someone whose authority you question (ask to accompany them to a police station if they insist), and don't ever let your passport out of your sight. Similarly, don't let your bag out of sight; never trust a "station-porter" who insists on carrying your bag or storing it in the baggage compartment or a "new friend" who offers to guard your bag while you buy a train ticket or use the restroom. Beware of **pickpockets** in city crowds, especially on public transportation. Also, be alert in public telephone booths. If you must say your calling card number, do so very quietly; if you punch it in, make sure no one can look over your shoulder.

DRUGS AND ALCOHOL

Recreational drugs are illegal in Spain, Portugal, and Morocco. Possession of small amounts of marijuana sometimes goes unpunished in Spain and Portugal, but any attempt to buy or sell will definitely land you in jail or with a heavy fine. Morocco is infamous as a supplier of hashish to the Iberian Peninsula; don't be surprised if you are stopped and searched on your way into Spain. The Moroccan government enforces drug laws more strictly than most, and foreigners with drugs have regularly been arrested and faced severe punishment.

HEALTH

Common sense is the simplest prescription for good health while you travel. Travelers complain most often about their feet and their gut, so take precautionary measures: drink lots of fluids to prevent dehydration and constipation, wear sturdy, broken-in shoes and clean socks, and use talcum powder to keep your feet dry.

BEFORE YOU GO

Preparation can help minimize the likelihood of contracting a disease and maximize the chances of receiving effective health care in the event of an emergency. For tips on packing a basic **first-aid kit** and other health essentials, see p. 24. In your **passport,** write the names of any people you wish to be contacted in case of a medical emergency, and also list any allergies or medical conditions of which you would want doctors to be aware. If you know you are going to be taking medicine during your trip, take the time to find its foreign equivalent before leaving.

IMMUNIZATIONS AND PRECAUTIONS. Travelers over two years old should be sure that the following vaccines are up to date: MMR (for measles, mumps, and rubella); DTaP or Td (for diptheria, tetanus, and pertussis); OPV (for polio); HbCV (for haemophilus influenza B); and HBV (for Hepatitis B), although HBV is really only recommended for stays nearing six months. Adults traveling to Morocco on trips longer than four weeks should consider getting a Hepatitis A (or immune globulin) and typhoid vaccine four to six weeks before leaving. See the **Essentials** section for Morocco (p.539) for more specific information on staying healthy during a stay in North Africa. For recommendations on immunizations and prophylaxis, consult the CDC (see below) in the US or the equivalent in your home country, and be sure to check with a doctor for guidance.

USEFUL ORGANIZATIONS AND PUBLICATIONS. The US **Centers for Disease Control and Prevention (CDC;** ☎877-FYI-TRIP; www.cdc.gov/travel) maintains an international fax information service and an international travelers hotline (☎404-332-4559). The CDC's comprehensive booklet *Health Information for International Travel*, an annual rundown of disease, immunization, and general health advice, is free online or US$25 via the Public Health Foundation (☎877-252-1200). For quick information on health and other travel warnings, call the **Overseas Citizens Services** (☎202-647-5225; after-hours 202-647-4000), contact a passport agency or an embassy or consulate abroad. US citizens can send a self-addressed, stamped envelope to the Overseas Citizens Services, Bureau of Consular Affairs, #4811, US Department of State, Washington, D.C. 20520. For information on medical evacuation services and travel insurance firms, see the US government's website at http://travel.state.gov/medical.html or the **British Foreign and Commonwealth Office** (www.fco.gov.uk). For detailed information on travel health, including a country-by-country overview of diseases, try the **International Travel Health Guide,** Stuart Rose, MD (Travel Medicine, US$24.95; www.travmed.com). For general health info, contact the **American Red Cross** (☎800-564-1234).

MEDICAL ASSISTANCE ON THE ROAD. The following section offers general advice about medical help while traveling; see the **Essentials** sections for **Spain** (p. 55), **Portugal** (p. 526), and **Morocco** (p. 671) for more detailed info on each country.

Those with medical conditions (diabetes, allergies to antibiotics, epilepsy, heart conditions) may want to obtain a stainless-steel **Medic Alert** ID tag (first-year US$35, US$15 annually thereafter), which identifies the condition and gives a 24-hour collect-call number. Contact the Medic Alert Foundation, 2323 Colorado Ave, Turlock, CA 95382, USA (☎800-825-3785; www.medicalert.org).

ONCE ABROAD

ENVIRONMENTAL HAZARDS

Neither Spain, Portugal, nor Morocco has a very extreme climate; the biggest environmental threat for most travelers is the sun. Stay aware of how much time you're spending lying on Spanish beaches or sweating in Moroccan sand dunes.

Heat exhaustion and dehydration: Heat exhaustion, characterized by dehydration and salt deficiency, can lead to fatigue, headaches, and wooziness. Avoid it by drinking plenty of fluids, eating salty foods (e.g. crackers), and avoiding dehydrating beverages (e.g. alcohol, coffee, tea, and caffeinated soda). Continuous heat stress can eventually lead to heatstroke, characterized by a rising temperature, severe headache, and cessation of sweating. Victims should be cooled off with wet towels and taken to a doctor.

Sunburn: If you're prone to sunburn, bring sunscreen with you (it's often more expensive and hard to find when traveling), and apply it liberally and often to avoid burns and risk of skin cancer. If you plan on spending time near water, in the desert, or in the snow, you are at risk of getting burned. Apply sunscreen liberally. If you get sunburned, drink more fluids than usual and apply Calamine or an aloe-based lotion.

High altitude: Allow your body a couple of days to adjust to less oxygen before exerting yourself. Note that alcohol is more potent and UV rays are stronger at high elevations.

INSECT-BORNE DISEASES

Be aware of insects in wet or forested areas, especially while hiking and camping. **Mosquitoes** are most active from dusk to dawn. Wear long pants and long sleeves, tuck your pants into your socks, and buy a mosquito net. Use insect repellents, such as DEET, and soak or spray your gear with permethrin (licensed in the US for use on clothing). Consider natural repellents that make you smelly to insects, like vitamin B-12 or garlic pills. To stop the itch after being bitten, try Calamine lotion or topical cortisones (like Cortaid), or take a bath with a half-cup of baking soda or oatmeal. **Ticks**—responsible for Lyme and other diseases—can be particularly dangerous in forested regions (in parts of northern Spain, for instance). Pause periodically while walking to brush off ticks using a fine-toothed comb on your neck and scalp. Do not try to remove ticks by burning them or coating them with nail polish remover or petroleum jelly.

Malaria: Extremely limited risk, only in some rural parts of Morocco. Transmitted by *Anopheles* mosquitoes that bite at night. The incubation period varies from 6-8 days to as long as months. Early symptoms include fever, chills, aches, and fatigue, followed by high fever and sweating, sometimes with vomiting and diarrhea. See a doctor for any flu-like sickness that occurs after travel in a risk area. Left untreated, malaria can cause anemia, kidney failure, coma, and death. To reduce the risk of contracting malaria, use mosquito repellent, particularly in the evenings and when visiting forested areas, and take oral prophylactics, like **mefloquine** (sold under the name Lariam) or **doxycycline** (ask your doctor for a prescription).

Tick-borne encephalitis: A slight risk in the few forested areas of Spain and Portugal. A viral infection of the central nervous system transmitted during the summer by tick bites (primarily in wooded areas) or unpasteurized dairy products. While a vaccine is available in Europe, the immunization schedule is impractical, and the risk of contracting the disease is relatively low, especially if precautions are taken against tick bites.

Lyme disease: Also a slight risk in forested areas of Spain and Portugal. A bacterial infection carried by ticks and marked by a circular bull's-eye rash of 2 in. or more. Later symptoms include fever, headache, fatigue, and aches and pains. Antibiotics are effective if administered early. Left untreated, Lyme can cause problems in joints, the heart, and the nervous system. If you find a tick attached to your skin, grasp the head with tweezers as close to your skin as possible and apply slow, steady traction. Removing a tick within 24 hours greatly reduces the risk of infection.

FOOD- AND WATER-BORNE DISEASES

Prevention is the best cure: be sure that everything you eat is cooked properly and that the water you drink is clean. Peel your fruits and veggies and avoid tap water (including ice cubes and anything washed in tap water, like salad). Watch out for food from markets or street vendors that may have been cooked in unhygienic conditions. Other culprits are raw shellfish, unpasteurized milk, and sauces containing raw eggs. Buy bottled water, or purify your own water by bringing it to a rolling boil or treating it with **iodine tablets.**

Traveler's diarrhea: Results from drinking untreated water or eating uncooked foods; a temporary (and fairly common) reaction to the bacteria in new food ingredients. Symptoms include nausea, bloating, urgency, and malaise. Try quick-energy, non-sugary foods with protein and carbohydrates to keep your strength up. Over-the-counter anti-diarrheals (e.g. Imodium) may counteract the problems, but can complicate serious infections. The most dangerous side effect is dehydration; drink 8 oz. of water with ½ tsp. of sugar or honey and a pinch of salt, try uncaffeinated soft drinks, or munch on salted crackers. If you develop a fever or your symptoms don't go away after 4-5 days, consult a doctor promptly. Consult a doctor for treatment of diarrhea in children.

Dysentery: Results from a serious intestinal infection caused by certain bacteria. The most common type is bacillary dysentery, also called shigellosis. Symptoms include bloody diarrhea (sometimes mixed with mucus), fever, and abdominal pain and tenderness. Bacillary dysentery generally only lasts a week, but it is highly contagious. Amoebic dysentery, which develops more slowly, is a more serious disease and may cause long-term damage if left untreated. Seek medical help immediately for both. A stool test can determine which kind you have. Dysentery can be treated with the drugs norfloxacin or ciprofloxacin (commonly known as Cipro). If you are traveling in Morocco (especially rural regions) consider obtaining a prescription before you leave home.

Hepatitis A: A viral infection of the liver acquired primarily through contaminated water. Symptoms include fatigue, fever, loss of appetite, nausea, dark urine, jaundice, vomiting, aches and pains, and light stools. The risk is highest in rural areas and the countryside, especially in Morocco, but it is also present in urban areas. Ask your doctor about the vaccine (Havrix or Vaqta) or an injection of immune globulin (IG).

Parasites: Microbes, tapeworms, etc. that hide in unsafe water and food. **Giardiasis,** for example, is acquired by drinking untreated water from streams or lakes all over the world, including Spain, Portugal, and Morocco. Symptoms include swollen glands or lymph nodes, fever, rashes or itchiness, digestive problems, eye problems, and anemia. Boil water, wear shoes, avoid bugs, and eat only thoroughly cooked food.

Typhoid fever: Caused by the salmonella bacteria; common in villages and rural areas in Morocco. While mostly transmitted through contaminated food and water, it may also be acquired by direct contact with another person. Symptoms include fever, headaches, fatigue, loss of appetite, constipation, and a rash on the abdomen or chest. Antibiotics can treat typhoid, but a vaccination (70-90% effective) is usually recommended.

OTHER INFECTIOUS DISEASES

Rabies: Really only a risk for those who may be exposed to wild or domestic animals during their travel. Transmitted through the saliva of infected animals; fatal if untreated. By the time symptoms appear, thirst and muscle spasms, the disease is in its terminal stage. If you are bitten, wash the wound and seek immediate medical care. A rabies vaccine, which consists of 3 shots given over a 21-day period, is only semi-effective.

Hepatitis B: A viral infection of the liver transmitted via bodily fluids or needle-sharing. Symptoms may not surface until years after infection. Vaccinations are recommended for health-care workers, sexually-active travelers, and anyone planning to seek medical treatment abroad. The 3-shot vaccination series must begin 6 months before traveling.

Hepatitis C: Like Hep B, but the mode of transmission differs. IV drug users, those with occupational exposure to blood, hemodialysis patients, and recipients of blood transfusions are at the highest risk, but the disease can also be spread through sexual contact or sharing items like razors and toothbrushes that may have traces of blood on them.

AIDS, HIV, STDS

For detailed information on **Acquired Immune Deficiency Syndrome (AIDS)** in Spain, Portugal, and Morocco, call the **US Centers for Disease Control's** 24-hour hotline at ☎800-342-2437, or the **Joint United Nations Programme on HIV/AIDS (UNAIDS),** 20 av. Appia 20, CH-1211 Geneva 27, Switzerland (☎41 22 791 36 66, fax 791 41 87). Council's brochure, *Travel Safe: AIDS and International Travel,* is available at all Council Travel offices and on their website (www.ciee.org/Isp/safety/travelsafe.htm). Spain, Portugal, and Morocco may deny long-term residence to those who test HIV-positive, but they generally do not deny tourist, student and work visa applications on the basis of HIV status, even when medical tests are required (as they usually are to obtain a Spanish visa). Contact the nearest consulate.

Sexually transmitted diseases (STDs) such as gonorrhea, chlamydia, genital warts, syphilis, and herpes are easier to catch than HIV and can be just as deadly. **Hepatitis B** and **C** are also serious STDs (see **Other Infectious Diseases,** above). Though condoms may protect you from some STDs, oral or even tactile contact can lead to transmission. Warning signs include swelling, sores, bumps, or blisters on sex organs, the rectum, or the mouth; burning and pain during urination and bowel movements; itching around sex organs; swelling or redness of the throat; and flu-like symptoms. If these symptoms develop, see a doctor immediately.

WOMEN'S HEALTH

Women traveling in unsanitary conditions are vulnerable to **urinary tract** and **bladder infections,** common and very uncomfortable bacterial conditions that cause a burning sensation and painful (sometimes frequent) urination. To try to avoid these infections, drink plenty of vitamin-C-rich juice and clean water, and urinate frequently, especially right after intercourse. Untreated, these infections can lead to kidney infections, sterility, and even death. If symptoms persist, see a doctor.

Vaginal yeast infections may flare up in hot and humid climates. Wearing loosely fitting trousers or a skirt and cotton underwear will help, as will over-the-counter remedies like Monostat or Gynelotrimin. Bring supplies from home if you are prone to infection, as it may be embarrassing, if not difficult, to explain your predicament to a foreign druggist. Since **tampons, pads,** and reliable **contraceptive devices** are sometimes hard to find when traveling, consider bringing supplies with you.

Abortions are illegal in Spain, Portugal, and Morocco, but women considering an **abortion** while traveling can contact the **International Planned Parenthood Federation (IPPF),** Regent's College, Inner Circle, Regent's Park, London NW1 4NS (☎020 7487 7900; fax 7487 7950; www.ippf.org), for guidance. In the US and Canada, the National Abortion Federation Hotline, (US ☎800-772-9100, Canada ☎800-424-2280; M-F 9am-7pm) provides referrals.

INSURANCE

Travel insurance generally covers four basic areas: medical or health problems, property loss, trip cancellation or interruption, and emergency evacuation. Prices for travel insurance purchased separately generally run about US$50 per week for full coverage; trip cancellation or interruption may be purchased separately at a rate of about US$5.50 per US$100 of coverage.

Medical insurance (especially university policies) often covers costs incurred abroad; check with your provider. **US Medicare** does not cover foreign travel. **Canadians** are protected by their home province's health insurance plan for up to 90 days after leaving the country; check with the provincial Ministry of Health or Health Plan Headquarters for details. **Homeowners' insurance** (or your family's coverage) often covers theft during travel and loss of travel documents (passport, plane ticket, railpass, etc.) up to US$500.

ISIC and **ITIC** (see p. 12) provide basic insurance benefits, including US$100 per day of in-hospital sickness for up to 60 days, US$3000 of accident-related medical reimbursement, and US$25,000 for emergency medical transport. Cardholders have access to a toll-free 24-hour helpline for medical, legal, and financial emergencies overseas (US and Canada ☎800-626-2427, elsewhere call US collect ☎713-267-2525). **American Express** (US ☎800-528-4800) grants most cardholders automatic car rental insurance (collision and theft, but not liability) and ground travel accident coverage of US$100,000 on flight purchases made with the card.

INSURANCE PROVIDERS. Council and **STA** (see p. 32) offer a range of plans that can supplement your basic coverage. Other private insurance providers in the **US and Canada** include: **Access America** (☎800-284-8300); **Berkely Group/Carefree Travel**

Insurance (☎800-323-3149; www.berkely.com); **Globalcare Travel Insurance** (☎800-821-2488; www.globalcare-cocco.com); and **Travel Assistance International** (☎800-821-2828; www.worldwide-assistance.com). Providers in the **UK** include **Campus Travel** (☎018 6525 8000) and **Columbus Travel Insurance** (☎020 7375 0011). In **Australia,** try **CIC Insurance** (☎9202 8000).

PACKING

Pack lightly: lay out only what you absolutely need, then take half the clothes and twice the money. If you plan to do a lot of hiking, also see **Outdoors,** p. 27. If you plan to cover most of your itinerary by foot, a sturdy **frame backpack** is unbeatable. (For the basics on buying a pack, see p. 27.) Toting a **suitcase** or **trunk** is fine if you plan to live in one or two cities and explore from there, but a very bad idea if you're going to be moving around a lot. In addition to your main piece of luggage, a **day-pack** (a small backpack or courier bag) is a must.

CLOTHING. No matter when you're traveling, it's a good idea to bring a warm jacket or wool sweater, a rain jacket (Gore-Tex® is both waterproof and breathable), sturdy shoes or hiking boots, and thick socks. Flip-flops or waterproof sandals are crucial for hostel showers. You may also want a nicer outfit than your jeans and t-shirt. Bringing light clothing is a wise idea since temperatures soar.

SLEEPSACK. Some hostels require that you either provide your own linen or rent sheets from them. Save cash by making your own sleepsack: fold a full-size sheet in half the long way, then sew it closed along the long side and one short sides.

CONVERTERS AND ADAPTERS. In Spain and Portugal, electricity is 220 volts AC; most of Morocco runs on 220V as well, though some smaller towns still have 110V outlets. **Americans** and **Canadians** should buy an **adapter** (which changes the shape of the plug) and a **converter** (which changes the voltage; US$20). **New Zealanders** and **South Africans** (who both use 220V at home) as well as **Australians** (who use 240/250V) won't need a converter, but will need a set of adapters.

TOILETRIES. Toothbrushes, towels, cold-water soap, deodorant, razors, tampons, and condoms are often available, but may be difficult to find, so bring extras along. **Contact lenses** may be expensive and difficult to find, so bring enough extra pairs and solution for your entire trip. Also bring your glasses and a copy of your prescription in case you need emergency replacements.

FIRST-AID KIT. For a basic first-aid kit, pack bandages, aspirin or other painkillers, antibiotic cream, a thermometer, a Swiss Army knife, tweezers, moleskin, decongestant, motion-sickness remedy, diarrhea or upset-stomach medication (Pepto Bismol or Imodium), an antihistamine (like Benadryl), sunscreen, insect repellent, and burn ointment.

FILM. Film and developing in Spain, Portugal, and Morocco can get expensive, so consider bringing along enough film for your entire trip and developing it at home. Despite disclaimers, airport security X-rays *can* fog film, so buy a lead-lined pouch at a camera store or ask security to hand inspect it. Always pack it in your carry-on luggage, since higher-intensity X-rays are used on checked luggage.

OTHER USEFUL ITEMS. For safety purposes, you should bring a **money belt** and small **padlock.** Quick repairs of torn garments can be done on the road with a needle and thread; also consider bringing electrical tape for patching tears. Doing your **laundry** by hand (where it is allowed) is both cheaper and more convenient than doing it at a laundromat. **Other things** you might forget: an umbrella; sealable **plastic bags** (for damp or dirty clothes, soap, food, shampoo, and other spillables); an **alarm clock;** safety pins; rubber bands; a flashlight; earplugs; and a small **calculator.**

ACCOMMODATIONS

For more specific information on accommodations, see the **Essentials** sections for **Spain** (p. 73), **Portugal** (p. 537), and **Morocco** (p. 671).

HOSTELS

Hostels are generally dorm-style accommodations, often in single-sex large rooms with bunk beds, although some hostels do offer private rooms for families and couples. They sometimes have kitchens and utensils for your use, bike or moped rentals, storage areas, and laundry facilities. There can be drawbacks: some hostels close during certain daytime "lockout" hours, have a curfew, don't accept reservations, and impose a maximum stay. See the **Essentials** sections for each country for more country-specific information on accommodations.

HOSTELLING INTERNATIONAL

Joining the youth hostel association in your own country (listed below) automatically grants you membership privileges in **Hostelling International (HI),** a federation of national hosteling associations, which offer accommodations at significantly cheaper prices than private lodgings. HI hostels are scattered throughout Spain and Portugal (though not Morocco) and many accept reservations via the **International Booking Network** (Australia ☎2 9261 1111; Canada ☎800-663-5777; England and Wales ☎1629 58 14 18; Northern Ireland ☎1232 32 47 33; Republic of Ireland ☎1 830 1766; New Zealand ☎9 379 4224; Scotland ☎541 55 32 55; US ☎800-909-4776). HI's umbrella organization's web page (www.iyhf.org). Other comprehensive websites include www.hostels.com and www.hostelplanet.com. All prices listed below are valid for **one-year memberships** unless otherwise noted.

Australian Youth Hostels Association (AYHA), 422 Kent St., Sydney NSW 2000 (☎2 9261 1111; fax 2 9261 1969; www.yha.org.au). AUS$49, under 18 AUS$14.50.

Hostelling International-Canada (HI-C), 400-205 Catherine St., Ottawa, ON K2P 1C3 (☎800-663-5777 or 613 237-7884; fax 613 237-7868; www.hostellingintl.ca). CDN$25, under 18 CDN$12.

An Óige (Irish Youth Hostel Association), 61 Mountjoy St., Dublin 7 (☎1 830 4555; fax 1 830 5808; www.irelandyha.org). IR£10, under 18 IR£4.

Youth Hostels Association of New Zealand (YHANZ), P.O. Box 436, 173 Cashel St., Christchurch 1 (☎3 379 9970; fax 3 365 4476; www.yha.org.nz). NZ$40, ages 15-17 NZ$12, under 15 free.

Hostels Association of South Africa, 3rd fl. 73 St. George's St. Mall, P.O. Box 4402, Cape Town 8000 (☎21 424 2511; fax 21 424 4119; www.hisa.org.za). SAR50, under 18 SAR25, lifetime SAR250.

Scottish Youth Hostels Association (SYHA), 7 Glebe Crescent, Stirling FK8 2JA (☎1786 89 14 00; fax 1786 89 13 33; www.syha.org.uk). UK£6, under 18 UK£2.50.

Youth Hostels Association (England and Wales) Ltd., Trevelyan House, 8 St. Stephen's Hill, St. Albans, Hertfordshire AL1 2DY, UK (☎1727 85 52 15; fax 1727 84 41 26; www.yha.org.uk). UK£12, under 18 UK£6, families UK£24.

Hostelling International Northern Ireland (HINI), 22-32 Donegall Rd., Belfast BT12 5JN, Northern Ireland (☎1232 32 47 33; fax 1232 43 96 99; www.hini.org.uk). UK£7, under 18 UK£3.

Hostelling International-American Youth Hostels (HI-AYH), 733 15th St. NW, #840, Washington, D.C. 20005 (☎202-783-6161 ext. 136; fax 202-783-6171; www.hiayh.org). US$25, under 18 free.

HOTELS, GUESTHOUSES, AND PENSIONS

Hotel singles in Spain cost about US$20 per night, doubles US$35-40. In Portugal rates run US$20-30. You'll typically share a hall bathroom; a private bathroom will cost extra, as may hot showers. Smaller **guesthouses** and **pensions** are often cheaper than hotels. If you make **reservations** in writing, indicate your night of arrival and the number of nights you plan to stay. The hotel will send you a confirmation and may request payment for the first night.

UNIVERSITY DORMS

Many **colleges and universities** open their residence halls to travelers when school is not in session; some do so even during term-time. These dorms are often close to student areas—good sources for information on things to do—and are usually very clean. See listings within individual towns.

HOME EXCHANGES & HOME RENTALS

Home exchange offers the traveler various types of homes (houses, apartments, condominiums, villas, even castles in some cases), plus the opportunity to live like a native and to cut down on accommodation fees. For more information, contact **HomeExchange.Com** (☎800-898-9660; www.homeexchange.com), **Intervac International Home Exchange** (in Spain ☎93 453 31 71; www.intervac.com), or **The Invented City: International Home Exchange** (US ☎800-788-CITY, elsewhere US ☎415-252-1141; www.invented-city.com). **Home rentals** are more expensive than exchanges, but they can be cheaper than comparably-serviced hotels.

CAMPING & THE OUTDOORS

For more specific information on camping, see the **Essentials** sections of **Spain** (p. 73), **Portugal** (p. 538), and **Morocco** (p. 672). An excellent general resource for travelers planning on camping or spending time in the outdoors is the **Great Outdoor Recreation Pages** (www.gorp.com).

USEFUL PUBLICATIONS & RESOURCES

A variety of publishing companies offer hiking guidebooks to meet the educational needs of novice or expert. For information about camping, hiking, and biking, write or call the publishers listed below to receive a free catalog. Campers heading to Spain and Portugal should consider buying an **International Camping Carnet.** Similar to a hostel membership card, it's required at a few campgrounds and provides discounts at others. It is available in North America from the **Family Campers and RVers Association** and in the UK from **The Caravan Club** (see below).

Automobile Association, A.A. Publishing. Orders and enquiries to TBS Frating Distribution Centre, Colchester, Essex, CO7 7DW, UK (☎01206 25 56 78; www.theaa.co.uk). Publishes *Camping and Caravanning: Europe* (UK£9) and *Britain & Ireland* (UK£8) as well as Big Road Atlases for Europe, France, Spain, Germany, and Italy.

The Caravan Club, East Grinstead House, East Grinstead, West Sussex, RH19 1UA, UK (☎01342 32 69 44; www.caravanclub.co.uk). For UK£27.50, members receive equipment discounts, a 700pp directory and handbook, and a monthly magazine.

Sierra Club Books, 85 Second St., 2nd fl., San Francisco, CA 94105, USA (☎415-977-5500; www.sierraclub.org/books).

The Mountaineers Books, 1001 SW Klickitat Way, #201, Seattle, WA 98134, USA (☎800-553-4453 or 206-223-6303; www.mountaineersbooks.org). Over 400 titles on hiking, biking, mountaineering, natural history, and conservation.

WILDERNESS SAFETY

THE GREAT OUTDOORS. Stay warm, stay dry, and stay hydrated. The vast majority of life-threatening wilderness situations can be avoided by following this simple advice. Prepare yourself for an emergency, however, by always packing raingear, a hat and mittens, a first-aid kit, a reflector, a whistle, high energy food, and extra water for any hike. Dress in wool or warm layers of synthetic materials designed for the outdoors; never rely on cotton for warmth, as it is useless when wet.

Check **weather forecasts** and pay attention to the skies when hiking, since weather patterns can change suddenly. Whenever possible, let someone know when and where you are going hiking, either a friend, your hostel, a park ranger, or a local hiking organization. Do not attempt a hike beyond your ability—you may be endangering your life. See **Health**, p. 19, for information about outdoor ailments and basic medical concerns.

CAMPING AND HIKING EQUIPMENT

Good camping equipment is both sturdy and light. Camping equipment is generally more expensive in Australia, New Zealand, and the UK than in North America.

Sleeping Bag: Most sleeping bags are rated by season ("summer" means 30-40°F at night; "four-season" or "winter" often means below 0°F). Sleeping bags are made either of **down** (warmer and lighter, but more expensive, and miserable when wet) or of **synthetic** material (heavier, more durable, and warmer when wet). Prices may range from US$80-210 for a summer synthetic to US$250-300 for a good down winter bag. **Sleeping bag pads** include foam pads (US$10-20), air mattresses (US$15-50), and Therm-A-Rest self-inflating pads (US$45-80). Bring a **stuff sack** to store your bag.

Tent: The best tents are free-standing (with their own frames and suspension systems), set up quickly, and only require staking in high winds. Low-profile dome tents are the best all-around. Good 2-person tents start at US$90, 4-person at US$300. Seal the seams of your tent with waterproofer, and make sure it has a rain fly. Other tent accessories include a **battery-operated lantern,** a **plastic groundcloth,** and a **nylon tarp.**

Backpack: Internal-frame packs mold better to your back, keep a lower center of gravity, and flex adequately to allow you to hike difficult trails. **External-frame packs** are more comfortable for long hikes over even terrain, as they keep weight higher and distribute it more evenly. Make sure your pack has a strong, padded hip-belt to transfer weight to your legs. Any serious backpacking requires a pack of at least 4000 cu. in. (16,000cc), plus 500 cu. in. for sleeping bags in internal-frame packs. Sturdy backpacks cost anywhere from US$125-420—this is one area in which it doesn't pay to economize. Either buy a **waterproof backpack cover,** or store all of your belongings in plastic bags inside your pack.

Boots: Be sure to wear hiking boots with good **ankle support.** They should fit snugly and comfortably over 1-2 pairs of wool socks and thin liner socks. Break in boots over several weeks first in order to spare yourself from painful and debilitating blisters.

Other Necessities: Synthetic layers, like those made of polypropylene, and a **pile jacket** will keep you warm even when wet. A **"space blanket"** will help you retain your body heat and doubles as a groundcloth (US$5-15). Plastic **water bottles** are virtually shatter- and leak-proof. Bring **water-purification tablets** for when you can't boil water. Although most campgrounds provide campfire sites, you may want to bring a small **metal grate** or **grill** of your own. For those places that forbid fires or the gathering of firewood (this includes virtually every organized campground in Europe), you'll need a **camp stove** (the classic Coleman starts at US$40) and a propane-filled **fuel bottle** to operate it. Also don't forget a **first-aid kit, pocketknife, insect repellent, calamine lotion,** and **waterproof matches** or a **lighter.**

...AND WHERE TO BUY IT

The mail-order/online companies listed below offer lower prices than many retail stores, but a visit to a local camping or outdoors store will give you a good sense of the look and weight of certain items.

Campmor, 28 Parkway, P.O. Box 700, Upper Saddle River, NJ 07458 (US ☎888-226-7667; elsewhere US ☎+1 201-825-8300; www.campmor.com).

Discount Camping, 880 Main North Rd., Pooraka, South Australia 5095, Australia (☎08 8262 3399; www.discountcamping.com.au).

Eastern Mountain Sports (EMS), 327 Jaffrey Rd., Peterborough, NH 03458, USA (☎888-463-6367 or 603-924-7231; www.shopems.com)

L.L. Bean, Freeport, ME 04033 (US and Canada ☎800-441-5713; UK ☎0800 891 297; elsewhere, call US ☎+1 207-552-3028; www.llbean.com).

Mountain Designs, P.O. Box 1472, Fortitude Valley, Queensland 4006, Australia (☎07 3252 8894; www.mountaindesign.com.au).

Recreational Equipment, Inc. (REI), Sumner, WA 98352, USA (☎800-426-4840 or 253-891-2500; www.rei.com).

YHA Adventure Shop, 14 Southampton St., London, WC2E 7HA, UK (☎020 7836 8541). The main branch of one of Britain's largest outdoor equipment suppliers.

KEEPING IN TOUCH

BY MAIL

SENDING MAIL HOME FROM ABROAD

See the individual **Essentials** sections for **Spain** (see p. 55), **Portugal** (see p. 526), and **Morocco** (see p. 668) for more detailed information about mailing from abroad. Sending airmail to Spain from the US requires between four and seven days. To Portugal, allow seven to 10 days. Airmail to Morocco usually requires around two weeks, but it could either go more quickly or much more slowly. Mailing from European locations to any of these countries is a few days faster; from Australia, New Zealand, or South Africa, a couple of days slower. Mail sent to smaller towns will take longer. Envelopes should be marked "air mail" or "par avion." There are several ways to arrange pick-up of letters sent to you while you are abroad.

Mail can be sent internationally through *Lista de Correos* in Spain, *Posta Restante* in Portugal, or *Poste Restante* in Morocco. The mail will go to a special desk in the central post office, unless you specify a post office by street address or postal code. As a rule, it is best to use the largest post office in the area, and mail may be sent there regardless of what is written on the envelope. It is usually safer and quicker to send mail express or registered. When picking up your mail, bring a form of photo ID, preferably a passport. There is generally no surcharge; if there is a charge, it should not exceed the cost of postage. If the clerks insist there is nothing for you, have them check under your first name as well. Mark the envelope "HOLD" and address it with the last name capitalized and underlined, as follows:

Spain: MARTINEZ, Román; Lista de Correos; City Name; Postal Code; SPAIN; PAR AVION.

Portugal: CALDERON, Teresita; Posta Restante; Post Office Street Address; City Name; Postal Code; PORTUGAL; PAR AVION.

Morocco: Moroccan post offices often misplace or automatically return held mail. If you want to try, mail should be addressed as follows: VELEZ, Andrés.; Poste Restante; Post Office Address; City Name; MOROCCO; PAR AVION.

AMERICAN EXPRESS. AmEx's travel offices throughout Iberia will act as a mail service for cardholders if you contact them in advance. Under this free **Client Letter Service,** they will hold mail for up to 30 days and forward upon request. Address the letter in the same way shown above. Some offices will offer these services to non-cardholders (especially those who have purchased AmEx Travelers Cheques), but you must call ahead to make sure. *Let's Go* lists AmEx office locations for most large cities. AmEx also has a free complete list (☎ 800-528-4800).

OTHER OPTIONS. If regular airmail is too slow, **Federal Express** (US ☎800-247-4747, Spain ☎900 10 08 71, Portugal ☎0800 24 41 44, Morocco ☎212 254 21 33, www.fedex.com) can get a letter from New York to Madrid in two days for a whopping US$50; rates among non-US locations are similarly expensive (London to Madrid, for example, costs upwards of US$35). For a cheaper alternative, try **DHL** (US ☎800-225-5345, Spain 902 12 24 24, Portugal 0218 10 00 99, Morocco 212 297 20 20), which can get a document from New York to Madrid in one to two days for US$39. By **US Express Mail,** a letter from New York would arrive within four days and would cost US$17.

Surface mail is by far the cheapest and slowest way to send mail. It takes one to three months to cross the Atlantic and two to four to cross the Pacific—appropriate for sending large quantities of items you won't need to see for a while. When ordering books and materials from abroad, always include one or two **International Reply Coupons (IRCs)**—a way of providing the postage to cover delivery. IRCs should be available from your local post office and those abroad (US$1.75).

BY TELEPHONE

CALLING FROM SPAIN, PORTUGAL, OR MOROCCO

For more country-specific information about telephones abroad, see the **Essentials** sections of **Spain** (p. 69), **Portugal** (p. 535), or **Morocco** (p. 668). Most useful communication information (including **international access codes, calling card numbers, country codes, operator** and **directory assistance,** and **emergency numbers**) is also listed on the inside back cover of this book.

Wherever possible, use a **calling card** (see below) for international phone calls, as the long-distance rates for national phone services are often exorbitant. You can usually make direct international calls from pay phones, but if you aren't using a calling card you may need to drop your coins as quickly as your words. Where available, prepaid phone cards and occasionally major credit cards can be used for direct international calls, but they are still less cost-efficient. Look for pay phones in public areas, especially train stations, as private pay phones are often more expensive. Although incredibly convenient, in-room hotel calls invariably include an arbitrary and sky-high surcharge (as much as US$10).

The expensive alternative to dialing direct is using an international operator to place a **collect call.** An English-speaking operator from your home nation can be reached by dialing the appropriate service provider listed above; they will usually typically place a collect call even if you don't have one of their phone cards.

CALLING SPAIN, PORTUGAL, AND MOROCCO FROM HOME

Let's Go lists the city **telephone code** under **Practical Information** in Portugal, and Morocco. Spain no longer has city or area codes. The bracketed 0 for Morocco codes is necessary only if you are calling from a different area code within the same country. If you are calling from another country, you will not need to dial the parenthesized number. For example, we have listed the telephone code for Asilah as (0)9. To reach Asilah from elsewhere in Morocco, dial 01, then the number. To reach Asilah from another country, dial 1, then the number. **Portugal has recently changed access to its telephone system** by adding a 2 to all previous city codes. See the **Essentials** section for **Portugal** (see p. 538) for more information on the change. **To place a direct international call,** dial:

1. The international access code of your home country. **International access codes** include: Australia 0011; Ireland 00; New Zealand 00; South Africa 09; UK 00; US 011. Country and city codes are sometimes listed with a zero in front (e.g., 033), but after dialing the international access code, drop successive zeros (e.g., with an access code of 011, dial 011 33).
2. The **country code:** Spain 034, Portugal 351, Morocco 212.
3. For Portugal or Morocco, the city code (see the city's **Practical Information** section).
4. The local number.

ESSENTIALS

CALLING HOME FROM SPAIN, PORTUGAL, AND MOROCCO

For more country-specific information about telephones abroad, see the **Essentials** sections of **Spain** (p. 74), **Portugal** (p. 538), or **Morocco** (p. 672). Most useful communication information (including **international access codes, calling card numbers, country codes, operator** and **directory assistance,** and **emergency numbers**) is also listed on the inside back cover of this book.

Wherever possible, use a **calling card** (see below) for international phone calls, as the long-distance rates for national phone services are often exorbitant. You can usually make direct international calls from pay phones, but if you aren't using a calling card you may need to drop your coins as quickly as your words. Where available, prepaid phone cards and occasionally major credit cards can be used for direct international calls, but they are still less cost-efficient. Look for pay phones in public areas, especially train stations, as private pay phones are often more expensive. Although incredibly convenient, in-room hotel calls invariably include an arbitrary and sky-high surcharge (as much as US$10).

The expensive alternative to dialing direct or using a calling card is using an international operator to place a **collect call.** An English-speaking operator from your home nation can be reached by dialing the appropriate service provider.

CALLING CARDS

Setting up a calling card account is probably your best and cheapest bet for making calls from overseas. **MCI WorldPhone** also provides access to MCI's Traveler's Assist, which gives legal and medical advice, exchange rate information, and translation services. Other phone companies provide similar services to travelers. **To obtain a calling card** from your national telecommunications service before you leave home, contact the appropriate company below.

Australia: Telstra Australia **Telstra Direct** (☎13 22 00).

Canada: Bell Canada **Canada Direct** (☎800-668-6878).

Ireland: Telecom Éireann **Ireland Direct** (☎800 40 00 00).

New Zealand: Telecom New Zealand (☎0800 00 00 00).

South Africa: Telkom South Africa (☎10 219).

UK: British Telecom **BT Direct** (☎800 34 51 44).

US: AT&T (☎888-288-4685), **Sprint** (☎800-877-4646), or **MCI** (☎800-444-3333).

PLACING INTERNATIONAL CALLS. To call Iberia or Morocco from home or to place an international call from abroad, dial:

1. The **international dialing prefix.** To dial out of **Australia,** dial 0011; **Canada** or the **US,** 011; the **Republic of Ireland, New Zealand, Morocco, Portugal, Spain** or the **UK,** 00; **South Africa,** 09.

2. The **country code** of the country you want to call. To call **Australia,** dial 61; **Canada** or the **US,** 1; **Morocco,** 212; **Portugal,** 351; the **Republic of Ireland,** 353; **New Zealand,** 64; **South Africa,** 27; **Spain,** 34; the **UK,** 44.

3. The **city** or **area code.** *Let's Go* lists the phone codes for cities and towns in Portugal and Morocco opposite the city or town name, alongside the following icon: ☎. If the first digit is a zero (e.g., 09 for Tangier), omit it when calling from abroad (e.g., dial 011 212 9 from Canada to reach Tangier).

4. The **local number.**

CALLING WITHIN SPAIN, PORTUGAL, AND MOROCCO

The simplest way to call within the country is to use a coin-operated phone. **Prepaid phone cards** (available at tobacco stores and newspaper kiosks), which carry a certain amount of phone time depending on the card's denomination, usually save time and money in the long run–in fact, some phones only accept cards. The computerized phone will tell you how much time, in units, you have left on your card. Another kind of prepaid telephone card comes with a Personal Identification

Number (PIN) and a toll-free access number. Instead of inserting the card into the phone, you call the access number. These cards can be used to make international as well as domestic calls. Phone rates tend to be highest in the morning, lower in the evening, and lowest on Sunday and late at night.

TIME DIFFERENCES

Greenwich Mean Time (GMT) is five hours ahead of New York time, eight hours ahead of Vancouver and San Francisco time, two hours behind Johannesburg time, ten hours behind Sydney time, and twelve hours behind Auckland time. Some countries ignore **daylight savings time,** and fall and spring switchover times vary.

Spain is two hours ahead of GMT in the summer during daylight savings time, and one hour ahead during the winter. Portugal keeps daylight savings time as well, and is one hour behind Spain year round (one hour ahead of GMT in summer and at GMT in winter). Morocco does not change time; they are always on GMT.

EMAIL AND INTERNET

Email is an attractive communication option and increasingly easy to access in Spain, Portugal, and, less so, Morocco. Though in some places it's possible to forge a remote link with your home server, in most cases this is a much slower (and thus more expensive) option than taking advantage of free **web-based email accounts** (e.g. www.hotmail.com and www.yahoo.com). Travelers with laptops can call an Internet service provider via a **modem.** Long-distance phone cards specifically intended for such calls can defray normally high phone charges; check with your long-distance phone provider to see if it offers this option. **Internet cafés** and the occasional free Internet terminal at a public library or university are listed in the **Orientation and Practical Information** sections of major cities.

GETTING THERE

For country-specific information on traveling, travel organizations, and travel discounts within Spain, Portugal, and Morocco, see the **Getting There and Around** sections for **Spain, Portugal,** and **Morocco.** Much of the following general information refers to planning your trip to and from these countries and for European travel.

Fares on all modes of transportation are either "single" (one-way) or "return" (round-trip). "Period returns" require you to return within a specific number of days; "day return" means you must return on the same day. Unless stated otherwise, *Let's Go* always lists single fares. Round-trip fares on trains and buses are generally 75% above the one-way fares.

BY PLANE

When it comes to airfare, a little effort can save you a bundle. If your plans are flexible enough to deal with the restrictions, courier fares are the cheapest. Tickets bought from consolidators and standby seating are also good deals, but last-minute specials, airfare wars, and charter flights often beat these fares. The key is to hunt around, to be flexible, and to ask persistently about discounts. Students, seniors, and those under 26 should never pay full price for a ticket.

AIRFARES

Airfares to Spain, Portugal and Morocco peak between mid-June and early September; holidays are also expensive. The cheapest times to travel are December and January. Midweek (M-Th morning) round-trip flights run US$40-50 cheaper than weekend flights, but they are generally more crowded and less likely to permit frequent-flier upgrades. Traveling with an "open return" ticket can be pricier than fixing a return date when buying the ticket. Round-trip flights are by far the cheapest; "open-jaw" (arriving in and departing from different cities, e.g. New

York-Madrid and Paris-New York) tickets tend to be pricier. Patching one-way flights together is an expensive way to travel. Flights between capitals or regional hubs—Madrid, Barcelona, Lisbon, Rabat and Casablanca—tends to be cheaper.

If Spain, Portugal and Morocco is only one stop on a more extensive globe-hop, consider a **round-the-world** (RTW) ticket. Tickets usually include at least 5 stops and are valid for about a year; prices range US$1200-5000. Try **Northwest Airlines/KLM** (US ☎800-447-4747; www.nwa.com) or **Star Alliance,** a consortium of 22 airlines including United Airlines (US ☎800-241-6522; www.star-alliance.com).

Fares for roundtrip flights to Madrid from the US or Canadian east coast cost US$500-700, US$400-600 in the off season; from the US or Canadian west coast US$800-1100/US$550-800; from the UK, UK£175-250/UK£130-225; from Australia, AUS$2000-2500/AUS$1700-2100.

BUDGET AND STUDENT TRAVEL AGENCIES

While knowledgeable agents specializing in flights to Spain, Portugal, and Morocco can make your life easy and help you save, they may not spend the time to find you the lowest possible fare—they get paid on commission. Students and under-26ers holding **ISIC and IYTC cards** (see p. 12), respectively, qualify for big discounts from student travel agencies.

usitWorld (www.usitworld.com). Over 50 **usit campus** branches in the UK (www.usitcampus.co.uk), including 52 Grosvenor Gardens, **London** SW1W 0AG (☎0870 240 1010); **Manchester** (☎0161 273 1880); and **Edinburgh** (☎0131 668 2221). Nearly 20 **usit now** offices in Ireland, including 19-21 Aston Quay, O'Connell Bridge, **Dublin** 2 (☎01 602 16 00; www.usitnow.ie), and **Belfast** (☎028 90 327 111; www.usitnow.com). Affiliated offices are also in both Spain and Portugal, including Plaza Callao 3, **Madrid** (☎902 25 25 75) and Rua Camilo Castelo Branco, 20, **Lisbon** (☎21 316 60 00). Other offices in Athens, Auckland, Brussels, Frankfurt, Johannesburg, Luxembourg, Paris, Sofia, and Warsaw.

Council Travel (www.counciltravel.com). US offices include: Emory Village, 1561 N. Decatur Rd., **Atlanta,** GA 30307 (☎404-377-9997); 273 Newbury St., **Boston,** MA 02116 (☎617-266-1926); 1160 N. State St., **Chicago,** IL 60610 (☎312-951-0585); 931 Westwood Blvd., Westwood, **Los Angeles,** CA 90024 (☎310-208-3551); 254 Greene St., **New York,** NY 10003 (☎212-254-2525); 530 Bush St., **San Francisco,** CA 94108 (☎415-421-3473); 424 Broadway Ave E., **Seattle,** WA 98102 (☎206-329-4567); and 3301 M St. NW, **Washington, D.C.** 20007 (☎202-337-6464). **For US cities not listed,** call ☎800 2-COUNCIL (226-8624). In the UK, 28A Poland St. (Oxford Circus), **London,** W1V 3DB (☎020 7437 7767).

CTS Travel (www.ctstravel.co.uk). 44 Goodge St., **London** W1 (☎020 7636 0031).

STA Travel, 7890 S. Hardy Dr., Ste. 110, Tempe AZ 85284 (24hr. reservations and info ☎800-777-0112; fax 480-592-0876; www.sta-travel.com). A student and youth travel organization with over 150 offices worldwide (check their website for a listing of all their offices), including US offices in Boston, Chicago, L.A., New York, San Francisco, Seattle, and Washington, D.C. Ticket booking, travel insurance, railpasses, and more. In the UK, walk-in office 11 Goodge St., **London** W1T 2PF or call 0870-160-6070. In New Zealand, 10 High St., **Auckland** (☎09 309 0458). In Australia, 366 Lygon St., **Melbourne** Vic 3053 (☎03 9349 4344).

Travel CUTS (Canadian Universities Travel Services Limited), 187 College St., **Toronto,** ON M5T 1P7 (☎416-979-2406; fax 979-8167; www.travelcuts.com). 60 offices across Canada. Also in the UK, 295-A Regent St., **London** W1R 7YA (☎0207-255-1944).

Wasteels, Skoubogade 6, 1158 Copenhagen K., (☎3314-4633, fax 7630-0865; www.wasteels.dk/uk). A huge chain with 165 locations across Europe. Sells Wasteels BIJ tickets discounted 30-45% off regular fare, 2nd-class international point-to-point train tickets with unlimited stopovers for those under 26 (sold only in Europe).Locations in Spain, Portugal, and Morocco are: Plaza de Cataluna, **Barcelona** (☎933 01 18 81); Blasco de Garay, 13, **Madrid** (☎915 43 12 03); Rua dos Caminhos de Ferro, 90, **Lisbon** (☎21 886 97 93); 25 Rue Leon l'Africain, **Casablanca** (☎02 314 060); 45 Bd. Mohamed V, **Meknes** (☎05 523 062).

FLIGHT PLANNING ON THE INTERNET. The internet is without a doubt one of the best places to look for travel bargains—it's fast and convenient, and you can spend as long as you like exploring options.

Many airline sites offer special last-minute deals on the Web. For Portugal, try TAP (www.tap-airportugal.pt); for Spain, check Iberia (www.iberia.com) and Spanair (www.spanair.com); for Morocco, Royal Air Moroc (www.royalair-moroc.com). Other sites do the compile the deals for you—try www.best-fares.com, www.onetravel.com, www.lowestfare.com, and www.travelzoo.com. **STA** (www.sta-travel.com), **Council** (www.counciltravel.com), and **StudentUniverse** (www.studentuniverse.com) provide quotes on student tickets, while **Expedia** (msn.expedia.com) and **Travelocity** (www.travelocity.com) offer full travel services. **Priceline** (www.priceline.com) allows you to specify a price, and obligates you to buy any ticket that meets or beats it; be prepared for antisocial hours and odd routes. **Skyauction** (www.skyauction.com) allows you to bid on both last-minute and advance-purchase tickets.

An indispensable resource on the Internet is the *Air Traveler's Handbook* (www.cs.cmu.edu/afs/cs/user/mkant/Public/Travel/airfare.html), a comprehensive listing of links to everything you need to know before you board a plane.

Just one last note—to protect yourself, make sure that the site you use has a secure server before handing over any credit card details. Happy hunting!

COMMERCIAL AIRLINES

The commercial airlines' lowest regular offer is the **APEX** (Advance Purchase Excursion) fare, which provides confirmed reservations and allows "open-jaw" tickets. Generally, reservations must be made 7 to 21 days ahead of departure, with 7- to 14-day minimum-stay and up to 90-day maximum-stay restrictions. These fares carry hefty cancellation and change penalties (fees rise in summer). Book peak-season APEX fares early; by May you will have a hard time getting your desired departure date. Use **Microsoft Expedia** (msn.expedia.com) or **Travelocity** (www.travelocity.com) to get an idea of the lowest published fares, then use the resources outlined here to try beat those fares. Low-season fares should be appreciably cheaper than the **high-season** (mid-June to early Sept.) ones listed here.

TRAVELING FROM NORTH AMERICA

Basic round-trip fares to Madrid range from roughly US$350-750. Standard commercial carriers like American (☎800-433-7300; www.aa.com) and United (☎800-241-6522; www.ual.com) will probably offer the most convenient flights, but they may not be the cheapest, unless you manage to grab a special promotion or airfare war ticket. You might find flying one of the following airlines a better deal, if any of their limited departure points is convenient for you.

Icelandair: ☎800-223-5500; www.icelandair.com. Stopovers in Iceland for no extra cost on most transatlantic flights.

Finnair: ☎800-950-5000; www.us.finnair.com. Cheap round-trips from San Francisco, New York, and Toronto to Madrid, Malaga and Lisbon; connections throughout Europe.

TRAVELING FROM THE UK & IRELAND

Because of the myriad carriers flying from the British Isles to the continent, we only include discount airlines or those with cheap specials here. The **Air Travel Advisory Bureau** in London (☎020 7636 5000; www.atab.co.uk) provides referrals to travel agencies and consolidators that offer discounted airfares out of the UK.

Aer Lingus: Ireland ☎01 886 88 88; www.aerlingus.ie. Return tickets from Dublin, Cork, Galway, Kerry, and Shannon to Madrid (IR£102-244/€130-310).

British Midland Airways: UK ☎0870 607 05 55; www.britishmidland.com. Departures from throughout the UK. London to Madrid and Barcelona(UK£90-110).

buzz: UK ☎0870 240 70 70; www.buzzaway.com. A subsidiary of KLM. From London to Jerez and Murcia (UK£50-80). Tickets can not be changed or refunded.

easyJet: UK ☎0870 600 00 00; www.easyjet.com. London to Barcelona, Madrid, Málaga, Palma, and Mallorca (UK£47-136). Online tickets.

Go-Fly Limited: UK ☎0845 605 43 21, elsewhere call UK +44 1279 66 63 88; www.go-fly.com. A subsidiary of British Airways. From London to seven locations in Spain and Portugal, including Barcelona and Faro (return UK£53-180).

TRAVELING FROM AUSTRALIA & NEW ZEALAND

Qantas Air: Australia ☎13 13 13, New Zealand ☎0800 808 767; www.qantas.com.au. Flights from Australia and New Zealand to London for around AUS$2400.

Singapore Air: Australia ☎13 10 11, New Zealand ☎0800 808 909; www.singaporeair.com. Flies from Auckland, Sydney, Melbourne, and Perth to Madrid.

Thai Airways: Australia ☎1300 65 19 60, New Zealand ☎09 377 38 86; www.thai-air.com. Auckland, Sydney, and Melbourne to Amsterdam, Frankfurt, and London.

TRAVELING FROM SOUTH AFRICA

Air France: ☎011 880 80 40; www.airfrance.com. Johannesburg to Paris; connections throughout Europe.

British Airways: ☎0860 011 747; www.british-airways.com/regional/sa. Cape Town and Johannesburg to the UK and the rest of Europe from SAR3400.

Lufthansa: ☎011 484 47 11; www.lufthansa.co.za. From Cape Town, Durban, and Johannesburg to Germany and elsewhere.

Virgin Atlantic: ☎011 340 34 00; www.virgin-atlantic.co.za. Flies to London from both Cape Town and Johannesburg.

AIR COURIER FLIGHTS

Those who travel light should consider courier flights. Couriers help transport cargo on international flights by using their checked luggage space for freight. Generally, couriers must travel with carry-ons only and must deal with complex flight restrictions. Most flights are round-trip only, with short fixed-length stays (usually one week) and a limit of a one ticket per issue. Most of these flights also operate only out of major gateway cities, mostly in North America. Courier flights to Spain are common; those to Portugal or Morocco are scarcer. Generally, you must be over 21. In summer, the popular destinations usually require an advance reservation of about two weeks (you can usually book up to 2 months ahead). Super-discounted fares are common for "last-minute" flights (3-14 days ahead).

TRAVELING FROM NORTH AMERICA

Round-trip courier fares from the US to Spain run about US$200-500. Most flights leave from New York, Los Angeles, San Francisco, or Miami in the US; and from Montreal, Toronto, or Vancouver in Canada. The first four organizations below provide their members with lists of opportunities and courier brokers worldwide for an annual fee (typically US$50-60). Alternatively, you can contact a courier broker (such as the last three listings) directly; most charge registration fees, but a few don't. Prices quoted below are round-trip.

Air Courier Association, 15000 W. 6th Ave. #203, Golden, CO 80401 (☎800-282-1202; www.aircourier.org). 10 departure cities throughout the US and Canada to Madrid (high-season US$150-360). 1yr. US$64.

International Association of Air Travel Couriers (IAATC), 220 South Dixie Highway #3, PO Box 1349, Lake Worth, FL 33460 (☎561-582-8320; www.courier.org). From North American cities to Western European cities, including Madrid. One-year US$45-50.

Global Courier Travel, PO Box 3051, Nederland, CO 80466 (www.globalcourier-travel.com). Searchable online database. 6 departure points in the US and Canada to Madrid. 1yr. US$40, 2 people US$55.

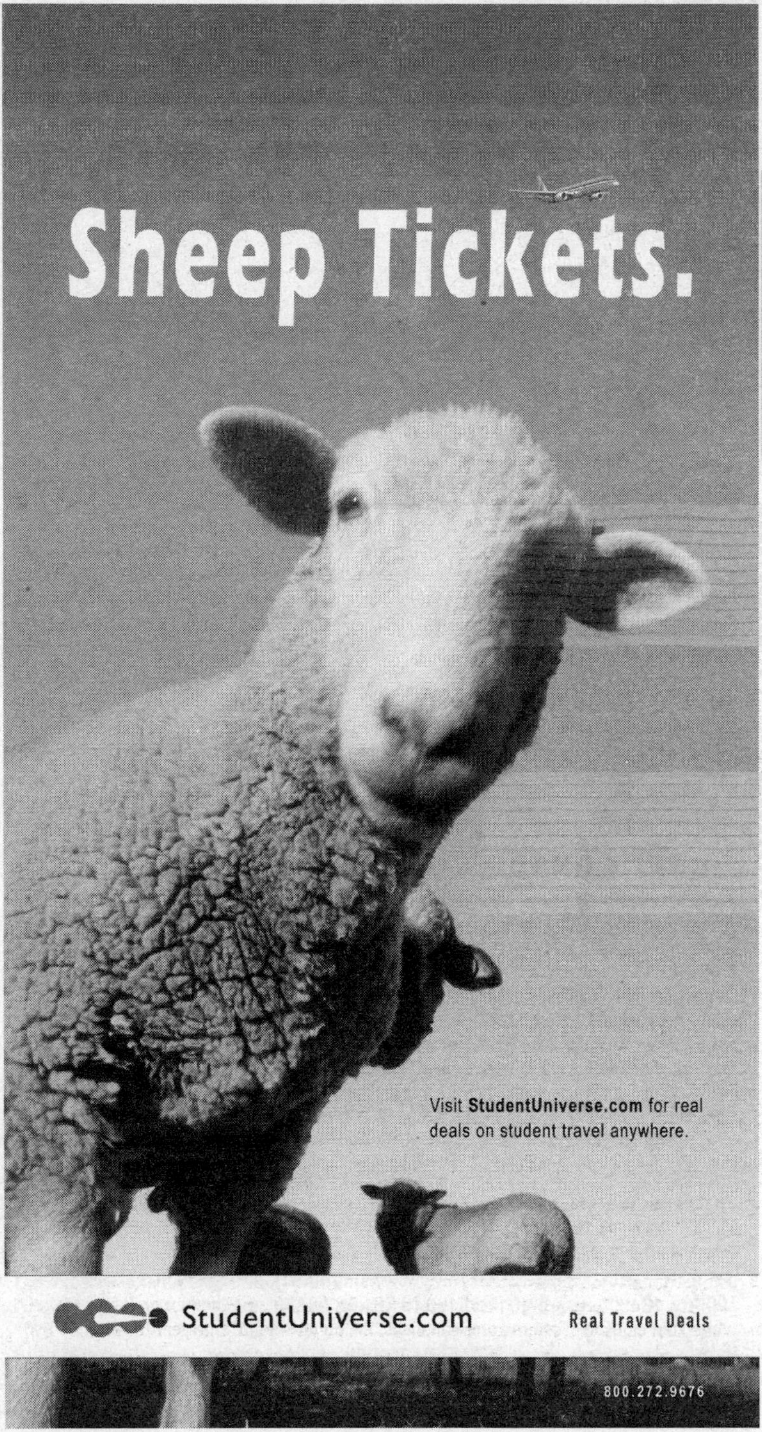

Sheep Tickets.

Visit **StudentUniverse.com** for real deals on student travel anywhere.

Real Travel Deals

800.272.9676

NOW Voyager, 74 Varick St. #307, New York, NY 10013 (☎212-431-1616; fax 219-1753; www.nowvoyagertravel.com). To Madrid (US$499-699). Usually 1wk. max. stay. 1yr. US$50. Non-courier discount fares also available.

FROM THE UK AND IRELAND

Although the courier industry is most developed from North America, there are limited courier flights in other areas. The minimum age for couriers from the **UK** is usually 18. **Brave New World Enterprises,** P.O. Box 22212, London SE5 8WB (www.nry.co.uk/bnw) publishes a directory of all the companies offering courier flights in the UK (UK£10, in electronic form UK£8). **Global Courier Travel** (see above) also offer flights from London and Dublin to continental Europe. **British Airways Travel Shop** (☎0870 606 11 33; www.british-airways.com/travelqa/booking/) arranges flights from London to destinations in continental Europe (specials as low as UK£60; no registration fee).

STANDBY FLIGHTS

Traveling standby requires considerable flexibility in arrival and departure dates and cities. Companies dealing in standby flights sell vouchers rather than tickets, along with the promise to get to your destination (or near your destination) within a certain window of time (typically 1-5 days). You call in before your specific window of time to hear your flight options and the probability that you will be able to board each flight. You can then decide which flights you want to try to make, show up at the appropriate airport at the appropriate time, present your voucher, and board if space is available. You may receive a monetary refund only if every available flight within your date range is full; if you opt not to take an available (but perhaps less convenient) flight, you can only get credit toward future travel. Carefully read agreements with any company offering standby flights as tricky fine print can leave you in a lurch. To check on a company's service record in the US, call the **Better Business Bureau** (☎212-533-6200). It is difficult to receive refunds, and clients' vouchers will not be honored when an airline fails to receive payment in time. One established standby company in the US is **Whole Earth Travel,** 325 W. 38th St., New York, NY 10018 (☎800-326-2009; fax 212-864-5489; www.4standby.com) and Los Angeles, CA (☎888-247-4482).

TICKET CONSOLIDATORS

Ticket consolidators, or **"bucket shops,"** buy unsold tickets in bulk from commercial airlines and sell them at discounted rates. The best place to look is in the Sunday travel section of any major newspaper (such as the *New York Times*), where many bucket shops place tiny ads. Call quickly, as availability is typically extremely limited. Not all bucket shops are reliable, so insist on a receipt that gives full details of restrictions, refunds, and tickets, and pay by credit card (in spite of the 2-5% fee) so you can stop payment if you never receive your tickets. For more info, see www.travel-library.com/air-travel/consolidators.html.

TRAVELING FROM THE US & CANADA

Travel Avenue (☎800-333-3335; www.travelavenue.com) searches for best available published fares and then uses several consolidators to attempt to beat that fare. **NOW Voyager,** 74 Varick St., Ste. 307, New York, NY 10013 (☎212-431-1616; fax 219-1793; www.nowvoyagertravel.com) arranges discounted flights, mostly from New York, to Barcelona, London, Madrid, Milan, Paris, and Rome. Other consolidators worth trying are **Interworld** (☎305-443-4929; fax 443-0351); **Pennsylvania Travel** (☎800-331-0947); **Rebel** (☎800-227-3235; www.rebeltours.com); **Cheap Tickets** (☎800-377-1000; www.cheaptickets.com); and **Travac** (☎800-872-8800; fax 212-714-9063; www.travac.com). Yet more consolidators on the web include the **Internet Travel Network** (www.itn.com); **Travel Information Services** (www.tiss.com); **TravelHUB** (www.travelhub.com); and **The Travel Site** (www.thetravelsite.com). Keep in mind that these are just suggestions to get you started in your research; *Let's Go* does not endorse any of these agencies. As always, be cautious before you hand over your credit card number.

TRAVELING FROM THE UK, AUSTRALIA, & NEW ZEALAND

In London, the **Air Travel Advisory Bureau** (☎0207-636-5000; www.atab.co.uk) can provide names of reliable consolidators and discount flight specialists. From Australia and New Zealand, look for consolidator ads in the travel section of the *Sydney Morning Herald* and other papers.

CHARTER FLIGHTS

Charters are flights a tour operator contracts with an airline to fly extra loads of passengers during peak season. Charter flights fly less frequently than major airlines, make refunds particularly difficult, and are almost always fully booked. Schedules and itineraries may also change or be cancelled at the last moment (as late as 48 hours before the trip, and without a full refund), and check-in, boarding, and baggage claim are often much slower. However, they can also be cheaper.

Discount clubs and **fare brokers** offer members savings on last-minute charter and tour deals. Study contracts closely; you don't want to end up with an unwanted overnight layover. **Travelers Advantage,** Trumbull, CT, USA (☎203-365-2000; www.travelersadvantage.com; US$60 annual fee includes discounts and cheap flight directories) specializes in European travel and tour packages.

ESSENTIALS

BY BOAT FROM THE UK & IRELAND

The following fares listed are **one-way** for **adult foot passengers** unless otherwise noted. Though standard return fares are in most cases simply twice the one-way fare, **fixed-period returns** (usually within five days) are almost invariably cheaper. Ferries run **year-round** unless otherwise noted. **Bikes** are usually free, although you may have to pay up to UK£10 in high-season. For a **camper/trailer** supplement, you will have to add anywhere from UK£20-140 to the "with car" fare. If more than one price is quoted, the quote in UK£ is valid for departures from the UK, etc. A directory of ferries in this region can be found at www.seaview.co.uk/ferries.html.

P&O Stena Line: UK ☎08706 00 06 11; from Europe 44 13 04 86 40 03; www.posl.com. **Dover** to **Calais** (1¼hr., every 30min.-1hr., 30 per day; UK£24).

Hoverspeed: UK ☎08702 40 80 70; France ☎03 21 46 14 54; www.hoverspeed.co.uk. **Dover** to **Calais** (35-55min., every hr., UK£24) and **Ostend, Belgium** (2hr., 5-7 per day, UK£28). **Folkestone** to **Boulogne, France** (55min., 3-4 per day, UK£24). **Newhaven** to **Dieppe, France** (2¼-4¼hr., 1-3 per day, UK£28).

SeaFrance: UK ☎08705 71 17 11; France ☎03 21 46 80 00; www.seafrance.co.uk. **Dover** to **Calais** (1½hr., 15 per day, UK£15).

DFDS Seaways: UK ☎08705 33 30 00; www.scansea.com. Call for prices. **Harwich** to **Hamburg** (20hr.) and **Esbjerg, Denmark** (19hr.). **Newcastle** to **Amsterdam** (14hr.); **Kristiansand, Norway** (19hr.); and **Gothenburg, Sweden** (22hr.).

Brittany Ferries: UK ☎0870 901 24 00; France ☎08 25 82 88 28; www.brittany-ferries.com. **Plymouth** to **Roscoff, France** (6hr., in summer 1-3 per day, off-season 1 per week, UK£20-58 or 140-300F/€22-46) and **Santander, Spain** (24-30hr., 1-2 per week, return UK£80-145). **Portsmouth** to **St-Malo** (8¾hr., 1-2 per day, 150-320F/€23-49) and **Caen** (6hr, 1-3 per day, 140-290F/€22-44), France. **Poole** to **Cherbourg** (4¼hr., 1-2 per day, 140-290F/€22-44). **Cork** to **Roscoff** (13½hr., Apr.-Sept. 1 per week, 340-650F/€52-100).

P&O North Sea Ferries: UK ☎0870 129 6002; www.ponsf.com. Online bookings. Daily ferries from **Hull** to **Rotterdam, Netherlands** (13½hr.) and **Zeebrugge, Belgium** (14hr.). Both UK£38-48, students UK£24-31, cars UK£63-78.

Fjord Line: www.fjordline.no. Norway ☎55 54 88 00, UK 0191 296 1313. **Newcastle, England** to **Stavanger** (19hr.) and **Bergen** (26hr.), Norway. Also between **Bergen** and **Egersund,** Norway, and **Hanstholm,** Denmark.

Irish Ferries: France ☎01 44 94 2040; Ireland ☎1890 31 31 31, UK ☎08705 17 17 17; www.irishferries.ie. **Rosslare** to **Cherbourg** (18hr., IR£57-82/€73-105); **Roscoff** (17hr., Apr.-Sept. 1-9 per week, 470-680F/€72-104); and **Pembroke, England** (3¾hr.). **Holyhead, England** to **Dublin** (2-3hr., return IR£20-60/€26-77).

Stena Line: UK ☎44 1233 64 68 26; www.stenaline.co.uk. **Harwich, England** to **Hook of Holland** (5hr., UK£25). **Fishguard** to **Rosslare** (1-3½hr., UK£22-30). **Holyhead** to **Dublin** (4hr., UK£18-20) and **Dún Laoghaire** (1-3½hr., £20-28). **Stranraer** to **Belfast** (1¾-3¼hr., Mar.-Jan., UK£18-24).

BY CHUNNEL FROM THE UK

Traversing 27 mi. under the sea, the Chunnel is undoubtedly the fastest, most convenient, and least scenic route from England to France.

BY TRAIN. Eurostar, Eurostar House, Waterloo Station, **London** SE1 8SE (UK ☎0990 18 61 86; US ☎800-387-6782; elsewhere call UK44 1233 61 75 75; www.eurostar.com; www.raileurope.com) runs a frequent train service between London and the continent. Ten to twenty-eight trains per day run to **Paris** (3hr., US$75-159, 2nd class), **Brussels** (3hr., 50min., US$75-159, 2nd class), and Eurodisney. Routes include stops at Ashford in England, and Calais and Lille in France. Book at major rail stations in the UK, at the office above, by phone, or on the web.

BY BUS. Both **Eurolines** and **Eurobus** provide bus-ferry combinations.

BY CAR. If you're traveling by car, **Eurotunnel** (UK ☎08000 96 99 92; www.eurotunnel.co.uk) shuttles cars and passengers between Kent and Nord-Pas-de-Calais. Return fares for vehicle and all passengers range from UK£219-299 with car, UK£259-598 with campervan, and UK£119-299 for a trailer/caravan supplement. Same-day return costs UK£110-150, five-day return UK£139-195. Book online or via phone. Travelers with cars can also look into sea crossings by ferry (see below).

BY TRAIN

Trains in Spain and Portugal are generally comfortable, convenient, and reasonably swift. Second-class travel is pleasant, and compartments, which seat two to six, are great places to meet fellow travelers. Trains, however, are not always safe; for safety tips, see next page. For long trips make sure you are in the correct car, as trains sometimes split at crossroads. Towns listed in parentheses require a train switch at the town listed immediately before the parenthesis.

You can either buy a **railpass,** which allows you unlimited travel within a particular region for a given period of time, or rely on buying individual **point-to-point** tickets as you go. Almost all countries give students or youths (usually defined as anyone under 26) direct discounts on regular domestic rail tickets, and many also sell a student or youth card that provides 20-50% off all fares for up to a year.

RESERVATIONS. While seat reservations are required only for selected trains (usually on major lines), you are not guaranteed a seat without one. Reservations are available on major trains up to two months in advance, and Europeans often reserve far ahead of time; you should strongly consider reserving during peak holiday and tourist seasons (at the very latest a few hours ahead). It will be necessary to purchase a **supplement** (US$10-50) or special fare for high speed or quality trains such as Spain's AVE.

OVERNIGHT TRAINS. Night trains have their advantages—you won't waste valuable daylight hours traveling, and you will be able to forego the hassle and considerable expense of securing a night's accommodation. However, night travel has its drawbacks as well: discomfort and sleepless nights are the most obvious; the scenery probably won't look as enticing in pitch black, either. **Sleeping accommodations** on trains differ from country to country, but typically you can either sleep upright in your seat (for free) or pay for a separate space. **Couchettes** (berths) typically have four to six seats per compartment (about US$20 per person); **sleepers** (beds) in private sleeping cars offer more privacy and comfort, but are considerably more expensive (US$40-150). If you are using a railpass valid only for a restricted number of days, inspect train schedules to maximize the use of your pass: an overnight train or boat journey uses up only one of your travel days if it departs after 7pm (you need only write in the next day's date on your pass).

SHOULD YOU BUY A RAILPASS? Railpasses were conceived to allow you to jump on any train in Europe, go wherever you want whenever you want, and change your plans at will. In practice, it's not so simple. You still must stand in line to validate your pass, pay for supplements, and fork over cash for seat and couchette reservations. More importantly, railpasses don't always pay off. If you are planning to spend extensive time on trains, hopping between big cities, a railpass would probably be worth it. But in many cases, especially if you are under 26, point-to-point tickets may prove a cheaper option.

JUST SAY NO If you are planning on traveling in just Spain and Portugal, do not buy a Eurailpass or Europass. Train travel in these countries is less expensive than the rest of Europe, where passes can save you from paying for expensive train fares. A Eurailpass/Europass only makes sense for those planning on traveling in other European countries as well.

EURAILPASS. Eurail is valid in most of Western Europe: Austria, Belgium, Denmark, Finland, France, Germany, Greece, Hungary, Italy, Luxembourg, the Netherlands, Norway, Portugal, the Republic of Ireland, Spain, Sweden, and Switzerland. It is not valid in the UK. Standard Eurailpasses, valid for a consecutive given number of days, are most suitable for those planning on spending extensive time on trains every few days. Flexipasses, valid for any 10 or 15 (not necessarily consecutive) days in a two-month period, are more cost-effective for those traveling longer distances less frequently. Saverpasses provide first-class travel for travelers in groups of two to five (prices are per person). Youthpasses and Youth Flexipasses provide parallel second-class perks for those under 26.

EURAILPASSES	15 days	21 days	1 month	2 months	3 months
1st class Eurailpass	US$554	US$718	US$890	US$1260	US$1558
Eurail Saverpass	US$470	US$610	US$756	US$1072	US$1324
Eurail Youthpass	US$388	US$499	US$623	US$882	US$1089

EURAIL FLEXIPASSES	10 days in 2 months	15 days in 2 months
1st class Eurail Flexipass	US$654	US$862
Eurail Saver Flexipass	US$556	US$732
Eurail Youth Flexipass	US$458	US$599

Passholders receive a timetable for major routes and a map with details on possible ferry, steamer, bus, car rental, hotel, and Eurostar discounts. Passholders often also receive reduced fares or free passage on many bus and boat lines.

EUROPASS. The Europass is a slimmed-down version of the Eurailpass: it allows five to 15 days of unlimited travel in any two-month period within France, Germany, Italy, Spain, and Switzerland. **First-Class Europasses** (for individuals) and **Saverpasses** (for people traveling in groups of 2-5) range from US$348/296 per person (5 days) to US$728/620 (15 days). **Second-Class Youthpasses** for those ages 12-25 cost US$233-513. For a fee, you can add **additional zones** (Austria/Hungary; Belgium/Luxembourg/Netherlands; Greece Plus, including the ADN/HML ferry between Italy and Greece; and/or Portugal): US$60 for one associated country, US$100 for two. You are entitled to the same **freebies** afforded by the Eurailpass (see above), but only when they are within or between countries that you have purchased.

Study Spanish & Portuguese

In Spain - Barcelona Madrid Granada Sevilla Marbella Salamanca
Many locations in Latin America, including Brazil

- Learn the RIGHT way FAST
- For all ages and levels
- Most programs start weekly
- Private tutor or small groups
- 3-8 hours per day
- Exciting excursions
- Pre-departure assistance
- Travel insurance
- Easy to book online
- All major credit cards accepted

¡Now Featuring!
University Semester Abroad Programs
Volunteer and Internship Placements

AmeriSpan programs can also be found at major travel organizations around the world: such as STA Travel (USA, UK, Australia & New Zealand), Council Travel (USA), Travel Cuts (Canada), Travel Active (Netherlands) & others.

For free information:
USA & Canada: 1-800-879-6640
Worldwide: 215-751-1100
Fax: 215-751-1986
Email: info@amerispan.com
WWWeb: http://www.amerispan.com

AmeriSpan Unlimited
THE BRIDGE BETWEEN CULTURES

SHOPPING AROUND FOR A EURAIL OR EUROPASS. Eurailpasses and Europasses are designed by the EU itself, and are purchasable only by non-Europeans almost exclusively from non-European distributors. These passes must be sold at uniform prices determined by the EU. However, some travel agents tack on a US$10 handling fee, and others offer certain bonuses with purchase, so shop around. Also, keep in mind that pass prices usually go up each year, so if you're planning to travel early in the year, you can save cash by purchasing before January 1 (you have three months from the purchase date to validate your pass in Europe).

It is best to buy your Eurail- or Europass before leaving; only a few places in major European cities sell them, and at a marked-up price. You can get a replacement for a lost pass only if you have purchased insurance on it under the Pass Protection Plan (US$10). Eurailpasses are available through travel agents, student travel agencies like STA and Council (see p. 32), and **Rail Europe,** 44 South Broadway, White Plains, NY 10601 (US ☎877-456-RAIL, Canada ☎800-361-RAIL; www.raileurope.com) or **DER Travel Services,** 9501 W. Devon Ave. #301, Rosemont, IL 60018 (US ☎888-337-7350; fax 800-282-7474; www.dertravel.com).

INTERRAIL PASS. If you have lived for at least six months in one of the European countries where InterRail Passes are valid, they prove an economical option. There are eight InterRail **zones,** one of which includes Spain, Portugal, and Morocco. The **Under 26 InterRail Card** allows either 14 days or one month of unlimited travel within one, two, three, or all eight zones; the cost is determined by the number of zones the pass covers (UK£159-259). If you buy a ticket including the zone in which you claim residence, you must still pay 50% fare for tickets inside your own country. Passholders receive **discounts** on rail travel, Eurostar journeys, and most ferries to Ireland, Scandinavia, and the rest of Europe. Most exclude **supplements** for high-speed trains. For info and ticket sales in Europe contact **Student Travel Center,** 24 Rupert St., 1st fl., London W1V 7FN (☎20 74 37 81 01; fax 20 77 34 38 36; www.student-travel-centre.com). Tickets are also available from travel agents or major train stations throughout Europe.

KINGSBROOK SINCE *1985*

LEARN SPANISH IN BEAUTIFUL BARCELONA BY THE SEA

Situated in heart of the city

* 12 – 18 HRS PER WEEK
* Accommodation Assistance
* Airport Pick-Up Service
* Teachers Training Course
* Groups of 4 to 12 students
* High Quality Teaching At All Levels
* Economic Rates
Job Opportunities
* cruise ship jobs
* Baby sitting jobs

Add: Travesera. de Gracia, 60, 1º 3ª
08006 Barcelona SPAIN

Tel: 34-93-209 37 63 www.kingsbrookbcn.com
Fax: 34-93-202 15 98 e-mail: kingsb@teleline.es

DISCOUNTED TICKETS

For travelers under 26, **BIJ** tickets (Billets Internationals de Jeunesse; a.k.a. **Wasteels, Eurotrain,** and **Route 26**) are a great alternative to railpasses. Available for international trips within Europe as well as most ferry services, they knock 20-40% off regular second-class fares. Tickets are good for 60 days after purchase and allow a number of stopovers along the normal direct route of the train journey. Issued for a specific international route between two points, they must be used in the direction and order of the designated route and must be bought in Europe. The equivalent for those over 26, **BIGT** tickets provide a 20-30% discount on 1st- and 2nd-class international tickets for business travelers, temporary residents of Europe, and their families. Both types of tickets are available from European travel agents, at Wasteels or Eurotrain offices (usually in or near train stations), or directly at the ticket counter in some nations. For more info, contact **Wasteels,** Plaza de Cataluna, **Barcelona** (☎933 01 18 81); Blasco de Garay, 13, **Madrid** (☎915 43 12 03); Rua dos Caminhos de Ferro, 90, **Lisbon** (☎21 886 97 93).

BY BUS

Though European trains and railpasses are extremely popular, in many cases buses prove a better option. In Spain, the bus and train systems are on par; in Portugal, bus networks are more extensive, efficient, and often more comfortable. In Morocco, buses are the easiest way to get around, even though some run somewhat infrequently. Please see the Essentials sections of Spain (see p. 55), Portugal (see p. 526), and Morocco (see p. 668) for details on country specific bus travel.

BY CAR

Cars offer speed, freedom, access to the countryside, and an escape from the town-to-town mentality of trains. Unfortunately, they also insulate you from the *esprit de corps* of rail traveling and driving in major cities can be hair-raising. Although a single traveler won't save by renting a car, four usually will. If you can't decide between train and car travel, you may benefit from a combination of the two; Rail Europe and other railpass vendors offer rail-and-drive packages for both individual countries and all of Europe.

Before setting off, know the laws of the countries in which you'll be driving. The **Association for Safe International Road Travel (ASIRT)** can provide more specific information about road conditions in Spain, Portugal and Morocco. It is located at 5413 West Cedar Lane #103C, Bethesda, MD 20814 (☎301-983-5252; fax 983-3663; www.asirt.org). Western Europeans use unleaded gas almost exclusively.

RENTING

You can rent a car from a US-based firm with European offices, from a European-based company with local representatives, or from a tour operator which will arrange a rental for you from a European company at its own rates. Multinationals offer greater flexibility, but tour operators often strike better deals. Most available cars will have standard transmission—cars with automatic transmission are difficult to find and much more expensive. Reserve well before leaving for the region and pay in advance if at all possible. It is always significantly less expensive to reserve a car from the US than from Spain, Portugal, or Morocco. Ask your airline about special fly-and-drive packages; you may get up to a week of free or discounted rental. The minimum age in Spain and Portugal is usually 25 with the larger agencies (Hertz, Avis) and 21 at smaller, local businesses. Minimum age in Morocco is almost always 21. At most agencies, all that's needed to rent a car is a US license and proof that you've had it for a year, although in Spain, you may need an international driver's license (see below).

RENTAL AGENCIES. You can generally make reservations before you leave by calling major international offices in your home country. However, occasionally the price and availability information they give doesn't jive with what the local offices in your country will tell you. Try checking with both numbers to make sure you get the best price and accurate information. Local desk numbers are included in town listings; for home-country numbers, call your toll-free directory.

Minimum age in Spain and Portugal is usually 25 with the larger agencies (Hertz, Avis), although policies vary from agency to agency. Small local operations occasionally rent to people under 21, but be sure to ask about the insurance coverage and deductible, and always check the fine print. At most agencies, all that's needed to rent a car is a US license and proof that you've had it for a year, although in Spain, you may need an international driver's license (see below). Rental agencies in Spain and Portugal include:

Alamo (☎800-GO-ALAMO, www.alamo.com). Alamo has 85 offices in Spain and 13 in Portugal, including the airports of Barcelona, Lisbon, Madrid and Sevilla. Frequent flyer deals can be had when flying with most major US airlines.

Auto Europe (in US ☎888-223-555, in UK 0800 89 9893; www.autoeurope.com). Offers car rentals in Spain, Portugal and Morocco, as well flight and hotel bookings. Also rents cell phones to US citizens traveling in Europe.

Budget (☎800-527-0700, www.budget.com). Rentals in Spain Portugal and Morocco.

Hertz (☎800-654-3001 in US, 08708 448844 in UK, 61 (3) 9698 2555 in Australia; www.hertz.com). Rentals in Spain, Portugal and Morocco; hand control cars available for travellers with disabilities in Madrid.

Europcar (☎800-227-3876 in US 877 940 6900 in Canada, 0870 607 5000 in UK; www.europcar.com, www.europcar.co.uk). Rentals in Spain, Portugal and Morocco. Europcar is one of the few services that will rent to those 21-24 in most locations.

Europe by Car (☎800-223-1516; www.europebycar.com). Student discounts.

COSTS & INSURANCE. Rental car prices start at around US$20 a day from national companies. Expect to pay more for larger cars and for 4WD, less for minis or at local agencies. Cars with **automatic transmission** are considerably more expensive than standard manuals (stick shift), and in some places, automatic transmission is hard to find in the first place. It is virtually impossible, no matter where you are, to find an automatic 4WD. National chains often allow one-way rentals, picking up in one city and dropping off in another. There is usually a minimum hire period and sometimes an extra drop-off charge of a few hundred dollars.

Be sure to ask any of a number of questions before leaving the agency: including the number of kilometers included with the rental cost, the cost of returning a car without a full tank of gas, and the type of insurance included with the rental fee. Most credit cards cover standard insurance, although you should double-check with your credit card company if you are using **American Express** or **Visa/Mastercard Gold or Platinum** to rent a car in Spain, Portugal or Morocco. If you rent, lease, or borrow a car, you will need a **green card,** or **International Insurance Certificate,** to certify that you have liability insurance and that it applies abroad. Green cards can be obtained at car rental agencies, car dealers (for those leasing cars), some travel agents, and some border crossings. Rental agencies may require you to purchase theft insurance in countries that they consider to have a high risk of auto theft. If you have a collision abroad, the accident will show up on your domestic records if you report it to your insurance company.

ON THE ROAD. Speed limits in Spain and Portugal are 60kph on main roads, 90kph on larger roads and 120kph on highways. Police are often on the lookout for speeding tourists, and if you're caught you will likely face an on the spot fine. Petrol (gasoline) prices vary, but average about 135ptas per liter. Road conditions are fairly good throughout Spain and Portugal with the most difficult conditions in the Pyrenees, although driving in Morocco can be difficult at times.

DRIVING PRECAUTIONS. When traveling in the summer or in the desert, bring substantial amounts of water (a suggested 5 liters of **water** per person per day) for drinking and for the radiator. For long drives to unpopulated areas, register with police before beginning the trek, and again upon arrival at the destination. Check with the local automobile club for details. When traveling for long distances, make sure tires are in good repair and have enough air, and get good maps. A **compass** and a **car manual** can also be very useful. You should always carry a **spare tire** and **jack, jumper cables, extra oil, flares, a torch (flashlight),** and **heavy blankets** (in case your car breaks down at night or in the winter). If you don't know how to **change a tire,** learn before heading out, especially if you are planning on traveling in deserted areas. Blowouts on dirt roads are exceedingly common. If you do have a breakdown, **stay with your car;** if you wander off, there's less likelihood trackers will find you.

DRIVING PERMITS & CAR INSURANCE

INTERNATIONAL DRIVING PERMIT (IDP). If you plan to drive a car while in the region, you should have an International Driving Permit (IDP), though Spain, Portugal and Morocco allow travelers to drive with a valid American, Canadian or EU member license. It may be a good idea to get an IDP, in case you're in a situation (e.g. an accident or stranded in a small town) where the police do not know English; information on the IDP is printed in ten languages, including Spanish, French, Portuguese, and Arabic. Your IDP, valid for one year, must be issued in your own country before you depart. When you are on the road, you will always be asked to present your regular license in addition to your IDP. An application for an IDP usually needs to include one or two photos, a current local license, an additional form of identification proving that you are over 18, and a fee. To apply, contact the national or local branch of your home country's Automobile Association.

Australia: Royal Automobile Club (RAC) or National Royal Motorist Association (NRMA) if in NSW or the ACT (☎08 9421 4444; www.rac.com.au/travel). Permits AUS$15.

Canada: Contact any Canadian Automobile Association (CAA) branch office or write to CAA, 1145 Hunt Club Rd., #200, Ottawa Ontario, K1V 0Y3. (☎613-247-0117; www.caa.ca/CAAInternet/travelservices/internationaldocumentation/idptravel.htm). Permits CDN$10.

Ireland: Contact nearest Automobile Association (AA) office or write to The Irish Automobile Association, 23 Suffolk St., Rockhill, Blackrock, Co. Dublin (☎01 617 9988; www.aaireland.ie). Permits IR£4.

New Zealand: Contact your local Automobile Association (AA) or their main office at 99 Albert St. Auckland (☎9 377 4660; www.nzaa.co.nz). Permits NZ$10.

South Africa: Contact the Travel Services Department of the Automobile Association of South Africa at P.O. Box 7118, Johannesburg 2000 (☎011 403 5320; fax 403 5438; www.aasa.co.za). Permits SAR28.50.

UK: To visit your local AA Shop, contact the AA Headquarters (☎0870 600 0371; www.theaa.com), or write to: The Automobile Association, International Documents, Fanum House, Erskine, Renfrewshire PA8 6BW. Permits UK£4.

US: Visit any American Automobile Association (AAA) office or write to AAA Florida, Travel Related Services, 1000 AAA Drive, Box 28, Heathrow, FL 32746 (☎407-444-4240; fax 444-4247; www.aaa.com). Permits US$10.

BY BICYCLE

Today, biking is one of the key elements of the classic budget Eurovoyage. With the proliferation of mountain bikes, you can do some serious natural sightseeing. If you are nervous about striking out on your own, **Blue Marble Travel** (in Canada ☎519-624 4760; in Paris ☎01 42 21 14 77; in US ☎973-326-8939; www.bluemarble.org) offers bike tours designed for adults aged 20 to 50.

Many airlines will count your bike as your second piece of luggage, and a few charge extra. The additional fee runs about US$60-110 each way. Airlines sell bike boxes at the airport (US$10), although it is easier and cheaper to get one from a local bike store. Most ferries let you take your bike for free or for a nominal fee. You can always ship your bike on trains, though the cost varies.

Riding a bike with a frame pack strapped on it or your back is about as safe as pedaling blindfolded over a sheet of ice; panniers are essential. The first thing to buy, however, is a suitable **bike helmet** (US$25-50). U-shaped **Citadel** or **Kryptonite locks** are expensive (starting at US$30), but the companies insure their locks against theft of your bike for one to two years. For mail order equipment, **Bike Nashbar,** 4111 Simon Rd., Youngstown, OH 44512 (☎800-627-4227; www.nashbar.com), beats all competitors' offers and ships anywhere in the US or Canada.

Renting a bike beats bringing your own if your touring will be confined to one or two regions. *Let's Go* lists bike rental shops for most larger cities and towns. Some youth hostels rent bicycles for low prices. Some train stations rent bikes and often allow you to drop them off elsewhere.

BY MOPED AND MOTORCYCLE

Motorized bikes don't use much gas, can be put on trains and ferries, and are a good compromise between the high cost of car travel and the limited range of bicycles. In Spain, they are an extremely popular method of transportation for locals, and they can be a fun alternative for tourist daytrips. However, they're uncomfortable for long distances, dangerous in the rain, and unpredictable on rough roads and gravel. Always wear a helmet, and never ride with a backpack. If you've never been on a moped, the windy roads of the Pyrenees and the congested streets of Madrid are not the place to start.

Before renting, ask if the quoted price includes tax and insurance, or you may be hit with an unexpected additional fee. Avoid handing your passport over as a deposit; if you have an accident or mechanical failure you may not get it back until you cover all repairs. Pay ahead of time instead.

BY THUMB

HITCHHIKERS BEWARE. *Let's Go* strongly urges you to consider seriously the risks before you choose to hitch. We do not recommend hitching as a safe means of transportation, and none of the information presented here is intended to do so. Women traveling alone should never hitch.

No one should hitch without careful consideration of the risks involved. Hitching means entrusting your life to a random person who happens to stop beside you on the road and risking theft, assault, sexual harassment, and unsafe driving. In spite of this, there are gains to hitching. Favorable hitching experiences allow you to meet local people and get where you're going, especially in areas where public transportation is sparse or unreliable. For instance, hitching in southern Spain, particularly in Andalucía, and northern Portugal is easier than hitching in Murcia and allows you to mingle with the locals. The choice, however, remains yours.

Where one stands is vital. Experienced hitchers pick a spot outside of built-up areas, where drivers can stop, return to the road without causing an accident, and have time to look over potential passengers as they approach. Hitching (or even standing) on super-highways is usually illegal: one may only thumb at rest stops or at the entrance ramps to highways. Finally, success will depend on what one looks like. Successful hitchers travel light and stack their belongings in a compact but visible cluster. Most Europeans signal with an open hand, rather than a thumb; many write their destination on a sign in large, bold letters and draw a smiley-face under it. Drivers prefer hitchers who are neat and wholesome.

Safety issues are always imperative, even for those who are not hitching alone. Safety-minded hitchers avoid getting in the back of a two-door car and never let go of their backpacks. They will not get into a car that they can't get out of again in a hurry. If they ever feel threatened, they insist on being let off, regardless of where they are. Acting as if they are going to open the car door or vomit on the upholstery will usually get a driver to stop. Hitchhiking at night can be particularly dangerous; experienced hitchers stand in well-lit places, and expect drivers to be leery of nocturnal thumbers (or open-handers).

SPECIFIC CONCERNS

WOMEN TRAVELERS

Women exploring on their own inevitably face some additional safety concerns, but it's easy to be adventurous without taking undue risks. If you are concerned, consider staying in hostels which offer single rooms that lock from the inside or in religious organizations with rooms for women only. Communal showers in some hostels are safer than others; check them before settling in. Stick to centrally located accommodations and avoid solitary late-night treks or metro rides.

When traveling, always carry extra money for a phone call, bus, or taxi. **Hitching** is never safe for lone women, or even for two women traveling together. Choose train compartments occupied by other women or couples; ask the conductor to put together a women-only compartment if he or she doesn't offer to do so first. Look as if you know where you're going (even when you don't) and approach older women or couples for directions if you're lost or feel uncomfortable.

Generally, the less you look like a tourist, the better off you'll be. Dress conservatively, especially in rural areas. Wearing a conspicuous **wedding band** may help prevent unwanted overtures. Some travelers report that carrying pictures of a "husband" or "children" is extremely useful to help document marriage status. Even a mention of a husband waiting back at the hotel may be enough in some places to discount your potentially vulnerable, unattached appearance.

Your best answer to verbal harassment is no answer at all; feigning deafness, sitting motionless, and staring straight ahead at nothing in particular will do a world of good that reactions usually don't achieve. The extremely persistent can sometimes be dissuaded by a firm, loud, and very public "Go away!" in the appropriate language. In Morocco, however, it is more advisable to simply ignore the advances, as local women do; rebuffs, or any kind of reaction, are often construed as coy or playing hard to get. Don't hesitate to seek out a police officer or a passerby if you are being harassed. Memorize the emergency numbers in places you visit, and consider carrying a whistle or airhorn on your keychain. A self-defense course will not only prepare you for a potential attack, but will also raise your level of awareness of your surroundings as well as your confidence (see **Self Defense,** p. 18). Refer to the **Essentials** section for Morocco (p.539) for information on traveling there.

TRAVELING ALONE

There are many benefits to traveling alone, including independence and greater interaction with locals. On the other hand, any solo traveler is a more vulnerable target of harassment and street theft. Lone travelers need to be well-organized and look confident at all times. Try not to stand out as a tourist, and be especially careful in deserted or very crowded areas. If questioned, never admit that you are traveling alone. Maintain regular contact with someone at home who knows your itinerary. For more tips, pick up *Traveling Solo* by Eleanor Berman (Globe Pequot Press, US$17) or subscribe to **Connecting: Solo Travel Network,** 689 Park Road, Unit 6, Gibsons, BC V0N 1V7 (☎604-886-9099; www.cstn.org; membership US$28).

Alternatively, several services link solo travelers with companions who have similar travel habits and interests; for a bi-monthly newsletter for single travelers seeking a travel partner (subscription US$48), contact the **Travel Companion Exchange,** P.O. Box 833, Amityville, NY 11701 (☎631-454-0880 or 800-392-1256; www.whytravelalone.com; US$48).

OLDER TRAVELERS

Senior citizens are eligible for a wide range of discounts on transportation, museums, movies, theaters, concerts, restaurants, and accommodations. If you don't see a senior citizen price listed, ask, and you may be delightfully surprised. The books *No Problem! Worldwise Tips for Mature Adventurers*, by Janice Kenyon (Orca Book Publishers; US$16) and *Unbelievably Good Deals and Great Adventures That You Absolutely Can't Get Unless You're Over 50*, by Joan Rattner Heilman (NTC/Contemporary Publishing; US$13) are both excellent resources. For more information, contact one of the following organizations:

ElderTreks, 597 Markham St., Toronto, ON M6G 2L7 (☎800-741-7956; www.eldertreks.com). Adventure travel programs for the 50+ traveler in Spain and Portugal.

Elderhostel, 11 Ave. de Lafayette, Boston, MA 02111 (☎877-426-8056; www.elderhostel.org). Organizes 1-4wk. "educational adventures" in Spain, Portugal and Morocco on varied subjects for those 55+.

The Mature Traveler, P.O. Box 15791, Sacramento, CA 95852 (☎800-460-6676). Deals, discounts, and travel packages for the 50+ traveler. Subscription$30.

Walking the World, P.O. Box 1186, Fort Collins, CO 80522 (☎800-340-9255; www.walkingtheworld.com), organizes trips for 50+ travelers to a variety of destinations, including Spain and Portugal.

BISEXUAL, GAY, AND LESBIAN TRAVELERS

Attitudes toward homosexuality in Spain, Portugal, and Morocco vary by region. Gay and lesbian travelers may feel out of place in the smaller, rural areas of Spain and Portugal, given the countries' strong Catholic religious heritage, but overt homophobia is extremely rare. The larger cities, especially Lisbon, Barcelona and Madrid, have well-developed gay men's scenes, and the lesbian scene is also growing rapidly. In Spain, Sitges and Ibiza in particular are internationally renowned as gay party destinations, and Madrid hosts annual Gay & Lesbian Pride marches. Most Spanish newsstands carry the *Guía Gay Visado,* a publication dedicated to gay bars, discos, and contacts in Spain; the Portuguese website www.portugal-gay.pt offers similar listings in Portuguese and English.

There is no gay community in Morocco. Lesbianism is almost unheard of and unrecognized; male homosexuality is illegal under Islamic and civil law.

Listed below are contact organizations, mail-order bookstores and publishers which offer materials addressing some specific concerns. **Out and About** (www.planetout.com) offers a bi-weekly newsletter addressing travel concerns and a comprehensive site addressing gay travel concerns.

Gay's the Word, 66 Marchmont St., London WC1N 1AB (☎+44 20 7278 7654; www.gaystheword.co.uk). The largest gay and lesbian bookshop in the UK, with both fiction and non-fiction titles. Mail-order service available.

Giovanni's Room, 1145 Pine St., Philadelphia, PA 19107 (☎215-923-2960; www.queerbooks.com). An international lesbian/feminist and gay bookstore with mail-order service (carries many of the publications listed below).

International Gay and Lesbian Travel Association, 4331 N. Federal Hwy., #304, Fort Lauderdale, FL 33308, USA (☎954-776-2626; fax 776-3303; www.iglta.com). An organization of over 1350 companies serving gay and lesbian travelers worldwide. The website offers good links to Spanish and Portuguese gay websites.

International Lesbian and Gay Association (ILGA), 81 rue Marché-au-Charbon, B-1000 Brussels, Belgium (☎+32 2 502 2471; www.ilga.org). Provides political information, such as homosexuality laws of individual countries.

FURTHER READING: BISEXUAL, GAY, & LESBIAN.

Spartacus International Gay Guide 2001-2002. Bruno Gmunder Verlag (US$33).

Damron Men's Guide, Damron's Accommodations, and *The Women's Traveller.* Damron Travel Guides (US$14-19). For more info, call 800-462-6654 or visit www.damron.com.

Ferrari Guides' Gay Travel A to Z, Ferrari Guides' Men's Travel in Your Pocket, and *Ferrari Guides' Inn Places.* Ferrari Publications (US$16-20). Purchase the guides online at www.ferrariguides.com.

The Gay Vacation Guide: The Best Trips and How to Plan Them, Mark Chesnut. Citadel Press (US$15).

TRAVELERS WITH DISABILITIES

Wheelchair accessibility varies widely in Iberia but is generally inferior to that in the United States. Access in Morocco is minimal. In Spain and Portugal, handicapped access is common in modern and big city museums. Check out www.geocities.com/Paris/1502 for general information on traveling for the disabled.

Those with disabilities should inform airlines and hotels of their disabilities when making reservations; some time may be needed to prepare special accommodations. Call ahead to restaurants, museums, and other facilities to find out about the existence of ramps, the widths of doors, etc. **Guide dog owners** should inquire as to the quarantine policies of each destination. At the very least, they will need to provide a certificate of immunization against rabies.

Rail is probably the most convenient form of travel for disabled travelers in Europe: many larger stations have ramps, and some trains have wheelchair lifts, special seating areas, and specially equipped toilets. Spain and Portugal's rail systems, however, have limited resources for wheelchair accessibility, especially in smaller stations. For those who wish to rent cars, some major **car rental** agencies (Hertz, Avis, and National) offer hand-controlled vehicles.

USEFUL ORGANIZATIONS

Mobility International USA (MIUSA), P.O. Box 10767, Eugene, OR 97440 (☎541–343-1284, voice and TDD; www.miusa.org). Sells *A World of Options: A Guide to International Educational Exchange, Community Service, and Travel for Persons with Disabilities* (US$35).

Moss Rehab Hospital Travel Information Service MossRehab Hospital, 1200 West Tabor Road, Philadelphia, PA 19141, USA (☎215-456-9900 or 800-CALL-MOSS; email netstaff@mossresourcenet.org; www.mossresourcenet.org). An information resource center on travel-related concerns for those with disabilities.

Society for the Advancement of Travel for the Handicapped (SATH), 347 Fifth Ave., #610, New York, NY 10016 (☎212-447-7284; www.sath.org). An advocacy group that publishes free online travel information and the travel magazine *OPEN WORLD* (US$18, free for members). Annual membership US$45, students and seniors US$30.

TOUR AGENCIES

Directions Unlimited, 123 Green Ln., Bedford Hills, NY 10507 (☎800-533-5343). Books individual and group vacations for the physically disabled; not an info service.

FURTHER READING

Wheelchair Through Europe, Annie Mackin. Graphic Language Press (US ☎760-944-9594; niteowl@cts.com; US$13).

MINORITY TRAVELERS

Because of demographic homogeneity, Spanish people experience little interaction with other races. The infrequent incidents of racism are rarely violent or threatening, just a little awkward. They occur out of naiveté or ignorance when meeting a non-Caucasian foreigner is most often curiosity rather than insensitivity. Portugal, with its rich ethnic composition, is actively anti-racist, and minority travelers have little to fear. Morocco encompasses a diverse cultural and racial spectrum; visitors are defined more by their foreign ways than by their skin color.

TRAVELERS WITH CHILDREN

Family vacations often require that you slow your pace, and always require that you plan ahead. When deciding where to stay, remember the special needs of young children; if you pick a B&B or a small hotel, call ahead and make sure it's child-friendly. If you rent a car, make sure the rental company provides a car seat for younger children. **Be sure that your child carries some sort of ID** in case of an emergency or in case he or she gets lost.

Museums, tourist attractions, accommodations, and restaurants often offer discounts for children. Children under two generally fly for 10% of the adult airfare on international flights (this does not necessarily include a seat). International fares are usually discounted 25% for children from two to 11. Finding a private place for **breast feeding** is often a problem while traveling, so plan accordingly.

TAKING THE KIDS ALONG The following books provide valuable information on how to prepare for a taking a trip with your kids.
Backpacking with Babies and Small Children, Goldie Silverman. Wilderness Press (US$10).
Take Your Kids to Europe, Cynthia W. Harriman. Cardogan Books (US$18).
How to take Great Trips with Your Kids, Sanford and Jane Portnoy. Harvard Common Press (US $10).
Have Kid, Will Travel: 101 Survival Strategies for Vacationing With Babies and Young Children, Claire and Lucille Tristram. Andrews McMeel Publishing (US$9).
Adventuring with Children: An Inspirational Guide to World Travel and the Outdoors, Nan Jeffrey. Avalon House Publishing (US$15).
Trouble Free Travel with Children, Vicki Lansky. Book Peddlers (US$9).

DIETARY CONCERNS

Spain and Portugal can be difficult places to visit as a strict vegetarian; in Spain in particular meat or fish is featured in the vast majority of popular dishes. Most restaurants serve salads, however, and there are also many egg-, rice- and bean-based dishes that can be requested without meat. Be careful, though, as some servers may interpret a "vegetarian" order to mean "with tuna instead of ham." Eating as a vegetarian in Morocco is slightly easier, as bean-based stews and *couscous* (a form of pasta) dishes are extremely widespread. The **North American Vegetarian Society,** P.O. Box 72, Dolgeville, NY 13329 (☎518-568-7970; www.navs-online.org), publishes information about vegetarian travel, including *Transformative Adventures, a Guide to Vacations and Retreats* (US$15).

If it's **kosher,** chances are it's difficult to find in Spain, Portugal, and Morocco. If you are strict in your observance, you may have to prepare your own food on the road. Your own synagogue or college Hillel should have access to lists of Jewish institutions across the nation. Travelers who keep kosher should contact synagogues in larger cities for information on kosher restaurants. A good resource is the *Jewish Travel Guide,* by Michael Zaidner (Vallentine Mitchell; US$17).

For more information, visit your local bookstore, health food store, or library, and consult *The Vegetarian Traveler: Where to Stay if You're Vegetarian,* by Jed and Susan Civic (Larson Publications; US$16) and *Europe on 10 Salads a Day,* by Greg and Mary Jane Edwards (Mustang Publishing; US$10).

ALTERNATIVES TO TOURISM

For an extensive listing of "off-the-beaten-track" and specialty travel opportunities, try the **Specialty Travel Index,** 305 San Anselmo Ave., #313, San Anselmo, CA 94960, USA (☎888-624-4030 or 415-455-1643; www.spectrav.com; US$6). **Transitions Abroad** (www.transabroad.com) publishes a bimonthly on-line newsletter for work, study, and specialized travel abroad.

STUDYING ABROAD

Spain is one of the most popular destinations in the world for study-abroad students. To find out more, contact US university programs and youth organizations that set students up at Spanish universities and language centers. Ask for the names of recent participants in the programs. Many of the programs cluster around Madrid and Sevilla. While Portugal is not as common a destination for study abroad, most universities in **Portugal** open their gates to foreign students, and foreigners can enter language and cultural studies programs at most of them. Study abroad is rare in **Morocco,** though it is somewhat common in Rabat.

Studying in **Spain** or **Portugal** requires a good deal of regulatory paperwork. Students planning to stay longer than three months must obtain a visa from their national consulate. Those students studying only for the summer (i.e., for less than three months) need only a passport. Individual universities and programs have their own requirements, most of which involve a basic knowledge of Spanish and a minimum grade point average.

UNIVERSITIES

Most American undergraduates enroll in programs sponsored by US universities. Those relatively fluent in Spanish or Portgugese may find it cheaper to enroll directly in a local university (though getting credit may be more difficult). Some schools that offer study abroad programs to foreigners are listed below.

Academic Programs International (API), 129 East Hopkins Street, Suite 101, San Marcos, TX, 78666, USA. (☎800-844-8124). Programs available in Granada, Sevilla, Barcelona, and Madrid. Classes include civilization studies, international business, Spanish literature, and Spanish studies among others.

American Institute for Foreign Study, College Division, River Plaza, 9 West Broad St., Stamford, CT 06902, USA (☎800-727-2437, ext. 5163; www.aifsabroad.com). Organizes programs for high school and college study in the Universities of Granada and Salamanca. Both programs offer courses in art history, economics, sociology, and Spanish language among others.

Central College Abroad, Office of International Education, 812 University, Pella, IA 50219, USA (☎800-831-3629 or 641-628-5284; studyabroad.com/central). Offers semester- and year-long programs in Granada. US$25 application fee. Classes include anthropology, art history, international studies, and music history among others.

Council on International Educational Exchange (CIEE), 205 East 42nd St., New York, NY 10017 (☎888-268-6245 or 800-407-8839; www.ciee.org/study) sponsors work, volunteer, academic, and internship programs in Spain and Portugal. Classes span from area studies and business administration to history and Spanish studies.

Institute of Spanish Studies. 17303 Southwest 80st Place, Miami, FL 33157, USA. (☎888-454-6777) Pick from history, Spanish language, and literature amongst others. Students live in family homes. Optional travel to Barcelona and Mallorca at extra cost.

LANGUAGE SCHOOLS

These programs are run by foreign universities, independent international or local organizations, and divisions of local universities. They generally cost anywhere from US$1000 per month and usually include food and lodging.

Eurocentres, 101 N. Union St. #300, Alexandria, VA 22314, USA (☎800-648-4809 or 703-684-1494; www.eurocentres.com) or in Europe, Head Office, Seestr. 247, CH-8038 Zurich, Switzerland (☎+41 1 485 50 40). Language programs for students at all levels with homestays in Spain and Portugal run approximately US$1132 a month.

Language Immersion Institute, 75 South Manheim Blvd., SUNY-New Paltz, New Paltz, NY 12561, USA (☎914-257-3500; www.newpaltz.edu/lii). 2-week summer language courses and some overseas courses in Spanish. Program fees are about US$295 for a weekend or US$750 per 2 weeks.

FURTHER READING & RESOURCES: STUDYING ABROAD.

StudyAbroad.Com Program Search (www.studyabroad.com)

Academic Year Abroad 2002-2003. Institute of International Education Books (US$47).

Vacation Study Abroad 2000-2001. Institute of International Education Books (US$43).

Peterson's Study Abroad 2002. Peterson's (US$30).

Peterson's Summer Study Abroad 2002. Peterson's (US$30).

Discover A New World Today!

Learn Spanish in Spain, Mexico, Central and South America ...

- Classes starting throughout the year
- Small group and private instruction
- Accommodations with host families
- Cultural Activities
- Excursions
- Academic Credit
- Airport Pickup
- Flight Info
- Country Info
- Plus Much More!

Spanish Abroad, Inc.
www.spanishabroad.com
1-888-722-7623
World wide: 602-778-6791 • Fax: 602-840-1545
5112 N. 40th St., #103 • Phoenix, AZ 85018 • USA

WORKING ABROAD

Obtaining a work permit in Spain is a complicated process. EU citizens, if they intend to stay for more than three months, must apply for a **residence card** (*tarjeta de residencia*) within 30 days of arrival. Application can be made at a regional police headquarters or a Foreigner's Registration Office, and you will need a contract of employment, three photos, and a passport. Non-EU citizens must first obtain a *visado especial* from the Spanish embassy in their country of residence, which requires a copy of the employment contract and a medical certificate. Portugal's regulations are similar, although both EU and non-EU citizens can obtain a work permit with a residence visa.

The most commonly available jobs continue to be in the areas of teaching (particularly English) and child care (especially *au pair* services, but also as private tutors). While jobs in those areas are generally available year-round (with September the best time to look for a teaching job), other, more tourist-specific jobs will often open up in the early summer. One favorite of seasoned work-travelers is "touting," which involves enticing tourists to enter a certain restaurant or club.

In **Spain,** the national employment service (*Oficinas de Empleo*) has a monopoly on the job-finding market, and is probably the best place to begin a search. Many seasoned travelers, however, go straight to a particular town's Yellow Pages (*Las Paginas Amarillas*) or even go door-to-door in the town in which they are staying. In **Portugal,** the English-language weekly newspaper *Anglo-Portuguese News* carries job advertisements. In **Morocco,** your best bet is to contact your national consulate for a list of schools with openings.

European Union citizens can work in Spain and Portugal, and if your parents were born in an EU country, you may be able to claim the right to a work permit. Friends in Spain or Portugal can often help expedite work permits or arrange work-for-accommodations swaps.

For US college students, recent graduates, and young adults, the simplest way to get legal work permission to work abroad is through Council Exchanges Work Abroad Programs (p. 50). Fees are from US$300-425. Council Exchanges can help you obtain a three to six month work permit/visa and also provides assistance finding jobs and housing.

AU PAIR ORGANIZATIONS

Accord Cultural Exchange, 750 La Playa, San Francisco, CA 94121, USA (☎415-386-6203); www.cognitext.com/accord). US$40 application fee.

InterExchange, 161 Sixth Ave., New York, NY 10013 (☎212-924-0446; fax 924-0575; www.interexchange.org). Participants must speak the local language.

Childcare International, Ltd., Trafalgar House, Grenville Pl., London NW7 3SA (☎020 8906 3116; fax 8906 3461; www.childint.co.uk). UK£100 application fee.

TEACHING ENGLISH

International Schools Services, Educational Staffing Program, P.O. Box 5910, Princeton, NJ 08543, USA (☎609-452-0990; www.iss.edu). Recruits teachers and administrators for American and English schools in Spain and Portugal. US$150 program fee.

Office of Overseas Schools, US Department of State, Room H328, SA-1, Washington, D.C. 20522 (☎202-261-8200; fax 261-8224; www.state.gov/www/about_state/schools/). Keeps a comprehensive list of schools abroad and agencies that arrange placement for Americans to teach abroad.

VOLUNTEERING

Volunteer jobs are readily available, and many provide room and board in exchange for labor. You can sometimes avoid high application fees by contacting the individual workcamps directly.

Earthwatch, 3 Clocktower Pl., P.O. Box 75, Maynard, MA 01754 (☎800-776-0188 or 978-461-0081; www.earthwatch.org). Arranges 1-3wk. programs in Spain to promote conservation of natural resources. Programs average US$1600.

Habitat for Humanity International, 121 Habitat St., Americus, GA 31709, USA (☎800-422-4828; www.habitat.org). Offers international opportunities in Portugal to live with and build houses in a host community. Costs range US$1200-3500.

Peace Corps, Office of Volunteer Recruitment and Selection, 1111 20th St. NW, Washington, D.C. 20526 (☎800-424-8580; www.peacecorps.gov). Opportunities in 78 developing nations including Morocco. Volunteers must be US citizens ages 18+ willing to make a 2-year commitment. A bachelor's degree is usually required.

Service Civil International Voluntary Service (SCI-IVS), 814 NE 40th St., Seattle, WA 98105, USA (☎/fax 206-545-6585; www.sci-ivs.org). Arranges placement in workcamps in Spain, Portugal and Morocco for those 18+. Registration fee US$65-150.

Volunteers for Peace, 1034 Tiffany Rd., Belmont, VT 05730, USA (☎802-259-2759; fax: 802-259-292; www.vfp.org). Arranges placement in workcamps in Spain, Portugal or Morocco. Annual *International Workcamp Directory* US$20. Registration fee US$200. Free newsletter.

FURTHER READING

How to Get a Job in Europe, Robert Sanborn. Surrey Books (US$22).

Work Abroad: The Complete Guide to Finding a Job Overseas, Clayton Hubbs. Transitions Abroad (US$16).

Teaching English Abroad, Susan Griffin. Vacation Work (US$17).

Overseas Summer Jobs 2001, Work Your Way Around the World, and **Directory of Jobs and Careers Abroad.** All *by* Peterson's (US$13-15 each).

OTHER RESOURCES

Let's Go tries to cover all aspects of budget travel, but we can't put *everything* in our guides. Listed below are books and websites that can serve as jumping off points for your own research.

USEFUL PUBLICATIONS

The Broadsheet, monthly magazine aimed at English speakers in Madrid. Features current cultural and social events, as well as news. Commercially oriented. Web edition at www.spainalive.com.

Focus Magazine, monthly online magazine about the Mediterranean world. Includes information on Morocco. www.focusmm.com.au or www.focusmm.com.

Contemporary Spain: A Handbook, Christopher Ross. Broad and informative discussion of Spanish politics, culture, society, and travel. (US$20/£13).

Culture Shock! Morocco, Orin Hargraves. An extremely helpful guide to the salient cultural characteristics of Morocco, the differences between this culture and ours, and how to manage those differences. (US$14/£10)

Worst Case Survival Handbook: Travel, Joshua Piven and David Borgenicht. Finally someone has filled the void: two experts offer advice on such things as how to stop a runaway camel or navigate a minefield. (US$15)

TRAVEL PUBLISHERS & BOOKSTORES

Hippocrene Books, Inc., 171 Madison Ave., New York, NY 10016 (☎212-685-4371; orders 718-454-2366; www.netcom.com/~hippocre). Free catalog. Publishes foreign language dictionaries and language learning guides.

Hunter Publishing, 130 Campus Dr., Edison, NJ 08818, USA (☎800-255-0343; www.hunterpublishing.com). Has an extensive catalog of travel guides and diving and adventure travel books.

Rand McNally, 150 S. Wacker Dr., Chicago, IL 60606, USA (☎800-234-0679 or 312-332-2009; www.randmcnally.com), publishes road atlases (each US$10).

Adventurous Traveler Bookstore, 245 S. Champlain St., Burlington, VT 05401, USA (☎800-282-3963 or 802-860-6776; www.adventuroustraveler.com).

Bon Voyage!, 2069 W. Bullard Ave., Fresno, CA 93711, USA (☎800-995-9716, from abroad 559-447-8441; www.bon-voyage-travel.com). They specialize in Europe but have titles pertaining to other regions as well. Free catalog.

Travel Books & Language Center, Inc., 4437 Wisconsin Ave. NW, Washington, D.C. 20016 (☎800-220-2665 or 202-237-1322; www.travelbks.com). Over 60,000 titles from around the world.

THE WORLD WIDE WEB

Almost every aspect of budget travel is accessible via the web. Within 10min. at the keyboard, you can make a reservation at a hostel in Spain, Portugal, or Morocco, get advice on travel hotspots from other travelers who have just returned, or find out how much a train from Madrid to Barcelona costs.

Listed here are some budget travel sites to start off your surfing; other relevant web sites are listed throughout the book. Because website turnover is high, use search engines (such as www.google.com) to strike out on your own. But in doing so, keep in mind that most travel web sites simply exist to get your money.

THE ART OF BUDGET TRAVEL

How to See the World: (www.artoftravel.com) A compendium of great travel tips, from cheap flights to self defense to interacting with local culture.

Rec. Travel Library: (www.travel-library.com) A fantastic set of links for general information and personal travelogues.

Lycos: (cityguide.lycos.com) General introductions to cities and regions throughout Spain, Portugal and Morocco, accompanied by links to applicable histories, news, and local tourism sites.

Backpacker's Ultimate Guide: (www.bugeurope.com) Tips on packing, transportation, and where to go. Also tons of country-specific travel information.

Backpack Europe: (www.backpackeurope.com) Helpful tips, a bulletin board, and links.

TravelPage: (www.travelpage.com) Links to official tourist office sites throughout Europe.

COUNTRY-SPECIFIC INFORMATION

All About Spain (www.red2000.com/spain/index.html) has an excellent photo tour of Spain, traveler's yellow pages, and information on major regions and cities.

Arab Net: (www.arab.net/morocco/morocco_contents.html) Good historical, cultural, and tourist information on Morocco, including a list of links.

Atevo Travel: (www.atevo.com/guides/destinations) Detailed introductions, travel tips, and suggested itineraries.

CIA World Factbook: (www.odci.gov/cia/publications/factbook/index.html) Statistics on Spanish, Portuguese and Moroccan geography, government, economy, and people.

CyberSpain: (www.cyberspain.com) Has a wide variety of tourist and cultural info as well as links to other good sites inside and outside of Spain.

Foreign Language for Travelers: (www.travlang.com) Provides free online translating dictionaries and lists of phrases, although it is loaded with advertisements.

Geographia: (www.geographia.com) Highlights, culture, and people of Morocco.

MadridMan: (www.madridman.com) A site devoted entirely to the city of Madrid, with tons of useful info for visitors as well as history, culture, and current events sections.

Microsoft Expedia: (expedia.msn.com) Everything you'd ever need to make travel plans on the web: compare flight fares, look at maps, make reservations. FareTracker, a free service, sends you monthly mailings about the cheapest fares to any destination.

Morocco Today: (www.morocco-today.com) A comprehensive source of information on Moroccan current events, government, and society.

MyTravelGuide: (www.mytravelguide.com) Country overviews, with everything from history to transportation to live web cam coverage.

PlanetRider: (www.planetrider.com) A subjective list of links to the "best" websites covering the culture and tourist attractions of Spain, Portugal and Morocco.

Portugal-info: (www.portugal-info.net) An excellent source for all types of information, from photos to wine descriptions to portuguese personals.

Sí, Spain: (www.sispain.org) Run by the Spanish Ministry of Foreign affairs, this site offers cultural and historical info, tourist info, and another great set of links, all available in German, French and English.

SpainAlive: (www.spainalive.com) From bars and concerts, to beaches and soccer, covers nightlife and recreation info for Spain's major tourism cities.

Spanish Culture: (www.spanishculture.miningco.com/culture/spanishculture) Offers a great set of links including everything cultural from Spanish proverbs to bullfighting to Flamenco music. Many of the links are in Spanish.

Spain Tourism: (www.tourspain.es) Run by the national tourist office, this site is rife with cultural and practical information including stats on national parks, museums, and links to the biggest Spanish newspapers online. In French, English, Spanish and German.

Tourism in Morocco: (www.tourism-in-Morocco.com) Helpful information on all aspects of traveling to and within Morocco, plus city-specific info.

TravelPage: (www.travelpage.com) Links to official tourist office sites throughout Spain, Portugal, and Morocco.

Turespaña: (www.tourspain.es) The official Spanish tourism site. It offers reams of national and city-specific info, an information request service, helpful links on all aspects of travel, and a nifty festival locator.

Xacobeo 99: (www.xacobeo.es) The Camino de Santiago's official website.

AND OUR PERSONAL FAVORITE...

Let's Go: www.letsgo.com. Our recently revamped website features photos and streaming video, info about our books, a travel forum buzzing with stories and tips, and links that will help you find everything you could ever want to know about Spain, Portugal or Morocco.

SPAIN

PESETAS	
US $1= 187.4PTAS	100PTAS=US $0.53
CDN $1= 127PTAS	100PTAS=CDN $0.79
EUR 1= 166.4PTAS	100PTAS=EUR 0.60
UK £1= 272.6PTAS	100PTAS=UK £0.37
IR £1= 211.3PTAS	100PTAS=IR £0.45
AUS $1= 108.2PTAS	100PTAS=AUS $0.92
NZ $1= 80.2PTAS	100PTAS=NZ $1.25
SAR 1= 26.9PTAS	100PTAS=SAR 3.73
MOR 1DH= 17.3PTAS	100PTAS=MOR 5.81DH
POR 1$=0.83PTAS	100PTAS= POR 120.49$

Country Code: 34. **International dialing prefix:** 00.

LIFE AND TIMES

Kiss me baby. Kiss me now like there is no tomorrow. Spain is the country to go to experience a Mediterranean sunset while sipping your *sangría*. As you walk through cobblestoned streets, immerse yourself in a luscious history marked by diverse peoples who once ruled Spain with an iron fist--Romans, Visigoths, Arabs, and French. Each rose in triumphant glory and each fell in tremendous defeat to the next wave of invaders. Nevertheless, in the period they ruled Spain, they each contributed to what makes Spain stand out from the rest of European nations---a vibrant people not to be found anywhere else.

HISTORY AND POLITICS

Some people confuse Portugal with Spain. Aside from being ignorant, these people are dangerous. But let us start from the beginning. Spain was lucky enough to witness man at his most ooga-ooga: in the region of the Bay of Biscay and western Pyrenees, caves are adorned with Paleolithic art that dates back to the 18,000-14,000 BC, displaying pictures of man engaged in hunting, fighting, and taking part in ceremonial activities. In 1100 BC, the Phonecians, well-established traders in the Mediterranean, arrived in Spain and left intricate gold ornaments behind. In 600 BC, the Greeks followed and they too left stuff behind: the potter's wheel along with ceramic vases that used this technology. In 200 BC, the Romans arrived and remained in the Iberian Peninsula close to seven centuries. During this time, they penetrated Spain not only geographically but also culturally; the Latin language was introduced as well as Roman architecture, roads, and irrigation techniques. In 312 AD, when Emperor Constantine officially recognized Christianity as the religion of the Roman Empire, everyone converted in Spain. Sadly, one afternoon in 406, while the Romans were dipping their bread in olive oil and basking in the sun, Germanic tribes, the Swabians, Vandals, and Alans, poured in through the Pyrenees. The Visigoths, however, emerged from the rest of the invading Germanic tribes, settled their court at Barcelona in 415.

THE MOORISH OCCUPATION (711-1492). Following Muslim unification and a victory tour through the Middle East and North Africa, a small force of Arabs, Berbers, and Syrians invaded Spain in 711. Practically welcomed by the divided Visigoths, the Moors encountered little resistance, and the peninsula soon fell under the dominion of the caliphate of Damascus. These events precipitated the infusion of Muslim influence, which peaked in the 10th century. The Moors set up their Iberian

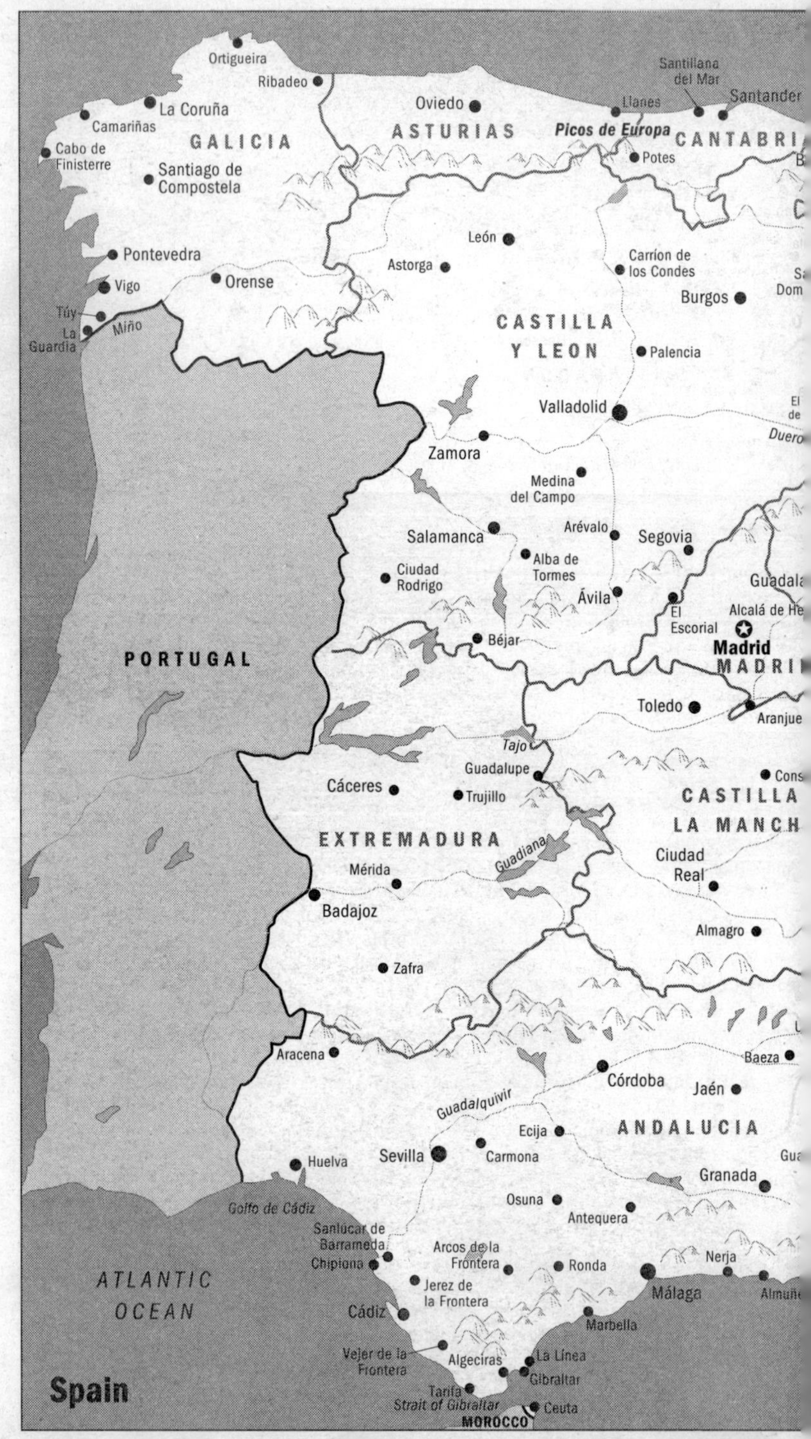
Ortigueira
Ribadeo
La Coruña
Camariñas
GALICIA
Cabo de Finisterre
Santiago de Compostela
Oviedo
ASTURIAS
Llanes
Santillana del Mar
Santander
Picos de Europa
Potes
León
Astorga
Carríon de los Condes
Burgos
Pontevedra
Vigo
Orense
Túy
La Guardia
Miño
CASTILLA Y LEON
Palencia
Valladolid
Duero
Zamora
Medina del Campo
Salamanca
Arévalo
Segovia
Alba de Tormes
Ciudad Rodrigo
Ávila
El Escorial
Alcalá de He
Madrid
Béjar
PORTUGAL
Toledo
Aranjue
Tajo
Guadalupe
Cáceres
Trujillo
CASTILLA LA MANCH
EXTREMADURA
Guadiana
Ciudad Real
Mérida
Badajoz
Almagro
Zafra
Aracena
Baeza
Córdoba
Jaén
Guadalquivir
Ecija
ANDALUCIA
Sevilla
Carmona
Huelva
Granada
Golfo de Cádiz
Osuna
Antequera
Sanlúcar de Barrameda
Chipiona
Arcos de la Frontera
Ronda
Nerja
Jerez de la Frontera
Málaga
ATLANTIC OCEAN
Cádiz
Marbella
Vejer de la Frontera
Algeciras
La Línea
Gibraltar
Tarifa
Strait of Gibraltar
Ceuta
MOROCCO
Spain

FRANCE
Hondarribia
Irún
Roncesvalles
NAVARRA
Ansó
Sangüesa
Tafalla
Olite
Tudela
Tarazona
Torla
Pq. Na. de Ordesa
Jaca
Castillo de Loarre
Ainsa
Huesca
ARAGON
Ebro
Zaragoza
Calatayud
Cariñera
Daroca
Vielha
ANDORRA
Puigcerdà
Seu d'Urgell
Núria
Ripoll
Portbou
Figueras
Empúries
Girona
Palafrugell
Tossa de Mar
CATALUÑA
Montserrat
Lérida
Barcelona
Vilanova i la Geltrú
Sitges
Tarragona
Balearic Sea
TO MENORCA
Morella
Albarracín
Teruel
Mora de Rubielos
Cuenca
Alcúdia
Palma
Mallorca
Sagunto
Golfo de Valencia
Valencia
VALENCIA
Úcar
Cullera
San Antonio Abad
ISLAS BALEARES
Gandía
Játiva
Denia
Calpe
Ibiza
S. Francisco Javier
Formentera
Albacete
Alicante
Menorca
Ciudadela
Mahón
Murcia
MURCIA
Manga del Mar Menor
Lorca
Mediterranean Sea
Águilas
Mojácar
ALGERIA
N
0
50 mi
0
75 km

JEWISH EXPERIENCE IN SPAIN Shortly after the fall of the second Temple in 70 AD, Jews already in Diaspora in the Mediterranean migrated to Spain. For centuries, **Jews** were peacefully settled throughout Iberia, living in peace with Muslims and Christians in a remarkable period known as the *convivencia*. During this time, Jews excelled as merchants, ambassadors, and politicians. However, resentment against Jewish control over trade grew in the 1200s, when **Pope Innocent II** issued a papal bull that made all Jews in Europe wear a special badge, which later came to be known as the **Badge of Shame.** In 1263, **King Jaime I** decided to hold a public debate between Pablo Christiani, a converted Jew, and the medieval Jewish scholar Nachmanides. It was the king's aim to prove publicly that Judaism was "wrong" and Christianity was "right." Nachmanides's refusal to agree with Pablo Christiani on anything promptly won him the prize of expulsion. **King Enrique de Trastámara** comprehensively enforced the papal bull in Spain in the 1300s. The **1391 pogroms** started soon after, as thousands of Jews were massacred and many more forcibly converted. Even those who did convert, called *conversos*, were persecuted and tortured. Jews and Christians had intermarried so much during the *convivencia* that some scholars now believe that most of the Spanish aristocracy had Jewish heritage.

capital in **Córdoba** (see p. 214). During **Abderramán III**'s rule in the 10th century, some considered Spain the wealthiest and most cultivated country in the world. Abderramán's successor, **Al Mansur,** snuffed out all opposition within his extravagant court and undertook a series of military campaigns that climaxed with the destruction of **Santiago de Compostela** (see p. 455), a Christian holy city, in 997.

THE CATHOLIC MONARCHS (1469-1516). It took almost 750 years, if you count the 718 victory of the Asturian Don Pelayo over a Muslim army in Covadonga as the start of the *Reconquista* or Reconquest of Spain, for the Christian kingdoms to "retake" Spain from the Moors. In 1469, the marriage of **Fernando de Aragón** and **Isabel de Castilla** joined Iberia's two mightiest Christian kingdoms. By 1492, the power couple had captured Granada (the last Moorish stronghold) and shuttled off Columbus to explore the New World. Jews and Muslims were forced to convert to Christianity or face expulsion. The Catholic Monarchs introduced the **Inquisition** in 1478, executing and then burning heretics, principally Jews (even those who had converted earlier). In approximately 50 years of rule, the Catholic Monarchs heightened Spain's position not only as the prime European exponent of Catholicism but also as a world economic, political, and cultural power—made even more enduring by lucrative conquests in the Americas.

THE HABSBURG DYNASTY (1516-1713) OR INBREEDING FABULOUS. So sometimes you feel attracted to your cousin. But you never go as far as going to bed with them. The Habsburgs did just this and many, many times. The Habsburgs in this section were the love children of couples who were kissing cousins or nieces that rapidly became Lolitas to their uncles. The daughter of Fernando and Isabel, **Juana la Loca** (the Mad), married **Felipe el Hermoso** (the Fair) of the powerful Habsburg dynasty. When Mr. Hottie passed away after a game of *jai alai* (a fun-yet apparently lethal combination of lacrosse and racquetball) Miss Nuts refused to believe that he had died and dragged his corpse through the streets screaming. But before the hunk was dead, Juana and Felipe engaged in mattress merengue and produced the half-Habsburg **Carlos I** (Charles V, 1516-1556), who reigned as the last Roman Emperor over an immense empire comprising modern-day Holland, Belgium, Austria, Spain, parts of Germany and Italy, and the American colonies. From here on, Habsburgs did other Habsburgs in bed.

But trouble was brewing in the Protestant Netherlands (then called the Low Countries and Flanders). After Carlos I died, his son **Felipe II** (1556-1598) was left holding Pandora's box: a handful of rebellious territories. Despite this, he decided to annex Portugal after its ailing King Henry died in 1580. One year later, the Dutch declared their independence from Spain, and Felipe began warring with the Protestants, spurring an embroilment with England. The war with the British ground to a halt when Sir Francis Drake and some unfortunate changes in the weather undid Spain's **Invincible Armada** in 1588.

Felipe III (1598-1621), preoccupied with religion and the finer aspects of life, allowed his favorite adviser, the Duque de Lerma, to pull the governmental strings. In 1609, Felipe III and the Duke expelled nearly 300,000 of Spain's remaining Moors. **Felipe IV** (1621-1665) painstakingly held the country together through his long, tumultuous reign. Emulating his great-grandfather Carlos I, Felipe IV discerningly patronized the arts (painter Diego Velázquez and playwrights Lope de Vega and Calderón de la Barca were in his court) and architecture (the Buen Retiro in Madrid), and donned extravagant black garb. Then the **Thirty Years' War** (1618-1648) broke out over Europe, and defending Catholicism drained Spain's resources. It ended with the marriage of Felipe IV's daughter, María Teresa, and Louis XIV of France. Felipe's successor **Carlos II** (1665-1700), known as the "*hechizado*" (bewitched), was the product of all the inbreeding booty-shakes: he was known to fly into fits of rages that precipitated epileptic spells. He was also born with a huge, misshapen head, an equally gargantuan chin, and a lethal case of impotence. From then on, little went right: when Carlos II died, he left no heirs because of his "problem" and chaos ensued as several people from all over Europe battled for the Spanish crown. The War of the Spanish Succession had begun.

BOURBONS, CONSTITUTIONS, AND LIBERALS (1713-1930). The 1713 Peace of Utrecht ended the Spanish Succession ordeal and seated **Felipe V** (1713-1746), a Bourbon grandson of **Louis XIV,** on the Spanish throne. The king built ostentatious palaces to mimic Versailles in France and cultivated a flamboyant, debaucherous court. Despite his lack of sexual self-restraint, Felipe competently administered the Empire, at last beginning to regain control of Spanish-American trade lost to northern Europeans. **Carlos III** (1759-1788) was probably Madrid's finest "mayor," founding academies and generally beautifying the capital. Spain's global standing recovered enough for it to team with France to help the American colonies gain independence from Britain, aid that was symbolized by Captain Gálvez's heroically engineered victories in the American South.

Napoleon then invaded Spain (1808-1814) as part of his world domination egoism trip. The French occupation ended, ironically enough, when the Protestant Brits beat up the Corsican's troops at Waterloo (1814). This victory led to the restoration of arch-reactionary **Fernando VII** (1814-1833), who sought to revoke the progressive *Constitución de Cádiz* of 1812. Galvanized by Fernando's ineptitude and inspired by liberal ideas in the new constitution, most of Spain's Latin American empire soon threw off its yoke. Domestically, parliamentary liberalism was restored in 1833 upon Fernando VII's death and survived the conservative challenge of the **Carlist Wars** (1833-1840); these would dominate Spanish politics until 1837, when the monarchy was so weakened that a **Spanish republic** was proclaimed. But even with this new tide of events, political anarchy ensued until **Primo de Rivera's** mild dictatorship in the 1920s. Despite the political anarchy, rapid industrialization and prosperity marked the last two decades of 19th-century Spain. It was during this period that the wealth produced by Catalunya's industrial-inspired *Renaixença* (Renaissance) financed Barcelona's **Modernista** movement in architecture and design. But Spain's defeat to the US in the 1898 **Spanish-American War** cost the Spanish the Philippines, Puerto Rico, Cuba, and any dreams left of Latin American wealth.

THE ROAD TO THE NATIONAL TRAGEDY (1931-1975). In April 1931, **King Alfonso XIII** (1902-1931), disgraced by his support for Rivera's dictatorship, shamefully fled Spain, thus giving rise to the **Second Republic** (1931-1936). Republican Liberals and Socialists established safeguards for farmers and industrial workers, granted women's suffrage, assured religious tolerance, and chipped away at traditional military dominance. National euphoria, however, faded fast. The 1933 elections split the Republican-Socialist coalition, in the process increasing the power of right wing and Catholic parties in the parliamentary

Cortes. Military dissatisfaction led to a heightened profile of the **Fascist Falange** (founded by Rivera's son José), which further polarized national politics. By 1936, radicals, anarchists, Socialists, and Republicans had formed a loose, federated alliance to win the next elections. But the victory was short-lived. Once **Generalísimo Francisco Franco** snatched control of the Spanish army, militarist uprisings ensued, and the nation plunged into war. The three-year **Civil War** (1936-1939) ignited worldwide ideological passions. Germany and Italy dropped troops, supplies, and munitions into Franco's lap, while the US and liberal European states were slow to aid the Republicans. The Soviet Union, somewhat indirectly, called for a **Popular Front** of Communists, Socialists, and other leftist sympathizers to battle Franco's fascism. But soon after, the West abandoned the coalition, and aid from the Soviet Union waned as Stalin began to see the benefits of an alliance with Hitler. All told, bombings, executions, combat, starvation, and disease took nearly 600,000 lives, and in 1939 Franco's forces marched into Madrid and ended the war.

FRANCO AND THE NATIONAL TRAGEDY (1939-1975). Brain-drain (as leading scientists, artists, and intellectuals emigrated or were assassinated en masse), worker dissatisfaction, student unrest, regional discontent, and international isolation characterized the first decades of Franco's dictatorship. Several anarchist and nationalist groups, notably the Basque ETA, resisted the dictatorship throughout Franco's reign, often via terrorist acts. In his old age, Franco tried to smooth international relations by joining NATO and encouraging tourism, but the **national tragedy** (as it was later called) did not officially end until Franco's death in 1975. King Juan Carlos I (1975-), grandson of Alfonso XIII and nominally a Franco protégé, carefully set out to undo Franco's damage. In 1978, under centrist premier Adolfo Suárez, Spain adopted a new constitution in a national referendum that led to the restoration of parliamentary government and regional autonomy.

TRANSITION TO DEMOCRACY (1975-2000). The post-Franco years have been marked by progressive social change. Divorce was finally legalized in 1981 and the percentage of women who vote has risen and they also comprise over 50% of universities' ranks. Charismatic **Felipe González** led the PSOE (Spanish Socialist Worker's Party) to victory in the 1982 elections. González opened the Spanish economy and championed consensus policies, overseeing Spain's integration into the European Community (EC; now the EU) in 1986. Despite unpopular economic stands, González was reelected in 1986 and continued a program of massive public investment. The years 1986 to 1990 were outstanding for Spain's economy, as the nation enjoyed an average growth rate of 3.8% a year. By the end of 1993, however, recession had set in. In 1993, González and the PSOE only barely maintained a majority in Parliament over the increasingly popular conservative *Partido Popular* (PP). Revelations of large-scale corruption led to a resounding Socialist defeat at the hands of the *Partido Popular* in the 1994 European parliamentary elections. Negative attention triggered losses in regional elections in the President's homeland and traditional Socialist stronghold, Andalucía. A second cascade of high-profile scandals in late 1994 further destabilized the PSOE government. Most damaging of these scandals was the arrest of four interior ministry officials charged with organizing an illegal undercover organization, GAL (Anti-terrorist Liberation Groups), in the 1980s to combat Basque separatists; González himself was eventually pestered into admitting his complicity in GAL "death squads." **José María Aznar** led the PP to power after González's support eroded and has managed to maintain a coalition with the support of the Catalán and Canary Islands regional parties. There was a point in mid-1999 when the PSOE seemed on the verge of regaining the majority, but it achieved the worst results in 20 years in the 2000 elections; the PP won an absolute majority, returning Aznar to office.

CURRENT EVENTS. The last three years have seen mixed progress in one of Spain's most pressing areas of concern, Basque nationalism and terrorism. On September 12, 1998, the federal government issued the **Lizarra Declaration,** which called for an open dialogue between all parties, including the militant ETA, the Freedom for the Basque Homeland terrorist group, and was endorsed by the Basque National Party (PNV). Six days later, ETA publicly declared a truce with the national government. Moreover, the newest Basque president, **Juan José Ibarretxe**, gained the support of Euskal Herritarok (the political wing of ETA) and the federal government, pledging to maintain and strengthen the peace. On December 3, 1999, however, ETA publicly declared an end to the 14-month cease-fire due to lack of progress with negotiations. The year 2000 saw a return of periodic terrorist murders of PP and PSOE members, journalists, and army officers, as well as numerous instances of arson. The cry of "Basque yes, ETA no" has been growing stronger as Basque nationalists themselves split over the issue of terrorism, and the problem has become a central focus point for government officials like Aznar as he begins his new term in office. As of June 2001, the ETA continues to place *coche bombas* or car bombs in places like San Sebastián to further the cause.

The Spanish economy is currently in good and improving shape. Over the past four years, unemployment has dropped from 23% to 15% with the creation of two million new jobs—half of the total employment increase for the entire European Union during that time. Aznar describes visions of "a new Spain" and plans to reduce unemployment even further, draw more women into the workforce, and improve the faltering birthrate by restructuring family and work arrangements. As for his involvement in world affairs, Aznar met with Yasir Arafat on late June 2001 to discuss the latest US-brokered truce between Palestine and Israel.

LANGUAGE

Spain's four regional languages and their various dialects differ far more than just cosmetically, although some spelling variations are merely superficial. **Castilian** (castellano), spoken almost everywhere, is Spain's official language. **Catalán** (catalá) is spoken in all of Catalunya. It has given rise through permutations to **Valencian** (valenciá), the regional tongue of Valencia in the east, and **Mallorquín,** the principal dialect of the Balearic Islands. The once-Celtic northwest corner of Iberia gabs in **Galician** (gallego), which is closely related to Portuguese. Although more prevalent in the countryside than cities, Galician is now spreading among the young, as is **Basque** (euskera), spoken in País Vasco and northern Navarra.

City and provincial names in this text are usually listed in Castilian first, followed by the regional language in parentheses, where appropriate. We have found it most useful, however, to adhere to the common usage, and if a town is almost exclusively referred to in its regional name, then we have written it as such. Information within cities (i.e. street or plaza names) on the other hand, is listed in the regional language. *Let's Go* provides a **phrasebook, glossary,** and **pronunciation guide** for all terms used recurrently throughout the text (see p. 733).

THE ARTS

PAINTING

Over its long history, Spanish painting has seen a series of luminaries separated by several lulls. Flemish, French, and Italian influences have often predominated, but such heavy hitters as El Greco, Diego Velázquez, Francisco Goya, and Pablo Picasso have forged a dazzling, distinctive, and hugely influential body of work.

EARLY AND RENAISSANCE. In the 11th and 12th centuries, fresco painters and manuscript illuminators adorned churches and their libraries along the Camino de Santiago and in León and Toledo. **Pedro Berruguete's** (1450-1504) use of traditional gold backgrounds in his religious paintings exemplifies the Italian-influenced style of early Renaissance works. Not until after Spain's imperial ascendance in the 16th century did painting reach its **Golden Age** (roughly 1492-1650). Felipe II imported foreign art and artists in order to jump-start native production and embellish his palace, El Escorial. Although he supposedly came to Spain seeking a royal commission, Cretan-born Doménikos Theotokópoulos, known as **El Greco** (1541-1614), was rejected by Felipe II for his intensely personal style. Confounding his contemporaries, El Greco (or The Greek) has received newfound appreciation in the 20th century for his haunting, elongated figures and dramatic use of light and color.

Felipe IV's foremost court painter, **Diego Velázquez** (1599-1660), is generally considered one of the world's greatest artists. Whether depicting Felipe IV's family or lowly court jesters and dwarves, Velázquez painted with naturalistic precision; working slowly and meticulously, he captured light with a virtually photographic quality. Nearly half of this Sevillian-born artist's works reside in the Prado, notably his famous Las Meninas (1656; see **Museo del Prado,** p. 111). Other noteworthy Golden Age painters include **José de Ribera** (1591-1652), **Francisco de Zurbarán** (1598-1664), and **Bartolomé Estebán Murillo** (1618-1682).

FROM MODERN TO AVANT-GARDE. During the era of Spain's waning power, **Francisco de Goya** (1746-1828) ushered European painting into the modern age. Hailing from provincial Aragón, Goya rose to the position of official court painter under the degenerate Carlos IV. Not bothering with flattery, Goya's depictions of the royal family come closer to caricature, as can attest Queen María Luisa's haughty, cruel jawline in Goya's famous The Family of Charles IV (1800). His series of etchings The Disasters of War (1810-1814), which includes the landmark El dos de mayo and El tres de mayo, records the horrific Napoleonic invasion of 1808. Deaf and despondent in his later years, Goya painted more nightmarish and wildly fantastic visions, inspiring expressionist and surrealist artists of the next century. The Prado museum has an full room of his chilling Black Paintings (1820-1823).

It is hard to imagine an artist who has had as profound an effect upon 20th-century painting as Andalucian-born **Pablo Picasso** (1881-1973). A child prodigy, Picasso headed for Barcelona, then a hothouse for Modernist architecture and political activism. Bouncing back and forth between Barcelona and Paris, Picasso in 1900 inaugurated his Blue Period, characterized by somber depictions of society's outcasts. His permanent move to Paris in 1904 initiated his Rose Period, during which he probed into the curiously engrossing lives of clowns and acrobats. With his French colleague Georges Braque, he founded **Cubism,** a method of painting objects simultaneously from multiple perspectives. His gigantic 1937 mural Guernica portrays the bombing of that Basque city by Nazi planes in cahoots with Fascist forces during the Spanish Civil War (see **The Tragedy of Guernica,** p. 424). A vehement protest against violence and fascism, Guernica now resides in the Centro de Arte Reina Sofía in Madrid.

Catalan painter and sculptor **Juan Miró** (1893-1983) created simplistic, almost child-like shapes in bright, primary colors. His haphazard, undefined squiggles became a statement against the authoritarian society of the post-Civil War years. By contrast, fellow Catalan **Salvador Dalí** (1904-1989) scandalized society and leftist intellectuals in France and Spain by supporting the Fascists. Dalí's name is synonymous with **Surrealism.** A self-congratulatory fellow, Dalí founded the Teatro-Museo Dalí in Figueres, the second-most visited museum in Spain after the Prado.

Since Franco's death in 1975, a new generation of artists has thrived. With new museums in Madrid, Barcelona, Valencia, Sevilla, and Bilbao, Spanish painters and sculptors once again have a national forum for their work. Catalan **Antonio Tapiès** constructs collages out of unusual and unorthodox materials and is a founding member of the self-proclaimed "Abstract Generation," while **Antonio López García** has distinguished himself for his hyperrealist paintings.

ARCHITECTURE

Spanish architecture is as impressive and wildly diverse as the various civilizations that have called the Iberian peninsula home. Continental trends tended to arrive here late, only to be transformed into distinct Spanish shapes and forms.

ANCIENT AND EARLY MODERN. Scattered **Roman ruins** testify to six centuries of colonization. Highlights include some of the finest remains in existence: the aqueduct in Segovia, the theater in Mérida, and the town of Tarragona. Other vestiges of the Roman past lie at the ruined towns of Itálica (near Sevilla), Sagunto (near Valencia), and Empúries (near Palafrugell).

After the invasion of 711, the **Moors** constructed mosques and palaces throughout southern Spain. Because the Koran forbade human and animal representation, architects lavished their buildings with stylized geometric designs, red-and-white horseshoe arches, ornate tiles, courtyards, pools, and fountains. The spectacular 14th-century **Alhambra** in Granada and the **Mezquita** in Córdoba, one-time capital of the Muslim empire, epitomize the Moorish style.

The combination of Islam and Christianity created two architectural movements unique to Spain: **Mozarabic** and **Mudéjar.** The former describes Christians under Muslim rule (Mozarabs) who adopted Arab devices like the horseshoe-shaped arch and the ribbed dome. The more common Mudéjar architecture was created by Moors in the years between Christian resurgence (11th century) and the Reconquista (1492). The first Gothic cathedral in Spain was Burgos (1221), followed closely by Toledo and León. The **Spanish Gothic** style, like those elsewhere in Europe, brought experimentation with pointed arches, flying buttresses, slender walls, airy spaces, and stained-glass windows.

THE RENAISSANCE. New World riches inspired the **Plateresque** ("in the manner of a silversmith") style, a flashy extreme of Gothic that transformed wealthier parts of Spain. Intricate stonework and extravagant use of gold and silver splashed 15th- and 16th-century buildings, most notably in Salamanca, where the university practically drips with ornamentation. In the late 16th century, **Italian Renaissance** innovations in perspective and symmetry arrived in Spain to sober up the Plateresque style. **El Escorial** (1563-1584), Felipe II's grand palace, was designed by one of Spain's most prominent architects, Juan de Herrera.

Opulence seized center stage once again in 17th- and 18th-century **Baroque** Spain. The Chirruguera brothers pioneered this style—called, appropriately, **Chirrugueresque**—which is equal parts ostentatious, ornamental, and difficult to pronounce. Wildly elaborate works with extensive sculptural detail and twisted columns help set this period apart in Spanish architecture.

In the late 19th and early 20th centuries, Catalunya's **Modernistas** burst on the scene in Barcelona, led by the eccentric genius of **Antoni Gaudí, Luis Domènich i Montaner,** and **José Puig y Caldafalch.** Modernista structures defied any and all previous standards with their voluptuous curves and abnormal textures. The new style was inspired partly by Mudéjar relics but far more so by organic forms and unbridled imagination. Spain's outstanding architectural tradition continues to this day with such trend-setters as **Josep María Sert, Ricardo Bofill, Rafael Moneo,** and **Santiago Calatrava,** who has become the most recent sensation with his steel-and-crystal buildings and unmistakable bridges in Sevilla, Mérida, and Bilbao.

LITERATURE

Spain's literary tradition first blossomed in the late Middle Ages (1000-1500). The 12th-century *Cantar de Mío Cid* (Song of My Cid), Spain's most important epic poem, chronicles national hero El Cid's life and military triumphs, from his exile from Castilla to his return to grace in the king's court. Fernando de Rojas's *La Celestina* (1499), a tragicomedy most noted for its strong, witch-like female character that helps two star-crossed lovers. was recently made into a film with Penélope Cruz in 1996. *La Celestina* helped pave the way for picaresque novels like *Lazarillo de Tormes* (1554) and *Guzmán de Alfarache* (1599), rags-to-riches stories about mischievous boys (*pícaros*) with mostly good hearts. This literary form surfaced during Spain's **Golden Age.** Poetry particularly thrived in this era. Some consider the sonnets and romances of **Garcilaso de la Vega** the most perfect ever written in Castilian. Along with his friend **Joan Boscán,** Garcilaso introduced the "Italian" (or Petrarchan) sonnet to Iberia. This period also bred outstanding dramas, including works from **Calderón de la Barca** and **Lope de Vega,** who wrote nearly 2000 plays. Both espoused the Neoplatonic view of love, claiming it changes one's life dramatically and eternally. **Miguel de Cervantes's** two-part *Don Quijote de la Mancha* (1605-1615)—often considered the world's first novel—is the most famous work of Spanish literature. Cervantes relates the hilarious parable of the hapless Don and his servant Sancho Panza, who think themselves bold caballeros (knights) out to save the world.

The 18th century brought a period of economic and political decline accompanied by a belated Enlightenment movement; one of the movement's most important figures was José Cadalso, author of the *Cartas Marruecas* (1789). The 19th century inspired contrasting variety, including the biting journalistic prose of **Mariano José de Larra, José Zorrilla's** romantic poem *Don Juan Tenorio* (1844), a reworking of Tirso de Molina's *El burlador de Sevilla,* **Benito Pérez Galdos's** prolific realism, and the naturalistic novels of **Leopoldo Alas ("Clarín").** Essayist **Miguel de Unamuno** (whose novel *El árbol de la ciencia* is still the most sold out book in Spain) and cultural critic **José Ortega y Gasset** led the **Generación del '98;** reacting to Spain's defeat in the Spanish-American War (1898), these nationalistic authors argued, through essays and novels, that each individual must spiritually and ideologically attain internal peace before society can do the same. Unamuno and Ortega y Gasset single handedly influenced the **Generación del 1927,** a group of experimental lyric poets who wrote Surrealist and avant-garde poetry. This group included **Jorge Guillén, Federico García Lorca** (assassinated at the start of the Civil War), **Rafael Alberti,** and **Luis Cernuda.**

In the 20th century, the Nobel Committee has honored playwright and essayist **Jacinto Benavente y Martínez** (1922), poet **Vicente Aleixandre** (1977), and novelist **Camilo José Cela** (1989; author of *La Familia de Pascal Duarte* (1942)). Female writers, like **Mercè Rodoreda** and **Carmen Martín Gaite,** have likewise earned critical acclaim. As Spanish artists are again migrating to Madrid, just as they did in the early part of the century, an avant-garde spirit—known as *La Movida*—has been reborn in the capital. **Ana Rossetti** and **Juana Castro** led a new generation of erotic poets into the 80s. This newest group of poets represents the first time in the panorama of Spanish literature that women have taken a place at the forefront.

MUSIC

Flamenco, one of the cultural aspects for which Spain is most famous, tis a combination of cante jondo (melodramatic song), guitar, and dancing. It originated among Andalucian gypsies and has continued as an extremely popular tradition that today hypnotizes audiences all over the world. While it is possible to buy all manner of flamenco recordings, nothing compares to seeing a live performance; the spontaneity of the singing and the improvisation for which the best performers are famous is what gives flamenco music its soul. **Andrès Segovia** (1893-1987) was the seminal force in the development of the guitar as a concert instrument; his goal was to invest the guitar with the same renown as the violin and the cello. **Paco de Lucía** (1947-) is one of the most well known names associated with the tradition.

Pablo Casals (1876-1973), Spanish cellist, conductor, composer, pianist, and humanitarian, was one of the most influential musicians of the 20th century. To promote world peace, Casals composed the oratorio *The Manger* (1960), which he conducted throughout the world. Barcelona-born **José Carreras** and **Plácido Domingo,** of "three Tenors" fame, are recognized as two of the world's finest opera singers. While American rock is coveted by youth throughout Spain, there is considerable national pride in Spanish rock, which is plentiful and widespread. **Mecano** enthralls audiences around the world, and disco-goers dance all night long to pulsing **bakalao** (comparable to American house). Barcelona band **El Último de la Fila** and big-forum **Héroes del Silencio** are well worth a listen. **Ella Baila Sola** tops the best-selling charts, and other popular groups and soloists are **Presuntos Implicados, Los Rodríguez,** and **Manolo Tena.** And we cannot forget **Julio Iglesias,** beloved the world over, and of course, his handsome offspring **Enrique Iglesias,** whose dark looks and crooked smile have captivated all of you ladies out there.

FILM

One of the greatest influences on Spanish film was not a filmmaker, but a politician: Franco's regime of censorship (1939-1975) defined Spanish film both during and after his rule. Early success, at least, did not elude Spanish cinema. Spain's first film, *Ría en un Café* (directed by Fructuos Gelabert), dates to 1897, and director **Segundo de Chomón** is recognized world-wide as a pioneer of early cinema. The Surrealist **Luis Buñuel,** close friends with **Salvador Dalí,** produced several early classics, most notably *Un Chien Andalou* (1929). Later, in exile from Francoist Spain, he produced a number of brilliantly sardonic films including *Belle du Jour* (1967). Meanwhile, in Spain itself, Franco's censorship stifled most creative tendencies and left the public with nothing to watch but cheap westerns and bland spy flicks. As government supervision slacked in the early 1970s, Spanish cinema showed signs of life, led by **Carlos Saura's** dark, subversive hits such as *El Jardín de las Delicias* (1970) and *Cría Cuervos* (1975).

In 1977, in the wake of Franco's death, domestic censorship laws were revoked, bringing artistic freedom along with financial hardship for Spanish filmmakers, who found their films shunned domestically in favor of newly permitted foreign films. Internationally, however, depictions of the exuberant excesses of a super-liberated Spain found increasing attention and respect. **Pedro Almodóvar's** *La ley del deseo* (1986), featuring **Antonio Banderas** as a gay man, perhaps best captures the risqué themes of transgression and sexuality most often treated by contemporary Spanish cinema. Almodóvar's *Mujeres al borde de un ataque de nervios* (1988) (that's Women on the Verge of a Nervous Breakdown in *español*) expresses post-Franco disillusion in an unrefined yet fashion-conscious Madrid. Almodóvar, probably the best known Spanish director of them all, has accumulated a long list of international awards, most recently crowned by a 2000 Oscar for his movie *Todo sobre mi madre.* Other directors to look for in Spain include **Bigas Luna,** director of the controversial *Jamón Jamón* (1992) and **Fernando Trueba** whose *Belle Epoque* won the Oscar in 1993 for Best Foreign Film. Other directors to watch out for are **Vicente Aranda** whose recent *Locura de amor* (2001) is based on how Juana la Loca, or the already mentioned Juana the Mad in the Habsburg section, actually became insane.

BULLFIGHTING

A visit to Spain would not be complete without the experience of a bullfight. The national spectacle that is bullfighting dates, in its modern form, to the early 1700s. With bullfighting growing in popularity, Roman amphitheaters like those in Sevilla and Córdoba were rebuilt and embellished, and bulls began to be bred to possess aggressive instincts. The techniques of the modern bullfighter (matador) were developed around 1914 by Juan Belmonte, considered one of the greatest matadors of all time (others include Joselito, Manolete, and Cristina, the first female matador). Belmonte made bullfighting both more exciting and more dangerous by emphasizing closeness to the horns and intricate capework over the kill itself.

A bullfight is divided into three principal stages: in the first, picadors (lancers on horseback) pierce the bull's neck muscles to lower his head for the kill; next, assistants on foot thrust banderillas (decorated darts) into his back to enliven the tiring animal for the final stage; finally, the matador has ten minutes to kill his opponent with a sword between the shoulder blades. He can be granted up to five extra minutes if necessary, but after that the bull is taken out alive, much to the matador's disgrace. On the other hand, if the matador has shown special skill and daring, the audience waves white handkerchiefs to implore the bullfight's president to reward him with the coveted ears (and, very rarely, the tail).

Although bullfighting has always had its critics—the Catholic Church in the 17th century felt that the risks made it equivalent to suicide—the late 20th century has seen an especially strong attack from animal rights' activists and social workers who feel that its prospect of social mobility leads too many young men to premature deaths. Whatever its merits and faults, however, bullfighting is an essential element of the Spanish national consciousness, and will almost certainly continue to be one. For an American take on the myth, meaning, and machismo of the bullfight, check out Ernest Hemingway's accounts in *Death in the Afternoon* (1932) and *The Sun Also Rises* (1926).

FOOD AND DRINK

Spanish food is characterized by a uber-use of olive oil in every dish imaginable. Be ready however, for the fact that taste often ranks above appearance. Spanish food becomes increasingly sophisticated and cosmopolitan, but fresh local ingredients are still an integral part of the cuisine; consequently it varies according to each region's climate, geography, and history. Most experts, in fact, argue that one can only speak of Spanish food in local terms.

LOCAL FARE

Andalucian cuisine is the one of the oldest in all of Spain—it was through Sevilla that New World products like corn, peppers, tomatoes and potatoes first entered Europe. Andalucians have since mastered the art of *gazpacho*, a cool, tomato-based soup perfectly suited to the hot southern climate. The area is also known for its *pescadito frito* (fried fish), *rabo de toro* (bull's tail), egg yolk desserts, sherry wines, and excellent tapas (see below). Spain's best cured ham, *jamón ibérico*, (as opposed to the more common jamón york) comes from the town of Jabugo, where black-footed Iberian pigs gain a special flavor from daily oak acorn feasts.

Sheep share space with more of these prized pigs in nearby **Extremadura,** where a pastoral lifestyle has lent itself to hearty stews (*cocidos*), cheeses, and unique breadcrumb-based meals (*migas*). This type of dry-land "shepherd's cuisine" dominates central Spain. **Castilla-La Mancha** is famous for its sheep's milk *queso manchego*, the most widely eaten cheese in Spain, and lamb and roasted game are an essential part of menus here and in **Castilla y Léon.** *Escabeche*, an Arab tradition of sautéing with lemon or vinegar, has become a Castilian specialty, as has *tortilla española* (potato omelette) and *menestra de verduras*, a succulent vegetable mix. **Madrid** rivals Andalucía with its tapas offerings and is also renowned for the heavy *cocido madrileño*, a mix of meats with cabbage, carrots, and potatoes.

Further north, **Galicia** surpasses every other region with its 800 miles of coastline; most Galician shellfish dishes are prepared simply to emphasize freshness. Octopus, spider crab, and mussels are particularly popular here, as is *empanada gallega*, the Galician pastry filled with everything from pork to chicken to fish. In **Asturias,** dried beans rule the kitchen; *fabada asturiana*, a bean and sausage stew, is the best-known hearty dish for regaining your strength back after a long day of work. Apples, cider, and cow's milk are also especially good here. **Cantabrian** sardines, tuna, and anchovies are among the best in Spain. Food in the **País Vasco** rivals that of Catalunya in national prominence. Particularly popular dishes include *bacalao* (salted codfish), *angulas* (baby eels), and squid prepared in its own ink. It was also in Basque country that Spain's first gastronomic society was founded on January 1, 1900; these all-male cooking groups have grown increasingly popular over the past century and now number over 1,000.

In **Catalunya,** the Roman trilogy of olives, vineyard, and wheat dominates, and seafood, grilling, and unique sauces are key elements of many meals. **Aragonese** cuisine reflects the huge size of the region and ranges from cured hams to egg dishes to candied fruits. **Navarra** boasts the best red peppers in Spain, as well as the famous Roncal cheese; cooked game, sausages, and caldron stews are popular here. **La Rioja** is known for its pork, vegetables and above all wine. **Valencia,** on the East Coast, has been the home of paella and oranges ever since Arab short-grain rice and American oranges were introduced to the area. Less than 200 years old, paella has evolved from a simple vegetable-rice dish to an increasingly elaborate mix of seafood, vegetables, poultry, and meats.

Tapas, small bite-sized dishes, are a popular alternative to full meals. Generally eaten with drinks or as a mid-morning or late-night snack, tapas range in price, size, and content, but essentially every component of Spanish cuisine makes some appearance in tapa form. Their name comes from the verb tapar, "to cover"—it is speculated that they started out as the ham (yes, ham), cheese, or bread used to top wine-glasses in the mid-18th-century to protect them from flies. From that humble beginning they have grown to be a major part of Spanish culture.

MEALS AND DINING HOURS

Discover the leisurely pace of the Spanish lifestyle through its dining hours. Spaniards start their day with a continental breakfast of coffee combos or thick, liquid chocolate and *bollos* (rolls), *churros* (lightly fried fritters), or other pastries. Midmorning they often have another café with a tapa to tide them over to the main meal of the day, *la comida*, generally eaten around 2 or 3pm. This traditionally consists of several courses: an appetizer of soup or salad; a main course of meat, fish, or a twist like *paella*; and a dessert of fruit, cheese, or some sweets. Supper at home, la cena, tends to be light, usually a sandwich or tortilla consumed around 8pm. Eating-out starts anywhere between 9pm and midnight. Going out for tapas is an integral part of the Spanish lifestyle; groups of friends will often spend several hours moving from bar to bar drinking, eating, and socializing leisurely.

EATING OUT

While some restaurants are open from 8am to 1 or 2am, most serve meals from 1 or 2 to 4pm only and in the evening from 8pm until midnight. Some hints: eating at the bar is cheaper than at tables, and the check won't be brought to your table unless you request it. ("*La cuenta, por favor.*") Service in Spain is for the most part notoriously slow and at times frustrating; don't expect subservient, overeager bus-boys. Most city tourist offices rate nearby *restaurantes* on a fork system, five forks meaning gourmet. Full restaurant meal prices range from about 800ptas (€5) to perhaps 1800ptas (€11) in a four-forker. *Cafeterías* are ranked by cups, one to three. Also, many *bar-restaurantes* (and some *hostales*) have cozy *comedores* (dining rooms) on the premises. Diners will repeatedly come across three options. **Platos combinados** (combination platters) include a main course and side dishes on a single plate, plus bread and sometimes a drink. The **menú del día**—two or three dishes, bread, wine/beer/mineral water, and dessert—is Spaniards' common choice for the *comida*, a good deal at roughly 800-1500ptas. (€5-9) Generally, you'll have several options, although advertised items are periodically not available. Those dining **á la carte** choose from individual entrées. Large tapas, often comparable in size to entrées, are called raciones.

DRINKY DRINKS

Cultivate your palate with the fine potpourri of Spanish wine. When in doubt among your choices, the *vino de la casa* (house wine) is an economical, often delectable choice. Also good are *vino tinto* (red wine), *vino blanco* (white wine), or *rosado* (rosé). For a taste, get a *chato* (small glass). Mild, fragrant reds are Spain's best vintages, but the crops of fine wines are vast. La Mancha's **Valdepeñas** are light, dry reds and whites, consumed without long aging. Catalunya's whites and **cavas** (champagnes) and Aragón's Cariñena wines pack bold punches. **Sidra** (alcoholic cider) from Asturias and País Vasco, and **sangría** (a red-wine punch with sliced peaches and oranges, seltzer, sugar, and a dash of brandy) are delicious alcoholic options. A popular light drink is *tinto de verano*, a cool mix of red wine and carbonated mineral water. **Jerez (sherry),** Spain's most famous wine, hails from Jerez de la Frontera in Andalucía. Try the dry *fino* and *amontillado* as aperitifs, or finish off a rich supper with the sweet dulce. The manzanilla produced in Sanlúcar has a salty aftertaste, ascribed to the region's salt-filled soil.

Wash down your tapas with a *caña de cerveza*, a normal-sized draft-beer. A *tubo* is a little bigger than a caña, and small beers go by different names—*corto* in Castilla, *zurito* in Basque. Pros refer to **mixed drinks** as *copas*. So impress your lady by ordering a *copa*. Beer and Schweppes is a **clara.** A **calimocho,** popular with young crowds, mixes Coca-Cola and red wine. Older drinkers prefer **sol y sombra** (brandy and anise). Spain whips up numerous non-alcoholic quenchers as well, notably **horchata de chufa** (made by pressing almonds and ice together) and the flavored crushed-ice **granizados.** Coffee and milk, however, do mix. Café solo means black coffee; add a touch of milk for a *nube*; a little more and it's a *café cortado*; half milk, half coffee and you have *café con leche.*

THE MEDIA

NEWSPAPERS AND MAGAZINES. *ABC*, tangibly conservative and pro-monarchist, is the oldest national daily paper. It jostles with the more liberal *El País* for Spain's largest readership. *El Mundo* is a younger left-wing daily renowned for its investigative reporting. Barcelona's *La Vanguardia* maintains a substantial Catalan audience, while *La Voz de Galicia* dominates the northwest. *Diario 16*, the more moderate counterpart to *El Mundo*, publishes the popular newsweekly *Cambio 16*, whose main competition is *Tiempo*. *Hola*, the original *revista del corazón* (magazine of the heart), caters to Spain's love affair with aristocratic titles, Julio Iglesias, and "beautiful" people. The nosier, less tasteful tabloid *Semana* has gossip galore and readers aplenty.

TELEVISION. Channel surf to the state-run *TVE1* and *La2* or private stations *Tele5* and *Antena3*. Each region has its own network, broadcast in the local vernacular. In Madrid, the local channel is *TeleMadrid* (TM3). *Canal Plus* is Spain's top-notch HBO equivalent. It appears scrambled during movies but features free sitcoms and music videos on Sunday mornings. Tune in to news at 3 and 8:30pm on most stations. Programming includes well-dubbed American movies, sports, melodramatic Latin American *telenovelas* (soaps), game shows (such as the popular and dangerous *Juego de la Oca*, or Game of the Goose), jazzed-up documentaries, and cheesy three-hour variety extravaganzas. If all else fails, *fútbol* games and bullfights are guaranteed to hold your attention.

SPORTS: THE CUP OF LIFE, BABY

¡Viva España! True to form, the beat and the glory go on for Spanish sports. **Miguel Indurain,** a Basque hero and Spain's most decorated athlete, may not have been able to win a sixth straight Tour de France title before his retirement, but he is remembered fondly by his fanatical fans. Several Spaniards, including old favorites like **Aranxta Sánchez-Vicario** and **Conchita Martínez** and up-and-comers like **Carlos Moya** and **Alex Corretja,** have made their names in tennis. Golfer **Chema Olazabal** is one of the world's best, with two Green Jackets in his closet to prove it, but the recent successes of **Seve Ballesteros** and **Sergio García,** "El Niño," have really brought the sport to national attention. As with cuisine, regional specialties spice the sports scene, including *cesta punta* (known internationally as *jai alai*) from Basque country, wind surfing along the southern coast, and skiing in the Sierra Nevadas and the Pyrenees. But the most popular sport is of course *fútbol*, a uniting passion for Spaniards. Their pride is well-warranted: despite a shocking early knock-out in the first round of the 1998 World Cup, the Spanish national team ranks with the finest in Europe. City teams are also powerful: in May 2000, *Real Madrid* won its 8th European League championship, beating Valencia in a first-ever same-country final match.

RECOMMENDED READING

English-speaking scribes have penned several first-class Spanish travel narratives. Richard Ford's witty, account, *Handbook for Travellers in Spain* and *Readers at Home*, remains a favorite. Most time-honored classics are region-specific, including Washington Irving's *Tales of the Alhambra* and Bloomsbury Circle-expatriate Gerald Brenan's *South from Granada.* For a recent bestsellers, look for Lucia Graves' account of her life in Mallorca titled *A Woman Unknown: Voices from a Spanish Life*, which was just published in September 2000.

FICTION, SPANISH AND FOREIGN. Start with the epic story of *Poema del Mío Cid.* Think Braveheart sans kilt and blue paint but with a heavy dose of medieval bad-mouthing at non-Spanish enemies. If you like reading about how a Spanish hunk steals the virtue of all the ladies in one medieval Spanish town, enjoy Tirso de Molina's *El burlador de Sevilla.* They all fall like flies, baby. Whet your palate with the uber-classic *Don Quijote* by Miguel de Cervantes. Be sure to get the abridged version or you'll never finish it. Ever. For gorgeous early 20th century prose, read Nobel-Prize winner Benito Pérez Galdós. His tale of friendship, love, and betrayal in *El Abuelo,* which was made into a movie and nominated for Best Foreign Film in the 2000 Academy Awards, will not only charm you with its prose but also make you weep in ecstasy for its characters' follies. To get a taste of Spain during Franco's regime, be sure to read Ana María Matute's wondrous account of growing up in *Primera Memoria.* Spain has also inspired a number of prominent American and British authors. Ernest Hemingway immortalized bullfighting, machismo, and Spain itself in *The Sun Also Rises* and *For Whom the Bell Tolls.*

SPAIN

ART AND ARCHITECTURE. The definitive work on Spanish art history is Bradley Smith's *Spain: A History in Art.* For late 20th-century art, check out William Dyckes' *Contemporary Spanish Art.* If you want to splurge a little, go for Fred Licht's *Goya,* a must-read for fans of the artist that should be published by fall of 2001. Books on Pablo Picasso, Salvador Dalí, and Antonín Gaudí can be found with minimal fuss. The standard text on Spanish architecture is Bernard Bevan's *History of Spanish Architecture.* For the latest (1980s and 90s) scoop, peruse Anatzu Zabalbeascoa's *The New Spanish Architecture.* However, if you really want to be called a *connoisseur* and know your *arquitectura,* run to the next bookstore and get your hands on *Spain: Contemporary Art and Architecture Handbook* by Sidra Stich.

HISTORY AND CULTURE. Written in 1968, James Michener's best-seller *Iberia* continues to captivate audiences with its thoroughness, insight, and style. *Barcelona,* by Robert Hughes, delves deep into the culture of Catalunya. George Orwell's *Homage to Catalonia,* a personal account of the Spanish Civil War, rivals *Iberia* and *Barcelona* in quality and fame. A handful of other historians and works stand out—Richard Fletcher's comprehensive *Moorish Spain,* J.H. Elliot's masterful *Imperial Spain 1469-1716,* Raymond Carr's *Spain 1808-1975,* and Stanley Payne's *The Franco Regime 1936-1975* on the modern era.

ESSENTIALS

The information in this section is mostly designed to help travelers get their bearings once they are in Spain. For information about general **travel preparations** (including passports and permits, money, health, packing, international transportation, and more), consult the **Essentials** section at the beginning of this book. **Essentials** also has important information about alternatives to tourism (**work** and **study** programs in Spain; see p. 49) and for those with specific concerns: **women travelers** (p. 45); **older travelers** (p. 46); **bisexual, gay, and lesbian travelers** (p. 47); **travelers with disabilities** (p. 47); **minority travelers** (p. 48); **travelers with children** (p. 48); and travelers with **dietary concerns** (p. 49).

TRANSPORTATION

Transportation to and within Spain is quite *excelente.* The easiest, quickest, and often cheapest method of entering Spain is by plane, although Barcelona is well-connected to the European rail system. Despite a romanticized view of European train travel, buses offer the most extensive coverage and are the best option for short trips. Spain's islands are accessible by both plane and ferry. For more specific information on island travel, see **Balearic Islands** (p. 55) and **Canary Islands** (p. 500). For general information on traveling in Europe, see **Getting There,** p. 31.

BY PLANE

All major international airlines offer service to Madrid and Barcelona, most serve the Balearic and Canary Islands, and many serve Spain's smaller cities. **Iberia** (in US and Canada ☎800 772-4642; in UK ☎45 601 28 54; in Spain ☎902 400 500; in South Africa (Johannesburg) ☎11 884 92 55; in Ireland (Dublin) ☎1 407 30 17; www.iberia.com) serves all domestic locations and all major international cities. **Aviaco,** a subsidiary of Iberia, covers mostly domestic routes, with a few connections to London and Paris. Some fares purchased in the US require a 21-day minimum advance purchase. Iberia's two less-established domestic competitors often offer cheaper fares and are worth looking into. **Air Europa** (in US ☎888 238-7672 or 718 244-6016; in Spain ☎ 902 30 06 00; www.air-europa.com) flies out of New York City and most European cities to Madrid, Málaga, Tenerife, and Santiago de Compostela. Discounts available for youth and senior citizens. No service Wednesdays or Sundays during the summer. **SpanAir** (in US ☎888 545-5757; in Spain ☎902 13 14 15; fax 971 49 25 53; www.spanair.com) offers international and domestic flights.

SpanAir Spain Pass: good for flying to any airport within Spain, including Mallorca and Menorca. No minimum stay; maximum stay 3 months. Reservations must be made before arriving in Spain. Valid for 1 year. Under 12 65% discount. 3 tickets US$195 (€228), 4 tickets US$240 (€280), 5 tickets US$295 (€345). Additional tickets US$50 (€58). **SpanAir Spain Pass B** is the same as Spain Pass A, but also includes Lanzarote, Gran Canaria, or Tenerife. 3 tickets US$245 (€286), 4 tickets US$290 (€340), 5 tickets US$345 (€400). Additional tickets US$50 (€58).

Iberia VisitSpain Airpass: 4 one-way coupons good for all mainland airports and the Balearic Islands. Reservations must be made before arriving in Spain. Maximum stay 60 days. Oct. 1-June 14 US$240 (€280); June 15-Sept. 30 US$260 (€300).

BY TRAIN

Spanish trains are clean, relatively punctual, and reasonably priced, but tend to bypass many small towns. Spain's national railway is **RENFE** (www.renfe.es). Avoid tranvía, semidirecto, or correo trains—they are very slow.

AVE (Alta Velocidad Española): High-speed trains dart between Madrid and Sevilla (hitting Ciudad Real and Córdoba). AVE trains soar above others in comfort and price, not just speed. The 10am and noon trains are cheapest; student discounts are available.

Talgo: Sleek trains zip passengers in air-conditioned compartments from Madrid to Málaga, Cádiz/Huelva, or Algeciras. It's more comfortable, possibly faster, and twice as pricey as Cercanías-Regionales trains.

Talgo 200: Talgo trains on AVE tracks. These currently service only Madrid-Málaga and Madrid-Cádiz/Huelva. Changing a Talgo 200 ticket carries a 20% fine.

Intercity: Cheaper than Talgo, but fewer stops. A/C and comfy. 5 lines: Madrid-Valencia, Madrid-Zaragoza-Barcelona, Madrid-Alicante, Madrid-Zaragoza-Logroño-Pamplona, and Madrid-Murcia-Cartagena.

Estrella: A pretty slow night train that has literas (bunks).

Cercanías: Commuter trains from large cities to suburbs and towns, with frequent stops.

Regional: Like cercanías but older; multi-stop, cheap rides to small towns and cities.

There is absolutely no reason to buy a Eurail pass if you are planning on traveling just within Spain and Portugal. Trains are cheap, so a pass saves little money. For the most part buses are an easier and more efficient means of traveling around Spain.

Spain Flexipass offers 3 days of unlimited travel in a 2-month period. 1st-class US$200 (€232); 2nd-class US$155 (€180). Each additional rail-day (up to 7) US$35 (€40) for 1st-class, US$30 (€35) for 2nd-class.

Iberic Railpass is good for 3 days of unlimited 1st-class travel in Spain and Portugal for US$205 (€240). Each additional rail-day (up to 7) US$45 (€53).

Spain Rail n' Drive Pass is good for 3 days of unlimited 1st-class train travel and 2 days of unlimited mileage in a rental car within a 2-month period. Prices US$255-365

(€298-430), depending on how many people are traveling and the type of car. Up to 2 additional rail-days and extra car days are also available, and a 3rd and 4th person can join in the car using only a Flexipass.

BY BUS

Bus routes, far more comprehensive than the rail network, provide the only public transportation to many isolated areas and almost always cost less than trains. They are generally quite comfortable, although leg room may be limited and few buses have bathrooms on board. For those traveling primarily within one region, buses are probably the best method of transport.

Spain has numerous private companies; the lack of a centralized bus company may make itinerary planning an ordeal. Companies' routes rarely overlap; it's unlikely that more than one will serve your intended destination. We list below the major national companies, along with the phone number of the Madrid or Igualada office; you will likely use other companies for travel within a region.

ALSA (☎902 42 22 42). Serves Madrid, Galicia, Asturias, and Castilla y León. Also to Portugal, Morocco, France, Italy, and Poland.

Auto-Res/Cunisa, S.A. (☎902 02 09 99). From Madrid to Castilla y León, Extremadura, Galicia, and Valencia.

Julia Tours (☎91 335 18 97). Runs throughout Iberia and Western Europe, and to Morocco.

Linebús (☎91 426 28 03). Runs to France, the UK, Netherlands, Italy, and Morocco.

Samar, S.A. (☎91 468 48 39). To Aragón, Toulouse (in France), Andorra, and Portugal.

BY CAR

For more info on renting and driving a car, see p. 42. Spain's highway system connects major cities by four-lane autopistas with plenty of service stations. Fast may be in vogue, but **speeders beware:** police can "photograph" the speed and license plate of your car, and issue a ticket without pulling you over. Purchase **gas** in super (97-octane), normal (92-octane), diesel, and unleaded. Prices are astronomical by North American standards: about 130-140ptas per liter (0.781-0.841$ per liter). **Renting** a car in Spain is considerably cheaper than in many other European countries. You may want to check with **Atesa,** Spain's largest national rental agency. The Spanish automobile association is **Real Automóbil Club de España (RACE),** C. José Abascal, 10, Madrid (☎91 594 74 75; fax 91 594 73 29).

BY THUMB

In Spain, hitchers report that Castilla and Andalucía offer little more than a long, hot wait, and that hitchhiking out of Madrid is virtually impossible. The Mediterranean Coast and the islands are much more promising. Approaching people for rides at gas stations near highways and rest stops purportedly gets results. Let's Go does not recommend hitchhiking.

MONEY

Banking hours in Spain from June through September are generally Monday through Friday 9am to 2pm; from October to May, banks are also open Saturday 9am to 1pm. Some banks are open in the afternoon as well. **Banco Central Hispano** often provides good rates, especially on traveler's checks. The following rates are from August 2002. For more information on money, see p. 13.

Tipping is not very common in Spain. In restaurants, all prices include service charge. Satisfied customers occasionally toss in some spare change—usually no more than 5%—but this is purely optional. Many people give train, airport and hotel porters a 100pta coin per bag, while taxi drivers sometimes get 5-10%. **Bargaining** is really only common at flea markets and with street vendors.

Spain has a 7% **Value Added Tax,** known as IVA, on all restaurant and accommodations. The prices listed in *Let's Go* include IVA unless otherwise mentioned.

Retail goods bear a much higher 16% IVA, although listed prices are usually inclusive. Non-EU citizens who have stayed in the EU fewer than 180 days can claim back the tax paid on purchases at the airport. Ask the shop where you have made the purchase to supply you with a tax return form.

SAFETY

MEDICAL EMERGENCY ☎ 112	**Local police:** ☎ 092. **National police:** ☎ 091. **Guardia Civil:** ☎ 061.

Spain has a low crime rate, but visitors can always fall victim to tourist-related crimes. Tourists should take particular care in Madrid, especially in El Centro, and in Barcelona around Las Ramblas. If visiting the Costa del Sol in a car, be aware of the fact that this area has seen increased car theft in recent years. If using a car in Spain you happen to experience car problems, be weary of people posing as "Good Samaritans." Drivers should be extremely careful about accepting help from anyone other than a uniformed Spanish police officer or *Guardia Civil* (Civil Guard.) Travelers who accept unofficial assistance should keep their valuables in sight and at hand. For those travelers using public transportation, it is essential to be on the lookout for potential muggings and pickpocketing. Scams such as squirting mustard on clothing and asking for street directions are often employed for such purposes. For more general safety tips, see p. 18.

Also of concern to the traveler in the northwestern corner of Spain is Basque terrorism, a highly controversial issue both domestically and internationally. The ETA, whose name stands for Basque Homeland and Freedom in the Basque language, was founded in 1959 to fight for Basque self-determination. Its separatist aims have been concentrated toward the pulling away of the Basque region as its own country, distinct from Spain and France. It has historically aimed its attacks at the police, military, and other Spanish government targets. In 1998, the government issued the Lizarra Declaración, which called for an open dialogue between all involved parties, and ETA publicly declared a truce eight days later. The cease-fire quickly ended as there were several assassinations of government officials afterwards. In March 2001, the ETA issued a bulletin announcing its intentions of attacking tourist areas. The U.S. State Department believes that although the ETA has targeted tourist areas in the past, these attacks were not intended to cause serious injury. While there may be some risk to the traveler, the attacks are very targeted and are not considered random terrorism.

HEALTH

There are no particular health risks associated with traveling in Spain. Be sure to be up to date on your vaccinations for tetanus-diphtheria, measles, and chicken-pox. If traveling during the flu season, which runs from November through April, add the flu shot to your case. For more general information on travel-related **health** concerns, see p. 19. The public health care system in Spain is very reliable; in an emergency, seek out the *urgencias* (emergency) section of the nearest hospital. For smaller concerns, it is probably best to go to a private clinic to avoid the frustration of long lines. Expect to pay cash up front (though most travel insurance will pick up the tab later) and bring your passport and other forms of identification. A single visit to a clinic in Spain can cost anywhere from 7700-19,300ptas (46-116$), depending upon the service. You can visit the following site for the most recent updates on travel-related health concerns in Spain: www.mdtravelhealth.com/destinations/europe/spain.html.

Farmacias in Spain are also very helpful. A duty system has been set up so that at least one farmacia is open at all times in each town; look for a lighted green cross. Spanish pharmacies are not the place to find your cheap summer flip-flops or greeting cards, but they sell contraceptives, common drugs and many prescription drugs; they can answer simple medical questions and help you find a doctor.

ACCOMMODATIONS

YOUTH HOSTELS

Red Española de Albergues Juveniles (REAJ), C. José Ortega y Gasset, 71, Madrid 28006 (☎91 347 77 00; fax 91 401 81 60), the Spanish Hostelling International (HI) affiliate, runs 165 youth hostels year-round. Prices depend on location (typically some distance away from town center) and services offered, but are generally 1500-2500ptas (9.0-15.0$) for guests under 26 and higher for those 26 and over. Breakfast is usually included; lunch and dinner are occasionally offered at an additional charge. Hostels usually lockout around 11:30am, and have curfews between midnight and 3am. As a rule, don't expect much privacy—rooms typically have from four to 20 beds in them. To reserve a bed in high se1ason (July-Aug. and during fiestas), call well in advance. A national **Youth Hostel Card** is usually required (see **Hostels,** p. 25). HI cards are also available from Spain's main youth travel company, **TIVE.** Occasionally, guests can stay in a hostel without one and pay extra, or pay 300ptas (1.8$) extra per night for six nights to become a member.

PENSIONES AND HOSTALES

Spanish accommodations have many aliases, distinguished by the different grades of rooms. The cheapest and barest options are **casas de huéspedes** and **hospedajes.** While **pensiones** and **fondas** tend to be a bit nicer, all are essentially just boarding houses. Higher up the ladder, **hostales** generally have sinks in bedrooms and provide sheets and lockers, while **hostal-residencias** are similar to hotels in overall quality. The government rates hostales on a two-star system; even establishments receiving one star are typically quite comfortable. The system also fixes each hostal's prices, posted in the lounge or main entrance. Hostal owners invariably dip below the official rates, especially in the off season (Sept.-May). In most cases, the owner lives in the same building.

The highest-priced accommodations are **hoteles,** which have a bathroom in each room but are usually too expensive for the budget traveler. The top-notch hoteles are the handsome **Paradores Nacionales**—castles, palaces, convents, and historical buildings that have been converted into luxurious hotels that often are interesting sights in their own right. For a parador, 12,000ptas (72.12$) per night is a bargain. If you have any trouble (with rates or service), ask for the **libro de reclamaciones** (complaint book), which by law must be produced on demand. The argument will usually end immediately, since all complaints must be forwarded to the authorities within 48 hours. Report any problems to tourist offices who may help resolve disputes for you. In less-touristed areas, **casas particulares** (private residences) may sometimes be the only option. **Casas rurales** (rural cottages) and **casas rústicas** (farmhouses), referred to as *agroturismo*, have overnight rates from 1000 to 3500ptas (6.0-21.0$). In the Pyrenees and Picos de Europa, there are several **refugios,** rustic mountain huts for hikers.

CAMPING

In Spain, **campgrounds** are generally the cheapest choice for two or more people. Most charge separate fees per person, per tent, and per car; others charge for a *parcela*—a small plot of land—plus per-person fees. Although it may seem like an inexpensive option, prices can get high for lone travelers, and even for pairs. Campgrounds are categorized on a three-class system, with rating and prices based on amenity quality. Like hostels, they must post fees within view of the entrance. They must also provide sinks, showers, and toilets. Most tourist offices provide information on official areas, including the hefty *Guía de campings.*

KEEPING IN TOUCH

Some useful **communication information** (including international access codes, calling card numbers, country codes, operator and directory assistance, and emergency numbers) is listed on the **inside back cover.**

TELEPHONES. The central Spanish phone company is *Telefónica*. Phone booths are marked by signs that say *Teléfono público* or *Locutorio*; most bars have pay phones, though they are often only coin-operated. The best way to make local calls is with a phone card, issued in denominations of 1000 and 2000ptas (€6-12) and sold at tobacconists (estancos or tabacos, identifiable by brown signs with yellow lettering and tobacco leaf icons) and most post offices. You can also ask tobacconists for calling cards known as *Phonepass*: for 1000ptas (€6.01) it gives you 62 minutes on the public phones for calls to the US. For an additional 1000ptas, get 150 minutes! American Express and Diner's Club cards now work as phone card substitutes in most pay phones. International calls can be made using phone cards but are very expensive; the best way to call home is with an international calling card issued by your phone company. Numbers for obtaining calling cards from home are in the **Essentials** section (see p. 29).

FAX. Most Spanish post offices have fax services. Some photocopy shops and telephone offices (*Telefónica*) also offer fax service, but they tend to charge more than post offices (whose rates are standardized by the government), and faxes can only be sent, not received. Cybercafés are also becoming increasingly popular places to send faxes at cheap rates.

MAIL. Air mail (*por avión*) takes five to eight business days to reach the US or Canada; service is faster to the UK and Ireland and slower to Australia and New Zealand. Standard postage is 115ptas (€0.70) to North America. Surface mail (por barco), while considerably less expensive than air mail, can take over a month, and packages will take two to three months. Registered or express mail (registrado or certificado), is the most reliable way to send a letter or parcel home, and takes four to seven business days. Spain's overnight mail is not worth the added expense, since it is not exactly "overnight." For better service, try private companies such as DHL, UPS, or the Spanish company SEUR; look under *mensajerías* in the yellow pages. Their reliability does, however, come at a high cost. Stamps are sold at post offices and tobacconists (*estancos* or *tabacos*). Mail letters and postcards from the yellow mailboxes scattered throughout most cities, or from the post office in small towns.

EMAIL. Email is easily accessible within Spain and much quicker and more reliable than the regular mail system. An increasing number of bars offer Internet access for a fee of 200-700ptas per hour (€1.20-4.20). Cybercafés are listed in most towns and all cities. In small towns, if internet access is not listed, your best bet is to check the library or the tourist office (where occasionally travelers may get access for a small fee). The website www.tangaworld.com lists nearly 200 cybercafés across Spain by location and name.

EMBASSIES AND CONSULATES

Embassies and consulates are usually open Monday through Friday, mornings and evenings, with *siestas* in between. Many consulates are only open in the mornings. Call for specific hours.

Australian Embassy: Pl. Descubridor Diego de Ordás, 3, **Madrid** 28003 (☎91 441 60 25; fax 91 441 93 00; information@embaustralia.es; www.embaustralia.es). **Consulates:** Gran Vía Carlos III, 98, 9th fl., **Barcelona** 08028 (☎93 330 94 96; fax 93 411 09 04); Federico Rubio, 14, **Sevilla** 41004 (☎95 422 09 71; fax 95 421 11 45).

British Embassy: C. Fernando el Santo, 16, **Madrid** 28010 (☎91 700 82 00; fax 91 700 83 11). **Consulate-General:** Edificio Torre de Barcelona, Av. Diagonal, 477, 13th fl., **Barcelona** 08036 (☎93 366 62 00; fax 93 366 62 21). **Consulates:** Marqués de la Ensenada, 16, 2nd fl., **Madrid** 28004 (☎91 308 52 01; fax 91 308 08 82);

Alameda de Urquijo, 2, 8th fl., **Bilbao** 48008 (☎94 415 76 00; fax 94 416 76 32); Pl. Mayor, 3D, **Palma de Mallorca** 07002 (☎971 71 24 45; fax 971 71 75 20); Av. Isidoro Macabich, 45, 1st. fl., Apartado 307, **Ibiza** 07800 (☎971 30 18 18; fax 971 30 19 72); Pl. Calvo Sotelo, 1-2, **Alicante** 03001 (☎96 521 60 22; fax 965 14 05 28); Po. Pereda, 27, **Santander** 39004 (☎942 22 00 00; fax 942 22 29 41); Edificio Eurocom, Bloque Sur, Calle Mauricio Moro Pareto, 2 **Málaga** 29006 (☎952 35 23 00; fax 952 35 92 11); Edificio Cataluña, C. Luis Morote, 6, 3rd fl., **Las Palmas** 35007 (☎928 26 25 08; fax 928 26 77 74).

Canadian Embassy: C. Núñez de Balboa, 35, **Madrid** 28001 (☎91 423 32 50; fax 91 423 32 51; www.canada-es.org). **Consulates:** Elisenda de Pinos, 10 **Barcelona** 08034 (☎93 204 27 00; fax 93 204 27 01); Edificio Horizonte, Pl. Malagueta, 3-1 **Málaga** 29016 (☎95 222 33 46; fax 95 222 40 23; concon@microcad.es).

Irish Embassy: Po. Castellana, 46, 4th fl., **Madrid,** 28046 (☎91 576 35 00; fax 91 435 16 77). **Consulate:** Gran Via Carlos III, 94, **Barcelona** 08028 (☎93 451 90 21; fax 93 411 29 21).

New Zealand Embassy: Pl. Lealtad, 2, 3rd fl., **Madrid** 28014 (☎91 523 02 26; fax 91 523 01 71). **Consulate:** Travesera de Gracia, 64, 2nd fl., **Barcelona** 08006 (☎93 209 03 99; fax 93 202 08 90).

South African Embassy: Claudio Coello, 91, 6th fl., **Madrid** 28006 (☎91 436 37 80; fax 91 577 74 14). **Consulates:** Teodora Lamadrid, 7-11, **Barcelona** 08022 (☎93 418 64 45; fax 93 417 36 54); Las Mercedes, 31, Las Arenas, **Vizcaya** 48930 (☎ fax 94 464 11 24); Calle Alvareda 54, 2nd floor **Las Palmas de Gran Canaria** 35008 (☎928 22 60 04; fax 928 22 49 75).

US Embassy: C. Serrano, 75, **Madrid** 28006 (☎91 587 22 00; fax 91 587 23 03). **Consulate General:** Paseo Reina Elisenda de Montcada, 23, **Barcelona** 08034 (☎93 280 22 27; fax 93 205 52 06). **Consulates:** Paseo de las Delicias, 7, **Sevilla** 41012 (☎95 423 18 85; fax 95 423 20 40); Edificio ARCA, C. Los Martínez Escobar, 3, Oficina 7, **Las Palmas** 35007 (☎928 27 12 59; fax 928 22 58 63); Dr. Romagosa 1, 2, J **Valencia** 46002 (☎ 96 351 69 73; fax 96 352 95 65); Cantón Grande, 6-8 E, **La Coruña** 15003 (☎981 21 32 33; fax 981 22 88 08); Av. Jaime III, 26, Entresuelo H-1, **Palma de Mallorca** 07012 (☎971 72 26 60; fax 971 71 87 55).

NATIONAL HOLIDAYS

The following table lists the national holidays for 2002, so that you don't find yourself stranded in say, Madrid, when everything is closed down, on say, Epiphany.

DATE	HOLIDAYS
January 1	New Year's Day
January 6	Epiphany
March 28	Maundy Thursday
March 29	Good Friday
March 31	Easter
April 1	Easter Monday
April 25	Liberation Day
May 1	May Day/*Fiesta del Trabajo* (Labor Day)
May 2	Autonomous Community Day
June 23	*Noche de San Juan*
August 15	*La Asunción* (Feast of the Assumption)
October 12	*Fiesta Nacional de España* (National Day)
November 1	All Saints Day
November 9	Virgen de la Almudena
December 6	*Día de la Constitución* (Constitution Day)
December 8	*La Inmaculada Concepción* (Feast of the Immaculate Conception)
December 25	*Navidad* (Christmas)
December 31	New Year's Eve

Travel Cheep.

Visit **StudentUniverse** for real deals on student and faculty airline tickets, rail passes, and hostel memberships.

StudentUniverse.com

Real Travel Deals

800.272.9676

MADRID

Life in Madrid is lived around the clock. The morning rush hour coincides with the move to after-hours clubs. In Madrid day are filled with fervent activity, evenings with calm cocktails, and the nights with packed clubs. *Madrileños* pause for meals, but life between is lived on the go. While tourists inundate the city, spending their days absorbing its "Old World" monuments, world-renowned museums, and raging nightlife, Madrid's population of 4.5 million roams the labyrinthine neighborhoods, living life with a simple and energetic joy.

Madrid's history does not read like that of rival European capitals. Although the city witnessed the coronation of Fernando and Isabel, Madrid did not gain importance until Habsburg King Felipe II moved the court here in 1561. Despite being far from vital ports and rivers, it immediately became a seat of wealth, culture, and imperial glory, serving as the center of Spain's 16th- and 17th-century Golden Age of literature, art, and architecture. In the 18th century, Madrid witnessed a Neoclassical rebirth as King Carlos III embellished the city with wide, tree-lined boulevards and scores of imposing buildings. In the 19th century, however, Madrid was scarred by the Peninsular Wars against Napoleon, the bloody inspiration for some of Francisco de Goya's most famous canvases.

In 1939, Madrid was the last city, save Valencia, to fall in the Spanish Civil War. Though it was hostile to Franco's nationalism, the city was forced to serve as the center of his government. This time, its location—smack in the center of the country—was considered its greatest strength. With Franco's death nearly 40 years later came an explosion known as *La Movida* ("Shift" or "Movement"). After decades of totalitarian repression, Madrid burst out laughing and crying in a breathtaking, city-wide release of inhibition. A 200,000-strong student population took to the streets and stayed there—they haven't stopped moving yet.

Today Madrid continues to serve as Spain's political, intellectual and cultural center. It is not as cosmopolitan as Barcelona nor as charming as Sevilla, but it is undeniably the *capital*—the wild, pulsing heart of Spain. Students, families and artists alike flock to the city in pursuit of their dreams, and Madrid continues to grow. Even its very architecture, with modern skyscrapers and shining industrial spaces expanding from narrow alleys and ancient plazas, seems to epitomize the mix of galvanizing history and passion for the present that so defines all of Spain.

INTERCITY TRANSPORT

All flights land at **Aeropuerto Internacional de Barajas** (☎90 235 35 70), 20 min. or 15km northeast of Madrid. A branch of the **regional tourist office** in the international arrivals area has maps and info. (☎90 220 00 07. Open M-F 8am-8pm, Sa 9am-1pm). Branches of the **Brújula accommodations service,** located in the airport and at the Bus-Aeropuerto stop, can help visitors find places to stay (see p. 90).

The **Barajas metro line,** inaugurated in June 1999, connects the airport to all of Madrid (145ptas/0.90€). From the airport, follow signs to the metro. Take line 8 (pink) to Mar de Cristal, and switch to line 4 (brown, towards Argüelles). From line 4, change to line 2 (red) at the Goya stop, and five stops later you will find yourself at Sol, smack in the middle of Madrid's best accommodations and sights. Another option is the green **Bus-Aeropuerto #89** (look for "EMT" signs just outside the doors), which leaves from the national and international terminals and runs to the city center (every 25min. 4:45am-6:17am; every 15min. 6:17am-10pm; every hr. 10pm-1:50am; 400ptas/2.40€). The bus stops underground beneath the Jardines del Descubrimiento in **Plaza de Colón** (M: Colón). After surfacing in Pl. Colón, walk toward the neo-Gothic statue that overlooks the **Paseo de Recoletos** on the opposite side of the gardens. The Colón metro station is across the street. Fleets of **taxis**

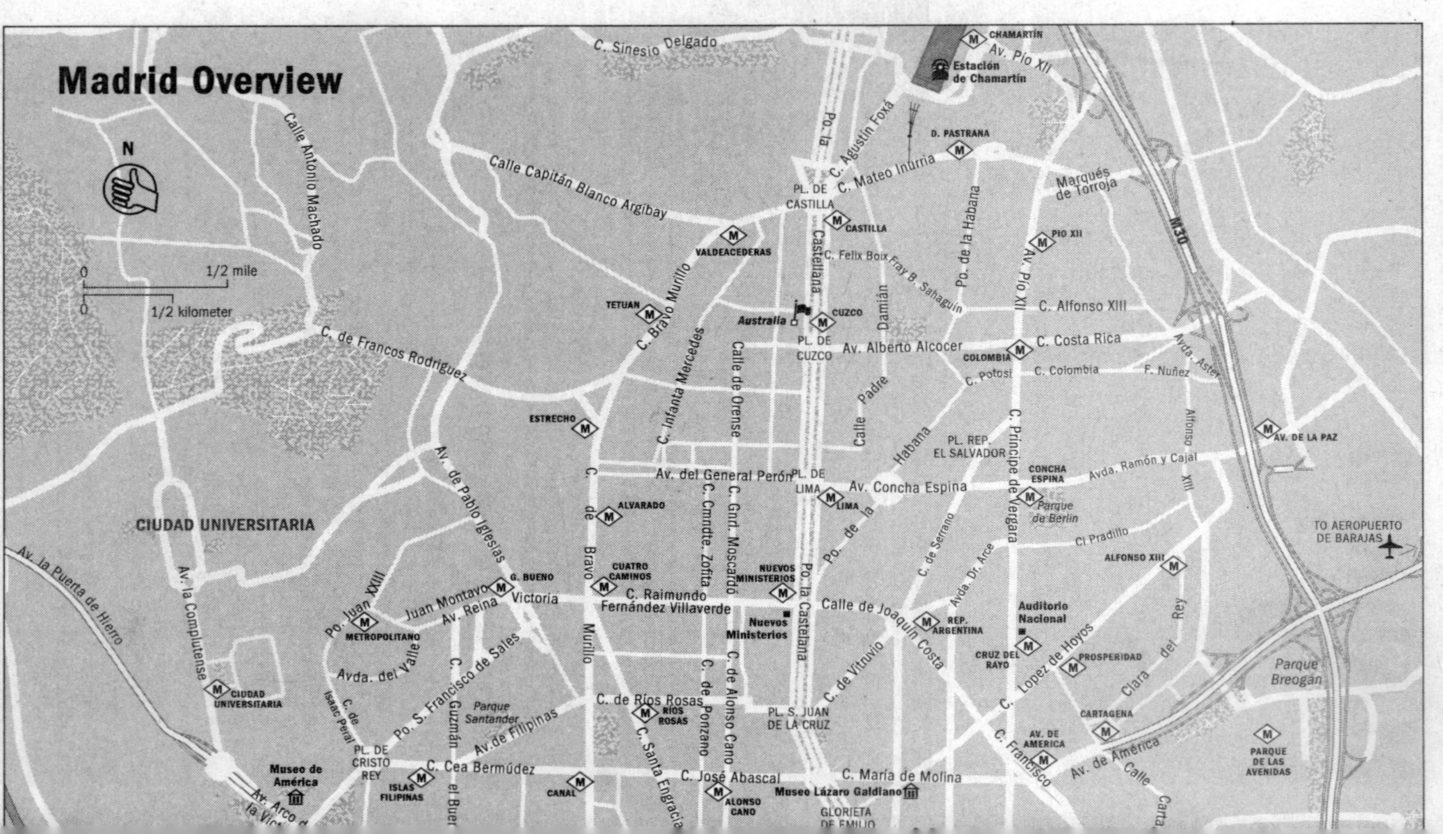
Madrid Overview
N
0
1/2 mile
0
1/2 kilometer
C. Sinesio Delgado
CHAMARTÍN
Av. Pío XII
Estación de Chamartín
Calle Antonio Machado
Calle Capitán Blanco Argibay
Po. la Castellana
C. Agustín Foxá
D. PASTRANA
C. Mateo Inurria
PL. DE CASTILLA
CASTILLA
Marqués de Torroja
M30
Po. de la Habana
PIO XII
Av. Pío XII
VALDEACEDERAS
C. Félix Boix
Fray B. Sahagún
TETUAN
C. Bravo Murillo
Australia
CUZCO
Damián
C. Alfonso XIII
PL. DE CUZCO
Av. Alberto Alcocer
COLOMBIA
C. Costa Rica
Avda. Aster
C. de Francos Rodríguez
C. Infanta Mercedes
Calle de Orense
C. Potosí
C. Colombia
F. Nuñez
Calle Padre
ESTRECHO
Habana
PL. REP. EL SALVADOR
C. Príncipe de Vergara
Alfonso XIII
AV. DE LA PAZ
Avda. Ramón y Cajal
Av. del General Perón
PL. DE LIMA
Av. Concha Espina
CONCHA ESPINA
LIMA
ALVARADO
C. Cmndte. Zofita
C. Gnrl. Moscardó
Po. de la
Parque de Berlín
CIUDAD UNIVERSITARIA
C. de Bravo Murillo
C. de Serrano
Cl Pradillo
TO AEROPUERTO DE BARAJAS
Av. la Puerta de Hierro
Av. la Complutense
Po. Juan XXIII
G. BUENO
CUATRO CAMINOS
NUEVOS MINISTERIOS
ALFONSO XIII
Avda. Dr. Arce
Juan Montavo
Av. Reina
Victoria
C. Raimundo Fernández Villaverde
Calle de Joaquín Costa
REP. ARGENTINA
Auditorio Nacional
METROPOLITANO
Nuevos Ministerios
Rey
CRUZ DEL RAYO
C. Lopez de Hoyos
PROSPERIDAD
Clara del
Parque Breogán
Avda. del Valle
C. Guzmán el Bueno
Po. S. Francisco de Sales
C. de Ríos Rosas
RÍOS ROSAS
C. de Ponzano
C. de Alonso Cano
C. de Vitruvio
CIUDAD UNIVERSITARIA
C. de Isaac Peral
Parque Santander
Av. de Filipinas
PL. S. JUAN DE LA CRUZ
CARTAGENA
PL. DE CRISTO REY
C. Santa Engracia
AV. DE AMERICA
C. Francisco
Av. de América
PARQUE DE LAS AVENIDAS
Museo de América
C. Cea Bermúdez
C. José Abascal
C. María de Molina
Calle Carta
ISLAS FILIPINAS
CANAL
ALONSO CANO
Museo Lázaro Galdiano
GLORIETA DE EMILIO
Av. Arco de la Vict

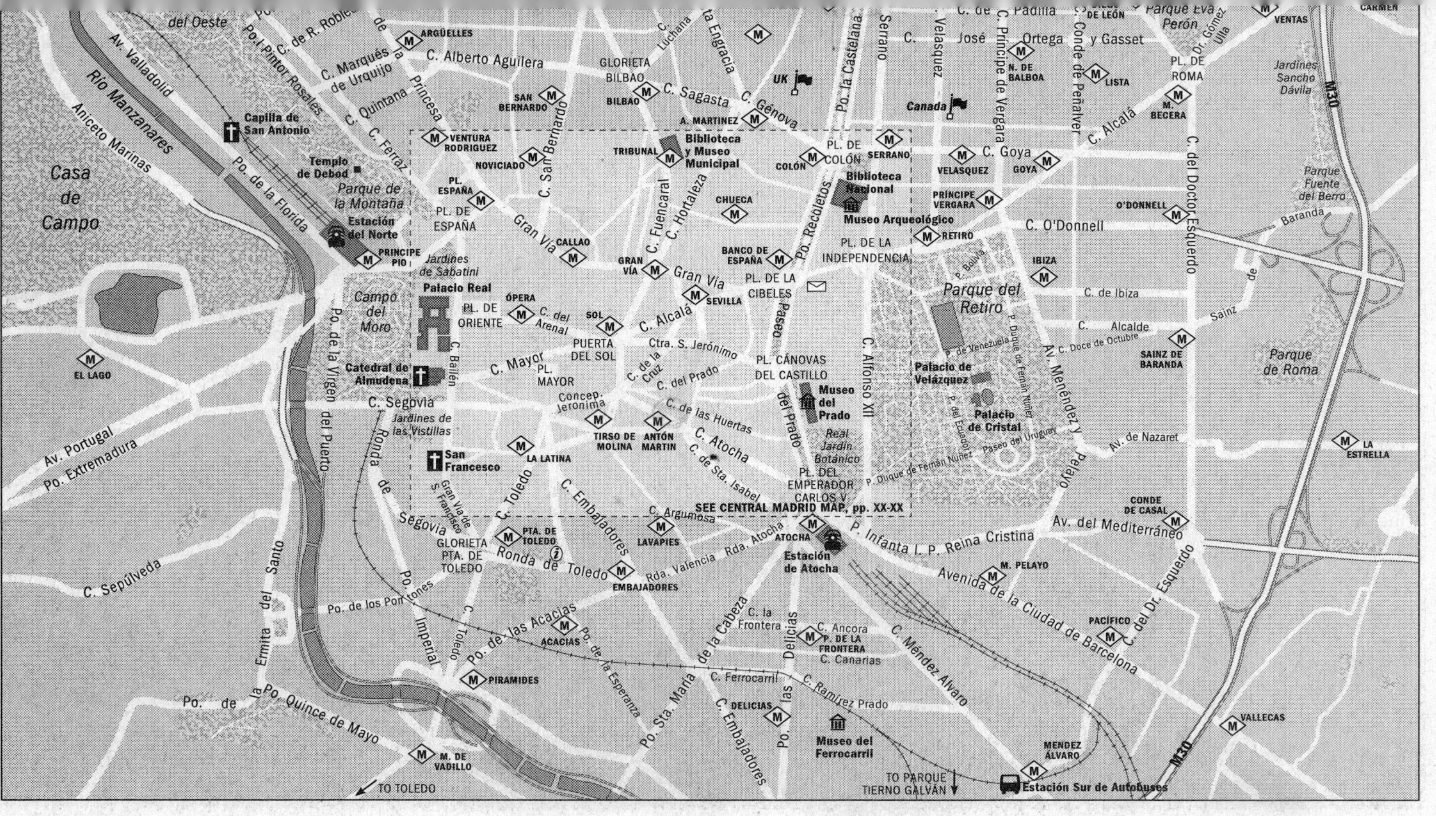
M30
Parque Fuente del Berro
Jardines Sancho Dávila
Parque de Roma
LA ESTRELLA
VENTAS
VALLECAS
C. del Doctor Esquerdo
C. del Dr. Esquerdo
PL. DE ROMA
M. BECERA
O'DONNELL
SAINZ DE BARANDA
LISTA
C. Conde de Peñalver
C. Alcalá
C. de Ibiza
C. Alcalde
C. Doce de Octubre
Av. de Nazaret
CONDE DE CASAL
Av. del Mediterráneo
PACÍFICO
Avenida de la Ciudad de Barcelona
Estación Sur de Autobuses
MENDEZ ALVARO
C. O'Donnell
IBIZA
Av. Menéndez y Pelayo
GOYA
C. Goya
N. DE BALBOA
C. Príncipe de Vergara
PRINCIPE VERGARA
RETIRO
VELASQUEZ
C. Velasquez
C. José Ortega y Gasset
Canada
Parque del Retiro
Palacio de Velázquez
Palacio de Cristal
P. Duque de Fernán Nuñez
P. de Venezuela
P. del Ecuador
Paseo del Uruguay
M. PELAYO
C. Méndez Alvaro
TO PARQUE TIERNO GALVÁN
Serrano
SERRANO
PL. DE COLÓN
Biblioteca Nacional
Museo Arqueológico
PL. DE LA INDEPENDENCIA
C. Alfonso XII
Museo del Prado
Real Jardín Botánico
P. Infanta I. P. Reina Cristina
Po. la Castellana
Po. Recoletos
COLÓN
UK
Paseo del Prado
PL. DE LA CIBELES
BANCO DE ESPAÑA
PL. CÁNOVAS DEL CASTILLO
PL. DEL EMPERADOR CARLOS V
SEE CENTRAL MADRID MAP, pp. XX-XX
ATOCHA
Estación de Atocha
C. Ancora
P. DE LA FRONTERA
C. Canarias
C. Ramírez Prado
Museo del Ferrocarril
Po. las Delicias
DELICIAS
C. Ferrocarril
C. Embajadores
C. Génova
C. Sagasta
Santa Engracia
A. MARTINEZ
Biblioteca y Museo Municipal
CHUECA
C. Hortaleza
Gran Vía
SEVILLA
C. Alcalá
Ctra. S. Jerónimo
C. del Prado
C. de las Huertas
C. Atocha
C. de Sta. Isabel
Rda. Atocha
C. Argumosa
LAVAPIES
Rda. Valencia
EMBAJADORES
Po. Sta. María de la Cabeza
C. la Frontera
C. Fuencarral
TRIBUNAL
GRAN VÍA
GLORIETA BILBAO
BILBAO
C. Luchana
SOL
PUERTA DEL SOL
C. de la Cruz
ANTÓN MARTIN
TIRSO DE MOLINA
Concep. Jerónima
Po. de la Esperanza
ACACIAS
Po. de las Acacias
C. San Bernardo
SAN BERNARDO
CALLAO
C. del Arenal
PL. MAYOR
C. Mayor
LA LATINA
C. Toledo
PTA. DE TOLEDO
Ronda de Toledo
PIRAMIDES
M. DE VADILLO
TO TOLEDO
C. Alberto Aguilera
NOVICIADO
VENTURA RODRIGUEZ
ÓPERA
PL. DE ORIENTE
Palacio Real
C. Bailén
San Francesco
Gran Vía de S. Francisco
GLORIETA PTA. DE TOLEDO
Po. Imperial
Po. de los Pontones
ARGÜELLES
C. Princesa
PL. ESPAÑA
PL. DE ESPAÑA
Jardines de Sabatini
Jardines de las Vistillas
C. Segovia
Ronda de Segovia
Catedral de Almudena
Campo del Moro
PRINCIPE PIO
Estación del Norte
Parque de la Montaña
Templo de Debod
C. Ferraz
C. Quintana
C. Marqués de Urquijo
Po. de la Virgen del Puerto
Po. de la Po. Quince de Mayo
Ermita del Santo
Po. de la Florida
Capilla de San Antonio
Po. Pintor Rosales
Po. del Oeste
Av. Valladolid
Río Manzanares
Aniceto Marinas
Casa de Campo
EL LAGO
Av. Portugal
Po. Extremadura
C. Sepúlveda

• Hostal Oriente.

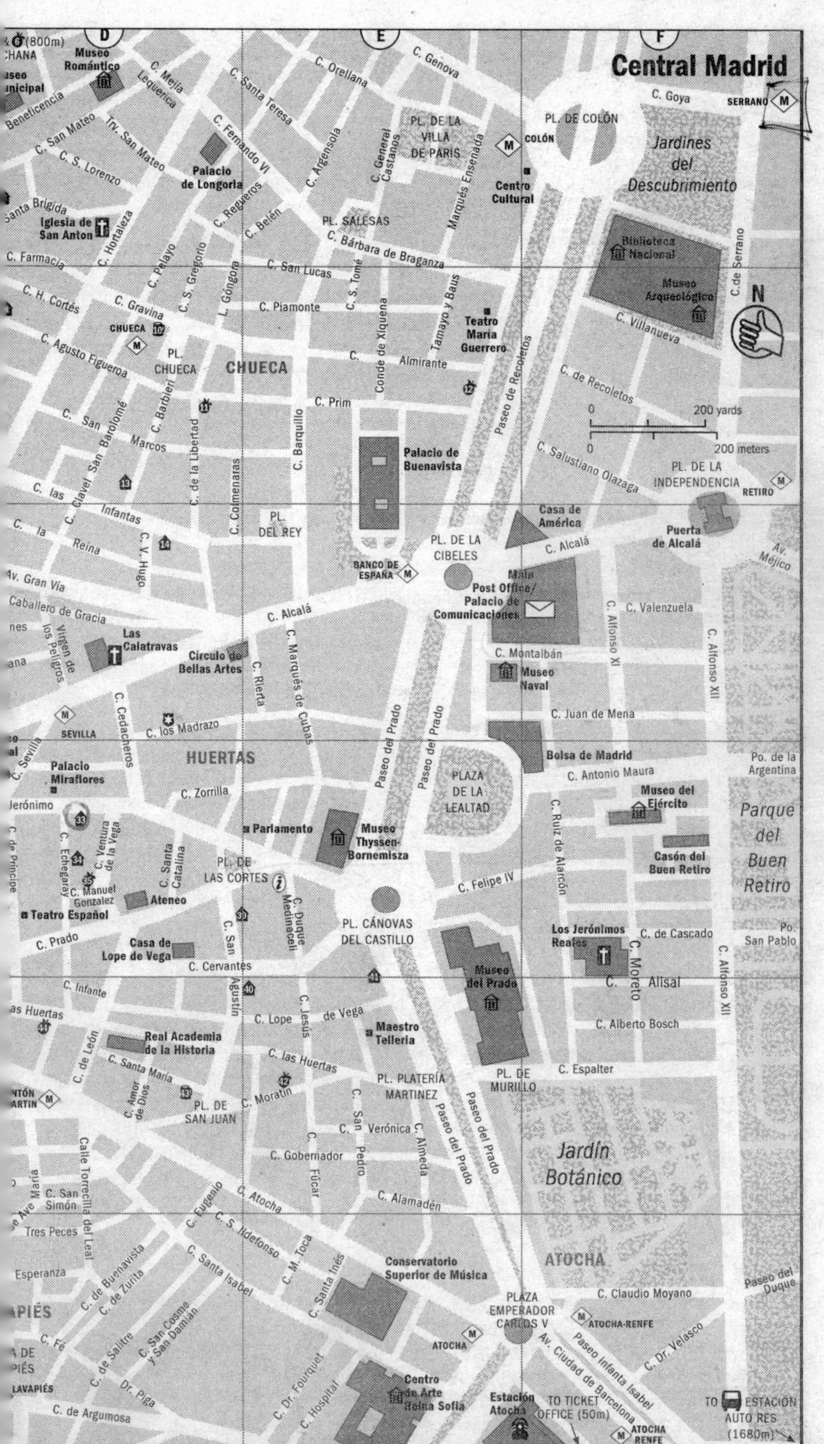

Central Madrid
D
E
F
Museo Romántico
Palacio de Longoria
Iglesia de San Anton
C. Genova
C. Orellana
C. Santa Teresa
C. Fernando VI
PL. DE LA VILLA DE PARIS
COLÓN
Centro Cultural
PL. DE COLÓN
C. Goya
SERRANO
Jardines del Descubrimiento
Biblioteca Nacional
Museo Arqueológico
C. de Serrano
C. Villanueva
C. de Recoletos
Paseo de Recoletos
PL. SALESAS
C. Bárbara de Braganza
C. San Lucas
C. Piamonte
Teatro María Guerrero
C. Almirante
C. Prim
CHUECA
PL. CHUECA
C. Gravina
C. Augusto Figueroa
C. San Marcos
Palacio de Buenavista
C. Salustiano Olazaga
PL. DE LA INDEPENDENCIA
RETIRO
Puerta de Alcalá
Casa de América
C. Alcalá
PL. DE LA CIBELES
BANCO DE ESPAÑA
Main Post Office/ Palacio de Comunicaciones
PL. DEL REY
C. Infantas
C. la Reina
Av. Gran Vía
Caballero de Gracia
Las Calatravas
Círculo de Bellas Artes
C. Marqués de Cubas
C. Valenzuela
C. Alfonso XI
C. Alfonso XII
C. Montalbán
Museo Naval
C. Juan de Mena
Bolsa de Madrid
C. Antonio Maura
Museo del Ejército
Casón del Buen Retiro
Parque del Buen Retiro
Po. de la Argentina
SEVILLA
C. los Madrazo
HUERTAS
Palacio Miraflores
C. Zorrilla
Parlamento
Museo Thyssen-Bornemisza
PLAZA DE LA LEALTAD
Paseo del Prado
PL. DE LAS CORTES
C. Felipe IV
C. Ruiz de Alarcón
Ateneo
Teatro Español
PL. CÁNOVAS DEL CASTILLO
Casa de Lope de Vega
C. Cervantes
C. Prado
Los Jerónimos Reales
C. de Cascado
C. Moreto
C. Alisal
Po. San Pablo
Museo del Prado
C. Alberto Bosch
Maestro Tellería
Real Academia de la Historia
C. Lope de Vega
C. las Huertas
PL. PLATERÍA MARTINEZ
PL. DE MURILLO
C. Espalter
PL. DE SAN JUAN
C. Moratín
C. Verónica
C. Gobernador
C. Alameda
Jardín Botánico
C. Atocha
C. Alamadén
ATOCHA
Conservatorio Superior de Música
PLAZA EMPERADOR CARLOS V
C. Claudio Moyano
ATOCHA-RENFE
Paseo del Duque
Av. Ciudad de Barcelona
Paseo Infanta Isabel
C. Dr. Velasco
Centro de Arte Reina Sofía
Estación Atocha
TO TICKET OFFICE (50m)
TO ESTACIÓN AUTO RES (1680m)
200 yards
200 meters
N

swarm the airport. Taxi fare to central Madrid should cost around 3000ptas/18€, including the 400ptas/€2.40 airport surcharge.

AIRLINES

Iberia: Santa Cruz de Marcenado, 2 (☎91 587 81 56). M: San Bernardo. Open M-F 9:30am-2pm and 4-7pm. 24hr. reservations and info (☎902 40 05 00). **Aviaco,** C. Maude, 51 (☎91 554 36 00), is a domestic affiliate. International affiliates, **Tap Air Portugal** (☎90 111 65 18) and **Portugalia** (☎91 541 77 78) fly to Portugal.

Air France: Pl. España, 18, 5th fl. (☎91 330 04 12; reservations ☎91 111 22 66; www.airfrance.es). M: Pl. España. Open M-F 9am-5pm.

American Airlines: Orense, 4, 1st fl. (☎90 211 55 70). Open M-F 9am-5:30pm. Reservations (☎91 453 14 00). Open M-F 9am-6:30pm, Sa 9am-2pm.

British Airways: Santiago de Compostela, 100 (☎91 387 43 00). Open M-F 9am-5pm. Reservations (☎91 376 96 66) open M-F 9am-7pm.

Continental: C. Leganitos, 47, 9th fl. (☎91 559 24 87). M: Pl. España. Open M-F 9am-6pm. Reservations open M-F 9am-7pm.

Lufthansa: Cardenal Marcelo Española, 2 (☎91 383 51 13; reservations ☎90 222 01 01), located outside city limits.

USAir: Alberto Aguillera, 38, 2nd fl. (☎90 099 33 08). Open M-F 9am-6pm.

BY TRAIN

Two *Largo Recorrido* (long distance) **RENFE** stations, **Madrid-Chamartín** and **Madrid-Atocha,** connect Madrid to the rest of Europe. Call RENFE (☎91 328 90 20 or 90 224 02 02; www.renfe.es) for reservations and info. **RENFE Main Office,** C. Alcalá, 44, at Gran Vía (M: Banco de España) sells tickets. Schedules and **AVE** (☎91 534 05 05) and **Talgo** tickets are also available. Open M-F 9:30am-8pm.

Estación Chamartín: (for international destinations 24hr ☎93 49 01 122; domestic destinations ☎90 224 02 02; Spanish only), Agustín de Foxá. M: Chamartín. Bus #5 runs to and from Sol (45min.); the stop is just beyond the lockers. Ticket windows open 8:30am-10:30pm. Chamartín services both international and domestic destinations in the Northeast and South. Most *cercanías* (local) trains leave from Chamartín; many stop at Atocha. To: **Barcelona** (7hr., 10 per day 7am-12:50am, 6785ptas/€41); **Lisbon** (10hr., 10:45pm, 6900ptas/€42); **Paris** (13hr., 7pm, 19,500ptas/€117); and **Nice** (22hr., 10am, 21,500ptas/€129). Chamartín is a mini-mall of useful services, including a **tourist office** (Vestíbulo, Puerta 14. ☎91 315 99 76. Open M-F 8am-8pm, Sa 9am-1pm), currency exchange, accommodations service, post office, car rental, police, and **lockers** (400-600ptas/€2.40-3.61).

Estación Atocha: (☎91 328 90 20). M: Atocha. Ticket windows open 6:30am-11:30pm. No international service. Trains to: **Andalucía, Castilla-La Mancha, Castilla y León, El Escorial, Extremadura, Sierra de Guadarrama,** and **Valencia. AVE** service (☎91 534 05 05) to the south of Spain, including **Córdoba** (1¾hr., 16 per day 7am-10pm, 5100-7200ptas/€31-43; cheaper on the Málaga route than the Sevilla route) and **Sevilla** (2½hr., 20 per day 7am- 9pm, 8600-10,000 ptas/€52-60) The cast-iron atrium of the original station has been turned into a simulated rainforest. Art galleries, boutiques, restaurants, and cafés serve as additional diversions. **Information office** in the main terminal (☎90 224 02 02). Open 7am-10pm daily. **Luggage storage** (400-600ptas/€2.40-3.61), follow signs for *cosigna*, by the rainforest.

BY BUS

Numerous private companies, each with its own station and set of destinations, serve Madrid; many buses pass through the **Estación Sur de Autobuses.** The Pl. Mayor tourist office has a comprehensive and oft-updated photocopy of most relevant inter-city bus information. Search for your destination below. (For more general information, see **By Bus,** p. 71.)

www.renfe.es

Central Madrid

ACCOMMODATIONS

Albergue Juvenil Santa Cruz de Marcenado (HI), **4**	B1
Hostal A. Nebrija, **16**	B2
Hostal Abril, **9**	D2
Hostal Aguilar, **33**	D4
Hostal Alcante, **25**	B4
Hostal Armesto, **39**	E4
Hostal Esparteros, **30**	C4
Hostal Excelsior, **19**	B2
Hostal Gonzalo, **40**	E5
Hostal Internacional, **34**	D4
Hostal Lauria, **19**	B2
Hostal Leones, **37**	C4
Hostal Lorenzo, **14**	D3
Hostal Madrid, **29**	C4
Hostal Margarita, **19**	B2
Hostal Medieval, **8**	D2
Hostal Paz, **23**	B3
Hostal Palacios, **15**	C2
Hostal-Residencia Alibel, **21**	C3
Hostal-Residencia Carreras, **36**	D4
Hostal-Residencia Cruz-Sol, **32**	C4
Hostal-Residencia Domínguez, **7**	D1
Hostal-Residencia Encarnita, **31**	C4
Hostal-Residencia Lamalonga, **17**	B2
Hostal-Residencia Lido, **34**	D4
Hostal-Residencia Luz, **27**	B4
Hostal-Residencia María, **20**	C3
Hostal-Residencia Miño, **25**	B4
Hostal-Residencia Mondragón, **33**	D4
Hostal-Residencia Regional, **36**	D4
Hostal-Residencia Rios, **1**	A1
Hostal-Residencia Rober, **24**	B3
Hostal-Residencia Sud-Americana, **41**	E5
Hostal Ribadavia, **15**	C2
Hostal R. Rodríguez, **38**	C4
Hostal Santillan, **18**	B2
Hostal Triana, **22**	C3
Hostal Villar, **36**	D4
Hotel Mónaco, **13**	D2

FOOD THUMB-PICKS

Ananias, **3**	A1
Arepas con Todo, **6**	D1
Café Gijón, **12**	E2
Casa Alberto, **44**	D5
Cáscaras, **2**	A1
Champagneria Gala, **42**	E5
El 26 de Libertad, **11**	D2
El Estragón, **45**	A5
La Granja Restaurante Vegetariano, **5**	C1
La Toscana, **35**	D4

NIGHTLIFE THUMB-PICKS

Acuarela, **10**	D2
El Barbu, **28**	B4
El Café de Sheherezade, **43**	D5
Palacio de Gaviria, **26**	C4

MADRID

Estación Sur de Autobuses: C. Méndez Alvaro (☎91 468 42 00). M: Méndez Álvaro. Info booth open daily 7am-11pm. **Empresa Galiano Continental** (☎91 745 63 00, 527 29 61) to **Toledo** (1hr.; M-Sa every 30min. 6:30am-10pm, Su every 30min. 8:30am-midnight; 605ptas/€3.61). **Empresa Larrea** (☎91 539 00 05, 530 48 00) to **Avila** (2hr.; M-F 8 per day 7:15am-8pm, Sa-Su 3 per day 10am-8pm; 950ptas/€5.71). **Empresa Autominibus Urbanos,** (☎91 530 46 06) to **Aranjuez** (1hr.; M-F about every hr. 7:15am-11pm, Sa 13 per day 8am-10pm, Su 9 per day 9am-10pm; 405ptas/€2.45).

Estación Auto Res: Pl. Conde de Casal, 6 (☎91 551 72 00; www.auto-res.net). M: Conde de Casal. Info booth open M-Th 6am-10pm, F, Sa 6am-1pm. Tickets can only be bought here from 6am-1pm daily. Reservations (☎90 202 09 99). To: **Badajoz** (5¼hr., 9-10 per day 8am-1am, 3245ptas/€20; express 4½hr., 3795ptas/€23); **Càceres** (4¾hr., 7-9 per day 8am-1am, 2420ptas/€15; express 3½hr., 2630ptas/€16); **Cuenca** (3hr.; M-F 8-10 per day 6:45am-10pm, Sa-Su 5-6 per day 8am-8pm; 1325ptas/€8; express 2½hr.; M-F, Su 10am & 6:30pm, Sa 10am; 1650ptas/€10); **Mérida** (4¼hr., 9 per day 8am-1am, 2420ptas/€15; express 4hr., 3305ptas/€20); **Salamanca** (3-3¼hr., 7 per day 8:30am-6pm, 1505ptas/€9; express 2½hr., 14-15 per day 7am-9:30pm, 2250ptas/€14); **Trujillo** (3¼hr., 11-12 per day 8am-1am, 2035ptas/€12; express 3hr., 2435ptas/€16); **Valencia** (5hr., 4 per day 1am-2pm, 2875ptas/€18; express 4hr., 9 per day 7am-10:30pm, 3175ptas/€19).

Estación Empresa Alacuber: (☎91 376 01 04), on Po. Moret. M: Moncloa. To: **El Pardo** (20min., every 15min. 6am-1:30am, 140ptas/€0.80).

Estación Empresa Continental Auto: C. Avenida de América, 34 (☎91 745 63 00). M: Cartagena. To: **Alcalá de Henares** (40min.; M-Sa every 15min. 6:15am-10:45pm, Su every 30min. 7-9am and every 20min. 9am-11pm; 260ptas/€1.55) and **Guadalajara** (1hr., every hr. 7am-midnight, 575ptas/€3.46).

Estación Empresa Larrea: Po. Florida, 11 (☎91 530 48 00). M: Príncipe Pío (via extension from M: Ópera). To: **Ávila** (2hr., 4 per day 7:15am-8pm, 950ptas/€5.71).

READ THIS The **Guía del Ocio,** available behind the counter of any news kiosk, should be your first purchase in Madrid (150ptas/€0.90). It has concert, theater, sports, cinema, and TV schedules. It also lists exhibits, restaurants, bars, and clubs. Although it is in Spanish, the alphabetical listings of clubs and restaurants are invaluable even to non-speakers. The *Guía* comes out on Thursday or Friday, so be sure that you are buying an up-to-date copy instead of last week's issue. For an English magazine with articles on new finds in and around the city, pick up **In Madrid,** distributed free at tourist offices and many restaurants. Live Music and Nightlife sections are basically an English translation of the *Guía.* **The Broadsheet,** free at bookstores, is a no-frills listing of English classifieds. The weekly **Segundamano,** on sale at kiosks, is essential for apartment or roommate seekers. COGAM publishes **Entiendes...?** which addresses gay issues in Spain and lists activities and nightspots for every town in Spain (see p. 88). **Minerva** keeps you up-to-date on the art scene.

Estación Herranz: on C. Princesa (☎91 896 90 28), in the Intercambio de Moncloa. M: Moncloa. To: **El Escorial** (50min., every 15min. 7am-9pm, 420ptas/€2.45) and **Valle de los Caídos** via El Escorial (20min.; 3:15pm, returns 5:30pm; 1030ptas/€6.20).

Estación La Sepulvedana: Po. Florida, 11 (☎91 547 52 61; 91 530 48 00). M: Príncipe Pío (via extension from M: Ópera). To: **Segovia** (1½hr., about every 30min. 6:30am-10:15pm, 840ptas/€5.05) and **Ávila** (1½hr.; M-F 8 per day 6am-7pm, Sa-Su 3 per day 10am-7pm; 930ptas/€5.60).

BY THUMB AND RIDESHARE

Hitchhiking is legal only on minor routes. The **Guardia Civil de Tráfico** picks up highway hitchhikers and deposits them at nearby towns or on a bus. No official organization arranges shared journeys; hitchhikers often try the message boards listed on p. 88 for rideshare offers. *Let's Go* does not recommend hitchhiking.

ORIENTATION

The "Kilómetro 0" sign in front of the police station in **Puerta del Sol** marks the intersection of eight of Madrid's most celebrated streets, and the starting point of the country's major highways. To make Madrid's infinite plazas and serpentine streets more navigable, our coverage of the city is broken down into five major neighborhoods: **Centro, Huertas, Malasaña and Chueca, Bilbao,** and **Argüelles.**

Most of Madrid's prominent sights, including the **Ópera** and **Plaza Mayor,** radiate from Sol in the Centro. Just west of Sol off C. Mayor, Plaza Mayor is the hub of activity for tourists and *madrileños* alike; the plaza houses both contemporary cafés and the churches and historical buildings of **Habsburg Madrid,** also known as **Madrid de los Asturias.** Farther west of Sol, by way of C. Arenal, lies the reigning monument of **Bourbon Madrid,** the Palacio Real. This section of Madrid, also known as **Ópera,** hosts fantastic gardens and churches.

To the south-east of Sol lies **Huertas,** once the literary district and now the center for exploring the city's three great museums (see **Museums,** p. 111) or the lush **Parque del Buen Retiro** (see p. 108). Bordered by C. Alcalá to the north, Po. Prado to the east, and C. Atocha to the south, the neighborhood is the home of traditional café, and theater life, as well as the some of the best nightlife in the city. Centered around **Plaza Santa Ana,** Huertas is crowded with some of the best budget accommodations in the city, as well as some of the best traditional *tapas* bars.

Also south of Sol and west of Huertas is the area around the metro stop **La Latina,** which has less prestige and fewer tourists than the rest of Old Madrid. Small markets line winding lantern-lit streets, perfect for an evening of gourmet tradition. **El Rastro,** a gargantuan ancient flea market, is staged here every Sunday morning. Farther south lies **Lavapiés,** a working-class neighborhood.

North of Sol, the grand avenue **Gran Vía** is the commercial center of Madrid, littered with fast-food joints and a handful of skyscraper. Linked to C. de Fuencarral, it acts as the southern border of **Malasaña** and **Chueca,** full of über-cool restaurants and shops. Beyond Gran Vía and east of Malasaña and Chueca lies modern Madrid. Running the length of Madrid from **Atocha** in the south to **Plaza de Castilla** in the north, **Paseo del Prado, Paseo de Recoletos,** and **Paseo de la Castellana** pass the Prado, the fountains at the **Plazas Cibeles** and **Colón,** and the elaborate skyscrapers beyond Pl. Colón, including the twin towers of the **Puerta de Europa.**

The area northwest of Sol holds the **Plaza de España** and the tall **Torre de Madrid,** the pride of 1950s Spain. Still farther northwest of Sol lie **Argüelles** and **Bilbao,** energetic neighborhoods spilling over from **Moncloa.** Both are student districts, filled with cheap eateries and neon nightclubs.

Madrid is much safer than other major European cities, but Sol, Pl. España, Pl. Chueca, and Malasaña's Pl. Dos de Mayo are still intimidating late at night. As a general rule, avoid the parks and quiet residential streets after dark and always watch out for thieves and pickpockets in crowds.

LOCAL TRANSPORTATION

MAPS

The *Plano de Madrid* (street map) and the *Plano y Guía de Transportes* (public transportation map), free at city tourist offices, are fantastic. **El Corte Inglés** (see p. 88) also offers convenient one-page maps of Madrid. For a comprehensive map with street index, pick up the *Almax* map (650ptas/€3.91) at any newsstand.

METRO

Safe, speedy, and spotless, Madrid's metro puts most major subway systems to shame. Trains run frequently; green timers above most platforms show increments of five minutes or less since the last train departed. The free *Plano del Metro* (available at any ticket booth) and the wall maps of surrounding neighborhoods are clear and helpful. Fare and schedule info is posted in every station.

Eleven lines connect Madrid's 164 stations, 40 of which are brand new as of 2000. Lines are distinguished by color and number. An individual metro ticket costs 145ptas/€0.87, but savvy riders opt for the **bonotransporte** (ticket of 10 rides for either the metro or bus system) at 760ptas/€4.57. Buy them at machines in any metro stop, *estanco* (tobacco shop), or newsstand. For more details, call **Metro info** (☎91 553 59 09) or ask at any ticket booth. Remember to hold on to your ticket or pass until you leave the metro—riding without one incurs an outrageous fine.

Trains run every day from 6am to 1:30am. Violent crime in the metro stations is almost unheard of, and women usually feel safe traveling alone. Do watch out for pickpockets in crowded cars. If you feel uncomfortable, avoid empty cars and ride in sight of the conductor. At night avoid the stations to the north, which tend to be less frequented. Metro stations Chueca, Gran Vía, La Latina, Plaza de España, Sol, and Tirso de Molina, surface in areas that can be intimidating after midnight.

BUS

While the metro makes the most sense for trips across Madrid, buses cover areas inaccessible by the metro and are a great way to see the city while getting where you need to be. Like the metro, the bus system is exceptionally organized. Most stops are clearly marked, but if you want extra guidance in finding routes and stops, try the handy *Plano de los Transportes*, free at the tourist office, or *Madrid en Autobús*, also free at bus kiosks.

The fare is 145ptas/€0.87. 10-ride *bonotransporte* passes are sold at newsstands and *estancos* for 750ptas/€4.51. Buses run from 6am to 11:30pm. From midnight until 3am, the night bus service, **búho** (owl), travels from Pl. Cibeles (and other marked routes) to the outskirts every 20min.; from 3-6am, they run every hour. Night buses (N1-N20), the cheapest form of transportation for late-night revelers, are listed in a special section of the *Plano*. For more info, call **Empresa Municipal de Transportes** (☎91 406 88 10. Spanish only. Open 6AM-midnight.)

TAXI

Madrid is filled with taxis around the clock. If one does not appear when you need it, or if you want to summon one to your door, call ☎91 371 21 31, 371 37 11, 445 90 08 or 447 32 32. A green *libre* sign in the window or a lit green light indicates availability. The base fare is 190ptas/€1.14, plus 50-75ptas/€0.30-0.45 per kilometer. Common fare supplements include: airport (400ptas/€2.40); bus and train stations (125ptas/€0.75); luggage charge (50ptas/€00.30 per bag); Sundays and holidays (6am-11pm, 125ptas/€0.75); nighttime (11pm-7am, 125ptas/€0.75). The fare from the city center to the airport is 2500-3000ptas/€15-18, depending on traffic.

Make sure that your driver turns on his meter. If you have a complaint or think you've been overcharged, demand a *recibo oficial* (official receipt) and *hoja de reclamaciones* (complaint form), which the driver is required to supply. Take down the license number, route taken, and fare charged. Drop off the forms and information at the **Ayuntamiento (City Hall),** Pl. Villa, 4 (☎91 447 07 15 or 447 07 14), to request a refund. To request **taxi service for the disabled,** call ☎91 547 85 00 or 547 86 00. Rates are identical to those of other taxis. If you leave possessions in a taxi, visit or call the **Negociado de Objetos Perdidos,** Pl. Legazpi, 7. (☎91 588 43 46. Open M-F 9am-2pm.) Drivers are obligated to turn in items within 48 hours.

CAR RENTAL

There is no reason to rent a car in Madrid. If congested traffic and nightmarish parking don't drive you into hysterics, aggressive drivers and annoying mopeds will. Don't drive unless you're planning to zoom out of the city, and even then bus and train fares will be cheaper. Tobacco shops sell parking permits. If driving to destinations outside of Spain, a larger car rental chain is your best bet. The tourist office has a complete list of car rental companies. See **Car Rental,** p. 86.

Europcar, Estación de Atocha (☎91 530 01 94; reservations 90 210 50 30; www.europcar.com), follow signs to the AVE terminal, near the rainforest. M: Atocha Renfe. Cheapest car 8900ptas/€54 per day, 49,800ptas/€300 per week. 400km per day included. Minimum age 21. Open daily 8am-midnight. Other offices in Madrid include the airport (☎91 393 72 35). Open 7am-midnight.

Avis, Estación de Atocha (☎91 530 01 68; reservations 91 213 55 31), follow signs to the AVE terminal, near the rainforest, across from Europcar. M: Atocha Renfe. Cheapest car 12,800ptas/€77 per day, 73,000ptas/€439 per week. 400km per day included. Minimum age 23. Open daily 8am-midnight. Other offices in Madrid include Gran Vía, 60 (☎91 548 42 03) and the airport (☎91 393 72 22).

MOPED RENTAL

Popular with Madrileños, mopeds are swift and convenient. A lock and helmet are necessary. With Madrid's stellar public transportation system, rentals are not popular. If you must compete for cool with the locals, rent from **Motocicletas Antonio Castro,** C. Conde Duque, 13 (☎91 542 06 57). M: San Bernardo. A Honda costs 4500ptas/€27 per day (8am-8pm) or 19,500ptas/€117 per week, including unlimited mileage and insurance. Deposit of 40,000ptas/€241 required (IVA not included). Renters must be at least 18. For mopeds larger than 125cc (for highway use, for example), an International Driver's Permit is required; for smaller models any driver's license is sufficient. Open M-F 8am-1:30pm and 5-8pm, Sa 9-11am.

PRACTICAL INFORMATION

TOURIST AND FINANCIAL SERVICES

Tourist Offices: English is spoken at all tourist offices. Those planning trips outside the Comunidad de Madrid can visit region-specific offices within Madrid; ask the tourist offices below for their addresses. **Regional/Provincial Office of the Comunidad de Madrid,** main office: Duque de Medinacelia, 2 (☎91 429 49 51; info line 90 210 00 07; www.comadrid.es/turismo). Brochures, transportation info, and maps for towns in

the Comunidad. **Municipal,** Pl. Mayor, 3 (☎91 366 54 77 or 588 16 36; fax 366 54 77). M: Sol. Hands out indispensable city and transportation maps and a complete guide to accommodations, as well as *In Madrid* and *Enjoy Madrid,* monthly activities and information guides. Open M-Sa 10am-8pm, Su 10am-2pm. **Secondary office** at Mercado Pta. de Toledo, Ronda de Toledo 1, stand #3134 (☎91 364 18 75). M: Pta. de Toledo. In a gallery with large banners on a plaza across from the metro station. Open M-F 9am-7pm, Sa 9:30am-1:30pm. **Other offices** at Estación Chamartín (see **By Train,** p. 82) and the airport (see **By Plane,** p. 82). Megastore **El Corte Inglés** has **free maps** and information (see p. 88).

General Info Line: ☎010. 20ptas/€0.14 per min. Run by the Ayuntamiento. They'll tell you anything about Madrid, from police locations to zoo hours. Ask for *inglés* and they will transfer you to an English-speaking operator. Outside Madrid dial ☎90 130 06 00.

Websites: www.madridman.com; www.iberica.com; www.red2000.com/spain/madrid.

Tours: Read the fine print before signing on. The following are given in English. Tourist office has details as well as offering their own **walking tours** of Habsburg Madrid every Saturday (Pl. Mayor office; 10am; 500ptas/€3). **Madrid Vision** (☎91 559 96 05) offers the most comprehensive tours. 1 or 2 day pass for guided tour in English from 900-2000ptas/€5.50-12. **Juliá Tours,** Gran Vía, 68 (☎91 559 96 05). M: Pl. de España. Offers tours of Andalucía, Portugal, and Morocco.

Budget Travel: Viajes TIVE, C. Fernando el Católico, 88 (☎91 543 74 12; fax 91 544 00 62). M: Moncloa. M: C. Isaac Peral, walk straight down C. Arcipreste de Hita, and turn left on C. Fernando el Católico; it's on your left. A resource for long-term visitors. ISIC 700ptas/€4.25, HI card 1800ptas/€10.85. Organizes group excursions and language classes. Lodgings and student residence info. English spoken. Open M-F 9am-2pm, Sa 9am-noon, information only. Arrive early to avoid long lines. If you don't need tickets try **Comunidad de Madrid, Dirección General de Juventud,** C. Gran Vía, 10 (☎91 580 42 42; www.comadrid.es/inforjoven). M: Banco de España. Offers many of the same services as TIVE, which it controls. Open M-F 9am-2pm and 5-8pm; in Aug. mornings only. **ASATEJ Group,** Fernardo el Católico, 60 (☎91 543 47 61; www.asatej.com). M: Arguelles. Backpackers sell other backpackers student airfares, tours, car rental, bus passes, ISIC cards, and other student travel needs. Open M-F 10am-8pm, Sa 4pm-7pm. **USIT,** Pl. Callao, 3 (☎902 25 25 75 or 91 524 70 40; www.unlimited.com). Part of a travel megaplex with other services. Arranges trips, car rentals, and documentation. Student friendly. **Viajes Barceló**, C. Princesa 3 (☎91 559 08 74; www.barcelo-viajes.es). M: Ventura Rodríguez or Pl. España. Student travel services. Open 10am-7pm.

Currency Exchange: Banco Central Hispano charges no commission on traveler's checks up to 100,000ptas. Offers the best rates on AmEx traveler's checks. **Main branch,** Pl. Canalejas, 1 (☎91 558 11 11). M: Sol. Follow C. San Jerónimo to Pl. Canalejas. Open Apr.-Sept. M-F 8:30am-2:30pm, Sa 8:30am-1pm; Oct.-Mar. M-Th 8:30am-4:30pm, F 8:30am-2pm, Sa 8:30am-1pm. **Banks** usually charge 1-2% commission (min. charge 500ptas/€3). Booths in Sol and Gran Vía, open as late as midnight and on weekends, have poor rates and are not a good deal for cashing traveler's checks, despite their charging commission. On the other hand, for small-denomination bills they may be the best option. **ATMs** are everywhere in Madrid and can be operated in English. **Servi Red, Servi Caixa,** and **Telebanco** machines accept bank cards with one or more of the Cirrus, PLUS, EuroCard, and NYCE logos. See **Cash Cards,** p. 16.

American Express: Pl. Cortés, 2 (☎91 527 03 03; info ☎91 322 54 00). M: Sevilla. From the metro stop, take a right on C. Alcala, another right down C. Cedacero and a left on C. San Jerónimo; it's on the left. The office has Agencia de Viajes written in big letters on the windows. Offers currency exchange (no commission on cash or AmEx traveler's checks; 750ptas set fee for non-AmEx traveler's checks), will hold mail for 30 days, and can help send and receive wired money. In an emergency, will cash personal checks up to US$1000 for cardholders. Open M-F 9am-5:30pm, Sa 9am-noon. 24hr. Express Cash machine outside. To report or cancel lost traveler's checks, call toll free ☎90 237 56 37. To report other problems, call ☎90 094 14 13 or 90 099 44 26.

LOCAL SERVICES

Message Boards: Tons of cheap travel tickets and rideshare offers at **TIVE** travel agency (see p. 87). Mostly rideshares at **Albergue Juvenil Santa Cruz** (see p. 95).

Luggage Storage: Barajas Airport. Follow the signs to *consigna.* 1 day 425ptas/€2.55, 2-15 days 530-740ptas/€3.15-4.50 per day, after day 15: 105-210ptas/€0.60-1.25 per day. **Estación Chamartín.** Self-serve, automatic lockers in the *consigna* area by the bus stop. Lockers 400-600ptas/€2.40-3.60 per day. Open daily 6:30am-12:30am. **Estación Atocha.** Same services, prices, and hours. Exit the *largo recorrido* area and the lockers are to the left. **Estación Sur de Autobuses.** Bags (800ptas/€4.85).

El Corte Inglés: C. Preciados, 3 (☎91 379 80 00). M: Sol. **C. Goya, 76** (☎91 432 93 00). M: Goya. **C. Princesa, 56** (☎91 454 60 00). M: Argüelles. **C. Raimundo Fernández Villaverde, 79** (☎91 556 23 00). M: Nuevos Ministerios. Various other locations in Madrid, and around Spain. *La mama grande* of department stores, the chain's official motto is: "A place to shop. A place to dream." Currency exchange with no commission but mediocre rates. Open M-Sa 10am-9:30pm, Su 11am-9pm.

English-Language Periodicals: International edition dailies and weeklies available at kiosks everywhere, especially on the Gran Vía, Paseos del Prado, Recoletos, and Castellana, and around Pta. Sol. If you're dying for the *New York Times* (425ptas/€2.55), try one of the **VIPS** restaurants (see **Red-Eye Establishments,** p. 97).

Language Service: Forocio (*Fo*reign *Ocio*), C. San Jerónimo, 18, 1st fl. (☎91 532 15 50 or 91 522 56 77; www.forocio.com). M: Sol. An organization dedicated to bringing foreigners and natives together to share languages and good times. Sponsors weekly international parties. Open M-F 10am-8pm, Sa 4-7pm.

Libraries: Bibliotecas Populares (info ☎91 445 98 45). 1 large branch at M: Puerta de Toledo (☎91 366 54 07). English-language periodicals. Open M-F 8:30am-8:45pm. **Washington Irving Center,** (☎ 91 587 22 00). In the American Embassy, C. Serrano, 75. M: Serrano or Colón. Anyone over 16 can check books out for 2 weeks by filling out a form. Allow 1 week for processing. Open M-F 2-6pm.

Religious Services: Our Lady of Mercy, C. Alfonso XIII, 165 (☎91 416 90 09), at Pl. Habana. Sunday mass in English 11am, followed by coffee and doughnuts. **Immanuel Baptist Church,** C. Hernández de Tejada, 4 (☎91 407 43 47). English services Su 11am and 7pm. **Community Church of Madrid,** C. Bravo Murillo, 85. M: Cuatro Caminos. At the Colegio El Porvenir. Multi-denominational Protestant services in English Su 10am. **British Embassy Church of St. George,** C. Núñez de Balboa, 43 (☎91 576 51 09). M: Velázquez. Services Su 8:30, 10, and 11:15am. **Sinagoga Beth Yaacov,** C. Balmes, 3 (☎91 591 31 31), near Pl. Sorolla. M: Iglesia. Services F 8pm, Sa 9:15am. Kosher restaurant can be reserved. Passport sometimes required. Spanish only. **Centro Islámico,** C. Alonso Cano, 3 (☎91 448 05 54). M: Iglesia. Services and language classes. Open M-F 10:45am-2pm.

Women's Services: Instituto de la Mujer (☎91 347 80 00). **Ministerio de Asuntos Sociales** (☎90 019 10 10). **Librería de Mujeres,** C. San Cristóbal, 17 (☎/fax 91 521 70 43; www.unapalabraotra.org/libreriamujeres.html), near Pl. Mayor. M: Sol. From Sol, C. San Cristóbal is the second left off C. Mayor. The shop's motto: *"Los libros no muerden, el feminismo tampoco."* ("Books don't bite, neither does feminism.") Books and gifts, but more of a resource for Spanish speakers. Helpful with finding local support and discussion groups. Open M-F 10am-2pm and 5-8pm, Sa 10am-2pm.

Gay and Lesbian Services: Colectivo de Gais y Lesbianas de Madrid (COGAM), C. Fuencarral, 37 (☎/fax 91 523 00 70). M: Gran Vía. Provides a wide range of services and activities of interest to gays, lesbians, and bisexuals. English usually spoken. Free screenings of gay-interest movies, COGAM youth group (25 and under), and HIV-positive support group (☎91 522 45 17; M-F 6-10pm). Reception daily M-Sa 5:30-9pm. Free counseling M-Th 7-9pm. Library open daily 7-9pm. Once every 2 months, COGAM publishes *Entiendes...?*, a magazine in Spanish about gay issues that also lists activities and nightspots for every town in Spain. **Berkana Librería Gai y Lesbiana** has guidebooks, contact information, and listings (see **Books,** p. 122). Most entertainment guides list gay and lesbian clubs. **GAI-INFORM,** a gay info line (☎91 523 00 70), provides information in Spanish (and sometimes French and English) about gay associations, leisure activities, and health issues. The same number has info on sports, workshops in French and English, dinners, and on **Brujulai,** COGAM's weekend excursion group. Open daily 5-9pm.

Laundromat: Many hostales provide some laundry services; if not, ask the owner for the nearest laundromat. Other options include: **Lavandería,** C. Cervantes 1. M: Puerta del Sol or Banco de España. From Pl. Santa Ana follow C. Prado, turn right on C. León and then left onto C. Cervantes. Wash 500ptas/€3, dry 100ptas/€0.60 for 9min. Open M-Sa 9am-8pm. **Lavandería Automática SIDEC,** C. Don Felipe, 4. M: Tribunal. Wash 700ptas/€4.21, detergent 25ptas/€0.15. Open M-F 10am-9pm.

EMERGENCY AND COMMUNICATIONS

Emergency: ☎112 (for all emergencies). ☎091 or 092 (national, local police).

Police: C. de los Madrazo, 9 (☎91 541 71 60). M: Sevilla. From C. Arenal a right onto C. Cedacneros and left onto C. los Madrazo. English forms available. To report crimes in the **metro,** go to the office in the Sol station (☎91 521 09 11). Open daily 8am-11pm. **Guardia Civil** (☎062 or 91 534 02 00). **Protección Civil** (☎91 537 31 00).

Crisis Lines: Poison Control (24hr. ☎91 562 04 20). **Rape Hotline** (☎91 574 01 10). Open M-F 10am-2pm and 4-7pm (other times machine-recorded instructions).

Help Lines: AIDS Info Hotline (☎90 011 10 00). Open M-F 10am-10pm. **Detox** (☎90 016 15 15). English spoken. Open daily 9am-9pm. **Alcoholics Anonymous,** C. Juan Bravo, 40-bis, 2nd fl. (English ☎91 309 19 47; Spanish ☎91 341 82 82). M: Núñez de Balboa. 20ptas/€0.14 per min. **English-Language Helpline** (☎91 559 13 93), trained volunteers offers confidential help. 20ptas/€0.14 per min. Open daily 7-11pm.

Late-Night Pharmacy: Dial ☎098 to find the nearest one. One located at **C. Mayor, 59** (☎91 548 00 14), near M: Sol. Listings of the nearest on-duty pharmacy are also posted in all pharmacy windows.

First Aid Stations: Scattered about the city, all open 24hr. C. Navas de Tolosa (☎91 521 00 25); General Ricardos, 14 (☎92 471 03 50); Avenida del Paseo de Extremadura, 147 (☎91 464 76 32).

Hospitals: Prompt appointments are hard to obtain, but public hospitals don't require advance payment. Emergency rooms are the best option for immediate attention. US insurance is not accepted as payment, but get a receipt and your insurance may pick up the tab when you get home. General emergency examination runs 18,000-24,000ptas/€144. For non-emergency concerns, **Anglo-American Medical Unit,** Conde de Aranda, 1, 1st fl. (☎91 435 18 23), is quick and friendly. M: Serrano or Retiro. Doctors, dentists, and optometrists. Run partly by British and Americans. Regular personnel on duty 9am-8pm. Not an emergency clinic. Initial visit 9000ptas/€54 for students, 10,000-15,000ptas/€60-90 for non-students. AmEx/MC/V. Embassies and consulates also keep lists of English-speaking doctors in private practice. **Hospital Clínico San Carlos** (☎91 330 30 00), on Pl. Cristo Rey. M: Moncloa. Open 24hr.

Anglo-American Medical Unit, Conde de Aranda, 1, 1st fl. (☎91 435 18 23), is quick and friendly. M: Serrano or Retiro. Doctors, dentists, and optometrists. Run partly by British and Americans. Regular personnel on duty 9am-8pm. Not an emergency clinic. Initial visit 9000ptas/€54 for students, 10,000-15,000ptas/€60-90 for non-students. AmEx/MC/V. Embassies keep lists of English-speaking doctors in private practice. **Hospital Clínico San Carlos** (☎91 330 30 00), on Pl. Cristo Rey. M: Moncloa. Open 24hr.

Emergency Clinics: In a **medical emergency,** dial ☎061. **Equipo Quirúrgico Municipal No. 1,** C. Montesa, 22 (☎91 588 51 00). M: Manuel Becerra. **Hospital Ramón y Cajal** (☎91 336 80 00), Ctra. Colmenar Viejo. Bus #135 from Pl. Castilla. **Red Cross** (☎91 457 77 00)

Telephones: Information ☎1003. No English spoken. 10ptas per min. (For further information, see **Keeping in Touch,** p. 28.)

Internet Access: New internet centers are surfacing everywhere. While the average is a reasonable 300ptas per hr., many opportunists are starting small shops in apartments and charging even less; keep a lookout.

Oficina13, C. Mayor, 1, 4th fl., office 13. M: Sol. Take the elevator up and buzz the office. A brand new office; friendly service and U2 songs abound. Unbeatably low 200ptas/€1.20 per hr., 150ptas/0.90 for 30min. Open daily 10am-11pm.

Interpublic, C. San Jerónimo 18, 1st fl. (☎/fax 91 532 15 50). M: Sol. On the same floor as ASATEJ travel and Forocio, young travelers stop by the airy room with international decor. 200ptas/€1.20 for 30min., 300ptas/€1.80 per hr. Open daily 9am-midnight.

Yazzgo Internet, Gran Vía, 84 & 69. (☎91 522 11 20; www.yazzgo.com). M: San Bernado or Pl. de España. A growing chain, check their website for new locations. Trendy work center open late. 300ptas/€1.80 per hour, 150ptas/€0.90. per 30min. Open daily 10am-1am.

Conéctate, C. Hilarión Eslava, 27 (☎91 544 54 65) M: Moncloa. A computer zone for students with over 300 flat-screens with service at the lowest price in Madrid. 150ptas/€0.90. per hour; less for larger blocks. Open 24hr.

La Casa de Internet, C. Luchana, 20 (☎91 594 42 00). M: Bilbao. 300ptas/€1.80 per hr. Open M-Sa noon-2am, Su 4pm-2am.

Post Office: Palacio de Comunicaciones, C. Alcala, 51 on Pl. Cibeles (☎90 219 71 97). M: Banco de España. Enormous, ornate palace on the far side of the plaza from the metro. Info (main vestibule) open M-Sa 8:30am–9:30pm. Windows open M-Sa 8:30am-9:30pm, Su 9am-2pm for stamp purchases, certified mail (main door), telex and **fax** service. Receive **Poste Restante** (Lista de Correos) at windows 80-82; passport required. Send packages at door N (enter from C. Montlaban). Postal Express is at door K (enter from Po. del Prado). **Postal Code:** 28080.

ACCOMMODATIONS

The demand for rooms in Madrid is always high and increases dramatically in summer. Never fear—the city is filled with hostels. Prices average about 2800ptas/€17 per person for a basic hostel room, a bit more for a two-star hostel, and slightly less for a bed in a *pensión*. Try negotiating the price if you plan on staying awhile.

Because there are so many reasonably priced hostels (*hostal*es) in Madrid, the listings here focus on them almost exclusively. Be aware that there are other accommodation options in Madrid: Hotels and *Pensiones*. In Madrid, the difference between a one-star *hostal* and a *pensión* is often minimal. A room in a one- or two-star *hostal* has at least the basics: bed, closet space, desk with chair, sink and towel, window, light fixture, fake flowers, a lock on the door, and the occasional religious icon. Winter heating is standard, air-conditioning is not. Unless otherwise noted, communal bathrooms (toilet and shower) are the norm. Most places accept reservations, but none require them. Reservations are, however, recommended in summer and on weekends year-round, especially in the Puerta del Sol area and at the first place *Let's Go* lists in each district. Hostels in Madrid are generally well-kept and comfortable. Owners are usually accustomed to opening the doors, albeit groggily, at all hours or providing keys for guests, but ask before club-hopping into the wee hours; late-night lockouts or confrontations with irate owners are never fun. *Pensiones* are like boarding houses: they sometimes have curfews and often host guests staying for longer periods of time. The best deals are found outside central locations, and Madrid's stellar public transportation makes virtually any place central.

RESERVATIONS SERVICE

Viajes Brújula: Estación Atocha (☎91 539 11 73), at the AVE terminal. For 400ptas/€2.40, they make reservations with any participating locale in Spain. You must go in person. You pay a deposit of one-third of the room price, which is then subtracted from the price of the accommodation. A good deal and a safe bet if you are tired and need a bed. English spoken. Open 8am-10pm. Another office at the **airport bus terminal** (☎91 575 96 80) in Pl. Colón (open daily 8am-10pm).

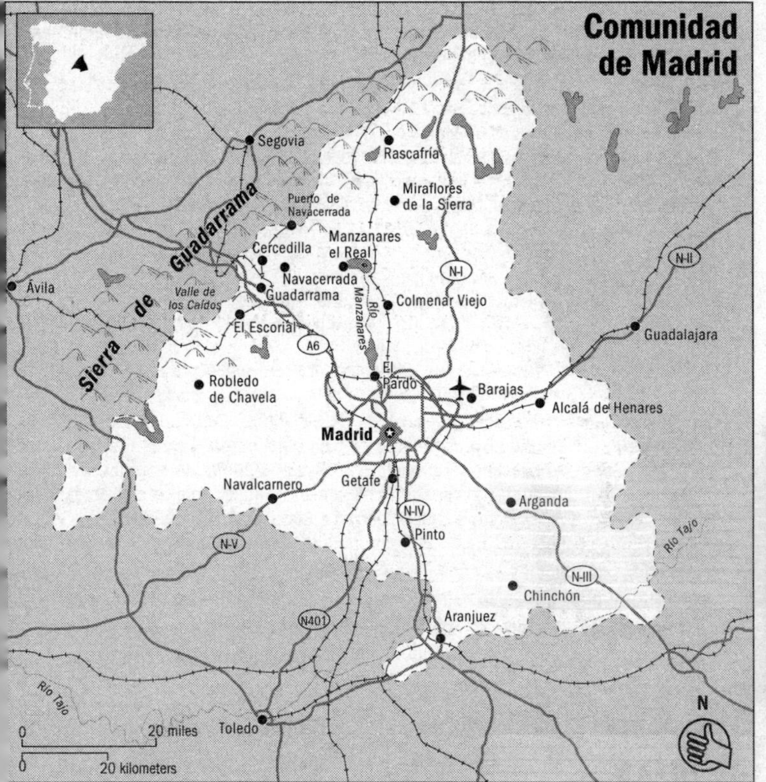

EL CENTRO: SOL, ÓPERA, AND PLAZA MAYOR

Puerta del Sol is the center of the city in the center of the country. All roads converge here (it's Spain's km 0) and most visitors ramble through at least once. Signs indicating *hostales* and *pensiones* stick out from flower-potted balconies and decaying façades on narrow, sloping streets. For better deals in quieter spots, stray several blocks from Sol. Don't be afraid to climb that extra flight of stairs; prices drop the higher up you go. The following listings fall in the area between the Sol and Ópera metro stops. Price and location in the Centro are as good as it gets, especially if you are planning to brave the nightlife. Buses #3, 25, 39, and 500 serve Ópera; buses #3, 5 (from Atocha), 15, 20, 50, 51, 52, 53, and 150 serve Sol.

Hostal Paz, C. Flora, 4, 1st and 4th fl. (☎91 547 30 47). M: Ópera. Don't be deterred by the dark street, parallel to C. Arenal, off C. Donados or C. Hileras. Wonderful owners rent peaceful rooms with large windows, satellite TV, A/C, and spotless, spacious bathrooms. Reservations advised. Laundry 1200ptas/€7.25. Singles 2500ptas/€15; doubles 4100-4800ptas/€24.50-29; triples 6000ptas/€36. MC/V.

Hostal-Residencia Luz, C. Fuentes, 10, 3rd fl. (☎91 542 07 59 or 91 559 74 18; fax 91 542 07 59), off C. Arenal. M: Ópera. 12, sunny, newly redecorated rooms exude comfort: hardwood floors, elegant furniture, beautiful curtains and bedspreads. Satellite TV, fax, and public phone. Laundry 1000ptas/€6. Singles 2500ptas/€15; doubles 3700ptas/€22.25; triples 5500ptas/€33. Discounts for longer stays.

Hostal Esparteros, C. Esparteros, 12, 4th fl. (☎/fax 91 521 09 03). M: Sol. Cheap, small, sparkling rooms with balcony or large windows (no fans). English-speaking owner ensures a terrific stay. Laundry 1000ptas/€6. Singles 2000-2200ptas/€12, with bath 2700ptas/€16.25; doubles 3200ptas/€19.25, with bath 3700ptas/€22.25; triples 4400ptas/€26.50, with bath 5500ptas/€33. Discounts for longer stays.

Hostal-Residencia Rober, C. Arenal, 26, 5th fl. (☎91 541 91 75). M: Ópera. Brilliant balcony views down Arenal. Smoking strictly prohibited. All 14 pristine rooms have their own tiny TVs and A/C. Singles with double bed and shower 3800ptas/€23, with bath 4800ptas/€29; doubles with bath 6000ptas/€36; triples with bath 7800ptas/€47.

Hostal-Residencia Cruz-Sol, Pl. Santa Cruz, 6, 3rd fl. (☎91 532 71 97; info@hostalcruz-sol.com). M: Sol. Modern rooms with parquet floors, double-paned windows, safes, heat, phones, internet jacks, and A/C. Vending machines satiate late-night munchies. Laundry 1000ptas/€6. Singles 3500ptas/€21, with bath 4000ptas/€24; doubles 6000ptas/€36; triples 8500ptas/€51; quads 9500ptas/€57. AmEx/MC/V.

Hostal Alcante, C. Arenal, 16, 2nd fl. on the left. (☎91 531 51 78). Spacious rooms, with TV, heat, and A/C. Beware the skimpy pillows. Singles 3500ptas/€21; doubles 5500ptas/€33, with bath 6500ptas/€39; triples with bath 9000ptas/€54. MC/V.

Hostal Madrid, C. Esparteros, 6, 2nd fl. (☎91 522 00 60; fax 91 532 35 10). M: Sol. Off C. Mayor. The backpacker's equivalent of a 5-star hotel. TVs, telephones, safes, A/C, and new bathrooms. Reservations 4 days ahead advised. Singles 7000ptas/€42; doubles 10,000ptas/€60; triple with balcony 13,000ptas/€78. AmEx/MC/V.

Hostal-Residencia Miño, C. Arenal, 16, 2nd fl. (☎91 531 50 79 or 91 531 97 89). M: Ópera. Don't be deterred by the deer's head at the entrance. Singles 4000ptas/€24; doubles 6000ptas/€36, with bath 6500ptas/€39; triples with bath 8100ptas./€49.

Hostal-Residencia Encarnita, C. Marqués Viudo de Pontejo, 7, 4th fl. (☎91 531 90 55). M: Sol. Above the María del Mar. Dim rooms, soft beds, cheap nature posters, rickety furniture, and a friendly family at the helm. Room TVs. Hot showers 200ptas, cold showers 100ptas. Singles 1700ptas/€10.25; doubles 2900ptas/€18, with bath 3400ptas/€20.50; triples 4500ptas/€27 or 1500ptas/€9 per extra person.

HUERTAS

Although *madrileños* have never settled on a nickname for this neighborhood, the area between C. San Jerónimo and C. de las Huertas is generally referred to as Huertas. Once a seedy neighborhood—and a Hemingway hangout—Huertas has shaped up to be a cultural hotbed of food and drink. Though quieter than El Centro, Malasaña and Chueca, **Pl. Santa Ana, C. Principe** and **C. Echegaray** offer some of the best bars in Madrid, and **C. Ventura de la Vega** some of the best restaurants. It's centrally located—Sol, Pl. Mayor, *el triángulo del arte*, and the Atocha train station are all within walking distance. Sol-bound buses stop near accommodations on C. Príncipe, C. Núñez de Arce, and C. San Jerónimo; buses #14, 27, 37, and 45 run along Po. Prado. The metro stops are Sol and Antón Martín.

Hostal Villar, C. Príncipe, 18, 1st-4th fl. (☎91 531 66 00; fax 91 521 50 73; www.arrakis.es/~h-villar). M: Sol. From the metro, walk down C. San Jerónimo and turn right on C. Príncipe. The 1970s stormed through this building, leaving 46 decidedly brown rooms in their wake. TV, phone, and A/C. Lounge for the young crowd. Singles 3000ptas/€18, with bath 3500ptas/€21; doubles 4000ptas/€24, with bath 5300ptas/€32; triples 5600ptas/€34, with bath 7400ptas/€44.50. AmEx/MC/V.

Hostal Gonzalo, C. Cervantes, 34, 3rd fl. (☎91 429 27 14; fax 91 420 20 07). M: Antón Martín. Off C. León, off C. Atocha. A budget traveler's dream: newly renovated rooms have pristine baths, firm beds, TVs, and fans in summer. Leather-plush lounge. Singles 5500ptas/€33; doubles 6500ptas/€39; triples 8500ptas/€51. AmEx/MC/V.

Hostal-Residencia Sud-Americana, Po. Prado, 12, 6th fl. (☎91 429 25 64), across from the Prado. M: Antón Martín or Atocha. Airy doubles facing the Prado with views of the Paseo. Singles 2800ptas/€17; doubles 5500ptas/€33; triples 7000ptas/€42.

Hostal Aguilar, C. San Jerónimo, 32, 2nd fl. (☎91 429 59 26 or 91 429 36 61; fax 91 429 26 61; www.hostalaguilar.com). M: Sol. More than 50 clean, expansive modern rooms with vast bathrooms, telephones, A/C, safe boxes, and TVs. Elegantly sparse lounge with deep couches serves as a meeting ground for clubbers. Perhaps the most social of Madrid's hostales. Singles 4000ptas/€24; doubles 6000ptas/€36; triples 8000ptas/€48, 2000ptas/€12 per extra person. MC/V.

Hostal R. Rodríguez, C. Núñez de Arce, 9, 3rd fl. (☎91 522 44 31), off Pl. Santa Ana. M: Sol. Reception decor makes even the cheapest of travelers feel like royalty. Clean shared baths and spacious rooms. 24hr. reception. English spoken. Singles 3300ptas/€20; doubles 5,000-6,000ptas/€30-36; triples 8000ptas/€48. AmEx/MC/V.

Hostal-Residencia Mondragón, C. San Jerónimo, 32, 4th fl. (☎91 429 68 16). M: Sol. Two sisters keep guests happy in this many-halled spot where Spain's first motion picture was filmed in 1898 (see p. 65). Ask for a room off the gardenia-filled terrace that overlooks the street. Hot water runs only in communal bathrooms. The best value around. Singles 2000ptas/€12; doubles 3000ptas/€18; triples 3900ptas/€23.50.

Hostal Armesto, C. San Agustín, 6, 1st fl. (☎91 429 90 31). M: Antón Martín. In front of Pl. Cortés. This small hostel offers a quiet night's sleep for the less boisterous. Some rooms have garden view; all have private baths, TVs, A/C. Older crowd. Singles 5800ptas/€35; doubles 6800ptas/€41; triples 8000ptas/€48. AmEx/MC/V.

Hostal-Residencia Carreras, C. Príncipe, 18, 3rd fl. (☎/fax 91 522 00 36). M: Antón Martín, Sol, or Sevilla. Off C. San Jerónimo, between Pl. Santa Ana and Canalejas. Be sure to ask for a room with a balcony—they tend to be larger. Rooms in the annex next door have modern baths. Small, central lounge. Singles 2500-3500ptas/€15-21, with bath 4500ptas/€27; doubles 4000-4500ptas/€24-27, with bath 5000ptas/€30; triples 6000-6300ptas/€36-38, with bath 6900ptas/€41.50 (IVA not included). Advance payment required. AmEx/MC/V.

Hostal-Residencia Regional, C. Príncipe, 18, 4th fl. (☎91 522 33 73). M: Antón Martín, Sol, or Sevilla. In the same building as Carreras. Dimly lit with cavernous showers. No A/C means stuffy rooms in summer. Singles 2600ptas/€15.75, with bath 3600ptas/€21.75; doubles 3600-4600ptas/€21.75-27.75; triples 5500ptas/€33.

Hostal Leones, C. Núñez de Arce, 14, 2nd fl. (☎91 531 08 89). A classic hostel with spartan rooms and spotless bathrooms. Singles 2500ptas/€21; doubles 4400ptas/€26.50, with bath 4800ptas/€29.

Hostal-Residencia Lido, C. Echegaray, 5, 2nd fl. (☎91 429 62 07). M: Sol. Off C. San Jerónimo near Pl. Canalejas. Comfy beds and quiet location. Avoid the windowless single. TV lounge. Long-term guests preferred. Ask to use kitchen. Breakfast 350ptas/€2. Singles 2500ptas/€15; doubles 3500ptas/€21, with bath 4500ptas/€27. Monthly: singles 45,000ptas/€270; doubles 75,000-80,000ptas/€450-480.

Hostal Internacional, C. Echegaray, 5, 2nd fl. (☎91 429 62 09 or 91 429 81 51). Across the hall from Lido; more bang for more buck. Simple rooms have heat and A/C. Common baths are plush and plentiful. Spacious TV lounge. Kitchen use intended for long-term guests, but accessible to all. Singles 3500ptas/€21; doubles 6000ptas/€36. Monthly: singles 40,000-50,000ptas/€240-300.

GRAN VÍA

The neon lights of Broadway and the Champs-Élysées have met their match in Gran Vía. It glows and pulsates with the sharp lights of sex shops, McDonald's, and five-star hotels, in a 24-hour parade of flashing cars, swishing skirts, and stack-heeled shoes. *Hostal* signs scatter the horizon, but accommodations here tend to be overpriced and less comfortable than in other areas. This is not a street you want to be returning to late at night or at less than your sharpest; El Centro and Huertas provide safer bargains. Buses #1, 2, 44, 46, 74, 75, 133, 146, 147, and 148 reach Callao; buses #1, 2, 3, 40, 46, 74, 146, and 149 service both Pl. España and Callao. The closest metro stops are Gran Vía and Callao.

Hostal A. Nebrija, Gran Vía, 67, 8th fl., elevator A (☎91 547 73 19). M: Pl. España. A grandson continues his grandparents' tradition with pleasant and spacious rooms in a very tidy building, heavily furnished in classic style. All rooms have TVs and fans. Singles 4500ptas/€27; doubles 5900ptas/€35.50; triples 8100ptas/€49. AmEx/MC/V.

Hostal Margarita, Gran Vía, 50, 5th fl. (☎/fax 91 547 35 49). M: Callao. Simple rooms with large windows, TV, and telephone; some with street views. Plush lounge and big kitchen. Laundry 1500ptas/€9. Reservations wise. Singles 3500ptas/€21; doubles 5400ptas/€32.50, with bath 5800ptas/€35; triples with bath 7500ptas/€45. MC/V.

Hostal Triana, C. de la Salud, 13, 1st fl. (☎91 532 68 12; fax 91 522 97 29; www.hostaltriana.com). M: Callao or Gran Via. From Gran Via, turn onto C. Salud, the sign is quite visible. Catering to those seeking a little more comfort than the standard hostal. All rooms have TV, fans, private baths. Reserve 2 weeks ahead. Singles 4900ptas/€30; doubles 6200ptas/€38 with A/C 6800ptas/€41.

Hostal Santillan, Gran Vía 64, 8th fl. (☎/fax 91 548 23 28). M: San Bernardo. If the Beatles, little dwarfs and familial portraits don't welcome you, the friendly management will. Simple rooms with showers and sinks. All have TV, fan, safety box and public phone. Single 4000ptas/€24; double 6500ptas/€39; triple 9000ptas/€54. MC/V.

Hostal-Residencia Lamalonga, Gran Vía, 56, 2nd fl. (☎91 547 26 31 or 91 547 68 94). M: Santo Domingo. All is neat and polished. Singles 5500ptas/€33; doubles 7500ptas/€45; triples 9500ptas/€57. 10% discount for stays over 5 days. MC/V.

Hostal-Residencia María, Miguel Moya, 4, 2nd fl. (☎91 522 44 77). M: Callao. Located just off Pl. Callao. Just beyond the electric ruckus of Gran Vía, location quickly becomes the greatest asset. All with TVs and private baths, some with fans. Singles 4500ptas/€27; doubles 6700ptas/€40; triples 8700ptas/€52.25. MC/V.

Hostal-Residencia Alibel, Gran Vía, 44, 8th fl. (☎91 521 00 51). M: Callao. Well-lit rooms with great views and TVs off tired hallways. Doubles 5000-5500ptas/€30-33, with bath 6000ptas/€36; triples 8000ptas/€48.

Hostal Lauria, Gran Vía, 50, 4th fl. (☎/fax 91 541 91 82; www.geocities.com/hostal lauria). M: Callao. Stare down the stuffed birds on the way, and you'll be alright. Sleeping quarters are more simplified, but are well endowed with large bed, baths, phones, fans and TVs. Lounge with couches, TV, and stereo. English spoken. Singles 4850ptas/€29.25; doubles 7000ptas/€42; triples 9500ptas/€57. MC/V.

Hostal Excelsior, Gran Vía, 50, 2nd fl. (☎91 547 34 00; fax 91 547 34 08). Low prices, low beds and the bare necessities make room-shopping crucial—if you don't get a good one, it may not be worth it. Singles 3210ptas/€19.25, with bath 3960ptas/€23.75; doubles with bath 6206ptas/€37.25; triples with bath 8345ptas/€38; quads with bath 9950ptas/€60. AmEx/MC/V.

MALASAÑA AND CHUECA

Split down the middle by C. Fuencarral, Malasaña and Chueca are both hard-core party pits for Madrid's alternative youth. Hostels and *pensiones* are almost as abundant as the clubs and boutiques and are usually located above the first floor of old buildings. Unless techno helps you sleep, make sure your room has sound-proof windows. Chueca is hip, fun, funky, and largely gay, but can be dangerous, especially for solo travelers. Buses #3, 40, and 149 run along C. Fuencarral and Hortaleza. Metro stops Chueca, Gran Vía, and Tribunal serve the area.

Hostal Palacios and **Hostal Ribadavia,** C. Fuencarral, 25, 1st-3rd fl. (☎91 531 10 58 or 91 531 48 47). M: Gran Vía. Run by the same cheerful family. Palacio (1st and 2nd fl.) offers large, tiled rooms with elegant modern furniture. Older Ribadavia (3rd fl.) has comfortable rooms with TVs. Singles 2500ptas/€18, with bath 4000ptas/€24; doubles 4000ptas/€24, with bath 5500ptas/€33; triples 6600ptas/€40, with bath 7500ptas/€45; quads with bath 8000-9000ptas/€48-54. AmEx/MC/V.

Hostal Lorenzo, C. las Infantas, 26, 3rd fl. (☎91 521 30 57; fax 91 532 79 78). M: Gran Vía. From the metro walk up C. Del Clavel, it's on the corner of the plaza. Slightly upscale from the standard hostal. Sound-proof windows muffle daytime traffic and the nighttime revelry below. Turning the knob by the bed produces music through ceiling speakers. Breakfast 350ptas/€2. Reservations recommended. Singles 5950ptas/€36; doubles 8500ptas/€51; triples 9700ptas/€58.50 (IVA not included). AmEx/MC/V.

Hostal-Residencia Domínguez, C. Santa Brígida, 1, 1st fl. (☎/fax 91 532 15 47). M: Tribunal. Down C. Fuencarral toward Gran Vía, left on C. Santa Brígida, and up a flight. Hospitable young owner ready with tips on local nightlife. English spoken. Singles 3000ptas/€18, with bath 4500ptas/€27; doubles with bath and A/C 6000ptas/€36.

Hostal Abril, C. Fuencarral, 39, 4th fl. (☎91 531 53 38). M: Tribunal or Gran Vía. Dorm style singles inclined to accommodate students. Sleepy rooms with balconies are surprisingly tranquil for the spicy location. Singles 2500-2700ptas/€15-16.25; doubles 3900ptas/€23.50, with bath 4500ptas/€27; triples with bath 6200ptas/€37.25.

Hostal Medieval, C. Fuencarral, 46, 2nd fl. (☎91 522 25 49). M: Tribunal. On the corner of C. Augusto Figueroa. TV lounge honors Real Madrid. Singles 3500ptas/€21; doubles 4500ptas/€27, with bath 5500ptas/€33; triples 6500ptas/€39.

Hotel Mónaco, C. Barbieri, 5 (☎91 552 46 30; fax 91 521 16 01). M: Chueca. From Pl. de Chueca, follow C. Barbieri all the way. Once a brothel catering to Madrid's high society, this hotel still encourages naughtiness. Frescoes of Eve-like temptresses tempt the imagination while hundreds of mirrors and *palacio*-sized beds allow the reality. Green-lit lounge and a lively bar/cafeteria area. Adventurous older crowd. Be ready to lighten your wallet. Simple singles 7490ptas/€45; doubles 10,700ptas/€64.25; triples 13,500ptas/€81; quads 15,000ptas/€90. AmEx/MC/V.

ELSEWHERE

Near the **Chamartín** train station budget lodgings are rare, as is the case in most of the residential districts located away from the city center. Near the **Atocha** train station are a handful of hostels, the closest of which are down Po. Santa María de la Cabeza. Be aware that this neighborhood is not as safe as those that are more central. The tourist office in Pl. Mayor has a full list of lodgings.

Albergue Juvenil Santa Cruz de Marcenado (HI), C. Santa Cruz de Marcenado, 28 (☎91 547 45 32; fax 91 548 11 96). M: Argüelles. From the metro, walk 1 block down C. Alberto Aguilera away from C. Princesa, turn right on C. Serrano Jóve, then left on C. Santa Cruz de Marcenado. Lounge is great for meeting people for a night out and late-night card playing. The 72 beds fill quickly, even in winter. English spoken. Rooms have cubbies; recommended lockers are outside the rooms (200ptas/€1.25 extra). Breakfast included. Sheets (but no towels) provided. 3-day max. stay. Quiet hours after midnight. Reception daily 9am-1:30pm. 1:30am curfew is strictly enforced. Reserve a space (by mail, fax, or in person only) in advance, or arrive early and pray. Closed Christmas and New Year's. An HI (YHA) card is required and can be purchased for 1800ptas/€10.85. Dorms 1200ptas/€7.25; over 26 yrs. 1820ptas/€11.

Hostal-Residencia Rios, C. Juan Álvarez Mendizábal, 44, 4th fl. (☎91 559 51 56). M: Ventura Rodríguez. Face the green shrubbery, walk 3 blocks left up C. Princesa to C. Rey Francisco, go 3 blocks to J. A. Mendizábal, and turn left again. Nothing fancy; just clean, cheap, comfortable rooms close to the park, some with A/C (1000ptas/€6). Singles 2000ptas/€12, doubles with shower 4000ptas/24, triples 6000ptas/€36.

CAMPING

Tourist offices can provide info about the 13 campsites within 50km of Madrid. Similar info is in the *Guía Oficial de Campings* (official camping guide), a big book which they gladly let you look through but don't give away (most bookstores carry it). The *Mapa de Campings* shows the location of every official campsite in Spain. Also ask for the brochure *Hoteles, Campings, Apartamentos,* which lists hotels, campsites, and apartments in and around Madrid. For further camping info, contact the *Consejería de Educación de Juventud* (☎91 522 29 41).

Camping Alpha (☎91 695 80 69; fax 91 683 1659), on a tree-lined site 12.4km down the Ctra. de Andalucía in Getafe. M: Legazpi. From the metro station take bus #447, which stops next to the Nissan dealership (10min., every 30min. until 10pm, 190ptas/

€1.25). Ask driver to let you off at the pedestrian overpass for the campsite. Cross the bridge and walk 1½km back toward Madrid along a busy highway; camping signs lead the way. Cars, trailers and tents crowd the lots. Alpha has a pool, showers, and laundry. 710ptas/€4.25 per person, 715ptas/€4.25 per tent and per car. (IVA not included.)

Camping Osuna (☎91 741 05 10; fax 91 320 63 65), on Av. Logroño. M: Canillejas. From the metro cross the pedestrian overpass, walk through the parking lot, and turn right along the freeway. Pass under 2 bridges (the 1st a freeway and the 2nd an arch) and look for campground signs on the right. Or grab the #101 bus from the metro toward Barajas and ask for the campsite. Closer than Alpha, but not quite as nice. Clean showers, laundromat, supermarket and bar (sandwiches 400ptas/€2.50, salads, 300ptas/€1.85.). 730ptas/€4.50 per person, per tent, and per car. 790ptas/ €2.85 for electricity. (IVA not included.) Reception open daily 8:30am-10pm.

FOOD

In Madrid, it's not hard to feed yourself without annihilating your wallet. You can't walk a block without tripping over at least five *cafeterías*, where a sandwich, coffee, and dessert sell for around 600ptas/€3.60. Vegetarians should check out the *Guía del Ocio* (150ptas/€.90), which has a complete listing of Madrid's vegetarian havens under the section *Otras Cocinas*, or the website www.mundovegetariano.com. Even carnivores may appreciate a veggie meal or two, given Madrid's indulgence in fatty meats and fried preparation.

For a full meal at a *restaurante*, one step up from the typical *cafetería*, expect to spend at least 1100ptas/€6.75. Most restaurants offer a *menú del día*, which includes bread, one drink, and one choice from each of the day's selections for appetizers, main courses, and desserts. For 1100-1500ptas/€6.75-9, it is a fantastic way to fill up keep in mind the following essential buzz words for quicker, cheaper *madrileño* fare: *bocadillo* (a sandwich on a long, hard role, 350-450ptas/€2-2.75); *sandwich* (a sandwich on sliced bread, ask for it *a la plancha* if you want it grilled, 300ptas/€1.85); *croissant* (with ham and cheese, 250ptas/€1.50); *ración* (a large *tapa*, served with bread 300-600ptas/€1.85-3.75); and *empanada* (a puff pastry with meat fillings, 200-300ptas/€1.25-1.85). See the **Glossary** p. 736, for additional useful translations.

In general, *restaurantes* are open from 1 to 4pm and 8pm to midnight; in the following listings, this is the case unless otherwise noted. More casual establishments such as *mesones*, *cafeterías*, *bares*, *cafés*, *terrazas*, and *tabernas* serve drinks and foodstuffs all day until midnight, though some are closed on Sundays.

FOOD SHOPPING

In general, groceries get cheaper the farther you get from the center. Specialty items may require a visit to a pricey store in the center, but for daily fare, slipping into any corner store will reward you with an inexpensive selection of standards at drastically lower prices than would be found in a major chain.

Groceries: %Dia and **Simago** are the cheapest city-wide supermarket chains. More expensive are **Mantequerías Leonesas, Expreso,** and **Jumbo.** Every **El Corte Inglés** (see p. 88) has a huge food market with an excellent selection (it shows in the price), located either on the basement or top floor.

Markets: Mercado de San Miguel, a covered market on Pl. San Miguel, off the northwest corner of Pl. Mayor, sells the finest seafood and produce in the city at high prices. A wide selection of tourists can be found on display between the bacalao and the tuna. Open M-F 9:30am-2:30pm and 5:15-8:15pm, Sa 9am-2:30pm. **Mercado de la Cebada,** at the intersection of C. Toledo and C. San Francisco, is larger, less expensive and caters to many more locals. Open M-Sa 8am-2pm and 5:30-8pm.

Specialty Shops: Pastry shops are everywhere. The sublime **Horno La Santiagüesa,** C. Mayor, 73, sells everything from *roscones de reyes* (sweet bread for the Feast of the Epiphany) to *empanadas* and pastries doused in rich chocolate. Don't pass through without trying the *tarta de santiago* (almond sweet bread, 1800ptas/€10.85). Open M-Sa 8am-9pm, Su 8am-8pm. **Horno San Onofre,** C. San Onofre, 4 (☎91 532 90 60), off C. Fuencarral, serves sumptuous fruit tarts and *suspiros de modistilla* (seamstress's sighs), a *madrileño* specialty. Open M-Sa 9am-9pm, Su 9am-8pm.

Red-Eye Establishments: *Guía del Ocio* lists late-night eateries under *Cenar a última hora*. The chain **VIPS,** at Gran Vía, 43 (☎91 542 15 78; M: Callao); Serrano, 41 (M: Serrano); Calle Princesa, 5 (M: Ventura Rodríguez); Fuencarral 101 (M: Tribunal); and other scattered locations are a standard late-night option. A diner with cushioned booths, average service, and overpriced burgers with cheese fries. VIPS also carries English books and magazines, records, and canned food. Open daily 9am-3am. **7-Eleven** stores are scattered about in Ópera, Alonso Martínez (C. Mejía Lequerida), and Av. America. **Hot & Cool,** C. Gaztambide in Moncloa-Argüelles, serves fresh *bocadillos* until 3am on weekends. **Street vendors** also sell cheap *bocadillos* late night on weekends. Open Cervecerías are not hard to find within a couple blocks until about 2am.

EL CENTRO: SOL, ÓPERA, AND PLAZA MAYOR

Flooded with tourists looking for "traditional" fare, this area abounds with mediocre food at high prices. Streets off M: Ópera teem with crowded cafés, markets, and restaurants. Places with menus in several different languages are tourist traps; avoid them like green *gambas*. Cruise to nearby Pl. Santa Ana for better deals, but don't miss the Museo del Jamón. The surrounding streets, especially those through the **Arco de los Cuchilleros** in the southwest corner of Pl. Mayor, house old specialty shops and renowned *mesones*. Head here for garlicky *tapas* and pitchers of *sangría* served in a festive, albeit touristy, atmosphere.

Museo del Jamón, C. San Jerónimo, 6 (☎91 521 03 46). M: Sol. 5 other much-loved locations throughout the city, including one at C. Mayor 7 (☎91 531 45 50). Dodge hooves and shanks at the sterile, metallic bar or head upstairs to the dining room (open at 1pm) for a sampling of the chef's specialties (600-1160ptas/€3.75-7). Succulent Iberian ham is served up in every form you could possibly desire, and the chicken is...chicken. *Menú* 1400ptas. Generous combo plates 650-950ptas/€4-5.75. Open M-Th 9am-12:30pm, F-Sa 9am-1am, Su 10am-12:30pm. AmEx/V.

El Cuchi, C. Cuchilleros, 3 (☎91 366 44 24). Just outside Plaza Mayor and better and cheaper than the restaurants inside it. Delicious Mexican food in festive setting. Entrées 900-2900ptas/€5.40-17.50. Open M-Sa 1pm-1am, Su 1-midnight. AmEx/MC/V.

Casa Lhardy, C. San Jerónimo, 8 (☎91 521 33 85), at C. Victoria. M: Sol. For dinner, get slicked-up and bring your wallet; this gorgeous restaurant, replete with original wallpaper and woodwork, is 150 years old and the house specialty *cocido* (4100ptas/€25) has won deserved fame as a *madrileño* specialty. Open M-Sa 1-3:30 and 8:30-11:30pm, Su 1-3:30pm. AmEx/MC/V.

Matador Parilla, C. De La Cruz, 13 (☎91 522 35 95), off C. San Jerónimo. They'll grill just about any meat or vegetable for you at this bull-and-*torero*-themed spot—and will have a rowdy good time while they're at it. 5 different *menús* 1400-2300ptas/€8.50-13.85 each. Open daily 1-4:30pm, Su-Th 8pm-midnight, F-Sa 8pm-1am.

HUERTAS

A popular place among locals at all hours of the day and night, Pl. Santa Ana is perfect for killing some time with a drink and snack. Straying slightly from its center, **Calles Echegaray, Ventura de la Vega,** and **Manuel Fernández González** offer the best food options; quality is high and prices are low. As the evening grows and wine flows, these streets become the first stop of a night out in Madrid.

Pizzaría Cervantes, C. Leon, 8 (☎91 420 12 98), off C. del Prado. Offering much more than pizza, this place is hands down the best cheap lunch in the area. A shockingly good *menú* (1100ptas/€6.60, available M-F) includes a selection of exquisite desserts. Most entrées 950ptas/€5.75. Open M, W-F 11am-12:30am, Tu 7pm-12:30am, Sa noon-1:30am, Su noon-12:30am. AmEx/MC/V.

Restaurante Integral Artemisa, C. Ventura de la Vega, 4 (☎91 429 50 92), off C. San Jerónimo. M: Sol. Second location in Pl. del Carmen, at Tres Cruces, 4 (☎91 521 87 21). Elegant veggie food served in a long, mellow dining area with A/C. Bulletin board at the entrance informs of yoga and other New Age activities. Veggie *menú* 1400ptas/€8.50. Open daily 1:30-4pm and 9pm-midnight. AmEx/MC/V.

Gula Gula, C. Infante 5 (☎91 420 29 19), off C. Echegaray near C. Huertas. M: Antón Martín. New location also at C. Gran Vía, 1 (☎91 522 87 64). All-you-can-eat buffet with salads, chicken, rice and pasta, a soup, and hot dishes (1500ptas/€9 at lunch; cold buffet plus an ordered hot dish 3100ptas/€18.75 at dinner). Waiters more exotic than the food perform themed drag, strip, and cabaret shows after the meal. Reserve for weekend dinners a week ahead. Open Tu-Su 1-5pm and 9pm-3am. AmEx/MC/V.

Al Natural, C. Zorrilla, 11 (☎91 369 47 09). From the metro stop, a left off of C. de Cedaceros, behind the Congress building. M: Sevilla. A unique offering of vegetarian Mediterranean dishes served in a lively, candle-lit atmosphere. Entrées (1200-1800) range from Hawaiian pizza to tofu. Open daily 1pm-4pm, M-Sa 7pm-12am.

LAVAPIÉS, LA LATINA AND ATOCHA

The neighborhoods south of Sol, bounded by C. Atocha and C. Toledo, are residential and working class. No caviar or champagne here, but you'll find plenty of *menús* for around 1000ptas/€6 and can get even better bargains by eating *a la carte*. **Calle Agurrosa** at Lavapiés has some funky outdoor eateries, and there are good restaurants up the hill toward Huertas.

MADRID

El Estragón, Pl. de la Paja, 10 (☎91 365 89 82). M: La Latina. From the metro, follow C. Duque de Alba, turn right through to Pl. Puerta de Moros and leave the church on your right; it's on the far side of Pl. de la Paja. Perhaps the best medium-priced restaurant–of any kind–in Madrid, with vegetarian food that could turn the most die-hard carnivores into switch-hitters. Treat yourself to *crepes a la Museliño*, the house specialty, or dine on the delicious and creative *menú (*M-F 1500ptas/€9; Sa-Su and evenings 2975ptas/€18). Open daily 1:30-4:30pm and 8pm-1am. AmEx/MC/V.

Champagneria Gala, C. Moratín, 22 (☎91 429 25 62). Down the hill on Moratín from C. Atocha. The *paella* buck stops here, with decor as colorful and varied as its specialty. *Menú* (1750ptas/€10.50) offers choice of *paella*, along with the usual salad, bread, wine, and dessert. Enjoy a romantic meal under the high, lit roof of the vine-covered interior garden. Reserve on weekends. Open daily 1:30-5pm and 9pm-12:30am.

El Granero de Lavapiés, C. Argumosa, 10 (☎91 467 76 11), off the plaza. M: Lavapiés. For 16 years, frescoes, inventive vegetarian specials, and fresh bread have kept this hideaway packed with locals. Vegetarian *menú* M-Sa 1200ptas/€7.25. Open daily 1-4pm, F-Sa 8:30-11pm. MV/V.

La Farfalla, C. Santa María, 17 (☎91 369 46 91). M: Antón Martín. One block from the metro along C. Huertas; look for the butterfly above the entrance. La Farfalla's specialty is Argentine-style grilled meat, but don't miss their thin-crust pizzas (750ptas/€4.50). Open for dinner Su-Th 9:30pm-3am, F-Sa 9:30pm-4am. AmEx/MC/V.

GRAN VÍA

If you came to Spain to escape fast-food chains, stay clear of Gran Vía. Luckily, **Calle Fuencarral** is lined with cheap eateries. If you must eat among all the lights, steel yourself for tchotchkes.

Museo Chicote, C. Gran Vía, 12 (☎91 532 97 80). M: Gran Vía. Lose yourself in the green leather booths amidst pictures of Spanish and International stars from Ava Gardener, John Wayne to Lola Flores or Luis Buñuel. Kick back a cocktail with Madrid's 40-something socialites after 11pm. Lunchtime *menú* 1400ptas/€8.50. Open M-Sa 8am-12:30am. Lunch served 1-4pm.

MALASAÑA AND CHUECA

Malasaña and Chueca, both above Gran Vía, are divided in atmosphere along C. Hortaleza. Closer to the Ópera, Malasaña's restaurants often feature new and adventurous menus filled with vegetarian options. Young locals congregate in hordes in **Plaza 2 de Mayo** on warm evenings. From its central plaza at the metro stop, Chueca's flamboyantly gay district boasts an assortment of colorful, fun places to wine and dine before a night out on the town.

MALASAÑA

La Granja Restaurante Vegetariano, C. San Andrés, 11 (☎91 532 87 93), off Pl. 2 de Mayo. M: Tribunal and Bilbao. Dimmed yellow light warms the atmosphere with plants, tiles, and pottery. Youthful crowd as light as the well-portioned nourishment. Lunchtime *menú* 1100ptas/€6.75. Open W-M 1:30-4:30pm and 9pm-midnight. V.

El Tazumal, C. Madera, 36 (☎91 522 79 82). M: Tribunal. From the station, walk down to C. Espiritú Santo, turn right, then left on C. Madera. Tasty and unique cuisine from El Salvador in a down-home setting. Entrées 275-1300ptas/€1.75-7.85. Open W-M 1:30-4:30pm and 8pm-midnight. AmEx/MC/V.

La Gata Flora, C. 2 de Mayo, 1 (☎ 91 523 10 26), across the street at C. San Vicente Ferrer, 33. M: Noviciado or Tribunal. You can't miss the pink exterior. Young people plus good, cheap food makes for a fun scene; most eat outside in the packed plaza. Stuffed pitas 550ptas/€3.50. *Sangría* 600-900ptas/€3.75-5.50. Open daily Su-Th 2-4pm and 8:30pm-12am, F-Sa until 1am. AmEx/MC/V.

MADRID

CHUECA

El 26 de Libertad, C. Libertad, 26 (☎91 522 25 22), off C. las Infantas. M: Chueca. Innovative and exotic Spanish cuisine. Dinner is served in a yellow room whose cheeriness helps you swallow the price (3000ptas/€18 before tax). Open M-Th 1-4pm and 8pm-midnight, F-Sa 1-4pm and 9pm-midnight, Su 1-4pm. MC/V.

La Sacristia, C. San Marcos, 8 (☎91 522 09 45). M: Gran Vía or Chueca. Colored, textured walls create a pleasant cave-like tavern where delicious creations and 60 types of *bacalao* are served. Dinner *menú* changes weekly (M-Th only, 2500ptas/€15). Open M-Sa 1-4pm and 8pm-1am, Su 8pm-1am. AmEx/MC/V.

La Gastroteca, Pl. de Chueca, 8 (☎91 532 25 64 or 91 522 88 04). M: Chueca. Look for the French owners in a mock-Egyptian portrait above the bar. Entrées 2400-2980ptas/€14.50-18. Open M-F 2-3:30pm and 9pm-1:30am, Sa 9pm-1:30am.

Chez Pomme, C. Pelayo, 4 (☎91 532 16 46), off C. Augusto Figueroa. M: Chueca. Quiet, artsy spot. French vegetarian cuisine perfectly presented. Delicious, creative salads 750-930ptas/€4.50-5.60. Light *menú* 1000ptas/€6. Open M-Th 1:30-4 and 8:30-11:30pm, F-Sa 1:30-4pm and 8:30pm-midnight.

La Carreta, C. Barbieri, 10 (☎91 532 70 42 or 91 521 60 97), off C. las Infantas. M: Gran Vía or Chueca. Small, friendly spot specializing in Argentinian, Uruguayan, and Chilean meals. Lunch *menú* 1650ptas/€9.92. Entrées 1300-1500ptas/€8-9. Occasional tango performances on weekends begin at 10pm. Reservations recommended. Open daily 1:30-5pm and 9pm-5am. AmEx/MC/V.

BILBAO

The area north of Glorieta de Bilbao, in the "V" formed by C. Fuencarral and C. Luchana and including Pl. Olavide, is the ethnic food extravaganza of Madrid; it overflows with bars, clubs, cafés, and restaurants of all nationalities. **C. Hartzenbusch** and **C. Cisneros** present endless options. Most serve splendid, cheap *tapas* to the youthful crowd that swarms the area at night. Lunch gets pricier farther north in a more gentrified area. The metro stop is Bilbao.

Arepas con Todo, C. Hartzenbusch, 19 (☎91 448 75 45), off C. Cardenal Cisneros, from C. Luchana. Hanging gourds and waitresses in festive dress fill this classic Colombian restaurant. A rotating *menú* (1600-2000ptas/€10-12) for every night of the month, and 60 fixed dishes (1800-2400ptas/€11-14.50). Only the live music repeats itself. For dinner, make reservations. Open M-W 2pm-1am. MC/V.

Collage, C. Olid, 6. (☎91 448 45 62), third street on your right off C. Fuencarral. M: Bilbao. A group of Swedish chefs mix and match in style. Only the hip need enter, and bring a full wallet. Entrées 1650-2850ptas/€10-17. Open Su-M 1:30-4pm, Tu-Sa 1:30-4pm and 8:30-midnight. AmEx/MC/V.

Tanger, C. Cardenal Cisneros, 11 (☎91 594 44 61). Middle-Eastern and Moroccan dishes, such as tahini-slathered meat (1000-1200ptas/€6-7.25), are served in a fantastic, mirrored dining room, replete with low, backless seats and engraved wooden tables. Midday *menú* 1100ptas/€6.75. Open Tu-Su 12:30pm-2am.

Bar Samara, C. Cardenal Cisneros, 13 (☎91 448 80 56). From M: Bilbao, walk up C. Luchana and take a quick left onto C. Cisneros. Bills itself as Egyptian, but offers Middle Eastern staples. Kebabs and other entrées 1675-2225ptas/€10-13.25. Open M 8:30pm-midnight, Tu-Th 2-4pm and 8:30-midnight; F-Su 2-4pm and 8:30pm-1am.

ARGÜELLES

Argüelles is a middle-class neighborhood near the Ciudad Universitaria. It's geared toward locals rather than tourists and is therefore full of inexpensive markets, moderately priced restaurants, and informal neighborhood bars. Check out the quiet *terrazas* on C. Pintor Rosales, overlooking the park.

Cáscaras, C. Ventura Rodríguez, 7 (☎ 91 542 83 36). M: Ventura Rodríguez. Facing the green outside the metro, take your first right off C. Princesa. Sleek interior enhances the dining experience. Popular for *tapas, pinchos,* and ice-cold Mahou beer in the early afternoon and evening. Exotic vegetarian entrées 800-985ptas/€4.85-6. Open M-F 7am-1am, Sa-Su 10am-1am. AmEx/MC/V.

Ananias, C. Galileo, 9 (☎91 448 68 01). M: Argüelles. From C. Alberto Aguilera, take a left onto C. Galileo. Swirling waiters serve Castilian dishes with a flourish. Authentic *torero* paraphernalia covers the walls in the front room, while finer diners and regulars enjoy the elegance of the back room. Entrées 1500-2500ptas/€9-15. Open Su-Tu, Th-F 1-4pm, 9-11:30pm, Sa 9-11:30pm. AmEx/MC/V.

La Crêperie, Po. Pintor Rosales, 28 (☎91 548 23 58). M: Ventura Rodríguez. The cherub decorations are almost as sweet as the dessert crepes (370-645ptas/€2.25-3.90). Eat the lunch and dinner crepes (535-805ptas/€3.25-5) on the chic Po. Rosales *terraza.* Open Su-Th 1:30-4:15pm and 8pm-1am, F-Sa 1:30-4:15pm and 8pm-1:30am.

La Vaca Argentina, Po. Pintor Rosales, 52 (☎91 559 66 05). M: Moncloa or Argüelles. Follow C. Marqués de Urquijo downhill, then take a left on Po. Rosales. Famous for its imported steak specialties and infamous for the cowhide wallpaper. Tender fillets 1100-4500ptas/€6.75-27. Open daily 1-4:30pm and 9pm-12:30am. AmEx/MC/V.

TAPAS

Not so long ago, bartenders in Madrid used to cover *(tapar)* drinks with saucers to keep the flies out. Later, servers began putting little sandwiches on top of the saucers, and there you have it: *tapas.* Hopping from bar to bar gobbling *tapas* is an active alternative to a full sit-down meal and a fun way to sample food you might never dream of even trying. Most *tapas* bars (a.k.a. *tascas* or *tabernas*) are open noon to 4pm and 8pm to midnight or later. Some, like **Museo del Jamón** (see p. 97), double as restaurants, and many cluster around **Plaza Santa Ana,** which is the place to be on Sundays, and **Plaza Mayor** (beware the tourist traps!). Authentic bars pack **C. Cuchilleros** and **C. de la Cruz.**

Casa Alberto, C. Huertas, 18 (☎91 429 93 56). M: Antón Martín. Patrons spill out into the night air to wait for a spot at the bar. Interior dining room decorated with bullfighting and Cervantine relics; Cervantes wrote the second part of "El Quijote" here. The *tapas* are all original house recipes. Get the feel of their *gambas al ajillo* (shrimp in garlic and hot peppers; 1250ptas/€7.50) or the filled *canapés* (275-350ptas/€1.75-2). Sit-down dinner is a bit pricey. Open Tu-Sa noon-1:30am, Su noon-4pm. AmEx/MC/V.

TAPAS So finally you've found a hostel, only been lost twice, and are ready to experience the *madrileño* lifestyle. Clearly, it's time for some drinks and *tapas*. The only problem is, what the hell are you going to order? To the untrained reader, *tapas* menus are often cryptic and undecipherable–if the bar has even bothered to print any. To make sure you don't end up eating the stewed parts of the oxen you rode in on, just keep the following words in mind. Servings come in three sizes: *pincho* (normally eaten with toothpicks between sips of beer), *tapa* (small plate), or *ración* (sizable, meal portion). *Aceitunas* (olives), *albóndigas* (meatballs), *anchoas* (anchovies), *callos* (tripe), *chorizo* (sausage), *croquetas* (croquettes), *gambas* (shrimp), *jamón* (ham), *patatas alioli y bravas* (potatoes with sauces), *pimientos* (peppers), *pulpo* (octopus), and *tortillla* (omelette) comprise any basic menu. More adventurous travelers should try *morcilla* (blood sausage) or *sesos* (cow's brains). Bartenders will often offer tastes of *tapas* with your drink and strike up a conversation in the spirit of Madrid's generosity and charm. To ensure full treatment and local respect, the house *cerveza* is always a good choice. *Sangría,* a mixture of wine and fruit juices, seems innocent but packs a kick–natives drink it by the jar and box in the sweltering summers.

La Toscana, C. Manuel Fernández González, 10-12 (☎91 429 60 31), at C. Ventura de la Vega. M: Sol. A local crowd hangs out over *tapas* of *mocillo asado* (1300ptas/€7.85). Despite the antique lettering and wrought iron, the range of dishes is anything but medieval. Spacious bar area jam-packed on weekends. Most *tapas* around 800ptas/€5. Open Th-Tu noon-4pm and 8pm-midnight.

Los Gabrieles, C. Echegaray, 17. (☎91 429 62 61 or 429 50 03). Near Villa Madrid. The tiled mural at the back depicts Spain's famous artists–from Velázquez to Goya–as stumble-drunks. The big draw here is the *laguita* (500ptas/€3), a fine sherry that helps wash away the cares of the day. Open daily 1pm-late.

Casa Amadeo, Pl. de Cascorro, 18 (☎91 365 94 39). M: La Latina. The jovial owner of 60 years supervises making of house specialty *caracoles* (snails; *tapas* 700ptas/€4.25, big *ración* 1500ptas/€9) and *chorizo* (sausage) made with snails (750ptas/€4.50). *Raciones* 350-900ptas/€2-5.50. Wild Sunday nights. Open M-F 10:30am-4pm and 7-10:30pm, Su 7-11pm.

La Trucha, C. Núñez de Arce, 6 (☎91 429 58 33). M: Sol. Impressive selection of seasonal veggies (800-1500ptas/€5-9) and daily specials are popular with locals. Don't skip the stewed bull's tail (*rabo de toro*; 1500ptas/€9). Entrées 2000-2500ptas/€12-15. Open M-Sa 12:30-4pm and 7:30pm-midnight. AmEx/MC/V.

Taberna del Alabarder, C. Felipe V, 6 (☎91 547 25 77 or 91 541 51 92) M: Ópera. Near Café Oriente in Pl. Oriente. Overlooking the glorious Palacio Real try the country-famous *patatas al pobre* (potatoes with garlic) or *tigres unidad* (fried muscles). Tapas from 600-1100ptas/€3.75-6.75. Open M-Sa 1pm-4pm, 7pm-12am. AmEx/MC/V.

La Princesita, C. Princesa, 80 (☎91 543 70 71). M: Argüelles. From open to closing, students crowd the bar to enjoy regional specialties, including *queso de Cabrales* (goat cheese; 175ptas/€1). Open M-Sa 10am-11:30pm.

Cafetería-Restaurante El Encinar del Bierzo, C. Toledo, 82 (☎91 366 23 89). M: La Latina. A neighborhood landmark. House specialties *conejo al ajillo* (rabbit with garlic, 2000ptas/€12) and *gambas a la plancha* (fried shrimp, 1100ptas/€6.75). Menú 1100ptas/€6.75, 1300ptas/€8 on Su. Open daily 1-4:30pm, 9pm-11:30pm. MC/V.

CAFÉS

Coffee in Madrid's cafés may be expensive (200-450ptas/€1.25-2.75), but included in the price are atmosphere, history, and image. It's customary to linger for an hour or two in these historic cafés, an economical way to soak up a little of Madrid's culture and finally write those postcards you bought a few days ago. You won't be bothered with the check until you ask.

Café Gijón, Po. Recoletos, 21 (☎91 521 54 25). M: Colón. On its 100th anniversary in 1988, Gijón was designated a historic site for its intellectual significance. Check out how smart you look in the mirrors and forget how much that cup of coffee costs. Coffees from 615ptas/€3.75. Open daily 9am-1:30am. AmEx/MC/V.

Café de Oriente, Pl. Oriente, 2 (☎91 547 15 64). M: Ópera. A beautiful, old-fashioned café catering to a ritzy, older crowd. Spectacular view of the Palacio Real from the *terraza,* especially at night when a spotlight illuminates the palace. Prices are significantly cheaper inside than on the patio. Specialty coffees (540-840ptas/€3.35-5) live up to their price. Open daily 8:30am-1:30am.

Eucalipto, C. Argumosa, 4. M: Lavapiés. You need not be a koala to enjoy the *zumos tropicales* (fresh fruit drinks; 400-550ptas/€2.40-3.30). Spike up the night with a *daiquiri* (600-650ptas/63.75-4) and enjoy a fantastic fruit salad for 2 (1000ptas/€6). Lively sidewalk seating. Open daily M-Th 6pm-2am, F-Sa 6pm-3am, Su 2pm-midnight.

Salón Del Prado, C. Del Prado, 4 (☎91 429 33 61). M: Sol. Head left down C. San Jerónimo, right down C. Príncipe to Pl. Santa Ana, and left on C. Del Prado. Interior as cool as the *granizado de limón* (frozen lemon drink; 400ptas/€2.50) and homemade ice cream it serves up. Open M-Th 2pm-2am, F-Sa 2pm-2:30am.

Café Comercial, Glorieta de Bilbao, 7 (☎91 531 56 55). M: Bilbao. Founded in 1887, Madrid's oldest café imports an old sports high ceilings, cushioned chairs, and huge mirrors perfect for people-watching. Frequented by artists and Republican aviators alike. The first anti-Franco protests took place here. Coffee 160ptas/€1 at the bar, 260ptas/€1.55 at a table. Open Su-Th 8am-12:45am, F-Sa 8am-1:45am.

El Café Sin Nombre, C. Conde Duque 10, (☎91 548 09 72). M: Ventura Rodríguez. From the metro and Duque de Lina take the stairs up through the little park up to Conde Duque; across from the Exhibition Center. After an afternoon of gallery viewing, sink into tapestry-covered couches for coffee-sipping or casual drinks. From Cuban *machiatos* to Brazilian *Capirinhas* (750ptas/€2.50.). Open M-F 9am-2am, Sa 8pm-3am.

SIGHTS

You need good shoes to walk around in.
— A shoemaker

Madrid, large as it may seem, is a walker's city. Its fantastic public transportation system should be used as little as possible. Although the word *paseo* refers to a major avenue—such as *Paseo de la Castellana* or *Paseo del Prado*—it literally means "a stroll." Do just that from Sol to Cibeles and from the Plaza Mayor to the Palacio Real—sights will kindly introduce themselves. The city's art and architecture and its culture and atmosphere convince wide-eyed walkers that it was once the capital of the world's greatest empire. While Madrid is perfect for walking, it also offers some of the world's best places to stop strolling. Whether soothing tired feet after perusing the *triángulo de arte* or suffering from a hangover after a night in Chueca, there's nothing better than a shady sidewalk café.

For hard-core visitors with a checklist of destinations, the municipal tourist office's *Plano de Transportes* map, which marks monuments as well as bus and metro lines, is indispensable. In the following pages, sights are arranged by neighborhood. Each section has a designated center from which all directions are given. If you are trying to design a walking tour of the entire city, it is best to begin in El Centro, the self-evident nucleus of Madrid. The neighborhoods naturally fall in geographical order from there; a good day of sightseeing might move from historic Madrid, to the cafés of Huertas, to the celebrated *paseos*, to a stroll through the Retiro. El Pardo falls last, as it is a separate trip.

EL CENTRO

The area known as El Centro, spreading out from the Puerta del Sol ("Gate of the Sun"), is the gateway to the history and spirit of Madrid. Although several rulers carved the winding streets, the Habsburg and Bourbon families left the Centro's most celebrated monuments. As a result, the Centro is divided into two major sections: Madrid de los Habsburgs and Madrid de los Borbones. All directions are given from the Puerta del Sol. For convenience, the metro stop closest to each sight (often not M: Sol) is also listed.

PUERTA DEL SOL

Kilómetro 0—the origin of six national highways fanning out to the rest of Spain—marks the country's physical and psychological center in the most chaotic of Madrid's numerous plazas, Puerta del Sol. Sol blazes all day and night with the lights of taxis, bars, street performers, and newsstands. A web of pedestrian-only tributaries originating at the Gran Vía leads a rush of consumers down a gallery of stores, funneling them into Sol.

It was not until the late 19th century that Sol became the true nucleus of Madrid. In the 16th century, an eastward-facing gate, known as the Gateway to the Sun, stood in Puerta del Sol. Today, government buildings dominate the plaza, where citizens and tourists alike converge upon *El oso y el madroño*, a bronze statue of a bear and a strawberry tree, now a symbol of Madrid. On New Year's Eve, citizens congregate in Sol to gobble up one grape per chime as the clock strikes midnight.

HABSBURG MADRID

"Old Madrid," the city's central neighborhood, is the most densely packed with both monuments and tourists. In the 16th century, the Habsburgs built **Plaza Mayor** and the **Catedral de San Isidro** from scratch. Many of Old Madrid's buildings, however, date from much earlier, some as far back as the Moorish empire. When Felipe II moved the seat of Castilla from Toledo to Madrid (then only a town of 20,000) in 1561, he and his descendants commissioned the court architects (including Juan de Herrera, the architect of the austere El Escorial) to update many of Madrid's buildings to the latest styles. After only a century of development and expansion, Madrid more than doubled in population. Today, central Madrid, from the celebrated street of Alcalá to the iron verandas of Plaza Mayor, still reflects the power of the Habsburgs and the architecture of Juan de Herrera.

PLAZA MAYOR. In 1620, Pl. Mayor was completed for Felipe III; his statue, installed in 1847, still graces the plaza's center. Though designed by Juan de Herrera, Pl. Mayor is much softer in style. Its elegant arcades, spindly towers, and pleasant verandas are defining elements of the "Madrid style" of architecture, which inspired architects across the city and throughout the country. With lances of exaggerated length, 17th-century nobles on horseback spent Sunday afternoons chasing bulls in the plaza. The nobility had such a jolly time that eventually everyone joined in the fun. Citizens, on foot and armed with sticks, also began running hither and thither after those pesky bulls. The tradition came to be known as a *corrida*, from the verb *correr* (to run).

Toward evening, Pl. Mayor awakens as *madrileños* resurface, tourists multiply, and café tables fill with lively patrons. Live performances of flamenco and music are a common treat. While the cafés are a nice spot for a drink, food is overpriced; save dinner for elsewhere. On Sunday mornings, the plaza holds a rare coin and stamp sale, marking the starting point of **El Rastro** (see p. 122). During the annual **Fiesta de San Isidro** (May 15-22, see p. 120), the plaza explodes with celebration. *(From Pta. Sol, walk down C. Mayor. The plaza is on the left. M: Sol.)*

CATEDRAL DE SAN ISIDRO. This cathedral, which commemorates San Isidro, protector of crops and patron saint of Madrid, has had a turbulent history. It was designed in the Jesuit Baroque style at the beginning of the 17th century; in 1769 San Isidro's remains were brought here. During the Civil War rioting workers burned the exterior—only the primary nave and a few Baroque decorations remain from the original. San Isidro, which has since been restored, reigned as *the* cathedral of Madrid from the late 19th century until the Catedral de la Almudena (see p. 105) was consecrated in 1993. *(From the Pta. Sol, take C. Mayor to Pl. Mayor, cross the plaza, and exit onto C. Toledo. The cathedral is located at the intersection of C. Toledo and C. Sacramento. M: Latina. Open for mass only at 9am, 10am, 11am, 12pm daily.)*

PLAZA DE LA VILLA. When Felipe II made Madrid the capital of his empire in 1561, most of the town huddled between Pl. Mayor and the Palacio Real; Pl. Villa marks the heart of what was once Old Madrid. Though only a handful of medieval buildings remain, the plaza still features a stunning courtyard (surrounding the statue of Don Álvara de Bazón), beautiful tile-work, and eclectic architecture. The horseshoe-shaped door on C. Codo is one of the few examples of Gothic-Mudéjar left in Madrid, and the 15th-century Torre de los Lujanes (on the left when looking from C. Mayor) is the sole remnant of the once lavish residence of the Lujanes family. Across the plaza is the 17th-century Ayuntamiento (Casa de la Villa), designed in 1640 by Juan Gómez de Mora as both the mayor's home and the city jail. Inside is Goya's *Allegory of the City of Madrid* (1819). The neighboring Casa de Cisneros, a 16th-century Plateresque house, also served as a government building when Habsburg officials annexed it for the city's growing bureaucracy. *(From Pta. Sol, go down C. Mayor, past Pl. Mayor. The plaza is on the left. M: Sol.)*

ALONG RÍO MANZANARES. Past the **Puerta de Toledo**, the triumphal arch commissioned by Joseph Bonaparte to celebrate his brother Napoleon, the Río Manzanares, Madrid's notoriously puny river, snakes its way around the city. The broad Baroque **Puente de Toledo** makes up for the river's inadequacies. Sandstone carvings on both sides of the bridge depict San Isidro and his family. The **Puente de Segovia,** which fords the river along C. Segovia, was conceived by Juan de Herrera. Both bridges afford gorgeous views and are popular with young couples. *(To reach Puente de Toledo from Pta. Sol, go down C. Mayor, through the Pl. Mayor, and onto C. Toledo; follow Toledo to the bridge. For the Puente de Segovia, take C. Mayor from Pta. Sol, turn left on C. de Bailén, and right on C. Segovia, which crosses the river. M: Sol.)*

OTHER SIGHTS. As the legend goes, the **Iglesia de San Pedro** began as a Mudéjar mosque. A 17th-century overhaul, commissioned by Felipe IV, infused the original structure with Baroque intricacies. *(From Pta. Sol, go down C. Mayor, through the Pl. Mayor onto C. Toledo, and right on C. Duque de Alba. M: La Latina. San Perdo is open for mass only, daily 9am,11am,7pm. Free.)* Next to the Iglesia de San Pedro is the **Museo de San Isidro** where the saint was said to have resided and home to the sarcophagus of San Isidro, the **Capilla de San Isidro.** *(Pl. de San Andre's. M: La Latina. Open Tu-F, 9:30am-8pm, Sa-Su 10am-2pm. Free.)*

BOURBON MADRID

Weakened by plagues and political losses, the Habsburg era in Spain ended with the death of Carlos II in 1700. Felipe V, the first of Spain's Bourbon monarchs, ascended the throne in 1714 after the 12-year War of Spanish Succession. Bankruptcy, industrial stagnation, and widespread moral disillusionment compelled Felipe V to embark on a crusade of urban renewal. His successors, Fernando VI and Carlos III, fervently pursued the same ends, with astounding results. Today, the lavish palaces, churches, and parks that remain are the most touristed in Madrid; a walk around them will require planning and patience.

PALACIO REAL. The impossibly luxurious Palacio Real lounges at the western tip of central Madrid, overlooking the Río Manzanares. Felipe V commissioned Giovanni Sachetti to replace the Alcázar, which had burned down in 1734, with a palace that would dwarf all others; he succeeded. When Sachetti died, Filippo Juvara took over the project, basing his new façade on Bernini's rejected designs for the Louvre. The shell took 26 years to build, and the decoration of its 2000 rooms (with a vast collection of porcelain, tapestries, furniture, armor, and art) dragged on for over a century. When Alfonso XIII abdicated in 1931, the Second Republic abandoned the costly construction. Today, the unfinished palace is only used by

King Juan Carlos and Queen Sofía on special occasions. Although only a fragment is complete, the palace stands as one of Europe's most grandiose residences.

The palace's most impressive rooms are decorated in the *Rococo* style. The **Salón de Gasparini**, site of the king's ceremonial dressing before the court, houses Goya's portrait of Carlos IV and a Mengs ceiling fresco. The **Salón del Trono** (Throne Room) also contains a ceiling fresco, painted by Tiepolo, outlining the qualities of the quintessential ruler. The **Real Oficina de Farmacia** (Royal Pharmacy) features crystal and china receptacles used to hold royal medicines, and the **Biblioteca** shelves first editions of *Don Quijote*. Also open to the public is the **Real Armería** (Armory), which displays the finest armor of the age, that of Carlos V and Felipe II, as well as other medieval weapons and artillery. *(From Pta. Sol, take C. Mayor, and turn right on C. Bailén. ☎91 454 88 00. M: Sol. Open Apr.-Sept. M-Sa 9am-6pm, Su 9am-3pm; Oct.-Mar. M-Sa 9:30am-5pm, Su 9am-2pm. 1000ptas/€6, with tour 1150ptas/€6.90; students 500ptas/€3, with tour 1150ptas/€6.90. EU citizens free W. Arrive early to avoid lines and skip M, when it is one of the only sights open.)*

CATHEDRAL DE LA ALMUDENA. Take a break from the cherub-filled frescoes of most cathedrals in Spain for refreshingly ultra-modern decor. Begun in 1879 and finished a century later, this cathedral—especially its interior—is a stark contrast to the gilded Palacio Real. After a 30-year hibernation, the building received a controversial face-lift. The reasons for the controversy are immediately apparent, as the cathedral's frescoes and stained glass windows contain a discordant mix of traditional and abstract styles: gray stone walls clash with the ceiling panels of brilliant colors and sharp geometric shapes. *(From Pta. Sol, go down C. Mayo and turn right on C. Bailén; the cathedral is just before the Palacio Real. Closed during mass. Open M-Sa 1-7pm. Free.)*

PLAZA DE ORIENTE. A minor architectural miscalculation was responsible for this sculpture park. Most of the statues were designed for the palace roof, but because they were too heavy and the queen had a nightmare about the roof collapsing, they were instead placed in this shady plaza. An equestrian statue of Felipe IV, sculpted by Pietro Tacca, dominates the plaza; other structures include the Teatro Real, inaugurated by Isabel II. Treat yourself to a pricey coffee at the elegant *terrazas* encompass the plaza. *(From Pta. Sol, take C. Arenal to the plaza.)*

OTHER SIGHTS. The **Jardines de Sabatini,** just to the right if you are facing the palace, is the romantic's park of choice. Below the Palace, the **Campo de Moro,** opened to the public just 13 years ago, is straight out of a fairy-tale. *(Enter from the side opposite the Palace. Both are free.)* The **Parque de las Vistillas,** named for the tremendous *vistillas* (views) of Palacio Real, Nuestra Señora de la Almudena, and the surrounding countryside, provides a stunning photo-op. Take precaution, as it can be dangerous at night. *(Located in the Pl. Gabriel Miró. From Pta. Sol, go down C. Mayor, turn left on C. Bailén, and then right on C. Morería into the plaza.)*

HUERTAS

The area east of Sol is a wedge bounded by C. de Alcalá to the north, C. Atocha to the south, and Po. Prado to the east. Off C. San Jerónimo a myriad of streets slope downward, outward, and eastward toward various points along Po. Prado and Pl. Cánovas de Castillo. **Plaza Santa Ana** and its *terrazas* are the center of this old literary neigborhood; all directions in this section start from there. Huertas's sights, from authors' houses to famous cafés, are reflections of its artistic past. Home to Cervantes, Góngora, Quevedo, Calderón, and Moratín at its heyday during the "Siglo de Oro" (see **Literature,** p. 63), Huertas enjoyed a fleeting return to literary prominence when Hemingway frequented the neighborhood in the 1920s.

CASA DE LOPE DE VEGA. Although Golden Age writers Lope de Vega and Miguel de Cervantes were bitter rivals, Vega's 17th-century house is ironically located on C. Cervantes. (Ironically still, Cervantes is buried on C. Lope de Vega.) A prolific playwright and poet, Lope de Vega spent the last 25 years of his life writing over two-thirds of his plays, in this house. *(C. Cervantes, 11. With your back to Pl. Santa Ana,*

MADRID

turn left on C. Prado, right on C. León, and left on C. Cervantes. ☎ 91 429 92 16. Open Tu-F 9:30am-2pm, Sa 10am-2pm. 200ptas/€1.20, students 100ptas/€.60, W free.)

CÍRCULO DE BELLAS ARTES. Designed by Antonio Palacios, this building encloses two stages and several studios for lectures and workshops run by prominent artists. The Círculo is the energetic hub of much of Madrid's art, sponsoring and organizing performances and shows around the city. Be sure to pick up their free monthly schedule, the *Minerva*, available at the entrance. Many facilities are for *socios* (members) only, but exhibition galleries for all media are open to the public. *(C. Alcalá, 42. From Pl. Santa Ana, go up C. del Príncipe, cross C. San Jerónimo, and continue towards C. Alcalá. Turn right on C. Alcalá; the building is on the right. ☎ 91 360 54 00. Hours and admission vary with exhibitions.)*

OTHER SIGHTS. Juan de Villanueva's simple **Real Academia de la Historia** houses a magnificent old library, another example of Madrid-style architecture. *(At the intersection of C. León and C. Huertas. From Pl. Santa Ana, take C. Príncipe and turn left on C. Huertas.)* Also impressive are the façades of the **Palacio Miraflores** and the **Palacio del Marqués de Ugena** designed by the 18th-century architect, Pedro de Ribera. *(Palacio Miraflores, C. San Jerónimo, 15. Palacio de Marqués de Ugena, Pl. Canalejas, 3.)*

GRAN VÍA

Urban planners paved the Gran Vía in 1910 to link C. Princesa with Pl. Cibeles, creating the cosmopolitan center of life in the city. After Madrid gained wealth as a neutral supplier during World War I, the city funneled much of its earnings into making the Gran Vía one of the world's great thoroughfares. Today, movie theaters and fast-food joints line the most Americanized street in Madrid. Still, Gran Vía is a sight in itself—be sure to stroll (quickly) among the shops and skyscrapers.

Sol's shopping streets converge at Gran Vía's highest elevation in **Plaza de Callao** (M: Callao), C. Postigo San Martín splits off southward, where you'll find the famed **Monasterio de las Descalzas Reales** (see p. 113). Westward from Pl. Callao (left when facing the conspicuous sex shop), the Gran Vía makes its descent toward **Plaza de España** (M: Pl. España), where a statue commemorates Spain's most prized fictional duo: Cervantes's *Don Quijote* and *Sancho Panza* (riding horseback and muleback, respectively). Next to Pl. España are two of Madrid's tallest skyscrapers, the **Telefónica building** (1929) and the **Edificio de España** (1953). Louis S. Weeks of the Chicago School designed the Telefónica building, the tallest concrete building in existence at the time (81m), and Franco's architect designed the Edificio de España. Tucked between the two skyscrapers on C. San Leonardo is the small **Iglesia de San Marcos,** a Neoclassical church composed of five intersecting ellipses—this Euclidean dream of a church doesn't have a straight line.

MALASAÑA AND CHUECA

The area between **Calle de Fuencarral** and **Calle de San Bernardo** is home to some of Madrid's most avant-garde architecture and current art exhibitions. Though not packed with historic monuments, the labyrinthine streets provide many spontaneous, undocumented "sights," from platform-shoe stores to street performers—they are an ultra-modern, funkafied relief for travelers weary of crucifixes and brushstrokes. By night, these districts bristle with Madrid's alternative scene.

IGLESIA DE LAS SALESAS REALES. Bourbon King Fernando VI commissioned this church in 1758 at the request of his wife, Doña Bárbara. The Baroque-Neoclassical domed church is clad in granite, with façade sculptures by Alfonso Vergaza and a dome painting by the brothers González Velázquez. The church's ostentatious façade and interior prompted critics to pun on the queen's name: "Barbaric queen, barbaric tastes, barbaric building, barbarous expense," they said, giving rise to the expression "*¡qué bárbaro!*" Today, the expression refers to absurdity, extravagance, or just plain craziness. For nightlife in surrounding streets that defines *¡qué bárbaro!*, see p. 114. *(C. Bárbara de Braganza, 1. M: Alonso Martínez.*

From the metro take a R off C. Genova onto C. Marqués de la Ensenada; a R on C. Barbara de Braganza will lead you to the entrance.)

ARGÜELLES

The 19th century witnessed the growth of several neighborhoods around the core of the city, north and northwest of the Palacio Real. Today, the area known as Argüelles and the zone surrounding **Calle San Bernardo** form a cluttered mixture of elegant middle-class houses, student apartments, and bohemian hangouts, all brimming with cultural activity. Heavily bombarded during the Civil War, Argüelles inspired Chilean poet Pablo Neruda, then a resident, to write *España en el corazón.* Directions in this section are given from the Argüelles metro stop.

TEMPLO DE DEBOD. Built by Pharaoh Zakheramon in the 4th century BC, it's the only Egyptian temple in Spain. In appreciation of Spanish archaeologists who helped rescue the Abu Simbel temples from the floods of the Aswan dam, the Egyptian government shipped the temple stone by stone to Spain. The **Parque de la Montaña** is home to the temple and two of its three original gateways and provides a peaceful haven with beautiful views of Madrid. *(M: Ventura Rodríguez. From the metro, walk down C. Ventura Rodríguez into Parque de la Montaña; the temple is on the left. ☎91 366 74 15. In summer Tu-Su 10am-1:45pm and 6–7:45pm; off-season Tu-F 10am-1:45pm and 4-6pm, Sa-Su 10am-2pm. 300ptas/€1.80, students 150ptas/€0.90. W and Su free.)*

ERMITA DE SAN ANTONIO DE LA FLORIDA. Although out of the way, the Ermita is worth the trouble. It contains Goya's pantheon—a frescoed dome arches above his buried corpse. Curiously enough, Goya's skull, apparently stolen by a phrenologist, was missing when the corpse arrived from France. Every 12th of June single *madrileñas* pay homage to this statue to beg of San Antonio's help in the husband-hunt *(M: Príncipe Pío. From the metro, go left on C. de Buen Altamirano, walk through the park, and turn left on Po. Florida; the Ermita is at the end of this street. ☎91 542 07 22. Open Tu-F 10am-2pm and 4-8pm, Sa-Su 10am-2pm. Free.)*

CASA DEL CAMPO. A sight in itself, take the **Teléferico** from Rosales into the city's largest park. Shaded by pines, oaks, and cypresses, large numbers of families, joggers and walkers roam the grounds by day. Early morning reveals evidence of questionable nighttime activities; it's wise to stay away after dark. Inside the amusement park **Parque de Atracciones,** you can relive your childhood on the roller coaster. *(M: Batán. Walk up the main street away from the lake and through the park. ☎91 526 80 31. Open Su-F noon-11pm, Sa noon-midnight. www.parquedeatracciones.es.)* The **Zoo/ Aquarium** is 5 min. away. *(☎91 512 37 70. M-F 10:30am-9pm, Sa-Su 10:30am-9:30pm. 1615ptas/€9.75, children under 8 1300ptas/€7.85)*

OTHER SIGHTS. Parque del Oeste is a large, sloping park known for the **Rosaleda** (rose garden) at its bottom. A yearly competition determines which award-winning rose will be added to the permanent collection. (M: Moncloa. From the metro, take C. Princesa. *Open daily 10am-8pm.)* A prime example of Fascist Neoclassicism, the arcaded **Cuartel General del Aire (Ejército del Aire)** commands the view on the other side of Arco de la Victoria (by the Moncloa metro station). The renovation of Felipe V's soldiers' barracks has produced one of Madrid's finest cultural centers, the **Centro Cultural Conde Duque,** which hosts travelling exhibitions. (C. Conde Duque, 11. ☎91 588 58 34. M: San Bernardo.) The fabulous **Museo de América** (see p. 113) is a bit farther down the avenue, past the **Arco de Moncloa.** The **Faro de Moncloa** is a 92m high metal tower near the museum that offers views of the city. From the tower, you can see El Escorial on a clear day. *(Avda. Arco de la Victoria, ☎90 215 19 12. Open M-Su 10am-1:45pm, 5-8:45pm. 200ptas/€1.25 to ascend the Faro de Moncloa.)*

RETIRO

Felipe IV intended the 300-acre **Parque del Buen Retiro,** once a hunting ground, to be a *buen retiro* (nice retreat). Today it's full of palm-readers, soccer players, and sunbathers. The northeast corner of the park enchants with medieval monastic ruins and waterfalls. On weekends, the promenades fill with musicians, families, and young lovers; on summer nights (when only the north gate remains open), the lively bars and cafés fill with teenagers, families, and couples. It is easily accessible from the Retiro metro stop, and all directions are given from there. Avoid venturing alone into the park after dark. *(M: Retiro.)*

ESTANQUE GRANDE. Overlooked by Alfonso XII's mausoleum, rowers crowd the rectangular lake in the middle of the park, the Estanque Grande. The lake has been the social center of the Retiro ever since aspiring caricaturists, fortune-tellers, sunflower-seed vendors, and drug pushers first parked their goods along its marble shores. *(M: Retiro. With your back to the metro stop, turn right on C. Alcalá and walk until you reach Pta. Alcalá; enter the park on Av. Mejico which leads to the lake. Boat rentals daily 10am-8:30pm. Paddle boats 575ptas/€3.50 for 4 people. Motorboats 165ptas/€1 per person.)*

PALACIO DE CRISTAL. Built by Ricardo Velázquez to exhibit Philippine flowers in 1887, this exquisite steel-and-glass structure hosts a variety of art shows, with subjects ranging from Bugs Bunny to Spanish portraiture. *(Open Tu-Sa 11am-2pm and 5-8pm, Su 10am-2pm. Admission varies, but often free.)*

MADRID

PALACIO DE VELÁZQUEZ. A place where all artists should dream of having their art displayed, this Velázquez creation has billowing ceilings, marble floors, and ideal lighting. The Palacio de Velázquez exhibits works in conjunction with the Museo de Arte Reina Sofía (see p. 112). *(From the metro, turn right on C. Alcalá, walk through Pta. Alcalá, pass the Estanque, and turn left on Po. Venezuela. ☎91 575 62 45. Open M-Sa 11am-8pm, Su 11am-6pm. Free.)*

CASÓN DEL BUEN RETIRO. Three minutes from the Prado sits the Casón del Buen Retiro, which, while closed for renovations, is still worth a peek from the outside. Once part of Felipe IV's Palacio del Buen Retiro, the Casón was destroyed in the Napoleonic wars. The rebuilt version normally houses the Prado's 19th- and 20th-century works, currently on loan to the Reina Sofía. *(C. Alfonso XXII, 28. ☎91 330 28 60. Closed for renovations until at least 2002.)*

OTHER SIGHTS. Bullets from the 1921 assassination of prime minister Eduardo Dato permanently scarred the eastern face of **Puerta de Alcalá** (1778), outside the Retiro's Puerta de la Independencia. To the south, the **Casón del Buen Retiro** faces the park (see p. 112); behind it sits the **Museo del Ejército** (see p. 114). The two buildings are remnants of Felipe IV's palace, which burned down in 1764.

EL PARDO

Built as a hunting lodge for Carlos I in 1547, El Pardo was enlarged by generations of Habsburgs and Bourbons. Though Spain's growing capital eventually engulfed El Pardo, it still stands as one of Spain's greatest country palaces. El Pardo gained attention in 1940 when Franco decided to make it his home; he resided here until his death in 1975. Although politics have changed, the palace is still the official reception site for distinguished foreign visitors. Renowned for its collection of **tapestries**—several of which were designed by Goya—the palace also holds a Velázquez painting and Ribera's *Techo de los hombres ilustres (Ceiling of the Illustrious Men)*. You can also see the bedroom cabinet in which Franco kept Santa Teresa's silver-encrusted hand. Entrance to the palace's **capilla** and the nearby **Casita del Príncipe,** created by Juan de Villanueva, of Museo del Prado fame, is free. *(Take bus #601 from the stop in front of the Ejército del Aire building above M: Moncloa; 15min., 150ptas/€0.90. ☎91 376 03 29. Palace open Apr.-Sept. M-F 10:30am-6pm, Su 9:25am-1:40pm; Oct.-Mar. M-F 10:30am-5pm, Su 9:55am-1:40pm. Compulsory 45min. guided tour in Spanish. 800ptas/€4.80, students 250ptas/€1.50. W free for EU citizens.)*

THE PASEOS: A WALKING TOUR

The most salient feature on any map of Madrid is the grand avenue at the center's eastern edge, running from Madrid-Atocha in the south to Madrid-Chamartín in the north. Madrid's great thoroughfare is really three fused segments, **Po. Prado, Po. Recoletos,** and **Po. Castellana,** that represent three eras of urban expansion. Carlos III, the city's urban visionary, laid the Po. Prado from 1775 to 1782. The road connects Atocha to Pl. Cibeles, passing the Museo del Prado (see p. 111), the Thyssen-Bornemisza (see p. 112), and the Ritz Hotel along the way. Along Po. Recoletos, extending from Pl. Cibeles to Pl. Colón, the newest members of the *clase alta* (upper class) congregate at luxuriously shaded *terrazas*. Contemporary Madrid stretches further north along Po. Castellana (lined with bank buildings from the 1970s and 80s) to Pl. Castilla's twin towers (Puerta de Europa). The *paseos* reveal a different side of Madrid's architecture from the sights of the center, providing a relief from the density of many neighborhoods. In the summer, a late afternoon stroll along the *paseos* should include a stop at one of the fabulous chic cafés of the Po. Castellana (see p. 110). Strolls along Po. Prado and Po. Recoletos combine well with a tour of Huertas or the Retiro; even a walk to the post office in Pl. Cibeles can incorporate the majority of the sights along the *paseos*.

PASEO DEL PRADO

Modeled after the Piazza Navona in Rome, Paseo del Prado is the center of Madrid's art district. Virtually every major museum is in the vicinity of this museum mile, known as the *triángulo de arte.* Directly across from the Estación de Atocha, the **Centro de Arte Reina Sofía** (see p. 112), home to Picasso's *Guérnica*, extols its glass elevators in Pl. Emperador Carlos V.

Walking up Po. Prado, you'll pass the **Jardín Botánico** on the right. Opened during Carlos III's reign, the garden showcases over 30,000 species of plants, ranging from traditional roses to medicinal herbs. Just about anyone will appreciate the garden's vast collection of imported trees, bushes, and flowers. *(Pl. de Murillo, 2, next to the Prado Museum. ☎91 420 30 17; www.ejb.scic.es. Open daily in summer 10am-8pm; in winter 10am-6pm; in spring and fall 10am-7pm. 250ptas/€1.50, students 100ptas/€0.60.)* Next to the Jardín Botánico is the world-renowned **Museo del Prado** (see p. 111) and behind it, on C. Ruiz de Alarcón, stands the **Iglesia de San Jerónimo,** Madrid's royal church. Built by Hieronymite monks and re-endowed by the Catholic Monarchs, the church has witnessed a few joyous milestones, including the coronation of Fernando and Isabel and the marriage of King Alfonso XIII. These days, only the highest of high-society weddings grace the church. *(Open daily 8am-1:30pm and 5-8:30pm.)* Back on Po. Prado, to the north in Pl. Lealtad, stands the **Obelisco a los Mártires del 2 de Mayo,** filled with the ashes of those who died in the 1808 uprising against Napoleon. Its four statues represent Constancy, Virtue, Valor, and Patriotism, and the flame burns continuously in honor of the patriots. Behind the memorial sits the colonnaded Greco-Roman-style **Bolsa de Madrid** (Stock Exchange), designed by Repullés. Ventura Rodríguez's **Fuente de Neptuno,** in Pl. Cánovas de Castillo, is one of three aquatic masterpieces along the avenue.

The arts of the Po. Prado transform into the Po. Recoletos at the tulip-encircled **Plaza de Cibeles.** Madrid residents successfully protected this emblem of their city (best viewed at dusk) during Franco's bomb raids by covering it with a pyramid of sandbags. The **Museo Naval** is to the right. *(Entrance at Po. Prado, 5. ☎91 379 52 99. Open Tu-Su 10am-1:30pm. Free.)* The spectacular **Palacio de Comunicaciones** (see p. 90), where you can mail your letters in true style, is also here. Antonio Palacios and Julián Otamendi of Otto Wagner's Vienna School designed the neo-Baroque structure in 1920. On the northeastern corner of the intersection (behind black gates) is the former **Palacio de Linares,** a 19th-century townhouse built for Madrid nobility. Long abandoned by its former residents and proven by a team of "scientists" to be inhabited by ghosts, it was transformed into the **Casa de América,** with a library and lecture halls for the study of Latin American culture and politics. It sponsors art

SEX IN THE CIBELES The Plaza de Cibeles, with its infamous marble fountain, has been Madrid's physical and spiritual axis since its construction in 1781. Depicting the fertility goddess's triumph over the emblematic Castilian lions, the fountain's image of Cybele has long captivated citizens. Legend has it that the fleet-footed Atlanta, one of Cybele's maids, would take as her lover only the man who could outrun her. No man was up to the challenge until one cunning suitor instructed his cohorts to scatter golden apples (as distractions) in Atlanta's path. The goddess Cybele, watching the prank, was overcome with wrath at men's evil ways. So, after punishing the plotters by turning them into lions, she hitched them up to her own carriage. This assertion of power and sexuality charmed Madrid, resulting in the proverb *"mas popular qué Cibeles"* (more popular than Cybele).

exhibitions, tours of the palace, and guest lectures. *(Po. de Recoletos, 2. M: Banco de España. ☎91 595 48 00. Open F 10-12:30, S-Su 10am-1:30pm.)* Looking to your right up C. Alcalá from the Palacio de Comunicaciones is Sabatini's triumphant **Puerta de Alcalá**, the 18th-century emblematic gateway and symbolic of the court.

PASEO DE RECOLETOS

Continuing north toward the brown **Torres de Colón** (Columbus Towers), you'll pass the **Biblioteca Nacional,** where the sleek **Museo del Libro** displays treasures from the monarchy's collection, including a first-edition copy of *Don Quijote. (Entrance at #20. Open Tu-Sa 10am-9pm, Su 10am-2pm. Free.)* Behind the library lies the huge **Museo Arqueológico Nacional** (see p. 114). The museum entrance is on C. Serrano, an avenue lined with expensive boutiques in the posh **Barrio de Salamanca.**

The museum and library huddle just beyond the modern **Plaza Colón** (M: Colón) and the adjoining **Jardines del Descubrimiento** (Gardens of Discovery). At one side huge clay boulders loom, inscribed with odd trivia about the New World, including Seneca's prediction of the discovery, the names of all the mariners on board the caravels, and passages from Columbus' diary. From a thundering fountain in the center of the plaza rises a neo-Gothic spire to Columbus. Concerts, lectures, ballets, and plays are performed in the **Centro Cultural de la Villa,** the underground municipal art center underneath the statue and the waterfall. *(☎91 575 60 80.)*

PASEO DE LA CASTELLANA

Nineteenth- and early twentieth-century aristocrats dislodged themselves from Old Madrid to settle along Paseo de la Castellana. During the Civil War, Republican forces used the mansions as barracks. Most were torn down in the 1960s when banks and insurance companies commissioned new innovative structures. Competition begot architectural excellence, offering the lowly pedestrian a rich man's spectacle of architecture and fashion. Some notables include: Rafael Moneo's **Bankinter,** #29, the first to integrate rather than demolish a townhouse; **Banco Urquijo,** known as "the coffeepot;" the Sevillian-tiled **Edificio ABC,** #34, the former office of the conservative, monarchical newspaper is now a shopping center; the pink **Edificio Bankunion,** #46; **Banca Catalana Occidente,** #50, which looks like an ice cube on a cracker; and the famous **Edificio La Caixa,** #61.

Just south of the American Embassy, between Pl. Colón and Glorieta de Emilio Castelar, is an **Open-air Sculpture Museum** displaying works by Miró, González, and Chillida. Look up—the works are hanging from the bridge as well.

A number of intimate private museums, including the **Museo Lázaro Galdiano** (see p. 113), are located just off Po. Castellana. At **Plaza de Lima** is the 110,000-seat **Estadio Santiago Bernabéu,** home to the beloved **Real Madrid,** winner of its 8th European Championship in 2000 and its 28th Spanish Championship in 2001 (M: Lima). Farther north, the **Puerta de Europa,** consisting of two 27-story leaning towers connected by a tunnel, dominates Pl. Castilla (M: Pl. Castilla). They were designed by American John Bergee as a doorway to the city.

MUSEUMS

Madrid's great museums need no introduction. If you plan on visiting the three famous ones, your best bet is the **Paseo del Arte** ticket (1275ptas/€7.66), which grants admission to the Museo del Prado, Museo Thyssen-Bornemisza, and Centro de Arte Reina Sofía. The pass is on sale at all three museums.

MUSEO DEL PRADO

Po. Prado at Pl. Cánovas del Castillo. M: Banco de España or Atocha. ☎ 91 420 37 68 or tel./fax 91 330 28 00; http://museoprado.mcu.es. Open Tu-Sa 9am-7pm, Su 9am-2pm. 500ptas/€3, students 250ptas/€1.50. Sa after 2:30pm and Su and holidays free.

The Prado is Spain's most eminent museum, as well as one of Europe's finest centers for art from the 12th-17th centuries. In 1785, architect **Juan de Villanueva** began construction of the Neoclassical building, following Carlos III's order for a museum of natural history and sciences. In 1819 Fernando VII transformed it into the royal painting archive; the museum's 7000 pieces are the result of hundreds of years of Bourbon art collecting. The walls are filled with Spanish and foreign masterpieces, including a comprehensive selection from the Flemish and Venetian schools. The museum is well-organized: each room is numbered and described in the museum's free guide. The sheer quantity of paintings means you'll have to be selective—walk past the rooms of imitation Rubens and Rococo cherubs and into the groves of the masters. The museum's guidebooks help you sift through the floors and offer extensive art history and criticism (100-3000ptas/€0.60-18).

DIEGO VELÁZQUEZ. The second floor houses Spanish and Italian works from the 16th and 17th centuries. The most notable of these are an unparalleled collection of works by Diego Velázquez (1599-1660), court painter and interior decorator for Felipe IV (portraits of the foppish monarch abound). Because of their unforgiving realism and use of light, Velázquez's works resonate even in the 20th century. Several of his most famous paintings are here, including *Las hilanderas (The Tapestry Weavers)*, *Los borrachos (The Drunkards)*, and *La fragua de Vulcano (Vulcan's Forge)*. With *Las lanzas (The Spears* or *The Surrender of Breda)*, Velázquez began to experiment with spatial perspective, developing the technique to imply continuous movement in the canvas. Smoke from a recent battle clears in the background as an anxious horse dominates the foreground. Velázquez's technique, called *illusionism*, climaxed in his magnum opus *Las meninas (The Maids of Honor)*, since dubbed an "encounter" rather than a painting. The "snapshot quality" of the figures transformed painting in the 17th century.

FRANCISCO GOYA. In 1785, Francisco de Goya y Lucientes (1746-1828) became the court portraitist. Perhaps the most interesting aspect of his works is that he managed to depict the royal family so unflatteringly and satirically without being expelled from court. Some suggest that he manipulated light and shadow to focus the viewer's gaze on the figure of the queen (rather than the centrally located king) in *La familia de Carlos IV*—a discreet way of supporting popular contemporary opinion about the true power behind the monarchy. The stark *Dos de Mayo* and *Fusilamientos de Tres de Mayo*, which depict the terrors of the Revolution of 1808, may be Goya's most recognized works. Also notable is the expressionless woman in *La maja vestida* and *La maja desnuda*. Perhaps the most evocative pieces in the Goya collection are the *Pinturas Negras (Black Paintings)*. These paintings were aptly named for the darkness of both the colors and the subject matter—Goya painted them in the house where he lived at the end of his life, deaf and alone. *Saturno devorando a su hijo (Saturn Devouring His Son)* stands out among the *Pinturas Negras*, a reminder from an ailing artist that time eventually destroys its creations. Goya violently captures the moment when Saturn eats his children upon hearing a prophesy that one of them would overthrow him.

ITALIAN, FLEMISH, AND OTHER SPANISH ARTISTS. The first floor of the Prado also displays many of **El Greco's** (Doménikos Theotokópoulos, 1541-1614) religious paintings. *La Trinidad (The Trinity)* and *La adoración de los pastores (The Adoration of the Shepherds)* are characterized by El Greco's luminous colors, elongated figures, and mystical subjects. On the second floor are other works by Spanish artists, including **Murillo's** *Familia con pájaro pequeño (Family with Small Bird)*, **Ribera's** *El martirio de San Bartholomeo (Martyrdom of Saint Bartholomew)*, and **Zurbarán's** *La inmaculada*.

The collection of **Italian** works is formidable, including **Titian's** portraits of Carlos I and Felipe II and **Raphael's** *El cardenal desconocido (The Unknown Cardinal)*. **Tintoretto's** rendition of the homicidal seductress Judith and her hapless victim Holofernes, as well as his *Washing of the Feet* are here as well. Some minor **Botticellis** and a slew of his imitators are also on display. Among the works by **Rubens,** *The Adoration of the Magi* bests reflect his voluptuous style.

As a result of the Spanish Habsburgs' control of the Netherlands, the **Flemish** holdings are also top-notch. **Van Dyck's** *Marquesa de Legunes* is here, as well as works by **Albrecht Durer.** Especially harrowing is **Peter Breughel the Elder's** *The Triumph of Death*, in which death drives a carriage of skulls on a decaying horse. **Hieronymus Bosch's** moralistic *The Garden of Earthly Delights* is a favorite, with detailed depictions of hedonism and the destiny that awaits its practitioners.

MUSEO NACIONAL CENTRO DE ARTE REINA SOFÍA

C. Santa Isabel, 52, opposite Estación Atocha at the south end of Po. Prado. M: Atocha. ☎ 91 467 50 62 or 468 30 02. Open M and W-Sa 10am-9pm, Su 10am-2:30pm. 500ptas/€3.01, students 250ptas/€1.50. Sa after 2:30pm, Su and holidays free.

Since Juan Carlos I decreed this renovated hospital a national museum in 1988, the Reina Sofía's collection of **20th-century art** has grown steadily. The second and fourth floors are a maze of permanent exhibits charting the Spanish avant-garde and contemporary movements. Rooms dedicated to Juan Gris, Joan Miró, and Salvador Dalí display Spain's vital contributions to the Surrealist movement. Miró's works show a sparse, colorful abstraction, while Dalí's paintings, including *Monumental Imperial a la mujer niña* and *El enigma sin fin*, portray the artist's Freudian nightmares and sexual fantasies.

Picasso's masterwork **Guérnica** is the centerpiece of the Reina Sofía's permanent collection. Now freed from its restrictive glass cover, it depicts the Basque town bombed by the Germans at Franco's request during the Spanish Civil War. Picasso denounced the bloodshed in a huge, colorless work of contorted, agonized figures. The screaming horse in the center represents war, and the twisted bull—an unmistakable national symbol—symbolizes Spain. When asked by Nazi officials whether he was responsible for this work, Picasso answered, "No, you are." He gave the canvas to New York's Museum of Modern Art on the condition that they return it to Spain when democracy was restored. In 1981, five years after Franco's death, Guérnica was delivered to Madrid's Casón del Buen Retiro. The subsequent move to the Reina Sofía sparked an international controversy—Picasso's other stipulation had been that the painting hang only in the Prado, to affirm his equivalent status with artists like Titian and Velázquez. Today, Basques want the painting relocated to the Guggenheim in Bilbao, but Madrid art officials declare it too delicate to move. The Reina Sofía surrounds Guérnica with its preliminary sketches and a myriad of other Picasso paintings and sculptures, testimony to his breadth of talent. Two other works of note are *Woman in Blue* and *Painter with Model.*

MUSEO THYSSEN-BORNEMISZA

On the corner of Po. Prado and C. San Jerónimo. M: Banco de España. Bus #6, 14, 27, 37, or 45. ☎ 91 369 01 51; www.museothyssen.org. Open Tu-Su 10am-7pm. No one admitted after 6:30pm. 700ptas/€4.2, seniors and students with ISIC 400ptas/€2.4, under 12 free.

Unlike the Prado and the Reina Sofía, the Thyssen-Bornemisza covers a wide range of periods and media, with exhibits ranging from 14th-century canvases to

20th-century sculptures. The museum is housed in the 18th-century **Palacio de Villahermosa** and contains the former collection of Baron Heinrich Thyssen-Bornemisza. The baron donated his collection in 1993, and today the museum, with over 775 pieces, is the world's most extensive private showcase. To view the collection in chronological order and observe the evolution of styles and themes, begin on the top floor and work your way down.

The top floor is dedicated to the **Old Masters** collection, which includes such notables as Hans Holbein's austere *Portrait of Henry VIII* and El Greco's *Annunciation*. The organization of the Thyssen-Bornemisza provokes natural comparisons across centuries—note how the representation of the body evolves from Lucas Cranach's *The Nymph of the Spring* to Titian's *Saint Jerome in the Desert* to Anthony van Dyck's *Portrait of Jacques Le Roy*. In both variety and quality, the Thyssen-Bornemisza's **Baroque** collection, including pieces by Caravaggio, José de Ribera, and Claude Lorraine, overshadows that of the Prado.

The movement from the dark canvases of the top floor to the vibrant ones below reflects the revolutionary command of light and the arbitrary use of color that became popular in the 17th century. During this period, Dutch works, such as Frans Hals's *Family Group in a Landscape*, began to display a mastery of natural light. The **Impressionist** and **Post-Impressionist** collections explode with texture and color—look for works by Renoir, Manet, Degas, Monet, van Gogh, Cézanne, and Matisse. Though less well-known, the **Expressionist** artists are well-represented, with noteworthy works by Nolde, Marc, and Beckmann. The museum is also home to Europe's only collection of North American 19th-century painting.

The highlight of the tour is the museum's **20th-century** collection. The modern artists represented include Picasso, Léger, Mondrian, Miró, Kandinsky, Gorky, Pollack, Rothko, Dalí, Hopper, Chagall, Ernst, Klee, and O'Keefe, among others.

OTHER MUSEUMS

MUSEO DE AMÉRICA. This under-appreciated museum recently reopened after painstaking renovations; it is now a must-see. It documents the cultures of America's pre-Columbian civilizations and the effects of the Spanish conquest with detail, insight, and dedication to making it come alive. Artifacts include solid gold Columbian ornaments and Mayan treasures. *(Av. Reyes Católicos, 6, next to the Faro de Moncloa. ☎91 549 26 41. M: Moncloa. Open Tu-Sa 10am-3pm, Su 10am-2:30pm. 500ptas/€3, students 250ptas/€1.50. Su free.)*

MUSEO DE LA REAL ACADEMIA DE BELLAS ARTES DE SAN FERNANDO. Following the example of Italy and France, Spain's Old Masters convinced Ferdinand VI to finally declare a royal academy in 1752 to train the country's most talented artists. The collection of Old Masters in this beautiful museum represents their legacy; it is surpassed only by the Prado. Goya's *La Tirana* and Velázquez's portrait of Felipe IV are masterpieces; the Raphael and Titian collections are also excellent. Other attractions include a room dedicated to Goya (a former academy director) and 17th-century canvases by Ribera, Murillo, Zurbarán, and Rubens. The top floor also has Picasso sketches. The **Calcografía Real** (Royal Print and Drawing Collection), in the same building, houses Goya's studio and organizes temporary exhibitions. The front desk has comprehensive guides for all collections. *(Alcalá, 13. ☎91 522 14 91. M: Sol or Sevilla. Open Tu-F 9am-7pm, Sa-M 9am-2:30pm. 400ptas/€2.40, students 200ptas/€1.20. W and Oct. 12, May 18, Dec. 6 free.)*

MUSEO LÁZARO GALDIANO. Among the riches of this private collection are an overwhelming display of Italian Renaissance bronzes and Celtic and Visigoth brasses. The paintings include Leonardo da Vinci's *The Savior* and Hieronymous Bosch's *Ecce Homo*, as well as works by the Spanish trifecta: El Greco, Velázquez and Goya. *(C. Serrano, 122. Turn right off Po. Castellana onto C. María de Molina. ☎91 561 60 84. M: Rubén Darío. Open Sept.-July Tu-Su 10am-2pm. 500ptas/€3. W free.)*

MONASTERIO DE LAS DESCALZAS REALES. In 1559 Juana of Austria, Felipe II's sister, converted the former royal palace into a convent; today it is home to 26

Franciscan nuns who watch over Juana's tomb. The **Salón de Tápices** contains 10 renowned tapestries based on cartoons by Rubens, as well as Santa Ursula's jewel-encrusted bones and *El viaje de Santa Úrsula y las once mil vírgenes (The Journey of Santa Úrsula and the Eleven Thousand Virgins)*. Claudio Coello's magnificent 17th century frescoes line the staircase. Lines are long in the summer; arrive early. *(Pl. Descalzas, between Pl. Callao and Pta. de Sol. ☎91 559 74 04/91 542 00 59. M: Callao or Sol. Open Tu-Th and Sa 10:30am-12:45pm and 4-5:45pm, F 10:30am-12:45pm, Su 11am-1:45pm. 800ptas/€4.81, students 400ptas/€2.40. W free for EU citizens.)*

MUSEO ARQUEOLÓGICO NACIONAL. After countless moves, Madrid's display of the history of the Western world settled in this huge museum in 1895. Founded by a decree of Isabel II, the museum houses an astounding collection of items from Spain's past, including the country's most famous archaeological find, *Dama de Elche*, a 4th-century funerary urn, Felipe II's astrolabe, and a 16th-century porcelain clock belonging to Lady Baza. Outside stands a replica of the Altamira caves and their Paleolithic paintings. *(C. Serrano 13, behind the Biblioteca Nacional. ☎91 577 79 12; www.man.es. M: Serrano. Open Tu-Sa 9:30am-8:30pm, Su 9:30am-2:30pm. 500ptas/€3, students 250ptas/€1.50. Sa after 2:30pm and Su free.)*

MADRID

CONVENTO DE LA ENCARNACIÓN. Designed by Juan de Herrera's disciple Juan de Gómez, the convent is an oasis in the middle of Madrid's bustle. Housed here are about 1500 relics of saints, including a vial of San Pantaleón's blood believed to liquify every year on July 27. According to the legend, if the blood does not liquify, disaster will strike Madrid. *(Pl. Encarnación, off C. Bailén just east of Palacio Real. ☎91 542 00 59. M: Ópera. Open Tu-Th and Sa 10:30am-12:45pm and 4-5:45pm, Su 11am-1:45pm. 425ptas/€2.55, students 225ptas/€1.35. W free for EU citizens.)*

MUSEO MUNICIPAL. An Isabelline façade leads to a collection on Madrid's history. Extensive displays include early documents and engravings of the city, including the first complete 16th-century map of Madrid. *(C. Fuencarral. ☎91 588 86 72. M: Tribunal. 300 ptas/€1.80. Open Tu-F 9:30am-8pm, Sa-Su 10am-2pm. W & Sa free.)*

MUSEO DEL EJÉRCITO. In this stately fragment of the Palacio del Buen Retiro stands a vast collection of military paraphernalia. Each room is dedicated to a different period or conquest; the most famous contains the *Tizona* sword of Cid Campeador and a fragment of the cross Columbus wore when he arrived in the New World. *(C. Méndez Núñez, 1, just north of Casón del Buen Retiro. ☎91 522 89 77. M: Retiro or Banco de España. Open Tu-Su 10am-2pm. 100ptas/€0.60, students 50ptas/€0.30, under 18, over 65 free. Sa free.)*

MUSEO CERRALBO. This palatial museum displays an eclectic collection of period furniture and ornamentation. The music room has a Louis XVI-style French piano, and the chapel houses El Greco's *The Ecstasy of Saint Francis*. *(C. Ventura Rodríguez, 17. ☎91 547 36 46. M: Ventura Rodríguez. Open Tu-Sa 9:30am-2:30pm, Su 10am-2pm. 400ptas/€2.40, students 200ptas./€1.20. W and Su free.)*

MUSEO ROMÁNTICO. Housed in a 19th-century mansion, this museum is a time capsule of the Romantic period's decorative arts. *(C. San Mateo, 13. ☎91 448 10 71; www.mcu.es/nmuseos/romantico. M: Alonso Martínez. Open Sept.-July Tu-Sa 9am-3pm, Su 10am-2pm. 400ptas/€2.40, students 200ptas/€1.20. Su free.)*

NIGHTLIFE

Simply put, *madrileños* like to party. Whether on a *terraza* in the summer or in a bar in the winter, the night hours are characterized by a steady stream of pedestrian traffic as revelers meander from place to place: *la marcha*. Proud of their nocturnal offerings—they'll tell you with a straight face that they were bored in Paris or New York—*madrileños* insist that no one goes to bed until they've "killed the night" and, in some cases, a good part of the following morning.

An average night includes several neighborhoods and countless venues; half the party is the in-between. A typical evening might start in the *tapas* bars of Huertas,

THE RIGHT TO PARTY After 40 years of Franco-imposed repression, Madrid was a cultural explosion waiting to happen. Franco's death in 1975 served as a catalyst for change; not a day passed before every newspaper printed a pornographic photo on its front page. *El Destapeo* ("the uncorking" or "uncovering" which followed Franco's regime) and *La Movida* ("the Movement," which took place a few years later) exploded in Madrid, inspiring political diversity, apolitical revelry, and eccentricity of all kinds. Filmmaker Pedro Almodóvar became a reflection of the movement and its most famous member, creating farcical films about loony grandmothers, outgoing young women, unapologetic homosexuals, and troubled students. Gradually, *La Movida* became too much for the city. Artists and club-rats were forced to give up their favorite pastimes for practical jobs—no one could afford to keep up the careless and eccentric lifestyle that *La Movida* represented. Remnants of *La Movida* are still visible, however, in today's outrageous clubs, ambitious bars, and in the excitement of young *madrileños* planning to *ir de marcha* ("to party," literally "to go marching").

moving to a first-session disco in Malasaña, and then to the wild parties of Chueca. Some clubs don't even bother opening until 4 or 5am; the only (relatively) quiet nights of the week are Sunday and Monday. For clubs and discos, life begins around 2am. Many discos have "afternoon" sessions for teens (7pm-midnight; cover 250-1000ptas/€1.50-6), but the "night" sessions (lasting until dawn) are when people really let their hair down. The *entrada* (cover) often includes a drink and can be as high as 2000ptas/€12; men may be charged up to 500ptas/€3 more than women, if women are charged at all. Keep an eye out for *invitaciones* and *oferta* cards—in stores, restaurants, tourist publications, tourist offices, and in the streets—that offer discounts or free admission.

MADRID

For the most up-to-date info on what's going on, scan Madrid's entertainment guides (see **Read This,** p. 84). The *Guía del Ocio* is an indispensable tool, featuring the latest information about virtually all of Madrid's nighttime establishments.

EL CENTRO: SOL, ÓPERA, AND PLAYA MAYOR

In the middle of Madrid and at the heart of the action are the grandiose and spectacular clubs of El Centro. With multiple floors, swinging lights, cages, and disco-balls, they fulfill even the wildest club-rat's expectations. The mainstream clubs found among these streets are often tourist hotspots; as a result, a night of fun here is the most expensive in the city. El Centro includes more territory than Madrid's other neighborhoods, so make a plan for your night and bring a map.

Palacio de Gaviria, C. Arenal, 9 (☎91 526 60 69.) M: Sol or Ópera. Pick a country to represent on International Thursdays when Palacio is at it's best. A grand red carpet leads to two huge ballrooms turned club spaces with dancers and blazing light shows; Cover starts at 2000ptas/€12. Open M-Sa 10:30pm-late, Su 8pm-late.

El Barbu, C. Santiago, 3 (☎91 542 56 98). M: Sol or Ópera. Chill to lounge music in a brick 3-room interior. Open Tu-Sa 8pm-3am. Su transforms the bar to "8th," a rave-like setting with popular local DJs. Cover 1000ptas/€6. Open 7pm-5:30am.

Mad Suite Café Club, Virgen de los Peligros, 4 (☎91 521 40 31), off C. de Alcalá. M: Sevilla. Nouveau *tapas* by day, sleek cocktails by night (900-1000ptas/€5.41-6). Upstairs rolls with house and ambience while the crowd downstairs at the bar makes its own music. Open daily 11am-3:30am.

Kathmandú, C. Señores de Luzón, 3 (☎91 541 52 53), a right off C. Mayor from Puerta del Sol, after Pl. Mayor and facing the Ayuntamiento. M: Sol. Jammed with locals dancing to high-energy techno and swarming with locals who begin the madness at 3am. Cover 800-1000ptas/€4.81-6, includes 1 drink. Open Th 12am-5am, F-Sa 12am-6am.

Heaven, C. Veneras, 2 (☎91 548 20 22). M: Santo Domingo. Facing out from the parking garage, take your second right towards Gran Vía. Heavenly drag performances and underwordly goth parties for a primarily gay crowd. Special "Groove Sundays." Drinks 800-1200ptas/€5-8. Cover 1000ptas/€6, includes 1 drink. Open daily 12am-dawn.

Refugio, C. Dr. Cortezo, 1 (☎91 869 40 38). Off C. Colegiata. Refugio is on C. Dr. Cortezo closest to C. Atocha. M: Tirso de Molina. Steel doors covered in steel vines lead to an outrageous gay scene. Cages and disco-ball dance floor get packed after 3am. Cover 1500ptas/€9, includes 1 drink. Open Th-Sa 12am-dawn.

HUERTAS

The heart of Huertas lies at **Plaza Santa Ana,** brimming with *terrazas*, bars, and live street music. Many bars convert to clubs as the night unfolds, spinning house and techno on intimate dance floors. With its variety of styles, Huertas is simply the best place to party. C. Príncipe is lined with smaller spots, but be sure to check out the larger *discotecas* on **Calle Atocha.** Most locals begin their evenings here and emerge, slightly worn out, from Malasaña and Chueca (see p. 117) in the morning.

DISCOTECAS

Kapital, C. Atocha, 125 (☎91 420 29 06), a block off Po. Prado. M: Atocha. Take the metro—it's the safest way here. The Prado of clubs: you'll probably get bored before you see the entire thing. From hip-hop to house, open *terraza* to cinema, 7 floors of overstimulation have necessitated a ground-floor directory. Dress to impress (the bouncer). Drinks 1500ptas/€9. Cover 2000ptas/€12, includes 1 drink. Open Th 12:30-6am, F-Sa 6-10:30pm and midnight-6am, but it's a ghost town until 2am.

No Se Lo Digas a Nadie, C. Ventura de la Vega, 7 (☎91 369 17 27), next to Pl. Santa Ana. M: Sevilla. Head through the garage doors onto the packed dance floor. Drinks 500-800ptas/€3-5. Open W-Sa until 3:30am.

Azúcar, Po. Reina Cristina, 7 (☎91 501 61 07). M: Atocha. Sweet, sweet salsa. No sneakers. Salsa classes daily 10:00-11pm. Su-Th cover 1000ptas/€6, includes 1 drink; F-Sa 1500ptas/€9, includes 1 drink. Open M-Sa 11pm-5am, Su 9pm-dawn.

Villa Rosa, Pl. Santa, 15 (☎92 429 36 89). American pop meets Moorish architecture in this Alhambra-inspired disco, which sports 4 bars and a raised dance floor. Frescoed and tiled walls compete with flat-screen TVs to stimulate your euphoria. Cover F, Sa 1000ptas/€6. Drinks 1000ptas/€6. Open M-Sa 10:30pm-6am.

BAR-MUSICALES

Cardamomo, C. Echegaray, 15 (☎91 369 07 57). M: Sevilla. Flamenco music spins all night. A local crowd dances flamenco occasionally, but come W nights to see professionals do it. Mondays bump with Brazilian and other exotic beats. Open 9pm-4am.

La Comedia, C. Príncipe, 16 (☎91 521 51 64). M: Sevilla. Americans feel at home in a crowd dancing to hip-hop, R&B, and reggae. Hit up DJ Jay with requests; he spins to please. Beer 600ptas/€3.60, drinks 1000ptas/€6. Open daily 9pm-4am.

Café Jazz Populart, C. Huertas, 22 (☎91 429 84 07). This intimate, smoke-filled scene hosts local and foreign talent. Live jazz, blues, reggae, and flamenco. Shows Su-W 11pm, F-Sa 11pm and 12:30am. Open Su-Th 6pm-12:30am, F-Sa 6pm-3am.

Café Central, Pl. Angel, 10 (☎91 369 41 43), off Pl. Santa Ana. M: Antón Martín or Sol. Art Deco meets old-world café in one of Europe's top jazz venues. Mesmerized listeners recline in each others' arms. An older audience. Shows nightly. Beer 300-500ptas/€1.80-3. Cover 1200-2500ptas/€7.21-15. Open daily 1:30pm-3:30am.

La Boca del Lobo, C. Echegaray, 11 (☎91 429 70 13). M: Sevilla. The wolf on the sign won't eat you, but waterfall mirrors in the bathrooms may drench you. Live shows of reggae, funk, blues and rock bands hit this two story joint, drawing a varied crowd. Cover 1000ptas/€6. Open daily 10pm-dawn.

BARS

El Café de Sheherezade, C. Santa María, 18 (☎91 369 24 74), a block from C. Huertas. M: Antón Martín. Recline on opulent pillows while sipping exotic infusions in a bohemian atmosphere. Surrounded by Middle Eastern music and decor, groups cluster around *pipas* (1100-1600ptas/€7-10) that filter sweet, incense-like smoke through whiskey or water. Late nights sometimes end with belly dancing. Open daily 7pm-5am.

Trocha, C. Huertas, 55 (☎91 429 78 61). M: Antón Martín or Sol. Come here for Brazilian *capirinhas* (lime, ice, rum, and sugar drinks; 725ptas/€4.36 at the bar, 750ptas/€4.51 seated). The delicious and potent drinks (ask for *flor de caña)* are served in a chill setting with jazz tunes, and cushioned wicker couches. Open Su-Th 8pm-3am, F-Sa 8pm-4am.

Viva Madrid, C. Manuel Fernández González, 7 (☎91 429 36 40), a sidestreet off C. Echegaray. M: Sol or Sevilla. *"Lo mejor del mundo"* (the best of the world) is the humble motto of this daytime café/nighttime foray, a longtime local favorite for a romantic evening. Cocktails 1100ptas/€7. Open Su-Th 12:30pm-2am, F-Sa 12:30pm-3am.

Mauna Loa, Pl. Santa Ana, 13 (☎91 429 70 62). M: Sevilla or Sol. Feels like Hawaii—birds fly freely between low chairs and the scantily clad dance to upbeat tunes. Sip on a *fuerte volcano* (1000-1700ptas/€6-10.22) through an enormous straw at this crowded pre-party destination. Open Su-Th 6pm-2am, F-Sa 6pm-3am.

Naturbier, Pl. Santa Ana, 9 (☎91 429 39 18). M: Sol or Sevilla. Join the locals who pour in for the excellent locally brewed *bier,* inspired by their motto "beer is important to human nutrition." Superior lager 300-700ptas/€1.80-4.21; it gets cheaper as you progress to the innermost of the 3 bars. Open daily 11am-2am.

GRAN VÍA

The deepest drum and bass pounds in the boisterous landmark clubs on the side streets of Gran Vía well into the early morning. Subtlety has never been a strong point for this area, nor is it exactly known for its safety; a mix of sketchy tourists and sketchier locals makes the Gran Vía less than ideal for late-night wandering.

Sugar Hill, C. Fundadores 7, M: Manuel Becerra or O'Donell. Named after the original, this is the only real hip-hop club in town. Those in the know arrive around 3:30am to a packed dance floor. Drinks 1000ptas/€6. Cover 1500ptas/€9, includes 1 drink. Open Sa only 12:45-5:30am. For more of the hip hop and funk scene, try **Bash,** Pl. Callao, 4 (☎91 531 01 32). Cover 1000ptas/€6. Open W only midnight-5:30am.

Cool Ballroom, C. Isabel la Católica, 6 (☎91 542 34 39). M: Santo Domingo. Survive the painfully cool entrance to watch the club dancers waggle their hips and purse their lips. Mesmerizing video projections give this club the production-value of international ve- nues, which fits with the mix of locals, Brits and Americans yelling to be heard over the latest house. Drinks 1300ptas/€8. Open daily 12am-late.

MALASAÑA AND CHUECA

The dark cafés and darker clubs of Malasaña and Chueca filter jazz and techno into the night and early morning. Known for their bohemian crowds, Malasaña's hotspots radiate from **Plaza 2 de Mayo** and **Calle San Vincente Ferrer.** People are high on life, drugs, and booze; be wary at night. **Calle de Pelayo** is the main drag in flamboyant and gay Chueca. The safest walking route at night is up C. Fuencarral from Gran Vía and right on C. Augusto Figueroa.

Acuarela, C. Gravina, 10 (☎91 522 21 43), on the corner of plaza behind next to Trocha. M: Chueca. A welcome alternative to the club scene. Buddhas and candles surround antique furniture. Spend hours just chilling. Coffees and teas (500-700ptas/€3-4.21). Liqueur 700ptas/€4.21. Open M–Su 3pm-3am.

Café la Palma, C. La Palma, 62 (☎91 522 50 31). M: San Bernardo or Noviciado. Slip back into the comfy pillows of this decadent setting for live music and late night whispering. Pick up a monthly program of shows (sometimes 800ptas/€5 cover) or call ahead. Beer 350ptas/€2.10. Mixed drinks 700ptas/€4.21. Open daily 4pm-3:30am.

Black & White, C. Libertad, 34 (☎91 531 11 41). From the plaza walk towards Gran Vía on C. Gravina. M: Chueca. A lively disco/bar with room to chat, mingle, and groove on packed dance floors. 2 floors of male fun for the gay crowd. Hot-body contest and international exchange night on W. Beer 500ptas/€3. Mixed drinks 1000ptas/€6. Open Su-Th 9pm-5am, F-Sa 9pm-6am.

Vía Láctea, C. Velarde, 18 (☎91 466 75 81). M: Tribunal. Dive into the Brit Underground scene every night from 8-9pm when soft drinks and beer on tap are 300ptas/€1.80 each. After midnight, a late 20s crowd gets groovy between the pink walls. Funk spins Th. The loudspeakers might leave you deaf. Open daily 8pm-3am.

Café Figueroa, C. Augusto Figueroa, 17 (☎91 521 16 73), on the corner of C. Hortaleza. M: Chueca. Smoke-filled, pink-walled café lit by dim chandeliers. Mostly gay clientele. Coffee 300ptas/€1.80. Open Su-Th 2:30pm-1am, F-Sa 2:30pm-2:30am.

Star's Café, C. Marqués de Valdeiglesias, 5 (☎91 522 27 12). M: Chueca. A stylish café during the week, a vivacious dance club on the weekends. Come well-dressed and don't forget to turn your cell phone ringer to high. Open Su-Th 10am-2pm, F-Sa 10am-4am.

El Truco, C. Gravina, 10 (☎91 532 89 21). M: Chueca. Classy bar featuring local artists' works and pop artist hits. Lesbian-friendly. Open Su-Th 8pm-2am, F-Sa 9pm-4am. Same owners run **Escape,** a club down the street. Both are strong enough for a man, but designed particularly for a woman. Open F-Sa midnight-7am.

Bolero Terraza, Po. Castellana, 33 (☎91 554 91 51). M: Rubén Darío. Flashy smiles and pressed collars yanked way up. *The* ultra-fashionable, yuppie *terraza*. Outside seating centered around a bar. Drinks 1000ptas/€6. Open daily 7:30pm-3am.

BILBAO

In the student-filled streets radiating from **Glorieta de Bilbao,** it's easy to find a cheap drink. Although discos are plentiful, revelers don't come here to dance: it's the *terrazas* that are packed late into the night with boisterous customers sipping icy Mahou on Pl. Olavide, C. Fuencarral, and C. Luchana.

Barnon, C. Santa Engracia, 17 (☎91 447 38 37). M: Alonso Martínez or Tribunal. Barnon actually bars many from its hip-hop scene if you're not as cool as the owner, Real Madrid's stud *fútbol* forward. Dress well and bring a blonde. Tu is salsa night, free lessons 11-12pm. Drinks 1600ptas/€9.61. Open Su-Th 11pm-4am, F-Sa 12am-5am.

Clamores Jazz Club, C. Albuquerque, 14 (☎91 445 79 38), off C. Cardenal Cisneros. M: Bilbao. Swanky, pink neon setting and some of Madrid's more interesting jazz. The cover (500-1500ptas/€3-9) gets slipped into the bill if you're there for the live jazz, starting around 10:30 every night but M. Check the posters outside and arrive early for a seat. Open Su-Th 7pm-3am, F-Sa 7pm-4am.

Big Bamboo, C. Barquillo, 42 (☎91 657 01 10). M: Alonso Martínez. Walk 3 blocks east of C. Pelayo on C. Gravina and turn left on C. Barquillo. Infiltrate the Rasta scene at this international club that jams to smooth reggae. Wed and Th theater shows. Drinks 400-500ptas/€2.40-3. Open 10:30pm-6am, F-Sa 10:30pm-7am.

MONCLOA

No more pencils, no more books, no more teachers' dirty looks: Moncloa is Madrid's student party zone. High-schoolers dominate the streets, sporting their favorite tight jeans, halter tops, denim jackets, and little black bags. The area is packed during grad week and mid-year school vacations but clears out weekdays in June (when exams hit) and everyday in August (during family vacations).

Unless you're Lolita, or looking for one, there are only two reasons to leave Madrid's better nighttime neighborhoods for Moncloa: **Los Bajos** and its incredibly **cheap drinks.** A virtual concrete megaplex of diminutive bars, with three tiers and two enormous courtyards, Los Bajos is more of a phenomenon than a nightspot. Even more than in the rest of Madrid, the real party here is among the swirling crowds outside. Visits to bars are barely long enough to down your drink, which in most cases is a *chupito* (shot) anyway—at 150ptas/€0.90, they're hard to turn down. Bars in Los Bajos are usually only open Friday and Saturday nights and generally close by 1 or 2am. They tend to be slightly grimy, if homey, and dance floors are small. To get to Los Bajos from M: Moncloa, cross C. Isaac Peral in front of the Plaza de Moncloa, passing under the gate onto C. Gatzambide, 35.

ENTERTAINMENT

Anyone interested in the latest on live entertainment—from music to dance to theater—should stop by the **Círculo de Bellas Artes,** C. Alcala, 42 (☎91 360 54 00; fax 91 523 28 12), at M: Sevilla or Banco de España. The six-floored building not only houses performance venues and art exhibits, but also serves as an organizing center for events throughout Madrid; it has virtually all current information on performances. Their monthly magazine, *Minerva*, is indispensable.

MUSIC

In summer, Madrid sponsors free concerts, ranging from classical and jazz to bolero and salsa, at Pl. Mayor, Lavapiés, Oriente, and Villa de París; check the *Guía del Ocio* for the current schedule. Many nightspots also have live music.

The **Auditorio Nacional,** C. Príncipe de Vergara, 146, home to the National Orchestra, features Madrid's best classical performances. (☎91 337 01 00. M: Cruz del Rayo. 800-4200ptas/€4.81-25.24.) The **Fundación Juan March,** C. Castelló, 77, hosts a university lecture series (Tu-W 7:30pm) and sponsors free weekend concerts. (☎91 435 42 40. M: Núñez de Balboa.) **Teatro Monumental,** C. Atocha, 65, is home to Madrid's Symphonic Orchestra. Reinforced concrete—a Spanish invention—was first used in its construction in the 1920s, so be prepared for unusual acoustics. (☎91 429 81 19. M: Antón Martín.) For opera and *zarzuela* (Spanish light opera), head for the ornate **Teatro de la Zarzuela,** C. Jovellanos, 4, modeled on Milan's La Scala. (☎91 524 54 00. M: Banco de España.) The city's principal performance venue is the prestigious **Teatro Real**, Pl. de Isabel II, features the city's best ballet and opera at a price to match. (☎91 516 06 06. M: Ópera.) The grand 19th-century granite **Teatro de la Ópera** (☎91 559 35 51), in Pl. Ópera, is the city's principal venue for classical ballet. Most theaters shut down in July and August.

MADRID

FLAMENCO

Flamenco in Madrid is tourist-oriented and expensive. A few nightlife spots are authentic (see **Cardamomo,** p. 116), but they too are pricey. **Casa Patas,** C. Cañizares, 10, offers excellent quality for a bit less than usual. Summer courses are taught in flamenco dance and song. (☎91 369 04 96; www.casapatas.com. M: Antón Martín. Call for prices and reservations.) **Café de Chinitas,** C. Torija, 7, is as overstated as they come. Shows start at 10:30pm and midnight, but the memories last forever—or at least they should, given the price. (☎91 547 15 02 or 91 559 51 35. M: Santo Domingo. Cover 4000ptas/€24 and up.) At **Corral de la Morería,** C. Morería, 17, by the Viaducto on C. Bailén, shows start at 9:45pm and last until 2am. (☎91 365 84 46. M: Ópera or La Latina. Cover 4000ptas/€24, includes one drink.) **Teatro Albéniz,** C. Paz, 11, hosts an annual *Certamen de Coreografía de Danza Española y Flamenco* that features original dance and music, including extraordinary flamenco. (☎91 521 99 98. M: Sol. Tickets 700-2000ptas/€4.21-12.)

FILM

In summer, the city sponsors free movies and plays, all listed in the *Guía del Ocio* and the entertainment supplements of Friday's newspapers. In July, look out for the **Fescinal,** a film festival at the Parque de la Florida. Most cinemas show three films per day, at around 4:30, 7:30, and 10:30pm. Tickets cost 700-900ptas/€2.40-5.40. Some cinemas offer weekday-only matinée student discounts for 600ptas/€3.61. Wednesday (sometimes Monday instead) is *día del espectador*, when tickets cost around 500ptas/€3—show up early. Check the *versión original (V.O. subtitulada)* listings in the *Guía del Ocio* for English movies subtitled in Spanish. Three excellent movie theaters cluster near M: Ventura Rodríguez, between Pl. España and Argüelles. **Princesa,** C. Princesa, 3 (☎91 541 41 00), shows mainstream Spanish films and subtitled foreign films. The theater/bar **Alphaville,** C. Martín de los Héroes, 14 (☎91 559 38 36), behind Princesa and underneath the patio, shows current alternative and mainstream Spanish titles.

Renoir, C. Raimundo Fernández Villaverde, 10 (☎91 541 41 00), shows highly acclaimed recent films, many foreign and subtitled. The state-subsidized *filmoteca española* in the Art Deco **Ciné Doré,** C. Santa Isabel, 3, is Madrid's finest repertory cinema. (☎91 549 00 11. M: Antón Martín. Tickets 200-400ptas/€1.20-2.40.)

THEATER

Huertas, east of Sol, is Madrid's theater district. In July and August, Pl. Mayor, Lavapiés, and Villa de París frequently host plays as theaters move outdoors. For a complete listing of theaters and shows, consult the *Guía del Ocio*. Seeing a play in Madrid is an entertaining way to participate in traditional culture and to practice your Spanish. Tickets to the shows worth going to start around 4000ptas/€24, but special deals for as low as 2000ptas/€12 are not uncommon. Theater-goers should consult the well-illustrated magazines published by state-sponsored theaters, such as **Teatro Español,** C. Príncipe, 25, in Pl. Santa Ana (☎91 429 62 97. M: Sol), **Teatro de la Comedia,** C. Príncipe, 14 (☎91 521 49 31. M: Sevilla), and the superb **Teatro María Guerrero,** C. Tamayo y Baus, 4 (☎91 319 47 69; M: Colón). Tickets can be purchased at theater box offices or at ticket agencies. (**FNAC** ☎91 595 62 00. **Librería Crisol** ☎91 322 47 00. **TelEntrada** ☎902 210 12 12.)

FÚTBOL

Spaniards obsess over *fútbol* (soccer to Americans). Each match is a blow out: the festivities start hours before the match as fans congregate in the streets, earphones and radio in hand and *cerveza* in the other, listening to the pregame commentary and discussing it with other die-hards. If either **Real Madrid** or **Atlético de Madrid** wins a match, count on streets clogged with honking cars. Every Sunday and some Saturdays between September and June, one of these two teams plays at home. Real Madrid plays at **Estadio Santiago Bernebéu,** Po. Castellana, 104. (☎91 457 11 12. M: Lima.) Atlético de Madrid plays at **Estadio Vicente Calderón,** C. Virgen del Puerto, 67. (☎91 366 47 07. M: Pirámides or Marqués de Vadillos.) Tickets cost 3000-7000ptas/18-42. Tickets sell out quickly so it's wise to plan in advance.

RECREATIONAL SPORTS

For **bicycle rental,** try **Karacol Sport,** C. Tortosa, 8, M: Atocha. (☎ 91 539 96 33. Open M-Su 10:30am-8pm, Th until 10pm, Sa until 2pm. Rental 2000ptas/€12 per day with 500ptas/€3 deposit and passport.) For **cycling info** and bicycle repair, spin over to **Usera Bike,** C. Usera, 26. (☎91 475 02 19. Open M-F 9am-2pm and 5-8pm, Sa 9am-2pm. M: Usera.) **Swimmers** splash in the outdoor pools at: **Casa de Campo,** on Av. Angel next to M: Lago (☎91 463 00 50); the indoor **Municipal de La Latina,** Pl. Cebada, 2, M: La Latina; and **Peñuelas,** on C. Arganda (☎91 474 28 08), M: Delicias or bus #18. (☎91 540 39 39 for pool information. All pools 520ptas/€3.13, ages 4-13 250ptas/€1.50. Open daily 10:30am-8pm.) Gallop over to the **Hipódromo de Madrid,** Ctra. de La Coruña, km 7800 (☎91 357 16 82), for **horse-racing.** Call the **Oficina de Información Deportiva** (☎91 463 55 63) for more information on outdoor recreation in Madrid. The tourist office's *Plano de las Instalaciones Deportivos Muncipales* lists areas open to the public.

BULLFIGHTS

Bullfighters are either loved or loathed. So too are the bullfights themselves. Nevertheless, bullfights are a Spanish tradition, and locals joke that they are the only things in Spain ever to start on time. Hemingway-toting Americans and true fans clog Pl. de Ventas for the events.

From May 15 to 22 every year, the **Fiestas de San Isidro** provide a *corrida* (bullfight) every day with top *matadores* and the fiercest bulls. The festival is nationally televised; those without tickets can crowd into bars. There are also bullfights every Sunday in summer from March to October; they occur less frequently during the rest of the year and the quality is not as good. Look for posters in bars and cafés (especially on C. Victoria, off C. San Jerónimo). **Plaza de las Ventas,** C. Alcalá, 237, east of central Madrid, is the biggest ring in Spain. (☎91 356 22 00. M: Ventas.) A seat runs 450-15,200ptas/€2.70-92, depending on whether it's in the sun (*sol*) or shade (*sombra*); shade is more expensive. Tickets are usually available the Friday and Saturday before and the Sunday of the bullfight. **Plaza de Toros Palacio de Vista Alegre,** a new ring in town, hosts bullfights and other cultural events. (☎91 422 07 80. M: Vista Alegre. Ticket window open M-F 10am-2pm and 5-8pm.) For younger *toreros*, **Saturday** fun, and the old college try, all at a **lesser price,** head to the **bullfighting school,** which has its own *corridas*. (☎91 470 19 90. M: Batán. Open Sa 7pm. Tickets 1000ptas/€6, children 500ptas/€3.) If you're intrigued by the lore but not the gore, head to the **Museo Taurino,** C. Alcalá, 237, at Pl. Monumental de Las Ventas. The museum displays a remarkable collection of capes and bullfighters' outfits. (☎91 725 18 57. Open M-F 9:30am-2:30pm, on fight days 10am-1pm. Free.)

FESTIVALS

The brochure *Las Fiestas de España*, available at tourist offices and the bigger hotels, contains historical background and general information on Spain's festivals. Madrid's **Carnaval** (February 5-12 in 2002) was inaugurated in the Middle Ages and prohibited during Franco's dictatorship. Now, however, the city bursts with street fiestas, dancing, and processions. In late April, the city bubbles with the renowned **International Theater Festival.** Starting May 15, the **Fiestas de San Isidro,** in honor of Madrid's patron saint, bring concerts, parades, and Spain's best bullfights. Throughout the summer, the city sponsors the **Veranos de la Villa,** an outstanding and varied set of cultural activities, including free classical music concerts, movies in open-air settings, plays, art exhibits, an international film festival, opera, *zarzuela* (light Spanish opera), ballet, and sports. The **Festivales de Otoño** (Autumn Festivals), from September to November, also bring an impressive array of music, theater, and film. On November 1, **Todos los Santos** (All Saints' Day), an International Jazz Festival, brings great musicians to Madrid. The **Día de la Constitución** (Day of the Constitution, or National Day) on December 6 heralds the arrival of the National Company of Spanish Classical Ballet in Madrid. Tourist offices have all the information.

SHOPPING

The swanky avenue in Madrid is **C. Serrano,** where fine boutiques and specialty stores line the street. Most stores in Madrid open from 10am to 2pm and 5 to 8pm. Some have begun to stay open on Saturday afternoon and during lunch. By law, *grandes almacenes* (department stores) may open only the first Sunday of every month, a vestige of the country's Roman Catholic heritage. Many small boutiques close in August, when practically everyone flees to the coast. Non-residents of the EU can shop tax-free at major stores, as long as you remember to ask for your VAT return form (☎60 043 54 82 for more information). **Inal** publishes a yearly *Guía Esencial para vivir en Madrid*, which includes descriptions of most stores. For funky gear, check out **Chueca's** boutiques; you can even find Madrid's crazy bright street-cleaning uniforms at **Azules de Vergara, S.L.,** C. Fuencarral, 150. (☎91 448 78 60. M: Quevedo. Open M-F 9:30am-1:30pm and 4:30-8pm, Sa 9:30am-1:30pm.)

MALLS

La Vaguada (M: Barrio del Pilar; bus #132 from Moncloa), in the northern neighborhood **Madrid-2,** is Madrid's first experiment in super-malls. It offers everything the homesick anglophone could want: 350 shops, including the Body Shop, Burberry's, a food court with Kentucky Fried Chicken and trusty McDonald's, multi-cinemas and a bowling alley (open daily 10am-10pm). **ABC,** C. Serrano, 61, in the old ABC Newspaper headquarters, has a modern complex of food courts and Spanish clothing chains from Zara to Mango. (M: Castellano, right next to metro stop. Open M-Sa 10am-9:30pm, Su until noon-8pm.) Madrid's outlet mall is **Las Rozas,** Juan Ramón Jiménez, a 20 min. drive from the center, with up to 60% off favorite brands. (☎91 640 49 08; www.valueretail.com.) By far the poshest shopping mall is the **Galería del Prado,** Pl.

Cortes, located beneath the Hotel Palace and across the Castellana from the Ritz. (M: Banco de España. Open M-Sa 10am-9pm.) And of course, there's always the unavoidable **El Corte Inglés** (see p. 88).

EL RASTRO (FLEA MARKET)

For hundreds of years, El Rastro has been a Sunday morning tradition in Madrid. From Pl. Mayor and its Sunday stamp and coin market, walk down C. Toledo to Pl. Cascorro (M: La Latina), where the market begins, and follow the crowds to the end, at the bottom of C. Ribera de Curtidores. In El Rastro you can find anything, from pots to jeans to antique tools to pet birds. Although the main street is a labyrinth of cheap jewelry, incense, and sunglasses, each side street has its own concert of vendors and wares. Antique-sellers contribute their peculiar mustiness to C. del Prado. *Tapas* bars and small restaurants line the streets and provide an air-conditioned respite. The flea market is a pickpocket paradise, so leave your camera in your room and turn that backpack into a frontpack. Police are everywhere if you have any problems. El Rastro is open Sundays and holidays from 9am to 2pm.

BOOKS

FNAC, C. Preciados, 28 (☎91 595 62 00). M: Callao. The best music and book selection in town. Books in English on 3rd fl. Open M-Sa 10am-9:30pm, Su noon-9:30pm.

Booksellers, C. José Abascal, 48 (☎91 442 79 59 or 91 442 81 04). M: Gregorio Marañón. A vast array of new books, videos and children's literature in English, plus American and English magazines. Open M-F 9:30am-2pm and 5-8pm, Sa 10am-2pm.

Librería de Mujeres, C. San Cristóbal, 17 (☎91 521 70 43), near Pl. Mayor. International bookstore. English spoken. (See **Women's Services,** p. 88.)

Berkana Librería Gai y Lesbiana, C. Gravina, 11 (☎/fax 91 532 13 93). M: Chueca. Gay and lesbian bookstore with loads of contact info for foreigners and a free map of gay Madrid. Open M-F 10:30am-2pm and 5-8:30pm, Sa noon-2pm and 5-8:30pm.

Altair, C. Gaztambide, 31 (☎91 543 53 00). M: Moncloa or Argüelles. Comprehensive travel bookstore, with the world's best travel guides and others. Knowledgeable staff. Open M-Sa 10:30am-2:30pm and 4:30-8:30pm. AmEx/MC/V.

COMUNIDAD DE MADRID

The Comunidad de Madrid is an autonomous administrative region shaped like an arrowhead and pointing right at the heart of Castilla y León. Historically, this area along with Madrid and Castilla La Mancha, was known as Castilla La Nueva (New Castile). Its small towns make interesting and refreshing daytrips from the city.

ALCALÁ DE HENARES

Residents of Alcalá (pop. 165,000) pride themselves on their town's distinguished offspring, including Miguel de Cervantes, and Golden Age authors Francisco de Quevedo and Lope de Vega, and the city's exceptional Renaissance architecture. With its famous history and proximity to Madrid, Alcalá is worth a peek.

TRANSPORTATION AND PRACTICAL INFORMATION. The **train station** is located on Po. Estación (☎91 563 02 02). **Cercanías** trains run to (50min.; every 10min. M-F 5:11am-11:26pm, Sa-Su 5:56am-11:26pm; 350ptas/€2.10) and from (M-F 5:22am-11:50pm, Sa-Su 5:44am-11:50pm) Madrid's **Estación Atocha.** The **Continental-Auto bus station,** Av. Guadalajara, 5 (☎91 888 16 22), runs between Alcalá and Madrid (45min., every 15min., 350ptas/€2.10). To reach the city center from the bus station, turn right on Av. Guadalajara and continue as it turns into C. Libreros. The **tourist office,** Callejón de Santa María, 1, at Pl. Cervantes, has a map, and a list of accommodations and restaurants. (☎91 889 26 94. Open daily June and Sept. 10am-2pm and 5-7:30pm; July-Aug. Tu-Sa 10am-2pm and 5-7:30pm; Oct.-May 10am-2pm and 4-6:30pm.) **Banco Central Hispano,** Pl. Cervantes, 4, has an **ATM**

Important phone numbers include **emergency** ☎112; **ambulance** ☎061; and **police** ☎91 881 92 63. **Alcal@.3**, on C. San Diego, 3, offers 15 speedy computers and friendly service. (☎91 883 40 24. 100ptas/€0.60 for 15min., 400ptas/€2.40 per hour. Open July-Aug M-Sa 10am-10pm; Sept.-June daily 10am-10pm.) The **post office,** Pl. Cervantes, 5, is inside Banco Argentina. (☎91 219 71 97. Open M-F 8:30am-7pm, Sa 9:30am-1pm.) The **postal code** ranges from 28801 to 28807.

ACCOMMODATIONS AND FOOD. Some of the least expensive rooms lie within **Hostal Jacinto,** Po. Estación, 2, 2nd staircase, 1-D. Pleasant tiled rooms all with sinks, floral bedspreads, TVs, and heat during the winter. (☎/fax 91 889 14 32. Singles 2800ptas/€17, with shower 3000ptas/€18; doubles with or without shower 5500ptas/€33, with bath 6000ptas/€36; triples 6500ptas/€39.) For food, Alcalá's famed *almendras garrapiñadas* (honey- and sugar-coated almonds) beg to be tried. Picnickers can stock up at the gigantic **Supermercado Champion** on Vía Complutense, located just behind the bus station or if you are coming from the train station take a left at the traffic circle (☎91 889 36 37. Open M-Sa 9:15am-9:15pm, Jun15-Sept15 open M-Sa 9am-10pm. MC/V.) For fantastically cheap *menús*, turn left on C. Mayor from Pl. Cervantes, and check out the restaurants on the right side of the street like **El Gringo Viejo**, on C. Ramón y Cajal, 8. Take C. Mayor from Pl. Cervantes, then your first left onto C. Ramón y Cajal and the entryway is on your right, (☎91 878 89 01. Mexican entrées 750-2800ptas/€5.71-17. Open M-Th 8:30am-12am, F 8:30am-1am, Sa 10:30am-1am, Su 11am-12am. MC/V.)

SIGHTS. Plaza de Cervantes, blessed with a statue of its namesake and filled with cafés and rose bushes, bursts with color in summer. At the end of the plaza opposite C. Libreros lie the **Ruinas de Santa María,** the remains of a 16th-century church destroyed during the Civil War. In the surviving Capilla del Oidor, art exhibits surround the fountain where Cervantes was christened. (Open Oct.-May Tu-Su noon-2pm and 6-9pm; June-Sept. Tu-Su noon-2pm and 5-8pm. Free.) Just before Pl. Cervantes in Pl. San Diego, take a left off C. Libreros onto C. Bedel, the college is straight ahead, sits the **Colegio Mayor de San Ildefonso** (☎ 91 889 04 00), center of the once illustrious humanist university and founded by Cardinal Cisneros in 1499, opened for classes in 1508. In the **Paraninfo,** where doctorates were once awarded, the king now presents the "Premio Cervantes," Spain's most prestigious literary award. The Paraninfo and **Capilla de San Ildefonso** both have spectacular Mudéjar ceilings, crafted wood pieces held together by pressure. (By tour only. June-Sept. M-F 11:30am, 12:30, 1:30, 5:30, and 6:30pm; Sa-Su 11, 11:45am, 12:30, 1:15, 2, 5, 5:45, 6:30, 7:15 and 8pm; Oct.-May M-F 11:30am, 12:30, 1:30, 4:30 and 5:30pm, Sa-Su 11, 11:45am, 12:30, 1:15, 2, 4, 4:45, 5:30, 6:15, 7pm. 350ptas/€2.10.) The town's **Catedral Magistral,** at the end of C. Mayor in Pl. de los Santos Niños, is one of two in the world with this title (the other is located Lovaina, Belgium); to be so named each priest must be a university professor. (Open M-Sa 9am-noon and 6:30-8:30pm, Su 9am-12:45pm and 6:30-9pm. Free.) Down C. Mayor from Pl. Cervantes is the **Casa de Cervantes,** the reconstructed house where the author was born. Currently under expansion, the house displays a variety of period furniture and editions of *Don Quijote* in languages Cervantes never knew. (☎91 889 96 54. Open Tu-Su 10:15am-1:30pm and 4-6:15pm. Free.) The **Convento de San Bernardo,** hides a gorgeous 17th-century elliptical interior behind a simple façade. (Required tour meets in the courtyard and leaves June-Sept. M-F 1:45 and 6:30pm; Sa-Su 12:30, 1:30, 5, 5:45, 6:30, 7:15, and 8pm; Oct.-May M-F 1:45 and 5:30pm, Sa-Su 12:30, 1:30, 4, 4:45, 5:30, 6:15 and 7pm. 350ptas/€2.10.)

SAN LORENZO DEL ESCORIAL ☎918

They called it the eighth wonder of the world and they were right. San Lorenzo's El Escorial—half monastery and half mausoleum—is the most popular daytrip from Madrid. Although Felipe II constructed El Escorial for himself and for God, today, the complex, with its magnificent library, palaces, and art treasures, seems as though it were made for tourists. Do not go on Monday, when the whole town is closed. Also, don't miss the Valle de los Caídos. Visits are especially popular during the Festivals of San Lorenzo (Aug. 10-20), when parades of giant figures line the streets and fireworks fill the sky, and on Romería a la Ermita de la Virgen de Gracia, the second Sunday in Sept., when folk dancing contests fill the forests.

TRANSPORTATION AND PRACTICAL INFORMATION. **Autocares Herranz buses** whisk passengers from Madrid's **Moncloa Metro station** (50min.; every 15min. M-F 7am-11:30pm, Sa 9am-10:15pm, Su 9am-11pm; 445ptas/€2.75) to El Escorial's Plaza Virgen de Gracia at the center of town. The **Autocares Herranz** office, C. Rey, 27 (☎918 96 90 28), sells return tickets (every 15min. M-F 6:15am-10:30pm, Sa 7:45am-9pm, Su 9am-10pm). El Escorial's **train station** (☎918 90 07 14; RENFE info 913 28 90 20), on Ctra. Estación, is 2km outside of town. Trains run to **Madrid-Atocha** and **Madrid-Chamartín** (1hr.; M-F every 30min., Sa-Su 1 per hr. 5:47am-10:15pm; round-trip 1000ptas/€6).

From the **bus station** pedestrian ramp, start left down the street above, turn right at the corner onto C. Juan de Leyva, and continue to its end. Left and down the steps across the street is the **tourist office** (underneath the walkway connecting the two buildings) and the monastery. (☎/Fax 918 90 53 13. Open M-Th 11am-6pm, F-Su 10am-7pm.) From the **train station,** take the shuttle to the bus station (M-F every 15-20min. 7:23am-10:38pm, Sa-Su every 20-60min. 9:44am-10:38pm; 145ptas/€0.90). In an **emergency** call 112 or the **police,** Pl. de la Constitución, 1 (☎ 918 90 52 23), inside the Ayuntamiento.

MADRID

ACCOMMODATIONS AND FOOD. El Escorial is usually done as a daytrip. However, for those wishing to stay, there are several budget options. **Hostal Cristina,** C. Calvario, 45, has private baths, TVs and phones. (☎918 90 19 61; fax 90 12 04. July-Aug. doubles 6950ptas/€42; low-season 6500ptas/€39. MC/V.) To reach **Residencia Juvenil El Escorial (HI),** C. Residencia, 14, from C. Rey, turn right on C. Tozas, left onto C. Claudio Coello, left again onto Po. Unamuno, then right onto C. Residencia. (☎918 90 19 61; fax 90 12 04. HI card required. Closed Sept. Laundry 300ptas/€1.80. Dorms 1200pta/€7.25, with dinner 1600ptas/€10, with lunch and dinner 2000ptas/€12; over 26 1700ptas/€10, with dinner 2200ptas/€13, 2700ptas/€16 with lunch and dinner. IVA not included. MC/V.) **Restaurante El Trillo,** C. Duque de Medinaceli, 11 (☎91 890 73 19), a straight shot uphill from the tourist office, serves a traditional *menú* indoors for 1200ptas/€7.25, outside for 1500ptas/€9. (Open 1:30-4:30pm and 8pm-midnight. MC/V.) Central cafés are bustling throughout the day. Self-caterers head to **Mercado Público,** C. Rey, 7, just off of the central plaza (open M-Sa 9am-2pm and 6-9pm).

EL ESCORIAL

☎918 90 59 03 or 90 59 04. Complex open Apr.-Sept. Tu-Su 10am-6pm; Oct.-Mar. Tu-Su 10am-5pm. Last admission to palaces, pantheons, and museums 1hr. before closing. Monastery 1000ptas/€6, students and seniors 500ptas/€3, guided tour 1150ptas/€7. Spanish tours leave every 15min., ask at the desk for the next English tour. W free for EU citizens.

THE MONASTERY. The **Monasterio de San Lorenzo del Escorial,** a gift from Felipe II to God, his people, and himself, was meant to commemorate his victory over the French at the battle of San Quintín in 1557 and includes a royal monastery and mausoleum. He commissioned Juan Bautista de Toledo to design the complex in 1561; when he died in 1567, Juan de Herrera inherited the job. Except for the Panteón Real and minor additions, the monastery was finished in just 21 years. According to tradition, Felipe oversaw much of the work from a chair-shaped rock, **Silla de Felipe II** (Felipe's Chair), 7km from the site.

Considering the resources that Felipe II commanded, the building is noteworthy for its austerity, symmetry, and simplicity; Felipe described it as "majesty without ostentation." Fulfilling the *desornamentado* style, the monastery is pieced together with granite hewn from the surrounding quarries. The entire structure is built around a gridiron pattern: four massive towers pin the corners, and a great dome surmounts the towers of the central basilica, giving the ensemble a pyramidal shape. At Felipe II's behest, steep slate roofs—the first of their kind in Spain—were introduced from Flanders. Slate spires lend grace to the grim structure, further mellowed by the glowing *piedra de Colmenar* stone.

GALLERIES AND LIVING QUARTERS. To avoid the worst of the crowds, enter El Escorial by the traditional gateway on the west side (C. Floridablanca), where you'll encounter a collection of Flemish tapestries and paintings. The collection exudes much of the same severity as the monastery, with dark paintings like El Greco's *Martirio de San Mauricio y la Legión* and Roger van der Weyden's glowing *Calvary.* The adjacent **Museo de Arquitectura and Pintura** has an exhibition comparing the construction of El Escorial to other related structures; there is also a display of wooden models of 16th-century machinery. Though masterpieces by Bosch, Dures, El Greco, Titian, Tintoretto, Zurbarán, Van Dyck, and others hang from the walls, the majority of the collection now lies in Madrid's Prado Museum.

The **Palacio Real,** lined with *azulejos* from Toledo, includes the **Salón del Trono** (Throne Room) and 2 dwellings: Felipe II's spartan 16th-century apartments and the more luxurious 18th-century rooms of Carlos III and Carlos IV. Pastoral images cover the **Puertas de Marguetería,** German doors made from 18 different species of wood. The **Sala de Batallas** (Battle Room) links the two parts of the palace with frescoes by Italian artists Grabelo and Castello. Castile and Spain's greatest victories—including Juan II's 1431 triumph over the Muslims at Higueruela, Felipe's II's successful expeditions in the Azores, and the Battle of San Quintín—are detailed on the walls and ceiling. Maps line the walls; the last one on the right portrays the world, as (mis)understood by the 16th century Europeans. Downstairs, in the royal chambers, Felipe II's miniscule bed attests to his asceticism.

LIBRARY. The **biblioteca** (library) on the second floor holds numerous priceless books and manuscripts (though several fires have reduced the collection). Alfonso X's *Cantigas de Santa María,* the Book of Hours of the Catholic monarchs, Saint Teresa's manuscripts and diary, the gold-scrolled *Aureus Codex* (by German Emperor Conrad III, 1039), and an 11th-century *Commentary on the Apocalypse* by Beato de Liébana are just a sampling of the manuscripts. Frescos of history's most prized academic figures cover the ceiling.

BASILICA. The lower cloister leads to the basilica. Marble steps lead up to an altar adorned by two groups of sculptures. The figures on the left represent assorted relatives of Felipe II, including his parents Carlos I and Isabel, his daughter María, and his sisters María (Queen of Hungary) and Leonor (Queen of France). Those on the right depict Felipe II with his three wives and his son Carlos. The **Coro Alto** (High Choir) has a magnificent ceiling fresco of an angel-filled heaven. The **cloister** shines under Titian's fresco of the martyrdom of St. Lawrence.

PANTHEONS. The nearby **Panteón Real,** filled with tombs of past monarchs, glistens with intricate gold and marble designs completed in 1654. Felipe II ordered that its design allow for mass to be conducted over his father's tomb. The connecting **Pudreria,** where bodies would dry before being buried, is thankfully out of commission. Two centuries later, the **Panteón de los Infantes** was constructed for the same purpose, and has space for over 50 babies. It is rumored that many of the royalty's illegitimate children, including a son of Charles V, lie within the crypts.

THE CASITAS

Commissioned by the Prince of Asturias, later to become Carlos IV, the **Casita del Príncipe** displays a collection of ornaments, including chandeliers, lamps, rugs, furniture, clocks, tapestries, china, and engraved oranges. Though the French roughed up the *casita* during the Napoleonic invasions, many rooms were later redecorated by Fernando VII in the then-popular Empire style. (Approx. 1 km from the monastery on the way to Madrid. Open Sa-Su 10:30am-1pm and 4-6:30pm. Visitors may only enter with a guided tour; every 30min., 10-person max. Call ahead for reservations

☎918 90 59 03. 575ptas/€3.50 per person; students and seniors 300ptas/€1.80.) Three kilometers toward Ávila, the simpler **Casita del Infante,** commissioned by Carlos's brother, Gabriel de Borbón, in the mid-16th century as a retreat, was meant to entertain guests with stunning views and musical performance. (Open *Semana Santa* and July-Sept. Tu-Su 10am-7pm; 500ptas/€3.)

NEAR EL ESCORIAL: EL VALLE DE LOS CAÍDOS

In a once-untouched valley of the Sierra de Guadarrama, 8km north of El Escorial, Franco forced prisoners to build the overpowering monument of Santa Cruz del Valle de los Caídos (Valley of the Fallen) as a memorial to those who gave their lives in the Civil War. Although ostensibly a monument to both sides, the massive granite cross (150m tall and 46m wide) implicitly honors only those who died "serving Dios and España," (i.e. the fascist Nationalists); many of the Republican prisoners-of-war died under the grueling conditions of its construction. To climb to the base of the cross, use the stairs adjacent to the automatic lift or follow the paved road up to the trailhead just past the monastery on the right. Apocalyptic tapestries line the cave-like **basilica,** where lies the ghost of fascist architecture, and death-angels carry swords and angry light fixtures. Behind the chapel walls lie a multitude (9 levels) of the dead. The high altar, located directly underneath the mammoth cross with its mammoth statues, is testimony to modern Spain's view of Franco—although Franco lies buried underneath, there is no mention of his tomb in tourist literature. El Valle de los Caídos is accessible only via El Escorial. (Mass M-Sa 11am, Su 11am, 12:30, 1, and 5:30pm. Entrance gate open Tu-Su 10am-6pm; Basilica open 10am-6:30pm. 800ptas/€5, seniors and students 400ptas/€2.50. W free for EU citizens. Funicular to the cross 400ptas/€2.50.) **Autocares Herranz** runs one bus to the monument (15min., leaves El Escorial Tu-Su 3:15pm and returns 5:30pm, round-trip plus admission 1150ptas/€6.30, funicular not included).

SIERRA DE GUADARRAMA

The Sierra de Guadarrama is a pine-covered mountain range halfway between Madrid and Segovia. With *La Mujer Muerta* (The Dead Woman) to the west, the *Sierra de la Maliciosa* (Mountain of the Evil Woman) to the east, and the less-imaginatively-named *Siete Picos* (Seven Peaks) between the two, the Sierra draws both summer and winter visitors to hike and ski.

CERCEDILLA ☎918

A picturesque chalet town full of budget accommodations and blessed with great weather, Cercedilla is the ideal base for venturing into the Sierras. In the summer, cooler temperatures and a relaxed pace lure sweltering city-dwellers; in the winter, skiers enjoy the nearby resorts. For those weary of Madrid's sights, Cercedilla has no monuments, churches, or museums, and the most exciting event in the town's history is its mention in Quevedo's 17th century novel, *El buscón*. Ahh.

TRANSPORTATION AND PRACTICAL INFORMATION. Cercedilla makes an easy daytrip from Madrid. The **train station** (☎918 52 00 57), at the base of the hill on C. Emilio Serrano, sends trains to: **El Escorial** via Villalba (1hr.; 19-30 per day M-F 6:41am-12:26am, Sa-Su 7:27am-12:26am; 170ptas/€1); **Los Cotos** (45min., every hr. Sa-Su, every 2hr. M-F; 9:35am-7:35pm, 550ptas/€3.25); **Madrid-Atocha** (1½hr.; over 30 per day M-F 6:07am-10:35pm, Sa-Su 6:37am-10:35pm; 550ptas/€3.25); **Puerto de Navacerrada** (30min., on the way to Los Cotos, 550ptas/€3.25); **Segovia** (45min., 8-9 per day 7:20am-9:20pm, 385ptas/€2.40); **Villalba** (30min.; M-Sa 6:07am-10:35pm, Sa-Su 6:37am-10:35pm; 170ptas/€1). The **bus station,** Av. José Antonio, 2 (☎918 52 02 39), sends buses to **Madrid** (M-F 29 per day 6am-8:45pm, Sa 15-17 per day 6:20am-8:45pm, Su 17 per day 8:30am-9:30pm; 430ptas/€2.50). Find info at the **Consejería de Medio Ambiente** (see **Hiking,** below). For **Cta. Las Dehesas,**

go straight uphill and stay left at the fork. Services include: **emergency** ☎112; **police** ☎91 852 02 00, and the **Centro Médico** (☎91 852 04 97).

ACCOMMODATIONS AND FOOD. On Ctra. Las Dehesas, two youth hostels afford views of the Sierras. Both are filled with summer camp groups from July-Aug.15 and closed from July 16-Sept. 15 for vacation. Reservations more than 15 days in advance should be made through the central office in Madrid (☎91 580 42 16). The closest to the train station is **Villa Castora (HI),** about 1km up Ctra. Las Dehesas on the left. (☎918 52 03 34; fax 52 24 11. All rooms with private bath. Reception daily 8am-10pm. Rooms and 3 meals 2000ptas/€12, with 2 meals 1600ptas/€9.50, only breakfast 1200ptas/€7.25; over 26 years old with three meals 2889ptas/€17.50, with two meals 2354ptas/€14, only breakfast 1819ptas/€11.) **Hostal La Maya,** C. Carrera del Señor, 2, has rooms with TVs, sofas, and modern private baths. (☎91 852 22 52. Doubles 6500ptas/€39. MC/V.) **Camping,** which is strictly controlled throughout the Sierra de Guadarrama, is prohibited throughout the area surrounding Cercedilla. A list of campsites is available at the Conserjería del Medioambiente (see Hiking, below). **Supermarket Gigante,** C. Doctor Cañados, 2, is in the town center off Av. Generalísimo. (☎918 52 23 19. Open M-Sa 9:30am-2pm and 5:30-9pm, Su 9:30am-2pm.)

HIKING. The **Consejería de Medio Ambiente,** Ctra. las Dehesas, a wooden chalet 2km up the road on the right, functions as a **tourist office** and offers hiking information. (☎/fax 852 22 13. Open daily 9am-6pm; English spoken during the week.) Most of the hiking around Cercedilla begins up the **Carretera las Dehesas,** near the Consejería. Atop the carretera, the **Calzada Romana,** (about 1.5km from the Consejería), offers hiking along a Roman road that once connected Madrid to Segovia.

PUERTO DE NAVACERRADA AND LOS COTOS

A year-round magnet for outdoorsy types, **Puerto de Navacerrada** offers bland **skiing** in the winter (late Dec.-earlyApr.) and beautiful **hiking** in the summer. Backpackers in search of challenging hikes often take the popular **Camino Schmid,** a 7km trail which goes from Navacerrada to Pradera de los Corralillos; from there it is another 3km to the Consejería in Cercedilla. For hiking information, try **Deporte y Montaña,** 1.5km from the train station. (☎918 52 14 35. Open Sa-Su 10:30am-5pm in summer.) To head straight for the trails, exit the train station, turn left at the highway, and turn left again (off the road) at the large intersection marking the pass. The dirt path leads uphill to several trailpaths through the pine forests. A **train** leaves for Navacerrada from the Cercedilla station (30min.; every hr. Sa-Su, every 2hrs. M-F; 9:35am-7:35pm; 550ptas/€3.50.) **Los Cotos** is another popular winter resort. For information, try the **Parque Nacional Peñalara** (☎915 2 28 743), a few km from the train station. **Valdesqui** (☎918 52 33 02) is a ski resort in nearby **Rascafria,** about a 2.5km hike from the Cotos station.

ARANJUEZ

Two rivers converge at the heart of green Aranjuez (pop. 42,000). Once a getaway for generations of Habsburg and Bourbon royalty, Aranjuez still maintains a pastoral elegance thanks to its dazzling gardens and palaces. Famed for its strawberries asparagus, and acres of gardens, this small city is pleasing to a variety of senses.

TRANSPORTATION. **Trains** (RENFE info ☎902 24 02 02) go to: **Cuenca** (2hr.; 4-5 per day M-F 6:10am-8:14pm, Sa-Su 9:23am-8:14pm; 1045ptas/€6.30); **Madrid** (45min.; *cercanías* to Atocha every 15-30min. M-F 5:30am-11:30pm, Sa-Su 6am-11:30pm; *regionales* to **Chamartín** (8-10 per day M-F 6:57am-9:27pm, Sa-Su 8:57am-9:27pm; 390-535ptas/€2.34); and **Toledo** (30min.; 7-10 per day; M-F 7:20am-9:12pm, Sa-Su 9:17am-9:12pm; 390ptas/€2.34). **AISA** runs from the **bus station,** Av. Infantas, 16 (☎918 91 01 83), to: **Madrid's Estación Sur de Autobuses** (45min.; M-F every 15-30min. 6am-9pm, Sa every 45min. 7:45am-9pm, Su 10 per day 8am-9pm; 415ptas/€2.50). For **taxis,** call ☎918 91 11 39 or 669 81 53 00 between 10pm and 6am.

PRACTICAL INFORMATION. The **tourist office,** is in Pl. San Antonio. (☎918 91 04 27. Open Tu-Su 10am-2pm and 4-6pm.) Local services include: **emergency,** ☎112; **police,** C. Infantas, 36 (☎918 91 00 22); and a **pharmacy,** on the corner of C. Capitán Gómez and C. Real. (Open M-F 9:30am-1:15pm and 5-8:30pm, Sa 9:30am-1:15pm. MC/V.) For **internet** access, head to **Zeroburning Cibercafé,** C. Valeras, 11-15. From Pl. San Antonio, head through the arch on the side of the plaza opposite the tourist office onto C. Av. San Antonio and take your second left onto C. Valeras, located a few blocks up on the left. (☎918 91 42 45. 100ptas/€0.60 for 15min., 300ptas/€1.80 per hour. Open M-Sa 11am-1am, Su 4pm-midnight.) The **post office** is on C. Peña Redonda, 3, off C. Capitán Gómez (☎918 91 11 32. Open M-F 8:30am-2:30pm, Sa 9:30am-1pm). **Postal code:** 28300.

ACCOMMODATIONS AND FOOD. Accommodations in Aranjuez tend to be expensive, but you get what you pay for. **Hostal Infantas,** Av. Infantas, 4-6, will be on your left with your back is to the bus station. All the rooms have sinks, TV, phones and doubles with shower or bath have A/C. (☎918 91 13 41; fax 91 66 43. Singles 2150ptas/€13, with shower 3200ptas/€20, with bath 4100ptas/€25; doubles 3850ptas/€23, with shower 6200ptas/€38, with bath 6600ptas/€40; triples 4900ptas/€30, with shower 8000ptas/€48, with bath 8500ptas/€51. MC/V.) **Camping Soto del Castillo,** across Río Tajo and off the highway to the right, sits amid lush fields and offers a restaurant, a small supermarket, and during the summer months, a swimming pool. (☎918 91 13 95. 650ptas/€3.90 per person, 575-700ptas/€3.46-4.21 per tent, 550ptas/€3.31 per car. Open year-round. MC/V.) For **groceries** try the municipal market on C. Andalucía. With your back to the tourist office go left through the arch; the market is on your left (open M-F 9am-2pm and 6-9pm, Sa 9am-2pm).

SIGHTS. The River Tajo water the palace's beautiful **gardens.** River walkways run from the **Jardín de la Isla,** which sprouts banana trees and a mythological statue garden, to the **Jardín del Príncipe,** built for the amusement of Carlos IV. (Both open daily Apr.-Sept. 8am-8:30pm; Oct.-Mar 8am-6:30pm. Free.) Inside the park, the **Casa del Labrador,** a mock cottage, is full of Neoclassical decorative arts. (3km down C. de la Reina. ☎918 91 03 05. Open June-Aug. Tu-Su 10am-6:15pm; Sept.-May Tu-Su 10am-5:15pm. 800ptas/€4.81, students and children under 16 400ptas/€2.40.) The **Falúas Reales,** once the quarters of the Tajo's sailing squad, stores royal gondolas. (Open June-Aug. Tu-Su 10am-6:15pm; Sept.-May Tu-Su 10am-5:15pm. 500ptas/€3, students and children under 16 250ptas/€1.51. W free for EU citizens.)

The stately **Palacio Real,** splendid in white brick, was originally designed by Juan de Herrera—chief architect of El Escorial—under the direction of Felipe II. In subsequent years, Felipe V, Fernando VI, and Carlos III all had the palace enlarged and embellished to suit their own tastes. The Oriental **porcelain room,** with three-dimensional wallpaper and Rococo ceramic work, and the Mozarabic **smoking room,** which bears a striking resemblance to the Alhambra, are particularly remarkable. (☎918 91 07 40. Open Apr.-Sept. Tu-Sa 10am-6:15pm; Oct.-Mar. Tu-Sa 10am-5:15pm. Compulsory 30min. tour in Spanish leaves about every 15min. 800ptas/€4.81, students 400ptas/€2.40. EU citizens free W.) A new museum, **Aranjuez, Una Gran Fiesta,** brings you behind the scenes of a bullfight. Wind in and out of the bullring as you follow the exhibit through the history of bullfighting. (Plaza de Toros. ☎918 92 16 43. Open Tu-Su Apr.-Sept. 11am-7:30pm, Oct.-Mar. 11am-5:30pm. 500ptas/€3, students, seniors, and children under 16 200ptas/€1.20.)

CENTRAL SPAIN

CASTILLA LA MANCHA

Cervantes chose to set Don Quijote's adventures in La Mancha (*manxa* means parched earth in Arabic, and *mancha* means stain in Spanish) in an effort to evoke a cultural and material backwater. While Castilla La Mancha is indeed one of Spain's least developed regions, no fantasy of the Knight of the Sad Countenance is needed to transform the austere beauty of this battered, windswept plateau. Its tumultuous history, gloomy medieval fortresses, and brooding cliffs present a landscape evoking both melancholy and reverence.

Long ago, this region was at the epicenter of conflict between Christians and Muslims. When Christian forces arrived in Muslim Spain, La Mancha became the domain of the military orders Santiago, Calatrava, Montesa, and San Juan, which were modeled after such crusading institutions as the Knights Templar, a society of powerful warrior-monks (see **Convento di Cristo,** p. 618). In the 14th and 15th centuries, the region saw fearsome struggles between the kingdoms of Castilla and Aragón. All this warring left La Mancha in a state of utter destruction.

The region is Spain's largest wine-producing area (Valdepeñas and Manzanares are popular table wines), and its abundant olive groves and hunting influence many local recipes. Stews, roast meats, and game are all *manchego* staples. *Gazpacho manchego* (a hearty stew of rabbit, lamb, chicken, and pork) and *queso manchego* (Castile's beloved cheese) are both indigenous specialties.

TOLEDO ☎925

For Cervantes, Toledo was a "rocky gravity, glory of Spain and light of her cities." Cossío called it "the most brilliant and evocative summary of Spain's history." To the architecture-lover, Toledo is paradise. Toledo has been successively a Roman settlement, capital of the Visigoth kingdom, stronghold of the Emirate of Córdoba, and imperial city under Carlos V. To the military historian, Toledo is equally interesting, as it produced swords for most of medieval Europe and conquistadors such as Francisco Pizarro. Modern-day Toledo (pop. 65,000) may be marred by armies of tourists and caravans of kitsch, but it remains a treasure trove of Spanish culture. The city's numerous churches, synagogues, and mosques share twisting alleyways, emblematic of a time when Spain's three religions coexisted peacefully. Visitors pay monetary homage to Toledo's Damascene swords and knives, colorful pottery, and almond-paste marzipan.

TRANSPORTATION

Trains: Po. Rosa, 2 (RENFE Info ☎902 24 02 02), in an exquisite neo-Mudéjar station just over the Puente de Azarquiel. One line to **Madrid** (1½hr.; 9-10 per day; M-F 6:30am-8:58pm, Sa-Su 8:25am-8:58pm; 780ptas/€4.70), usually via Aranjuez (35min.; 8-9 per day; M-F 6:30am-8:58pm, Sa-Su 8:25am-8:58pm; 390ptas/€2.34).

Buses: (☎925 21 58 50), 5min. from the city gate. From Pl. Zocodóver, take C. Armas and its extension to the Puerta de Bisagra; as you exit the old city turn right following Ronda de Granadal to the next traffic circles. Just before the bridge, take a left and the station is straight ahead. Information booth open daily 7am-11pm. Despite multiple companies, destinations are few. **Continental-Auto** (☎925 22 36 41) runs to **Madrid** (1½hr.; every 30min. M-F 5:15am-10pm, Sa 6am-10:30pm, Su 8:30am-11:30pm; 605ptas/€3.75). **ALSINA** (☎925 21 58 50 or 963 49 72 30) to **Valencia** (5½hr., M-F 3pm, 2600ptas/€16; buy the ticket on the bus).

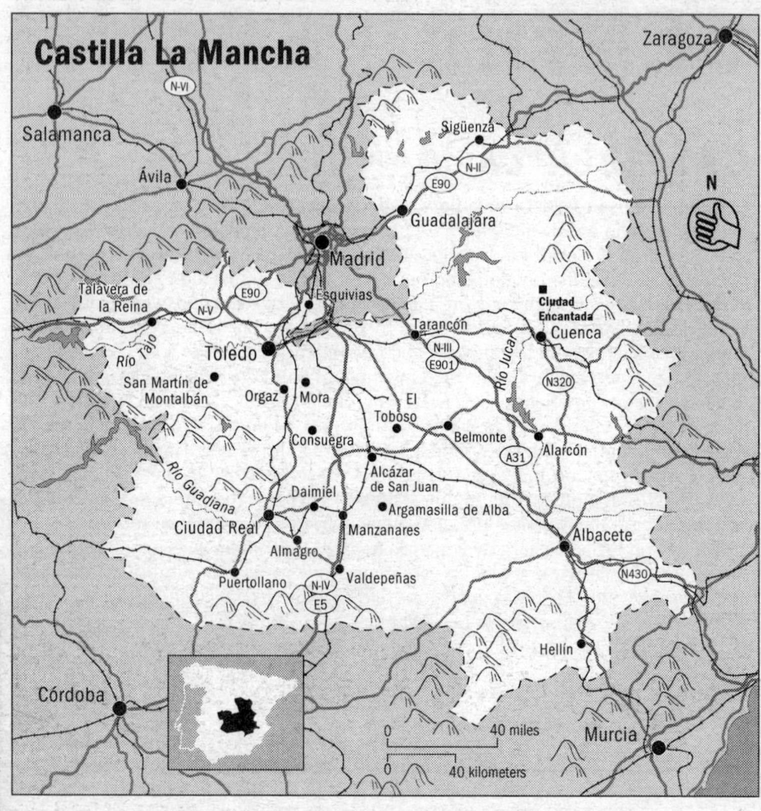

CASTILLA LA MANCHA

Public Transportation: Buses #5 and 6 stop to the right of the train station and across the street from the bus station on their way to Pl. Zocodóver (120ptas/€0.72).

Taxis: ☎925 25 50 50 or 22 70 70.

Car Rental: Avis C. Venancio González 9 (☎925 21 45 35 or 21 57 94). From about 9300ptas/€56 per day. Min. age 23. Open M-F 9:30am-2pm and 4:30-8pm, Sa 9:30am-2pm. **Hertz** (☎925 25 38 90), at the train station. From about 8000ptas/€48 per day. Open M-F 9am-1:30pm, 4:30-7pm; Sa 9am-1pm. Including IVA and insurance.

ORIENTATION AND PRACTICAL INFORMATION

Toledo is an almost unconquerable maze of narrow streets where pedestrians and cars battle for sovereignty. To get to Plaza de Zocodóver in the town center, take bus #5 or 6 (120ptas) from the stop on the right after you exit the train station. On foot from the train station, *do not* take the big bridge across the Tajo. Instead, turn right after leaving the station and follow the left fork uphill to a smaller bridge, Puente de Alcántara. Cross the bridge to the stone staircase (through a set of arches); after climbing the stairs, turn left and continue upward, veering right at C. Cervantes to Pl. Zocodóver. From the bus station, exit from the restaurant, head straight toward the traffic circle, and take the first right along the steep highway that surrounds the city. Despite well-labeled streets, visitors are likely to lose their way—and discover Toledo's back-street beauty.

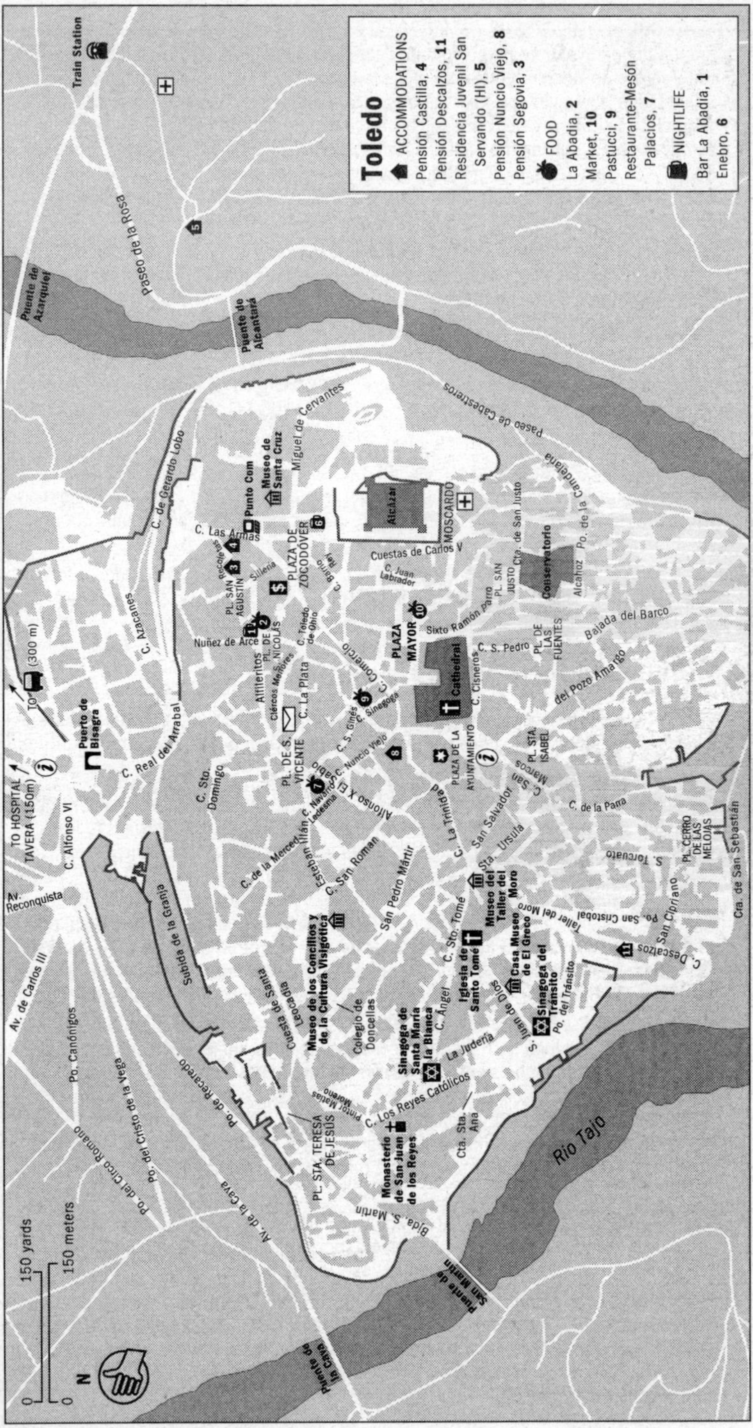

Toledo

ACCOMMODATIONS
Pensión Castilla, **4**
Pensión Descalzos, **11**
Residencia Juvenil San Servando (HI), **5**
Pensión Nuncio Viejo, **8**
Pensión Segovia, **3**

FOOD
La Abadia, **2**
Market, **10**
Pastucci, **9**
Restaurante-Mesón Palacios, **7**

NIGHTLIFE
Bar La Abadia, **1**
Enebro, **6**

Tourist Office: (☎925 22 08 43; fax 25 26 48), just outside the Puerta Nueva de Bisagra, on the north side of town. From Pl. Zocodóver, take C. Armas downhill and through the **Puertas de Bisagra** gates; the office is across the intersection (10min.). From the train station, turn right and take the busy right-hand fork across the bridge (Puente de Azarquiel), following the city walls until you reach the second traffic circle; the office is across the road, outside the walls. English-speaking staff offers handy maps. Open July-Sept. M-Sa 9am-7pm, Su 9am-3pm; Oct.-June M-F 9am-6pm, Sa 9am-7pm, Su 9am-3pm. **Second office** in Pl. Ayuntamiento (☎925 25 40 30), opposite the cathedral, English spoken. Open Tu-Su 10:30am-2:30pm and 4:30-7pm.

Currency Exchange: Banco Central Hispano, C. Comercio, 47 (☎925 22 98 00). No Commission and a 24hr. **ATM.** Open Apr.-Sept. M-F 8:30am-2:30pm; Oct.-Mar. M-F 8:30am-2:30pm, Sa 8:30am-1pm.

Luggage Storage: At the **bus station** (100-200ptas/€0.60-1.20). Open daily 7am-11pm. At the **train station** (500ptas/€3). Open daily 7am-9:30pm.

Emergency: ☎112. **Police:** ☎092, where Av. Reconquista and Av. Carlos III meet.

Pharmacy: (☎925 22 17 68), Pl. Zocodóver. Posted list of late-night pharmacies.

Hospital: Hospital Virgen de la Salud (☎925 26 92 00), Av. Barber.

Internet Access: Punto Com, C. Armas, 4, 2nd floor (☎925 25 62 08), in Pl. Zocodóver just as you begin to walk downhill on the right. The cheapest and most convenient connection in town. 150ptas/€0.90 for 15min., 250ptas/€1.50 for 30min., 400ptas/€2.40 per hr. Open M-Sa 11:30am-10pm, Su 4-10pm.

Post Office: C. Plata, 1 (☎925 22 36 11; fax 21 57 64). Take C. Comercio from Pl. Zocodóver and turn right on C. Toledo de Ohio which turns into C. Plata. **Lista de Correos.** Open M-F 8:30am-8:30pm, Sa 9am-2pm. **Postal Code:** 45070.

ACCOMMODATIONS AND CAMPING

Toledo is chock-full of accommodations, but finding a bed during the summer can be a hassle, especially on weekends. Try the tourist office if you run into trouble.

Residencia Juvenil San Servando (HI), Castillo San Servando (☎925 22 45 54). Cross the street from the station, turn left, then immediately right up Callejón del Hospital. When the steps reach a road, turn right, then right again, following the signs to Hospital Provincial. The steep walk uphill past the hospital leads to the 14th-century castle. From the bus station, exit the restaurant, head toward the traffic circle, and continue straight up the hill; cross the footbridge to the left and make your way up to the castle. Attractive, monumental building has 38 rooms, each with 2-4 bunk beds and private bath, some with views. Gorgeous pool in summer. TV room. Say yes to the sheets (they are free). Reception open 7-9:40am, 10am-7:40pm, 8-11:50pm. Dorms 1400ptas/€8.50, with breakfast 1500ptas/€9; over 26 1800ptas/€10.82, with breakfast 2000ptas/€12.

Pensión Descalzos, C. Descalzos, 30 (☎925 22 28 88), down the steps off Po. del Tránsito, near the Sinagoga de Tránsito. Recently refurbished hostel in a quiet part of town with stunning views of the surrounding hills. Modern rooms with TV, A/C, full bath, and phone, some with balconies. Rooms #41 and 42 are favorites. Breakfast 225-800ptas/€1.35-4.80. With the small pool/big jacuzzi combo in the backyard you may never want to leave your hostel. Apr.-Oct. singles 4000ptas/€24; doubles 6420-7250ptas/€39-44. Oct.-Mar. singles 3750ptas/€23; doubles 5600-6500ptas/€34-39. IVA not included. MC/V.

Pensión Castilla, C. Recoletos, 6 (☎925 25 63 18). Take C. Armas downhill from Pl. Zocodóver, then the first left up C. Recoletos (opposite the Caja Madrid bank); the hostel is up the stairs in the corner. Comfortable rooms feature high, wood-beamed ceilings. Singles 2200ptas/€14; doubles with bath 3900ptas/€24.

Pensión Segovia, C. Recoletos, 2 (☎925 21 11 24). Continuing around the bend from *Castilla* (above), *Segovia* is on your left. Simple but spacious rooms with decent beds and sinks. 3 common baths for 8 rooms. Singles 2400ptas/€15; doubles 3200ptas/€20; triples 4500ptas/€27.

Pensión Nuncio Viejo, C. Nuncio Viejo, 19, 3rd fl. (☎925 22 81 78). 7 rooms opposite the tourist office may be cramped, but they're bright and clean. Their motherly owner is a great cook. Breakfast 250ptas/€1.50. Meals 950ptas/€5.75. One single 2400ptas/ €15; doubles 4300ptas/€26, with bath 4900ptas/€30.

Camping: Out of town sites bring quiet and shade; in town trade convenience for noise.

El Greco (☎925 22 00 90), 1½km from town on Ctra CM-400, km 0.7. Bus #7 (from Pl. Zocodóver) stops at the entrance. Shady, wooded site between the river and an olive grove. Restaurant, bar, and supermarket. Pool during the summer Open year-round. 670ptas/€4.02 per person, 650ptas/€3.90 per tent, 650ptas/€3.90 per car. IVA not included. MC/V.

Circo Romano, Av. Carlos III, 19, (☎925 22 04 42), through Puerta de Bisagra, off the 2nd "spoke" of the traffic circle as you walk to the right. Closer but noisier. Popular pool area (600ptas/€3.61 per person per day). Restaurant and bar. 670ptas/€4.03 per person, 650ptas/€3.91 per tent, 50ptas/€0.30 per car. Open year-round. MC/V.

FOOD

Toledo grinds almonds into marzipan of every shape and size; from colorful fruity nuggets to half-moon cookies, *pastelería* windows beckon on every corner. If your pocket allows, dining out in Toledo can be a pleasant culinary experience (*menús* 1400-1600ptas/€8.41-9.62). Alternatively, grab fresh fruit and the basics from **Alimentación Pantoja**, C. Arrabal, 30, just inside the Puerta de Bisagra, across from the tourist office. (Open June-Aug. M-Sa 9am-11pm, Su 9am-3pm; rest of the year M-Sa 9am-10pm and Su 9am-3pm.) The **market** appears in Pl. Mayor, behind the cathedral (open M-Sa 9am-8pm).

La Abadía, Pl. San Nicolás, 3 (☎925 25 07 46). With your back to the McDonald's in Pl. Zocodover, take C. Sillería (to the left of the pharmacy), then bear left when the road splits. When you reach a small plaza, Abadía will be to your right. The exquisite dining room is a maze of connected cave-like underground rooms. While dinner prices are exorbitant, the delicious *menú* is a steal (1375ptas/€8.30). Upstairs lounge offers miniature tables, *tapas* (225ptas/€1.35), wine (150ptas/€0.90), and beer (175ptas/ €1.05). Open M-Th 8am-midnight, F 8am-1:30am, Sa noon-2:30am, Su noon-midnight. AmEx/MC/V.

Pastucci, C. Sinagoga, 10 (☎925 21 48 66), where pizza and pasta is the name of the game. From Pl. Zocodóver take C. Comercio; keep to the right through the underpass. Periwinkle walls, lots of light, and a cheerful atmosphere. Pastas 800-1000ptas/€4.81-6. Over varieties of pizza (1000ptas/€6). 10% discount with your *Let's Go* guide. Open daily 12:15pm-midnight. MC/V.

Restaurante-Mesón Palacios, C. Alfonso X El Sabio, 3 (☎925 21 59 72), off C. Nuncio Viejo. Its cool, dim interior is a popular escape from the heat. Two daily menús loaded with meat, fish, and egg options. Toledo's famous partridge dish is an option in the more expensive menú (1000 or 1700ptas/€6-10.22). Entrées 1200-2000ptas/€7.21-12. Open M-Sa 1-4pm and 7-11pm, Su noon-4pm. AmEx/MC/V.

SIGHTS

Toledo's excellent collection of museums, churches, synagogues, and mosques, make the city almost impossible to see in just one day. Within its fortified walls, (attributed to 7th-century King Wamba), Toledo's major attractions form a belt around its middle. An east-west tour, beginning in Pl. Zocodóver, is mostly downhill. Most sights are closed on Mondays.

CATHEDRAL. Built between 1226 and 1498, Toledo's grandiose cathedral boasts five naves, delicate stained glass, and unapologetic ostentation. Noteworthy pieces include the 14th-century Gothic *Virgen Blanca* by the entrance, El Greco's *El Espolio*, and Narciso Tomés's *Transparente*, a Spanish-Baroque whirlpool of architecture, sculpture, and painting. In the **Capilla Mayor,** the massive Gothic altarpiece stretches to the ceiling. The tomb of Cardinal Mendoza, founder of the

EL GRECO'S THREE MISTAKES Upon a visit to the sacristy of Toledo's cathedral, the eye is quickly drawn to the large El Greco painting at the end of the room. El Greco painted *El Espolio*—his first painting—specifically for the cathedral, although neither party had thought to negotiate costs before the completion of the work. The cathedral's clergy were unhappy with the painting due to three mistakes El Greco had inadvertently made. The first is an anachronism: the scene depicts the point in the Bible at which the Roman soldiers are about to remove Jesus' gown, but the soldier standing to his left is wearing distinctly 16th-century armor. El Greco's second mistake was painting three women in the bottom left corner; according to the New Testament, no women were present at that moment. The clergy's final complaint was that the artist painted ordinary men's heads above the head of Jesus; even in art, Christ is more holy than mere humans. The two parties went to court over the matter, eventually working out a compromise. In the end, El Greco won something more valuable than money—the court battle threw him into the spotlight, earning him a slew of new commissions and spreading his reputation.

Spanish Inquisition, lies to the left. Beneath the dome is the **Capilla Mozárabe,** the only place where the ancient Visigoth mass (in Mozarabic) is still held. The **treasury** flaunts interesting ornamentations, including a replica of one of Columbus's ships and a 400-pound, 16th-century gold monstrosity lugged through the streets during the annual Corpus Christi procession. The **sacristy** is home to 18 El Grecos and two Van Dycks, along with the portrait of every archbishop of Toledo. The red hats hanging from the ceiling mark the cardinals' tombs. *(At Arco de Palacio, up C. Comercio from Pl. Zocodóver. ☎925 22 22 41. Cathedral open daily June-Aug. 10am-noon and 4-7pm; Sept.-July 10am-noon and 4-6pm. Cathedral is free, but it's worth the extra money to see the Sacristy and the capillas, open June-Aug. M-Sa 10am-7pm, Su 2-6pm; Sept.-May M-Sa 10:30am-6pm, Su 2-6pm. 800ptas/€4.81. 450ptas/€2.70 for the audio guide available in English, French, and Italian. Tickets sold at the store opposite the entrance. Conservative dress required.)*

CASTILLA LA MANCHA

ALCÁZAR. Toledo's most formidable landmark, the Alcázar served as military stronghold of the Romans, Visigoths, Moors, and Spaniards. Much of the building was reduced to rubble during the Civil War, when Fascist troops besieged by Republicans used the Alcázar as their refuge. Don't miss the room detailing Colonel Moscardó's refusal to surrender the Alcázar, even at the cost of his son's life. You can also visit the dark, windowless basement refuge where over 500 civilians hid during the siege. The rooms above ground have been turned into a national military museum complete with armor, swords, guns, knives, and comparatively benign dried plants. *(Cuesta Carlos V, 2, a block down from Pl. Zocodóver. ☎925 22 30 38. Open Tu-Su 9:30am-2:30pm. Doors close at 2pm. 200ptas/€1.20. Free W.)*

EL GRECO. Greek painter Doménikos Theotokópoulos (more commonly known as El Greco) spent most of his life in Toledo. Many of his works are displayed throughout town, but the majority of his masterpieces have long since been carted off to the Prado and other big-name museums. On the west side of town, the **Iglesia de Santo Tomé** houses his famous *El entierro del Conde de Orgaz (The Burial of Count Orgaz)*. The stark figure staring out from the back is El Greco himself, and the boy is his son, Jorge Manuel, who built Toledo's city hall. *(Pl. Conde. ☎925 25 60 98. Open daily Mar.-Oct.15 10am-6:45pm; Oct.16-Feb. 10am-5:45pm. 200ptas/€1.20; children under 18, students and seniors 150ptas/€0.90.)* Downhill and to the left lies the **Casa Museo de El Greco,** containing 19 works by El Greco, including a copy of the detailed *Vista y plano de Toledo* (Landscape of Toledo). *(C. Samuel Levi, 2. ☎925 22 40 46. Open Tu-Sa 10am-2pm and 4-6pm, Su 10am-2pm. 200ptas/€1.20; students, under 18, and over 65 free. Sa and Su afternoons free.)* Outside handsome Puerta Nueva de Bisagra, on the way to Madrid, 16th-century **Hospital Tavera** displays five El Grecos as well as several works by his mentor, Titian. *(Cardenal Tavera, 2. ☎925 22 04 51. Near the tourist office. Open daily 10:30am-1:30pm and 3:30-6pm. 500ptas/€3)*

THE OLD JEWISH QUARTER. Samuel Ha Leví, diplomat and treasurer to Pedro el Cruel, built the **Sinagoga del Tránsito** (1366). Its simple exterior hides an extraordinarily ornate sanctuary with Mudéjar plasterwork and an *artesonado* (intricately designed wood) ceiling. The walls decorated with Hebrew inscriptions are mostly taken from the Psalter. Inside, the **Museo Sefardí** is packed with artifacts, including a Torah (parts of which are over 400 years old) and a beautiful set of Sephardic wedding costumes. *(C. Samuel Leví. ☎925 22 36 65. Open Tu-Sa 10am-1:45pm and 4-5:45pm, Su 10am-2pm. 400ptas/€2.40, students and under 18 200ptas/€1.20. Free Sa after 4pm and Su.)* **Sinagoga de Santa María la Blanca,** down the street to the right, was originally built to be a mosque, but was then purchased by Jews and used as the city's principal synagogue; in 1492 it was converted into a church. Now secular, its Moorish arches and tranquil garden make for a pleasant retreat. *(☎925 22 72 57. Open daily June-Aug. 10am-1:45pm and 3:30- 6:45pm; Sept.-May 10am-1:45pm and 3:30-5:45pm. 200ptas/€1.20; students, children under 16, seniors 150ptas/€0.90.)*

MONASTERIO DE SAN JUAN DE LOS REYES. At the far western edge of the city stands the Franciscan Monasterio de San Juan de los Reyes, commissioned by Isabel and Fernando to commemorate their victory over the Portuguese in the Battle of Toro (1476). The light-filled cloister, covered with the initials of the *Reyes Católicos*, melds Gothic and Mudéjar architecture. The Catholic monarchs had planned to use the church as their burial place but changed their minds after their victory over Granada. *(☎925 22 38 02. Open daily Apr.-Sept. 10am- 1:45pm and 3:30-6:45pm; rest of the year 10am-1:45pm and 3:30-6pm. 200ptas/€1.20.)*

OTHER SIGHTS. Toledo was the seat of Visigoth rule and culture for three centuries prior to the 711 Muslim invasion. The **Museo del Taller del Moro,** on C. Bulas near Iglesia de Santo Tomé, features outstanding woodwork, plasterwork, and tiles. *(Taller de Moro, 200. ☎925 22 45 00. Open Tu-Sa 10am-2pm and 4-6:30pm, Su 10am-2pm. 100ptas/€0.60.)* The exhibits at the **Museo de los Concilios y de la Cultura Visigótica** pale in comparison to their beautiful setting in a 13th-century Mudéjar church. *(C. San Clemente, 4. ☎925 22 78 72. Open Tu-Sa 10am-2pm and 4-6:30pm, Su 10am-2pm. 100ptas/€0.60, students 50ptas/€0.30.)* The impressive and untouristed **Museo de Santa Cruz** (1504) exhibits a handful of El Grecos in its eclectic art collection. Oddly enough, it also holds the remains from archaeological digs throughout the province. *(C. Cervantes, 3, off Pl. Zocodóver. ☎925 22 14 02. Open Tu-Sa 10am-6:30pm, Su 10am-2pm. Usually free.)*

NIGHTLIFE

For nightlife, head through the arch and to the left from Pl. Zocodóver to **C. Santa Fé,** brimming with beer and local youth. **Trébol**, C. Sante Fe, 1 (☎925 21 37 02) has excellent *tapas*; their *bombas* (stuffed potato bombs) are famous and deservedly so (375ptas/€2.25). Open M-Sa 10am-3:30pm and 7pm-midnight, Su 1-3:30pm and 7pm-midnight. Look for **Enebro,** tucked away on small Pl. Santiago Balleros off C. Cervantes, whose claim to fame is free evening *tapas*. (☎925 22 21 11. Beer 200ptas/€1.20. No cover. Open daily 11am-4pm and 7pm-2:30am.) **C. Sillería** and **C. Alfileritos,** west of Pl. Zocodóver, are home to more upscale bars and clubs, including **Bar La Abadía,** Pl. San Nicolás, 5. (See directions above. ☎925 25 07 46. Open M-Th 8am-midnight, F 8am-1:30am, Sa noon-2:30am, Su noon-midnight. AmEx/MC/V.) **O'Brien's Irish Pub**, C. Armas, 12, fills with twenty-somethings later in the evening. There is live music on Thursdays at 10:30pm. (☎925 21 26 65. Open Su-Th noon-12:30am, Sa-Su noon-4am. MC/V.)

DAYTRIPS FROM TOLEDO

CONSUEGRA

Samar buses (☎925 22 39 15) depart for Consuegra from the Toledo bus station (1¼hr.; M-F 10 per day 9:15am-8:30pm, Sa 5 per day 9:15am-11pm, Su 3 per day 10:30am-11pm; 545ptas/€3.30). Buses return to Toledo from C. Castilla de la Mancha (1¼hr.; M-F 8 per day

6:45am-5:45pm, Sa 3 per day 7am-1:30pm, Su 3 per day 7am-6pm). In Toledo, buy tickers at the office; upon return, buy tickets from the driver.

Of all Manchegan villages, tiny Consuegra provides the most raw material for an evocation of Quijote's world. The village **castle,** called *Cresteria Manchega* by locals, was a Roman, then Arab, then Castilian fortress. It keeps erratic hours, but the view of the surrounding plains justifies a climb any time. **El Cid's** only son, Diego, died in the stable; you can visit a lavish monument in his honor near the Ayuntamiento. Though small, Consuegra is home to a palace, a Franciscan convent, and a Carmelite monastery. The **tourist office,** located on the same road as the castle, about halfway up on the left, will gladly provide more information (☎925 47 57 31. Open June-Sept. M-F 9:30am-2pm and 4:30-7pm, Sa 10:30am-2pm and 4:30-7pm, Su 10:30am-2pm; in winter, afternoon hours 3:30-6pm.) Plan around bus departure times so you don't have to spend the night.

DRIVING SOUTH

Though the following stops are not on a public transportation route, Don Quijote buffs will love them, and they break up the monotony of driving through dry, sun-scorched plains.

A hop, skip, and jump south of Toledo lands you at the small **San Martín de Montalbán,** home to a castle poised on an enormous pile of gray granite rocks and leaning out over the abysmal gorge of the River Torión. The castle was first Visigothic territory, then an Arab fortress, and later an enclave of the mysterious Knights Templar. Legend has it that a treasure lies buried within its walls.

Cervantes fans come to La Mancha to follow in the footsteps of the writer and his characters. Cervantes met and married Catalina de Palacios in the main church in **Esquivias** in 1584 and supposedly began writing his masterpiece while imprisoned in the **Argamasilla de Alba's Cueva del Medrano.** It was in **El Toboso,** 100km southeast of Toledo, that Quijote fell in love with Dulcinea. El Toboso is also home to the **Casa Cervantes,** which displays Cervantes memorabilia, including translations of *Don Quijote* in 30 different languages. (Pl. Cervantes. ☎925 54 66 32 or 52 01 61. Open Tu, Th, F 10am-1pm and 3-6pm; Sa-Su 10am-1:30pm; hours change frequently; call ahead, especially for winter visits.)

ALMAGRO ☎926

City slickers seeking quiet and solace will find sleepy Almagro appealing. For most of the year, the life of this small town (pop. 8500) belongs to the locals. For the first three weeks in July, however, a classical theater festival of international renown attracts hundreds of visitors, bringing life to the narrow cobblestone streets and purpose to the 16th-century theatrical monuments.

TRANSPORTATION. Find the **train station** at Po. Estación (☎926 86 02 76), outside the city center, at the end of the tree-lined pedestrian street. To get from the station to the Pl. Mayor, walk down Po. Estación and turn left onto C. Rondo de Calatrava; turn right onto C. Madre de Dios (a sign points to the Centro Urbano), which becomes C. Feria and leads to the plaza. To: **Aranjuez** (2hr., 2 per day, 1400-1600ptas/€8.41-9.62); **Ciudad Real** (15min., 5 per day 8:40am-9pm, 270-800ptas/€1.65-4.81); **Madrid-Atocha** (2¾hr., 2:59 and 6:05pm, 1860-2135ptas/€11.27-12.77). Change at Ciudad Real for Córdoba, Sevilla, Granada, and Valencia. **Buses** (☎926 86 02 50) stop at a brick building at the far end of Ejido de Calatrava, left of the Hospedería Municipal de Almagro. **AISA** buses go to **Ciudad Real,** the connection point for most other cities (20min.; M-F 7 per day 7am-7pm, Sa 1 and 5pm; 230ptas/€1.35); and **Madrid** (2¼hr., M-F 5 per day 7am-6:45pm, 1700ptas/€10.22).

ORIENTATION AND PRACTICAL INFORMATION. The center of Almagro is the long, arcaded Pl. Mayor. To get to Pl. Mayor from the bus station, turn left on C. Madre de Dios and take the road straight to the plaza. The **tourist office,** C. Bernardas, 2, is inside the newly renovated Palacio del Conde de Valdeparaíso.

From Pl. Mayor, take a right on C. Mayor de Carnicerías and another right on C. Bernardas. (☎926 86 07 17. Open Apr.-June and Sept. Tu-F 10am-2pm and 5-8pm, Sa 10am-2pm and 5-7pm, Su 11am-2pm; July-Aug. same hours except Tu-F 7-9pm and Sa 6-9pm; Oct.-Mar. same hours except Tu-F 5-7pm, Sa 10am-2pm and 4-6pm.) **Banks** and **ATMs** line C. Mayor de Carnicerías. In case of an **emergency** ☎926 86 00 33 or contact the **police,** on C. Mercado, 1 (☎609 01 41 36), adjacent to the Pl. Mayor. The **Centro de Salud (health clinic)** is on C. Mayor de Carnicerías, 11 (☎926 86 10 26). The **post office,** on C. Mayor de Carnicerías, lies across from Caja Rural. (☎926 86 00 52. Open M-F 8:30am-2:30pm, Sa 9:30am-1pm.) **Postal code:** 13270.

ACCOMMODATIONS AND FOOD. **Hospedería de Almagro,** Ejido de Calátrava, resembles the austere decor of the monastery to which it is attached. The rooms themselves are bright, cheery, and spacious, and many overlook a pleasant courtyard. Clean bathrooms, phones, and TVs also provide for a comfortable stay. Reservations months ahead are needed for the theater festival. (☎926 88 20 87; fax 88 21 22. Aug.-June singles with bath 3250ptas/€20; doubles with shower 4500ptas/€27, with bath 5500ptas/€33. July singles 3750ptas/€22.54; doubles with bath 5500ptas/€33.36, with shower 6500ptas/€39. MC/V.) Outdoor **restaurants** crowd on Pl. Mayor; they offer some of the best (and only) food in town. If you wish to choose your own food adventure, fresh fruits and veggies are sold at the outdoor **market.** From the Pl. Mayor, walk down C. de San Agustín for one block, then turn left on C. Mercado. (Open Tu-W and F-Su 8am-3pm.)

SIGHTS AND ENTERTAINMENT. The center of Almagro, the **Plaza Mayor,** is also the city's cultural hub. There you can find the **Corral de Comedias,** an open-air multilevel theater resembling Shakespeare's Globe. This theater is the only one left intact from the "Golden Age" of Spanish drama, and its stage was home to the works of such literary masters as Cervantes and Lope de Vega. (☎926 86 15 39. Open Apr.-June and Sept. Tu-F 10am-2pm and 5-8pm, Sa 11am-2pm and 5-8 pm, Su 11am-2pm and 4-6pm; July-Aug. Tu-Sa 10am-2pm and 6-9pm, Su 11am-2pm and 5-7pm; Oct.-Mar. same hours except Tu-F 4-7pm, Sa-Su 4-6pm. 300ptas/€1.80, children and groups of 15 or more 150ptas/€0.90.) Directly across the plaza from the *corral* and through a few arches, the new **Museo Nacional del Teatro** displays the history of Spanish drama. (☎/fax 926 88 22 44. Closed for renovations during summer 2001, but scheduled to reopen in fall; call for new hours.) The final stop on the theater tour is the **Teatro Municipal,** C. San Agustín, 20. Follow C. San Agustín out of Pl. Mayor and look for a crimson building on the right. Inside is a renovated theater as well as a collection of elaborate costumes. (☎926 86 13 61. Open Apr.-June and Sept. Tu-F 10am-2pm and 5-8pm, Sa 11am-2pm and 5-8pm, Su 11am-2pm; July-Aug. same hours except Tu-F 6-9pm, Sa 10am-2pm and 6-9pm; Oct.-Mar. same hours except Tu-F 4-7pm, Sa 10am-2pm and 4-6pm. A single ticket, available at any of the sights, allows entrance to all three.)

Every July, prestigious theater companies and players from around the world descend on Almagro for the **Festival Internacional de Teatro Clásico de Almagro** (July 4-28 in 2002). Daily performances of Spanish and international classics take place in the Corral de Comedias, Teatro Hospital de San Juan de Dios, Teatro Municipal, Claustro de los Domínicos, Teatro Infantil, Teatro en la Calle, and Seminarios. The **box office** is in the Palacio de los Medrano, C. San Agustín, 7. (☎902 10 12 12; www.festivaldealmagro.com. Open May-June Th 11am-1:30pm; July daily 11:30am-2pm and 7-10:30pm. MC/V.) There are daily shows in July at 10:45pm; tickets are 1700-2400ptas/€10.22-15 (Tu half-price) and should be purchased before the festival. The festival also has an office in Madrid at C. Príncipe, 14 (☎915 21 07 20), and the 2002 program is listed online.

CUENCA

☎969

Cuenca (pop. 47,000) owes its fame to its location. Perched atop a hill, the vertical city is flanked by two rivers and the stunning rock formations they have created. These natural boundaries have served the city well; Muslims and then Christians settled in Cuenca because it was a nearly impenetrable fortress. Yet the city now strains against its boundaries, it's modern commercial life spilling down the hill into New Cuenca. The enchanting old city still safeguards most of Cuenca's unique charm, including the famed *casas colgadas* (hanging houses), dangling high above the Río Huécar, and the colorful Plaza Mayor.

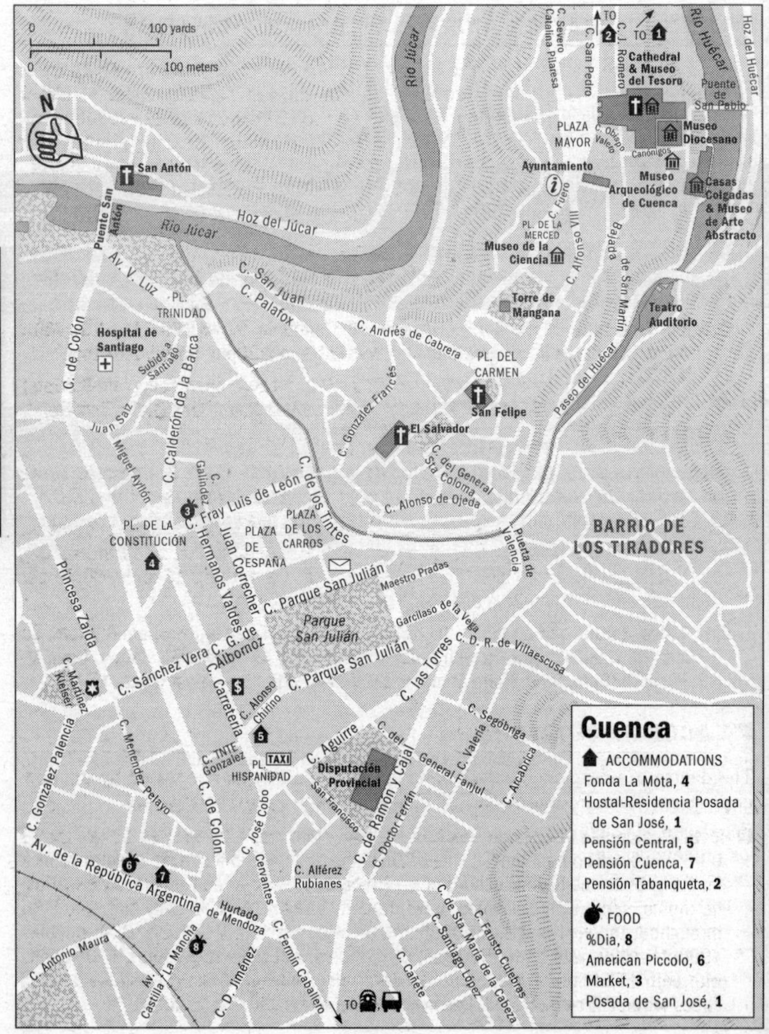

TRANSPORTATION

Trains: C. Mariano Catalina, 10 (☎902 24 02 02), in the new city. Trains to: **Aranjuez** (2hr., 5-6 per day 7:05am-6:55pm, 1045ptas/€6.30); **Madrid** (2½-3hr., 5-6 per day 7:05am-6:55pm, 1430ptas/€8.60); **Valencia** (3-4hr.; 3-4 per day, M-F 7:40am-6:40pm, Sa-Su 11:19am-6:40pm; 1575ptas/€9.50).

Buses: C. Fermín Caballero, 20 (☎969 22 70 87). Info open M-F 7am-10pm, Sa-Su 7am-9pm. **SIAL** (☎969 22 27 51) to: **Barcelona** (3½hr.; M-Sa 9:30am, July-Aug. extra bus Su at 2pm; 4550ptas/€27). **AutoRes** (☎969 22 11 84) to: **Madrid** (2½hr.; 8-9 per day, M-Sa 7:30am-8pm, Su 8am-10pm; 1370-1695ptas/€8.20-10.15). **AISA** to: **Toledo** (3hr., M-F 5:30am, 1620ptas/€9.75).

Taxis: Radio-Taxi (☎969 23 33 43). From the train station to Pl. Mayor 600ptas/€3.60.

ORIENTATION AND PRACTICAL INFORMATION

Upon exiting the train station, the back of the bus station will be directly in front of you; head up the steps to C. Fermín Caballero and turn right. To reach **Pl. Mayor** in the old city from either station, take a left on to C. Fermín Caballero, following it as it becomes C. Cervantes, C. José Cobo, and finally, bearing slightly left through Pl. Hispanidad, main **C. Carretería.** Alternately, take #1 bus (every 20min., 85ptas/€0.50) to the last stop in the old city. From C. Carretería, turn right on C. Fray Luis de León; it's a grueling walk to Pl. Mayor and the old city (20-25min.).

Tourist Office: (☎969 23 21 19; www.aytocuenca.org). Located in Pl. Mayor, on the downhill side of the archway. Some English spoken. Open July-Sept. M-Sa 9am-9pm, Su 9am-2pm; Oct.-June M-Sa 9am-2pm and 4-6pm, Su 9am-2pm.

Currency Exchange: Banco Central Hispano, C. Carretería, 23 (☎969 211 726). **ATM.** Apr.-Sept. M-F 8:30am-2:30pm; Oct.-Mar. M-F 8:30am-2:30pm, Sa 8:30am-1pm.

Luggage Storage: At the **train station** (500ptas/€3 per day; open daily 7am-9:30pm) and the **bus station** (300ptas/€1.80 per day; open M-F 7am-10pm, Sa-Su 7am-9pm).

Emergency: ☎112. **Police:** C. Martínez Kleyser, 4 (☎091 or 092).

Pharmacy: Farmacia Castellanos, C. Cervantes, 20 (☎969 21 23 37), located at the corner of C. Alferez Rubianes. A list of late-night pharmacies posted in the window.

Internet Access: La Repro, C. Jorge Torner, 39 (☎ 969 24 01 36). From the bus station, take C. Fermín Caballero toward the city center; turn right at the 1st stop light, walking up C. Julio Larrañaga 1 block. It's on the corner at the 1st left. 100ptas/€0.60 per 30min. Open M-F 10am-2pm and 5-8:30pm, Sa 10am-2pm.

Post Office: Parque de San Julián, 16 (☎969 22 90 16). Open M-F 8:30am-8:30pm, Sa 9:30am-2pm. Smaller **branch** with fewer services right next to **RENFE** station. Open M-F 8:30am-2:30pm, Sa 9:30am-1pm. **Postal Code:** for the large post office, 16004.

ACCOMMODATIONS

The dearth of cheap accommodations in the old city is compensated by the new city's abundance. Rooms on the hill charge for their spectacular views.

Hostal-Residencia Posada de San José, C. Julián Romero, 4 (☎ 969 21 13 00; fax 23 03 65), a block up from the left side of the cathedral. Cash in that extra traveler's check for cushy beds, the historic echoes of a 17th-century convent, and gorgeous views. Rustic rooms, some with balconies, have modern baths with sinks. July-Aug. and F-Sa throughout the year singles 3000ptas/€18, with full bath 6400ptas/€39; doubles 4900ptas/€29, with bath 9500ptas/€57; triples with bath 12,800ptas/€77; quads with bath 15,200ptas/€92. *Semana Santa* prices higher; weeknight and low season prices lower. IVA not included. Reservations recommended. AmEx/MC/V.

Pensión Tabanqueta, C. Trabuco, 13 (☎969 21 12 90). Head up C. San Pedro from the cathedral past Pl. Trabuco. Rooms on the side of the gorge have fabulous views and sinks. The bar below with its popular terrace shouldn't be missed. One single 2000ptas/€12; doubles 4000ptas/$24; triples 6000ptas/€36.

Fonda La Mota, Pl. Constitución, 6, 1st fl. (☎969 22 55 67), at the end of C. Carretería. Cheerful modern rooms have sinks and TVs. Breakfast 250ptas/€1.50. Doubles 4500ptas/€27, with bath 5500ptas/€33. Singles occasionally available in winter.

Pensión Central, C. Alonso Chirino, 7, 2nd fl. (☎969 21 15 11), off C. Carretería. Clean, old-fashioned rooms with big windows, high ceilings and sinks. Be prepared to wait in line for the common bathroom. Breakfast 200ptas/€1.20. Lunch or dinner 900ptas/€5.40. July-Sept. singles 1800ptas/€10.80; doubles 3000ptas/€18; triples 4200ptas/€25. Sept.-June prices 200ptas/€1.20 lower.

Pensión Cuenca, Av. República Argentina, 8, 2nd fl. (☎969 21 25 74), in the new city. From the bus station, take the third left off C. Fermín Caballero onto C. Hurtado de Mendoza, which becomes Av. República Argentina. Smallish rooms have good beds, new furniture, and sinks. TV lounge. Showers 350/€2.10. Singles 2000ptas/€12, with shower 2300ptas/€14; doubles 3000ptas/€18, with shower 4000ptas/€24.

FOOD

Restaurants around Pl. Mayor are expensive and mediocre. Budget eateries line **C. Cervantes** and **C. República Argentina,** but the cafés off **C. Fray Luis de León,** near the market, are even cheaper. *Resoli*, a liqueur of coffee, sugar, orange peel, and eau-de-vie, and *alajú*, a nougat of honey, almonds, and figs are a heavenly match. The **market** is on C. Fray Luis de León, near Pl. Constitucíon (open M-Sa 8:30am-2pm). Grab **groceries** at **%Día,** Av. Castilla La Mancha and Av. República Argentina (open M-Th 9:30am-2pm and 5:30-8:30pm, F-Sa 9am-2:30pm and 5:30-9pm).

Meson-Bar Tabanqueta, C. Trabuco, 13 (☎ 969 21 12 90), beneath the pension of the same name. This little joint bustles with patrons enjoying the views of the gorge over cheap food and drink. Wide range of options including *a menú del dia (*1200ptas/€7.20) and sandwiches (400-700ptas/€2.40-4.20). Open Tu-Su noon-2am.

Posada de San José, C. Julián Romero, 4 (☎969 21 13 00). Interior features wood beams and earthenware pots. Outdoor wooden terrace offers spectacular views. Soak in the ambiance with a serving of *pisto* (stew made of tomatoes, peppers, and onions; 575ptas/€3.45). *Bocadillos* and omelettes 300-600ptas/€1.80-3.60. Open Tu-Su 8am-11am and 6-10:30pm. AmEx/MC/V.

American Piccolo, Av. República Argentina, 14 (☎969 21 28 55). Ignore the cheesy sign and enjoy the photos and prints covering the walls of this cheerful *trattoria*. Wide range of pizzas 850-1250ptas/€5.10-7.50. Pastas 925-1270ptas/€5.55-7.60. Weekday lunch *menú* 1350ptas/€8.10. Open Th-Tu 1:30-4pm and 8pm-midnight. MC/V.

SIGHTS

CASAS COLGADAS. Cuenca draws its fame from the gravity-defying *casas colgadas* (see **Living on the Edge,** above) that have dangled over the riverbanks for six centuries. In his memoirs, Surrealist filmmaker Luis Buñuel recalls a pre-war visit to one of the *casas* in which he spied birds flying beneath the toilet seat. Walk across the Puente de San Pablo bridge (not for anyone suffering from vertigo) at sunset to get a spectacular view of the *casas* and the surrounding cliffs. Two hiking trails along the Hoz del Júcar and Hoz del Huécar (the steep river gorges on either side of the narrow old city) present fantastic views of Cuenca settled upon its perch. Maps are available from the municipal tourist office.

MUSEO DE ARTE ABSTRACTO ESPAÑOL. Inside one of the *casas*, the award-winning Museo de Arte Abstracto Español exhibits works by the odd yet internationally renowned "Abstract Generation" of Spanish painters. All pieces, most by

Canogar, Tápies, Chillida, and Fernando Zóbel, were chosen by Zóbel himself. Don't miss the "White Room" upstairs. Striking views of the gorge are an added plus. *(Pl. Ciudad de Ronda. ☎969 21 29 83. Open Tu-F and holidays 11am-2pm and 4-6pm, Sa 11am-2pm and 4-8pm, Su 11am-2:30pm. 500ptas/€3, students and seniors 250ptas/€1.50.)*

CATHEDRAL. Constructed under Alfonso VIII six years after he conquered Castile, the cathedral dominates Pl. Mayor. A perfect square, 25m on each side, it is the only Anglo-Norman Gothic cathedral in Spain. A Spanish Renaissance façade and tower were added in the 16th and 17th centuries, only to be torn down when deemed aesthetically inappropriate. A 1724 fire prevented a subsequent attempt to build a front, leaving the current exterior incomplete and strangely reminiscent of a Hollywood set. Wonderfully colorful stained-glass windows illuminate the entrance like a sunset. Inside, the **Museo del Tesoro** houses some late medieval psalters and oodles of gold jewelry. More impressive is the **Sala Capitular** and its delightful ceiling. *(Cathedral and museum open Tu-Sa 9am-2pm and 4-6pm, Su 9am-2pm. Mass daily 9:20am, plus Su noon and 1pm. Cathedral free, museum 200ptas/€1.20.)*

OTHER SIGHTS. Down C. Obispo Valero, the **Museo Arqueológico de Cuenca** is a treasure trove of archeological finds, including Roman mosaics, ceramics, coins, and excellent Visigoth jewelry. *(☎969 21 30 69. Open June-Sept. Tu-Sa 10am-2pm and 5-7pm, Su 11am-2pm; Oct.-July Tu-Sa 10am-2pm and 4-7pm, Su 10am-2pm. 200ptas/€1.20, students 100ptas/€0.60. Sa afternoon and Su free.)* Perhaps the most beautiful of the museums along this street is the **Museo Diocesano,** whose exhibits include Juan de Borgoña's altarpiece from local Convento de San Pablo, many colossal Flemish tapestries, splendid rugs, and two El Grecos—*Oración del huerto* and *Cristo con la cruz*. *(☎969 22 42 10. Open July-Sept. Tu-Sa 11am-2pm and 5-8pm, Su 11am-2pm; Oct.-June Tu-Sa 11am-2pm and 4-7pm, Su 11am-2pm. 300ptas/€1.80.)*

ENTERTAINMENT

New Cuenca's nighttime bar scene extends into the wee hours of the morning. Several bars with young, snazzily dressed crowds line C. Galíndez, off C. Fray Luis de León, a long, dark walk down the hill from Old Cuenca; a taxi will be about 600ptas/€3.60. Check out the bar under **Pensión Tabanqueta** on C. Trabuco. For more nightlife, take the winding street/staircase just off Pl. Mayor across from the cathedral toward the Río Júcar. Cuenca rings with song during the **Festival of Religious Music,** a famous international celebration the week before *Semana Santa*.

SIGÜENZA ☎949

Perched on a hill in what seems to be the middle of nowhere, sleepy Sigüenza (pop. 5000) is small-town Spain at its best. Pinkish stone buildings and red-roofed houses cluster around a storybook Gothic cathedral and castle. During the Civil War, the Republicans seized the cathedral and the Nationalists the castle, making for one hell of a shoot-out. Fortunately, Sigüenza's medieval architecture has been painstakingly restored, and a walk through Sigüenza's neighborhoods, beginning at the castle, carry visitors through time—from the 12th-century medieval city to the 18th-century Baroque neighborhoods. Tourists come in trickles instead of droves, making Sigüenza an excellent daytrip escape from Madrid.

PRACTICAL INFORMATION. The **train station** (☎949 39 14 94) is at the end of Av. Alfonso VI. Trains run to: **Madrid-Chamartin** (1½-2hr.; 6-7 per day, M-F 6:52am-8:05pm, Sa 9:11am-8:05pm, Su 10:08am-10:53pm; 1145-2600ptas/€6.90-16); **Soria** (1½hr., daily 9:45am and 8:33pm, extra train F at 5:05pm, 805ptas/€4.80); and **Zaragoza** (2hr., 3-4 per day 9:19am-11:35pm, 2400-2500ptas/€14-15). For a **taxi** call ☎949 39 14 11. **Luggage storage** is at the train station (400ptas/€2.40 per locker). To get to the **tourist office** follow Av. Alfonso VI to the first intersection after Parque de la Alameda (on the left). The office is just around the corner in the restored Ermita. (☎949 34 70 07. Open M-F 10am-2:30pm and 4-6:30pm, Sa 9:30am-3pm and 3:30-7pm,

LIVING ON THE EDGE Very little is known about Cuenca's unique 14th-century *casas colgadas*. They were supposedly built to house kings; one is even named Casa del Rey. Casa de la Sirena, the only other remaining original hanging house, got its name from the siren-like screams emitted by a Cuenca *señorita* when she flung herself out of the window after her son was killed by her lover. Despite their striking appearance, the *casas* did not become famous until recently. Indeed, the *casas* were completely run down when the city of Cuenca decided to rehabilitate them early in this century, transforming them into magnificent museums. Now one of Central Spain's greatest tourist attractions, the houses draw thousands of visitors each year.

Su 9:30am-3:30pm. Closed M from Oct.-Apr.) Across the intersection sits **Banco Hispano Central,** Av. Calvo Siteco, 9, with a 24hr. **ATM** (open M-F 8:30am-2:30pm). **Internet** is at **Locutorio,** C. Humilladero, 15, half a block up on the continuation of Av. Alfonso VI. (☎949 39 15 83. 150ptas/€0.90 per 15min., 250ptas/€1.50 per 30min. Open Tu-Su 8:30am-2pm and 5:30-8:30pm.) Services include: **emergency** (☎949 30 00 19); **Red Cross** (☎949 39 13 33), Ctra. Madrid; and **police** (☎949 39 01 95), Ctra. de Atienzo. **Post office:** C. Villaviciosa, 10, off Pl. Hilario Yabén. (☎949 39 08 44. Open M-F 8:30am-2:30pm, Sa 9:30am-1pm.) **Postal code:** 19250.

ACCOMMODATIONS AND FOOD. Although you can "do" Sigüenza in a couple of hours, it can be a fun place to spend the night. **Pensión Venancio,** C. San Roque, 3, is charming. From the station, follow Av. Alfonso VI, turn left at the first intersection onto Av. Pio XII, then take the first right. (☎949 39 03 47. Singles 2200ptas/€13; doubles 4200ptas/€25; triples 5400ptas/€32.) Cheap places to eat are everywhere. **Bar-Restaurante Sánchez,** C. Humilladero, 11, has an incredibly cheap and delicious *menú* for 1100ptas/€6.60. (☎949 39 05 45. Open daily 2-4pm and 10pm-midnight.) **Autoservicio Matin Ruiz**, C. Cardenal Mendoza, 10, sells groceries (open M-Sa 9am-2pm and 4:30-8pm).

SIGHTS. The tourist office offers guided tours of the city, including entrance to all parts of the cathedral, for 1000ptas/€6. From the bottom of the hill, two buildings jut out from Sigüenza's low skyline: the cathedral and the fortified **castle,** a 12th-century castle-turned-*parador* (luxury hotel). Restored in the 1970s, the castle merits an uphill stroll through the cobblestone streets, even just for a peek into the luxuriously decorated *parador* and its marvelous view. To get to the magnificent **cathedral,** follow Av. Alfonso VI uphill (it changes to C. Humilladero), then take a left onto C. Cardenal Mendoza. Work on the cathedral began in the mid-12th century and continued until the 16th century; it combines Romanesque, Mudéjar, Plateresque, and Gothic styles. One of the structure's most renowned features is the 15th-century Tumba del Doncel, commissioned by Isabel in memory of a favorite page who died fighting the Muslims in Granada. The sacristry's elaborate Renaissance ceiling boasts 304 stone portraits carved by Alanso de Covarrubias. The 3700 faces belong to Christians and Moors, monks and countesses, dandies and dames. The adjoining chapel houses an El Greco, *Anunciación*, and a ceiling so magnificent that the church has a mirror on the floor to help you view it. (☎619 36 27 15. Cathedral open M-Sa 9am-1:30pm and 4:30-8pm, Su 9:30am-1:30pm and 4:30-7pm. Free. To enter the sacristy and the chapel, you must take a tour in Spanish: year-round Tu-Sa 11am, noon, 12:45, 4:30, 5:30pm; June-Nov. 12 Su 5:30pm; in winter Su noon, 1, 4:30pm. 300ptas/€1.80.) Opposite the cathedral, the small **Museo de Arte Antiguo** (Museo Diocesano) houses medieval and early modern religious works, including a Ribera and a Zurbarán. (☎949 39 10 23. Open Tu-Su 11am-2pm and 4-7pm. 300ptas/€1.80.)

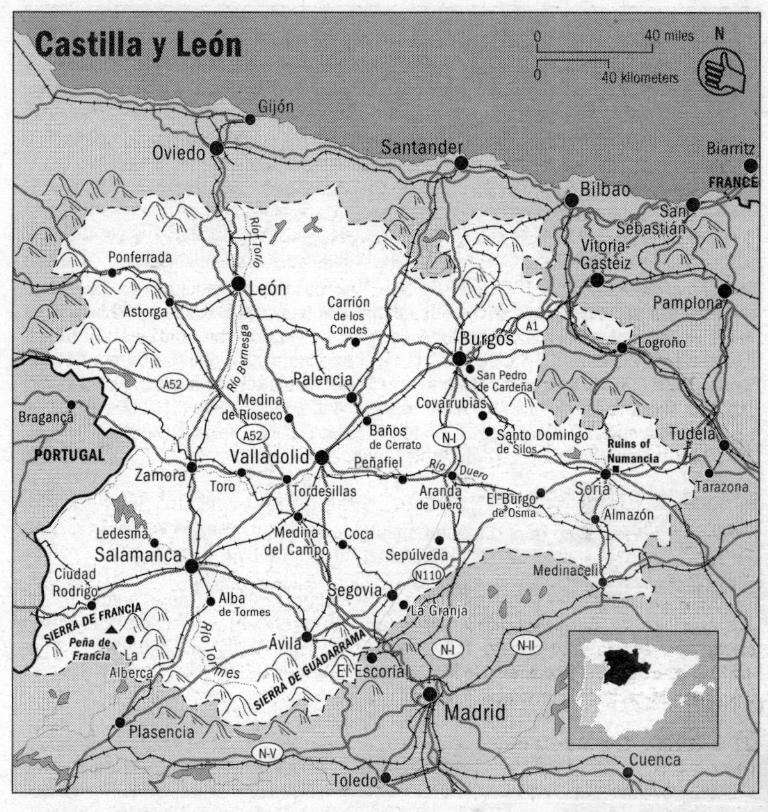

CASTILLA Y LEÓN

Castilla y León's hilltop cities rise as green oases from a desert of burnt sienna. At the center of these red-tiled towns are the monuments and legacies of Castilla's royal and divine past. These monuments—the Gothic cathedrals of Burgos and León, the Romanesque belfries along Camino de Santiago, the sandstone of Salamanca, and the city walls of Ávila—have all become regional and national images.

Well before Castilla's famous 1469 confederation with Aragón, when Fernando of Aragón and Isabel of Castilla were united in world-shaking matrimony, it was clear that Castilla had its act together. In the High Middle Ages, the region emerged from obscurity to lead the Christian charge against Islam. Castilian nobles, sanguine from the spoils of combat, introduced the concept of a unified Spain (under Castilian command, of course), and *castellano* ("Spanish") became the dominant language throughout the nation. Imperious León, Castilla's comrade in arms, though chagrined to be lumped with Castilla in a 1970s provincial reorganization, has much in common with its co-province.

SEGOVIA ☎921

Legend has it that the devil built the famed aqueduct in Segovia (pop. 55,000) in one night, all in an effort to win the soul of a Segovian water-seller named Juanilla. When the shocked Juanilla awoke to find the aqueduct almost complete, she prayed to the Virgin Mary, who hastened the sun to rise in order to foil the Devil's scheme. Segovia's aqueduct may not have won Juanilla's soul, but it has intrigued visitors even since Roman times. During its period of greatest prosperity, in the 12th and 13th centuries, Segovia had claim to the largest number of Romanesque monuments in Europe. Its remaining castles and cathedrals represent Castilla at its finest. Twisted alleyways lead to streets lined with shopping stalls. Such old-town charm comes with a price tag; food and accommodations are more expensive here than in Madrid.

TRANSPORTATION

Trains: (☎921 42 07 74), Po. Obispo Quesada. To: **Madrid** (2hr.; 7-9 per day, M-F 5:55am-8:55pm, Sa-Su 8:55am-8:55pm, 805ptas/€4.85); **Villalba** (1hr., 525ptas/€3.25) the transfer for El Escorial, Ávila, León, and Salamanca.

Buses: Estacionamiento Municipal de Autobuses, Po. Ezequiel González, 12 (☎921 42 77 07), at the corner of Av. Fernández Ladreda. **La Sepulvedana** (☎921 42 77 07) to: **La Granja** (20min.; 9-12 per day, M-Sa 7:40am-9:30pm, Su 10:30am-10:30pm; round-trip 230ptas/€1.40); **Madrid** (1½hr.; M-F every 30min. 6-11am, 9:30pm-midnight; 855ptas/€5.50). **Renfe-Iñigo** (☎921 44 12 52) to: **Ávila** (1hr.; M-F 10:30am, 2pm and 7:30pm, Sa 2pm, Su 7:45pm; 625ptas/€3.76). **Linecar** (☎921 42 77 06) to: **Valladolid** (2hr.; 6-13 per day M-Sa 6:45am-9pm, Su, 9am-9pm; 900ptas/€5.49); **Auto Res** (921 42 77 05) to: **Salamanca** (3hr., M-Th 8:50am, 1:30pm & 5:30pm, F-Sa 8:50am, 1:30pm and 5:45pm, Su 5:45pm; 1320ptas/€7.95).

Public Transportation: Transportes Urbanos de Segovia, Pl. Mayor, 8 (☎921 46 03 29). Bus tickets 105ptas/€0.60, 10-trip pass 650ptas/€4 sold at the office.

Taxis: Radio Taxi (24hr. ☎921 44 50 00). Taxis pull up by the train and bus stations.

Car Rental: Avis, C. José Zorrilla, 123 (☎921 42 25 84). Min. age 23. small vehicles 13,500ptas/€81 per day; insurance and IVA included. Open M-F 9-1:30pm and 4:30-7:30pm; Sa 9:30am-1:30pm.

ORIENTATION AND PRACTICAL INFORMATION

Take any bus from the train station (105ptas/€0.62) to **Pl. Mayor,** the city's historic center, or to **Pl. del Azogeojo,** just downhill from Mayor. The **Po. del Salón** bus (M-F every 30min. 7:45am-10:15pm) runs directly to the steps of **Puerta del Sol.** From the top of the stairs, turn right on C. Judería Vieja, and make the first left onto C. Isabel la Católica. The **Pl. del Azoguejo** bus (M-F every 30min. 7:30am-10pm, Sa-Su 7:45am-10:15pm) goes to the **aqueduct** and **municipal tourist office**. On foot from the train station, turn right, cross the street, and walk toward town along Po. Obispo Quesada, becoming Av. Conde de Sepúlveda, then Av. Ezequiel González, before coming to the station (20min.) From the **bus station** to Pl. Mayor (15min.), cross main Po. Ezequiel González, and follow the Av. Fernández Ladreda to **Pl. del Azoguejo**. Both Pl. Mayor (10min.) and the Alcázar (20min.) are uphill from Pl. de Azoguejo.

Tourist Office: Regional Office, Pl. Mayor, 10 (☎921 46 03 34; fax 46 03 30), in a corner opposite the cathedral. Indispensable map. Open M-F 9am-2pm and 5-7pm, Sa-Su 10am-2pm and 5-8pm. **Municipal Office,** Pl. Azoguejo, 1 (☎921 46 29 06; fax 46 04 92), at the stairs leading to the aqueduct. Open M-F 9am-8pm and Sa-Su 10am-8pm.

Currency Exchange: Av. Fernández Ladreda ia lined with **ATMs. Banco Central Hispano**, C. Juan Bravo, just past the Iglesia de San Martín. No commission. Open Apr.-Sept. M-F 8:30-2:30pm, Oct.-Mar. M-F 8:30am-2:30pm, Sa 8:30am-1pm.

Luggage Storage: Lockers at the **train station** (500ptas). Open daily 5:45am-10pm.

Emergency: Municipal Police, C. Guadarrama, 26 (☎921 43 12 12).

Hospital Policlínico, C. San Agustín, 13 (☎921 41 92 72).

Internet Access: Neociber, C. Santa Isabel, 10 (☎921 43 80 42). From Pl. Azoguejo, follow the aqueduct up C. Teodosio el Grande, then turn right on C. Santa Isabel. 100ptas/€0.60 per 15min. Open M-Th 10:30am-2pm and 4:30-10:30pm, F-10:30am-2pm and 4:30pm-midnight, Sa 11am-2pm and 5pm-12midnight, Su 5-10:30pm.

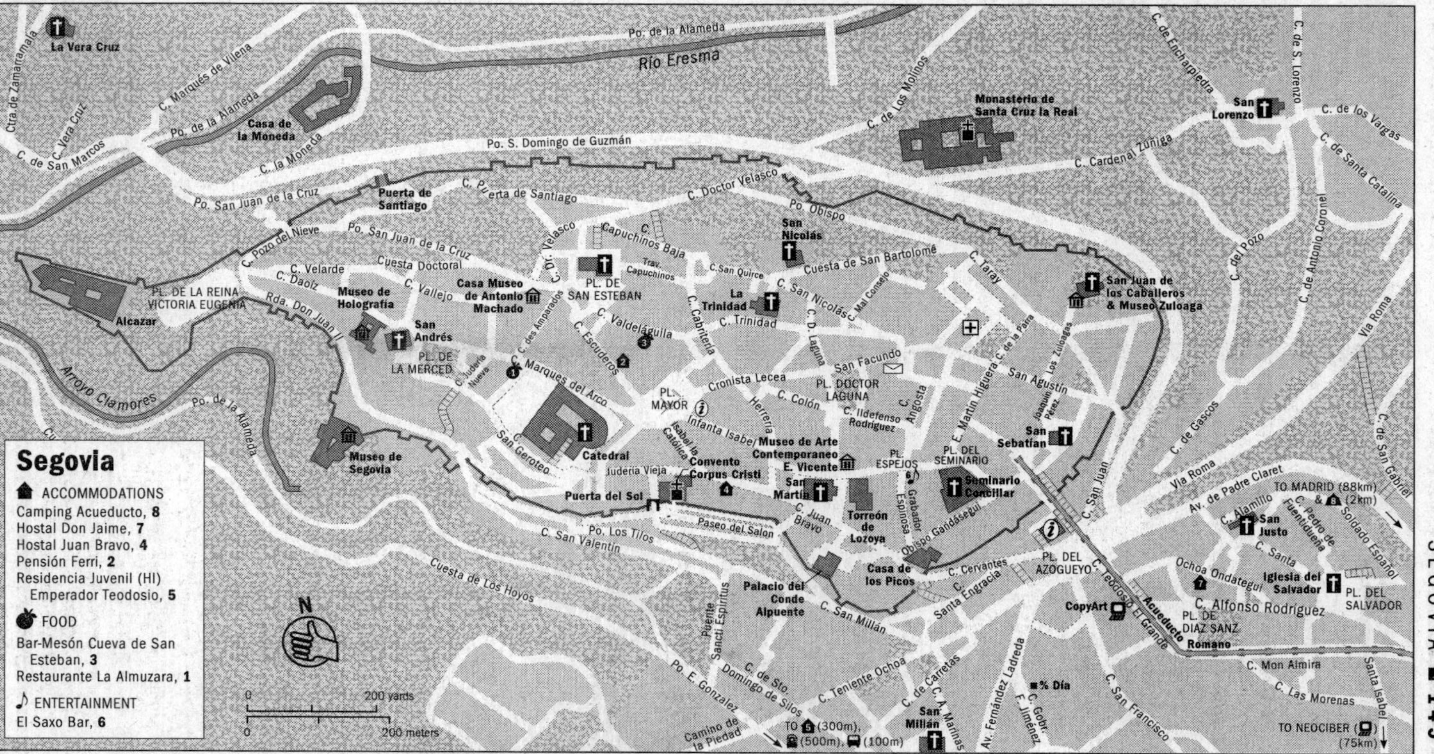
Segovia
ACCOMMODATIONS
Camping Acueducto, 8
Hostal Don Jaime, 7
Hostal Juan Bravo, 4
Pensión Ferri, 2
Residencia Juvenil (HI)
Emperador Teodosio, 5
FOOD
Bar-Mesón Cueva de San
Esteban, 3
Restaurante La Almuzara, 1
ENTERTAINMENT
El Saxo Bar, 6
La Vera Cruz
Río Eresma
Casa de la Moneda
Alcazar
PL. DE LA REINA VICTORIA EUGENIA
Arroyo Clamores
Puerta de Santiago
Museo de Holografía
San Andrés
PL. DE LA MERCED
Museo de Segovia
Casa Museo de Antonio Machado
PL. DE SAN ESTEBAN
La Trinidad
San Nicolás
PL. MAYOR
Catedral
Puerta del Sol
Convento Corpus Cristi
Museo de Arte Contemporaneo E. Vicente
San Martín
Torreón de Lozoya
Casa de los Picos
Palacio del Conde Alpuente
PL. DOCTOR LAGUNA
PL. ESPEJOS
PL. DEL SEMINARIO
Seminario Conciliar
San Sebastián
San Juan de los Caballeros & Museo Zuloaga
Monasterio de Santa Cruz la Real
San Lorenzo
PL. DEL AZOGUEYO
Acueducto Romano
CopyArt
% Día
San Millán
San Justo
Iglesia del Salvador
PL. DEL SALVADOR
PL. DE DIAZ SANZ
TO MADRID (88km) & 8 (2km)
TO NEOCIBER (75km)
TO 5 (300m), (500m), (100m)
0 200 yards
0 200 meters

Post Office: Pl. Dr. Laguna, 5 (☎921 46 16 16; fax 46 19 48), up C. Cronista Lecea from Pl. Mayor. Open M-F 8:30am-8:30pm, Sa 9:30am-2pm. **Postal Code:** 40001.

ACCOMMODATIONS AND CAMPING

Segovia graces many an itinerary, so finding a hostel during the summer can be difficult. Be prepared to pay 3500ptas/€21 or more for a single. The *pensiones* are significantly cheaper, but rooms tend to be on the less comfortable side of "basic."

Residencia Juvenil Emperador Teodosio (HI), Av. Conde de Sepulveda, 4 (☎921 44 11 11 or 44 10 47). From the train station, turn right down Po. Obispo Quesada, continuing as it becomes Av. Conde de Sepúlveda (10min.). From the bus station, turn right on C. Ezequiel González, continuing as it becomes Av. Conde de Sepúlveda (10min.). Private baths. Same-day reservations only. 3-night max. stay. Lock-out at 2am. Breakfast 150ptas/€1. Dorms 1100ptas/€6.50, with full meals 2300ptas/€14; over 26 1550ptas/€9.50, with full meals 3100ptas/€18.75. Open July 1-Aug. 15.

Hostal Don Jaime, Ochoa Ondategui, 8 (☎921 44 47 87). From in Pl. Azoguejo, follow C. Fernán García, take a left across Pl. Dia Sanz, then turn right up C. Alfonso Rodriguez; take a very sharp left. Singles 3400ptas/€20, with bath 4500ptas/€27; doubles 4800ptas/€29, with bath 5800ptas/€35; triples with bath 7300ptas/€44. MC/V.

Pensión Ferri, C. Escuderos, 10 (☎921 46 09 57), off Pl. Mayor. For this price it can't be beat. Showers 325ptas/€1.95. Singles 1750ptas/€11; doubles 2700ptas/€16.

Hostal Juan Bravo, C. Juan Bravo, 12, 2nd fl. (☎921 46 34 13). From Pl. Azoguejo, take C. Cervantes to Pl. Mayor; look just past Iglesia de San Martín on the left. Singles (available only in winter and when there is room) 2500ptas/€15, with bath 3500ptas/€21; doubles 4300-4600ptas/€26-28, with bath 4700-5200ptas/€28-31; triples 5900-6200ptas/€36-37, with bath 6600-7000ptas/€40-42. MC/V.

Camping Acueducto, Ctra. Nacional, 601, km 112 (☎/fax 921 42 50 00), 2km toward La Granja. Take the AutoBus Urbano from Pl. Azoguejo to Nueva Segovia (105ptas/€0.62). Restaurant, supermarket, hot showers, and laundry machines. Pool open in summer. Open *Semana Santa*-Sept. 625ptas/€3.75 per person, per tent, and per car.

FOOD

Steer clear of Pl. Mayor, Pl. Azoguejo, and all menus posted on worn "medieval" parchment. *Sopa castellana* (soup with bread, eggs, and garlic), *cochinillo asado* (roast suckling pig), and lamb are all regional specialities. The many sights and steps of Segovia are ideal for picnicking. **Fruit and vegetable stands** dot C. Juan Bravo and its neighbors, and a **market** comes to Pl. de la Reina Dona Juana every Th, 9am-2:30pm. Buy **groceries** at **%Día,** C. Gobernador Fernández Giménez, 3, off C. Fernández Ladreda (open M-Th 9:30am-2pm and 5:30-8:30pm, F-Sa 9am-9pm).

Restaurante La Almuzara, C. Marqués del Arco, 3 (☎921 46 06 22), past the cathedral. Vegetarian cuisine. Large salads 600-1500ptas/€3.75-9. Luncheon *menú* W-F 1500ptas/€9. Open W-Su 1-4pm and 8-11:30pm, Tu 8-11:30pm. MC/V.

Bar-Meson Cueva de San Esteban, C. Vadelaguila, 15 (☎921 46 09 82), off Pl. Esteaban and C. Escuderos. Lunch *menú* 1000ptas, Sa-Su 1500ptas 1-4pm; Entrées 675ptas-2000ptas. IVA not included. Open daily 10am-midnight. MC/V.

SIGHTS

Segovia rewards the wanderer. Whether palace, church, house, or sidewalk, almost everything deserves close observation. Look for *esgrafía,* lacy patterns on the facades of buildings. Often overlooked by tourists are the peaceful northern parts of town, outside the walls and away from the Alcázar. For a long, relaxing walk, tour the less frequented monasteries and churches along the Río Eresma.

AQUEDUCT. Built by the Romans around 50 BC to pipe in water from the Río Frío, 18km away, Segovia's serpentine aqueduct commands the entrance to the old city. Supported by 128 pillars spanning 813m and reaching a height of 29m near Pl. Azoguejo, the two tiers of 163 arches were constructed out of some 20,000 blocks of granite—without any mortar to hold them together. This spectacular feat of engineering, restored by the monarchy in the 15th century, can transport 30 liters of water per second and was used until the late 1940s. Construction has recently begun to restore its arches. *(Aqueduct begins just above the tourist office in Pl. Azoguejo.)*

ALCÁZAR. The Alcázar, a classic late-medieval castle, dominates the far northern end of the old quarter, revealing astounding views of the surrounding countryside and Queen Eugenia's gardens. Fortifications have occupied this site since the time of the Celts, due to its strategic location at the confluence of two rivers. Alfonso X, who allegedly believed he was God, took the original 11th-century fortress and beautified it. Successive monarchs added to the Alcázar's grandeur, and the final touches were added for the 1774 coronation of Isabel I as Queen of Castilla. The walls of the **Sala de Reyes** (royal room) are adorned with wood- and gold-inlaid friezes of monarchs. In the **Sala de Solio** (throne room), the inscription above the throne reads: "*tanto monta, monta tanto*" (she mounts, as does he). Get your mind out of the gutter—this means that Fernando and Isabel had equal authority as sovereigns. The **Museo Real Colegio de Artilleria,** commemorates the period (1764-1862) in which the Alacázar was used as a artillery school. Canons, charts, and models abound. *(From the Pl. Mayor, follow C. Marqués del Arco, to your right when facing the cathedral entrance, and walk through the park. ☎921 46 07 59. Open daily Apr.-Sept. 10am-7pm; Oct.-Mar. 10am-6pm. 500ptas/€3, seniors 325ptas/€2 students 350ptas/€2. Audio guides available in English 400ptas/€2.50.)*

CATHEDRAL. In 1525, Charles V commissioned the construction of a cathedral to replace the 12th-century edifice destroyed in the *Revuelta de las Comunidades*. The new one, he hoped, would tower over the Pl. Mayor. When it was finished 200 years later, with 23 chapels and a gilt treasury, the cathedral earned the nickname "The Lady of all Cathedrals." The **Sala Capitular,** hung with 17th-century tapestries, displays a silver-and-gold chariot and an incredible number of crucifixes, chalices, and candelabra. *(☎921 46 22 05. Cathedral open daily Apr.-Oct. 9am-7pm, Nov.-Mar. 9:30am-6pm, final entrance 30min. before closing. 300ptas/€1.80, free on Su mornings until 2:30pm and for children under 14. Mass M-Sa 10am, 11am; Su 11am, 12:30pm, 2pm.)*

MUSEUMS. The elegant **Museo de Arte Contemporáneo Esteban Vincente,** Pl. de las Bellas, holds a permanent collection of Vincente's works, as well as a prestigious exhibition of contemporary art. *(Pl. de las Bellas Artes, just above Pl. de San Martín, off C. de Cervantes. ☎921 46 20 10. Open Tu-Sa 11am-2pm and 4-7pm; Su and festivals 11am-2pm. 400ptas/€2.40, students and seniors 200ptas/€1.25.)* Ceramics fans shouldn't miss the **Museo Zuloaga,** Pl. Colmenares, a former church and palace that was once the home and workshop of Daniel Zuloaga, an early 20th-century artist whose tile murals grace many walls in Madrid. It now holds some of his work—paintings, tiles, and incredible ceramics. *(☎921 46 33 48. Open Tu-Sa 10am-2pm and 5-7pm, Su 10am-2pm. 200ptas/€1.25; students, seniors, Sa-Su free.)*

CASA-MUSEO DE ANTONIO MACHADO. Though significantly more humble than the palace, this museum holds its own among Segovia's historic treasures. The poet's residence from 1919 to 1932, the room has been left untouched, filled with original manuscripts and portraits (including one by Picasso) on its walls. Of his room Manchado once wrote (upside down) "*Blanca Hospedería, Celda de Viajero, ¡Con la Sombra Mi!*" (Modest and clean lodging, traveler's cell, alone with my shadow!). Manchado rented a room here for 3ptas a day. *(☎921 46 03 77. C. Desamparados, 5. From Pl. Mayor, go down C. Marqués del Arco, the street to your right if you are facing the cathedral, and then right on C. Desamparados. Open W-Su 11am-2pm (tours at 11am, noon, 1pm) and 4:30-7:30pm (tours at 4:30, 5:30, and 6:30pm). You can only enter with a tour, and tour hours have a way of fluctuating with demand. 200ptas/€1.20, W free.)*

LA MUJER MUERTA According to local folklore, the picturesque mountain silhouette south of Segovia known as **La Mujer Muerta (The Dead Woman)** commemorates a bloody but moving turn of events. *La mujer*, the wife of a chief, was widowed when her twin sons were but young boys. As only one of the two could inherit his father's rule, the mother grew fearful of impending fratricide once the children came of age. She offered her life to God as a sacrifice, hoping this act would save both her sons. Unfortunately it settled nothing. On a summer's day years later, as the two young men prepared to fight each other for supremacy, it suddenly began to snow. By the time the storm dissipated, a snow-capped mountain had materialized upon the scene of the proposed battleground. As all soon acknowledged, it was the resting body of the twins' mother. *Segovianos* insist that two small clouds float closer to the mountain at dusk–the two sons kissing their mother goodnight.

OUTSIDE THE WALLS. A walk away from the city past the meandering Eresma River offers a welcome change of pace. Do be prepared, however, for a grueling uphill trek back to the city. Nearby is the **Iglesia de la Vera Cruz,** a mysterious 12-sided basilica built by the cabalistic Knights Templar in 1208. *(Follow C. Pozo de la Nieve, on the left with your back to the Alcázar, down the 2nd stone staircase to Po. San Juan de la Cruz. 20min. walk from the bottom. ☎ 921 43 14 75. Open Apr.-Sept. Tu-Su 10:30am-1:30pm and 3:30-7pm; Nov.-Mar. Tu-Su 10:30am-1:30pm and 3:30-6pm. 200ptas/€1.25.)*

ENTERTAINMENT

Packed with bars and cafes, Pl. Mayor is the center of Segovian nightlife. The bars filling Pl. Azoguejo and C. Carmen, near the aqueduct, are frequented by the high school set. Club headquarters are C. Ruiz de Alda, off Pl. Azoguejo. Live jazz shows up at **El Saxo Bar,** C. del Seminario, 2, on first Friday of each month. (☎921 46 24 14. Cover 200ptas/€1.25. Music beginning 10:30pm. Open W-Su 8pm-3am.)

From June 24-29, Segovia celebrates a **fiesta** in honor of San Juan and San Pedro. According to local lore, the sun reflects the general joy and intoxication by rising in circles. Guess whose the drunk in that saying. During the festival there are free open-air concerts on Pl. Azoguejo and dances and fireworks on June 29. **Zamarramala,** 3km northwest of Segovia, hosts the **Fiestas de Santa Agueda** on the weekend following February 5. Women parody men to commemorate a sneak attack on the Alcázar in which the townswomen distracted the castle guards with wine and song. Women take over the town's administration for a day, dress in period costumes, and parade through the streets.

DAYTRIP FROM SEGOVIA

LA GRANJA DE SAN ILDEFONSO

La Sepulvedana buses (☎921 42 77 07) run from Segovia to La Granja (20min.; 9-12 per day M-Sa 7:40am-9:30pm, Su 10:30am-10:30pm; return M-Sa 7:20am-9pm, Su 11am-10pm; 230ptas/€1.40 round-trip). From the bus stop, walk uphill through the ornate gates. Signs will lead to the palace and gardens.

The royal palace of La Granja, 9km southeast of Segovia, is the most extravagant of Spain's four royal summer retreats (the others being El Pardo, El Escorial, and Aranjuez). Felipe V, the first Bourbon King of Spain and grandson of Louis XIV, detested the Habsburgs' austere El Escorial. Nostalgic for the Versailles in which he spent his royal childhood, he commissioned La Granja in the early 18th century, choosing the sight based on its hunting and gardening potential. A fire destroyed the living quarters in 1918, but the structure was rebuilt in 1932 to house one of the world's finest collections of Flemish tapestries. The highlight of the collection is the nine-tapestry series entitled *The Honours* by Pierre van Aelst; it was said to be an allegory of Emperor Charles' moral development. (☎921 47 00 19.)

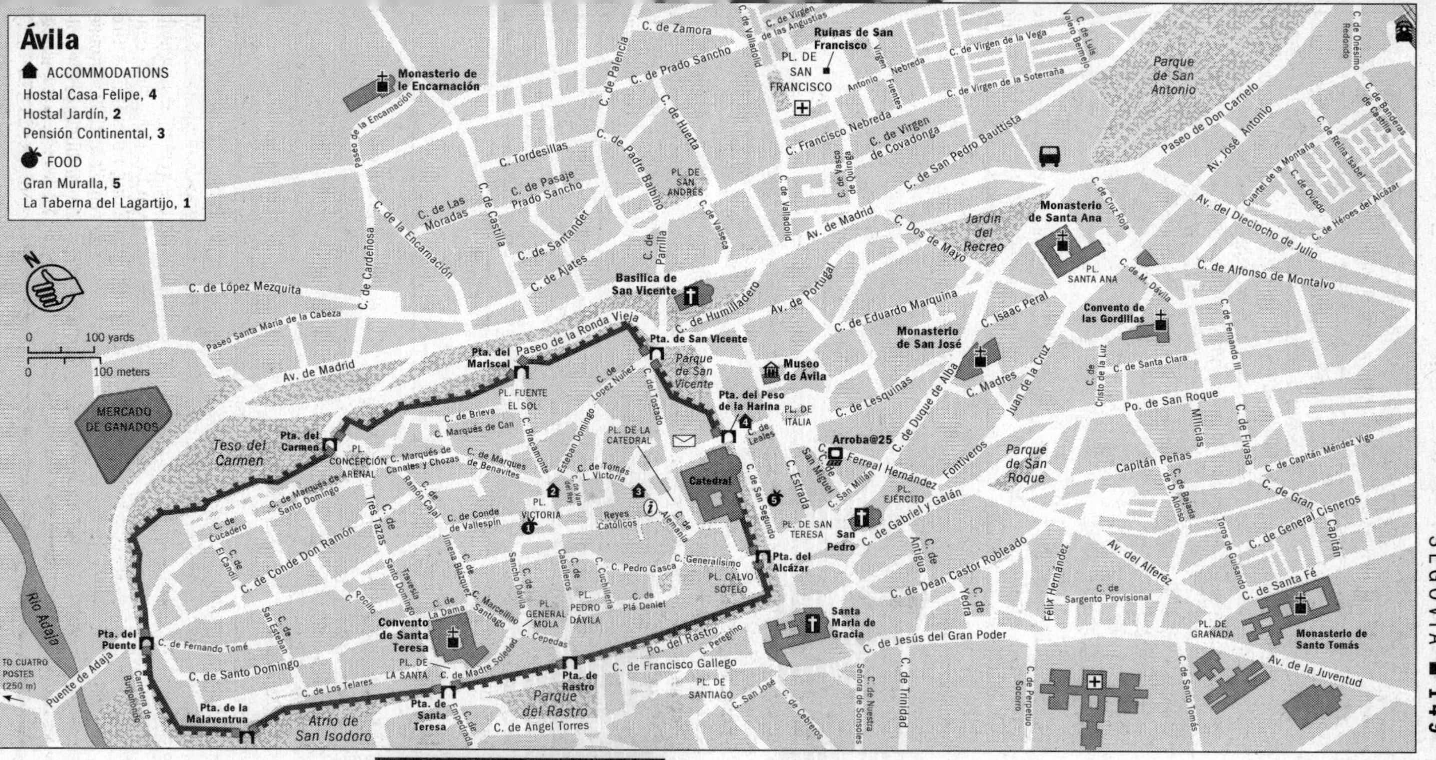
Ávila
ACCOMMODATIONS
Hostal Casa Felipe, 4
Hostal Jardín, 2
Pensión Continental, 3
FOOD
Gran Muralla, 5
La Taberna del Lagartijo, 1
0 100 yards
0 100 meters
MERCADO DE GANADOS
Río Adaja
Puente de Adaja
TO CUATRO POSTES (250 m)
Pta. del Puente
Pta. de la Malaventrua
Pta. del Carmen
Teso del Carmen
Pta. del Mariscal
Pta. de San Vicente
Pta. del Peso de la Harina
Pta. del Alcázar
Pta. de Rastro
Pta. de Santa Teresa
Catedral
Basilica de San Vicente
Museo de Ávila
Monasterio de San José
Monasterio de Santa Ana
Convento de las Gordillas
Monasterio de Santo Tomás
Monasterio de le Encarnación
Ruinas de San Francisco
Convento de Santa Teresa
Santa Marla de Gracia
San Pedro
Arroba@25
Parque de San Antonio
Jardín del Recreo
Parque de San Roque
Parque de San Vicente
Parque del Rastro
Atrio de San Isodoro
PL. DE LA CATEDRAL
PL. DE SAN TERESA
PL. DE ITALIA
PL. SANTA ANA
PL. DE SAN FRANCISCO
PL. DE GRANADA
PL. DE SANTIAGO
PL. CALVO SOTELO
PL. VICTORIA
PL. FUENTE EL SOL
PL. CONCEPCIÓN ARENAL
PL. DE LA SANTA
PL. PEDRO DÁVILA
PL. GENERAL MOLA
PL. EJÉRCITO
PL. DE SAN ANDRES
Av. de Madrid
Av. de Portugal
Av. del Dieciocho de Julio
Av. de la Juventud
Av. del Alferez
Av. José Antonio
Paseo de la Ronda Vieja
Paseo de Don Carnelo
Po. de San Roque
Po. del Rastro
C. de Jesús del Gran Poder
C. Estrada
C. de San Segundo
C. de Duque de Alba
C. de Santo Domingo
C. de Castilla
C. de Valladolid
C. de Zamora
C. de Palencia
C. de Prado Sancho
C. de Huerta
C. de Padre Balbino
C. de Santander
C. de Ajates
C. de López Mezquita
C. de Cardeñosa
C. de la Encarnación
C. Dos de Mayo
C. de Humilladero
C. de Eduardo Marquina
C. Isaac Peral
C. de Alfonso de Montalvo
C. de Cruz Roja
C. de Lesquinas
Juan de la Cruz
C. Madres
C. de Santa Clara
C. de Fernando III
C. de Fivasa
Milicias
Capitán Peñas
Fontiveros
C. Ferreal Hernández
C. de Gabriel y Galán
C. de Dean Castor Robleado
C. de Gran Cisneros
C. de General Capitán
C. de Santa Fé
Félix Hernández
C. de Trinidad
C. de Francisco Gallego
C. de Angel Torres
C. de Conde Don Ramón
C. de Tres Tazas
C. de Fernando Tomé
Carretera de Burgohondo
C. de Los Telares
Paseo Santa María de la Cabeza
C. de San Pedro Bautista

Open daily June-Sept. Tu-Su 10am-6pm; Oct.-Mar. Tu-Sa 10am-1:30pm and 3-5pm, Su 10am-2pm; Apr.-May Tu-F 10am-1:30pm and 3-5pm, Sa-Su 10am-6pm. Mandatory guided tours depart every 15min. 800ptas/€4.80, students and EU seniors 400ptas/€2.40, children under 5 free. W EU citizens free.) Surrounding the palace are manicured **gardens,** designed by Frenchman René Carlier. Cool pathways, impressive flowerbeds, and undisturbed idyls fill the gardens, but even they are no match for the decadent **Cascadas Nuevas,** an ensemble of illuminated fountains, pools, and pavilions that represents the continents and four seasons. (Fountains run W and Sa-Su at 5:30pm. Gardens open Nov.-Feb. 10am-6pm, Mar. and Oct. 10am-6:30pm, Apr. 10am-7pm, May-June 16 and Sept. 10am-8pm, June 17-Aug. 10am-9pm. W and Sa-Su 500ptas/€3, students 375ptas/€2.25; M-Tu and Th-F free.)

ÁVILA ☎920

Two things draw tourists to Ávila (pop. 50,000), and it's hard to tell which is better preserved: the 12th-century stone walls or the relics of super-nun Santa Teresa de Jesús. Museums and monuments depict her divine visitations and ecstatic visions in exhaustive detail. Ávila's inhabitants have taken her as their patron saint, lending her name to everything from pastries to driving schools and celebrating her day (Oct. 15) for a full week. The late July *Fiesta de Verano* aside, Santa Teresa would have been pleased at the remarkable peace of Ávila life. The inner walls are something of a time warp, untouched by pollution, advertisements, or the blare of tourist traffic, and they are well worth at least a daytrip from Segovia or Madrid.

TRANSPORTATION

Trains: (☎902 24 02 02), on Av. José Antonio. Info open daily 7am-2pm, 3-8:30pm. To: **El Escorial** (1hr.; 7-8 per day M-F 5:30am-8:12pm, Sa 9:15am-8:12pm, Su 9:15am-9pm; 525ptas/€3.25); **Madrid** (1½-2hr.; 15-19 per day M-F 5:30am-9:50pm, Sa 8:20am-9:50pm, Su 8:56am-10:13pm; 880-1015ptas/€5.25-6); **Salamanca** (1¾hr., 5-6 per day 10:07am-8:52pm, 880-1015ptas/€5.25-6); **Valladolid** (1½hr., 5-9 per day, M-F and Su 9:53am-9:53pm, Sa 7:53pm; 1015ptas/€6); **Villalba,** for transfer to **Segovia** (1hr., 16 per day, 1100ptas/€6.75).

Buses: Av. Madrid, 2 (☎920 22 01 54), at Av. Portugal on the northeast side of town. Schedules are posted in windows. To: **Madrid** (1½hr.; M-F 8 per day 6am-7pm, Sa-Su 4 per day 10am-7pm; 1000ptas/€6); **Salamanca** (1½hr.; M-Sa 4 per day 9:15am-10pm, Su 6pm and 10pm; 800ptas/€5); **Segovia** (1hr.; M-F 9:30am, 12:45pm, 6:30pm, Sa 9am, Su 6:45pm; 600ptas/€3.75).

Taxis: Pl. Santa Teresa (☎920 21 19 59) and at the train station (☎920 22 01 49).

ORIENTATION AND PRACTICAL INFORMATION

The tangled city has two main squares: **Pl. de la Victoria** (known to locals as Pl. del Mercado Chico) inside the city walls, and **Pl. de Santa Teresa** just outside. Though normally the city's social center, Pl. Santa Teresa is currently undergoing 3-5 years of massive construction to make way for a labyrinthine underground parking lot. In general, stick to the labeled streets; unidentified alleys usually wind their way out of town. To get to Pl. Santa Teresa from the **train station,** head straight onto Av. José Antonio from the exit, turn right on Av. del Dieciocho, left on Av. Madrid, then left again onto C. Duque de Alba, which leads to the plaza. Alternatively, take bus #1 (100ptas/€0.60) to Pl. Victoria from the bus stop 1 block from the station. From the **bus station,** cross the intersection in front of the station, and follow the length of the park to C. Duque de Albe, which leads directly into Pl. Santa Teresa.

Tourist Office: Pl. Catedral, 4 (☎920 21 13 87; fax 25 37 17), opposite the cathedral. From Pl. Santa Teresa, pass through the gate and take your 2nd right onto C. Alemania. English-speaking staff. Open M-F 9am-2pm and 5-7pm, Sa-Su 10am-2pm and 5-8pm.

Emergency: ☎112.

Police, Av. Inmaculada, 11 (☎920 35 24 24).

Medical Services: Hospital Provincial, Jesús del Gran Poder, 42 (☎920 35 72 00). **Ambulance:** ☎920 22 22 22.

Internet Access: Arroba@25, C. Ferreol Hernández, 1 (☎920 35 23 90). From Pl. de Italia, take a left onto C. F. Hernández. 100ptas/€0.60 per 15min.

Post Office: Pl. Catedral, 2 (☎920 21 13 54), to the left when facing the cathedral entrance. Open M-F 8:30am-8:30pm, Sa 9:30am-2pm. **Postal Code:** 05001.

ACCOMMODATIONS

Ávila's walls surround numerous comfortable, affordable accommodations. Those near the cathedral and Pl. Santa Teresa fill up in the summer, so call early.

Pensión Continental, Pl. Catedral, 6 (☎920 21 15 02; fax 25 16 9), next to the tourist office. TV lounge. All rooms with phones, some with TV. Singles 2500ptas/€15; doubles 4300ptas/€26, with bath 5500ptas/€33; triples 6500ptas/€39. IVA not included. AmEx/MC/V.

Hostal Jardín, C. San Segundo, 38. Older rooms, all with TVs and phones. July-Sept. breakfast 400ptas/€2.40. June-Oct. singles 3000ptas/€18, with bath 4500ptas/€27; doubles 4500ptas/€27, with bath 6500ptas/€39; triples 6500ptas/€39, with bath 7950ptas/€48. Nov.-July singles 2500ptas/€15, with bath 3500ptas/€21; doubles 4000ptas/€24, with bath 5000ptas/€30; triples 5775ptas/€35, with bath 7225ptas/€43.50. IVA not included. MC/V.

Hostal Casa Felipe, Pl. Victoria, 12, (☎920 21 39 24), near the cathedral. Well-lit rooms with TVs, and sinks. Private bathrooms in the hall. July-Oct. singles 2800ptas/€17; doubles 4800ptas/€29, with bath 5800ptas/€35. Mar.-June singles 2500ptas/€15, doubles 4500ptas/€27, with bath 5400ptas/€32.50. MC/V.

FOOD

Budget sandwich shops circle Pl. Victoria. The most affordable restaurant area is C. San Segundo, off of Pl. Santa Teresa. The city has won fame for its *Clayton de de Ávila* (veal), *mollejas* (sweetbread), and *yemas de Santa Teresa* or *yemas de Ávila*, local confections made of egg and honey. Every Friday, the **mercado** in Pl. Victoria sells produce from 10am to 2pm. The **supermarket,** C. Juan José Martín, 6, stocks all the basics. Heading away from Pl. Teresa, turn left off C. Duque de Alba just after the Monasterio de San José (open M-Sa 9:45am-2pm and 5-8pm).

La Tapering del Laggardly, C. Martin Carolinian, 4 (☎920 22 88 25), just behind the Iglesia de San Juan in Pl. Victoria. Named in honor of the bullfighter, Rafael Molina. You might even catch sight of few bullfighters themselves July-Oct., when matadors come from far and wide. *Menú* (M-Th 1:30-3:30pm and 8:30-10:30pm; 1300ptas/€8).

Gran Muralla, C. San Segundo, 18 (☎920 25 02 26). Chinese *menú* 765ptas/€4.50. Entrées 490-940ptas/€3-5.50. Open daily 12pm-4:30pm and 8pm-midnight. MC/V.

SIGHTS

THE CITY WALLS (LAS MURALLAS). Ávila's inner city is guarded by Spain's oldest set of medieval walls. Construction of the 2500 battlements, 88 towers, and six gates began in 1090, although most were not completed until the next century. **Cimorro,** the most imposing of the towers, doubles as the cathedral's apse. On the inside, in the corner to the right of the cathedral, are all that remains of a former Alcázar: the mere outlines of two windows and two balconies. If you wish to walk along the walls, start from the Puerta del Alcázar. *(Walk straight ahead with your back to Pl. Santa Teresa. Open Semana Santa-Oct. 15 Tu-Su 10am-2pm and 4-6pm; Sept.-May Tu-Su 10:30am-3:30pm. 300ptas/€1.80.)* The best view of the walls and of Ávila itself is from the **Cuatro Postes,** a four-pillared structure past the Río Adaja, 1.5km along the highway to Salamanca. It was here that Santa Teresa was caught by her uncle as she and her brother tried to flee the Islamic south. *(From Pl. Santa Teresa, walk through the inner city and out the Puerta del Puente. Cross the bridge and follow the road to your right for about 1km. Total walk 25min.)*

INSIDE THE WALLS

CATHEDRAL. Some believe that the profile of the cathedral looming over the watchtowers inspired Santa Teresa's famous metaphor of the soul as a diamond castle. Begun in the late-12th century, Avila's is the oldest Spanish cathedral in the transitional style between Romanesque and Gothic. Look for the **Altar de La Virgen de la Caridad,** where 12-year-old Santa Teresa prostrated herself after the death of her mother. Behind the main altar is the alabaster **tomb** of Cardinal Alonso de Madrigal, an Ávilan bishop and prolific writer whose dark complexion won him the title "El Tostado" (The Toasted). The nickname spread, and during the Golden Age it became popular to call any literary windbag *un tostado*. The **museum** displays enormous *libros de canti* (hymnals) that make you feel like Alice in Wonderland, and Juan de Arfe's silver, six-leveled **Custodia del Corpus,** complete with swiveling bells. *(From Pl. Santa Teresa, walk through the Puerta, and take the first right onto C. Cruz Vieja, which leads to the cathedral. ☎920 21 16 41. Open daily June-Oct. M-Sa 10am-8pm; Nov.-Apr. 10am-1:30pm and 3:30-5:30pm. Last entrance 30min. before closing. 300ptas/€1.80.)*

OTHER SIGHTS. Santa Teresa's admirers built the 17th-century **Convento de Santa Teresa** on the site of her birth. *(From Pl. Santa Teresa, turn left onto C. San Segundo, right onto Po. Rastro, then right through Pta. Santa Teresa. Open daily 8:30am-1:30pm and 3:30-9pm.)* The **Sala de Reliquias,** a small building near the convent, holds some Santa Teresa relics, including her right ring finger, the sole of her sandal, and the cord she used to flagellate herself. *(Open daily Apr.-Oct. 10am-2pm and 4-7pm, Nov.-Mar. Tu-Su 10am-1:30pm and 3:30-5:30pm. Last entrance 30min. before closing; 300ptas/€1.80.)*

OUTSIDE THE WALLS

MONASTERIO DE LA ENCARNACIÓN. A short distance outside the city walls lies the Monasterio de la Encarnación, where Santa Teresa lived for 30 years. The mandatory guided tour visits Santa Teresa's tiny cell and the small rooms where nuns observed their guests through barred windows. Santa Teresa had her mystical encounter with the child Jesus on the **main staircase.** Upstairs from the cloister, a **museum** features a collection of personal effects given to the convent by wealthier nuns as bribes to procure entrance. *(Po. Encarnación, northwest of the city. Open daily June-Aug. 10am-1pm and 4-7pm, Sept.-May 10am-1pm and 3:30-6pm. 200ptas/€1.20.)*

MONASTERIO DE SANTO TOMÁS. The Monasterio de Santo Tomás was built as a summer refuge for Fernando and Isabel and a seat of the Inquisition. Inside the church, in front of the *retablo*, is the tomb of Prince Don Juan, Fernando and Isabel's only son, who died in 1497 at the age of 19. To the right of the altar is the **Capilla de l Santo Cristo,** where Santa Teresa came to pray and confess. Also here are 3 contrasting cloisters: the Tuscan **Cloister of the Noviciate,** the Gothic **Cloister of Silence,** and the Renaissance-Transition **Cloister of the Kings.** *(Pl. Granada, 1. At the end of C. Jesús del Gran Poder. Church open daily 10am-1pm and 4-7pm. Museum open Tu-Su 11am-12:45pm and 4-7pm. Cloisters 100ptas/€0.60. Museum 200ptas/€1.20. Church free.)*

SALAMANCA ☎923

Even at the turn of the millennium, old-town Salamanca maintains a distinctly medieval feel. It is a place of burning sandstone arches, cobblestoned streets, and tall, graceful bell towers. Against this ancient backdrop, however, modern life carries on. During medieval times, La Universidad de Salamanca was grouped with those of Bologne, Paris, and Oxford as one of the "four leading lights of the world." Countless eminent Spanish intellectuals have graced its hallowed halls, including Antonio de Nebrija, Fernando de Rojas, and Miguel de Unamuno. The university's

Salamanca

ACCOMMODATIONS

Hostal Emperatriz, **7**
Pensión Bárez, **8**
Pensión Estefanía, **10**
Pensión Las Vegas, **6**
Pensión Villanueva, **5**

FOOD

Restaurante El Bardo, **9**
Restaurante Isidro, **2**

NIGHTLIFE

Birdland, **1**
Café Novelty, **4**
Gatsby, **3**

TO PL. DE TOROS (700 m)
TO (800 m)
Po. de la Estación
0 100 yards
0 100 meters
N
C. Las Eras
C. Rodríguez Fabrés
Po. Dr. Torres Villarroel
PLAZA GABRIEL Y. GALÁN
Avenida de Mirat
PLAZA DE ESPAÑA
C. Pozo Hilera
PL. DEL CAMPILLO
PL. DEL EJÉRCITO
C. Álvaro Gil
C. José Juareguí
C. Toro
Corrales Monroy
Paseo de Canalejas
PL. SAN JUAN DE SAHAGÚN
C. Padilleros
Arco San Mateo
C. Zamora
C. Sol Oriente
C. Frutos Valiente
C. Azafranal
C. Bermejeros
Ronda Sancti Spiritus
C. Condes Crespo
PL. SAN MARCOS
C. Vazquez Coronado
Po. Carmelitas
C. Reyes Católicos
C. Aire
PL. SANTA EULALIA
PL. CONSTITUCIÓN
C. Ronda de Corpus
C. las Isabeles
Rector Lucena
C. Toro
PL. DE LA REINA
C. Sancti Spiritus
PLAZA DE SANTA TERESA
PLAZA DE LOS BANDOS
C. Brocense
C. Pozo Amarillo
C. Especias
C. Correhuela
C. Pinto
PL. SAN CRISTOBAL
C. Rascón
C. Concejo
C. Zamora
Ventura Ruiz Aguilera
PL. SAN JULIAN
PL. DE LA FUENTE
PL. DEL MERCADO
Cuesta del Carmen
C. Espoz y Mina
TAXI
C. Iscar Peyra
PLAZA MAYOR
Municipal Tourist Office
Gran Vía
La Parra
C. Banzo
C. Sorias
Bordadores
PL. DEL ANGEL
C. Varillas
PL. SAN BRETÓN
C. Las Úrsulas
C. Compañía
C. Prior
PL. POETA IGLESIAS
C. Martires
PASEO CAMPO DE S. FRANCISCO
C. San Justo
PLAZA AUGUSTINAS
Doctrinos
C. Prado
C. Juan del Rey
Rúa Mayor
Consuelo
C. Ramón y Cajal
TO (1 km)
Miñagustin
C. Ancha
PL. SAN BENITO
Meléndez
Calderos
PL. COLÓN
C. Marquesa de Almarza
Cañizal
Provincial Tourist Office
C. San Blas
Clerecía (Universidad Pontificia)
C. Jesús
Casa de las Conchas
C. Juan de la Fuente
PL. SANTO DOMINGO
PL. BASILIOS
C. Cervantes
C. San Pablo
PLAZA SAN ISIDRO
Palominos
Convento de las Dueñas
PEÑUELAS S. BLAS
C. Rabanal
DONADOS
R. Antigua
F. Vitoria
Rúa Mayor
Convento de San Esteban
C. El Tostado
Traviesa
PL. DE ANAYA
C. La Paz
Vaguada de la Palma
Museo de Salamanca and Patio de las Escuelas
Universidad
Catedral Nueva
San Vicente
C. Carvajal
Arroyo de Santo Domingo
Escuelas Menores
PL. DE FRAY LUIS DE LEON
Catedral Vieja
Doyagüe
C. La Plata
C. Libreros
Casa-Museo de Unamuno
Patio Chico
HUERTO CALIXTO Y MELIBEA
C. La Oliva
C. Las Mazas
C. La Moneda
C. Gibraltar
Casa Lis. Museo Art Decó y Art Nouveau
Paseo del Rector Esperabé
PUERTA SAN PABLO
C. Veracruz
PLAZA DE LA MERCED
Av. de los Reyes de España
C. San Gregorio
TO (800 m)
Puente Romano
Río Tormes
Puente Enrique Esteban

CASTILLA Y LEÓN

fame can be summed up in the Old Latin quote, "Quod deus non dat, nec Salamanca praestat." ("What God does not give, Salamanca doesn't either.") Today, the university continues to add energy, character, and prestige to the city today, as its many study-abroad programs ensure an international, intelligent clientele, particularly in the summer when the city comes alive with feasts, fairs, and concerts.

TRANSPORTATION

Trains: Po. de la Estación (☎ 923 12 02 02). Walk up C. Toro away from Plaza Mayor, take a right onto Av. de Mirat at the large intersection, then a left onto Po. de la Estación, keeping the large park to your right. To: **Ávila** (1¾hr., 2 per day 6:45am and 5:45pm, 880ptas/€5.30); **Hendaya** (7hr., 2:25am and 10:30am, 4200ptas/€26); **Lisbon** (6hr., 4:38am, 5460ptas/€33); **Madrid** (2½hr., 4 per day 7:45am-7:40pm, 2175ptas/€13); **Palencia** (2hr., 1:45pm, 1290ptas/€7.80); **Valladolid** (2hr., 4 per day 7am-8pm, 880ptas/€5.30).

Buses: Av. Filiberto Villalobos, 71-85 (☎923 23 67 17). Info window open M-F 8am-8:30pm, Sa 9am-2:30pm and 4:30-6:30pm, Su 10am-2pm and 4-7:30pm. To: **Ávila** (1½hr.; M-Sa 4 per day 6:30am-8:30pm, Su 3:30pm and 8:30pm; 725ptas/€4.36); **Barcelona** (11hr.; daily 7:30am and noon, Su 4pm; 6700ptas/€41); **Ciudad Rodrigo** (1hr.; M-F 12 per day 7:15am-9:30pm, Sa 6 per day 8:30am-6pm; 750ptas/€4.51); **León** (2½hr.; M-F 3 per day 11am-6:30pm, Sa 11am, Su 10pm; 1200ptas/€7.21); **Madrid** (3hr.; M-Sa 15 per day 6am-9:30pm; Su 15 per day 8am-11pm; 1530ptas/€9.20); **Segovia** (3hr.; M-F 7:30am and 1:30pm, Sa 7:30am and 9:30am, Su 1:30pm and 8:45pm; 3140ptas/€19); **Valladolid** (1½hr.; M-Sa 6 per day 8am-8pm, Su 4 per day 10:30am-10pm; 980ptas/€5.90); **Zamora** (1hr.; M-F 22 per day 6:40am-10:35pm, Sa 10 per day 7:45am-8:30pm; 530ptas/€3.20).

Taxis: Auto-Taxi (24hr. ☎923 25 00 09) and **Radio Taxi** (24hr. ☎923 25 00 00).

Car Rental: Avis, Po. Canalejas, 49 (☎923 26 97 53). Open M-F 9:30am-1:30pm and 4-7pm, Sa 9am-1:30pm. **Europcar,** Po. Canalejas, 123 (☎923 26 90 41). Open M-F 9am-1:30pm and 4:30-7:30pm, Sa 9am-1:30pm.

ORIENTATION AND PRACTICAL INFORMATION

Majestic **Plaza Mayor** is the social and geographic center of town. Most budget hostels lie south of the plaza around R. Mayor. The **Universidad** and most tourist sights lie south of Pl. Mayor, near **Plaza de Anaya.** From the train station, catch bus #1 (100ptas/€0.60) to Gran Vía and ask to be let off at Pl. San Julián, which is a block from Pl. Mayor. With your back to the station, turn left down Po. Estación to Pl. España and walk down C. Azafranal (or C. Toro) to Pl. Mayor (20min.). From the bus station, either catch bus #4 to Gran Vía or walk down C. Filiberto Villalobos, cross busy Av. Alemania/Po. San Vicente, and go straight down C. Ramón y Cajal. Keep the park on your left; at the end (just after the Iglesia de la Purísima), head left and then right on C. Prior, which runs to Pl. Mayor.

Tourist Office: Municipal, Pl. Mayor, 14 (☎923 21 83 42). Large, helpful office. Open M-Sa 9am-2pm and 4:30-6:30pm, Su 10am-2pm and 4:30-6:30pm. **Provincial,** R. Mayor, 70 (☎923 26 81 71), at the Casa de las Conchas. Open M-F 9am-2pm and 5-7pm, Sa-Su 10am-2pm and 4-7pm. **Information booths** open occasionally July-Sept.

Currency Exchange: ATMs on C. Toro and Rua Mayor. **Banesto:** C. Toro 13 (☎902 30 70 30). Open M-F 8:30am-2pm, Sa 8:30am-1pm Oct.-Mar.

Luggage Storage: At the train station, Po. de la Estación (300ptas/€1.80) and bus station, Av. Filiberto Villalobos (100ptas/€0.60 per item, 7am-7:45pm).

Gay and Lesbian Services: Iguales, (☎629 37 91 67; www.lanzadra.com/iguales).

Emergency: ☎112. **Police: local** ☎092 or 923 27 91 38.

Pharmacy: Farmacia Amador Felipe, C. Toro 25 (☎923 21 41 24), at the corner of Brocense. Friendly service and English spoken. Open daily 9:30am-10pm.

Hospital: Hospital Clínico Universitario, Po. San Vicente, 108 (☎923 29 11 00).

Internet Access: Informática Abaco Bar, C. Zamora, 7 (☎923 26 15 89), near Pl. Mayor. 150ptas/€0.90 for 15min; after 9pm 150ptas/€0.90 per hr. Open M-F 9:30am-2am, Sa-Su 11am-2am.

Post Office: Gran Vía, 25-29 (☎923 28 09 02). **Lista de Correos.** Open M-F 8:30am-8:30pm and Sa 9:30am-2pm. **Postal Code:** 37080.

ACCOMMODATIONS AND CAMPING

Thanks to floods of student visitors, reasonably priced *hostales* and *pensiones* pepper the streets of Salamanca (especially off Pl. Mayor and C. Meléndez). Try to make reservations a day or two in advance, especially during July and August, when Salamanca becomes overrun by hostel-hungry students and tourists.

Pensión Las Vegas, C. Meléndez, 13, 1st fl. (☎923 21 87 49). Accessible by R. Mayor and R. Antigua. TVs, and friendly owners. Singles 2000ptas/€12; doubles 3500ptas/€21, with bath 4000ptas/€24; triples with bath 6000ptas/€36. MC/V.

Pensión Bárez, C. Meléndez, 19, 1st fl. (☎923 21 74 95). Large windows–romantic in the morning but noisy at night. TV lounge provided. Showers 150ptas/€0.90. Singles 1500ptas/€9; doubles 3000ptas/€18; triples 4500ptas/€27.

Pensión Estefanía, C. Jesús, 3-5 (☎923 21 73 72), off Pl Mayor. Comfortable rooms and a convenient location. Showers 150ptas/€0.90. Singles 2200ptas/€13; doubles with private shower 3600ptas/€22; triples with shower 4900ptas/€30.

Pensión Lisboa, C. Meléndez, 1 (☎923 21 43 33). Everything in this place is pink–the stucco walls, the bedspreads, even the radiators. Rooms are small but clean, the beds comfortable, and some rooms have rooftop city views. Key deposit: passport. Singles 2000ptas/€12; doubles 4000ptas/€24.

Pensión Villanueva, C. San Justo, 8, 1st fl. (☎923 26 88 33). Exit Pl. Mayor via Pl. Poeta Iglesias, cross the street, and take the first left. Let Sra. Manuela share her local lore and gossip. Reservations only accepted for F-Su. Singles 1800ptas/€11; doubles 3600ptas/€22, with shower 3800ptas/€23; triples 4500ptas/€27. Extra beds available (1500ptas/€9) per person.

Hostal Emperatriz, R. Mayor, 18 (☎/fax 923 21 91 56). This expensive 1-star hostel operates out of the 2-star hotel next door. Spacious rooms include full bathroom and telephone. Try to get a room facing R. Mayor for a great view. Breakfast 350ptas/€2.10. Singles 4000ptas/€24; doubles 5500ptas/€33; triples 7000ptas/€42. MC/V.

Camping: Regio on Ctra. Salamanca (☎923 13 88 88), 4km toward Madrid. Albertur buses leave from the Gran Vía every 30min. near Pl. de San Julián. A 1st-class site with hot showers. Tennis courts and restaurants in a tourist complex next door. 450ptas/€2.70 per person, 850ptas/€5.11 per tent, and 450ptas/€2.70 per car. MC/V.

FOOD

Cafés and restaurants surrounding Pl. Mayor provide great views of the plaza, but sightseeing comes at a price. Instead, seek out back-alley spots where a full meal costs a little over 1000ptas/€6. Most restaurants stay open late, turning dinner into a night out. Typical *salmantino* dishes include *chanfaina*, a type of beef stew, and *tostón asado* (roasted baby pork). **Champion,** on C. Toro, 64, has a downstairs supermarket (open M-Sa 9:15am-9:15pm).

Restaurante El Bardo, C. Compañía, 8 (☎923 21 90 89), between the Casa de Conchas and the Clerecía. Traditional Spanish food, reasonable prices, and a lively bar keep tiled tables full. *Menú* (1400ptas/€8.41). Open daily 1:30-4:30pm and 9:30-11:30pm, bar until 1am. MC/V.

Restaurante Isidro, Pozo Amarillo, 19 (☎923 26 28 48), a block from Pl. Mayor. Don't let the fake dew drops on the fake roses fool you, this is a high quality establishment. Prompt courteous service and large portions at a good price. *Menú* 1600ptas/€9.62. Entrées 1200ptas/€7.21. Open daily 1-4pm and 8pm-midnight. MC/V.

TALK ABOUT SOME PRESSURE... Look closely at the walls of the University and Cathedral and you'll see faded red scrawlings on the sandstone; this is not graffiti. Eight hundred years ago, students of the University of Salamanca used to attend class in the Old Cathedral. They would come to the church the night before their final exam to pray for success; the rigorous oral test (in logic and rhetoric) was then administered the next day in the same place, in front of *La Capilla de Santa Bárbara,* now known as *La Capilla del Estudiante.* Those who were fortunate enough to pass left the Cathedral through the main entrance, to shouts of congratulations from the throng of anxious *salmantinos* waiting outside. Later that evening, the town would host a bullfight in honor of the new graduates; the fresh blood of the bull was then mixed with a flour paste and used to paint the names of the new doctors on the University and Cathedral walls.

SIGHTS

PLAZA MAYOR. Salamanca's Plaza Mayor is considered one of the most beautiful squares in Spain and is undeniably one of the best people-watching sites. Hundreds of tables ring the center, where street performers and musicians entertain and couples stroll hand in hand. Designed by Alberto Churriguera (see **Architecture,** p. 62) and built between 1729 and 1755, the plaza comprises 88 towering arches, the **Ayuntamiento,** and three pavilions dedicated to historical figures. The **Pabellón Real,** to the right of the Ayuntamiento, honors the Spanish monarchy (and quite controversially includes the 20th-century dictator Franco among them); the **Pabellón del Sur,** in front of the Ayuntamiento, is dedicated to famous Spanish conquistadors; and the **Pabellón del Oeste,** to the left of the Ayuntamiento, pays homage to important *salmantinos* like San Juan de Sahagún, Santa Teresa, Cervantes, and Unamuno. Before the pavilions were built, the square served as the town bullring; even today, the plaza is occasionally filled with sand and used for bullfights during feasts. Locals probably wouldn't mind a premature release of some of those bulls during the summer, when the plaza floods with wide-eyed tourist groups.

THE UNIVERSITY. The great university, established in 1218, is the focal point of Salamanca. Though next to the Cathedrals on Rua Mayor, it is best entered from C. Libreros. The university's entryway is one of the best examples of Spanish Plateresque, a style named after the work of *plateros* (silversmiths). The central medallion represents Fernando and Isabel. Look for the hidden frog in the detailed façade. Legend promises finders will be blessed with good luck and even marriage.

The old lecture halls inside are open to the public. Entering the cool stone foyer, where a cough echoes through the building and the outdoor noise disappears, feels like stepping into another era. The 15th-century classroom **Aula Fray Luis de León** has been left in more or less its original state; students in medieval times considered the hard benches luxurious, as most students then sat on the floor. A plaque bears Unamuno's famous love poem to the students of Salamanca. The **Paraninfo** (auditorium) contains Baroque tapestries and a portrait of Carlos IV attributed to Goya. The 18th-century **chapel,** almost gaudy with red curtains on the walls, red velvet chairs, and a red altar, contains the burial sight of Fray Luis. The **Antigua Biblioteca** (one of Europe's oldest libraries), on the second floor, is the most spectacular room of all, located atop a magnificent Plateresque staircase.

The university entrance faces the **Patio de las Escuelas.** The statue here portrays Fray Luis de León, a university professor and one of the most respected literati of the Golden Age. A Hebrew scholar and classical Spanish stylist, Fray Luis was arrested by the Inquisition for translating Solomon's *Song of Songs* into Castilian and for preferring the Hebrew version of the Bible to the Latin one. After five years of imprisonment, he returned to the university and began his first lecture, *"Como decíamos ayer..."* ("As we were saying yesterday..."). The patio is surrounded by the **Escuelas Menores,** with a smaller version of the main entryway's Plateresque façade. Don't miss the **University Museum,** through the lefthand corner of the patio. The reconstructed **Cielo de Salamanca,** the library's famous 15th-century fresco of the zodiac painted on the ceiling by the celebrated Fernando Gallego, is preserved here in all its splendor. Take a peek at the intricate strongbox with its many locks. *(From Pl. Mayor follow R. Mayor, veer right onto R. Antigua, then left onto C. Libreros; the university is on the left. University ☎923 29 44 00. Museum ☎923 29 12 25. Open M-F 9:30am-1:30pm and 4-7:30pm, Sa 9:30am-1:30pm and 4-7pm, Su 10am-1:30pm. University and museum 300ptas/€1.80, students and seniors 150ptas/€0.90.)*

CATEDRAL NUEVA. Rome wasn't built in a day, and neither was this. In fact, it took 220 years (1513-1733) to construct this striking Gothic Spanish cathedral. While several architects decided to retain the original late Gothic style, they could not resist adding touches from later periods, most notably to its Baroque tower, one of the tallest in Spain. Inside, the cathedral is separated into many small chapels dedicated to various saints or important locals. These surround a center chapel and the enormous organ, whose pipes rise up toward the high ceiling. *(From Pl. Mayor, walk down R. Mayor into Pl. Anaya; the Catedral Nueva is in front of you. Open daily Apr.-Sept. 9am-2pm and 4-8pm; Oct.-Mar. 9am-1pm and 4-6pm. Free.)*

CATEDRAL VIEJA. The smaller Catedral Vieja (1140) was built in the Romanesque style. Apocalyptic angels separate the sinners from the saved inside the arresting cupola. The oldest original part of the cathedral is the **Capilla de San Martín,** with brilliantly colored frescoes dating from 1242. Look for the image of the Virgen de la Vega, patron saint of Salamanca. The **Capilla de Santa Bárbara,** also called the Capilla del Título, was what students used to face as they took their final exams. Other points of interest include a document signed by El Cid Campeador and the crucifix he held at his death. The **museum** features a paneled ceiling by Fernando Gallego and houses the Mudéjar Salinas organ (one of the oldest in Europe). Be sure to check out the famed **Patio Chico,** behind the cathedral, where students congregate to chat and play music. It is ideal for getting a splendid view of both cathedrals. *(Enter through the Catedral Nueva. Museum ☎923 21 74 76. Cathedral open daily Apr.-Sept. 10am-1:30pm and 4-7:30pm. Cathedral, cloister, and museum 300ptas/€1.80, students 250ptas/€1.50, children 200ptas/€1.20.)*

CASA LIS MUSEO ART NOUVEAU Y ART DECO. Cross the threshold of this odd-looking building and enter the bizarre. Salamancan industrialist Miguel de Lis collaborated with modernist architect Joaquín Vargas to design the building, which now showcases Lis's eclectic art collection. Exhibits range from the elegant (fans signed by such noteworthies as Salvador Dalí) to the odd (porcelain dolls with two faces), to the racy (small sculptures of animals and people in compromising positions). *(C. Gibraltar, 14, behind the cathedrals. ☎923 12 14 25. Open Apr.-Oct.15 Tu-F 11am-2pm and 5-9pm, Sa-Su 11am-9pm; Oct. 16-Mar. 31 Tu-F 11am-2pm and 4-7pm, Sa-Su 11am-8pm. 300ptas/€1.80. Students 200ptas/€1.20. Children and Tu mornings free.)*

CONVENTO DE SAN ESTEBAN. While on a fundraising endeavor, Columbus spent time in one of Salamanca's most dramatic monasteries, the Convento de San Esteban, off of C. San Pablo and Palominos. When illuminated by the afternoon sun, the stoning of St. Stephen and the crucifixion of Christ come alive on its façade. The beautiful **Claustro de los Reyes** (Kings's Cloister), with its Gothic interior and Plateresque exterior, is visibly the product of two different eras. José Churriguera's central altarpiece (1693) is a masterpiece of Spanish Baroque. Also worth seeing is the **Panteón de los Teólogos,** home to the remains of the most decorated Dominican theologians of the University. *(☎923 21 50 00. Open Apr.-Sept. Tu-Su 9am-1pm and 4-8pm; Oct.-Mar. 9am-1pm and 4-6pm. 200ptas/€1.20, free W mornings.)*

CASA DE LAS CONCHAS. From Pl. Mayor, exit onto pedestrian R. Mayor (through the archway opposite the clock). Follow this street until you reach a second plaza with a water fountain. Take a right and look up at the face of the building on your right. Yup, those are sandstone shells. The 15th-century Casa de las Conchas

(House of Shells), with over 300 large scallop halves, is one of Salamanca's most famous landmarks. Pilgrims who journeyed to Santiago de Compostela (see p. 455) traditionally wore shells to commemorate their visit to the tomb of St. James the Apostle. According to legend, the owner of the *casa*, created this monument either to honor the renowned pilgrimage, or to honor his wife, whose family shield was decorated with scallops. The building now serves as a public library and houses the provincial tourist office. *(C. Compañía, 39. Library ☎923 26 93 17. Open M-F 9am-9pm, Sa-Su 9am-2pm and 4-7pm. Free.)*

LA CLERECÍA. Directly across from the Conchas is the Clerecía (Royal College of the Holy Spirit), the private faculty of the Universidad de Salamanca. When Saint Ignatius of Loyola, founder of the Jesuits, arrived in Salamanca in the early 16th century, he was imprisoned for 20 days for heresy. Once the Jesuits were finally recognized by the Church, Loyola decided to claim recompense for his mistreatment by creating an enormous church and college of the Jesuit Order. Founded in 1611 with the financial aid of Queen Margarita de Austria (Felipe III's wife), the college actually owes its name to King Carlos III, who expelled the Jesuits from Spain and made the institute property of the Real Clerecía in the 18th century. The building has a unique U-shaped groundplan, allowing visitors to peer over the Cloister of Studies into the lower gallery and courtyard. Legend has it that the Jesuits leveled every house in the area to build the college; the Casa de las Conchas was the only one that would not let itself be bought, despite the Jesuits' shady offer of one gold coin for every sandstone shell. *(☎923 26 46 60. Open for mass M-Sa 1:15 and 7pm, Su noon. Free.)*

MUSEO DE SALAMANCA. Across from the university in the Patio de Escuelas, the Museum of Salamanca, also known as the museum of fine art, occupies an astounding 15th-century building that was once home to Alvarez Albarca, physician to Fernando and Isabel. Along with the Casa de las Conchas, this structure is among Spain's most important examples of 15th-century architecture. The museum has an intriguing collection of painting and sculpture as well as some temporary exhibits in archaeology and ethnology. Its most important canvases are Juan de Flandes' portrait of Saint Andrew and Luis de Morales' *Llanto por Cristo muerto*, both from the 16th century. *(Po. de Escuelas, 2. ☎923 21 22 35. Open Tu-Sa 8am-2pm and 4:30-8pm, Su 9:30am-2:30pm. 200ptas/€1.20.)*

CASA MUSEO DE UNAMUNO. Miguel de Unamuno, Rector of the University at the beginning of this century, is revered as one of the founding figures of the Spanish literary movement known as the "Generation of '98." Unamuno passionately opposed dictatorship and encouraged his students to do so as well. His stand against General Primo de Rivera's 1923 *coup d'état* led to his dismissal from the rector's post; he was triumphantly reinstated some years later. Unamuno lived in this house during his years as rector and his original furniture has been preserved, along with many framed photos and letters. *(To the right of the university's main entrance. ☎923 29 44 00, ext. 1196. Open July-Sept. Tu-F 9:30am-1:30pm, Sa-Su 10am-1:30pm; Oct.-June Tu-F 9:30am-1:30pm and 4-6pm, Sa-Su 10am-2pm. Research room open M-F 9am-2pm. Mandatory tour in Spanish every 30min., 300ptas/€1.80. Ring bell if house appears closed.)*

PUENTE ROMANO. This 2000-year-old Roman bridge, spanning the scenic Río Tormes at the edge of the city, was once part of an ancient Roman road called the *Camino de la Plata* (Silver Way). The *Camino* ran from Mérida in Extremadura to Astorga and was heavily traveled during the Roman occupation of Spain. In medieval times, the *Camino de la Plata* was the route most Andalucian and Castilian Christians took to complete their pilgrimage to Santiago de Compostela. The bridge is guarded at its end by a headless granite bull called the **Toro Ibérico.** Though it dates back to pre-Roman times, the bull gained fame in the 16th century when it appeared in *Lazarillo de Tormes*, the prototype of the picaresque novel and a predecessor of *Don Quijote;* in one episode the novel's hero gets his head slammed into the bull's stone ear after he cheats his employer.

ENTERTAINMENT

Lugares, a free, slim pamphlet distributed at the tourist office and at some bars, lists everything from movies and special events to bus schedules. Posters at the **Colegio Mayor** (Palacio de Anaya) advertise university events, free films, and student theater. During the summer, Salamanca sponsors the **Verano Cultural de Salamanca,** with silent movies, contemporary Spanish cinema, pop singers, and theater groups. On June 12, in honor of San Juan de Sahagún, there is a **corrida de toros** charity event in **La Plaza de Toros** en Plaza Glorieta to the northeast of old city as well as parades and instant craft fairs throughout the city. From Sept. 8 to 21, Salamanca indulges in festivals and exhibitions, most honoring the bullfight that has made the region's *ganaderías,* or bull farms, the best in all Spain. This is also a fun place to be during *Semana Santa,* with local traditions like **Lunes de Aguas,** celebrated the Monday after Easter. This feast remembers the tradition of banishing local prostitutes across the river during the 40 days of Lent; they used to return triumphantly on *Lunes de Quasimodo,* when eager *salmantinos* would picnic along the bridge to await their arrival. One thing led to another and...

NIGHTLIFE

Plaza Mayor is *the* social center of Salamanca. It's packed day and night with locals, students, and tourists who come to lounge in its cafés, watch the sunset, or take a stroll. At night, members of various local college or graduate-school **tunas** (medieval-style student troubadour groups) often finish their rounds here. Dressed in traditional black capes, they strut around the plaza with guitars, mandolins, *bandurrias,* and tambourines, serenading women. Student nightlife spreads out to **Gran Vía, C. Bordadores,** and side streets. Spacious discos/bars, or *pafs,* blast music into the wee hours of the morning. **C. Prior** and **C. Rúa Mayor** are full of bars; locals gather in the charming *terrazas* on **Pl. de la Fuente,** off Av. Alemania. More intense partying occurs off **C. Varillas,** where *chupiterías* (bars that mostly serve shots) take precedence over *pafs.*

Birdland, C. Azafranal, 57, facing Pl. España. Drink to modern funk jazz. Take a break from the club scene to enjoy a lower-decibel conversation. Beer 250-400ptas/€1.50-2.40. Mixed drinks 500-1000ptas/€3-6. Open Su-Th 4pm-3am, F-Sa 4pm-4:30am, opens at 6:30pm during summer months.

Café Novelty, (☎923 21 99 90) on Pl. Mayor, underneath the flags. Café by day, pub by night, this place stakes its claim as the oldest café in town and is a popular meeting place for students and professors. Grab an ice cream and stroll the plaza. Beer 200ptas/€1.20. Mixed drinks 400ptas/€2.40. Open daily 8am-2am.

Gatsby, C. Bordadores, 6 (☎923 21 72 74) Across the street from Camelot, this club draws American and Salamancan students from their rooms with its disco beat. Beer 300ptas/€1.80. Sangría 350ptas/€2.10. Mixed drinks 700ptas/€4.21. Specials nearly every night. Open Su-Th 10pm-4am, F-Sa 7pm-6:30am.

LA TUNA... MORE FRAT THAN FISH In Spain, it's not dolphins who are threatened by the "tuna industry." According to legend, it is young women who need to watch out, lest their hearts be captured unawares by a charming bard. *Las tunas* are university student music bands dating back to King Alfons X the Wise, in 1215. Originally founded by students who needed to earn money for their studies, they have become a form of social competition in modern universities, as well as paid entertainment for private parties and high-class restaurants. To become *tunos,* candidates *(pardillos)* must prove their wit and artistic ability in a series of tests culminating with a bowl of The Soup of Charity, a painfully fiery concoction mixed by veteran tunos. The chosen ones take an oath over a tambourine, the symbol of the tuna, and are given a tuna sash and nickname for life.

CASTILLA Y LEÓN

DAYTRIPS FROM SALAMANCA

CIUDAD RODRIGO

Buses come from the Salamanca bus station, Av. Filiberto Villalobos, 71-85 (1hr.; M-F 13 per day 7am-9:30pm, Sa 6 per day 8:30am-6pm, Su 4 per day 11am-10pm; 760ptas/€4.57.) Buy tickets in Salamanca from La Pilar, windows 23 & 24. Last bus leaves Ciudad Rodrigo at 7:30pm.

The hushed, labyrinthine streets and 18th-century ramparts of Ciudad Rodrigo, a sleepy town just 27km from Portugal, harbor myriad sandstone cathedrals, Roman ruins, and medieval masonry. Although the town was originally a Roman outpost, today it is known for its namesake, Conde Rodrigo González Girón, the count who brought the site back to life in 1100 after the destruction of the Moorish invasions. The **cathedral** is the town's masterpiece. Originally a Romanesque church commissioned by Fernando II of León, it was later modified in the 16th-century Gothic style. The **coro** (choir) was the masterpiece of Rodrigo Alemán, who worked on it from 1498 to 1504. Look for the sculptor's signature—a carving of his head hidden among the rest of the carvings. The two 16th-century organs star in a series of concerts every August. The cathedral's **claustro** (cloister) alone merits a trip to Ciudad Rodrigo. The columns are covered with figures doing everything from making love to playing peek-a-boo, even flirting with cannibalism. The cathedral's **museum** is filled with strange but interesting pieces, including an ancient clavichord, the cathedral's "ballot box," richly embroidered robes and slippers worn by bishops and priors, and Velázquez's *Llanto de Adán y Eva por Ariel muerto.* (Cathedral open daily 10am-1pm and 3:30-7pm. Free. Cloister and museum open daily 10am-1pm and 3:30-7pm. 200ptas/€1.20. Tours in Spanish.) To reach the cathedral from the tourist office (see below for more information on the tourist office), turn left onto Pl. Amayuelas into town, and then take your first right onto Pl. de San Salvador. The cathedral is to your left.

Also of note is the 14th-century **Castillo de Enrique II de Trastámara,** built by Gonzalo Arias de Genizaro. Ciudad Rodrigo was once the site of a bloody face-off between Trastámara and Pedro I El Cruel; today the castle serves as a more tranquil *parador* (luxury hotel). The castle's ramparts and garden (ask the concierge to let you in if it's locked) affords a good view of the Río Agueda and the **ancient Roman bridge** that spans it. In front of the castle, an ancient **verraco** (pig), stands guard, Ciudad Rodrigo's only other remnant of its ancient Roman settlers.

The **bus station** (☎923 46 10 09) is on Campo de Toledo, 3-25. From the station entrance, take a left onto Campo de Toledo (with the station behind you) and then the second right onto Av. Yurramendi (uphill), and pass through the stone arch; the **tourist office,** Pl. Amayuelas, 5, is immediately on your left, across the street and before the cathedral. (☎923 46 05 61. Open M-F 9am-2pm and 5-7pm, Sa-Su 10am-2pm and 5-8pm. French also spoken.) Most **restaurants, bars, and cafés** in town cluster on Plaza Mayor. From the tourist office, continue straight on Pl. de Amayuelas into town, then turn left onto C. del Cardenal Pacheco just before Pl. de San Salvador; Pl. Mayor is at the end of this street.

ZAMORA

Zamora is most easily reached by bus, which are more frequent and travel to more cities than trains. Trains leave from Zamora's C. de Estación (24hr. ☎980 52 11 10) at the end of C. Alfonso Peña and go to: Madrid (3hr.; 3 per day 3:50am, 2:23 and 6:20pm; 3500ptas/€21.08) and Valladolid (1½hr., 8:32am and 7:40pm, 1045ptas/€6.30).

Alone atop a serrated cliff over the Río Duero, Zamora (pop. 65,000) is a beguiling mix of modern and medieval: 11th-century churches rub shoulders with Mango and Zara, 15th-century palaces harbor internet cafés and luxury hotels, tangled and narrow streets empty onto grand *avenidas,* and the magnificent 12th-century cathedral overlooks modern subdivisions and steel bridges in the distance. While locals clearly enjoy the town's modern conveniences, it is Zamora's history as one of the most powerful cities in medieval Castile that constantly lures busloads of

Spanish tourists. In nearly every plaza and street, monuments stand to Zamora's infamous figures, from Viriato, the fierce Roman warrior born in Zamora, and El Cid, the Spanish hero who played fugitive here, to Sancho II, who died here during his attempt to overthrow his sister Doña Urraca and claim the House of Castile as his own. Fortunately, Zamora is only a short bus ride from Salamanca, making it an easy—and worthwhile—daytrip.

Zamora's foremost monument is its Romanesque **cathedral,** built from the 12th to 15th centuries. Its Byzantine cupola is notable for its **Bishop's Door**, an entrance in the side of the dome that can only be reached by a vertigo-inducing flight of stairs running up the side of the building. Inside, the cathedral's highlights are its intricately carved choir stalls (complete with seated apostles laughing and singing) and the main altar, an ornate structure made of marble and gold. Golden angels keep watch from a flawless blue sky above. Inside the cloister, the **Museo de la Catedral** features the priceless 15th-century **Black Tapestries,** which tell the story of the Trojan War and Achilles's defeat. (☎980 53 06 44. Cathedral and museum open Tu-F 10am-2pm and 4-8pm, Sa-Su 10am-8pm. Mass daily at 10am, also Sa 6pm and Su 1pm. Cathedral free; museum 300ptas/€1.80.) To reach the cathedral from Pl. Mayor, walk left (with your back to the *Ayuntamiento*) up C. Ramón Carrión, following it until its name changes to R. de Los Francos and R. de Los Notarios. After R. de Los Notarios curves to the left, it will bring you to Pl. de la Catedral. Behind the cathedral is the **Parque del Castillo,** a great spot for an afternoon picnic.

Twelve striking **Romanesque churches** remain within the walls of the old city, gleaming in the wake of recent restoration. Almost all these churches were built in the 11th and 12th centuries; their ornate altars, however, were usually added in the 15th and 16th centuries. Most visitors follow the **Romanesque Route,** a self-guided tour of all of the churches available from the tourist office. With their gray stone, dark interiors, and sculptures of Christ in the sepulcher, all twelve churches do tend to blend together. There are, however, a few standouts. In Pl. Mayor, the **Iglesia San Juan** is notable for its luminescent, marble-veined windows. **La Magdalena,** straight up C. Ramón Carrión from Pl. Mayor, features an intricately carved south door; it also houses a Mary Magdalene icon, one of the most revered religious works of art in Zamora. Across the street from La Magdalena on C. Ramón Carrión is the **Convento del Transitó,** a convent of Carmelite nuns who watch over *La Virgen del Transitó*, the patron saint of Zamora; she is credited with miracles ranging from bringing rain during a drought to protecting El Cid.

Farther up C. Ramón Carrión on the left is **Iglesia San Ildefonso,** noted for its bright green-and-orange organ and its statues of *La Virgen Amor y Hermosa*, another important Zamoran saint. Finally, **Iglesia Santa María La Nueva** was the site of one of Zamora's most significant historical events, *El Motín de la Trucha;* in 1158 villagers set the church on fire (with Zamoran nobility inside) to protest a law giving noblemen priority over plebeians in buying trout. It may sound silly, but the event was one of the first in a series that led to the rise of the Spanish bourgeoisie. To get to the church from Pl. Mayor, walk up C. Sacramento and then turn right onto C. Barandales; the church is in Pl. Santa María la Nueva. (All open Tu-Sa 10am-1pm and 5-8pm. Free.) The **Museo de Semana Santa,** Pl. Santa María La Nueva, 9, is a rare find. Hooded mannequins stand guard over elaborately sculpted floats that depict the stations of the Via Crucis. These mannequins were used during the *romerías*, processions honoring *Semana Santa*; Zamora has one of the most decorated Easter celebrations in all of Spain. To reach the museum from Pl. Mayor, take C. Sacramento and turn right on C. Barandales. (☎980 53 22 95. Open M-Sa 10am-2pm and 5-8pm, Su 10am-2pm. 450ptas/€2.70.) The **train** and **bus stations** are both a 15min. walk from Pl. Mayor. The **tourist office** is at C. Santa Clara, 20. (☎980 53 18 45; fax 53 38 13. Open M-Sa 9am-2pm and 5-7pm.)

LEÓN ☎987

The residents of León (pop. 506,000) are justifiably proud of their riverside oasis. From the tangled streets of the *barrio gótico* to the stunning cathedral, locals boast that their city is the best in Castille, if not in Spain. It's fitting, then, that the city's unofficial mascot is the oh-so-proud lion—images of lions are everywhere and *leones*, the local moniker for natives of the area, literally means "lions" in Spanish. Strangely enough, though, the city's name has nothing to do with lions—it stems rather from *legio* (Latin for legion), a name that the Seventh Roman Legion gave the town in AD 68. During the Middle Ages, the city was as an important stop on the pilgrim's route to Santiago de Compostela—and continues to be, as attested to by the gold shells marking the *camino*'s path through the city center—and it served as an essential defense point against Moorish invaders during the *Reconquista.* Today the city is best known for its cathedral, whose spectacular blue stained-glass windows have earned León the nickname *La Ciudad Azul* (The Blue City). While history provides León with its local prominence, it is the city's serene parks and vibrant outdoor nightlife that make it worth exploring.

TRANSPORTATION

Trains: RENFE, Av. Astorga, 2 (☎902 24 02 02). With Pl. Guzmán el Bueno behind you, cross the river and continue on Av. Palencia as it curves to the right; the station is on your left. Open 24hr. Trains to: **Barcelona** (9½hr.; Su-F 3 per day 12:25am, 1:20, 11:47pm, Sa 2 per day 12:25am and 1:20pm; 7650ptas/€46); **Bilbao** (5½hr., 1 per day 3:10pm, 4000ptas/€24); **Burgos** (2-3hr.; Su-F 3 per day 1:20am-9:27pm, Sa 2 per day 1:20am and 3:10pm; 1240ptas/€7.45); **La Coruña** (7hr., express 4½hr.; M, W, F 2 per day 4:35am and 2:07pm; Tu, Th, Sa-Su 3 per day 4:35am, 2:07, and 5:08pm; 4100ptas/€25); **Madrid** (4½hr., M-Sa 7 per day midnight-6:12pm, 3420ptas/€21); **Oviedo** (2½hr.; M-F 7 per day 4:45am-8:52pm, Sa 6 per day 4:45am-8:52pm, Su 5 per day 11:52am-7:40pm; 1200ptas/€7.21); **Palencia** (1½hr.; Su-F 13 per day 12:15am-10:35pm, Sa 12 per day 12:25am-10:35pm; 1100ptas/€6.61); **Valladolid** (2½hr., M-Sa 10 per day 12am-10:35pm, 1510ptas/€9.10). **FEVE,** Av. Padre Isla, 48 (☎987 22 59 19), north of Pl. Santo Domingo, sends trains to local destinations. Train and bus schedules are printed daily in *Diario de León* (110ptas/€0.65).

Buses: Estación de Autobuses Po. Ingeniero Sáenz de Miera, (☎987 21 00 00). Info open M-Sa 7:30am-9pm. To: **Madrid** (4½hr.; M-F 12 per day 2:30am-10:30pm, Sa-Su 8 per day 2:30am-7:30pm; 2680ptas/€16.10); **Santander** (5hr., F 3:30pm and Su 7:30pm, 2700ptas/€16.23); **Valladolid** (2hr., 8 per day 2:30am-10:30pm, 1100ptas/€6.61); **Zamora** (2½hr.; M-F 9 per day 8am-9:15pm, Sa 6 per day 8am-5pm, Su 4 per day 10:15am-7pm; 1185ptas/€7.12).

Taxis: Radio Taxi (☎987 24 24 51 or 24 12 11). 24hr. service.

Car Rental: Hertz, C. Sampiro, 20 (☎987 23 19 99). From Pl. Glorieta Guzmán el Bueno when facing the river, walk right up Po. de Condesa de Sagasta; C. Sampiro is the last street on your right before Pl. San Marcos. Must be at least 25 and have had a license for 1yr. or more. Open M-F 9am-2pm and 4-7pm, Sa 9am-1pm.

ORIENTATION AND PRACTICAL INFORMATION

Most of León, including the old city (called *León Gótico*) and modern commercial district, lies on the east side of the **Río Bernesga.** The bus and train stations are across the river in the west end. Av. Palencia (a left out of the main entrance of the bus station or right out of the main entrance of the train station) leads across the river to **Pl. Glorieta Guzmán el Bueno,** where, after the rotary, it becomes **Avenida de Ordoño II** and leads to León's cathedral. Av. Ordoño II then bisects the new city and at Pl. Santo Domingo becomes **Calle Ancha,** which splits the old town in two.

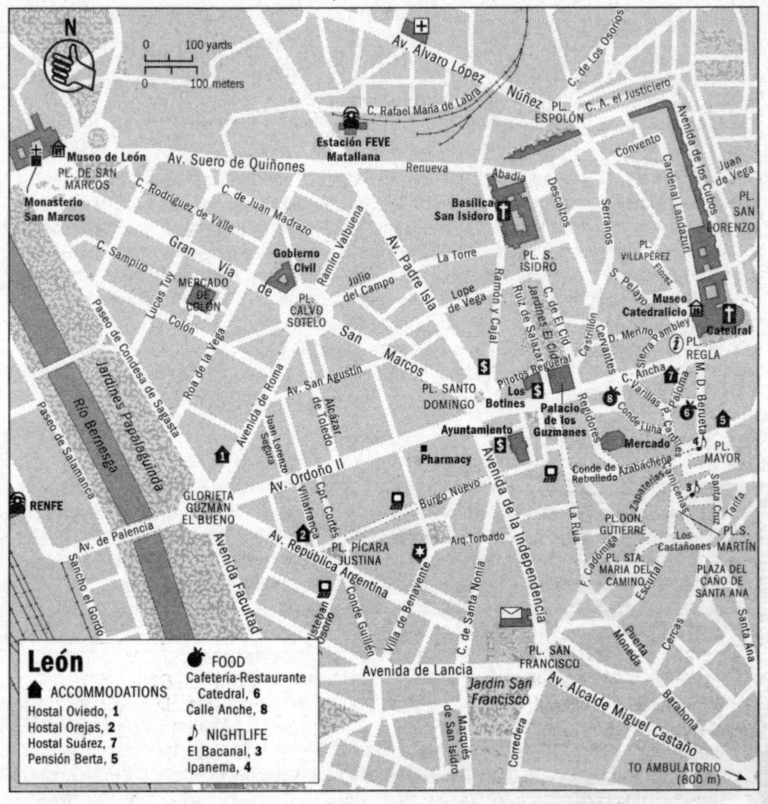

Tourist Office: Pl. Regla, 3 (☎987 23 70 82; fax 27 33 91), in front of the cathedral. Free city maps, regional brochures, and accommodations guide. Open M-F 9am-2pm and 5-7pm, Sa-Su 10am-2pm and 5pm.

Currency Exchange: ATMs and **banks** line Pl. Santo Domingo. **Banco Central Hispano,** Pl. Santo Domingo (☎902 24 24 24). Follow Av. Ordoño II into the plaza. Open M-F 8:30am-2:30pm. **Citibank,** at the corner of Av. de la Independencia and C. Legión VII. Open M-F 8:30am-2pm.

Luggage Storage: At the **train station.** Lockers 500ptas/€3. Open 24hr. At the **bus station,** 25ptas/€0.15 per bag. Open M-F 9am-8pm, Sa 9am-2pm.

Emergency: ☎112. **Police:** C. Villa Benavente, 6 (☎987 20 73 12).

Medical Services: Hospital Virgen Blanca (☎987 23 74 00). **Medical emergency:** ☎987 22 22 22.

Pharmacy: Although pharmacies are on every block, only **Farmacia Mata Espeso,** Ave. Ordoño II, 3, is open all night. Open M-F 9:30am-2pm, 4:30-8pm, and 10pm-9:30am, Sa-Su 10pm-9:30am.

Internet Access: NovegaWeb, C. Burgo Nuevo, 15. From the Pl. Glorieta Guzmán El Bueno rotary, walk up Ave. República Argentina; at Pl. Pícara Justina, turn left onto C. Burgo Nuevo. 400ptas/€2.40 per hr. Open daily 10am-11pm.

Post Office: Jardín San Francisco (☎987 23 90 79; fax 87 60 78). From Pl. Santo Domingo, go down Av. Independencia; the post office is on the right just before Ave. de Lancia. **Lista de Correos** (windows #12-13) and **fax** service available. Open M-F 8:30am-8:30pm, Sa 9:30am-2pm. **Postal Code:** 24004.

ACCOMMODATIONS

Budget beds are fairly easy to come by in León, thanks to the yearly influx of pilgrims on their way to Santiago, but pensiones do tend to fill during the June fiestas. Many accommodations cluster on **Av. de Roma, Av. Ordoño II,** and **Av. República Argentina,** which lead into the old town from Pl. Glorieta Guzmán el Bueno. The tourist office has a free brochure listing all accommodations in town.

Hostal Orejas, C. Villafranca, 6, 2nd fl. (☎987 25 29 09; janton@usarios.Retecal.es). Just down Av. República Argentina from Pl. Glorieta Guzmán el Bueno. Brand-new rooms, complete with bath, shower, and cable TV. Free internet access. Singles 4500ptas/€27.05; doubles 5500ptas/€33.06; triples 8500ptas/€51.09; quads 9800ptas/€58.90. V.

Hostal Oviedo, Av. Roma, 26, 2nd fl. (☎987 22 22 36), off Pl. Glorieta Guzmán el Bueno. Street-side rooms have terraces. Shared bathrooms are kept impeccably clean. Singles 2200ptas/€13.22; doubles 3700ptas/€22.24; triples 5700ptas/€34.26.

Hostal Suárez, C. Ancha, 7 (☎987 25 42 88). Prime location, seconds away from the cathedral. Rooms are spacious with high ceilings and soft beds. Kitchen. No heat. Doubles 3000ptas/€18.03; triples 3600ptas/€21.64. Open Apr.-Nov.

Pensión Berta, Pl. Mayor, 8, 2nd fl. (☎987 25 70 39). From Pl. Santa Domingo, walk up C. Anche, and turn right on C. Mariano Domínguez Berrueta, just before the cathedral. When you reach Pl. Mayor, turn left onto the first walkway; the pension is on your left. Berta is centrally located in the midst of the *barrio humidor,* with all-night bars right at the doorstep. Singles 1800ptas/€10.82; doubles 3200ptas/€19.23.

FOOD

Inexpensive eateries fill the area near the cathedral and on the small streets off C. Ancha; also check Pl. San Martín, near Pl. Mayor. Meat-lovers will rejoice, as many variations of pork top the local menus. In June, León's 3500km of trout-fishable streams draw the **International Trout Festival.** Fresh produce as well as bread, cheese, and milk are available at the **Mercado Municipal del Conde,** Pl. Conde, off C. General Mola. From Pl. Santo Domingo, walk up C. Anche, and then turn right onto C. Regidores, which empties into the market. (Open M-Sa 9am-3:30pm).

Cafetería-Restaurante Catedral, C. Mariano Domínguez Berrueta, 17 (☎987 21 59 18). From Pl. Santo Domingo, walk up C. Anche and turn right onto C. Mariano Domínguez Barreuta. Huge portions, garlic-laden trout, and otherworldly flan. *Menú del día* 1300ptas/€7.81. Open daily 1-4pm and 9-11:30pm. AmEx/MC/V.

Calle Ancha, C. Ancha, 11 (☎987 21 01 83). Between C. Regidores and C. Conde Luna, a 2min. walk from the cathedral. *Everything* comes with *ajo* (garlic) at this bright café. The *menú del día* (1100ptas/€6.61) comes with a bottle of wine. Open daily noon-4pm and 9:15pm-midnight, F-Sa until 3:30am. MC/V.

SIGHTS

CATHEDRAL. The 13th-century Gothic cathedral, *La Pulchra Leonina,* is arguably the most beautiful cathedral in Spain. It is also one of Spain's best examples of Gothic architecture. The exceptional façade depicts smiling saints amidst bug-eyed monsters munching on the damned. But the real attractions are its stained-glass windows, which feature angelic saints and brilliant flowers, and the elaborate altar painting of the stations of the Via Crucis. In summer 2001, extensive renovations began on the cathedral; call ahead to confirm that the cathedral and museum are open. *(On Pl. Regla. ☎987 87 57 70. From Pl. Santo Domingo, walk straight up C. Anche. Cathedral open in summer daily 8:30am-1:30pm and 4-8pm; in winter daily 8:30am-1:30pm and 4-7pm. Free. Museum open in summer daily 9:30am-1:30pm and 4-6:30pm; in winter M-Sa 9:30am-1pm and 4-6pm. 500ptas/€3.01 Claustro 100ptas/€0.60.)*

BASÍLICA SAN ISIDORO. The Romanesque Basílica San Isidoro was dedicated in the 11th century to San Isidoro of Sevilla. After his death his remains were brought from Muslim-dominated Andalucía to the Christian stronghold of León. The corpses of countless royals rest in the impressive Panteón Real, where the ceilings are covered by vibrant 12th-century frescoes. The unusual Annunciation and Roman agricultural calendar are particularly noteworthy. Admission to the pantheon includes entrance to the library, which houses a 10th-century handwritten Bible, and to the treasury, home of Doña Urraca's famous agate chalices. *(On. Pl. San Isidoro. From Pl. Santo Domingo, walk up C. Ramón y Cajal; the basilica is up the flight of stairs on the right just before C. La Torre. Open M-Sa 9am-8pm, Su 9am-2pm. 400ptas/€2.40.)*

OTHER SIGHTS. The **Museo de León** displays an extensive archaeological collection with pieces dating from the Paleolithic era; particularly stunning are the 4th-century Roman mosaics. *(Pl. San Marcos. From Pl. Santo Domingo, walk up Gran Vía de San Marcos to its end at Pl. San Marcos. ☎987 24 50 61. Open May-Sept. Tu-Sa 10am-2pm and 5-8:30pm, Su 10am-4pm; Oct..-April Tu-Sa-10am-2pm and 4:30-8pm, Su 10am-4pm. 200ptas/€1.20. Free for students and Sa-Su.).* **Los Botines** is one of the few buildings outside Cataluña designed by modernist architect Antoni Gaudí, the Catalunyan who popularized modernist architecture in Spain. The relatively restrained structure contains hints of his later style in its turrets and windows (see **Barcelona,** p. 299). It now serves as offices for the Caja de España bank and is not open to the public. *(From Pl. Santo Domingo, walk up C. Anche toward the cathedral; Los Botines is immediately on your left in front of Pl. San Marcelo.)* Some of Leon's most enjoyable attractions are its myriad parks and promenades where locals spend their evenings strolling, picnicking, and sucking face. Two of the most peaceful are the **Jardines El Cid,** directly behind Los Botines on Pilotos Tegueral between El Cid and Ruiz de Salazar, and the **Jardines Papalaguinda,** running along the river from Pl. San Marcos in the north to the Plaza de Toros in the south.

ENTERTAINMENT AND NIGHTLIFE

Festivals commemorating **San Juan** and **San Pedro** occur from June 21 to 30. Highlights include a *corrida de torros* (bullfight) and the feast days of San Juan on June 23 and San Pedro on June 30. King Juan Carlos I and his wife Sofía attend the fiestas and the cathedral's **International Organ Festival** every year on October 5.

For nearby bars, discos, and techno music, head to the *barrio húmedo* (drinker's neighborhood) around **Plaza de San Martín** and **Plaza Mayor.** To get to the *barrio*, walk up C. Ancha toward the cathedral and take a right on C. Varillas (which becomes Platerías Candiles). To reach P. San Martín, take a right where the street ends at C. Carnicerías; to reach Pl. Mayor, take a left onto C. Plegaria at the end of C. Platerías Candiles. All the bars here are open until 2am daily and until 5-6am on Friday and Sunday. In Pl. San Martín, **El Bacanal,** C. Mulhacín, 5, attracts crowds to its Caravaggio-covered walls. (☎987 21 38 51.) Around Pl. Mayor, Leon's hippest partyers flock to **Ipanema,** C. Plegarias, 8; the upstairs is a dim, bossa nova-infused café, while the downstairs dance floor sticks to the standard Spanish disco beats. After 2am, the crowds weave to **Calle Lancia** and **Calle Conde de Guillén,** both heavily populated with discos and bars.

DAYTRIP FROM LEÓN

ASTORGA

Astorga is most easily reached by **bus** *from León, Po. Ingeniero Saenz de Miera (45min.; M-F 16 per day 6:15am-9:30pm, Sa 7 per day 8:30am-8:30pm, Su 6 per day 8:30am-8:30pm; 430ptas/€2.58). RENFE runs* **trains** *to Astorga from León (45min.; M-Tu and Th-F 5 per day 2:04am-8:29pm, W 6 per day 2:04am-8:29pm, Sa 4 per day 2:04am-8:29pm, Su 3 per day 2:15am-8:29pm; 500ptas/€3.01), but the station is a 30min. walk uphill from the main sights.*

Astorga reached its peak in the 15th century as an important stopping point on both *La Ruta de la Plata*, the Roman silver route, and *El Camino Santiago*, the pilgrim's path toward Santiago de Compostela that begins in the French Pyrenees. In the early 17th century it became one of the world's main centers of chocolate making; a few die-hards still produce bars of authentic *chocolate de Astorga*.

Today Astorga is perhaps most distinguished by the **Palacio Episcopal,** designed in the late 19th century by Antoni Gaudí. The palace's turrets, main entryway, and beveled stone exterior are most characteristic of Gaudí's style. Gaudí built the palace to replace the one which burned down in 1886, but no bishop has actually ever lived there. Now the palace houses the fascinating **Museo de los Caminos,** dedicated to the various paths toward Santiago de Compostela that converge in 2000-year-old Astorga. (☎987 61 88 82. Open M-Sa 10am-1:30pm and 4-7:30pm, Su 10am-1:30pm. 500ptas/€3.) The **cathedral,** directly to the left when facing Gaudí's palace, is definitely worth a quick visit. While it is not as well-preserved or as opulent as León's cathedral, its emptiness—there are no pews, chapel gates, or candle tables—affords a rare opportunity to experience the airiness and immensity of Gothic architecture. Flocks of birds à la Hitchcock make their nest here, adding to the dramatic atmosphere. The cathedral's **museum** has ten rooms filled with religious relics, although over half are closed for refurbishing as of summer 2001. Even so, the museum's series of paintings depicting the temptations of St. Anthony—including several panels of his gruesome attack by demons—are well worth the small admission fee. (Cathedral and museum open daily 10am-2pm and 4-8pm. Cathedral free; museum 250ptas/€1.50, 400ptas/€2.40 for a joint ticket with the Museo de los Caminos.) Kids and sweet-toothed should stop by the **Museo de Chocolate,** C. José María Goy, 5. From the Palacio Episcopal, walk up Los Sitios to Pl. Obispo Alcolea; veer to the right onto C. Lorenzo Segura and C. José María Goy is on the right. (Open Tu-Sa 10:30am-2pm and 4:30-8pm, Su 10:30am-2pm. 400ptas/€2.40.) The museum sells chocolates by the dozen, but you can also purchase their types of sugary delights next door at the **Confitería la Mallorquina,** C. Lorenzo Segura, 7. (Open daily 10am-2pm and 4-7pm.) Visiting Astorga without buying a box of the famous *milagritos* or *hojaldres* pastries just might classify as a sin.

The **bus station,** Av. las Murallas, 54 (☎987 61 93 51), faces the back of the Palacio Episcopal. From the station's main entrance, cross Av. las Murallas and the new-age Parque de "El Melgar"; the stairs in the city walls will lead you straight up to the cathedral and palace. To get to the town center from the RENFE **train station** (☎987 84 21 22), Pl. Estación, cross the parking lot in front of the station and follow C. Pedro de Castro until it crosses Puerta de Rey. A large building (Casa Granell) is on the right. Walk through the city wall onto C. Enfermas and turn right onto Los Sitios, which will bring you to the palace. With your back to the palace, the **tourist office,** Glorieta Eduardo de Castro, 5, is directly in front of you across the plaza. (☎987 61 82 22. Open Sa-M 9am-8:30pm, Tu-F 10am-2pm and 4-8:30pm.)

VALLADOLID ☎983

For nearly 300 years, Valladolid was the most important town in the Kingdom of Castile; when Fernando and Isabel were married here in 1469, it stood at the forefront of Spanish politics, finance, and culture. Explorers Magellan and El Cano came to Valladolid to discuss their plans for voyages to circumnavigate the globe, newly discovered to be round. Miguel de Cervantes, creater of the romantic hero Don Quijote, lived here; in 1506, famous explorer Christopher Columbus died here. Close to a century later, shady dealings by minister Conde Duque de Lerma brought the city's glory days to an end. In return for a whopping bribe, Lerma took Valladolid (then capital of Castile) out of the running for capital of Spain. Madrid won, and history moved on. Today, the city has little to offer visitors beyond its sculpture museum and relics of a Renaissance past. It does, however, offer a glimpse of the unaffected Spanish urban life.

TRANSPORTATION

Flights: Villanubla Airport, León Highway (N-601), km 13 (☎983 41 54 00). Daily trips to Barcelona and Paris. June-Oct. service to the Balearic Islands. Info open daily 8am-8pm. **Iberia,** at the airport (☎983 56 01 62). Open daily 8am-8pm. Taxi to airport 1800-2000ptas/€11-12.

Trains: Estación del Norte, C. Recondo s/n (☎902 24 02 02), at the end of Campo Grande. Info open daily 7am-8pm. Trains to: **Barcelona** (9¾-11hr.; Su-F 9:18 and 9:30am, Sa 8:10pm; 5900ptas/€35.50); **Bilbao** (4hr.; M, W, F 6:27pm; 2400ptas/€14.50); **Burgos** (1¾-2½hr.; M-F 11 per day 7am-1:42am, Sa-Su 7 per day noon-11:45pm; 975-1070ptas, €6-6.50); **León** (2-3hr.; M-Sa 8 per day 10:26am-1:42am, Su 7 per day 10:26am-5:25pm; 1000-1300ptas/€6-8); **Lisbon/Oporto** (7¾hr., 2:51am, 6500ptas/€40); **Madrid** (3-3¾hr.; M-F 13 per day 4am-8:41pm, Sa 12 per day 4am-8:41pm, Su 11 per day 7am-9pm; 1500-2500ptas/€9-15); **Oviedo** (4-5½hr; M-Sa 1:42 and 10:27am, Su 5:25pm; 3100ptas/€19); **Paris** (11hr., 9:20pm, 13,700ptas/€ 83.50); **Salamanca** (1¾-2¾hr.; M-F 7 per day 7:15am-10:02pm, Sa 7 per day 9:45am-8:15pm, Su 6 per day 7:05am-10:02pm; 975-1070ptas/€6-6.50); **Santander** (3-6hr.; M-F 7 per day 9:35am-1:42am, Sa 8 per day 7:15am-1:42am, Su 7 per day 7:15am-6:40pm; 1800-2350ptas/€11–14); **San Sebastián** (5hr.; 3:41am, 11:47am, 12:25pm; 3120ptas/€19); **Zamora** (2hr., 8:36am, 1080ptas/€6.50).

Buses: Puente Colgante, 2 (☎983 23 63 08). Info open daily 8am-10pm. **La Regional** runs to Palencia and Zamora; **ALSA** serves all others. Info open M-Sa 6am-10pm, Su 8am-10pm. To: **Barcelona** (10hr.; 9:45am, and 12:15, 9:45pm; 6085ptas/€36.75); **Bilbao** (5hr.; M-Th and Sa 1:35 and 5:30pm, F 1:35, 3:30, and 5:30pm, Su 5:30 and 7:15pm; 2900ptas/€17.43); **Burgos** (1¾-2¾hr., Su-Th 5 per day 9:45am-9:45pm, 1120ptas/€6.75); **León** (2hr.; M-F 9 per day 2:45am-12:45am, Sa 7 per day 2:45am-12:45am, Su 6 per day 2:45am-9:45pm; 1165ptas/€7); **Madrid** (2¼hr.; M-Sa 18 per day 4:15am-12:30am, Su 19 per day 10:15am-10pm; 1655ptas/€10); **Oviedo** (3¼-4¼hr., 4 per day 2:15am-7pm, 2260ptas/€13.50); **Palencia** (45min.; M-F hourly 7am-9pm, Sa 6 per day 8am-8:15pm, Su 3 per day 10am-10pm; 440ptas/€3); **Santander** (4hr.; M-Th and Sa 9:45am and 4:45pm, F and Su 4:45 and 8pm; 2250ptas/€13.50); **Zamora** (1½hr.; M-F 7 per day 7am-6:30pm, Sa 5 per day 8am-5:30pm, Su 10:30am, 5pm, and 10pm; 870ptas/€5.25).

Taxis: Agrupación de Taxistas de Valladolid 24hr. ☎983 20 77 55.

ORIENTATION AND PRACTICAL INFORMATION

The bus and train stations sit on the southern edge of town, beneath the Parque de Campo Grande. To get from the **bus station** to the **tourist office,** (15min.) exit at the corner of Paseo del Arco de Ladrillo and C. San José (do not exit onto the corner of Po. del Arco de Ladrillo and C. de Puente Colgante). Turn left onto Po. del Arco de Ladrillo, and keep right onto C. Ladrillo at the rotary. Follow C. Ladrillo to Po. de Los Filipinos; at the edge of the Campo, take the pedestrian path through the park; the office will be straight ahead through a metal archway. When you reach Pl. de Zorrilla at the end of the park, C. Santiago—the street the tourist office is on—will be directly across the rotary. From the front entrance of the **train station,** (10min.) take the sidewalk to your left onto C. Estación del Norte, following it to Plaza de Colón. Follow the rotary to the right; C. Acera de Recoletos will be the third street on your right, running alongside the park, and will take you directly to Pl. de Zorilla. C. Santiago is the second street to the right from this rotary (10min.). **Plaza Mayor** is straight up C. Santiago from the tourist office; the **cathedral** and **sculpture museum** are 10min. to the north.

Tourist Office: C. Santiago, 19 (☎983 34 40 13). Open daily 9am-2pm and 5-7pm.

Currency Exchange: Banco Central Hispano, C. Perú, 6 (☎902 24 24 24), on the corner of Av. Acera Recoletos. Open M-F 8:30am-2:30pm. **Citibank,** C. Miguel Iscar, 7, off Pl. Zorrilla. Open M-F 8am-2pm.

Luggage Storage: At the **train station** 24hr. (lockers 400ptas/€2.50). At the **bus station** (100ptas/€0.60 per bag). Open M-Sa 8am-10pm.

Emergency: ☎091 or 092. **Local Police:** In the Ayuntamiento (☎983 42 61 07).

Medical Services: Ambulance/emergencies: ☎061. **Hospital Pío del Río Hortega,** Rondilla de Santa Teresa, s/n (☎983 42 04 00). **Red Cross** (*Cruz Roja* ☎983 22 22 22).

Pharmacy: Daytime pharmacies line C. Santiago. **Lcda. López,** Po. Zorrilla, 85, is the only all-night pharmacy. Open Sa-Th 10pm-9:30am, F 10pm-10am.

Internet Access: Ciberc@fé Segafredo, Po. de Zorrilla, 46 (☎983 33 80 63). From Pl. de Zorrilla, walk down Po. de Zorrilla alongside the park; the café is on the right just before Av. García Morato. Exact change needed to feed machines. 100ptas/€0.60 per 15min. Open daily 8am-midnight.

Post Office: Pl. Rinconada, s/n (☎983 33 02 31). From Pl. Mayor, take C. Jesús to the left of the Ayuntamiento. **Faxes** and **Lista de Correos.** Open M-Sa 8:30am-8:30pm, Su 8:30am-2pm. **Postal Code:** 47001.

ACCOMMODATIONS

Cheap lodgings with winter heating are easy to come by. The dusty and construction-filled streets off Av. Acera Recoletos near the train station are packed with pensiones, as are those near the cathedral and behind Pl. Mayor at Pl. Val.

Pensión Dani, C. Perú, 11, 1st fl. (☎983 30 02 49). Following the directions from the train station to the tourist office, turn right onto C. Perú before Pl de Zorrilla. Singles 1700ptas/€10.25; doubles 3000 ptas/€18; triples 4300ptas/€26.

Pensión Dos Rosas, C. Perú, 11, 2nd fl. (☎983 20 74 39). The rooms at Dos Rosas are just as spacious and well-kept as those at Dani. Portable heaters in winter. Singles 1700ptas/€10.25; doubles 3000ptas/€18; triples 4300ptas/€26.

Hostal Residencia Val II, Pl. Val, 6, 1st fl. (☎983 37 57 52). From Pl. Mayor, turn left onto Pl. Corrillo, two streets to the right when facing the Ayuntamiento. Walk up C. Val, the third street on the right in the plaza. TV common area and quiet lounge. Huge rooms with eclectic quilts open onto private terraces. Apr.-Sept. singles with bath 3500ptas/€21.04, with toilet 2500ptas/€15.03; doubles with bath 5000ptas/€30.05, with toilet 4000ptas/€24.04. Oct.-Mar. singles with bath 3000ptas/€18.03, with toilet 2000ptas/€12.02; doubles with bath 4500ptas/€27.05, with toilet 3500ptas/€21.01.

FOOD

Though bars and cafés abound, the search for a meal beyond *tapas* may leave visitors filled with angst but with an empty stomach. Search for eateries between Pl. Mayor and Pl. Val and explore the area near the cathedral for *tapas.* The **Mercado del Val,** in Pl. Val just off Pl Mayor, has fresh foods. (open M-Sa 6am-3pm).

Restaurante Chino Gran Muralla, C. Santa María, 1 (☎983 34 23 07), to the right off C. Santiago, north of Pl. Zorrilla. Neon dragons welcome patrons to this stock. Four-course *menú del día* (725ptas/€4.25). Open daily 11:30am-5pm and 7pm-12:30am.

Casa San Pedro Regalad, Pl. Ochavo, 1 (☎983 34 45 06). From Pl. Mayor, walk up C. Lencería and turn left onto C. Lonja, which runs into Pl. Ochavo. Descend into the cavernous depths of this 16th-century *bodega* to enjoy elegant dining. *Menú* 1200ptas/€7.25. Open daily 1:30-3:30pm and 8-11:30pm. AmEx/MC/V.

SIGHTS

CATHEDRAL METROPOLITANA. Although this Romanesque cathedral was partly designed by Juan de Herrera, creator of El Escorial (see p. 124), it is still an excellent example of Herrera's *desornamentado* style of plain masonry. Apparently, other architects felt the need to ornament the cathedral; ranks of gargoyles leer down at parishioners. The extensive **Museo Diocesano,** in the cathedral's Gothic addition, houses the remains of the original 11th- to 13th-century structure as well as Herrera's model of the basilica. *(C. Arribas, 1, in Pl. Universidad. From Pl. Mayor, walk up C. Ferrari. After 2 blocks, veer left onto Bajada de la Libertad. At Pl. Libertad, turn right; the cathedral is directly in front of you. ☎983 30 43 62. Cathedral and museum open Tu-Sa 10am-1:30pm and 4:30-7pm, Su 10am-2pm. Cathedral free. Museum 400ptas/€2.50.)*

CASA DE CERVANTES. The supposed home in which Cervantes penned his epic "El Quijote" from 1603-1606, the *casa* houses an amusing collection of old books and furniture; the medieval bed-warmer is its only unique highlight. *(☎983 33 88 10. C. Rastro. From Pl. de Zorrilla, walk up C. Miguel Iscar; C. Rastro will be two block up on your right. Open Tu-Sa 9:30am-3:30pm, Su 10am-3pm. 400ptas/€2.50, students with ID 200ptas/€1.25. Under 18 and over 65 free. Su free.)*

ENTERTAINMENT

Valladolid's cafés and bars are lively, though nothing to write home about. A student crowd fills the countless bars on **C. Paraíso,** just beyond the cathedral. From Pl. de la Universidad at the cathedral, turn left onto C. Duque de Lerma, then right onto C. Marqués del Duero; C. Paraíso will be on the right. For pubs, try **Pl. San Miguel** (from P. Mayor, walk up Pl. Corrillo, turn left onto C. Val, and after the plaza, continue straight onto C. Zapico; at Pl. Los Arces, turn left onto C. San Antonio de Padua, which brings you to Pl. San Miguel) and **C. Santa María,** off C. Santiago. Cafés on **C. Vincente Moliner** draw an older crowd; from Pl. Mayor, walk up C. Ferrari, and at Pl. Fuente Dorada, C. Vicente Moliner is on the left. The neighborhood around **Pl. Martí Monsó,** however, is the most central nightlife in Valladolid. In addition to its numerous all-night *tapas* bars—such as **El Concho,** C. Correos, 2 (open daily 8:30pm-2:30am)—and chic wine bars—like **Vino Tinto,** C. Calixto Fernández de la Torre, 4 (open M-Sa 7pm-4am)—this neighborhood also houses Valladolid's two best dance clubs. **TinTin,** C. Campañas, 12, deserves its title as most popular bar in Valladolid. From Pl. Mayor, walk up Calixto Fernández de la Torre (to the left when facing the Ayuntamiento), turn right onto Pl. Martí Monso, then right again onto C. Campanas. (Open Tu-Sa 10pm-sunrise.) **Club 38,** C. Mayor, 30 (☎983 74 52 82), is also a dance hotspot.(Open 7pm-late.)

With over 12 movie theaters, Valladolid has one of the highest cinema-to-citizen ratios in all Spain. Each movie theater features a different genre of film. **Cines Casablanca,** C. Platerias, 1 (☎983 33 89 14), features *film noir* classics, while the **Cines Coca,** Pl. Marti Monso, 10 (☎983 33 02 90), shows recent British and American films. (Tickets 1100ptas/€6.75.) The **International Cinema Week** (Oct. 21-31) features indie European films. The week of September 21 marks the **Fiesta Mayor,** which features bullfights, carnivals, and parades.

CASTILLA Y LEÓN

PALENCIA ☎979

Although Palencia (pop. 180,000) lacks the attractions and pizazz of its fellow Castillian capitals, it is, of course, rich in history and religious monuments. After being catapulted to Spanish fame for fending off the Duke of Lancaster's 14th-century attack, Palencia underwent a surge of construction. As a result, its historical center is riddled with 14th to 16th-century churches. While not as well-known as the cathedrals in Leon or Burgos, they do provide an interesting glimpse at the development of Romanesque and Gothic architecture. Most travelers should skip Palencia, but those with time to spare can explore its compact city center--peppered with a series of modern sculptures—or join the locals in an afternoon of sunbathing in the riverside Perque Islas dos Aguas.

TRANSPORTATION. Trains depart from Parque Los Jardinillos, s/n (☎979 74 30 19 or 902 24 02 02). Trains to: **Barcelona** (8½-9hr.; daily 1:30am, 2:21, 11pm; 5500ptas/€33); **Bilbao** and **San Sebastián** (3¾hr., 4:13pm, 2700-3100ptas/€16.25-18.75); **Burgos** (1hr.; M-F 9 per day 7:45am-1:30am, Sa-Su 8 per day 11:38am-1:30am;

1400ptas/€11); **La Coruña** (8hr.; 3:25am, 1, and 4pm; 4800ptas/€29); **León** (1¼hr., 11 per day 8:10am-9:35pm, 945-1700ptas/€10.25); **Madrid** (3-5hr., M-F 14 per day 2:24am-8:24pm, 2600-3600ptas/€16-22); **Oviedo** (4-5hr.; M-F 5 per day 3:19am-5:56pm, Sa 4 per day 3:19am-5:56pm, Su 3 per day 10:53am-5:56pm; 2000-2600ptas/€12-16); **Salamanca** (2½hr., M-Sa 8am and 1:10pm, 2000-2300ptas/€12-14); **Santander** (3-3¾hr.; M-F 6 per day 3:56am-7:52pm, Sa 7 per day 3:56am-7:24pm, Su 6 per day 7:49am-7:24pm; 1650-2400ptas/€10-14.50); **Valladolid** (45min., 12 per day 7:33am-9:15pm, 410-1100ptas/€2.50-7); **Zamora** (2hr., M-Sa 8am, 1750ptas/€11). **Buses** depart from Jardinillos de la Estación, s/n (☎979 74 32 22) Info booth open M-F 8am-10:30pm, Sa-Su 8am-1:30pm and 5-10:30pm. To: **Burgos** (1½hr.; M-F 9am, 2, 3 7pm, Sa 9am and 2pm; 625ptas/€3.75) and **Valladolid** (45min.; M-F every hr. 7am-10pm, Sa 6 per day 8am-7:30pm, Su 11am, 4, 9pm; 440ptas/€2.75).

PRACTICAL INFORMATION. The **tourist office,** C. Mayor Principal, 105, a 15min. walk down C. Mayor Principal from Pl. de León. (☎979 74 00 68. Open M-F 9am-2pm and 5-7pm, Sa-Su 1am-2pm and 5-8pm.) Services include: **Banco Central Hispano,** C. Mayor, 37 (☎904 24 24 24; open M-F 8:30am-2:30pm.); **emergency** ☎091, 092; **local police,** C. Ortega y Gasest, s/n (☎979 71 82 00); **medical emergency,** dial ☎979 70 21 00 or 71 29 00. **Clínica Virgen de la Salud,** Av. Simón Nieto, 31 (☎ 979 74 77 00). The two **post offices,** one at Pl. León, 2 (☎979 74 21 80; fax 74 22 60), send and receive **faxes.** The office next to the train station (☎979 74 21 77) provides **Lista de Correos.** (Both open M-F 8:30am-8:30pm, Sa 9:30am-2pm.) **Postal code:** 34001.

ACCOMMODATIONS AND FOOD. Pickings are slim for rooms in Palencia. Fortunately, while *pensiones* and *hostales* near C. Mayor Principal are few, even the most expensive have fairly cheap rooms. One of the best is **Pensión Gredos,** C. Valentín Calderón, 18. Downstairs is a restaurant and patio. (☎979 70 28 33 or 609 29 46 84. Reception 24hr. Breakfast 350ptas/€2; lunch and dinner 1000ptas/€6 each. Singles 1800ptas/€11; doubles 3500ptas/€21; triples 6000ptas/€36.) At the youth hostel, **Victorio Macho (HI),** in the Campo de Juventud on C. Dr. Fleming, s/n, hordes of Spanish teenagers enjoy the common room with TV, kitchen and dining hall, and athletic facilities. Bus B from the corner of Pl. de León and Ave. Calvo Sotelo (every 15min., 70ptas/€0.45) saves trekkers a hike. (☎979 72 04 62; fax 72 98 73. HI members only. Breakfast 100-150ptas/€0.60-0.90. 1000ptas/€6; over 26 1450ptas/€9. Open July-Aug. 15.) There are very few reasonably priced restaurants in Palencia. Fortunately, there's a **Champion Supermarket** at the corner of C. Menéndez Pelayo and C. Pedro Romero. From Pl. de León, walk down C. Mayor Principal and turn right onto C. Patrio del Castaño, which turns into C. Pedro Romero. (☎979 74 96 56. Open M-F 9:15am-9:15pm.)

ENTERTAINMENT. Palencia's biggest attraction is its Gothic cathedral, **Santa Iglesia de San Antolín,** where 14-year-old Catherine of Lancaster married 10-year-old Enrique III in 1388. *Sick.* Built between the 14th and 16th centuries with predominantly Gothic features, the cathedral has a precious sandstone and pastel interior. During the Spanish tour, guides illuminate the various altars and then lead visitors down a stone staircase to the spooky **Cripta de San Antolín,** a 7th-century sepulchre. The cathedral's **museum** houses El Greco's famed *San Sebastián* and some spectacular 16th-century Flemish tapestries—not to mention a tiny caricature of Carlos V. From Pl. de León. Walk down C. Eduardo Dato, and at Pl. Carmelitas turn left onto C. Santa Teresa de Jesús; the cathedral is at the end of this street in Pl. de la Inmaculada Concepción. (Cathedral ☎979 70 13 47. Cathedral and museum open M-Sa 9am-1:30pm and 4:30-7pm, Su 9am-1:30pm. Cathedral free, museum 300ptas/€2. Tours in Spanish M-Sa 10:30am and 4pm, Su 11:15pm. 100ptas/€0.60.) Of the other churches in town, the favorite of El Cid fans is **Iglesia de San Miguel.** According to legend, it was here that El Campeador wed Doña Jimena. Its most notable feature is the 13th-century Gothic tower graced with tall openwork windows. Much of the church was under construction in summer 2001; check at the tourist office to see if construction is complete. To reach the church from the cathedral, walk down C. San Pedro from Pl. de Inmaculada Concepción, and turn left onto C. General Mola, which takes you directly to San Miguel. (☎979 74 07 69. Open M-F 9:30am-noon, 12:30-1:30pm and 6-7:30pm.)

DAYTRIP FROM PALENCIA: CARRIÓN DE LOS CONDES

Estabanez AJA ***buses*** *(☎979 74 32 22) carry day-trippers to Carrión from the Palencia bus station, Jardinillos de la Estación, s/n (30min.; M-F 1:30 and 6:30pm, Sa 8:30am and 1:30pm; return buses M-F 8:30am, 5, 7:30pm, Sa 5:30pm; 330ptas/€2).*

From the bus stop, tiny Carrión (pop. 1000) doesn't look like much: a café, a few benches, and a crumbling church. Wandering up into the tiny town, however, reveals some of the most important sights on the Palencian segment of the Camino de Santiago. When not paying their respects at Carrion's numerous churches, the pilgrims lounge and socialize at the **Café-Bar España,** giving Carrión de los Condes much of its liveliness and draw for summertime visitors. The Camino first winds past the **Convento de Santa Clara,** also known as **Las Clarisas,** on the south side of town. The convent's **museo** shelters local religious artifacts as well as information about the pilgrimage itself. To enter, ring the bell and ask for the keeper. From the bus stop at the corner of C. Santa María and Highway N-120, walk downhill on C. Santa María, which becomes Ave. de los Peregrinos. The convent will be on the left. (☎979 88 01 34. Open in summer Tu-Su 10:30am-2pm and 4:30-8pm. 200ptas/€1.25.) Back uphill on C. Santa Maria is the 12th-century **Iglesia de Santa María** (☎979 88 00 72), notable for its southern façade's depiction of the legendary tribute of four Carrión maidens to Moorish conquerors. Santa María foiled the transaction by sending four menacing bulls to gore the Moors. (Open daily 9:30am-2pm and 4:30-9pm.) Continuing up C. Santa María and turning right onto Pl. de Generalísimo Franco brings travelers to the **Iglesia de Santiago,** a 12th-century Romanesque church and the most important religious structure in Carrión. The church's **museum** features relics and icons from throughout the diocese's history. (Open daily 10am-2pm and 5-7pm. Museum 200ptas/€1.25.) On the far side of the Río Carrión looms the secularized **Monasterio de San Zoilo.** Although the monastery now serves as a *parador,* visitors can still tour the building's Renaissance cloister to see its architecture and ornate frescoes of saints and Popes staring down at devotees. Near the exit are the tombs of the notorious Infantes de Carrión. In the *Cantar del Mío Cid,* they married, deflowered, beat, and then abandoned El Cid's daughters in the middle of the forest. From the Iglesia de Santiago, walk into Pl. de Generalísimo Franco (towards the Ayuntamiento) and turn right onto C. de José Girón. Follow this street as it winds its way down to the river, then cross the bridge to your left and follow the signs for the Restaurant Las Vegas. (☎979 88 09 02. Open daily May-Oct. 10:30am-2pm and 4-8pm; Nov.-Apr. M-F 10:30am-2pm, Sa-Su 10:30am-2pm and 4-6:30pm. 200ptas/€1.25.) Carrión's **tourist office** is in a wood-frame hut on C. Santa Maria, across from Café-Bar España (office hours vary).

BURGOS ☎947

The first thing one sees upon entering Burgos (pop. 346,000) is, of course, its cathedral: the magnificent Gothic spires tower over even the remotest *calle* and *plaza.* While this architectural and religious landmark is the city's claim to fame, there is much more to the town than transepts and altars. From its duck-filled riverbanks to its elegant denizens sipping *sangría* in sidewalk cafés, Burgos emits an aura of vivacity, prosperity, and elegance. Perhaps modern Burgos' ease and confidence is due to its 500-year stint as Castille's capital. After all, every street seems to mark some historical legacy, from the return of Christopher Columbus from the new world to the various conquests of El Cid Campeador, and nearly every plaza and paseo is graced with an architectural marvel, such as the Puente de Santa María and the Monasterio de Las Huelgas. Perhaps the heroes and kings of yore just knew a good thing when they saw it: what with its debaucherous nightlife and delectable cuisine, not even the King of Spain himself could deny that even from the most out-of-the-way alley, Burgos is simply splendid.

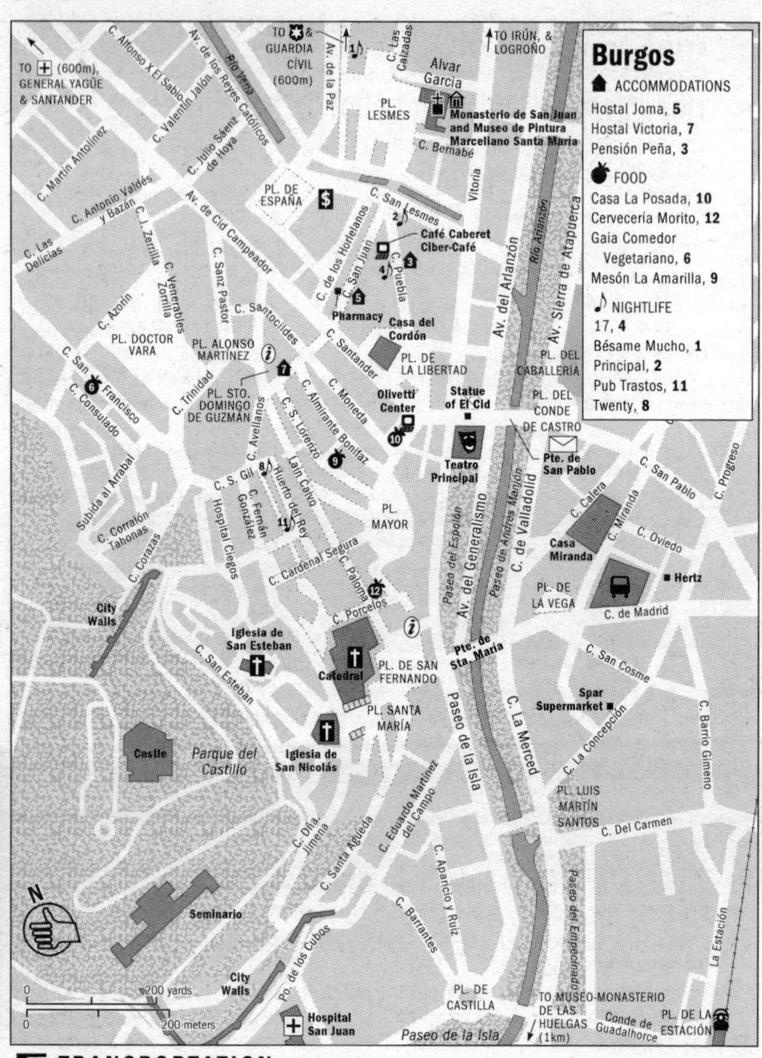

TRANSPORTATION

Trains: Av. Conde Guadalhorce, s/n (☎947 20 35 60). 10min. walk or a 500ptas/€3 taxi ride to the city center. Info open daily 7am-10pm. To: **Barcelona** (9-13¾hr., 4 per day 2:17am-11:40pm, 5100ptas/€30.50); **Bilbao** (2½-4hr.; M-F 5 per day 3:17am-6:44pm, Sa 4 per day 3:17am-6:44pm, Su 3 per day 12:57-6:44pm; 2200ptas/€13.25); **La Coruña** (6-9hr.; daily 2:38am, 12:13 and 3:16pm; 4900-5300ptas/€29.50-32); **León** (2-3hr.; M-Sa 4 per day 2:38am-3:16pm, Su 3 per day 2:38am-3:16pm; 2200ptas/€13.25); **Lisbon** (8-10hr., daily at 1:32pm, 5700ptas/€34.50); **Madrid** (3-5½hr.; M-F 10 per day 2:20am-11:07pm, Sa-Su 9 per day 2:20am-11:07pm; 3060-3500ptas/€18.50-21); **Palencia** (45min.; M-F 8 per day 2:38am 8:20pm, Sa-Su 6 per day 2:38am-8:20pm; 515-1200ptas/€3.25-7.25); **Oviedo** (5hr., M-Sa 6:48am and 3:16pm, 3200ptas/€19.25); **San Sebastián** (3-3½hr., 8 per day 5:12am-6:44pm, 2095-2500ptas/€13-15); **Valladolid** (1-2hr., 12 per day 1:44am-11:07pm, 975-1700ptas/€6-10.25)

Buses: C. Miranda, 4 (☎947 28 88 55). To: **Barcelona** (7½hr.; 11:45am, 3, 11:59pm, 5110ptas/€30.75); **Bilbao** (2-3hr., M-F 4 per day 8:30am-7pm, 1445ptas/€9); **La Coruña/Santiago** (7hr., 10am, 4650ptas/€28); **León** (3½hr., M-Sa 10:45am, 1725ptas/€10.50); **Madrid** (2¾hr., M-F 19 per day 7:30am-3:45am, 1975ptas/€12); **Oviedo** (4-5hr., 4:45am and 4pm, 1810ptas/€11); **Salamanca** (4hr., M-Sa 10:45am, 1765ptas/€10.75); **San Sebastián** (4-5hr., 7 per day 7:15am-3:15am, 1810ptas/€11); **Santander** (2¾hr., 4 per day 10:30am-3:15am, 1375/ptas/€8.50); **Valladolid/Zamora** (2hr., M-Sa 5 per day 10:15am-4:30pm, 1060ptas/€6.50); **Vitoria-Gasteiz** (1¾hr., 9 per day 7:15am-3:15am, 975ptas/€6).

Taxis: Abutaxi (☎947 27 77 77) or **Radio Taxi** (☎947 48 10 10). 24hr. service. Taxis line up by Pl. de Santo Domingo de Guzmán, Pl. de Vega, and Pl. de Conde Jordana.

Car Rental: Hertz, C. Progreso, 5 (☎947 20 16 75, reservations ☎902 40 24 05). From the main entrance of the bus station, turn left onto C. Miranda, left again onto C. de Madrid, and left again onto C. Progreso. Min. age 25; credit card in driver's name required for deposit. Small cars with unlimited mileage 11,000ptas/€66 per day, longer rentals less. Open M-F 9am-1pm and 4-7pm, Sa 9am-1pm. AmEx/MC/V.

ORIENTATION AND PRACTICAL INFORMATION

The Río Arlanzón splits Burgos north-to-south. While the **train** and **bus stations** are on the south side, the **Santa Iglesia Cathedral** and most other sights of interest are located to the north. From the **train station** at Av. Conde de Guadalhorce (s/n), follow Av. Conde de Guadalhorce away from the station, then turn right onto C. La Merced before the river. At the second bridge, **Puente de Santa María,** turn left. Continuing through the gate will bring you to the cathedral, while turning right onto the **Po. del Expolón** leads to Plaza Mayor and **Pl. de la Libertad,** both on the left. From the main entrance of the **bus station,** C. Miranda, 4, turn left onto C. Miranda and right onto C. Madrid across the river and to the cathedral.

Tourist Office: Pl. Alonso Martínez, 7 (☎947 20 31 25; fax 27 65 29). Open M-F 9am-2pm and 5-7pm, Sa-Su and holidays 10am-2pm and 5-8pm.

Currency Exchange: Banco Central Hispano, Plaza de España, 6 (☎904 24 24 24). Open M-Th 8:30am-6:30pm, F 8am-3pm.

Emergency: ☎091 or 092. **Guardia Civil,** Av. Cantabria, 87-95; ☎062 or 947 22 22 63. **Police,** Av. Cantabria, s/n; ☎947 28 88 39.

Pharmacy: Farmacia Natividad Combarro Rodríguez, C. San Juan, 25 (☎947 20 12 89). Open M-F 9:45am-2pm and 5-8pm, Sa 10:15am-2pm. All pharmacies post a list of late-night and Su pharmacies in their windows.

Medical Services: Ambulance ☎947 23 22 22. **Hospital General Yagüe,** Av. del Cid, 96 (☎947 28 18 00).

Internet Access: Café Cabaret Ciber-Café, C. La Puebla, 21 (☎947 20 27 22). 500ptas/€3 per 30min. 300ptas/€2 per each additional 30min. Printing 10ptas/€0.06 per page. Open M-Th 4pm-2am, F 4pm-4am, Sa 5pm-4am, Su 5pm-2am.

Post Office: Pl. Conde de Castro, s/n (☎947 26 27 50, info ☎902 19 71 97; fax 26 57 11). From Pl. de la Libertad, cross the river on Puente de San Pablo; post office will be directly on your right. **Lista de Correos** and **fax** services (1850ptas/€11.12 first page, 500ptas/€3 each additional page). Open M-F 8:30am-8:30pm, Sa 9:30am-2pm. **Postal Code:** 09070.

ACCOMMODATIONS AND CAMPING

Inexpensive *pensiones* line the streets near **Pl. Alonso Martínez.** The C. San Juan area is also dotted with reasonably priced hostels. Otherwise, the tourist office distributes a complete list of Burgos's accommodations. Reservations are crucial on summer weekends, for the festivals in June and July, and in August.

Pensión Peña, C. La Puebla, 18, 2nd fl. (☎947 20 63 23). From the Puente de Santa María, turn right onto C. Vitoria, then left at Pl. del Cid. Cross Pl. de la Libertad to your right and turn left onto C. La Puebla will be directly in front of you. Singles 1700ptas/€10.25, with sink 1800ptas/€11; doubles 2900ptas/€17.50, 3000ptas/€18.

Hostal Joma, C. San Juan, 26, 2nd fl. (☎947 20 33 50). From Puente de Santa María, turn right onto C. Vitoria, and at Pl. del Cid, turn left onto C. Santander. Spotless rooms in a large, modern building. June-Sept. singles 1800ptas/€11; doubles 3200ptas/€19.25. Oct.-May singles 1600ptas/€9.75; doubles 2700ptas/€16.25.

Hostal Victoria, C. San Juan, 3, 2nd fl. (☎/fax 947 20 15 42). From Puente de Santa María, turn right onto C. Vitoria. At Pl. del Cid, turn left onto C. Santander; C. San Juan is the 2nd left. Sunny rooms have big beds, desks, and sinks. Public phone and luggage storage. July-Sept. singles 300ptas/€18; doubles 4500ptas/€27. Oct.-June singles 2600ptas/€16; doubles 4000ptas/€24. Extra bed 1750ptas/€10.50.

Camping Fuentes Blancas, Pl. Vega, 6, 1st floor (☎947 20 54 57). The "Fuentes Blancas" bus leaves from Pl. España (July-Sept. 15 9:30am, 12:30, 4:15, 7:15pm; 75ptas/€0.45). Swimming pool, showers, restaurant, and currency exchange on site. 560ptas/€3.50 per person, 495ptas/€3 per tent and per car. Open Apr.-Sept. MC/V.

FOOD

Burgos natives take pride in their delicious *queso de Burgos*, a cheese usually served with honey or in a *tarte* as dessert, and *morcilla*, a sausage made from tripe, blood, and rice. The area around **Pl. Alonso Martínez** is laden with restaurants serving these staples, while C. San Lorenzo is *tapas* heaven. **Mercado de Abastos (Sur),** on C. Miranda next to the bus station, sells fresh meat and bread. (Open M-Sa 7am-3pm, or until the vendors sell out.) **Spar Supermercado,** C. Concepción, 14, near the train station, carries all the staples. (☎947 26 00 07. Open M-Th 9am-2pm and 5:30-8:30pm, F 9am-2:30pm and 5:30-8:30pm, Sa 9am-2:30pm.)

Gaia Comedor Vegetariano, C. San Francisco, 31 (☎947 23 76 45). From Pl. Alonso Martínez, walk up C. Trinidad and turn right onto C. San Francisco. The earth goddess herself would be delighted by this vegetarian, counter-cultural luncheonette. Four-course *menú* (1000ptas/€6). Open M-Sa 1:30-4pm.

Casa La Posada, Pl. Santo Domingo de Guzmán, 18 (☎947 20 45 78). The oh-so-fancy *menú de la casa* (1800ptas/€11) features a rotating local dish of the day. Open daily 1-4pm and 9-11pm. AmEx/MC/V.

Cervecería Morito, C. Porcelos, 1 (☎947 21 73 21). From Pl. Mayor, walk up C. Sombrería, and C. Porcelos will be on your right. Be prepared to fight for a table on this popular *tapas* bar's terrace. *Raciones* (225-925ptas/€1.50-5.50). Open M-Sa 7pm-2am.

SIGHTS

SANTA IGLESIA CATHEDRAL. Officially named a UNESCO World Heritage Sight and unofficially named the most beautiful cathedral in Spain, the **Catedral Santa Iglesia** is deserving of its notoriety. Its magnificent spires find their way into every view of the city, and its Gothic interior is equally remarkable. Originally a Romanesque church built in the 13th century by *Reconquista* hero Fernando III (El Santo), the cathedral was transformed during the following three centuries into a Gothic marvel. Devout visitors can enter the Chapel of Christ, the cathedral's holiest and most infamous arch: the crucified Jesus is constructed of real human body parts. Fortunately, the cathedral has other wonders for those not attending services: the 16th-century stained-glass dome of the Capilla Mayor; the eerily lifelike papamoscas (fly-catcher), a strange creature high up near the main door in the central aisle that tolls the hours by opening its mouth and gulping; and, under the transept and marked only by a small brick, the remains of El Cid and Doña Jimenez. Within the cloister, the cathedral's museum displays a Visigoth Bible and El Cid's nuptial documents. *(☎947 20 47 12. Open M-Sa 9:30am-1pm and 4-7pm, Su 9:30-11:45am and 4-7pm. Cathedral free. Museum 600ptas/€3.75, students 400ptas/€2.50. Recorded histories in English 100ptas/€0.45.)*

MUSEO-MONASTERIO DE LAS HUELGAS REALES. Built by King Alfonso VIII in 1188, the austere Museo-Monasterio de las Huelgas Reales is slightly out of the way, but certainly worth the trip. Once a summer palace for Castilian kings and later an elite convent for Cistercian nuns, today's monastery-as-museum allows visitors a glimpse of the austerity and glory of medieval Castillian royalty. In fact, the monastery has been closely associated with Spanish royalty since the Middle Ages; the abbess of Las Huelgas has traditionally served as a personal advisor to the king. Burial wardrobes can be viewed in the **Museo de Telas** (Textile Museum). *(Take the "Barrio del Pilar" bus from Pl. España to the Museo stop (80ptas/€48). ☎947 20 56 87. Open Apr.-Sept. Tu-F 11am-1:15pm and 4-5:15pm, Sa 11am-1:15pm and 4-5:45pm, Su 10:30am-2:15pm; Oct.-Mar. Tu-Sa 10:30am, 1:15 and 3:30-5:45pm, Su 10:30am-2:15pm. 800ptas/€4.80, students and under 14 400ptas/€2.50, under 5 and EU passport-bearers free. W free. Obligatory tours in Spanish every 30min.)*

PARQUE DEL CASTILLO. Atop a hill high above the cathedral, the ruins of a medieval castle and a sprawling, tangled park preside over Burgos. Sections of the walls and building demolished by Napoleonic troops are still undergoing reconstruction. The bleached castle rocks offer astounding views of the red roofs of Burgos below and the surrounding countryside. *(From the front entrance of Iglesia San Esteban, climb the 200 steps directly across the street.)*

CASA MIRANDA. This sprawling 16th-century mansion houses four floors of provincial Burgalese art and archaeology. Included in the exhibits are the remains of Cluny, a piece of the front façade of the monastery at Santo Domingo de Silos, and the sepulchre of Don Juan de Padilla. While the provincial art tends toward the usual devotional images, the first floor archaeological collection is a fascinating collection of artifacts and bones. *(C. Miranda, 13. ☎947 26 58 75. Open Tu-F 10am-2pm and 4:30-8pm, Sa 10am-2pm and 4:45-8:15pm, Su 10am-2pm. 200ptas/€1.25, under 18, senior citizens, and students with ID free. Sa-Su free.)*

CASA DEL CORDÓN. The restored Casa del Cordón—named for the Franciscan Friar's belt that hangs from the doorway—was built by Castilian constables in the 15th century. On April 23, 1497, Columbus met with Fernando and Isabel here after his second trip to America, and here Felipe el Hermoso breathed his last ragged breath after an exhausting game of *pelota* (jai-alai). Upon his death, his wife Juana dragged his corpse through the streets, earning her nickname, Juana la Loca (the Mad). *(On C. Santander, on the other side of the statue of El Cid, on the right.)*

ENTERTAINMENT AND NIGHTLIFE

Like a typical Spanish town, Burgos' nightlife starts late into the night. By midnight C. Avellanos (across from Pl. Alonso Martínez) fills with night owls, migrating from C. Avellanos onto nearby C. Huerto del Rey. If you have to hit the sack early on a Saturday night, wake up Sunday to join the crowds still dancing at *discotecas* along C. San Juan, C. La Puebla, and in the disco complex on Pl. San Lesmes. Nightlife shifts into overdrive during the last week in June, when Burgos honors its patron saints with concerts, parades, fireworks, bullfights, and dances. The day after **Corpus Christi** (May 30th in 2002), citizens parade through town with the *Pendón de las Navas*, a banner captured from the Moors in 1212.

Twenty, Pl. Huerto del Rey, 20 (☎947 26 46 92). Easily the most popular and crowded stop on the Huerto del Rey clubhopping route. Techno predominates the multi-level dance floor. Beer 300ptas/€2. Open M-Sa 7pm-5am, Su 7pm-midnight.

17, C. La Puebla, 17. Burgos's trendsetters enjoy evenings at this cavernous bar. If the barman bores you, entertain yourself with the caveman-like drawings of "couples" on the bright orange walls. Open Tu-Sa 4pm until the last person leaves.

Principal, C. La Puebla, 40, at the corner of C. San Juan and C. San Lesmes. Sleek limestone-and-glass bar attracts an older, low-key crowd. Open daily 5pm-3am.

Pub Trastos, Pl. Huerto del Rey, 7-9. Cheap liquor keeps backpackers dancing until dawn. Arrive after 1am. Beer 250ptas/€1.50. Open daily 7pm-5am, later F-Sa.

SHOVE IT UP YOUR APSE After a few Castillian towns, the regions cathedrals and churches often blend together, and unless you're an art history major or an aficionado of Catholic churches, all the terms—Romanesque and Gothic, apse and transept—mean little, and the building's themselves even less. So here's a quick lesson in cathedral architecture. Every Catholic cathedral is built in the shape of the cross. The vertical arm of the cross is called the **nave;** the horizontal arm of the cross is the **transept.** Where the transept and nave meet is usually where the **altar** stands; below the altar in the nave are the **choir stalls.** The segment of the nave above the transept is the **apse**, usually the site of several **chapels,** or altars in honor of saints and apostles other than the patron of the cathedral. Underneath the main floor is the **sepulchre,** or **catacomb,** a burial place for royal and holy figures. The **cloister** is situated off the apse or the transept and is a square structure with a garden in the middle.

As for the architectural styles, **Romanesque**, dating from the 11th to 13th centuries, is the older of the two. Based on Roman architecture (hence the name), Romanesque relied on strict geometric shapes mathematically proven to support the weight of the building. Therefore, the hallmarks of a Romanesque structure, are perfectly round arches, walls of even thickness, and a scarcity of windows. Columns are all symmetrically placed, and vaults—the arched ceilings—are never more than half the width of the height they support. In other words, Romanesque churches are dark, blocky, and full of right angles and perfect circles.

Gothic architecture, named after the Visigoths as an insult, defied all the rules of Romanesque geometry. Due to the invention of flying buttresses and ribbed vaults, Gothic architects were able to make taller and brighter cathedrals. The walls of the cathedral were freed from supporting the entire weight of the building—a job now given over to the buttresses and the ribbings—and the result was more windows and a less visible structure. In fact, it is none other than Gothic cathedrals that are renowned for their enormous and elaborate stained glass windows. Thanks to rib vaulting, the cathedrals could also be taller than Romanesque churches, creating imposing new spires on local skylines. While in practice Gothic cathedrals may seem as dark and geometrically rigid as the Romanesque, they are in theory lighter, brighter, and taller, helping their parishioners to be just a little bit closer to God.

DAYTRIP FROM BURGOS

SANTO DOMINGO DE SILOS

To get from Burgos to Santo Domingo de Silos (50km) by car, take N-234 toward Salas de los Infantes to Hortigüela. From there, C-110, which borders the Arlanza River, will pass the monastery of San Pedro de Arlanza before arriving at Covarrubias; it's only 17km farther. Arcoredillo runs a ***bus*** *to Santo Domingo from Burgos, Miranda, 4 (1½hr.; departs Burgos M-F 5:30pm; departs Santo Domingo M-F 8:30am; 650ptas/€4).*

Since 1993, the Benedictine monks of Santo Domingo de Silos (pop. 380) have sold 5 million recordings, including the Gregorian chant album that reached #1 on global charts. In the **Abadía de Santo Domingo de Silos,** listeners are transported back in time as black-cloaked monks chant along with the organ and the soothing echoes of their own voices. You can sit in at morning song at high mass at 9am (Su at noon), vespers at 7pm (Th in summer at 8pm), and compline at 9:40pm. (☎947 39 00 68. Open Tu-Sa 10am-1pm and 4:30-6pm, Su-M 4:30-6pm. 250ptas/€1.50) Perhaps more interesting than the monastery itself are the **museum** and **cloister** next door, where highlights include an ancient pharmacy of 300-year-old chemicals, skulls, and preserved animal parts. Beyond Santo Domingo de Silos, the sole option for entertainment is hiking in the hills. Ask for directions to **La Yecla** (2.5km from Silos) where a precarious walkway leads through a narrow river gorge. Rooms are easy to find in this friendly (though pricy) little town—a good thing since visitors without cars are almost obligated to stay the night. **Hostal Cruces,** Plaza Mayor, 20, offers clean, sunny rooms with baths. (☎947 39 00 64. Singles 3000ptas/€18; doubles 5000ptas/€30. V.) Near the bus station, **Hostal Santo Domingo,** C. Santo Domingo, 14-16, has well-kept, air-conditioned rooms with full baths, phones, and TVs. (☎947 39 00 53. Singles 3500ptas/€21; doubles 4900-7500ptas/€30-45.)

SORIA

Though modern development has finally invaded provincial Soria (pop. 34,000), the city still preserves its leisurely pace. Men sporting berets tote bundles of local bread past Romanesque churches, and Soria's inhabitants still religiously observe their evening *paseo*, strolling and chatting with friends and neighbors before dinner. Although the city proper is best used as a base for exploring surrounding towns, the two intriguing architectural anomalies of Monasterio de San Juan de Duero and the Ermita San Saturio on its outskirts are well worth a visit.

TRANSPORTATION

Trains: Estación El Cañuelo (☎975 23 02 02), Ctra. de Madrid. Shuttle buses run from Pl. Mariano Granados to the station 20min. before each train departs (about 75ptas/€0.45), and then shuttles arrivals back to the city. To: **Madrid** (3hr.; M-F 7:40am and 5:25pm, Sa 8:40am and 5:25pm, Su 8:45am, 5:25pm, and 7:30pm; 1860ptas/€11.25) via **Alcalá de Henares** (2¾hr., 1575ptas/€9.50).

Buses: Av. Valladolid (☎975 22 51 60), at Av. Gaya Nuño. Info open M-Sa 7am-10pm, Su 9am-10pm. **Therpasa** (☎975 22 20 60) to: **Zaragoza** (2¼hr.; 3-6 per day M-Sa 7:30am-8pm, Su noon-9pm; 1230ptas/€7.50) via **Tarazona** (1hr., 630ptas/€3.75). **La Serrana** (☎975 24 09 13) to: **Burgos** (2½hr.; 2-3 per day M-F 7am-6:30pm, Sa 7am-2:15pm, Su 2pm and 6pm; 1345ptas/€8.25). **Linecar** (☎975 22 15 55) to: **Valladolid** (3hr.; 3 per day M-Sa 9:45am-6:45pm, Su 11:15am-6:45pm; 1685ptas/€10.25). **Continental Auto** (☎975 22 44 01) to: **Logroño** (1½hr.; 4-7 per day M-Th, Sa 11am-10:15pm, F-Su 11am-12:15am; 845ptas/€5.25); **Madrid** (2½hr.; 6-9 per day M-Th and Sa 9:15am-8:45pm, F and Su 9:15am-11:45pm; 1805ptas/€10.82); **Pamplona** (2hr.; 4-7 per day M-Th and Sa 10:45am-10:15pm, F and Su 10:45am-12:15am; 1625ptas/€10).

Taxis: (☎975 21 30 34). Stands at Pl. Mariano Granados and bus station.

Car Rental: Europcar, C. Angel Terrel, 3-5 (☎975 22 05 05), off C. Sagunto. Min. age 21. Must have credit card, passport, and license valid for at least one year. 11,355ptas/€68.25 per day, 55,855ptas/€335 per week (plus IVA; insurance included). Open M-F 9:30am-1:30pm and 4:30-8pm, Sa 10:30am-1pm.

ORIENTATION AND PRACTICAL INFORMATION

The city center is about a 15min. walk from the **bus station.** From the traffic circle outside the station, Av. Valladolid runs downhill to the *centro ciudad.* Keep walking for 5 blocks, then bear right at the fork onto Po. Espolón, which borders the **Parque Alameda.** When the park ends, **Pl. Mariano Granados** will be directly in front of you. To reach the center from the **train station,** either take the shuttle or turn left onto C. Madrid and follow the signs to *centro ciudad.* Continue on C. Almazán as it bears left and becomes Av. Mariano Vicen, follow the road for 6 blocks, keep left at the fork onto C. Alfonso VIII until you reach Pl. Mariano Granados. From the side of the plaza opposite the park, C. Marqués de Vadillo leads to pedestrian C. El Collado, the main shopping street that cuts through the old quarter to **Plaza Mayor.**

Tourist Office: Pl. Ramón y Cajal (☎/fax 975 21 20 52; www.sorianitelaimaginas.com), on the side of Pl. M. Granados opposite the park. English-speaking staff usually present only on weekends. Open M-F 9am-2pm and 5-7pm, Sa-Su 10am-2pm and 5-8pm.

Currency Exchange: Banco Hispano Central, C. Collado, 56 (☎975 22 02 25). Open April-Sept. M-F 8:30am-2:30pm; Oct.-May M-F 8:30am-2:30pm, Sa 8:30am-1pm.

Luggage Storage: At the **bus station.** 1st day 100ptas/€0.60, 25ptas/€0.15 each additional day. Open M-Sa 7am-10pm and Su 9am-10pm.

Emergency: ☎112 or 062.

Municipal Police: C. O. Augustín, 1 (☎092 or 975 21 18 62).

Medical Services: Hospital General, Po. Santa Barbara (☎975 23 43 00).

Internet: Café-Bar Carambola, C. Santa Maria, (☎975 23 17 73). With your back to the tourist office, take a right from Pl. Mariano Grandos onto C. Ferial, take a right after

1 block, then a quick left onto C. Santa Maria; the bar is a couple blocks up on left. Two coin-operated computers in a cyberspace loft above the bar. 200ptas/€1.25 for 15min., 700ptas/€4.25 per hour. Open M-Sa 9:30am-1:30am.

Post Office: Po. Espolón, 6 (☎ 975 23 35 70; fax 23 35 61), off Pl. Mariano Granados. Open M-F 8:30am-8:30pm, Sa 9:30am-2pm. **Postal Code:** 42070.

ACCOMMODATIONS AND CAMPING

Affordable hostels fill the streets around Pl. Olivo and Pl. Salvador, both near Pl. Mariano Granados.

Residencia Juvenil Juan Antonio Gaya Nuñoz, Po. San Francisco, (☎975 22 14 66). With your back to the tourist office, take C. Nicolás Rabal from Pl. Mariano Granados. Halfway along the park, take your 2nd left onto C. Luisa Marillac and look for the half-yellow dorms ahead. Open for HI members only from July 3-Aug. 15. Doubles with private bath. 3-night max. stay when full. Breakfast 150ptas/€1. Dorms 1100ptas/€6.75, over 26 1550ptas/€9.50.

Pension Ersogo, C. Alberca, 4 (☎975 21 35 08). The 1st right on C. Alberca off Pl. Ramón y Cajal. 7 4th floor rooms with 2 common baths. Singles 2300ptas/€14; doubles 3400ptas/€20.50; triples 4800ptas/€29.

Casa Diocesana Pío XII, C. San Juan, 5 (☎975 21 21 76; fax 24 02 78). The tall building set back from the street. From Pl. Marciano Granados, go up C. El Collado and right on C. San Juan, just after Pl. San Blas y el Rosel. Public telephone and laundry. July-Aug. singles 1890ptas/€11.25, with bath 3000ptas/€18; doubles 2760/€16.50, with bath 4150ptas/€25. Sept.-June singles 1470ptas/€8.75, with bath 2520ptas/€15; doubles 2390ptas/€14.50, with bath 3700ptas/€22.25. MC/V.

Camping Fuente la Teja (☎975 22 29 67), 2km from town on Ctra. Madrid (km 233). Swimming pool open Jun28-Aug. 500ptas/€3 per person, 525/€3.25 per car, and 600ptas/€3.75 per tent (IVA not included). Open *Semana Santa*-Sept. MC/V.

FOOD

Soria's specialties include *chorizo* and *migas* (fried bread crumbs). C. M. Vicente Tutor is peppered with bars and inexpensive restaurants. Buy fresh foods at the small **market** in Pl. Bernardo Robles on C. Estudios, left off C. Collado. (Open M-Sa 8:30am-2pm). The **supermarket** is **SPAR,** Av. Mariano Vicen, 29, 4 blocks from Pl. M. Granados toward the train station. (Open M-Sa 9am-2pm and 5:30-8:30pm. MC/V.)

La Parilla, C. Tejera, 20 (☎975 21 44 32). From Pl. Mariano Granados, take C. Ferial and continue 3 blocks up the hill to C. Tejerat. Popular *menú* available at every meal except Sa night (1300ptas/€8). Entrées 1100-2000ptas/€6.60-12. Open M-F and Su 1-3:30pm and 8:30-11pm, Sa 1-3:30pm and 9pm-midnight. MC/V.

Café-Bar Don Quijote, Av. Mariano Vicen, 37 (☎975 22 29 27), on the way to the train station. Locals crowd the café-bar, exchanging daily tidbits between bites of *tapas*. Luncheon menú (1450ptas) served M-Sa 1:30-4pm in a pleasant dining room. MC/V.

SIGHTS

The great 20th-century poet Antonio Machado once likened the **Río Duero** to a drawn bow arching around Soria. To find the river from Pl. M. Granados, walk past the sign for Restaurant Nueva York and straight down C. Zapatería. C. Zapatería changes to C. Real; follow this road to Pl. San Pedro, and the bridge lies ahead.

ERMITA DE SAN SATURIO. Soria's biggest draw is actually across the river and is well worth the trek. The 17th-century Ermita de San Saturio, built into the side of a cliff, is a heavenly retreat where light seeps into the caves through stained-glass windows. *(1.5km downstream. Turn right with the road after crossing the bridge. Open May-Sept. Tu-Su 10:30am-2pm and 4:30-7pm; Oct.-Apr. Tu-Su 10:30-6:30pm. Free.)*

MONASTERIO SAN JUAN DE DUERO. The Monasterio San Juan de Duero sits quietly by the river amid cottonwoods and grass. The church itself, dating from the 12th century, is quite simple. It's graceful arches combining Romanesque and Islamic styles, are all that remain of the 13th-century cloister. Inside, a small museum displays medieval artifacts. *(Turn left after crossing the bridge. Museo Numantino ☎975 22 13 97 for info. Open June-Aug. Tu-Sa 10am-2pm and 5-9pm, Su 10am-2pm; Sept.-Oct. and Apr.-May Tu-Sa 10am-2pm and 4-7pm, Su 10am-2pm; Nov.-Mar. Tu-Sa 10am-2pm and 3:30-6pm, Su 10am-2pm. 100ptas/€0.60; under 18, over 65, and students free; Sa-Su free.)*

MUSEO NUMANTINO. The museum exhibits an impressive collection of Celto-Iberian and Roman artifacts excavated from nearby Numancia. *(Po. Espolón, 8. ☎975 22 13 97. Open June-Sept. Tu-Sa 9am-2pm and 5-9pm, Su 9am-2pm; Oct.-May Tu-Sa 9am-8:30pm, Su 9am-2pm. 200ptas; under 18, over 65, and students free; Sa-Su free.)*

ENTERTAINMENT

As the moon rises, revelers of all ages crowd **Pl. Ramón Benito Aceña** and the adjacent **Pl. San Clemente,** off C. Collado. The intimate tables of **Bar Ogham**, C. Nicolás Rabal, 3 draw a young crowd (open M-Th 12pm-3am, F-Sa 12pm-4:30am, Su 3pm-2:30am). Late-night disco-bars center around the intersection of Rota de Calatañazer and C. Cardenal Frías, near Pl. Toros.

DAYTRIPS FROM SORIA

RUINS OF NUMANCIA

Getting to Numancia without a car proves a problem. The bus to Garray comes within 1km of the ruins (15min., summer M-F 1 and 6pm; winter M-F 1pm, F also 6pm, Su and holidays 4:15pm; 130ptas/€0.75), but the only return buses run in summer M-F 9:45am and 1:30pm, Su and holidays 1:30pm; low-season M-Sa 9:45am only, Su 1:30pm.

Archaeology fans will enjoy the ruins of Numancia, a hilltop settlement 7km north of Soria dating back more than over 4000 years. The Celto-Iberians settled here by the 3rd century BC and resisted Roman conquest. It took 10 years of the Numantian Wars and the direction of Scipio Africanus to dislodge them. Scipio encircled the town in a system of walls 9km long, 3m tall, and 2½m thick in order to starve its residents. After his victory, he kept 50 survivors as trophies, sold the rest into slavery, burned the city, and divided its lands among his allies. Numancia, however, lived on as a metaphor for patriotic heroism in Golden Age and Neoclassical tragedies, and the ruins, though battered, are worth a visit. (☎975 22 1397. Open June-Aug. Tu-Sa 10am-2pm and 5-9pm, Su 10am-2pm; Sept.-Oct. and Apr.-May Tu-Sa 10am-2pm and 4-7pm, Su 10am-2pm; Nov.-Mar. Tu-Sa 10am-2pm and 3:30-6pm, Su 10am-2pm. 100ptas/€0.60, under 18, over 65, and students free; Sa-Su free.)

EL BURGO DE OSMA

Gonzalo Ruiz (☎975 22 20 60) sends buses to and from Soria (50min.; M-Sa 1:30 and 6:30pm, Su 6pm; returning M-Sa 8:45am and 3:35pm, Su 8pm; 500ptas/€3).

Situated 55km southwest of Soria, **El Burgo de Osma** (pop. 5100), is only worth the trip for those with a car. Two of the town's more attractive buildings are the **Hospital de San Agustín** and **Casa Consistorial.** Monk Don Pedro de Osma erected the magnificent 13th-century **cathedral** on the site of an earlier church. Its two interior **museums** feature an important collection of codices, including a richly illuminated Beato de Liébana commentary on the Apocalypse and a 12th-century charter, considered one of the earliest written examples of Castilian vernacular. (☎975 34 03 19. Open Nov.-June Tu-Su 10:30am-1pm and 4:30-6:30pm; July-Oct. 10am-1pm and 4-7pm. Entrance to cathedral free; tour of museums 400ptas/€2.50.)

EXTREMADURA

The aptly named Extremadura is a land of harsh beauty and cruel extremes. Arid plains bake under the intense summer sun, relieved only by scattered patches of sunflowers. Yet the traveler who braves the Extremaduran plains is rewarded with stunning ruins and peaceful towns. Compared to the hectic pace of nearby Madrid, life in Extremadura is unhurried and far less modern, as though the region's history still dominated its present character. Though these are the lands that hardened New World conquistadors like Hernán Cortés and Francisco Pizarro, Extremadura itself has remained unexplored by most Spaniards. Mérida's Roman ruins and the hushed ancient beauty of Trujillo and Cáceres are only beginning to draw their flocks of admirers, coming to see what the traditional Spanish countryside has to offer. Beyond the regions's rugged landscape, its hearty pastoral cuisine is especially appealing; local specialties include rabbit, partridge, lizard with green sauce, wild pigeon with herbs, and *migas (*fried bread) with hot chocolate. Thick *cocido* (chick pea stew) warms *extremeños* in winter, while the many varieties of gazpacho (including an unusual white soup) cool in summer.

CÁCERES ☎927

Founded by Romans in 34 BC, this thriving provincial capital (pop. 90,000) is the closest Extremadura comes to a big city. Named a World Heritage City in 1986, Cáceres's *barrio antiguo* offers plenty of architectural wonder. Between the 14th and 16th centuries, rival noble families vied for social and political control, each building a miniature palace to demonstrate their power and wealth. As a result, the old city is a wonderful maze of palaces, museums, and churches. Although Cáceres's newer areas are less interesting, the *Parque del Principe* and a healthy nightlife provide ample amusement for a short stay. From Cáceres it is possible to enter Portugal by bus or train via Badajoz, or by train via Valencia de Alcántara.

TRANSPORTATION

Trains: (☎927 23 50 61), on Av. Alemania, 3km from the old city across the highway from the bus station. Info window open daily 9am-10pm. Trains to: **Mérida** (1hr., 5 per day 8:19am-6:40pm, 575-1700ptas/€3.50-10.20); **Badajoz** (2hr.; noon, 1:44pm, 6:40pm; 1100-2200ptas/€6.60-13); **Madrid** (4hr.; 3-4 per day; M-F 7:10am-4:28pm, Sa 7:10am-2:28pm, Su 10:05am-5:55pm; 2435-4800ptas/€15-29); **Lisbon** (6hr., 2:59am, 4900ptas/€29); **Sevilla** (4hr.; 8:19am, 2pm; 2200ptas/€13).

Buses: (☎927 23 25 50), on Ctra. Sevilla, across from the train station. Info window open M-F 7:30am-11:30pm, Sa-Su 8:30am-11:30pm. Buses to: **Badajoz** (1½hr.; M-Sa 12:45pm and 6:45pm, Su 12:45pm and 10:45pm; 1080ptas/€6.50); **Madrid** (4-5hr.; 6-7 per day; M-F 6am-6pm, Sa 6am-3:30pm, Su 8:15am-7pm; 2500ptas/€15); **Mérida** (1hr.; M-F 8 per day 6:30am-9:30pm, Sa 4 per day 1pm-9:30pm, Su 9:30pm; 675ptas/€4.05); **Salamanca** (4hr.; 3-6 per day; M-Sa 7am-6pm, Su 5-6:45; 1760ptas/€10.55); **Sevilla** (4hr.; daily 2pm and 7pm, F and Su extra bus at 3:30am, 2190ptas/€13); **Trujillo** (45min.; 4-7 per day M-F 6am-6pm, Sa 6am-2pm, Su 8:15am-7pm; 425ptas/€2.55); **Valencia de Alcántara** (2½hr.; M-F 4 per day 12:15-6:30pm, Sa 2:30pm, Su 8pm; 1100ptas/€6.60); **Valladolid** (5½hr., daily at 2 and 5:25pm, 2630ptas/€16).

Taxis: Stands at Pl. Mayor and bus and train stations. **Radio Taxi** (☎927 23 23 23).

Car Rental: Avis (☎927 23 57 21), in the bus station. On the right when you face the station from the outside. One-day rental starting at 12,000ptas/€72. Minimum age 23. Open M-F 9am-1pm and 4:30-7:30pm (in winter 5-8pm); Sa 9am-1pm.

ORIENTATION AND PRACTICAL INFORMATION

Ciudad Monumental (old city) and the commercial street **Av. de España** flank **Pl. Mayor** (a.k.a. Pl. General Mola). The plaza is 3km from the **bus** and **train stations,** which face each other across the rotary intersection of Av. Hispanidad and Av. Alemania. The best way to get to the center of town is via the #1 bus; hop off at Pl. Obispo Galarza, next to the big blue and red "FLEX" sign (100ptas/€0.60). Facing the bus stop, start right and take your first left down the steps. At the first intersection turn right, then left to continue downhill. When you reach the arches, Pl. Mayor will be to your left. Bus #2 stops on Av. Hispanidad, around the corner to the right as you emerge from the bus station, and runs to **Pl. de América,** hub of the new downtown area (100ptas/€0.60). From there, "Ciudad Monumental" signs point up the tree-lined Av. España (Po. Canovas) toward Pl. Mayor.

Tourist Office: Pl. Mayor, 10 (☎927 62 50 47). English spoken. Open Oct.-June M-F 9am-2pm and 4-6pm, Sa-Su 9:45am-2pm; July-Sept. M-F 9am-2pm and 5-7:30pm, Sa-Su 9:45am-2pm. The **Patronato de Turismo** (☎927 25 55 97), C. Amargura, in the Palacio de Caravajal, in the old city, provides quality maps of the monuments. From Pl. Mayor, pass under Arco de la Estrella into the old city and continue straight until you face the Catedral; it's opposite the left side. Open M-F 8am-9:30pm, Sa-Su 10am-2pm.

Currency Exchange: Banks line Av. España and the streets leading to Pl. Mayor.

Luggage Storage: At the train station (500ptas/€3 per day) and bus station (100ptas/€0.60 per item per day).

Emergency: ☎112. **Police: Municipal,** C. Diego M. Crehuet (☎927 24 84 24).

Late-Night Pharmacy: The 4 pharmacies in Pl. Mayor all post the *farmacias de guardia* (24hr. pharmacies) list in their windows.

Hospital: Hospital Provincial (☎927 25 68 00), on Av. España, off Pl. Mayor.

Internet Access: Ciberjust, C. Diego M. Crehuet, 7 (☎927 21 46 77). Plenty of speedy computers. From Pl. Mayor take C. Pintores to Pl. San Juan and continue down C. Rosa de Luna to Pl. Marron; C. Diego M. Carhuet is the third left. 300ptas/€1.80 per hr. Open M-Sa 10am-2am, Su noon-2am.

Post Office: C. Miguel Primo de Rivera (☎927 62 66 81; fax 21 42 16), off Av. España on the left from Pl. de América. Open for stamps and Lista de Correos M-F 8:30am-8:30pm, Sa 9:30am-2pm. **Postal Code:** 10071.

ACCOMMODATIONS

Hostales are scattered throughout the new city and line Pl. Mayo in the old town. Prices rise during festivals and advance reservations are recommended on summer weekends. Late-night arrivals never fear—24hr. reception is the norm.

Hostal Residencia Almonte, C. Gil Cordero, 6 (☎927 24 09 25; fax 24 86 02). Heading away from Pl. Mayor on Av. España, C. Gil Cordero is right off Pl. de América, the traffic circle at the end of the park. A/C 400ptas/€2.40 extra. Parking garage for 3 lucky cars 500ptas/€3. Singles 3100ptas/€19; doubles 4800ptas/€29; triples 5800ptas/€35; quads 6800ptas/€41. MC/V.

Pensión Castilla, Rios Verdes, 3 (☎927 24 44 04). From Pl. Mayor, take C. General Ezponda (opposite the tourist office), and then the first right. Good for a quieter night near the old city. Singles 2000ptas/€12; doubles 4000ptas/€24. IVA not included.

Pensión Carretero, Pl. Mayor, 22 (☎927 24 74 82). Spacious TV lounge. No winter heating. Singles 2000ptas/€12; doubles 3500ptas/€21; triples 4500ptas/€27; quads 6000ptas/€36. MC/V.

Pension Marquez, Gabriel y Galán, 2 (☎927 24 99 60), off Pl. Mayor, opposite the town hall. The owner will make Marquez feel like home. No winter heating. Doubles 3000ptas/€18; triples 4500ptas/€27. Winter singles 2000ptas/€12.

FOOD

Like every Pl. Mayor, the one in Cáceres is full of restaurants and cafés serving up cheap *bocadillos* (400-600ptas/€2.40-3.60), *raciones* (300-800ptas/€1.80-4.80), and *menús* (1000-1300ptas/€6-7.80). Explore the side streets for less touristed local bars and pastry shops. For groceries, hit up the big **Hiper Tambo,** C. Alfonso IX, 25. From Pl. de America follow the left side of Av. de España to its extension. (☎927 21 17 71. Open M-Sa 9:30am-9pm.)

Cantina Taqueria Doña Lupita, C. Sánchez, 9 (☎927 22 62 25). A great change of pace from the *comida tipica* of the plaza. Entrées 600-2000ptas/€3.60-12. Open M-F 12:30-4pm and 8:30pm-midnight. MC/V.

El Toro, C. General Ezponda, 2 (☎927 21 15 48). Serves yuppified Spanish cuisine in a terra cotta and marble setting. Entrées 1100-2500ptas/€6.60-15. *Menú* 1500-2000ptas/€9-12. Open Tu-Sa 11am-5pm and 8pm-1am. MC/V.

SIGHTS AND ENTERTAINMENT

BARRIO ANTIGUO. Golden, stork-filled Old Cáceres is home to one of the most varied architectural ensembles in Europe. Roman, Arabic, Gothic, Renaissance, and even Incan influences (brought back by the conquistadors along with all that gold) can be detected throughout the old city. The main attraction is the neighborhood as a whole, since most buildings don't open their doors to tourists; the best way to experience the *barrio antiguo* is to suppress your internal compass and wander among the narrow, winding streets. Though the area is small, a tourist office map will come in handy. *(From Pl. Mayor, take the stairs from the left of the tourist office to the Arco de la Estrella, the entrance into the walled old city.)*

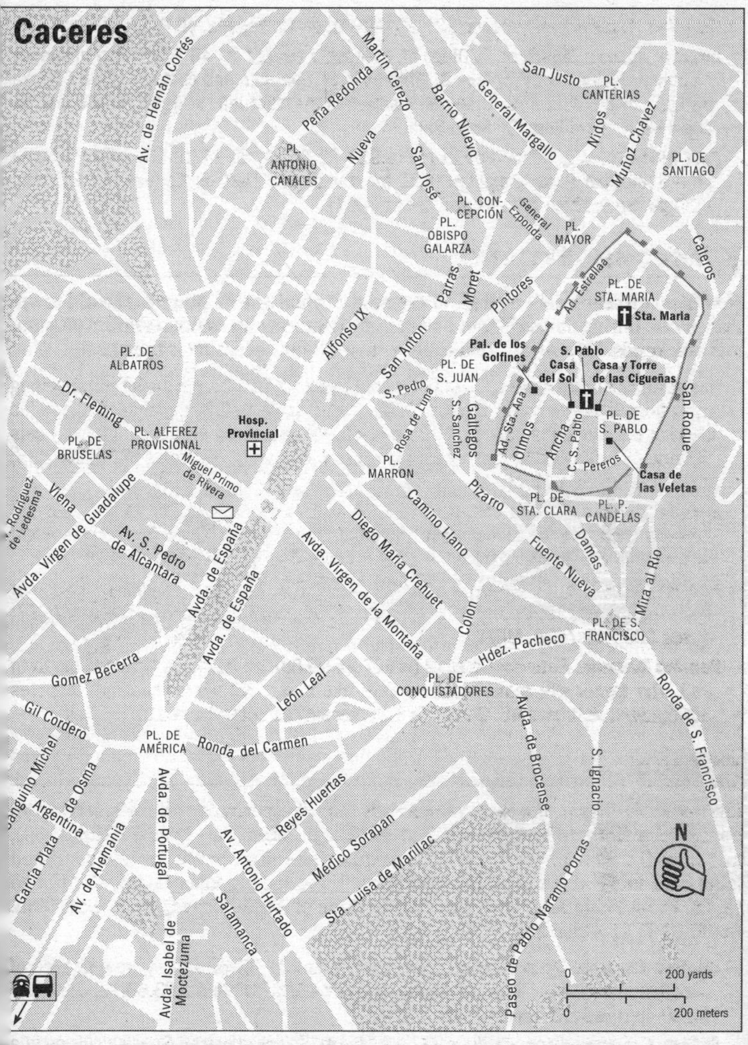

MUSEO DE CÁCERES. A must see. Inside the Casa de los Caballos, Museo de Cáceres houses a tiny but brilliant who's-who of Spanish art, featuring originals by El Greco, Picasso, Miró, and recent abstractionist stars, along with rotating exhibitions. Also called the Museo Arqueológico Provincial, the **Casa de las Veletas** (House of Weathervanes), in front of the Casa de los Caballos, displays Celtiberian stone animals, Roman and Visigothic tombstones, and crafts. *(Across from the Casa y Torre de las Cigueñas. ☎927 24 72 34. Open Apr. 14-Sept. Tu-Sa 9am-2:30pm and 5-8:15pm, Su 10:15am-2:30pm; Oct.-Apr. 13 Tu-Sa 9am-2:30pm and 4-7:15pm. 200ptas/€1.20; students, seniors, EU citizens free. Su free for all.)*

CATEDRAL DE SANTA MARÍA. A statue of San Pedro de Alcántara, one of Extremadura's two patron saints, eyes the plaza from a corner pedestal of the Catedral de Santa María. His shiny boots are the result of years of good-luck toe-rubbing. Built between 1229 and 1547, the Romanesque and Gothic cathedral has a Renaissance ceiling. *(Mass daily M-Sa 1 and 7:30pm; Su 10am, noon, 1, 7:30pm.)*

THE THINGS WE DO FOR LOVE Legend has it that the daughter of the Moorish King of Cáceres fell head over heels for the Christian conqueror, Alfonso IX, then vying for control over Cáceres. Alfonso was badly disadvantaged, but his sweetheart gave him the keys to the walled city, enabling a successful surprise attack. Every April 22, the day before St. George's Day (the patron saint of the city), the legend is reenacted by citizens of Cáceres who break into groups of Christians and Moors and act out the battle, casting a dragon into fake flames at its finish.

CASA Y TORRE DE LAS CIGUEÑAS. Cáceres's aristocracy were a rather war-like lot. The city's monarchs removed all battlements and spires from local lords' houses as punishment for their violent quarreling. Due to his loyalty to the ruling family, however, Don Golfín's Casa y Torre de las Cigueñas (House and Tower of the Storks) was the lone estate allowed to keep its battlements. Storks nest atop its spires each spring. *(From the Arco, take a right up the hill, a left onto C. del Arco de Santa Ana, another right, then a quick left onto C. Condes. Pass through Pl. de San Mateo to Pl. de Conde Canilleros; La Casa is on your left.)* Nearby **Convento de San Pablo** is late Gothic eye-candy for architecture addicts. *(To the left of Casa y Torre de las Cigueñas.)*

OTHER SIGHTS. The 16th-century **Casa Del Sol** is the most famous of Cáceres's numerous mansions; its crest is the city's emblem. The **Casa de Toledo-Moctezuma** was built by the grandson of the Aztec princess Isabel Moctezuma (Tecuixpo Istlaxochitl) to represent a unification of the old and new worlds. *(In Pl. de San Mateo, to the left as you enter the Arco de la Estrella.)* On October 26, 1936, in the **Palacio de los Golfines de Arriba,** yet another Golfín family palace, Francisco Franco was proclaimed head of the Spanish state and General of its armies. *(Sandwiched by C. Olmos and C. Adarve de Santa Ana.)*

ENTERTAINMENT. Weekend revelry starts in the **Pl. Mayor** and along **C. Pizarro,** lined with live-music bars. Later on, the party migrates to the area called **La Madrila,** near Pl. Albatros in the new city. From the Pl. Mayor, take Av. España, make a right onto Primo de Rivera, cross the intersection onto C. Dr. Fleming, then make another right into La Madrila.

DAYTRIP FROM CÁCERES

GUADALUPE (2½HR.)

Transportation to and from Guadalupe can be somewhat tricky; most visitors arrive via tour bus or in their own cars. ***Empresa Mirat*** *(☎927 23 48 63) sends buses from Cáceres to Guadalupe via Trujillo (2½hr., M-F 1:30 and 5:30pm, 1245ptas/€7.50) and back (M-F 6:30am and 7:30am). Bus schedules quite regularly force an overnight stay in Guadalupe, but the pleasant calm can be a relief from bigger cities.*

Two hours east of Trujillo and four hours southwest of Madrid, Guadalupe rests on a mountainside in the Sierra de Guadalupe. Particularly for pilgrims and backpackers, the **Real Monasterio de Santa María de Guadalupe,** with its eclectic history and decadent architecture, is a worthy daytrip. The fairy-tale monastery has even been nicknamed "the Spanish Sistine Chapel." At the Battle of Salado in 1340, Alfonso XI, aided by the Virgin Mary, defeated a much superior Muslim army. As a token of his gratitude, he commissioned the lavish Real Monasterio. Years later it became customary to grant licenses for foreign expeditions on the premises; in fact, Columbus finalized his contract with Fernando and Isabel here. To pay homage to the city, he named one of the islands he discovered Guadalupe (now known as Turugueira). The most prominent object in the basilica is the **Icon of the Virgin,** carved of wood, blackened with age, and cloaked in robes of silver and gold. (Monastery open daily 9:30am-1pm and 3:30-6:30pm. 300ptas/€1.80.)

The **tourist office** in **Plaza Mayor** posts information on the door; follow signs from the bus station. (☎927 15 41 28. Open Tu-Su 10am-2pm and 5-7pm.) Travelers looking for food or beds should head to Pl. Mayor.

TRUJILLO ☎927

The gem of Extremadura, hill-top Trujillo (pop. 10,000), is an unspoiled joy. Often called the "Cradle of Conquistadors," Trujillo furnished history with over 600 explorers and plunderers of the New World, including Peru's conqueror Francisco Pizarro and the Amazon's first European explorer, Francisco de Orellana. Scattered with medieval palaces, Roman ruins, Arabic fortresses, and churches of every era, Trujillo is a hodgepodge of histories and cultures. Its most impressive monument is also its highest: its 10th-century Moorish castle commands a stunning panoramic view of the surrounding plains. Twentieth-century residents take pride in the well-preserved beauty of their churches, palace, and castle, adorning them with lovely gardens and flowering vines.

TRANSPORTATION. The **bus station** (☎927 32 12 02) is at the corner of C. de las Cruces and C. del M. de Albayada; look for the **AutoRes** sign. As most buses stop only en route to larger destinations, there are not always seats available—check ahead. Buses run to: **Badajoz** (2hr.; 9-10 per day; M-Th, Sa 11:10am-11:50pm, F, Su 11:10am-12:20am; 1255ptas/€7.55); **Cáceres** (45min.; 5-7 per day; M-Th and Sa 11:15am-10:25pm, F and Su last train 12:20am; 445ptas/€2.70); **Madrid** (2½hr.; 12-14 per day; M-F 6:40am-8:25pm, Sa 6:40am-6:15pm, Su 8:55am-8:25pm; 2100ptas/€13).

PRACTICAL INFORMATION. The English-speaking **tourist office** is in the Plaza Mayor. Info is posted in the windows when it's closed. (☎927 32 26 77. Open June-Sept. 9:30am-2pm and 4:30-7:30pm; Oct.-May 9:30am-2pm and 4-8pm.) **Currency exchange** and 24hr. **ATM** are at **Banco Central Hispano,** Pl. Mayor, 25. (☎927 24 24 24. Open Oct.-Mar. M-F 8:30am-2:30pm and Sa 8:30am-1pm; Apr.-Sept. M-F 8:30am-2:30pm.) In a **medical emergency** call ☎112 or 927 32 20 16, or the **police,** C. Carniceria, 2 (☎927 32 01 08 or 608 70 65 17), just off Pl. Mayor. The **post office,** Po. Ruiz de Mendoza, 28, is on the way from the station to Pl. Mayor. (☎927 32 05 33. Open M-F 9am-2:30pm, Sa 9:30am-1pm.) **Postal code:** 10200.

ACCOMMODATIONS AND FOOD. The pleasant **Pensión Boni,** C. Mingo de Ramos, 11, is off Pl. Mayor to the right of the church. Close to the plaza without the noise, Boni has airy patio rooms and a comfy TV lounge. (☎927 32 16 04. Singles 2000ptas/€12; doubles 3500ptas/€21, with bath 5000ptas/€30; triples with full bath and A/C 6500-7000ptas/€39-42.) Get medieval at **Hostal Trujillo,** C. de Francisco Pizarro, 4-6. From the bus station, turn left on C. de las Cruces, right on C. de la Encarnación, then right again onto C. de Francisco Pizarro. The armor, lance, and shield-bedecked halls of this renovated 15th-century hospital lead to simple but comfortable rooms with full bath, A/C, and TV. (☎927 32 26 61; ☎/fax 32 22 74. Singles 3424ptas/€21; doubles 5564ptas/€33; triples 7062ptas/€42.) The best spot for a meal in Trujillo is a shaded table in the garden of **Meson Alberca**, C. Victoria, 8. Enjoy a three-course *menú* (1850ptas/€11.10) with traditional options like *migas* and *gazpacho* in this tourist-free sanctum. (☎927 32 22 09. Open Su-Tu, Th-Sa, 11am-5pm and 8:30pm-1am. AmEx/MC/V.)

SIGHTS. An afternoon stroll through Trujillo's *barrio* may be the best in Extremadura. All sights cost 200ptas/€1.20 and are open June-Sept. daily 10am-2pm and 5-8:30pm, Oct.-May 9:30am-2pm and 4:30-7:30pm, except where otherwise indicated. A "bono" ticket (700ptas/€4.20), available at the tourist office, allows entrance to the Casa-Museo de Pizarro, the Arab castle, and Iglesia de Santiago and includes a guide book available in English. The tourist office also offer tours of the old city, including the Museo del Traje. (Tours leave daily at 11:30am and 6pm; schedule may vary in the winter. 1000ptas/€6.)

Trujillo's **main plaza** was also the inspiration for the Plaza de Armas in Cuzco, Perú, which was constructed after Francisco Pizarro defeated the Incas. Palaces, arched corridors, and sprawling cafés surround the central fountain and the Estatua de Pizarro. The gift of an American admirer of Pizarro, the bronze statue was erected in 1929 and, like the plaza, has a twin in Lima, Perú. Festooned with stork nests, Iglesia de San Martín dominates the plaza's northeastern corner. The church has several historic tombs, but contrary to local lore, Francisco de Orellana does not rest here. (Church opens 20min. before mass. Mass M-Sa at 7:30pm, Su 1pm and 7:30pm. Free.) Across the street, the seven chimneys of the **Palacio de los Duques de San Carlos** reputedly symbolize the religions conquered in the New World. (Open daily 9:30am-1pm and 4:30-6:30pm. Entrance 200ptas/€1.20.)

The Gothic **Iglesia de Santa María** is still farther up the hill. According to legend, the giant soldier Diego García de Paredes picked up the fountain (now located next to the rear door) at age 11 and carried it to his mother; the giant was buried here after a fatal fall from a horse. (Commonly known as the "Extremaduran Samson," the giant is referenced in chapter 32 of Cervantes' *Don Quijote.*) The church's 25-panel Gothic altar-piece was painted by master Fernando Gallego in 1480. (Open May-Oct. 10am-2pm and 4:30-8pm, Nov.-Apr. 10am-2pm and 4-7pm, 200ptas/€1.20. Mass Su at 11am.) To the left of the church is the restored **Museo de la Coria,** which explores the relationship between Extremadura and Latin America. (Open Sa-Su 11:30am-2pm. Free.) To the right of the church is the Museo del Traje, exhibiting the spectacular evening gowns worn by royalty and famous actresses from the 17th century to present day inside a restored convent. (Open 10am-2pm and 5-8:30pm. 250ptas/€1.50.) To get to the **Casa-Museo de Pizarro,** walk uphill on the stone road to the right of the Iglesia de Santa María. The bottom floor of the house is a reproduction of the living quarters of a 15th-century nobleman), while the top floor is dedicated to the life and times of Francisco Pizarro. Crowning the hill are the spectacular ruins of a 10th-century **Arab castle.** Pacing the battlements and ramparts is like playing in your best Lego creation. A field-fresh breeze complements a view of the unspoiled landscape, with Trujillo on one side and fields scattered with ancient battlements on the other.

MÉRIDA ☎924

For quality of Roman ruins per square foot, it doesn't get any better than Mérida (pop. 60,000). In 26 BC, as a reward for services rendered to the Roman Empire, Augustus Caesar granted a heroic group of veteran legionnaires a new city in Lusitania, a province comprised of Portugal and part of Spain. The veterans chose a lovely spot surrounded by several hills on the banks of the Río Guadiana to found their new home, which they named "Augusta Emerita." Not content to rest on their laurels and itching to gossip with fellow patricians in Sevilla and Salamanca, soldiers proceeded to build the largest bridge in Lusitania, now the Puente Romano. The nostalgic crew adorned their "little Rome" with baths, aqueducts, temples, a hippodrome, an arena, and a famous amphitheater. Modern Mérida not only copied the Romans' buildings, but also complemented them with walkways, small plazas, and the world-class Museo Romano. In July and August, the spectacular *Festival de Teatro Clásico* presents some of Europe's finest classical and modern theater and dance, performed among the ruins.

TRANSPORTATION

Trains: (RENFE info ☎902 24 02 02), C. Cardero. Info window open daily 7am-10pm. Trains to: **Badajoz** (1hr.; M-Sa 7:12am-10:16pm, Su 2:18pm-10:16pm; 420-1600ptas/€2.50-9.60); **Cáceres** (1hr., 3-4 per day 9:06am-9pm, 525-1700ptas/€3.16-10.22); **Madrid** (4hr.; M-F, Su 1:26 and 9pm, Sa 1:26pm; 3005-4400ptas/€18-26); **Sevilla** (4½hr., 9:25am, 1700ptas/€10.20); **Zafra** (1hr., 9:25am, 525ptas/€3.16). Trains to **Lisbon** transfer in Cáceres.

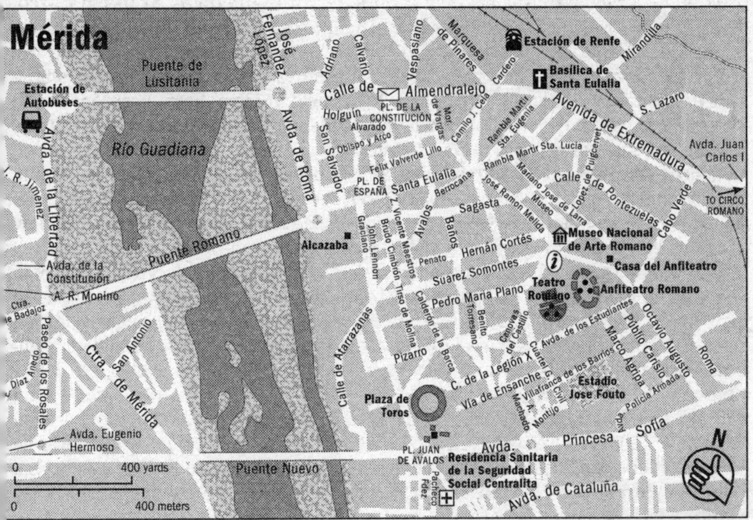

Buses: (☎924 37 14 04), Av. Libertad, in the Polígono Nueva Ciudad. Info booth open M-F 7am-11pm, Sa-Su 7am-1pm and 3:15-11pm. **LEDA** (☎924 37 14 03) sends buses to: **Badajoz** (1hr.; 4-9 per day; M-F 8am-12:30am, Sa 8:45am-10:50pm, Su 11:40am-10:50pm; 610ptas/€3.65); **Cáceres** (1hr.; 2-4 per day; M-Th 9:10am-9:15pm, F-Sa 9:10am-3:50pm, Su 5:50pm-8:30pm; 675ptas/€4); **Sevilla** (3hr.; 7-9 per day; M-F 7am-8:30pm, Sa 7am-6pm, Su 9am-8:30pm; 1625ptas/€9.75); **Zafra** (1¼hr.; M-Sa 11 per day 7am-9:50pm, Su 8:30 and 10:20pm; 600ptas/€3.60). **Alsa Grupo** (☎902 42 22 42) sends buses to: **Salamanca** (5hr.; 4-5 per day, M-Sa 9:15am-1:30am, Su 9:15am-12:10am; 2285ptas); **Sevilla** (3hr., 6-8 per day 5:05am-10:45pm, 1625ptas/€9.75). **AutoRes** (☎924 37 19 55) goes to **Madrid** (5½hr.; 7-8 per day, M-F 8:45am-7:15pm, Sa 8:45am-4:45pm, Su 9:45am-7:15pm; 2800-3300ptas/€17-20).

Taxis: Teletaxi (24hr. ☎924 31 57 56).

Car Rental: Avis (☎924 37 33 11 or 909 26 32 32), at the bus station. From 8000ptas/€48 per day plus IVA. Insurance included. Min age 23. Open M-F 9am-1pm and 5-8pm, Sa 9:30am-1pm.

ORIENTATION AND PRACTICAL INFORMATION

Plaza de España, the town center, is two blocks up from the Puente Romano and easily accessible from the **Teatro Romano.** Walking outward from the center, cafés and shops around the plaza quickly transform into quiet residential neighborhoods, and streets often lose their signs. From the **bus station** to Pl. España, cross the suspension bridge and turn right onto Av. de Roma. Continue along the river until you reach the Puente Romano, then turn left onto C. Puente, which leads straight into Pl. España. From the **train station** to Pl. España, take C. Cardero (on your left as you exit the station) and its continuation, C. Camilo José Cela; bear right onto C. Felix Valverde Lillo, following it to Pl. España (5-10min.).

Tourist Office: (☎924 31 53 53), on Av. Álvarez Saez de Buruaga, across from the Museo Romano and to the right of the Teatro Romano. From central Pl. España, head up C. Santa Eulalia, then bear right (as the hill peaks) on C. J. Ramon Melida at the little circle with the statue. The tourist office is at the end of the street to the right. English-speaking staff doles out theater schedules. Open in summer M-F 9am-1:45pm and 5-7:15pm, Sa-Su 9:30am-1:45pm; winter M-F 9am-1:45pm and 4-6:15pm, Sa-Su 9:30am-1:45pm.

Emergency: ☎112. **Police:** ☎092, on Av. Almendralejo, between Vespiano and Calvario. **Medical Emergency:** ☎924 38 10 18.

Hospital: Residencia Sanitaria de la Seguridad Social Centralita (☎924 38 10 00). From Pl. España, face the Banco de Extremadura and take the street to its left, curving right onto C. Graciano. Follow this through its multiple name changes; the hospital is on the right after Pl. de Toros.

Internet Access: Escuela de Idiomas Santa Eulalia, C. Santa Eulalia, 19, 2nd fl. (☎924 31 19 60). The closest internet connection to Pl. España. 1hr. minimum. 100ptas/€0.60 per 30 min. Open July-Sept. M-Sa 10am-2pm and 7-10pm; Oct.-June M-Sa 10am-3pm and 5-10pm.

Post Office: (☎924 31 24 58; fax 30 24 56), Pl. Constitución. From Pl. España, take C. Félix Valverde Lillo, turn a quick left onto C. Trajano, go through the arch, and follow the road to the right; the post office is in the left corner. Open Sept. 16-July 14 M-F 8:30am-8:30pm, Sa 9:30am-1pm; July 15-Sept. 15 M-F 8:30am-2:30pm, Sa 9:30am-1pm. **Postal Code:** 06800.

ACCOMMODATIONS

Despite Mérida's crowds of visor-sporting tourists, there are still several centrally located budget accommodations. Check the tourist office for complete listings.

Hostal-Residencia Senero, C. Holguín, 12 (☎924 31 72 07; hostalsenero@oem.es). From Pl. España, take the street just to the left of Hotel Emperatriz until it bisects C. Holguín. A/C 700ptas/€4.20 extra. Apr.-Oct. and Dec. 22-31 singles 2600ptas/€16, with bath 3200ptas/€19; doubles with bath 5100ptas/€31. Low-season singles 2400ptas/€14, with bath 3000ptas/€18; doubles with bath 4600ptas/€28. MC/V.

Hostal Salud, C. Vespasiano, 41 (☎/fax 924 31 22 59). From the train station, follow C. Cardero to the 1st intersection and take a sharp right onto C. Marquesa de Pinares. C. Vespasiano is your 3rd left. From the bus station, cross the bridge, head straight up Av. Almendralejo, and take your third left onto C. Vespasiano. Large, nicely furnished rooms with TV and private bath. Singles 2800ptas/€17; doubles 4800ptas/€29, with A/C 5800ptas/€35. Oct.-Mar. singles 2500ptas/€15; doubles 4200ptas/€25, with A/C 4800ptas/€29. AmEx/MC/V.

Hostal Nueva España, Av. Extremadura, 6 (☎924 31 33 56 or 31 32 11). Spotless private baths. Parking garage 900ptas/€5.40 per car. Apr.-Sept. singles 3400ptas/€20; doubles 5100ptas/€31; triples 6800ptas/€41. Low-season singles 2900ptas/€17; doubles 4600ptas/€28; triples 6200ptas/€37. MC/V.

FOOD

Plaza de España is filled with overpriced outdoor cafés. Self-catered picnics are the cheapest way to go. The **market** is on C. San Francisco, the street connecting C. Félix Valverde Lillo and C. Santa Eulalia. From Pl. España, take C. Félix Valverde Lillo; C. San Francisco is your second right. (Open M-Sa 8am-2pm.) For **groceries, El Arbol**, C. Félix Valverde Lillo, 8, is 1½ blocks from Pl. España (☎924 30 13 56. Open M-Sa 9:30am-2pm and 6-8:30pm. MC/V.)

Restaurante-Pizzeria Galileo, C. John Lennon, 28 (☎924 31 55 05). A glass-floored dining room reveals the Roman ruins below. 34 creative pizza flavors, fresh salads, and pastas. Entrées 640-100ptas/€3.85-6. Open Th-Tu 9am-12pm. MC/V.

Casa Benito, C. San Francisco, 3 (☎924 31 55 00). From Pl. España take C. Santa Eulalia for 2 blocks. The ivy-walled terrace is the perfect place for a beer. *Tapas* 100-500ptas/€0.60-3, *bocadillos* 350-900ptas/€2.10-5.40. Open M-Sa 9am-midnight.

SIGHTS

From the **Puente Romano** to the astrological mosaics, Mérida offers Spain's best view of Roman civilization in Iberia. A **combined ticket,** valid for all the sights below—except the Museo Nacional de Arte Romano—can be purchased at any one of the sights. (1200ptas/€7.20, EU students 600ptas/€3.60. Valid for several days and includes a guide book to the ruins.) The ruins are all open June-Sept. daily 9:30am-1:45pm and 5-7:15pm; Oct.-May 9:30am-1:45pm and 4-6:15pm.

MUSEO NACIONAL DE ARTE ROMANO. Enormous, elegant galleries under brick arches house all the Roman memorabilia you could ask for: statues, dioramas, coins, and other relics. The **Cripta** displays parts of an ancient Augusta Emerita street found when the museum was beginning construction. *(Follow C. Santa Eulalia from Pl. España; at the traffic circle turn right on C. Juan Ramón Melida. ☎ 924 31 16 90. Open Oct.-May Tu-Sa 10am-2pm and 4-6pm, Su and holidays 10am-2pm; June-Sept. Tu-Sa 10am-2pm and 5-7pm, Su and holidays 10am-2pm. 400ptas/€2.40; EU students 200ptas/€1.20. Sa afternoon and Su free.)*

ANFITEATRO ROMANO AND TEATRO ROMANO. Inaugurated in 8 BC, the *anfiteatro* was used for contests between any combination of animals and men, so long as blood be shed. *(In the park across from the Museo Nacional. 850ptas/€5.10 covers Teatro as well.)* The spectacular *teatro* was a gift from Agrippa, a Roman administrator, to the city in 16 BC. Its 6000 seats face a *scaenaefrons*, an incredible marble colonnade built upstage. Today the stage features performances of Teatro Clásico. *(Performances almost daily July-Aug. 10:45pm. Performance info ☎ 924 317 847; www.festivaldemerida.com. Tickets 1500-6000ptas/€9-36.)*

CASA DEL MITREO AND CASA DEL ANFITEATRO. These ruins of Roman homes showcase some of the world's finest Roman mosaics. Of special note is the Casa del Mitreo's **Mosaico Cosmólogico,** depicting the ancient Romans' conception of the world and the forces of nature. *(To reach Casa del Mitro from the entrance of the Teatro Romano, follow the right side of the ruins down Av. Alvarez Saenz de Buruaga and take a right onto Vía Ensarele. Casa del Anfiteatro is located between the Anfiteatro Romano and the Museo de Arte Romano. Admission to each 425ptas/€2.55.)*

OTHER RUINS. At the end of C. Rambla Mártir Santa Eulalia stand the **museo, basílica,** and **iglesia de Santa Eulalia,** all commemorating the child martyr. In 1990, in the midst of repairs to the 6th-century church, layers of previous construction were uncovered to reveal the ruins of Roman houses dating from the 3rd to 1st centuries BC, a 4th-century necropolis, and a basilica dedicated to Santa Eulalia. *(From Pl. España, take C. Santa Eulalia to the traffic circle and bear left onto C. Rambla. Admission to the museum and basilica 425ptas/€2.55. Church open daily during services at 8:30am and 8pm. Free.)* Near the theater complex is the **Circo Romano,** or the hippodrome. Diocles, the most famous Lusitanian racer, had his start here; he ended his career with a whopping 1462 victories, including three Winston Cup championships. Once filled with spectators, the arena (capacity 30,000) is currently under excavation and is closed to the public—though the view from the outside is still worth the trip. Next to the Circo stand the remains of the **Acueducto de San Lázaro.** *(With your back to the Teatro Romano entrance, follow the road to the right, turn left on C. Cabo Verde, and take the pedestrian walkway underneath the train tracks.)* Built from materials discarded by the Visigoths, the **Alcazaba** was designed by the Moors to guard the Roman bridge. *(Down the banks of the Guadiana and near Pl. España. 425ptas/€2.55.)*

BULLBOARDS Staring glassy-eyed out the window of your preferred mode of transportation, you may notice rather unusual monuments along the highway: massive, black paper cut-outs of solitary bulls. Once upon a time (in the 1980s) these cut-outs were advertisements for *Soberano Coñac* (cognac). In the early 1990s, however, billboards were prohibited on national roads. A plan was drafted to take the bulls down, but Spaniards protested, as the lone bull towering along the roadside had become an important national symbol. After considerable clamoring and hoofing, the bulls were painted black and left to loom proudly against the horizon. The familiar shape now decorates t-shirts and pins in souvenir shops, but the real thing is still impressive. Keep your eyes peeled as you whiz through the countryside.

DAYTRIP FROM MÉRIDA

ZAFRA

LEDA sends buses to Zafra (1¼hr.; M-Sa 11 per day 7am-9:50pm, Su 8:30 and 10:50pm; 600ptas/€3.60) and back (M-F 10 per day 7am-11:30pm, Sa 8 per day 7:20am-9:40pm, Su 10:30am and 11:30pm).

Known as "little Sevilla" for its gaiety and resemblance to the famous Andalucian city, Zafra is one of the better known *pueblos blancos,* a series of glowing white-washed villages scattered throughout Extremadura and Andalucía. Zafra is home to charming plazas and 17th- and 18th-century mansions like the **Casa de los Marqueses de Solanda,** a Renaissance Alcázar, but most of the "sights" don't hold up against the rest of Extremadura. If you're in the area, drop your bags at the Zafra station (50ptas/€0.30), swing through town for an hour or two between buses, and be sure to check out the **Convent de Santa Clara** for its immaculate confections. Exiting the **bus station** (☎924 55 02 15), cross the street and head straight down Av. Principe until it bisects C. López Asme. Take a left and follow the bend around the Alcázar, leaving it on your right and Pl. de España on your left. The **tourist office,** Pl. de España, 30, provides maps in English. (☎924 55 10 36. Open M-F 9:30am-2pm and 5-8pm, Sa-Su 10am-2pm. Zafra has a **train station** (RENFE info ☎902 24 02 02), but it's a hike from town.

BADAJOZ ☎924

Badajoz (pop. 120,000) is little more than a necessary stop en route to or from Portugal. Nonetheless, the contemporary art museum is worth a visit if you're in the area, and the Moorish ruins and 13th-century cathedral provide for an afternoon's distraction. The city has made great strides in cleaning up the industrial pollution that once plagued it—making layovers a more pleasant experience. While most people are just passing through, some have been here for a long time: archeological evidence suggests that humans first settled in Badajoz during the Lower Paleolithic period, giving them plenty of time to develop a raging nightlife. Street parties erupt in the evening in the Pl. de España and along the river; jealous Portuguese revelers often cross the border to partake in the fun.

TRANSPORTATION

From Badajoz, buses to Portugal are faster and more convenient than trains.

Flights: Aeropuerto de Badajoz (☎902 40 15 01), Carretera Madrid-Lisboa, 10km east of the city. This small airport is forever closing or changing airline companies—be sure to ask the tourist office or a travel agency if flights are running. **AirEuropa** currently sends flights to Madrid. From Pl. España, a taxi to the airport is about 2500ptas/€15.

Trains: Av. Carolina Coronado (☎924 27 11 70). From the train station to Pl. Libertad, take bus #1 (100ptas/€0.60). Info booth open daily 6am-9pm. Trains to: **Cáceres**

(2½hr.; Su-F 8:10am and 2:40pm, Sa 8:10am; 1900-2200ptas/€11.45-14); **Madrid** (5hr.; Su-F 3 per day 8:10am-2:40pm, Sa 8:10am and 12:30pm; 4200-4800ptas/€25-29); **Mérida** (1½hr., 7 per day 6:40am-7:40pm, 420-1600ptas/€2.50-9.65).

Buses: Central Station, C. José Rebollo López, 2 (☎924 25 86 61). Info booth open daily 7:45am-1am. Buses #3, 6a, 6b, and 9 run between the station and Pl. Libertad (100ptas). **Alsa** sends buses to **Cáceres** (1½hr.; M 3 per day 8am-4:30pm, Tu-Sa 9:30am and 4:30pm, Su 4:30pm; 1080-1280ptas/€6.50-7.70) on its way to **Salamanca** (5hr., 2745-3040ptas/€17-19); **Lisbon** (3½hr., daily at 3:45am and 4pm, 2375ptas/€15). **AutoRes** (☎924 23 85 15 or 902 02 09 99) to: **Lisbon** (2½hr.; daily 5pm and 2am, plus F 8:30pm; 2025ptas/€12); **Madrid** (4hr.; 7-8 per day, M-F and Su 8am-6:30pm, Sa 8am-4pm; 3355-3905ptas/€20-24); **Trujillo** (2hr.; 6 per day, M-Th and Sa 8am-4pm, F 8am-6:30pm, Su 9am-6:30pm; 1255ptas/€7.55). **Caballero** (☎924 25 57 56) to: **Cáceres** (1½hr.; M-F 8:30am and 4pm, Sa 8:30am and 2pm, Su 6pm; 885ptas/€5.30). **Damas** to: **Sevilla** (4½hr.; M-F 6:45am-8pm, Sa-Su 9am-8pm; 1815ptas/€10.95). **LEDA** (☎924 23 34 78) to: **Mérida** (1½hr.; M-F 8 per day 8am-9pm, Sa 6 per day 9:30am-9pm, Su 7:30 and 9:30pm; 610ptas/€3.65); **Zafra** (1hr.; 6-8 per day, M-F 6:45am-8:15pm, 6:45am-6pm, Su 9am-8:15pm; 745ptas/€4.50).

Taxis: At bus and train stations and Pl. de España. **Radio-Taxi** (24hr. ☎924 24 31 01).

ORIENTATION AND PRACTICAL INFORMATION

Across the Río Guadiana from the **train station** and home to the municipal tourist office, **Plaza de España** is the heart of Badajoz. From the plaza, C. Juan de Ribera and C. Valdivia lead to Pl. Dragones Hernan Cortes; one block to the right is **Pl. Libertad** (5min.) and the regional tourist office. Between Pl. de España and Pl. Libertad is the small park of **Po. San Francisco** (also right off C. Juan Ribera), home to the **post office, supermarket,** and a variety of **restaurants.** From the train station, follow Av. Carolina Coronado straight to the Puente de Palmas, cross the bridge, then continue straight on C. Prim and its continuation. Turn left onto C. Juan de Ribera at Pl. Minayo to get to Pl. de España, or right to Pl. Libertad (35min.). The #1 bus runs from the train station to Pl. Libertad, stopping directly across from the **Regional Tourist Office.** From the **bus station** entrance, turn left, take a quick right, then turn left onto C. Damión Tellez Lafuente. Pass straight through Pl. Constitución and Pl. Dragones Hernan Cortes, to the Plaza de España (20min.).

Tourist Office: Municipal Tourist Office, Pasaje San Juan (☎924 22 49 81). Facing the Ayuntamiento from Pl. España, take C. San Juan to its left; the tourist office is tucked into a small passageway on the right. The English-speaking staff offer the standard amps and info. Open M-F 10am-2pm and 6-8pm, Sa 9:30am-1:30pm; Sept.-May M-F afternoon hours 5-7pm. **Regional Tourist Office,** Pl. Libertad, 3 (☎924 22 27 63), across the street from Champion grocery store. No English. Open M-F 9:30am-2pm and 5-7:30pm, Sa-Su 10am-2pm; Sept.-May M-F afternoon hours 4-6:30pm. For tips on nightlife, visit the **Oficina de Información Juvenil**, Ronda de Pilar, 20 (☎924 21 01 54).

Luggage Storage: In the bus station (100ptas/€0.60) and train station (500ptas/€3).

Emergency: ☎112. **Police:** Av. Ramón y Cajal (☎091 or 924 23 02 53) off Pl. Libertad.

Hospital: Hospital Provincial, Pl. Minayo, 2 (☎924 20 90 00). From Pl. de España, walk down C. Juan de Riberato Pl. Minayo; it's on your left.

Post Office: Po. San Francisco, 4 (☎924 22 25 48). **Lista de Correos.** M-F 8:30am-8:30pm, Sa 9am-2pm. **Postal Code:** 06001.

ACCOMMODATIONS AND FOOD

Hotels line the streets originating in Pl. España. For **groceries,** head to **Simago,** next to the post office on Pl. San Francisco. (Open M-Sa 9:15am-9:15pm. MC/V.) Beyond Pl. España, cafés and eateries crowd **Po. San Francisco.**

Pension Pintor, C. Arco-Agüero, 26 (☎924 22 42 28). From Pl. de España take C. San Blas downhill, then take your first right onto C. Arco-Agüero. You may need to ring the bell across the street at #33. One single with bath 3000ptas/€18; doubles 3800ptas/€23, with bath, TV, and A/C 5500ptas/€33.

Hostal Niza II, C. Arco-Agüero, 45 (☎924 22 38 81 or 22 31 73; hniza@coeba.es) down the street from Pension Pintor. Large rooms with A/C, TV, private bath, and an owner eager to provide maps, brochures, and history. Singles 3750ptas/€23; doubles 6250ptas/€38; triples 7900ptas/€47.

Hostal Beatriz, C. Abril, 20 (☎/fax 924 23 35 56). Head downhill from Pl. España on C. Juan de Ribera, take the first right onto C. Juan Carlos Rey de España, then the 5th left onto C. Abril. Singles 2650ptas/€16; doubles 4450ptas/€27. MC/V.

Restaurante La Buena Pasta, C. Muñoz Torrero, 3 (☎924 22 03 64), one block off Pl. España, in a romantic setting. Pastas 650-1000ptas/€3.90-6, and pizzas 1100-1400ptas/€6.60-8.40. Open daily, except Tu, 1-4pm and 8:30-midnight.

SIGHTS AND ENTERTAINMENT

In 1995, Badajoz renovated its high-security prison to make way for the **Museo Extremeño e Iberoamericano de Arte Contemporáneo.** Five floors exhibit recent works from Spain, Portugal, and Latin America. The permanent collection includes a few controversial pieces, including Marta María Pérez Bravo's photograph of a woman's breasts as a communion offering. From Pl. de España, head down C. Juan Ribera, continuing as it turns into Av. Europa; the museum is on the left after Pl. Constitución. (☎924 26 03 84. Open Tu-Sa 10am-1:30pm and 5-8pm, Sun 10am-1:30pm. Free.) The old quarter of Badajoz, including **Plaza de España** and **Po. San Francisco,** is rich with history. With one Renaissance, one Gothic, and one Plateresque window, the 13th-century **cathedral** in Pl. de España (a converted mosque) is an artistic time line. (Open 11am-1pm. Free.) The ruins of the **Alcazaba,** a Moorish citadel, stand at the top of the hill. (Ruins free. Archeological museum open Tu-Su 10am-3pm. Free.) Badajoz **nightlife** draws partiers from as far as Portugal to **Pl. Santa Marta's** C. Francisco Lujan and C. Rafael Lucenqui. From Pl. España head downhill past Pl. Constitucion, and take the 2nd right onto C. General Palafox, which becomes C. Francisco Lujan. Keep your wits about you on the late-night party scene; this town is known for its rough spots.

ANDALUCÍA

Andalucía is what most everyone comes to Spain to see, whether they know it or not. This area derives its spirit from an intoxicating amalgam of cultures. The ancient kingdom of Tartessus—the same Tarshish mentioned in the Bible for its fabulous troves of silver—grew wealthy off the Sierra Nevada's rich ore deposits. The Greeks and Phoenicians established colonies and traded up and down the coast, and the Romans later cultivated wheat, olive oil, and wine from the fertile soil watered by the Guadalquivir. In the 5th century AD, the Vandals flitted through the region on their way to North Africa leaving little more than a name—Vandalusia (House of the Vandals). The Moors provided a more enduring influence. Arriving in AD 711 and establishing a yet unbroken link to Africa and the Muslim world, they bequeathed the region with far more than the flamenco music and gypsy ballads proverbially associated with southern Spain.

Under Moorish rule, which lasted until 1492, Sevilla and Granada reached the pinnacle of Islamic arts, and Córdoba matured into the most culturally influential city in Islam. The Moors preserved, perfected, and blended Roman architectural techniques with their own, creating a style that became distinctively and uniquely Andalucian. Intriguing patios, garden oases with fountains and fish ponds, and alternating red brick and white stone bands are its hallmarks. Two descendent peoples, the Mozarabs, Christians of Muslim Spain, and later the Mudéjares, Moors who remained in Spain after the *Reconquista*, made further architectural impacts, the former with horse-shoe arches and the latter with intricate wooden ceilings. The mingling of Roman and Moorish influences sparked the European Renaissance, merging Classical wisdom and science with that of the Arab world.

Andalucía has been the source of the many popular images of Spanish culture sent the world over by advertising campaigns, filled with bullfighting, flamenco, white-washed villages, sherry *bodegas*, sandy beaches, and the blazing sun. Beyond these obvious attractions lie Spain's most vivacious and warm-hearted residents. Despite (or perhaps because of) the poverty and high unemployment in their homeland, Andalucians have always maintained a passionate, unshakable dedication to living the good life. The *festivales*, *ferias*, and *carnavales* of Andalucía are world-famous for their extravagance.

SEVILLA ☎954

If Spain's three great cities were siblings, Madrid would be the stern breadwinner, Barcelona the rebellious hipster, and Sevilla the beloved baby sister who can do no wrong. Once the site of a Roman acropolis founded by Julius Caesar, later the capital of the Moorish empire, and a focal point of the Spanish Renaissance, the Sevilla of today is the guardian of traditional Andalucian culture, by far the best place for a taste of southern Spain. Flamenco, *tapas*, and bullfighting are at their best here, and the city's cathedral is stunning. Sevilla's yearly *Semana Santa* and *Feria de Abril* are among the most extravagant celebrations in all of Europe, and in the summer crowds gather to drink and dance along the Guadalquivir River.

INTERCITY TRANSPORTATION

BY PLANE

All flights depart and land at **Aeropuerto San Pablo** (☎954 44 90 00), 12km out of town on Ctra. Madrid. A taxi ride from the town center costs about 2000ptas/€12. **Los Amarillos** (☎954 98 91 84) runs a bus from outside the Hotel Alfonso XIII at the Pta. Jerez (6:15am-11pm, M-F every 30-45min., Sa-Su every hr.; 350ptas/€2.10).

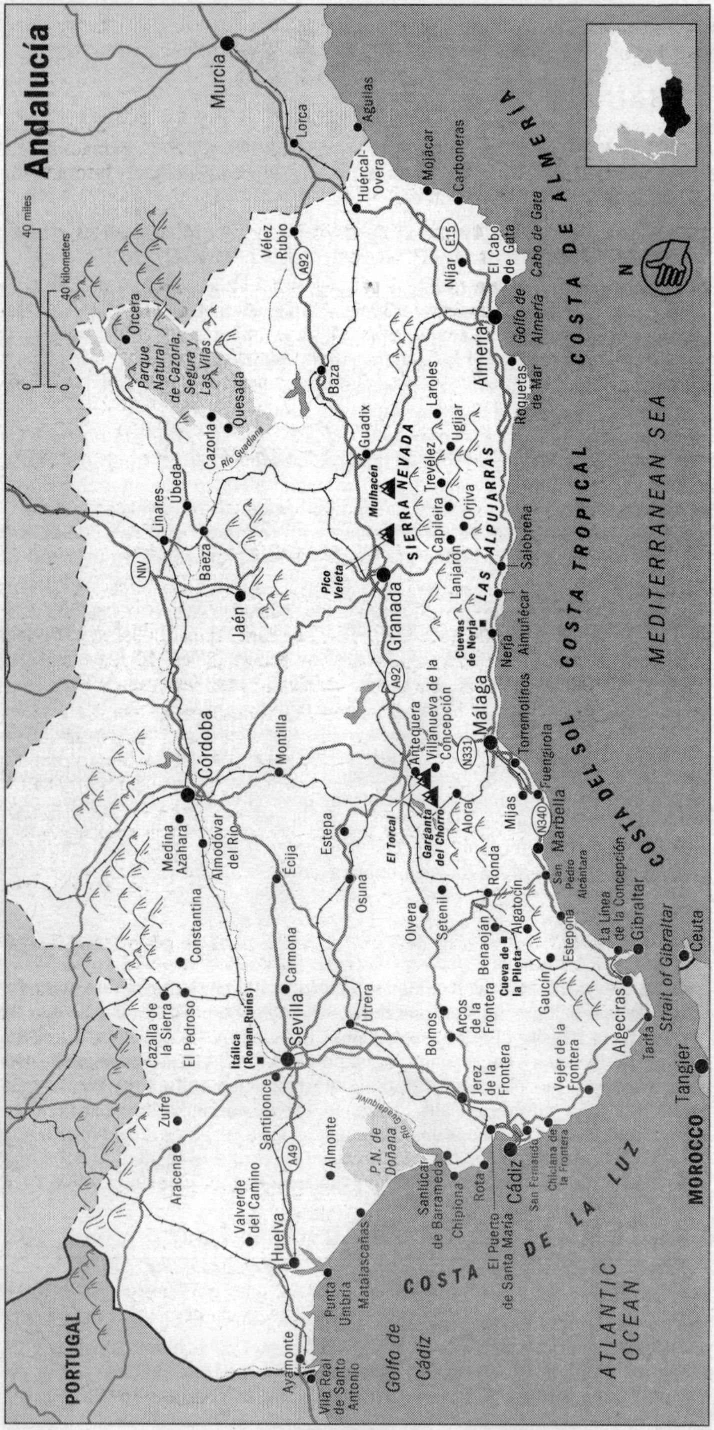

Andalucía

0 40 miles
0 40 kilometers

N

PORTUGAL
MOROCCO
ATLANTIC OCEAN
MEDITERRANEAN SEA
COSTA DE LA LUZ
COSTA DEL SOL
COSTA TROPICAL
COSTA DE ALMERÍA
Golfo de Cádiz
Golfo de Almería
Cabo de Gata
Strait of Gibraltar
SIERRA NEVADA
LAS ALPUJARRAS
Río Guadiana
Río Guadalquivir
P.N. de Doñana
Parque Natural de Cazorla, Segura y Las Vilas

Murcia
Lorca
Águilas
Huércal-Overa
Vélez Rubio
Mojácar
Carboneras
Níjar
El Cabo de Gata
Almería
Roquetas de Mar
Orcera
Quesada
Cazorla
Baza
Guadix
Laroles
Ugíjar
Trevélez
Mulhacén
Capileira
Órjiva
Lanjarón
Salobreña
Almuñécar
Úbeda
Linares
Baeza
Jaén
Pico Veleta
Granada
Cuevas de Nerja
Nerja
Torremolinos
Málaga
Fuengirola
Mijas
Marbella
San Pedro Alcántara
Estepona
Antequera
Villanueva de la Concepción
El Torcal
Garganta del Chorro
Álora
Córdoba
Montilla
Medina Azahara
Almodóvar del Río
Écija
Estepa
Osuna
Olvera
Setenil
Ronda
Benaoján
Algatocín
Cueva de la Pileta
Gaucín
La Línea de la Concepción
Gibraltar
Ceuta
Algeciras
Tarifa
Tangier
Constantina
Cazalla de la Sierra
El Pedroso
Carmona
Sevilla
Itálica (Roman Ruins)
Utrera
Bornos
Arcos de la Frontera
Jerez de la Frontera
Vejer de la Frontera
Zufre
Aracena
Santiponce
Almonte
Sanlúcar de Barrameda
Chipiona
Rota
Cádiz
San Fernando
Chiclana de la Frontera
El Puerto de Santa María
Valverde del Camino
Huelva
Matalascañas
Punta Umbría
Ayamonte
Vila Real de Santo António

NIV
A92
A49
E15
N331
N340

Iberia, C. Guaira, 8 (☎954 22 89 01; nationwide 902 400 500; open M-F 9am-1:30pm) books flights to **Barcelona** (55min., 6 per day) and **Madrid** (45min., 6 per day).

BY TRAIN

Sevilla's is served by **Estación Santa Justa** (☎954 41 41 11), Av. Kansas City. Services include **luggage storage** and **ATM.** In town, the **RENFE** office, C. Zaragoza, 29, is near Pl. Nueva. (☎954 54 02 02. Open M-F 9am-1:15pm and 4-7pm.) International bookings must be made at this office.

AVE trains run to: **Córdoba** (45min., 17 per day 6:30am-9pm, 2400-2800ptas/€15-17) and **Madrid** (2½hr., 20 per day 6:30am-9pm, 8400-9900ptas/€51-60).

Talgo trains run to: **Almería** (5½hr., 3 per day 7am-5:40pm, 4345ptas/€26); **Antequera** (2hr., 5 per day 7am-6pm, 1630ptas/€9.78); **Barcelona** (12hr.; M-F 8, 9am, 9:30pm; 8500ptas/€51); **Cáceres** (5½hr., 4:30pm, 3000ptas/€18); **Cádiz** (2hr., 12 per day 6:35am-9:30pm, 1450ptas/€8.70); **Córdoba** (1½hr., 6 per day 7:50am-7:50pm, 1250ptas/€7.50); **Granada** (3hr., 5 per day 7am-6pm, 2660ptas/€16); **Huelva** (1½hr., 3 per day M-F 8:50am-8:20pm, 1100ptas/€6.60); **Jaén** (2hr., 6:46pm, 2300ptas/€14); **Málaga** (2½hr., 5 per day 7:40am-9:10pm, 2130ptas/€13); **Valencia** (8½hr., 4 per day 8:11am-9:50pm, 5600ptas/€34).

BY BUS

The bus station at **Prado de San Sebastián,** C. Manuel Vázquez Sagastizabal, (☎954 41 71 11), serves Andalucía. Look carefully; the station is not marked on the street.

Transportes Alsina Graells (☎954 41 88 11). Open daily 6:30am-11pm. To: **Almería** (7hr., 3 per day 7am-midnight, 4039ptas/€24); **Córdoba** (2hr., 10-13 per day 8am-9pm, 1350ptas/€8.10); **Granada** (3hr., 9 per day 8am-11pm, 2500ptas/€15); **Jaén** (4hr., 3-4 per day 7:30am-6pm, 2365ptas/€14); **Málaga** (2½hr., 10-12 per day 7am-midnight, 2100ptas/€13); **Murcia** (8hr., 3 per day 8-11am, 4850ptas/€.29).

Transportes Comes (☎954 41 68 58). Open M-Sa 6:30am-9:30pm, Su 7:15am-10:30pm. To: **Algeciras** (3½hr., 4 per day 9am-8pm, 2195ptas/€13); **Cádiz** (1½hr., 12 per day 7am-8:45pm, 1445ptas/€9); **Jerez de la Frontera** (2hr., 6 per day 11:30am-8:30pm, 935ptas/€6); **Tarifa** (3hr., 4 per day 9am-8pm, 2165ptas/€13.)

Los Amarillos (☎954 98 91 84). Open M-F 7:30am-2pm and 2:30-8pm, Sa-Su 7:30am-2pm and 2:30-8pm. To: **Arcos de la Frontera** (2hr.; 8am, 4:30pm; 980ptas/€5.88); **Marbella** (3hr., 1-2 per day 8am-8pm, 1050ptas/€6.30); **Ronda** (2½hr., 3-5 per day 7am-5pm, 1395ptas/€8.37); **Sanlúcar and Chipiona** (2hr., 5-10 per day 7am-9pm, 960ptas/€5.76).

Enatcar-Bacoma (☎902 42 22 42). Open daily 9:30am-9pm. To **Valencia** (10hr., 2 per day 9am and 4:30pm, 6700ptas/€40). The bus station at Plaza de Armas, on the river bank at the Puente del Cachorro, serves destinations beyond Andalucía, including **Portugal.** (☎954 90 77 37. Open daily 5:30am-1:30am). Buses C1, C2, C3, and C4 stop nearby.

Socibus (☎954 90 11 60 or 902 22 92 92; fax 954 90 16 92). Open daily 8:30am-12:45am. To: **Lagos** (6hr.; 1 daily Jan.-May Th-Su, June-Oct. Tu-Su 7:30am or 4:30pm; from 2460ptas/€15); **Madrid** (6hr., 15 per day 1pm-midnight, 2745ptas/€17).

Damas (☎954 90 80 40). Open M-F 8am-1:30pm and 4:30-10:45pm, Sa-Su 10:30am-1:30pm and 8-10:45pm. To: **Badajoz** (3½hr., 3-5 per day 6:45am-8pm, 1815ptas/€11); **Huelva** (1¼hr., 18-30 per day, 940ptas/€5.64); **Lisbon** (9hr.; M,W,F noon, Th 12:30pm, Sa-Su 1:35pm; 4800-5200ptas/€29-31).

Alsa Internacional (☎954 90 78 00 or 902 42 22 42). July-Sept. 1000ptas more. Under 26 and seniors 10% discount, under 12 50% discount. July-Sept Sa, Th 1 per day to: Geneva, Lyon, Toulouse; Zurich. In Spain, daily 6:30am-9pm, to: **Cáceres** (4¼hr., 5 per day, 5255ptas/€31.53); **León** (13hr., 3 per day, 5400ptas/€32.40); **Salamanca** (9½hr., 5 per day, 3735ptas/€22.41).

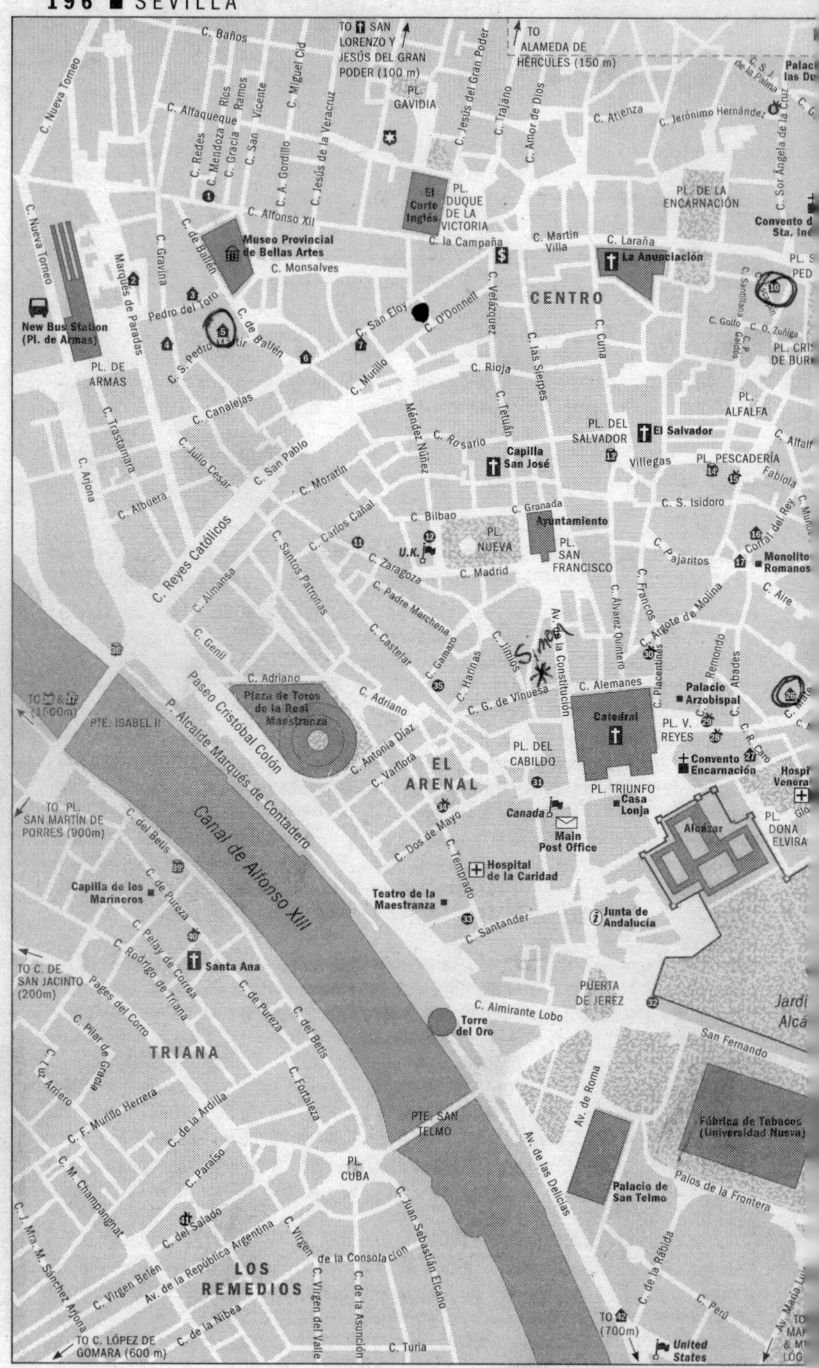

C. Baños
TO SAN LORENZO Y JESÚS DEL GRAN PODER (100 m)
TO ALAMEDA DE HÉRCULES (150 m)
PL. GAVIDIA
C. Jesús del Gran Poder
C. Trajano
C. Amor de Dios
C. Atienza
C. Jerónimo Hernández
C. S. J. de la Palma
C. Sor Angela de la Cruz
C. Nueva Torneo
C. Alfaqueque
C. Redes
C. Mendoza Ríos
C. Gracia
C. San Vicente
C. Miguel Cid
C. A. Gordillo
C. Jesús de la Veracruz
El Corte Inglés
PL. DUQUE DE LA VICTORIA
PL. DE LA ENCARNACIÓN
Convento de Sta. Inés
C. Alfonso XII
Museo Provincial de Bellas Artes
C. de Baltén
C. Gravina
Marqués de Paradas
C. Monsalves
C. la Campaña
C. Martín Villa
C. Laraña
La Anunciación
CENTRO
C. Santillana
C. Golfo
C. O. Zuñiga
C. P. Galdós
PL. CRISTO DE BURGOS
New Bus Station (Pl. de Armas)
Pedro del Toro
C. S. Pedro Mártir
C. San Eloy
C. O'Donnell
C. Velázquez
C. Cuna
C. las Sierpes
PL. DE ARMAS
C. Murillo
C. Rioja
C. Canalejas
Méndez Núñez
C. Tetuán
PL. ALFALFA
C. Trastamara
C. Julio César
C. San Pablo
C. Rosario
PL. DEL SALVADOR
El Salvador
Capilla San José
Villegas
PL. PESCADERÍA
C. Alfalfa
Fabiola
C. Arjona
C. Albuera
C. Moratín
C. S. Isidoro
C. Bilbao
C. Granada
Ayuntamiento
PL. NUEVA
C. Carlos Cañal
U.K.
PL. SAN FRANCISCO
C. Pajaritos
Corral del Rey
Monolitos Romanos
C. Reyes Católicos
C. Santos Patronas
C. Zaragoza
C. Madrid
C. Almansa
C. Padre Marchena
C. Álvarez Quintero
C. Francos
C. Argote de Molina
C. Aire
C. Genil
C. Castelar
C. Gamazo
C. Harinas
C. Jimios
Av. de la Constitución
C. Placentines
C. Remondo
C. Abades
C. Adriano
Plaza de Toros de la Real Maestranza
C. G. de Vinuesa
C. Alemanes
Catedral
Palacio Arzobispal
PL. V. REYES
TO (1500m)
PTE. ISABEL II
Paseo Cristóbal Colón
P. Alcalde Marqués de Contadero
C. Antonia Díaz
C. Varflora
EL ARENAL
PL. DEL CABILDO
C. R. Caro
Convento Encarnación
Hospital Venerables
PL. TRIUNFO
Casa Lonja
Canada
Main Post Office
Alcázar
PL. DOÑA ELVIRA
TO PL. SAN MARTÍN DE PORRES (900m)
C. del Betis
Canal de Alfonso XIII
C. Dos de Mayo
C. Temprado
Hospital de la Caridad
Capilla de los Marineros
C. de Pureza
Teatro de la Maestranza
Junta de Andalucía
C. Santander
C. Pelay de Correa
C. Rodrigo de Triana
Santa Ana
TO C. DE SAN JACINTO (200m)
Pages del Corro
C. de Pureza
C. del Betis
PUERTA DE JEREZ
C. Almirante Lobo
Torre del Oro
San Fernando
C. Pilar de Gracia
TRIANA
C. Luz Arriero
C. Fortaleza
C. F. Murillo Herrera
C. de la Ardilla
PTE. SAN TELMO
Av. de Roma
Av. de las Delicias
Fábrica de Tabacos (Universidad Nueva)
C. M. Champangnat
C. Paraíso
PL. CUBA
Palacio de San Telmo
Palos de la Frontera
C. J. Mra. M. Sánchez Arjona
C. del Salado
Av. de la República Argentina
C. Virgen de la Consolación
C. Juan Sebastián Elcano
C. de la Rábida
C. Virgen Belén
LOS REMEDIOS
C. Virgen del Valle
C. de la Asunción
C. Perú
C. de la Nibea
TO C. LÓPEZ DE GOMARA (600 m)
C. Turia
TO (700m)
United States
Av. María Luisa

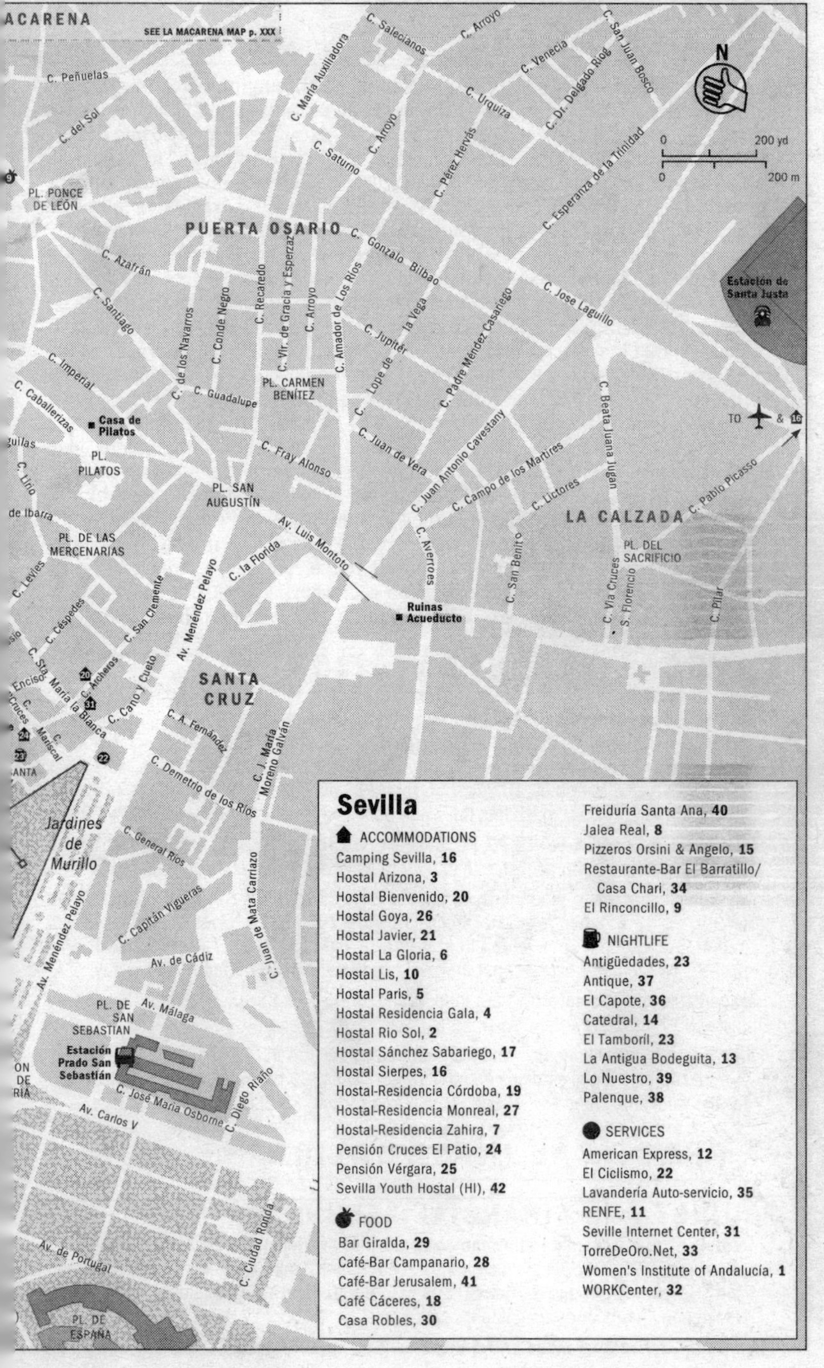
Sevilla
ACCOMMODATIONS
Camping Sevilla, 16
Hostal Arizona, 3
Hostal Bienvenido, 20
Hostal Goya, 26
Hostal Javier, 21
Hostal La Gloria, 6
Hostal Lis, 10
Hostal Paris, 5
Hostal Residencia Gala, 4
Hostal Rio Sol, 2
Hostal Sánchez Sabariego, 17
Hostal Sierpes, 16
Hostal-Residencia Córdoba, 19
Hostal-Residencia Monreal, 27
Hostal-Residencia Zahira, 7
Pensión Cruces El Patio, 24
Pensión Vérgara, 25
Sevilla Youth Hostal (HI), 42
FOOD
Bar Giralda, 29
Café-Bar Campanario, 28
Café-Bar Jerusalem, 41
Café Cáceres, 18
Casa Robles, 30
Freiduría Santa Ana, 40
Jalea Real, 8
Pizzeros Orsini & Angelo, 15
Restaurante-Bar El Barratillo/ Casa Chari, 34
El Rinconcillo, 9
NIGHTLIFE
Antigüedades, 23
Antique, 37
El Capote, 36
Catedral, 14
El Tamboril, 23
La Antigua Bodeguita, 13
Lo Nuestro, 39
Palenque, 38
SERVICES
American Express, 12
El Ciclismo, 22
Lavandería Auto-servicio, 35
RENFE, 11
Seville Internet Center, 31
TorreDeOro.Net, 33
Women's Institute of Andalucía, 1
WORKCenter, 32
ACARENA
SEE LA MACARENA MAP p. XXX
N
0 200 yd
0 200 m
PUERTA OSARIO
LA CALZADA
SANTA CRUZ
PL. PONCE DE LEÓN
PL. CARMEN BENÍTEZ
PL. SAN AUGUSTÍN
PL. PILATOS
Casa de Pilatos
PL. DE LAS MERCENARIAS
PL. DEL SACRIFICIO
Ruinas Acueducto
Estación de Santa Justa
TO & 16
Jardines de Murillo
PL. DE SAN SEBASTIAN
Estación Prado San Sebastián
PL. DE ESPAÑA
C. Peñuelas
C. del Sol
C. Azafrán
C. Santiago
C. Imperial
C. Caballerizas
C. Lirio
C. Levíes
C. Céspedes
C. San Clemente
C. Cano y Cueto
C. Archeros
C. Sta. María la Blanca
C. Mariscal
C. de los Navarros
C. Conde Negro
C. Recaredo
C. Vír. de Gracia y Esperanza
C. Arroyo
C. Amador de Los Ríos
C. Guadalupe
C. Fray Alonso
C. la Florida
Av. Menéndez Pelayo
Av. Luis Montoto
C. María Auxiliadora
C. Saturno
C. Salecianos
C. Urquiza
C. Pérez Hervás
C. Venecia
C. Dr. Delgado Ríos
C. San Juan Bosco
C. Esperanza de la Trinidad
C. Gonzalo Bilbao
C. Jose Laguillo
C. Júpiter
C. Lope de la Vega
C. Padre Méndez Casariego
C. Juan de Vera
C. Juan Antonio Cavestany
C. Campo de los Martires
C. Lictores
C. Beata Juana Jugan
C. Pablo Picasso
C. Averroes
C. San Benito
C. Vía Cruces
S. Florencio
C. Pilar
C. A. Fernández
C. J. María Moreno Galván
C. Demetrio de los Ríos
C. General Ríos
C. Capitán Vigueras
C. Juan de Mata Carriazo
Av. de Cádiz
Av. Málaga
C. José María Osborne
C. Diego Riaño
Av. Carlos V
Av. de Portugal
C. Ciudad Ronda

ORIENTATION

The **Río Guadalquivir** flows roughly north to south through the city. Most of the touristed areas of Sevilla, including the **Barrio de Santa Cruz** and **El Arenal,** are on the east bank. The historic and prideful **Barrio de Triana,** the **Barrio de Santa Cecilia, Los Remedios,** and the Expo '92 fairgrounds occupy the west bank. The cathedral, next to Barrio de Santa Cruz, is Sevilla's centerpiece. If you're disoriented, look for the conspicuous Giralda (the minaret-turned-bell tower). **Avenida de la Constitución,** home of the tourist office, runs alongside the cathedral. **El Centro,** a busy commercial pedestrian zone, lies north of the cathedral, starting where Av. Constitución hits **Plaza Nueva,** site of the Ayuntamiento. **Calle Tetuan,** a popular street for shopping, takes off from Pl. Nueva and runs northward through El Centro.

To reach El Centro from the train station, catch bus #32 to Plaza de la Encarnación, several blocks north of the cathedral. To get to Barrio Santa Cruz from the train station, take bus C-2 and transfer to C-3 at the Jardines del Valle; it will drop you off at the Jardines de Murillo. Walk right one block past the gardens; C. Santa María la Blanca is on the left. Coming to El Centro from the Prado de San Sebastián, take a right on Av. Carlos V Enramadilla, and follow it through Pl. Juan de Austria onto C. San Fernando. Continue along C. San Fernando to Puerta de Jerez and turn right onto Av. de la Constitución, which leads to the cathedral.

Bus C4 connects the bus station at the Plaza de Armas to Pr. San Sebastián. To walk to El Centro from Pl. Armas, walk along the river (on your left) three blocks and make a right onto C. Alfonso XII. To walk to the cathedral (20min.), exit right onto Po. Cristóbal Colón along the river (on your right) and take the first left onto C. Adriano. This street leads to C. García Vinuesa, which ends at the cathedral.

LOCAL TRANSPORTATION

Public Transportation: TUSSAM (☎900 71 01 71), the city bus network. Most lines run every 10min. (6am-11:15pm) and converge on Pl. Nueva, Pl. Encarnación, or in front of the cathedral. Night service departs from Pl. Nueva (every hr., midnight-2am). Fare 125ptas/€0.75, *bonobús* (10 rides) 650ptas/€3.90. Useful are C3 and C4, which circle the center, and 34, which hits the youth hostel, university, cathedral, and Pl. Nueva.

Taxis: TeleTaxi (☎954 62 22 22). **Radio Taxi** (☎954 58 00 00). Base rate 360ptas/€2.15, Su 25% surcharge. Extra charge for luggage and night taxis as well.

Car Rental: Hertz, Av. República Argentina, 3 (☎954 27 88 87), and at the airport (☎954 51 47 20). Min. age 25. From 10,000ptas/€60 a day. Open M-F 9am-1:30pm and 4-7pm, Sa 9am-1pm. **Triana Rent A Car,** C. Almirante Lobo, 7 (☎954 56 44 39 or 954 33 68 97). Min. age 21, but they will negotiate. From 5100ptas/€31 a day.

Moped Rental: Alkimoto, C. Fernando Tirado, 5 (☎954 58 49 27), near Est. Santa Justa. 3500ptas/€21 per day. Open M-F 9am-1:30pm and 5-8pm.

Bike Rental: El Ciclismo, Po. Catalina de Ribera, 2 (☎954 41 19 59), off Menéndez Pelayo, at the end of the Jardines de Murillo. 1500ptas/€9 per weekday, 2500ptas/€15 for the weekend. Open M-F 10am-1:30pm and 6-8pm, Sa 10am-1pm.

PRACTICAL INFORMATION

TOURIST AND FINANCIAL SERVICES

Tourist Offices: Centro de Información de Sevilla, Av. Constitución, 21B (☎954 22 14 04; fax 954 22 97 53), 1 block from the cathedral. English spoken. Open M-F 9am-7pm, Sa 10am-2pm and 3-7pm, Su 10am-2pm. **Info booths** in Est. Santa Justa and Pl. Nueva carry maps and bus guides.

Currency Exchange: Banco Central Hispano, C. Sierpes, 55 (☎954 56 26 84). Open M-F 8:30am-2:30pm, Sa 8:30am-1pm.

Banks and **ATMs:** All along Av. Constitución and near Pl. Nueva.

American Express: Pl. Nueva, 7 (☎954 21 16 17). Open M-F 9:30am-1:30pm and 4:30-7:30pm, Sa 10am-1pm.

LOCAL SERVICES

Luggage Storage: At Pr. San Sebastián bus station (250ptas/€1.50 per day; open 6:30am-10pm), Pl. Armas bus station (300ptas/€1.80 per day), and Santa Justa train station (300-500ptas/€1.80-3 per day).

English Bookstore: Vértice, C. San Fernando, 33 (☎954 21 16 54), near Pta. Jerez. Open M-F 9:30am-2pm and 5-8:30pm, Sa 10am-1:30pm. July closed Sa. **Librería Beta,** a chain with stores all over Sevilla, has an English-language section.

VIPS: C. República Argentina, 25 (☎954 27 93 97), 3 blocks from Pl. Cuba, in Triana. International newspapers, liquor, non-perishable groceries, and a restaurant that serves a popular American breakfast. Open Su-Th 8am-2am, F 8am-3am, Sa 9am-3am.

Women's Institute of Andalucía: C. Alfonso XII, 52 (☎955 03 49 53). Info on feminist and lesbian organizations, plus legal and psychological services for rape victims. Employment listings for women. Open M-Th 8am-8:30pm, F 8am-3pm.

Gay and Lesbian Services: COLEGA (Colectiva de Lesbianas y Gays de Andalucía), Cuesta del Rosario, 8 (☎954 18 65 10). Open M-F 10am-2pm.

Laundromat: Lavandería Auto-servicio, C. Castelar, 2 (☎954 21 05 35). From the cathedral, walk 2 blocks down C. Vinuesa and turn left. Wash and dry (1hr.) 1000ptas/€9. Open M-F 9:30am-1:30pm and 3-8:30pm, Sa-Su 9am-2pm.

EMERGENCY AND COMMUNICATIONS

Emergency: ☎112. **Police:** Po. Delicias, 15 (☎954 61 54 50).

Late-Night Pharmacy: Check list posted at any pharmacy for those open 24hr.

Medical Assistance: Ambulatorio Esperanza Macarena (☎954 42 01 05). **Hospital Universitario Virgen Macarena** (☎954 24 81 81), Av. Dr. Fedriani. English spoken.

Internet Access: TorreDeOro.Net, C. Núñez de Balboa, 3 (☎954 50 28 09), next to the Teatro Maestranza, at Po. Cristóbal Colón. Coin-operated computers. 300ptas/€1.80 per hr. Open daily 8:30am-1am. **Seville Internet Center,** C. Almirantazgo, 2, 2nd fl. (☎954 50 02 75), across from the cathedral. 200ptas/€1.20 per 30min. Open M-F 9am-10pm, Sa-Su noon-10pm.

Post Office: Av. Constitución, 32 (☎954 21 64 76), opposite the cathedral. Lista de Correos and fax. Open M-F 10am-8:30pm, Sa 9:30am-2pm. **Postal Code:** 41080.

ACCOMMODATIONS

During **Semana Santa** and **Feria de Abril,** rooms vanish and prices soar; it would be wise to make reservations many months ahead. The tourist office has lists of *casas particulares* that open for visitors on special occasions.

BARRIO DE SANTA CRUZ AND EL ARENAL

The narrow streets east of the cathedral around C. Santa María la Blanca are full of cheap hostels with virtually identical rooms. The neighborhood is overwhelmingly touristed, but its disorienting streets and shady plazas are all within a few minutes' walk of the cathedral, the Alcázar, and El Centro.

Pensión Vergara, C. Ximénez de Enciso, 11, 2nd fl. (☎954 21 56 68), at C. Mesón del Moro. 12 rooms of varying size with exposed beams. Up to 4 people in each room. All rooms have fans. Towels provided on request. 2500ptas/€15 per person.

Hostal-Residencia Monreal, C. Rodrigo Caro, 8 (☎954 21 41 66). From the cathedral, walk up C. Mateos Gago and take the 1st right. Air-conditioned rooms, many with verandas overlooking a nearby plaza. Singles 3000ptas/€18; doubles 6000ptas/€36, with bath 8000ptas/€48; triples 11,000-12,000ptas/€66-72. MC/V.

Hostal Sierpes, C. Corral del Rey, 22 (☎954 22 49 48; fax 954 21 21 07), on the continuation of C. Argote de Molina. Rooms all with baths and phones, many with A/C. Parking 2500ptas/€15. Singles 4500-9000ptas/€27-54; doubles 6000-11,000ptas/€36-66; triples 7500-15,000ptas/€45-90; quads 9000-19,000ptas/€54-114. MC/V.

Hostal Sánchez Sabariego, C. Corral del Rey, 23 (☎954 21 44 70). Hostal Sierpes's less flashy neighbor. A/C upstairs, fans in all other rooms. Singles 4000ptas/€24; doubles with bath 8000-10,000ptas/€48-60; triples with bath 9000-11,000ptas/€54-66.

Pensión Cruces El Patio, C. Cruces, 10 (☎954 22 96 33 or 954 22 60 41). The cheapest place to crash in Santa Cruz. Fans provided on request. Up to 6 people in a room. Laundry 1500ptas/€9. 2000ptas/€12 per additional person. Singles 2000ptas/€12; doubles 5000ptas/€30, with bath 6000ptas/€36.

Hostal-Residencia Córdoba, C. Farnesio, 12 (☎954 22 74 98), off C. Fabiola. Beautifully maintained patio. Air-conditioned rooms are immaculate and spacious. Singles with shower 5000ptas/€30; doubles 6500ptas/€39, with shower 7500ptas/€45.

Hostal Goya, C. Mateos Gago, 31 (☎954 21 11 70; fax 954 56 29 88), 3 blocks from the cathedral. All rooms have A/C and showers. Doubles 7500ptas/€45, with bath 8000ptas/€48; triples 10,500ptas/€63, with bath 12,000ptas/€72. MC/V.

Hostal Bienvenido, C. Archeros, 14 (☎954 41 36 55). Reasonably priced, but a 5min. walk from the center of Santa Cruz. Spacious roof-top terrace. Singles 3000ptas/€18; doubles 5000ptas/€30; triples 2500ptas/€15 per person. AmEx/MC/V.

Hostal Javier, C. Archeros, 16 (☎954 41 23 25), down the road from Hostal Bienvenido. Rooms with framed prints and floral-patterned bed sheets. Singles 3500ptas/€21, with bath 4000ptas/€24; doubles 5000/€30, with bath 6000ptas/€36. MC/V.

EL CENTRO

El Centro, a mess of narrow streets radiating from Pl. Encarnación, is a bustling shopping district during the day, but most streets are deserted at night.

Hostal Lis, C. Escarpín, 10 (☎954 21 30 88), on an alley near Pl. Encarnación. Glistening bathrooms. All rooms have fans. Singles 3000ptas/€18; doubles 6000ptas/€36, with bath 7000ptas/€42; triples with bath 9000ptas/€54.

Hostal La Gloria, C. San Eloy, 58, 2nd fl. (☎954 22 26 73), at the end of a lively shopping street. Faded white rooms of irregular shape. Singles 2500ptas/€15; doubles 4000ptas/€24, with bath 4500ptas/€27; triples 6000ptas/€36.

Hostal-Residencia Zahira, C. San Eloy, 43 (☎954 22 10 61; fax 954 21 30 48). Hotel-sized lobby disguises simple rooms beyond. All rooms have bath and A/C. Lounge with TV. Singles 3500-5000ptas/€21-30; doubles 6000-8000ptas/€36-48. AmEx/MC/V.

NEAR ESTACIÓN PLAZA DE ARMAS

Most hostels near the Pl. Armas bus station center on C. Gravina, parallel to C. Marqués de las Paradas and two blocks from the station. These are the most convenient for exploring El Centro and C. Betis on the west bank of the river.

Hostal Río Sol, C. Márquez de Parada, 25 (☎954 22 90 38), 1 block from Plaza de Armas bus station. A/C. Singles with sink 2000ptas/€12, with bath 3000-4000ptas/€18-24; doubles with bath 6500ptas/€39; triples with bath 9000ptas/€54. MC/V.

Hostal Paris, C. San Pedro Mártir, 14 (☎954 22 98 61 or 21 96 45; fax 21 96 45), off C. Gravina. Pricey but comfortable. All rooms have baths, A/C, phones, TVs. Singles 5500ptas/€33; doubles 7500ptas/€45; triples 10,500ptas/€63. AmEx/MC/V.

Hostal Residencia Gala, C. Gravina, 52 (☎954 21 45 03). Clean rooms with framed prints and spacious bathrooms. Singles 3000ptas/€18, with bath 4500ptas/€27; doubles 6500ptas/€39, with bath 7000ptas/€42; triples with bath 8500ptas/€51.

Hostal Arizona, C. Pedro del Toro, 14 (☎ 954 21 60 42), off C. Gravina. Some rooms have balconies. Singles 2000-2500ptas/€12-15; doubles 4000ptas/€24, with bath 4500ptas/€27; triples 5000-6000ptas/€30-36.

ELSEWHERE AND CAMPING

Sevilla Youth Hostel (HI), C. Isaac Peral, 2 (☎954 61 31 50; fax 954 61 31 58). Take bus #34 across from the tourist office near the cathedral; the 5th stop is behind the hostel. Isolated and difficult to find. Up to 4 per room. A/C. Many private baths. Breakfast included. Dorms 2050ptas/€12.30, over 26 2675ptas/€16.05. Non-members can pay an additional 500ptas/€3 a night for 6 nights to become members.

Camping Sevilla, Ctra. Madrid-Cádiz, km 534 (☎954 51 43 79), near the airport. From Pr. San Sebastián, take bus #70 (stops 800m away at Parque Alcosa). Hot showers, supermarket, and pool. 475ptas/€2.85 per person, per car, and per tent.

Club de Campo, Av. Libertad, 13, Ctra. Sevilla-Dos Hermanas (☎954 72 02 50), 8km out of town. Los Amarillos buses leave from C. Infante Carlos de Borbón, at the back of Pr. San Sebastián, to Dos Hermanas (every 45min., 140ptas). Lots of grass and a pool. 515ptas/€3.09 per person, per car, and per tent, children 410ptas/€2.46.

FOOD

Sevilla is a city of *tapas;* locals prepare and devour them with a vengeance. Other favorites include *caracoles* (snails), *cocido andaluz* (a thick soup of chick peas), *pisto* (tomato and eggplant hash), *espinacas con garbanzos* (spinach with chick peas), and all manner of fresh seafood. *Pescado frito,* lightly fried fish, is a particular specialty of Sevilla. One of the most enjoyable aspects of eating in Sevilla is a long evening spent wandering between *tapas* bars, sampling dozens of offerings. Defying the need for hydration, many locals imbibe only Sevilla's Cruzcampo beer, a light, smooth pilsner. **Mercado del Arenal,** near the bullring on C. Pastor y Leandro, between C. Almansa and C. Arenal, has fresh meat and produce (open M-Sa 9am-2pm). For a supermarket, try **%Día,** C. San Juan de Ávila, near El Corte Inglés (open M-F 9:30am-2pm and 6:30-9pm, Sa 9am-1pm).

BARRIO DE SANTA CRUZ AND EL ARENAL

Restaurants near the cathedral cater almost exclusively to tourists. Beware the unexceptional, omnipresent *menús* featuring *gazpacho* and *paella* for 1000ptas. Food and prices improve in the backstreet establishments between the cathedral and the river in El Arenal, and along side streets in the Barrio Santa Cruz.

Restaurante-Bar El Baratillo/Casa Chari, C. Pavía, 12 (☎954 22 96 51), on a tiny street off C. Dos de Mayo. A local favorite. Call or ask at least an hour in advance for the tour-de-force: homemade *paella* with a jar of wine, beer, or *sangría* (2500ptas/€15 for 2). *Menú* 650ptas/€3.90. Open M-F 9am-11pm, Sa noon-5pm.

Café-Bar Campanario, C. Mateos Gago, 8 (☎954 56 41 89), ½ block from the cathedral, on the right. Mixes the best (and strongest) jugs of *sangría* around (1200-1500ptas/€7.20-9). *Tapas* 275-350ptas/€1.65-2.10, *raciones* 650-1000/€3.90-6. Open daily noon-midnight.

Café Cáceres, C. San José, 24. The closest thing to a buffet-style breakfast in Sevilla. Choose from spread of cheeses, jams, and countless condiments. *Desayuno de la casa* (orange juice, coffee, ham, eggs, toast) 650ptas/€3.90. Open daily 7:30am-8pm.

EL CENTRO

This area belongs to professionals and shoppers by day and young people at night. Inexpensive *tapas* bars line the streets radiating from **Pl Alfalfa.**

Pizzeros Orsini & Angelo, C. Luchana, 2 (☎954 21 61 64), 2 blocks from Pl. del Salvador. Crisp and filling pizza served straight from the oven. Romantic outdoor seating in front of a Baroque church. Pizzas 400-950ptas/€2.40-5.70 and salads 400-700ptas/€2.40-4.20. Open daily 1-4pm and 8pm-1am.

Jalea Real, Sor Ángela de la Cruz, 37 (☎954 21 61 03). From Pl. Encarnación, walk 150m on C. Laraña, then turn left at Iglesia de San Pedro. Fabulous vegetarian cuisine.

LOYALTY REMEMBERED During the civil wars of the 1270s, King Alfonso X the Wise was betrayed by his own son Don Sancho, who wrestled from his father all of Castile, León, Galicia, Extremadura, and Andalucía—with the sole exception, that is, of Sevilla, whose people remained loyal to the old king. Alfonso is recorded as having sighed in gratitude *"No m'a dejado"* ("She has not forsaken me"). To remind generations to come of the city's loyalty, the king added a new logo to the city shield which has since become the emblem and motto of Sevilla: a NO and DO with a double knot in between, similar to "NO&DO." *Nudo* in Spanish means "knot," and *madeja* means "skein." The rebus reads *No m'a dejado* perfectly and is a particularly clever word play which proud Sevillians have emblazoned all over the city, from the sides of buses to government buildings.

Smells of zesty seasonings. Salads 800ptas/€4.80, *menú* 1400ptas/€8.40. Open M-F 1:30-5pm and 8:30-11:30pm, Sa 8:30-11:30pm. Closed Aug.

El Rinconcillo, C. Gerona, 40 or C. Alhóndiga, 2 (☎954 22 31 83), behind the Church of Santa Catalina. Founded in 1670, when Spain's empire stretched from the Philippines to America, this bodega continues to attract loyal patrons. Sip *cerveza* and savor *olivas* on top of ancient wine barrels. *Tapas* 185-300ptas/€1.11-1.80, *raciones* 225-1850ptas/€1.35-11.10. Open daily 1pm-2am, closed W. MC/V.

TRIANA AND BARRIO DE SANTA CECILIA

This old maritime neighborhood, on the far side of the river, was once a separate village. Avoid overpriced C. Betis and plunge down the less expensive side streets, where fresh seafood and *caracoles* abound. *Tapas* bars cluster around **Pl. San Martín** and along **C. San Jacinto.**

Café-Bar Jerusalém, C. Salado, 6, at C. Virgen de las Huertas. Bar with an international crowd and creative *tapas*. Chicken, lamb, or pork and cheese *shwarmas* called a *bocadillo hebreo*—it's not kosher, but it sure is tasty. Open daily 8pm-3am.

Freiduría Santa Ana, C. Pureza, 61 (☎954 33 20 40), parallel to C. Betis, 1 block from the river. A local institution, combination fish market and restaurant. Tasty fried seafood is their *raison d'être*. Seafood served by the kg. Open Sept.-July Tu-Su 7pm-midnight.

SIGHTS

While it is Sevilla's ambience which lingers longest in travelers' memories, there are plenty of postcard-worthy monuments in Barrio de Santa Cruz.

THE CATHEDRAL. Legend has it that the *reconquistadores* in 1401 wished to demonstrate their religious fervor by constructing a church so great, they said, that "those who come after us will take us for madmen." With 44 individual chapels, the Cathedral of Sevilla is the third largest in the world, after St. Peter's Basilica in Rome and St. Paul's Cathedral in London, and the world's biggest Gothic edifice ever constructed. Not surprisingly, it took more than a century to build.

In 1401, the 12th-century Almohad mosque was destroyed to clear space for a massive cathedral. All that remains is the **Patio de Los Naranjos,** where the faithful would wash before prayer, and the famed minaret **La Giralda,** built in 1198. The tower and its twins in Marrakesh and Rabat are the oldest and largest surviving Almohad minarets, with the lower walls standing 2.5m thick. There are 35 ramps inside leading to the top of the tower; once these allowed the *muezzin* to climb up on his horse for the call to prayer; today they enable tourists to take pictures.

In the center of the cathedral, the **Capilla Real** (main chapel), built in Renaissance style, stands opposite dark wooden **choirstalls** made of mahogany recycled from a 19th-century Austrian railway. The **retablo mayor** (altarpiece), one of the largest in the world, is a golden wall of intricately wrought saints and disciples. Nearby is the **Sepulcro de Cristóbal Colón** (Columbus's tomb). The black and gold coffin-bearers represent the eternally grateful monarchs of Castilla, León, Aragón, and Navarra. There is considerable mystery surrounding the actual whereabouts of Columbus's remains, since he has four alleged resting places throughout the world. The Sepulcro was inaugurated in 1902, 396 years after Columbus died; chances are this tomb isn't the jackpot.

Farther on and to the right stands the cathedral's treasury, the **Sacristía Mayor,** which holds gilded panels of Alfonso X "El Sabio", done by Juan de Arefe, as well as works by Ribera and Murillo and a glittering Corpus Christi icon, **La Custodia Processional.** A small, disembodied head of John the Baptist eyes visitors who enter the gift shop and overlooks keys presented to the city of Sevilla by Jewish leaders after King Fernando III ousted the Muslims in 1248. In the northwest corner of the cathedral lie the architecturally stunning **Sala de Las Columnas** and **Cabildo.** *(☎954 21 49 71. Open M-Sa 10am-5pm, Su 2-7pm. Tickets sold until 1hr. before closing. 800ptas/€4.80, seniors and students 200ptas/€1.20, under 12 free. Su free. Mass held in the Capilla Real M-F 8:30, 9, 10am; Sa 8:30, 10am, 8pm; Su 8:30, 10, 11am, noon, 1pm.)*

ALCÁZAR. If you can't make it to the Alhambra in Granada, at least come to Sevilla's Alcázar; the Moorish architecture and gardens are nothing short of magnificent. Originally constructed by the Moors in the 7th century, the palace was embellished greatly during the 1400-1500s and now serves as the residence of the King and Queen of Spain during their stays in Sevilla. Visitors enter through the **Patio de la Montería,** directly across from the intricate Almohad façade of the Moorish palace. Through the archway lies the Arabic residences, including the **Patio del Yeso** and the exquisitely carved **Patio de las Muñecas** (Patio of the Dolls), so named because of its miniature proportions. Of the Christian additions, the most notable is the **Patio de las Doncellas (Maids' Court).** Court life in the Alcázar revolved around this colonnaded quadrangle, which is encircled by archways adorned with glistening tilework. The astonishing, golden-domed **Salón de los Embajadores** is allegedly the site where Fernando and Isabel welcomed Columbus back from America. Nearby, the **Corte de las Muñecas** contains the palace's private quarters, decorated with the building's most exquisite carvings. Stunning, peaceful **gardens** stretch from the residential quarters in all directions. *(Pl. Triunfo, 7. ☎954 50 23 23. Open Tu-Sa 9:30am-7pm, Su 9:30am-6pm. 700ptas/€4.20; students, disabled, over 65, and under 16 free. Worthwhile audio guides in several languages give anecdotes, historical info, and a clearly marked route through the buildings and gardens; 400ptas/€2.40.)*

CASA LONJA. Between the cathedral and the Alcázar stands the 16th-century Casa Lonja, built by Felipe II as a *Casa de Contratación* (commercial exchange) for trade with the Americas. In 1785, Carlos III converted the building into the **Archivo General de las Indias (Archive of the Indies).** Today it contains a collection of over 44,000 documents relating to the discovery and conquest of the New World. Among its books is Juan Bautista Muñoz's "definitive" history of the conquest, commissioned by Carlos III. Other highlights of the collection include Juan de la Costa's wildly inaccurate *Mapa Mundi* and letters from Columbus to Fernando and Isabel, as well as a 1590 letter from Cervantes (pre-*Don Quijote*) requesting employment in America. *(☎954 21 12 34. Exhibits open M-F 10am-1pm. Free. Full access to documents is restricted to scholars.)*

BARRIO DE SANTA CRUZ

The tourist office has a detailed map of the winding alleys, wrought-iron gates, and courtyards of the Barrio de Santa Cruz. King Fernando III forced Jews in flight from Toledo to live in this former ghetto. The fragrance of jasmine lingers at sunset and every street corner echoes with legend. On **Calle Susona,** a glazed skull above a door evokes the tale of beautiful Susona, a Jewish girl who fell in love with a Christian knight. When Susona learned that her father and friends planned to kill several inquisitors, including her knight, she warned her lover. A bloody reprisal was unleashed on the Jewish ghetto, during which Susona's entire family was slaughtered. She requested that her skull be placed above the doorway in atonement for her betrayal, and the actual skull supposedly remained until the

18th century. C. Susona leads to **Plaza Doña Elvira,** where Sevillian Lope de Rueda's works, precursors to the dramas of Spain's Golden Age, were staged. A turn down C. Gloria leads to Pl. Venerables, site of the 17th-century **Hospital de los Venerables,** a hospital-church adorned with art from the Sevillian school. *(☎954 56 26 96. Open daily for guided visits 10am-2pm and 4-8pm. 600ptas/€3.60.)*

Calle Lope de Rueda, off C. Ximénez de Enciso, is graced with two noble mansions, beyond which lies the charming and fragrant **Plaza de Santa Cruz.** South of the plaza are the **Jardines de Murillo,** a shady expanse of shrubbery and benches. **Convento de San José** cherishes a cloak and portrait of Santa Teresa of Ávila. *(C. Santa Teresa, off Pl. Santa Cruz. Open daily 9-11am.)* The church in Pl. Santa Cruz houses the grave of the artist Murillo, who died in what is now known as the **Casa Murillo** after falling from a scaffold while painting frescoes in Cádiz's Iglesia de los Capuchinos. The house has information on Murillo's life and work. *(C. Santa Teresa, 8. ☎954 22 12 72. Open M-F 8am-3pm and 4-8pm. Free.)* **Iglesia de Santa María la Blanca** was built in 1391 on the foundation of a synagogue. It features red marble columns, Baroque plasterwork, and Murillo's *Last Supper*. *(C. Santa María la Blanca. Open M-Sa 10-11am and 6:30-8pm, Su 9:30am-2pm and 6:30-8pm.)*

SIERPES AND THE ARISTOCRATIC QUARTER

Originating from the Pl. San Francisco, **Calle Sierpes** cuts through the Aristocratic Quarter. At the beginning of this pedestrian street lined with shoe stores, fan shops, and chic boutiques, a plaque marks the spot where the royal prison once loomed. Some scholars believe Cervantes began writing *Don Quijote* here.

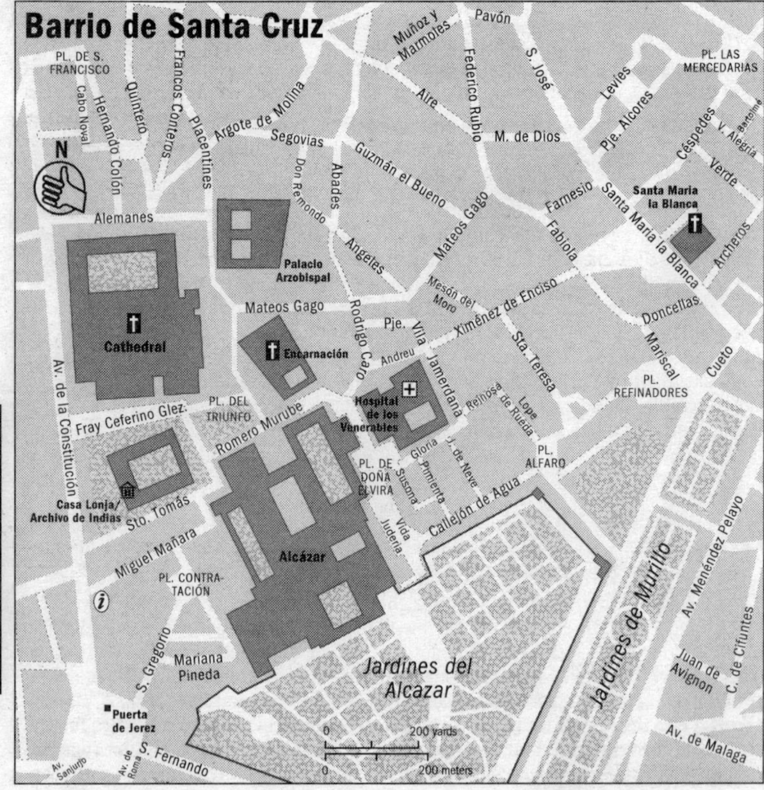

PILATE IN SEVILLA? When most people hear the name Pilate, they think biblical Jerusalem, not 17th-century Spain. At the time of the Inquisition, Pilate was not a name frequently chosen for children, let alone plazas and palazzos. By what heresy were Casa de Pilatos and the adjoining Plaza de Pilatos named? Local legend has it that the central courtyard of the palace was modeled after that of Pilate's villa in Jerusalem. Given the utter lack of resemblance between the two, this seems hardly plausible. Most likely, Casa de Pilatos—officially named the Palacio de San Andrés—received its epithet because of the role it played in annual Good Friday processions; each year worshippers would gather by a large wooden cross outside the palace to recreate Jesus' appearance before Pontius Pilate.

CASA DE PILATOS. Inhabited continuously by Spanish aristocrats since the 15th century, this private residence has only recently been opened to the bourgeois public. Mudéjar patios displaying Roman artifacts alternate with tropical gardens. The second floor, open for guided visits every half hour, features rooms decorated over the centuries with oil portraits, sculptures, and tapestries. Use the bell if the gate is closed during visiting hours. *(Pl. Pilatos. ☎954 22 52 98. Open daily 9am-7pm. 500ptas/€3 ground level only, 1000ptas/€6 ground level and upper chambers.)*

IGLESIA DEL SALVADOR. Fronted by a Montañés sculpture, this 17th-century church is built on the foundations of what was once the city's main mosque. The courtyard and the belfry's base are remnants of the old mosque. As grandiose as a cathedral, it is adorned with outstanding baroque *retablos* (altarpieces), sculptures, and paintings, including Montañés's *Jesús de la pasión*. *(Pl. Salvador, 1 block from C. Sierpes. Open daily 6:30-9pm.)*

OTHER SIGHTS. A few blocks southeast of Pl. Salvador stand the excavated ruins of an old **Roman temple.** The remaining columns rise 15m from below street level and offer a glimpse of the literal depth of Sevilla's history; river sediment that accumulated after the construction of the temple caused the ground level to rise. *(C. Mármoles.)* The **Ayuntamiento** has 16th-century Gothic and Renaissance interior halls, a richly decorated domed ceiling, and a Plateresque façade. *(It often displays art exhibitions; check with the tourist office for information. Pl. San Francisco. ☎954 59 01 01. Open Tu-Th 5:30-6:30pm, Sa-Su 11:30am-12:30pm.)* The interesting **Iglesia de la Anunciación** features a pantheon honoring illustrious *sevillanos*, including poet Gustavo Adolfo Bécquer. *(Pl. Encarnación, enter on C. Laraña. Open daily 9am-1pm.)*

EL ARENAL, TRIANA, AND PASEO ALCALDE MARQUÉS DE CONTADERO

Immortalized by *Siglo de Oro* (Golden Age) writers Lope de Vega, Quevedo, and Cervantes, Triana was Sevilla's chaotic 16th- and 17th-century mariners' neighborhood. El Arenal was once a stretch of sand by the harbor on the opposite bank, exposed when the river was diverted to its present course. The inviting riverside esplanade Po. Marqués de Contadero stretches along the banks of the Guadalquivir from the base of the Torre del Oro. Bridge-heavy boat tours of Sevilla leave from in front of the tower (1hr., 700ptas/€4.20).

MUSEO PROVINCIAL DE BELLAS ARTES. Cobbled together from decommissioned convents in the mid-1800s, this museum contains Spain's finest collection of works by painters of the Sevilla school, most notably Murillo, Valdés Leal, and Zurbarán, as well as El Greco and Dutch master Jan Breughel. Spanning patios and chapels, the grounds are a work of art. *(Pl. Museo, 9, off C. Alfonso XII. ☎954 22 07 90. Open Tu 3-8pm, W-Sa 9am-8pm, Su 9am-2:30pm. 250ptas/€1.50, EU citizens free.)*

PLAZA DE TOROS DE LA REAL MAESTRANZA. A tiled boardwalk leads to Pl. Toros de la Real Maestranza, Spain's most beautiful and renowned bullring. Home to one of the two great bullfighting schools (the other is in Ronda), the plaza fills to capacity for the 13 *corridas* of the *Feria de Abril* as well as for weekly fights.

Multilingual tour guides take visitors behind the ring to a chapel where *matadors* pray before each fight and a medical emergency room is used when their prayers go unanswered. *(☎954 22 45 77. Open on non-bullfight days 9:30am-2pm and 3-7pm, on bullfight days 9:30am-3pm. Tours every 30min., 500ptas./€3. See* **bullfights,** p. 210, *for tickets.)*

HOSPITAL DE LA CARIDAD. A 17th-century complex of arcaded courtyards, this hospital was founded by Don Miguel de Marañe, believed to be the model for legendary Sevillian Don Juan. This notorious playboy converted to a life of piety and charity after allegedly stumbling out of an orgy into his own funeral cortège. Don Miguel's body rests inside the crypt of the **Iglesia de San Jorge,** part of the hospital. The church's walls display paintings and frescos by Valdés Leal and Murillo, who couldn't refrain from holding his nose when he saw Leal's morbid *Finis Gloria Mundi*, which depicts corpses of a peasant, a bishop, and a king beneath a rendition of Justice and the Seven Deadly Sins. *(C. Temprado. ☎954 22 32 32. Open M-Sa 9am-1:30pm and 3:30-7:30pm, Su 9am-1pm. 400ptas/€2.40.)*

TORRE DEL ORO. The 12-sided Torre del Oro (Gold Tower), built by the Almohads in 1200, overlooks the river from Po. Cristóbal Colón. Glistening golden tiles once covered the entire tower; today a tiny yellow dome is all that remains. Inside is the **Museo Náutico,** a storehouse of naval relics with illustrations of Sevilla as a bustling 17th-century port. *(☎954 22 24 19. Open Sept.-July Tu-F 10am-2pm, Sa-Su 11am-2pm. 100ptas/€0.60. Tu free.)* On the far bank of the river, the **Torre de la Plata** (Silver Tower) used to be connected to the Torre de Oro by underwater chains designed to protect the city from river-borne trespassers. With piracy no longer a concern, the Torre de la Plata has since been absorbed by a bank building, but one side is still visible near the corner of C. Santander and C. Temprado.

OTHER SIGHTS. The **Capilla de los Marineros** in Triana was constructed in the 18th century to worship the Esperanza de Triana, who, along with the Virgin Mary and the "Macarena," is one of the most adored figures of Sevilla. *(C. Pureza, 53.)* One block farther inland, midway between Puente de Isabel II and Puente de San Telmo, stands the **Iglesia de Santa Ana,** Sevilla's oldest church and the focal point of the exuberant July fiestas that take over the area in July. *(Open M and W 7:30-8:30pm.)* The terraced riverside promenade **Calle Betis** is an ideal spot from which to view Sevilla's skyline and sparkling nights.

LA MACARENA

La Macarena is the virgin of the city and namesake of an enchanting church and neighborhood northwest of El Centro.

CONVENTS. The founder of **Convento de Santa Inés,** as legend has it, was pursued so insistently by King Pedro the Cruel that she disfigured her face with boiling oil so that he would leave her alone. Cooking liquids are used more positively today—the cloistered nuns sell patented puff pastries and coffee cakes through the courtyard's revolving window. *(C. María Coronel.)* **Convento de Santa Paula** includes a church with Gothic, Mudéjar, and Renaissance elements, a magnificent ceiling, and sculptures by Montañés. *(Pl. Santa Paula. ☎954 53 63 30. Open Tu-Su 10:30am-12:30pm and 4:30-6:30pm.)* The **museum** next door has Ribera's *St. Jerome*. Nuns here peddle scrumptious homemade marmalades and angel-hair pastry. *(Pl. Santa Paula, 11. Open Tu-Su 11am-noon and 4:30-6:30pm.)*

CHURCHES. Opposite the belfry of the Iglesia de San Marcos rises **Iglesia de Santa Isabel,** featuring an altarpiece by Montañés. Nearby stands the exuberantly Baroque **Iglesia de San Luis,** crowned by octagonal glazed-tile domes. The site of the church was the endpoint of a 12-step prayer route based on the ascent to Golgotha. More recently, it has been immortalized by the Cruzcampo beer logo. *(C. San Luis. ☎954 55 02 07. Open W-Th 9am-2pm, F-Sa 9am-2pm and 5-8pm.)* A stretch of **murallas** (fortress walls) created in the 12th century runs between Pta. Macarena and Pta. Córdoba on the Ronda de Capuchinos road. Flanking the west end of the walls, the **Basilica Macarena** houses the venerated image of *La virgen de la Macarena*, who

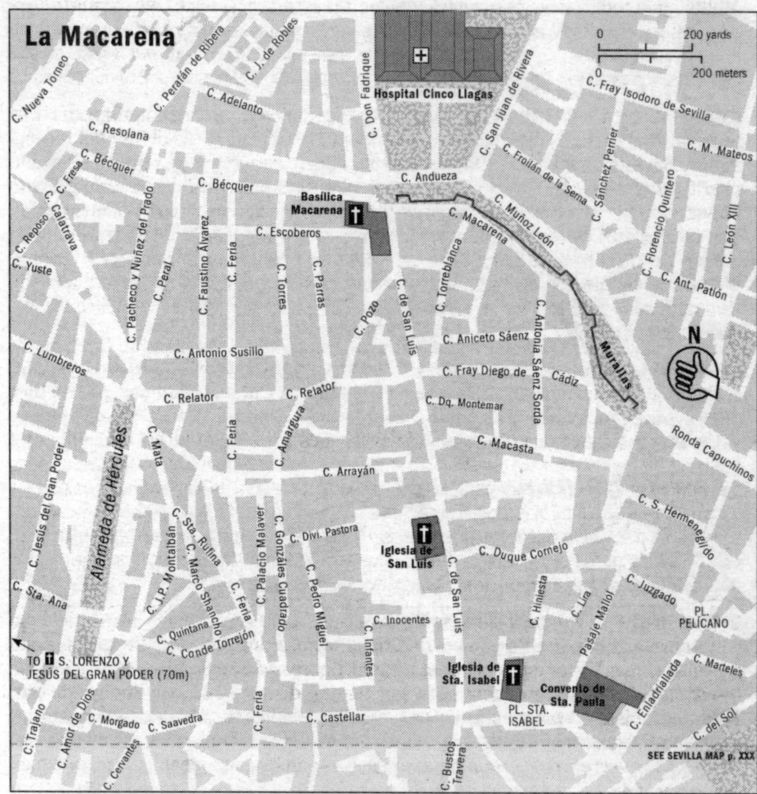

is borne through the streets, her emeralds a-tremble, in the climax of the *Semana Santa* processions. A **treasury** glitters with the virgin's jewels and other finery. *(Pl. San Gil. ☎954 37 01 95. Basilica open daily 9:30am-1pm and 5-9pm. Free. Treasury open daily 9:30am-1pm and 5-8pm. 400ptas/€2.40.)* Toward the river is **Iglesia de San Lorenzo y Jesús del Gran Poder,** with Montañés's remarkably lifelike sculpture *El Cristo del gran poder*. Worshipers kiss Jesus' ankle. *(Pl. San Lorenzo. ☎954 38 45 58. Open Sa-Th 8am-1:45pm and 6-9pm, F 7:30-10pm. Free.)*

OTHER SIGHTS. A large garden beyond the *murallas* and the basilica leads to the **Hospital de las Cinco Llagas,** a spectacular Renaissance building recently renovated to host the Andalucian parliament. Toward the river is the **Alameda de Hércules,** a leafy promenade that hosts the tremendous Sunday morning *Rastro* (flea market) but by nightfall fills with prostitutes and other shady types.

ELSEWHERE

PARQUE DE MARÍA LUISA. In 1929, Sevilla made elaborate plans for an Ibero-American world fair. Though plans for the fair were interrupted by the stock market crash, the lovely landscapes of the Parque de María Luisa remained, framed by Av. Borbolla and the river. Innumerable courtyards, turquoise-tiled benches, and tailored tropical gardens make for a perfect place to take a *siesta*. On the park's northeast edge, the twin spires of **Plaza de España** tower above the city skyline. Horse-drawn carriages still clatter in front of the plaza and rowboats can be rented to navigate its narrow moat. Mosaics depicting every provincial capital in Spain line the crumbling colonnade. The balconies above offer a beautiful view of the surrounding gardens. *(Park open daily 8am-10pm. Boat rides 500ptas/€3 for 1-3 people.)*

NIGHTLIFE

The tourist office distributes *El Giraldillo*, a free monthly magazine with complete listings on music, art exhibits, theater, dance, fairs, and film. Sevilla's reputation for partying is tried and true. A typical Sevillian sampling of *la marcha* (going out) begins with visits to several bars for *tapas* and *copas*, continues with dancing at *discotecas*, and culminates with an early morning breakfast of *churros con chocolate*. Most clubs don't get crowded until well after midnight; the real fun often starts after 3am. Popular bars can be found around C. Mateos Gago near the cathedral, C. Adriano by the bullring, and C. Betis across the river in Triana. Sevilla is also famous for its *botellón*, the (mostly student) tradition of getting drunk in massive crowds in plazas or at bars along the river to start the night. In the winter, the most popular places to *botellón* are in Pl. Alfalfa and Pl. del Salvador. In summer, the crowds sweep toward the river in hopes of a breeze, and even on "slow" nights, most *terrazas* stay open until 4am. New locations open every summer; check with the Centro de Información de Sevilla for the latest info.

BARRIO DE SANTA CRUZ

Terraza Chile, Paseo de las Delicias, at the intersection of Avda. Uruguay and Avda. Chile. Salsa and Spanish pop keep this breezy dance club packed and pounding throughout the early morning hours. Young *Sevillano* professionals mingle with Euro-chic American exchange students. *Botellón* pervades the surrounding streets. Beer 300-400ptas/€1.80-2.40. Mixed drinks 700ptas/€4.20. Open summer, M-Sa 9pm-6am.

La Carbonería, C. Levies, 18 (☎954 21 44 60), off C. Santa María La Blanca. Don't let the staid baronial entrance hall deter you—beyond lies a popular bar with free live flamenco and a massive outdoor patio replete with banana trees and guitar strumming Romeos. Mostly a backpacker crowd. Beer 200-275ptas/€1.20-1.65. Flamenco (of unpredictable quality) nightly at 10:30pm. Open M-Sa 8pm-3:30am, Su 8pm-2:30am.

El Tamboril, Pl. Santa Cruz (☎954 56 15 90). Come see *sevillanas* and *rumbas* with well-to-do Spaniards in this intimate Santa Cruz hideaway. Midnight music and dancing. *Sangría* 400ptas/€2.40 a glass, beer 300ptas/€1.80. Open daily 10pm-dawn. MC/V.

EL CENTRO AND TRIANA

El Capote, next to Pte. Isabel II, at the intersection of C. Arjona and C. Reyes Católicos. A hugely popular outdoor bar with live music performances throughout the summer. Experience *botellón* as you make your way toward the river, past throngs of young *Sevillanos* swigging cuba libres. Open daily during the summer 11pm-3am.

La Antigua Bodeguita, Pl. del Salvador, 6 (☎954 56 18 33). The crowds can't be contained at any hour of the day in this bustling bodega. Beer 125ptas/€0.75, *tapas* 200ptas/€1.20. Open daily 12:30-4pm and 8pm-midnight.

Lo Nuestro, C. Betis, 31A, in Triana. A local hangout in an area plagued by touristy bars. Images of bulls and matadors plaster the chic rust-colored walls. *Sevillanas* are spontaneous and frequent. Mixed drinks 300-900ptas/€1.80-5.40. Open daily 10pm-dawn.

Catedral, Cuesta del Rosario, 12, 1 block from Pl. del Salvador. Underground disco whose metal, stone and wood décor feels straight out of New York City. No cover for women and those who arrive with coupons (available in stores, restaurants, and hostels). Tends to be an older crowd. Cover for men 1000ptas/€6, includes 1 drink or 2 beers. Open Th-Tu midnight-8am, W midnight-6am. Sporadic summer hours.

CARTUJA '93

A bit of a jaunt from the center of Sevilla, the area across the Guadalquivir from Pte. de la Barqueta is still definitely worth an evening foray during the summer. Forged from the idle remnants of Expo '92, the massive clubs located here form

SEVILLANAS When in Sevilla, do as the *sevillanos* do. *Sevillanas* is the widely popular folk form of flamenco. While elegant flamenco dancers must study technique for years, just about anyone can perform *sevillanas.* In little bars in Sevilla, yuppie couples, chic young women, and toothless old men take the dance floor side-by-side when the guitar begins to play its song. A partnered dance, *sevillanas* consists of four segments that act out a courting ritual. The basic step is easy to pick up; ask sweetly for an impromptu lesson, and before long you'll be twisting your wrists like a native. During the *Feria de Abril* the whole city takes to the streets, stomping their feet, flipping their skirts, and holding their heads high as they turn and sashay. If you can't catch the dancing live, check out Carlos Saura's movie *Sevillanas.*

part of a surreal landscape of spaceship replicas, abandoned gondolas, pork vending stands, and innumerable empty rum bottles. (The A2 night bus runs at midnight, 1am, and 2am from Pl. Nueva; ask to be let off near Pte. de la Barqueta. Cabs from Pl. Nueva to the clubs listed below should cost around 700ptas/€4.20.)

Palenque, Avda. Blas Pascal, on the grounds of Cartuja '93. From Pte.de la Barqueta, follow C. Materatico Rey, turn left and walk toward the spaceship on the horizon. Once a stadium-sized auditorium, now the largest dance club in Sevilla. Multiple floors with salsa and American pop. Mainly *Sevillano* university crowd. Mixed drinks 700ptas/€4.20. Cover 1000ptas/€6. Open summer, Th, F, Sa 11pm-7am.

Antique, C. Materatico Rey Pastor. Cross Pte. de la Barqueta, it's on the left. Ottoman pavilions doubling as bars dot the yard and patio. Somewhat older crowd. Transforms during the winter into one of the city's most popular indoor dance clubs. No cover for women, cover for men 2000ptas/€12, includes 1 drink. Open W-Su, 11pm-4am.

ENTERTAINMENT

THEATERS

Cine Avenida, C. Marqués de las Paradas, 15 (☎954 22 15 48) and **Cines Warner Lusomundo,** Co. Comercial, Pl. Legión (☎902 23 33 43) show predominantly American films dubbed in Spanish. **Corona Center,** Pagés del Corro y Paraíso, in the mall between C. Salado and C. Paraíso in Barrio de Triana, screens subtitled films, often in English. (☎954 27 80 64. M-F movies 450ptas, Sa-Su 550ptas.) For more information, check under "Cinema" in *El Giraldillo.*

Sevilla is a haven for the performing arts. The venerable **Teatro Lope de Vega** (☎954 59 08 53), near Parque María Luisa, has long been the city's leading stage. Ask about scheduled events at the tourist office or check the bulletin board in the university lobby on C. San Fernando. If you can't see a show, at least stop by for a drink at **Casino,** the popular *terraza* outside. **Sala la Herrería** and **Sala la Imperdible** put on avant-garde productions in Pl. San Antonio de Padua. (Both ☎954 38 82 19.) **Teatro de la Maestranza,** on the river next to Pl. Toros, is a splendid concert hall accommodating both orchestral performances and opera. (☎954 22 33 44. Box office open M-F 10am-2pm and 6-9pm.) On spring and summer evenings, *barrio* fairs are often accompanied by free **open-air concerts** in Santa Cruz and Triana.

FLAMENCO

The lightning-quick *zapateado* of Andalucía's flamenco dancers dazzle the eyes, while the wailing *cantaores* delight the ears. Three tourist-ridden venues feature comparably flashy shows, though a more affordable option would be to visit the more casual flamenco bars (see above). Small and intimate **Los Gallos,** Pl. Santa Cruz, 11, is probably the best tourist show in Sevilla. Buy tickets in advance at hostels or stores in Barrio Santa Cruz and arrive early. (☎954 21 69 81. Shows nightly 9 and 11:30pm. Cover 3500ptas/€21, includes one drink.) **El Arenal** is also a *tablao-restaurante,* so you can eat a meal while watching. (Shows nightly 9:30 and

11:30pm. Cover 4300ptas/€26, includes one drink.) Though somewhat farther afield, **Las Brujas,** Gonzalo de Bilbao, 10, is certainly worth the trek. (☎954 413 651. Shows M-Sa 8:30pm and 11pm. Cover 3800/€232 includes one drink.)

FÚTBOL

Sevilla has two wildly popular pro teams within its city limits. The pride of the Guadalquivir is **Betis,** who play in Estadio Benito Villamarín (☎954 61 03 40), downstream on Av. Palmera. To the humiliation of its fans, team **Sevilla** was recently demoted to second division following unfortunate coaching changes. Sevilla plays in the Estadio Sámche Pizjuán (☎954 53 53 53), east of Av. Menéndez Pelayo on Av. Eduardo Dato. Tickets can be purchased at the respective stadiums; price and availability depend on the quality of the match-up. Even if you can't make it yourself, you'll know who's won by the colors worn by the crowds in the streets (Betis wears green and white, Sevilla white and red).

BULLFIGHTS

Sevilla's bullring is generally considered to be the most beautiful in Spain. The cheapest place to buy tickets is at the ring on Po. Marqués de Contadero. However, when there's a good *cartel* (line-up), the booths on C. Sierpes, C. Velázquez, and Pl. Toros might be the only source of advance tickets. Ticket prices, depending on the quality of both seat and matador, can run from 3000ptas for a *grada de sol* (nose-bleed seat in the sun) to 13,000ptas for a *barrera de sombra* (front-row seat in the shade). Buying a ticket from a scalper usually adds 20% to the ticket price. *Corridas de toros* (bullfights) or *novilladas* (apprentice bullfighters and younger bulls) are held on the 13 days around the *Feria de Abril* and into May, every Sunday in June, more often during Corpus Christi in June and early July, and again during the *Feria de San Miguel* near the end of September. During July and August, they occur on occasional Thursdays. It's obvious when a top-notch *matador* is scheduled to fight: hours before the big event, the ring is surrounded by throngs of young female fans who donning their most seductive dresses and alluring lipstick in hopes of catching the eye of their hero. Some of the most popular Sevillian bullfighters include Emilio Muñoz, known as "El Espártaco" (Spartacus), and the aging Curro Romero. (For current info and **ticket sales,** call ☎954 22 35 06. For more info on **Bullfighting,** see p. 65.)

FESTIVALS

Sevilla swells with tourists during the *fiestas*, and with good reason—they are insanely fun. If you're in Spain during any of the major festivals, head straight to Sevilla—you won't regret it (if you can remember it, that is).

SEMANA SANTA. Sevilla's world-famous *Semana Santa* lasts from Palm Sunday to Easter Sunday (March 24-31 in 2002). In each neighborhood of the city, thousands of penitents in hooded cassocks guide *pasos*, stunning, extravagant floats, through the streets, illuminated by hundreds of candles. The climax is Good Friday, when the entire city turns out for the procession along the bridges and through the oldest neighborhoods. Book rooms well in advance, and expect to pay triple the usual price. The tourist office has a helpful booklet of advice on where to eat and sleep during the week's festivities.

FERIA DE ABRIL. Two or three weeks after Semana Santa (Apr. 16-21 in 2002) the city rewards itself for its Lenten piety with the *Feria de Abril.* Begun as part of a 19th-century revolt against foreign influence, today circuses, bullfights, and flamenco shows roar into the night in a showcase of local customs and camaraderie. A spectacular array of flowers and lanterns decorates over 1000 kiosks, tents, and pavilions, collectively called *casetas*. Each has the elements necessary for a rollicking time: small kitchen, bar, and dance floor. Locals stroll from one to the next, sharing drinks and good food amid the lively music and dance. The majority of *casetas* are privately owned by families and businesses and the only way to get invited is by making friends with the locals. There are a few large public *casetas* where you can find drink and dancing. Either way, people-watching from the sidelines can be almost as exciting, as costumed girls dance *sevillanas* and men parade on horseback through the streets of Sevilla. The fairgrounds are on the southern end of Barrio Los Remedios.

ROMERÍA DEL ROCÍO. Folklore and religion unite in the *Romería del Rocío* which takes place 50 days after Easter on Pentecost and involves the veneration of the *Virgen del Rocío*. More than 70 brotherhoods of pilgrims from around the world make their way to the small town of Almonte, near Huelva, from all points in Spain. They arrive in flower-decorated carriages or on horses saddled in typical Andalucian style wearing traditional gypsy costumes. In the best Spanish fashion, the Romería is half penitence, half party. The solemnity of the days are broken with singing, dancing, and drinking around campfires from dusk until dawn.

DAYTRIPS FROM SEVILLA

OSUNA

Trains from Sevilla (1hr., 8 per day 6:40am-9:40pm, 1000ptas/€6). Empresa Dipasa/Linesur (☎954 98 82 22) runs buses to and from Sevilla's Prado de San Sebastián station (1½hr.; 5-11 per day 6:15am-7:40pm; 830ptas/€5 one-way, 1580ptas/€9.50).

Julius Caesar founded Osuna (pop. 17,500), naming it after the *osos* (bears) that once lumbered about its hills. Most sites of interest are found on the hill which rises above town. The **Colegiata de Santa María de la Asunción** (☎954 81 04 44), from Pl. Mayor to Pl. Duquesa Osuna and uphill was commissioned by the Dukes of Osuna in the Renaissance style and now houses the **Museo de Arte Sacro Panteón Ducal.** The Colegiata contains a spectacular array of paintings, including religious artifacts and five Riberas. (Knock to enter. Open May-Sept. 10am-1:30pm and 4-7pm; Oct.-Apr. Tu-Su 10am-1:30pm and 3:30-6:30pm. 300ptas/€1.80.) On the right side of the church sits the university and **Convento de la Encarnación,** a Baroque church founded by the Duke of Osuna in the 17th century and lavishly decorated in the 18th. A resident nun will show you room upon room of polychromed wooden sculptures, silver crucifixes, painted tiles, and handmade Christ-doll clothes. Make sure to knock and wait until the previous tour group finishes. (☎954 81 11 21. Open Tu-Su 10am-1:30pm and 3:30-6:30pm. 250ptas/€1.50.)

To reach Pl. Mayor from the **train station** (☎/fax 954 81 03 08; open 7am-8pm) walk up Av. Estación, curving right on C. Mancilla. At Pl. Salitre, turn left on C. Carmen and then right on C. Sevilla, which leads into the plaza. The **bus station** is on Av. Constitución. (☎954 81 01 46. Open M-F 6:50-9am, 10:15am-2:30pm and 3:30-7:40pm; Sa 7:30-9am and 10:30am-2pm; Su 3:30-4:30pm and 7-7:40pm). To get to Pl. Mayor from the bus station, walk downhill on C. Santa Ana past Pl. Santa Rita; continue on Av. Arjona until the plaza. The **tourist office** is in Pl. Mayor (☎955 82 14 00. Open M-F 10am-1:30pm and 4-7pm, Sa 10am-2pm and 4-7pm, Su 10am-3pm).

ITÁLICA

Take Empresa Casal's bus (☎954 41 06 58) toward Santiponce from the Pl. Armas bus station, platform 34. Tell the driver you're going to Itálica, and get off at the last stop (30min.; M-Sa every 30min. 6:30am-midnight, Su every hour, on the half hour 7:30am-11:30pm, 125ptas/€0.75). Pay onboard. When returning to Sevilla, wait at the bus sign in front of the entrance to Itálica, the bus will turn around in the neighboring gas station.

Just 9km northwest of Sevilla and right outside the village of Santiponce (pop. 6200) lie the excavated ruins of Itálica, the first important Roman settlement in Iberia. Itálica, founded as an outpost for legionnaires in 206 BC, was the birthplace of emperors Trajan (AD 53) and Hadrian (AD 76). During the fourth and fifth centuries AD, the city burgeoned into a cosmopolitan trading center, but by the early 500s, Sevilla had become the regional seat of power. Archaeological excavations began in the 18th century and continue today, although the oldest neighborhoods in Itálica are still buried under downtown Santiponce and may never be recovered. The **Casa**

del Planetario (The House of Planets), has intricate **mosaic floors** depicting the seven gods that represent planets and whose names are given to the days of the week. There are also reconstructed patios and a bakery depicting life as it was during the decline of the city. The **anfiteatro,** among Spain's largest, seats 25,000. It was once used to stage fights between gladiators and lions; today it hosts more mellow classical music performances in the summer. (☎955 99 73 76. Open June-Aug. Tu-Sa 8:30am-8:30pm, Su 9am-3pm; Sept-May Tu-Sa 9am-5:30pm, Su 10am-4pm. 250ptas/€1.50, EU citizens free.) For info on the annual **Festival Internacional de Itálica,** which brings dance, classical music, and theater to Itálica in July and August, check Sevilla's *El Giraldillo*. While the restaurant directly across the road from Itálica is less than inspiring, wonderful *hornos* populate the left side of the road back to Santiponce. Not for the vegetarian, these grilles serve delicious meat-and-potato entrées best washed down with a jug of *tinto de verano*.

CARMONA

Take the bus to Carmona from Sevilla (1hr., M-F 25 per day 6:15am-8:30pm, Sa 10 per day 6:30am-8:30pm, Su 7 per day, 8am-8:30pm, 315ptas/€1.89, pay on the bus.) departing from Prado de San Sebastián station, platform 25. In Carmona, buses return to Sevilla from the main square, along Av. Jorge Bonsor (23 per day, 6:15am-9pm).

Thirty-three kilometers east of Sevilla, ancient Carmona (pop. 25,000) dominates a tall hill overlooking the countryside. Founded by the Carthaginians, it became an important trade city during Roman occupation in later centuries and a Moorish stronghold thereafter. Moorish palaces mingle with Renaissance mansions in a network of streets partially enclosed by fortified walls. The **Puerta de Sevilla,** a horseshoe-shaped passageway with both Roman and Arab architectural elements, and the Baroque **Puerta de Córdoba,** on the opposite end of town, once linked Carmona to the east and west. From the bus stop, walk directly away from the back end of the bus onto C. San Pedro. Cross the roundabout and walk through the Puerta de Sevilla noting on your way the **Iglesia de San Pedro,** whose Mudéjar tower is a scaled-down copy of Sevilla's Giralda. Enter the **Alcázar de la Puerta Sevilla** through the tourist office on your right. The Alcázar originally served as a Carthaginian fortification against Roman attack. During the reign of Augustus, the structure was expanded to its current size. (☎954 19 09 55. Open M-Sa 10am-6pm, Su 10am-3pm. 300ptas/€1.80, students, seniors and children under 12 150ptas/€0.90. Tours M-Sa 11am, noon, 1, 4, and 5pm.) From the Alcázar, take C. Prim and then C. Martín to find Pl. Marqués de las Torres, where the late-Gothic **Iglesia de Santa María** (☎954 14 13 30) was built over an old mosque. The splendid **Patio de los Naranjos** remains from Moorish days. An even older Visigothic liturgical calendar graces one of the columns. (Open Tu-Sa 11am-2pm and 5-7pm. Mass Tu-Sa 9-11am and 7-9pm, Su 9am-12:30pm and 7-9pm.) The **Alcázar del Rey Don Pedro,** an old Almohad fortress and now a ritzy hotel, guards the eastern edge of town.

In the opposite direction from the bus stop, along C. Enmedio, lie the ruins of the **Necrópolis Romana,** Av. de Jorge Bonsor, 9 (☎954 14 08 11). Highlights include the **Tumba de Servilia** and **Tumba del Elefante,** where depictions of Mother Nature and Eastern divinities are overshadowed by the presence of a giant stone elephant. The **Museo Arqueológico** has remains from over a thousand tombs unearthed at the necropolis. (Both open June-Aug. Tu-F 8:30am-2pm, Sa 10am-2pm; Sept.-May Tu-F 9am-5pm, Sa-Su 10am-2pm. 250ptas/€1.50, EU citizens free.)

The **tourist office,** on Arco de la Puerta de Sevilla, is located at the Puerta de Sevilla, down C. San Pedro from the bus stop (☎954 19 09 55; fax 19 00 80. Open M-Sa 10am-6pm, Su 10am-3pm). The **police** (☎954 14 00 08), are in Pl. San Fernando, and you can find **medical assistance** on C. Paseo de La Feria (☎954 14 09 97).

HUELVA ☎959

A provincial capital and industrial port, there is little appealing about Huelva (pop. 140,000) other than its proximity to the towns from which Columbus mustered men. That said, however, travelers heading to or from Portugal shouldn't shy away from an opportunity to spend the night in a place truly free of tourism.

TRANSPORTATION. RENFE trains on Av. de Italia, (☎959 24 56 14), run to: **Córdoba** (2¼hr., 4:55pm, 2700ptas/€16.25); **Madrid** (4¼hr., 4:55pm, 8500ptas/€51); and **Sevilla** (1½hr., 3 per day 7:15am-7:20pm, 995ptas/€5.90). **Buses** depart from Av. Dr. Rubio (☎959 25 69 00) to: **Cádiz** (5hr., 10am, 2440ptas/€14.70); **Faro, Portugal** (2½hr., 4 per day 9am-6pm, 720-1080ptas/€4.35-6.50); **Lisbon** (6½hr.; M, W, and F 1:15pm; 4000ptas/€24); **Madrid** (6hr., 3 per day 9:45am-10:45pm, 3360ptas/€20.20); and **Sevilla** (1hr., 20 per day 6am-8:00pm, 940ptas/€5.65).

ORIENTATION AND PRACTICAL INFORMATION. The central axis of the city is **Av. Martín Alonso Pinzón** (a.k.a. Gran Vía). From the train station, go out the front door, cross the street, and go straight down the street directly in front of you, C. Alonso XII. From the bus station, exit across Av. Alemania. Take C. Gravina, turn left onto C. M. Núñez, then right onto C. Concepción. Follow C. Concepción for three blocks then turn left. One block over is Av. Martín Alonso Pinzón. The **tourist office** is at Av. de Alemania, 12, across the street from the bus station and half a block to the right. (☎959 25 74 03. Open M-F 9am-7pm, Sa 10am-2pm.) The bus station has large backpack-sized lockers for **luggage storage** (300ptas/€1.80 per day). **Police** are located on Av. Tomás Domínguez de Ortiz, 2 (☎959 24 93 50). For **internet access,** go to C. Vázquez López, Galería Comercial 10-12, across from the Gran Teatro. (☎959 25 14 10. Open M-Sa 10am-10pm. 400ptas/€2.40 per hr.) The **post office** is at Av. Tomás Domínguez de Ortiz, 1 (☎959 24 74 88).

ACCOMMODATIONS AND FOOD. Most of the accommodations in Huelva cluster between the train station and Av. Martín Alonso Pinzón. A decent option is the somewhat out of the way **Albergue Juvenil Huelva** on Av. Marchena Colombo, 14. (Take city bus #6 from the central bus station. ☎902 51 00 00. 1500-2200ptas/€9-13.20 per person. 500ptas/€3 extra per day for nonmembers. MC/V.) **Hostal Residencia Calvo,** C. Rascón, 31, is a spartan but spacious small-scale hotel, closer to the city center. (☎959 24 90 16. Prices rise in summer. Singles 1100-1200ptas/€6.60-7.20; doubles 2200-2400ptas/€13.20-14.40; triples 3300-3600ptas/€19.80-21.60.) **Mercado de Carmen,** the town's market is at the intersection of C. Barcelona, C. Carmen, and C. Duque de la Victoria. **Restaurante Trattoria Camilo e Pepone,** Isaac Peral, 3, offers generous portions of pizza and pasta. (☎959 24 13 63. Open June-Aug. F-Su; Sept.-May 12:30-5pm and 8:30pm-midnight.) **Bar La Prensa,** Gran Vía, 15, vaguely resembles a Parisian hangout (☎959 24 02 11). **Helados La Ibense,** C. Concepción, 10, is the best *heladería* in Huelva (☎959 24 96 47. Cones 90-340ptas/€0.55-2.05). At night locals gather at the bars around **Av. Pablo Rada.**

DAYTRIP FROM HUELVA

LA RÁBIDA

Buses leave from the main bus station in Huelva 9am-8pm for Porto de la Frontera via La Rábida. From the bus stop in La Rábida, cross the road and follow the dirt path up a small hill to the monastery of La María de La Rábida. 125ptas/€0.75.

When the King of Portugal refused to foot the bill for a trading expedition across the unknown expanses of the Atlantic, **Christopher Columbus** decided to try his luck in Spain. Fortunately for the Genoese navigator, Isabella I, Queen of Castille, proved much more receptive to his advances. At the Franciscan monastery of **Santa María de La Rábida**, Columbus found a powerful advocate in the person of Fray Juan Pérez. Enticed by missionary prospects in the East Indies, Pérez helped to ensure royal support for a western voyage to India—thus landing Columbus a permanent place in elementary school textbooks throughout the Americas.

Tours of the 14th-century monastery of Santa María de La Rábida are offered in Spanish by Franciscan monks. Make sure not to miss the room where Columbus first discussed his plans with Pérez or the chapel where he prayed just before his departure. (☎959 35 04 11. Tours Tu-Su 10, 10:45, 11:45am, 1pm, 4, 4:45, 5:30, 6:15, and 7:00pm. Donations accepted.) Nearby, the **Muelle de las Carabelas** is an open air museum with life-size replicas of the Niña, Pinta, and Santa María. Explore the caravels before visiting **La Isla del Encuentro,** a recreated Amerindian village replete with anatomically correct mannequins. (☎959 53 05 97. Open Apr.-Sept. Tu-F 10am-2pm and 5-8pm; Oct.-Mar. 10am-8pm. 500ptas/€3, students 200ptas/€1.20.)

CÓRDOBA ☎957

No longer the largest city in western Europe, Córdoba (pop. 315,000) nevertheless continues to entrance those who travel to its gates. Nowhere else are the remnants of Spain's Islamic, Jewish, and Catholic heritages so visibly intermixed. For three centuries, Córdoba was the hub of the Moorish Empire, whose legacy is visible in the famed Mezquita and its dazzling *mihrab* (prayer niche). The Judería is one of Spain's oldest Jewish quarters, containing one of the few synagogues in the Iberian peninsula, while the 14th-century Palacio del Marqués de Viana anticipates Spain's Golden Age of the 16th-17th centuries, when literary luminaries such as poet Luís de Góngora resided here. Springtime festivals, flower-filled patios, and whitewashed houses, combine with Córdoba's historical patrimony to make a visit to the city as rewarding as it is simple.

TRANSPORTATION

Trains: Plaza de las Tres Culturas, Av. América (☎957 40 02 02). To: **Algeciras** (AVE 4hr., 10:20am, 3400ptas/€20; regular 5½hr., 5am and 10:15pm, 2800-3300ptas/€17-20); **Barcelona** (10-11hr., 3 per day 9:45am-10:20pm, 6100-8400ptas/€37-50); **Cádiz** (AVE 2¾hr., 12:15am and 6pm, 3700ptas/€22; regular 3-4hr., 5 per day 6am-8pm, 2370-3700ptas/€14-22); **Madrid** (AVE 2hr., 18 per day 7:15am-10:45pm, 5100-6100ptas/€31-37; regular 2-6hr., 14 per day 2am-11:15pm, 3700-6000ptas/€22-36); **Málaga** (AVE 2¼hr., 5 per day, 2000-2200ptas/€12-13; regular 3hr., 9 per day 6:40am-10:10pm, 1650-3000ptas/€10-18); **Sevilla** (AVE 45min., 18 per day 8:40am-11:40pm, 2300ptas/€14). For international tickets, contact **RENFE,** Ronda de los Tejares, 10 (☎957 49 02 02).

Buses: Estación de Autobuses, Glorieta de las Tres Culturas (☎957 40 40 40; fax 40 44 15), across from the train station.

Alsina Graells Sur (☎957 27 81 00) covers most of Andalucía. To: **Algeciras** (5hr., 2 per day, 2805ptas/€17); **Almería** (5hr., 8am, 2890ptas/€18); **Antequera** (2½hr., 3 per day 9am-7pm, 1075ptas/€6.50); **Cádiz** via Los Amarillos or Comes Sur (4-5hr., 7am, 2120ptas/€13); **Granada** (3hr., 8-11 per day 5:20am-8:30pm, 1605-1710ptas/€9.50-10.20); **Málaga** (3-3½hr., 5 per day 8am-7pm, 1630ptas/€9.75); **Sevilla** (2hr., 10-13 per day 7am-10pm, 1330ptas/€7.90). **Bacoma** (☎957 45 65 14) goes to: Baeza, Ubeda, Valencia, and **Barcelona** (10hr., 6:25pm, 8475ptas/€51). **Secorbus** (☎902 22 92 92) provides exceptionally cheap service to **Madrid** (4½hr., 7 per day 1pm-8pm, 1675ptas/€10), departing from Camino de los Sastres in front of Hotel Melía.

Transportes Ureña (☎957 40 45 58) runs to **Jaén** (2hr., 7 per day 7:30am-8pm, 990ptas/€5.95). Intra-provincial buses depart from Av. República and Po. Victoria: **Autocares Priego** (☎957 40 44 79), **Empresa Carrera** (☎957 40 44 14), and **Empresa Rafael Ramírez** (☎957 42 21 77) runs buses to surrounding towns and camping sites.

Local Public Transportation: 12 bus lines (☎957 25 57 00) cover the city, running from the wee hours until 11pm. **Bus #3** makes a loop from the bus and train stations through Pl. Tendillas, along the river, and up C. Doctor Fleming. **Bus #10** runs from the train station to Barrio Brillante. Purchase tickets onboard for 125ptas/€0.75.

Taxis: Radio Taxi (☎957 76 44 44) has stands at most busy intersections throughout the city. Be sure that the meter is turned on before you start off. From the Judería to the bus and train stations about 500ptas/€3; to Barrio Brillante about 600ptas/€3.60.

Car Rental: Hertz (☎957 40 20 60), in the train station. Car 9200ptas/€55 per day. Min. age 25. Open M-F 8:30am-9pm, Sa 9am-1pm and 3:30-7pm, Su 9am-1pm.

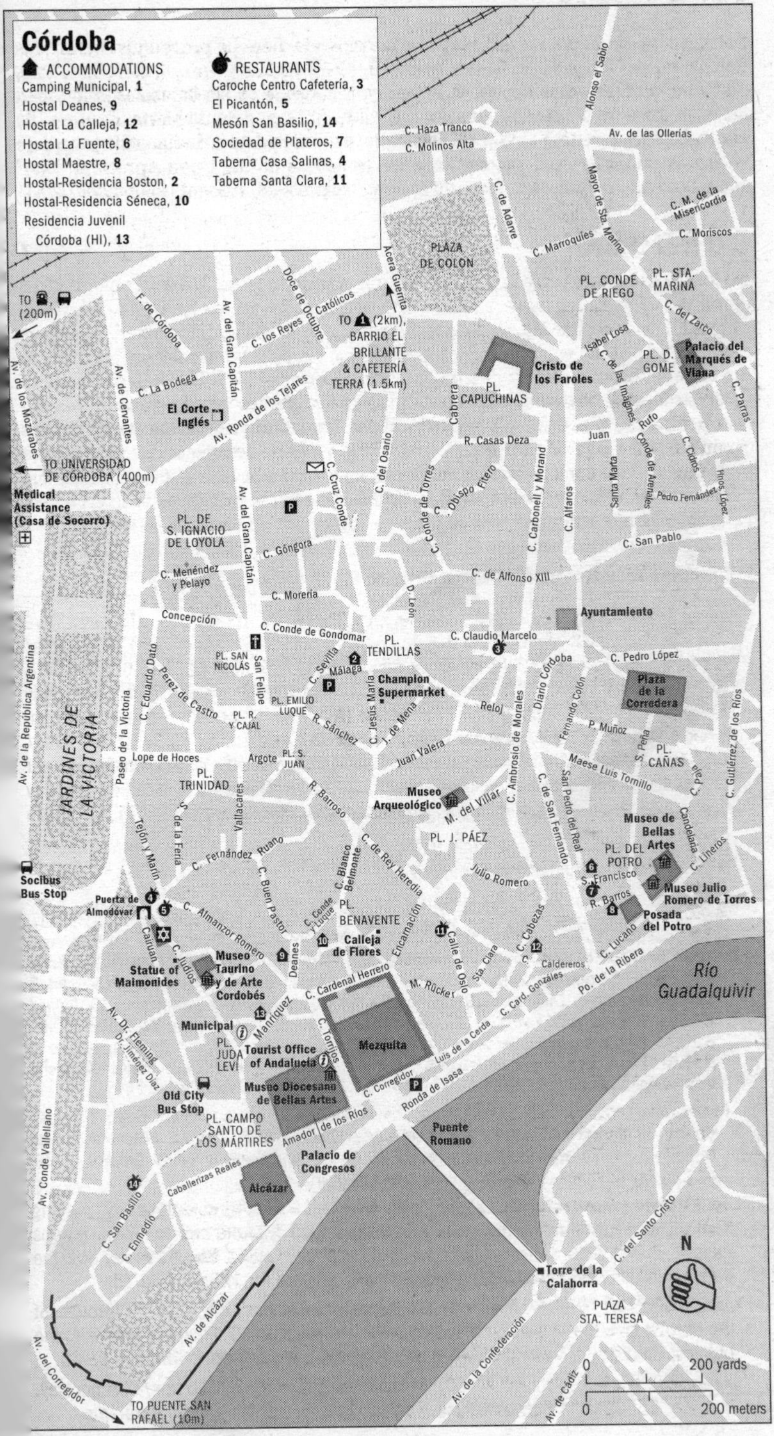

Córdoba

ACCOMMODATIONS

- Camping Municipal, **1**
- Hostal Deanes, **9**
- Hostal La Calleja, **12**
- Hostal La Fuente, **6**
- Hostal Maestre, **8**
- Hostal-Residencia Boston, **2**
- Hostal-Residencia Séneca, **10**
- Residencia Juvenil Córdoba (HI), **13**

RESTAURANTS

- Caroche Centro Cafetería, **3**
- El Picantón, **5**
- Mesón San Basilio, **14**
- Sociedad de Plateros, **7**
- Taberna Casa Salinas, **4**
- Taberna Santa Clara, **11**

ORIENTATION AND PRACTICAL INFORMATION

Córdoba is split between two parts: the old city and the new. The modern and commercial northern half extends from the train station on Av. América down to **Plaza de las Tendillas**, the center of the city. The old section in the south is a medieval maze known as the **Judería** (Jewish quarter). This tangle of beautiful and disorienting streets extends from Pl. Tendillas to the banks of the Río Guadalquivir, winding past the **Mezquita** and **Alcázar**. The easiest way to reach the old city from the train station and the bus station is to take city bus #3 to **Campo Santo de los Mártires** (125ptas/€0.75) Alternatively, the walk is about 20 minutes. From the train station, with your back to the platforms, exit left, cross the parking plaza and make a right onto Av. de los Mozárabes. When you reach the Roman columns, turn left and cross Gta. Sargentos Provisionales. Make a right on Paseo de la Victoria and continue until you reach Puerto Almodóvar and the old city.

Tourist Offices: Oficina Municipal de Turismo y Congresos Pl. Judá Leví, (☎957 20 05 22; fax 20 02 77). Open M-F 8:30am-2:30pm. **Tourist Office of Andalucía,** C. Torrijos, 10 (☎957 47 12 35; fax 49 17 78), in the Junta de Andalucía, across from the Mezquita. From the train station, take bus #3 along the river until a stone arch appears on the right. Office is 1 block up C. Torrijos. General information on Andalucía. English-speaking staff with good free map of the monument section. Open May-Sept. M-F 9:30am-8pm, Sa 10am-7pm, Su 10am-2; Oct.-Apr. M-F 9:30am-6pm, Su 10am-2pm.

Currency Exchange: Banco Central Hispano Pl. Tendillas, (☎957 47 42 67), charges no commission. Open June-Aug. M-F 8:30am-2:30pm; Sept.-May M-F 8:30am-2:30pm, Sa 9am-1pm. **Banks** and **ATMs** dot Pl. Tendillas.

Luggage Storage: Lockers at the train and bus stations open 24 hr. (300-600ptas/€1.80-3.61). Also at **Champion** supermarket, C. Jesús María, between Pl. Tendillas and C. J. de Mena. Open M-Sa 9:15am-9:15pm.

El Corte Inglés: Av. Ronda de los Tejares, 30 (☎957 47 02 67), on the corner of Av. Gran Capitán. Department store with supermarket (5th fl.). Sells an excellent traffic map (575ptas/€3.45). Open M-Sa 10am-10pm.

Emergency: ☎092. **Police:** Av. Medina Azahara (☎957 47 75 00).

Late-Night Pharmacy: On a rotating basis. Refer to the list posted outside the pharmacy in Pl. Tendillas or the local newspaper.

Medical Assistance: Red Cross Hospital (emergency ☎957 22 22 22, main line 42 06 66), Po. Victoria. English spoken. **Ambulance:** ☎957 29 55 70.

Internet Access: El Burladero Café Internet, C. Llanos del Pretorio, 1 (☎957 49 75 36), at the intersection of Av. América and Paso del Brillante. 300ptas/€1.80 for 30min., 500/€3 per hr. 300ptas/€1.80 minimum charge. Open daily 8am-4pm and 5pm-3am.

Post Office: C. Cruz Conde, 15 (☎902 19 71 97), 2 blocks up from Pl. Tendillas. **Lista de Correos.** Open M-F 8:30am-8:30pm, Sa 9:30am-2pm. **Postal Code:** 14070.

ACCOMMODATIONS AND CAMPING

Hostels cluster between the **Mezquita** and **C. de San Fernando.** Córdoba is especially crowded during *Semana Santa* and from May-Sept.—you may have to call two to three months in advance for reservations. Prices are higher in summer.

IN AND AROUND THE JUDERÍA

The Judería's whitewashed walls, narrow, twisting streets, and proximity to major sights make it the nicest area in which to stay. During the day, souvenir booths and cafés keep the streets lively, but at night, the area feels desolate, lit only by streetlights. Take bus #3 from the train station to Campo Santo de los Mártires and walk up C. Manríques to reach the heart of the neighborhood.

Residencia Juvenil Córdoba (HI), Pl. Juda Leví, (☎957 29 01 66; fax 29 05 00), next to the municipal tourist office and a 2min. walk from the Mezquita. A backpacker's utopia. Large, sterile rooms, either doubles or quads, all with bath. A/C. Public telephones. Internet service (100ptas/€0.60 for 15 minutes). Breakfast included, lunch and dinner 750ptas/€4.50. Towels 175ptas/€1. Wheelchair accessible. 24hr. reception. Reservations recommended. 2050ptas/€12 per person; ages 26 and up 2675ptas/€16. 500ptas/€3 extra per day for nonmembers for 6-night stay to gain membership. MC/V.

Hostal Deanes, C. Deanes, 6 (☎957 29 37 44). From the top left corner of the Mezquita take C. Cardenal, then a sharp right onto C. Romero which becomes C. Deanes. In a 16th-century home with an elegant *cordobés* patio. Only five rooms and cavernous baths. 24hr. reception. Requires reservations 1-2 months in advance. Doubles 5000ptas/€30; triples 6500ptas/€39; quad 8000ptas/€48. AmEx/MC/V.

Hostal-Residencia Séneca, C. Conde y Luque, 7 (☎/fax 957 47 32 34). Follow C. Céspedes 2 blocks from the Mezquita. Slightly older, non-backpacker crowd during the summer. Breakfast included. Reservations recommended. All rooms have fans; 1200ptas/€7.20 extra for A/C. Singles with sink 2300-2550ptas/€14-15, with bath 3500-4000ptas/€21-24; doubles with sink 4800ptas/€29, with bath 6000ptas/€36; triples with exterior bathroom 6150-6600ptas/€37-40.

BETWEEN THE MEZQUITA AND C. DE SAN FERNANDO

Hostal La Fuente, C. San Fernando, 51 (☎957 48 78 27 or 48 14 78; fax 48 78 27), between C. San Francisco and C. Julio Romero. Relax amidst the tiled splendor of La Fuente's traditional Andalucian courtyard. All rooms with bath, some with TV. Half of the building has A/C (at no extra charge) so be sure to ask for it. Breakfast 275ptas/€1.65. Parking 1000ptas/€6. Singles 4000 ptas/€24; doubles 6500ptas/€39; 1800ptas/€10.80 per person for large groups. AmEx/MC/V.

Hostal La Calleja, Calleja de Rufino Blanco y Sánchez, 6 (☎/fax 957 48 66 06), at the intersection of C. Calereros and C. Cardenal González. Spacious rooms, many with private bathrooms and patios. All rooms have TVs and A/C. 24hr. reception. Singles 2800ptas/€17; doubles 4200ptas/€25, with bath 4800ptas/€29. AmEx/MC/V.

Hostal Almanzor, C. Cardenal González, 10 (☎/fax 957 48 54 00), 3 blocks from the Mezquita at the end of C. Rey Heredía closest to the river. Ambiance for a good price. All singles have king-sized beds. Spotless rooms with balconies and TVs and A/C. Parking included. 24hr. reception. Singles 1500-2000ptas/€9-12; doubles with bath 3000-5000ptas/€18-30. AmEx/MC/V.

Hostal Maestre, C. Romero Barros, 4-5 (☎957 47 53 95), off C. de San Fernando. Not to be confused with the neighboring Hotel Maestre. Immaculate and pleasantly decorated, most rooms have private bath, some have TVs; 500ptas/€3 turns that fan into A/C. English spoken. Parking 1000ptas/€6 per day. Singles 2500-2850ptas/€15-17; doubles 4000-5000ptas/€24-30; triples 5000-6500ptas/€30-39. AmEx/MC/V.

OTHER AREAS

Hotel Residencia Boston, C. Málaga, 2 (☎957 47 41 76; fax 47 85 23), on the corner of Pl. Tendillas, near the new town. A/C, TV, phone, and bath. Breakfast 425ptas/€2.55. Laundry service. Parking nearby. Singles with bath 3500-4100ptas/€21-25; doubles with bath 5600-6700ptas/€34-40; triples 6500ptas/€39. AmEx/MC/V.

Camping Municipal, Av. Brillante, 50 (☎957 28 21 65). From the train station, turn left on Av. América, left on Av. Brillante, and walk uphill for about 20min, or take bus #10 or 11 from Av. Cervantes. Pool, currency exchange, supermarket, restaurant, free hot showers, laundry service. Camping equipment for rent. Wheelchair accessible. IVA not included. 400ptas/€2.40 per individual tent, 560ptas/€3.35 per family tent.

FOOD

The Mezquita area falls flat with many hyper-touristed restaurants, but a five-minute walk in any direction yields local specialties at reasonable prices. In the evenings, locals converge at the outdoor terrazas between C. Severo Ochoa and C. Dr. Jiménez Díaz for drinks and *tapas* before dinner. Cheap eateries cluster farther away from the Judería in **Barrio Cruz Conde,** and around **Av. Menéndez Pidal** and **Pl. Tendillas.** Regional specialties include *salmorejo* (a gazpacho-like cream soup topped with hard-boiled eggs and pieces of ham) and *rabo de toro* (bull's tail simmered in tomato sauce). **Supermarket Champion,** C. Jesús María, lies half a block from Pl. Tendillas (open M-Sa 9:15am-9:15pm).

Taberna Santa Clara, C. Osio, 2 (☎957 47 43 05). From the Mezquita, follow R. Encarnación to C. de Rey Heredia and turn right. Removed from the heart of the Judería, but still convenient. Spacious patio dining and exquisitely prepared meals. 2 pages of meat-free dishes. Fresh fish on Fridays. *Menú* 1250ptas/€7.50. Entrées 800-1800ptas/€4.80-10.80. Salads 650ptas/€3.90. Open Tu-Su 9-11pm. MC/V.

Mesón San Basilio, C. San Basilio, 19 (☎957 29 70 07), to the left of the Alcázar, past Campo Santo de los Mártires. The locals love it, and so will you. Dine on one of two floors surrounding a breezy patio or have a drink at the bar. *Menú* M-F 1000ptas/€6, Sa-Su 1500ptas/€9. *Raciones* 450ptas/€2.70 and up. Meat and fish dishes 800-1750ptas/€4.80-10.50. Open daily 1-4pm and 8pm-midnight. AmEx/MC/V.

Taberna Casa Salinas, Puerto Almodóvar (☎957 29 08 46). A few blocks from the synagogue, up C. Judíos and to the left. Pepe Salinas has been running this place for over 35 years and it's quite popular. Eschew the jam-packed bar and request a table on the romantic outdoor patio to sample the *raciones* (500-800ptas/€3-4.80) and fine wines (100ptas/€0.60). Open Sept.-July Th-Tu 11:30am-5pm and 8:30pm-12:30am.

El Picantón, C. F. Ruano, 19, 1 block from the Puerta de Almodóvar. From the right corner of the Mezquita, walk up Romero and turn left. No seats. Take ordinary *tapas*, pour on a *salsa picante,* stick it in a roll, and voilà, you've got a cheap and hearty meal for only 150-300ptas/€0.90-1.80. Open daily 10am-3pm and 8pm-midnight.

Sociedad de Plateros, C. San Francisco, 6 (☎957 47 00 42), between C. San Fernando and Pl. Potro. White-haired Spanish men play dominoes as tourists cool off in the shaded patio. A Córdoba mainstay since 1872. *Media-raciones* and *raciones* 400-1000ptas/€2.40-6. Bar open Tu-Su 8am-4:30pm and 8pm-12:30am, restaurant 1-4pm and 8pm-midnight. Open M-Sa in summer, Tu-Su in winter. MC/V.

Caroche Centro Cafetería, García Lovera, 7 (☎957 49 25 71). From Pl. Tendillas, walk 1 block down C. Claudio Marcelo. A large-screen TV and blustery air-conditioning make this a good place to take a break from the heat. *Menú* 900ptas/€5.40. *Raciones* 300-600ptas/€1.80-3.60. Open daily 7:30am-4am.

SIGHTS

LA MEZQUITA

☎957 47 05 12. Open Apr.-June daily 10am-7:30pm; July-Oct. daily 10am-7pm; Nov.-Mar. daily 10am-6pm. 1000ptas/€6, ages 8-13 500ptas/€3. Same ticket valid for Museo Diocesano de Bellas Artes. Last ticket sold 30min. before closing. Opens M-Sa 8:30am for mass starting at 9:30am; Su mass 11am, noon, and 1pm.

Built in 784 on the site of a Visigothic Basilica, this architectural masterpiece is considered the most important Islamic monument in the Western world. Over the course of the next two centuries, the Mezquita was enlarged to cover an area the size of several city blocks with more than 850 columns, making it the largest mosque in the Islamic world at the time of its completion. Carved from granite and marble, the pillars are capped by the characteristic banded Mudejar arches of different heights. Visitors enter through the **Patio de los Naranjos,** an arcaded courtyard featuring carefully spaced orange trees, palm trees, and fountains, where the dutiful would wash before prayer. The **Torre del Alminar** encloses remains of the minaret from where the *muezzín* would call for prayer.

The most elaborate additions, consisting of the dazzling **mihrab** (prayer niche) and the triple **maksourah** (caliph's niche), were created in the 10th century. The mihrab, which faces Mecca, formerly housed a gilt copy of the Koran; worn stones evince where pilgrims knelt in reverence. Estimated at close to 35 tons, the intricate gold, pink, and blue marble Byzantine mosaics shimmering across the arches of the mihrab were given by the Emperor Constantine VII to the caliphs.

At the far end of the Mezquita lies the **Capilla Villaviciosa,** where Caliphal vaulting appeared for the first time. Completed in 1371, it was the first Christian chapel to be built in the mosque, thus beginning the transition of the Mezquita to a place of Christian worship. In 1523, Bishop Alonso Manrique, an ally of Carlos V, proposed the construction of a cathedral in the center of the mosque. The town rallied violently against the idea, promising painful death to any worker who helped tear down the Mezquita. Nevertheless, a towering **crucero** (transept) and **coro** (choir stall), were eventually erected, incongruously planting a richly adorned baroque cathedral amidst far more austere environs. The townspeople were less than pleased, and even Carlos V regretted the changes to the Mezquita, lamenting, "You have destroyed something unique to create something commonplace." What remains, though, is far from commonplace, for the juxtaposition of the two architectural styles and programs accentuates the individual qualities of each one.

IN AND AROUND THE JUDERÍA

A combined ticket for the Alcázar, Museo Taurino y de Arte Cordobés, and Museo Julio Romero (see Outside the Judería, below) is available at all three locations. 1075ptas/€6.45, students 550ptas/€3.30.

ALCÁZAR. Along the river on the left side of the Mezquita lies the Alcázar. Built in 1328 during the Reconquest, the building was both a fortress and residence for Alfonso XI. Fernando and Isabel bade Columbus farewell here, and from 1490 to 1821, it served as a headquarters for the Inquisition. Its walls enclose a magnificent garden with terraced flower beds, ponds, palm trees, and fountains. Inside, the museum displays 1st-century Roman mosaics and a 3rd-century Roman marble sarcophagus. Don't miss the Arab bath turned Counter-Reformation interrogation chamber in the basement. *(☎957 42 01 51. Open May-Sept. Tu-Sa 10am-2pm and 6-8pm, Su 9:30am-3pm; Oct.-Apr. Tu-Sa 10am-2pm and 4:30-6:30pm, Su 9:30am-3pm. Illuminated gardens open July-Aug. 8pm-midnight. Admission 300ptas/€1.80, students 150ptas/€0.90. F free.)*

SINAGOGA. On C. Judíos, near the statue of Maimonides. Built in 1315, the Sinagoga is a hollow remnant of Córdoba's once vibrant Jewish community. Adorned with Mozarabic patterns and Hebrew inscriptions, the walls of the temple have been restored to much of their original intricacy, although little else has been preserved. The only other synagogues to survive the 1492 expulsion of the Jews from Spain are in Toledo. *(C. Judíos, 20. ☎957 20 29 28. Open Tu-Sa 10am-2pm and 3:30-5:30pm, Su 10am-1:30pm. Currently free because of restoration.)*

MUSEO TAURINO Y DE ARTE CORDOBÉS. The museum is dedicated to the history and lore of the bullfight. The main exhibit includes a replica of the tomb of Spain's most famous matador, the dashing Manolete, and the hide of the bull that killed him. *(Pl. Maimónides. ☎957 20 10 56. Open May-Sept. Tu-Sa 10am-2pm and 5:30-7:30pm, Su 9:30am-3pm; Oct.-Apr. M-Sa 10am-2pm and 5-7pm, Su 9:30am-2:30pm. 450ptas/€2.70, students 225ptas/€1.35, seniors free. F free.)*

MUSEO DIOCESANO DE BELLAS ARTES. Once the home of Córdoba's bishops while the Inquisition raged within the Alcázar, this 17th-century ecclesiastical palace houses a modest collection of Renaissance and Baroque religious art. *(C. Torrijos, across from the Mezquita in the Palacio de Congresos. ☎957 47 93 75. Open June-Sept. M-F 9:30am-3pm, Sa 9:30am-1:30pm; Oct.-Mar. M-F 9:30am-1:30pm and 3:30-5:30pm, Sa 9:30am-1:30pm. 150ptas/€0.90, under 12 free, free with admission to Mezquita.)*

OTHER SIGHTS. Townspeople take great pride in their traditional **patios,** many dating from Roman times. These open-air courtyards—tranquil havens of orange and lemon trees, flowers, and fountains—flourish in the old quarter. Among the streets of exceptional beauty are **Calleja del Indiano,** off C. Fernández Ruano at Pl. Angel Torres, and the aptly named **Calleja de Flores**, off C. Blanco Belmonte where lustrous geraniums in full bloom crowd along the white walls of the alley. In Pl. Tiberiades, rub the toes of the statue of **Maimonides** to gain his knowledge. The statue was used as the model for the face of the New Israeli Shekel.

OUTSIDE THE JUDERÍA

MUSEO JULIO ROMERO DE TORRES. Spice up your life with Romero's sensual portraits of Cordoban women, exhibited in the artist's former home. Only the Andalucian sun gets hotter than this. *(Pl. Potro, 5-10min. from the Mezquita. ☎957 49 19 09. Open May-Sept. Tu-Sa 10am-2pm and 5:30-7:30pm, Su 9:30am-2:30pm. Last entrance 30min. before closing. 450ptas/€2.70, students 225ptas/€1.35, seniors free.)*

MUSEO DE BELLAS ARTES. Across the courtyard from the Museo Julio Romero de Torres. This museum now occupies a building that served as a hospital during the reign of Fernando and Isabel. Its small collection displays Renaissance sketches and works by modern Cordoban artists. Don't miss the sculptures by Mateo Inurria and Juan de Mesa on the ground floor. *(Pl. Potro, 5-10 min. from the Mezquita. ☎957 47 33 45. Open Tu 3-8pm, W-Sa 9am-8pm, Su 9am-3pm. Enter 15min. before closing. 250ptas/€1.50; EU citizens free.)*

PALACIO DEL MARQUÉS DE VIANA. An elegant 14th-century mansion, the palace displays 12 quintessentially Córdoban patios complete with sprawling gardens and majestic fountains, as well as tapestries, furniture and porcelain. *(Pl. Don Gome, 2. A 20min. walk from the Mezquita. ☎957 48 01 34. Open June 16-Sept. M-Sa 9am-2pm; Oct. 1-May M-Sa 10am-1pm and 4-6pm; closed June 1-15. Patio only 200ptas/€1.20. Guided tours every hr. 500ptas/€3, children 200ptas/€1.20.)*

OTHER SIGHTS. Near the Palacio del Marqués de Viana in Pl. Capuchinos (a.k.a. Pl. Dolores) and next to the monastery is the **Cristo de los Faroles** (Christ of the Lanterns). This is one of the most famous religious icons in Spain and is the site of frequent all-night vigils. The eight lanterns that are lit at night symbolize the eight provinces of Andalucía. Facing the Museo de Bellas Artes and the Museo Julio Romero de Torres is the **Posada del Potro,** a 14th-century inn mentioned in *Don Quijote*. Across the river from the Mezquita stands the **Torre de la Calahorra,** a Muslim military tower which was built in 1369 to protect the Roman bridge and now houses a museum that covers Cordoba's cultures during the Middle Ages.

ENTERTAINMENT

For the latest cultural events, pick up a free copy of the *Guía del Ocio* at the tourist office. Cheap flamenco isn't easy to come by in Córdoba. Tourists fill the **Tablao Cardenal,** C. Torrijos, 10, facing the Mezquita, where national prize-winning dancers perform passionate *flamenco puro*. Reserve seats at the Tablao or your hostel. (☎957 48 33 20. Shows Tu-Sa 10:30pm. 2800ptas/€17, includes 1 drink.) Another option is **La Bulería,** C. Pedro López, 3, which has shows every night at 10:30pm. (☎957 48 38 39. 1500ptas/€9, includes 1 drink).

From the first weekend of June until the heat subsides, the cool **Barrio Brillante,** uphill from Av. América, is the place to be at night. Throngs of well-dressed, young *cordobeses* walk the streets, hopping from one packed outdoor bar to another until reaching a dance club. Bus #10 goes to Brillante from the train station until about 11pm; a taxi should cost 500-900ptas/€3-6. If you're walking, head up Av. Brillante passing along the way **El Rocio, Pub BSO,** and **El Navegante** at C. Llanos de Pretorio. Right around the corner is **Brujas Bar,** where every Tuesday and Thursday witches can tell your fortune. Once in Barrio Brillante, where C. Poeta Emilia Prados meets C. Poeta Juan Ramón Jiménez, go through **Cafetería Terra** to discover a massive open-air patio where the backs of nearly ten bars (**Havanna, Canaveral,** and **El Puerto** to name a few) converge. Across the street is **La Torre,** an outdoor nightclub that plays a mix of well-known Latin music and Spanish pop. Along Av. Brillante run a string of popular nightclubs, including **El Cachao, Pub La Mondoa, Club Pon Luis, Club Kachomba,** and **Bar Chicote**. To get home, catch a taxi at the corner of Av. Brillante and C. Las Acacias. During the cooler months of winter, nightlife tends to center around the Universidad de Córdoba, especially pubs on C. Antonio Maura and C. Camino de los Sastres. From there, the crowds move on to Av. Gran Capitán, Av. Ronda de los Tejares and C. Cruz Conde.

DAYTRIP FROM CÓRDOBA

MEDINA AL-ZAHRA

Medina al-Zahra can be hard to reach. The 0-1 ***bus*** *(☎957 25 57 00, or see the list in the tourist office) leaves from Av. República Argentina in Córdoba for Cruce Medina Al-Zahra, 3km from the site (10 past every hr., 125ptas/€0.75) and from Puerta del Puente (every hour, 125ptas/€0.75). From the bus stop, it's a 45min. walk (mostly uphill). The return bus stops along the highway at the cross, on the opposite side of the street from the gas station. A* ***taxi*** *from Córdoba to the entrance of the site costs about 2000ptas/€12.*

Built in the **Sierra Morena,** Córdoba's mountain range, by Abderramán III for his favorite wife, Zahra, this 10th-century medina was considered one of the greatest palaces of its time before it was sacked by Berbers in 1010. Long thought to be mythical, Medina al-Zahra was rediscovered in the mid-19th century and excavated in the early 20th century. Today, it is one of Spain's most impressive archaeological sites. The palace was constructed in three terraces: one for the nobility, another for servants, and a third for an enclosed garden and almond grove. After moving from Granada, Zahra missed the Sierra Nevada; to win her affections, Abderramán planted the white-blossoming almond groves as a substitute for her beloved snow. The Salón de Abd al-Rahman III, also known as the *salón rico*, on the lower terraces, is being restored to its original geometric beauty.

A complete tour of the ruins takes between 20-45min., depending on your level of interest. (☎957 32 91 30. Open May-Sept. Tu-Sa 10am-2pm and 6-8:30pm, Su 10am-2pm; Oct.-Apr. Tu-Sa 10am-2pm and 4-6:30pm, Su 10am-2pm. 250ptas/€1.50, EU citizens free.) **Córdoba Visión** offers transportation and a 2½-hour guided visit to the sight in English, Spanish, or French. (☎957 23 17 34; fax 23 73 94. Tours May-Sept. Tu-Sa 10:30am-6pm, Su 10:30am; Oct.-Apr. Tu-Sa 10:30am-4pm, Su 10:30am. 2500ptas/€15. Meets at Triunfo de San Rafael near the mosque.)

JEREZ DE LA FRONTERA ☎956

Jerez de la Frontera (pop. 200,000) is the cradle of three staples of Andalucian culture: flamenco, Carthusian horses, and, of course, *jerez* (sherry). It is the sheer quantity and quality of this third staple that draws in the tourists, most of whom are older, well-to-do Europeans. The city also makes a good departure point for the *ruta de los pueblos blancos*, but those not particularly interested in winery tours or horse shows would be better off spending their time elsewhere.

TRANSPORTATION

Flights: Airport, Ctra. Jerez-Sevilla (☎956 15 00 00), 7km from town. Taxi to the airport 1500-2000ptas/€9-12. **Iberia** (☎956 18 43 94) and **British Airways** (☎956 15 00 93) both have their offices at the terminal. Flights operate regularly to and from Madrid and Barcelona, as well as other major European cities.

Trains: Pl. Estación (☎956 34 23 19), at the end of C. Medina after it becomes C. Cartuja. **RENFE,** C. Larga, 34 (☎956 33 48 13). To: **Barcelona** (12hr., 7:30pm, 8500-9000ptas/€52); **Cádiz** (45min., every 30min. 6:40am-10:30pm, 430ptas/€2.58); **Madrid** (4½hr., 2 and 5pm, 7900-11,000ptas/€48-66); **Sevilla** (1¼hr., 12 per day 6:30am-8:30pm, 930ptas/€5.58).

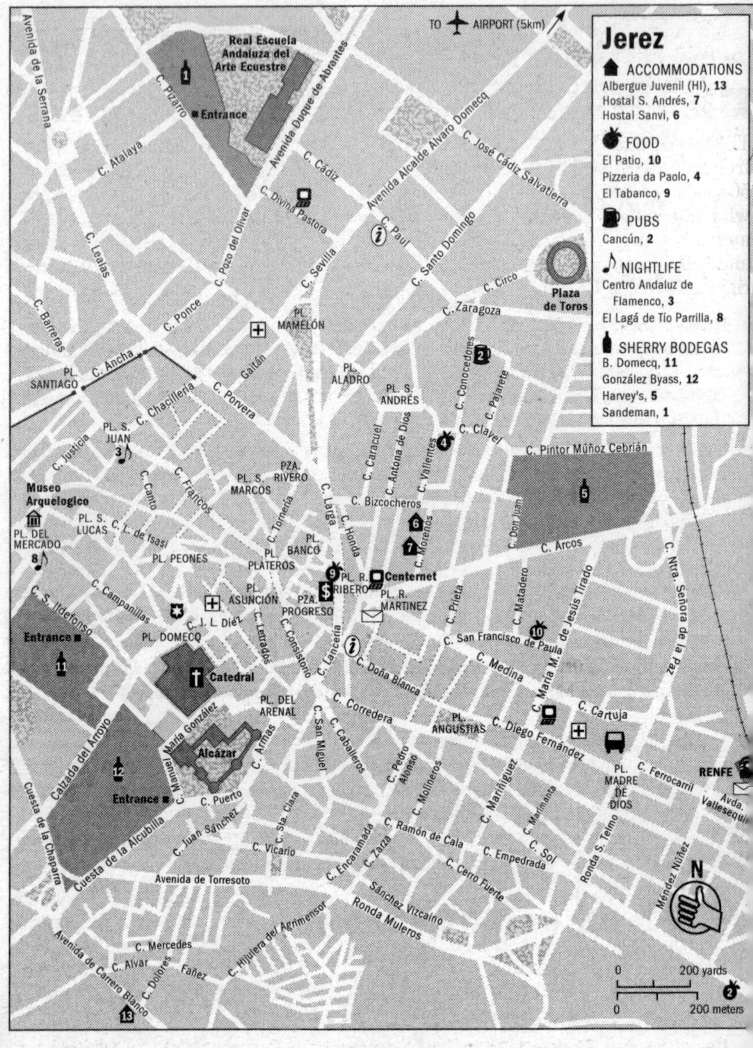

Buses: C. Cartuja (☎956 34 52 07), at the corner of C. Madre de Dios, 2 blocks from the train station. **Transportes Generales Comes** (☎956 21 17 63). To: **Cádiz** (1hr., 19 per day 7am-10pm, 380ptas/€2.28); **Puerto Santa María** (30min., 5 per day 8am-9pm, 190ptas/€1.14); **Ronda** (2¾hr., 4 per day 7:45am-3:30pm, 1375ptas/€8.25). **Los Amarillos** (☎956 32 93 47) goes to **Arcos de la Frontera** (30min., 8-17 per day 7:15am-8:15pm, 330ptas/€1.98) and **Córdoba** (4hr., 6pm, 2040ptas/€12.24). **Linesur** (☎956 34 10 63) to: **Algeciras** (2hr., 7-9 per day 7am-9:45pm, 1140ptas/€6.84); **Chipiona** (1hr., 12 per day 7am-10pm, 310ptas/€1.86); **Sanlúcar** (30min. every hr. 7am-10pm, 225ptas/€1.35); **Sevilla** (1½hr., 7-13 per day 6:30am-11pm, 800ptas/€4.80). **Secorbus** (☎902 22 92 92) goes to **Madrid** (7hr., 6 per day 8:50am-11:50pm, 3130ptas/€18.78). **City Buses:** Each of the 12 lines runs every 15min., most passing through Pl. Arenal and by the bus station. One ride 125ptas/€0.75. **Info office** (☎956 34 34 46) in Pl. Arenal.

Car Rental: Niza, C.N. IV Madrid-Cádiz, KM, 637; Av. Alvaro Domecq (☎956 30 28 60). Starts at 8000ptas/€48 per day. Min. age 21. Open daily 8:30am-1pm and 4:30-8pm.

ORIENTATION AND PRACTICAL INFORMATION

The labyrinthine streets of Jerez are difficult to navigate without a map. Get one free from the tourist office or buy one at any bookstore or newsstand (around 500ptas). To reach the town center from the **bus station,** exit left onto C. Cartuja, which becomes C. Medina, which leads into **Pl. Romero Martínez** (the city's commercial center). From here, walk left on C. Cerrón, which leads to C. Santa María and C. Lencería, heading into **Plaza del Arenal.** From the **train station,** exit to the right and take C. Cartuja to the bus station, then follow the directions above.

Tourist Office: Edif. Scritium, C. Paul (☎956 33 11 50; fax 33 17 31). Near Bodegas Sandeman and the Real Escuela del Arte Ecuestre. English-speaking staff has free maps and info on sherry production, *bodegas* tours, and horse shows. Open June-Aug. M-F 9am-7pm, Sa-Su 10am-2pm and 5-7pm; Sept.-May M-F 8am-3pm and 4-7pm, Sa-Su 10am-2pm and 5-7pm.

Currency Exchange: Banco Central Hispano, C. Largo, 11 (☎902 24 24 24), charges no commission. Open M-F 8:30am-2:30pm.

Emergency: ☎112. **Police:** ☎091 or 956 33 03 46.

Medical Assistance: Ambulatorio de la Seguridad Social C. José Luis Díaz, (☎956 34 84 68).

Internet Access: Centernet, C. Arcos 3 (☎956 32 49 39). 250ptas/€1.50 per hr. Open daily 10am-2pm and 4:30pm-midnight. **Cypercentro**, C. Mariñuez Local H. 300ptas/€1.80 per hr. Open 10am-2pm and 6-10pm.

Post Office: Main Office, C. Cerrón, 2 (☎956 34 22 95), off Pl. Romero Martínez. **Lista de Correos.** Open M-F 8:30am-8:30pm, Sa 9am-2pm. **Postal Code:** 11480.

ACCOMMODATIONS

Finding a place to crash is as easy as finding a cork to sniff, though few are cheap. Look along C. Medina, near the bus station, and C. Arcos, which intersects C. Medina at Pl. Romero Martínez. The area is close to the fountains and *terrazas* of C. Larga. Prices increase during Jerez's festivals.

Albergue Juvenil (HI), Av. Carrero Blanco, 30 (☎956 14 39 01; fax 14 32 63), in an ugly suburb, a 25min. walk or 10min. bus ride from downtown (bus L-8 from the bus station, bus L-1 from Pl. Arenal). One of Jerez's very few budget options. Clean and modern, with spacious doubles, a pool (open July-Aug.), tennis and basketball courts, small soccer field, library, TV/VCR room, and rooftop terrace. Laundry service available (300ptas/€1.80.) Call ahead. Dorms 1725ptas/€10.35, over 26 2375ptas/€14.25.

Hostal Sanvi, C. Morenos, 10 (☎956 34 56 24). Take C. Fontana (off C. Medina), for 1 block, then turn left; C. Morenos is the first right. Newly renovated rooms. Private bathrooms. Fans available on request. Singles 3000-3500ptas/€18-21; doubles 4200-4500ptas/€25-27; triples 6500-7000ptas/€39-42.

Hostal/Hotel San Andrés, C. Morenos, 12 (☎956 34 09 83; fax 34 31 96). Follow direction for Hostal Sanvi. Rambling hallways adorned with vines and Andalucian tile enclose two charming patios. Stay at the spartan, bare-walled hostal or splurge on a "hotel" room with bath and TV. Singles 2800ptas/€16.80, with bath and TV 3410ptas/€20.46; doubles 3960ptas/€23.76, with bath and TV 5520ptas/€33.12.

FOOD

Tapas-hoppers bounce around Pl. Arenal, C. Larga and in the old town around Pl. del Banco. Supermarket **Cobreros** sells the basics on the second floor of the Centro Comercial, C. Larga (open daily 9am-2pm and 5:30-9:30pm).

El Patio, C. San Francisco de Paula (☎956 34 07 36). Savor sumptuous traditional fare in a dining room with brightly colored oil paintings. Loaded with eggs, sausage and loads of garlic, the sizzling *sopa de ajo* (600ptas/€3.60) is a meal in itself. *Raciones* 800-1500ptas/€4.81-9.02. Open M-Sa 1:30-4pm and 8-11:30pm.

El Tabanco, Pl. Rafael Rivero (☎956 33 40 24). Tapas bar in an unrivaled setting. Outdoor plaza seating with frequent flamenco performances in the summer. *Tapas* 200-250ptas/€1.20-1.50. *Raciones* 800-1200ptas/€4.80-7.20. Next door, **Antigua Abaceria de San Lorenzo** serves an exquisite almond tart *postre* (250ptas/€1.50). Both open summer daily 7:30pm-2am, winter daily 7:30-midnight.

Pizzeria da Paolo, C. Clavel at C. Valientes. The best pizza in Jerez. Pizza 800-950ptas/€4.80-5.70. Open Tu-Su 1-4:45pm and 8:30pm-midnight. MC/V.

SHERRY BODEGAS

People come to Jerez for the *jerez.* Multilingual tour guides distill the sherry-making process for you, then give you free samples. The best time to visit is early September during the harvest; the worst is August when many *bodegas* close down. *Bodegas* are plotted on any map, and the tourist office can help find the right one for you. Group reservations for tours must be made at least one week in advance; reservations for individuals are usually unnecessary. Call ahead for exact times.

B. Domecq, C. San Idelfonso, 3 (☎956 15 15 00). Founded in 1730, Domecq is the oldest and largest *bodega* in town. Tours include an informative 15min. video followed by a stroll through some of the warehouses and gardens that comprise the sprawling complex. With unlimited sampling from 3 sherries and 2 brandies, Domecq's tasting is by far the most generous in Jerez. Celebrity visitors include Franco and Alexander Fleming. Open M-F 10am-1pm, 500ptas/€3; Sa 12pm 750ptas/€3.74. MC/V.

González Byass, C. Manuel María González, 12 (☎956 35 70 16. The Disneyworld of sherry *bodegas*: uncomfortably commercial and definitely overblown, but worth visiting at least once to get the mouse's signature. Motorized trolleys whisk visitors past the largest weathervane in the world and a storage room designed by Gustave Eiffel (of Eiffel Tower fame). At the end of the tour, a trained mouse climbs a miniature ladder to sip a glass of *oloroso.* Celebrity visitors include Margaret Thatcher and Orson Welles. Tours in English M-Sa 11:30am-5:30pm. Su 11:30am-1:30pm. 1000ptas/€6. MC/V.

Sandeman, C. Pizarro, 10 (☎956 31 29 95), next to the Royal Andalusian School of Equestrian Art. Although most associated with port, the House of Sandeman is also a leading sherry producer. Their labels sport the stylish black-caped Don. Tours M,W,F 10:30am-2:30pm; Tu,Th 10:30am-3pm; Sa 11:30am-1:30pm. 500ptas/€3. MC/V.

Harvey's, C. Arcos, 54. (☎956 34 60 04; fax 33 86 74). Makers of Harvey's Cream, the best selling sherry in the world. Entrance includes a videotape of the wine-making process and a guided tour featuring peacocks, countless oak barrels, and a crocodile. Open M-F 10am and 12pm. 500ptas/€3. Reservations required for groups. MC/V.

SIGHTS

ALCÁZAR. Seized by Christian knights under Alfonso X during the reconquest of Jerez in 1255, the Alcázar has slowly changed over the centuries. During the 1300s, the Moorish governor's private mosque was transformed into a chapel to commemorate the intercession of the Virgin Mary on behalf of Christian raids into the Kingdom of Granada. Later, in the 17th century, the neighboring Arab baths became servants quarters for the Palacio de Villavicencio, where the **Cámara Oscura** resides today. Designed along a model by Leonardo Da Vinci, the Cámara Oscura uses reflective lenses to project panoramas of the city. *(☎956 31 97 98. Open May-Sept. 16 M-Sa 10am-8pm, Su 10am-3pm; Sept. 17-Apr. 30 daily 10am-6pm. Alcázar only 400ptas/€2.40, students 100ptas/€0.60; Alcázar and Cámara Oscura 500ptas/€3, students 400ptas/€2.40.)*

LIQUOR FOR LINGUISTS The Islamic prohibition against consumption of alcohol did not prevent Jerez's Moorish merchants from exporting wine to the infidel English in the 12th century. "Sherry," an anglicization of Shir-az, the Arabic name for Jerez, is a legacy of this early commerce. Today, only wines produced in Jerez, Sanlúcar de Barrameda, and El Puerto de Santa María are considered sherries. There is no vintage sherry; wines from various years are continuously mixed together in what is known as the *solera* process. Less-than-diligent maintenance of this process results eventually in the creation of cognac. Unable to use the term for the same reason that wineries in other regions cannot call their products sherry, Jerez's merchants have settled with "brandy," another English bastardization, this time of the Dutch word "brandewyn," meaning "burnt wine." Impress your friends at dinner parties by knowing the trinity of major sherry types: **Fino:** A dry, light colored sherry served chilled and sipped with tapas. Most popular in Andalucía. Manzanilla, a type of fino from Sanlúcar de Barrameda, is slightly salty in taste. **Amontillado:** Somewhat sweeter and amber in color. Excellent with white meat and cheese. **Oloroso dulce:** A dessert wine, dark in color, with a raisin-like taste. Go ahead, be pretentious. You know you want to.

REAL ESCUELA ANDALUZA DE ARTE EQUESTRE. Jerez's love for wine is almost matched by its passion for horses. During the first or second week of May, the Real Escuela Andaluza de Arte Equestre (Royal Andalusian School of Equestrian Art), on Av. Duque de Abrantes, sponsors a **Feria del Caballo** (Horse Fair) with shows, carriage competitions, and races of Jerez-bred Carthusian horses. During the rest of the year, weekly shows feature a troupe of horses dancing in choreographed sequences. Dress rehearsals are almost as impressive. *(☎956 31 80 08. Dress rehearsals M, W, and F 10am-1pm. 1000ptas/€6. Shows June-Oct. Tu noon, Th noon; Nov.-May Th noon. 2000-3000ptas/€12-18, children and students 40% off. MC/V.)*

ENTERTAINMENT AND NIGHTLIFE

FLAMENCO. Rare footage of Spain's most highly regarded flamenco singers, dancers, and guitarists is available for viewing at the **Centro Andaluz de Flamenco,** in Palacio Pemartín, on Pl. San Juan. *(☎956 34 92 65; fax 32 11 27. Open M-F 9am-2pm. Audio-visuals every hr., 9am-2pm. Free.)* Most *peñas* and *tablaos* (clubs and bars that host flamenco) hide in the old town and host special performances during July and August. Ask for details in the tourist office or look for posters along the main streets. For more frequent (and touristy) shows, make the trek to **El Lagá de Tío Parrilla,** Pl. Mercado. *(☎/fax 956 33 83 34. Shows M-Sa 10:30pm. Cover 1200-1500ptas/€7.20-9, includes 1 drink.)*

FESTIVALS. Autumn, in addition to being grape harvest season, is festival season, when Jerez showcases its best equine and flamenco traditions. The **Fiesta de la Bulería** in September celebrates flamenco, as does the September **Festival de Teatro, Música, y Baile.** These festivals are collectively known as the **Fiestas de Otoño,** occurring from September 10 until October 13. The largest **horse parade** in the world, with races in Pl. Arenal, is the highlight of the final week. Ask for details at the tourist office; schedules are available in September for the upcoming year.

NIGHTLIFE. Visitors to Jerez tend to be on the older side; *tapas* bars are more popular than dance clubs here, although plenty of people go out on weekends. For bars and *terrazas*, look around the triangle formed by **C. Santo Domingo, C. Salvatierra,** and **Av. Méjico.** Also of interest is Pl. Canterbury, a mini-mall of nightspots located on C. Paul at C. Santo Domingo. **Cancún,** C. Pajarete, 18, a huge, trendy *bar-musical* off C. Zaragoza (a block from Pl. Canterbury), features Caribbean themes, but the usual techno-pop blasts from the speakers. *(☎956 33 17 22. Couples, ladies, and "members" only. Free.)*

SANLÚCAR DE BARRAMEDA ☎956

Sanlúcar de Barrameda (pop. 62,000), at the mouth of the Río Guadalquivir, borders both the **Parque Nacional Coto de Doñana** (see **Mother Nature and Family,** p. 227) and some pristine beaches. Home to a handful of sherry *bodegas* and a few palaces, Sanlúcar is a cross between a Spanish *pueblo blanco* and a European seaside resort. Its industrial outskirts are a bit of an eyesore, but it boasts superbly fine sands, forming the seaside corner of the illustrious "sherry triangle," along with Jerez and El Puerto de Santa María.

TRANSPORTATION. **Los Amarillos** (☎956 38 50 60), on Pl. Pradillo at the end of C. San Juan, runs **buses** to: **Cádiz** (1hr., 10 per day 6:15am-6:15pm, 400ptas/€2.40); **Chipiona** (30min., every hr. 8:15am-10:40pm, 120ptas/€0.72); and **Sevilla** (2hr., 13 per day 6:45am-9:15pm, 1000ptas/€6). **Linesur La Valenciana** (☎956 34 10 63) is two blocks toward the beach from Pl. Cabildo. Buses run to **Chipiona** (30min., every hr. 8am-9pm,120ptas/€0.72) and **Jerez** (45min., every hr. 7:20am-10:20pm, 250ptas/ €1.50). Buy tickets on the bus. For **taxis,** call ☎956 36 11 02 or 36 00 04.

PRACTICAL INFORMATION. The **tourist office** is on Calzada del Ejército, which runs perpendicular to the beach. English-speaking staff has info on the **Parque Nacional de Doñana.** (☎ 956 36 61 10; fax 956 36 61 32. Open June-Aug. M-F 9am-2pm and 6-8pm, Sa-Su 10am-2pm; Sept.-May M-F 10am-2pm and 5-7pm, Sa 10am-1pm.) Services include: **emergency** ☎112; **Ambulatorio de la S.S.** on Calzada del Ejército, (☎956 36 71 65); **police** Av. Constitución, (☎956 38 80 11); and the **post office,** C. Correos and Av. Cerro Falcón, toward the beach from the tourist office. (☎956 36 09 37. Open M-F 8:30am-2:30pm, Sa 9am-1pm.) **Postal code:** 11540.

ACCOMMODATIONS AND FOOD. Few true bargains exist in Sanlúcar; it may be worth it to inquire at doorway signs reading *"se alquilan habitaciones"* (rooms for rent). **Hostal La Blanca Paloma,** Pl. San Roque, 15, keeps spacious, clean rooms, a few with balconies. (☎956 36 36 44. Singles 2150-2500ptas/€12.90-15; doubles 3210-4000ptas/€19.26-24) Sanlúcar is famous for its *langostinos* (king prawns). For a sit-down meal, head for the side streets off C. San Juan. *Terrazas* fill Pl. San Roque and Pl. Cabildo, its tree-lined neighbor. **Bar-Restaurante El Cura,** C. Amargura, 2, between the two plazas, serves up divine *paella* (600ptas/€3.60) and entrées. (☎956 36 29 94. Open daily 7:30am-3am.)

SIGHTS AND ENTERTAINMENT. Two impressive palaces compete with the enormous 14th-century **Iglesia de Nuestra Señora de la O,** Pl. Paz, for the attention of sun-struck tourists. (☎956 36 05 55. Open 30min. before and after mass. Mass M-Sa 7:30pm, Su noon and 8pm. Free.) The **Palacio Medina Sidonia** is inhabited by the Duque de Medina Sidonia. (☎956 36 01 61. Call to arrange group visits on Sunday or Monday. Free.) The 19th-century **Palacio Infantes de Orleans** now houses the Ayuntamiento. (☎956 38 80 00. Open for guided visits F-W 11am-1:30pm 100ptas/€0.60.) Several **bodegas** tower over Sanlúcar's small streets. Check at the tourist office for their revolving schedules. (Tours M-Sa 12:30pm, 300ptas/€1.80.) For 500ptas/€3 per person, the tourist office organizes tours of the monuments and *bodegas*. Locals celebrate their sherry during the **Feria de la Manzanilla** (late May or early June). In August, **Carreras de Caballos** (horse races) thunder along the beach, and the **Festival de la Exaltación del Río Guadalquivir** (end of Aug.) brings poetry readings, a flamenco competition, dancing, and bullfights.

CHIPIONA ☎956

A quiet seaside village for most of the year, Chipiona (pop. 15,000) takes a summertime somersault into domestic tourism. This phenomenon began 200 years ago, when nearby salty and mineral-filled waters were reputed to have medicinal powers. Despite its popularity, Chipiona retains a traditional charm; wildflowers

MOTHER NATURE AND FAMILY Bust out your binoculars—the 60,000 acre **Parque Nacional Coto de Doñana** on the Río Guadalquivir delta is home to flamingos, vultures, and thousands more of your feathered favorites, along with geese (and mongeese), wild boars, and lynx. Despite a huge mining spill on a tributary of the Guadalquivir River in April of 1998 that threatened to be one of Spain's biggest ecological disasters, the park has done surprisingly well, and tourist visits have continued relatively unaffected. If ornithological delights don't entice you, the salt marshes, sand dunes, wooded areas, and beach might. Nature purists beware, though, lest you stumble upon the lair of the dreaded species *turgrupus touristicus*—the park borders the town of Matalascañas, with a concrete shopping center and hotel complex.

Access to most of the park is restricted and back-country hiking and camping are prohibited. The western end of the park is accessible from Huelva and Matalascañas. Also, boat tours on **S.S. Real Fernando** depart from **Sanlúcar.** (☎956 36 38 13. 4hr; Apr.-Aug. Tu-Su 9:30am and 5pm; Sept.-Mar. Tu-Su 10am.) Call or visit the office in the old ice factory by the dock on Av. Bajo de Guía. Those more interested in sand than life on the wild side can take the launch across the bay (8am-8pm, 400ptas/€2.40) to one of the few *chiringuitos* (refreshment stands) free beaches in Spain. To get a taste of Doñana, stop by the **Visitor Center,** also in the ice factory. (☎956 38 16 35. Open daily June-Aug. 9am-8pm; Sept.-May 9am-2:30pm and 4-7pm.)

line misty cobblestoned streets and each morning, before the throngs of sunbathers arrive, fishermen dig for shellfish along the shores of golden sand.

TRANSPORTATION AND PRACTICAL INFORMATION. Los Amarillos buses (☎956 37 70 10), run to: **Cádiz** (1½hr., 9 per day 6am-6:30pm, 500ptas/€3); **Sanlúcar** (30min., 15 per day 6am-8pm, 120ptas/€0.72); and **Sevilla** (2hr., 10 per day 6:30am-8pm, 1100ptas/€6.60). **Linesur La Valenciana** buses (☎956 37 12 83) go to **Jerez de la Frontera** (1hr., 14 per day 8am-10:20pm, 310ptas/€1.86). Both companies use a poorly located bus station on Av. de La Constitución, about 1km from the beach. The **tourist office,** C. Larga, 74, dispenses beach info. To get there from the bus station, take a left from the rotary onto **Av. de Rota** and continue for ¾km until a courthouse appears on the right at the intersection with C. Victor Pradera. Cross C. Victor Pradera to **C. Pozo,** which turns into **C. Cuatro Esquinas,** and take a right onto **C. Larga;** the tourist office will be on the right. (☎956 37 71 50; fax 37 22 56. Open M-F 10am-2pm and 6-8pm.) Services include: **emergency** ☎112; **police,** C. Camacho Baños (☎956 37 10 88); and the **post office,** C. Padre Lerchundi, 15, near Pl. Pío XII. (☎956 37 14 19. Open M-F 8:30am-2:30pm, Sa 9am-1pm.) **Postal code:** 11550.

ACCOMMODATIONS AND FOOD. Accommodations in Chipiona seem to have conspired against budget travelers; consider sleeping in Jerez and commuting to the beach. One luxurious option is the quaint **Hostal Gran Capitán,** C. Fray Baldomero, 3, off C. Isaac Peral, which sports a charming patio and large rooms with baths and TVs. (☎956 37 09 29; fax 37 43 35. Singles 3000-3600ptas/€18-21.60; doubles 5200-7000ptas/€31.20-42.) The municipal campground, **El Pinar de Chipiona,** on Ctra. Rota at 3km, 800m from the beach, has a supermarket on-site. (☎956 37 23 21. 575ptas/€3.45 per person and per tent; 500/€3 per car; electricity 450ptas/€2.70.) C. Isaac Peral and the small streets nearby are dotted with bars and restaurants specializing in non-Spanish cuisine. More indigenous eateries line Po. Cruz del Mar (at the end of C. Isaac Peral) and the area around Pl. Juan Carlos I and Pl. Pío XII. In the latter, try the scrumptious *pan montadito* (mini sandwiches on hot bread; 200ptas/€1.20) at **El Rincón de Jabugo. Bar Toro,** Po. Marítimo Cruz del Mar, 24, along the beachfront, serves *tapas* (250-300ptas/€1.50-1.80) and entrées (750-1500ptas/€4.50-9) both indoors and out. (☎956 37 03 04. Open daily 9am-12:30am.) The **market,** is on C. Víctor Pradera (open M-Sa 9am-2pm).

SIGHTS AND NIGHTLIFE. Constructed in the 16th century, **Iglesia de Nuestra Señora de la O** stands in the gorgeous Pl. Juan Carlos I (open M-F shortly before 8pm mass, Su before 9, 11am, noon, and 8:30pm mass). There are two things to do in Chipiona: sunbathe and party. **Bugui II** in Zona Central, **Picoco** on Po. Marítimo, and **Mohama Palladium** next to the lighthouse on Av. de Faro are the most popular discos (open summer weekends 10pm-8am). Bars cluster around these clubs, as well as opposite the tourist office on Pl. Andalucía.

ARCOS DE LA FRONTERA ☎956

The Spanish novelist Azorín once described Arcos (pop. 33,000) by saying: "Imagine a long, narrow ridge, undulating; place on it little white houses, clustered among others more ancient; imagine that both sides of the mountain have been cut away, dropping downward sheer and straight; and at the foot of this wall a slow, silent river, its murky waters licking the yellowish stone, then going on its destructive course throughout the fields...and when you have imagined all this, you will have but a pale image of Arcos." The most popular of Spain's *pueblos blancos*, Arcos is a historic and romantic gem. Emanating like gossamer strings from the Plaza del Cabildo, the convoluted medieval streets lead visitors to bump into geranium-lined balconies and tranquil farmer's markets lying unperturbed in the sun.

TRANSPORTATION

Buses: C. Corregidores. **Transportes Generales Comes** (☎956 70 20 15). To: **Cádiz** (1½hr., 6 per day 7:20am-7:15pm, 675ptas/€4.05); **Costa del Sol** (3-4hr., 4pm, 1535-2060ptas/€9.21-12.36); **Jerez** (30min., 7 per day 7:20am-7:15pm, 200ptas/€1.20); **Ronda** (1¾hr., 3 per day 8:20am-3:30pm, 950ptas/€5.70). **Los Amarillos buses** (☎956 70 02 57) go to **Jerez** (15min., 8-18 per day 6:30am-7:15pm, 300ptas/€1.80) and **Sevilla** (2hr., 7am and 5pm, 905ptas/€5.43).

Taxis: RadioTaxi (24hr. ☎956 70 13 55). Taxis cluster around C. Debajo del Corral.

ORIENTATION AND PRACTICAL INFORMATION

To reach the town center from the bus station, exit left, turn left, then continue uphill for two blocks on C. Josefa Moreno Seguro, taking a right on C. Muñoz Vásquez. From there it's a 20min. walk uphill. Continue straight until reaching Pl. de España, then veer left onto Debajo del Corall, which quickly changes into C. Corredera. After 500m, the old quarter will appear. Mini-buses run every 30min. from the bus station to C. Corredera (130ptas/€0.78); a taxi costs 600ptas/€3.60.

Tourist Office: on Pl. Cabildo (☎956 70 22 64). Open June-Aug. M-Sa 10am-3pm and 4-8:30pm, Su 10:30am-3pm; Sept.-May M-F 9am-2pm and 5-7pm, Sa 10am-2pm and 5-6:30pm. Also offers tours of the old city. M-F 10:30am, 12:30, 5, and 6:30pm; Sa 10:30am, 12:30, and 6:30pm; Su 12:30pm. 400ptas/€2.40, children free.

Emergency: ☎112. **Police:** C. Nueva, (☎956 70 16 52).

Medical Emergency: ☎956 70 04 98, **Hospital: Centro de Salud,** C. Rafael Benat Rubio (☎956 70 0787), Barrio Bajo.

Pharmacy: Ldo. Ildefonso Guerrero Seijo, C. Corredera 11 (☎956 70 02 13). Open M-F 9:30am-1:30pm and 5-9pm.

Post Office: C. Murete, 24 (☎956 70 15 60), overlooking the cliffs and the river. Open M-F 8:30am-2:30pm, Sa 9:30am-1pm. **Postal Code:** 11630.

ACCOMMODATIONS

Arcos has only a few budget hostels; call ahead during *Semana Santa* and in the summer to be safe. As usual, the tourist office has a list of accommodations.

Hostal San Marcos, C. Marqués de Torresoto, 6 (☎956 70 07 21), past C. Dean Espinosa and Pl. Cabildo. Run by a friendly young family and crowned by a scenic rooftop terrace. Bright, modern rooms with well-apportioned private baths. The restaurant below serves one of the cheapest *menús* in town (900ptas/€5.40.) Singles 2500-3000ptas/€15-18; doubles 4000-5000ptas/€24-30. MC/V.

Pensión El Patio, C. Dean Espinosa, 4 (☎956 70 23 02), shaded by the buttresses of Iglesia de Sta. María. Eat, sleep, and get your hair cut all under one roof: entrepreneurial owner runs a hostel in addition to a restaurant and barbershop on the ground floor. Spotless rooms, some with TVs and A/C. Singles 3000-3500ptas/€18-21; doubles 4000ptas/€24, with bath 6000ptas/€36. MC/V.

FOOD

Restaurants huddle at the bottom end of C. Corredera, while *tapas* nirvana can be found uphill in the old quarter.

Bar Típico Alcaraván, C. Nueva, 1 (☎956 70 33 97), down from Pl. Cabildo. Located in a 900-year-old cave draped with bougainvillea. The perfect place for a romantic *tête-a-tête*. *Tapas* 250-450ptas/€1.50-2.70, *raciones* 1000-1500ptas/€6-9. Open Tu-Su 12-4pm and 7:45pm-midnight. MC/V.

Los Faraones, C. Debajo del Corral, 8 (☎956 70 06 12), downhill from C. Corredera. Exquisite Arab cuisine and hearty Spanish staples prepared by a friendly Egyptian-Spanish couple. Extensive vegetarian *menú* 900ptas/€5.40. Immense *bocadillo de falafel* 450ptas/€2.70 (available on request). A/C. Open Tu-Su 9am-midnight.

Cafetería Albéniz, C. Muñoz Vázquez, 10 (☎956 70 14 99). A good view of the valley and plenty of outdoor seating make this café an extremely popular rest-stop. Coffee 125-150ptas/€0.75-0.90. Open M-Sa noon-3pm and 7-11pm.

MADRE DE DIOS! Foremost among the *pueblos blancos* of Andalucía, Arcos de la Frontera is most associated by travelers with quaint streets and a tranquil pace of life. Things here were not always so serene, however. In the early 18th century a great controversy arose over which of the town's main churches, Iglesia Santa María or Iglesia San Pedro, was to become the seat of the local diocese. Parish allegiances fractured bonds of local fraternity, turning neighbor against neighbor. At San Pedro, the congregation refused even to pronounce the words, "Mary, Mother of God," substituting in their place "The Divine Shepherdess," or more inexplicably, "San Pedro, Mother of God." Only intervention by the Vatican resolved the great schism when in 1764 a papal decree proclaimed Santa María the oldest and most distinguished church in Arcos. Relations between the two parishes have since improved; there are tentative plans for a **joint bake sale** next year during Semana Santa.

SIGHTS AND ENTERTAINMENT

The most beautiful sights in Arcos are the winding white alleys, Roman ruins, and hanging flowers of the old quarter, combined with the view from **Plaza Cabildo.** The plaza earned the nickname *Balcón de Coño* because the view is so startling that people often exclaim *¡coño!* (*#%&*$!) in disbelief. In this square stands the **Iglesia de Santa María,** a mix of Baroque, Renaissance, and Gothic styles, built between the 15th and 18th centuries. Its most impressive attribute is the 14th-century mural painting. A symbol of the Inquisition—a circular design within which exorcisms were once performed—is still etched into the ground on the church's left side. (Open M-F 10am-1pm and 3:30-6:30pm, Sa 10am-2pm. 150ptas/€0.90.) The late-Gothic **Iglesia de San Pedro** was built on the site of an Arab fortress in the old quarter. An assortment of Murillos, Zurbaráns, and Riberas decorate the interior. (Open M-F 10am-1pm and 4-7pm, Sa 10am-1:30pm. 150ptas/€0.90.)

An artificial **lake** made in 1960 laps at Arcos's feet, its gentle waters inviting overheated travelers to take a dip; most choose to swim near Porto Alegre, a beach-like strip on the lake. Urban buses descend to the beach, **Mesón de la Molinera** (4 per day, 9:15am-8:15pm, 130ptas/€0.78). For further information on water sports at the lake, call the **Oficina de Deportes** (☎956 70 30 11).

Festivals in Arcos are highly spirited. A favorite is the **Toro de Aleluya,** held on the last Sunday of *Semana Santa.* Two bulls run rampant through the steep, cobbled streets as residents drink and dance flamenco.

CÁDIZ ☎956

Cádiz makes for an interesting sandwich: with a powerful ocean on one side, a placid bay on the other, and a whole lot of history in between. Founded by the Phoenicians in 1100 BC, Cádiz (pop. 155,000) is thought to be the oldest inhabited city in Europe. From the 16th to the 18th century, the Spanish colonial shipping industry transformed the port into one of the wealthiest in Europe. When the New World fervor subsided, liberal politics took over as the hallmark of Cadisian life. In 1808, the city's decisive resistance to Napoleon was crucial in preserving the Spanish nation. Residents subsequently designed the Constitución de Cádiz (1812), an assertion of democratic ideals that inspired a wave of Latin American nationalism. Sadly, it proved ineffectual in its own land. Cadisian liberalism was thwarted again during the Civil War when it fell quickly, and hard, to Franco's Nationalist army. As a fitting retaliation, Cádiz continued to rekindle its immortal spirit once a year, celebrating its extravagant *Carnaval*, the only festival of its size and kind not suppressed by Franco's regime. Perhaps Spain's most dazzling party, *Carnaval* makes Cádiz an imperative destination on February itineraries. During the rest of the year, the city offers a little of everything to visitors—a metropolis trimmed by golden sand beaches that put its pebble-strewn eastern neighbors to shame.

TRANSPORTATION

Trains: RENFE Pl. Sevilla (☎956 25 43 01), off Av. Puerto. Although it is still possible to buy tickets from the main station, all trains now leave from Cádiz-Cortadura station in the new city. A free shuttle bus runs between the two stations every half hour. To: **Córdoba** (5hr., 10-12 per day 8am-6:45pm, 2465ptas/€15); **Granada** (6hr., 3 per day 6am-3:10pm, 3700ptas/€22); **Jerez** (40min., 20-35 per day 6:40am-10:10pm, 390ptas/€2.34); **Madrid** (5hr., 8am and 4:25pm, 8100ptas/€49); **Sevilla** (2hr., 12 per day 6:35am-9:30pm, 1315ptas/€7.89).

Buses: Transportes Generales Comes, Pl. Hispanidad, 1 (☎956 22 78 11). To: **Arcos de la Frontera** (1½hr., 6 per day 7am-6pm, 710ptas/€4.27); **Algeciras** (3hr., 10 per day 7am-8:30pm, 1315ptas/€7.90); **Córdoba** (5hr., 5pm, 2420ptas/€15); **Granada** (6hr., 1:30 and 9pm, 3985ptas/€24); **Jerez de la Frontera** (1hr., 7-18 per day, 380ptas/€2.28); **La Línea** (3hr., 4 per day 8am-8:30pm, 1565ptas/€9.40); **Málaga** (4hr.; 6am, 7pm, 9pm, 2765ptas/€17); **Sevilla** (2hr., 11 per day 7am-9:30pm, 1445ptas/€8); **Vejer de la Frontera** (1½hr., 6-10 per day 7am-10pm, 595ptas/€4).

Transportes Los Amarillos (☎956 28 58 52) depart from beside the port, off Pl. San Juan de Dios. Purchase tickets on the bus or at the office on nearby Av. Ramón de Carranza (open M-F 9:30am-1pm and 5-8:30pm, alternate Sa 10am-1pm). To: **Arcos de la Frontera** (1hr., 2-3 per day 12:15-7:15pm, 605ptas/€3.63); **Chipiona** (1½hr., 5-11 per day 7:15am-7:30pm, 505ptas/€3.30); **Sanlúcar** (1hr., 5-11 per day 7:15am-9:30pm, 410ptas/€2.46). **Secorbus** (☎902 22 92 92) has service to **Madrid** (8hr., 6 per day 8:10am-11:10pm, 3075ptas/€18.48). Buses leave from next to Estadio Ramón de Carranza, just past Pl. Glorieta Ingeniero, in new Cádiz.

Ferry: El Vapor (☎956 87 02 70), departs from a dock next to the Comes station and runs to **Pto. de Sta. María** (Tu-Su 45min., 4 per day 10am-6:30pm, 275ptas/€1.65).

Catamaran: (☎670 69 79 05). Leaves from Estación Marítima near Plaza de España for **Pto. de Sta. María** (25min., 5-8 per day 7:50am-9pm, 400ptas/€2.40).

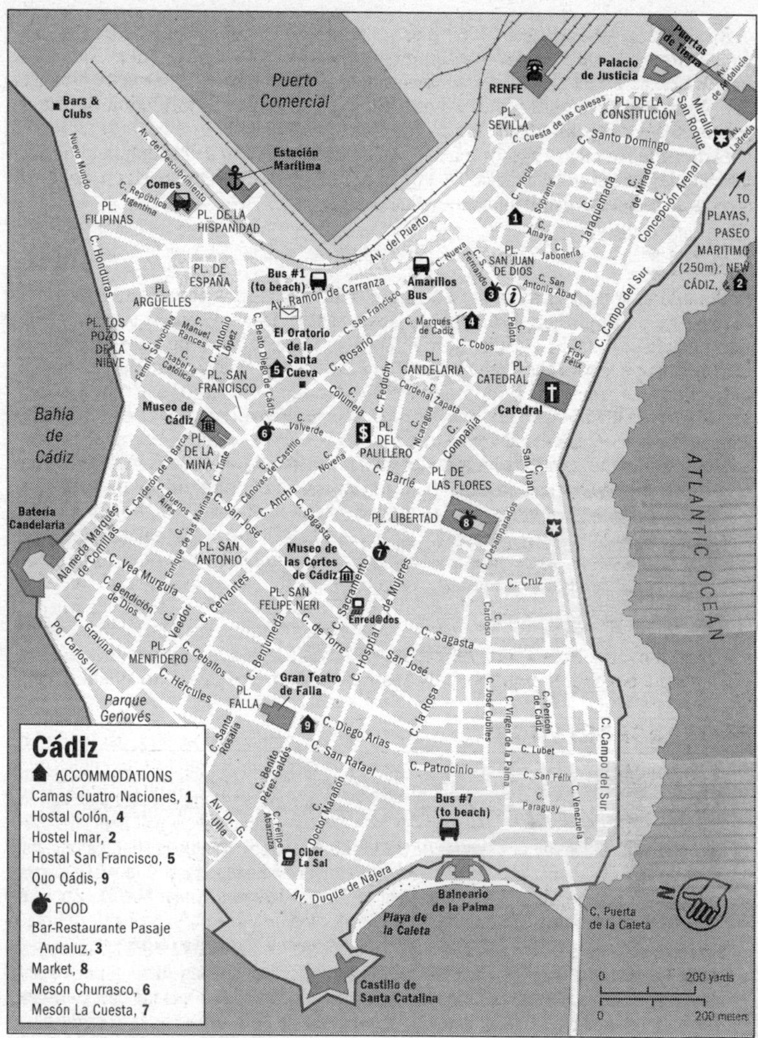

Municipal Buses: (☎956 26 28 06). Pick up a map/schedule and *bonobus* (discount packet of 10 tickets for 900ptas/€5.40) at the kiosk across from the Comes bus station. Most lines run through Pl. España. Beach bums' favorite bus #1 (Cortadura) runs along the shore to new Cádiz (every 10min. 6:40am-1:10am, 120ptas/€0.72). Bus #7 runs the same route, leaving from **Playa de la Caleta.**

Taxis: ☎956 21 21 21.

ORIENTATION AND PRACTICAL INFORMATION

Cádiz's old town was built on the end of the peninsula, and the new town grew up behind it farther inland. The old town hosts most of the cheap hostels and historic sights (not to mention the bus and train stations), while the new town is home to high-rise hotels, numerous bars and restaurants, kilometers of lovely sand, and deep blue seas. To reach **Plaza San Juan de Dios** (the town center) from the **Comes bus station,** walk along Av. Puerto for about 5min., keeping the port on the left; the plaza lies to the right, just after a park. From the **Los Amarillos bus stop,** walk inland about 100m. From the **train station,** walk past the fountain, keeping the port on the right, for about two blocks; Pl. San Juan de Dios is the first plaza on the left. The tangled *casco viejo* is disorienting—a map is necessary. When you take the bus into new Cádiz (down the main avenue), hop off at the square with the McDonald's and the modern-looking Hotel Victoria. This square is called **Glorieta Ingeniero.**

Tourist Office: Municipal, Pl. San Juan de Dios, 11 (☎/fax 956 24 10 01). Bright yellow "i" marks the spot. Useful free map. English spoken. Open M-F 9am-1pm and 5-8pm. On weekends, a kiosk opens in front of the main office (open Sa-Su and holidays 10am-1pm and 5-7:30pm). **Junta de Andalucía,** Av. Ramón de Carranza (☎956 25 86 46) Free map of Cádiz. Open M and Sa 9am-2pm, Tu-F 9am-7pm.

Currency Exchange: Banco Central Hispano, C. Ancha, 29 (☎956 22 66 22). Open M-F 8:30am-2pm. On weekends, try major hotels or **Gades Tour,** Pl. España, 1 (☎956 22 46 08). Open M-F 10am-1pm and 5:30-8:30pm, Sa 9am-1:30pm.

Luggage Storage: Lockers at train station (400ptas/€2.40), to the right on the way out to the platforms. Open daily 8am-11pm.

Emergency: ☎112. **Municipal police:** ☎091. In Campo del Sur in the new city.

Medical Assistance: Ambulatorio Vargas Ponce (☎062 or 956 28 38 55). **Hospital: Centro de Salud,** Av. Ana de Viya (☎956 24 21 00).

Internet Access: Enred@dos, C. Sacramento, 36 (☎956 80 81 81). Open M-Sa 9am-3pm and 7-10pm. **Ciber La Sal,** C. Dr. Marañón, 14 (☎956 21 15 39). Enter on C. Felipe Abarzuza. Computers 400ptas/€2.40 per hr. Open M-Sa 9am-10pm.

Post Office: (☎956 21 39 45), the red building in Pl. Flores, next to the market. Open M-F 8:30am-8:30pm, Sa 9:30am-2pm. **Postal Code:** 11070.

ACCOMMODATIONS

Most hostels huddle around the harbor, in Pl. San Juan de Dios, and just behind it on C. Marqués de Cádiz. Others are scattered throughout the old town. Singles and private bathrooms are scarce. Call months in advance to find a room during February's *Carnaval;* calling a few days ahead during the summer should be fine.

Quo Qádis, C. Diego Arias, 1 (☎/fax 956 22 19 39), 1 block from Pl. Falla. Clean rooms, roof terrace, TV room, and laundry facilities. Offers flamenco classes, planned excursions, and vegetarian dinners. Breakfast included. Sheets 200ptas/€1.20. Lockout 11am-5pm for dorms. Dorms 1000ptas/€6; singles 2100ptas/€12.60; doubles 4000ptas/€24; triples 6000ptas/€36. 10% discount if you arrive by bike.

Hostal Colón, C. Marqués de Cádiz, 6 (☎956 28 53 51), off Pl. San Juan de Dios. Spotless rooms with sinks and colorful tiles. All rooms have balconies, but the best view—the cathedral surrounded by hundreds of TV antennas—is from the terrace. 2 windowless singles 2500ptas/€15; doubles 4000ptas/€24; triples 6000ptas/€36.

Hostal San Francisco, C. San Francisco, 12 (☎956 22 18 42), 2 blocks from Pl. España. Conveniently located near the bus and train stations. Spacious rooms surround a Spanish patio with Japanese decor. Large communal bathrooms. Singles 2500-2600ptas/€15-15.60; doubles 3700-4250ptas/€22.22-25.50, with bath and TV 4800-5850ptas/€28.80-35.10. AmEx/MC/V.

Hostel Imar, Pl. Glorieta Ingeniero, 3 (☎956 26 05 00), on the main square in new Cádiz. The only semi-budget place next to Cádiz's best beach, Playa de la Victoria. Reservations a must. Doubles 6500ptas/€39, with bath 8100ptas/€48.60. V.

Camas Cuatro Naciones, C. Plocia, 3 (☎956 25 55 39), in a corner of Pl. San Juan de Dios. One of the cheapest places to stay in Cádiz. Rooms are simply furnished, but some have sunny terraces onto the street below. Welcome to the *budget* part of budget travel. Singles 1700ptas/€10.20; doubles 3500ptas/€21.

FOOD

Once you leave Pl. San Juan de Dios, finding eateries can be a trying experience. Opt for cafés and *heladerías* around Pl. Flores, near the post office and the municipal **market.** If you detest seafood, head to **Supermarket Champion,** next to the municipal market, off Pl. Flores (open M-Sa 9:15am-9:15pm).

Mesón Churrasco, C. San Francisco, 3 (☎956 22 72 81), 1 block from Pl. San Francisco. Traditional *bodega* packed with locals and legs of ham. Opt for the hearty *menú* (900ptas/€5.40); comes with free olives and bread. Open daily noon-11pm.

Mesón La Cuesta, C. Sacramento, 16 (☎956 22 59 92). Friendly waitstaff and tasty fried seafood make Juan "El Kuki" Rodríguez's new restaurant definitely worth a visit. *Menú* (1000ptas/€6). Open daily 12-4pm and 7:30pm-1am.

Bar-Restaurante Pasaje Andaluz, Pl. San Juan de Dios, 9 (☎956 28 52 54). Sip *café con leche* (175ptas/€1.05) and sit on the plaza where the Constitución de Cádiz was proclaimed in 1812. Open daily 12:30-4:30pm and 8-11:30pm.

SIGHTS

CATHEDRAL. This gold-domed 18th-century masterpiece is considered the last great cathedral built by colonial riches. Its treasury bulges with valuables—the *Custodia del Millón* is said to be set with a million precious stones. *(From Pl. San Juan de Dios, follow C. Pelota. ☎956 28 61 54. Museum open Tu-F 10am-12:45pm and 4:30-6:45pm, Sa 10am-12:45pm. 500ptas/€3, children 200ptas/€1.20. Cathedral open M-F 5:30-8pm. Mass W,F 7:30pm, Su at noon. Free.)*

PASEO. Cádiz's seaside *paseo* runs around the old city and along the Atlantic; walking the path is a good way to get a feel for the layout of the city. Stupendous views of ships leaving the harbor recall Spain's golden age; at the end of the *paseo*, infinite rows of antennae rising from the rooftops recall the 1950s. Exotic trees, fanciful hedges, and a few chattering monkeys enliven the adjacent **Parque Genovés.** *(Paseo accessible via Pl. Argüelles or C. Fermín Salvochea, off Pl. España.)*

MUSEO DE CÁDIZ. Thanks to the fusion of a Fine Arts and Provincial Archaeological Museum, Murillo, Rubens, and Zurbarán live here in unholy union with Phoenician sarcophagi. *(Pl. Mina. ☎956 21 22 81. Open for guided tours Tu 9am-2:30pm; for public Tu 2:30-8pm, W-Sa 9am-8pm, Su 9:30am-2:30pm. 250ptas, EU citizens free.)*

ENTERTAINMENT AND NIGHTLIFE

Carnaval insanity is legendary. The gray of winter gives way to dazzling color as the city hosts one of the most raucous *carnavales* in the world (Feb. 7-17 in 2002). Costumed dancers, street singers, ebullient residents, and spectators from the world over take to the streets in a week-long frenzy that makes New Orleans' Mardi Gras look like Thursday night bingo at the old folks' home.

For the café scene, try the area around **Pl. Mina,** which is especially lively on winter weekends. **Calle de Manuel Rances,** nearby off C. Antonio López, lines up some of the hippest bars in the old city. In the new city, C. General Muñoz Arenillas off Pl. Glorieta Ingeniero and the **Paseo Marítimo,** the main drag along Playa Victoria, have some of Cádiz's best bars. **La Jarra,** C. José G. Agullo (☎956 26 57 74), is one such hotspot, blaring *música española* and American top-40 late into the night. Club-rats will prefer **Punto de San Felipe,** a strip of almost 10 bars and clubs reached by walking north along the sea from Pl. España, just beyond the Comes station (take a right before the tunnel); these spots don't get going until 4 or 5am. Look for signs on the boardwalk advertising theme parties.

BEACHES

As Cádiz was built on a peninsula, the exhaust-spewing ships on one coast don't pollute the pristine beaches on the other. **Playa de la Caleta** is the beach most convenient to the old city. Better sand and more space can be found in the new city, serviced by bus #1, leaving from Pl. España (120ptas/€0.72). The first beach beyond the rocks is the unremarkable **Playa de Santa María del Mar.** Next to it, **Playa de la Victoria** has earned the EU's *bandera azul* (blue flag) for cleanliness. Get off bus #1 at Pl. Glorieta Ingeniero in front of McDonald's. A more natural landscape, with fewer hotels and straw mats, belongs to **Playa de Cortadura**, where the coveted *bandera azul* also flaps proudly. Take bus #1 until it almost reaches the highway, where the bus turns around. The boardwalk ends here, and sunbather density falls steadily the farther one walks.

VEJER DE LA FRONTERA ☎956

Glistening white above a sea of golden wheat, beautiful Vejer (pop.13,000) is one of Andalucía's most enchanting *pueblos blancos.* Fourteenth-century homes line cobblestoned alleys and gray-haired men discuss politics on street corners. The hike up to town is nothing short of painful, but pure relaxation awaits at the top. A mere village, Vejer is best a daytrip from Cádiz or a stop en route to Tarifa.

TRANSPORTATION. Getting to Vejer can be difficult. While some buses stop at the end of **Avenida de Los Remedios,** which leads uphill into La Plazuela (10min.), many just leave you by the highway at **La Barca de Vejer,** a small town at the base of the hill. Take one of the numerous taxis waiting by the bus stop (800ptas/€4.80). The alternative, an arduous 20min. uphill climb, is extremely difficult with a backpack. If you do make the trek, climb the cobbled track to the left of the restaurant. When you reach the top, keep walking straight; all roads lead to quiet **Plaza de España,** not to be confused with La Plazuela, which is a tiny intersection (where Av. Los Remedios and C. Juan Bueno meet).

For **bus** info, visit either the tourist office or the telephone kiosk just off La Plazuela toward Av. Los Remedios, where tickets are sold (☎956 44 71 46). Short-distance buses run from Av. Los Remedios to: **Cádiz** (1½hr., 8 per day 6:15am-7:15pm, 595ptas/€3.57); **Málaga** (4hr., 2 per day 8am and 5pm, 2030ptas/€12); and **Sevilla** via **Jerez** (3½hr., 1 per day 6:45am, 1790ptas/€10.75). For other destinations, descend the hill to La Barca de Vejer, with service to: **Algeciras** (2hr., 9 per day 8am-10pm, 750ptas/€4.50); **Cádiz** (1½hr., 8 per day 8am-7:15pm, 595ptas/€3.57); **Sevilla** (3½hr., 5 per day 8:30am-5:45pm, 1700ptas/€10.20); and **Tarifa** (1hr., 9 per day 8am-10pm, 500ptas/€3). For a **taxi,** call ☎956 45 04 08.

PRACTICAL INFORMATION. The staff at the **tourist office,** C. Marqués de Tamarón, 10, speak English. (☎956 45 01 91; fax 45 16 20. Open June-Aug. M-F 10:30am-2pm and 6-9pm, Sa 10:30am-2pm; Sept.-May M-F 9am-2:30pm and 5-9:30pm.) Services include: **Banco Central Hispano,** C. Juan Bueno, 5 (open M-F 8:30am-2:30pm); **Centro de Salud,** Av. Andalucía (☎956 44 76 25); **police** ☎956 45 04 00; and the **post office** at C. Juan Bueno, 22. (☎956 45 02 38. Open M-F 8:30am-2:30pm, Sa 9:30am-1pm.) **Postal code**: 11150.

ACCOMMODATIONS AND FOOD. The best places to stay in Vejer are in *casas particulares* (private houses). Two such *casas* are on C. San Filmo, up a stone staircase from Av. Los Remedios. The friendly Sra. Rosa Romero owns **Casa Los Cántaros,** C. San Filmo, 14, a beautifully restored Andalucían home with a grape-vined patio. The spotless suites have sitting rooms, antique furniture, private bathrooms, and kitchen access. (☎956 44 75 92. Doubles 2500-4000ptas/€15-24) Sra. Luisa Doncel keeps tidy little rooms with common bathrooms in **Calle San Filmo, 12.** If Doña Luisa is not at #12, try #16. (☎956 45 02 46. Singles 2000-

2500ptas/€12-15; doubles 2500-3500ptas/€15-21.) Where you stay may depend on which woman you meet first. The cheapest eats are *tapas* or *raciones* at the bars around the Plazuela. Renowned for its *jamón ibérico*, family-run **Mesón Pepe Julián,** C. Juan Relinque, 7, prepares the best tapas in town (100-200ptas/€0.60-1.20) and serves reasonably priced entrées (700-1500ptas/€4.20-9) in a warmly lit dining room. Open summer daily noon-4pm and 6:30pm-midnight, closed W in winter. MC/V. At peaceful **Bar El Cura,** Po. Cobijadas, 1, near the bottom of C. Juan Bueno, locals place bets on who can make the solemn owner laugh (or at least crack a smile). Enjoy the view around the corner while sipping *fino* (dry sherry) for a mere 75ptas/€0.45. (☎956 45 07 76. Open daily 7am-3pm and 5:30pm-late.)

SIGHTS. The best way to enjoy Vejer is by wandering along the labyrinthine streets and cliffside *paseos*, stopping occasionally for drinks or *tapas*. As for monuments, the **Castillo Moro,** down C. Ramón y Cajal from the church, offers the usual assortment of battlements and crenelated walls. (Open July-Aug. roughly M-Sa 11am-2pm and 6-9pm; Sept.-June M-Sa 10am-2pm. The gates open only when a Boy Scout troop is available to lead tours.) **Iglesia del Divino Salvador,** behind the tourist office, is a choice blend of Romanesque, Mudéjar, and Gothic styles (mass daily 8:30pm.) Ten kilometers from Vejer on the road to Los Caños lies **El Palmar,** 7km of fine white sand and clear waters easily accessible by car. Many beach-goers hitch rides at the bend of Av. Los Remedios or catch the bus to **Conil de la Frontera** and walk southeast along the beach for 3-4km. For information on the town and outdoor activities, consult **Discover Andalucía,** Av. Los Remedios, 45b. (☎956 44 75 75. Bikes from 2000ptas/€12 per day. Surfboards from 1000ptas/€6 per day. Open M-F 10:30am-2pm and 6-9pm, Sa 10:30am-2pm. AmEx/MC/V.)

NIGHTLIFE. Vejer's old quarter hops at night. Leave another little piece of your heart at **Bar Janis Joplin,** on C. Marqués de Tamarón, 6. Sit on plush wicker chairs and keep an eye out for Bobby McGee. (Open nightly 9:30pm-late.) Several popular pubs lie downhill from the Plazuela on C. Sagasta and C. Santísimo. From July to August, everyone dances among the thatched huts at *discoteca* **La Carpa** in Parque de Los Remedios, behind the bus stop. Stupendous terrace views make **Café-Bar El Arriate,** C. Corredera, 55 (☎956 44 71 70 or 45 13 05), a good place for a *copa* anytime. Vejer throws brilliant *fiestas*. Soon after the **Corpus Christi** revelry in June comes the **Candelas de San Juan** (June 23), climaxing with the midnight release of the *toro de fuego* (bull of fire) at midnight. A local (obviously one with a death wish) dressed in an iron bull costume charges the crowd as the firecrackers attached to his body fly off in all directions. The town demonstrates its creativity again during the delirious **Semana Santa** celebrations, when a *toro embolao* (sheathed bull), with wooden balls affixed to the tips of his horns, is set loose through the narrow streets of Vejer on the Sunday of the Resurrection. The good-natured **Feria de Primavera** (2 weeks after *Semana Santa*) is a bit tamer, with people dancing *sevillanas* and downing cupfuls of *fino* until sunrise.

TARIFA ☎956

When the wind picks up in Tarifa (pop. 15,000), the southernmost city in continental Europe, visitors can easily understand why it is known, even to locals, as the Hawaii of Spain. Shelter-seeking residents and tourists leave miles of white sandy beaches desolate but for the few, the proud—the windsurfers. You'll see more frame backpacks, stickered vans, Quicksilver attire, and Reefs than you could ever imagine. Still, there is more to Tarifa than just windsurfing—sandy beaches and an enchanting old city make for pleasant afternoon and evening walks.

TRANSPORTATION. Transportes Generales Comes buses roll in from C. Batalla del Salado, 19. (☎956 67 57 55. Open M-F 2:30-7pm, Sa-Su 3-8pm.) **Buses** run to: **Algeciras** (30min., 7-12 per day 6:30am-8:15pm, 245ptas/€1.47); **Cádiz** (2¼hr., 9 per day 7:25am-8:55pm, 1085ptas/€6.50); and **Sevilla** (3hr., 3 per day 7:55am-5:10pm,

2150ptas/€13). **Ferries** leave from the **FRS** at the port (☎956 68 18 30) for **Tangier** (35min.; M-Th and Sa 11:30am, 1:30pm, and 6pm; F 11:30am and 1:30pm; Su 9am, 11:30am, and 1pm; 3500ptas/€21, children 1750ptas/€10.50.) Prices and travel length for the return trip are the same, though the schedule is not. (M-Th and Sa 8am, 10:30am, and 5pm; F 8am, 10:30, and 6pm; Su 8am, 10:30am, 3pm, and 5pm.)

PRACTICAL INFORMATION. The **tourist office,** Po. Alameda, has good adventure sports information. From the bus station, exit toward the castle-shaped arch, follow C. Batalla del Salado for 2½ blocks, turn right before the arch on Av. Andalucía, and then left after the park onto tree-lined Alameda. The tourist office is the small glass building under the stairwell. (☎956 68 09 93 or 68 04 31. Open daily July 15-Aug. 10:30am-2pm and 6-8pm; Sept.-July 14 M-F 10am-2pm and 5-7pm.) Services include: **emergency** ☎091; **police,** Pl. Santa María (☎956 68 41 86); and **Centro de Salud** ☎956 68 15 15. Find **internet access** at **Planet,** C. Santísima Trinidad, 20. (10ptas/€0.06 per min. Open M-Sa 11am-3pm and 5pm-midnight, Su 5pm-12am.) The **post office,** C. Coronel Moscardó, 9, is near Pl. San Maleo. (☎956 68 42 37. Open M-F 8:30am-2:30pm, Sa 9:30am-1pm.) **Postal code:** 11380.

ACCOMMODATIONS AND FOOD. Affordable rooms line main C. Batalla del Salado. Prices rise significantly in summer; those visiting in Aug. should call ahead and arrive early. Comfortable **Hostal Villanueva,** Av. Andalucía, 11, features a rooftop terrace with an ocean view. (☎956 68 41 49. Singles 2500-3000ptas/€15-18; doubles 4500-6000ptas/€27-36.) The dining room downstairs serves speciality *paella* for 1100ptas/€6.60. (Open Tu-Su 1-4pm and 8-11pm.) Uphill, where Av. Andalucía becomes C. Amador de los Ríos, **Hostal El Asturian** keeps tiled rooms with full baths. A deluxe quad is part of the Arab castle adjoining the hostel. (☎956 68 06 19. Doubles 4000-8000ptas/€24-48; triples 7000-13,000ptas/€42-78; quads 15,000-18,000ptas/€90-108.) Official **campgrounds** lie a few kilometers west on the beach (600-700ptas/€3.60-4.20 per person); ask the bus driver to let you off. Serving a wide variety of *bocadillos* (500-600ptas/€3-3.60) and specialty drinks to locals and backpackers, **Café-Bar Central,** C. Sancho IV El Bravo, has one of the few wind-free *terrazas* in town (☎956 68 05 90. Open daily 9am-2am.) Up the street, **Ali-Baba,** C. Sancho IV El Bravo, 8, serves falafel and kebab (400-500ptas/€2.40-3) to go. (Open daily 1:30-4pm and 7pm-1am.)

SIGHTS AND ENTERTAINMENT. Next to the port and just outside the old town, stand the ruins of the **Castillo de Guzmán el Bueno.** In the 13th century, the Moors kidnapped Guzmán's son and threatened his life if Guzmán didn't relinquish the castle. Surprisingly, the father didn't surrender, even after his son's throat was slashed before his eyes. (Open daily 11am-2pm. 10am-2pm and 6-8pm. 300ptas/€1.80; free Su afternoon.) At night, sunburned travelers mellow out in the old town's many bars, which range from jazz to psychedelic to Irish. Follow the crowds as they bar-hop, or ask the young tourist office staff for tips on the latest *terrazas* and discos. Those with something more tranquil in mind can head 200m south to the **Playa Lances,** 5km of the finest white sand on the Atlantic coast. Bathers should be aware of the occasional high winds and a strong undertow. Adjacent to the Playa Lances on the Mediterranean, **Playa Chica** is smaller but more sheltered from the winds. **Tarifa Spin Out Surfbase** (☎956 23 63 52), 9km up the road toward Cádiz, rents windsurfing boards and instructs all levels, and many campgrounds and hotels along CN-340 between km 70 and km 80 provide instruction and gear for outdoor sports. Pick up a guide at the tourist office.

ALGECIRAS ☎956

Franco dreamt of transforming Algeciras into a burgeoning southern metropolis, one that would eclipse Gibraltar as the commercial center of the southwestern Mediterranean and force the Royal Army out of Iberia. Innumerable concrete wharfs and slapdash highrises remain, but so too, do the British. Hidden beyond

Algeciras's seedy port is a more serene old neighborhood, worthy of visiting for those with a few hours to spare. For most travelers, however, this is a city to be seen in transit. Gateway to Morocco, Algeciras also serves as an excellent base for daytrips to Tarifa and Gibraltar, each only a short (40min.) bus ride away.

TRANSPORTATION

Trains: RENFE (☎902 24 02 02), Ctra. Cádiz, down C. Juan de la Cierva. To: **Granada** (4hr., 3 per day 7am-4:25pm, 2465-2715ptas/€14-17); **Ronda** (1½hr., 4 per day 7am-6:25pm, 1020ptas/€6). Also to **Bobadilla** (1630ptas/€10), with connections to: **Córdoba** (5hr., 4 per day 11:25am-9:35pm, 2585-3400ptas/€15-21); **Madrid** (6hr., 4 per day 11:25-9:35, 5300-9500ptas/€31-57); **Málaga** (3½hr., noon and 3:55pm, 2100ptas/€13); **Sevilla** (6hr., 4 per day 7am-3:55pm, 3050-3200ptas/€18-19).

Buses: Buses depart from the separate addresses as indicated.

Empresa Portillo, Av. Virgen del Carmen, 15 (☎956 65 10 55). To: **Córdoba** (6hr., 3-4 per day 8am-3:15pm, 3030ptas/€18); **Granada** (5hr., 4 per day 10:30am-5pm, 2655ptas/€16); **Málaga** (1¾-3hr., 8-9 per day 8am-8pm, 1450ptas/€8.70); **Marbella** (1hr., 8-9 per day 8am-9pm, 805ptas/€4.85).

Transportes Generales Comes, C. San Bernardo, 1 (☎956 65 34 56), by Hotel Octavio. To: **Cádiz** (2½hr., 10 per day 7am-10:30pm, 1315ptas/€7.90); **La Línea,** for **Gibraltar** (45min., every 30min. 7am-9:30pm, 245ptas/€1.47); **Madrid** (8hr., 5 per day 8:10-9:45pm, 3530ptas/€21); **Sevilla** (4hr., 4 per day 7:30am-4:45pm, 2195ptas/€13); **Tarifa** (40min., 7-10 per day 7:05am-9pm, 240ptas/€1.44).

Empresa Bacoma, Av. Marina, 8 (☎956 66 50 67), left of Banco Zaragozano. To **Barcelona** (19hr., 7 per day 7am-11pm, 10,895ptas/€66).

Ferries: From the bus and train stations, follow C. San Bernardo to C. Juan de la Cierva, and turn left at its end; the port entrance will be on your right. Tickets are overpriced at the train station; book at a travel agency in town or at the port. Only **Trasmediterránea,** at the entrance of the port, offers Eurail discounts. *Embarcaciones rápidas* (fast ferries), depart for Ceuta, a Spanish enclave in North Africa; normal ferries leave for the Moroccan port of Tangier (see p. 674). Allow 30min. to clear customs and board, 90min. with a car. Summer ferries to **Ceuta** (35min., 18 per day 6:30am-10pm, 3400ptas/€21; under 12 1700ptas/€10.20; car 9800ptas/€59; motorcycle 3175ptas/€19) and **Tangier** (2½hr., 12 per day 6am-10pm, 3740ptas/€22; under 12 1870ptas/€11; car 11,540ptas/€69; motorcycle 3560ptas/€21; at Trasmediterránea, adult fare 2992ptas/€18 with Eurail pass.) Limited service in winter.

ORIENTATION AND PRACTICAL INFORMATION

Lined with travel agencies, banks, and hotels, **Av. de la Marina** runs along the coast, eventually turning into Av. Virgen del Carmen north of the port. **C. Juan de la Cierva** runs perpendicular to the coast from the port, becoming **C. San Bernardo** as it nears the **train** and **bus stations.** To reach the **tourist office** from either one, follow C. San Bernardo along the abandoned tracks toward the port, past a parking lot on the left. From the **port,** take a left onto Av. Virgen del Carmen, then a quick right onto C. Juan de la Cierva; the office is on the left. All services necessary for transit to Morocco cluster about the port, accessible by a single gate and driveway. Be wary of imposters peddling ferry tickets.

Tourist Office: (☎956 57 26 36; fax 57 04 75), C. Juan de la Cierva, in the tube-shaped, pink glass building. Provides maps (free for Algeciras, 100ptas/€0.60 for maps of other cities). Some English spoken. Open M-F 9am-2pm.

Currency Exchange: Banco Central Hispano, Av. Virgen del Carmen, 9-11. Changes travelers checks without commission. Open June-Aug. M-F 8:30am-2:30pm; Sept.-May M-F 8:30am-2:30pm, Sa 9am-1pm. For a daytrip to Tangier, buying **dirhams** may not be necessary; many places accept *pesetas* and you will not be able to convert them back to *pesetas.* For longer trips, change money in Morocco.

Luggage Storage: At **Empresa Portillo bus terminal,** lockers 400ptas/€2.40 per day. Open daily 7:40am-9:50pm. At **RENFE,** 400ptas/€2.40 per day. Open daily 5:30am-10:30pm. At the **port,** lockers 400ptas/€2.40. Open daily 7am-9:30pm.

Camping Gear: Adventura Sport, Ventura Morón, 5 (☎956 66 92 34), off Pl. Alta. Hiking boots, tents, sleeping bags, etc. Open June-Aug. M-F 10am-1:30pm and 5:30-9pm, Sa 10:30am-2pm; Sept.-May M-F 10am-1:30pm and 5:30-8:30pm, Sa 10:30am-2pm.

Emergency: ☎112. **Police: Local** C. Ruiz Zorilla, (☎956 66 01 55).

Medical Assistance: Ambulatorio Central, Pl. Menéndez Tolosa (☎956 66 19 56).

Post Office: Ruiz Zorilla, 42 (☎956 66 36 48). **Lista de Correos.** Open M-F 8:30am-2:30pm, Sa 9:30am-1pm. **Postal Code:** 11203.

ACCOMMODATIONS

Hostels line **C. José Santacana,** parallel to the seafront along Av. Marina and about a 10 min. walk from the bus and train stations. From either station, follow C. San Bernardo, turning left before the bush-lined median; take a right onto Av. Segismundo Moret and then take the 3rd left, C. José Santacana. Ask for back rooms—local teenagers cruise the narrow streets on Vespas at ungodly hours.

Hostal Rif, C. Rafael de Muro, 11 (☎956 65 49 53). Follow C. José Santacana into the small market square, bear left around the large kiosk and continue up C. Rafael del Muro for 1 block. In a restored 18th-century home with a palm-shaded patio. Backpackers share stories on the rooftop. Simple rooms with pastel walls and high ceilings. Communal showers. Info available on forays into Morocco. Laundry 700ptas/€4.20. Singles 1300ptas/€7.80; doubles 2600-2800ptas/€15.60-16.80; triples 4000ptas/€24.

Hostal Residencia González, C. José Santacana, 7 (☎956 65 28 43). Reasonably priced and close to the port. Rooms have cheerful blankets and oddly partitioned bathrooms. Run by a formidable matron. Singles 2000ptas/€12, with shower 2500ptas/€15; doubles 4000ptas/€24, with shower 4500ptas/€27; triples 6000ptas/€36, with bath 7500ptas/€45; quads 8000ptas/€48, with bath 10,000ptas/€60.

Hostal Residencia Versailles, C. Moutero Rios, 12 (☎/fax 956 65 42 11), off C. Cayetano del Toro. The Sun King might not have stayed here, but he would have been close to the bus station. Well-sized rooms, all with phones and baths, some with TVs. Singles with shower 2500ptas/€15; doubles with shower 3500-4000ptas/€21-24, with bath 5000ptas/€30; triples with shower 5500ptas/€33, with bath 6000ptas/€36.

FOOD

Outdoor cafés line C. Regino Martínez, Aleciras' main drag. Celebrate your return from Morocco with *pollo asado* (baked chicken) on Av. Virgen del Carmen, near the port, or C. Juan de la Cierva. There is a **supermarket** on the corner of C. José Santacana and C. Maroto. (Open daily 9am-2pm and 5-8pm.) The outdoor **market** at Pl. Palma is one block from Av. Virgen del Carmen. (Open M-Sa 8:30am-2pm.)

La Alegría, C. José Santacana, 6 (☎956 66 65 09). Whopping portions of Moroccan cooking. No written menu; choose from chicken, lamb, and vegetarian plates. Entrées 800ptas/€4.80. Open daily 9am-midnight.

La Buganvilla (☎930 55 05 25), C. García de la Torre. From the Banesto bank corner of Pl. Alta, head down C. Joaquín Costa and take an immediate left down an alley. The sign is obscured by branches; look for the purple door. Eclectic bar draws a young crowd. *Tapas* from 100ptas/€0.60. Open M-Sa 11am-4pm and 7pm-1am.

GIBRALTAR

Emerging from the morning mist, the Rock of Gibraltar craggy face menaces those who pass by its shores. Bastion of an empire, Jerusalem of Anglophilia, hangover of a bygone age, this 3mi. stretch of rock is among history's most contested plot of land.

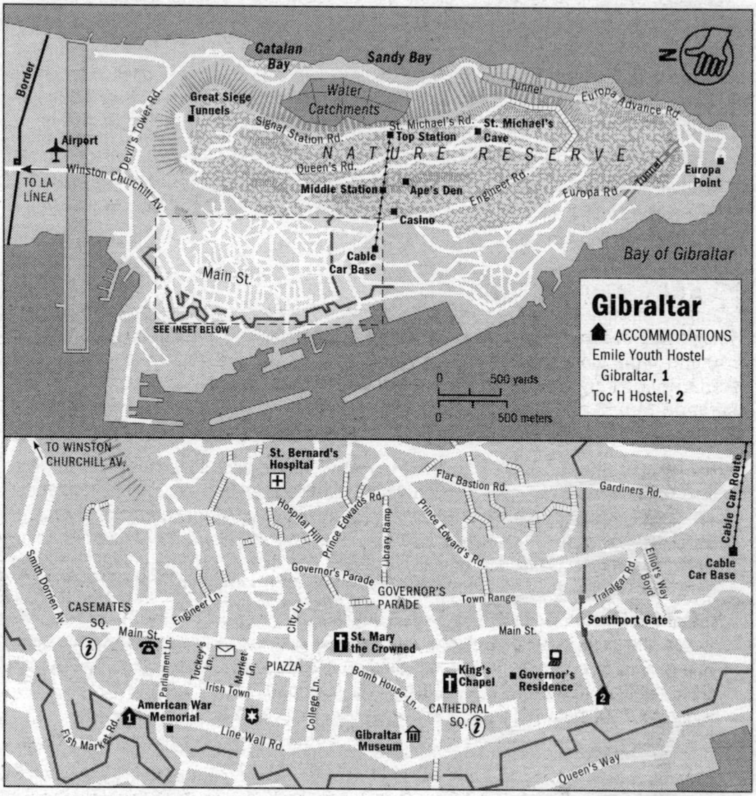

Gibraltar

ACCOMMODATIONS
Emile Youth Hostel Gibraltar, **1**
Toc H Hostel, **2**

Known affectionately to locals as "Gib," it is home to more fish 'n' chips plates and pints of bitter per capita than anywhere else in the Mediterranean. Ancient seafarers called the Rock of Gibraltar one of the Pillars of Hercules, believing that it marked the end of the world. Derived from *Gibel Tark* (Tarik Hall), in honor of the 8th-century Moorish king Tarik-Ibn-Zeyad, the term "Gibraltar" was not adopted until Islamic times. English troops stormed Gibraltar during the War of the Spanish Succession (1702-1713); in 1713, their advances were solidified under the Treaty of Utrecht. When a 1969 vote showed that Gibraltar's populace favored its colonial ties to Britain (a near-tie: 12,138 to 44), Franco sealed off the border. After 16 years of isolation and a decade of negotiations, the border re-opened on February 4, 1985. Tourists and residents now cross with ease, but Gibraltar remains culturally detached from Spain.

Although definitely worth visiting, Gibraltar is a tourist trap. Cross the border, spend a day exploring the Rock and stocking up on duty-fee liquor and tobacco, and then scurry back to Spain.

POUNDS, PESETAS, EUROS Although **pesetas** are accepted everywhere (except in pay phones), **the pound sterling (£)** is the preferred method of payment in Gibraltar. Merchants sometimes charge a higher price in *pesetas* than in the pound's exchange equivalent. Change is often given in English currency rather than Spanish. As of press date, **1£ = 264ptas = €1.58.**

TRANSPORTATION

Flights: Airport (☎730 26). **British Airways** (☎793 00) flies to **London** (2½hr., £100-200/€163-326) for those scared to set foot back in Spain.

Buses: From **La Línea,** on the Spanish border, to: **Algeciras** (40min., every 30min. 7:45am-10:15pm, 245ptas/€1.47); **Cádiz** (3hr., 5 per day 6:30am-8pm, 1565ptas/€9.39); **Granada** (5-6hr., 7:15am and 2:15pm, 2580ptas/€15.48); **Madrid** (7hr., 12:10pm and 10:15pm, 3435ptas/€20.61); **Málaga** (3¼hr., 4 per day 7:15am-5pm, 1325ptas/€7.95); **Marbella** (1¾hr., 4 per day 7:15am-5pm, 725ptas/€4.35); **Sevilla** (6hr., 3 per day 7am-4:15pm, 2755ptas/€16.53).

Ferries: Turner & Co., 5/67 Irish Town. (☎783 05; fax 720 06). To: **Tangier** (1¼hr.; M-Sa 8:30am, return M-Sa 1pm, Su 5pm; £15/€24.45, under 11 £9/€14.67).

Public Transport: Most bus lines run from one end of the Rock to the other. Buses #9 and 10 go between the border and the Rock for 40 pence or 100ptas/€0.60.

Taxis: ☎700 27.

ORIENTATION AND PRACTICAL INFORMATION

Buses from Spain terminate in the nearby town of **La Línea.** From the bus station, walk directly toward the Rock; the border is five minutes away. After bypassing the line of motorists, Spanish customs, and Gibraltar's passport control, catch bus #9 or 10 or walk across the airport tarmac (look both ways and hold hands) to the highway into town (20min.). Stay left on Av. Winston Churchill when the road forks with Corral Lane. Gibraltar's **Main Street,** a commercial strip lined with most services, begins at the far end of a square, past the Burger King on the left.

Tourist Office: (☎450 00; fax 749 43; tourism@gibraltar.gi), Duke of Kent House, Cathedral Square, across from Gibraltar Museum. Open M-F 9am-5:30pm. 2nd office (☎749 82), in Watergate House, Casemates Sq. Open M-F 9am-5:30pm, Sa-Su 10am-4pm.

American Express: Bland Travel (☎770 12), Irish Town St. Open M-F 9am-6pm.

Luggage Storage: Lockers at the bus station (400ptas/€2.40). Open daily 7am-10pm.

Bookstore: Gibraltar Bookshop, 300 Main St. (☎718 94). The best English bookstore on the Iberian Peninsula. Open M-F 10am-6:30pm, Sa 11:30am-2:30pm. AmEx/MC/V.

Emergency: ☎199. **Police:** 120 Irish Town St. (☎725 00).

Hospital: St. Bernard's Hospital on Hospital Hill, (☎797 00).

Telephone Code: From Britain (00) 350. From the US (011) 350. From Spain 9567.

Internet Access: At the **John McIntosh Hall Library,** 308 Main St., 2nd fl. 75 pence/€1.22 per 30min. Open M-F 9:30am-11pm.

Post Office: 104 Main St. (☎756 62). Possibly the world's easiest **Poste Restante** address: BOSCA, Carlo. Poste Restante, Gibraltar (Main Post Office). Open June-Aug. M-F 9am-2:15pm, Sa 10am-1pm; Sept.-May M-F 9am-4:30pm, Sa 10am-1pm.

ACCOMMODATIONS AND FOOD

Gibraltar is best done as a daytrip. The few accommodations in the area are often full, especially in the summer, and camping is illegal. At worst, you can crash across the border in **La Línea.** Back on the Rock, **Emile Youth Hostel Gibraltar,** Montague Boston, off Line Wall Rd., has cramped bunkbeds but clean communal bathrooms. (☎511 06. Breakfast included. Lock-out 10:30am-4:30pm. Dorms £12/€19; singles £15/€24; doubles £26/€42.) **Toc H Hostel,** Line Wall Rd., is a maze of plants. (☎734 31. Warm showers during the day. Singles £6/€9.75; doubles £12/€20.) International restaurants are easy to find, but you may choke on the prices. As a backup, there's the **Safeway** supermarket in the Europort complex. (Open 8am-8pm.)

SIGHT

THE ROCK OF GIBRALTAR

Top of the Rock Nature Reserve is accessible by car or cable car. Cable cars depart every 10min. M-Su 9:30am-5:15pm. It's possible to buy a ticket for only the cable car (£4/€6.50, children £2.30/€3.75), but if you plan on visiting any of sights highlighted below, it's better to buy a combined admittance ticket, including one-way cable car ride for £6/ €9.78, children £5/€8.15. The walk down takes an hour. Tickets sold until 5:15pm.

About halfway up the Rock is the infamous **Apes' Den,** where a colony of Barbary monkeys cavorts on the sides of rocks, the tops of taxis, and tourists' heads. These disturbingly tail-less monkeys have inhabited Gibraltar since the 18th century. When the ape population nearly went extinct in 1944, Churchill ordered reinforcements from North Africa; now they are proliferating at such at rate that population control has become an issue. At the northern tip of the Rock, facing Spain, are the **Great Siege Tunnels.** Originally used to fend off a combined Franco-Spanish siege at the end of the American Revolution, the tunnels were later expanded during World War II to span 33 miles underground. The eerie chambers of **St. Michael's Cave,** located ½km opposite the siege tunnels, were cut into the rock by thousands of years of water erosion. At the southern tip of Gibraltar, guarded by three machine guns and a lighthouse, **Europa Point** commands a view of the straits. Nearby the **Ibrahim-Al-Mosque,** Europe's largest, and the **Shrine of Our Lady of Europe** face each other in pluralistic harmony. (Take bus #3 or 1B from Line Wall Rd., just off Main St., all the way to the end. Departs every 15min., 40 pence/€0.65)

COSTA DEL SOL

The coast has sold its soul to the Devil and now he's starting to collect. Artifice covers its once-natural charms as chic promenades and swanky hotels burgeon between small towns and the shoreline. The Costa del Sol officially extends from Tarifa in the southwest to Cabo de Gata, east of Almería; post-industrial Málaga lies smack in the middle. To the northeast, costal hills dip straight into the ocean, where rocky beaches have helped to preserve some of the shore's natural beauty. To the southwest, waves seem to wash up onto more concrete than sand. That said, nothing can take away from the coast's major attraction: eight months of spring and four months of summer. News of Costa del Sol's fantastic weather has spread far and wide, and July and August bring swarms of pale-skinned Brits and thick-walleted German tourists. Make reservations days in advance to avoid having to sleep on the beach (not recommended for solo travelers and women). Alternatively, ask around for *casas particulares*. June is the best time to visit, when summer has already hit the beach but tourists haven't. Private bus lines offer connections along the coast itself—trains only go as far as Málaga and Fuengirola. Railpasses are not valid on the Costa del Sol, but train prices are reasonable.

MÁLAGA ☎952

Once celebrated by the likes of Hans Christian Andersen, Málaga (pop. 531,140) has since lost much of its charm. In the hundred years since Andersen and other Romantics discovered the city, 19th-century villas have been replaced by 70s high-rises, and the beach is better known for its bars than sand. The second-largest city in Andalucía and a critical transportation hub for the province, Málaga has all the requisite historical monuments—fortress, cathedral, bullring—but they are best seen in passing, en route to more enjoyable coastal stops.

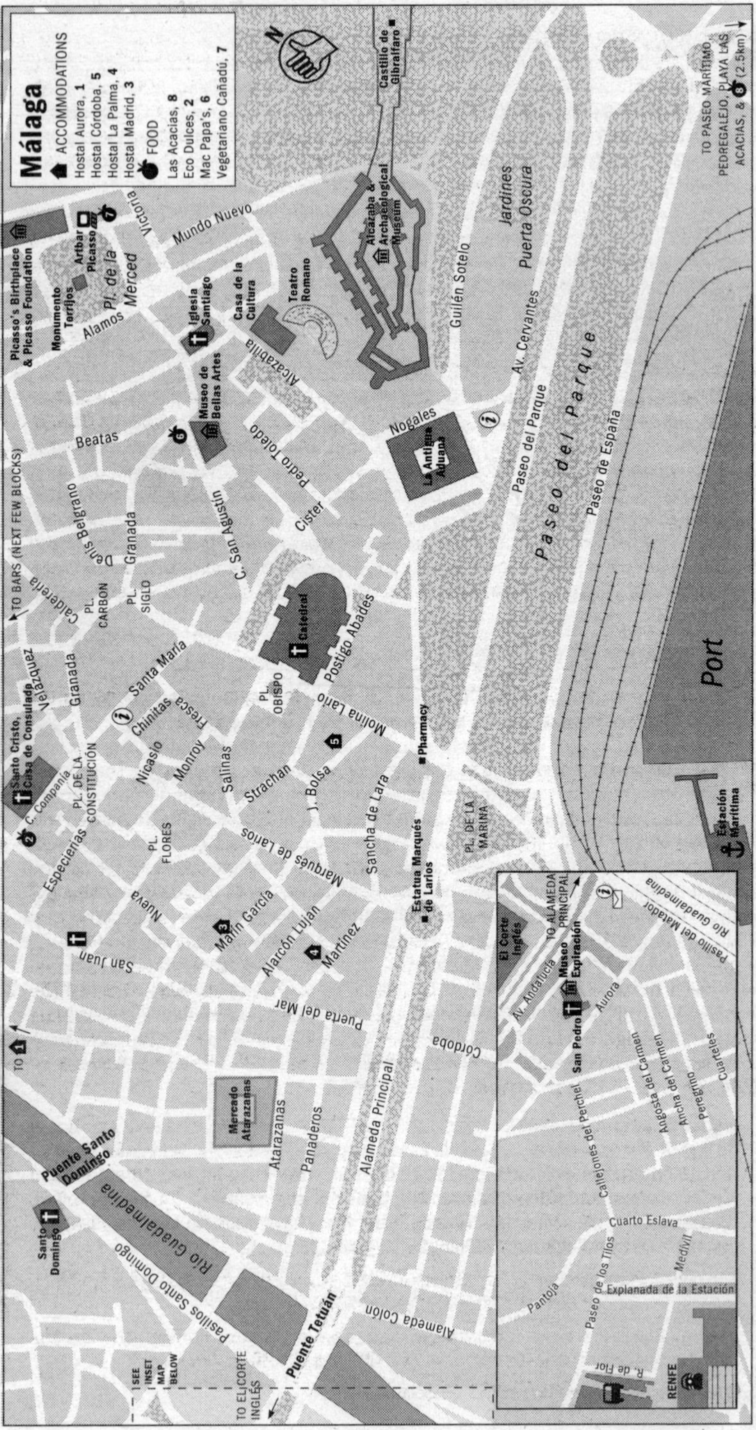

Málaga

ACCOMMODATIONS
Hostal Aurora, 1
Hostal Córdoba, 5
Hostal La Palma, 4
Hostal Madrid, 3

FOOD
Las Acacias, 8
Eco Dulces, 2
Mac Papa's, 6
Vegetariano Cañadú, 7

Picasso's Birthplace & Picasso Foundation
Monumento Torrijos
Artbar Picasso
Pl. de la Merced
Victoria
Mundo Nuevo
Alamos
Iglesia Santiago
Casa de la Cultura
Teatro Romano
Alcazaba & Archaeological Museum
Castillo de Gibralfaro
Museo de Bellas Artes
Alcazabilla
Beatas
Pedro Toledo
Nogales
La Antigua Aduana
Guilén Sotelo
Jardines Puerta Oscura
Av. Cervantes
Paseo del Parque
Paseo de España
TO BARS (NEXT FEW BLOCKS)
Denis Belgrano
Granada
Calderería
PL. CARBON
PL. SIGLO
C. San Agustín
Cister
Catedral
Postigo Abades
Santo Cristo, Casa de Consulado
Velázquez
Santa María
Chinitas
Fresca
PL. OBISPO
Molina Larío
Pharmacy
PL. DE LA CONSTITUCIÓN
C. Compañía
Nicasio
Monroy
Salinas
Strachan
J. Bolsa
Sancha de Lara
Estatua Marqués de Larios
PL. DE LA MARINA
Port
Estación Marítima
TO PASEO MARÍTIMO PEDREGALEJO, PLAYA LAS ACACIAS, & 8 (2.5km)
Especierías
PL. FLORES
Marqués de Larios
Nueva
Marín García
Alarcón Luján
Martínez
San Juan
Puerta del Mar
Córdoba
TO 1
Mercado Atarazanas
Atarazanas
Panaderos
Alameda Principal
Puente Santo Domingo
Santo Domingo
Río Guadalmedina
Pasillos Santo Domingo
Puente Tetuán
Alameda Colón
SEE INSET MAP BELOW
TO EL CORTE INGLÉS
El Corte Inglés
TO ALAMEDA PRINCIPAL
Av. Andalucía
Museo Expiración
San Pedro
Aurora
Pasillo del Matador
Río Guadalmedina
Callejones del Perchel
Angosta del Carmen
Ancha del Carmen
Peregrino
Cuarteles
Cuarto Eslava
Medivil
Paseo de los Tilos
Pantoja
Explanada de la Estación
R. de Flor
RENFE

TRANSPORTATION

Flights: (☎952 04 88 04). From the airport, bus #19 (every 30min., 200ptas/€1.20) runs from the City Bus sign stopping at the bus station and the corner of C. Molina Lario and Postigo de los Abades behind the cathedral. RENFE's train connecting the city and the airport is cheaper (135ptas/€0.81) and quicker (12min.). **Iberia,** C. Molina Larios, 13 (☎952 13 61 66; 24hr. reservations 902 400 500).

Trains: Estación de Málaga, Esplanada de la Estación (☎952 36 02 02). Take bus #3 at Po. Parque or #4 at Pl. Marina to the station. **RENFE** office, C. Strachan, 4 (☎902 24 02 02), off C. Molina Lario. To: **Barcelona** (13hr., 7:05am and 9pm, 6500-8000ptas/ €39-48); **Córdoba** (2hr., 11 per day 6:45am-9pm, 2000-3000ptas/€12-18); **Fuengirola** (30min., every 30min. 5:45am-10:30pm, 335ptas/€2); **Madrid** (5hr., 5 per day 9am-6pm, 8400ptas/€50); **Sevilla** (3hr., 6 per day 7:45am-8:08pm, 2175ptas/€13); **Torremolinos** (20min., every 30min. 5:45am-10:30pm, 165ptas/€1).

Buses: Po. Tilos (☎95 235 00 61), 1 block from the RENFE station along C. Roger de Flor. To: **Algeciras** (3hr., 17 per day 5am-9:45pm, 1400-1450ptas/€8.40-8.70); **Alicante** (8hr., 5 per day 8:30am-midnight, 4700ptas/€28); **Antequera** (1hr., 12-14 per day 7am-8:45pm, 600ptas/€3.60); **Cádiz** (5hr., 3 per day 7:30am-3:30pm, 2765ptas/€17); **Córdoba** (3hr., 5 per day 9am-7pm, 1630ptas/€9.75); **Fuengirola** (30min., every 40min., 325ptas/€1.95); **Granada** (2hr., 16 per day 7am-9pm, 1255ptas/€7.55); **La Línea** (3hr., 4per day 7am-5pm, 1325ptas/€7.95); **Madrid** (7hr., 10 per day 8:30am-1am, 2770ptas/€17); **Marbella** (1½hr., every hr. 7am-8:45pm, 700ptas/€4.20); **Murcia** (6hr., 5 per day 8:30am-midnight, 3950ptas/€24); **Nerja** (1hr., every hr. 7am-9:30pm, 500ptas/€3); **Ronda** (3hr., 4 per day 8:15am-5:15pm, 1275ptas/€7.65); **Sevilla** (3hr., 6-10 per day 7am-3am, 2030ptas/€12); **Torremolinos** (20min., every 15min. 6:15am-9:15pm, 155ptas/€0.95).

Taxis: Radio-Taxi (☎952 32 00 00 or 33 33 33). A taxi from the town center to the waterfront costs 950ptas/€5.70 and to the airport 1400ptas/€8.40.

ORIENTATION AND PRACTICAL INFORMATION

The bus and train station lie a block away from each other along C. Roger de Flor. To get to the town center from the **bus station** (20min.), exit right onto C. Perchel, walk straight through the big intersection with Av. Aurora, take a right on Av. Andalucía, and cross the bridge, Puente Tetuán. From here, **Alameda Principal** leads into **Plaza de la Marina.** Or take bus #4 or #21 along the same route (130ptas/ €0.78). From Pl. Marina, C. Molina Lario leads to the **cathedral** and the old town. C. Marqués de Larios connects Pl. Marina to **Plaza de la Constitución,** while Po. Parque leads past the **Alcazaba.** Farther on, seaside Po. Marítimo stretches toward the lively beachfront district **El Pedregalejo** (bus #11 or a 40min. walk). After dark, be wary of the neighborhoods of **Alameda de Colón, El Perchel** (toward the river from the train and bus stations), **Cruz del Molinillo** (near the market), and **La Esperanza/ Santo Domingo** (up the river from El Corte Inglés).

Tourist Offices: Municipal, Av. Cervantes, 1 (☎/fax 952 60 44 10), a little gray house along Po. Parque. Also has a kiosk in front of the post office on Av. Andalucía. Open M-F 8:15am-2:45pm and 4:30-7pm, Sa 9:30am-2:30pm; Oct.-May Sa 9:30am-1:30pm and 4:30-7pm. **Junta de Andalucía,** Pasaje de Chinitas, 4 (☎952 21 34 45), off Pl. Constitución at the corner of C. Nicasio. Enter the alley through the arch and take the 1st right. Open M-F 8:30am-8:30pm, Sa-Su 10am-2pm.

Currency Exchange: Banco Español de Crédito, Alameda Principal, 8 (☎952 21 15 41), at the intersection with Pta. Mar. Open M-F 8:30am-2pm.

Luggage Storage: Lockers at the **train station** (open daily 7am-10:45pm) and **bus station** (open daily 6:30am-11pm). Both 300-600ptas/€1.80-3.60 per day.

Emergency: ☎112. **Police:** ☎952 12 65 00.

Foreign Language Bookstore: Rayuela Idiomas, Pl. de la Merced, 17 (☎952 22 48 10). A wide range of classic literature and contemporary novels. The best foreign bookstore within 100km. Open M-F 9:30am-2pm and 4:30-7pm, Sa 10am-2pm.

Pharmacy: Farmacia y Laboratorio Laza, C. Molina Lario, 2 (☎952 22 75 97). Open M-F 9:30am-1:30pm and 5-8:30pm, Sa 10:30am-1:30pm.

Medical Services: ☎952 30 30 34. **Medical Emergency:** ☎061.

Internet Access: Artbar Picasso, Pl. de la Merced, 20 (☎952 22 62 41). 100ptas/€0.60 per 30min. Student discounts. Open daily 11am-4am.

Post Office: Av. Andalucía, 1 (☎952 35 90 08), just over the Puente Tetuán. **Lista de Correos.** Open M-F 8:30am-8:30pm, Sa 9:30am-2pm. **Postal Code:** 29080.

ACCOMMODATIONS

Most budget establishments are in the old town, between Pl. Marina and Pl. Constitución. Try bargaining if prices seem too much (above 3000ptas/€18 for a single, 4700ptas/€28.20 for a double); excluding August, the market is usually slow.

Hostal La Palma, C. Martínez, 7 (☎952 22 67 72), off C. Marqués de Larios. Spotless, with a great family atmosphere. Downstairs rooms share communal baths; upstairs doubles are brand new with A/C, mini-terraces, and private baths. Singles 2000-3000ptas/€12-18; doubles 4000-6500ptas/€24-39; triples 4500-7000ptas/€27-42.

Hostal Córdoba, C. Bolsa, 11 (☎952 21 44 69), off C. Molina Lario. Decently-sized rooms with antique furniture surround a patio filled with clothes-lines. Spotless common bathrooms. Singles 2000ptas/€12; doubles 4000ptas/€24; triples 6000ptas/€36.

Hostal Madrid, C. Marín García, 4 (952 22 43 92), on a quiet street off C. Nueva. Black leather sofas and framed pastoral vistas fill the lobby. Unadorned rooms with common bathrooms. Singles 2000-3000ptas/€12-18; doubles 3000-4000ptas/€18-24.

Hostal Aurora, Muro de Puerta Nueva, 1 (☎95 222 40 04), 5min. from Pl. Constitución, away from the busiest areas. Not to be confused with Hostal Aurora II, which is run by the owner's son. Rooms in this quiet home are cool, airy, and clean. Shared bath. Singles 4000ptas/€24; doubles 6500ptas/€39.

FOOD

Along Po. Marítimo in **El Pedregalejo,** beachfront restaurants specialize in fresh seafood. For a cheap snack, grab some sardines roasted over an open flame (usually in old rowboats) on the beach. The eateries around C. Granada near Pl. Constitución specialize in land creatures. Fresh produce fills the **market** on C. Afaranzas (open daily 8am-2pm), and you can buy groceries at **El Corte Inglés.**

Vegetariano Cañadú, Pl. de la Merced, 21 (☎952 22 90 56). A huge variety of hearty meatless fare. Entrées 700-1000ptas/€4.20-6. Open Su-Th 1:30-4pm and 8-11pm, F-Sa 1:30-4pm and 8pm-midnight. AmEx/MC/V.

La Acacias, Playa Las Acacias (☎952 29 89 46), El Pedregalejo. Frantic waiters, cheap food, and gusty sea breezes make this one of the liveliest eateries on the waterfront. Entrées 600-1200ptas/€3.60-7.20. Open daily 7pm-1am. AmEx/MC/V.

Mac Papa's, C. San Augustín, 23, at the intersection with C. Granada. Savor a delicious grilled sandwich by moonlight in one of Málaga's more picturesque neighborhoods. Outdoor seating. Sandwiches 300-450ptas/€1.80-2.70. Open daily 6pm-2am.

Eco Dulces, C. Compañía (☎952 22 77 94). A perfect stop for breakfast, picnics, afternoon snacks, or a simple repose from seafood. *Bocadillos* 175ptas/€1.05. Desserts 70-130ptas/€0.42-0.78. Open M-Sa 8:30am-2pm and 5-9pm.

SIGHTS

ALCAZABA. Featuring 10 impressive towers inside its walls, the Alcazaba is Málaga's most imposing sight. Guarding the east end of Po. Parque, this 11th-century structure was originally built as a fortified palace for Moorish kings. Perched above a highway tunnel, it now protects the ruins of a Roman theater and a **museum** of Moroccan art. There's an incredible view of the harbor from the ramparts. *(Open Tu-Su 9:30am-8pm. Free.)*

PICASSO FOUNDATION. Picasso may have high-tailed it out of Málaga when he was quite young, but according to local officials, he always "felt himself to be a true *malagueño.*" The painter's birthplace now houses the Picasso Foundation, which organizes a series of exhibitions, concerts, and lectures throughout the year. *(Pl. Merced. ☎952 21 50 05. Open M-Sa 11am-2pm and 5-8pm, Su 11am-2pm. Free.)*

CASTILLO DE GIBRALFARO. An Arab lighthouse was built in this Phoenician castle, which offers sweeping views of Málaga and the Mediterranean. Exploring the grounds alone can be dangerous. *(Buses to Castillo leave every hr. from the plaza below; otherwise it's an uphill hike. Open daily 9:30am-8pm.)*

CATHEDRAL. Málaga's cathedral is a blend of Gothic, Renaissance, and Baroque styles. The cathedral's second tower, under construction from the 16th to 19th century, was never completed—hence the cathedral's nickname *La Manquita* (One-Armed Lady). The organs date from 1781. *(C. Molina Larios. ☎952 21 59 17. Open M-Sa 10am-6:45pm. 300ptas/€1.50.)*

MUSEO DE BELLAS ARTES. The local fine arts museum, newly reopened in the Palacio Buenavista. Collections include Renaissance religious works, and a wing devoted to Picasso. *(C. Alcazabilla, 2. Open Tu 3-8pm, W-F 9am-8pm, Sa-Su 9am-3pm.)*

NIGHTLIFE

In summer, young *malagueños* crowd the boardwalk bars in El Pedregalejo. The **Nocturno 1 bus** takes over the Pedragalejo line nightly from 12:45 to 5:45am (every hr.). **La Tortuga,** El Pedregalejo, redefines "international relations" as Spanish-language students practice their lessons over mixed drinks and beer. (Drinks 400-1000ptas/€2.40-6. Open daily 10pm.) An older crowd drinks *copas* on C. Bolivia and a few blocks up from the beach. Stop by **Donde Bolivia 41,** C. Bolivia, 97, to mellow out among shrubbery, and pillows. On weekends, crowds invade the bars in the area between C. Comedias and C. Granada, which leads out of Pl. Constitución. **O'Neill's,** C. Luis de Velázquez, 3 (☎952 60 14 60), has dark wooden decor, pints of Guinness (550ptas/€3.30), and bartenders imported from the Emerald Isle.

DAYTRIP FROM MÁLAGA

TORREMOLINOS

Portillo Buses (☎95 238 24 19) and C-1 local trains (☎95 238 57 64) connect Torremolinos to Málaga, Fuengirola, and other destinations.

Cast from concrete and steel in the late 1950s, modern-day Torremolinos holds the dubious distinction of being the Costa del Sol's oldest package-holiday destination. English is spoken everywhere; the only trace of Spain is the pottery and lace spilling from souvenir shops. By day, visitors bask in the sun on wide, sandy beaches; by night they wander along **Av. Palma de Mallorca,** the main thoroughfare, or join the hordes that fill the countless bars and discos below the town center, along **Playa de La Carihuela** and **Playa de Bajondillo.** Exit the **train station** and turn right onto Av. Palma de Mallorca; 50 meters to the right is the pedestrian C. San Miguel. To reach the beach, turn right onto C. Stos. Arcángeles and take another quick right on Camino de la Playa. From the **bus station,** exit to the right and follow

C. Hoyo to Pl. Costa del Sol and Av. Palma de Mallorca; C. San Miguel is on the left. The **tourist office** is on Pl. Pablo Ruiz Picasso, uphill from Av. Palma de Mallorca. The staff speaks English, German, and French. (☎95 237 11 59. Open daily 9:30am-2:30pm.) Hostels in Torremolinos tend to get lost amid towering hotels and apartment complexes; look on Cuesta de Tajo and streets off Pl. Costa del Sol. Prices surge in August. A few doors down from the post office, **Hostal La Palmera,** Av. Palma de Mallorca, 37, has breezy rooms, some with views of the sea. Serge, the trilingual (French, Spanish, English) owner, will regale you with tales of his RV travels across Canada and the US. (☎95 237 65 09. Breakfast 350ptas/€2.10. Reservations suggested. All rooms with shower and sink. Singles 3500-4000ptas/€21-24; doubles 4000-5000ptas/€24-30; triples 6000-7000ptas/€36-42.)

MARBELLA ☎95

Like your vacation spots shaken, not shtirred? Scottish smoothie Sean Connery and a host of other jet-setters choose Marbella (pop. 100,000) for a vacation home. While there may be more yachts here than hostels, it's possible to visit on a budget. The controversial mayor, a self-proclaimed Franco enthusiast, has "cleaned up" many of the town's "marginal" elements (drug dealers, prostitutes, dogs, fellow politicians, etc.); best come visit before he sets his sights on backpackers.

TRANSPORTATION

Buses: Av. Trapiche, (☎95 276 44 00). To: **Algeciras** (1½hr., 9 per day 6:10am-8:30pm, 825ptas/€4.95); **Cádiz** (4hr., 6 per day 7:30am-8:45pm, 2140ptas/€13); **Fuengirola** (1hr., every 35min. 6:45am-10:30pm, 320ptas/€1.95); **Granada** (4hr., 7 per day 8:30am-6:55pm, 1895ptas/€11.35); **Madrid** (7½hr., 10 per day 7:30am-11:30pm, 3060ptas/€18); **Málaga** (1½hr., every 30min. 7am-8:45pm, 670ptas/€4); **Ronda** (1½hr., 8 per day 8:30am-8:55pm, 640ptas/€3.85); **Sevilla** (4hr., 3 per day, 2065ptas/€12.39).

Taxis: Radio Taxi ☎95 277 44 88, with service to Marbella center and Puerto Banús.

ORIENTATION AND PRACTICAL INFORMATION

Marbella, 56km south of Málaga, can only be reached by bus. The **bus station** surveys the sea from atop Av. Trapiche. To reach the main strip, exit the train station and walk left, make the first right onto Av. Trapiche, and turn right at the end of the road onto C. Salvador. Continue downhill on Av. del Mercado and turn left on C. Castillejos, which leads to the perpendicular Av. Ramón y Cajal. This becomes Av. Ricardo Soriano on the way to the super-swanky harbor of **Puerto Banús.** C. Peral curves up from Av. Ramón y Cajal around the **casco antiguo.**

Tourist Office: Pl. Naranjos (☎95 282 35 50), in the old town. From C. Castillejos, pass through Pl. Victoria and follow C. Estación into Pl. Naranjos. **Second office** is located at C. Glorieta de la Fontanilla (☎95 277 14 42). English spoken. Both open June-Aug. M-F 9.30am-9pm; Sept.-May M-F 9:30am-8pm, Sa 10am-2pm.

Currency Exchange: Banco Central Hispano, Av. Ramón y Cajal, 9 (☎95 277 08 92). Good exchange rates. Open June-Sept. M-F 8:30am-2:30pm; Oct.-May M-F 8:30am-2:30pm, Sa 8:30am-1pm. **ATMs** abound, especially near the *casco antiguo.*

Luggage Storage: At the **bus station** (400ptas/€2.40). Open daily 6:30am-11:30pm.

Emergency: ☎112. **Police:** Pl. Naranjos, 1 (☎95 282 24 94).

Medical Emergency: ☎092. **Hospital: Comarcal,** CN-340, km187 (☎95 286 27 48).

Pharmacy: Farmacia Espejo, Pl. Naranjos, 4 (☎95 277 12 99). Open M-F 9:30am-2pm and 5:30-9:30pm (in the winter, same morning hours, but open 4-8:30pm).

Internet Access: Neotel Locutorios, Pl. Puente de Ronda, 6 (☎655 54 73 11, fax 952 82 43 21), 100ptas/€0.60 per 10min. Open daily 10am-2pm and 4pm-midnight. MC/V.

Cibercafé, C. Miguel Cano, 6, 2nd fl. (☎952 90 00 13). 850ptas/€5.10 per hr., students 700ptas/€4.20 per hr. Open daily 10am-midnight.

Post Office: C. Jacinto Benavente, 26 (☎95 277 28 98), uphill from C. Ricardo Soriano. Open M-F 8:30am-2:30pm, Sa 9:30am-1pm. **Postal Code:** 29600.

ACCOMMODATIONS AND CAMPING

If you are reservationless, especially from June through September, arrive early and pray for a miracle. The area around **Pl. Naranjos** is loaded with hostels.

Hostal del Pilar, C. Mesoncillo, 4 (☎95 282 99 36), off C. Peral. Run by an accommodating Scotsman, this 17th-century inn is a Hogarthian haven for backpackers. Crackling fires warm the downstairs bar during winter. Immaculate white-walled rooms. Hearty English breakfast 800ptas/€4.80. Rooms 2000ptas/€12 per person, July-Aug. 3000ptas/€18 per person; roof mattresses available in the summer 2000ptas/€12.

Albergue Juvenil (HI), Av. Trapiche, 2 (☎95 277 14 91; fax 286 32 27). Exit left from the bus station, cross the highway and follow Av. del Trapiche for ½km. Like a proper hotel, only affordable. Facilities include a large pool, garden, TV room, and basketball court. Doubles and quads, many with private bathrooms. 2050ptas/€12.30 per person; over 26 2675ptas/€16.05. 500ptas/€3 fee for non HI-members. MC/V.

El Castillo, Pl. San Bernabé, 2 (☎95 277 17 39, fax 282 11 98), in the *casco antiguo*, a few blocks uphill from Pl. Naranjos. Older guests enjoy the medieval decor. Faded prints adorn patio walls. Sunny rooms with high ceilings and spacious baths. Singles 2000-35000ptas/€12-21; doubles 4000-5500ptas/€24-33. MC/V.

Princesa, C. Princesa (☎95 282 00 49). Chivalrous owner addresses his lodgers with courtly deference. Smaller than but similar to Aduar, with a rose-lined courtyard and pleasant, bright white rooms. Common baths. Doubles 4000-4500ptas/€24-27.

Pensión Aduar, C. Aduar, 7 (☎95 277 35 78). A courtyard brimming with flowers reflects sunlight into the well-kept rooms. Hot water can be sporadic in the ground level common bath; try upstairs if you find yourself shivering. Singles 2300-3000ptas/€13.80-18; doubles 3300-4000ptas/€19.80-24; triples 4500-6000ptas/€27-36.

Camping Marbella Playa (☎95 283 39 98), 2km east on N-340, on the Marbella-Fuengirola bus line; ask the bus driver to stop at the campground. 340-630ptas/€2.04-3.78 per person, 570-1050ptas/€3.42-6.30 per tent. Open year-round.

FOOD

The *terrazas* filling Pl. Naranjos are not particularly budget-friendly—the multilingual menu spells tourist trap. Restaurants farther uphill are less picturesque but easier on the wallet. Locals retreat to Av. Nabeul for cheap eats while seaside **Av. Miguel Cano** and **Av. Pta. Mar** host more lively bars and cafés. The municipal **market** is on Av. Mercado, uphill from C. Peral. (Open M-Sa 8am-2pm.) The **24-hr. minimarket** at the corner of C. Pablo Casals and Av. Fontanilla is a beacon in the night.

El Gallo, C. Lombatos, 44 (☎952 82 79 98). A perennial favorite with backpackers; serves up tasty meals for next to nothing. Ultra-cheap *tapas* (from 100ptas/€0.60). Battered chicken with fries (600ptas/€3.60). Open daily except Th, 8am-midnight.

Bar Avenida, Av. Miguel Cano, 11 (☎952 86 23 73). The freshest seafood at market prices. This local dive is an untainted relic of Marbella's fishing village days. *Raciones* 600-1200ptas/€3.60-7.20. Open daily noon-midnight. MC/V.

Pizzería Mama Rosa, Po. Marítimo (☎952 82 00 11), at Av. Miguel Cano. Pizza and pasta served alongside a popular beachfront promenade. An echelon of tightly-clad waitresses fill in for the matronly namesake. Pizza 775-1100ptas/€4.65-6.60, pasta 900-1500ptas/€5.40-9. Open daily noon-1am. MC/V.

Picobello, C. Miguel Cano (☎952 86 19 93), 2 blocks from the beach. Offering an affordable selection of pastries, cheeses, and sandwiches. A good choice for breakfast or lunch. Teas 200ptas/€1.20. Coffee 140ptas/€0.84. Open daily 8am-11pm.

SIGHTS

Although most visitors come to Marbella for the year's 320 days of sunshine, no visit to the city would be complete without a stroll through the **casco antiguo,** a maze of cobbled streets and white-washed façades trimmed with wild roses. The **Museo del Grabado Español Contemporáneo,** C. Hospital Bazán (☎952 82 50 35), in a restored hospital for the poor, is a treasure-trove of engravings by Miró, Picasso, Dalí, Goya, and contemporary artists. (Open Oct.-May M-F 10:15am-2pm and 5:30-8:30pm; June-Sept. Tu-Sa 10am-2pm and 6-8pm, 300ptas/€1.80.) To the northeast is the **Parque Arroyo de la Represa,** site of the **Museo del Bonsai.** (☎95 286 29 26. Open daily 10am-1:30pm and 4-7:30pm. 500ptas/€3, under 12 200ptas/€1.20.)

NIGHTLIFE

Nightlife in Marbella begins and ends late. The rowdiest corner of the *casco antiguo* is where C. Mesoncillo meets C. Peral. Loud music and cheery Spaniards spill from **El Güerto,** C. Peral, 9, and **The Tavern,** C. Peral, 7. (Both open at 8:30pm; El Güerto closed Th.) A mellower ambience suffuses the **Townhouse Bar,** C. Alamo, tucked down an alley off C. Nueva, downhill from Pl. Naranjos. (Open daily at 10pm.) Ask for a shot of apple pie; it ain't mama's. At cavernous **Kashmir,** C. Rafina, 8, off C. Aduar, a young international crowd gathers to hear the latest funk and house. (Open daily at 11pm). On the way to the beach, the suggestively decorated **Bar Incognito,** Av. Miguel Cano, 15, serves women half-priced beer and wine from 8pm until midnight. Between the beach and the *casco antiguo*, C. Puerta del Mar is home to several gay bars, including **Ojo,** C. Puerta del Mar, 9 (open daily at 11pm), and the younger **Bocaccio,** C. Puerta del Mar, 17 (opens at 10pm).

While the *casco antiguo* gets crowded on weekends, the elite scene at **Puerto Banús** is hopping all week long. The bars and clubs lining the yacht port and C. Ribera are hard to miss. Buses run there on the hour all night from Av. Ricardo Soriano (destination San Pedro, 145ptas/€0.87). Taxis from Marbella (1400ptas/€8.40) stop near the port's most popular celebrity-sighting hangout, **Sinatra Bar.** (Mixed drinks 700-1200ptas/€4.20-7.20. Open daily 11pm.) Around 4am, the action shifts to the clubs: **Comedia,** (terrace-level, C. Ribera) draws a younger crowd, and **Flicks Bar,** further down C. Ribera, rocks until dawn. (Cover for men 2000ptas/€12.)

BEACHES

City buses along Av. Richard Soriano (destination San Pedro or Hipercor, 145ptas/€0.87) bring you to chic and trendy **Puerto Banús** where beautifully clean beaches are buffered by imposing white yachts and row upon row of boutiques and fancy restaurants. On exceptionally clear days, the Moroccan coast is barely visible. The port has been frequented by the likes of Sean Connery, King Fahd of Saudi Arabia (who built a palace modeled on the White House), Antonio Banderas, and even the late Princess Diana; throngs of Euro-chicks mill about the marina, in search of well-banked husbands. With 22km of **beach,** Marbella offers a variety of settings, from its chic promenade to **Playa de las Chapas,** 10km east via the Fuengirola bus. **Funny Beach,** a 10min. bus ride, is a paradise of beach games, including jet-skiing and volleyball. Because of the mountains nearby, Marbella's winter temperatures tend to be 5-8°F warmer than Málaga's, and beach season lasts at least 10 months.

NERJA ☎952

Renowned for its beaches and caves, Nerja (pop. 15,000) offers all the comforts and clutter of a coastal resort town. Spectacular beaches are crowded with bikini-clad tourists and flip-flopped Anglophones. At the **Balcón de Europa,** hordes gather to catch a glimpse of one of the Costa del Sol's most stunning ocean views.

PRACTICAL INFORMATION. The **bus station,** C. San Miguel, 3 (☎952 52 15 04), sends buses to: **Almería** (4hr., 6 per day 8am-7:50pm, 1530ptas/€9.18); **Almuñécar** (30min., 9 per day 4am-8:30pm, 320ptas/€1.92); **Granada** (2¼hr.; 6:30am, 4:45, 7:15pm; 1200ptas/€7.20); **Málaga** (1½hr., 17 per day 6:30am-9:45pm, 500ptas/€3); **Sevilla** (4hr., 2 per day 7:30am and 4:30pm, 2300ptas/€13.80). The multilingual **tourist office,** Pta. del Mar, 2, is beside the Balcón de Europa. (☎952 52 15 31. Open June-Aug. M-F 10am-2pm and 5-8pm, Sa 10am-1pm; Sept.-May M-F 10am-2pm and 5-8pm, Sa 10am-1pm.) Services include: **pharmacy,** P. De San Cristóbal (☎958 63 06 98); **emergency** ☎112; **medical emergency,** C. Carlos Millón, 1 (☎952 52 09 35); **police** C. Virgen del Pilar 1 (☎952 52 15 45); and the **post office,** C. Almirante Ferrándiz, 6. (☎952 52 17 49. Open M-F 8:30am-2:30pm, Sa 9am-1pm.) **Postal code:** 29780.

ACCOMMODATIONS AND FOOD. It's worth breaking a sweat for **Hostal Estrella del Mar,** C. Bellavista, 5. From the bus station, follow Av. de Pescia past the traffic circle and take a right on C. Andalucía. Make another right on C. Asensio Cabanillas and then a left on C. Bellavista; the hostal is on your right. Spacious rooms with baths and terraces, many with ocean views. Guests lounge around the outdoor pool table in the evening. (☎952 52 04 61. Breakfast 400ptas/€2.40. Singles 3000-4000ptas/€18-24; doubles 4000-5300ptas/€24-31.80.) Otherwise, **Hostal Residencia Mena,** C. El Barrio, 15, conveniently located off the Balcón de Europa, has comfortable, if bare, rooms. (☎952 52 05 41. July-Sept. singles 3200ptas/€19.20; doubles 4500ptas/€27. Oct.-June singles 2500ptas/€15; doubles 3500ptas/€21.) Overpriced restaurants near and along the Balcón de Europa tempt passersby with views. On Playa de Burriana, **Merendero Montemar** serves fresh fish, English breakfasts (400ptas/€2.40), and *paella* (800ptas/€4.80). At night, the most happening place in town is the unfortunately named **C. Tutti Frutti,** where young Brits congregate at lively local bars. A **market** two blocks up C. San Miguel sells produce. (☎95 252 01 81. Open daily 8am-2pm.)

SIGHTS. To get to the **Balcón de Europa,** a promenade that overlooks Playa de la Caletilla, follow Av. de Pescia from the bus station to the traffic circle and turn right on C. Pintada, which leads downhill to the *balcón.* Below the cliff are some **caves** worthy of exploration, best approached from the **Paseo de los Carabineros** (off the stairs to the right of the tourist office). The walkway winds along the rocky shore to the east, past **Playa de Calahonda, Playa Carabeo,** and **Playa Burriana.** To reach the sprawling **Playa de la Torrecilla** from the *balcón,* cut west through town to the Playa de la Torrecilla apartments and follow the shoreline from there (15min.). Much closer but more crowded is **Playa del Salón,** accessible through an alley off the *balcón,* to the right of Restaurante Marisal.

ALMUÑÉCAR ☎958

In the 4th century BC, a booming fish-salting industry brought prosperity to this Phoenician port town known as **Sexi.** The Romans seized control a century later, constructing temples and a massive aqueduct. Though not quite as exciting as its Phoenician name suggests, Almuñécar entices visitors with expansive boardwalks and an alluring tropical environment. Understatedly sexy, baby.

PRACTICAL INFORMATION. The **bus station** (☎958 63 01 40) is at the corner of Av. Fenicia and Av. Juan Carlos I. Buses run to: **Nerja** (30min., 10 per day 7am-9:15pm, 320ptas/€1.92); **Málaga** (1½hr., 8 per day 7am-9:15pm, 800ptas/€4.80); **Granada** (1½hr., 10 per day 6:30am-9pm, 895ptas/€5.37); and **Madrid** (7hr., 1 per day, 2525ptas/€15.15). The **tourist office** is in a mauve mansion on Av. Europa, off Av. Costa del Sol. From the bus station, exit right and follow Ctra. Concepción through the rotary to Av. Costa del Sol; turn left onto Av. Europa and walk past the park. (☎958 63 11 25. Open daily 10am-2pm and 5-8pm.) **Luggage storage** at lockers in the bus station. 300ptas/€1.50. Open daily 6:30am-9:30pm). Services include:

THE FIFTH BOMB In the 1960s, as Spain was debating whether to join NATO, a USAF B-52 bomber carrying five hydrogen bombs blew up during an in-flight refueling mishap over the village of Palomares, 20km north of Mojácar. Locals looked on as US personnel in radiation suits combed the town in search of the bombs. Four were recovered and identified; the fifth supposedly emerged wrapped in a plastic tarp and without a serial number (Spanish Greenpeace still doubts that it was ever found). Much of Spain boycotted the area's produce (primarily tomatoes), and anti-NATO sentiment reached new heights. To downplay the accident, the US Ambassador and Franco's Minister of the Interior staged a seaside photo-op, swimming in the water before a dozen CIA agents. To top it off, the US built a health clinic in the town. Palomares has since prospered, with copious harvests of tomatoes, leeks, and melons, but some locals still blame defects and illnesses on the mysterious fifth bomb.

emergency ☎112; **police** at the Ayuntamiento in Pl. Constitución, (☎958 83 86 14); and **medical emergency** (☎958 63 20 63).

ACCOMMODATIONS AND FOOD. Several reasonably priced hostels lie on Av. Europa. Situated across from the tourist office and along Av. Europa, **Hotel Goya,** Av. Europa, 31, has comfortable rooms with dark wood furniture, baths and phones. (☎958 63 05 50 or 63 11 92; fax 63 11 92. Singles 2000-3500ptas/€12-21; doubles 3000-6000ptas/€18-36. MC/V.) **Residencia Tropical,** Av. Europa, 39, a half-block from the beach, has a bar and spotless, well-furnished rooms with private bathrooms. (☎958 63 34 58. Singles 3500ptas/€21; doubles 6200ptas/€37.20. MC/V.) Plenty of beach-front *terrazas* line Po. Puerta del Mar and Po. San Cristóbal, providing the place to savor the catch of the day. Locals frequent **Bar Avenida Lute y Jesús,** Av. Europa, 24, which specializes in *fritura de pescado* (650-1000ptas/€3.90-6). (☎958 63 42 76. *Menú* 800ptas/€4.80. Open daily 8am-1:30am.)

SIGHTS AND BEACHES. Alumuñécar's historical protagonists, the Phoenicians, Romans, and Moors, all fought over this subtropical paradise, and each left a distinct mark. The Moorish **Castillo de San Miguel** rests atop a massive hill at the front of Pl. Puerte del Mar. Bombarded by the British during the Napoleonic Wars, it was cleared of rubble and converted to a cemetery before finding its most recent incarnation as a museum. (Open Tu-Su 10:30am-1:30pm and 6:30pm-9:30pm. 325ptas/€1.95, children 225ptas/€1.35.) The 1900-year-old, 8km long **aqueduct** watered the ancient Roman town; parts of it are still in use. Almuñécar is also home to nearly 100 different species of birds, which nest in the **Parque Ornitológico Loro Sexi** beside El Castillo de San Miguel, 100m from the beach. (☎958 88 08 65. Open daily June-Aug. 11am-2pm and 5-8pm; Sept.-May 10am-2pm and 5-9pm. 500ptas/€3.) Uphill from the tourist office, **Parque El Majuelo** has 400 varieties of imported plants and great views of Roman ruins (free).

Located on the **Costa Tropical,** Almuñécar is known by Spaniards for its excellent beaches. Jutting into the sea, **Peñón del Santo,** a point of land crowned by a giant cross, separates the two main beaches. Both **Playa San Cristóbal** and **Playa del Mar** feature gray sands and stunning views of the surrounding sea cliffs in the afternoon. To reach either beach, follow Av. Europa to the sea; San Cristóbal is on the right, del Mar is on the left. Beyond Puerta del Mar lies beautiful and less frequented **Playa de Velilla.** Buses to Málaga go through **La Herradura** (15min., 11 per day 7am-9:15pm, 120ptas/€0.72) a suburb/beach frequented by windsurfers and scuba divers. The largest **nude beach** on the Costa Tropical is **Playa Cantarriján.**

ALMERÍA

Exciting nightlife, flowery promenades, and extensive coastline have turned the once-poor city of Almería into a choice spot for weekend getaways or even a destination for new residents. The cranes, bulldozers, and other construction equipment that frame the city are a testimonial to its growing popularity. Despite the ugly sprawl of the city's outskirts, the beautiful plazas, streets, and port of the center more than make up for it. A huge Moorish fortress presides over the city, but the best parts of Almería are the kilometers of sand stretching along the sea toward Cabo de Gata, at the eastern edge of the Costa del Sol.

TRANSPORTATION. The **airport** (☎950 21 37 00), 9km out of town, has daily flights to Madrid and Barcelona. **Trains** (☎902 24 02 02), Pl. Estación, run to: **Barcelona** (14hr.; W,F, Sa 7:30am; 6400ptas/€38.45); **Granada** (2hr., 4 per day 6am-6:10pm, 1645-1810ptas/€9.90-10.90); **Madrid** (7hr., 7:15am and 3:45pm, 5700-7200ptas/€34.25-43.25); **Sevilla** (6hr., 3 per day 6am-2:40pm, 4345ptas/€26.15); and **Valencia** (8hr.; W, F, Sa 7:30am; 5500ptas/€33). **Buses** (☎902 42 22 42) leave from Pl. Estación. **Entacar/Also** goes to: **Barcelona** (14hr., 4 per day 9:30am-9:30pm, 7440ptas/€44.70); **Mojácar** (1½hr., 6 per day 6:30am-8pm, 850ptas/€5.10); **Murcia** (3hr., 6 per day 6:30am-8pm, 2200ptas/€13.20); and **Valencia** (8hr., 4 per day 9:30am-9:30pm, 4285ptas/€25.75). **Alsina Graells** sends buses to: **Córdoba** (6hr., 1 per day, 3030ptas/€18.80); **Granada** (2hr., 12 per day 7am-8pm, 1425ptas/€8.55); **Málaga** (3½hr., 10 per day 6:30am-11pm, 2600ptas/€15.60); and **Sevilla** (5½hr., 3 per day, 3905ptas/€23.45). **Almeraya** goes to **Madrid** (8hr., 4 per day 9:30am-midnight, 3000ptas/€18).

ORIENTATION AND PRACTICAL INFORMATION. The city revolves around **Puerta de Purchena,** a six-way intersection just down C. Tiendas from the old town. To reach Pta. Purchena from the **bus station** or the connected **train station** on Pl. Estación, walk a block straight out the front door and take a left onto Av. Estación; turn right onto Av. Federico García Lorca, then left onto Rbla. Obispo Orbera. Po. Almería runs out of Pta. Purchena to the port—any services including banks with **ATMs,** can be found on Po. Almería or just off it. The **tourist office,** is in Parque Nicolás Salmerón. Follow Po. Almería out of Pta. Purchena toward the port, and turn right onto Parque de Salmerón. (☎950 27 43 55. Open M-F 9am-7pm, Sa-Su 10am-2pm.) **Emergency** ☎112; **police,** C. Santos Zarate ☎92; **Hospital Torre Cardenas** ☎950 01 60 00. **Internet access** can be found at **DC-9 Ciberclub,** C. Martínez Almagro, 8, several blocks behind the post office. Fax service and coffee bar also available. (☎950 25 71 96. Internet 350ptas/€2.10 per hr., faxes 250ptas/€1.50 each. Open M-Th 9am-10:30pm, F 9am-2am, Sa 10:30am-2am, Su 3:30-11pm.) **Post office,** Pl. Juan Cassinello, down Po. Almería. (☎950 24 02 31. Open M-F 8:30am-8:30pm, Sa 9:30am-2pm.) **Postal code:** 04080.

ACCOMMODATIONS AND FOOD. Rooms in Almería tend to be rather uninspiring—high prices are charged for average quality. The tourist office provides a list of accommodations, most of which surround Pta. Purchena. **Hostal Americano,** Ave. Estación, on the corner of C. Federico García Lorca, is one of the simpler hostels in town. (☎950 28 10 15. Singles 2800-3000ptas/€16.80-18, with bath 3500-4100ptas/€21-24.65; doubles 5100-5500/€30.65-33, with bath 6000-6550ptas/€36-39.37.) Though only a few blocks from the beach, **Albergue Juvenil (HI),** C. Isla de Fuerteventura, is a 30min. walk from everything else. Doubles with private baths and common lounges provide incentive to stay. From Pl. Estación, take C. Ronda, turn left onto Av. Cabo de Gata, then continue straight as it becomes C. Bilbao. Turn left onto C. Vinaroz, then right on C. Úbeda; Fuerteventura is on the left. (☎950 26 97 88. 1350-2050ptas/€8.10-13.30 per person including breakfast. MC/V.) Cafés line Po. Almería. With ham chandeliers and over 70 types of *tapas* (all 100ptas/€0.60), **Casa Puga,** C. Jovellanos, 7, in the old quarter, packs them in. (☎950 23 15 30. Open M-Sa 11am-4pm and 8pm-midnight. V.) The local supermarket is **Champion,** Po. Almería. (☎950 23 28 00. Open M-Sa 9:15am-9:15pm.)

ANDALUCÍA

SIGHTS AND NIGHTLIFE. Built in 995 by order of Abderramán III of Córdoba, the **Alcazaba,** a magnificent 14-acre Moorish fortress, spans two ridges overlooking the city and the sea. In its heyday, it was said to have housed 20,000 men and their ammunition. (From Pl. Carmen next to Pta. Purchena, follow C. Antonio Vico. ☎950 27 16 17. Open daily 9am-8:30pm. 250ptas/€1.50, free with EU passport.) The **cathedral,** in the old town, resembles a fortress due to repeated raids by Berber pirates. Though scabby on the outside, the inside is all Renaissance with a touch of Baroque on the altar. (☎609 57 58 02. Open M-F 10am-4:30pm, Sa 10am-1pm, and during mass. 300ptas/€1.80.)

Pubs, bars, and discos fill the small streets behind the post office where throngs of students and adults can be seen partaking in *"la movida"* as early as 11pm. By far the most popular hot spot is the disco **Dolce Vita,** Po. Mediterraneo, where several cavernous dance floors, numerous bars, and pulsating music keeps the tight-bodied crowd going until nearly 6am. (M-F no cover, Sa cover 1000ptas/€6, Su cover 800ptas/€4.80, both include one drink. Mixed drinks 800ptas/€4.80, beer 400ptas/€2.40. Open nightly 11pm-6:30am.) Student-aged partiers start the night off at the bar **Babel,** San Pedro, 7, where the owner offers free dance lessons M and T from 10pm-1am. (Mixed drinks 650ptas/€3.90, beer 350ptas/€2.10. Open Su-Th 3pm-3am, F-Sa 3pm-4am.) and their next stop is **Enebro,** C. San Pedro, which features loud Spanish pop. (Mixed drinks 650ptas/€3.90, beer 400ptas/€2.40. Open nightly until 4am.) **Chupitería Dalia,** C. Dalia, 3, serves up a variety of not-so-subtly-named shooters such as *orgasmo de manga.* (☎950 26 25 84. Cocktail shots 1200ptas/€7.20, shots 200ptas/€1.20, *copas* 600ptas/€3.60.) Those too old to giggle at a *buttery nipple* gather at the outdoor tables and by the bar at **The Irish Tavern,** C. Antonio González Eges, 4 (mixed drinks 700ptas/€4.20, beer 350-500ptas/€2.10-3; open daily 3pm-3am), then head over to dance at **Velvet,** C. Trajana at the corner of C. San Pedro (no cover; mixed drinks 550ptas/€3.30, open Th-Sa 11pm-4am).

DAYTRIP FROM ALMERÍA: CABO DE GATA

Alsina Graells (☎950 23 51 68) goes to San Miguel de Cabo de Gata (1hr., M-F 6 per day 8am-9pm, Sa-Su 4 per day 8am-8pm; 275ptas/€1.65); Autocares Bernardo (☎950 25 04 22) runs to San José (45min.; M-F 1:15 and 6:30pm, Sa 2:15pm; returns M-F 7am, 3 and 9pm, Sa 7am; 415ptas/€2.50).

Thirty kilometers east of urban Almería lies pristine **Parque Natural de Cabo de Gata-Níjar,** a 60km stretch of protected coast and inland environs. The near-desolate peninsula juxtaposes tropical and barren climates: flamingos flock to the area's salt marshes, while a desert and mountains farther inland draw visitors for hiking. The park has served as movie set for *The Good, the Bad, and the Ugly* and *Lawrence of Arabia*. Many come to Cabo de Gata to dive at **Mermaid's Reef** or windsurf off **Nijar. Grupo J. 126** (☎950 38 02 99) and **Ocio y Mar** (☎608 05 64 77) provide info and tours of the park; contact them a day or two before arriving. Long, sandy shores await in the low-key fishing town of **San Miguel de Cabo de Gata** (or simply **Cabo de Gata**). As Cabo de Gata has nary a budget lodging, it's best to head back to Almería for the night. Farther south, the little resort of **San José** boasts an even more pristine beach, and serves as a base for exploring the park.

MOJÁCAR

Mojácar is the kind of vacation spot one might expect to see on a postcard: a white-stoned, picture-perfect hilltop village with 17km of smooth coastline and a firecracker nightlife. Stunning sunsets find tourists and residents alike relaxing on the numerous outdoor terraces or strolling along the stone boardwalk by the beach. During the day, the village clears out as the tourists head downhill to the turquoise Mediterranean to escape the heat. The beachfront resorts fill up quickly in July and August when hordes of international visitors join the large contingent of expats who have made Mojácar their home—don't be surprised to hear more English than Spanish from both visitors and residents alike.

TRANSPORTATION. The bus station is in front of the shopping plaza near the beach. **Alsa/Enatcar** buses (☎902 42 22 42) leave for **Almería** (1½hr.; M-Sa 7 per day,

Su 2 per day, 7:50am-11:10pm; 850ptas/€5.10); **Barcelona** (12hr., 2 per day, 6595ptas/€39.65); **Madrid** (8hr., 1-2 per day, 4340ptas/€26.10); and **Murcia** (2½hr.; M-F 8 per day, Sa-Su 4-5 per day, 7:05am-9:35pm; 1350ptas/€8.10). For a **taxi** call ☎950 47 81 84, or wait at the stop in Pl. Nueva. The tourist office has a list of **car rental** agencies—with so many tourists around, there are a slew to choose from.

ORIENTATION AND PRACTICAL INFORMATION. Most buses stop both at the "official" stop in front of the shopping plaza by the beach, as well as at the lowest point of the village itself—since most budget lodging is in town, get off uphill. If you're stuck at the bus stop, wait for a yellow **Transportes Urbanos** bus running from town to beachfront. (2 per hr. 9:30am-1:30pm and 5pm-midnight, 1 per hr. 1:30-5pm; 100ptas/€0.60.) Mojácar is split into two parts: the beach, lined with pricey hotels, tourist-oriented restaurants, and the best nightlife spots, and the *pueblo*, where everyday life centers around Pl. Nueva. The 30min. hike up the mountain from the beach or the main bus stop to Pl. Nueva is not for the faint of heart. The **tourist office** (☎/fax 950 61 50 25; open M-F 8am-3pm, Sa 10:30am-1:30pm), **police** ☎950 47 20 00, and **post office** (open M-F 8:30am-2:30pm, Sa 9:30am-1pm) are all in Pl. Nueva. **Postal code:** 04638.

ACCOMMODATIONS AND FOOD. Finding a bed at the last minute in Mojácar can be difficult. The simple but pleasant accommodations at **Casa Justa,** C. Morote, 7, give you the most for your money. From Pl. Nueva, take a right on C. Alcalde Jacino, a left on C. Estacion Nueva, a right on C. Esteve, a sharp right again and go down the hill to C. Morote; the hostal is on the left. (☎950 47 83 72. Singles 2500ptas/€15, doubles 4000-7000ptas/€24-42.) The five elegant bedrooms at **Pensión Torreón,** C. Jazmín, 4, are decorated with a resort aesthetic, which is fortunate because they open onto fantastic oceanfront views. From Pl. Nueva, follow C. Indalo out of Pl. Nueva, and take the second right on C. Enmedio, a left downhill along C. Unión, and a right at the end of the hill onto C. Jazmín. (☎950 47 52 59. Call early to reserve a room. Doubles with shared bath 6000ptas/€36.) **Hostal Esquinica,** C. Esquinica, is another great option, with small but comfortable rooms. From Pl. Flores follow C. Arrabal to the right. (☎950 47 50 09. July-Aug. singles 3000ptas/€18, doubles 6000ptas/€36, slightly less in the low season.) For food, you'll find more variety and better value in town than at the beach, although the fresh seafood restaurants that have their feet in the sand are occasionally worth the splurge. **Pizzeria Pulcinella,** C. Puntica, 5, three blocks from Pl. Nueva (follow the large green signs), most definitely caters to the tourist but still manages to prepare some of the best Italian cuisine in town. (☎950 47 84 01. Pizzas 775-1250ptas/€4.66-7.50, pasta 975ptas/€5.85. Open Tu-Su 8pm-midnight. MC/V.)

ENTERTAINMENT AND BEACHES. Tourists come to Mojácar for one thing—the beaches. Buses run twice an hour between the town and beach and along the shore (see **practical information,** above). In town, buses leave from the stop below Pl. Nueva. From the beach, get on at one of the stops along Av. Mediterránea. There are a slew of beaches to choose among, from the crowded **Playa del Cantal** and **Playa del Cueva del Lobo** to the more sedate **Playa Piedra Villazar. Playa de las Ventanicas** marks the start of a gorgeous palm-lined pathway that stretches for several kilometers to the west. In general, the best beaches are to the right at the bottom of the hill from town.

Mojácar pulses with nightlife. Tented *chiringuitos* (beach bars) sprawl out along the water and are by far the most popular place to begin (or end) a night. Go by car if you can; buses stop running at 11pm, taxis disappear at sundown, and walking the poorly lit highway is a dangerous alternative. Some of the best *chiringuitos* include **Tito's,** on Playa de las Ventanicas; **El Cid,** on Playa del Cantal; and **El Patio,** on Pl. del Cantal. A popular discoteca is **Paschá,** on Po. Mediterráneo, where palm trees grace the bar, and **Tuareg Disco,** Caratera Mojácar-Carboneras, which doesn't even start getting crowded until 5am. For a midnight dip to sober up before bed, the pool at **Master Disco** (☎950 46 81 33), on the highway between the beach and the town, is open until 5am. Back in town, expats run more laid-back watering holes. **Time and Place,** in Pl. Flores, serves soothing drinks to a sunburnt crowd. (☎950 47 25 38. Open W-M 7pm-1:30am.) Guinness flows freely at **La Sartén** (a.k.a. Gordon's), on C. Estación Nueva, behind the church. Because Mojácar has more than 19 pubs and discos and over 11 beach bars, the "in" place seems to constantly be changing; pick up the free *Mojácar Viva* leaflet at the tourist office for more detailed info. In the second week of June, Mojácar goes haywire with the **Festival de Moros y Cristianos,** a week filled with beautiful costumes, loud parades, and revelry. War and reconciliation are recreated as "hostile" troops surround the city, fire rockets, make speeches, and later join the night-long fiesta in peace.

RONDA ☎952

Divided in half by a 100m gorge, Ronda (pop. 38,000) was a pivotal commercial center in Roman times. Fortunes dwindled under Moorish rule after Al Mutadid ibn Abbad drowned the ruling lord in his bath and annexed the city for Sevilla. More recently, Ronda—the birthplace of modern bullfighting—has attracted such forlorn artists as Rainer Maria Rilke, who wrote his Spanish Elegies here, and Orson Welles, whose ashes are buried on a bull farm outside of town. Brimming with sights, Ronda makes an excellent base for exploring the *pueblos blancos*.

TRANSPORTATION

The **train** and **bus stations** are in the new city three blocks away from each other on Av. Andalucía. To reach the tourist office and the town center from the **train station,** turn right on Av. Andalucía and follow it through Pl. Merced past the **bus station** (it becomes C. San José) to its end.

Trains: Av. Alférez Provisional (☎952 87 16 73). **Ticket office,** C. Infantes, 20 (☎952 87 16 62). Open M-F 10am-2pm and 6-8:30pm. To: **Algeciras** (2hr., 4 per day 7am-8:30pm, 930ptas/€6). Change at Bobadilla for: **Granada** (3hr., 3 per day 8:44am-5:58pm, 1645ptas/€10); **Málaga** (2hr., 4 per day 7:50am-5:58pm, 1270ptas/€8).

Buses: Pl. Concepción García Redondo, 2 (☎952 18 70 61 or 87 22 62), near Av. Andalucía. To: **Cádiz** (4hr., 5 per day 7am-7pm, 1700ptas/€10); **Málaga** (2½hr., 5 per day 6:30am-7:30pm, 1275ptas/€7.65); **Marbella** (1½hr., 5 per day 6:30am-8:30pm, 670ptas/€4); **Sevilla** (2½hr., 5 per day 7am-7pm, 1395ptas/€8.25).

Taxis: (☎952 87 23 16). From the train station to Pl. de España costs 400ptas/€2.40.

ORIENTATION AND PRACTICAL INFORMATION

The 18th-century **Puente Nuevo** (new bridge) connects the Ronda's old and new sections. On the new side of the city, **Carrera Espinel** (the main street, including the pedestrian walkway known as **C. la Bola**) runs perpendicular to C. Virgen de la Paz. Cra. Espinel intersects C. Virgen de la Paz between the bullring and Pl. España.

Tourist Office: Paseo Blas Infante, across from the bullring (☎952 18 71 19; fax 18 71 47). In a sleek black building. **Regional Tourist Office:** Pl. España, 1 (☎95 287 12 72). Open M-F 9am-2pm and 4-7pm, Sa-Su 10am-3pm.

Currency Exchange: Banco Central Hispano, Cra. Espinel, 17, near C. Remedios. Open June-Sept. M-F 8:30am-2:30pm; Oct.-May M-F 8:30am-2:30pm, Sa 9am-1:30pm.

Luggage Storage: At the **bus station** (400ptas/€2.40 per day). Open daily 8am-10pm.

Emergency: ☎112. **Police:** Pl. Duquesa de Parcent (☎952 87 13 69).

Medical Emergency: ☎951 06 52 18. **Centro de Salud** (☎951 06 50 00), on the road to El Burgo.

Internet Access: Zaidín Cervecería, C. Pozo, 11 (☎952 87 93 77), off Pl. Merced. 300ptas/€1.80 per 30min., 400ptas/€2.40 per hr. Open daily 7am-midnight.

Post Office: C. Virgen de la Paz, 20 (☎95287 25 57), across from Pl. Toros. **Lista de Correos.** Open M-F 8:30am-2:30pm, Sa 9:30am-1pm. **Postal Code:** 29400.

ACCOMMODATIONS

Most budget lodgings are concentrated in the new city near the bus station, along the streets perpendicular to Carrera Espinel—try C. Naranja and C. Lorenzo Borrego. Expect room shortages during the *Feria de Ronda* in September.

Hostal Ronda Sol, C. Almendra, 11 (☎952 87 44 97). Spotless, pleasant rooms surround a leafy patio. The best budget deal in town. Singles 1700ptas/€10.20; doubles 2800ptas/€16.80; triples 4000ptas/€24.

Hotel Morales, C. Sevilla, 51 (☎952 87 15 38; fax 18 70 02). With its myriad framed maps, the lobby is a cartographer's fantasy. New rooms, all with baths, some with TVs. Worth the splurge. Singles 3000/€18; doubles 5000-6000ptas/€30-36. MC/V.

Pensión La Purisma, C. Sevilla, 10 (☎952 87 10 50). Greco-Roman statuary greets lodgers at the entrance. Parking 1200ptas/€7.20. Singles 2500ptas/€15; doubles 4000ptas/€24; triples 6000ptas/€36. MC/V.

FOOD

Restaurants and cafés abound in Ronda, although many are geared to tourists and tend to be overpriced. Stay away from Pl. España and check out some of the listings below. Rabbit and stewed bull's tail are local specialties.

Restaurante Hnos. Macías, C. Pedro Romero, 3 (☎95 287 42 38). On a quaint pedestrian thoroughfare. Delicious and hearty cuisine elegantly served. Exquisite pork entrées and rice desserts. *Menú* 975ptas/€5.85. Open daily 11am-2am. MC/V.

Bodega San Franciso, C. Ruedo Alameda, 32 (☎95 287 81 62). Follow C. Imágenes past Iglesia del Espíritu Santo and down the hill. A favorite with locals, located beyond the Old City and refreshingly free of tourists. Cheap, tasty *tapas* 100-200ptas/€0.60-1.20. Open F-W 12-5pm and 8pm-2am. MC/V.

Carmelitas Descalzas, Pasaje S. Juan de la Cruz, 1 (☎95 287 29 65), to the left of the church entrance. A divine pastry shop. Place your money on the round table and a cloistered nun will fill your order. 200-300ptas/€1.20-1.80 for ¼kg of pastries. Open daily 10:15am-1:15pm and 4:45pm-6:45pm.

SIGHTS

BRIDGES. Carved by the Río Guadalevír, Ronda's gorge falls 100m below the **Puente Nuevo,** across from Pl. España. Arrested highwaymen were once held in a cell beneath the center of bridge; during the Civil War, political prisoners were thrown from the top. Two other bridges span the gap: the innovative **Puente Viejo** was rebuilt in 1616 over an earlier Arab bridge, and the **Puente San Miguel** (a.k.a. **Puente Árabe**) is a prime Andalucian hybrid of a Roman base and Arab arches.

CASA DEL REY MORO. A colonnaded walkway leads to the Casa del Rey Moro (House of the Moorish King), which, despite its name and Moorish façade, actually dates from the 18th century. Sixty meters below the palace lies an Islamic well constructed during the 1300s. Four hundred Christian prisoners were once employed in the arduous task of drawing water; today visitors climb down a series of passageways and stone steps to survey the ravine's depths. Don't miss the view of the surrounding countryside from the serene Forestier gardens, laid in 1915 and located near the museum exit. *(C. Cuesta de Santo Domingo, 9. ☎952 18 72 00. Open daily summer 10am-8pm; winter 10am-7pm. 600ptas/€3.60, children 300ptas/€1.80.)*

IGLESIA DE SANTA MARÍA. Begun following the Christian reconquest of Ronda in 1485, this church was slowly assembled over the next two centuries. Part

A WHOLE LOT OF BULL Bullfighting aficionados charge over to Ronda's **Plaza de Toros** (☎952 87 41 32), Spain's oldest bullring (est. 1785) and cradle of the modern *corrida.* The **Museo Taurino** inside tells the story of local hero Pedro Romero, the first matador to brave the beasts *a pie* (on foot), and to use the red cape. (Open daily June-Sept. 10am-8pm; Oct.-May 10am-6pm. 500ptas/€2.50.) Romero killed his first bull at age 17 in 1771, the start of a glorious career: "From 1781-1799, it can be said that I killed in each year 200 bulls, whose sum totals 5600 bulls, yet I am persuaded that there may have been more." Though no mathematician (if you're a nerd, do the math and see how he relied on hyperbole rather than reality), Romero certainly knew his way around the ring. The museum displays heads of bulls legendary for their ferocity and bloodied matador shirts, including the shirt of Francisco Rivera ("Paquirri"), who was gored to death in 1984. Elaborate *trajes de luces,* the traditional costumes of the bullfighters, are kept behind glass cases. An exhibit on 20th-century bullfighting showcases photos of Orson Welles and Ernest Hemingway. In early September, the Plaza de Toros hosts *corridas goyescas* (bullfights in traditional costumes) as part of the **Feria de Ronda.** The town fills to capacity–book rooms months ahead.

Gothic, part Renaissance, part Baroque, its incense filled nave provides a timeline of architectural evolution. A small Moorish arch near the entrance and a verse from the Koran engraved behind the sacristy are the last vestiges of the mosque which once stood in its place. *(Off C. Marqués de Salvatierra. ☎95 287 22 46. Open daily summer 10am-8pm; winter 10am-6pm. 335ptas/€2, groups 250ptas/€1.50 per person.)*

PALACIO DE MONDRAGÓN. Originally inhabited by Don Fernando Valenzuela, a prominent minister under Carlos III, this 17th-century palace has since been transformed into a fascinating anthropological museum. Exhibits on ancient life in the area fill former sitting rooms and libraries. No doubt Don Fernando would not have approved of the Neolithic hut replicated in his bedroom. *(☎952 87 84 50. Open summer M-F 10am-7pm, Sa-Su 10am-3pm; winter M-F 10am-6pm, Sa-Su 10am-3pm. 300ptas/€1.80, students and groups 150ptas/€0.90 per person, under 14 and disabled free.)*

OTHER SIGHTS. Frequented by Hemingway and widely regarded as the world's most beautiful bullring, Ronda's **Plaza de Toros** was inaugurated in 1785, making it among the oldest in Spain. Fights take place in September; tours are available year. *(Virgen de la Paz, 15. ☎952 87 15 39; fax 87 03 79. Open daily Nov.-Feb. 10am-6pm, Mar.-Apr. 10am-7pm, May-Oct. 10am-8pm. 600ptas/€3.60.)* For something just as bloody, visit the **Museo del Bandolero,** C. Armiñán, 59, dedicated to presenting "pillage, theft, and rebellion, in Spain since Roman times." *(☎952 87 77 85. Open daily summer 10am-9pm, winter 10am-6pm. 400ptas/€2.40.)* The **Museo de Caza** displays hunting trophies from four continents to the melodious strains of Spanish soft rock. With its mountains of taxidermy, it's definitely not a good place for vegetarians. *(C. Armiñán, 59. ☎952 87 78 62. Open daily 11am-7pm. 200ptas/€1.20.)*

NIGHTLIFE

At night, Rondans congregate in the pubs and *discotecas* along C. Jerez and the streets behind Pl. Socorro, including C. Pozo. **Disco-Bar Niágara,** C. Jerez, 17, with its tropical cave decor, is the closest thing in town to a dance club, although the place is still small by most standards. (☎929 84 41 82. Open daily 4pm-late.) Somewhat less trendy, but equally popular with young Spaniards, is **Bar Antonio,** C. San José 4, outside of which crowds form between midnight and 1am. (Open M-Sa 7am-1:30am.) For a more tranquil evening, head to **Tetería Al-Zahra,** C. Tiendas, 19, where patrons sip tea from all over the world. The Islamic decor, floor pillows, and soothing New Age tunes invite long stays. (☎952 87 16 98. Open W-M 4pm-late.)

DAYTRIP FROM RONDA

CUEVAS DE LA PILETA (25 MIN.)

*By **car**, take highway C-339 north (Ctra. Sevilla from the new city). The turnoff to Benaoján and the caves is about 13km out, in front of an abandoned restaurant. **Taxis** will go round-trip from Ronda for 6000ptas/€36. A cheaper way to reach Cuevas de la Pileta is by train, via the town of Benaoján. **Trains** run to Benaoján from Ronda (7am, 9:38am, and 3:48pm and return at 12:49pm, 5:39pm, and 7:51pm. Round-trip 540ptas/€3.24). From the train station at Benaoján, it's a tough but scenic 1hr. climb to the caves. With your back to the train, exit left and follow the road parallel to the tracks for 100m until the sign for Hotel Molino del Santo. Take a right and continue past the hotel until you see a sign on the left for the caves. Follow the wide path for 1km up to a dilapidated farm; on the right, just after the abandoned refrigerator, is a goat path leading upward (look for goat dung if you lose your way), to the hill. There, near the summit is a narrow highway; turn left and follow the road for 500m. **Caves** open daily 10am-1pm and 4-6pm. Tours last 1¼hr. Groups up to 8 1000ptas/€6 per person; 9 or more 900ptas/€5.40 per person.*

Twenty-two kilometers west of Ronda are the **Cuevas de la Pileta** (☎952 16 73 43 or 16 72 02), a dark expanse of stalactites and Paleolithic paintings, stretching for over a mile underground. More than 22,000 years ago local inhabitants took refuge in these caves, painting the walls with cryptic symbols and animal imagery. The highlights are the *Yegua preñada* (pregnant mare) and the beautifully preserved *Pez* (fish). The abstract depiction of human genitalia in the *sala finale* is somewhat more open to criticism. The chamber walls are darkened with soot and small human bones have been discovered in a number of locations; it's believed that the caves held special ceremonial significance during Neolithic times and were the scene of child sacrifices. Today, children are still welcome (400-500ptas/€2.40-3), although to preserve the interior climate, only 25 people are admitted at a time. Guides lead gas-lantern tours in Spanish and English. Wear comfortable shoes and dress warmly; even in the summer the caves are 30°F colder than outside.

ANTEQUERA ☎952

Few sunsets rival those seen from atop the old Moorish fortress at the crossroads of Andalucía, with Antequera's (pop. 41,000) whitewashed houses spread out below. The Romans gave Antequera its name, but older civilizations preceded them—pre-Roman *dólmenes* (funerary chambers built from rock slabs, the oldest in Europe) lie on the outskirts of town. The alluring Sierra del Torcal, a Mars-like wasteland of eroded rock, is 15km of Antequera. Wise travelers kick back here for a few days of inland visual splendor.

TRANSPORTATION

Trains: on Av. Estación (☎902 24 02 02). To: **Algeciras** (4hr., 3 per day 8:35am-7:25pm, 1810ptas/€10.86); **Granada** (2hr., 3 per day 9:50am-6:55pm, 1020ptas/€6.12); **Málaga** (1½hr., 3 per day, 855ptas/€5.13) via **Bobadilla; Ronda** (1½hr., 3 per day 8:35am-7:25pm, 855ptas/€5.13); **Sevilla** (2½hr., 5 per day 8:30am-8:45pm, 1630ptas/€9.78) via **Bobadilla.**

Buses: Po. García del Olmo (☎952 84 13 65), near the Parador Nacional. To: **Almería** (5hr., 2am and 9:30am, 2420ptas/€14.52); **Córdoba** (2¼hr., 9:45am and 5:45pm, 1150ptas/€6.90); **Granada** (2hr., 5 per day 6:30am-1am, 1050ptas/€6.30); **Málaga** (45min., 3 per day 9:30am-7pm, 560ptas/€3.36); **Murcia** (5½hr., 9:45am, 3350ptas/€20.10); **Sevilla** (2¼hr., 5 per day 4:10am-6:45pm, 1570ptas/€9.42).

Taxis: Taxi Radio Antequera (☎952 84 55 30) services Antequera and will go to Sierra de Tocal. From the town center to either station costs 600ptas/€3.60.

ORIENTATION AND PRACTICAL INFORMATION

From the train station at the base of Av. de la Estación, it's a 10min. hike up a shadeless hill (on Av. Estación) to the town center. At the top, continue straight past the market, turn right on C. Encarnación, and go past the Museo Municipal to reach **Plaza San Sebastián.** The **bus station** is at the intersection of Campillo Alto and Paseo García del Olmo atop a neighboring hill. To reach Pl. San Sebastián from the bus station, exit onto Campillo Alto and take a left on C. Porterías. Turn right onto C. Cruz Blanca and veer right at the fork onto Lucena. Continue for 5-10 min. until you reach Pl. San Sebastián and the **tourist office.**

Tourist Office: Pl. San Sebastián, 7 (☎/fax 952 70 25 05). Open June-Sept. M-Sa 10am-2pm and 5-8pm, Su 10am-2pm; Oct.-May M-Sa 9:30am-1:30pm and 4-7pm, Su 10am-2pm.

Banks: Banco Central Hispano, C. Infante Fernando, 51 (☎952 84 04 61). Open June-Aug. M-F 8:30am-2:30pm; Sept.-May M-F 8:30am-2:30pm, Sa 9am-1pm.

Emergency: ☎112. **Medical Emergency:** ☎952 84 19 66. **Municipal Police:** on Av. Legión (☎95 270 81 04).

Pharmacy: on C. Encarnación, near C. Calzada. Open M-F 9:30am-1:30pm and 5-8:30pm, Sa 10am-1:30pm.

Laundry: Pressto, Merecillas, 7 (☎952 84 55 44).

Hospital: Hospital Comarcál, C. Polígono Industrial, 67 (☎952 84 62 63).

Post Office: C. Nájera (☎952 84 20 83). Open M-F 8am-2pm, Sa 9:30am-1pm. **Postal Code:** 29200.

ACCOMMODATIONS

Pensión Toril, C. Toril, 3-5 (☎/fax 952 84 31 84), off Pl. San Francisco. Grandfatherly owner lets bright, clean rooms. Locals gather on the patio to chat over dominos. The restaurant downstairs has entrées for 500ptas/€3, and a filling *menú* accompanied by a bottle of wine for 900ptas/€5.40. Meals served daily 1-4pm and 8-9:30pm. Singles 1600ptas/€9.60, with bath 2000ptas/€12; doubles with bath 4000ptas/€24.

Pensión Madrona, C. Calzada, 25 (☎952 84 00 14), through Bar Madrona. Newly renovated, with A/C, hand-made quilts, and heating in every room. Restaurant/bar downstairs offers a tasty *menú* (900ptas/€5.40). Singles 1600ptas/€9.60, with bath 2750ptas/€16.50; doubles with bath 3850ptas/€23.10. MC/V.

Hotel/Pensión Colón, C. Infante Fernando, 29 (☎/fax 952 84 00 10). The comforts of a small hotel for a fraction of the price. Spotless rooms with hardwood floors and traditional furniture; many have A/C and TVs. Singles 1000-1600ptas/€6-9.60, with bath 2000-25000ptas/€12-15; doubles 2000-3200ptas/€12-19.20, with bath 4000-5000ptas/€24-30. AmEx/MC/V.

FOOD

For traditional Spanish cuisine, your best bet is to sample a *menú* at one of the pensions listed above. Other options exist for those weary of pork and seafood. Get fresh produce at the **market,** in Pl. San Francisco (open M-Sa 8am-3pm). Ten-aisle **Mercadona,** C. Calzada, 18, has all the basics. (Open M-Sa 9am-9pm. MC/V.)

La Espuelados, C. San Agustín, 1 (☎952 70 34 24), on a narrow street off C. Infante Fernando. An elegant Italian restaurant serving pizza and pasta (650-1200ptas/€3.90-7.20), and bonified veggie options (600-1000ptas/€3.60-6). *Menú* 1500ptas/€9. Open daily noon-4pm and 8-11:30pm. MC/V.

Manolo Bar, C. Calzada, 14 (☎952 84 10 15), downhill from the market. Filled with cowboy paraphernalia and good-humored patrons. Ultra-cheap *tapas* (150ptas/€0.90). Open Tu-Th 4:30-11:30pm, F-Sa 4:30pm-3am.

SIGHTS

LOS DÓLMENES. Antequera's three ancient caves are the oldest in Europe. Once burial chambers with storerooms for the riches of the dead, they were long ago looted but remain highly worthy of spelunking. Marvel at the 200-ton roof hauled five miles to the **Cueva de Menga** (2500 BC). Carved millennia ago, the four figures engraved on the chamber walls typify Mediterranean Stone Age art. **Cueva de Viera** (2000 BC), uncovered in 1905, begins with a narrow passageway leading deep into the darkness of the earth. Somewhat farther afield, **Cueva de Romel** (1800 BC) is still explored by visitors with gas lamps. Relive eighth-grade *Tom Sawyer* fantasies amidst the gentle sizzle of gas and the warmly illuminated domed ceilings of the interior. *(To reach the Cuevas de Menga and Viera, follow signs toward Granada from the town center (20min.) and watch for a small sign on past the gas station. To reach Cueva de Romeral from the other caves, continue on the highway to Granada for another 3km. On the left side of the street, across from Hotel Restaurante Camas, a gravel road leads to a narrow path bordered by cyprus trees. Take this path across the tracks to reach the cave. Sometimes the guard falls asleep; if the gate is locked, give a shout. All three caves open Tu 10am-2pm, W-F 9am-3:30pm, Su 9:30am-2pm. Free.)*

OTHER SIGHTS. Back in town, all that remains of the **Alcazaba** are its two towers, the wall between them, and some well-trimmed hedges. The view of the city at dusk is magnificent. Next door, the towering **Colegiata de Santa María** was the first church in Andalucía to incorporate Renaissance style. *(Open Tu-Th 10:30am-2pm and 9-11pm, F-Sa 10:30am-2pm, Su 11:30am-2pm. Free.)* The plaza in front of the church offers views of the massive **Peña de los Enamorados (Lovers' Rock),** which looks exactly like the Sphinx lying down, if you tilt your head sideways. Legend has it that a Christian man and his Moorish girlfriend, fearing separation by invading soldiers, leaped to their deaths from atop the rock. Downhill, the **Museo Municipal** exhibits avant-garde 1970s paintings by native son Cristóbal Toral alongside dozens of Roman artifacts, including the graceful **Efebo,** a rare bronze statue of a Roman page; the postcards don't do him justice. *(☎952 70 40 21. Open Tu-Th 10am-1:30pm and 9-11pm, F-Sa 10am-1:30pm, Su 11am-1:30pm. 200ptas/€1.20.)* The new **Museo Conventual de las Descalzas** is housed in the Convento de las Carmelitas Descalzas and exhibits 16th- and 17th-century paintings, sculptures, and bronze works. *(Open Tu-F 10am-1:30pm and 6-8pm, Sa-Su 10am-12:30pm. 350ptas/€2.10.)*

DAYTRIP FROM ANTEQUERA

SIERRA DE TORCAL

Two-thirds of the 13km to the Sierra de Torcal can be covered by bus; ask the driver to let you off at the turnoff for El Torcal. Casado ***buses*** *(☎95 284 19 57) leave from Antequera (M-F 1pm, 180ptas/€1.08); the return bus leaves from the turnoff (M-F 4:15pm). You can also take a* ***taxi*** *(the tourist office will call one for you) to the refugio (round-trip 3000ptas/€18) and have the driver wait.*

A garden of wind-sculpted boulders, the Sierra de Torcal glows like the surface of a barren and distant planet. The central peak **El Torcal** (1369m) takes up most of the horizon, but the surrounding clumps of eroded rocks are even more extraordinary. Several trails circle the summit. The green arrow path (1½km) takes about 45min.; the red arrow path (4½km) takes over 2hr. All but the green path require a guided tour; call the **Centro de Información** for more details. (☎952 03 13 89. Open daily 10am-2pm and 4-6pm.) Each path begins and ends at the *refugio* (lodge) at the mountain base. Try to catch the sunset and the spectacular mountain view from the striking **Mirador de las Ventanillas.**

GRANADA ☎958

When Moorish ruler Boabdil fled Granada, the last Muslim stronghold in Spain, his mother berated him for casting a longing look back at the Alhambra, saying, "You do well to weep as a woman for what you could not defend as a man." A spectacular palace celebrated by poets and artists throughout the ages, the Alhambra continues to inspire melancholy in those who depart from its timeless beauty. The age-old saying holds true: *"Si has muerto sin ver la Alhambra no has vivido"* (If you have died without seeing the Alhambra, you have not lived).

Conquered by invading Muslim armies in 711, Granada eventually blossomed into one of Europe's wealthiest, most refined cities. As Christian armies turned back the tide of Moorish conquest in the 13th century, the city became the last Muslim outpost on the peninsula, surrounded by a unified Christian kingdom. In the latter decades of the 15th century, Fernando and Isabel's troops continually besieged the city. Meanwhile, ruling Sultan Moulay Abul Hassan, obsessing over one of his concubines, ignored his civic duties. When Queen Aïcha caught on, she drummed up local support, had her husband deposed, and thrust her young son Boabdil on the throne. Fernando and Isabel capitalized on the chaos by finally capturing Boabdil and the Alhambra on the momentous night of January 1, 1492. Although the Christians torched all the mosques and the lower city, embers of Granada's Arab essence still linger. The Albaícin, an enchanting maze of Moorish houses and twisting alleys, is Spain's best-preserved Arab quarter and the only part of the Muslim city to survive the *Reconquista* intact.

TRANSPORTATION

Flights: Airport (☎958 24 52 37), 17km west of the city. A **Salidas** bus (☎958 13 13 09) runs from Gran Vía, in front of the cathedral (M-Sa 5 per day 8:15am-5:30pm, Su 5:30 and 7pm; 425ptas/€2.55). A **taxi** to the airport costs 2000ptas/€12. **Iberia** (☎902 40 05 00) flies to **Barcelona** (1¼hr., 2-3 per day) and **Madrid** (45min., 2-3 per day). Open M-F 9am-1:45pm and 4-7pm.

Trains: RENFE Station Av. Andaluces (☎902 24 02 02). From Pl. Isabel la Católica, follow Gran Vía to the end, then bear left on Av. Constitución; or take bus #3, 4, 5, 6, 9, or 11 from Gran Vía to the stop marked Constitución 3. Turn left on Av. Andaluces; RENFE is at the end. To: **Algeciras** (5-7hr., 3 per day 7:15am-5:50pm, 2715ptas/€16.29); **Almería** (3hr., 4 per day 10:00am-9:05pm, 1810 ptas/€10.86); **Antequera** (2hr., 3 per day 7:15am-5:50pm, 1020ptas/€6.12); **Barcelona** (12-13hr.; M-Su 10:10pm, M, Th, Sa 8:30am; 6300-7700ptas/€38-46); **Madrid** (5-6hr., 7:55am and 4:40pm, 4300-5300ptas/€26-32); **Ronda** (3-4hr., 3 per day 7:15am-5:50pm, 1800ptas/€10.80); **Sevilla** (4-5hr., 4 per day 8:18am-8:15pm, 2715ptas/€16).

Buses: All major bus routes originate from the new **bus station** on the outskirts of Granada on Ctra. Madrid, near C. Arzobispo Pedro de Castro.

Alsina Graells (☎958 18 54 80) to: **Almería** (2¼hr., 12 per day 6:45am-9:30pm, 1425ptas/€8.55); **Almuñecar** (1½hr., 11 per day 7:30am-8pm, 850ptas/€5.10); **Antequera** (2hr., 3-5 per day 3pm-7pm, 970ptas/€5.82); **Cádiz** (4hr., noon and 3:30pm, 3925ptas/€23.55); **Córdoba** (3hr., 10 per day 7:30am-8pm, 1605ptas/€9.63); **Jaén** (1½hr., 15 per day 7am-9:30pm, 970ptas/€5.82); **Málaga** (2hr., 16 per day 7am-9pm, 1255ptas/€7.53); **Sevilla** (3hr., 9 per day 8am-3am, 2480ptas/€14.88).

La Línea runs to: **Algeciras** (5hr., 6 per day 9am-8pm, 2705ptas/€16.23); the villages in **Las Alpujarras** (10:30am, noon, 5:15pm; 1000-2000ptas/€6-12); **Gibraltar** (4½hr., 8am and 3pm, 2580ptas/€15.48); **Madrid** (5hr., 14 per day 7am-1:30am, 2075ptas/€12.45).

Bacoma (☎958 15 75 57). To: **Alicante** (6hr., 5 per day, 3510ptas/€21.06); **Barcelona** (14hr., 3 per day, 8300ptas/€49.80); **Valencia** (8hr., 4 per day, 5145ptas/€30.87). All buses run 10:15am-1:45am.

Junta de Andalucía, the regional government, charters buses regularly to **Veleta** from the Granada bus station. Call ahead (☎630 95 97 39) for reservations and additional information. (45 min.; 5-7 per day 9am-6:40pm; 500ptas/€3 one-way, 800ptas/€4.80 round-trip.) Under three years old, free; 50% discount for seniors and children under 9.

Public Transportation: (☎958 81 37 11). Important buses include: "Bus Alhambra" from Pl. Nueva; #10 from the bus station to the youth hostel, C. de Ronda, C. Recogidas, and C. Acera de Darro; and #3 from the bus station to Av. Constitución, Gran Vía, and Pl. Isabel la Católica. Rides 130ptas/€0.78, bonobus (10 tickets) 1000ptas/€6.

Taxis: Teletaxi, (24hr. ☎958 28 06 54), with service to Granada and environs.

Car Rental: Atasa, Pl. Cuchilleros, 1 (☎958 22 40 04). Cheapest car 46,000ptas/€276 per week with unlimited mileage and insurance. Prices rise with shorter rentals. Min. age 20, and must have had a license for at least 1 year.

ORIENTATION AND PRACTICAL INFORMATION

Municipal **buses** cover practically the entire city, but the best way to explore is on foot. The geographic center of Granada is the small **Pl. de Isabel la Católica,** the intersection of the city's two main arteries, **C. de los Reyes Católicos** and **Gran Vía de Colón.** On Gran Vía, you'll find the **cathedral.** Two short blocks uphill on C. Reyes Católicos sits Pl. Nueva. Downhill, also along C. Reyes Católicos, lie Pl. Carmen, site of the **Ayuntamiento,** and Puerta Real, the six-way intersection of C. Reyes Católicos, C. Recogidos, C. Mesones, C. Acera de Darro, C. Angel Gavinet, and C. Acero del Casino. The **Alhambra** commands the steep hill up from Pl. Nueva.

Tourist Office: Oficina Provincial, Pl. Mariana Pineda, 10 (☎958 24 71 28; fax 22 89 16). From Pta. Real, turn right onto C. Angel Ganivet, then take a right 2 blocks later to reach the plaza. English spoken. Open M-F 9:30am-7pm, Sa 10am-2pm. **Junta de Andalucía** (☎958 22 10 22; fax 22 39 27; email otgranada@andalucia.es), C. Mariana Pineda. From Pta. Real, take C. Reyes Católicos to Pl. Carmen; C. Mariana Pineda is the 1st left. Hotel guide (800ptas/€4.80) and brochures on hiking, hunting, and golf (400ptas/€2.40). Open M-Sa 9am-7pm, Su 10am-2pm.

Currency Exchange: Banco Central Hispano, Gran Vía, 3 (☎958 21 73 00), off Pl. Isabel la Católica. Exchanges money and AmEx traveler's checks; no commission. Open May-Sept. M-F 9am-2pm; Oct.-Apr. M-Sa 9am-2pm.

American Express: C. Reyes Católicos, 31 (☎958 22 45 12), between Pl. Isabel la Católica and Pta. Real. Open M-F 9am-1:30pm and 2-9pm, Sa 10am-2pm and 3-7pm.

Gay and Lesbian Organizations: Juvenós, C. Lavadero de las Tablas, 15, organizes weekly activities for gay youth. **Información Homosexual Hotline** ☎958 20 06 02.

Luggage Storage: At the **train** and **bus stations** (400ptas/€2.40). Open daily 4-9pm.

El Corte Inglés: C. Genil, 20 and 22, (☎958 22 32 40). Follow C. Acera del Casino from Pta. Real to C. Genil. Good map for 475ptas/€2.85. Open M-Sa 10am-10pm.

Foreign Language Bookstore: Metro, C. Gracia, 31 (☎958 26 15 65). Vast foreign language section. Open M-F 10am-9pm, Sa 10am-2pm.

Laundromat: C. La Paz, 19. From Pl. Trinidad, take C. Alhóndiga, turn right on C. La Paz, and walk 2 blocks. Wash 500ptas/€3; dry 150ptas/€0.90 per 15min. Open M-F 9:30am-2pm and 4:30-8:30pm, Sa 9am-2pm.

Emergency: ☎112. **Police:** C. Duquesa, 21 (☎958 24 81 00). English spoken.

Pharmacy: Farmacia Gran Vía, Gran Vía, 6 (☎958 22 29 90). Open M-F 9:30am-2pm and 5-8:30pm.

Medical Assistance: Clínica de San Cecilio, C. Dr. Oloriz, 16 (☎958 28 02 00 or 27 20 00), on the road to Jaén. **Ambulance:** ☎958 28 44 50.

Internet Access: Net (☎958 22 69 19) has 3 locations: #1) C. Santa Escolástica, 13, up C. Pavaneras from Pl. Isabel la Católica; #2) Pl. de los Girones, 3, 1 block away from first locale; #3) C. Buensucesco, 22, 1 block from Pl. Trinidad. English spoken. 200ptas/€1.20 per hr. All open M-Sa 9am-1am, Su 3pm-1am.

Post Office: Pta. Real (☎958 22 48 35; fax 22 36 41), on the corner of C. Acera de Darro and C. Angel Ganinet. **Lista de Correos** and **fax** service. Open M-F 8am-9pm, Sa 9:30am-2pm. Wires money M-F 8:30am-2:30pm. **Postal Code:** 18009.

ACCOMMODATIONS AND CAMPING

NEAR PLAZA NUEVA

Hostels line Cuesta de Gomérez, the street leading uphill to the Alhambra, to the right of Pl. Nueva. Crashing in this area is wise for those planning to spend serious time at the Alhambra complex, but these spots tend to fill up the quickest.

Hostal Venecia, Cuesta de Gomérez, 2, 3rd fl. (☎958 22 39 87). Cozy abode is the most appealing bargain in town. Rooms near the street can be noisy. Singles 2000ptas/€6; doubles 4000ptas/€24; triples and quads 1800ptas/€11 per person.

Hostal Residencia Britz, Cuesta de Gomérez, 1 (☎/fax 958 22 36 52), on the corner of Pl. Nueva. Laundry 600ptas/€3. 24hr. reception. Singles 2500ptas/€15, with bath 4000ptas/€24; doubles 4100ptas/€24.60, with bath 5700ptas/€34.20. MC/V.

Hostal Navarro-Ramos, Cuesta de Gomérez, 21 (☎958 25 05 55). Watercolors and memorabilia from Queen Elizabeth's silver jubilee cover the walls of this pension near the walls of the Alhambra. Showers 150ptas/€0.90. Singles 1700ptas/€10.20; doubles 2700ptas/€16.20, with bath 4500ptas/€27; triples with bath 6000ptas/€36.

Hostal Gomérez, Cuesta de Gomérez, 10 (☎958 22 44 37). Spartan rooms with hall baths. Multilingual owner will assist guests planning longer stays. Laundry 1000ptas/€5 per load. Singles 2500ptas/€15; doubles 3500ptas/€21; triples 4500ptas/€27.

NEAR THE CATHEDRAL/UNIVERSITY

Hostels surround Pl. Trinidad, at the end of C. Mesones when coming from Pta. Real. Many *pensiones* around C. Mesones cater to students during the academic year but free up during the summer. The ones listed below are open year-round.

Hospedaje Almohada, C. Postigo de Zarate, 4 (☎958 20 74 46). From Pl. Trinidad, follow C. Duquesa to C. Málaga and take a right; it's the red door with the small sign on your right. A successful experiment in communal living: guests cook for each other with produce from a local market and fraternize over Cruzcampo and olives in the cozy den. Simple white rooms with sinks and cheerful furniture. Laundry 700ptas/€4.20 per load. Dorms 1800ptas/€10.80; singles 2200ptas/€13.20; doubles 3900ptas/€23.

Hostal-Residencia Lisboa, Pl. Carmen, 29 (☎958 22 14 13 or 22 14 14; fax 22 14 87). Take C. Reyes Católicos from Pl. Isabel la Católica; Pl. Carmen is on the left. TVs, and fans. Singles 2700ptas/€16, with bath 4000ptas/€24; doubles 4000ptas/€24, with bath 5800ptas/€35; triples 5400ptas/€32, with bath 7800ptas/€47. MC/V.

Hostal Zurita, Pl. Trinidad, 7 (☎958 27 50 20). Bright rooms with floral sheets and sound-proof balcony doors. High-quality beds, A/C, and 24hr. hot water. Singles 2500ptas/€15; doubles 4500ptas/€27, with baths 5500ptas/€33; triples 6500ptas/€39, with bath 7500ptas/€45.

ALONG GRAN VÍA DE COLÓN

Hostels are sprinkled along Gran Vía. In all cases, rooms with balconies over the street are much noisier than those that open onto an inner patio.

Hostal Antares, C. Cetti Meriém, 10 (☎958 22 83 13), on the corner of C. Elvira, 1 block from the cathedral. Winter heating. Singles 2500ptas/€15; doubles 4000ptas/€24, with bath 5500ptas/€33; triples 5250ptas/€31.50. Rooms with A/C and TVs available upstairs: doubles 6000ptas/€36; triples 10,500ptas/€63.

Hostal Gran Vía, Gran Vía, 17 (☎958 27 92 12), about 4 blocks from Pl. Isabel la Católica. Singles with shower 3000ptas/€18; doubles 3500ptas/€21, with shower 4000ptas/€24, with bath, 5000ptas/€30; triples with shower 6000ptas/€36, with bath 7000ptas/€42.

Hostal-Residencia Londres, Gran Vía, 29, 6th fl. (☎958 27 80 34). Perched atop a fin-de-siecle edifice with multiple patios. One large bath for every 2 bedrooms. Singles 3000ptas/€18; doubles 3500ptas/€21; 1500ptas/€9 per each additional person.

Pensión Olympia, Alvaro de Bazán, 6 (☎958 27 82 38). From Pl. Isabel, walk 6 blocks down Gran Vía and turn right. A simple standard. Singles 2500ptas/€15; doubles 3000ptas/€18, with shower 4000ptas/€24, with bath 5000ptas/€30. MC/V.

ELSEWHERE

Albergue Juvenil Granada (HI), Ramón y Cajal, 2 (☎958 00 29 00 or 00 29 01; fax 00 29 08). From the bus station take #10; from the train station #11; ask the driver to stop at "El Estadio de la Juventud." A cross the field on the left. 24hr. reception. Towels 175ptas/€1.50. Dorms 1725-2050ptas/€10-12, over 26 2375-2675ptas/€14-16. Non-HI guests can join by paying an extra 500ptas/€3 per night for 6 nights.

CAMPING

Buses serve five campgrounds within 5km of Granada. Check the departure schedules at the tourist office, sit up front, and ask bus drivers to alert you to your stop.

Sierra Nevada, Av. Madrid, 107 (☎958 15 00 62; fax 15 09 54). Take bus #3 or 10. Lots of shady trees, modern facilities, a large outdoor pool, and free hot showers. If you arrive when the town fair is here, stay elsewhere or you'll have clown nightmares. 630ptas/€3.78 per person, children under 10 525ptas/€3.15. Open Mar.-Oct.

María Eugenia, Ctra. Nacional, 342 (☎958 20 06 06, fax 20 94 10), at km 436 on the road to Málaga. Take the Santa Fé or Chauchina bus from the train station (every 30min.). 500ptas/€3 per person, children 400ptas/€2.40. Open year-round.

FOOD

Granada offers a variety of ethnic restaurants to revive those who have had a bit too much fish. North African cuisine can be found around the **Albaicín,** while more typical *menú* fare awaits in Pl. Nueva and Pl. Trinidad. The adventurous eat well in Granada—*tortilla sacromonte* (omelette with calf's brains, bull testicles, ham, shrimp, and veggies), *sesos a la romana* (batter-fried calf's brains), and *rabo de toro* (bull's tail) are common. Picnickers can gather fresh fruit and vegetables at the **market** on C. San Augustín. Get groceries at **Supermercado T. Mariscal,** C. Genil, next to El Corte Inglés (open M-F 9:30am-2pm and 5-9pm, Sa 9:30am-2pm).

NEAR PLAZA NUEVA

The places around Pl. Nueva offer *tapas* for **free** (with a drink).

Restaurant Sonymar, (☎958 27 10 63), Pl. Boquero, 6. Relish the nouveau Moorish decor of this secluded neighborhood eatery. *Menú* 850ptas/€5.10. Entrées 1200-2100ptas/€7.20-12.60. Open daily 1-4pm and 8-11:30pm. AmEx/V.

La Nueva Bodega, C. Cetti Meriém, 9 (☎958 22 59 34), out of Pl. Nueva on a street off C. Elvira. Locals stake out the bar as tourists dine on hearty traditional cuisine. *Menús* 1000-1100ptas/€6-6.60. *Bocadillos* 275ptas/€1.65. Open daily noon-midnight.

Bodega Castañeda, (☎958 21 54 64), C. Almireceros 1-3. Plenty of A/C and tourists. Traditional *bodega* atmosphere. Legs of ham and wine barrels line the walls. *Bocadillos* 400ptas/€2.40. Open daily 8am-4pm and 6pm-1am, Sa-Su noon-4pm and 6pm-3am.

THE ALBAICÍN

Wander the romantic, winding streets of the Albaicín and you'll discover a number of budget bars and restaurants on the slopes above Pl. Nueva. C. Calderería Nueva, off C. Elvira leading from the plaza, is crammed with teahouses and cafés.

El Ladrillo II, C. Panaderos, 13 (☎958 29 26 51), off Cuesta del Chapiz near the Iglesia El Salvador, high on the Albaicín. This time, it's worth checking out the sequel. Feast under the stars on seafood while listening to the romantic strains of *sevillanas*. *Menú* claims—with some credibility—to offer "the biggest portions in Spain." Entrées 1100-2000ptas/€6.60-12. Open daily 12:30pm-1:30am. MC/V.

Naturi Albaicín, C. Calderería Nueva, 10 (☎958 22 06 27). Excellent vegetarian restaurant with a serene Moroccan ambience. Tasty options include *berenjenas rellenas* (stuffed eggplant), quiche, and *kefir* (a yogurt drink). No alcohol served. *Menús* 950-1150ptas/€5.70-6.90. Open Sa-Th 1-4pm and 7-11pm, F 7-11pm.

Medina-Zahara, C. Calderería Nueva, 12 (☎958 22 15 41). A North African take-out joint distinguished by its inauthentic but delicious *samosas* (275-325ptas/€1.65-1.95) and exceptional falafel (325ptas/€1.95). Open daily 9pm-2am.

GRAN VÍA AND ELSEWHERE

Botánico Café, C. Málaga, 3 (☎958 27 15 98), 2 blocks from Pl. Trinidad. Manhattan minimalism meets Spanish modernity at this student hangout where a fusion of cultural food traditions brings new life to Spanish favorites. Entrées 800-1500ptas/€4.80-9. Open M-Th 10am-3am, Su noon-1am.

Restaurante Chino Estrella Oriental, C. Alvaro de Bazán, 9 (☎958 22 34 67), 5 blocks down Gran Vía from Pl. Isabel la Católica. Bright-red Pagoda façade welcomes all to cheap, tasty *menús* (650ptas/€3.90). Free delivery with orders of 1500ptas/€9 or more. Open daily 12:30-4:30pm and 8:00pm-12:30am. MC/V.

SIGHTS

THE ALHAMBRA

To reach the Alhambra, take C. Cuesta de Gomérez off Pl. Nueva, and be prepared to pant (20min.; no unauthorized cars 9am-9pm). Or take the cheap, quick Alhambra-Neptuno micro-bus (every 5min., 130ptas/€0.78) from Pl. Nueva. ☎958 22 15 03. Open Apr.-Sept. daily 8:30am-8pm; Oct.-Mar. M-Sa 9am-5:45pm. Nighttime visits June-Sept. Tu, Th, Sa 10-11:30pm; Oct.-May Sa 8-10pm. All visits 1000ptas/€6, free for the handicapped and children under 8. Limited to 7700 visitors per day June-Sept., 6300 Oct.-May, so get there early to stand in line. Enter the Palace of the Nazarites (Alcázar) during the time specified on your ticket, but stay as long as desired. It is possible to reserve tickets a few days in advance at banks for a 125ptas/€0.75 service charge; this is recommended especially July-Aug. and Semana Santa. *Reservations ☎902 22 44 60. Audioguides available, narrated by Washington Irving in Spanish, English, French, German, and Italian (500ptas/€3).*

From the streets of Granada, the Alhambra, in Arabic, "the red one," appears simple, blocky, faded—a child's toy castle planted in the foothills of the Sierra Nevada. Up close, however, you will discover an elaborate and detailed piece of architecture; one that magically unites water, light, wood, stucco, and ceramics to create a fortress-palace of rich aesthetic and symbolic grandeur.

THE ALCAZABA. The Christians drove the first Nazarite King Alhamar from the Albaicín to this more strategic hill, where he built the fortress Alcazaba. A dark, spiraling staircase leads to the **Torre de la Vela** (watchtower), where visitors get a great 360° view of Granada and the surrounding mountains. The tower's bells were rung to warn of impending danger and to coordinate the Moorish irrigation system. During an annual festival, custom dictates that any local girl who scrambles up the tower and rings the bell by hand will receive a wedding proposal within a year. Exit through the **Puerta del Vino,** the original entrance to the medina, where inhabitants of the Alhambra once bought tax-free wine (alas, no more).

THE ALCÁZAR. Follow signs to the *Palacio Nazaries* to see the Alcázar, a royal palace built for the Moorish rulers Yusuf I (1333-1354) and Muhammed V (1354-1391). Yusuf I was murdered in an isolated basement of the Alcázar, and his son Muhammed V was left to complete the palace.

The entrance leads into the **Mexuar,** a great, pillared council chamber. Note the glazed tile arrangements that reiterate the Nazarite mantra: "There is no victor but God." The Mexuar adjoins the **Patio del Cuarto Dorado (Patio of the Gilded Hall).** Off the far side of the patio, foliated horseshoe archways of diminishing width open onto the **Cuarto Dorado (Gilded Hall),** decorated by Muhammed V. Its painstakingly carved wooden ceiling, inlaid with ivory and mother-of-pearl, displays polygonal figures and colorful ceramic *dados*.

Next is the **Patio de los Arrayanes (Courtyard of Myrtles),** an expanse of emerald water filled with goldfish and bubbling fountains. Stand at the top of the patio for a glimpse of the 14th-century **Fachada de Serallo,** the palace's elaborately carved façade. The long and slender **Sala de la Barca (Boat Gallery),** with an inverted boat-hull ceiling, flanks the courtyard.

In the elaborate **Sala de los Embajadores (Hall of Ambassadors),** adjoining the Sala de la Barca to the north, Granada was formally surrendered to the Catholic Monarchs and Fernando and Columbus discussed finding a new route to India. Every surface of this magnificent square hall is intricately wrought with symbolic inscriptions and ornamental patterns. The Mozarabic dome, carved of more than 8000 pieces of wood and inlaid cedar, depicts the seven skies of paradise mentioned in the Koran. From the Patio de los Arrayanes, the Sala de los Mozárabes leads to the **Patio de los Leones (Courtyard of the Lions),** the grandest display of Nazarite art in the palace, where a rhythmic arcade of marble columns borders the courtyard, and a fountain supported by 12 marble lions babbles in the middle.

Moving counter-clockwise around the courtyard, the next room is the **Sala de los Abencerrajes.** Here, Sultan Abul Hassan piled the heads of his first wife's 16 sons so that Boabdil, son by his second wife, could inherit the throne. The rust-colored stains in the basin are said to mark the indelible traces of the butchering; evidently none of this bothered the Emperor Charles V, who dined here during the construction of his neighboring *palazzo*. Light bleeds into the room through the intricate domed ceiling, which features an eight-pointed star—a design said to represent terrestrial and heavenly harmony.

Through stalactite archways, at the far end of the courtyard from the Patio de los Leones, lies the **Sala de los Reyes (Hall of Kings).** Fixed to the walls with bamboo pins, detailed sheepskin paintings depict important assemblies and hunts. On the remaining side of the courtyard, the resplendent **Sala de las Dos Hermanas (Chamber of the Two Sisters)** has a honeycombed Mozarabic dome comprised of thousands of tiny cells. From here a secluded portico, **Mirador de Daraxa (Eyes of the Sultana),** overlooks the Jardines de Daraxa.

Passing the room where American author Washington Irving resided in 1829, a courtyard leads to the 14th-century **Baños Reales (Royal Baths),** the center of court social life. Light shining through star-shaped holes in the ceiling once refracted through steam, creating indoor rainbows. Unfortunately, the baths are currently closed during summer for conservation studies and archaeological bubble baths.

TOWERS AND GARDENS. Just outside the east wall of the Alcázar in the **Jardines del Partal,** lily-studded pools stand beside rose-laden terraces. The **Torre de las Damas (Ladies' Tower)** soars above it all. The series of six towers traverses the area between the Alcazaba and El Generalife, one for captives, one for princesses, etc.

EL GENERALIFE. Over a bridge, across the **Callejón de los Cipreses** and the shady **Callejón de las Adelfas,** are the vibrant blossoms, towering cypresses, and streaming waterways of El Generalife, the sultan's vacation retreat. In 1313 Arab engineers changed the Darro's flow by 18km and employed dams and channels to prepare the soil for Aben Walid Ismail's design of El Generalife. Over the centuries, the estate passed through private hands until it was finally repatriated in 1931. The two buildings of El Generalife, the **Palacio** and the **Sala Regia,** connect across the **Patio de la Acequia (Courtyard of the Irrigation Channel),** embellished with a narrow pool fed by fountains that form an aquatic archway. Honeysuckle vines scale the back wall, and shady benches invite long rests.

PALACIO DE CARLOS V. After the *Reconquista* drove the Moors from Spain, Fernando and Isabel restored the Alcázar. Little did they know that two generations later Emperor Carlos V would demolish part of it to make way for his Palacio, a Renaissance masterpiece by Pedro Machuca (a disciple of Michelangelo). Although it is incongruous with the surrounding Moorish splendor, scholars concede that the palace is one of the most beautiful Renaissance buildings in Spain. A square building with a circular inner courtyard wrapped in two stories of Doric colonnades, it is

THE HEADLESS MOORISH HORSE In 1829, after an undistinguished legal career and a brief stint as United States Ambassador to Spain, Washington Irving traveled to Granada, where he stayed for several months in the Alhambra as a guest of the royal governor. Enchanted by his surroundings, Irving later published a collection of short stories entitled *Tales of the Alhambra* (1832). Particularly memorable is the legend of the eerie but innocuously headless Moorish horse who "issues forth in the dead of the night and scours the avenues of the Alhambra and the streets of Granada." In later years, Irving again took up the theme of phantasmagorical decapitation, although he was no less inspired by the beauty of the Andalucían countryside. A girl's transformation into womanhood, he wrote, "is like passing from the flat, bleak, uninteresting plain of La Mancha, to the voluptuous valleys and swelling hills of Andalucía." Perhaps it's time the regional tourism board adopt a new slogan. Tales of the Alhambra *is available at El Corte Inglés (650ptas/€3.90) and countless souvenir shops throughout Granada. If you're willing to risk an encounter with the headless Moorish horse,* ***tours of the Alhambra under moonlight*** *are romantic and unforgettable. June-Sept. Tu, Th, Sa 10-11:30pm; Oct.-May Sa 8-10pm (1000ptas/€6).*

Machuca's only surviving design. Inside, the **Museo de La Alhambra** contains the only original furnishings remaining from the Alhambra. *(☎958 22 62 79. Open Tu-Sa 9am-2pm. 250ptas/€1.50, free for EU citizens.)* Upstairs, the **Museo de Bellas Artes** displays religious sculptures and paintings of the Granada School dating from the 16th century to the present. *(☎958 22 48 43. Open April-Sept. Tu 2:30-6pm, W-Sa 9am-6pm, Su 9am-2:30pm; Oct.-March Tu 2:30-7:45pm, W-Sa 9am-7:45pm, Su 9am-2pm.)*

IN THE CATHEDRAL QUARTER

CAPILLA REAL. Downhill from the Alhambra's Arab splendor, the Capilla Real (Royal Chapel), Fernando and Isabel's private chapel, exemplifies Christian Granada. During their prosperous reign, the Catholic Monarchs funneled almost a quarter of the royal income into the chapel's construction (which lasted from 1504 to 1521) to produce a proper burial place. Their efforts did not go unrewarded; intricate Gothic masonry and meticulously rendered figurines, as well as **La Reja,** the gilded iron grille of Master Bartolomé, grace the resting place of the couple. Behind La Reja lie the almost lifelike marble figures of the royals themselves. Fernando and Isabel are on the right, when facing the altar; beside them sleeps their daughter Juana la Loca (the Mad) and her husband Felipe el Hermoso (the Fair). To the horror of the rest of the royal family, Juana insisted on keeping the body of her husband with her for an unpleasantly long time after he died. The lead caskets, where all four monarchs were laid to rest, lie directly below the marble sarcophagi in a crypt accessible by a small stairway on the left. The smaller, fifth coffin belongs to the hastily buried child-king of Portugal, Miguel, whose death allowed Carlos V to ascend the throne.

THE ALBAICÍN. A labyrinth of steep streets and narrow alleys, the Albaicín was the only Moorish neighborhood to escape the torches of the *Reconquista* and remains a key stop in Granada. After the fall of the Alhambra, a small Muslim population remained here until being expelled in the 17th century. Today, with its abundance of North African cuisine and the recent construction of a mosque near Pl. San Nicolás, the Albaicín attests to the persistence of Islamic influence in Andalucía. Spectacular sunsets over the surrounding mountains can be seen from C. Cruz de Quirós, above C. Elvira. Although generally safe, the Albaicín is disorienting and should be approached with caution at night. *(Bus #12 runs from beside the cathedral to C. Pagés at the top of the Albaicín.)*

The best way to explore this maze is to proceed along C. Acera de Darro off Pl. Nueva, climb the Cuesta del Chapiz on the left, then wander through Muslim ramparts, cisterns, and gates. On Pl. Nueva, the 16th-century **Real Cancillería** (or **Audiencia**), with a beautiful arcaded patio and stalactite ceiling, was the Christians' Ayuntamiento. Farther uphill are the 11th-century **Arab baths.** *(C. Acera de Darro, 31.*

☎958 02 78 00. Open Tu-Sa 10am-2pm. Free.) The **Museo Arqueológico** showcases funerary urns, Classical sculpture, Carthaginian vases, Muslim lamps, and ceramics. *(C. Acera de Darro, 41. ☎958 22 56 40. Open Tu 3-8pm, W-Sa 9am-8pm, Su 9am-2:30pm. 250ptas/€1.50, free for EU members.)* The terrace adjacent to **Iglesia de San Nicolás** affords the city's best view of the Alhambra, especially in winter when snow adorns the Sierra Nevada behind it.

SACRISTY. Next door in the sacristy, Isabel's private **art collection,** the highlight of the chapel, favors Flemish and German artists of the 15th century. The glittering **royal jewels**—the queen's golden crown and scepter and the king's sword—shine in the middle of the sacristy. Nearby are the Christian banners which first fluttered in triumph over the Alhambra. *(☎958 22 92 39. Capilla Real and Sacristy both open M-Sa 10:30am-1pm and 4-7pm, Su 11am-1pm and 4-7pm; 350ptas/€2.10.)*

CATHEDRAL. Construction of the cathedral began upon the smouldering embers of Granada's largest mosque and was not completed until 1704. The first purely Renaissance cathedral in Spain, its massive Corinthian pillars support a 45m vaulted nave. Full scale restoration efforts are currently underway. *(☎958 22 29 59. Open Apr.-Sept. M-Sa 10:45am-1:30pm and 4-7pm, Su 4-7pm; Oct.-Mar. M-Sa 10:30am-1:30pm and 3:30-6:30pm, Su 11am-1:30pm. Closed Su morning. 350ptas/€2.10.)*

OTHER SIGHTS. The 16th-century **Hospital Real** is divided into 4 tiled courtyards. Above the main staircase, the Mudéjar-coffered ceiling echoes those of the Alhambra. *(C. San Juan de Dios. Open M-F 9am-2pm. Free.)* The 14th-century **Monasterio de San Jerónimo** is around the corner. Though badly damaged by Napoleon's troops, it has since been restored. *(☎958 27 93 37. Open Apr.-Sept. M-Sa 10am-1:30pm and 4-7pm, Su 11am-1:30pm; Oct.-Mar. M-Sa 10am-1pm and 3-6:30pm, Su 11am-1:30pm. 350ptas/€2.10.)*

NIGHTLIFE

Entertainment listings are at the back of the daily paper, the *Ideal*, under *Cine y Espectáculos;* the Friday supplement lists bars and special events. The *Guía del Ocio*, sold at newsstands (100ptas/€0.60), lists clubs, pubs, and cafés.

FLAMENCO AND JAZZ

The most "authentic" flamenco performances, which change monthly, are advertised on posters around town. A list of the nightly *tablaos* is available at the tourist office. Everyone loves **Los Jardines Neptuno,** C. Arabial, near the Neptuno shopping center at the base of C. Recogidas where rows of plastic chairs fill an enclosed theater. (☎958 52 25 33. Cover 3800ptas/€23, includes 1 drink and a bus ride to Albaicín.) A smoky, intimate setting awaits at **Eshavira,** C. Postigo de la Cuna, in an alley off C. Azacayes, between C. Elvira and Gran Vía. This joint is *the* place to go for flamenco, jazz, or a fusion of the two. Photos of Nat King Cole and other jazz greats plaster the walls. (☎958 29 08 29. Min. 1 drink. Call for schedule.)

PUBS, BARS, AND CLUBS

Pubs and bars spread across several neighborhoods, genres, and energy levels. The most boisterous crowds hang out on C. Pedro Antonio de Alarcón, running from Pl. Albert Einstein to Ancha de Gracia, while hip new bars and clubs line C. Elvira from Cárcel to C. Cedrán. A few gay bars cluster around Carrera del Darro, while a more openly gay scene can be found at the Parque del Triunfo and the Paseo del Salón. A full list of gay establishments is available at the tourist office.

Camborio, Camino del Sacromonte, 48 (☎958 22 12 15), a 20min. walk uphill from Pl. Nueva. Gypsies and highwaymen once roamed the caves of Sacromonte, now the domain of scantily-clad clubbers. American and Spanish pop echoes through labyrinthine dance floors to the rooftop terraces above. Striking, if blurry-eyed, view of the Alhambra at sunrise. Can seem empty on Tuesdays and Wednesdays. 700ptas/€4.20 cover on F and Sa. Beer 300-500ptas/€1.80-3. Open Tu-Sa 11pm-dawn.

Granero, Pl. Luis Rosales (☎958 22 89 79), near Pl. Isabel Católica. A New Age barn loft bulging with grooving Spanish yuppies. The place to go for a night on the town early in the week. Salsa and Spanish pop pervade. Beer 400ptas/€2.40, mixed drinks 500-700ptas/€3-4.20. Open daily 10pm-dawn.

Planta Baja, C. Horno de Abad, 11 (☎958 25 35 09). Live bands play regularly within the concrete confines of this techno dance club. Wildly popular with students. Beer 300ptas/€1.80. Cover 500ptas/€3. Open from fall until early July, Th-Sa 10pm-6am.

Disco 10, C. Carcel Baja, 3 (☎958 22 40 01). Movie theater by evening, raging dance club by night. Perhaps the most opulent disco you'll ever see (at least in Granada). Best for after hours on weekends. Open daily. 1000ptas/€6 cover Th-Sa includes one drink.

Kasbah, C. Calderería Nueva, 4 (☎958 22 79 36). Relax amidst the comforts of this candlelit café. Silky pillows and romantic nooks abound. Arab pastries and an exhaustive selection of Moroccan teas (300ptas/€1.80). Open daily 3pm-3am.

Fondo Reservado, Cuesta de Sta. Inés, off Carrera del Darro. A popular gay bar with a fun, mixed crowd that parties hard. Beer 400ptas/€2.40, mixed drinks 600ptas/€3.60. Opens daily at 11pm.

El Angel Azul, C. Lavadero de las Tablas, 15. Well established gay bar with a basement dance floor and curtained booths. Monthly drag shows and striptease contests. Beer 400ptas/€2.40. Open daily midnight-5am.

ENTERTAINMENT

Festivals sweep Granada in the summer. The **Corpus Christi** celebrations, processions, and bullfights are famous (May 30 in 2002). Every May, avant-garde theater groups from around the world make a pilgrimage to Granada for the **International Theater Festival** (☎958 22 93 44). The **Festival Internacional de Música y Danza** (mid-June to early July) sponsors open-air performances of classical music, ballet, and flamenco in the Alhambra's Palacio de Carlos V and other outdoor venues. (☎958 22 18 44. Tickets 1000-6000ptas/€6-36, senior and youth discounts available.)

DAYTRIPS FROM GRANADA

FUENTE VAQUEROS

Buses run hourly between Av. Andaluces in front of the Granada train station and Fuente Vaqueros (25min.; 9am-9pm, returns 8am-8pm; 180ptas/€1.10). From the bus stop in Fuente Vaqueros, turn right onto Po. Prado, then onto C. Poetra Lorca, the museum is #4. Buy tickets around the corner on C. Manuel de Falla, the next left off Po. Prado.

Poet and playwright Federico García Lorca, known for his works *Bodas de Sangre* and *Romancero Gitano*, was born outside the tiny town of Fuente Vaqueros. Killed by right-wing forces near Granada at the outbreak of the Civil War, he is recognized as one of Spain's greatest writers. The restored **Casa-Museo,** Lorca's house-turned-museum, has everything from the piano where the master played to the bed in which he was born, in addition to the more staid museum fare of letters, poetry, and other writings. The upper level of the **granero** (granary) features photos of Lorca with his close friend Salvador Dalí and costumes from performances of his plays around the world. (☎958 51 64 53. Open only for tours on the hour; Apr.-June Tu-Sa 10am-1pm and 5-7pm, July-Sept. Tu-Sa 10am-1pm and 6-8pm, Oct.-Mar. Tu-Sa 10am-1pm and 4-6pm. 200ptas/€1.20. 15 people max per hr.; call ahead for reservations.) Each June, the town celebrates Lorca's birthday (June 5), with a 4-day long **fiesta** that culminating in concerts, plays, and other festivities.

VELETA

The Autocares Bonal bus (☎958 27 31 00) between the bus station in Granada and Veleta is a bargain (9am, returns 5pm from Albergue; round-trip 900ptas/€5.40).

Near the foot of the Alhambra, the highest road in Europe begins its gradual ascent to Veleta, one of Europe's greatest peaks. The road starts off in the arid countryside before scaling the daunting face of the Sierra to the stark summit at 3470m. Due to snow, cars can cruise to the very top of Veleta only in August and September; be sure to check current road conditions before starting off (☎958 24 91 19). Veleta has 39 slopes and 61 sq. km of skiing area, with a vertical drop of 1300m. Lift tickets go for 2325ptas/€14. **Ski rentals** are available in the Gondola Building and in Pl. Prado Llano (full equipment 2500ptas/€15.03 per day). This ski resort is the southernmost in Europe—wear sunscreen or suffer. The cheapest accommodation is the **Albergue Universitario** (☎958 48 01 22), the yellow building at the bus stop. (Singles 2200ptas/€13; doubles 5200ptas/€31.)

Ski season runs from December to April. The mountains are less attractive in summer, but tourists still come to paraglide and hike. **Cetursa** (☎958 24 91 11) has info on outdoor activities. If you plan to hike extensively, stop first at **Librería Flash** in Granada for their indispensable 800pta/€4.80 map of the Sierra (see p. 261).

LAS ALPUJARRAS

The *pueblos blancos* (white villages) of Las Alpujarras are seated along the southern slopes of the Sierra Nevada. Although the roads are now paved and the towns well-traveled, a medieval Berber influence is still evident in the region's architecture; the low-slung houses rendered from earth and slate quite closely resemble those in Morocco's Atlas Mountains. The fall of Granada in 1492 is traditionally seen as the mark of the end of Moorish rule in Iberia, but the Berbers in fact relocated to the Alpujarras and Christian-Muslim conflict continued until 1610, when John of Austria finally ousted the Moors. The legacy of Moorish defiance lives on every June during Trevélez's Fiestas de Moros y Cristianos. Settlers from Galicia made the Alpujarras their home after the Moors were ousted, and they brought with them Celtic and Visigothic traditions found nowhere else in Andalucía.

Although tourists have recently discovered the beauty of these settlements and the region's numerous hiking trails, the Alpujarras remain one of Spain's poorest areas. Until the 1950s, travel was possible only by foot or mule, and the region still suffers from unemployment and low literacy rates. Nevertheless, the villages' slow-paced lifestyle, well-preserved beauty, and rooted cultural traditions, not to mention temperate climate, make for a refreshing visit. For the more active tourist, the mountains themselves offer plenty of climbing and hiking opportunities.

Alsina Graells buses—the only available form of transportation—travel from Granada to many of the high-altitude towns, and bus drivers will often stop to let travelers off at intermediate points (**buses** leave Granada at 10:30am, noon, and 5:15pm for the villages, and begin the return trip from the farthest town, Alcutar, at 5am and 5pm). The buses trace switchback after unnerving switchback, claiming the scenic road—the drive through the mountains is often one of the highlights of a visit to the Alpujarras. Some hard-core visitors hike from place to place, and the locals, well aware of the transportation problem, often sympathize with hitchers.

PAMPANEIRA

As the road winds in serpentine curves up to the high Alpujarran villages, the landscape quickly becomes harsh. Pampaneira (pop. 360, 1059m) is the first in a trio of hamlets overlooking the **Poqueira Gorge,** a massive ravine cut by the Río Poqueira; the town makes a great springboard for climbing to **Bubión** (30min.) and **Capileira** (1¾hr.). The trail to both begins from behind the church at the very top of town; a sign points the way. For more info on the region's natural wonders, visit the local organization **Nevadensis** in the main square; between arranging rural accommodations and horseback riding, they serve as the town's main tourist information center. (☎958 76 31 27; fax 76 33 01; www.nevadensis.com. Open Tu-Sa 10am-2pm and 4-6pm, Su-M 10am-3pm.) **Hostal Pampaneira,** just off the highway in front of the bus stop, has large rooms with private baths. (☎958 76 30 02. Singles 2500ptas/€15;

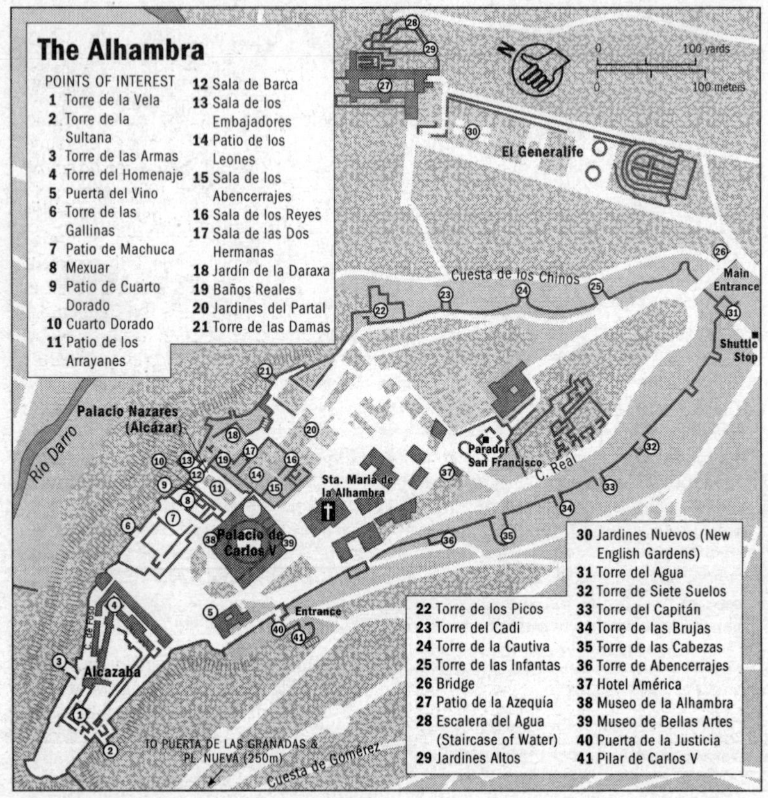

doubles 4000ptas/€24; triples 4500ptas/€27. MC/V.) The hostel **restaurant** tends to be busy when all others aren't, and the food certainly lives up to expectations. (Entrées 650-1200ptas/€3.90-7.20. MC/V.)

BUBIÓN

Bubión, a steep 3km (30min.) hike from Pampaneira, is resplendent with Berber architecture, village charm, and enough *artesanía* to make your head spin. For tourist info, stop by **Rustic Blue,** Barrio La Ermita. The helpful staff organizes excursions and rural lodging. (☎958 76 33 81; fax 958 76 31 34. English and French spoken. Open M-F 10am-2pm and 5-8pm, Sa 11am-2pm.) **Las Terrazas,** Pta. Sol, has several flower-filled terraces that overlook the valley. (☎958 76 30 34. Singles 3000ptas/€18; doubles 4200ptas/€25.25.) An extremely pleasant meal can be had at **Restaurante La Artesa,** on the main road in front of the bus stop. (☎958 76 30 82. *Menús* 1100-1500ptas/€6.60-9. Open daily 1-4pm and 8-11pm.)

CAPILEIRA

Capileira (1436m), perched atop the Poqueira Gorge (2½hr. from Granada and a 1hr. hike on the trail from Bubión), makes a good base for exploring the neighboring villages and the back side of the Sierra Nevada. Cobblestone alleys rest between looming peaks and the distant valley below. Enjoy small luxuries in the tiled **Hostal Paco Lopez,** Ctra. de la Sierra, 5, with balconies, TVs, and bathrooms in every room. (☎958 26 39 76. Singles 2500ptas/€15, doubles 5000ptas/€30.) A filling *menú* is served at **Restaurant Poqueira,** C. Dr. Castillo, 6 (open Tu-Su).

TREVÉLEZ

Jamón serrano, and lots of it, characterizes Trevélez, continental Spain's highest community (1476m). The town is probably best known for its cured pork, whose special qualities will probably elude all but the true connoisseur. The ham gets its unique flavor from being cured in the cool, dry winter and sweated (mmm—think about it: sweating pork) in the hot summer months, and everything about this tiny town revolves around the ham industry. Steep roads weave through three *barrios* and water rushes down Moorish irrigation systems still intact from 1000 years ago.

Trevélez is a logical base for the ascent to **Mulhacén.** Every August, throngs of locals climb to pay homage to the **Virgen de las Nieves (Virgin of the Snow).** Summit-bound travelers should head north on the trail leaving the upper village from behind the church; avoid the trail that follows the swampy Río Trevélez. Continue past the Cresta de los Postreros for a good 4-5hr. until you reach the **Cañada de Siete Lagunas** (the largest lake should be directly in front of you); go right to see a famous cave refuge. To reach Mulhacén, go up the ridge south of the refuge (3-4hr. farther). It is not advisable to hike Mulhacén the same day you visit the lake.

Budget beds aren't hard to find in Trevélez. **Hostal Gonzalez,** Pl. Francisco Abellán, behind the restaurant of the same name, has perfectly comfortable, clean rooms waiting past the grungy exterior. (☎958 85 85 31. Singles 2000ptas/€12; doubles 3500ptas/€21.) If you like ham, you're in luck—nearly every **restaurant** in town either advertises ham specials or has the meat hanging from the ceiling. Any one of the restaurants in the main plaza by the bus station serves up a variety of tasty local dishes, most often made of—you guessed it—ham. Non-pork options exist as well, although the *menú* options (around 1100ptas/€6.60) tend to include it.

JAÉN

Spain's "olive capital" is more of a transportation hub than a destination in itself, but half a day waiting for a bus to Baeza can be profitably spent among the winding hillside streets and crowded shopping avenues. Popular with Andalucian tourists as well as those from farther afield, Jaén is a fine place for an afternoon stroll.

TRANSPORTATION. Trains (☎902 24 02 02) depart from Po. Estación at the bottom of the slope and run to: **Córdoba** (1½hr., 8am, 1200ptas/€7.21); **Madrid** (4-5hr., 3 per day 6am-5pm, 3120ptas/€19); **Sevilla** (3hr., 8am, 2300ptas/€14). **Buses,** Pl. Coca de la Piñera (☎953 25 50 14), head to: **Baeza** (1hr., 12 per day 8:30am-8:45pm, 455ptas/€2.70); **Cazorla** (2hr., noon and 4:30pm, 1000ptas/€6); **Granada** (1½hr., 14 per day 7:30am-9pm, 930ptas/€5.56); **Málaga** (3hr., 3 per day 7:30am-noon, 2040ptas/€13); **Úbeda** (30min., 12 per day 8:30am-8:45pm, 580ptas/€3.50).

ORIENTATION AND PRACTICAL INFORMATION. Jaén centers around **Plaza de la Constitución.** From the plaza, **C. Bernabé Soriano** leads uphill to the cathedral and the old section of town. **C. Maestra,** home to the tourist office, is up several blocks to the right. To reach the town center from the bus station, exit from the bus depot and follow Av. Madrid uphill to Pl. Constitución (5min.). From the train station, turn right on Po. Estación, which becomes C. Roldán y Marín. If you're not up for the 25min. walk, take the #1 bus along Po. Estación (90ptas/€55) or take a taxi (500ptas/€3). The **tourist office,** C. Maestra, 13, is near the cathedral. (☎/fax 953 24 26 24. Open M-F 10am-7pm, Sa-Su 10am-1pm.) Other services include: **Banco Central Hispano,** in Pl. Constitución (☎902 24 24 24; open M-Th 8:30am-5pm, F 8am-3pm); **luggage storage** at the bus station (300ptas/€1.80 for 24hr.); **emergency** ☎112; **police** at ☎953 21 91 05. **Internet access** is available at **Cu@k Internet,** C. Cobo Medina, 11. (300ptas/€1.80 per hr. Open M-F 10:30am-2:30pm and 5pm-12:30am, Sa-Su 11am-3pm and 5pm-12:30am.)

ACCOMMODATIONS AND FOOD. Jaén has surprisingly few lodging options for a city of its size. The prime location of **Hostal Carlos V,** Av. Madrid, 4, 3rd fl., downhill from Pl. Constitución, make up for its tiny rooms. (☎953 22 20 91.

Singles 2500ptas/€15; doubles 4000ptas/€24.) Another option is **Hostal Martín,** C. Cuatro Torres, 5, off Pl. Constitución. (☎953 24 50 51. Singles 2500ptas/€15; doubles 4000ptas/€24, with bath 4500ptas/€27.) The extensive menu of **Colon Cafetería,** C. Navas de Tolosa, s/n, along the main pedestrian walkway, includes everything from *churros* (125ptas/€0.75), to *batidos helados* (frappes, 360ptas/€2.20). Prices are slightly higher at outside tables.

SIGHTS AND ENTERTAINMENT. The Renaissance **Catedral de Santa María,** on C. Bernabé Soriano uphill from Pl. Constitución, was designed by Andrés de Vandelvira. (☎953 23 42 33. Open M-Sa 8:30am-1pm and 5-8pm, Su 8:30am-1pm and 6-8pm. Free.) The **Museo de la Catedral** displays sundry objects of interest, among them candlesticks by Maestro Bartolomé. (☎953 22 46 75. Open daily 10am-1pm and afternoons when the cathedral is open. 200ptas/€1.20.) Jaén's most imposing and least accessible sight is the **Castillo de Santa Catalina,** a 5km climb from the center of town. (☎953 21 91 16. Open Th-Tu 10am-2pm. Free.) Those preferring to avoid a sweaty walk may take a taxi (900ptas/€5.41) from the bus station. The Renaissance **Palacio de Villadompardo,** in Pl. Santa Luisa Marillac, at the end of C. Maestra, contains incredible 11th-century baths—Spain's largest—and an art museum. Follow C. Maestra from the cathedral to C. Martínez Molina. (☎953 23 62 92. Open Tu-F 9am-8pm, Sa-Su 9:30am-2:30pm. Free.) Uphill from the cathedral, **Peña Flamenca Jaén,** C. Maestra, 11, serves up drinks and flamenco. (☎953 23 17 10. Open M-F noon-4pm and 8pm-1am, Sa-Su noon-1am.)

GUADIX

A hangover from an earlier age of Spanish history, Guadix is not only encrusted with remnants of Jewish, Muslim, and Catholic culture, but is also home to the world's largest community of *cueva-casas* (cave houses). Often a haven of retreat from Granada during the conflicts of Moorish Spain, Guadix's natural stronghold offered unparalleled protection. Almost 10,000 residents live in the cave houses, which range from incredible stone palaces to smaller and more run-down dwellings. A walk through the cave neighborhood alone warrants a visit to the city.

TRANSPORTATION. From the station on C. Santa Rosa, **Maestra buses** (☎958 66 06 57) depart for: **Almería** (1½hr., 3 per day 8am-6pm, 1035ptas/€6.20); **Granada** (1hr.; M-Sa 11 per day 6:45am-6:45pm, Su 6 per day 9:45am-8:30pm; 600ptas/€3.60); and **Jaén** (1½hr., 11am and 6pm, 1140ptas/€6.25).

ORIENTATION AND PRACTICAL INFORMATION. The central point in town, **Pl. de las Américas,** lies at the foot of the massive cathedral. Ave. Mariana Pineda, the main street, radiates from the plaza. The **tourist office,** on Av. Mariana Pineda, is several blocks to the left when your back is facing the cathedral. (☎958 66 26 65. Open M-F 8am-3pm.) The bus station provides **luggage storage** (daily until 6pm). Services include: **emergency** ☎112; **police** ☎092; and **Centro de Salud** (☎958 66 06 47). **Internet** access is available at **CiberGu@dinet,** C. Josefa Segovia. (☎958 66 91 30. 300ptas/€1.80 per hr. Open Su-Th 10am-2pm and 5-10pm, F 10am-2pm and 5pm-midnight, Sa 10am-2pm and 4pm-midnight.) The **post office** is in Pl. Constitución.

ACCOMMODATIONS AND FOOD. Despite Guadix's impressive attractions, the city itself remains apart from the tourist scene: accommodations are scarce but prices remain reasonable. Experience *Flintstone* living for yourself at **Chez Jean & Julia,** Ermita Nueva, 67, in the *barriada cueva.* Groups can rent mini-cave apartments complete with kitchens and bathrooms. (☎958 66 91 91. Cave quads 8000ptas/€48, for 6 people 10,000ptas/€60. Regular, cave-less doubles and triples 5000ptas/€30.) **Hostal El Retiro,** C. Granada, 40, one block farther from the tourist office along the main street, has simple, clean, rooms. (☎652 91 02 08. Singles 2000ptas/€12.) Several blocks uphill, **Cafeteria-Bar Granada,** C. Granada, 7, is as local and cheap as it gets, with *comida típica* and a loyal crowd of regulars. (☎958 66 32 40. *Menú* 1000ptas/€6. Open daily 6am-late.)

SIGHTS. Guadix's sights are split into two major zones: the **zona de cuevas** and **casco antiguo.** The *zona de cuevas* is a 10min. walk uphill from the cathedral; signs point the way up winding streets. The well-preserved cave serves as the **Museo de Alfarería,** C. San Miguel, 47. (☎958 66 47 67. Open M-F 10am-2pm and 4-8pm, Sa-Su 10am-noon. Adults 300ptas/€1.80, children 100ptas/€0.60.) More preserved rock formations can be seen at the **Cueva Museo,** on the right off C. Canada de las Perales. (Open M-F 10am-2pm and 4-8pm, Sa-Su 10am-noon. Adults 210ptas/€1.25, children 105ptas/€0.63.) The best way to visit the **zona de cuevas** itself is to simply wander the city's streets or to splurge on a **burro taxi;** the burro taxi stand is by the Cueva Museo (rides 200-1000ptas/€1.20-6). Back in town, the *casco antiguo* begins in the center of town at the impressive **Catedral.** Up any of the uphill side streets to the left, you'll find the **Alcazaba Arabe,** built of impressive 11th-century turrets that command an amazing view of the town and surrounding hills. (Open M-F 10am-2pm. Adults 205ptas/€1.20, children 105ptas/€0.63.)

BAEZA

If you're looking for a taste of quintessential old Spain, look no further. A former Moorish capital and the first Andalucian town to fall during the *Reconquista,* Baeza (pop. 17,000) flaunts its Renaissance heyday with well-preserved monuments, still unspoiled by modern life. Nearby Ubeda may have similar architecture and attractions, but Baeza's overall small-town feel makes it a more desirable destination. Antonio Machado, a poet who taught in Baeza, immortalized the village in his works when he wrote, "*Campo de Baeza, soñaré contigo cuando no te vea*" ("Countryside of Baeza, I shall dream of you when I see you no more").

TRANSPORTATION. **Trains** leave from **Estación Linares-Baeza** (☎902 24 02 02), 13km out of town on the road to Madrid, for **Madrid** (3hr., 5 per day 7am-6pm, 2625ptas/€16) and **Málaga** (4hr., 2:45 and 5pm, 3000ptas/€18). At the top of Av. Alcalde Puche Pardo, as it becomes C. Julio Barrel, the **bus station** (☎953 74 04 68) offers service to: **Cazorla** (1½hr., 1 and 5:30pm, 550ptas/€3.30); **Granada** (2-3hr., 7 per day 7:55am-6:55pm, 1395ptas/€8.40); **Jaén** (1hr., 11 per day 7:10am-6:55pm, 470ptas/€2.85); and **Úbeda** (15min., 15 per day 8:20am-9pm, 110ptas/€0.65).

ORIENTATION AND PRACTICAL INFORMATION. Marking the center of town, **Pl. de España** leads downhill to **Pl. Constitución.** To get to Pl. España from the bus station, follow C. Julio Burrel to C. San Pablo, and continue to the plaza. The **tourist office,** Pl. Pópulo, offers guided tours of the town M-F at 11am. (☎953 74 04 44. Open M-F 9am-2pm and 5-7:30pm, alternating Sa 10am-1pm.) Services include: **emergency** ☎112; **police,** C. Cardenal Benavides, 5 (☎953 74 06 59); **Centro de Salud Comarcal,** Av. Alcalde Puche Pardo (☎953 74 29 00). For **Internet access** try **Microware,** Po. Tundidores, 13, in Pl. Constitución. (☎953 74 70 10. 300ptas/€1.80 per hr. Open Tu-Su 10:30am-2pm and 5-10pm.) The **post office** is on C. Julio Burell, 19. (☎953 74 08 39. Open M-F 8:30am-2:30pm, Sa 9am-1pm.) **Postal code:** 23440.

ACCOMMODATIONS AND FOOD. Baeza hides its hostels throughout the city; the two listed below are by far the most central. **Hostal El Patio,** C. Romanones, 13, has the cheapest rooms in town and a location, in the middle of the *barrio monumental,* that's hard to beat. (☎953 74 02 00. Singles 1500ptas/€9, with shower 2000ptas/€12; doubles 3000ptas/€18, with bath 4000ptas/€24.) Directly uphill from Pl. Constitución, **Hostal Comercio,** C. San Pablo, 12, has cozy rooms, all with private bathrooms. (☎953 74 01 00. Singles 2000ptas/€12; doubles 4000ptas/€24.) Several bars and restaurants line Pl. Constitución, although almost all serve *comida típica.* A popular choice with locals is the bar **Guadalquivir,** C.

San Pablo, 44. (☎953 74 15 29. *Bocadillos* 275-350ptas/€1.65-2.10, *raciones* 800-1000ptas/€4.80-6. Open daily noon-4pm and 8:30pm-midnight.)

SIGHTS. Baeza's main attraction is the **Barrio Monumental.** With your back to the tourist office, walk up the stairs to your right, then take a left on C. Romanones; at the street's end stands the **Antigua Universidad** (founded in 1595) whose courtyard served as an outdoor classroom where poet Antonio Machado taught French. (Open Tu-Su 10am-1pm and 4-6pm. Free.) (Open Tu-Su 10am-1pm and 4-6pm. Free.) Across the plaza from the *palacio* looms the 13th-century **Iglesia de Santa Cruz,** Baeza's oldest church, with its frescoes of La Virgen, Santa Catalina, and the martyr San Sebastián (open M-Sa 11am-1pm, Su noon-2pm). Adjacent to the *palacio*, the **seminario's** façade bears the names of some egotistical graduates and a caricature of an unpopular professor, rumored to be painted in bull's blood. Across the Pl. Santa María from the seminary towers, the **Santa Iglesia Catedral,** houses *La Custodia de Baeza*, Spain's second-most important (after Toledo's) Corpus Christi icon. (Open daily June-Aug. 10:30am-1pm and 4:30-6:30pm; Sept.-May 10:30am-1pm and 4:15-6pm.) Fabulous views of the olive-carpeted Guadalquivir Valley unfold from the intersection of Po. Murallas and C. Argentina.

ÚBEDA

Úbeda is a city of two faces: the cobbled streets of its monument district dip between the ivied medieval walls of old churches and palaces, while modern sprawl envelops the rest of the city. A stop on the crucial 16th-century trade route linking Castilla to Andalucía, the town (pop. 33,000) prospered from American gold. Today, the *barrio antiguo* stands as one of the best-preserved gems of Spanish Renaissance architecture, attracting visitors from around the world.

TRANSPORTATION. There is **no train service** to Úbeda; the nearest station is **Estación Linares-Baeza** (☎953 65 02 02), 40min. northwest by bus. **Buses** leave Úbeda from C. San José, 6 (☎953 75 21 57). **Alsina Graells** travels to: **Baeza** (15min., 17 per day 7am-7:30pm, 110ptas/€0.65); **Cazorla** (1hr., 4 per day 10am-6pm, 475ptas/€2.85); **Estación Linares-Baeza** (30min., 8 per day 7:45am-9pm, 275ptas/€1.65); **Granada** (2-3hr., 7 per day 7:45am-6:45pm, 1505ptas/€9); and **Jaén** (1hr., 13 per day 7am-6:45pm, 580ptas/€3.50). **Bacoma** buses go to **Córdoba** (2½hr., 6 per day 5am-8:40pm, 1425ptas/€8.56) and **Sevilla** (5hr., 6 per day 5am-8:40pm, 2755ptas/€16.53).

ORIENTATION AND PRACTICAL INFORMATION. Úbeda centers around **Plaza de Andalucía,** currently under construction to create an underground parking garage. From the plaza, the **barrio antiguo** stretches downhill along C. Doctor Quesada (which leads to C. Real) and surrounding streets. To reach Pl. Andalucía from the **bus station,** bear right from the front of the station, walk downhill one block, then turn left on Av. Cristo Rey, which turns into C. Obispo Cobos and then C. Mesones, and continue to the plaza (5min.). The **tourist office** is in the **Palacio Marqués de Contadero,** C. Baja del Marqués, 4, but right in the middle of the main tourist attractions. From Pl. Andalucía, follow the directions to the *barrio antiguo*. From the back of the *ayuntamiento*, take a right onto C. Corazón de Jesús, then the first right onto C. Baja del Márquez; the tourist office is on the left. (☎953 75 08 97; fax 79 26 70. Open M-F 8:30am-7:30pm, Sa-Su 10am-2pm.) **Banco Central Hispano,** Pl. Andalucía, 13, has an **ATM.** (☎953 75 04 43. Open May-Sept. M-F 8:30am-2pm, Oct.-Apr. M-F 8:30am-2pm and Sa 8:30am-1pm.) Local services include: **luggage storage** at the bus station (300ptas/€1.80 per day); **emergency** ☎112; **police** ☎953 75 00 23; **Centro de Salud,** C. Esplanada (☎953 75 11 03), off Av. Ramón y Cajal; and the **post office,** C. Trinidad, 4, along the Hospital de Santiago. (☎953 75 00 31. Open M-Sa 9am-2pm.) **Postal code:** 23400.

ACCOMMODATIONS AND FOOD. Indulge at **Hostal Victoria,** C. Alaminos, 5, 2nd fl. From the bus station, walk down C. Mesones past Hospital de Santiago and turn right on C. Sagasta, then left on C. Alaminos. Glistening private bathrooms, color TVs, and A/C make for a pleasant stay. (☎953 75 29 52. Singles 2500-2800ptas/€15-17; doubles 4700-5000ptas/€28-30.) Cheaper, but less central rooms can be found at **Hostal Castillo,** Av. Ramón y Cajal, 20, with a popular bar/restaurant downstairs. (☎953 75 04 30 or 953 75 12 18. Singles 2200ptas/€13, with bath 2500ptas/€15; doubles 3600ptas/€21.64, with bath 4600ptas/€28; triples from 6300ptas/€38.) Leading from Pl. Andalucía, C. Rastro is lined with *terrazas* offering combination platters (1000ptas/€6) and entrées (600-800ptas/€3.61-4.81). The **market** is down C. San Fernando from Pl. Andalucía (open M-Sa 7am-2:30pm).

SIGHTS AND ENTERTAINMENT. A walk through historic Úbeda begins right out of the bus at the **Hospital de Santiago,** adjacent to the station, which houses a modern art museum. (☎953 75 08 42. Open M-F 8am-3pm; evening hours 5:30-10pm in summer, 4:30-10pm in winter, Sa 8am-3pm. 225ptas/€1.65, children and seniors 75ptas/€0.45.) From Pl. Andalucía, C. Real leads downhill to C. Juan Montilla, which then continues to **Plaza de Vázquez de Molina** and the center of Úbeda. Two stone lions guard the **Palacio de las Cadenas,** now the *Ayuntamiento.* Across the way is the Gothic **Colegiata de Santa María de los Reales Alcázares,** its side chapels embellished with wrought-iron grilles; you can't enter, but the façade alone is worth the visit. Uphill from Pl. Vásquez de Molina and along C. Juan Ruíz Gonzales, Pl. 1 de Mayo runs in front of **Iglesia de San Pablo** (open 7-9pm and during mass). The **Museo Arqueológico,** C. Cervantes, 6, uphill from the church, narrates Úbeda's history through prehistoric, Roman, Moorish, and Castilian times. (☎953 75 37 02. Open Tu 3-8pm, W-Sa 9am-8pm, Su 9am-3pm. 250ptas/€1.50, EU citizens free with passport.) In the basement of the *Ayuntamiento,* the small but charming **Museo de Alfarería** (*artesanía* or handcrafts), displays pottery and local arts. (Open Tu-Sa 10:30am-2pm and 5:30-8pm. 305ptas/€1.60.) A walk downhill along C. Baja del Salvador leads to a stunning view of the olive-laden **Guadalquivir Valley.** Kick back, relax, and enjoy some *cerveza* at **Casablanca Café,** on the corner of C. Redonda de Santiago and Ave. Ramón y Cajal. (☎953 79 27 88. Open daily 4pm-3am. Beer 175ptas/€1.05, mixed drinks 450ptas/€2.70 and up.)

CAZORLA ☎953

Nestled between foreboding cliffs and two ancient castles, Cazorla (pop. 9000) keeps quietly to itself, paying little heed to the trickle of tourists passing through on their way to the **Parque Natural de las Sierras de Cazorla, Segura, y las Villas** (1hr. away). The national park's 210,000 hectares of protected mountains and waterways offer some of the best hiking in Andalucía. For those not interested in exploring the natural park, the town itself offers little other than café. Nonetheless, the tranquility of this *pueblo blanco* makes for a nice weekend getaway.

ORIENTATION AND PRACTICAL INFORMATION. To reach **Pl. de Corredera** from the bus stop, face the peaks and walk down the narrow C. Dr. Muñoz to the right. Farther downhill are Pl. Santa María and the **barrio antiguo. Buses** (☎953 75 21 57) depart from Pl. Constitución for: **Granada** (4hr.; M-Sa 7am and 5:30pm, Su 8am and 5:30pm; 1930ptas/€11.57); **Jaén** and **Úbeda** (2hr., 4 per day 7am-5:30pm, 1000ptas/€6 and 450ptas/€2.70). Buy tickets in the tiny ticket office across from the plaza bus depot. The **tourist office,** Po. Santo Cristo, 17, is up a garden-lined walkway from Pl. Constitución. (☎953 71 01 02; fax 72 00 60. Open M-F 10am-2pm and 5-9pm.) Services include: **emergency** ☎112; **police** on Pl. Corredera (☎953 72 01 81); **Centro de Salud,** Av. Ximénez de Rada, 1 (☎953 72 10 61); and the **post office,** C. Mariano Extremera, 2, uphill from Pl. Corredera. (☎953 72 02 61. Open M-F 8:30am-2:30pm, Sa 9am-1pm.) **Postal code:** 23470.

ACCOMMODATIONS AND FOOD. From the far end of Pl. Corredera, walk uphill on C. Carmen to reach the **Albergue Juvenil Cazorla (HI),** Pl. Mauricio Martínez, 6. This hostel has a TV lounge, basketball/soccer court, and a heaven-sent pool, although it's only open for swimming mid-June through mid-Sept. (☎953 72 03 29; fax 72 02 03. 24hr. security guard. Breakfast included; sheets provided. HI members Oct.-May 1350ptas/€8.11, over 26 1800ptas/€10.82; June-Sept. 1725ptas/€10.37, over 26 2375ptas/€14.27.) **Hostal Betis,** Pl. Corredera, 19, has incredible views of the valley from most rooms. (☎953 72 05 40. Singles with bath 1500-17000ptas/€9-10.22; doubles 3000-3200ptas/€18-19, with bath 3200-3400ptas/€19-21.) Open-air bar-restaurants serving traditional platters such as *rin-ran* (a cold soup of potatoes, red peppers, olives, and fish) line Pl. Corredora and Pl. Santa María. Perhaps the best bargain in town is **La Taberna,** C. Nueva, s/n, on a side street off Pl. Corredera, where brightly tiled walls and a casual environment attract a range of patrons. (☎953 71 01 22. Open daily 9am-midnight.) The **market** is at Pl. Mercado, downstairs from C. Dr. Muñoz (open M-F 9am-noon), and a larger **supermarket** sits in Pl. Corredera (open M-F 9am-noon and 6-9pm, Sa 9am-noon).

SIGHTS AND HIKING. The majority of visitors to Cazorla come for the **Parque Natural de las Sierras de Cazorla, Segura, y las Villas.** The truly adventurous can take a 9hr. round-trip hike from Cazorla, past the **Castillo de la Yedra,** and through the park; stop by the tourist office for a map. Begun by Romans builders, the castle provides a pretty view of town from its solitary turrets. (☎953 71 00 39. Open Tu 3-8pm, W-Sa 9am-8pm, Su 9am-3pm. 250ptas/€1.50. EU citizens free.) For information on longer or guided excursions through the park, stop by **Quercus,** C. Juan Domingo, 2. Tours can be arranged with an English-speaking guide. (☎953 72 01 15. Open daily 9am-2pm and 5-9pm, holidays 10am-2pm and 6-9pm. Map 375ptas/€2.25. Half-day tours 2800-5900ptas/€17-36.) **Buses** run from Cazorla to the park (1hr.; June-Aug. M-Sa 6:30am and 2:40pm, Sept.-May 5:45am and 3pm; 400ptas/€2.40), but service is subject to change. **Carecesa** buses depart Pl. Constitución for the **Torre del Vinagre Visitor Center** (☎953 71 30 40), near the trailhead of the popular **Sendero Cerrada de Elias/Río Borosa,** from which 4- or 12km trails lead up the river canyon punctuated with natural pools. The center rents **horses** (1500ptas/€9 per hr., in groups of 4 or more) and **mountain bikes** (1200ptas/€7.20 per half-day, 2000ptas/€12 per day). Those with a car can drive further into the park to the source of the **Rio Guadalquivir,** where breathtaking waterfalls and scenic trails wind alongside the river. The last bus back to Cazorla leaves Torre del Vinagre at 4:30pm; tickets can be bought on the bus.

EAST COAST

VALENCIA

With a coastline of popular beaches and a rolling interior, Valencia is something of a natural wonder. The farmlands are a patchwork of orange orchards and vegetable fields, all fed by Moorish irrigation systems. Bordering the lush heart of Valencia, the 466km of Mediterranean shoreline alternate between soft dunes and agged promontories. Valencia's nature has found a place even in its cities, where carefully landscaped gardens employ ornate fountains and exotic plants.

Valencia's past is a tangle of power struggles between the whole cast of usual suspects. Phoenicians, Carthaginians, Greeks, Romans, and Moors have all battled across the land. The region first fell under Castillian control when El Cid expelled he Moors in 1094; he ruled it in the name of Alfonso VI until his death in 1099. Without El Cid's powerful influence, the region again fell to the Moors, remaining an Arab stronghold until 1238. In the 1930s, Valencia was again besieged, this time by Franco's troops. The *valencianos* resisted with characteristic strength; Valencia was the last region incorporated into Franco's Spain. In 1977, with the reinstitution of the monarchy, the region finally regained its autonomy.

Valenciano, the regional language spoken sparingly in the north and inland, is similar to Catalan. Although Valencia's regionalism is not as intense as Cataluña's, the Generalitat's recent mandate that all students enroll in one course of *valenciano* reflects a resurgence of regional pride. Valencia's festivals are some of the raziest in Spain, and its culinary heritage has had a pronounced impact on Spanish cuisine: *Paella*, now considered a quintessential Spanish dish, was first concocted somewhere in the region's rice fields, and Valencian oranges are widely accepted as the best in the nation, if not the world.

VALENCIA ☎963

pain's third largest city is a stylish and cosmopolitan nerve center that stands in triking contrast to the surrounding orchards and mountain ranges. A long, winding strip of parks and gardens completely surround the city center. Along with the soft-sanded beaches nearby, they manage to balance out Valencia's frenetic days. he local government has been pouring money into making Valencia attractive to ourists, and the city now displays some of Spain's most innovative architecture. he wide variety of museums found here may not live up to their big-time counterparts in Barcelona and Madrid, but they're certainly among the best in the country.

TRANSPORTATION

Flights: Airport (☎961 59 85 00), 8km from the city. **Cercanías** trains run between the airport and train station (30min.; M-F every 30min., Sa-Su every hr. 7:03am-10:03pm; 165ptas/€1). Many flights to the Balearic Islands. **Iberia,** C. La Paz, 14 (☎963 52 75 52 or 24hr. info and reservations 902 40 05 00). Open M-F 9am-2pm and 4-7pm.

Trains: Estación del Nord, C. Xàtiva, 24 (☎963 52 02 02), 3 blocks down Av. Marqués de Sotelo from Pl. Ayuntamiento. Ticket windows open 7:30am-9:30pm. **RENFE** (24hr. ☎902 24 02 02) to: **Alicante** (2-3hr., 9 per day 10am-9pm, 1430-4100ptas/€8.58-25); **Barcelona** (3hr., 12 per day 6:35am-8:05pm, 5200ptas/€31); **Madrid** (3½hr., 9 per day 6:45am-8:15pm, 4700ptas/€28); **Sevilla** (8½hr., 11:30am, 5600ptas/€34). **Cercanías** trains run throughout the day at least twice an hr. to: **Gandía** (1hr., 525ptas/€3.15); **Játiva** (45min., 405ptas/€2.43); **Sagunto** (30min., 335ptas/€2.01).

Buses: Estación Terminal d'Autobuses, Av. Menéndez Pidal, 13 (☎963 49 72 22) across the river, a 25min. walk from the city center. Municipal bus #8 (130ptas, €0.78) runs between Pl. Ayuntamiento and the bus station. **Auto Res** (☎963 49 2 30) goes to **Madrid** (4hr., 13 per day 7am-3am, 3470ptas/€20.82). **ALSA** (☎902 4 22 42) to: **Alicante** via the **Costa Blanca** (4½hr., 13 per day 6:30am-6pm, 2000ptas, €12); **Barcelona** (4½hr., 15 per day 1am-10pm, 3135ptas/€19); **Granada** (8hr., per day 1-10:30pm, 5145ptas/€31); **Málaga** (11hr., 5 per day 1-10:30pm 6340ptas/€38); **Sevilla** (11hr., 4 per day 2:45-10:30pm, 6725ptas/€40).

Ferries: Trasmediterránea, Estació Marítima (☎902 45 46 45). Take bus #4 from P Ayuntamiento or #1 or 2 from the bus station. Boats run to Mallorca and Ibiza (1-2 pe day, 5000-11,500ptas/€30-69, depending on speed of ferry and class). There is on 15hr. ferry to Menorca each week (Sa 11:30pm, prices vary). Buy tickets at a trave agency, or on the day of departure at the port. Ask a travel agent about **Baleari** (☎902 16 01 80) Denia-Eivissa service. See **By Boat,** p. 475.

Public Transportation: EMT Office, C. En Sanz, 4 (☎963 52 83 99). Open M-F 8am-2pm. Many buses pass through the Pl. Ayuntamiento. Bus #8 runs to the bus station. Buses #10, 21, 22, and 23 go to Las Arenas and Malvarrosa along Po. Marítimo. Buy tickets (130ptas/€0.78) on board; 10-ride ticket (740ptas/€4.44) or 1-day pass (500ptas/€3) available at newsstands. Service stops at 10:30pm. Late-night buses go through Pl. Ayuntamiento (every 45min. 11pm-1:38am).

Taxis: ☎963 70 33 33 or 57 13 13.

ORIENTATION AND PRACTICAL INFORMATION

Since **Estación del Nord** penetrates Valencia's sprawl to bring you close to the city's center, it is best approached by train. **Av. Marquéz de Sotelo** runs from the train station to **Pl. del Ayuntamiento,** the center of town. Just about everything of interest, except for the university and beaches, is in the **casco antiguo** (old quarter), nestled in a bend of the Río Turia, which loops around the center of the city. Because of Valencia's size, it's best to take advantage of the extensive bus system to see more than just the small area in walking distance from the center.

Tourist Office: Regional, Estación del Nord, C. Xàtiva, 24 (☎963 52 85 73), on the right of the train tracks as you disembark. The main regional **branch** is on C. Paz, 46-48 (☎963 98 64 22). Open M-F 10am-6pm, Sa 10am-2pm. **City office,** Pl. Ayuntamiento, 1 (☎963 51 04 17). Open M-F 8:30am-2:15pm and 4:15-6:15pm, Sa 9am-12:45pm.

Budget Travel: Barceló Viajes: C. Paz, 38 (☎963 51 47 84). From Pl. Reina, facing the cathedral, go left on C. Paz. Can organize travel to the Balearic Islands and any other world destination. ISIC 700ptas/€4.20. Open M-F 9:30am-1:30pm, Sa 9:30am-1pm.

Currency Exchange: Banco Central Hispano, C. Barcas, 8 (☎963 53 81 00), offers decent exchange rates. 24hr. **ATMs** are everywhere.

American Express: Duna Viajes, C. Cirilo Amorós, 88 (☎963 74 15 62; fax 34 57 00). From the tip of Pl. Ayuntamiento, take C. Barcas, which becomes C. Don Juan de Austria, then C. Sorní. When you reach Pl. América, take C. Cirilo Amorós on the right. No commission on AmEx traveler's checks. Will hold mail and provide fax service for cardholders. Open M-F 9:30am-2pm and 5-8pm, Sa 10am-1pm.

Luggage Storage: At the **bus station,** lockers 300-500ptas/€1.80-3. At the **train station,** lockers 400-750ptas/€2.40-4.50. Both good for 24hr., same hours as stations.

Laundromat: Lavandería **El Mercat,** Pl. Mercado, 12 (☎963 91 20 10). Full-service wash and dry in 2-3hr. 1500ptas. Open M-F 10am-2pm and 5-9pm, Sa 10am-2pm.

Emergency: ☎112. **Ambulance:** ☎085.

Late-Night Pharmacy: Rotates daily. Check listing in the local paper *Levante* (125ptas/€0.75) or check the *farmacias de guardia* schedule posted outside any pharmacy.

Hospital: Hospital Clínico Universitario, Av. Blasco Ibañez, 17 (☎963 86 26 00), at the corner of C. Dr. Ferrer. Take bus #41, 71, or 81 from Pl. Ayuntamiento. An English-speaking doctor is often on duty.

Internet Access: Fundación Bancaixa, Pl. Tetuán, 23 (☎963 87 58 64). Free 1hr. per day on somewhat slow computers. Passport or student ID required. Open M-F 9am-2pm and 4-9pm, Sa 9am-2pm. **Confederación,** C. Ribera, 8 (☎963 94 03 11), off Pl. Ayuntamiento. 46 ultra-modern computers. 300ptas/€1.80 per 30min., 500ptas/€3 per hr.

Post Office: Pl. Ayuntamiento, 24 (☎963 51 67 50). Open M-F 8:30am-8:30pm, Sa 9:30am-2pm. **Postal Code:** 46080.

ACCOMMODATIONS

Hostels may clutter Valencia's streets, but during weekends, especially in summer, finding a room isn't always easy—it's best to call in advance. Reservations are especially needed during the *papier-mâché* orgy of *Las Fallas* (Mar. 12-19). The best deals cluster around **Pl. del Ayuntamiento** and **Pl. del Mercado.**

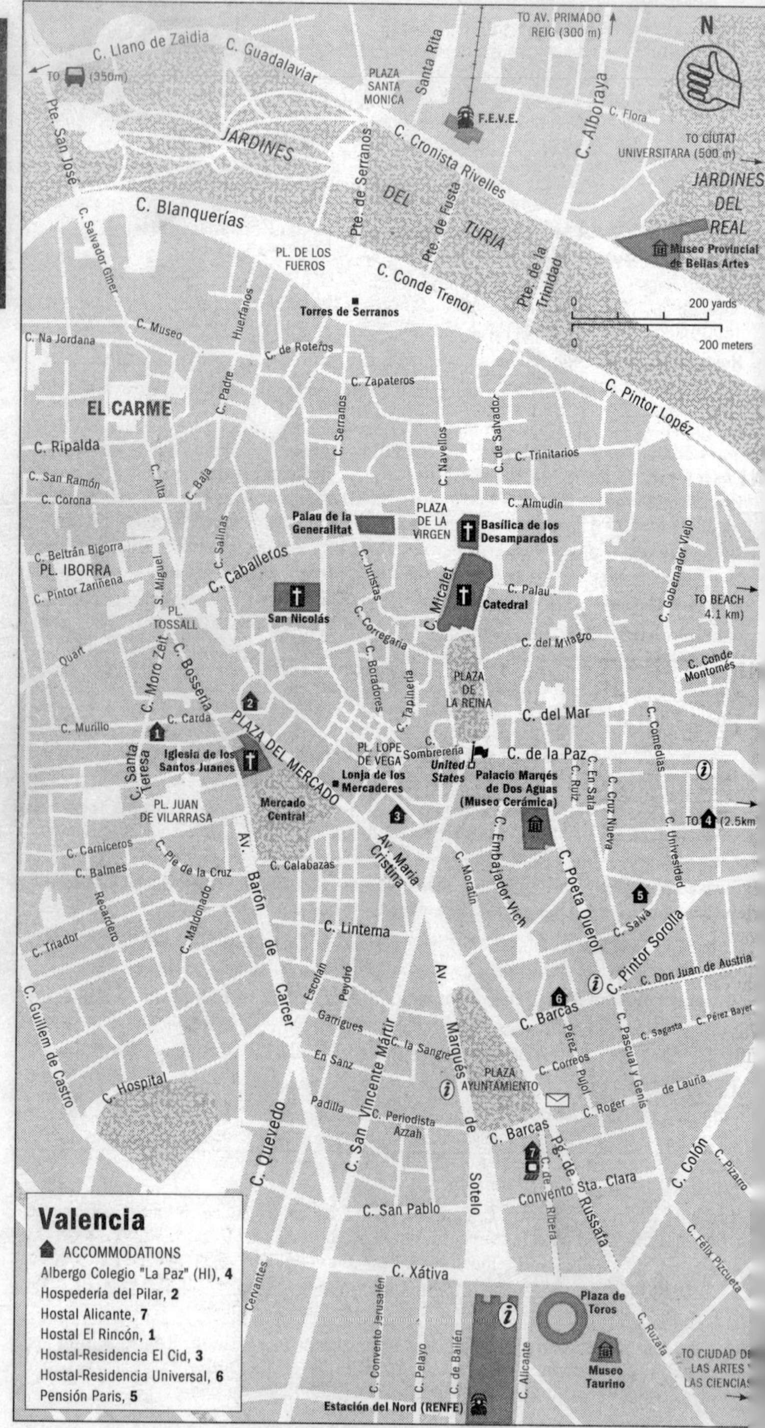
C. Llano de Zaidia
C. Guadalaviar
TO (350m)
PLAZA SANTA MONICA
Santa Rita
TO AV. PRIMADO REIG (300 m)
N
F.E.V.E.
C. Alboraya
C. Flora
Pte. San José
JARDINES DEL TURIA
C. Cronista Rivelles
Pte. de Serranos
Pte. de Fusta
TO CIUTAT UNIVERSITARA (500 m)
JARDINES DEL REAL
C. Blanquerías
Museo Provincial de Bellas Artes
C. Salvador Giner
PL. DE LOS FUEROS
C. Conde Trenor
Pte. de la Trinidad
200 yards
200 meters
Torres de Serranos
C. Museo
Huerfanos
C. Na Jordana
C. de Roteros
C. Zapateros
C. Pintor Lopéz
EL CARME
C. Padre
C. Serranos
C. de Salvador
C. Ripalda
C. Navellos
C. Trinitarios
C. San Ramón
C. Alta
C. Baja
C. Corona
C. Almudin
Palau de la Generalitat
PLAZA DE LA VIRGEN
Basílica de los Desamparados
C. Salinas
C. Beltrán Bigorra
PL. IBORRA
C. Pintor Zariñena
S. Miguel
C. Caballeros
C. Juristas
C. Gobernador Viejo
C. Micalet
C. Palau
San Nicolás
Catedral
TO BEACH 4.1 km)
PL. TOSSALL
C. Corregaria
Quart
C. Moro Zeit
C. Bossería
C. del Milagro
C. Conde Montornés
C. Boradores
C. Tapinería
PLAZA DE LA REINA
C. Carda
C. del Mar
C. Murillo
PLAZA DEL MERCADO
PL. LOPE DE VEGA
C. Sombrerería
C. de la Paz
C. Comedias
C. Santa Teresa
Iglesia de los Santos Juanes
United States
C. En Sala
C. Ruiz
Lonja de los Mercaderes
Palacio Marqés de Dos Aguas (Museo Cerámica)
C. Cruz Nueva
PL. JUAN DE VILARRASA
Mercado Central
TO (2.5km
C. Universidad
C. Carniceros
Av. Maria Cristina
C. Embajador Vich
C. Balmes
C. Pie de la Cruz
C. Calabazas
C. Moratín
C. Poeta Querol
Av. Barón de Carcer
Recardero
C. Maldonado
C. Salvá
C. Triador
C. Linterna
C. Pintor Sorolla
C. Don Juan de Austria
C. Guillem de Castro
Escolan
Peydro
Garrigues
Av. Marqués de Sotelo
C. Barcas
C. Pérez Bayer
C. Sagasta
C. San Vincente Mártir
C. la Sangre
Pérez Pujol
En Sanz
C. Pascual y Genis
C. Hospital
C. Correos
PLAZA AYUNTAMIENTO
de Lauria
Padilla
C. Periodista Azzah
C. Roger
C. Barcas
C. Quevedo
Pg. de Russafa
C. de Ribera
C. Colón
C. Pizarro
Convento Sta. Clara
C. San Pablo
C. Félix Pizcueta
C. Xátiva
Cervantes
Plaza de Toros
C. Convento Jerusalén
C. Pelayo
C. de Bailén
C. Alicante
Museo Taurino
C. Ruzafa
TO CIUDAD DE LAS ARTES Y LAS CIENCIAS
Estación del Nord (RENFE)
Valencia
ACCOMMODATIONS
Albergo Colegio "La Paz" (HI), 4
Hospedería del Pilar, 2
Hostal Alicante, 7
Hostal El Rincón, 1
Hostal-Residencia El Cid, 3
Hostal-Residencia Universal, 6
Pensión Paris, 5

NEAR PLAZA DEL AYUNTAMIENTO

Pensión Paris, C. Salvá, 12 (☎963 52 67 66). From Pl. Ayuntamiento, turn right at C. Barcas, left at C. Poeta Querol, and take the 2nd right onto C. Salvá. 13 spotless rooms complemented by balconies. Singles 2600ptas/€16; doubles 4000ptas/€24, with shower 4600ptas/€28; triples 5700ptas/€34, with shower 6500ptas/€39.

Hostal-Residencia El Cid, C. Cerrajeros, 13 (☎/fax 963 92 23 23). From the train station, pass Pl. Ayuntamiento and take the 2nd left off C. Vicente Mártir. Room quality varies—some have TVs and A/C, others just a fan. Singles 1800ptas/€11; doubles 3400ptas/€21, with shower 4000ptas/€24, with bath 4900ptas/€30. AmEx/MC/V.

Hostal-Residencia Universal, C. Barcas, 5 (☎963 51 53 84), off Pl. Ayuntamiento. Clean, pastel-painted rooms with large windows and quilted bedspreads make up for the slightly dingy hallway showers. 24hr. access. Singles 2600ptas/€16; doubles 4000ptas/€24, with shower 4600ptas/€28; triples 5700ptas/€34.

Hostal Alicante, C. Ribera, 8 (☎963 51 22 96), on the pedestrian street off Pl. Ayuntamiento. As central as it gets, with clean, well-lit rooms and firm beds. Hugely popular with backpackers. Singles 3000ptas/€18, with bath 4000ptas/€24; doubles 4500ptas/€27, with bath 5000ptas/€30. MC/V.

NEAR PLAZA DEL MERCADO

Hostal El Rincón, C. Carda, 11 (☎963 91 79 98). From Pl. Ayuntamiento, Pl. Mercado extends past the market and continues as C. Carda. Bright hallways lead to bare-walled but clean rooms. Singles €10, with bath €13; doubles €18, with bath €24. MC/V.

Hospedería del Pilar, Pl. Mercado, 19 (☎963 91 66 00), past the market and Llonja. Singles 1600ptas/€9.62, with bath 2500ptas/€15; doubles 3000ptas/€18, with bath 3850ptas/€23; triples 4500ptas/€27, with bath 6000ptas/€36.

NEAR THE BEACH

Alberg Colegio "La Paz" (HI), Av. Puerto, 69 (☎96 369 01 52), nearly halfway between the city and the port. Take bus #19 from Pl. Ayuntamiento (next to Citibank) and get off at the 8th stop on Av. Puerto (20min. walk to the beach). 2-4 people and a bathroom in every room. Breakfast included. Sheets 500ptas/€3. Reception daily 3pm-2am. Dorms 2000ptas/€12, over 26 1600ptas/€9.61. Open July-Sept. 15.

FOOD

Paella may be the most famous dish, but it is actually just one of 200 Valencian rice dishes. Oh boy! Other specialties include *arroz a banda* (rice and fish with garlic, onion, tomatoes, and saffron), *all i pebre* (eels fried in oil, paprika, and garlic), and *sepia con salsa verde* (cuttlefish with garlic and parsley). Valencia's restaurants are generally cheap and perfect for people on the run. Bushels of fresh fish, meat, and fruit are sold at the **Mercado Central,** on Pl. Mercado (open M-F 7am-3pm). For **groceries,** stop by the basement of **El Corte Inglés,** C. Colón, or the fifth floor of the C. Pintor Sorilla building. (☎963 51 24 44. Open M-Sa 10am-10pm.)

La Pappardella, C. Bordadores, 5 (☎963 91 89 15). Face the cathedral and the restaurant is on the left. Two floors of pasta bliss. Vast, delicious *menú* offers dishes ranging from basic spaghetti, oil, and garlic, to exotic pastas complemented by fresh veggies, meats and seafood (entrées 700-1000ptas/€3.50-6). *Menú* 1200ptas/€7.20. Open daily 2-4:30pm and 9pm-midnight.

La Lluna (☎963 92 21 46), C. Sant Ramón, in El Carme district. From Pg. Guillém de Castro, take C. Corona, then the 1st left onto C. Beneficia; C. Sant Ramón is on the right. A veggie restaurant to moon over. Stuffed peppers and eggplant are the specialties. 4-course *menú* (served weekday afternoons) 900ptas/€5.40. Entrées 400-650ptas/€2.40-3.90. Open M-Sa 1:30-3:30pm and 9-11:30pm.

SIGHTS

Touring Valencia on foot is a good test of stamina. Most of the sights line the Río Turia or cluster near Pl. Reina, which is linked to Pl. Ayuntamiento by C. San Vicente Mártir. EMT bus #5, dubbed the **Bus Turistic** (☎963 52 83 99), makes a loop around the old town sights (130ptas/€0.78; 1-day pass 500ptas/€3 for all buses).

CIUDAD DE LAS ARTES Y LAS CIENCIAS. Modern, airy, and thoroughly fascinating, Valencia's latest urban creation dedicated to the arts and sciences has raised quite a stir. Built along the dried-up bed of the Río Turia, this mini-city has already become the fourth biggest tourist destination in Spain. The complex is divided into four large attractions, all surrounding a reflecting pool. Even the parking garage is a work of art, with a garden terrace on the roof. **L'Hemisfèric** wows the eyes with its IMAX theater, laser shows, and planetarium. **L'Oceanografic** is an underground water-world, recreating diverse aquatic environments. The **Palau de les Arts,** which is scheduled to be completed by 2002, will house stages for opera, theater, and dance. The **Museu de Les Ciencies Principe Felipe** is packed with students and tourists learning through hands-on exhibits on science and technology. *(South along the riverbed off the highway to Salér. Bus #35 runs from Pl. Ayuntamiento. ☎902 10 00 31; www.cac.es. IMAX shows 1100ptas/€6.60, weekdays children and students 800ptas/€4.80. Museum and aquarium open M-Th 10am-8pm, F-Su 10am-9pm, admission to each 1000ptas/€6, weekdays children and students 700ptas/€4.20.)*

CATHEDRAL. Begun in the 13th century and completed in 1482, this magnificent cathedral is the region's most impressive building. The three different entrances display a mélange of Gothic, Baroque, and Romanesque architectural styles. French novelist (not mathematician) Victor Hugo once counted 300 bell towers in Valencia from atop the **Miguelete** (the cathedral tower); there are actually only about a hundred. The interior is lined with altars, each with its own design and character. The **Museo de la Catedral** squeezes a great many treasures into three tiny rooms—one for the Gothic period, one for the Renaissance, and the last for Mannerism. Check out the overwrought tabernacle made from 1200kg of gold, silver, platinum, emeralds, and sapphires, a Holy Grail, two Goyas, and the Crucifijo de Marfil (crucifix) statues depicting "man's passions." *(Pl. Reina. Cathedral ☎963 91 01 89. Open daily 8am-2pm and 5-8pm. Closes earlier in winter. Free. Tower open daily 10am-1pm and 4:30-7pm. 200ptas/€1.20. Museum ☎963 91 81 27. Open Mar.-May and Oct.-Nov. M-F 10am-1pm and 4:30-6pm, June-Sept. 10am-1pm and 4:30-7pm, Dec.-Feb. 10am-1pm. Sa-Su open 10am-1pm year-round. 200ptas/€1.20.)*

MUSEU PROVINCIAL DE BELLES ARTES. One of Valencia's finer attractions, this museum features a wide array of paintings, with one floor dedicated to 14th- to 16th-century Valencian art, and another to more recent works. The museum itself has been labeled one of Spain's premier art galleries. The collection also includes works by Spanish and foreign masters, including El Greco's *San Juan Bautista*, Velázquez's self-portrait, Ribera's *Santa Teresa*, and a slew of Goyas. Check out the sculpture pavilion. *(C. Sant Pius V, next to the Jardines del Real. ☎963 60 57 93. Open Tu-Sa 10am-2:15pm and 4-7:30pm, Su 10am-7:30pm. Free.)*

INSTITUT VALENCIÁ D'ART MODERN (IVAM). See everything from classic avant-garde art to 1970s clash. This museum is also home to a permanent collection of abstract works by 20th-century sculptor Julio González, among others. The rotating temporary exhibits are extremely popular. *(C. Guillém de Castro, 118, west across the old river. Bus #5 stops right in front. ☎963 86 30 00. Open Tu-Su 10am-7pm. 350ptas/€2.10, students 175ptas/€1.05; Su free.)*

PARKS. Well-manicured parks lie on the outskirts of the historic district. Horticulturists will marvel at the **Jardín Botánico,** a university-maintained garden that cultivates 43,000 plants of 300 international species. *(C. Quart, 80, on the western end of Río Turia. ☎963 91 16 57. Open Tu-Su 10am-9pm, closes earlier in winter. 50ptas/€0.30.)* One block farther on, a series of manicured recreation areas define the banks of the

PYROMANIAC'S PARADISE Fire, fire! If you can choose any time of year to come to Valencia, make it March 12 to 19, when Valencia's most illustrious event, *Las Fallas,* grips the city. The city explodes with festivity, including parades, bullfights, fireworks, and street dancing. Neighborhoods compete to build the most elaborate and satirical *papier-mâché* effigy; over 300 such enormous *ninots* spring up in the streets. On the final day–*la nit del foc* (fire night)–Valencians burn all the *ninots* simultaneously in one last, clamorous inferno meant to bring luck for the agricultural season and exorcize the social ills satirized by the *papier-mâché* giants.

now-diverted Río Turia. Next to the Museo Provincial de Bellas Artes is the popular **Jardines del Real,** home to ponds, caged birds, fountains, and greenhouses.

OTHER SIGHTS. The elliptical **Basílica Virgen de los Desamparados** houses a resplendent golden altar. *(Behind the cathedral on Pl. Virgen. Open for mass M-F 7am-2pm and 5-9pm, Su 7:30am-2:30pm and 5-9:30pm. Free.)* The old **Lonja de la Seda (Silk Exchange)** is one of the foremost examples of Valencian Gothic architecture and a testament to Valencia's prominence in the medieval silk trade. *(Pl. Mercado. ☎963 52 54 78. Open Tu-Sa 9:15am-2pm and 5:30-9pm, Su 9am-1:30pm. Free.)*

ENTERTAINMENT AND NIGHTLIFE

Valencia's most famous festival is **Las Fallas,** March 12-19 (see **Pyromaniac's Paradise,** p. 283). During **Semana Santa,** the streets clog with monks enacting Biblical scenes and children performing the miracle plays of St. Vincent Ferrer. **Corpus Christi** follows soon after with its display of *rocas* or huge carriages symbolizing Biblical mysteries. The **Festiu de Juliol** (July Fair) brings fireworks, riverside concerts, bullfights, and a *batalla de flores*—a violet skirmish in which flowers are tossed between parade-goers and girls on passing floats.

Use your siesta wisely—Valencia's nightlife will keep you drinking and dancing until sunrise. Bars and pubs in **El Carme** district, just beyond the market, start up at 11:30pm. Follow Pl. Mercado and C. Bolsería (bearing right) to Pl. Tossal, where outdoor terraces, upbeat music, and *agua de Valencia* (orange juice, champagne, and vodka) energize the masses.

American students frequent **Finnegan's,** at Pl. Reina, 19, in front of the cathedral, an Irish pub with a hip atmosphere. (☎963 91 05 03. Pints of Guinness and Irish beers 500ptas/€3. Open Su-Th 12:30pm-1am, F-Sa 12:30pm-3am.) An older crowd fills the spacious bar **Fox Congo,** C. Caballeros, 35. (☎963 92 55 27. Beer 600ptas/€3.60, mixed drinks 900ptas/€5.40. Open daily 7pm-3:30am.) Discos, which normally don't draw a crowd until at least 3am, dominate the university area, particularly on **Av. Blasco Ibañez.** There are a few smaller discos in El Carme district, most of which are popular with both gay and straight patrons. In summer, however, the only places to be seen are the outdoor discos at Playa de Malvarrosa. **Caballito de Mar,** C. Eugenia Viñes, 22 (☎963 71 07 63), is the most popular and heats up with a psychedelic tunnel and huge outdoor deck. For more info, consult the *Qué y Dónde* weekly magazine (150ptas/€0.90) or the weekly entertainment supplement, *La Cartelera* (125ptas/€0.75), both available at newsstands.

BEACHES

Sand-seekers can join the topless by bouncing down to the expansive and packed beaches on Valencia's coast. The sand and water quality are less than spectacular, but the blistering heat converts everyone into sea-lovers. The most popular beaches are **Las Arenas** and **Malvarrosa,** connected by a bustling boardwalk. Buses #20, 21, 22, and 23 all pass by the sands. Equally crowded but more attractive is **Salér,** a pine-bordered strand 14km from the city that divides a lagoon from the sea. Cafeterias and snack bars line the shore. **Autobuses Buñol** (☎963 49 14 25) go to Salér (on the way to El Perello) from the intersection of

Gran Vía Germanías and C. Sueca. To get to the bus stop, exit the train station, and take the street to the right (between the station and the bullring stadium) to Gran Vía Germanías. The bus stop is one block down (25min., every 30min. 7am-10pm, 150ptas/€0.90).

DAYTRIPS FROM VALENCIA

SAGUNTO (SAGUNT)

*Frequent RENFE Cercanías **trains** (☎962 66 07 28) from Valencia (the C-6 line) stop in Sagunto (30min.; M-F 37 per day 6:10am-10:30pm, Sa-Su 15 per day 7:20am-10:30pm; M-F 345ptas/€2.07, Sa-Su 360ptas/€2.16), as do ALSA **buses** (☎964 66 18 50. 45min., every 30min. 7am-10:15pm, 290ptas/€1.74).*

The residents of Sagunto are thought to be the most courageous in Spain. Their reputation dates back to the 3rd century BC, when the citizens of Phoenician-controlled Sagunto (called Saguntum) held out for an eight-months siege by Hannibal's Carthaginians. Some sources say that on the brink of annihilation, Sagunto's women, children, and elderly threw themselves into a burning furnace; others insist that the residents chose starvation over defeat. The architectural medley of Sagunto's monuments reflects a long list of conquering forces. The highlight of the old town is its refurbished **medieval castle,** declared a national monument in 1931. (Open June-Sept. Tu-Sa 10am-8pm, Su 10am-2pm; Oct.-May Tu-Sa 10am-2pm and 4-6pm, Su 10am-2pm. Free.) Along the way into town is the **Roman Theater,** which has survived a controversial restoration process to become an impressive modern performance stage, built entirely on the skeleton of the original Roman structure. Ask at the **tourist office** in Pl. Cronisto Chabret, at the far end from the ayuntamiento, for a list of performances. (☎962 66 22 13; fax 66 26 77; www.sagunt.com/turismo. Open M-Th 8am-3pm and 4:30-7pm, F 8am-3pm and 4-6:30pm, Sa 8:45am-1:45pm.) By the port, (4km from the town center), Sagunto's **beaches** attract summer travelers. **Puerto de Sagunto** is the recent recipient of an EU beach award. **Buses** to the beaches leave from Av. Santos Patronos next to the tourist office (every 30min. 7am-9:30pm, 100ptas/€0.60).

CULLERA

Cullera lies on the Cercanías train line between Valencia and Gandía (35min.; M-F every 30min., Sa-Su every hr. 6:23am-10:38pm; 525ptas/€3.15). From the train station, take the bus into the city (105ptas/€0.63). Ask the bus driver to let you off near Pl. Virgen and point you toward Pl. Mercado; from there climb the stairs to C. Calvari and continue uphill.

38km south of Valencia, the rapidly expanding town of Cullera has spread beyond the protective watch of its 13th-century **castle,** recently reopened but still undergoing reconstruction. Built upon the ancient ruins of an Islamic castle, the current structure still bears the architectural vestiges of its predecessor. Those who complete the zig-zagging 15-minute hike are rewarded with a 360-degree view of surrounding mountains, verdant rice paddies, sea, river, and the city beyond. Attached to the castle, the 19th-century **Santuari de la Verge** displays sundry religious treasures "collected" by castle residents over the years. *(Both castle and sanctuary open June-Aug. daily 10:30am-1:30pm and 4:30-8:30pm. Free.)*

L'ALBUFERA

Autobuses Buñol buses (☎963 49 14 25) depart from the intersection of Gran Vía de Germanía and C. Sueca in Valencia, stopping in L'Albufera en route to El Perello (40min., every 30min., 175ptas/€1.05). To catch the return bus, walk with your back to the lagoon and cross the bridge on your right.

Spain's largest lagoon, L'Albufera, 15km south of Valencia, and the surrounding **Parc Natural de L'Albufera,** are a nature-lovers' paradise. Trails for biking and hiking ring the lake, while small fishing boats hide amid tall wetland reeds. L'Albufera, one of the wettest regions in the Iberian peninsula, is a prime spot for bird watching—

over 250 migrant species make temporary camp along its shores. Ask at a Valencia tourist office for information on boat tours or cultural excursions.

MORELLA ☎964

The medieval fortress town of Morella (pop. 3000) is straight out of a fairy tale. Centuries-old stone walls surround the mountaintop city, various storybook towers rising above Cataluña's lush countryside, and Morella's prized castle high above it all. The city's picturesque stone walls once served a purpose other than providing tourists with glorious photo opportunities: protecting Morella from its many invaders. Celts, Romans, and Moors have all used the mountaintop as a natural stronghold at different points in its history.

PRACTICAL INFORMATION. Morella is hard to get to. Most visitors arrive via Valencia, though the city is accessible from Barcelona as well. Travelers must make a connection at **Castelló,** on the **Cercanías train** line from Valencia (1hr.; M-F 36 per day 6:10am10:30pm, Sa-Su 15 per day 7:20am-10:30pm; M-F 525ptas/€3.15, Sa-Su 550ptas/€3.30). From Barcelona, the **RENFE** Mediterranean goes to Castelló (2½hr., 17 per day 8am-9pm, 2300-3800ptas/€14-23). **Autos Mediterráneo buses** (☎964 22 00 54 or 22 05 36) depart from the bus stop outside of Castelló's train station for **Morella** (2½hr.; to Morella M-F 7:30am and 3:45pm, Sa 3:45pm; returns M-F 7:30am and 4pm, Sa 4pm; 1115ptas/€7.20). The bus from Castelló doesn't originate at the bus stop, however, and only stops there briefly, so keep an eye out. Morella's **tourist office,** Pl. San Miguel, 3, is right by Puerta San Miguel, the enormous arched entrance to the city. (☎964 17 30 32; fax 17 30 32. www.morella.net. Open July-Aug. daily 10am-2pm and 4-7pm, Sept.-June Tu-Sa 10am-2pm and 4-6pm.) In an **emergency,** dial ☎112. For **medical assistance,** call ☎964 16 09 62.

ACCOMMODATIONS AND FOOD. Once you pass through the Moorish archways of Morella, you may never want to leave. **Hostal La Muralla,** C. Muralla, 12, has rooms with TV and private bath. (☎964 16 02 43. Breakfast 400ptas/€2.40. Singles 3000ptas/€18; doubles 4200ptas/€25. MC/V). Live like budget royalty at **Hostal El Cid,** Port Sant Mateu, 3, one block to the right of the bus station when facing the city wall. The gigantic rooms come with TV, phone, and bathtub; some even have balconies. (☎964 16 01 25. Singles 3300-3600ptas/€20-22; doubles 5400-5800ptas/€33-35. V.) The town's gourmet cuisine is filled with *trufas* (truffles) dug up from under the local turf. Specialties include *paté de trufas* (truffle pâté) and *cordero relleno trufado* (lamb with truffle stuffing). Eating out in Morella is somewhat pricey, and options are limited—most eateries are located on shop-lined Don Blasco de Alagón, Morella's main thoroughfare. **Restaurante Cardenal Ram**, Cuesta Suner, 1, in the hotel and off C. Don Blasco de Alagón, serves up delicious local favorites including hen, quail, rabbit, and truffle-stuffed lamb (1100-1600ptas/€6.60-9.60) in a beautiful dining room with views of the countryside. (☎964 17 30 85. *Menú* 1750ptas/€10.50. Open daily 1:30-3:15pm and 8:30-10:15pm. MC/V.) Those looking to escape the truffle madness run to **Restaurante Lola,** Blasco de Alagón, 21, for the best Italian cuisine in town. (☎964 16 03 87. Entrées 700-1000ptas/€4.20-6. Open M-Sa noon-4:30pm and 8:30pm-2am.)

SIGHTS. Perched atop a massive rock, the **Castell de Morella** dazzles even the most seasoned of castle-goers. Celts, Romans, and Moors have all defended Morella's walls as their own. El Cid stormed the summit in 1084, and Don Blasco de Aragón took the town in the name of Jaume I in 1232. Civil wars in the 19th century and an internal explosion have damaged the castle, but the resulting craters only add to the intrigue. Artillery walls surround the exterior, with openings just wide enough for the sights of battling archers or the lens of your Nikon. Inspect the **Cadro guardhouse** and the **Catxo dungeon,** where the prince of Vienna was imprisoned in the 15th century. (☎964 17 31 28. Entrance on C. Hospital, uphill from the basilica and through the Convent of St. Frances. Open M-F 10:30am-2pm and 4-7:30pm, Sa-Su 10:30am-7:30pm; in winter until 6:30pm. 300ptas/€1.80, students 200ptas/€1.20.) In Pl. Arciprestal, on the way to the castle, the ceiling of gothic **Basílica Santa María la Mayor** hovers over a winding stairwell, an overgrown organ, and the ghostly statue of Nuestra Señora de la Asunción. Bracketed by golden chandeliers, the altar is almost as breathtaking as the Basílica's original 14th-century stained glass windows. (Open June-Aug. daily 11am-2pm and 4-7pm; Sept.-May noon-2pm and 4-6pm. Mass M-F 7pm; Sa 8:15pm; Su 10am, 5, 6:30pm. Basilica free. Musuem inside 150ptas/€0.90) Exit the city from Puerta de San Miguel, turn left, and walk five minutes to the remnants of the Gothic **aqueduct,** whose arches once spanned 16 towers and 6 gates.

ALICANTE (ALACANT) ☎965

Few cities blend beach life, nightlife, and city life as well as Alicante (pop. 285,000), a place where anyone can find activities catering to their tastes. History buffs get lost in the streets of the *casco antiguo*, peruse the modern art museum in its midst, and check out the castle overlooking the entire city. Beach bums catch rays on the crowded shores mere blocks away from the city center, or find refuge on a secluded stretch of coastline just a bus ride away. Partiers marvel at the center's array of pubs, bars, and port-side discos. Every facet of Alicante's vibrant energy crescendoes for one wild week at the end of June when the city celebrates the festival of Sant Joan with a unfriendliness *fiesta*.

TRANSPORTATION

Flights: Aeroport Internacional El Altet (☎966 91 90 00), 10km from town. **Iberia** (24hr. ☎902 40 05 00) and **Air Europa** (☎902 24 00 42) have daily flights to Madrid, Barcelona, and the Balearic Islands, among other destinations. **Alcoyana** (☎965 16 79 11) bus C-6 runs to the airport from Pl. Luceros (every 40min., 140ptas/€0.84).

Trains: RENFE, Estació Término (☎902 24 02 02), on Av. Salamanca, at the end of Av. Estación. Info open daily 7am-midnight. To: **Barcelona** (4½-6hr., 9 per day 6:55am-6:30pm, 6000-10400ptas/€36.00-62.40); **Elche** (30min., every hr. 6:05am-10.05pm, 245-260ptas/€1.47-1.56); **Madrid** (4hr., 9 per day 7am-8pm, 5600-8600pta/€33.60-51.60); **Murcia** (1½hr., every hr. 6:05am-10:05pm, 575-600ptas/€3.45-3.60); **Valencia** (1½hr., 10 per day 6:55am-10:20pm, 1430-5300ptas/€8.58-31.80). **Ferrocarriles de la Generalitat Valenciana,** Estació Marina, Av. Villajoyosa, 2 (☎965 26 27 31), on Explanada d'Espanya, by the beach. Service along the Costa Blanca day and night (see **Costa Blanca: Getting There and Away,** p. 291). In summer the **Trensnochador** (night train; ☎965 26 27 31) runs to beaches near **Alicante,** including Altea and Benidom, with some continuing to Dénia (July-Aug. F-Sa every hr. 9pm-5am, Su-Th 4 per night 9pm-5am 150-700ptas/€0.90-4.20).

Buses: C. Portugal, 17 (☎965 13 07 00). To reach Explanada d'Espanya from the station, turn left on C. Italia and continue walking; the street will turn into C. San Fernando. Any right runs directly to the waterfront. **Alsa** (☎965 13 06 73) to: **Altea** (1hr., 18 per day 6:30am-7:30pm, 560ptas/€3.36); **Barcelona** (7hr., 11 per day 1am-10:30pm, 4790ptas/€28); **Calpe** (1½hr., 17 per day 6:30am-7:30pm, 665ptas/€3.99); **Dénia** (2½hr., 10 per day 6:30am-8pm,1065ptas/€6.39); **Granada** (6hr., 7 per day 1:15am-10:45pm, 3510ptas/€21); **Jávea** (2hr., 7 per day 8am-9pm, 930ptas/€5.58); **Madrid** (5hr., 9 per day 8am-midnight, 3465-5000ptas/€20-30); **Málaga** (8hr., 7 per day 1:15am-10:45pm, 4705ptas/€28); **Sevilla** (10hr., 6 per day, 6000ptas/€36); **Valencia** (2½hr., 10 per day 7am-9pm, 1980ptas/€11.88). **Mollá** (☎965 13 08 51) to: **Elche** (30min.; M-F 2 per hr. 7am-10pm, Sa every hr. 8am-10pm, Su 8 per day 9am-9:30pm; 230ptas/€1.38).

Ferries: Balearia Eurolines Maritimes (☎902 16 01 80) departs from nearby Dénia (see p. 292).

Taxis: ☎965 25 25 11.

Public Transportation: TAM (☎965 25 82 82). Buses #21 and 22 run from the train station in Alicante to Playa San Juan. 125ptas/€0.75.

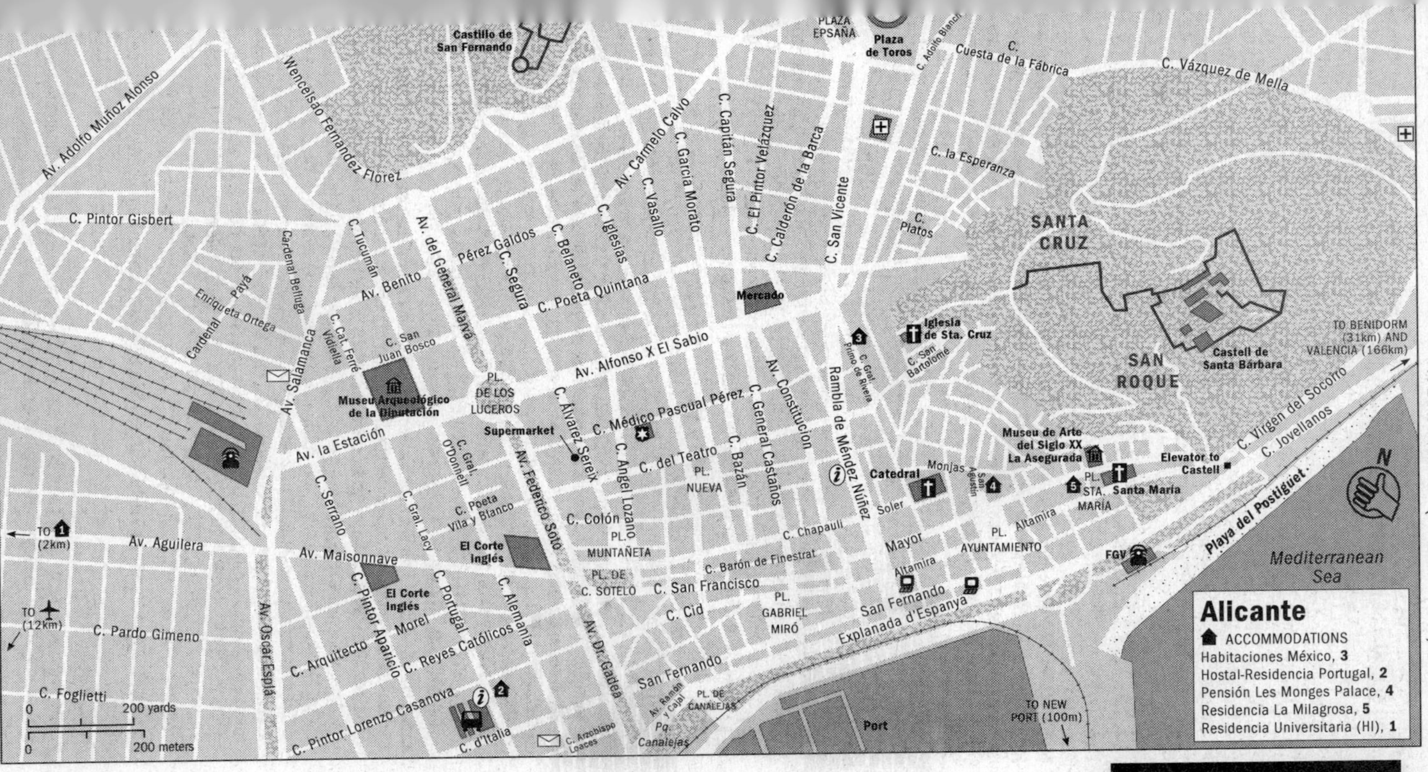
Alicante
ACCOMMODATIONS
Habitaciones México, 3
Hostal-Residencia Portugal, 2
Pensión Les Monges Palace, 4
Residencia La Milagrosa, 5
Residencia Universitaria (HI), 1
Mediterranean Sea
Playa del Postiguet
TO BENIDORM (31km) AND VALENCIA (166km)
C. Jovellanos
C. Virgen del Socorro
Castell de Santa Bárbara
SAN ROQUE
SANTA CRUZ
Elevator to Castell
Santa María
PL. STA. MARÍA
Museu de Arte del Siglo XX La Asegurada
San Agustín
Iglesia de Sta. Cruz
C. San Bartolomé
Catedral
PL. AYUNTAMIENTO
Mayor
Altamira
Monjas
Soler
FGV
TO NEW PORT (100m)
Port
Explanada d'Espanya
San Fernando
Rambla de Méndez Núñez
C. Gral. Primo de Rivera
C. San Vicente
C. Calderón de la Barca
C. El Pintor Velázquez
Mercado
Plaza de Toros
PLAZA EPSAÑA
C. Adolfo Blanch
C. Vázquez de Mella
C. Cuesta de la Fábrica
C. la Esperanza
C. Platos
C. Capitán Segura
C. García Morato
Av. Carmelo Calvo
C. Vasallo
C. Iglesias
C. Belaneto
C. Poeta Quintana
C. Segura
Pérez Galdós
Castillo de San Fernando
Av. Constitucion
C. General Castaños
C. Bazán
PL. NUEVA
C. del Teatro
Av. Alfonso X El Sabio
C. Médico Pascual Pérez
C. Angel Lozano
C. Chapauli
C. Barón de Finestrat
PL. GABRIEL MIRÓ
C. San Francisco
C. Cid
PL. MUNTAÑETA
C. Colón
PL. DE C. SOTELO
C. Álvarez Sereix
Av. Dr. Gadea
PL. DE CANALEJAS
Av. Ramón y Cajal
Pq. Canalejas
C. Arzobispo Loaces
Av. Federico Soto
PL. DE LOS LUCEROS
Supermarket
El Corte Inglés
C. Alemania
C. Portugal
C. Reyes Católicos
C. d'Italia
C. Pintor Lorenzo Casanova
Av. del General Marvá
C. Gral. O'Donnell
C. Poeta Vila y Blanco
C. Gral. Lacy
Av. Benito
C. San Juan Bosco
Museu Arqueológico de la Diputación
C. Tucumán
C. Cat. Ferré Vidiella
Av. la Estación
C. Serrano
Av. Maisonnave
C. Pintor Aparicio
C. Arquitecto Morel
Wenceslao Fernandez Florez
Av. Salamanca
Cardenal Belluga
Enriqueta Ortega
Payá
Cardenal
Av. Oscar Esplá
Av. Aguilera
C. Pardo Gimeno
C. Foglietti
C. Pintor Gisbert
Av. Adolfo Muñoz Alonso
TO 1 (2km)
TO (12km)
0 200 yards
0 200 meters

ORIENTATION AND PRACTICAL INFORMATION

Originating at the train station, **Av. de la Estación** becomes **Av. Alfonso X el Sabio** after passing through Pl. Luceros. **Explanada d'Espanya** stretches along the waterfront between Rbla. Méndez Núñez and Av. Federico Soto; the two reach back up to Av. Alfonso X El Sabio. This grid of streets constitutes the center of town.

Tourist Office: Main city office, C. Portugal, 17 (☎965 92 98 02), at the bus station. Open June-Aug. M-Sa 9am-2pm and 4-8pm. **Regional office,** Rbla. de Méndez Nuñez, 23 (☎965 20 00 00; fax 20 02 43). Info on the entire coast. English spoken. Open June-Aug. M-F 10am-8pm; Sept.-May M-F 10am-7pm, Sa 10am-2pm and 3-7pm. Also at the **airport** (☎966 91 91 00) and the **Ayuntamiento** (☎900 21 10 27).

Budget Travel: TIVE, Pl. San Cristóbal, 8 (☎965 21 16 86). ISIC 700ptas/€4.20. HI card 1800ptas/€10.80. Open M-F 9am-1:30pm and 5-8pm.

Luggage Storage: At the **bus station** (200-500ptas/€1.2-3 per bag) and the **train station** (400ptas/€2.40 per bag). Open M-Sa 8am-8:30pm, Su 10am-1pm, 3:45-7pm.

Emergency: ☎112. **Police:** Comisaría, C. Médico Pascual Pérez, 27 (☎965 10 72 00).

Hospital: Hospital General, C. Maestro Alonzo, 109 (☎965 93 83 00).

Internet Access: Fundación BanCaja, Rbla. Méndez Nuñez, 4, on the corner of C. San Fernando, 2nd fl. Sometimes a wait. Open M-F 9am-2pm and 4-9pm, Sa 9am-2pm. Free hr. per day with ISIC. **Yazzgo,** Explanada, 3. Open M-Sa 8am-11pm, Su 9am-11pm. 8am-4pm 250ptas/€1.50 per hr.; 4pm-11pm 500ptas/€3 per hr.

Post Office: Corner of C.Arzobispo Loaces and C. Alemania (☎965 21 99 84), near the bus station. Open M-F 8:30am-8:30pm, Sa 9:30am-2pm. **2nd branch,** Bono Guarner, 2 (☎965 22 78 71), next to the RENFE Station. Same hours. **Postal Code:** 03070.

ACCOMMODATIONS AND CAMPING

Although hostels seem to wait round every corner, finding a desirable room may pose a challenge. Good accommodations require an early arrival or a reservation, especially during the festival at the end of June.

Hostal Les Monges Palace, C. San Agustín, 4 (☎965 21 50 46), behind the Ayuntamiento. Excellent rooms with TVs, paintings, and A/C (700ptas/€4.20 per day). Winter heating. Parking 1000ptas/€6 per day. Singles 3000ptas/€18, with shower 2600ptas/€15.60, with bath 5000ptas/€30, with sauna and jacuzzi 8000ptas/€48 doubles with shower 5500ptas/€33, with bath 8000ptas/€48, with sauna and jacuzzi 13,000ptas/€78; triples with shower 7000ptas/€42, with bath 9500ptas/€57, with sauna and jacuzzi 15,000ptas/€90. MC/V.

Habitaciones México, C. General Primo de Rivera, 10 (☎965 20 93 07), off the end of Av. Alfonso X El Sabio. Small but cozy rooms. Free internet access and kitchen use Laundry 800ptas/€4.80 per load. Singles 2200ptas/€13; doubles 4000ptas/€24 with bath 5000ptas/€30; triples 5400ptas/€33, with bath 6000ptas/€36.

Residencia La Milagrosa, C. Villa Vieja (☎965 21 69 18), across from the art museum From C. Rambla Méndez Nuñez, turn left on C. Mayor and continue straight. Thirty sparkling rooms blocks from the beach. Huge rooftop terrace has a view of the castle. Free kitchen use. Rooms 2500-3000ptas/€15-18 per person.

Residencia Universitaria (HI), Av. Orihuela, 59 (☎965 11 30 44). Take bus #03 (125ptas/€0.75). Individual rooms with private bath and A/C, snack bar, big-screen TV, free laundry, and foosball. 3-day max. stay. Dorms 800ptas/€4.80, with breakfast 900ptas/€5.40, with 3 meals 1900ptas/€11.40; over 26 dorms 1100ptas/€6.60 with breakfast 1400ptas/€8.40, with 3 meals 2400ptas/€14. Open July-Sept. only.

Hostal-Residencia Portugal, C. Portugal, 26 (☎965 92 92 44), across from the bus station. Dining room-cum-lounge has a color TV. Ask for a room facing the street with a balcony. In-room TV 400ptas/€2.40. Singles 2500-2700ptas/€15-16; doubles 3900-4200ptas/€23-29, with bath 4700-4900ptas/€28-29; triple prices negotiable.

Camping: Playa Mutxavista (☎965 65 45 26), right by the beach. Hop bus #21 from the city center (125ptas/€0.75). Restaurant and supermarket on site. June-Sept. 570ptas/€3.42 per person, 1845ptas/€11.07 per tent; Oct.-May 350ptas/€2.10 per person, 1250ptas/€7.50 per tent.

FOOD

Most visitors refuel along the main pedestrian streets; prices are reasonable despite the crowds of tourists. The smaller, cheaper, family-run *bar-restaurantes* in the old city have less visitors but also less variety. The **market** is near Av. Alfonso X El Sabio (open M-Sa 8am-2pm). Buy basics at **Supermarket Mercadona,** C. Alvarez Sereix, 5, off Av. Federico Soto. (☎965 21 58 94. Open M-Sa 9am-9pm.)

Kebap, C. Italia, 2 (☎965 22 92 35), near Av. Dr. Gadea. Mouth-watering Middle Eastern cuisine. Most popular dish, *kebaps* (pita with meat, or veggies; 390ptas/€2.34). Heaping entrées (950-1000ptas/€5.7-6). Open daily 1-4pm and 8pm-midnight.

Cafetería Mediterráneo, C. Altamira, 8 (☎965 14 08 40), 2 blocks from the *Explanada*. A café bursting with locals at all hours of the day. Chrome bar displays array of raw fish. 4-course *menú* 1000ptas/€6. Open M-Sa 7am-10pm.

Restaurante El Buen Comer, C. Mayor, 8 (☎965 21 31 03). Fabulous *menú* options; choose from 6 first courses and 5 second courses (1295ptas/€7.70). Entrées are pricy. Open daily 10am-midnight.

SIGHTS AND BEACHES

With drawbridges, dark passageways, and hidden tunnels, the **Castell de Santa Bárbara** keeps silent guard over Alicante's beach. Built by the Carthaginians, the 200m high fortress boasts a dry moat, dungeon, and ammunition storeroom. The *Albacar Vell*, or lower zone, constructed during the Middle Ages, holds a vast sculpture garden with exhibits from Spanish greats. A paved road from the old section of Alicante leads to the top, although most people opt for the **elevator** rising from a hidden entrance on Av. Jovellanos—just across the street from Playa Postiguet and near the white crosswalk. (☎965 26 31 31. Open Apr.-Sept. 10am-7:30pm; Oct.-Mar. 9am-6:30pm. Free. Elevator 400ptas/€2.40.) The **Museu de Arte del Siglo XX La Asegurada,** Pl. Santa Maria, 3, at the eastern end of C. Mayor, showcases Valencian modernist art pieces, including several works by Picasso and Dalí. The museum offers free guided tours if reserved in advance. (☎965 14 07 68. Open May 15-Sept. 14 M-F 10am-2pm and 5-9pm, Sa-Su 10:30am-2:30pm; Sept. 15-May 14 M-F 10am-2pm and 4-8pm, Sa-Su 10:30am-2:30pm. Free.)

Alicante's **Playa del Postiguet,** just meters to the left of the New Port, is perpetually packed with sunbathers, volleyball players, and children on the loose. For more peaceful shores, the 6km. of **Playa de San Juan** and **Playa del Mutxavista** are the nearest options. Both **Playa del Postiguet** and **Playa de San Juan** wave the EU *bandera azul* for great waters. The **Costa Blanca's** gorgeous shores extend to the north along the Alicante-Dénia train line. (To San Juan, take TAM buses #21, 22, or 31. For Mutxavista, take #21. Each departs every 15min., 25ptas/€0.75. The Alicante-Dénia train leaves from the main station every hr., 25ptas/€0.75.)

ENTERTAINMENT AND NIGHTLIFE

The bars, discos, and port-side pubs of Alicante make for a vibrant and varied nightlife. Most night owls kick off the evening by bar-hopping in the *casco antiguo*. **Pl. Sant Cristofol,** one block toward the castle from Rbla. Méndez Nuñez, offers several popular bars; others line the streets heading down toward the water. For a famous *mojito* (lemon, rum, mint, and sugar; 350ptas/€2.10), head to **Coscorrón,** C. Tarifo, 3, open since 1936 and claiming status as the oldest bar in Alicante (open Su-Th 10:30pm-2:30am, F-Sa 11pm-4:30am). Alicante's **main port** also houses a complex of bars overlooking the water; they tend to fill up a bit

WE LIKE TO PARTY Everyone knows that Spain loves to party. During the rollicking June 20-29 **Festival de Sant Joan,** Alicante takes it to the next level. Only Pamplona's running of the bulls even comes close. During the *fiesta*, streets are more packed at five in the morning than five in the evening as—for one week straight—young and old fill the streets from midnight 'til dawn, dancing and drinking in one dizzy outdoor fiasco. The craziness culminates on the seventh day, when citizens light fire to the huge *papier-maché* creations towering over the streets. Firefighters then proceed to soak everyone nearby, and the party continues until dawn—wet.

later than the bars in town. A dance-happy crowd fills the discos on the **Puerto Nuevo,** to the left when facing the water; people always love **Puerto Di Roma.** Clubs in Alicante sometimes have a drink minimum but rarely a cover charge. For yet wilder nightlife, **Benidorm,** 45min. away, rocks out with several huge *discotecas*: **Space, KU, KM, and Pachá**, all accessible in July and August by FGV's special **Trensnochador** trains from Estació Marina (see **Trains,** p. 288, for more info). During July and August, la Playa de San Juan becomes a stage for **ballet and musical performances,** part of the *Plataforma Cultural* series. (Open nightly until 9am. Cover from 1500ptas/€9.)

From June 20 to 29, hedonism rules the **Festival de Sant Joan.** *Fogueres* (symbolic or satiric effigies) are erected around the city, only to be burned in the streets on the 24th. The revelry continues with street decorations and nightly fireworks. The culmination is the firehouse-drenching *Banya*. The **Verge del Remei** procession begins in Alicante on August 3rd; pilgrims then trek to the monastery of Santa Faz the following Thursday. Alicante honors *La Virgen del Demedio* all summer during the **Fiestas del Verano,** when numerous concerts and theatrical performances are held in the new open-air theater on the port.

DAYTRIPS FROM ALICANTE

ELCHE (ELX)

*RENFE **trains** run from Alicante every hr. 6:05am-10:05pm, 245-260ptas/€1.47-1.56. Mollá **buses** (☎965 13 08 51) leave Alicante M-F 2 per hr. 7am-10pm, Sa every hr. 8am-10pm, Su 8 per day 9am-9:30pm; 230ptas/€1.38.*

A lush oasis of a city, 23km from Alicante, surrounded by one of Europe's only palm forests, Elche is a refreshing change from the monochrome cities lining the rest of the *Costa Blanca*. Elche's parks make for a great daytrip; heading to nearby beaches is also an option, although better beaches lie further north. At the corner of Av. Ferrocarril and Po. Estación begins the **Parque Municipal,** where palm trees, grassy promenades, and playgrounds make for a cheerful, family-oriented park. (Open daily June-Aug. 7am-midnight; Sept.-May 7am-9pm). Of Elche's parks and public gardens, by far the most beautiful is **Hort del Cura (Orchard of the Priest),** where magnificent trees shade colorful flower beds. (Open June-Aug. 9am-9pm, Sept.-May 9am-6pm. 300ptas/€1.80.) Both the **train station** (**Estación Parque**) and the **bus station** (☎965 45 58 58), are located along Av. Libertat. To get to the town center from the bus and train stations, bear left when leaving either station, then left again on Po. Estación. The **tourist office** is on Pl. Parc, at the end of Po. Estación. (☎965 45 27 47. Open M-F 10am-7pm, Sa 10am-2:30pm, Su 10am-2pm.)

ISLA TABARCA

Cruceros Kon Tiki (☎965 21 63 96) sends ferries daily from the dock on the Explanada d'Espanya to the island (high-speed 30min., regular 1hr.; Sept.-June. 11am, July-Aug. 3-4 per day 10:30am-3:30pm; round-trip 2000ptas/€12). Ferries return July-Aug. 3-4 per day noon-6pm and Sept.-June 5pm.

Still a quiet fishing village, this tiny island 15km south of Alicante offers an old fort, several fresh seafood restaurants, a rocky beach with beautiful turquoise water...and not much else. Despite its petite proportions, tourists have recently begun to make the island a choice daytrip destination. Most attractions are immediately visible from the dock. The only **beach** is straight ahead; rent beach chairs and umbrellas for the day from an attendant (chairs 800ptas/€4.80 per day, 2 chairs and umbrella 1600ptas/€9.60). To the left, the remnants of the tiny **fort,** once a jail for Spanish exiles, overlooks the ocean on three sides. A variety of seafood **restaurants** line the narrow strip between the fort and the beach—all serve the same typical—yet delicious—*comida típica* with *menús* ranging from 1200-1500ptas/€7.20-9. For **tourist information** and the **police** call ☎965 96 00 58.

COSTA BLANCA

You could while away a lifetime touring the charming resort towns of the Costa Blanca. The "white coast" that extends from Dénia through Calpe to Alicante derives its name from the fine, white sand of its shores. A varied terrain of hills blanketed with cherry blossoms, jagged mountains, lush pine-layered hillsides, and natural lagoons surrounds densely inhabited coastal towns. Altea, Calpe, Dénia, and, especially, Jávea offer relief from the disco-droves that energize Alicante and Benidorm, although even these towns are not tourist-free.

COSTAL TRANSPORTATION

TRAINS. Ferrocarrils de la Generalitat Valenciana (☎965 92 02 02, in Alicante 965 26 27 31) hits up almost every town and beach along the coast with its Alicante-Dénia line. Trains run from Alicante to: **Altea** (1½hr., every hr. 6am-9pm except noon, 580ptas/€3.48); **Calpe** (1¾hr., 8 per day 6am-9pm, 720ptas/€4.32) and **Dénia** (2¼hr., 8 per day 6am-9pm, 1050ptas/€6.30). From Dénia and Calpe, trains return to **Alicante** every two hours (6:25am-7:25pm), while from Altea trains depart every hour. (6:24am-10:24pm). **Trensnochador** (☎965 26 22 33), the night train running out of Alicante, runs July-Sept. to **Benidorm, Altea, Calpe,** and **Dénia** (F-Sa hourly to Altea and Benidorm, 3 per night to Calpe and Dénia; Su-Th 4 per night to Altea and Benidorm, 3 per night to Calpe and Dénia; 10:20pm-6am).

BUSES. ALSA (☎902 42 22 42) runs inexpensive **buses** between Alicante and Valencia, stopping in towns along the Costa Blanca. Buses are the easiest and most cost-efficient way to get around the Costa Blanca. Not all buses that leave Valencia or Alicante stop in every town or continue all the way to the other end of the coast. From **Valencia** buses run to: **Alicante** (4½hr., 13 per day 6:30am-6pm, 2000ptas/€12); **Altea** and **Calpe** (3-3½hr., 12 per day 6:30am-6pm, 1315-1420ptas/€7.89-8.52); **Dénia** (2hr., 9 per day 6:30am-9:15pm, 1070ptas/€6.42); **Gandía** (1hr., 13 per day 6:30am-9:15pm, 735ptas/€4.41); and **Jávea** (2hr., 7 per day 8am-9:15pm, 1080ptas/€6.48). From **Alicante** buses run to: **Altea** (1¼hr., 18 per day 6:30am-9pm, 560ptas/€3.36); **Calpe** (1½hr., 18 per day 6:30am-9pm, 675ptas/€4.05); **Dénia** (2½hr., 10 per day 6:30am-8pm, 1065ptas/€6.29); **Jávea** (2½hr., 7 per day 8am-9pm, 930ptas/€5.58); and **Valencia** (4 to 4½ hr., 10 per day 6:30am-6pm, 2000ptas/€12).

ALTEA

Unlike the majority of towns lining *Costa Blanca*, Altea's sun-drenched coastline betrays little of its growing tourism industry. Restaurants remain modest and cheap, daily life appears relatively uninterrupted, and huge hotels have yet to spring up. A long bouldered path separates the Mediterranean from Altea's calm stretch of shoreline, and pebbly beaches fan out along either coast. From the beach, narrow cobblestone streets and steps wind up to **Pl. de la Iglesia.** Shaded by the cobalt dome of the church of the **Virgen del Consuelo,** the square commands breathtaking views of the turquoise Mediterranean. The main drag, **Comte d' Altea,** is filled with snack shops and beachware. During the last week of September the city erupts with music, gunpowder, and dance for the **Fiestas de Moros y Cristianos.**

While in Altea, be prepared to shell out. **Hostal Paco,** Jaime I, 7-A, just off Comte d' Altea, provides A/C, full baths, TVs, and wide windows. (☎965 84 05 41. Singles 5000ptas/€30; doubles 8000ptas/€48.) For breakfast, lunch, or dinner head to C. Jaime I, parallel to the water, and its sidestreets. Both **trains** and **buses** stop at the foot of the hill on C. La Mar (coming out of the station, head left to go toward the center). If you're arriving by bus from Alicante, get off at the 1st stop; if arriving from Valencia, get off at the second stop.

The **tourist office** sits on C. Sant Pere, 9, parallel to C. La Mar and right by the water. From the train station or the bus stop, walk toward the sea to C. Sant Pere. (☎965 84 41 14; fax 84 42 13. Open June-Aug. M-Sa 10am-2pm and 5-8:30pm; Sept.-May M-Sa 10am-2pm and 5-7:30pm. Services include: **emergency** ☎112; **police** ☎965 84 05 25; and **ambulance** ☎965 84 35 32; **internet access** at **Red Attack,** C. Garganes, 9 (☎966 88 12 91. 200ptas/€1.20 per 30min.; open June-Aug. M-F 11am-2pm and 6pm-2am, Sa-Su 6pm-2am; Sept.-May M-F 10am-2am, Sa-Su noon-2am); and the **post office,** C. Jaime I, 13 (☎965 84 01 74; open M-F 8:30am-2:30pm, Sa 9:30am-1pm.).

CALPE (CALP)

With T-shirt stores lining the streets and beaches packed with foreigners escaping the summer heat, Calpe at first seems the classic tourist trap—yet the yearly flocks of visitors descend for good reason. The **Peñó d'Ifach** (327m), a massive, flat-topped rock formation whose precipitous face edges right on the sea, towers above the beach and town. Farther north, from the cliffs and caves of the easterly **Cabo de la Nao,** Ibiza can be seen in the distance on a clear day. Around the bend from the *cabo*, a castle and watch-tower have protected the old fishing village of **Moraira** from pirates for centuries. And of course, Calpe's beaches, the little town's main attraction, lure visitors with kilometers of white sand.

Calpe's main avenue, **Gabriel Miró,** descends to the blue-flagged (EU praised) **Platja Arena-Bol.** Beyond the Peñó, both **Platja Levante** and the cove of **Calalga** bear the same *bandera azul*. To hike to the **Peñó d'Ifach** (2½hr. round-trip), walk past the tourist office, then turn right on Av. del Port, and left on C. Isla Formentera, following the signs. **ALSA buses** (☎965 83 90 29) stop 2km from the beach at C. Capitán Pérez Jorda (See **Transportation,** p. 291). From the station, set out straight down Av. Masnou (toward the rotary), which curves around to the left before turning into C. Goleta and leading ultimately into Pl. Constitución. From the plaza to the water, turn right down Av. Gabriel Miró, and follow the smell of the sea. Taking the **Autobuses Ifach bus** past the bus station to the beach is a less strenuous option (1 per hr., 115ptas/€0.69). If all else fails, call a **taxi** (☎965 83 78 78).

With your back to the bus station, turning right will lead you downhill to a neighborhood of gorgeous Mediterranean architecture. A 20min. beach walk along the street running from the old town leads to the **tourist office,** Av. Ejércitos Españoles, 62. (Open June-Aug. M-Sa 9am-9pm, Su 10:30am-2pm; Sept.-May M-F 9am-2pm and 4-8pm, Sa 9am-2pm.) The **police,** Av. Ejércitos Españoles (☎965 08 90 00), are several doors down. **Internet Center Perlamar,** C. Benidorm, 1, is right off Gabriel Miró, 3 blocks from the beach. (☎965 83 93 83. Coin-operated computers 200ptas/€1.20 for 30min. Open daily 10am-midnight.) For a comfortable bed, try the tiny **Pensión Céntrica,** Pl. Ifach. All rooms have sinks, but the toilets are relegated to hallway bathrooms. (☎965 83 55 28. 1500ptas/€9 per person.) The most reasonably priced **restaurants** in Calpe line the incline toward the old town.

DÉNIA ☎966

Set halfway between Valencia and Alicante along the Golfo de Valencia, Dénia (named by the Greeks for Diana, goddess of the hunt, the moon, and purity) is an upscale family resort. Though the town has little to offer budget travelers in the way of bargains, its beautiful beaches, water-sports, and tasty restaurants are enough to tempt even the most thrifty to splurge. Dénia's harbor serves as an important ferry connection to the Balearic Islands. Come summertime, the town goes nutty with several wild festivals.

ORIENTATION AND PRACTICAL INFORMATION. The **train station** (☎965 78 04 45) is located on C. Calderón. The **bus station** is on Pl. Arxiduc Carles. For train and bus schedules, see **Transportation,** p. 291. Local buses (☎966 42 14 08) depart from the tourist office for nearby beaches. Take the bus marked "Marina" or "Calma" for the best beaches; the bus marked "Rotas" heads in the opposite direction (Marinas and Rotas depart hourly 8am-8pm; Calma 6 per day 9am-9pm; 105ptas/€0.63.) To reach the Balearics by sea, consult **Balearia Eurolinies Maritimes,** in Pl. Oculista Burgues, next to the tourist office. (☎902 16 01 80; www.balearia.com.) Ferries run from Dénia to **Palma** and **Ibiza** (6295-10,055ptas/€38-60). For full ferry info, see Baelaric Islands **By boat,** p. 475. For **taxis,** call 965 78 65 65. Most local services, including local **buses, trains, ferries,** and the **post office,** are located along **C. Patricio Fernández,** which runs straight to the port. The **tourist office** sits on Pl. Oculista Baigues, 9, 30m inland from Estació Marítima. (☎966 42 23 67; www.denia.net. Open M-Sa 9:30am-1:30pm and 4:30-7:30pm, Su 10am-2pm.) To get to the tourist office from the bus depot, turn left out of the plaza onto C. Patricio Fernandez; from the train station, start straight ahead, then veer to your right. Three blocks over from C. Patricio Fernández, shop and restaurant-lined **C. Marqués de Campo** is the main tourist strip. In an emergency, contact the **police** ☎092. **Internet access** is found at **CiberDeni@,** C. Senija). From C. Patricio Fernández take C. Sagunto; C. Senjira is the second left. (☎966 43 14 81. 480ptas/€2.88 per hr.)

ACCOMMODATIONS AND FOOD. Dénia certainly doesn't cater to budget travelers, especially in the lodging department. Be prepared to shell out 5000ptas/€30 or more for a single room in the summer. **Hostal L'Anfora,** Explanada de Cervantes, 8, has some of the most inexpensive rooms in town. (☎966 43 01 01. Deposit required. Oct.-June singles 3500ptas/€21; doubles 6000ptas/€36. July-Sept. singles 5000ptas/€30; doubles 8000ptas/€48. MC/V.) With A/C, TVs, and private baths, **Hostal Comercio,** C. de la Vía, 43, may appear more of a hotel than a hostal. (☎/fax 965 78 00 71. Oct.-May singles 3800ptas/€23; doubles 4900ptas/€29. June singles 5000ptas/€30; doubles 7900ptas/€47. July-Sept. singles 5300ptas/€32; doubles 8200ptas/€49. MC/V.) **Camping Las Marinas,** C. Les Bovetes Nord, 4, is a 3km bus ride (125ptas/€0.75) from Platja Jorge Joan. Hot water, supermarket, restaurant, and beach-side locale are all added bonuses. (☎966 47 41 85 or 75 51 88. 690ptas/€4.14 per person and per tent. Open year-round.) **Restaurants** line C. Marqués de Campo and the Explanada de Cervantes, though most cater to the ubertourist. Cheaper eateries sit merely a block or two away off the main drags. Despite its portside location, **Khyber I,** Pl. Fontanella, 4 serves up reasonably priced and authentic curries and other Indian cuisine—definitely a standout amidst the sundry Spanish and Italian restaurants nearby. (Entrées 800-1000ptas/€4.6-6. ☎965 78 56 04. Open daily 1-4pm and 9-11pm.) The **supermarket,** C. Carlos Senti, 7, is just off C. Patricio Fernández. (☎965 78 22 61. Open M-Sa 9am-8:30pm.)

SIGHTS AND ENTERTAINMENT. An 18th-century **castle** sprawls across the hill overlooking the marina. James II enforced the 1304 separation between the town below and the castle above by displacing all of Dénia's inhabitants to the *villa vella*, or old quarter, beyond the castle walls. (☎966 42 06 56. Open daily Nov.-March 10am-1pm and 3-6pm, April-May 10am-1:30pm and 3:30-7pm, June 10am-1:30pm and 4-7:30pm, July-Aug. 10:30am-1:30pm and 7-8:30pm, Sept. 10:30am-1:30pm and 5-8pm, Oct. 10am-1pm and 3-6:30pm. 300ptas/€1.80.) A tourist train chugs to the castle from the tourist office (every 30min. 10am-1pm and 5-8pm; 500ptas/€3 includes entrance to the castle), or you can walk by way of the stairs next to the town hall. Dénia's biggest attraction, however, is its 14km of glorious **beaches.** Windsurfers skip over the waves off **Playa Els Molins,** while scuba divers explore the depths off **Las Playas Area Les Rotes.** Beyond beaches, **Montgó Natural Park** (☎966 42 32 05) has plenty of trails. Dénia holds a mini **Fallas festival** Mar. 16-20, burning effigies on the final midnight. During **Festa Major** (early July), locals prove they're just as gutsy as their countrymen in Pamplona—bulls and fans dive as one into a pool of water, a feat known as **Bous a la mar.** In mid-July, the **Fiestas de la Santísima Sangre** feature street dances, concerts, mock battles, and fireworks over the harbor. The parades and religious plays of the **Fiesta de Moros y Cristianos** celebration also take place between Aug. 14 and 17.

JÁVEA (XÀBIA)

Jávea's harbors host tranquil waters free from rambunctious tourists—while British families venture here in the summer, backpackers tend to head to more popular and younger destinations. Although a municipal bus runs 2km inland to the port, then on to a larger beach, Jávea's real beauties—its coves, capes, and cliffs—are only accessible by car, bike, or foot. A number of secluded coves also line the coast south of the port. Jávea's most popular beaches, **Playa La Granadella, Playa de Ambolo,** and **Playa La Barraca,** are all serene and accessible. The **Fiesta de Moros y Cristianos** erupts during the second half of July; fireworks jolt wide-eyed tourists roaming among costumed Moors and Christians.

Inconvenient transportation to Jávea has spared the town from the bane of heavy tourist loads. **ALSA buses** stop at C. Príncipe de Asturias, but arrive only five times per day (see **Transportation,** p. 291.). To get to the port, take the **municipal bus** (☎966 42 14 08. June-Sept. every 30min., Oct.-May every hr., 8am-2pm and 4-10pm; 110ptas/€0.66.) If you don't feel like waiting, continue down Av. Alicante, which runs directly to the port (20min.). **Autocarres Carrió** (☎965 58 10 36) runs between Denia and Jávea (15min., 6 per day 8am-7pm, 140ptas/€0.84). Jávea has three tourist offices—the most convenient are those near the port (☎965 79 07 39), Pl. Almirante Bastarreche, 24, or by the *ayuntamiento*, Pl. de la Iglesia, 6 (☎965 79 43 56). All are open M-F 9am-2pm and 5-9pm, Sa 10am-2pm and 5-9pm, Su 10am-1pm. Jávea's remote location may necessitate an overnight stay. **Pensión La Favorita,** C. Magallanes, 4, is as good as it gets; follow the signs to the tourist office (☎965 79 04 77. Singles 3000ptas/€18; doubles 4000-6200ptas/€24-37, with bath 5000-6700ptas/€30-40). **Restaurants** line C. Andrés Lambert, leading away from the port.

JÁTIVA (XÀTIVA)

Trains are the best way to get in and out of Játiva. RENFE (☎963 52 02 02) runs from Valencia to Játiva (1hr., every 30min. 6am-10pm, 435ptas/€2.61). From Játiva, trains run to Valencia (6am-10pm) and Alicante (1hr., 6 per day, 2500ptas/€15).

Once the second most populated city in Valencia, Játiva, a place of palaces and churches, was burned to the ground by Felipe V in the 18th century. Today it is simply a quiet town with little to offer other than its impressive castle. **Alameda de Jaume I** divides the town into the new and the old villages, starting from the foot of a hill topped by an awe-inspiring castle. The **castle** above has two sections: the **castell machor,** on the right as you enter, and the pre-Roman **castell chicotet.** The former, used from the 13th through the 16th century, bears the scars of siege and earthquake. Its vaulted **prison** has held some famous wrongdoers, including King Fernando el Católico and the Comte d'Urgell, would-be usurper of the Aragonese throne. The Comte is now buried in its chapel. To get there, it's a 30min. walk uphill. A tourist train chugs up to the castle at 12:30 and 4:30pm. (Open Tu-Su 10am-7pm; in winter Tu-Su 10am-6pm. 300ptas/€1.5, students and seniors 150ptas/€0.75.) Held since 1250, Jativa's annual **Fira festival** storms the city from August 15th to 20th with live music, bullfights, and pulling contests.

To reach the old village from the train station, walk straight up Baixada de L'Estació and turn left at its end. The **tourist office,** Alameda Jaume I, 50, is across from the Ajuntament. English is spoken. (☎962 27 33 46. Open June 15-Sept. 15 Tu-F 10am-2:30pm and 5-7pm, Sa-Su 10am-2pm; Sept. 16-June 14 Tu-F 9am-2pm and 4-6pm, Sa-Su 10am-2pm.) In an **emergency,** call ☎112.

GANDÍA

Centuries before the EU began blue-flagging beaches, the powerful Borjas family of Valencia had already discovered Gandía and transformed it into a center of noble beach bumming. Five centuries later, the Gandía still gets most of its income from visitors seeking the peace of a seaside vacation. Fine sands stretch for kilometers; here, there's little else to do but sunbathe. Departing from the tourist office, **La Marina buses,** Marqués de Campo, 14 run to the **beach** along Pg. Marítimo (every 15min.; last bus 1am in summer, 11:30pm in winter; 145ptas/€0.87).

The majority of services in Gandía are located near the train station on **Marqués de Campo;** everything else is by the beach. The **tourist office,** Marqués de Campo, is across from the train station. (☎962 87 77 88. English spoken. Open June-Aug. M-F 9:30am-1:30pm and 4:30-7:30pm, Sa 10am-1:30pm; Sept.-May M-F 9:30am-1:30pm and 4-7pm, Sa 10am-1pm.) Services include: **emergency** ☎112; **police** ☎962 87 88 00; and **Internet** at **Cibercafé,** C. Cibeles, 46 (☎962 84 00 97; 300ptas/€1.80 per hr.; open daily 10am-1am.) The **post office,** Pl. Jaume I, 7, is a few blocks behind the *Ayuntamiento.* (☎962 87 10 91. Open M-F 8:30am-2:30pm.) **Postal code:** 46700.

Gandía is full of expensive hotels; those who want to stay here on the cheap should make reservations well in advance. **Habitaciones Rosmar,** C. Cullera, 8, has the cheapest rooms and is only a 3min. walk from the beach. (☎962 84 31 96. Singles 3200ptas/€19, doubles 5500ptas/€33. Open Apr.-Sept.) **El Nido,** C. Alcoy, 22, is right off the beach but is pricier. (☎962 84 46 40. Sept.-June doubles 6000ptas/€36, July doubles 7000ptas/€42, Aug doubles 8000ptas/€48.) Stock up on groceries at **Supermarket Macedona,** C. Perú (open M-Sa 9am-9pm).

RENFE trains (☎902 24 02 02) run from **Valencia** (1hr., every 30min. 6am-10pm, 550ptas/€3.30). **ALSA,** C. Magistrado Catalán, 3 (☎962 96 50 66) runs **buses** to: **Valencia** (1hr., 9-12 per day, 735ptas/€4.41); and **Alicante** (3hr., 9-12 per day, 235ptas/€7.41). Buses to Alicante stop in **Altea** (675ptas/€4.05), **Calpe** (560ptas/€3.36), and **Dénia** (335ptas/€2.01).

NEAR GANDÍA: PLATJA DE PILES

Just 10km south of Gandía, Platja de Piles offers vast stretches of beach. From Gandía, **La Amistad,** Av. Marqués de Campo, 9 (☎962 87 44 10), runs to and from Platja de Piles (M-Sa 4-5 per day 8:45am-8:30pm, 125ptas/€0.75). Buses depart from outside the train station, across from the supermarket. While in Platja, spend the night at **Alberg Mar i Vent (HI),** C. Dr. Fleming. Walk down the street from the bus stop, then follow the signs to the hostel. The beach is out the back door. The owner organizes **bike** (1000ptas/€6 per day) and **kayak rental,** as well as **windsurfing** lessons (☎962 83 17 48 or 83 17 25. 3-day max. stay, flexible if uncrowded. Curfew weeknights 2am, Sa 4am. Usually closed in Dec. and Jan. Sheets 300ptas/€1.8 for entire stay. Dorms 800ptas/€4.60, over 26 1100ptas/€6.60.).

MURCIA

The tiny province of Murcia, bordered by Valencia to the north, the Mediterranean to the east, and Andalucía to the west, may be in the shadow of more touristed regions, but its sunny, warm climate, tiny beach resort towns, and thriving capital city give it more than its share of character. Four centuries ago, a bizarre wave of plagues, floods, and earthquakes wreaked havoc throughout Murcia. Along with the utter destruction of some areas, the earthquakes uncovered a rich supply of minerals and natural springs. Today, thermal spas, pottery factories, and paprika mills pepper the lively coastal towns, and orange and apricot orchards bolster Murcia's reputation as the "Huerta de Europa" (Europe's Orchard).

MURCIA

Residents of Murcia will tell you that their city is a pleasant place to visit from fall, until spring, when the city thrives off the energy of its university. In summer, from mid-July to mid-September, Murcia becomes a ghost town; even the most patriotic of residents flee the oppressive heat of Murcia for the nearby Mediterranean. A few museums and other sights might spark some interest, but the main tourist attraction of Murcia is simply the same thing it offers residents—clean, tree-lined streets, cute cafés, and a sense that everyone in the city is happy to be there.

TRANSPORTATION. **Aeropuerto San Javier** (☎968 17 20 00) has flights to Barcelona, Madrid, and London. **RENFE trains** (☎902 24 02 02), at Pl. Industria, head to: **Alicante** (1½hr., 9-17 per day, 600ptas/€3.60); **Barcelona** (7-10hr., 2 per day, 6500ptas/€39); **Lorca** (1hr., every hr., 555ptas/€3.33); **Madrid** (4-5hr., 3 per day, 5400ptas/€33); and **Valencia** (3½hr., 3 per day, 2000-3500ptas/€12-21). **Buses** (☎968 29 22 11) leave from C. San Andrés, behind the Museo Salzillo, to: **Alicante** (1½hr., 7 per day 8:15am-8:15pm, 600ptas/€3.60); **Almería** (3½hr., 9 per day 5:30am-8:30pm, 2250ptas/€14); **Barcelona** (8½hr., 11 per day, 5275ptas/€32); **Denia** (3½hr., 4 per day 2am-9:10pm, 1515ptas/€9.05); **Granada** (4-5hr., 5 per day 8:30am-10pm, 2525ptas/€15); **La Manga de Mar Menor** (1hr.; Sept.-June 2 per day, July-Aug. every hr.; 385ptas/€2.30); **Lorca** (1½hr., 12 per day 7am-9pm, 555ptas/€3.33); **Madrid** (5-6hr., 12 per day, 7am-midnight, 3285ptas/€20); **Málaga** (6hr., 6 per day 2:30am-11pm, 4010ptas/€24); **Sevilla** (7-9hr., 3 per day 11:30am-10pm, 4850ptas/€29); **Valencia** (3¾hr., 4-12 per day 8am-9:30pm, 1895ptas/€11.40). Municipal buses (110ptas/€0.70) cover the city and outskirts; bus #9 runs past the train and bus stations.

ORIENTATION AND PRACTICAL INFORMATION. The **Río Segura** divides the city, with sights and services to the north half and the train station to the south (take bus #9 or 11 between the two). The cathedral is in **Pl. Cardenal Belluga**, at C. Trapería's end, while the bus station is a 10min. walk to the west of town. **Gran Vía** is the main thoroughfare, connecting to Pl. Circular, home to the post office. The **tourist office,** C. San Cristóbal, 6, is in Pl. Romea. (☎968 36 61 00. Open M-F 9am-2pm and 5-7pm.) The bus station provides **luggage storage** (300ptas/€1.80 per day). **Emergency** ☎112; **police** on Av. San Juan de la Cruz, ☎968 26 66 00; and **Hospital Morales Meseguer,** Av. Marqués de Vélez, 22 (☎968 36 09 00). For **Internet** access, visit **Cyber Forum,** C. Vinader, on the pedestrian path off the street behind Pl. Santa Isabel. (☎968 90 18 04. 200ptas/€1.20 per 30min., 350ptas/€2.10 per hr. Open M-Sa 10:30am-4:30pm and 4pm-12:30am, Su 4pm-12:30am.) The **post office,** on Pl. Circular, 8a, is located where Av. Primo de Ribera connects to the plaza. (☎968 24 10 37. Open M-F 8:30am-8:30pm, Sa 9:30am-2pm.) **Postal code:** 30008.

ACCOMMODATIONS AND FOOD. When Murcia steams up and empties out in summer, finding a room is the only breeze in town; winter competition is a bit stiffer. The only decent budget option is **Hostal-Residencia Murcia,** C. Vinader, 6, off Pl. Sta. Isabel; take bus #11 from the train station. Rooms have TVs, phones, and A/C. (☎968 21 99 63. Singles 3000ptas/€18, with bath 3500ptas/€21; doubles 6000ptas/€36, with bath 7000ptas/€42.) Sample the Murcian harvest at the **market** on C. Verónicas (open M-Sa 9am-1pm). Although ice cream shops and outdoor cafés seem to be everywhere, finding a decent meal is a bit harder. The area around **Pl. San Juan,** near the river, is home to a good number of popular restaurants and *tapas* bars. **Foster's Hollywood,** Pl. Santa Catalina, 4, one block off Gran Vía, serves up globalized favorites and has a *menú* for 1250ptas/€7.50. (Open M-Th 1-5pm and 8:30pm-midnight, F-Su 1-5pm and 8:30pm-12:30am.)

SIGHTS AND ENTERTAINMENT. The palatial **Casino de Murcia** (Casino Cultural), C. Trapería, 18, began as a gentlemen's club for the town's 19th- and 20th-century bourgeoisie. Current membership has use of all the building, from its lounges to its libraries. The rooms were each designed according to a particular theme, including the Versailles ballroom, English billiard room, Arabic patio, and Oxford library. (☎968 21 22 55. Open daily 10am-9pm. 200ptas/€1.20.) Murcia's **Museo de Bellas Artes,** C. Obispo Frutos, 12, is the region's largest art museum, with over 1,000 works and an extensive collection of local art. (☎968 23 93 46. Open M-F 9am-2pm and 5-8pm, Sa 10am-2pm. 200ptas/€1.20.) The **Museo Taurino,** C. Alfaro, 6, displays bullfighting memorabilia, *matador* costumes, and mounted bulls' heads that pay homage to particularly valorous beasts. Of particular importance is the shrine to José Manuel Calvo Benichon's shredded, bloody shirt, worn the day he was gored to death in Sevilla by his 598kg opponent. (☎968 28 59 76. Open June-Aug. M-F 10am-2pm and 5-8pm; Sept.-May 10am-2pm and 5-8pm, Su 11am-2pm. Free.) Just outside of Murcia, the Río Espuña courses through the rocky mountains, pines, and sagebrush of the **Parque Natural Sierra Espuña**. The flowers explode into dazzling color in springtime, the best season to visit the park. Much of Murcia's nightlife centers around the numerous plazas that dot the city. The *tapas* bars in Pl. San Juan, two blocks from the river by Pl. Cruz Roja, are a great place for starting the night. **Café-Pub Pura Vida,** Pl. Periodista Jaime Campmany, a left off C. Isidoro de la Cierva, is one of the more popular spots. (Mixed drinks 500-600ptas/€3-3.60. Open M-Sa 4pm-2:30am). On the day before Easter, the **Fiesta de Primavera** starts a week-long harvest celebration that brings jazz and theater.

DAYTRIPS FROM MURCIA

ÁGUILAS

*RENFE Cercanías **trains** (☎902 24 02 02) leave from Lorca (5 per day, 140ptas/€0.80) and from Murcia (740ptas/€4.45). **Buses** from Murcia via Lorca (9 per day, 845ptas/ €5.10).*

EU blue-flagged beaches line the shores of Águilas, the easternmost town along *la Costa Cálida*, and frequent buses and trains make it the most easily accessible beach getaway from Murcia. Águilas' beaches and turquoise waters are clearly the main draw, although the **Tower of Cope** and **Castillo de San Juan de las Águilas,** both featuring incredible views of the coastline, are popular stops. **Playa de Levante Puerto,** the closest *bandera azul* beach to town, is to the left of the port when facing the water. At the next cove over, **Playa Delicias** is cleaner and more popular. **Pl. España,** the center of town and home to the *ayuntamiento*, is halfway between the bus and train stations. To get there from the bus station, head toward the ocean and take your second left; from the train station, head toward the beach, take a right by the water, and another right at the pier onto C. Coronel Pareja. *Paella* is the beachfront favorite, and any number of cafés and restaurants along the water serve up the steaming platters. Head back to Murcia for the night, however, for accommodations are limited and quite expensive. The **tourist office,** C. Coronel Pareja, is a block toward the water from the plaza. (☎968 41 33 03. Open M-F 9am-2pm and 6-8pm, Sa 10am-2pm.)

LORCA

*RENFE Cercanías **trains** (☎902 24 02 02) run to Lorca Sutullena Station, Av. Estació (1hr., every hr. 6:45am-9:45pm, 575ptas/€3.46). The bus station (☎968 46 92 70) receives Trapemusa **buses** to Murcia (every hr., 555ptas/€3.33) and Aguilas (30min.; M-F 9 per day, Sa-Su 2-3 per day; 290ptas/€1.75).*

A stroll through Lorca, from the modern train station to the crumbling medieval castle, leads you through centuries of aesthetic and economic variety. Medieval ghettos, Renaissance artistry, post-Franco urban expansion, and contemporary elitism all flavor the town's neighborhoods. Ancient and medieval battles left Lorca without the orchards that extend through the rest of the region. Yet each conquering force left its own peculiar imprint on the **castillo** atop Lorca's central hill, a 20min. walk from Pl. Espanya. The castle is being converted into a pricey hotel, but the façade is the real attraction. The Moors built the **Torre Espolón** shortly before the city fell to Alfonso el Sabio of Castilla, who in a fit of self-adulation ordered the construction of the **Torre Alfonsín.** The ruins of the **Ermita de San Clemente,** deteriorate at the castle's eastern edge. When Granada fell in 1492, inhabitants moved to the bottom of the slope, leaving in their wake three idyllic churches—**Santa María, San Juan,** and **San Pedro.** Starting anew, Lorcans erected six monasteries and the **Colegiata de San Patricio.** One of many well-preserved private residences, the **Casa de Guevarra,** features a pre-19th century pharmacy. (Open M-F 11am-1pm and 5-7pm. Free.) Lunch can be had at **Don Jamón,** C. Museo Valiente, 2, off C. Juan Carlos I, where *tapas* start at 250ptas/€1.50.

(☎968 47 07 89. Open M-Sa noon-4pm and 8pm-1am, Su 8pm-1am.) The **tourist office** is just before the Casa de Guevarra on C. Lópes Gisbert. (☎968 46 61 57. Open M-F 9am-2pm and 5-7:30pm, Sa 11am-2pm.) **Luggage storage** is available in the bus station.

LA MANGA DEL MAR MENOR

A geographic fluke created the popular vacation spot known as La Manga (the sleeve) of the Mar Menor. Centuries of marine deposits settled over a small volcanic ridge and then solidified into a 19km strip of land separating the Mar Menor from the Mediterranean. Beach-lovers and windsurfers take advantage of the white sands and crystal waters of the Mediterranean. Local **buses** zip back and forth along La Manga (every 20-30min., after 4am every hr., 150ptas/€0.90). **Autobuses Gimenez Hermanos/Lycar** (☎968 29 22 11) runs to **Murcia** (5-6 per day, 700ptas/€4.20) and makes several stops along the strip. **Autocares Costa Azul** (☎968 50 15 43) goes to **Alicante** (2½hr., 9:30am, 980ptas/€5.90). The **tourist office** is on Gran Vía, Salida 2 (☎968 56 33 55). **Serma, C.B.** (☎968 56 41 19), in Pl. Cavanna, rents **bikes** for 1400ptas/€8.40 per day (open daily 10am-2pm and 5-9pm). The **Escuela de Vela Pedruchillo,** km 8-9, sells water sports equipment. (☎968 14 04 12. Open daily 10am-2pm and 4-8pm.) The closest thing to a budget accommodation on La Manga is the **Albergue Juvenil Deportivo,** Urbanización Hawaii V, km 8-9 (☎968 14 07 42), in the Grimanga Club. (Dorms 1700ptas/€12.20, with 3 meals 3600ptas/€22.)

BARCELONA

If you make it until 6am, you'll see the quietest side of Barcelona. While the city is dark, the occasional street worker battles Catalan separatist graffiti, the empty streets are scrubbed by hulking machines, and pigeons and parrots share the same branch, cooing with their heads under their wings. Enjoy the calm—it won't last.

When the sun comes up, you'll see a different city. Street vendors tug produce and popsicles onto every corner; cash boxes ring with the sounds of commerce and style; tourists marvel at medieval monsters that residents mistake for buildings; museums fill with tomorrow's avant-garde; pedestrians salivate at plates of exotic delicacies; beaches overflow with bronzed nudity; a white gorilla delights spectators; street protesters demand independence. On this side of 6am, Barcelona is sensory overload: only the attentive will notice that the Modernist masterpieces change colors slightly at every moment, and that no two *tapas* bars waft quite the same scent. After a day immersed in Barcelona's schizophrenic personalities and a night rubbing elbows with her even more schizophrenic nightlife, Barcelona will have exhausted herself—and when 6am rolls around again, you'll be glad for the quiet.

Barcelona is a gateway city: the gateway to Catalunya, to Spain, to the Mediterranean, to the Pyrenees. Pack your swimsuit and your skis, your art history book and your clubbing shoes, an extra bag to fill up with souvenirs (everything from fake poop to emus), and don't worry about the fact that you don't speak Spanish: neither does Barcelona.

INTERCITY TRANSPORT

BY PLANE

Domestic and international flights land at **El Prat de Llobregat** airport (☎932 98 38 38; www.aena.es/ae/bcn/homepage), 12km southwest of Barcelona. The **Aerobus** links the airport to Pl. Catalunya, the center of Barcelona (40min.; every 15min.; Barcelona M-F 6am-midnight and Sa-Su 6:30am-midnight, to the airport M-F 5:30am-11:15pm and Sa-Su 6am-11:20pm; 525ptas/€3).

RENFE (24hr. info ☎934 91 31 83; www.renfe.es) trains provide cheaper airport transport (20-25min.; every 30min.; 6:13am-11:15pm from airport, 5:43am-11:24pm from Sants; 350ptas/€2.10). The most useful stops are **Estació Barcelona-Sants** and **Plaça Catalunya.** Tickets are sold at the red machines. In Sants, buy tickets at the "Aeroport" window (open 5am-11pm). After 11pm, get them from the ticket machines or the Recorridos Cercanías window.

The city **bus** offers inexpensive night service. Take bus EN (called EA during the day) from the airport to Pl. Espanya (every hr.; departs airport 6:20am-2:40am, departs Pl. Espanya 7:10am-3:15am; 160ptas/€2). The Pl. Espanya stop is on the corner of Gran Via and Av. Reina María Cristina. A **taxi** ride between Barcelona and the airport costs 3000-4500ptas/€18-27.

Three **national airlines** are popular carriers. **Iberia/Aviaco,** Pg. de Gràcia, 30 (☎934 01 32 82; ☎902 40 05 00), has extensive coverage and student discounts. **Air Europa** (☎902 40 15 01; www.air-europa.com) and **Spanair,** Pg. de Gràcia, 57 (☎932 16 46 26; ☎902 13 14 15) offer cheaper fares.

All major **international airlines** serve Barcelona, including **British Airways,** airport office ☎932 98 34 55, 24hr. info 902 11 13 33; open 6am-7pm) and **Delta** (☎901 11 69 46; www.delta-air.com). **Easy Jet** (☎902 29 99 92; www.easyjet.com) also offers flights from Barcelona to Amsterdam, Geneva, and London.

BY TRAIN

Barcelona has two main stations which serve different destinations. When in doubt, go to Estació Barcelona-Sants; while all domestic trains leaving Estació

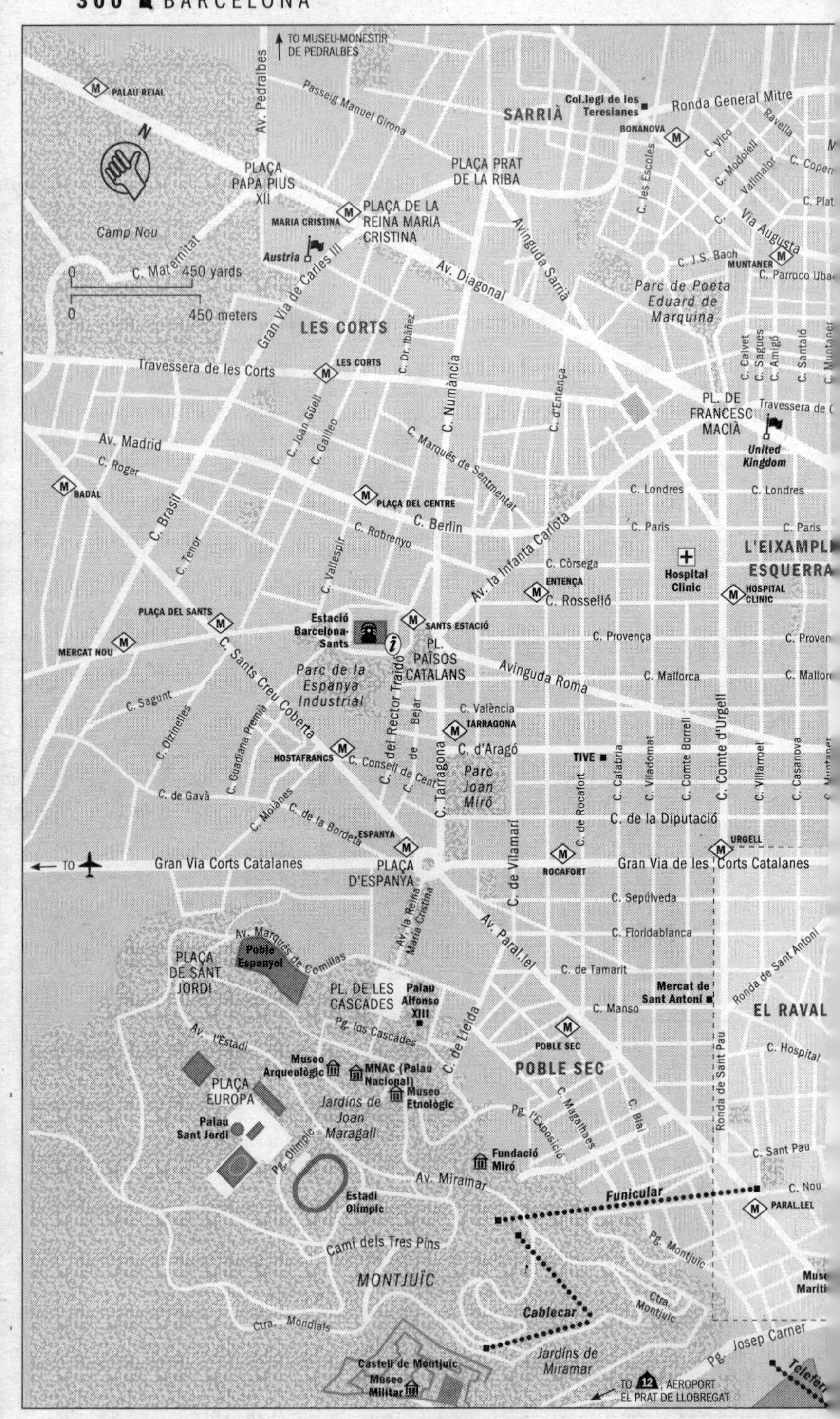
TO MUSEU-MONESTIR DE PEDRALBES
PALAU REIAL
Av. Pedralbes
Passeig Manuel Girona
Col.legi de les Teresianes
SARRIÀ
Ronda General Mitre
BONANOVA
PLAÇA PAPA PIUS XII
PLAÇA PRAT DE LA RIBA
PLAÇA DE LA REINA MARIA CRISTINA
MARIA CRISTINA
Camp Nou
Austria
C. Maternitat
450 yards
450 meters
Gran Via de Carles III
Av. Diagonal
Avinguda Sarrià
Parc de Poeta Eduard de Marquina
C. J.S. Bach
MUNTANER
C. Parroco Uba
Via Augusta
LES CORTS
Travessera de les Corts
LES CORTS
C. Dr. Ibáñez
C. Numància
C. d'Entença
PL. DE FRANCESC MACIÀ
Travessera de
United Kingdom
Av. Madrid
C. Roger
BADAL
C. Joan Güell
C. Galileo
C. Marquès de Sentmenat
PLAÇA DEL CENTRE
C. Berlin
C. Londres
C. Paris
C. Brasil
C. Tenor
C. Robrenyo
C. Vallespir
Av. la Infanta Carlota
C. Còrsega
ENTENÇA
C. Rosselló
Hospital Clinic
HOSPITAL CLINIC
L'EIXAMPLE ESQUERRA
PLAÇA DEL SANTS
MERCAT NOU
Estació Barcelona-Sants
SANTS ESTACIÓ
PL. PAÏSOS CATALANS
C. Provença
C. Mallorca
Avinguda Roma
Parc de la Espanya Industrial
C. Sants Creu Coberta
C. Sagunt
C. Olzinelles
C. Guadiana Premià
C. del Rector Triadó
C. València
TARRAGONA
C. d'Aragó
TIVE
Parc Joan Miró
HOSTAFRANCS
C. Consell de Cent
C. Tarragona
C. de Rocafort
C. Calabria
C. Viladomat
C. Comte Borrell
C. Comte d'Urgell
C. Villarroel
C. Casanova
C. de Gavà
C. Moianes
C. de la Bordeta
ESPANYA
C. de la Diputació
URGELL
ROCAFORT
TO
Gran Via Corts Catalanes
PLAÇA D'ESPANYA
Gran Via de les Corts Catalanes
C. de Vilamarí
C. Sepúlveda
C. Floridablanca
Av. la Reina Maria Cristina
Av. Paral.lel
Av. Marquès de Comillas
Poble Espanyol
PLAÇA DE SANT JORDI
PL. DE LES CASCADES
Palau Alfonso XIII
C. de Tamarit
Mercat de Sant Antoni
C. Manso
Ronda de Sant Antoni
EL RAVAL
Pg. los Cascades
Av. l'Estadi
C. de Lleida
POBLE SEC
Museo Arqueològic
MNAC (Palau Nacional)
Museo Etnològic
PLAÇA EUROPA
POBLE SEC
C. Hospital
Jardins de Joan Maragall
Palau Sant Jordi
Pg. Olímpic
C. Magalhaes
Pg. l'Exposició
C. Blai
Ronda de Sant Pau
Fundació Miró
C. Sant Pau
Av. Miramar
Estadi Olímpic
Funicular
C. Nou
PARAL.LEL
Camí dels Tres Pins
Pg. Montjuïc
MONTJUÏC
Ctra. Montjuïc
Cablecar
Ctra. Mondials
Pg. Josep Carner
Castell de Montjuïc
Museo Militar
Jardins de Miramar
TO 12, AEROPORT EL PRAT DE LLOBREGAT

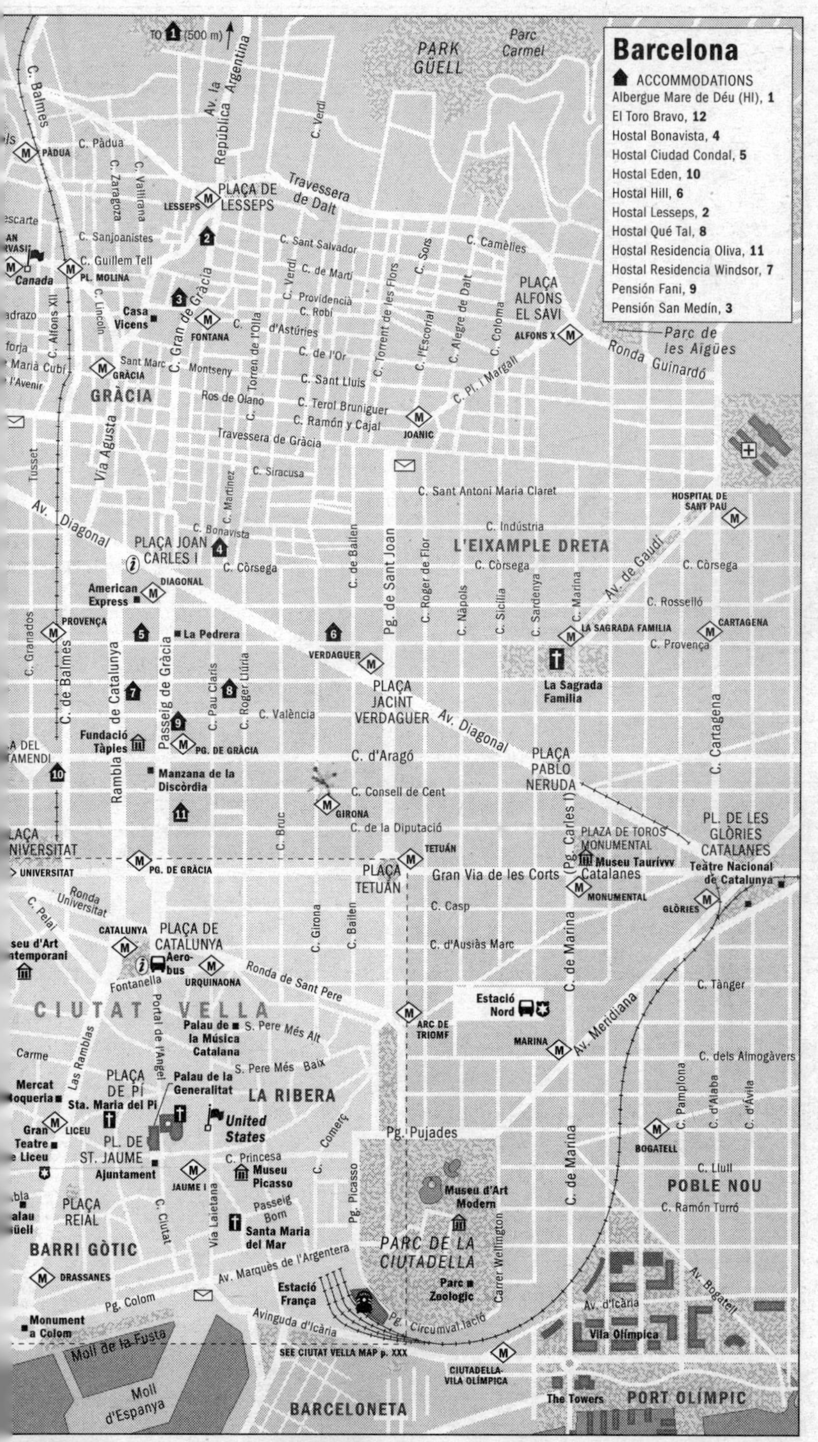

Barcelona
ACCOMMODATIONS
Albergue Mare de Déu (HI), 1
El Toro Bravo, 12
Hostal Bonavista, 4
Hostal Ciudad Condal, 5
Hostal Eden, 10
Hostal Hill, 6
Hostal Lesseps, 2
Hostal Qué Tal, 8
Hostal Residencia Oliva, 11
Hostal Residencia Windsor, 7
Pensión Fani, 9
Pensión San Medín, 3
PARK GÜELL
Parc Carmel
GRÀCIA
L'EIXAMPLE DRETA
CIUTAT VELLA
LA RIBERA
BARRI GÒTIC
POBLE NOU
BARCELONETA
PORT OLÍMPIC
PARC DE LA CIUTADELLA
PLAÇA DE LESSEPS
PLAÇA ALFONS EL SAVI
PLAÇA JOAN CARLES I
PLAÇA JACINT VERDAGUER
PLAÇA PABLO NERUDA
PLAÇA TETUÁN
PLAÇA DE CATALUNYA
PL. DE LES GLÒRIES CATALANES
PLAÇA DE PI
PL. DE ST. JAUME
PLAÇA REIAL
La Sagrada Familia
Casa Vicens
La Pedrera
Fundació Tàpies
Manzana de la Discòrdia
American Express
Estació Nord
Estació França
Museu d'Art Modern
Parc Zoologic
Vila Olímpica
The Towers
Teatre Nacional de Catalunya
Museu Taurívvv
Palau de la Música Catalana
Palau de la Generalitat
Sta. Maria del Pi
United States
Canada
Museu Picasso
Santa Maria del Mar
Ajuntament
Monument a Colom
Mercat Boqueria
Gran Teatre Liceu
SEE CIUTAT VELLA MAP p. XXX

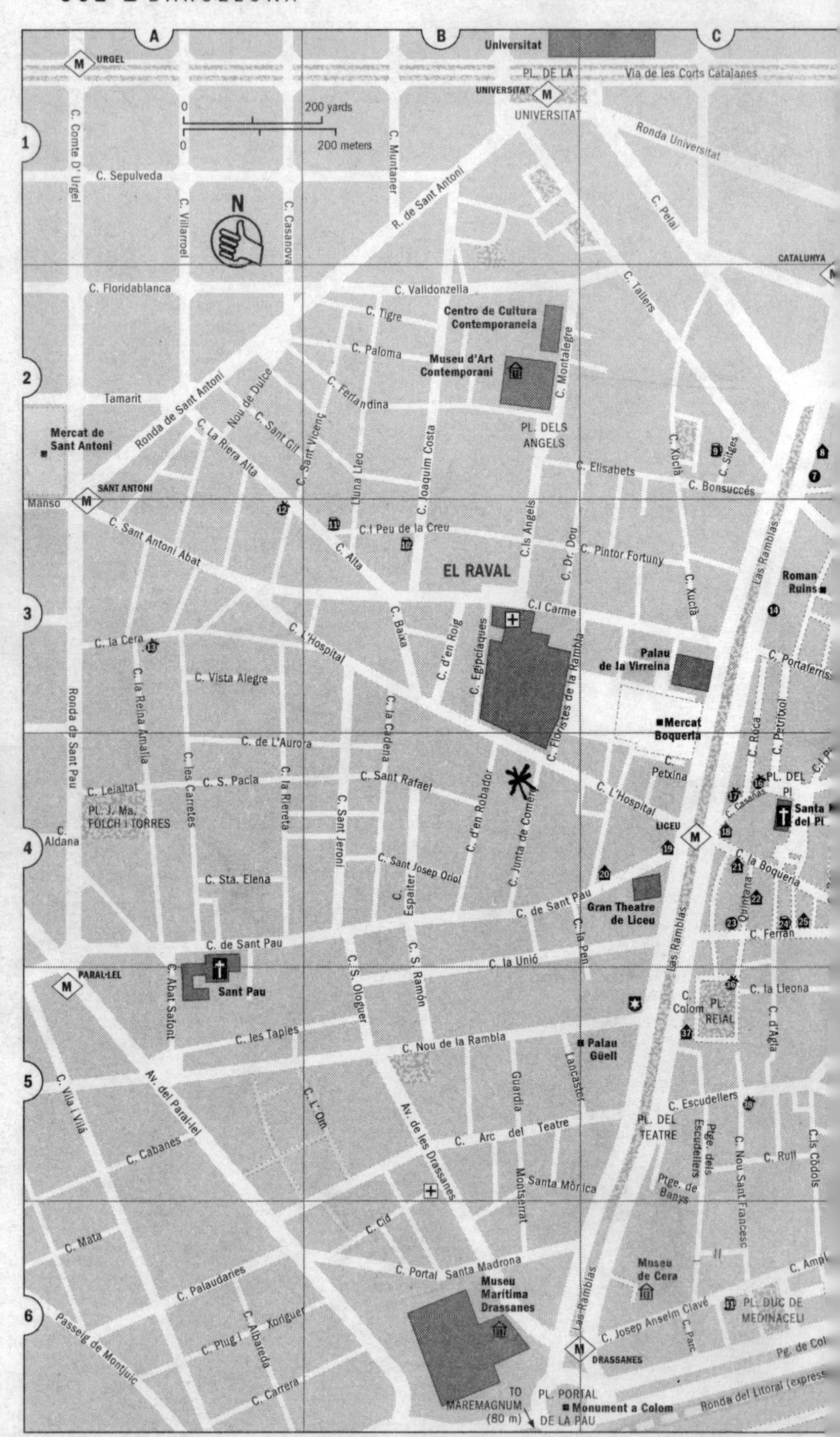

Universitat
URGEL
PL. DE LA UNIVERSITAT
UNIVERSITAT
Via de les Corts Catalanes
Ronda Universitat
200 yards
200 meters
C. Comte D' Urgel
C. Sepulveda
C. Villarroel
C. Casanova
C. Muntaner
R. de Sant Antoni
C. Pelai
CATALUNYA
C. Floridablanca
C. Valldonzella
C. Tallers
C. Tigre
Centro de Cultura Contemporaneia
C. Paloma
Museu d'Art Contemporani
C. Montalegre
Tamarit
Ronda de Sant Antoni
Nou de Dulce
C. Sant Gil
C. Ferrandina
Mercat de Sant Antoni
C. La Riera Alta
C. Sant Vicenç
Lluna Lleo
C. Joaquim Costa
PL. DELS ANGELS
C. Xucla
C. Sitges
C. Elisabets
C. Bonsuccés
SANT ANTONI
Manso
C. Sant Antoni Abat
C.I Peu de la Creu
C. Alta
C.ls Angels
C. Dr. Dou
C. Pintor Fortuny
Las Ramblas
EL RAVAL
Roman Ruins
C.I Carme
C. Baixa
C. d'en Roig
C. Egipciaques
C. L'Hospital
C. la Cera
C. Vista Alegre
C. la Reina Amalia
C. Floristes de la Rambla
Palau de la Virreina
C. Portaferrissa
C. Petritxol
Ronda de Sant Pau
C. la Cadena
Mercat Boqueria
C. de L'Aurora
C. Roca
C. les Carretes
C. S. Pacia
C. la Riereta
C. Sant Rafael
C. d'en Robador
C. Petxina
PL. DEL PI
C. Leialtat
PL. J. Ma. FOLCH I TORRES
C. Sant Jeroni
C. Junta de Comerç
C. L'Hospital
C. Casañas
Santa Maria del Pi
C. Aldana
LICEU
C. Sant Josep Oriol
C. la Boqueria
C. Sta. Elena
C. Espalter
C. de Sant Pau
Gran Theatre de Liceu
Quintana
C. Ferran
C. la Pen.
C. de Sant Pau
C. S. Ramón
C. S. Ologuer
C. la Unió
PARAL·LEL
Sant Pau
C. Abat Safont
C. la Lleona
C. Colom
PL. REIAL
C. d'Aglá
C. les Taples
C. Nou de la Rambla
Palau Güell
C. Vila i Vilá
Av. del Paral-lel
C. L'Om
Guardia
Lancaster
C. Escudellers
Av. de les Drassanes
C. Arc del Teatre
PL. DEL TEATRE
Ptge. dels Escudellers
C. Nou Sant Francesc
C.ls Còdols
C. Cabanes
Montserrat
Santa Mònica
C. Rull
Ptge. de Banys
C. Mata
C. Cid
C. Palaudaries
C. Portal Santa Madrona
Museu de Cera
C. Ample
Museu Marítima Drassanes
C. Josep Anselm Clavé
PL. DUC DE MEDINACELI
C. Albareda
C. Xoriguer
C. Plug I
Passeig de Montjuic
C. Parc
DRASSANES
Pg. de Colom
C. Carrera
TO MAREMAGNUM (80 m)
PL. PORTAL DE LA PAU
Monument a Colom
Ronda del Litoral (express

D
E
F
PASSEIG DE GRACIA
Via de les Corts Catalanes
PL. TETUÁN
TETUÁN
C. Pau
C. Roger
C. I Bruc
C. Girona
C. Bailén
Passeig de Gràcia
C. Casp
L'EIXAMPLE
Pg. de Sant Joan
CATALUNYA
PL. CATALUNYA
Ronda de Sant Pere
URQUINAONA
PL. D'URQUINAONA
El Corte Ingles
C. d'Ausiàs
C. Fontanella
C. d' Alí-Bei
TO ESTACIO NORD VILLANOVA (300 m)
C. Estruc
C. les Moles
C. les Jonqueres
C. Trafalgar
C. d'Ortigosa
C. Méndez Núñez
ARC DE TRIOMF
C. Comtal
Via Laietana
C. Sant Pere Mes Alt
Palau de la Música Catalana
C. d'en Monec
Pg. Lluís Companys
Arc de Triomf
C. Montsió
PL. SANT PERE
Avinguda Portal d l'Àngel
C. Durán i Bas
C. Sant Pere Mitja
C. I Rec Comtal
C. Sant Pere Mes Baix
C. d'en Cortinas
C. Dr. J. Pou
C. Sagristans
C. Jaume Giralt
PL. DEL COMERÇ
C. Boters
PL. NOVA
Av. de la Catedral
PL. ANTONI MAURA
Av. de Francesc Cambó
Grat. Alvarez
C. Fonollar
C. I Portal Nou
PL. DE LA SEU
Palau Real
C. Avella
LA RIBERA
Catedral de la Santa Creu
Museu Frederic Marès
Mercat Santa Caterina
Palau Generalitat
C. I Bisbe
C. de la
Museu d'Història de la Ciutat
C.Is Carders
Pg. de Pujades
C. Tantarantana
C.Is Assaonadors
Cascada Fountains
C.Is Corders
C. Llibreteria
PL. DE L'ANGEL
Museu de Zoologia
PL. DE SANT JAUME
C. Jaume I
C. Princesa
C.Is Flassaders
C. I Comerç
Museu d'Art Modern
JAUME I
Museu Textil i d'Indumentària
C. Montcada
Pg. de Picasso
PL. DE SANT MIQUEL
C. Ciutat
Daguería
C. I Argentería
C. Banys Vells
Museu Picasso
C. Fussina
Ajuntament
Via Laietana
C. I Rec
BARRI GÒTIC
C. Lledó
C. Manresa
Antic Mercat del Born
Museu de Geologia
C. la Nau
C. Mosques
Comtessa
C. Regomir
C. Is Sots
Santa Maria del Mar
Pg. del Born
Parc de la Ciutadella
C. d'Ataulf
C. Espasería
C. Vidreria
C. la Ribera
Canvis Nous
TO ZOO (50 m)
C. Gignas
C. la Fustería
C. I Consolat de Mar
Av. Marquès de L'Argentera
C. Marquet
PL. DEL PALAU
Parc Zoològic
C. Simó Oller
la Mercè
C. Plata
Pg. d'Isabel II
Gobierno Civil
PL. D'ANTONI LOPEZ
Canvis Vells
Estació de França
Pg. Circumvallació
BARCELONETA
TO VILA OLIMPICA (800 m)
Moll de la Fusta
TO MOLL D'ESPANYA (50 m)
Av. D'Icària

França pass through here, not all trains leaving Barcelona-Sants pass through Estació França. A taxi between either station and the Pl. Catalunya will cost about 1000ptas/€6. For general information about trains call RENFE (☎902 24 02 02).

Estació Barcelona-Sants, Pl. Països Catalans. M: Sants-Estació. Buses to the station include #30 from Pl. Espanya, 44 from La Sagrada Família, and N2. For late arrivals, the N14 Nitbus shuttles to Pl. Catalunya (every 30min. 10:30pm-4:30am, 160ptas/€2.80). Currency exchange (open 8am-9:30pm), pharmacy, tourist office, luggage storage, and shopping. Station open M-F 4:30am-midnight, Sa-Su 5am-midnight.

Estació França, Av. Marquès de l'Argentera (☎902 24 02 02). M: Barceloneta. Buses include #17 from Pl. de Catalunya and N6. Open daily 7am-10pm. Serves regional destinations, including Girona, Tarragona, and Zaragoza, and some international arrivals.

RENFE (☎902 24 02 02; international 934 90 11 22; www.renfe.es. Phones open daily 7am-10pm.) The prices listed are for *turista* class only. Non-smokers (and non-chain-smokers) should buy a *no-fumador* (non-smoking) seat in advance, as they may sell out. (For details on routes, ask for an *horario*—schedule). To: **Alicante** (4-5hr., 8 per day, 6000-6700ptas/€36-41); **Bilbao** (8-9hr., 3 per day, 5000-5200ptas/€30-32); **Granada** (11-12hr., 2 per day, 6300-7700ptas/€32-44); **Madrid** (7-8hr., 7 per day, 5100-6900/€30-41); **Pamplona** (6-7hr., 4 per day, 4300-4400ptas/€26-27); **Salamanca** (10-12hr., 3 per day, 5800-6000ptas/€35-36); **San Sebastián** (8-9hr., 3 per day, 5000ptas/€30); **Sevilla** (11-12hr., 3 per day, 6400-10,200ptas/€39-61); **Valencia** (3-5hr., 16 per day 7am-9pm, 3120-5200ptas/€20-33). International destinations include **Milan** (through **Nice**) and **Montpellier** with connections to **Geneva** and **Paris.**

Ferrocarrils de la Generalitat de Catalunya (FGC) (☎93 205 15 15; www.fgc.catalunya.net.) Commuter trains. Two interlocking "V"s mark connections with the Metro. FCG costs the same as the Metro (160ptas/€2) until Tibidabo, where rates rise by zone: zone 2 destinations cost 240ptas/€1.50 and zone 3 costs 340ptas/€2. Metro passes are valid in zone 1. Information office at the Catalunya station, open M-F 7am-9pm.

BY BUS

Most buses arrive at **Barcelona Nord Estació d'Autobuses,** C. Ali-bei, 80. The station has food, money exchange, and luggage storage. (☎932 65 61 32. M: Arc de Triomf, exit to Nàpols. Info office open daily 7am-9pm.) Buses include #54 along Gran Via (a block from Pl. Catalunya) and N11. A taxi from Pl. Catalunya will cost about 700ptas/€4. Other buses, particularly **international buses,** arrive at the **Estació d'Autobuses de Sants** station, next to the train station in Pl. Països Catalans (see above). The following companies operate out of Estació Nord:

Enatcar (☎902 422 242; www.enatcar.es). To: **Alicante** (9hr., 5 per day, 4650ptas/€28); **Madrid** (8hr., 18 per day, 2690ptas/€16); **Valencia** (4hr., 16 per day, 2690ptas/€16). Open daily 7am-1am.

Sarfa (☎902 30 20 25; www.sarfa.com). Sarfa buses stop at many beach towns along the Costa Brava, north of Barcelona. To: **Cadaqués** (2½hr., 10:45am and 7:45pm, 2250ptas/€14); **Palafrugell** (2hr., 13 per day); **Tossa de Mar** (1½hr., 9 per day 8:15am-8:15pm, 1070ptas/€6.50). Open daily 8am-8:30pm.

Linebús (☎932 65 07 00). Discounts for travelers under 26 and over 60. To **London** (25hr., 3 per week, 14,650ptas/€88) and **Paris** (15hr.; 8pm M-Sa; 12,800-23,600ptas/€77-142). Daily service to Morocco. Open M-F 8am-2pm and 3-8pm, Sa 8:30am-1:30pm and 4:30-8pm.

Alsa (☎902 422 242; www.alsa.es). To: **Lisbon** (17hr., F 2:30pm, 12,000ptas/€72); **Naples** (24hr., 5:15pm, 18700ptas/€113); **Zaragoza** (4½hr., 2 per day, 1655ptas/€10); **Zurich** (17hr., F 12:45am, 13250ptas/€80).

BY FERRY

Barcelona is an ideal gateway to the **Balearic Islands,** renowned for their beaches, raging clubs, and resorts. The main ferry station is **Estació Marítima,** in Port Vell.

Central Barcelona

ACCOMMODATIONS

Name	Grid
Albergue de Juventud Kabul, 37	C5
Albergue Juvenil Palau, 33	D5
Casa de Huéspedes Mari-Luz, 34	D5
H.-R. Lausanne, 4	D3
H.-R. Rembrandt, 15	D3
Hostal Aviñyó, 39	D5
Hostal Fernando, 25	C4
Hostal Fontanella, 2	D2
Hostal Layetana, 27	D4
Hostal Levante, 35	D5
Hostal Paris, 18	C4
Hostal Residencia Opera, 20	C4
Hostal Rey Don Jaume I, 26	D4
Hotel Toledano & H.-R. Capitol, 8	C2
Mare Nostrum, 19	C4
Pensión Aris, 1	D2
Pensión Bienestar, 22	C4
Pensión Dalí, 21	C4
Pensión Santa Anna, 6	C2
Residencia Victoria, 3	D2

SERVICES

Name	Grid
Net Movil, 7	C2
Pharmacy, 14	C3
Tintorería Ferran, 23	C4

FOOD

Name	Grid
Colibri, 12	A3
Els Quatre Gats, 5	D3
Irati, 16	C4
Juicy Jones, 17	C4
La Habana Vieja, 29	E5
Las Caracoles, 38	C5
Le Quinze Nits, 36	C5
Restaurante Bidasoa, 40	D6
Restaurante Can Lluís, 13	A3
Terrablava, 31	D5
Txirimira, 28	E4

NIGHTLIFE

Name	Grid
Casa Almirall, 10	B3
El Cafe que pone Muebles Navarro, 11	B3
Harlem Jazz Club, 32	D5
La Oveja Negra, 9	C2
Margarita Blue, 41	C6
Mudanzas, 30	E5
Schilling, 24	C4

Trasmediterránea, Estació Marítima-Moll Barcelona, Moll de Sant Bertran (☎902 454 645; fax 93 295 91 34; www.trasmediterranea.es). M: Drassanes. Head down Las Ramblas to the **Monument a Colom** (see p. 318). Columbus points toward the Estació Marítima. Cross the street and walk right, along the waterfront, until you see the large Trasmediterránea building on your left. In the summer only to: **Ibiza** (9hr.; 1 per day, 2 per day M, F, Sa); **Mallorca** (3hr., 3 per day); **Menorca** (1 per day starting mid-June). One way trips start at 8000ptas/€48 and quickly rise to over 10,000ptas/€60. Tickets are available at any travel agency, but the station office is open daily 10am-4pm.

ORIENTATION

Barcelona's layout is simple. Imagine yourself perched on Columbus' head at the **Monument a Colom** (on **Passeig de Colom,** along the shore), viewing the city with the sea at your back. From the harbor, the city slopes upward to the mountains. From the Columbus monument, **Las Ramblas** (see p. 317), the main thoroughfare, runs from the harbor up to **Plaça de Catalunya** (M: Catalunya), the city's center. The **Ciutat Vella** (Old City) is the heavily-touristed historical neighborhood, which centers around Las Ramblas and includes the Barri Gòtic, La Ribera, and El Raval. The **Barri Gòtic** is east of Las Ramblas (to the right, with your back to the sea), enclosed on the other side by **Via Laietana.** East of Via Laietana lies the maze-like neighborhood of **La Ribera,** which borders Parc de la Ciutadella and the Estació França train station. To the west of Las Ramblas (with your back to the sea) is **El Raval.**

BARCELONA

Beyond La Ribera, (farther east, outside the Ciutat Vella) is the **Poble Nou** neighborhood and the **Vila Olímpica,** with its twin towers (the tallest buildings in Barcelona) and an assortment of discos and restaurants. Beyond El Raval (to the west) rises **Montjuïc,** crammed with gardens, museums, the 1992 Olympic grounds, Montjuïc castle, and other attractions. Directly behind the Monument a Colom is the **Port Vell** (Old Port) development, where a wavy bridge leads across to the ultramodern shopping and entertainment complexes **Moll d'Espanya** and **Maremagnum** (see p. 333). Beyond the Ciutat Vella, is **l'Eixample,** the gridded neighborhood created during the expansion of the 1860s, which runs from Pl. Catalunya toward the mountains. **Gran Via de les Corts Catalanes** defines its lower edge and **Passeig de Gràcia,** l'Eixample's main street, bisects the neighborhood. **Avinguda Diagonal** marks the border between l'Eixample and the **Zona Alta** ("Uptown"), which includes Pedralbes, Gràcia, and other older neighborhoods in the foothills. The peak of Tibidabo, the northwest border of the city, offers the most comprehensive view of the city.

LOCAL TRANSPORT

MAPS

El Corte Inglés has a good free map, distributed in their stores (see p. 329) and at mobile and stationary info centers. The Barcelona **tourist office** (in Pl. de Catalunya or Pl. Sant Jaume) also has maps with a good enlarged inset of the Barri Gòtic.

METRO AND BUS

Barcelona's public transportation (info ☎010, claims ☎933 18 70 74) is quick and cheap. The *Guia d'Autobuses Urbans de Barcelona,* free at tourist offices and Metro stations, maps out the city's bus routes and five Metro lines; the *Guia Facil del Bus per Mour't per Barcelona,* also free, describes the routes in more detail.

If you plan to use public transportation, there are several *abonos* (passes) available, which work interchangeably for the Metro, bus, zone 1 FGC trains, and the Nitbus. The **T-1 pass** (885ptas/€5) is valid for 10 rides and saves you nearly 50% the cost of single tickets. The **T-Día** pass (670ptas/€4) is good for a full day of unlimited travel, while the **T-Mes** (5825ptas/€35) offers the same for a month. The **T-50/30** (3700ptas/€22) buys 50 trips in a 30-day period. For short stays, the **3 Dies** pass (1700ptas/€10) gets you three days of unlimited travel; the **5 Dies** (2600ptas/€16) is good for five days. Both save money if you use the Metro more than three times per day.

Metro: (☎93 486 07 52; www.tmb.net). Vending machines and ticket windows sell Metro passes. Red diamonds with an "M" inside mark stations. Hold on to your ticket during the ride–riding without a ticket carries a fine of 5000ptas/€30. Trains run M-Th 5am-11pm, F-Sa 5am-2am, Su 6am-midnight. 160ptas/€1 for a *sencillo* (single ride).

Buses: Go just about anywhere, usually from 5am-10pm. 160ptas/€1.

Nitbus: (☎901 511 151). 16 different lines run 10:30pm-4:30am, every 20-30 min., depending on the line; a few run until 5:30am. All buses depart from the Pl. Catalunya; a Metro pass is valid on the Nitbus. The buses stop in front of most of the club complexes and work their way through the Ciutat Vella and the Zona Alta. Maps are available at *estancos* (tobacco shops) and marked by signs in Metro stations.

Bus Turístic: The Bus Turístic stops at 26 sites along 2 routes (red for the north-bound buses, blue for south-bound); a ticket comes with an info guide in 6 languages about each sight. A full ride on both routes takes about 3½ hours, but you can get on and off as often as you wish. The easiest place to hop on the Bus Turístic is Pl. Catalunya, in front of El Corte Inglés (see p. 329). Many sights covered are closed on Mondays. Purchase tickets on the bus, the Pl. Catalunya tourist office, or at Estació Barcelona-Sants. Runs daily except Dec. 25 and Jan. 1; every 10-30min., 9am-9:30pm; 1-day pass 2200ptas/€13, children aged 4-12 1300ptas/€8, 2-day pass 2800ptas/€17.)

TAXIS

On weekend nights, you may wait up to 30min. in some locations; long lines form at popular club spots like the Port Olímpic. A *lliure* or *libre* sign or a lit green light on the roof means vacant; yellow means occupied. To call a cab, try **RadioTaxi** (☎932 25 00 00), or **Servi Taxi** (☎933 30 03 00). Disabled travelers should call 93 420 80 88.

CAR RENTAL

Docar, C. Montnegre, 18 (☎934 39 81 19). M: Les Corts. Free delivery and pickup. From 2300ptas/€14 per day with 1500ptas/€9 insurance, 25ptas/€0.15 per km. Open M-F 8:30am-2pm and 3:30-8pm, Sa 9am-2pm.

Hertz, C. Tuset, 10 (☎932 17 8076). M: Diagonal or FCG: Gràcia. Branch in El Prat de Llobregat airport (☎93 298 3637; see p. 299).

Tot Car, C. Berlin, 97 (☎934 30 01 98). Free delivery and pickup. From 4500ptas/€27 per day, 21ptas/€0.13 per km. Open M-F 8am-2pm and 3-8pm, Sa 9am-1pm.

BICYCLE AND MOPED RENTAL

Everyone who's anyone in Barcelona has a motorcycle; it's probably the most popular method of transport. Be wary of speeding suits and grannies on *motos*.

Vanguard Rent a Car, C. Londres, 31 (☎934 39 38 80). Mopeds start at Tu-Th 4760ptas/29 per day, F-M 7280ptas/€44 per day. 2-person motos start at 6200ptas/€37 per weekday. Insurance, helmet, and IVA included. Min. age 19 to rent.

Over-Rent S.A., Av. Josep Terradellas, 42 (☎934 05 26 60). Call at least a week ahead to reserve a vehicle. Motorcycles 2500-8200ptas/€15-50 per day. Min. age 23 to rent.

PRACTICAL INFORMATION

TOURIST AND FINANCIAL SERVICES

Tourist Offices: Informació Turística Plaça Catalunya, Pl. Catalunya, 17S, below Pl. Catalunya. M: Catalunya. Open daily 9am-9pm. **Informació Turística Plaça Sant Jaume,** Pl. Sant Jaume, 1, off of C. Ciutat. M: Jaume I. Open M-Sa 10am-8pm, Su 10am-2pm. **Oficina de Turisme de Catalunya,** Pg. de Gràcia, 107 (☎93 238 40 00; fax 93 292 12 70; www.gencat.es/probert). M: Diagonal. Open M-Sa 10am-7pm, Su 10am-2pm. **Estació Barcelona-Sants,** Pl. Països Catalans. M: Sants-Estació. Station open M-F 4:30am-midnight, Sa-Su 5am-midnight. **Aeroport El Prat de Llobregat** (☎93 478 05 65), international terminal. Open daily 9am to 9pm. English-speaking agents offer information, maps, and hotel reservations. **Mobile information offices** dot the city in the summer. Open Mar.-June 10am-8pm.

Tours: In addition to the Bus Turístic (see **Metro and Bus,** p. 306), the Pl. Catalunya tourist office offers walking tours of the Barri Gòtic. Call 906 301 282. Sa-Su at 10am in English and noon in Catalan and Spanish. Tour group size is limited; buy tickets in advance. 1100ptas/€6.60, children aged 4-12 500ptas/€3.

Budget Travel Offices: usit UNLIMITED, Ronda Universitat, 16 (☎934 12 01 04; fax 12 39 84; www.unlimted.es). Open M-F 10am-8:30pm and Sa 10am-1:30pm.

Centre d'Informació Assesorament per a Joves, C. Ferrán, 32 (☎93 402 78 00; www.bcn.es/ciaj), M: Liceu. One block off Las Ramblas. No tickets for sale, but free advice and youth opportunities. Library of travel guides. Open M-F 10am-2 and 4-8pm.

Currency Exchange: As always, **ATMs** give the best rates (with no commission). The next best rates are available at banks. General banking hours M-F 8:30am-2pm. **Banco de Espanya,** Pl. Catalunya, 17 (☎934 82 47 00) and the **American Express** office (see below) charge no commission on traveler's checks.

American Express, Pg. de Gràcia, 101 (☎900 994 426). M: Diagonal. Open M-F 9:30am-6pm, Sa 10am-noon. Also at Las Ramblas, 74 (☎933 01 11 66). Open daily 9am-8pm.

LOCAL SERVICES

Luggage Storage: Estació Barcelona-Sants. M: Sants-Estació. Open 5:30am-11:00pm. **Estació França.** M: Barceloneta. Open 7am-10pm. **Estació del Nord.** M: Arc de Triomf. Open 24hr. Large lockers 700ptas/€4.20 for 24hr., small 500ptas/€3.

El Corte Inglés: Pl. Catalunya, 14 (☎933 06 38 00). M: Catalunya. Behemoth department store. **Free map** of Barcelona at the information desk. Also has English books, salon, cafeteria, supermarket, and the *oportunidades* discount department. Open M-Sa and first Su of every month 10am-10pm. Branches: Portal de l'Angel, 19-2 (M: Catalunya); Av. Diagonal, 471-473 (M: Hospital Clinic); Av. Diagonal, 617, (M: Maria Cristina).

English Bookstores: Llibreria del Raval, C. Elisabets, 6 (☎933 17 02 93). M: Catalunya, in **El Raval,** off Las Ramblas. Books in four languages (Catalan, Spanish, English, and French). Catalan/Spanish and Catalan/English dictionaries (1100ptas/€7). Open M-F 10am-8:30pm; Sa 10am-2:30pm and 5-8pm. **LAIE,** Av. Pau Claris, 85 (☎93 318 17 39). M: Urquinaona. Small English book section with travel guides and a café. Bookstore open M-F 10am-9pm, Sa 10:30am-9pm. Café open M-F 9am-1am, Sa 10am-1am.

Libraries: Biblioteca Sant Pau, C. de l'Hospital, 56 (☎933 02 07 97). M: Liceu. Take C. Hospital off Las Ramblas and walk down to a castle on your right; walk to the far end of the courtyard; the library is on the left. Do not confuse it with the Catalan library you'll see first, which requires permission to enter. Open in summer M and Th 10am-2pm; M-F 3:30-8:30pm, Sa 10am-2pm. Closed for 3 weeks in Sept. **Institut d'Estudis Norteamericans,** Via Augusta, 123 (☎93 240 51 10). Open Sept.-July M-F 9am-2pm and 4-7pm.

Religious Services: Comunidad Israelita de Barcelona (Jewish services), C. Avenir, 29 (☎932 00 61 48). **Comunidad Musulmana** (Muslim services), Mosque Toarek Ben Ziad, C. Hospital, 91 (☎934 41 91 49). Services daily at prayer times. **Església Catedral de la Santa Creu** (Catholic services), in Pl. Seu, up C. Bisbe from Pl. St. Jaume. M: Jaume I. Cathedral open daily 8am-1:30pm and 4-7:30pm.

Gay and Lesbian Services: Cómplices, C. Cervantes, 2 (☎934 12 72 83). M: Liceu. From C. Ferran, take a left onto C. Avinyó and then the 2nd left. A bookstore with publications in English and Spanish and a decent selection of LGB films. Also provides an **informative map** of Barcelona's LBG bars and discos. Open M-F 10:30am-8:30pm, Sa noon-8:30pm.

Laundromats: Tintorería Ferrán, C. Ferrán, 11. M: Liceu. Full service 1500ptas/€9. Open daily 8:30am-2pm and 4:30-7:30pm. **Tintorería San Pablo,** C. San Pau 105 (☎933 29 42 49). M: Paral.lel. Wash, dry, and fold 1800ptas/€11; do-it-yourself 1400ptas/€8.40. Open M-F 9am-1:30pm and 4-8:30pm.

EMERGENCY AND COMMUNICATIONS

Emergency: ☎112. **Local Police:** ☎092. **National police:** ☎091. **Medical:** ☎061.

Police: Las Ramblas, 43 (☎933 44 13 00), across from Pl. Reial and next to C. Nou de La Rambla. M: Liceu. Tourists should visit the department labeled "Tourist attention," where there are multilingual officers. Open 24hr., tourist assistance open 8am-2am. Other offices beneath the Pl. Catalunya on the Banco Nacional side, and at Barcelona-Nord bus station.

Crisis Lines: Oficina Permanente de Atención Social (24hr. toll-free ☎933 19 00 42). **AIDS Information: Association Ciutadana Anti-SIDA de Catalunya,** C. Junta de Comerç, 23 (☎933 17 05 05). AIDS information. Open M-F 10am-2pm and 4-7pm.

Late-Night Pharmacy: Pharmacies open 24hr. on a rotating basis. Check pharmacy windows for current listings.

Hospitals: Hospital Clinic, Villarroel, 170 (☎932 27 54 00). M: Hospital Clinic. Main entrance at the intersection of C. Roselló and C. Casanova. **Hospital de la Santa Creu i Sant Pau** (☎932 91 90 00, emergency ☎932 91 91 91), at the intersection of C. Cartagena and C. Sant Antoni Moria Claret. M: Hospital de Sant Pau. **Hospital Vall d' Hebron** (☎932 74 60 00) M: Vall d'Hebron.

Internet Access:

Easy Everything, Las Ramblas, 31. M: Liceu. 200ptas/€1.20 for about 40min.—fluctuates with the number of computers in use. Open 24hr. Also on Ronda Universitat, 35, next to Pl. Catalunya.

bcnet (Internet Gallery Café), Barra de Ferro, 3 (☎932 68 15 07), down the street from the Picasso museum. M: Jaume I. 250ptas/€1.50 per 15min., 600ptas/€4 per hr.; 10hr. ticket available for 3000ptas/€18. Open daily 10am-1am.

Conèctate, C. Aragó, 283 (☎934 67 04 43). M: Pg. de Gràcia. One block to the right of the Metro, facing away from Pl. de Catalunya. No Telnet. Internet midnight-9am 200ptas/€1.20 for 2hr., 6pm-9pm 200ptas/€1.20 for 45min., other times 200ptas/€1.20 per hr. Open 24hr.

Internet Exchange, Las Ramblas, 130. M: Catalunya. 10ptas/€0.06 per minute; 2000ptas/€12 for 5hr., 4500ptas/€27 for 20 hr.; students 2500ptas/€15 for 10hr., 5000ptas/€30 for 30hr.

Cybermundo Internet Centre, Bergara, 3 and Balmes, 8 (☎933 17 71 42). M: Catalunya. Off Pl. Catalunya, behind the Triangle mall. 30min. 300ptas/€2, 1hr. 490ptas/€3; students 30min, 250ptas/€1.50, 1hr 350ptas/€2.

Telephones: Get phone cards at tobacco stores, tourist offices, and newsstands. **Private phone service** (☎/fax 934 90 76 50), at Estació Barcelona-Sants. M: Sants-Estació. Open M-Sa 8am-9:45pm. **Directory Assistance:** ☎1003 for numbers within in Spain, ☎1008 for numbers within in Europe, ☎1005 for numbers outside Europe.

Post Office: Lista de Correos, Pl. de Antoni López (☎902 197 197: general info). M: Jaume I or Barceloneta. Fax and **lista de correos.** Open M-F 8:30am-9:30pm. A little shop in the back of the post office building, across the street, wraps packages for mailing (about 300ptas/€2). Shop open M-Sa 9am-2pm and 5-8pm. **Postal Code:** 08003.

ACCOMMODATIONS

The area between Pl. Catalunya and the water—the **Barri Gòtic, El Raval,** and **La Ribera**—offers budget beds, but except for a few places that subside on walk-ins, reservations are a must. Last-minute travelers can crash in **Gràcia** or **l'Eixample,** outer boroughs with more vacancies that are easily accessible to the rest Barcelona.

LOWER BARRI GÒTIC

The following hostels are in the lower part of the Barri Gòtic, between C. Ferran and the water. Backpackers flock here to be close to hip Las Ramblas, an ideal place to experience the old city. Guard your pocket book in the Pl. Reial and C. Escudellers.

UNDER 2500PTAS/€15 FOR ONE PERSON

Hostal Fernando, C. Ferran, 31 (☎/fax933 01 79 93). M: Liceu. So clean it shines; fills from walk-ins. Dorms with lockers 2500ptas/€15; doubles 5000-6000ptas/€30-36, with bath 7000-8000ptas/€42-48; triples 8500-9500ptas/€51-57. MC/V.

Casa de Huéspedes Mari-Luz, C. Palau, 4 (☎/fax933 17 34 63). M: Liceu. From Las Ramblas, follow C. Ferran, go right on C. Avinyó, left on C. Cervantes, and right on C. Palau. The owners make their hostel feel like home. Kitchen June-Aug. (open only 8-10:30am). Laundry 800ptas/€4.80. Dorms with lockers 1900ptas/€11.50; doubles June 21-Aug. 15 6000ptas/€36, Aug.16-June 20 4800ptas/€29. MC/V.

Albergue Juvenil Palau (HI), C. Palau, 6 (☎934 12 50 80). M: Liceu. A budget refuge. Kitchen (open 7-10pm), dining room, and 45 clean dorms with lockers (3-8 people each). Breakfast included. Showers 8am-noon and 4-10pm. Sheets 200ptas/€1.20. Reception 7am-3am. Curfew 3am. No reservations. Dorms 1900ptas/€12.

Hostal Avinyó, C. Avinyó, 42 (☎933 18 79 45; fax 18 68 93). M: Drassanes. With annual renovations, owners are on a mission to make it the most modern spot in the Barri Gòtic. 28 bedrooms with couches, fans, in-room safes, and stained glass windows. Singles 2500ptas/€15; doubles 4000-4600ptas/€12-14, with bath 5000-6000ptas/€15-18.

Hostal Marmo, C. Gignàs, 25 (☎933 10 59 70). M: Jaume I. A right off Via Laietana from the Metro. 17 rooms in an old house bedecked with plenty of plants, lacy curtains, and tiled floors. All rooms have balconies. Reservations only accepted 2 days in advance. Singles 2200-2400ptas/€13.50-14.50, with bath 2500-2700ptas/€15-16.30; doubles 4200-4600ptas/€25-28, with bath 4500-4900ptas/€27-€30.

Pensión Bienestar, C. Quintana, 3 (☎933 18 72 83). M: Liceu, a left off C. Ferran, coming from Las Ramblas. The entrance looks utterly uninviting and brown is the dominant color inside, but many of the mattresses are new and the rooms are cheap. Singles 2500ptas/€15; doubles 3500ptas/€21; triples 7000ptas/€42.

UNDER 5000PTAS/€30 FOR ONE PERSON

Hostal Levante, Baixada de San Miguel, 2 (☎933 17 95 65; fax 17 05 26). M: Liceu. Walk down C. Ferran, turn right onto C. Avinyó, and take the 1st left onto Baixada de San Miguel. Large, tastefully decorated rooms with balconies or fans. Ask for a renovated room. Singles 4000ptas/€24; doubles 6500ptas/€39, with bath 7500ptas/€45. Suites also available for 4-8 people each (kitchen, living room, laundry machines) 4000ptas/€24 per person per night. MC/V.

Hotel Rey Don Jaume I, C. Jaume I, 11 (☎/fax 933 10 62 08; r.d.jaume@atriumhotels.com). M: Jaume I. The building has seen better days but maintains a touch of opulence, with marble stairs and a tapestry-filled TV lounge. Stark rooms have balconies, phones, and bath. Safes available. Reservations recommended 1-2 months ahead. Singles 6000ptas/€36; doubles 9000ptas/€54; triples 12,000ptas/€72. AmEx/MC/V.

Albergue de Juventud Kabul, Pl. Reial, 17 (☎933 18 51 90; fax 933 01 40 34). M: Liceu. Head to the port on Las Ramblas, pass C. Ferran, and go left on C. Colon Pl. Reial; Kabul is on the near right corner of the plaça. Legendary coed dorm rooms can pack 200 frat boys. Common area includes TV, snack bar, Internet (100ptas/€0.60 per 20min.), pool, pop music, and beer vending machines. Key deposit 1000ptas/€6. Free in-room lockers. Sheets 300ptas/€1.80. Laundry 900ptas/€5.50. No reservations. June-Sept. dorms 2900ptas/€17.50, Oct.-May 1900ptas/€11.50.

UPPER BARRI GÒTIC

This section of the Barri Gòtic is between C. Fontanella and C. Ferran. **Portal de l'Angel** is a pedestrian avenue running through the middle. Accommodations are pricier than in the lower Barri Gòtic, but more serene. Early reservations are obligatory in summer. The nearest Metro stop is Catalunya, unless otherwise specified.

UNDER 4000PTAS/€24 FOR ONE PERSON

Hotel Toledano/Hostal Residencia Capitol, Las Ramblas, 138 (☎933 01 08 72; fax 934 12 31 42; www.hoteltoledano.com). Split-level hotel/hostel borders on luxurious. Hotel rooms include bath, hostel rooms don't. English-speaking owner. 4th-floor Hotel Toledano: singles 4600ptas/€28; doubles 7900ptas/€48; triples 9900ptas/€60; quads 11000ptas/€66. 5th-floor Hostel Residencia Capitol: singles 3400ptas/€21; doubles 5400ptas/€33, with shower 6200ptas/€37; triples 6900ptas/€42, with shower 7700ptas/€47; quads 7900ptas/€48, with shower 8700ptas/€52. Reservations can be made over the website; book early. AmEx/MC/V. Wheelchair accessible.

Hostal Benidorm, Las Ramblas, 37 (☎933 02 20 54). M: Drassanes. With phones and baths in every neat room and balconies, this could be the best value on Las Ramblas. Singles 4000ptas/€24; doubles 5500ptas/€33; triples 7000ptas/€42; quads 9000ptas/€54; quints10,500ptas/€63.

Hostal Campi, C. Canuda, 4 (☎/fax 933 01 3545). The first left off Las Ramblas coming from M: Catalunya. A great bargain for the quality and location. The rooms are spacious, with light, comfortable furniture and lacy curtains. Rooms with bath have TVs. Reservations accepted 9am-8pm. Singles 3000ptas/€18; doubles 6000ptas/€36, with bath 7000ptas/€42; triples 8000ptas/€48, with bath 9000ptas/€54.

Hostal Fontanella, Via Laietana, 71 (☎/fax 933 17 59 43). M: Urquinaona. Tasteful floral waiting room and wood furniture in the rooms. Reservations require a credit card. Singles 3300ptas/€20, with bath 4300/€26; doubles 5500ptas/€23, with shower 6500ptas/€39, with bath 7500ptas/€45; triples 7700ptas/€46, with bath 9100ptas/€55; quads 9650ptas/€58, with bath 11,000ptas/€66. AmEx/MC/V.

Hostal Residencia Rembrandt, C. Portaferrissa, 23 (☎/fax 933 18 10 11). M: Liceu. Each pastel room is themed differently; ask for a balcony. Fans 300ptas/€2 per night. Singles 4000ptas/€24, with bath 5500ptas/€33; doubles 6500ptas/€39, with bath 8800ptas/€53; triples 9000ptas/€54, with bath 10,000ptas/€60. One suite (12,000ptas/€72) with a balcony, marble tub, and sitting area.

Hostal Parisien, Las Ramblas, 114 (☎933 01 62 83). M: Liceu. In the middle of the excitement (and noise) of Las Ramblas, 13 well-kept rooms keep young guests happy. Balconies showcase the street's daily spectacle. Quiet after midnight. Singles 3500ptas/€21, with bath 4000ptas/€24; doubles 7500ptas/€45, with bath 8500ptas/€51.

Pensión Aris, C. Fontanella, 14 (☎933 18 10 17). Right off Pl. Catalunya. 13 huge, clean, sparse rooms with fans and white-washed walls. Furniture could be sturdier, but the prices are impossible to beat for the location. Laundry 500-1000ptas/€3-6. Singles 2500ptas/€15; doubles 5000ptas/€30, with bath 6000ptas/€36.

Hostal Layetana, Pl. Ramón Berenguer, 2 (☎/fax 933 19 20 12). M: Jaume I. Walk up Via Laietana toward the mountains. Look for the multinational flags on the third-floor balcony. A peaceful, clean hostel. Singles 3400ptas/€21; doubles 5100ptas/€31, with bath 7350ptas/€44; triples 8000ptas/€48, with bath 10,200ptas/€61. MC/V.

Hostal Paris, Cardenal Casañas, 4 (☎933 01 37 85; fax 934 12 70 96). M: Liceu. The yellow sign is visible from Las Ramblas, across from the Metro. 42 well-kept rooms overlooking the street. Rooms on the inside patio have A/C; all others have fans. Rooms with bath have TVs. Singles 3300ptas/€20, with bath 3700ptas/€22; doubles 6000ptas/€36, with shower 7000ptas/€42, with bath 9000ptas/€54. No reservations. MC/V.

Residencia Victoria, C. Comtal, 9 (☎933 17 45 97). From Pl. Catalunya, walk down Av. Portal de l'Angel and take a left on C. Comtal. Lounge with terrace and kitchen. Basic but spacious. Laundry 400ptas/€2.50. Singles 3500-4000ptas/€21-24; doubles 5500-6000ptas/€33-36; triples 8000ptas/€48.

Hostal Marítima, Las Ramblas, 4 (☎933 02 31 52). M: Drassanes, down a tiny alley off the port end of Las Ramblas. Follow the signs to Museu de Cera, which is next door. Nothing to write home about, convenient and comfortable. No reservations. Laundry 800ptas/€4.80 (no dryer). Singles, doubles, and triples 3000ptas/€18 per person.

Pensión Noya, Las Ramblas, 133 (☎933 01 48 31). M: Catalunya, above the noisy Núria restaurant. This 10-room hostel has time-warped back to the colors and styles of the 1950s. Bathrooms and hallways are cramped. No heat in winter. Hot water 8am-midnight. Singles 3000ptas/€18; doubles 5800ptas/€35; triples 7500ptas/€45.

Pensión Santa Anna, C. Santa Anna, 23 (☎/fax 933 01 22 46). Tight quarters, but the floors and bathrooms are spotless and the cheap, light bedroom furniture is easy on the eyes. All rooms have fans, and guests get keys. Singles 3000ptas/€18; doubles 6000ptas/€36, with bath 8000ptas/€48; triples 9000ptas/€54.

UNDER 7500PTAS/€45 FOR ONE PERSON

Hostal Plaza, C. Fontanella, 18 (☎/fax 933 01 01 39 or 17 91 08). Savvy Texan owners and quirky rooms. Drink/breakfast bar, kitchen, and Internet. Laundry 1500ptas/€9 for 5kg. 24hr. reception. Singles 7000ptas/€42, with bath 9000ptas/€54; doubles 9000ptas/€54, with bath 10,000ptas/€60; triples 12,000ptas/€72, with bath 13,000ptas/€78. Discount in Nov. and Feb. AmEx/MC/V.

Pensión Dalí, C. Boqueria, 12 (☎933 18 55 90; fax 18 55 80). M: Liceu; off Las Ramblas. Designed by Domènech i Montaner, Pensión Dalí has the stained glass and gaudy iron of its youth. Internet (100ptas/€0.60 per 4min.). Singles 4400ptas/€267, with bath 6000ptas/€36; doubles 6500ptas/€39, with bath 7500ptas/€45; triples 10,200ptas/€62; quads 12,800ptas/€77. AmEx/MC/V.

Hotel California, C. Rauric, 14 (☎933 17 77 66). M: Catalunya, a right off C. Ferran coming from Las Ramblas, in the Barri Gòtic. Such a lovely place. Caters to a gay clientele. Sparkling, pleasant rooms with TV, phone, bath and A/C. Breakfast included. Singles 7500ptas/€45; doubles 12,000ptas/€72; triples 15,000ptas/€90. AmEx/MC/V.

Mare Nostrum, Las Ramblas, 67 (☎933 18 53 40; fax 934 12 30 69). M: Liceu. Chill in A/C or on a balcony and love life. Breakfast included, served 8am-11am. Doubles 7950ptas/€50, with bath 9500ptas/€57. Additional person 2800ptas/€17. MC/V.

Hostal-Residencia Lausanne, Av. Portal de l'Angel, 24 (☎933 02 11 39 or 02 16 30). M: Catalunya, between Zara display windows. Overlooks a popular pedestrian street. Singles 4500ptas/€27; doubles 6500ptas/€39, with shower 8000ptas/€48, with bath 12,000ptas/€72; triples 12,000ptas/€72; quads 16,000ptas/€96.

Hostal Palermo, C. Boqueria, 21 (☎/fax 933 02 40 02). M: Liceu. Large, party-conducive rooms. Small, plastic-chaired turquoise TV room and white-washed walls. Laundry 700ptas/€4.20, safe 200ptas/€1.20 per day. Singles 5500ptas/€33, with bath 7500ptas/€45; triples 13,500ptas/€81, with bath 18,000ptas/€1089. MC/V.

LA RIBERA

Hostal Orleans, Av. Marqués de l'Argentera, 13 (☎933 19 73 82). M: Barceloneta. Spotless and comfortable, private baths. Singles 3000-4500ptas/€18-27; doubles 8500ptas/€50, with A/C 9000ptas/€54; triples 9500-10000ptas/€56-60; quads 12000ptas/€72. AmEx/D/MC/V.

Hostal de Ribagorza, C. Trafalgar, 39 (☎933 19 19 68; fax 19 12 47). M: Urquinaona. With your back to Pl. Urquinaona, take Ronda Sant Pere and go right 1 block on C. Méndez Núñez. Homey doubles in a Modernist building. Oct.-Feb. 4000ptas/€24; with bath 6000ptas/€36; Mar.-Sept. 5500ptas/€33; with bath 7500ptas/€45. MC/V.

Hostal Nuevo Colón, Av. Marqués de l'Argentera, 19 (☎933 19 50 77). M: Barceloneta. Follow Pg. Joan de Borbó and go right on Av. Marqués de l'Argentera. Clean rooms and a TV area. Singles 3900ptas/€24.40; doubles 5900ptas/€35, with bath 7900ptas/€47. 6-man apartments (with kitchen) 18,000ptas/€110. MC/V.

Pensión Ciutadella, C. Comerç, 33 (☎933 19 62 03). M: Barceloneta. From Pg. Joan de Borbó, turn right on Av. Marqués de l'Argentera; C. Comerç is the 6th left. Spacious doubles with balcony. Oct.-May 5000ptas/€30, with bath 6000ptas/€36; June-Sept., 6000ptas/€36, 7500ptas/€45 June-Sept. Additional person 1500ptas/€9.

Pensión Lourdes, C. Princesa, 14 (☎933 19 33 72). M: Jaume I. Cross Via Laietana and follow C. Princesa. Adequate rooms with telephones. Common area with TV. Singles 3500ptas/€21; doubles 5000ptas/€30, with bath 6700ptas/€40.

EL RAVAL

Be careful in the areas nearer to the port and farther from Las Ramblas.

Pensión L'Isard, C. Tallers, 82 (☎933 02 51 83; fax 02 01 17). M: Universitat. Exit Metro at C. Pelai, left at end of the block, and left at the pharmacy. Simple, elegant, and clean. Singles 2800ptas/€16,80; doubles 4900ptas/€30, with bath 6500ptas/€39; triples 7300ptas/€44, with bath 8500ptas/€51.

Hostal Australia, Ronda Universitat, 11 (☎933 17 41 77). M: Universitat. Guests are family at this hostel; all rooms have curtains, balconies, artwork, and fans. Be prepared for the family-style quiet time starting at 10pm. Curfew 4am. Singles 3300ptas/€20; doubles 5400ptas/€33, with bath 7000ptas/€42. MC/V.

Hostal La Terrassa, Junta de Comerç, 11 (☎933 02 51 74; fax 01 21 88). M: Liceu. From the Metro, take C. Hospital and turn left after Teatre Romea. A minimalist experience. Singles 2700ptas/€16.20; doubles 4200ptas/€25.20, with bath 5200ptas/€31.20; triples 5700ptas/€34.20, with bath 6600ptas/€40. MC/V.

Hostal Opera, C. Sant Pau, 20 (☎933 18 82 01). M: Liceu, off Las Ramblas. Like the opera house next door, the hostal has been recently renovated, making its sunny rooms feel new. Rooms come with bath, telephone, and A/C. Singles 5000ptas/€30.10; doubles 8000ptas/€48.20; triples 10,000ptas/€60.30. No reservations. MC/V.

Pensión 45, C. Tallers 45 (☎933 02 70 61). M: Catalunya. From Pl. Catalunya, take the first right off Las Ramblas onto Tallers. Lacking in name-choice originality, full of charm. Singles 3100ptas/€19; doubles 5000ptas/€31, with bath 6000ptas/€40.

L'EIXAMPLE

Hostal Ciudad Condal, C. Mallorca, 255 (☎932 15 10 40). M: Diagonal, just off Pg. de Gràcia, 2 blocks from La Pedrera. Rooms with bath and phones. 24hr. reception. Must reserve with a credit card for late arrivals. Singles 8500ptas/€51; doubles 13,000-14,000ptas/€78-84. Prices often drop in winter. MC/V. Wheelchair accessible.

Pensión Fani, C. València, 278 (☎932 15 36 45) M: Catalunya. Oozes character; birds in the sunroom. Rents by month or night. Shared baths, kitchen, TV room, and laundry room. Bring a towel. Singles 42,000ptas/€252 per month; doubles 80,000ptas/€480 per month; triples 120,000ptas/€720 per month. 1 night 3000ptas/€18 per person.

Hostal Residencia Oliva, Pg. de Gràcia, 32 (☎934 88 01 62 or 88 17 89; fax 93 487 04 97). M: Pg. de Gràcia, at C. Diputació. Classy ambiance. Reservations a must. Laundry 2000ptas/€12. Singles 3500ptas/€21; doubles 6500ptas/€39, with bath 7500ptas/€45; triple with bath 10,500ptas/€63.

Hostal Eden, C. Balmes, 55 (☎934 52 66 20; fax 52 66 21). M: Pg. de Gràcia. Walk down C. Aragó to C. Balmes and turn left. Stained-glass and floral tiles. May-Oct.: singles 4815ptas/€29, with bath 6420ptas/€38; doubles 5885ptas/€35, with bath 8560ptas/€50. Nov.-Apr.: singles 3815ptas/€23, with bath 5350ptas/€32; doubles 4815ptas/€29, with bath 7500ptas/€45. AmEx/MC/V.

Hostal Residencia Windsor, Rambla de Catalunya, 84 (☎932 15 11 98). M: Pg. de Gràcia, on the corner of C. Mallorca. Carpeted hallways, gilded mirrors, and a plush TV room. Rooms with sleep sofas and heat in winter. Singles 4500ptas/€27, with bath 5400ptas/€33; doubles 7200ptas/€43, with sink and shower 7800ptas/€47, with bath 8500ptas/€51; extra beds 1600ptas/€9.50 each.

Hostal Hill, C. Provença, 323 (☎934 57 88 14), between C. Girona and C. Bailen. M: Verdaguer. A great deal. Singles 3900ptas/€24, with bath 4900ptas/€30; doubles 6000ptas/€36, with bath 7300ptas/€44. V.

Hostal Qué Tal, C. Mallorca, 290 (☎/fax 934 59 23 66). M: Pg. de Gràcia. Gay and lesbian hostel. Singles 5500ptas/€33; doubles 8200ptas/€49, with bath 10,500ptas/€63; triples 11,000ptas/€66.

GRÀCIA

Gràcia is Barcelona's "undiscovered" quarter, but natives have definitely discovered its lively nightlife. Last-minute arrivals may find vacancies here.

Hostal Lesseps, C. Gran de Gràcia, 239 (☎932 18 44 34; fax 17 11 80). M: Lesseps. Spacious rooms sport red velvet wallpaper. 16 rooms have TV and bath, 4 have A/C (600ptas/€3.61 extra per day). Singles 5000ptas/€30; doubles 8000ptas/€48; triples 10,500ptas/€63; quads 12,500/€75. MC/V.

Pensión San Medín, C. Gran de Gràcia, 125 (☎932 17 30 68; fax 934 15 44 10; www.sanmedin.com). M: Fontana. Curtains and tiling abound. Singles 4000ptas/€24, with bath 5000ptas/€30; doubles 7000ptas/€42, with bath 8000ptas/€48. MC/V.

Hostal Bonavista, C. Bonavista, 21 (☎932 37 37 57). M: Diagonal. No reservations. Singles 2700ptas/€16; doubles 4100ptas/€24, with bath 5200ptas/€32.

Albergue Mare de Déu (HI), Pg. Mare de Déu del Coll, 41-51 (☎932 10 51 51; fax 10 07 98). From M: Vallcarca, walk up Av. República d'Argentina and cross bridge at C. Viaducte de Vallcarca; signs point the way. Breakfast included. Sheets 350ptas/€2. 3-day max. stay. Reception 8am-3pm, 4:30pm-11:30pm. Lockout 10am-1:30pm. Midnight curfew. Dorms 2000ptas/€12; over 25 2700ptas/€16. AmEx/MC/V.

CAMPING

For info, contact **Associació de Càmpings de Barcelona,** Gran Vía, 608 (☎934 12 59 55).

El Toro Bravo, Autovía Castelldefells km11 (☎936 37 34 62; fax 37 21 15). Bus L95 (200ptas/€1.20) from Pl. Catalunya 11km. Reception 8am-7pm. Sept. 1-June 14 725ptas/€4 per person, 775ptas/€5 per site, 725ptas/€4 per car, 575ptas/€3.50 for electricity. June 15-Aug. 31 760ptas/€5 per person, 810ptas/€5 per site, 760ptas/€5 per car, 575 ptas/€3.50 for electricity. AmEx/MC/V.

FOOD

The following listings represent a variety of regional, vegetarian, and international cuisine in the most tourist-trafficked areas. It is impossible to list every great restaurant in the city, so strike out on your own too. As always, the *Guía del Ocio* (available at newsstands) is an invaluable source of suggestions. The following is a breakdown of what's hot in neighborhood's without listings: Port Vell and Port Olímpic are great places to head for seafood; Las Ramblas has plenty of good and visible, albeit touristy and expensive options. The restaurants on C. Aragó by Pg. de Gràcia, have great lunchtime *menús*, and the Pg. de Gràcia has beautiful outdoor dining. Gràcia's Pl. Sol and La Ribera's Santa Maria del Mar are the best places to head for *tapas* (if you don't mind standing), while the other northern areas like Sarrià and Horta have great Catalan cuisine, if you know where you're going ahead of time, and as for Montjuïc... pack a lunch.

BASICS

If you want to live cheap and do as *barceloneses* do, buy your food fresh at a *mercat* (marketplace), hit up a grocery store for other essentials.

Markets: La Boqueria (Mercat de Sant Josep), off Las Ramblas, outside M:Liceu. Wholesale prices for fruit, cheese, and wine. **Mercat de la Concepi,** on C. València between C. Bruc and C. Girona. M: Girona. Smaller version of La Boquería.

Supermarkets: Champion Supermarket, Las Ramblas, 11. M: Liceu. Open M-Sa 9am-9pm. **El Corte Inglés,** Pl. Catalunya, 14. M: Catalunya. Supermarket in basement. Open M-Sa and first Su of month 10am-10pm.

LOWER BARRI GÒTIC

Great restaurants are scattered on C. Escudellers and C. Clave. Lively hangouts surround Santa Maria del Pi.

Les Quinze Nits, Pl. Reial, 6. M: Liceu. One of the most popular restaurants, with nightly lines that move quickly. Stylish decor and Catalan entrées at unbelievable prices (500-1200ptas/€3-7). No reservations. Open daily 1-3:45pm and 8:30-11:30pm. MC/V.

Los Caracoles, C. Escudellers, 14. M: Drassanes. What started as a snail shop in 1835 is now a Catalan restaurant. Dishes taste as good as they look; specialties include the *caracoles* (snails; 1900ptas/€11.50), suckled pig (2900ptas/€18), and chicken (1900ptas/€11.50). Expect a wait. Open daily 1pm-midnight. AmEx/MC/V.

Irati, C. Cardenal Casañas, 17. M: Liceu. Basque *tapas* (160ptas/€1 each). Keep your toothpicks for your bill. Bartenders pour *sidra* (cider) behind their backs (150ptas/€1). Starters 1500ptas/€9. Entrées 2500-3000ptas/€15-18. Open Tu-Sa noon-midnight, Su noon-4:30pm. *Tapas* served noon-3pm and 7-11pm. AmEx/MC/V.

Restaurante Bidasoa, C. Serra, 21. M: Drassanes. Follow C. Clavé to the 3rd left. Fresh Catalan food is good, cheap, and plentiful. Most dishes 500ptas/€3. Open Tu-Su 1:30-4pm and 8pm-midnight. Closed Aug.

Juicy Jones, Cardenal Casañas, 7 (group dinner reservations ☎606 20 49 06). M. Liceu. A touch of flower-power in Barcelona. Vegan *menú* (1175ptas/€7) features rice, veggies, soups, and salad (after 1pm only). Fresh juices 300-500ptas/€2-3. Dining room in the back. Open daily Oct.-April 10am-11:15pm, May-Sept. 8am-11:15pm.

L'Antic Bocoi del Gòtic, Baixada de Viladecols, 3. M: Jaume I, at the end of the street that starts as C. Daguería, a left off C. Jaume I coming from Pl. de l'Angel (it changed names 3 times). Complete with Roman wall, it's what one imagines in the "Gothic Quarter." Salads and sausages about 1000ptas/€6, artisan cheeses 1500-2000ptas/€9-12. Wine 1500-3000ptas/€9-18 a bottle. Open M-Sa 8:30pm-midnight. AmEx/MC/V.

UPPER BARRI GÒTIC

Els Quatre Gats, C. Montsió, 3. M: Catalunya; the 2nd left off Portal de l'Angel. Picasso's old Modernist hangout; he designed a personalized menu (on display at Museu Picasso;

see p. 325). Reproductions of his works and more adorn the walls. Food is expensive (entrées around 2000ptas/€12); *tapas* are the best way to go (200-600ptas/€1.50-3.60). Coffee is cheap (150ptas/€1) and wicked good. Live piano and violin 9pm-1am. Open M-Sa 9am-2am, Su 5pm-2am. Closed Aug. AmEx/MC/V.

Betawi, C. Montsió, 6. M: Catalunya, directions above. A peaceful Indonesian restaurant; food verges on gourmet in taste and size. *Menú* 1275ptas/€8. Entrées 1200-1500ptas/€7-9. Open M-Sa 1-4pm, Tu-Th 8-11pm, and F-Sa 8-11:30pm. AmEx/MC/V.

Govinda, Pl. Vila de Madrid, 4. M: Catalunya. Vegetarian Indian food served a few feet from a row of Roman tombs nearly 2000 years old. *Thali* (traditional Indian "sampler" meals with a variety of dishes on one platter; 2500-3000ptas/€15-18). Salad bar 700-1000ptas/€4-6. M-F *menú* 1300ptas/€7.80. Entrées around 1200ptas/€7. Open for lunch daily 1-4pm, for dinner Tu-Th 8-11pm and F-Sa 8-11:45pm. AmEx/MC/V.

La Colmena, Pl. de l'Angel, 12. M: Jaume I. After more than 120 years in the Pl. de l'Angel, this divine pastry/candy shop has earned its prime location. Be prepared to buy—you won't be able to resist. Open daily 9am-9pm. AmEx/MC/V.

Terrablava, Via Laietana 55. A buffet of fresh salads, veggies, pasta, pizza, meat dishes, fruit, and coffee. Food also available to go. Buffet M-F 12:30-6pm 1095ptas/€7, 6pm-1am and Sa-Su 1395ptas/€9. Open daily 12:30pm-1am.

LA RIBERA

East of Via Laietana, La Ribera is home to numerous bars and small restaurants. The few tourists who walk over are well rewarded. The area around Santa María del Mar and the Mercat del Born is crawling with *tapas* bars.

La Habana Vieja, C. Banys Vells, 2. M: Jaume I. C. Cuban music sets the mood for large portions, perfect for sharing. Cuban rice 600-900ptas/€4-5; meat dishes 1600-2000ptas/€102-112. Open daily 10am-4:30pm and 8:30pm-1am. AmEx/D/MC/V.

Xampanyet, C. Montcado, 22. M: Jaume I. Cross Via Laietana, walk down C. Princesa, and turn right on C. Montcado. Xampanyet is on the right after the Museu Picasso. The house special *cava* served at a colorful bar. Glasses 120ptas/€1. Bottles 900ptas/€5. Open Tu-Sa noon-4pm and 7-11:30pm, Su 7-11:30pm. Closed Aug. MC/V.

Va de Vi, C. Banys Vells,16. M: Jaume I; take C. Princesa, a right on C. Montcada, a right on C. Barra de Ferro, and a left on C. Banys Vells. Candle lit wine bar. Wine (glasses from 275-675ptas/€2-4), cheeses (500-1200ptas/€3-7), and *tapas* (450-900ptas/€3-5). Open daily June-Sept. 7pm-2am, Sept.-June noon-3pm and 7pm-2am.

Tèxtil Café, C. Montcada, 12. M: Jaume I. In the Museu Tèxtil courtyard; patrons swarm for coffee or a meal. M-F lunch *menú* 1400ptas/€8. Wine and *cava* 250-350ptas/€1.50-2 per glass. Sandwiches 360-1250ptas/€2-8. Open Tu-Su 10am-midnight.

EL RAVAL

Students and blue-collar workers congregate in Catalan joints west of Las Ramblas. Restaurants are fairly inexpensive: most have simple decor, basic food, and lots of noise, although trendier places have started to move in as well.

Bar Ra, Pl. Garduña (☎933 01 41 63). M: Liceu, behind Las Ramblas' Boqueria market. Everything about Ra exudes cool. A mixture of traditional Spanish and trendy California cuisine. *Menú* 1300ptas/€8. Open M-Sa 1:30-4:pm, 9:30-2am. Dinner by reservation.

Buenas Migas, Pl. Bonsuccés, 6. M: Catalunya, off Las Ramblas. Enjoy coffee (120-160ptas/€1) at a shaded table, or stay indoors with *focaccia* (thick Italian bread; 300-500ptas/€2-3). Cakes (350ptas/€2). Open Su-W 10am-10pm, Th-Sa 10am-midnight.

Colibri, C. Riera Alta. M: Liceu. Take C. Carme of Las Ramblas and make your 6th right onto Riera Alta; Colibri is 2 blocks up on the left. Freshness, flair, and service. Dishes 1700-4000ptas/€10.20-24. Open M-F 1:30-6:30, 8:30-11:30pm. MC/V.

Restaurante Can Lluís, C. Cera, 49. M: Sant Antoni. Head down Ronda S. Pau and take the 2nd left on C. Cera. A defining force in Catalan cuisine, overflowing with delicacies like *cabrit* (goat) and *conill* (rabbit). Daily *menú* 1600ptas/€9.60. Entrées 1350-2500ptas/€8-€15.10. Open M-Sa 1:30-4pm and 8:30-11:30pm. V.

Pla dels Angels, C. de Ferlandina, 23. The funky decor fitting for its proximity to Barcelona's contemporary art museum. Pastas 500ptas/€3, entrées 800-900ptas/€4.90-5.60. Open M 1:30-4pm; Tu-Th 1:30-4pm, 9-11pm; F-Sa 9pm-midnight.

mamacafé, C. Joaquim Costa, a right off C. Hospital. Healthy vegetarian and meat options with an exotic twist. Casual not divey, artsy not pretentious. Entrées 1200-1800ptas/€7-10. *Menú* 1175ptas/€7. Open Tu-Sa 1pm-1am, M 1pm-5pm.

Silenus, C. dels Angels, 8. From M: Catalunya, a right off C. Carme. As much an art gallery as restaurant. Entrées include fish and meat (1775ptas/€11) and the exotic *filete de kangoo*: yep, kangaroo (2400ptas/€15). Open M-Sa 1-5pm, 9pm-1am. MC/V.

L'EIXAMPLE

L'Eixample is full of good places to spend a long, enjoyable dinner, but restaurants are spread out widely. Most tourists never make it past the Pg. de Gràcia, which caters to a wealthy clientele. Be prepared to pay well for the food and atmosphere.

El Racó d'en Baltá, C. Aribau, 125. M: Hospital Clinic. Mediterranean fare and Catalan dishes like *fideua* noodles (1200ptas/€7). Appetizers and salads 950-1200ptas/€6-7. Fish and meat entrées 1575-2300ptas/€10-14. Bottles of wine 600-2600ptas/€3.50-16. Open M 9pm-11pm and Tu-Sa 1-4pm and 9-11pm. AmEx/D/MC/V.

Comme-Bio, C. Gran Vía, 603. M: Catalunya on the corner of Gran Vía and Rambla de Catalunya. Fresh salad, hummus, tofu, yogurt, and juice. Restaurant, food-to-go, and grocery store all in one. Pasta, rice, and pizzas around 1000ptas/€6. Salads 800-1000ptas/€5-6. Open daily 9am-11:30pm. MC/V.

Mandalay Café, C. Provença, 330. M: Verdaguer. Asian cuisine in a room featured in decorating books. F-Sa night trapeze artist 11pm. *Menú* 1200ptas/€7. Entrées 1500-2000ptas/€9-12. Open Tu-Sa 1-4pm and 9-11pm. MC/V.

Laie Llibreria Café, C. Pau Claris, 85. M: Urquinaona. An ultra-cool lunch spot. Indulge in the cheap, fresh all-you-can-eat buffet lunch (1250ptas/€8) in the open, bamboo-draped lunch room, then grab a coffee or drink at the bar on the way out. Vegetarian dinner *menú* 2250ptas/€14. Open M-F 9am-1am, Sa 10am-1am. AmEx/MC/V.

Café Miranda, C. Casanova, 30 (☎934 53 52 49). M: Universitat. Lavish gay restaurant features drag performers. Mediterranean delicacies, friendly waitstaff, and mixed crowd make it a popular place; reservations recommended. Take a peek at the bathrooms. *Menú* 3300ptas/€20. Open daily 9pm-1am. MC/V.

Txapela (Euskal Taberna), Pg. de Gràcia, 8-10 (☎934 12 02 89). M: Catalunya. For the *tapas*-clueless who want to learn: place mats have pictures with the description of each *tapa*, 150ptas/€1 each. Open M-Th 8am-1:30am, F-Su 10am-2am. MC/V.

GRÀCIA

La Gavina, C. Ros de Olano, 17. Funky pizzeria complete with life-size patron saint. Pizzas go for 750-1450ptas/€5-9. Open Tu-Su 2pm-1am, F-Sa 2pm-2am.

La Buena Tierra, C. Encarnació, 56. M: Joanic. Follow C. Escorial for 2 blocks and turn left on C. Encarnació. Vegetarian delicacies! Choose from an eclectic range of entrées like *moussaka* or tortellini with roquefort (650-1050ptas/€4-6.50) and feast in the backyard terrace. Open M-Sa noon-4pm and 8pm-1am. Disover.

Ikastola, C. La Perla 22. M: Fontana, off C. Verdi. Ikastola (Basque for "nursery school") serves mostly vegetarian dishes (350-600ptas/€2-3.50) and is also a popular bar. Draw on the chalkboard walls. Open M-F 11am-1am, Sa-Su 5pm-3am.

SIGHTS

Architecturally, Barcelona is defined by its unique Modernist treasures. Las Ramblas—a bustling avenue smack in the city center—and the Barri Gòtic, Barcelona's "old city," are the traditional tourist areas. But don't neglect vibrant La Ribera and

El Raval, the upscale avenues of l'Eixample, the panoramic city views from Montjuïc and Tibidabo, Gaudí's Park Güell, and the harbor-side Port Olímpic.

RUTA DEL MODERNISME

For those with a few days and an interest in seeing all the biggest sights, the Ruta del Modernisme is the cheapest and most flexible option. The Ruta del Modernisme isn't a tour in the sense that it doesn't offer a guide or transportation; it's a ticket which gives discounted entrance to Modernist sites. Passes (600ptas/€4; students and over 65 400ptas/€2; groups over 10 people 500ptas/€3 per person) are good for a month and give holders a 50% discount on entrance to Palau Güell, La Sagrada Família, Casa Milà, Palau de la Música Catalana, Casa-Museu Gaudí, Fundació Tàpies, the Museu d'Art Modern, El Hospital de la Santa Creu i Sant Pau, tours of the façades of La Manzana de la Discòrdia (Casas Amatller, Lleó Morera, and Batlló), and other attractions. The pass also comes with a map and a booklet which give a history of the movement and prioritize the sites. Purchase passes at **Casa Amatller,** Pg. Gràcia, 41 (☎934 88 01 39. M: Pg. de Gràcia). Many of these sights have mandatory tours that only leave on the hour; visiting all of them on the same day is impossible.

LAS RAMBLAS

M: Catalunya, Liceu, or Drassanes. Addresses with low numbers lie towards the port, while higher numbers head towards Pl. Catalunya.

Las Ramblas' pedestrian strip is an urban carnival, where street performers dance, human statues shift poses, vendors vend birds, and artists sell caricatures—all for the benefit of droves of tourists and all, of course, for a small fee. The wide, tree-lined thoroughfare dubbed Las Ramblas is actually composed of five distinct *ramblas* (promenades) that together form one long boulevard, about 1km long.

The first segment, by Pl. Catalunya, is **La Rambla de les Canaletes,** named for the **Font de les Canaletes,** recognizable by it four faucets and the Catalan crest. Legend has it that visitors who sample the water will fall in love with the city and are bound to return to Barcelona. Because of its central location in the city, La Rambla de les Canaletes sees a fair deal of political demonstrations.

You'll hear the squawking from next section of Las Ramblas, **La Ramblas dels Estudis,** before you see it. This stretch, which extends to C. Carme and C. Portaferrissa, is also called La Rambla dels Ocells—the **Rambla of the Birds.** Stalls here sell birds of nearly every kind: roosters, parrots, doves, and even baby emus. Other caged critters are also available. The official name of this stretch of *rambla* comes from the university that used to be located here; "*estudis*" is Catalan for "studies."

Screeching bird stalls lead to the roses of **La Rambla de Sant Josep,** a.k.a. **La Rambla de les Flors** (the Rambla of the Flowers). In April, flower stands are joined by book vendors for the **Día de Sant Jordi** (April 24), a Catalan holiday when couples exchange flowers and books. The stone building at C. Carme is the Església de Betlem, a baroque church burned during the Civil War. Farther down is the traditional market, **La Boquería,** and the infamous **Museu de l'Eròtica** (see p. 326). The Boquería market is officially name **El Mercat de Sant Josep;** the market and the *rambla* are named for the same saint. At Pl. Boqueria, before the Metro station, you'll walk across Joan Miró's circular mosaic, now a popular meeting point.

Miró's street mosaic marks **La Rambla dels Caputxins.** Across from the renovated opera house (the **Liceu;** see below), restaurants with outdoor seating offer decent but unremarkable and fairly expensive food in prime people-watching perches.

The last stretch of *rambla* could be nicknamed *La Rambla de las Prostitutas;* instead, it's called **La Rambla de Santa Mónica.** After nightfall, women of the night patrol this area by the port, beckoning with loud kissing noises. During the day, the street distinguishes itself with skilled practitioners of a different art. Roving galleries and artists sell landscapes, caricatures, and portraits. La Rambla de Santa Monica is also home to the **Centre d'Art de Santa Mónica** and the **Museu de Cera**. Las Ramblas ends at the seafront-end of La Rambla de Santa Monica with one very visible statue.

MONUMENT A COLOM. Ruis i Taulet's Monument a Colom towers at the port end of Las Ramblas. Ninteenth-century Renaixença enthusiasts convinced themselves that Columbus was Catalan, from a town near Girona. The fact that Columbus points proudly toward Libya, not the Americas, doesn't help the claim; historians agree that Columbus was from Italy. Take the elevator to the top and get a stunning view. *(Portal de la Pau. M: Drassanes. Elevator open June-Sept. 9am-8:30pm; Oct.-Mar. M-F 10am-1:30pm and 3:30-6:30pm, Sa-Su 10am-6:30pm; Apr.-May 10am-1:30pm and 3:30-7:30pm, Sa-Su 10am-7:30pm. 300ptas/€1.80, children and over 65 200ptas/€1.20.)*

LA BOQUERÍA. One of the cheapest ways to get food in the city, la Boquería is a traditional Catalan market located right on Las Ramblas. Specialized vendors sell their goods—produce, dairy, meat—from independent stands. A wonderland of fresh foods for wholesale prices; butcher displays are not for the faint of heart. *(Las Ramblas, 95. M: Liceu, Mercat exit. Open M-Sa 8am-8pm.)*

GRAN TEATRE DEL LICEU. Once one of Europe's leading stages, the Liceu has been ravaged by anarchists, bombs, and fires. It is adorned with palatial ornamentation, gold façades, sculptures, and grand side rooms—a Spanish hall of mirrors. *(Las Ramblas, 51-59, by C. Sant Pau. Office open M-F 2-8:30pm and 1hr. before performances. ☎934 85 99 13. Guided tours 9:30-11am, reservation only (call 934 85 99 00). 800ptas/€4, students 600ptas/€4.)*

PALAU DE LA VIRREINA. This 18th-century palace houses temporary photography, music, and graphics exhibits. Also on display are the 10-15ft. tall dolls who have been in the city's Carnival celebrations since 1320. The imposing couple Jaume and Violant, dressed in regal robes, are the undisputed king and queen of the Carnival parade. The cultural institute here, **ICUB,** serves as information headquarters for Barcelona's cultural festivals. Be sure to also check out the famous rainbow stained-glass façade of the **Casa Beethoven** nextdoor at no.97, now a well-stocked music store. *(Las Ramblas 99, on the corner of C. Carme. M: Liceu.)933 16 10 00. Open Tu-Sa 11am-8:30pm and Su 11am-3pm. Free.)*

BARRI GÒTIC

The Barri Gòtic offers everything that Barcelona's Modernist architecture and l'Eixample do not. Its narrow, winding streets have developed out of centuries of architectural and cultural mixing, from early Roman through modern times. In 1714, the neighborhood waged campaign for Catalan independence against Felipe V. As punishment, Felipe V built walls around the Barri Gòtic, turning it into a ghetto. It was not until a cholera epidemic in the 1850s that the Spanish government permitted the walls to be torn down. The narrow streets are crowded with an endless array of historical sights, shops, and eateries. The Barcelona Tourist Office leads professional **walking tours** from the information office in Pl. Catalunya; buy tickets there or at the Ajuntament in Pl. St. Jaume. *(For walking tours, call 906 301 282. Sa-Su at 10am in English and noon in Catalan and Spanish. Buy tickets in advance. 1100ptas/€7, children under 12 500ptas/€3.)*

ESGLÉSIA CATEDRAL DE LA SANTA CREU. La Catedral de la Santa Creu is one of Barcelona's most popular monuments. Three separate buildings have existed on the site: a fourth-century basilica, an 11th-century Romanesque church, and the present Gothic cathedral, begun in 1298. The façade comes from another era; it was tacked on to the main structure by architect Josep Mestres in 1882. The first thing you will see upon entering is the **choir.** Beyond the choir are the the altar with the bronze **cross** designed by Frederic Marès in 1976, and the sunken **Crypt of Santa Eulalia,** one of Barcelona' s patron saints. Completed in 1334, the crypt holds a white marble sarcophagus which depicts scenes from the saint's martyrdom at age 13. Also at rest is **Saint Olegario,** who died in 1137. His preserved body, in full regalia, is visible through glass by the **Chapel of El Santo Cristo de Lepanto.** Outside of the sacristy are the **tombs** of Ramon Berenguer I and his wife. To the right of the tombs is the **cloister,** home to 13 white geese, reminders of Sta. Eulalia's age at her death. At the right corner of the cloister, coming from the cathedral, you will find the **cathedral museum,** whose most notable holding is Bartolomé Bermejo's *pietà*, the image of Christ dying in the arms of his mother. The front of the cathedral is the place to catch a performance of the **sardana,** the traditional Catalan dance. Performances occur Sunday after mass at noon and 6:30 pm. *(M: Jaume I. In Pl. Seu, up C. Bisbe from Pl. St. Jaume. Cathedral open daily 8am-1:30pm and 4-7:30pm. Cloister open 9am-1:15pm and 4-7pm. Elevator to roof open M-F 10:30am-12:30pm and 4:30-6pm, Sa-Su 10:30am-12:30pm, 225ptas/€1.50. 150ptas/€1. Sala capitular 100ptas/€1.)*

PLAÇA DE SANT JAUME. Plaça de Sant Jaume has been Barcelona's political center since Roman times. Two of Catalunya's most important buildings have dominated the square since 1823: the **Palau de la Generalitat,** the headquarters of Catalunya's autonomous government, and the **Ajuntament,** the city hall. *(Palau de la Generalitat open the 2nd and 4th Su of each month 10am-2pm. 30min. Mandatory tours in English, French, Spanish, and Catalan. Ajuntament open Sa-Su 10am-1:45pm. Free.)*

TEMPLE OF AUGUSTUS. Inside the protective walls of the **Centre Excursionista Catalunya,** an outdoors club, are four columns from the Roman **Temple of Augustus.** Built on the former summit of Mont Tàber 2000 years ago, the now eye-level columns have not moved from their original position. *(M: Jaume I. Enter Pl. St. Jaume from C. Bisbe, and a sharp left to C. Paradís. Inside the Centre Excursionista de Catalunya building. The protective gate opens Tu-Su 10am-2pm, but the remains are visible through the gate as well.)*

OTHER SIGHTS. Palaces and museums congregate on C. Comtes. The former royal home, the **Palau Reial,** is the pearl of the plaça, which also holds the **Museu d'Història de la Ciutat** (see p. 326) and **Museu Frederic Marès.** *(Admission to the history museum includes the royal palace.)* Lively student hangout **Plaça del Pí** and the old **Església del Pí** are just off Las Ramblas. *(From Las Ramblas, follow C. Cardenal Casañas.)*

LA RIBERA

As the stomping ground of fishermen and merchants, La Ribera has always had a plebian feel; recently, the neighborhood has evolved into Barcelona's bohemian nucleus, with art galleries, chic eateries, and exclusive bars.

PALAU DE LA MÚSICA CATALANA. In 1891, the Orfeó Catalan choir society commissioned Modernist Lluís Domènech i Montaner to design this must-see concert venue. The music hall glows with stained-glass, an ornate chandelier, marble reliefs, intricate woodwork, and ceramic mosaics. Concerts given at the Palau include all varieties of symphonic and choral music in addition to more modern of pop and jazz. *(C. Sant Francese de Paula, 2. ☎932 95 72 00; www.palaumusica.org. M: Jaume I. Off Via Laietana by Pl. Urquinaona. Entrance only with a tour. Reserve ahead at the gift shop next door. Palau open daily 10am-3:30pm, Aug. 10am-6pm. Box office open M-Sa 10am-9pm, Su from 1hr. before concert. Check the Guía del Ocio for listings. 800ptas/€5, students and seniors 600ptas/€4. Concert tickets 1300-26000ptas/€8-125. MC/V.)*

SANTA MARIA DEL MAR. Built in the 14th century in a quick 55 years, Santa Maria del Mar (Mary of the Sea) was important to the growing population of sailors living in La Ribera at the time. At a distance of 13m apart, the supporting columns span a width greater than any other medieval building in the world. A fascinating example of the limits of Gothic architecture—were it 2 ft.higher, it would collapse from structural instability. Church holds classical, gospel, and folk concerts; call for information. *(☎933 10 23 90. Open M-Sa 9am-1:30pm and 4:30-8pm, Su 9am-2pm and 5-8:30pm. For concert info, call 933 19 05 16.)*

OTHER SIGHTS. Museums, art galleries, and palaces of 16th-century bureaucrats crowd **C. Montcada.** The **Museu Picasso** (see p. 325) inhabits several such mansions, and the **Galería Maeght** (C. Montcada, 26;), an art gallery, was once a medieval manor. Also worth a look is Antoni Tàpies' **Homenatge a Picasso,** a sculpture on Pg. Picasso in front of the Museu Geologia. The 1983 jumble of wood and steel was

MATING GAME. You've seen him in your dreams. You can feel his presence. Finally, it's time for a private audience. Though some call him Snowflake, in his native Catalan he's Floquet de Neu (Floquet to his friends), the world's only white gorilla, who bears more than a passing resemblance to Willie Nelson. Taken from the forest in west Africa in the 60s, Floquet has been the toast of Barcelona ever since.

Spend some time at the zoo (see p. 320), and you may observe a behavior common to both captive and wild gorillas–coprophagy, or eating one's own excrement. Vitamin D is not available in the gorillas' natural habitat, but is produced by bacteria in their hind gut; eating everything twice helps satisfy their nutritional needs. Floquet has made an art form of the practice, and often spends minutes on end smearing and sampling, strange expressions passing over his countenance all the while.

Stay longer, and you may see a behavior not common in the wild–incest. With gorillas and the other apes in endangered species status, zoos are making concerted efforts to aid breeding. Because of Floquet's dashing good looks, special measures are taken in his case. In an effort to breed another white gorilla (Floquet's blue eyes mean he is not an albino, but lucistic), he has been encouraged to breed with his daughters. With over a dozen offspring to date, there is still no Floquet Jr.; Floquet de Neu may be the last of his kind, all the more reason for a pilgrimage to Barcelona.

inspired by Picasso's comment that "A picture is not something to decorate a sitting room, but a weapon of attack and of defense against the enemy."

PARC DE LA CUITADELLA

Barcelona's military resistance to the Bourbon monarchy in the early 18th century convinced Felipe V to quarantine Barcelona's influential citizens in the Ciutadella, a large citadel on what is now Pg. Picasso. The city razed the fortress in 1868 and replaced it with the peaceful promenades of Parc de la Ciutadella. Host of the 1888 Universal Exposition, the park now harbors several museums, well-labeled horticulture, the wacky **Cascada** fountains, a pond, and a zoo. Buildings of note include Domènech i Montaner's Modernist **Castell dels Tres Dragons** (now **Museu de Zoología**), the **geological museum** (a few buildings down Pg. Picasso from M. Zoología), and Josep Amergós's **Hivernacle.** Expo '88 also inspired the **Arc de Triomf,** just across Pg. Pujades from the park. *(M: Barceloneta or Arc de Triomf.)*

PARC ZOOLÒGIC . Quarters are cramped for the zoo's residents, but the zoo still draws park-goers young and old. Stately and saucy **Floquet de Neu** (Snowflake), the world's only white gorilla, titillates tourists of all ages, although the elephants, hippos, seals also draw crowds. The zoo also features an aquarium, petting zoo, and the famous **Senyoreta del Paraigua** sculpture. *(M: Ciutadella. Follow C. Wellington out of the Metro to a separate entrance. Inside the park, the entrance is next to the Museu d'Art Modern. ☎932 25 67 80. Open Nov.-Feb. 10am-5pm, Mar. and Oct. 10am-6pm, Apr. and Sept. 10am-7pm, May-Aug. 9:30am-7:30pm. Entrance 1600ptas/€10; children under 12 1025ptas/€6; over 65 925ptas/€5.50. After 5pm May-Sept., entrance 1050ptas/€6, children 625ptas/€4, and seniors 575ptas/€3.50. AmEx/D/MC/V.)*

EL RAVAL

PALAU GÜELL. Gaudí's Palau Güell (1886)—haunting Modernist residence built for patron Eusebi Güell (of Park Güell fame)—has one of Barcelona's most spectacular interiors. Güell and Gaudí spared no expense on this home. The 20 unique rooftop chimneys display Gaudí's first use of the *trencadis*—the covering of surfaces with irregular shards of ceramic. *(C. Nou de La Rambla, 3-5. ☎933 17 39 74; fax 17 37 79. M: Liceu, two blocks from the Opera Liceu, off Las Ramblas. Visits by tour only, every 15min. Open M-Sa 10am-1pm and 4:15-7pm. 400ptas/€2.40; students 200ptas/€1.20.)*

L'EIXAMPLE

The Catalan Renaissance and the growth of Barcelona during the 19th century pushed the city past its medieval walls and into modernity. Ildefons Cerdà drew up a plan for a new neighborhood which called for a geometric grid of squares, softened by octagonal intersections with cropped corners. Cerdà envisioned both an escape from the stress that had festered in the overcrowded Barri Gòtic as well as a new city where people of all social classes could live side by side. He called each 10-block area a *massa (*neighborhood) and allotted each its own school, marketplace, and park. However, l'Eixample (pronounced luh-SHOMP-luh) did not thrive as a utopian community but rather as a playground for the bourgeois.

LA SAGRADA FAMÍLIA. Only Antonio Gaudí could draw thousands of tourists to an unfinished church. He gave 43 years of his life to the task, living in the basement before his death in 1926. Since, construction has been erratic and controversial. Of the three proposed façades, only the first (a smaller one), the Nativity Façade, was finished under Gaudí. A furor has arisen over recent additions, especially sculptor Josep Subirach's Cubist Passion Façade on C. Sardenya, which is criticized for being inconsistent with the Gaudí-endorsed Nativity Façade. The churches' staircases and towers are not for anyone with a fear of heights or closed spaces. The **museum** displays artifacts relating to the building's construction. *(C. Mallorca, 401. M: Sagrada Família. ☎932 07 30 31. Open Nov.-Feb. 9am-6pm, elevator 9:30am-5:45pm; Mar., Sept., and Oct. 9am-7pm, elevator 9:30am-6:45pm; April-Aug. 9am-8pm, elevator 9:30am-7:45pm. Guided tours Apr.-Oct. daily 11:30am, 1pm, 4pm, and 5:30pm; Nov.-Mar. F-M 11:30am and 1pm; 500ptas/€3. Tickets 850ptas/€5, students 650ptas/€4.50.)*

LA MANZANA DE LA DISCÒRDIA. A short walk from Pl. Catalunya, the odd-numbered side of Pg. Gràcia between C. Aragó and Consell de Cent is popularly known as *la manzana de la discòrdia* (block of discord), referring to the stylistic clashing of the three buildings. Regrettably, the bottom two floors of **Casa Lleó i Morera,** by Domènech i Montaner, were destroyed to make room for a fancy store, but you can buy the **Ruta del Modernisme pass** (see p. 317) there and take a tour of the upstairs, where sprouting flowers, stained glass, and legendary doorway sculptures adorn the interior. Puig i Cadafalch opted for a geometric, Moorish-influenced pattern on the façade of **Casa Amatller** at #41. Gaudí's balconies ripple like skulls, and tiles sparkle in blue-purple glory on **Casa Batlló,** #43. The most popular interpretation of Casa Batlló is that the building represents Catalunya's patron Sant Jordi (St. George) slaying a dragon; the chimney plays the lance, the roof, the scaly roof is the dragon's back, and the bony balconies are the remains of his victims. Also of interest is **Fundació Tàpies** (seep. 326), designed by Domènech i Montaner, around the corner from *la manzana.*

CASA MILÀ (LA PEDRERA). Modernisme buffs argue that the spectacular Casa Milà apartment building, an undulating mass of granite popularly known as *La Pedrera* (the Stone Quarry), is Gaudí's most refined work. Note the intricate ironwork around the balconies and the irregularity of the front gate's egg-shaped window panes. The roof sprouts chimneys that resemble armored soldiers, one of which is decorated with broken champagne bottles. Rooftop tours provide a closer look at the "Prussian helmets" (spiral chimneys inspired by the helmets worn in Wagner's operas). The winding brick attic (recently restored along with the rooftop in a multi-million-*peseta* project) has been transformed into the **Espai Gaudí,** a multimedia presentation of Gaudí's life and works. A refurnished and restored apartment awaits one floor below, as an example of the fine, captivating interior of Gaudí homes. *(Pg. Gràcia, 92. ☎934 84 59 95. Open daily 10am-8pm. 1000ptas/€6; students and over 65 500ptas/€3. Free guided tours M-F 5:30pm in English and Catalan, 6pm in Spanish, Sa-Su 11am in English and Catalan, and 11:30pm in Spanish.)*

HOSPITAL DE LA SANTA CREU I SANT PAU. The Modernist Hospital de la Santa Creu i Sant Pau was Domènech i Montaner's (of Palau fame) masterpiece. In 1905, Domènech i Montaner designed pavilions that would serve only 28 patients. The interior is painted in shades of green is full of natural light. Domènech i Montaner studied wind patterns and put infectious wards at the back of the hospital, at the end of the current. He also built underground tunnels for staff, to keep the grounds feeling as unlike a hospital as possible. The most interesting attraction is the main administrative building, which is steeped in symbolism. The sculptured figures on

FAR-OUT FAÇADE Gaudí was religious, and his plans for La Sagrada Família (see p. 321) called for elaborate symbolism in almost every element of the church. On the left of the **Passion Façade,** a snake lurks behind Judas, symbolizing the disciple's betrayal of Jesus. The 4x4 box of numbers next to him contains 310 combinations of four numbers, each of which adds up to 33, Christ's age at death. The faceless woman in the center of the façade, **Veronica,** represents the Biblical woman with the same name and the miraculous appearance of Christ's face on the cloth she wiped him with. The cypress tree on the **Nativity Façade** has been interpreted as a stairway to heaven (cypress trees do not put down deeper roots with time but still grow taller); the tree is crowned with the word "Tau," Greek for the name of God. The top of the eight finished towers carries the first letter of one of the names of the apostles. Inside, on the **Portal of the Rosary,** overt references to modern life lurk amongst more traditional religious imagery: the Temptation of Man is represented in one carving by the devil handing a bomb to a terrorist and in another by his waving a purse at a prostitute.

the front façade represent faith, hope, charity, and work, and the multi-domed ceiling of the entrance foyer is covered with the symbols of Catalunya. *(Entrance at corner of C. Cartagena and C. St. Antonia Maria Claret. M: Hospital de St. Pau. ☎934 88 20 78. 50min. tours Sa-Su 10am-2pm every 30min., in Catalan, Spanish, or English. 700ptas/€4, students and over 65, 500ptas/€3.)*

AROUND THE PORT

Barcelona's drive to refurbish its seafront resulted in the expansion of Port Vell, the port complex, and waterfront area near Monument a Colom that clamors with seaside eateries, loud discos, and overpriced shops. After moving the coastal road underground, the city opened **Moll de la Fusta,** a pedestrian zone that leads down to the docks past the **Museu d'Història de Catalunya** (see p. 326). The wavy bridge **Rambla de Mar** links Moll de la Fusta with the bright **Maremagnum** mall (see p. 333).

L'AQUÀRIUM DE BARCELONA. This aquarium—the largest in Europe—is an aquatic wonder, featuring copious amounts of octopi and a plethora of penguins. The highlight is an 80m-long glass tunnel through an ocean tank of sharks, sting rays, and one two-dimensional fish. *(Moll d'Espanya, next to Maremagnum. M: Drassanes. ☎932 21 74 74. Open daily July-Aug. 9:30am-11pm; Sept.-June 9:30am-9pm. 1550ptas/€9; children under 12 and seniors 950ptas/€6.)*

BOAT TOURS. Las Golondrinas, Portal de la Pau (☎934 42 31 06). M: Drassanes, at the foot of the Monument a Colom. Ferries chug around the Port Vell. (35min.; July-Aug. daily every 35min. 11:30am-7:30pm, Sept.-June every hr. M-F noon-6pm and Sa-Su noon-7:30pm; 525ptas/€3, children 275ptas/€2.) A longer excursion includes a **tour of Port Olímpic.** (1½hr.; July-Aug. daily every 45min. 11:30am-7:30pm, Sept.-June 3 per day 11am-4:30pm; round-trip 1325ptas/€8, seniors and students 950ptas/€6, kids ages 4-10 575ptas/€3.50.)

VILA OLÍMPICA. The Vila Olímpica was built to house athletes and entertain tourists for the 1992 Summer Olympics. Today it is home to parks, a mall, and offices. Toward the Mediterranean, **Port Olímpic** is an L-shaped complex flaunting twin towers, a metallic fish sculpture, docked sailboats, and upscale discos and restaurants. **Barceloneta's** (see p. 329) mediocre beaches—good for a tan or drooling over naked Spaniards—stretches out from the port. *(From M: Ciutadella/Vila Olímpica, walk along the waterfront on Ronda Litoral toward the 2 towers.)*

MONTJUÏC

Throughout Barcelona's history, whoever controlled Montjuïc (Hill of the Jews) controlled the city. Dozens of despotic rulers have modified the **fortress,** built atop the ancient Jewish cemetery; Franco made it one of his "interrogation" headquarters. Somewhere in the recesses of the structure, his *beneméritos* ("honorable ones") shot Catalunya's former president, Lluís Companys, in 1941. The fort was not available for recreation until Franco rededicated it to the city in 1960. A huge stone monument expresses Barcelona's (forced) gratitude for the return of the fortress. Since reacquiring the mountain, Barcelona has made it a tourist attraction, and it was chosen as the site of the 1992 Olympics. To get to **Parc de Montjuïc,** take the Metro to Pl. Espanya (M: Espanya) and catch bus #50 either at Av. Reina María Cristina (flanked by 2 large brick towers) or as it heads up the hill (every 10min.). Outdoor escalators lead up to the Montjuïc from the Palau Nacional.

CASTELL DE MONTJUÏC. A visit to this historic fortress and its **Museum Militar** is a great way to get an overview of the city—both of its layout and its history. From the castle's exterior *mirador*, gaze over the city. Enjoy coffee at the café while cannons stare you down. *(M: Paral.lel. Take the funicular to Av. Miramar and then the Teleféric de Montjuïc. The funicular runs from inside M: Paral.lel at Av. Paral.lel and Nou de la Rambla. Teleféric open M-Sa 11:15am-9pm. Alternatively, walk up the steep slope on C. Foc, next to the funicular station. Open Mar. 15-Nov. 15 Tu-Su 9:30am-8pm, Nov. 16-Mar. 14 Tu-Su 9:30am-5pm. Museum 400ptas/€2.50. Mirador only, 100ptas/€0.60.)*

FONTS LUMINOSES. The "Illuminated Fountains" run along Av. Reina Maria Cristina and are dominated by the central **Font Mágica** (Magic Fountain). The fountains are visible from Pl. Espanya, in front of hilltop **Palau Nacional** (home of the MNAC; see **Museums,** p. 326). On weekends, colored lights and cheesy music bring the fountains to life in a spectacular display. *(Shows June-Sept. Th-Su every 30min., 9:30pm-12:30am; Oct.-May F-Sa 7-8:30pm. Free.)*

ANELLA OLÍMPICA. The "Olympic Ring" is the area of Olympic facilities Barcelona inaugurated in 1929 with the **Estadi Olímpic de Montjuïc** in its failed bid for the 1932 Games. Over 50 years later, architects Federic Correa and Alfons Milà finished the esplanade in preparation for the 1992 Olympics. *(☎934 26 20 89. Open daily 10am-8pm. Free.)* Designed by Japanese architect Arata Isozaki, the **Palau d'Esports Sant Jordi** is the most technologically sophisticated of the Olympic structures. *(☎934 26 20 89. You must call in advance to visit.)* Test your swimming mettle in the **Olympic pools** (see p. 329) or visit the **Galeria Olímpica** exposition on the games at the south end of the stadium. *(☎934 26 06 60. Open Oct.-Mar. M-F 10am-1pm and 4-6pm; Apr.-May M-F 10am-2pm and 4-7pm; June M-Sa 10am-2pm and 4-7pm, Su 10am-2pm; July-Sept. M-Sa 10am-2pm and 4-8pm, Su 10am-2pm. 400ptas/€2.40; students 350ptas/€2; seniors 170ptas/€1. Combined visit with Poble Espanyol 1200ptas/€7.)*

POBLE ESPANYOL. Built for the International Exhibition in 1929, this tourist-oriented "town" features replicas of sights from every region of Spain. During the day, Poble Espanyol is a souvenir bazaar with mediocre restaurants, but at night the disco scene brings new meaning to the word "party." *(On Av. Marqués de Comillas, to the right when facing the Palau Nacional. M: Espanya, up the escalators. ☎935 08 63 00. Open Su 9am-midnight, M 9am-8pm, Tu-Th 9am-2am, F-Sa 9am-4am. 975ptas/€5.80; students 775ptas/€5; seniors 600ptas/€3.50; children 7-12 550ptas/€3; guided tour 500ptas/€3. MC/V.)*

GRÀCIA

PARK GÜELL. Eusebi Güell commissioned the Gaudí to fashion a garden city in the tradition of Hampstead Heath in England; the English spelling of "park" is a nod to the Anglo gardens. Intended by Güell as a housing development, the park was to have 60 houses; only three houses went up before Gaudí passed away.

As a housing development, it was a failure; as a park, it is fantastic. Combining natural influences with Catalan and religious symbolism, Park Güell is dreamy and whimsical, organic and tactile. The most eye-catching structures are by the entrance on C. Olot. The entrance's **Palmetto Gate** is flanked by two dwarfish buildings, inspired by a *Hansel and Gretel*; the spire-topped construction belonging to the children and the other, crowned with a red poisonous mushroom, belonging to the witch. Up the double staircase, tourists jostle for a photo with the gaping **lizard** fountain, drooling into the basin below. The stairs lead to the **Hall of One Hundred Columns (Teatro Griego),** which actually only has 86 columns. The hall's multicolored medallions, designed by Gaudí's right-hand man Josep Marià Jujol, are made with bits of mirror, glasses, and even porcelain dolls. Stairs next to the hall lead up to the **Pl. de la Naturalesa,** surrounded by the **Serpentine bench,** the longest park bench in the world. The shape of the bench is not only aesthetic, but comfy. The park's summit commands tremendous views of the city.

To the right of the lizard fountain when walking up the stairs, follow the wide path past the flower beds and continue to the right as smaller paths branch off and the path twists uphill to the pink **Casa-Museu Gaudí.** Farther ahead, the **Pont dels Enamorats** offers views of the city all the way to the sea. Along the left-hand side, Gaudí's **stone trees**—tall columns topped with plants—are interspersed with benches which seem to hang in midair. Around the next curve is **Casa Trias** (1905), which is owned by Trías Domènech's family. *(Bus #24 from Pl. Catalunya stops at the upper entrance. From M: Vallarca, walk down Av. l'Hospital Militar for 4 blocks, turn left onto Baixada de la Glòria, and take the escalators to the park's back entrance. Park ☎932 19 38 11. Free. Open daily May-Sept. 10am-9pm; Mar.-Apr. and Oct. 10am-7pm; Nov.-Feb. 10am-6pm.)*

PLAÇAS. Gràcia has several notable plaças. The first of these is **Plaça Rius i Taulet,** home to the **Torre del Reloj** (Clocktower), an emblem of the Revolution of 1868. **Plaça del Diamant,** on nearby C. Astúries, was made famous by Catalan author Mercè Rodoreda's novel of the same name. **Plaça del Sol** is full of cafés and bars and crowded with locals at night. Protest graffiti fills the plaça, touching on everything from Catalan independence to the Zapatista uprising in Chiapas, Mexico.

CASA VICENS. One of Gaudí's earliest projects, Casa Vicens was designed for a local tile manufacturer, is fittingly decorated with blocks of cheerful ceramic tiles. The *casa* illustrates the influence of Arabic architecture and a rigidness that is uncharacteristic of Gaudí's later works. The hard lines contrast with Gaudí's trademarkn fluid ironwork on the balconies and façade. *(C. Carolines, 24-26. M: Fontana, walk uphill Gran de Gràcia and turn left onto C. Carolines.)*

ELSEWHERE IN THE ZONA ALTA

MONESTIR DE PEDRALBES. The artistic high-water of this Gothic church and 14th-century cloister is in the **Capella Sant Miguel,** where murals by Ferrer Bassa depict the seven joys of Mary, as well as several of her sorrows. The monastery also received a part of the Thyssen-Bornemisza collection in 1993. *(Baixada del Monestir, 9. FGC: Reina Elisenda. A 10min. walk down Pg. Reina Elisenda. ☎932 03 92 82. 600ptas/€4; students 300ptas/€2. Combined ticket with art collection 800ptas/€5; students 500ptas/€3. Open Oct.-Apr. Tu-Su, 10am-2pm. June-Sept. 10am-3pm.)*

PARC DE COLLSEROLA. People come to these 16,000 acres of greenery to hike, bike, and horseback ride. Before entering the park, be sure to stop at the **Centre d'Informació** (the FGC train to the Baixador de Vallvidrera stop and follow the sandstone steps for 10min.), which has loads of info on all the park's attractions.

The park is full of natural and man-made sights worth tracking down. Numerous lookout points in the park offer good views of the city and surrounding hills, especially the **Mirador de Vila Paula.** Take the FGC train from Pl. Catalunya to the Peu del Funicular stop, walk up the hill from the station on Av. de Vallvidrera, follow it along the tight, immediate left turn, then a right turn, and then a few smaller twists and curves (about 15min.); it will be up the hill on your right. Also inside the park are more than 50 notable archaeological finds. The **Cova de l'Or,** the oldest cave dwelling in the park, dates back to the Neolithic period, 6000 BC (although it could not be visited at the time of publication). The terraced remains of a 4th-to-6th century BC Laietana dwelling can be seen on **La Penya del Moro** hillside. **Castellciuró,** a castle built in the 14th century over 12th-century remains, doubles as a particularly good lookout point. *(Tourist office: Carretera de l'Església, 92. ☎932 80 35 52. Office open daily 9:30am-3pm except Dec. 25-26 and Jan. 1 and 6.)*

MUSEUMS

When I was a child, my mother said to me, "If you become a soldier, you'll be a general. If you become a monk, you'll end up as the Pope." Instead, I became a painter and wound up as Picasso.

—Pablo Picasso

Barcelona has always been on the cutting edge of defining what can be included in the category of "art;" the city's museums range from Surrealist art and classical masterpieces to historical exhibits and one-of-a-kind curiosities. Culture vultures should invest in the **Articket,** which gives half-price admission to six of Barcelona's premier art centers, including the Museu Nacional d'Art de Catalunya (MNAC; see p. 326), the Fundació Miró (see p. 325), the Fundació Tàpies (see p. 326), the Centre de Cultura Contemporània de Barcelona (CCCB; see p. 327), and the Museu d'Art Contemporani (MACBA; seep. 326). The ticket, available at tourist offices (see p. 307) and at the museums, goes for 2496ptas/€15, and is valid for three months.

MUSEU PICASSO. This incredible museum traces the development of Picasso as an artist, with a collection of his early works that weaves through five connected mansions once occupied by nobility. Although the museum offers little from Picasso's well-known middle years, it boasts the world's best collection of work from his formative period in Barcelona. The collection also includes lithographs and pencil sketches by an 11-year-old Picasso, and an excellent display of the artist's Cubist interpretations of Velázquez's *Las Meninas*, which hangs in the Prado in Madrid. *(C. Montcada, 15-19. ☎933 19 63 10. M: Jaume I. Walk down C. Princesa from the Metro, and turn right on C. Montcada. Open Tu-Sa 10am-8pm, Su 10am-3pm. 800ptas/€5; students and seniors 400ptas/€2.50; under 16 free. Free first Su of each month.)*

MUSEU DEL FÚTBOL CLUB BARCELONA. A close second to the Picasso Museum as Barcelona's most visited museum, the FCB museum merits all the attention it gets. Sports fans will appreciate the storied history of the team; The high point is the chance to enter the stadium and take in the enormity of Camp Nou, see p. 328. *(C. Aristides Maillol, next to the stadium. ☎93 496 36 08. M: Collblanc. Enter through access gates 7 or 9. Museum entrance 575ptas/€4; with 45min. stadium tour 1300ptas/€8; children under 13 425ptas/€4; with stadium tour 700ptas/€4.50. Tours begin at 10:30am, 11:30am, 12:30, 3, 4, and 5pm. Open M-Sa 10am-6:30pm, Su 10am-2pm.)*

FUNDACIÓ MIRÓ. Designed by Miró's friend Josep Luís Sert and tucked into the side of Montjuïc, the Fundació links interior and exterior spaces with massive windows and outdoor patios. Sky lights illuminate an extensive collection of statues, paintings, and tapestries from Miró's career, including the stunning Barcelona Series, which depicts Miró's personal reaction to the Spanish Civil War and several paintings from Miro's Las Constelaciones series, a reaction to Nazi invasion during World War II. His best-known pieces in the museum include *El Carnival de Arlequin*, *La Masia*, and *L'or de L'azuz*. Room 13 displays experimental work by young artists. The Fundació also sponsors music recitals and film festivals. *(Av. Miramar, 71-75. ☎934 43 94 70. Take the funicular from inside the M: Paral.lel station at Av. Paral.lel and Nou de la Rambla. When you get off, turn left out of the funicular station; the museum is a 5min. walk up on the right. Open July-Sept. Tu-W and F-Sa 10am-8pm, Th 10am-9:30pm, Su 10am-2:30pm; Oct.-June Tu-W and F-Sa 10am-7pm, Th 10am-9:30pm, Su 10am-2:30pm. 1200ptas/€7; students and seniors 650ptas/€4.)*

MUSEU D'ART MODERN. This museum, a part of MNAC (see below), houses of paintings, sculptures, and furniture by 19th-century Catalan artists. Works include Ramon Casas's *Plein Air*, Josep Llimona's *Desconsol*, Isidre Nonell's paintings of Gypsy women, and a room of Josep Clará's *Noucentiste* sculptures. The museum also displays furniture designed by Gaudí for Casa Battló (see p. 321). Also of note are two of Dalí's early portraits, his only paintings in Barcelona. *(Pl. D'Armes. M: Arc de Triomf. Follow Pg. Til.les to the statue of General Prim at the roundabout and turn left toward Pl. D'Armes; signs point the way. ☎933 19 57 28. 500ptas/€3, students and children 350ptas/€2. Free first Th of every month. Open Tu-Sa 10am-7pm, Su 10am-2:30pm.)*

MUSEU D'ART CONTEMPORANI (MACBA). The MACBA was a collaboration between Barcelona's mayor and the Catalan government to improve El Raval by making it a cultural focalpoint. Architect Richard Meier created a building whose sparse decor would allow the art to speak for itself. The MACBA has received acclaim for its focus on avant-garde art between the two world wars; exhibits focus on three-dimensional art, photography, and video. *(Pl. dels Angels, 1. M: Catalunya. ☎934 12 08 10. Open July-Sept. M, W, F 11am-8pm; Th 11am-9:30pm; Sa 10am-8pm, Su 10am-3pm. Oct.-June M-F 11am-7:30pm, Sa 10am-8pm, Su 10am-3pm. Closed Tu. 800ptas/€5, students 550ptas/€3.50.)*

MUSEU D'HISTORIA DE LA CIUTAT. Exhibits display the history of Barcelona, from its Roman foundations in the 1st-century BC through the sixth-century Visigoth takeover and medieval development to the modern day. The history of the city unfolds as you descend to the original Roman ruins in the basement and continue on toward former royal palaces. The upper floors are home to the **Capella de Santa Agueda,** which stored king's holy relics. *(In Pl. del Rei. M: Jaume I. Walk up C. Jaume I and take the first right. Enter on C. Verguer. ☎933 15 11 11. Open June-Sept. Tu-Sa 10am-8pm, Su 10am-2pm; Oct.-May Tu-Sa 10am-2pm and 4-8pm, Su 10am-2pm. Closed Jan. 1, May 1, June 24, and Dec. 25-26. 600ptas/€4, students 300ptas/€2. Multimedia show 200ptas/€1.20.)*

MUSEU DE L'ERÒTICA. This museum examines the anthropological and sociological insights which can be gleaned from a careful examination of societies' erotica. Um, yeah, okay. Just show us the fly honeys! Exhibits include vintage porn flicks from the 1930s and saucy international sculptures and sketches, depicting more sexual acrobatics than thought humanly possible. Wince at the rather medieval-looking "pleasure chair" and giggle at the sex phones. *(Las Ramblas, 96. ☎933 18 98 65. Open daily 10am-10pm. 1200ptas/€7; students 1000ptas/€6.)*

MUSEU NACIONAL D'ART DE CATALUNYA. Inside the **Palau Nacional,** the MNAC houses the world's finest collection of Catalan Romanesque art and Gothic altarpieces from Catalunya's medieval churches. The museum's Gothic art corridor displays murals from homes in Mallorca; paintings give a political history of the time. *(M: Espanya, walk up Av. Reina María Cristina to the escalators. ☎936 22 03 60; Open Tu-Sa 10am-7pm, Su 10am-2:30pm. 800ptas/€5; 1000ptas/€6 with temporary exhibits; students and seniors 550ptas/€4; 700ptas/€4 with temporary exhibits. Free first Th of every month.)*

FUNDACIÓ TÀPIES. Tàpies's wire sculpture atop Domènech i Montaner's red brick building announces this collection of abstract art. Tàpies's art is characterized by his use of unconventional materials like sand and glue to show the eloquence inherent in simplicity. Most of his works include a "T" in some form. The symbolism of the "T" has been variously interpreted: as a religious cross, sexual penetration, and his own signature. Most of his works are interpreted as protests against the dictatorship and its urban alienation. The other floors feature exhibits of other modern artists. *(C. Aragó, 255, around the corner from the Manzana de la Discòrdia. M: Pg. Gràcia. ☎934 87 03 15. Open Tu-Su 10am-8pm. 700ptas/€4, students 350ptas/€3.)*

MUSEU DEL ARQUEOLÒGIA DE CATALUNYA. The exhibits cover prehistoric times up to the constitution of Catalunya. Several rooms feature a collection of Carthaginian art from Ibiza and excavated relics from the Greco-Roman city of Empúries. *(Pg. Santa Madrona, 39-41. ☎934 23 21 49. From M: Espanya, take bus #55 up the hill to the Palau Nacional. When facing the Palau Nacional, the museum is to the left. Open Tu-Sa 9:30am-7pm and Su 10am-2:30pm. 400ptas/€2.40; students and seniors 300ptas/€1.80.)*

MUSEU D'HISTÒRIA DE CATALUNYA. This high-tech, hands-on museum guides visitors through Catalunya's history, from Roman times through the 20th century. Computer screens, original film clips, and music stations help narrate the region's tumultuous past. *(Pl. Pau Vila, 3, on the waterfront. M: Drassanes. ☎932 25 47 00. 500ptas/€3; students and seniors 350ptas/€2. Open Tu-Sa 10am-7pm, W 10am-8pm, Su 10am-2:30pm.)*

MUSEU DE CERA (WAX MUSEUM). 300 wax celebrities and legends will keep visitors guessing which figures are wax and which are just creepy-looking tourists. *(Las Ramblas, 4, on the left as you face the port. M: Drassanes. ☎933 17 26 49. Open daily, 10am-10pm. 1100ptas/€7; children under 11 625ptas/€4.)*

CENTRE DE CULTURA CONTEMPORÀNIA DE BARCELONA (CCCB). This cultural center investigates modern urban design and sponsors temporary exhibits, dance performances, concerts, workshops, and lectures; check the *Guia del Ocio* for a schedule. *(Casa de Caritat, C. Montalegre, 5. M: Catalunya, next to the MACBA. ☎933 06 41 00. Open Tu-Sa 11am-8pm, Su 11am-3pm. 600ptas/€3.80, students 400ptas/€2.20.)*

MUSEU TAURÍ. This dense collection commemorates the tradition of bullfighting, with pictures of fights and fighters, old posters and stamps, a colorful exhibit on the evolution of the bullfighter's costume throughout time, and a good handful of stuffed bulls' heads on the walls. For tickets to a bullfight, see p. 328. *(Gran Vía de les Corts Catalanes, 749. M: Monumental. ☎932 45 58 04. Open M-Sa 10:30am-2pm and 4-7pm, Su 10:30am. 450ptas/€2.70; children 300ptas/€1.80.)*

MUSEO DEL CALCAT. This hip new museum runs through time with shoes from the first to the 20th century. Adding just a pinch of Hollywood, the museum also displays a number of shoes that have covered celebrity feet. *(Pl. Sant Felip Neri, 5. ☎933 01 45 33. M: Jaume I. Open Tu-Su 11am-2pm. 300ptas/€2.)*

ART GALLERIES

One of the capitals of cutting-edge art, Barcelona showcases many of the latest artistic trends. Many private showings display the works of both budding artists and renowned masters. Most of Barcelona's galleries are located in **La Ribera** around C. Montcada. Three of the best-known in the La Ribera area include: **Gallery Surrealista**, **Galeria Maeght,** and **Galeria Montcada**. For more in-depth gallery info check the *Guía del Ocio*. The **Palau de la Virreina** also has information on cultural events. *(Las Ramblas, 99. Between La Boquería market and C. Carme. M: Liceu. ☎933 01 77 75. Open M-F 10am-2pm and 4-8pm.)*

ENTERTAINMENT

Barcelona has everything from outdoor activities, sports, and bullfights to shopping, cinema, and festivals. Consult the oh-so-informative **Guía del Ocio,** available at newsstands, for info on movies, live concerts, nightlife, and cultural events.

THEATER, MUSIC, AND DANCE

Barcelona offers many options for aficionados, although most performances are in Catalan (*Guía del Ocio* lists the language). Reserve tickets through **Tel Entrada** (24hr. ☎902 10 12 12; www. telentrada.com) or any branch of **Caixa Catalunya** bank (open M-F 8am-2:30pm). The Grec-Barcelona summer festival turns Barcelona into an international theater, music, and dance extravaganza from late June to mid-August (www.grec.bcn.com). For information about the festival, which takes place in venues across the city, ask at the tourist office or swing by the Institut de Cultura de Barcelona (ICUB), Palau de la Virreina, Las Ramblas, 99. (☎933 01 77 75. Open for info year-round M-F 10am-2pm and 4-8pm. Ticket sales M-Sa 10am-9pm. Prices vary, but most performances cost 4000ptas/€24.) Another resource for tickets is the Internet: www.travelhaven.com/activities/barcelona/barcelona.html provides 10% discounts for performances at: Palau de la Música Catalana, Gran teatre del Liceu, and Tablao Flamenco.

Palau de la Música Catalana, C. Sant Francese de Paula, 2 (☎932 95 72 00; www.palaumusica.org). M: Jaume I. Off Via Laietana near Pl. Urquinaona. Head up Via

Laietana to the intersection of C. Ionqueres. Box office open M-Sa 10am-9pm, Su from 1hr. prior to the concert. No concerts in Aug. Tickets 1300-26,000ptas/€8-125. MC/V.

Centre Artesá Tradicionarius, C. Trav. de Sant Antoni, 6-8 (☎932 18 44 85; www.personal4.iddeo.es/tramcat). M: Fontana. Catalan folk music Sept.-June F, 10pm. Tickets 1500ptas/€9. Classes in Catalan music and dance (4000ptas/€24) offered each trimester; call for information. Open M-F 11am-2pm, 5pm-midnight. Closed Aug.

Gran Teatre del Liceu, Las Ramblas, 51-59 (☎934 85 99 13; www.liceubarcelona.com. 24hr. ticket sales, ☎902 33 22 11), on **Las Ramblas.** M: Liceu. Highlights for the 2002 season will include Monteverdi's *L'Orfeo* in February and Mozart's *Die Zauberflöte* (The Magic Flute) in July. Tickets begin at 1000ptas/€6 and rise fast, be sure to reserve tickets well in advance.

El Patio Andaluz, C. Aribau 242 (☎932 68 90 70; fax 68 90 62). M: Diagonal. From the Metro, take a left on Diagonal and a right on C. Aribau. Flamenco dancing. Show and 1 drink 4500ptas/€27; show and *menú del día* from 7950ptas/€48. Daily shows at 9:30pm and midnight. Call 9am-7pm for reservations.

El Tablao de Carmen, Av. Marqués de Comillas, inside Poble Espanyol (☎933 25 68 95). M: Espanya, up the escalators, to the right when facing the Palau Nacional. Restaurant and flamenco show. Open Tu-Su from 8pm; shows Su-Th 9:30pm and 11:30pm, F-Sa 9:30pm and midnight. Call ahead for reservations, which include entrance into Poble Espanyol (see p. 323). Dinner and show 8400ptas/€50; drink and show 4450ptas/€27. MC/V.

FILM

Most screens display the latest Hollywood features, some of which are in the original English. The *Cine* section in *Guía del Ocio* denotes these subtitled films with *V.O. subtitulada (versión original);* other foreign films are dubbed, usually in Catalan. Many theaters have a bargain ticket day (usually Monday). **Filmoteca,** Av. Sarrià, 33, screens classic, cult, and otherwise exceptional films. (☎934 10 75 90. M: Hospital Clínic. 400ptas/€2.40.) **Méliès Cinemas,** Villarroel, 102, shows classics. (☎934 51 00 51. M: Urgell. Tu-Su 600ptas, M 400ptas/€2.40). For new releases and no English, try **Maremagnum,** which has eight screens. (☎934 05 22 22. Tu and Th-Su 750ptas/€4.50, W 600ptas/€3.60.) **Icària-Yelmo,** C. Salvador Espira, 61, in the Olympic Village, boasts 15 screens and V.O. (☎932 21 75 85. Tu-Su 850ptas/€5; M, matinees, and students 600ptas/€4.) The new **IMAX Port Vell** on the Moll d'Espanya next to the aquarium and Maremagnum, has an IMAX screen, an Omnimax 30m in diameter, and 3-D projection. Get tickets at the door, through **ServiCaixa** automatic machines, or by phone. (☎932 25 11 11. Tickets 1000-1500ptas/€6-9.)

FÚTBOL

For the record, the lunatics covered head to toe in red and blue didn't just escape from an asylum—they are **F.C. Barcelona** fans. Grab some face paint and head to **Nou Camp,** which has a box office on C. Aristedes Maillol, 12-18. Get tickets early! **R.C. Deportivo Espanyol,** a.k.a. *los periquitos* (parakeets), Barcelona's second professional soccer team, spreads its wings at **Estadi Olímpic,** Pg. Olímpic, 17-19. This team is not as renowned as the FCB, but it is a great time, and it's **free.** Obtain tickets for both from Banca Catalana or by phoning TelEntrada (24hr. ☎902 10 12 12).

BULLFIGHTS

Although the best bullfighters rarely venture out of Madrid, Sevilla, and Málaga, Barcelona's **Plaza de Toros Monumental,** Gran Via de les Corts Catalans, 743 is an excellent facility, complete with Moorish influences. (☎932 45 58 04. M: Monumental.) Bullfights take place during the summer tourist season, since tourists are about the only people who go (June-Oct. Su at 7pm; doors open at 5:30pm). Tickets are available at travel agencies or ServiCaixa ("la Caixa" banks; ☎902 33 22 11; 2400-12,500ptas/€15-69). The box office also sells tickets before the start of the fight. The cheapest seats are in the Andanada section, in the sun.

RECREATIONAL SPORTS

The tourist offices can provide info about swimming, cycling, tennis, squash, sailing, hiking, scuba diving, white-water rafting, kayaking, or just about any other sport. Though Barcelona tends to ignore its beaches, there's plenty of nearby sand.

Piscines Bernat Picornell, Av. Estadi 30-40 (☎934 23 40 41; fax 26 78 18), to the right when facing the stadium. Test your swimming in the Olympic pools—two gorgeous facilities nestled in stadium seating. 700ptas/€4 for outdoor pool, 1300ptas/€8 for workout facilities including sauna, massage parlor, and gym. Outdoor pool open M-Sa 9am-9pm and Su 9am-8pm. Workout facilities open M-F 7am-midnight, Sa 7am-9pm and Su 7:30am-8pm. **Club Sant Jordi,** C. París 114 (☎934 10 92 61). M: Sants. Passes available for other facilities, including sauna, weights, and stairmaster. Bring your passport. Pool 515ptas/€3 per hr. Open M-F 7am-10pm, Sa 8am-6pm, Su and holidays 9am-2pm. Closed Aug. 1-15.

Beaches: The entire strip between Vila Olímpica and Barceloneta is a long public beach accessible from M: Ciutadella or Barceloneta. The closest and most popular is **Platja Barceloneta,** off Pg. Marítim. Beware (or aware) of nudity on Platja San Sebastià.

BARCELONA

SHOPPING

Many of Barcelona's stores are out of the budget range, but there's nothing wrong with window shopping. Expensive designer shops line **Passeig de Gràcia, Rambla de Catalunya,** and **Portal de l'Angel.** For right off-the-runway style, Barcelona's signature stores include **Zara** (Pg. de Gràcia) and **Mango** (Pg. de Gràcia). Fashion-snobs can be found roaming the avenues of **l'Eixample** while the fashion-smart go for some of the smaller boutiques hidden in side streets off **Las Ramblas.** Funky art, knick-knacks, and jewelry can be found all over **La Ribera.** Barcelona's most unique jewelry shop is probably **Carali** (on C. Cecila right near La Sagrada Família). Antiques get their 15 minutes of fame on **C. Rosa** and **C. Banys Nous** (off Pl. Pi). For more of a mall experience, Pl. Catalunya hosts a number of places like **El Corte Inglés** and **VIPS. Maremagnum,** at Port Vell, has dozens of varied shops.

Bargains abound if you know where to go. One place to try is **Calle Girona,** between C. Casp and Gran Via, in **l'Eixample,** where you'll find a small line-up of discount shops offering girl's clothing, men's dress clothes, shoes, bags, and accessories, and even a coveted Mango outlet. (M: Tetuán. Walk two blocks down Gran Via and take a left on C. Girona.) Another area to try for discounts is the **Mercat Alternatiu (Alternative Market)** on C. Riera Baixa in **El Raval** (M: Liceu. Take C. de l'Hospital—a right off Las Ramblas if you're facing the ocean—and follow it to C. Riera Baixa, the seventh right, shortly after the stone hospital building.) This street is crammed with second-hand and thrift stores covering everything from music to clothes. The area around C. Banys Nou (M: Jaume I), in **La Ribera,** is a great place to look for antiques. Flea markets are a mess of shopping options and great places to find deals. Hold your wallets in **Fira de Bellcaire** and visit **El mercado de Sant Antoni** (M: Sant Antoni. Visit M,W, F, or Sa for the best stuff).

FESTIVALS

Festas abound in Barcelona. Before Christmas, the **Feria de Santa Llúcia** fills Pl. Catedral and the area around the Pl. Sagrada Família with stalls and booths. City residents celebrate **Carnaval** on February 7 to 13, but many head to even more raucous celebrations in Sitges and Vilanova i la Geltrù. Also in February is the **Festa de San Medir,** when neighbors gather at the base of Tibidabo mountain to be caught in a candy-shower orchestrated by men riding down the mountain on horses. Soon thereafter, the **Festa de Sant Jordi** (St. George), April 24, brings feasts in honor of Catalunya's patron saint. This is Barcelona's St. Valentine's Day; men give women roses, and women give men books. On May 11, the **Fira de Saint Ponç,** a traditional market of aromatic and medicinal herbs and honey, sets up in Carrer Hospital, close to Las Ramblas. Barcelona erupts on June 23, the night before **Día de Sant Joan.** Bonfires roar throughout the city, unsupervised children play with fireworks, and the fountains of Pl. Espanya and Palau Reial light up in anticipation of fireworks on Montjuïc.

HOLY SHIT. Christmas in Barcelona is pretty crappy. If you're in the city in December, don't be startled by what appears to be feces in the windows of pastry shops and in the hands of young children. These marzipan cakes, called ***tifas,*** are a popular Christmas treat, disgustingly realistic, but by all reports tasty.

The Catalan have an affinity for the scatological, which the Christmas season brings to the forefront. On Christmas Eve, Catalan families place under their tree a delightful little treat called the *Caga Tío*—the "Shit Log:" a box filled with candy, covered by a blanket. The children then beat the shit out of it (pardon the pun) with sticks, chanting in Catalan: "Shit, log, shit, you don't shit, I'll bash you with my stick!" The log bursts open, rewarding the delighted children for their brutal attack on the defenseless log.

Visitors are also surprised by the infamous *caganer* ("shitter"), a fixture of Catalan nativity scenes. The traditional figures are all there: the baby Jesus, Mary, Joseph, the kings, the shepherds...and so is the *caganer*, a ceramic guy with his pants down, squatting to do his business—and yes, there even is a ceramic business beneath him.

While this character may seem shocking, to outsiders, Catalans swear the little dude has the best intentions. Catalans value regularity and regard the well-formed stool as a sign of fertility and fortune; the *caganer* fertilizes the earth and ensures the health of the land. Stool is a potent, if bizarre, symbol in Catalan culture. The *caganer* has even been officially sanctioned in the world of art through the works of Joan Miró, one of Catalunya's most renowned artists, who seems to have a special liking for the *caganer*.

On August 15-21, city folk jam at Gràcia's **Fiesta Mayor.** Lights blaze in the plazas and streets, and rock bands play all night. On September 11, the **Fiesta Nacional de Catalunya** brings traditional costumes, dancing, and Catalan flags hanging from balconies. The **Feria de Cuina i Vins de Catalunya** draws wine and *butifarra* (sausage) producers to the Rbla. Catalunya. For one week you can sample fine food and drink for a small fee. On September 24, during the **Festa de la Verge de la Mercè,** fireworks light up the city while the traditional *correfocs* (parades of people dressed as devils) whirl pitchfork-shaped sparklers and the city's residents hurl buckets of water at the demons. The beginning of November marks the **Fiesta del Sant Çito,** when locals and tourists alike roll up their sleeves and party on Las Ramblas. Finally, from October through November, the **Festival Internacional de Jazz** hits the city's streets and clubs.

NIGHTLIFE

The whole world knows that Madrid sleeps less than any other city in Europe. Clearly, whoever's counting forgot to take their survey to Barcelona; as in Madrid, nightlife here begins with a 5pm stroll and doesn't wind down until nearly 14 hours later—if even then. Following the afternoon *siesta*, the masses stroll to their favorite *tapas* bars, crowded *plaças*, or outdoor cafés for drinks or a snack with friends. Most people dine between 9 and 11pm, the bar scene picks up around 10pm, and discos start to fill around 2am. Places on Las Ramblas tend to be tourist-dominated, as do the Maremagnum Mall and most portside establishments. L'Eixample is famous for its gay nightlife, and Poble Nou (the neighborhood inland from Port Olímpic) has a good alternative music scene.

BARS AND DISCOS

The Barcelona evening can be divided into thirds, starting with the *bares-restaurantes* or *cervecerías*, moving to the *bares-musicales*, and finishing up with a bang at the *discotecas*. *Cervecerías* ranging from deli-like, *fútbol*-obsessed pubs to elegant lounges fill up on Las Ramblas and in the nearby Barri Gòtic and El Raval. As a general rule, the farther from Las Ramblas and the narrower the street, the less-touristed the bar. The trendiest *bares-musicales* are concentrated in Gràcia. Barcelona's *discotecas* don't heat up until around 2am and usually stay full until dawn, if not later. If you are planning on clubbing, dress the part: no backpacker attire allowed. Also expect to be overcharged for drinks (around 600ptas/€4 for a beer and

1000ptas/€6 and up for mixed drinks unless otherwise listed). Below are some of Barcelona's best bars and discos, but keep in mind that what's popular changes on a daily basis—talk to locals for an up-to-the-minute report.

BARRI GÒTIC

Here, cookie-cutter *cervecerías* and *bares-restaurantes* can be found every five steps. Nightlife in the Barri Gòtic is perfect for chit-chatting your night away, sipping *sangría*, or scoping out your next dance partner.

El Bosq de les Fades. M: Drassanes, in an alley off Las Ramblas, next to the Museu de Cera. From the maniacal geniuses who brought you the wax museum, El Bosq de les Fades (the Forest of Fables) is a fairy tale world, complete with gnarly trees, waterfalls, gnomes, and plush side rooms. Open M-Th until 1:30am, F-Sa until 2:30am.

Jamboree, Pl. Reial, 17. M: Liceu, in the corner immediately to your right coming from Las Ramblas. Once a convent, now a popular music venue. Jazz or blues daily 11pm-1am (M-F 1000ptas/€6 with one drink, Sa-Su 1500ptas/€9, some performances 2000ptas/€12; 200ptas/€1.20 discount if you buy ahead of time at a ServiCaixa machine). At 1:30am, the brick basement turns into a hip-hop club (open until 5am). Upstairs, the attached club **Tarantos** plays pop and salsa for an older crowd. Jamboree cover Su-Th 1200ptas/€7 (includes one drink); F-Sa 2000ptas/€12. Cash only.

New York, C. Escudellers, 5. M: Drassanes, right off Las Ramblas. Once a strip joint, now the biggest club in the Barri Gòtic, with plenty of drink tables overlooking the red-and-black, strobe-lit dance floor. Crowds don't arrive until well after 3am; music includes reggae and British pop. Cover 11:30pm-2am 900ptas/€5.40 (includes 1 beer); 2-5am 1400ptas/€11.40, includes any drink. Open Th-Sa 11:30pm-5am. Cash only.

Molly's Fair City, C. Ferran, 7. M: Liceu. With blaring music and a location next to the Pl. Reial, Molly's has become *the* meeting place for English speakers in the Barri Gòtic. Guinness on tap 800ptas/€5. Open M-F 8pm-2:30am and Sa-Su 7pm-3am. Cash only.

Dot Light Club, C. Nou de Sant Francesc, 7. M: Drassanes, the second right off C. Escudellers coming from Las Ramblas. The atmosphere in this tiny 2-room bar/club is all about funky lighting and cutting edge DJ action. The bouncer outside is not actually looking to bounce; until it gets full, just nod hello and he'll let you in. Th night indie film screenings 10:30pm-midnight. Open Th-Su 10:30pm-2:30am, F-Sa 10:30pm-3am.

Schilling, C. Ferran, 23. M: Liceu. Though chandeliers, marble tables, and tinted windows cry out "exclusive," Schilling is surprisingly diverse and has a lot more breathing space than most bars in the Barri Gòtic. Mixed gay and straight crowd. Excellent *sangría* (pitcher 2000ptas/€12). Mixed drinks 700ptas/€4.20. Wine 250ptas/€1.50. Beer 300ptas/€1.50. Open M-F 9am-2am and Sa-Su 11am-2am. Cash only.

Margarita Blue, C. J. A. Clavé, 6. M: Drassanes, off Las Ramblas, 1 block from the port. With blue margaritas and retro 80s pop tunes, this Mexican-themed bar draws a flamboyant crowd of locals and tourists alike. Su night magic shows, Tu night drag queen performances (around 11:30pm/midnight). Creative Mexican food accompanies the tequila; most dishes run 800-1000ptas/€4.80-6. Blue margaritas 500ptas/€3. Beer 450ptas/€2.70. Tequila shots 300ptas/€1.80. Open Su-W 7pm-2am, Th 7pm-2:30am, F-Sa 7pm-3am (kitchen closes Su-Th at 1am, F-Sa at 1:30am). MC/V.

Fonfone, C. Escudellers, 24. M: Liceu or Drassanes. Atmospheric lighting and good sounds draw 1am crowds here, another bar/club mix with plenty of white leather couches and a small dance area. A different DJ every night. Music includes lounge, house, free style, garage, and more. Open Su-Th 10pm-2:30am, F-Sa 10pm-3am.

Café Royale, C. Nou de Zurbano, 3. M: Liceu, on the tiny street leading out of the corner of Pl. Reial occupied by Jamboree (go left out of the plaça if you're facing Las Ramblas). The self-proclaimed "only" place in the city to chill out to soul and funk, spun by DJ Fred Guzzo. Arrive by midnight if you want one of the velveteen or leather seats; after that, chances are you'll wait up to 1hr to get in. Mixed gay and straight crowd. Open daily 6pm-3am. V; minimum charge 4000ptas/€24.

Glaciar Bar, Pl. Reial, 3. M: Liceu, in the near left corner coming from Las Ramblas. A hidden treasure in a sea of tourist bars. Laid-back, lots of local patrons, plenty of outside tables, and winter photo exhibits. Beer 325ptas/€2. Drinks 650ptas/€4. Jar of *sangría* 1600ptas/€10. Open M-Sa 4pm-2:30am and Su 8am-2:30am. Cash only.

LA RIBERA

In La Ribera, the name of the game is *tapas* bars, where crowds gather to soak up artsy flavor. La Ribera is more of a place to mingle—you may want to brush up on your n your Spanish or Catalan before giving one of these bars a try.

Plàstic Café, Pg. del Born, 19. M: Jaume I, follow C. Princesa and turn right on C. Comerç and right again on Pg. del Born. 'Café' is a misnomer for this packed, trendy bar, with a mix of international, house, and 80s pop spinning in the background. Friendly bartenders do fancy tricks with bottles. Open Su-Th 10pm-2:30am, F-Sa 10pm-3am.

Palau Dalmases, C. Montcada, 20. A self-labeled 'Baroque space' in a 17th century palace fittingly decorated with lavish oil paintings, candelabras, and statues. Romantic candle-lit tables complete the atmosphere. Thursday is opera night with live performances at 11pm (3000ptas/€18, includes one drink). Mixed drinks 900-1500ptas/€5.40-9. Fresh juices 1200ptas/€7.20. MC/V.

Mudanzas, C. Vidreira, 15. M: Jaume I. Everything is black, even the suits. The only color comes from illuminated bottles lining the wall behind the bar. Wide selection of rum, whiskey, and wines (200-800ptas/€2-5). Open Su- F 10am-2am, Sa 11am-2am.

EL RAVAL

Though traditionally El Raval has been home to a local, unpretentious set of bars, this neighborhood to the west of Las Ramblas is rapidly becoming a hotspot for funky new lounge-style hangouts.

La Oveja Negra, C. Sitges, 5. M: Catalunya; go down Las Ramblas and take the 1st right onto C. Tallers; C. Sitges is the 1st left. Gossip (in English) about your European romp over foosball and pitchers of *sangría*. Pitchers of beer 1000ptas/€6, of *sangría* 1500ptas/€9. Open M-Th 9am-2:30am, F 9am-3:30am, Sa-Su 5pm-3am.

London Bar, C. Nou de la Rambla, 34. M: Liceu, off of Las Ramblas. Rub shoulders with unruly, fun-loving expats at this smoky Modernist tavern, around since 1910. Live music nightly, usually rock or blues. Beer 400ptas/€2.40; wine 300ptas/€1.80; absinthe 500ptas/€3. Open F-Sa 7pm-5am, Su, Tu-Th 7pm-3am. Closed M.

(El Café que pone) Muebles Navarro, Riera Alta, 4-6. Friends get friendlier on huge, comfy couches. Beer and wine 300ptas/€1.80. Mixed drinks 600-800ptas/€3-5. Snacks 225-600ptas/€1.30-4. Open Tu-Th 6pm-1am, F-Sa 6pm-2:30am.

Casa Almirall, C. Joaquím Costa, 33. A cavernous space with a decaying ceiling and weathered couches, the laid-back Casa Almirall is Barcelona's oldest bar. The staff will walk you through your first glass of *absenta* (absinthe; 500ptas/€3)–and cut you off after your second. Beer 300ptas/€1.50, mixed drinks 600-800ptas/€3.80-5. Open daily 7pm-3am.

L'EIXAMPLE

L'Eixample has upscale bars and the some of the best gay nightlife in Europe.

La Fira, C. Provença, 171. M: Hospital Clinic. A mix of fun house and circus castaways. Bartenders pour drinks under the big top for a hip crowd in red pleather booths or dangling from carousel swings. Fun house mirrors and clowns complete the picture. DJs spin a mix of funk, disco, and oldies. Open M-Th 10pm-3am and F-Sa 10pm-4:30am.

Dietrich, C. Consell de Cent, 255. M: Pg. de Gràcia. An unflattering painting of Marlene Dietrich greets a mostly gay crowd. Bartenders are scantily clad; 1am nightly drag/strip show. Open Su-Th 10:30pm-2:30am and F-Sa 10:30pm-3:30am.

Buenavista Salsoteca, C. Rosselló, 217. FGC: Provença. This salsa club attracts a laid-back, mixed crowd. The music is irresistible and the dancers are not shy. Free salsa and merengue lessons W, and Th at 10:30pm. Free Su-Th; cover F-Sa 1500ptas/€9 (includes 1 drink). Open W-Th 11pm-4am, F-Sa 11pm-5:30am, Su 8pm-1am.

Salvation, Ronda de St. Pere, 19-21, between C. Bruc and Pl. Urquinaona. M: Urquinaona. A popular gay club with 2 dance floors and pounding house music. Su is a mixed crowd; F and Sa women need special passes, which they can request, midnight-3am at Dietrich (see above). Cover 1500ptas/€9 (includes 1 drink). Open F-Su midnight-6am.

La Boîte, Av. Diagonal, 477. M: Hospital Clinic, club is in courtyard. Big names come to perform in this intimate disco setting. Live jazz, funk, and blues nightly midnight-2am. Music cover 1000-3500ptas/€6-21. Disco free entrance Su-Th after 2am, cover 1800ptas/€11 F-Sa after 2am (includes one drink). Open daily 11:30pm-5am.

POBLE NOU

Poble Nou is the place to be for the untouristed alternative scene in Barcelona. **DIXI 724** (C. Pallars, 97; open F-Su 6pm-3am) boasts cheap beer, a bizarre shark-turned-airplane hanging from the ceiling and tons of space. **Bar Coyote & Co.** (C. Pere IV, 68; open F-Su 6pm-3am) offers a Western twist. **Q3** (C. Pere IV, 49; open F-Sa 6pm-6am), a blasts heavy metal while **Bóveda** (C. Pallars, 97; open F-Sa 6pm-10pm and midnight-6am, Su 6pm-10pm) is club with dance beats. On the same street, **Garatge Club** (C. Pallars, 195) rolls up its door as a venue for rock concerts.

La Ovella Negra (Megataverna del Poble Nou), C. Zamora, 78. From M: Marina, walk 2 blocks along C. Almogàvers and turn right onto C. Zamora. Cavernous medieval tavern; the brother of La Oveja Negra in El Raval and is *the* place to come for the first few beers of the night, at a mere 300ptas/€1.80 per mug. Pool and foosball. Open Th-Su 5pm-3am, disco open Sept.-May. Wheelchair accessible. MC/V.

Razzmatazz, C. Pamplona, 88. 2½ blocks from M: Marina following C. Almogàvers. A 2-in-1 club: choose the front entrance for 3 rooms *or* the back entrance for 2. Cover 1200ptas/€7, includes 1 drink. Open F, Sa, and holidays 1-5am. MC/V.

PORT OLÍMPIC

Port Olímpic caters to tourists with money to burn. A long strip of glitzy clubs fling open their doors at night, and the walkway becomes a carnival of skimpily dressed dance fiends and late-night eaters and drinkers. Mixed drinks are expensive (1000-1200ptas/€6-7). **Pachito** is attracts exorbitantly dressed drag queens, while the **Kennedy Irish Sailing Club** is popular with those who prefer pubbing to clubbing. **There is no cover anywhere.** If you don't like the music in one club, just shove your way out and choose another; the range includes salsa, techno, hip-hop, and plenty of American pop. The complex is open 5pm-6am. Other options line Pg. Marítim.

Luna Mora, C. Ramón Trias Fargas, on the corner with Pg. Marítim. This planetarium-like disco is by far the best place for late-night dancing on the beach. Th no cover, F-Sa 2000ptas/€12. Open Th-Sa 11:30pm-6am; the local crowd doesn't arrive until 3am.

Baja Beach Club, Pg. Marítim, 34. If Baywatch were a club, this would be it. Cover 2000ptas/€12; Su free for ladies, free if you eat dinner. Open June-Sept. M-W 1pm-1am, Th and Su 1pm-5am, F-Sa 1pm-6am; Oct.-May M-W 1-5pm, Th-Sa 1pm-1am.

MAREMAGNUM

Like Dr. Jekyll, Barcelona's biggest mall has more than one personality. At midnight, the complex turns into a tri-level maze of clubs, complete with escalators to cut down on navigating effort. Each club plays its own music for international students, tourists, and the occasional Spaniard. This is not the most "authentic" experience in Barcelona, but it is an experience. No one charges cover; clubs make their money from exorbitant drink prices. Good luck catching a cab home.

MONTJUÏC

Lower Montjuïc is home to Barcelona's epic "disco theme park."

Tinta Roja, C. Creu dels Molers, 17 (☎93 443 32 43). M: Poble Sec. Walk 4 blocks down Av. Paral.lel, away from Montjuïc. Tinta Roja features tango dance shows (F-Sa 12:30am, 1800ptas/€11), tango lessons (Tu 8:30-9:30pm, 3000ptas/€18 each), and a tapas bar. Call for reservations. Open Tu-Th and Su 5pm-1am, F-Sa 5pm-3am.

La Terrazza/Discothèque, Av. Marqués de Comillas. M: Espanya, in Poble Espanyol. By the front gates of Poble Espanyol. Shake it in La Terrrazza's outdoor plaza; the club heads inside (Oct.-May) and becomes Discothèque. Open Th-Su midnight-6am. Cover Th 1800ptas/€12; F 2000ptas/€12 Sa 2500ptas/€15, 1500ptas/€9 Su.

Torres de Ávila, next to the main entrance of Poble Espanyol. M: Espanya. Going strong as one of the city's hottest night spots–complete with glass elevators, 7 bars, and a rooftop terrace. House and techno. Drinks 800-1400ptas/€4,80-8,40. Dress to impress. Cover (includes 1 drink) 2000ptas/€12. Open Th-Sa midnight-6:30 or 7am.

ZONA ALTA

The area around C. de Marià Cubí is great some nightlife, with its eclectic mix of bars and clubs. They are all a substantial walk from FCG: Muntaner (that's why taxis exist). The following listings are some of "Uptown's" happenin' spots.

Otto Zutz, C. Lincoln, 15. FGC: Pl. Molina. Walk downhill on Via Augusta and take C. Lincoln when it splits off to the right. The place to see and be seen. Groove to house, hip hop, funk, and rap beats while Japanimation lights up the top floor. Occasional live music. 2500ptas/€15 cover includes 1 drink, but look for Otto Zutz cover discount cards at bars and upscale hotels all over the city. Open Tu-Sa midnight-6:30am.

Lizard, C. Plató, 15. FGC: Muntaner. Walk uphill on C. Muntaner 2 blocks and turn right. 1 dance floor, 2 bars. Rap, hip-hop, and funk. No cover. Open Th-Sa midnight-3:30am.

Buda, C. Torrent de L'Olla, 134. M: Fontana. Follow C. Astúries and turn right on C. Torrent de L'Olla. Dungeon-esque bar with pool table and darts; a chill spot to unwind. Beer 350ptas/€2, drinks 600ptas/€3.50. Open M-Th 9pm-2:30am, F-Sa 9pm-3am.

Row, C. Roselló, 208. FGC: Provença. Trendy Spaniards and tourists converge on the multi-level, über-hip Row club, grinding to house and techno beats. Door policy leans toward snooty. Cover 2000ptas/€12, drinks 500-800ptas/€3-5. Open W-Sa 11pm-5:30am.

Up and Down, C. Numància, 179, at Diagonal. M: Les Corts. 2-in-1 club has something for everyone. Thirtysomethings live it up in the posh upstairs. Kids go downstairs to 80s and pop. Jacket required. Hardly anyone goes downstairs before 3am. Up: cover 2500ptas/€15, Open Tu-Sa 12am-6am. Down: cover 1500ptas/€9. Open Th-Sa 12am-6am.

NEAR BARCELONA

MONTSERRAT

A 1235m peak protruding from the Río Llobregat Valley with a colorful interplay of limestone, quartz, and slate stone, Montserrat (Sawed Mountain) inspires poets, artists, and travelers. A millennium ago, a wandering mountaineer had a vision of the Virgin Mary; as story spread, pilgrims flocked to the mountain. The monastery to the virgin, founded in 1025 by the opportunistic Bishop Oliba, is today tended by 80 Benedictine monks. During the Catalan *Renaixença* (renaissance) of the 19th century, politicians and artists like poets Joan Maragall and Jacint Verdaguer turned to Montserrat as a source of Catalan legend and tradition. Under Franco, it became a center for Catalan resistance. Today, the site attracts devout worshipers and tourists who come to see the Virgin of Montserrat, her ornate basilica, the art museum, and the panoramic views of the mountain's awesome rocks.

TRANSPORTATION. FGC (☎932 05 15 15) line R5 connects to Montserrat from M: Espanya (1hr.; every hr. 8:36am-5:36pm; roundtrip including cable car 1875ptas/€11); get off at Aeri de Montserrat, not Olesa de Montserrat. From there, catch the **Aeri cable car** to the monastery. (July-Aug. every 15min. daily 9:25am-1:45pm and 2:20-6:35pm;

price included in FCG fare or 975ptas/€6 by itself. Schedules change frequently; call 938 77 7701 to check.) **Autocars Julià** buses to the monastery, from near Estació Sants. (Leaves Barcelona daily at 9am and returns at 5pm. Call 933 17 64 54 for reservations. 1500ptas/€9. MC/V.) If you plan to use the funiculars to hike, consider the **Tot Montserrat** available at tourist offices or in M: Espanya: it covers tickets for the FGC, cable car, mountain funiculars, the Museu de Montserrat (see below), and a meal, all for 5400ptas/€33 (3250ptas/€20 if you buy it at Montserrat without the FCG fare.) Call 938 35 03 84 for a **taxi** from the mountain.

PRACTICAL INFORMATION. Montserrat is not a town, but a monastery with adjacent lodging and food for religious and camera-toting pilgrims. Visitor services are in Pl. Creu, the area straight ahead from the top of the Aeri cable car steps. The **info booth** in Pl. Creu provides free maps, schedules of religious services, and advice on mountain navigation. (☎938 77 72 01. Open daily July-Sept. 9am-7pm; Oct.-June M-F 10am-6pm, Sa-Su 9am-7pm.) For more detailed information, buy the *Official Guide to Montserrat* (900ptas/€5) or the guide to the museum (1000ptas/€6). Services include: **ambulance** or the **mountain rescue team,** ☎904 105 555; **ATMs;** and a **post office** (open daily 10am-1pm).

ACCOMMODATIONS AND FOOD. For room reservations, contact the **Central de Reserves i Informació** (☎938 77 77 01; fax 77 77 24; www.abadiamontserrat.net). The apartment administration office, **Administració de les Delles,** is in the corner of the plaça. (Open daily 9am-1pm and 2-6pm; after 6pm they're at the Hotel Abat Cisneros reception. 2-day minimum stay, 7-day in July and August.) **Abat Marcet** has rooms with bath, TV, heat, and a kitchen. (Singles 1750-4820ptas/€11-29; doubles 3500-6170ptas/€21-37.) **Abat Oliva** has rooms for 2-7 people, but there are only hotplates, and there is no heat, so it closes in winter. (Doubles 3775-4100ptas/€23-25 quads 5925-6460ptas/€36-39). The **Hotel Abat Cisneros,** next to the basilica, has comfortable bedrooms. (Singles 3825-7000ptas/€23-42; doubles 6450-12,200ptas/€39-74. Breakfast included.) The **campsite** is a 5min. walk uphill from the Sta. Cova funicular. (☎938 35 02 51. Open Apr.-Oct. Office open daily 8am-9pm. 400ptas/€2.30 per person, under 12 300ptas/€1.50; 350ptas/€2 per tent. No fires.)

If you want to take food hiking with you, try the 2-aisle **Queviures supermarket** in Pl. Creu. For a quick meal, **Bar de la Plaça** is next to the supermarket (*bocadillos* and hamburgers 400-450ptas/€2.30-2.70; open 9:30am-5pm), and the **cafeteria** is at the top of the cable car steps (open daily Apr.-Nov. 8:15am-8pm, Dec.-Mar. 8:15am-5pm; MC/V). The **self-service cafeteria** for *Tot Montserrat* card-holders is up the hill to the right from the cable car steps (open daily noon-4pm; closed Jan.), as is **Restaurant de Montserrat.** (*Menú del día* 1750ptas/€11 kids 725ptas/€4. Open daily Mar. 15-Nov. 15 noon-4pm. MC/V). The **Restaurant Hotel Abat Cisneros** offers an expensive *menú* (3500ptas/€21) in a nice setting. (Open daily 1-3:30pm and 8-9:45pm. AmEx/MC/V.)

SIGHTS. Above Pl. Creu, the **basilica** looks onto Pl. Santa Noría. Next to the main chapel, a route through side chapels leads to the 12th-century Romanesque **La Moreneta** (the black Virgin), an icon of Mary. (Walkway open Nov.-June M-F 8-10:30am and noon-6:30pm, Sa-Su 8-10:30am, noon-6:30pm, and 7:30-8:30pm; July-Sept. daily 8-10:30am, noon-6:30pm, and 7:30-8:30pm.) Legend has it that St. Peter hid the figure, carved by St. Luke, in Montserrat's caves. The solemn little figure is now showcased in an silver case. For luck, rub the orb in Mary's hand. If you can, catch the renowned **Escalonia boys' choir** sing in the basilica. (Daily at 1pm, except July.) Also in Pl. Santa María, the **Museo de Montserrat** has a variety of art, from a mummified Egyptian to Picasso's *Sardana of Peace*, painted for Montserrat. The Impressionist paintings are its highlights; Ramon Casas' *Madeline Absinthe* is one of the evocative portraits. (Open Nov.-June M-F 10am-6pm, Sa-Su 9:30am-6:30pm; July-Sept. M-F 10am-7pm, Sa-Su 9:30am-7pm. 600ptas/€3.50, students and over 65 400ptas/€2.50.) The **Espai Audiovisual,** at the top of the cable car steps, offers a view of the life of a monk. (125ptas/ €1. Open daily 9am-6pm.)

WALKS. Some of the most beautiful areas of the mountain are accessible only on foot. The **Santa Cova funicular** descends from Pl. Creu to paths which wind to ancient hermitages. (Apr.-Oct. daily every 20min. 10am-6pm; Nov.-Mar. Sa-Su only, 10am-5pm. Roundtrip 400ptas/€2.40.) Take the **St. Joan funicular** for inspirational views of Montserrat. (July-Aug. daily every 20min. 10am-7pm; Sept.-Oct. and Apr.-June 10am-6pm; Nov.-Mar. M-F 11am-4:15pm, Sa-Su 10am-4:25pm. Roundtrip 975ptas/€6. Joint roundtrip ticket with the Sta. Cova funicular 1100ptas/€6.50.) The dilapidated **St. Joan monastery** and **shrine** are only a 20min. tromp from the highest station. The real prize is **Sant Jerónim** (the area's highest peak at 1235m), with its views of Montserrat's mystical rocks. The serrated outcroppings are named for human forms, including "The Bewitched Friars" and "The Mummy." The hike is about 2½ hours from Pl. Creu or a one-hour trek from the terminus of the St. Joan funicular. The paths are long and winding but not all that difficult—after all, they were made for guys wearing long robes. En route, take a sharp left when, after about 45min., you come to the little old chapel—otherwise, you're headed straight for a helicopter pad. On a clear day the hike offers views of Barcelona and surrounding areas. For **guided visits** and hikes, call 938 77 77 01 two weeks in advance. (Hiking tour in English 1000ptas/€6, museum tour 800ptas/€5, joint tour 1400ptas/€14. In Spanish, hiking and museum tour 600ptas/€4 each, joint tour 1100ptas/€7.) For rock-climbing and more athletic hiking in the area, call Marcel Millet at ☎938 35 02 51 or stop by his office next to the Montserrat campsite.

SITGES

Forty kilometers south of Barcelona, beachy Sitges deserves its self-given title "jewel of the Mediterranean," with prime tanning grounds, lively festivals, and a atmosphere of tolerance. A thriving gay community mingles with daytripping Spaniards, tourist families, and twentysomething partyers, all in search of sun and a good time. The climate, with over 300 sunny days a year, sees to the former, while a vibrant nightlife helps with the latter. Through it all, Sitges has not fallen into the commercial traps of typical resort towns; despite booming tourism, the old town somehow has kept traces of its fishing village past, with narrow cobblestoned streets and 19th century architecture. Sitges is the ideal daytrip for when the crowded city beaches just aren't cutting it, and is well worth a couple of days' stay.

TRANSPORTATION. **Cercanías Trains** (☎934 90 02 02) run from Estació Sants to Sitges (40min.; every 15-30min. 5:25am-11:00pm; 350ptas/€2) and continue to **Vilanova** (7min.; every 15-30min. until 11:45pm; 160ptas/€1). The last train from Sitges to Barcelona is at 10:25pm. Rent a car at **Car Office,** Oasis Local, 14 (☎938 11 12 12), at the corner of C. Vilafranca and Vilanova. For a **taxi,** call 938 94 13 29.

PRACTICAL INFORMATION. The train station is on Av. Carbonell, a five minute walk from the center of town. Take a right as you leave the station, and then your third left onto C. Sant Francesc, which leads to the old town, and C. Parellades, the main commercial path, parallel to the ocean. From here, all streets lead to water; Pg. Ribera runs along the central beaches. For a free map, stop by the **tourist office,** Sínia Morera, 1. From the station, turn right onto C. Carbonell and take the first big right. The office is across the street, to the left—look for the sign with the big "i." (☎938 94 50 04. Open in summer 9am-9pm; in winter W-M 9am-2pm, 4-6:30pm.) In summer, a branch opens on C. Fonollar. (☎938 94 42 51. Open 10am-1:30pm, 5-9pm.) **Internet** and **fax** service are available at **Sitges Internet Access,** C. Espanya, 7. 750ptas/€4.50/hr, 15min. 195ptas/€1.20. Open daily 11am-2am. Services include: **medical assistance** (☎938 94 64 26); **emergency** (☎938 94 39 49), on C. Samuel Barrachina; **Super Avui,** Carbonell, 24, is a supermarket across from the train station. (Open M-Sa 9am-9pm, Su 10am-2pm.) The **post office** is in Pl. Espanya. (☎93 894 12 47. Open M-F 8:30am-2:30pm, Sa 9:30am-1pm.) **Postal code:** 08870.

ACCOMMODATIONS AND FOOD. Rooms are expensive and scarce on summer weekends, so reserve early. **Hostal Parellades,** C. Parellades, 11, is close to the beach and offers standard rooms that are dirt cheap for Sitges. (☎938 94 08 01. Singles 3000ptas/€18; doubles 5000ptas/€30, with bath 6000ptas/€36; triples with bath 7200ptas/€44.) **Hostal Casa-Bella,** Av. Carbonell, 12, has clean, modern rooms with bath that border on sterile. (☎938 94 43 22. Take a right as you leave the train station. Singles 5000ptas/€30; doubles 8000ptas/€48.) **Hostal Internacional,** C. Sant Francesc, 52, off Carbonell, provides bright rooms. (☎938 94 26 90. Doubles 5500ptas/€33, with shower 6500ptas/€39.) **Izarra,** C. Mayor, 24, behind the museum area, is a Basque *tapas* bar for a quick food fix before a hard night of club-hopping. (*Tapas* 120ptas/€1. Entrées 700ptas/€4 and up. Open daily.) **Restaurante La Oca,** C. Parellades, 41, roasts chickens that attract lines of hungry tourists. Try the succulent *half-pollo al ast* (roasted chicken) for 795ptas/€5; add sauce for 895ptas/€5.50. (Open daily 1pm-midnight.) **Restaurante El Pozo,** C. Sant Pau, 3, off C. Parellades, is a throwback to the town's days as a fishing village and features seafood. (Entrées 1100-2000ptas/€7-12. Open F-W 1-4pm and 7:30-11pm. MC/V.)

SIGHTS. The pedestrian **C. Parellades,** with shopping, eating, and drinking galore, is the center of attention. Sitges has some can't-miss attractions, including Morell's whimsical **Modernist clock tower,** Pl. Cap de la Vila, 2, above Optica at the intersection of Parellades and Sant Francesc. From the beach, the parish church on the waterfront is the city's most distinctive sight. Behind it, on C. Fonollar, the **Museu Cau Ferrat** hangs over the water. Once home to Santiago Rusinyol and a meeting point for other young Catalan artists Picasso and Ramon Casas, the building is a shrine to Modernist work (☎938 94 03 64). Next door, the **Museu Maricel del Mar** has a collection of Romanesque and Gothic art (☎938 94 03 64). Further into town, the **Museu Romàntic,** C. Sant Gaudenci, 1, off C. Parellades, is a 19th-century house filled with period pieces like music boxes and 17th-century dolls. (☎938 94 29 69. All 3 museums open in summer Tu-Su 10am-2, 5-9pm; rest of the year Tu-F 10am-1:30, 3-6:30pm, Sa 10am-7pm, Su 10am-3pm. Combo entrance 900ptas/€5.40, students 500ptas/€3; otherwise 500ptas/€3 per museum, students and seniors 250ptas/€1.50.) Across the street from the museums, the stately **Palau Maricel,** on C. Fonollar, built in 1910 for American millionaire Charles Deering, wows visitors with its sumptuous halls and gardens. Guided tours are available on summer nights and include a glass of *cava* (8pm; 900ptas/€5.40); on Friday, Saturday, and Sunday nights, a piano and soprano concert complete the evening of luxury (1200ptas/€7 for tour, *cava*, and concert). Call for reservations (☎938 11 33 11).

NIGHTLIFE AND FESTIVALS. The place to be is **C. Primer de Maig** (which runs from the beach) and its continuation, **C. Marquès Montroig.** Bars line the street, blasting music until 3am. The clubs are wide-open and accepting, with a mixed crowd. There's no cover, making for great bar/club-hopping. Beers go for about 500ptas/€3, mixed drinks 1000ptas/€6. Crazier is the "disco-beach" **Atlántida,** in Sector Terramar, and the legendary **Pachá,** on Pg. Sant Didac in nearby Vallpineda. Buses run all night to the two discos from C. Primer de Maig (midnight to 4am).

Sitges shines especially bright in its gay nightlife scene. **Parrot's Pub** on C. Primer de Maig is a place to relax with a drink before hitting the clubs. Ask for the **plano gay,** the free map of gay establishments in Sitges. **Mediterráneo,** C. Sant Bonaventura, 6, off C. Sant Francesc, shakes every summer night with two floors of drinking and dancing (open 10pm-3:30am). After hours, **Trailer,** C. Angel Vida, 36, is the hottest disco party in town, with foam parties W and Su (opens at 2am).

Sitges celebrates holidays with all-out style. During the **Festa de Corpus Christi** in June, townspeople collaborate to create intricate fresh-flower carpets. For *papier-mâché* dragons, devils, and giants dancing in the streets, visit during the **Festa Major,** held August 22-27 in honor of the town's patron saint Bartolomé. Nothing compares to the **Carnaval,** on Sunday and Tuesday, in preparation for Catholic fasting during the first week of Lent (usually mid-February). Spaniards crash the town for a frenzy of dancing, outrageous costumes, and vats of alcohol. On the first Sunday of March, a pistol shot starts the **Rally de Coches de Epoca,** an antique car race from Barcelona to Sitges. June brings the **International Theater**

Festival (1500-3500ptas/€9-21 per show), and July and August the **International Jazz Festival** (1700ptas/€10 per concert). In mid-October, the one- to two-week **Festival Internacional de Cine Fantástico de Sitges** showcases the scarier side of film, with a varied menu of horror and gore flicks. From September 15 to 17, competitors tread on grapes for the annual **Grape Harvest.**

DAYTRIP FROM SITGES: VILANOVA I LA GELTRÙ

Cercanías trains run from Vilanova to Sitges (10min., every 15-30min., 160ptas/€1), continuing to Barcelona (50min., 350ptas/€2). Mon Bus (☎938 93 70 60) connects Vilanova to Sitges (200ptas/€1.20), and Barcelona (480ptas/€3). The train station doubles as the bus station. Taxis from Vilanova to Sitges are 1500-2000ptas/€9-€12.

Vilanova i la Geltrù are actually two cities in one: an industrial center and a well-groomed beach town. There is little in the uptown area except for old churches and stone façades; most visitors spend the day on the beach (10min. from the train station). In the evening, Vilanovans generally forgo late-night madness for beach volleyball or soccer at Parc de Ribes. To get to the **beaches,** exit the station, turn left on C. Forn de Vidre, take the third left onto the thoroughfare Rambla de la Pau, head under the overpass, and follow the *rambla* all the way to the port. The **tourist office,** with an excellent **map,** is about 50m to the right, in a small park called **Parc de Ribes Roges.** (☎938 15 45 17. Open July-Aug. M-Sa 10am-8pm, Su 10am-2pm; Sept.-June 10am-2pm and sometimes 4-7pm.) To the right, past the tourist office, is the wide **Platja de Ribes Roges;** to the left is the smaller **Platja del Far.**

If you decide to stay in town, the popular **Can Gatell,** C. Puigcerdà, 6-16, has clean rooms and full baths. With your back to the station, head down C. Victor Balaguer, the leftward of the two parallel streets; at the end, turn right onto La Rambla. Ventosa, and hang a quick left at the sign. (☎938 93 01 17. Doubles 7000ptas/€43; triples 9500ptas/€57.) The hostel's *menú* (1300ptas/€8; served M-F) is popular with locals. A less expensive alternative is **Supermarket Orangután,** Rambla de la Pau, 36, on the way to the beach (open M-Sa 9am-1:30pm, 5-8:30pm).

NORTHEASTERN SPAIN

CATALUÑA(CATALUNYA)

From rocky Costa Brava to smooth Costa Dorada, the lush Pyrenees to chic Barcelona, Cataluña is a vacation in itself. It has also been graced with many of the nation's richest resources, making it the most prosperous region in Iberia. *Catalanes* are famous for their resourcefulness and work ethic. As the saying goes, *"El Català de les pedres fa pa"* (a Catalan can make bread out of stones).

Colonized first by the Greeks and the Carthaginians, Cataluña was later one of Rome's favored provinces. Only briefly subdued by the Moors, Cataluña's counts achieved independence in AD 987. Cataluña grew powerful as she joined the throne of Aragón in 1137; while this union empowered Cataluña to pursue her own empire for a time, it also ultimately doomed her to be subjugated to subsequent Spanish rule. King Felipe V was finally able to fully suppress Cataluña in the early 18th century when the Catalans sided against him in the War of Spanish Succession (1702-1714). In the late 18th century, the region's fortunes revived when it developed into one of Europe's premier textile manufacturers, opening trade with the Americas. Nineteenth-century industrial expansion nourished arts and sciences, ushering in an age known as the Catalan Renaixença (Renaissance). The 20th century gave birth to the Modernist movement and an all-star list of artists and architects, including Picasso, Miró, Dalí, Antoni Gaudí i Comet, Lluís Domènech i Montaner, and Josep Puig i Cadafalch. Home to staunch opponents of the Fascists during Spain's Civil War, Cataluña lost its autonomy in 1939. During his regime, Franco suppressed Catalan language instruction (except in universities) and limited Catalan publications.

Since Cataluña regained regional autonomy in 1977, Catalan media and arts have flourished. Today, Catalan is once again the region's official language. While some worry that the use of the regional dialect will discourage talented Spaniards from working or studying in Cataluña, effectively isolating the region, others argue that extensive regional autonomy has generally led to progressive ends. Many *catalanes* will answer inquiring visitors in Catalan, even if asked in Castilian (the politically correct name for "Spanish"). Lauded throughout Spain, Catalan cuisine boasts *pa amb tomaquet*, bread smeared with olive oil, tomato, and garlic, and *ali-oli*, a garlic and olive oil sauce.

COSTA DORADA

TARRAGONA

Tarragona's strategic position made the city a provincial Roman capital under Augustus; today an amphitheater and other ruins pay homage to the city's imperial days. These vestiges of Tarragona's august past are the city's most compelling attractions, but plenty of visitors are satisfied with a sight-seeing-light and beach-heavy stay in Catalunya's second most important port city.

TRANSPORTATION

Trains: Station Pl. Pedrera (☎977 24 02 02), by the water. Info open daily 6am-9pm. Trains to: **Alicante** (3hr., 7 per day, 4500ptas/€27); **Barcelona** (1hr., 30-40 per day, 675ptas/€4); **Madrid** (7hr., 4 per day, 6000ptas/€36); **Sitges** (45min., 23 per day, 420ptas/€2.50); **Valencia** (2-3hr., 15 per day, 1860ptas/€12); **Zaragoza** (3hr., 8 per day, 2000ptas/€12). Trains are the better transport option from Tarragona.

Buses: Pl. Imperial Tarraco, (☎977 22 91 26). **Transportes Bacoma** (☎977 22 20 72) serves most destinations. To: **Barcelona** (1½hr., 8 per day, 1220ptas/€7.30) and **Valencia** (3½hr., 5 per day, 2500ptas/€15).

Public Transportation: EMT Buses (☎977 54 94 80) run all over Tarragona. Buses run daily 6am-11pm. 125ptas/€1, 10-ride *abono* ticket 700ptas/€4.20.

Taxi: Radio Taxi (☎977 22 14 14).

ORIENTATION AND PRACTICAL INFORMATION

Most sights are clustered on a hill, surrounded by remnants of Roman walls. At the foot of the hill, **La Rambla Vella** and **La Rambla Nova** (parallel to one another and perpendicular to the sea) are the main thoroughfares of the new city. La Rambla Nova runs from **Passeig de les Palmeres** (overlooking the sea) to **Plaça Imperial Tarraco,** the monstrous rotunda and home of the bus station. To reach the old quarter from the train station, turn right and walk 200m to the killer stairs parallel to the shore.

Tourist Office: C. Major, 39 (☎977 24 52 03; fax 24 55 07), below the cathedral steps. Crucial **free map**. Open June-Sept. M-F 9:30am-8:30pm, Sa 9:30am-2pm and 4-8:30pm, Su 10am-2pm; Oct.-May M-F 10am-2pm and 4:30-7pm, Sa-Su 10am-2pm.

Tourist Information booths: Pl. Imperial Tarraco, at the bottom of la Rambla Vella, just outside the bus station; another at the intersection of Av. Catalunya and Vía de l'Impera Romi. Open daily July-Oct. 10am-2pm and 4-8pm; Nov.-June Sa-Su 10am-2pm.

Luggage Storage: 24hr. at the train station. June-Aug. 400ptas/€2.40; Sept.-May 600ptas/€3.60.

Emergency: ☎112. **Police: Comisaria de Policía** (☎977 23 33 11), on Pl. Orleans. From Pl. Imperial Tarraco on the inland end of La Rambla Nova, walk down Av. Pres. Lluís Companys, and take the 3rd left to the station.

Medical Assistance: Hospital de Sant Pau i Santa Tecla, La Rambla Vella, 14 (☎977 25 99 00). **Hospital Joan XXIII** (☎977 29 58 00), on C. Dr. Mallafré Guasch.

Internet Access: Futureland, C. Estanislao Figueras, 19 (☎977 22 08 52), off the Imperial Tarraco rotunda. 500ptas/€3 per hr. Open M-F 10:30am-2:30pm and 4:30-10:30pm; Sa-Su 10am-2pm and 4:30-11pm. **Biblioteca Pública,** C. Fortuny, 30 (☎977 24 05 44). Public library; free use of computers with a passport.

Post Office: Pl. Corsini, 12 (☎977 24 01 49), below La Rambla Nova off C. Canyelles. Open M-F 8:30am-8:30pm, Sa 9am-2pm. **Postal Code:** 43001.

CATALUÑA

ACCOMMODATIONS AND CAMPING

Most of the city's accommodations are two- to four-star hotels near the center. Pl. Font in the old quarter (parallel to La Rambla Vella) is filled with quality lodging.

Pensión Noria, Pl. de la Font, 53 (☎977 23 87 17), in the heart of the historic town. Enter through the restaurant. Clean and bright rooms with pretty-in-pink bathrooms. Singles with bath 3400ptas/€21; doubles with bath 5900ptas/€36.

Hostal Forum, Pl. de la Font, 37 (☎977 23 17 18), upstairs from the restaurant. Clean rooms and bathrooms don't leave space for spreading out, but a decent place to sleep for the night. Singles with bath 3000ptas/€18; doubles with bath 6000ptas/€36.

Camping: Several sites line the beach-side road toward Barcelona (Vía Augusta or CN-340). Take bus #9 (every 20min., 105ptas/€1) from Pl. Imperial Tarraco. **Tarraco** (☎977 29 02 89) is closest, at Platja de l'Arrabassada. Well-kept facilities near the beach. 24hr. reception. 555ptas/€3 per person, per car, and per tent. Open Apr.-Sept.

FOOD

Pl. Font and Las Ramblas Nova and Vella are full of cheap *menús* (800-1200ptas/€5-7) and greasy *platos combinados.* Tarragona's indoor **Mercado Central** (market) takes place in Pl. C[illegible] Flea market Tu and Th.) For **groceries,** head to **Champion,** C. Augusta at Comte de Rius, between Las Ramblas Nova and Vella. (Open M-Sa 9:15am-9:15pm.) **El Serrallo,** the fisherman's quarter right next to the harbor, has the best seafood. Try your food with Tarragona's typical *romesco* sauce, simmered from red peppers, toasted almonds, and hazelnuts.

La Teula, C. Mercería, 16 (☎977 23 99 89), in the old city off Pl. Santiago Rusinyol, the plaça in front of the cathedral. Great for salads (500-750ptas/€3-€4.50) and toasted sandwiches with interesting veggie/meat combos (975-1100ptas/€6-€7). Lunch *menú* 1100ptas/€7. Open M-Sa 1-4pm and 8pm-midnight. MC/V.

Restaurant El Caserón, Trinquet Nou, 4 (☎977 23 93 28), parallel to La Rambla Vella. Looks like a diner; home-style food. Entrées 800-1400ptas/€4.80-€8.40. Daily *menú* 1200ptas/€7.20. Open M-Sa 1-4pm and 8:30-11pm, Su 1-3:30pm.

SIGHTS AND BEACHES

Tarragona's status as provincial capital transformed the small military enclosure into a glorious imperial port. Countless Roman ruins stand silently amid 20th-century hustle and bustle.

ROMAN RUINS. Below Pg. Palmeres and set amid gardens above the beach is the **Roman Amphitheater** (☎977 44 25 79), where gladiators killed wild animals and each other; this popular activity dates back to the founding of the city. In 259, the Christian bishop Fructuosus and his two deacons were burned alive here; in the sixth century, these martyrs were honored with a basilica built in the arena.

Above the amphitheater, across Pg. Sant Antoni, is the entrance to the excellent **Museu de la Romanitat** (☎977 24 19 52), which houses the **Praetorium Tower,** the former administrative center of the region, and the **Roman Circus,** the site of chariot races and other spectacles. Visitors descend into the long, dark tunnels which led fans to their seats, and see a model reconstruction of what the complex looked like. The Praetorium was the governor's palace in the first century BC. Rumor has it that the infamous hand-washer Pontius Pilate was born here.

CATALUÑA

The scattered **Fòrum Romà,** with its reconstructed columns, lies near the post office on C. Lleida. Once the center of the town, its distance clearly demonstrates how far the walls of the ancient city had extended. To see what remains of the second-century BC walls, stroll through the **Passeig Arqueològic.** The walls originally stretched to the sea and fortified the entire city. *(Nearly all monuments and museums open June-Sept. Tu-Su 9am-9pm; Oct.-May Tu-Su 10am-1:30pm and 4-6:30pm. Admission to each 300ptas/€2; students 100ptas/€1.)*

MUSEUMS. The **Museu Nacional Arqueològic,** across Pl. Rei from the Praetorium, displays ancient utensils, statues, and mosaics. *(☎977 23 62 09. 400ptas/€2.40, students 200ptas/€1.20; includes admission to the Necropolis.)* For a bit of the macabre, creep over to the **Museu i Necròpolis Paleocristians,** Av. Ramón y Cajal, 78, at Pg. Independència on the western edge of town. The huge early Christian burial site has yielded a rich variety of urns, tombs, and sarcophagi, the best of which are in the museum. *(☎977 21 11 75. 400ptas/€2.40, students 200ptas/€1.20; includes admission to Museu Arqueològic.)* If you've had too much Roman roamin,' descend the steps in front of the cathedral and take the third right onto C. Cavellares to visit the **Casa-Museu Castellarnau.** It housed the Viscounts of Castellarnau, 18th-century nobles. *(☎977 24 22 20. 300ptas/€1.80.)*

OTHER SIGHTS. The **Pont del Diable (Devil's Bridge)**, a Roman aqueduct 10min. outside of the city, is visible on the way in and out of town by bus. Take municipal bus #5 (every 20min., 105ptas/€1) from the corner of C. Christòfer Colom and Av. Prat de la Riba or from Pl. Imperial Tarraco. Lit by octagonal windows flanking the cross is the Romanesque-Gothic **cathedral.** The interior contains the tomb of Joan d'Aragó. *(C. Major near Pl. Seu. 300ptas/€2, students 100ptas/€1. Open June-Aug. M-Sa 10am-7pm; Sept.-May M-Sa 10am-12:30pm and 3-6pm.)*

BEACHES. Access to **Platja del Miracle,** the town's main beach, is hidden along Baixada del Miracle, beyond the Roman theater: walk away from the theater until you reach the underpass under the train tracks. Though the beach is not on par with other Costa Dorada stops—nor even with the beaches of Barcelona—it's not bad for a few hours of relaxation. A bit farther away are **Platja l'Arrabassada,** with its dirt-like sand, and the windy **Platja Llarga** (take bus #1 or 9 from Pl. Imperial Tarraco or any of the other stops).

ENTERTAINMENT AND NIGHTLIFE

July and August usher in the **Fiesta de Tarragona** (☎977 24 47 95; 24hr. tickets ☎902 33 22 11). The **Auditori Camp de Mart** near the cathedral holds film screenings, as well as music, dance, and theater performances. A booth on Av. Catalunya at Portal del Roser sells tickets until 9pm for the 10:30pm performances (1000-2500ptas/€6-€15).

Arrive at least one hour early. On even-numbered years, the first Sunday in October brings the **Concurs de Castells,** an important regional competition featuring tall human towers, as high as seven to nine "stories," called *castells*. *Castells* also appear amid beasts and fireworks during the annual **Fiesta de Santa Tecla** (Sept. 23). If you're unable to catch the *castellers* in person, don't miss the monument to the *castellers* on La Rambla Nova, an impressive life-size *castell* of bronze Tarragonans.

Weekend nightlife in Tarragona is on a much smaller scale than that of its northern neighbors Sitges and Barcelona. Between 5 and 9pm, Las Ramblas Nova and Vella (and the area in between) are packed with strolling families. After 9pm, the bars start to liven up; around 10pm on Saturdays in summer, fireworks brighten the skies. The most popular place to be is at **Port Esportiu,** a portside plaza full of restaurant-bars and mini-*discotecas*. Heading up La Rambla Nova away from the beach, take a left onto C. Unió; bear left at Pl. General Prim and follow C. Apodaca to its end. Cross the tracks; the fun will be to the left.

COSTA BRAVA ☎972

Skirting the Mediterranean Sea from Barcelona to the French border, the Costa Brava's jagged cliffs and pristine beaches draw throngs of European visitors, especially in July and August. Early June and late September can be remarkably peaceful; the water is already warm and the beaches much less crowded. In the winter Costa Brava lives up to its name, as fierce winds sweep the coast, leaving behind tranquil, near empty beach towns. Unlike its counterparts, Costa Blanca and Costa del Sol, Costa Brava offers more than just high-rises and touristy beaches. The rocky shores have traditionally attracted romantics and artists, like Marc Chagall and Salvador Dalí, a Costa Brava native. Dalí's house in Cadaqués and his museum in Figueres display the largest collections of his work in Europe.

TOSSA DE MAR

Falling in love in (or in love with) Tossa de Mar is easy. In 1934, French artist Marc Chagall commenced a 40-year love affair with this seaside village, deeming it "Blue Paradise." When *The Flying Dutchman* was filmed here in 1951, Ava Gardner fell hard for Spanish bullfighter-turned-actor Mario Cabrera, much to the chagrin of Frank Sinatra, her husband at the time. (A statue of the actress in Tossa's old city commemorates her visit.) Like many coastal cities, Tossa (pop. 4000) suffers from the usual tourist industry blemishes: souvenir shops, inflated prices, and crowded beaches. That said, it resists a generic beach town ambiance, drawing from its historical legacy and cliff-studded landscape to preserve a unique small-town feel. Raised in the 12th century as a fortified medieval village, the sun-baked walls of Vila Vella overlook Tossa's blue Mediterranean water.

TRANSPORTATION

Buses: Av. Pelegrí at Pl. Nacions Sense Estat. **Pujol i Pujol** (☎610 50 58 84) to **Lloret del Mar** (20min.; June-Aug. every 30min., Sept.-May every hr. 8am-9:15pm; 180ptas/€1). **Sarfa** (☎972 34 09 03) to **Barcelona** (1½hr.; 15 per day 7:40am-7:40pm, 1150ptas/€7) and **Girona** (1hr.; 2 per day, offseason 1 per day; 580ptas/€4).

Car Rental: Viajes Tramontana, Av. Costa Brava, 23 (☎972 34 28 29; fax 34 13 20). **Avis** (☎902 13 55 31) and their affiliate, **Olimpia** (☎972 36 47 10), operate from the same storefront. Min. age 21. Have a major credit card, driver's license (int'l driver's license required for longer rentals), and passport ready. 6700-17,000ptas/€40-102. Open daily July-Aug. 9am-9pm, Apr.-June, Sept.-Nov. 9am-3pm and 4-8pm.

Mountain Bike and Moped Rentals: Jimbo Bikes, La Rambla Pau Casals, 12 (☎972 34 30 44). Staff gives bike route information. Bring license for moped rental. Mountain bikes 500-700ptas/€3-4 per hr., 2500-3500ptas/€15-21 per day. Open M-Sa 9am-9pm and Su 9:30am-2pm and 4-8pm. AmEx/MC/V.

Boat rentals: Kayaks Nicolau, (☎972 34 26 46) on Mar Menuda, offers 1½hr. kayak excursions to Cala Bona (10am, noon, and 4pm; 1700ptas/€10.30). Kayak 800ptas/€4.80 per hr., paddle boats 1000ptas/€6. Open daily Apr.15-Oct.15 9am-6pm.

Taxis: ☎972 34 05 49. Cluster outside the bus station.

ORIENTATION AND PRACTICAL INFORMATION

Buses arrive at **Plaça de les Nacions Sense Estat** where **Avinguda del Pelegrí** and **Avinguda Ferrán Agulló** meet; the town slopes gently down from there to the waterfront. Walk away from the station down Av. Ferrán Agulló, turn right on Av. Costa Brava, and continue until your feet get wet (10min.). **Passeig del Mar,** at the end of Av. Costa Brava, curves along the **Platja Gran** (Tossa's main beach) to the old quarter.

Tourist Office: Av. Pelegrí, 25 (☎972 34 01 08; fax 34 07 12; www.tossademar.com), in the bus terminal at Av. Ferrán Agulló and Av. Pelegrí. Grab a map. English spoken. Open June 15-Sept. 15: M-Sa 9am-9pm, Su 10am-2pm and 4-8pm. Apr.-May and Oct.: M-Sa 10am-2pm and 4-8pm, Su 10:30am-1:30pm. Mar. and Nov.: M-Sa 10am-1pm and 4-7pm. Dec.-Feb. M-F 10am-1pm and 4-7pm, Sa 10am-1pm.

Currency Exchange: Bancos Central Hispano, C. Ferrán Agilló, 2 (☎972 34 10 65). Open Apr.-Sept. M-F 8:30am-2:30pm; Oct.-Mar. also Sa 8:30am-1pm. **ATM.**

Police: Municipal police, Av. Pelegrí, 14 (☎972 34 01 35), down the street from the tourist office. English spoken. They'll escort you to the **24hr. pharmacy.**

Medical Services: Casa del Mar (☎972 34 18 28 or 34 01 54), Av. Catalunya. Primary health services and immediate attention. Nearest hospital is in **Blanes,** 30min. south.

Internet Access: Cyber-Café Bar La Playa, C. Socors, 6 (☎972 34 09 22), off the main beach. 200ptas/€1.20 per 15min., 400ptas/€2.40 per 30min. Open daily May-Oct. 15 9:30am-midnight. **Scuba Libre,** Av. Sant Raimón de Penyafort, 11 (☎972 34 20 26). Dive shop and café has several Internet terminals. 600ptas/€3.65 per hr. Open daily May-Oct. 8am-3am, Nov.-Apr. Sa-Su 8am-6pm.

Post Office: C. María Auxiliadora (☎972 34 04 57), down Av. Pelegrí from tourist office. Open M-F 8:30am-2:30pm, Sa 9:30am-1pm. **Postal Code:** 17320.

ACCOMMODATIONS

Tossa is a seasonal town, and therefore many hostels, restaurants, and bars are open only from May to October. During the summer and festivals, Tossa fills quickly. Make reservations in advance, as some establishments are booked solid in July and August. The **old quarter** hotels are the only ones really worth considering.

Fonda/Can Lluna, C. Roqueta, 20 (☎972 34 03 65; fax 34 07 57). From Pg. del Mar; turn right onto C. Peixeteras, veer left on C. Estalt, walk uphill until the dead-end, turn left, and then head straight. Immaculate single, double, and triple rooms with private bath. Breakfast included. Coin wash 600ptas/€3.60. Booked months in advance July-Aug., Oct.-Mar. 2500ptas/€15 per person. Mar.-June and Sept. 2000ptas/€12.

Pensión Carmen Pepi, C. Sant Miguel, 10 (☎972 34 05 26). Turn left off Av. de Pelegrí onto María Auxiliadora, then veer immediately to your right through the Pl. de l'Antic Hospital onto C. Sant Miguel. Great location, though the high-ceilinged rooms with private bath are somewhat beyond their prime. Breakfast 300ptas/€1.50. July-Aug. 31 singles 3000ptas/€18; doubles 6000ptas/€36. May-July 1 singles 2700ptas/€16; doubles 5300ptas/€32. Sept.-June singles 2200ptas/€13; doubles 4400ptas/€26.

L'Hostalet de Tossa, Pl. de l'Església, 3 (☎972 34 18 53; fax 34 29 69), in front of the Sant Vicenç church. Clean, hotel-quality rooms. Many of L'Hostalet's double rooms overlook its orange tree terrace and face the church. Rooms have baths and include breakfast. Apr.-May and Oct. 5800ptas/€35; June and Sept. 6800ptas/€14; *Setmana Santa* (Holy Week) and July-Aug. 8200ptas/€50. MC/V.

Camping: Closest site is **Can Martí** (☎972 34 08 51; fax 34 24 61), at the end of La Rambla Pau Casals, off Av. Ferrán Agulló, 15min. from the bus station. Showers, swimming pool, and restaurant. June 20–Aug. 31. 900ptas/€5.40 per person, 925ptas/€5.50 per tent, 525ptas/€3.20 per car; May 12-June 19 and Sept. 1-16 725ptas/€4.40 per person, 800ptas/€4.80 per tent, 425ptas/€2.60 per car.

FOOD

The old quarter has the best cuisine and ambiance in Tossa. Restaurants catering to tourists serve up *menús* at reasonable prices; most specialize in local seafood. If you need groceries, head to **Megatzems Palau,** C. Enric Granados 4. (☎972 34 08 58. Open daily June-Sept. 8am-9pm.)

Restaurant Marina, C. Tarull, 6 (☎972 34 07 57). Faces the Església de Sant Vincenç and has outdoor seating for prime people-watching. A nice family restaurant. Multilingual menu features pizza, meat, and fish dishes, and lots of *paella*. Entrées 600-1600ptas/€3.60-9.60. *Menús* 1200ptas/€7.20 and 1500ptas/€9. Open daily *Semana Santa* (Holy Week) to Oct. daily 11:30am-11:30pm. MC/V.

Pizzeria Anna, Pont Vell, 19 (☎972 34 28 51). Turn right onto Pont Vell from Pg. Mar; it's on the left. Homesick Italians might be disappointed, but seafood-sick travelers will be in heaven. Seating inside and out. Pasta 700-900ptas/€4.22-5.40; pizza 850-1100ptas/€5-6.60. Open daily Apr.-Sept. noon-4pm, 7:30-11:30pm. AmEx/MC/V.

La Taberna de Tossa, C. Sant Telm, 26 (☎972 34 14 47). In the heart of the old quarter, right off La Guardia. Serves inexpensive wine, *tapas,* and provincial meat and fish specialities (entrées 725-1325ptas/€4.30-8). Set *menús* 1095-1295ptas/€7-8. Open daily Apr.-Sept. 1pm-4 and 7pm-1am, Oct.-Mar. F-Su 1pm-4 and 7pm-1am. V.

SIGHTS AND ENTERTAINMENT

Inside the walled fortress of the Vila Vella, a spiral of medieval alleys leads to tiny Pl. Pintor J. Roig y Soler, where the **Museu Municipal** has a wonderfully displayed collection of 1920s and 1930s art, including one of the few Chagall paintings still in Spain. Tossa's Roman mosaics (dating from the 4th-1st century BC), and other artifacts from the nearby Vila Romana are displayed in 12th-century palace turned museum. (☎972 34 30 81. Open June 1-15 M-F 11am-1pm and 3-5pm, Sa-Su 11am-6pm; June 16-Sept. 15 10am-8pm; Sept. 16-30 M-F 11am-1pm and 3-5pm, Sa-Su 11am-6pm; Oct. M-F 11am-1pm and 3-5pm, Sa-Su 11am-5pm. 500ptas/€3, students and seniors 300ptas/€1.80.) From the museum, it's a picturesque stroll uphill to the remains of the **Vila Vella** and gorgeous Mediterranean views.

Tossa's main beach, **La Platja Gran,** is surrounded by cliffs and draws the majority of beach-goers. To escape the crowds, visit some of the neighboring *calas* (small coves), accessible by foot. Hiking and mountain-biking [illegible] cross the area and offer [illegible]. The tourist office pam[illegible] lots of information. Several companies, like **Fonda Cristal,** send glass-bottomed boats to nearby beaches and caves. Tickets are available at booths on the Platja Gran. (☎972 34 22 29. 1hr., 17 per day, 1100ptas/€7 per person.) **Club Aire Libre,** on the highway to Lloret, organizes various excursions and rents equipment for water sports. (☎972 34 12 77. Canoeing, kayaking 2200ptas/€13. Water skiing 4400ptas/€26 for 2 lessons. Scuba diving 44,000ptas/€264 for 5-day certification course. Sailing 1800ptas/€11 per hr. Windsurfing 1700ptas/€10 per hr.)

NIGHTLIFE

Bars line the streets of the old quarter and offer live music from time to time. **Bar El Pirata,** C. Portal, 32, and its companion bar **Piratín** have outdoor tables overlooking the sea. (☎972 34 14 43. Open daily Apr.-Oct. 2pm-3am.) **Bar Trinquet,** C. Sant Josep 9, has a lovely tree-filled interior courtyard. DJs spin acid jazz and house on weekend nights. (☎659 61 39 30. Open daily Apr.-Oct. 7pm-3am.) For live music try

Don Pepe, C. Estolt, 6, a small, less-touristed bar which showcases a flamenco guitarist every night. (☎972 34 22 66. Open daily Apr.-Oct. 10pm-4:30am.)

PALAFRUGELL ☎972

In 988, inhabitants of the beach town of Llafranc founded inland Palafrugell, seeking refuge from the constant plundering of Mediterranean pirates. Today, budget travelers come here to flee the wallet-plundering of seaside hotels and restaurants. Forty kilometers east of Girona, Palafrugell serves as a base for trips to the nearby beach towns **Calella, Llafranc,** and **Tamariu,** that cater to wealthy Europeans whose idea of budget accommodation is any hotel that doesn't leave mints on the pillow. To save some *pesetas*, stay in bland and beachless Palafrugell and daytrip to the beaches, connected by the **Camino de Ronda** footpaths.

TRANSPORTATION

Buses: Sarfa, C. Torres Jonama, 67-79 (☎972 30 06 23). Prices rise on weekends. To: **Barcelona** (2hr., 12 per day, 1750ptas/€10.50); **Calella** and **Llafranc** (12-24 per day, in winter 4-5 per day; 160ptas/€0.96); **Figueres** (1½hr., 3-4 per day, 800-950ptas/€4.80-5.70); and **Girona** (1hr., 15 per day, 515-600ptas/€3.60).

Taxis: Radio Taxi (☎972 61 00 00). 24hr. service.

ORIENTATION AND PRACTICAL INFORMATION

To get from the bus station to the center of town, turn right and walk down C. Torres Jonama to C. de Pi i Maragall. Turn right and walk past the Guardia Civil and the market until you hit **Pl. Nova,** the main square of the town, off which are C. San Sebastià and C. Cavallers. On your way you'll pass the **Pl. l'Església** on the right. To get to the nearby beach towns of Calella, Llafranc, and Tamariu, take a bus (see above), or spin away on moped or mountain bike.

Tourist Office: Can Rosés, Pl. l'Església (☎972 61 18 20; fax 61 17 56), the first right off C. Cavallers heading away from Pl. Nova. The *Guía Municipal* guide is indispensable. A **larger branch** is at C. Carrilet, 2 (☎972 30 02 28; 61 12 61). From the bus station, go left on C. Torres Jonama, left again at the traffic circle, and walk about 200m. Both open Apr.-Sept. M-Sa 10am-1pm and 5-8pm, Su 10am-1pm; Oct.-Mar. M-Sa 10am-1pm and 4-7pm, Su 10am-1pm; Carrilet branch also open July-Aug. M-Sa 9am-9pm and Su 10am-1pm.

Currency Exchange: Banco Central Hispano, the corner of C. Valls and C. Cavallers off Pl. Nova. **ATM.** Open M-F 8:30am-2:30pm; Oct.-Mar. also Sa 8:30am-1pm.

Emergency: ☎112. **Police:** ☎088. **Municipal police:** ☎972 61 31 01, Av. Josep Pla and C. Cervantes. Call them for **24hr. pharmacy** info.

Medical Services: Centro de Atención Primaria, C. d'Angel Guimerà, 6 (☎972 61 06 07 Emergencies/ambulance: ☎972 60 00 03). Open 24hr.

Internet Access: Internet Papereria Palé, C. Cavallers 16 (☎972 30 12 48). 175ptas/€3 per 15min., 550ptas/€3 per hr. Open Aug.-Sept. M 5-9pm, Tu-Sa 9am-1pm and 5-9pm, and Su 9am-1pm; Oct.-July Tu-Sa 9am-1pm and 5-9pm, Su 9am-1pm.

Post Office: C. Torres Jonama, 14 (☎902 197 197). **Lista de Correos.** Open M-F 8:30am-2:30pm, Sa 9:30am-1pm. **Postal Code:** 17200.

ACCOMMODATIONS

Though options are few, accommodation prices are reasonable and room quality high in Palafrugell. Be sure to call ahead on summer weekends.

Fonda l'Estrella, C. Quatre Cases, 13-17 (☎972 30 00 05), at the corner of C. La Caritat, a right off C. Torres Jonama. Even the common baths are gorgeous. Singles 3000ptas/€18 (available Apr.-May and Sept.-Oct.); doubles 6000ptas/€36.

Hostal Plaja, C. Sant Sebastià, 34 (☎972 30 05 26), off of Pl. Nova. Grand foyer gives way to a courtyard surrounded by spotless rooms, all with balconies. For not much more, rooms with bathrooms are a significant jump in luxury. Breakfast 1000ptas/€6. Singles 3000ptas/€18, with bath 4000ptas/€24; doubles with bath 8000ptas/€48.

Residencia Familiar, C. Sant Sebastià, 29 (☎689 26 95 38), off Pl. Nova. Mattresses are on the saggy side, but rooms have sinks. No private baths. Singles 3000ptas/€18; doubles 6000ptas/€36; less for longer stays and for families.

Camping: Camping Moby Dick, C. Costa Verda, 16-28 (☎972 61 43 07). Take the Sarfa bus to Calella and ask the driver to let you off. No white whale in sight, but it is close to the water. Nice showers. 600ptas/€3.60 per adult, 430ptas/€2.50 per child; 660ptas/€4 per tent; 600ptas/€4 per car. Open Apr. 10-Sept. 30.

CATALUÑA

FOOD

Restaurants near the beach are predictably expensive, making meals in Palafrugell proper a wiser option. Pickup **groceries** for daytrips at **MAXOR,** C. Torres Jonama, 33. (Open M-Th 8:30am-2:30pm, 4:40-8:30pm; F-Sa 8:30am-8:30pm; Su 9am-2pm.) For some reason, the town has a disproportionately high number of pizzerias and Italian restaurants. Shrugs one local, "We just really like pizza." **L'Arcobaleno,** C. Mayor, 3, brings a touch of Tuscany to Catalan classics. The delicious lunchtime *menú* has everything from roast chicken (1200ptas/€7) to lasagna. (Open daily noon-4pm and 7pm-midnight. AmEx/MC/V.) Ice cream shops and restaurants with terraces dominate the Pl. Nova, including **Can Moragas,** a pizzeria and *crêpería*. Follow your individual pizza (1100ptas/€6.60) with one of many specialty *crêpes* with fruit and liqueur toppings for only 300-500ptas/€2.40. (Open daily 8:30am-midnight. MC/V.)

SIGHTS AND ENTERTAINMENT

Palafrugell boasts one of the world's few cork museums. The **Museu del Suro,** C. Tarongeta, 31, has everything you ever (never?) wanted to know about cork. From Plaça Nova, face C. Sant Sebastià, take a left onto C. Pi i Margall, and the second right onto C. Tarongeta; the museum is at the end of the block. (☎972 30 39 98. Open June 15-Sept. 15 daily 10am-2pm and 4-10m; Sept.16-June 14 Tu-Sa 5-8pm and Su 10:30am-1:30pm. 200ptas/€1.20, students and seniors 100ptas/€1.)

A Palafrugell Friday evening stroll ends up at the *plaça,* where young and old often dance the traditional Catalan *sardana* around 10:30pm in July and August. The tourist office prints a monthly bulletin of upcoming events; also check the *Guía Municipal.* The town's biggest party takes place July 19th to the 21st, when the dance-intensive **Festa Major** bursts into the streets. Calella honors **Sant Pere** on June 29 with *sardana* dancing, and Tamariu celebrates on August 15, coinciding with the Assumption of the Blessed Mother. The **festivals of the** [illegible] Dance the night away at **Discoteca Xarai,** C. Barris i Buixo, 42. No athletic gear allowed. Take a right off C. Sant Sebastià onto C. Barris i Buixo and look for the lime-green and orange building. (Open F-Sa only.)

DAYTRIPS FROM PALAFRUGELL

CALLELA, LLAFRANC, AND TAMARIU

Take a Sarfa bus from Palafrugell to ***Calella*** *(15min., 12-24 per day, 160ptas/€1.50). From Calella, follow the Camino de Ronda (see below) and walk 20min. or so to* ***Llafranc.*** *From Llafranc,* ***Tamariu*** *is a 2hr. walk farther along the path.* ***Tourist Office*** *at Tamariu, C. Riera. ☎972 62 01 93. Open June-Sept. M-Sa 10am-1pm and 5-8pm, Su 10am-1pm.*

The three beaches grow quieter the farther you walk from Callela; Tamariu is the most peaceful. In Callela, **Jardí Botànic de Cap Roig,** the botanical garden in front of Hotel Garbí, provides an excellent view of the coast. (☎972 61 53 45. Open daily June-Aug. 9am-8pm; Sept.-May 9am-6pm. 300ptas/€1.80.) Russian Nicolas Voevodsky built the garden's **seaside castle** after fleeing the Bolshevik Revolution. He and his wife planted and pruned the splendid maze of paths and flower beds with their own hands. The first sign for the castle points to the right at the fork of Av. Costa Daurada and C. Consolat del Mar—it also hosts the **Festival de Jazz de la Costa Brava** in July and August. Callela's **tourist office,** C. Voltes, 6, provides maps of walking paths that criss-cross the area, including the **Camino de Ronda,** a popular climb along the coast from Callela to Llafranc. (☎972 61 44 75. Open daily July-Aug. 10am-1pm and 5-9pm; Apr-June and Sept. 10am-1pm and 5-8pm.)

L'ESCALA ☎972

L'Escala (pop. 5000, in summer 75,000) is a good launching point for the numerous coves and beaches in the area. Once a fishing village that made it big with anchovies, L'Escala's old quarter has pleasant pedestrian paths and tree-lined promenades, and the beaches and the Greek and Roman ruins of nearby **Empúries** make the town a very worthwhile trip from Palafrugell. Less cosmopolitan than some of its Costa Brava neighbors, L'Escala attracts mostly local tourists and day trippers.

ORIENTATION AND PRACTICAL INFORMATION. For **Sarfa buses,** call 972 77 02 18. Buses to: **Figueres** (55min., 5 per day 7:10am-7:05pm, 485ptas/€2.90); **Girona** (1hr., 7:30am and 2:30pm, 555ptas/€3.40); and **Palafrugell** (35min., 5 per day 7:10am-6:55pm, 365ptas/€2.20). Buses stop in front of the tourist office; buy tickets on board. With your back to the tourist office, the ruins are to the left (walk down Rda. del Pedró) and the center is straight ahead (down Av. Ave María). L'Escala is a compact, walkable town; its main thoroughfare, Av. Ave María runs from Pl. Escoles (tourist office) downhill to the water in several long blocks. The Alberg d'Empúries youth hostel arranges **mountain bike rental** if you contact them in advance, and **Emporda Bikes,** Av. Ave María, 9, rents by the day. (☎972 77 40 42. 500ptas/€3 per hr., 1900ptas/€11.42 per day; 10% discount when renting 2 or more bikes. Open June-Sept. daily 9am-1pm and 5-8pm; Oct.-June Tu-Sa 9am-1pm and 5-8pm.) The **tourist office,** Pl. Escoles, 1, has **fax** service. (☎972 77 06 03; fax 77 33 85. Open June-Sept. M-Sa 9am-8:30pm, Su 10am-1pm; Oct.-May M-Sa 9am-1pm and 4-7pm and Su 10am-1pm.) The **Banco Central Hispano,** C. Maranges, 16 has an **ATM** (open Apr.-Oct. M-F 8:30am-2:30pm; Oct.-Mar. M-F 8:30am-2:30pm and Sa 8:30am-1pm). Services include: **medical emergency** (☎908 09 43 33); **municipal police,** C. Pintor Joan Massanet, 24 (☎972 77 48 18); and the **post office,** next to the tourist office. (Open M-F 8:30am-2:30pm, Sa 9:30am-1pm.) **Postal code:** 17130.

ACCOMMODATIONS AND FOOD. Finding a cheap room in L'Escala can be difficult, especially during the summer. **Alberg de Empúries,** Les Coves, 41, is a short walk from the Empúries ruins and beaches. Facing the tourist office, follow the road on the right toward the coast. When you get to the headless male statue, take a left down the small lane and into the wooded area. (☎972 77 12 00. Reception hours 10am-1pm and 7-8:30pm. Mar.-June dorms 2000ptas/€12; over 25 2700ptas/€16; July-Sept. dorms 2350ptas/€14; over 25 3000ptas/€18; Oct.-Feb. dorms 1775ptas/€11; over 25 2400ptas/€15. AmEx/MC/V. **Pensió Torrent,** C. Riera, 28, has whitewashed rooms with clean bathrooms. From Pl. Escoles, walk downhill 1 block on C. Pintor, turn left, and follow the street around the corner. (☎972 77 02 78. Doubles 4500ptas/€27; off-season 3000ptas/€18.)

From May to September, the town **market** is held daily 7am-2pm in **Pl. Victor Català** (Oct.-Apr. Tu, Th, Sa-Su 7am-2pm). Alternatively, fill your basket at **MAXOR,** Pl. Escoles, 2, across the street from the tourist office (open M-F 8am-2pm and 4:30-9pm, Sa 8:30am-9pm, Su 9am-2pm). Former fishermen's hangout, **Restaurante-Bar Cal Galán,** C. La Torre, 18, offers a lunch and dinner *menú* (1175ptas/€7 and 1500ptas/€9) Entrées 525-850ptas/€3-5. Open daily Oct.-May M and W-Su 8:30am-midnight. Closed Nov. MC/V.) Vegetarians will rejoice over the Italian-Mediterranean fare at **Pizzeria del Port,** C. de Port, 9. (*Menú* 1595ptas/€9.60; pastas 750-1100ptas/€4.50-6.60. Open daily May-Oct. 11am-4pm and 7pm-midnight; Nov.-Apr. Su-Tu, Th-Sa 11am-4pm and 7pm-midnight. MC/V.)

DAYTRIP FROM L'ESCALA: EMPÚRIES

To get to Empúries, walk 20-30min. north, following C. Mirador del Pedró to Cami Forestal (at the headless male statue), or take the little train, Carrilet (☎937 65 47 84), which stops across the street from the tourist office, to St. Martí d'Empúries and ask to get off at the ruins (June 15-Sept. 15 on the hr., every hr. 8am-9pm, 250ptas/€1.50). ***Ruins and museum*** *(☎972 77 02 08; www.mac.es). Open daily June-Sept. 10am-8pm; Oct.-May 10am-6pm. 400ptas/€2.40; students and seniors 300ptas/€3.60. Audio-visual program screened every 30min. from 10:30am until closing; 300ptas/€3.60.* ***Aquatic tour*** *(☎609 136 00 04). Open 10am-7pm daily. 600ptas/€3.60 or 525ptas/€3.20 with ticket to ruins. Look for the CASC hut on the beach in front of the ruins; bring your swimsuit.*

Just 1km north of L'Escala are the ruins of Empúries. In the 7th century BC, Greek traders landed on a small island on the northeast Iberian coast. As the settlement grew, it moved to the mainland and became the prosperous colony of Emporion (meaning "marketplace"); four centuries later, it fell into Roman hands. Mostly knee-high remnants of Greek and Roman cities, including some gorgeous mosaic floors and a Visigoth basilica, fill Empúries's 40 hectares of ruins. Excavation continues, backed by profits from the 1992 Olympic Games. (The Olympic torch first formally entered Spain through this ancient Greek port city, commemorated by the headless male statue.) A winding road at the entrance takes you through the remarkable ruins, from which the careful layout of the great ancient cities is visible. The small **Museu Monogràfic d'Empúries** showcases a large collection of ceramics and Etruscan wares. Explanatory signs in a variety of languages throughout the ruins indicate the ancient urban plan amid the fountains, mosaics, and columns set against cypress trees and the breezy Mediterranean. If you can't get enough of Empúries, the **Centre d'Arqueològia Subaquática de Catalunya** (CASC) offers snorkeling tours of the remains of 2000 year old submerged ships off the city's shore.

CATALUÑA

GIRONA ☎972

Girona (pop. 70,000) is a world-class city that the world has yet to notice. A Roman settlement and then an important medieval center, Girona was one of the few Spanish cities where Christians, Arabs, and Jews were able to peacefully coexist—for a time. Girona was the founding place of the renowned *cabalistas de Girona*, a group of 12th-century rabbis who created an oral tradition called the *Kabbala* based on numerological readings of the Torah (see The Jewish Sepharad, p. 353). The city is divided by the Riu Onyar, which separates the medieval alleys and Romanesque buildings of the old quarter from the Spanish dwellings of the new.

TRANSPORTATION

Trains: RENFE (☎972 24 02 02; www.renfe.es), in Pl. Espanya. Info open daily 6:30am-10pm. To: **Barcelona** [illegible] ptas/€5.00); **Figueres** (30-40min., 24 per day 6:15am-10:44pm, 390ptas/€2.30); **Madrid** (10½hr., 8:21pm, 6800ptas/€41); **Portbou** (50min.-1hr., 12 per day 6:15am-10:44pm, 525ptas/€3.20); and **Paris** (11hr., 10:17pm, 17,700ptas-19,300ptas/€107-€116).

Buses: Station police ☎972 21 23 19. Station right next to the train station. **Sarfa** (☎972 20 17 96; open M-F 6:45am-9:15pm, Sa 6:45am-1pm and 4:30-8pm, Su 6:45am-noon and 3:45-8pm; 10% discount for students) runs to **Palafrugell** (1¼hr., 17 per day, 590ptas/€3.50), for connections to Begur, Llafranc, Calella, and Tamariu and to **Tossa de Mar** (40min.; July-Aug. 2 per day, Sept.-June 1 per day; 580ptas/€3.50). **Teisa** (☎972 20 02 75; open M-F 9am-1pm and 3:30-7:15pm, Sa-Su 9am-1pm; cash only) drives to: **St. Feliu** (45min., 9-14 per day, 490ptas/€3); **Olot** (1¼hr., 9 per day, 720ptas/€4.30); **Ripoll** (2hr., 3 per day, 1240ptas/€7.50); **Lerida** (3½hr.; 2 per day; 2375ptas/€14.30, for students 2140ptas/€13). **Barcelona Bus** (☎972 20 24 32; M-F 7-10am, 11am-2pm, and 4:30-7pm; MC/V) express to **Barcelona** (1¼hr., 3-6 per day, 1345ptas/€8.10) and **Figueres** (50min., 2-6per day, 540ptas/€3.30).

Taxis: ☎972 22 23 23 or 22 10 20. Try Pl. Independència and Pont de Pedra.

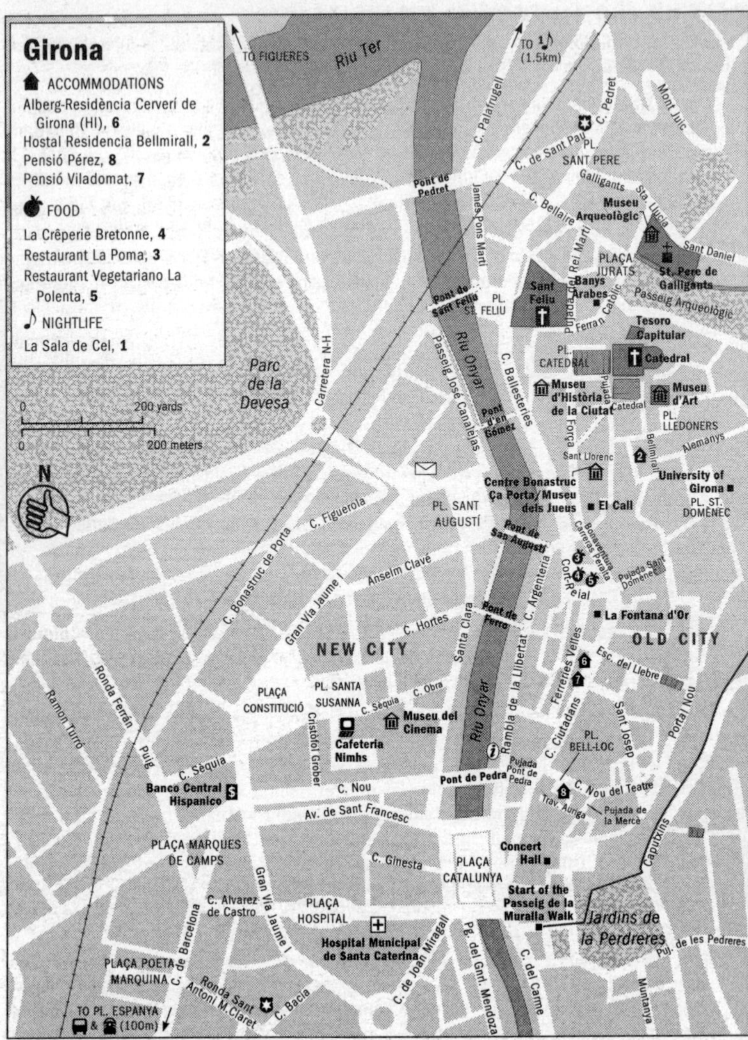

Car Rental: Europcar, inside the train station. Other companies cluster around C. Barcelona, right outside. Must be 21+ (for most) and have 1-2yr. license record. **Hertz,** C. Bailen, 2 (☎972 41 00 68). Walk through the parking lot away from the train station; C. Bailen leads off diagonally to your left. Min. age 25. Rentals from 7000ptas/€42, plus 10ptas/€0.06 per km after the first 300km. Open M-F 8am-1pm and 4-8pm, Sa 8am-1pm. AmEx/MC/V; credit cards only.

ORIENTATION AND PRACTICAL INFORMATION

The **Riu Onyar** separates the new city from the old. The **Pont de Pedra** bridge connects the two banks and leads into the old quarter by way of C. Ciutadans, C. Peralta, and C. Força, which lead to the cathedral and **El Call,** the historic Jewish neighborhood. The **RENFE** and **bus terminals** are situated off C. de Barcelona, in the modern neighborhood. To get to the old city, head straight out through the parking lot, turning left on C. Barcelona. Follow C. Barcelona for two blocks until it forks at the traffic island. Take the right fork via C. Santa Eugenia to Gran Vía de Jaume I, and continue across the Gran Vía to C. Nou, which leads to the Pont de Pedra.

Tourist Office: Rambla Llibertat, 1 (☎972 22 65 75; fax 22 66 12), in a yellow building directly on the left as you cross Pont de Pedra from the new town. Open M-F 8am-8pm, Sa 8am-2pm and 4-8pm, Su 9am-2pm. The **train station branch** (☎972 20 70 93) is to the right of the RENFE ticket counter. Open July-Sept. M-Sa 8am-1pm and 3-8pm.

Currency Exchange: Banco Central Hispano, on the corner of C. Nou and Gran Vía. Another on Pujada Pont de Pedra, beyond the bridge in the old city). **ATMs.** Open Oct.-Mar. M-F 8:30am-2:30pm, Sa 8:30am-1pm; Apr.-Sept. 30 M-F 8:30am-2:30pm.

Luggage Storage: Lockers in train station (700ptas/€4.20 per 24hr.) Open M-F 6:30am-10pm.

Travel Bookstore: Ulysseus, C. Ballesteries, 29 (☎/fax 972 21 17 73), on the left-hand side of the street as you walk up Ballesteries toward the Pl. Cathedral. Very thorough offering of regional guides to Spain, as well as country guides for most of Europe; some in English (3000-4500ptas/€18-27). Open M-Sa 10am-2pm and 4:30-8:30pm. MC/V.

Supermarket: Hipercor: (☎972 18 84 00), on C. Barcelona; take a right out of the train station (15min.). El Corte Inglés' not-so-chic cousin. Groceries, clothing, telephones, currency exchange, English books, and cafeteria. Open M-Sa 10am-10pm.

Emergency: ☎112. **Police: Policía Municipal,** C. Bacià, 4 (☎092). From Banco Central Hispano, turn right on the Gran Vía, then right on Bacià.

Hospital: Hospital Municipal de Santa Caterina, Pl. Hospital, 5 (☎972 18 26 00).

Internet Access: Corado Telephone, C. Barcelona, 31 (☎972 22 28 75), across from the train station. 300ptas/€1.80 per hr. Open M-Sa 9am-2pm and 5-9pm. **Cafeteria Nimhs,** C. Sèquia, 5 (☎972 22 03 86), next to Museu del Cinema. 200ptas/€1.20 for 15min., 500ptas/€3 per hr. Open M-F 8am-10pm.

Post Office: Av. Ramón Folch, 2 (☎972 22 21 11), at the start of Gran Vía de Jaume I. Turn right on Gran Vía coming from the old city. **Second office,** Ronda Ferrán Puig, 17 (☎972 22 34 75). **Lista de Correos** only. Both open M-F 8:30am-8:30pm and Sa 9:30am-2pm. **Postal Code:** 17070.

ACCOMMODATIONS

Pensió Viladomat, C. Ciutadans, 5 (☎972 20 31 76; fax 20 31 76), next to the youth hostel. Bright rooms and a dining area with balcony. Singles 2500ptas/€15; doubles 5000ptas/€30, with bath 7500ptas/€45; triples with bath 9500ptas/€57.

Hostal Residencia Bellmirall, C. Bellmirall, 3 (☎972 20 40 09). With the cathedral directly behind you, C. Bellmirall is ahead to the left; look for the blue sign. Expensive but delightful rooms [illegible] included. Make reservations. Closed Jan.6-Feb. 28. Singles 5300ptas/€32; doubles 8200ptas/€49, with bath 9200ptas/€55,50; triples 12,495ptas/€75,30; family room (for 4) 16,000ptas/€97.

Albergue-Residència Cerverí de Girona (HI), C. Ciutadans, 9 (☎972 21 80 03; fax 21 20 23). From the new city, cross Pont de Pedra and take a left on Ciutadans; it's a block up on your left. The sterile walls and blue bunks in this college dorm may cause summer camp flashbacks. Sitting rooms with TV/VCR; rooms of 3 and 8 beds with lockers. Breakfast included. Sheets 350ptas/€2.10. Laundry 500ptas/€3. **Members only.** HI cards for sale. Make reservations at the Barcelona office (☎934 83 83 63). Dorms 2000ptas/€12, over 25 2700ptas/€16.30. MC/V.

Pensió Pérez, Pl. Bell-lloc, 4 and **Pensió Borras,** Trav. Auriga, 6 (☎972 22 40 08). Cross Pont de Pedra into the old quarter and head straight on C. Nou; Pl. Bell-lloc is on the right. To Pensió Borras from Pérez, take a right out the door and follow the street around the corner, making a left at its end; Pérez is on the 2nd floor of the last building on your right. Spartan pensions owned by the same woman. Singles 2000ptas/€12; doubles 3500ptas/€21, with bath 4000ptas/€24; triples 4700ptas/€28.

FOOD

Girona's specialties are its *botifarra dolça* (sweet sausage of with pork, lemon, cinnamon, and sugar) and *xuixo* (sugar-sprinkled pastries filled with cream). The best place to find good, cheap food is on C. Cort Reial, at the top of C. Argenteria. La Rambla is home to tourist cafés with ubiquitous terrace seating. In summer, an open **market** comes to Parc de la Deversa (open Tu and Sa 8am-3pm). Get your **groceries** at **Caprabo,** C. Sequia, 10, one block from C. Nou. (Open M-Sa 9am-9pm.)

La Crêperie Bretonne, C. Cort Reial, 14. Potent proof of Girona's proximity to France, this popular *crêpe* joint offers funky atmosphere in addition to good taste. *Menú* 1350ptas/€8.10. *Crêpes* 350-875ptas/€2.10-5.30. Unusual salads 850-925ptas/€5.10-5.60. Open M 1-4pm and Tu-Sa 1-4pm and 8pm-midnight. MC/V.

Restaurante La Poma, C. Cort Reial, 16. Internationally-influenced sandwiches, *crêpes*, pasta, pizza, and salads at unbelievable prices, in a friendly restaurant decked out in primary colors. Salads and pasta 650-750ptas/€3.90-4.50. Pizza 675ptas/€4. *Crêpes* 500-600ptas/€3-3.40. Open W-M 7:30pm-midnight.

Restaurant Vegetariano La Polenta, C. Cort Reial, 6. Vegetarian *menú del día* with an international accent and innovative rice, tofu, and polenta dishes (1400ptas/€9). Fills up at lunchtime but maintains a pleasant atmosphere. Open M-F 1-4pm. MC/V.

SIGHTS

Available at any one of the following museums, a combined ticket gains access to all 6 city museums for only 800ptas/€4.80 (good for a month).

The narrow, winding streets of the medieval old city, interspersed with steep stairways and low arches, are ideal for wanderers. Start your self-guided historical tour at the **Pont de Pedra** and turn left at the tourist office down tree-lined **Rambla de la Llibertat.** Continue on C. Argenteria, bearing right across C. Cort Reial. Up the flight of stairs, C. Forçà begins on the left.

EL CALL. The part of the old town around C. Forçà and C. Sant Llorenç was once the center of Girona's medieval Jewish community ("call" comes from *kahal*, for "community" in Hebrew.) The site of the last synagogue in Girona now serves as the **Centre Bonastruc Ca Porta,** named for Rabbi Moshe Ben-Nahman (Nahmanides), a scholar of Jewish mysticism (*Kabbala*) and the oral tradition (see **The Jewish Sepharad,** p. 353). The center includes the **Museu d'Història dels Jueus Girona,** notable for its detailed wooden model of the original Call, as well as its collection of inscribed Hebrew tombstones. *(Entrance to the center is off C. Força, halfway up the hill. ☎972 21 67 61. Center and museum open June-Oct. M-Sa 10am-8pm, Su 10am-2pm; Nov.-May M-Sa 10am-6pm, Su 10am-3pm. Museum 300ptas/€1.80, students and over 65 150ptas/€1, under 16 free. The tourist office also offers guided tours of El Call in July and Aug. for 1000ptas/€6 during the day and 2000ptas/€12 at night.)*

CATHEDRAL COMPLEX. Farther uphill on C. Forçà and around the corner to the right, Girona's imposing Gothic **cathedral** rises a record-breaking 90 steps (its stairway is the largest in Europe) from the plaça. The **Torre de Charlemany** (bell tower) and **cloister** are the only structures left from the 11th and 12th centuries; the rest of the building dates from the 14th-17th centuries. The world's widest Gothic **nave** (22m) is surpassed in sheer size only by St. Peter's in Rome. A door on the left leads to the trapezoidal cloister and the **Tesoro Capitular (treasury),** home to some of Girona's most precious possessions. The *tesoro's* (and possibly Girona's) most famous piece is the **Tapis de la Creació,** an 11th-century tapestry depicting the story of creation. *(Tesoro ☎972 21 44 26. Cathedral and Tesoro open July-Sept. Tu-Sa 10am-2pm and 4-7pm, Oct.-Mar. Tu-Sa 10am-2pm and 4-6pm, Mar.-June Tu-Sa 10am-2pm and 4-7pm; open Su-M and holidays 10am-2pm. Tesoro and cloister 500ptas/€3.)*

THE JEWISH SEPHARAD Though Girona has a reputation for tolerance, the Jews of Girona were still victims of discrimination, ostracism, and eventual expulsion. Despite it all, they contributed ineradicably to the city's culture. The *aljama* (Jewish quarter) in Girona, once populated by 300 people, became a leading center for the study of the **Kabbala,** a mystical reading of the Torah in which number values are assigned to each Hebrew letter and numerical sums are interpreted to reveal spiritual meaning. Operating like a tiny, independent country within the city (inhabitants answered to their King, not the city government), El Call was protected by the crown of Catalunya in exchange for financial tribute. Until the 11th century, Christians and Jews coexisted peacefully, even intermarrying. Unfortunately, this did not last. Historical sources cite attacks and looting of the Jewish quarter in eight separate years, the first in 1276 and the last in 1418. Eventually, almost every entrance to El Call was blocked off. The reopening of the streets of El Call began only after Franco's death in 1975. In recent years, eight Spanish mayors have created a network called *Caminos de Sepharad,* an organization aimed at restoring Spain's Jewish quarters and fostering a broader understanding of the Sephardic legacy.

WALKS. Girona's renowned **Passeig de la Muralla,** not for the faint of heart, begins at the bottom of La Rambla in Pl. de la Marvà. Take the steps up to the guard's rampart atop the old Roman defense walls and follow them around the entire eastern side of the old town. The walk ends behind the Cathedral, where the equally beautiful **Passeig Arqueològic** begins. Partly lined with cypresses and flower beds, this path skirts the northeastern medieval wall and also overlooks the city. (Passeig de la Muralla is open daily 8am-10pm.) For the less athletically inclined, a small trolley gives a 30min. guided tour of the main sights of the old town, including the town hall, Cathedral, St. Feliu church, El Call, and the walls. (In summer, leaves daily every 20-25min. from the Pont de Pedra, 10am-8pm or so. In winter, it runs less frequently, sometimes only weekends; check in the tourist office. Available in English. 500ptas/€3, for students 400ptas/€2,40.)

MUSEU DEL CINEMA. This unusual collection documents the rise of cinema from the mid-17th to the 20th century, with a few pieces from as early as the 11th century (Chinese shadow theater). It walks you through the chronological development of the camera obscura (9th-12th century), magic lantern (1659), panorama (1788), diorama (1822), Thomas Edison's kinetoscope (1891), and more, with several hands-on visual displays and a short film at the end. *(C. Sèquia, 1, one block north of C. Nou off C. Santa Clara. ☎972 41 2 777. Open Oct.-Apr. M-F 10am-6pm, Sa 10am-8pm, Su 11am-3pm; May-Sept. daily 10am-8pm. Museum entrance 500ptas/€3, for students and over 65 250ptas/€1.50. Guided tours available in multiple languages. AmEx/MC/V.)*

OTHER MUSEUMS. The **Museu d'Història de la Ciutat** [illegible] first settlers in Catalunya to the present day; check out the festival giants and the room dedicated to the Napoleonic War. (C. Força 27. ☎972 22 22 29. Open Tu-Sa 10am-2pm and 5-7pm, Su and holidays 10am-2pm. Some descriptions in English. 200ptas/€1.20, under 16 free.) To get to the **Banys Arabs** from the cathedral, with your back to the stairs, take a right on C. Ferran Catòlic. Inspired by Muslim bath houses, the graceful 12th-century structure once contained saunas and baths of varying temperatures; now they occasionally host art outdoor art exhibits. (☎972 21 32 62. Open Apr.-Sept. M-Sa 10am-7pm, Su 10am-2pm; Oct.-Mar. daily 10am-2pm. 250ptas/€1.50, students 100ptas/€0.60.) Next to the cathedral, the **Museu d'Art** holds medieval and modern art, including themed rooms on glass, ceramics, and liturgical art. (☎972 20 38 34. Open Tu-Sa Mar.-Sept. 10am-7pm, Oct.-Feb. 10am-6pm; Su and holidays 10am-2pm. 300ptas/€1. 80, for students and over 65 225ptas/€1.40. *(Combined tickets provide access to all 6 city museums for only 800ptas/€4,80. Good for a month—available at any of the musuems).*

ENTERTAINMENT AND NIGHTLIFE

During the latter half of May, government-sponsored **flower exhibitions** spring up all over the city; local monuments and pedestrian streets swim in blossoms, and the courtyards of Girona's fine old buildings open to the public. Summer evenings often inspire spontaneous *sardana* dancing in the city *plaças*. Like the rest of Catalunya, Girona also lights up for the **Focs de Sant Joan** on June 24, an outdoor party of fireworks and campfires.

The only concentrated nightlife locales are **Pl. de Independència,** the old quarter, and in summer, the expansive, impeccably designed **Parc de la Devesa,** which explodes with *carpas*, temporary outdoor bars. (Across the river from the old town, several blocks to the left. Open June-Sept. 15 Su-Th 10pm-3am and F-Sa 10pm-4:30am. Drinks 700-900ptas/€4.20-5.40.) The bars and cafés in the old quarter are particularly mellow and relaxing, a good way to start the evening. **Platea,** behind the post office on C. Fontclara, is a popular early morning dance spot on weekends. **La Sala del Cel,** C. Pedret, 118, a 15min. walk up-river from the Pont de St. Feliu, on the old town side, has 3 techno and house-blasting dance floors, a huge hangout area with black leather couches, and a pool and slide. (Cover 2000ptas/€12. Open F-Sa midnight-5:30am. MC/V.)

CATALUÑA

FIGUERES (FIGUERAS) ☎972

In 1974, the mayor of Figueres (pop. 35,000) asked native Salvador Dalí to donate a painting to an art museum the town was planning. Dalí refused to donate a painting; he was so flattered by his hometown's recognition that he donated an entire museum. With the construction of the Teatre-Museu Dalí, Figueres was catapulted to international fame; ever since, a multilingual parade of Surrealism fans has been awed and entranced by Dalí's bizarre perspectives and erotic visions. Though it is a beachless sprawl, Figueres hides other quality museums and some pleasant cafés. If you choose to extend your visit beyond Dalí's spectacle, the town's lovely Rambla is a good place to start for food, accommodations, and further sightseeing.

TRANSPORTATION

Trains: ☎902 24 02 02. To: **Barcelona** (1½hr., 21 per day 6:11am-8:58pm, 1200ptas/€7); **Girona** (30min., 21 per day 6:11am-8:58pm, 390ptas/€2.30); **Portbou** (30min., 12 per day 6:42am-11:16pm, 300ptas/€1.80).

Buses: Buses leave from the **Estació Autobuses** (☎972 67 33 54), in Pl. Estació. **Sarfa** (☎972 67 42 98; www.sarfa.com) runs to **Llançà** (25min.; July-Aug. 4 per day, Sept.-June 2 per day; 330ptas/€2) and **Cadaqués** (1¼hr.; July-Aug. 5 per day, Sept.-June 2-3 per day; 540ptas/€3.50). **Barcelona Bus** (☎972 50 50 29) drives to **Barcelona** (2¼hr., 4-6 per day, 1885ptas/€11) and **Girona** (1hr., 4-6 per day, 540ptas/€3.50).

Taxis: (☎972 50 00 08). Taxis line the Rambla and the train station.

Car Rental: Hertz, Pl. Estació, 9 (☎902 40 24 05). Min. age 24. All-inclusive rental from 8900ptas/€54 per day. AmEx/D/MC/V.

ORIENTATION AND PRACTICAL INFORMATION

Trains and buses arrive at **Plaça de Estació** on the edge of town. Cross the plaza and bear left on C. Sant Llàtzer, walk several blocks to Carrer Nou, and take a right to Figueres' tree-filled Rambla. To reach the **tourist office,** walk up the Rambla and continue on C. Lasauca straight out from the left corner. The blue, all-knowing **"i"** beckons across the rather treacherous intersection with Ronda Frial.

Tourist Office: Main office, Pl. Sol (☎972 50 31 55). Open July-Aug. M-Sa 9am-9pm and Su 9am-3pm; Apr.-June and Oct. M-Sa 9am-2pm, 4:30-8pm; Sept. and Nov.-Apr.

M-F 9am-3pm. Two add'l **branch offices** in summer, one at Pl. Estació (open mid-July to mid-Sept. M-Sa 9:30am-1:30pm and 4:30-7pm), and the other in a yellow mobile home in front of the Dalí museum (open July-Sept. 15 M-Sa 10am-2:30pm and 4-7pm).

Currency Exchange: Banco Central Hispano, La Rambla, 21. **ATM.** Open Apr.-Oct. M-F 8:30am-2pm; Nov.-Mar. M-F 8:30am-2pm, Sa 8:30am-1pm.

Luggage Storage: Large lockers at the **train station** 600ptas/€3.60. Open daily 6am-11pm. At the **bus station** 300ptas/€1.80. Bus station open daily 6am-10pm.

Emergency: ☎112. **Police: Mossos d'Esquadra** (☎972 67 50 89), on C. Ter.

Internet Access: Pizza Fono, C. Sant Antoni, 27 (☎972 61 00 55). 5 computers and takeout pizza. 30min. 300ptas/€1.80; 1hr. 500ptas/€3. Open Tu-Su 2-11pm.

Post Office: C. Santa Llogaia, 60-62 (☎972 50 54 31). Open M-F 8:30am-2:30pm, Sa 9:30am-1pm. **Postal Code:** 17600.

ACCOMMODATIONS

As most visitors make Figueres a daytrip from Barcelona, affordable accommodation abounds. Most lodging tends to be on the upper floors of small bars or restaurants. Some cluster on C. Jonquera, around the Dalí museum, while others are closer to La Rambla and C. Pep Ventura.

Hostal La Barretina, C. Lasauca, 13 (☎972 67 64 12). From the train station, walk up the left side of La Rambla to its end and look for C. Lasauca ahead. A luxury experience—rooms with TV, A/C, and bath. Reception downstairs in the restaurant. Reservations recommended. Singles 3500ptas/€21; doubles 6000ptas/€36. AmEx/MC/V.

Pensión Mallol, C. Pep Ventura, 9 (☎972 50 22 83). Follow the Rambla toward the tourist office, turn right on Castell at its end, and take the 2nd left. Spacious, clean, and simply decorated rooms with shared bathrooms and firm mattresses; a very good value. Singles 2200ptas/€13; doubles 3700ptas/€22.

Pensión San Mar, C. Rec Arnau, 31 (☎972 50 98 13). Follow C. Girona off La Rambl, continuing as it turns into C. de la Jonquera; turn right onto Travessera Rec Arnau, then right again onto C. Rec Arnau. Enter through the bar. Decorated with plants and no-frills furniture, some of the cheapest rooms in town, all with bath. Singles 2000ptas/€12, doubles 4000ptas/€24. 30% deposit required for reservation.

FOOD

Restaurants near the Dalí museum serve overcooked *paella* to the masses; better choices surround the Rambla on smaller side streets. The **market** is at Pl. Gra (open Tu, Th, and Sa 5am-2pm. Widest selection on Th). Supermarket **MAXOR,** Pl. Sol, 5. (Open July-Sept. M-Sa 9am-10pm; Oct.-June M-Sa 9am-9pm. MC/V.)

La Llesca, C. Mestre Falla, 15, just beyond Pl. Sol. Family-run restaurant specializes in *llesques*, toasted sandwiches [illegible] 1100ptas/€6.60, salads 450-675ptas/€3-4. Open M-Sa 7am-midnight, Su 6pm-midnight. AmEx/MC/V.

La Churraskita, C. Magre, 5. Hammocks adorn the walls of this Argentinian restaurant. A romantic outdoor terrace hides out back. Wide selection of grilled meats (625-1550ptas/€3.60-9) as well as plenty of vegetarian options like pizza and salads (450-950ptas/€2.80-5.80). Open Tu-Su 1-4pm and 8pm-midnight. AmEx/MC/V.

Restaurante La Pansa, C. l'Empordá, 8. A comfortable, slightly more upscale restaurant serves meat and fish dishes and a popular 4-course *menú*. *Menú* 1200ptas/€7.20. Open M-Sa 1-4pm and 8-10pm, Su 1-4pm. AmEx/MC/V.

SIGHTS AND ENTERTAINMENT

TEATRE-MUSEU DALÍ. Welcome to the world of the Surrealist master. This building was the municipal theater for the town of Figueres before it burned down in 1939—hence the name Teatre-Museu ("theater-museum") Dalí. When Dalí decided to donate a museum to Figueres, he insisted on using the ruins of the old theater,

CATALUÑA

IS THAT A MELTING CANDLE IN YOUR POCKET, OR ARE YOU JUST A ROTTING DONKEY? From an early age, Salvador Dalí was plagued by nightmares and insecurities. By age 15, he already had high hopes for himself: "I'll be a genius and the world will admire me." Although Dalí appeared to be confident in his talents, he was not equally confident in other aspects of his life. Sexually inexperienced until a late age, Dalí was sexually ambiguous and had a fear of close contact and impotence. This fear was one of the two central subjects of his work; the other, interestingly enough, was landscapes. Dalí was also influenced by Sigmund Freud, and sought to connect the unconscious with the conscious in his paintings. Surrealism itself attempted to explore the language of dreams in order to tap the unconscious. Although Dalí's paintings can be confusing at first, aspects of their symbol-language are consistent enough to be translated. Here a few examples:

Look carefully at Dalí's **women.** Those that are portrayed in a cubist style are that way because they pose no threat to Dalí.

Most of Dalí's **landscapes** are of the rocky shores of Cadaqués.

A rotting **donkey** or **fish** is Dalí's symbol of the bourgeoise.

The **crutches** propping up bits of soft flesh are symbols of masturbation.

The **grasshopper** is a symbol of terror, as Dalí had a great fear of the insect.

Staircases are a Freudian image, representing the fear of intercourse.

A **melting candle** is a symbol of impotence.

Lions represent animal aggression and **knives** are meant to be phallic symbols.

A **fish hook** (found in Dalí's head) is a symbol of his entrapment.

When asked about the **clocks** he said, "the famous soft watches are nothing else than the tender, extravagant, solitary, paranoia-critical Camembert of time and space." (*Conquest of the Irrational,* 1969.)

which was where he showed his first exposition as a teenager. The resulting homage to his first gallery is the reconstructed theater, covered in sculptures of eggs and full of Dalí's painting, sculptures, other creations, and his own tomb.

Despite his reputation as a fascist self-promoter, Dalí's personally designed mausoleum/museum/monument to himself should be approached as a multimedia experience, an electrifying tangle of sculpture, painting, music, and architecture. It's all here: Dalí's naughty cartoons, his dramatically low-key tomb, and many paintings of Gala, his wife and muse, one of which, when viewed through a telescope (10ptas/€0.01), transforms into a portrait of Abraham Lincoln. Careful when you look up at this work; if you're on the ground level, you're actually standing on Dalí's grave. The treasure trove of paintings includes, among others, the remarkable *Self Portrait with a Slice of Bacon*, *Poetry of America*, *Galarina*, and *Galatea of the Spheres*. Don't miss the spectacular *Sala de Mae West*, created by Dalí for the museum; when viewed from the lookout in the plastic camel, the furnished room resembles the face of actress Mae West. Other works include the surreal appearance of his own Cadillac in the middle of the museum. There is also a small offering of works by other artists selected by Dalí himself, including pieces by El Greco, Marcel Duchamp, and the architect Peres Piñero. While the museum is full of interesting art, not all the works are on the walls; look up as well. *(☎972 67 75 00; fax 50 16 66; www.salvador-dali.org. From the Rambla, take C. Girona from the end farthest from the tourist office, which goes past Pl. Ajuntament and becomes C. de la Jonquera. Steps by a Dalí statue lead to the pink, egg-covered museum. Open daily Tu-Su Oct.-May 31 10:30am-5:45pm, June 10:30am-5:45pm, July-Sept. 9am-7:45pm. 1200ptas/€7; students 800ptas/€4.80.)*

OTHER SIGHTS. Delight once again in the wonders of your favorite childhood toys at the **Museu del Joguet,** winner of Spain's 1999 National Prize of Popular Culture. A colorful collection of antique dolls, blocks, board games, comics, rocking horses, toys for the blind, *caganers*, and more. *(Hotel Paris, La Rambla, 10; enter on St. Pere. ☎972 50 45 85; www.mjc-figueres.net. Open June-Sept. M-Sa 10am-1pm and 4-7pm, Su*

11am-1:30pm and 5-7:30pm; Oct.-May Tu-Sa 10am-1pm and 4-7pm, Su 11am-1:30pm. 750ptas/€4.50; under 12 600ptas/€3.60.) Ten minutes from the Museu Dalí, the 18th-century **Castell de Sant Ferran** commands a view of the countryside and is the largest stone fortress in Europe at 12,000 square meters. *(Av. Castell de Sant Ferran; follow Pujada del Castell from the Teatre-Museu Dalí. ☎972 50 60 94. Open daily July-Sept. 30 10:30am-7pm; Oct. 1-June 30 Tu-Su 10:30am-2pm. 350ptas/€2.10.)*

FESTIVALS. In September, classical and jazz music come to Figueres during the **Festival Internacional de Música de l'Empordà.** (Tickets available at Caixa de Catalunya. Call 97 210 12 12 or get a brochure at the tourist office.) From September 9th to 12th, the **Mostra del Vi de L'Alt Empordà,** a tribute to regional wines, brings a taste of the local vineyards to Figueres. Around May 3, the **Fires i Festes de la Santa Creu** sponsors cultural events, art and technology exhibitions, and general merrymaking at the **Festa de Sant Pere,** held June 28-29, which honors the town's patron saint.

CATALUÑA

CADAQUÉS AND PORT LLIGAT

The whitewashed houses and small bay of Cadaqués (pop. 2000) have attracted artists, writers, and musicians ever since **Dalí** built his summer home in neighboring Port Lligat in the 1930s. Cadaqués is the bigger of the two overlapping towns (Port Lligat is basically just Dalí's house). To preserve the towns' authentic Mediterranean flavor, an affluent crowd of property owners and renters have kept at bay the commercial influx of sprawling condos, big hotels, and trains. Cadaqués has not been immune, however, to the trendy influence of French tourist hordes who flock here in summer, and the droves of Dalí-seeking day trippers from Barcelona; chic galleries and shops have cropped up to suit the cosmopolitan crowd. The rocky beaches and dreamy landscape attract their share of tourists, but Cadaqués preserves a pleasantly laid-back atmosphere. Be forewarned: if you're traveling to Cadaqués in between September and May, it's best to make it a daytrip only, as most food and entertainment options close in the off season.

PRACTICAL INFORMATION. The bus to Cadaqués halts at a small stone tower beneath a miniature Statue of Liberty. With your back to the Sarfa office, walk right and downhill on Av. Caritat Serinyana to the waterfront square, **Plaça Frederic Rahola,** where a signboard map with indexed services and accommodations will orient you. Cadaqués has no train station, but Sarfa **buses** (☎972 25 87 13) run to: **Figueres** (1hr., 5-7 per day, 540ptas/€3.30); **Girona** (2hr., 1-2 per day, 1040ptas/€6.10); and **Barcelona** (2½hr., 4-6 per day, 2365ptas/€14.20). On the beach, in front of the tourist office, **Escola de Vela Ones** rents **mountain bikes, kayaks,** and **wind-surfing** gear. (☎937 53 25 12. Open daily July-Sept. 15 10am-8pm). Farther down the beach on Platja Es Poal, **Animal Area Cadaqués** also has rentals. (☎972 25 80 27. Kayaks 1200ptas/€7,20 per hr., 3000ptas/€1[illegible] [illegible] per day. Scooters 4900ptas/€29 per half day, 6900ptas/€41 per day. Mountain bikes 700ptas/€4 per 2hrs., 1300ptas/€7,80 half day, 2000ptas/€12 full day.) The **tourist office,** C. Cotxe, 2, off Pl. Frederic Rahola, is opposite the *passeig.* (☎972 25 83 15; fax 15 94 42. Open July-Aug. M-Sa 9am-2pm and 4-9pm, Su 10:30am-1pm; Sept.-June M-Sa 9am-2pm and 4-7pm.) **Banco Central Hispano** is on C. Caritat Serinyana, 4. (☎972 25 83 62. Open Oct.-Mar. M-F 8:30am-2:30pm, Sa 8:30am-1pm; Apr.-Sept. M-F 8:30am-2:30pm.) Services include: **local police** (☎972 15 93 43), Pl. Frederic Rahola, by the promenade; **medical assistance** (☎972 25 88 07); and the **post office,** Av. Rierassa off C. Caritat Serinyana. (☎972 25 87 98. Open M-F 9am-2pm, Sa 9:30am-1pm.) **Postal code** is 17488.

ACCOMMODATIONS AND FOOD. As Cadaqués is a beach town, many accommodations are open only during the summer. **Hostal Cristina,** C. Riera, is right on the water, to the right of Avda. Caritat Serinyana. Bright, newly renovated rooms; a rooftop terrace overlooks the water. (☎972 25 81 38. Summer prices include breakfast. May-Sept. singles 4000ptas/€24; doubles 6000ptas/€36, with bath 8000ptas/€48, with TV 9000ptas/€54. Oct.-Apr. singles 3000ptas/€18; doubles 4000ptas/€24, with bath or terrace 6000ptas/€36, with TV 8000ptas/€48. MC/V.) **Pensión Ranxo,** Avda. Caritat Serinyana, 13, is on the right as you walk down from the bus stop. Potted plants and whitewashed hallways lead to clean and comfortable rooms. (☎972 25 80 05. July-Sept. 15: singles 4000ptas/€24; doubles 8000ptas/€48. Sept. 15-June: singles 3000ptas/€18; doubles 6000-7000ptas/€36-42. MC/V.) **Camping Cadaqués,** Ctra. Portlligat, 17, is 100m from the beach on the way to Dalí's house; follow the signs for Hotel Port Lligat. Popular and crowded campsite; relatively clean. Amenities include pool, supermarket, and bungalows (from 3925-5370ptas/€24-32). (☎972 25 81 26; fax 15 93 83. 655ptas/€4 per person; 820ptas/€5 per tent; 655ptas/€4 per car. No dogs allowed. Open late Mar.- late Sept.)

Cadaqués harbors the usual slew of overpriced, unexciting waterfront tourist restaurants—wander into the back streets for more interesting options. **Groceries** can be purchased at **Super Auvi,** C. Riera. (Open July 15-Aug. M-Sa 8am-2pm and 4:30-9pm, Su 8am-2pm; Sept.-July 14 M-Sa 8:30am-1:30pm and 4:30-9pm.) **Can Tito,** C. Vigilant, 8, is an exceptional historic and culinary experience. The stone archway at the entrance to this elegant restaurant is 1 of 5 portals dating back to AD 1100 when Cadaqués was still a fortified village at the mercy of roving pirates. 3-course lunchtime *menú* 1800ptas/€11. (Fish and meat entrées 800-2300ptas/€4.80-14. Open daily Mar.-Jan. 1-3pm and 8-10:30pm. MC/V.) 2nd floor **Restaurant Vehí,** C. de l'Església, 6, serves Catalan fare with a side of panorama. (*Menús* 1400-1750ptas/€8.40-10.50. Entrées 950-2300ptas/€5.80-14. Open from Mar.-Oct.)

CATALUÑA

SIGHTS AND ENTERTAINMENT. Església de Santa María, is a 16th-century gothic church with a baroque altar. Nearby, the **Museu de Cadaqués,** C. Narcis Monturiol, 15, displays rotating exhibits, often with a Dalí theme. (☎972 25 88 77. Open daily mid-June to Sept. 10:30am-1:30pm and 3-8pm. 750ptas/€4.50; students 500ptas/€3.) From the museum, it's pleasant walk (30min.) to **Casa-Museu Salvador Dalí,** in Port Lligat, the home where Dalí and his wife Gala lived until her death in 1982. With your back to the Statue of Liberty, take the right fork and follow the signs to Port Lligat until Casa de Dalí signs appear. At C. President Lluís Companys, where signs point to the house in two different directions, follow the one to the right—the left is the auto route. This modest fisherman's abode was transformed to meet the artist's aesthetic and eccentric needs. The egg-covered building flaunts Dalí's favorite lip-shaped sofa and more stuffed snakes than you bargained for. Though only two (unfinished) Dalí originals remain in the house, the decorating is a work in itself. (☎972 25 10 15. Open June 15-Sept. 15 daily 10:30am-9pm; Mar. 15-June 14 and Sept. 16-Nov. Tu-Su 10:30am-6pm. Make reservations for a tour—the only way to see the house—1-2 days in advance. Multilingual tours every 10min. Ticket office closes 45min. prior. 1300ptas/€7.80; students, seniors, and children 800ptas/€4.80.) **Boat rides** in his *Gala* depart from the front of the house on the hour for a 55min. trip to Cap de Creus (☎617 46 57 57. Open 10am-7pm. 1500ptas/€9).

CATALAN PYRENEES

While beach-goers and city-dwellers flock to Barcelona and the Costa Brava, Cataluña's portion of the Pyrenees draws a different breed of tourist. Bikinis and black pants are tossed aside for slightly better insulation as hikers and high-brow skiers, mostly from Spain and France, come for the refined ski resorts and some of Spain's wildest mountain scenery. Meanwhile, history and architecture buffs, notebooks in hand, eagerly explore the tranquil mountain towns filled with well-preserved Romanesque buildings. Early June to late September is the best time for trekking in the Pyrenees; any earlier, avalanches are a potential danger, and later, it can get prohibitively cold. Tourist offices distribute pamphlets with information on scenic areas and outdoor activities. Skiers will find the *Snow in Catalonia* or *Ski España* guides most useful, and the website www.pirineo.com is a fantastic general planning resource (for skiing and hiking both) for those who can read Spanish. The Pyrenees are best explored with a car, as public transportation links are few and far between. Either way, entry from the east begins in Ripoll.

RIPOLL

Although the sleepy town of Ripoll (pop. 11,000) may be trapped in a permanent time-warp (don't expect to see too many up-and-coming commercial establishments), it continues to attract visitors in search of Spain's Romanesque architectural legacy; the elaborately carved portal of the **Monasterio de Santa María** is one of the most famous in all of Spain. Ripoll also serves as a convenient base for excursions to the nearby town of **Sant Joan de las Abadesses.**

TRANSPORTATION. RENFE, Pl. Mova, 1 (☎972 70 06 44), runs **trains** to **Barcelona** (1½hr., 8-12 per day M-F 6:32am-8:00pm, 805ptas/€4.81) and **Puigcerdà** (1hr., 6 per day 8:56am-8:56pm, 420ptas/€2.5). The bus station next door sends **Teisa buses** (☎972 20 48 68) to: **Barcelona** (4hr., 1 per day, 1700ptas/€10.22); **Girona** (2hr., 2-6 per day, 1240ptas/€7.33), via **Olat** (where passengers must switch buses); **Sant Joan de las Abadesses** (15min., 6-9 per day, 265ptas/€1.55).

PRACTICAL INFORMATION. The **tourist office,** next to the monastery on Pl. Abat Oliba, hands out maps to navigate Ripoll's many plazas. (☎972 70 23 51. Open M-Sa 9:30am-1:30pm and 4-7pm, Su 10am-2pm; additional evening hours June-Sept. Su 4-7; Aug. daily 4-8pm. Services include: **Banco Central Hispano,** on Pl. Sant Eudald, off Pl. Gran. (Open Oct.-Mar. M-F 8:30am-2:15pm; Apr.-Sept. Sa 8:30am-1:30pm.); **emergency** ☎112; **police,** Pl. Ajuntament, 3 (☎972 71 44 14); **internet access** at **Xarxtel,** Pl. d'Espanya, 10, (☎972 70 45 03. 600ptas/€3.61 hr., with 15min. minimum. Open M-Sa 10am-2pm, 5-pm.); and the **post office,** on Paseo St. Joan, facing the tree-lined park on the train-station-side of the river (☎972 70 07 60. Open M-F 8:30am-2:30pm, Sa 9:30am-1pm.). **Postal code:** 17500.

ACCOMMODATIONS AND FOOD. The large cream-colored rooms of **Habitaciones Paula,** C. Berenfuer, 4. (☎972 70 00 11), on Pl. Abat Oliba, behind the Red Cross from the tourist office, have comfortable beds, TVs, lots of light, and spacious, tiled bathrooms. Call ahead during owners' scheduled Oct. vacation slot. (Singles 3320ptas/€19.90; doubles 5350ptas/€32.15. IVA not included. MC/V.) Restaurants surround **Pl. Gran**. Follow your nose down C. Bisbe Morgades, and take a right before the river on C. Mossen; the plaza is to the left. **Las Graelles,** C. d'Olot, 9. (☎972 70 24 51) offers an incredibly generous *menú del día:* three plates, bread, wine, dessert, and the *cuenta* for only 1100ptas/€6.61. (Open M-Th 10am-6pm and F-Sa 11am-5pm and 8pm-midnight. MC/V.) Stock up on **groceries** at **Champion,** C. Progress, 33-37, across the street and to the left of the train station. (☎972 70 26 3[illegible] Open M-Th 8:30am-2pm and 4:30 [illegible] [illegible] the monastery, try **Urgantún Supermarket,** C. Vinyes, 7. (☎902 16 09 25. Open M-F 9am-1pm, 5-8pm; Sa 9am-1:30pm, 5-8:30pm).

SIGHTS. Most visitors to Ripoll come to see the incredibly intricate 11th-century portal of the **Monasterio de Santa María.** To reach the monastery, take a left on C. Progrés from the train and bus stations, following it until it merges with C. Estació. Take the first left after the colorful modern "metal dancers" onto Pont d'Olot, cross the river, then continue straight on C. Bisbe Morgades to the Pl. Ayuntament and Pl. Abat Oliba. Founded in AD 879 by Count Guifré el Pelú (Wilfred the Hairy), the Santa María monastery was once the most powerful in all of Cataluña. The curved doorway, nicknamed the "Stone Bible," depicts survival scenes from the Old and New Testaments as well as a hierarchy of the cosmos and a 12-month calendar. Panels (in Catalan) attempt to decode the doorway. Adjoining it is a beautiful two-story Romanesque and Gothic **cloister.** (Church open daily 8am-1pm and 3-8pm. Free. Cloister open 10am-1pm and 3-7pm. 100ptas/€0.60)

DAYTRIP FROM RIPOLL: ST. JOAN DE LAS ABADESSES

TEISA buses (☎972 74 02 95) connect Sant Joan to Ripoll (15min., 5-7 per day, 265ptas/€1.60). The tourist office, Pl l'Abadia, 9, is next door to the monastery alongside a lovely 15th-century cloister. (☎972 72 05 99. Open daily 10am-2pm, 4-7pm).

Wilfred the Hairy was nothing if not an equal-opportunity employer. After founding Ripoll's first monastery, he went on to endow a convent 10km away, to which he appointed his daughter Emma as the first abbess in 887. Sant Joan de las Abadesses (pop. 3700) developed around the nuns, but unfortunately some of The Hairy's successors were not so keen on female independence; after their community was ousted in the 11th century, it took 100 years before anyone was allowed to move back. The Augustinians who eventually took over turned the convent into a **monastery.** Today it contains a Romanesque **church** with the **Santíssim Misteri,** a 13th-century seven-piece colored sculpture. One section depicts Christ's removal from the cross; on his forehead is a snippet of Holy Bread, supposedly preserved for 700 years. (Monastery open daily Mar.-Apr. and Oct. 10am-2pm and 4-6pm; May-June and Sept. 10am-2pm and 4-7pm; July-Aug. 10am-7pm; Nov.-Feb. M-F 10am-2pm, Sa 10am-2pm, 4-6pm; 300ptas/€1.80; price includes attached museum.)

CATALUÑA

NÚRIA AND QUERALBS

A family-oriented, newly-renovated mountain resort set in a small valley near the French border, Núria is best known for its hiking trails. The surrounding mountains are inaccessible by train or car, and for centuries, only the pious and infertile (see Our Virgin of Fertility Drugs, p. 361) made it through the high passes to the Santuario de Sant Gil. However, the *Cremallera* (Zipper) railway, installed in 1931, make Núria a major ski resort. In recent years, its popularity has been revived, offering right-at-your-doorstep hiking, skiing, archery, horseback-riding, mini-golf, and even canoeing and boating on an artificial lake. The most popular hikes climb to the snow-capped peaks of **Puigmal** (2913m; 5-6hr.) and **Eina** (1000m; 3hr.). Less ambitious trekkers can follow the path to neighboring village of **Queralbs** (2-3hr.), passing alongside waterfalls and gorges carpeted with wildflowers—be warned that uphill return to Núria is significantly more challenging than the way down. In winter, 10 ski trails offer slopes ranging from *molt facil* (very easy) to *molt difficil* (expert). Call ☎972 73 20 20 or visit www.valldenuria.com for further details on available activities.

To get to Núria and the surrounding slopes, take a train, bus, or car from Ripoll and stop in the tiny villages of **Ribes de Freser** or **Queralbs,** past which vehicles cannot continue. The *Cremallara* stops in Queralbs for passenger drop off/pick up before climbing the final 1000m through virgin mountainpasses. (☎972 73 20 20. 45min. ride from Ribes de Freser, 20min. from Queralbs; 6-11 per day; round-trip 1950ptas/€11.72. Closed Nov.) If you want to spend the night, a cable car (included in the price of a *Cremallera* ticket) whisks passengers straight to **Alberg de Joventut Pic de l'Aliga (HI),** a chalet-type hostel complete with roaming cows, a full-service bar, and magnificent views. The alternative route is an arduous 20-minute climb. (Info ☎972 73 20 48, reservations ☎934 83 83 63. Breakfast included. Reservations recommended. April and Oct. dorms 1775ptas/€10.67, over 25 or with breakfast 2400ptas/€15, full board 2550ptas/€14, over 25 3500ptas/€21; weekends and May-Sept. dorms 2350ptas/€14, over 25 3000ptas/€18, with breakfast 3325ptas/€20, full board 4400ptas/€27.) The **Bar Finistrelles,** downstairs from the souvenir store in the main complex, sells sandwiches (600ptas/€3.61). The complex also offers **ski rentals, ATMS, telephones,** and **lockers** (300ptas/€1.80).

Escape to the cliff-side mountain village of **Queralbs** (pop. 80 in winter, 500 in summer) for sublime views, medieval rubble, and a lovely 10th-century Romanesque church. The one official *pensión* in town, **Hostal L'Avet,** C. Mayor, 21, captures the warmth and simplicity of a rural lodge. (☎972 72 73 77. Doubles w/bath, breakfast and dinner 5500ptas/€33.06 Open weekends only Nov.-May.) **Cans Constans,** just off the main road at the entrance to Queralbs, rents four-person apartments with fireplaces. (☎972 72 70 13. Quad 6000ptas/€36.06) The *Cremallera* stops in Queralbs on its way between Ribes and Núria.

OUR VIRGIN OF FERTILITY DRUGS The Vall de Núria was just another remote mountain pass when recluse Gil of Nimes settled here in 700. At some point he carved an elaborate statue of the Virgin and child. Almost 400 years later, that statue, along with Gil's bell and cooking pot, were discovered by a local shepherd, and the hermit's isolated sanctuary became a pilgrimage destination. In a twist of events on which it is best not to speculate, some daredevil pilgrim discovered that her fertility increased if she put her head in the pot while simultaneously ringing the bell. Ever since, barren women have been doing the same—one chime for each desired child. Visitors today can stick their own heads in the progeny-producing pot, but please do not hold *Let's Go* responsible for the consequences.

CATALUÑA

PUIGCERDÀ

A challenge for foreign tongues, the town of Puigcerdà (pop. 7000) itself almost isn't worth the pronunciation effort. Its view of the valley is undeniably beautiful, however, and it can serve as a particularly cheap base for hiking, biking, or skiing the surrounding hillsides. Puigcerdà is perhaps best known for appearing in the 1993 *Guinness Book of World Records* for the world's longest *butifarra* (sausage), a Freudian nightmare (or dream come true) measuring 5200m.

TRANSPORTATION

Trains: RENFE (☎972 88 01 65) to: **Barcelona** (3hr., 6 per day 6:33am-6:50pm, 1145ptas/€6.91); **La Molina** (20min., 6 per day 6:33am-6:50pm, 180ptas/€1.10); **Núria** (6 per day, 6:33am-6:50pm; round-trip train and *Cremallera* ticket 2510ptas/€15.08); **Ripoll** (1¼hr., 6 per day, 400ptas/€2.40).

Buses: Depart from P. Barcelona. **Alsina Graells buses** (☎973 35 00 20) to: **Barcelona** (3hr.; 7:15am, 1:15pm; 1970ptas/€11.85) and **La Seu d'Urgell** (1hr.; 7:30am, 3:10pm, 5:45pm; 670ptas/€4.05). From La Seu there is passage to **Andorra.** Buses pass by the train station of their way out of town. Purchase tickets on board. Schedule with more destinations posted in **Bar Estació,** on the right as you enter the train station.

Taxis: (☎972 88 00 11). Waiting for a flag-down on Pl. Cabrinetty.

Bike Rental: Top Bikes Pl. d'Avenes, 21 (☎972 88 20 42) is on the right, 10min. along the highway toward Barcelona. Bikes 800ptas/€4.81 per hr., 1500ptas/€9.02 per 4hr., 2500ptas/€15.03 per day. Open daily 9am-1pm, 4-8pm. MC/V.

ORIENTATION AND PRACTICAL INFORMATION

Puigcerdà's center sits at the top of its own hill. Off the main plaza, **Plaça Ajuntament** is nicknamed *el balcón de* [illegible] **train station** is at the foot of the western slope. Buses stop at the train station and then Pl. Barcelona, where it's best to get off. To reach Pl. Ajuntament from the inconvenient train station, walk past the stairs in the station's *plaça* until you reach the first real flight of stairs (between 2 buildings). Turn right at the top, then look for the next set of stairs on your left, just before a sign for C. Hostal del Sol. Turn left at the top onto C. Raval de les Monges where the final set of stairs winds up to the right (make sure not to take the prior set). From the *plaça* walk one block on Carrer Alfons I to **Carrer Major,** the principal commercial street. Turn left on C. Major to Pl. Santa María. From Pl. Santa María with your back to the bell tower, head out diagonally to the left to Pl. Barcelona.

Tourist Office: C. Querol, 1 (☎/fax 972 88 05 42). Just off of Pl. Ajuntament, Open June 16-Sept. 10 M-Sa 9am-2pm and 3-8pm, Su 10am-2pm; Sept. 11-June 15, M 9am-2pm and 3-8pm, Tu-F 10am-1pm and 4-7pm, Sa 10am-1:30pm and 4:30-8pm.

Banco Central Hispano: Located on Pl. Cabrinetty. Open Oct.-Mar. M-F 8:30am-2:30pm, Sa 8:30am-1pm; Apr.-Sept. M-F 8:30am-2:30pm. 24hr. **ATM** available.

Library: Pg. 10 d'Abril (☎972 88 03 04). Located right next to the church. Inexpensive internet service for the patient. A sign up sheet hangs inside. Open T, Th, Sa 10am-1:30pm; M,F 4-9pm. 200ptas/€1.20 per hr.

Emergency: ☎091. **Municipal police,** Pl. Ajuntament, 1 (☎972 88 19 72). **Hospital: Hospital de Puigcerdá** in Pl. Santa María (☎972 88 01 50), behind the *campanari*.

Internet: Punt Com, C. d'Espanya, 10 (☎972 88 31 55). Open 10am-1pm and 4-8pm, June-Sept. until 8:30pm, 400ptas/€2.40 hour.

Post office: Av. Coronel Molera, 11 (☎972 88 08 14). Located 1½ blocks down Av. C. Molera from Pl. Barcelona (look for the pink movie theater). Open M-F 8:30am-2:30pm, Sa 9:30am-1pm. **Postal code:** 17520.

ACCOMMODATIONS AND CAMPING

Mainly daytrip destination, Puigcerdá tends to have plenty of rooms (not always on the cheap). Inexpensive *pensiones* crowd Pl. Santa María in the old town.

Hostel Muntanya, C. Molera, 1 (☎973 88 02 02), just off of Pl. Barcelona (with your back to the famous pink movie theater, look diagonally to the left). Mint green walls, a neatly folded pile of white, white towels, and refreshing hospitality. 2500ptas/€15.33 per person, 3000ptas/€18.03 with bath.

Mare de Déu de les Neus (HI), Ctra. Font Canaleta (☎972 89 20 12, reservations ☎934 83 83 63). 500m from the La Molina RENFE station and 4km from the slopes. Modern facilities and a beautiful rural location. Buses climb the slopes every 30 minutes in winter. Breakfast included. Sheets 350ptas. Jan.-Nov. dorms 1900ptas/€11.42, over 25 2500ptas/€15; Dec. dorms 2250ptas/€13.52, over 25 2800ptas/€17. AmEx/MC/V.

Camping Stel, (☎972 88 23 61). 1km from Puigcerdà on the road to Llivia. Full-service camping with benefits of a chalet-style restaurant-bar and lounge. Open June 19-Sept. 29 and weekends in winter. Site with tent and car 2150ptas/€12.92, 680ptas/€4.10 per person, 220V electricity for 480ptas/€2.90.

FOOD

The neighborhood off C. Alfons I is filled with open-air markets and inexpensive restaurants. For fresh fruits and vegetables try the weekly **market** held on Sundays at P. 10 d'Abril. Grab some **groceries** at **Bonpreu**, C. Colonel Molera, 12, the small supermarket diagonally across from the post office. (Open M-Sa 9am-1pm and 5-9pm, Su 10am-2pm. MC/V.) Or kick back with a margarita at **Cantina Restaurant Mexicà,** P. Cabrinetty, 9, and take in some excellent tacos, fajitas, and quesadillas. (☎972 88 16 58. Entrées 500-2000ptas/€3-12. Open M-W, F 1:30-4pm and 9-11:30pm, and Sa-Su 1:30-11:30pm. MC/V.)

SIGHTS AND SLOPES

Puigcerdà calls itself the "capital of snow." **Ski** in your country of choice (Spain, France, or Andorra) at one of 19 ski areas within a 50km radius. The closest and cheapest slope on the Spanish side is **La Molina.** The Puigcerdà area is also popular for **biking;** the tourist office hands out a brochure with 17 potential routes mapped out. Between ski runs and two-wheeled exploration, dash over to the **campanario,** the octagonal bell tower in Pl. Santa María. This 42m high 12th-century tower is all that remains of the **Església de Santa María,** and remains an eerie reminder of the destruction wreaked by the 1936 Civil War. (Open daily July-Sept. 11am-2pm and 4-8pm; Oct.-June weekends only. Free.) **Església de Sant Domènec,** on Pg. 10 d'Abril, contains several Gothic paintings considered to be among the best of their genre. (Open 9:30am-8pm, but often closed at midday. Free.)

PARC NACIONAL D'AIGÜESTORTES

The full name of Cataluña's only national park is actually Parc Nacional d'Aigüestortes i Estany de Sant Maurici, a reference to the park's distinct halves. In the east lies the valley of the Riu Escrita and the park's largest lake, the **Estany de Sant Maurici;** in the west, the wild tumbling of the Riu de Sant Nicolau through its own valley has earned it the nickname "Aigües Tortes" ("Twisted Waters"). On a sunny spring day, the park's snow-capped peaks, wildflower-dusted meadows, and ice-cold glacial lakes (more than 100 of them) are a sight to behold. With over 10,000 hectares to be explored, the park merits at least two days—if you rely on public transportation, it's hard to do it in fewer than three.

Don't rely on the free park maps from the **tourist office;** it's worth the extra cash to buy a better, more detailed map (1000ptas in the office; also available in area stores for a bit more). The red *Editorial Alpina* guides, one each for Montardo, Vall de Boí, and Sant Maurici, are also a useful option (775ptas). One particularly popular hike is to make is the east-west traverse through the park from Espot to Boí (see below for more on the towns themselves). From **Espot** to the **Estany de Sant Maurici** is about 8km (2hr.) and from the lake a path climbs 2½km to the **Portarró d'Espot,** the gateway between the park's two halves and a prime spot for viewing the scenery. Those with a car may opt for half the hike by parking in the last public access lot inside the park. From the pass it is nearly 2km to the **Estany Llong** and the **Aigüestortes** themselves (about 3½hr. from the Estany de Sant Maurici). Near the western tip of the Estany Llong lies the park's first *refugio*, also called **Estany Llong** (☎973 69 61 89. Open mid-June to mid-Oct. and winter weekends. 1200ptas per person.) Finally, to get to the western park entrance from the Estany Llong is a 3.5km hike, and to **Boí** itself another 6½km. The entire hike takes around nine hours but can be shortened by taking a jeep from Espot to the Sant Maurici lake or a taxi from the western entrance to Boí.

For more detailed hiking information, contact the park **tourist offices** (in Espot ☎973 62 40 36; in Boí ☎973 69 61 89). The park's five *refugios* (1500-2000ptas per person) and *Casas de Pagés* (pension-like lodging in private homes) are good accommodation options for those planning multi-day treks. The mountains are deceptively calm from afar, but the region's notoriously unpredictable weather can be quite dangerous, especially in winter. Wandering around to discover the environment is not recommended. Though the main trails are clearly marked, it is easy to become lost should one stray into the wild mountainsides.

ESPOT AND ESTANY DE SANT MAURICI

The official gateway to the eastern half of the park, and the best point of entrance from the direction of Barcelona, is the quiet little town of **Espot.** Espot is a good 4.5km from the actual entrance, but the walk to the park is quite scenic.

TRANSPORTATION. A four-wheel-drive **jeep service** (Dec.-Mar. 9am-5pm, July-Sept. 15 9am-8pm, 9am-7pm during the rest of the year) navigates the bumping mountain back roads from Espot to: **Amitges** (round-trip 2200ptas/€13.22 per person), a view-blessed site near the park's biggest and best **refugio** (see below), **Estany Negre de Pegura** (2700ptas/€16.23 per person, a much less frequented area of the park), **Estany de Ratera** (round-trip 1600ptas/€9.62 per person, dropping off passengers to hike down to the waterfall, then picking them up below), and **Estany Sant Maurici** (each way 600ptas/€3.61 per person). Unfortunately for those relying on public transportation, the **Alsina Graells bus** (☎973 26 85 00) from Barcelona (3hr., M-Sa 1:30pm, 3000ptas/€18.03)—the only mass transit in the area—only comes within 7km of Espot, on Highway C-147 at the La Torrassa crossing. Ask to be dropped off in **la Guingueta d'Aneu**, where you can call the jeep service for pickup. (☎973 62 41 05, 1500ptas/€9.02 for the ride to Espot. Jeeps seat 7-8.)

PRACTICAL INFORMATION. The bustling **park information office**, on Espot's main road (on the right as you enter town), provides good brochures and trekking advice. (☎973 62 40 36. Open daily Apr.-Oct. 9am-1pm and 3:30-7pm; Nov.-Mar. M-Sa 9am-2pm and 3:30-6pm.) In a medical **emergency** call ☎973 62 10 05.

ACCOMMODATIONS AND CAMPING. Many local residences take in travelers; the tourist office has a listing of local lodging possibilities. Cross the main bridge over to **Residència Felip** (☎973 62 40 93) for comfortable rooms with lace curtains. Follow the bridge road for two blocks, and then take a left; the Residència is just behind Hotel Roya. (Oct.-June singles 2000ptas/€13.22, with bath 2500ptas/€15.33; doubles 3000ptas/€18.03, with bath 4000ptas/€24.04. July-Sept. and holidays doubles jump 1000ptas/€6.01.) In the park proper is **Refugi d'Amitges** (☎973 25 00 07 or 25 01 09. Open Feb. 10-25, April 7-16 and 29-May 1, June-Sept., Oct. 12-14, Nov. 1-4, and Dec. 6-9. **Casa Peret de Peretó** and **Camping Solau** (☎973 62 40 68) run a joint establishment, offering spacious sunny rooms inside, and 22 campsites outside on the sprawling front yard. (Rooms Sept.-June 2000ptas/€12.02 per person, July-Aug. and holidays 2500ptas/€15.33. Campsites 600ptas/€3.61 per person, per tent, and per car.) Located 1.3 km down the park entrance road on the right, **Camping Vora Parc** offers the closest camping to the park itself, with sites right along the riverbank. (☎973 62 41 08. 650ptas/€3.91 per person, per tent, per car. MC/V.) **Càmping la Mola** (☎973 62 40 24) and **Càmping Sol i Neu** (☎973 62 40 01), both on the way to Espot, provide comparatively "cushy" camping with laundry, market, and bar. (Open June-Sept. and *Semana Santa.* 650ptas/€3.91 per person, per tent, per car; electricity 600ptas/€3.91. MC/ V.)

CATALUÑA

AIGÜESTORTES AND VALL DE BOÍ

The village of Boí is the most convenient base from which to explore the western half of the park. **Public transportation** from the east to the medieval village is difficult but possible through **Vielha,** or through **Lleida** via Pont de Suert. From Leida, catch the Alsina line's 9am bus from Barcelona on its way to Pont de Suert. From July-Sept. 15, catch the 11:15am connecting bus from Pont de Suert to Boí; in winter a school bus makes the run W, F at 2pm and M, T, Th at 5:30pm. From Boí's main *plaça* it's an easy taxi ride to the park. (☎973 69 63 14, in winter ☎629 20 54 89. 600ptas/€3.91 per person.) Boí's helpful **park information office** is near the bus stop on the *plaça.* (☎973 69 61 89. Open daily Apr.-Oct 9am-1pm and 3:30-7pm, Nov.-Mar. M-Sa 9am-2pm and 3:30-6pm.) The **Guardia Civil** can be reached at ☎973 69 08 15. In an **emergency** call ☎973 69 11 59.

Despite the nearby ski resort in **Taüll,** Boí has retained a pastoral feel. Low arches and cobblestone streets lend the village its charm. Green RCP (Residencias Casa de Payés) indicate the many local residences offering traveler accommodation. Inquire at the tourist office for a comprehensive price listing of local hostels and houses. Most of these private residences do not accept credit cards. Relax on the sun-drenched patio of **Casa Cosán,** C. de la Roca. Exit the plaça through the stone archway, turn right through the next arch, then bear right at the fork. At road's end, take your first right, then a second right onto C. de la Roca. (☎973 69 60 18. July-Aug. 2000ptas/€16; Sept.-June 1800ptas/€10.82 per person.) The owners of **Casa Guasch** let simple rooms, and welcome visitors to make use their kitchen. Exit the plaza through the stone arch, turn right through the next arch, then bear left and turn left again where the street ends; the entrance is on the left. (☎973 69 60 42. Singles 2000ptas/€12.02; doubles 3500ptas/€21.04.)

VAL D'ARAN

Some of the Catalan Pyrenees's most dazzling peaks cluster around green Val d'Aran, Cataluña's northernmost valley. Val d'Aran's main river flows into France and is hemmed in tightly by the highest peaks in the eastern range; consequently, the area's original native language is not Catalan but Aranese, a dialect close to *langue d'oc,* the medieval Romance language spoken in southern France. Today, modern transportation and the tourist industry have made substantial inroads into the valley's unique isolation, but it is still well worth exploring.

SWM SEEKING... Tall, dark, handsome, rich, famous, powerful, and searching for life partner. Enjoys water sports (competed on the Olympic sailing team). Educated at Georgetown. Looking for that special someone—attractive, charismatic, and preferably of noble lineage—to share interests and raise a family. His name is Felipe, the Prince of Asturias and heir to the Spanish throne. With his 30th birthday just behind him and his two elder sisters recently married, all eyes are on Felipe. Whom will he choose to be his queen when he takes over one of Europe's few powerful monarchies? The competition is fierce. Lovely ladies from wealthy families are stalking the streets of Madrid and the slopes of the Val d'Aran, but so far there are no front-runners. Cross your fingers and pack something nice—you could be the next queen of Spain.

CATALUÑA

BAQUIERA-BERET

Baquiera-Beret is Spain's most chic ski resort; after all, the Spanish royal family's favorite slopes are here. Girls, it's probably as good a place as any to have a chance encounter with the very eligible Prince Felipe. Currently, about 80 alpine trails and a few cross-country ones wind down the surrounding peaks. Although budget accommodations have disappeared at the ski station itself, the town of **Salardú,** a few kilometers away, has an enormous youth hostel, the **Albergue Era Garona (HI).** The hostel is accessible in the high season by shuttle bus from Vielha and offers dorms of four and six beds, as well as bike and ski rentals through the reception desk. (☎973 64 52 71. Breakfast included. Sheets 350ptas/€2.10. Beds Jan.-April 2350ptas/€14.12, over 25 3000ptas/€18.03; Dec. 2000ptas/€12.02 over 25 2700ptas/€16.23; low-season 1775ptas/€10.67, over 25 2400ptas/€14.42.) Upstairs above the umbrella tables of Bar Montanha, the colorful rooms of **Pensión Montanha,** C. Major, 8 offer a bit more privacy. With your back to the central pizzeria, begin a forward march up the front-facing side street, keeping an eye out for signs pointing the way to Bar Montanha. (☎973 64 41 08. Singles 2500ptas/€15.03, with bath 3500ptas/€21.04; doubles 3500ptas/€21.04, with bath 4500ptas/€27.05.) While in town, don't miss Salardú's 13th century church of **Sant Andreu**, and its incredible garden view. The town of Vielha is only 12km from Bacquiera-Beret, and the two are connected by a shuttle bus in July and August. Check at the tourist office for schedules. For skiing information and reservations, contact the **Oficeria de Baquiera-Beret** (☎973 64 44 55; fax 64 44 88).

VIELHA

The biggest town in the Val d'Aran, Vielha (pop. 3500) combines the warmth of its small old quarter with the bustling activity of the main commercial thoroughfare. From its prime location, Vielha welcomes hikers and skiers to its lively streets with every sort of service the outdoorsy-type might desire.

PRACTICAL INFORMATION. [illegible] (☎[illegible] 27 14 70 or 932 65 68 66) runs buses from Vielha to **Barcelona** (5½hr.; 5:30am, 1:30pm; 3725ptas/€23). For a **taxi** call ☎973 64 01 95. The **tourist office,** C. Sarriulèra, 6, is one block up-river from the Plaça de la Iglesia (look for the bright yellow sign.) Staff assists hikers, skiers, and Romanesque-seekers alike. (☎973 64 01 10; fax 973 64 03 72. Open Sept.-July M-Sa 10am-1pm, 4:30-7:30pm; Aug. daily 9am-9pm.) **ATMs** pepper main Av. Castiéro, which intersects the river before turning into Av. Pas d'Arró. Services include: **emergency** ☎112; **police** ☎973 64 09 72; **Internet access** at **CCV Informática,** C. Aneto, 7a. (☎973 64 12 88. Open M-F 9:30am-1:30pm, 4:30-8:30pm; Sa 9:30am-1:30pm. ½ hr. 350ptas/€2.10, 1hr. 700ptas/€4.21. MC/V.). The **post office,** C. Sarviulèra, 2, is by the tourist office. (☎973 64 09 12. Open M-F 8:30am-2:30pm, Sa 9:30am-1pm.) **Postal code:** 25530.

ACCOMMODATIONS AND FOOD. Budget travelers in need of a treat can put their feet up at the elegant, yet home style **Hotel El Cierco,** Pl. San Orencio. Standing on the bridge with your back to the tourist office, head downhill to the left. Upon entering the plaza, turn left to face the hotel's light green, mural-bedecked exterior. Wind down surrounded by harmonious color combinations or —for a childhood lift—slide stocking-footed across hard-wood floors. (☎973 64 01 65; fax 64 20 77. Apr.-Oct. singles 3000ptas/€18.03 doubles 5500ptas/€33.36; Dec.-Mar. singles 4000ptas/€24.04, doubles 7000ptas/€42.07. Closed for Nov. and the last two weeks in June. Several other inexpensive *pensiones* also fill the end of Camin Reiau, off Pg. Libertat (which intersects Av. Casteiro at Pl. Sant Antoni). With its cream-colored walls, great mattresses and modern furnishings, **Casa Vicenta,** C. Reiau, 3, comes highly recommended. (☎973 64 08 19. Sept.-June singles 2500ptas/€15.33; doubles 4000ptas/€24.04. July-Aug. singles 3000ptas/€18.03; doubles 4500ptas/€27.05.) Enjoy a sampling of every tortilla under the sun at the inviting **Restaurant Basteret,** C. Mayor 6B, tucked into a corner facing the tourist office, just across the river. Friendly staff and a well-priced daily *menú* (1400ptas/€8.41, including a glass of wine) make this a great spot. (☎973 64 07 14. Open daily June 1-Sept. 15 1-4:30pm and 8-11pm. Closed during the last two weeks of Oct. and Mondays from Sept.16-May. MC/V.) **Eth Breç,** Av. Castiero, 5 just beneath the green Fuji film sign along the main road heading toward, serves incredible pastries and a fabulous selection of teas. (☎64 00 50. Open daily 9am-1:30pm and 4-8:30pm. MC/V.)

CATALUÑA

SIGHTS AND ENTERTAINMENT. The **Iglesia de San Miguel,** a simple 12th-century Romanesque church, houses the intricate *Crist de Mijaran.* (Open daily 11am-8pm.) Also in Vielha is the **Museu de Val d'Aran,** on C. Mayor, whose ethnographic collection attempts to shed light on Aranese culture. (☎973 64 18 15. Open Tu-Sa 10am-1pm, and 5-8pm; Su 10am-1pm. 200ptas/€1.20.) Vielha is also, above all else, a good base for all sorts of outdoor activities. **Camins,** Av. Pas d'Arro, 5, in the shopping gallery, is a great place to start planning. Staff can answer questions, organize **treks** into the Aigüestortes National Park and the surrounding mountains (starting at 2500ptas/€15.53), lead **rafting** and **horseback trips,** and rent **mountain bikes.** (Bikes half-day 2200ptas/€13.22 and full-day 2900ptas/€18; ask about the popular ½day bike trip (26km one-way) to Camino Real/ Vielha-Les, promising a great workout and spectacular views.) In conjunction with the **Escola Snowboard Val d'Aran,** Camin can also teach you how to **snowboard** (Escola: ☎973 64 24 44; fax 973 64 24 97. Open M-F 9am-1pm and 4-8:30pm; try calling on weekends.)

LÉRIDA ☎973

Lérida (pop. 115,000) doesn't attract tons of tourists, but even so, a fair number of camera-toting visitors pass through this energetic but unassuming city to see the impressive cathedral of Seu Vella. Alongside the Rio Segre, Lérida's modern avenues run around its exterior, while narrows streets surround the cathedral.

TRANSPORTATION. RENFE trains (☎902 24 02 02), Pl. Berenguer IV. Trains to: **Barcelona** (2-4hr., 18 per day 5am-8:48pm, 1290-2900ptas/€7.74-18); **Huesca** (2hr., 7 per day 7:30am-9:30pm, 1100ptas/€6.60); **Madrid** (5hr., 6 per day 8:56am-1:25am, 5500-7300ptas/€33-44); **Tarragona** (1½-2hr., 11 per day 2:48am-5:55pm, 650-2500ptas/€3.90-15); and **Zaragoza** (2-4hr., 12 per day 8:56am-2:49am, 2200-3800ptas/€13-23). Central **Buses** (☎973 26 85 00), which stop one block from Av. Madrid near the intersection with Av. Catalunya. Buses to: **Barcelona** (2¼-2¾hr., 15 per day 6am-7:30pm, 2190ptas/€13); **Girona** (3½hr., 7:30am and 5:30pm, 2275ptas/€14); **Tarragona** (2hr.; M-F 6 per day 7:30am-9:15pm, Sa-Su 9:30am and 9:15pm; 620ptas/€3.75); **Zaragoza** (2 1/4hr., 5 per day 8am-6pm, 2250ptas/€14). Yellow **city buses** (☎973 27 29 99) run various routes throughout the city; the tourist office has a complete map and schedule. The most useful are the "Exterior" bus (#10) from the train station toward the center, which stops along Av. Madrid, and #15 between the train station and Seu Vella (110ptas/€0.66). For a **taxi,** call **Radio Taxi** (☎973 20 30 50) .

ORIENTATION AND PRACTICAL INFORMATION. Bordered by the Rio Segre, Lérida sprawls up the hilly incline toward Seu Villa. **A. Major,** one block in from the river, is the city's principle commercial street. Major banks and the post office line **Rbla. Ferran,** near the train station. Av. Madrid, Av. Catalunya, Rumbla d'Aragó, and Seu Villa frame the center of the city. Pl. Sant Joan, at the end of C. Major, is for all practical purposes the tourist's center, with several hostels. Lérida has two main **tourist offices.** For city information, head to the office at C. Major, 31, the street parallel to the river and one block inland. (☎973 70 03 19. Open M-F 11a-8pm, Sa 10am-8pm, Su 10am-1:30pm.) The office at Av. Madrid, 36, has regional information. (☎973 27 09 97, fax 27 09 49. Open June-Sept. M-F 9am-2pm and 3-8pm, Sa 9am-2pm; Oct.-May M-F 9am-2pm and 3-7pm, Su 10am-2pm.) **Banks** with 24hr. **ATMs** line Rbla. Ferran and are scattered throughout the city. Other services include: **luggage storage,** at the train station (700ptas/€3.50 for 24hr.); **emergency,** ☎112; **police,** Gran Passeig de Ronda, 52 (☎973 26 47 99); **Arnan de Vilanova Hospital,** Av. Alcalde Rovira Roure, 80 (☎973 24 81 00); **Cafetó Internet,** C. Bonaire, 8. (☎973 72 50 20; 400ptas/€2.40 per hr.; open M-F 9am-2pm and 4pm-midnight, Sa 9am-2pm and 4pm-2am, Su 5pm-midnight); and the **post office,** C. Rambla Ferran, 16, toward town from the train station. (☎973 24 70 00. M-F 8:30am-8:30pm, Sa 9:30am-2pm.) **Postal code:** 25007.

ACCOMMODATIONS. Most of Lérida's budget accommodations (including those listed) double as student housing, so term-time space is limited (Oct.-June). Rooms at the central **Hostal Mundial,** Pl. Sant Joan, 4, range widely in size and comfort. (☎973 24 27 00; fax 24 26 02. Singles 2000ptas/€12; doubles with shower 3200ptas/€19.20, with bath 4000ptas/€24. Breakfast 300ptas/€1.8. M-F *menú* 1000ptas/€6. Parking 9pm-9am 600ptas/€3.60.) Lérida's youth hostal, **Alberg Sant Anastasi (HI),** Rbla. d'Aragó, 11, offers clean, 4-person rooms, free internet, two TV lounges, and a game room. (☎973 26 60 99. Under 25 2000ptas/€12; over 25 2700ptas/€16.25.).

FOOD. Lérida's local specialty is *caragoles* (snails), and the city manages to consume over 12 slimy tons of them each year, most notably during their popular May gastronomic festival, *Aplec del Caragol.* The tourist office has a list of restaurants that serve a special *menú Xec Caragol* (4000ptas/€24) composed entirely of various snail dishes—some of the more popular dishes are snails cooked on a *llauna* (grill), served with *allioli* (mayonaise and garlic), cooked with veggies on a stone tile, and *a la gormanta* (fried with seasonings). Snail-less **restaurant** options are somewhat disappointing—most are closed on Sundays, and the few that offer *comida típica* are pricey. Check out the area surrounding C. Bonaire for basic food; the area around Seu Vella has a variety of tiny hole-in-the-wall digs that serve African cuisine. To satisfy your sweet tooth, hop over to the tiny **Crepes & Gofres,** C. Camp de Mart, 1, serves dessert crepe options (250-350ptas/€1.50-2.10) that are a delight (open Su-M 6-10:30pm, Th-Sa 6pm-3:30am).

SIGHTS. High above the city, **Seu Villa,** Lérida's amazing 14th-century cathedral and cloister was built upon the grounds of a Muslim mosque. When the city was conquered by Felipe V, both the mountaint[illegible] [illegible] military occupation lasted until 1947. Two of the **bell tower's** seven bells are Gothic originals from the 15th century *(To the cathedral, take bus #15 from the train station or walk up C. Cavallers, turn right at the market, and follow the stairs up the hill. ☎973 23 06 53. Open daily June -Sept. 10am-1:30pm and 4-7:30pm, Oct.-May 10am-1:30pm and 3-5:30pm. Bell tower closes 30min. before the rest of the complex. 400ptas/€2.40, over 65 and under 21 300ptas/€1.80.)* Lérida's intricate Romanesque ayuntamiento, the **Palau de la Paeria,** houses a small basement museum dedicated to art and archaeology of the city. *(C. Major. Museum open M-Sa 11am-2pm and 5-8pm, Sa 11am-2pm. Free.)* The tiny and free **Museu d'Arte Jaume Morera** houses a rotating display of 19th and 20th-century works; the permanent collection includes paintings by Morera himself. *(C. Cavallers, 15, 2nd fl. ☎973 27 36 65. Open June 15-Sept. 15 Tu-Sa 10am-1pm, 6-9pm; Su 10am-1pm; Sept. 15-June 15. Tu-Sa 11am-2pm, 5-8pm; Su 11am-2pm.)*

CATALUÑA

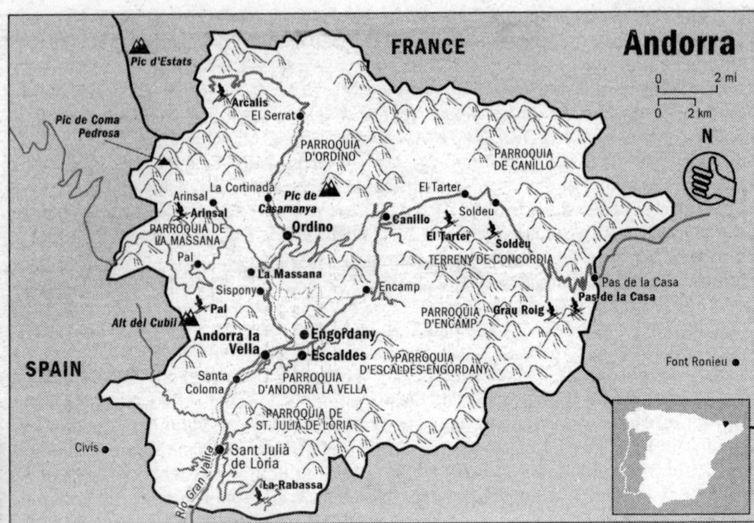

ANDORRA

Welcome to Andorra, the forgotten European nation, where stunning landscapes vie for attention with a neon-lit capital. Pragmatists say Andorra (pop. 65,000; 464 sq. km) offers the best of both worlds, though many may beg to differ. According to legend, Charlemagne founded Andorra in 784 as a reward to the valley's inhabitants for having led his army against the Moors. For the next 12 centuries, the little country played the rope in a game of tug-o'-war between the Spanish Counts of Urgell, the Church of Urgell, and the French King. Not until 1990 did the country create a commission to draft a democratic constitution, adopted on March 14, 1993. Andorra today is far less progressive than other western European nation. In the 1993 election, only the 10,000 native Andorrans (out of 65,000 total inhabitants) were granted the vote; women have had only had suffrage since 1970.

Sandwiched between France and Spain, Andorra's citizens are comfortably trilingual, though Catalan is the official language. The country has no currency of its own—all establishments are required to accept both *pesetas* and *francs* (*pesetas* are more prevalent). Currency still seems to flow like water, as the absence of a sales tax (and the abundance of duty-free shops) draws consumers from all over Europe. With Andorran towns spaced mere minutes apart and an extensive local bus system, a single day can include wading through aisles of duty-free perfume, hiking through a pine-scented valley, eating in an informal country restaurant, and relaxing in a luxury spa.

TRANSPORTATION

The only way to get to Andorra is by car or bus. Visitors must show a valid passport or EU identity card to enter the country. All traffic from Spain enters through the town of La Seu d'Urgell; the gateway to France is Pas de la Casa.

BY BUS

Andor-Inter/Samar buses (in Madrid ☎914 68 41 90; in Toulouse ☎561 58 14 53; in Andorra 82 62 89) run to **Madrid** (9hr.; Tu, F, Sa, and Su at 11am; W, Th, and Su at 10pm; 5200ptas/€31.25) as does **Eurolines** (Andorra ☎80 51 51; Madrid ☎915 06 33 60;

Tu 10am, F 10pm, Su 2:30pm; 5250ptas/€32). **Alsina Graells** (Andorra ☎ 82 65 67) runs to **Barcelona** (4hr., daily 6am, 7am, 10:30am, 3pm, 5pm, 2855ptas/€17.25), as does **Eurolines** (3hr 15min., daily at 6am, 10:30am, 3:30pm, and 8:15pm; F, Su and holidays buses also at 1:15pm and 6pm; 2975ptas/€17.50). All buses arrive at and depart from **Estació d'Autobusos,** on C. Bonaventura Riberaygua. To get to the station from Pl. Princep Benlloch, follow Av. Meritxell past the tourist office to the other side of the river. Make an immediate right after crossing the river, then an immediate left. Take the fourth right and go continue straight for four to five blocks (20min.) To go anywhere in Spain other than Madrid or Barcelona, you must first go to the town of La Seu d'Urgell on a **La Hispano-Andorra** bus (☎ 82 13 72; 30min., 5-7 buses per day, 400ptas/€2.50), departing from Av. Meritxell, 11. From La Seu, Alsina Graells buses continue into Spain via Puigcerdà (1hr., 2 per day, 570ptas/€3.50) and Lérida (2½hr., 2 per day, 1650ptas/€10).

BY CAR

Driving in Andorra la Vella is a nightmare. The main road turns into a parking lot, and drivers will find a map totally useless—it's best to follow signs and desert the car as soon as possible in one of the city's parking lots. Efficient intercity buses connect the villages along the three major highways that converge in Andorra la Vella. Since most towns are only 10 minutes apart, the country can be seen in a single day via public transportation. Bus rides are 100-300ptas/€0.60-1.85. All buses make every stop in the city, so don't worry about finding the right bus—just pay attention to the direction sign in the front window. Bus stops are easy to find.

ANDORRA LA VELLA

Andorra la Vella (pop. 23,000), the country's capital, is little more than a narrow, cluttered road flanked by shop after duty-free shop and sprinkled with American fast-food chains. This city is anything but *vella* (old), as most of the old buildings have been upstaged by shiny new electronics and sporting goods stores. After doing a little shopping, you're best off escaping to the countryside.

ORIENTATION AND PRACTICAL INFORMATION. Avinguda Meritxell, the main artery, runs through the city, beginning at Pl. Princep Benlloch in the heart of the tiny **barri antic** (old quarter) and continuing across the Riu Valira to become the main highway to parishes northeast of the capital. West of Pl. Princep Benlloch (to the right when facing the Eglésia de Sant'Esteve), Av. Meritxell becomes **Avinguida Princep Belloch.** The **tourist office** is on Av. Doctor Villanova. From the bus stop on Av. Princep Benlloch, continue east (away from Spain) past the *plaça* on your left, and take C. Dr. Villanova, as it curves to the right; the office is on the left before the hill. Multilingual staff offers the free *Sports Activities* and *Hotels i Restaurants* guides. (☎ 82 02 14; fax 82 58 23. Open daily July-Aug. [illegible] June [illegible] currency at **Banc Internacional,** Av. Meritxell, 32. (☎ 88 47 05. Open M-F 9am-1pm and 3-5pm, Sa 9am-noon.) In a **medical emergency** call 116 or the **police,** Prat de la Creu, 16 (☎ 87 20 00). For **weather and ski conditions,** call 86 43 89. **Taxi** answer at ☎ 86 30 00.

To make a **telephone call,** buy an STA *teletarjeta* (telecard) at the tourist office or the post office (500ptas/€3 minimum); collect calls to most countries—including the US—are not possible from Andorra. For directory assistance dial ☎ 111 or 119 (international). The **country code** is **376.** The **post office,** Carrer Joan Maragall, 10, is across the river from Pl. Princep Benlloch. (☎ 902 19 71 97. Lista de Correos upstairs. Open M-F 8:30am-2:30pm, Sa 9:30am-1pm.) Check your **email** at **Baviera,** Pl. Rotunda, across from the tourist office. (☎ 81 26 12. 600ptas/€3.75 for 30min. 1100ptas per hr. Open daily 8:30am-1am.)

ACCOMMODATIONS AND FOOD. The sunny doubles of **Hotel Viena,** C. de la Vall, 3 are a steal for two. From C. Major, turn left onto C. de la Vall; the hotel is on the left. (Breakfast 500ptas/€3 per person. Singles 4500ptas/€27;

doubles 5000ptas/€30. MC/V.) To reach the large, sunny rooms of **Hotel del Sol,** Pl. Guillemó, take a left onto C. Les Canals after the Pyrenees department store on the main road, then follow the signs for Spain until you reach the plaza with a water fountain. (☎82 37 01. 2000ptas/€12 per person. MC/V.) Shaded **Camping Valira,** Av. Salou, behind the **Estadi Comunal d'Andorra la Vella,** has video games, hot showers, and an indoor pool. Handicap accessible. (☎82 23 84. 575ptas/€2.75 per person, per tent, and per car. Call ahead.) Check out one of the three-story supermarket monstrosities in nearby Santa Coloma or the **Grans Magatzems Pyrénées,** Av. Meritxell, 11, the country's biggest department store, where an entire aisle is dedicated to chocolate bars. (Open Sept.-July M-F 9:30am-8pm, Sa 9:30am-9pm, Su 9:30am-7pm; Aug. and holidays M-Sa 9:30am-9pm, Su 9:30am-7pm.)

EXCURSIONS. The best thing to do in Andorra la Vella is drop your bags in a hostel and get out. The **Caldea-Spa,** in nearby **Escaldes-Engordany,** is the largest in all of Europe, with luxurious treatments and prices to match. (☎80 09 95. Open daily 10am-11pm. 2950ptas/€18 for 3hr., plus fees for each service.) The parish of **Ordino** bucks the Andorran trend of "bigger is better" with its quirky **Microminiature Museum,** Edifici Coma. Using intense yogic breathing, Nikolai Siadristy has created amazingly small objects, including the tiniest inscription ever made. (☎83 83 38. Open Tu-Sa 9:30am-1:30pm and 3:30-7pm, Su 9:30am-1:30pm. 300ptas/€1.80.) On the other side of the spectrum, the town of **Canillo** is home to the colossal **Palau de Gel D'Andorra,** a recreational complex complete with swimming pool, ice-skating rink ("ice disco" by night), and squash courts, all open to the public. (☎80 08 40. "Palace" open daily 10am-11:30pm; each facility has its own hours. 750ptas/€4.50 each or 1450ptas/€8.75 for all in one day. Equipment rental 425ptas/€2.50)

ANDORRA

HIKING AND THE OUTDOORS. An extensive network of hiking trails traverses Andorra. The free, multilingual, and extremely helpful tourist office brochure *Sports Activities* includes 52 suggested itineraries, potential routes, and bike rental locations, as well as cabin and refuge locations within the principality. (☎73 70 80. Open July-Aug. M-Sa 8am-7pm, Su 9am-5pm; Sept.-June M-Sa 9am-1pm and 3-7pm, Su 9am-1pm.) La Massana is home to Andorra's tallest peak, **Pic Alt de la Coma Pedrosa** (2946m). For organized hiking trips, try the **La Rabassa Sports and Nature Center** (☎32 38 68 or 32 62 22), in the parish of Sant Julià de Lòria, in southwest Andorra. In addition to *refugio*-style accommodations, the center has mountain biking, guided hikes, horseback riding, archery, and other field sports.

SKIING. With five outstanding resorts within its boundaries, Andorra offers skiing opportunities galore. **Pal** (☎73 70 00; fax 83 59 04), 10km from La Massana, is accesible by bus from La Massana (4 per day, last returning at 5pm, 255ptas/€1.50). Seven buses run daily from La Massana to nearby **Arinsal,** the last returning at 7:45pm (200ptas/€1.25). On the French border, **Pas de la Casa Grau Roig** (☎85 69 92) offers 600 hectares of skiable land, lessons, two medical centers, night skiing, and 27 lifts serving 48 trails for all levels of ability. **Soldeu-El Tarter** (☎89 05 00) occupies 840 hectares of skiable area between Andorra la Vella and Pas de la Casa. **Free buses** pick up skiers from their hotels in Canillo. The more horizontal **La Rabassa** (☎32 38 68) is Andorra's only cross-country ski resort, offers sleighing, skiing, horse rides, and a children's snow park. Andorra's tourist office publishes a winter edition of *Andorra.* Call **SKI Andorra** (☎86 43 89; www.skiandorra.ad) or the tourist offices with any questions.

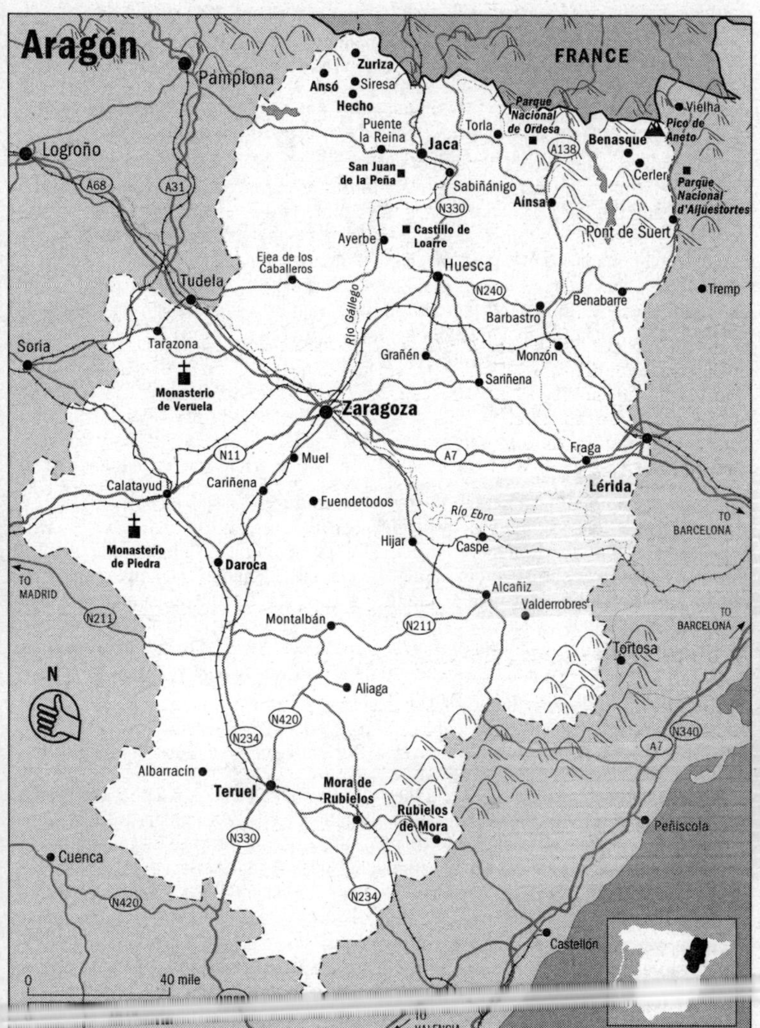

ARAGÓN

A striking collage of semi-deserts and lush mountain peaks, Aragón's landscape reflects the influence of both Mediterranean and Continental climates. In the south, a sun-baked assemblage of hardworking towns and flaxen plains scattered with fine examples of ornate *Mudéjar* architecture. In the center, prosperous and industrious Zaragoza is Aragón's capital and the fifth largest city in Spain. To the north, the stunning snow-capped peaks of the Pyrenees peer down at tiny medieval towns tilled with Romanesque architecture. Spain's largest river, the Ebro, carves a rushing line between these vastly different terrains.

Aragón's harsh climate, coupled with the region's strategic location, has produced a predominantly martial culture. Established as a kingdom in 1035 and united with enterprising Cataluña in 1137, Aragón forged a far-flung Mediterranean empire that brought Roussillon, Valencia, Murcia, the Balearic Islands, Naples, Sicily, and even the Duchy of Athens under its sway. The region retained the privileges of internal governance even after its union with Castilla in 1469, and it held those privileges until Felipe II marched into Zaragoza in 1591, bringing the region to its knees. Economic decline followed political humiliation; as eyes turned to the New World, people (and capital) moved to the coast in search of wealth. Today, Aragón is back on its feet economically, while still remaining relatively tourist-free. Only some areas of the rural Pyrenees and the Parque Nacional Ordesa y Monte Perdido, with its dramatic peaks and diverse hiking and skiing opportunities, attract many visitors, and even those are mostly urban Spaniards escaping the city heat during July and August.

Aragonese cuisine is as hearty as those who prepare it. *Migas de pastor* (bread crumbs fried with ham) and lamb chops are ubiquitous; more surprising treats include *chilindrón* (lamb and chicken stewed with red peppers) and *melocotones al vino* (sweet native peaches steeped in wine). The *Guía de servicios turísticos de Aragón*, available at any tourist office in the province, makes roaming easy, with information on accommodations and tourist offices.

ZARAGOZA ☎976

The political and cultural nexus of Aragonese culture, Zaragoza (pop. 603,000) is one of Spain's lesser-known beauties. Augustus founded the city in 14 BC as a retirement colony for Roman veterans, modestly naming it Caesaraugusta, after himself. Eventually shortened to 'Zaragoza', the city gained everlasting fame years later when the Virgin Mary dropped in for a visit; it has been a pilgrimage site ever since. Zaragoza's many leafy *paseos* and modern sprawl provide a sharp contrast to the narrow, winding streets of its *casco antiguo*. Blessed by a beloved patron saint, *Nuestra Señora del Pilar*, and humming with prosperity, Zaragoza is making its way into the competitive world of Spanish tourism.

TRANSPORTATION

Airplanes: Airport (☎976 34 90 50). **Iberia,** C. Canfranc, 22 (☎976 23 38 16; reservations 976 21 82 50). Open M-F 9:30am-2pm and 4-7pm, Sa 9:30am-1:30pm. **Ebrobus,** Pl. Aragón, 10 (☎976 32 40 09), off Pl. Paraíso at the beginning of Po. Independencia, runs to the airport (30-45min.; M-F 7-8 per day 6am-9:45pm, Sa 4 per day 6am-5:45pm, Su 5 per day noon-10:50pm; 250ptas/€1.50). A taxi to the airport costs about 2000ptas/€12.

Trains: Estación Portillo (24hr. ☎976 21 11 66), at Av. Anselmo Clavé. Take a taxi to Pl. Pilar (500ptas/€3); bus #21 from Po. María Agustín also stops at Pl. España. Info open daily 8am-9pm. **RENFE office,** C. San Clemente, 11 (☎976 28 02 02). From Pl. Paraíso, follow Po. Independencia 4 blocks, then turn right. Open M-F 9am-1:30pm and 4:30-8pm, Sa 9:30am-1pm. Trains to: **Barcelona** (4hr., 15 per day 1:50am-7:05pm 3600-4600ptas/€22-28); **Jaca** (3hr.,7:15am and 3:20pm, 1405ptas/€8.50); **Lérida** (1½hr., 10 per day 2:30am-7:05pm, 2500-3200ptas/€15-19); **Logroño** (2¼hr., 4 per day 6:30am-7:30pm, 1450ptas/€8.71); **Madrid** (3hr., 14 per day 7am-3:33am, 3500-4500ptas/€21-27); **Pamplona** (2¼hr., 3 per day 6:30am-4:15pm, 1290-2200ptas/€7.74-13); **San Sebastián** (4hr., 5pm and 2am, 3400ptas/€21); **Teruel** (3hr., 3 per day 8am-7:14pm, 1405ptas); **Tudela** (45min., 7-15 per day 6:30am-9:05pm, 515ptas/€3); **Valencia** (6hr., 8:05am and 4:05pm, 2575ptas/€15.45).

Buses: Various bus companies dot the city, each with private terminals.

Agreda Automóvil, Po. María Agustín, 7 (☎976 22 93 43). Bus #21 stops in front. From the station, turn right and follow Po. María Agustín to Pl. Paraíso. Info open daily 7:30am-9pm. To: **Barcelona** (3½hr., 16-19 per day 1-10:30pm, 1655ptas/€10); **Madrid** (3½hr., 15-18 per day 1:15pm-10:30pm, 1750ptas/€11); **Soria** (2½hr.; M-Sa 5 per day 7:30am-4:30pm; Su 9am; 1230ptas/€7.40). **Second Terminal,** Av. Valencia, 20 (☎976 55 45 88.) Enter on C. Lérida (bus #38). Buses to **Lérida** (2½hr.; M-Sa 4 per day 6:45am-8:30pm; 1200ptas/€7.20).

La Oscense, Po. María Agustín, 7 (☎976 22 93 43). Shares a terminal with Agreda Automóvil. To **Jaca** (2¼hr., 3-4 per day 10:55am-9:40pm, 1490ptas/€9).

Therpasa, C. General Sueiro, 22 (☎976 22 57 23). From the station, turn left and follow C. General Sueiro for 1½ blocks, then turn left again onto C. San Ignacio; turn right after 2 blocks into Pl. Paraíso. Goes to **Tarazona** (1½hr., 5 per day 10:30am-8:30pm, 805ptas/€4.85).

CONDA, Av. Navarra, 81 (☎976 33 33 72). To get to Pl. Paraiso and Pl. Aragón from the station, turn right on Av. Navarra, bearing left onto Av. Madrid. Cross the highway on the pedestrian bridge. After 2 blocks, turn right on Po. María Agustín and continue along Po. Pamplona to Pl. Paraiso. Or take bus #25 to Po. Pamplona. To: **Pamplona** (2hr., 6 per day 7:15am-8:30pm, 1760ptas/€10.60); **San Sebastián** (3¼hr., 3 per day 7:15am-7pm, 2600ptas/€16); **Tudela** (1hr., 6 per day 7:15am-8:30pm, 760ptas/€4.50).

Grupo Autobús Jiménez, C. San Juan Pablo Bonet, 13 (☎976 27 61 79). To get to the station, take bus #33 from Pl. España and watch for the road sign for C. San Juan Pablo Bonet after 2 stops on Po. Sagasta. To: **Logroño** (2½hr., 6 per day 7am-7pm, 1375ptas/€8.25) and **Teruel** (3hr., 4 per day 7am-4pm, 1195ptas/€7.20).

Public Transportation: Red **TUZSA buses** (☎976 59 27 27; www.tuzsa.es) cover the city (85ptas/€0.55; 10-ride pass 550ptas/€3.30; tickets available at any kiosk). Bus #21 runs from near the train station to Po. Pamplona, Pl. Paraíso, Pl. Aragón, Pl. España, Pl. Pilar, and up C. San Vincente de Paúl. Bus #33 is more central, passing through Po. Sagasta, Pl. Paraíso, Po. Independencia, and Pl. España.

Taxis: Radio-Taxi Aragón (☎976 38 38 38). Train station to Pl. Pilar (500ptas/€3).

Car Rental: Avis, Po. Fernando El Católico, 9 (☎976 55 50 94). From Pl. Paraíso, take Gran Vía, following it as it becomes Po. Fernando El Católico. 14,000ptas/€84 per day, includes insurance and 400km. 23+; must have credit card and valid license. Open M-F 8am-1pm and 4-7pm, Sa 8am-12:30pm. MC/V. Several other rental agencies have offices at the train station.

ORIENTATION AND PRACTICAL INFORMATION

ARAGÓN

Bordered to the north by the Río Ebro, Zaragoza is laid out like a slightly damaged bicycle wheel. Five spokes radiate from the hub of **Pl. Basilio Paraíso.** Facing the center of the plaza with the IberCaja bank building at your back, the spokes going clockwise are: Po. Sagasta; Gran Vía, which becomes Po. Fernando el Católico; Po. Pamplona, which leads to Po. María Agustín and the **train station;** Po. Independencia, which ends at **Pl. de España** (the entrance to the *casco viejo*); and Po. Constitución. To get to Pl. Paraíso from the train station, start upstairs, bear right down the ramp, and walk across Av. Anselmo Clavé. Head one block down C. General Mayandía and turn right onto Po. María Agustín. Continue 7 blocks until the street becomes Po. Pamplona and ends at Pl. Paraíso. The *casco viejo* lies at the end of Po. Independencia and stretches between Pl. España and **Pl. del Pilar.** To reach Pl. Pilar from Pl. Paraíso, walk down Po. Independencia, turn right at Pl. España, and continue left down C. Don Jaime I; Pl. Pilar is at the end on the left.

Tourist Office: Main Branch (☎976 20 12 00; fax 20 06 35), Pl. Pilar, in the black glass cube across from the basilica. Multilingual staff. Open daily 10am-8pm. In the summer, tiny [illegible] of many of the major sights, offer tourist information and free guided tours (hours vary by location).

Currency Exchange: Banks line Po. Independencia, with **ATMs** everywhere. **Banco Central Hispano,** Pl. Aragón, 6, has good rates on traveler's checks.

American Express: Viajes Turopa, Po. Sagasta, 47 (☎976 38 39 11; fax 25 42 44). Enter around the corner, 6 blocks from Pl. Paraíso. Cannot cash traveler's checks, but can give cash advances for AmEx credit card holders. Bus #33 from Pl. España stops nearby. Cardholder mail held. Open M-F 9am-1:30pm and 4-7:30pm.

El Corte Inglés: Po. Sagasta, 3 (☎976 21 11 21), and a smaller store at Po. Independencia, 11 (☎976 23 86 44). Open M-Sa 10am-10pm.

Luggage Storage: At the **train station** (small 400ptas/€1.80, large 500ptas/€3.00). Open 24hr. At **Agreda Automóvil** bus station, Po. María Agustín, 7 (200ptas/€1.20). Open M-F 10am-1:30pm and 4-7:30pm, Sa 10am-1:30pm. At the other **Agreda Automóvil,** Av. Valencia, 20 (100ptas/€0.60 per piece per day). Open M-F 10am-2:30pm and 4:30-8pm. At **Therpasa** bus station (100ptas/€0.60). Open M-F 9am-1pm and 4:15-7:30pm, Sa 9am-12:45pm.

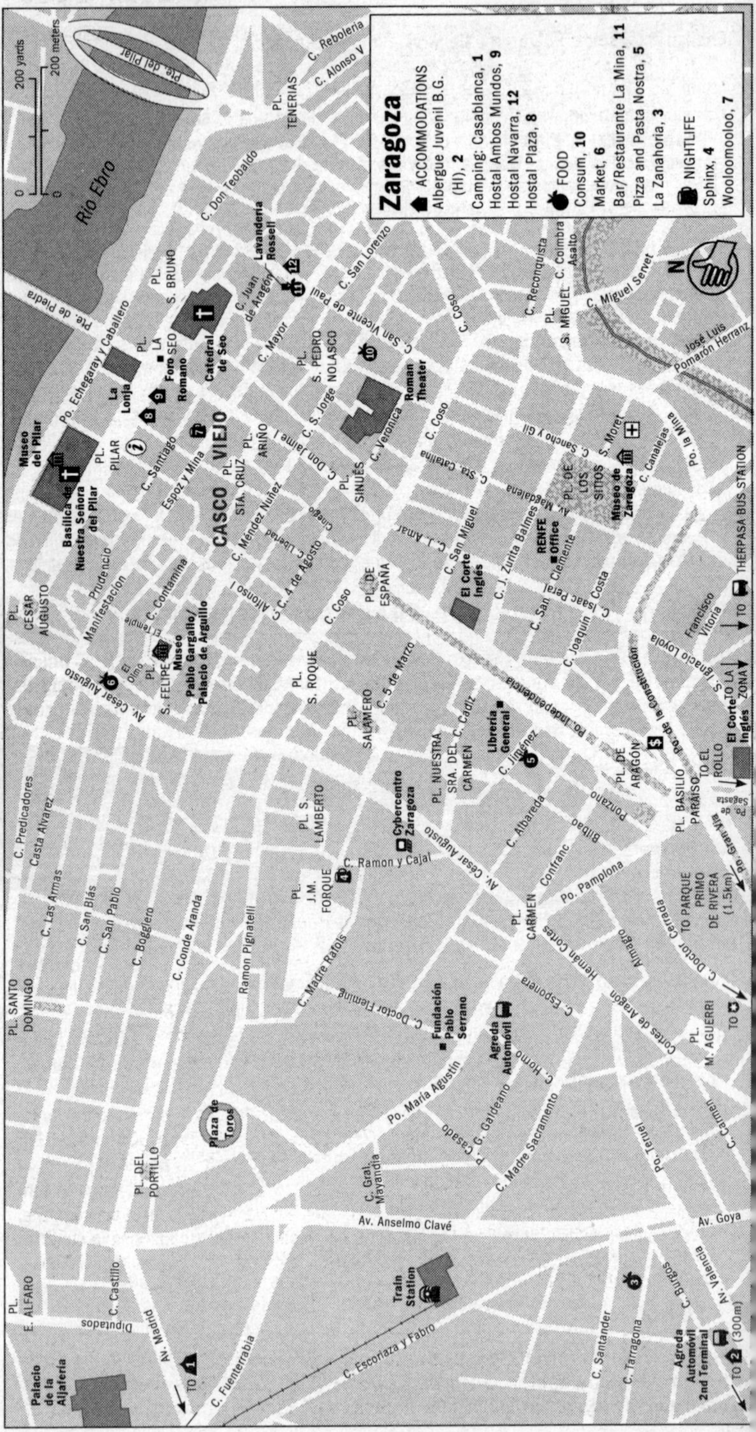

Zaragoza

ACCOMMODATIONS
Albergue Juvenil B.G. (HI), **2**
Camping: Casablanca, **1**
Hostal Ambos Mundos, **9**
Hostal Navarra, **12**
Hostal Plaza, **8**

FOOD
Consum, **10**
Market, **6**
Bar/Restaurante La Mina, **11**
Pizza and Pasta Nostra, **5**
La Zanahoria, **3**

NIGHTLIFE
Sphinx, **4**
Wooloomooloo, **7**

English Bookstore: Librería General, Po. Independencia, 22 (☎976 22 44 83; fax 976 22 89 48). Under the rainbow awning. Open June 15-Aug. M-F 9:30am-1:30pm, 5-9pm, Sa 10am-2pm; Sept.-June 14 M-Sa 9:30am-1:30pm, 4-8:30pm. AmEx/MC/V.

Laundromat: Lavandería Rossell, C. San Vicente de Paul, 27 (☎976 29 90 34). From Pl. España, turn right onto C. Coso, continue 4 blocks, and head left on C. San Vicente for another 4½ blocks. Wash and dry small 990ptas/€6, medium 1400ptas/€8.40, large 1900ptas/€11.40. Open M-F 8:30am-1:30pm and 5-8pm, Sa 8:30am-1:30pm.

Emergency: ☎112. **Police:** ☎091 or 092, on Domingo Miral.

Medical Services: Hospital Miguel Servet, Po. Isabel La Católica, 1 (☎976 35 57 00). **Emergency: Ambulatorio Ramón y Cajal,** Po. María Agustín, 12 (☎976 43 41 11).

Internet Access: Cybercentro Zaragoza (☎976 46 96 10), C. Ramón y Cajal. From Pl. Aragón, walk toward Pl. España, take a left on C. Ibareda, then a right at the big intersection on Av. César Augusto. Bear left onto C. Ramon y Cajal and look for the yellow awning on your right. 225ptas/€1.35 for 30min. Open daily 10am-2pm and 4-11pm.

Post Office: Po. Independencia, 33 (☎976 22 80 09 or 22 01 78), 1 block from Pl. Aragón on the right. **Fax** and **Lista de Correos** downstairs. Open M-F 8:30am-8:30pm, Sa 9:30am-2pm. Another **branch** next to the train station at C. Clavé. Open M-F 8:30am-8:30pm, Sa 9:30am-1pm. **Postal Code:** 50001.

ACCOMMODATIONS AND CAMPING

Small hostels and *pensiones* pepper the narrow streets of the central *casco viejo*, especially within the rectangle bounded by C. Alfonso I, C. Don Jaime I, Pl. España, and Pl. Pilar, along **C. Madre Sacramento,** perpendicular to Av. Anselmo Clavé, and near the train station. Be wary the week of October 12, when Zaragoza celebrates the *Fiesta de la Virgen del Pilar*. Make reservations as early as possible and expect to pay as much as double the rates listed below. *Ferias* (trade shows) are held from February through April (www.feriazaragoza.com), during which advance reservations are essential.

Hostal Plaza, Pl. Pilar, 14 (☎976 29 48 30 or 28 48 39; fax 39 94 06). Glistening modern bathrooms, TV, and phone; interior rooms have A/C. English and French spoken. July-Aug. singles with shower 4500ptas/€27; doubles with shower 6900ptas/€42, with bath 7900ptas/€48. Sept.-June singles with shower and sink 3900ptas/€24; doubles with shower 4900ptas/€30, with bath 5900ptas/€36. MC/V.

Albergue-Juvenil Baltasar Gracián (HI), C. Franco y López, 4 (☎976 55 15 04, reservations 71 47 97). Take bus #22 from the train station. On foot, turn right out of the station onto Av. Clavé, take the 2nd right onto C. Burgos, following it for 6 blocks as it becomes C. Obispo Covarrubias, then turn right onto C. Franco y Lopez. 55 beds in rooms of 2 and 4. Quite out of the way, but a real deal. Sheets and breakfast included. Midnight curfew. Dorms 1400ptas/€8.40, over 26 1800ptas/€10.80.

Hostal [illegible] [illegible] (☎976 29 97 04; fax 29 97 02), at C. Don Jaime I. Basic rooms some with balconies. Breakfast 400ptas/€2.40; other meals 1200ptas/€7.20. Singles 2600ptas/€16; doubles 5000ptas/€30.

Hostal Navarra, C. San Vicente de Paul, 30 (☎976 29 16 84). Comfortable rooms, some with balconies. TV lounge. Singles 2500ptas/€15, with bath 3000ptas/€18; doubles 4000ptas/€24, with bath 5000ptas/€30, with shower 4500ptas/€27.

Camping: Casablanca (☎976 75 38 70), Barrio Valdefierro, down Cra. Madrid. Bus #36 from Pl. Pilar or Pl. España to the suburb of Valdefierro. Ask the driver to let you off at the campsite, as it's notoriously difficult to find. Supermarket, bar, restaurant, and pool open in summer. July-Aug. 640ptas/€3.85 per person, per tent, and per car; Sept.-June 615ptas/€3.70 each.

FOOD

Zaragoza considers itself Spain's unofficial "*tapas* capital." (Check out tourist office-provided pamphlet, *Guía de Tapas*.) The side streets flanking C. Don Jaime I and the *tapas* bar-laden zone known as *El Tubo* (bordered by C. Mártires,

ARAGÓN

SAINTLY SOUVENIR Although she is frequently overshadowed by the amazing deeds of her internationally-acclaimed son, the original Madonna had some adventures of her own. Sure, painters like to portray her meditating serenely, but there was a tough, rugged side to the Virgin Mary as well. One of history's most illustrious backpackers (much like yourself, perhaps), the blue-clad Virgin hiked it from Jerusalem to Spain, arriving in the Roman city of Caesaraugustus (present-day Zaragoza) on January 2, AD 40. And she didn't pack light: Mary carried with her the sacred pillar that still stands, encased in silver, in Zaragoza's awe-inspiring cathedral. In honor of this journey and gift, the people of Aragón proudly sing that "she did not do anything like this with any other nation," reminding others that her visit was an actual "coming" rather than a mere spiritual apparition.

C. Cinegio, C. 4 de Agosto, and C. Estébanes) are traditional dinner areas. More expensive and varied restaurants fill the streets branching off from Po. Independencia. The **market** is in the long green building on Av. César Augusto off Pl. Pilar. (Open M-F 9am-2pm and 5-8pm, Sa 9am-2pm.) Famed *frutas de Aragón*, chocolate-dipped and candied fruits in colorful wrappers, are available at almost any candy shop, souvenir store, or *carnicería*. Stock up at **Consum** C. San Jorge 22, the continuation of C. Merdeo Núñez (open M-Sa 9am-9pm), or at the supermarket at **El Corte Inglés** (see **Practical Information,** above).

La Zanahoria, C. Tarragona, 4 (☎976 35 87 94). From Pl. Paraíso, start down Gran Vía, turn right onto Av. Goya, then take the 1st left after crossing Av. Teruel/Valencia. Popular with locals and nearby college students. Excellent salads and vegetable quiches (600-950ptas/€3.60-5.70). *Menú* 1050ptas/€6.30. Entrées 950ptas/€5.75. Open daily 1:30-4pm and 9-11:30pm. MC/V.

Pizza and Pasta Nostra, C. Marqués de Casa Jiménez, 8 (☎976 15 85 04). Pizzas and freshly made pasta dishes are leaps and bounds above those of its competitors. Pizzas 800-1300ptas/€4.80-11.80. Pasta dishes 800-1600ptas/€4.80-9.60. Open Su-Th 1-4pm and 8:30pm-midnight, F-Sa 1-4pm and 8:30pm-1am. MC/V.

Bar-Restaurante La Mina, C. San Vicente de Paul, 29 (☎976 39 17 68). Hearty and filling *menú* 1100ptas/€6.60. Fish dishes 900-1200ptas/€5.40-7.20. Meat dishes 900-1900ptas/€5.40-11.40. Open daily 8am-midnight.

SIGHTS

PLAZA DEL PILAR

A vast square surrounded by a unique fusion of architectural styles, Plaza del Pilar is Zaragoza at its best. The central square is the perfect place to begin a city tour.

BASÍLICA DE NUESTRA SEÑORA DEL PILAR. This massive Baroque structure (begun in 1681, although a few of the towers weren't completed until the mid-20th century) is Zaragoza's defining landmark. The interior walls feature frescoes by Goya, González Velázquez, and Francisco Bayeau. Two bombs (now on display) were dropped on the basilica during the Spanish Civil War in 1936 but failed to explode, purportedly due to the divine intervention of the Virgin. The **Museo del Pilar** exhibits the glittering *joyero de la Virgen* (Virgin's jewels) and preliminary paintings of the ceiling frescoes. Don't leave without taking in the breathtaking panorama of Zaragoza from one of the towers. *(Open daily 5:45am-9:30pm. Free. Museum ☎976 29 95 64. Open daily 9am-2pm and 4-6pm. 200ptas/€1.20. Elevator open June-Aug. Sa-Th 9:30am-2pm and 4-7pm; Sept.-May Sa-Th 9:30am-2pm and 4-6pm. 200ptas/€1.20.)*

OTHER SIGHTS. On the left as you exit the basilica is Zaragoza's **ayuntamiento**. Next door is the Renaissance **La Lonja,** host to occasional cultural exhibits (art, photography, etc.) and featuring the intricately vaulted ceiling of many a Zaragoza postcard. *(☎976 39 72 39. Open Tu-Sa 10am-2pm and 5-9pm, Su 10am-2pm. Free.)*

In front of La Lonja, statues portray scenes from Goya's paintings. On the other side of C. Don Jaime I, a large marble-and-glass cube houses the entrance to the **Foro Romano,** one of three nearby museums dedicated to Zaragoza's classical past. Excavated ruins from 1 BC-AD 1 await underground. The **Museo de las Termas Públicas de Caesaraugusta,** San Juan y San Pedro, 3-7, and the **Caesaraugusta River Port Museum,** Pl. San Bruno, 8, display archeological remains of baths and buildings from the same time period. *(Main office for all three at Pl. La Seo, 2. ☎976 39 97 52. Open Tu-Sa 10am-2pm and 5-8pm, Su 10am-2pm. Prices include admission museums. Guided visits begin on the hr. 600ptas/€3.60, students 400ptas/€2.40, over 65 and under 8 free.)*

BEYOND PLAZA DEL PILAR

PALACIO DE LA ALJAFERÍA. Following the Muslim conquest of the Iberian Peninsula in the 8th century, a crisis over succession smashed the kingdom into petty tributary states called *taifas.* Weighty renovations have somewhat encumbered the building's original grace, but its awesome stone exterior and refined interior are still impressive. The ground floor has a distinctly Moorish flavor that bears stark contrast with the Gothic second floor. The fortified tower imprisoned *el trovador* in García Gutierrez's drama of the same name, the inspiration for Verdi's opera *Il Trovatore. (C. Castillo. Take bus #21 or 33. Or head left on C. Coso from Pl. España; facing the casco viejo, continue onto Conde Aranda, make a right onto Pl. Maria Agustín, then a left onto C. Aliaferia. ☎976 28 95 28. Open June-Aug. daily 10am-2pm and 4:30-8pm; Sept.-May M-W and Sa 10am-2pm and 4:30-6:30pm, F 4:30-6:30pm, Su 10am-2pm. 300ptas/€1.80, students and seniors 150ptas/€0.90, under 12 free.)*

MUSEO DE ZARAGOZA. Archaeology buffs will love the extensive collection of artifacts that fill the museum's ground floor. The second story documents Aragonese painting up through the early 20th century. The room dedicated to Goya is the most popular, although many of the others are more impressive. *(Pl. Los Sitios, 6. From Pl. España, follow Po. Independencia about 4 blocks, turn left on C. Joaquín Costa and continue 3 more blocks; the museum is on the left after Pl. Los Sitios. ☎976 22 21 81. Open Tu-Sa 10am-2pm and 5-8pm, Su 10am-2pm. Free.)*

MUSEO PABLO GARGALLO. Dedicated to one of the most innovative Aragonese sculptors of the 1920s, the Museo Pablo Gargallo houses a small collection of his works in the graceful **Palacio de Arguillo,** built in 1670. *(Pl. San Felipe, 3. ☎976 39 20 58. From Pl. España, walk down C. Don Jaime I and turn left on C. Menéndez Nuñez. The museum is 5 blocks down in Pl. San Felipe. Open Tu-Sa 10am-2pm and 5-9pm, Su 10am-2pm. Free.)*

MUSEO PABLO SERRANO. This modern building houses bronze sculptures by the fascinating Pablo Serrano (1908-1985). Look for *Gran pan partido* (Big Bread Parted) and sculptural reinterpretations of works by Picasso, Velázquez, and Goya. Smaller halls feature [illegible] *[illegible] Open Tu-Sa 10am-2pm and 4-8pm, Su 10am-2pm. Free.)*

ENTERTAINMENT

The Zaragozan nightlife scene is almost strictly limited to weekends; even the most popular of *tapas* bars don't see more than a trickle of visitors before Friday night. Most locals begin their nights in **La Zona**—the streets bounded by Po. Constitución, C. León XIII, Po. Damas, and Camino de las Torres. Gulping beer from *litros* (about 400ptas) is the primary sport around **El Rollo,** the area bounded by C. Moncasi, C. Bonet, and C. Maestro Marquina at the southern end of Po. Sagasta. University students storm Po. Sagasta and its offshoot, C. Zumalacárregui. Around midnight, herds of party-goers crowd the market area around Pl. San Felipe. Gay bars and discos center around the west side of the *casco viejo;* mixed gay and straight crowds let loose on the small dance floor of **Sphinx,** C. Ramón y Caja, one block down from C. Conde Aranda. (Cover F-Su 2000ptas/€12. Open daily 11pm-5am.) Twenty-somethings of all nationalities issue odd mating calls at the Australian bar/disco, **Wooloomooloo,** C. Espoz y Mina, 19. (☎976 39 63 76. Open daily 6pm-4am.) **La Casa del Loco,** C. Mayor, 10-12, has frequent concerts and a range of music for its international crowd. (No cover. Open daily 10pm-5am.)

The city erupts for a week of unbridled craziness around October 12 in honor of *La Virgen Santa del Pilar*, one of the few remaining full-blown autumn *fiestas* in Spain; a schedule of events is available at the tourist office. City patrons **San Valero** and **San Jorge** are celebrated on January 29 and April 23, respectively.

DAYTRIPS FROM ZARAGOZA

Ask at the Zaragoza tourist office for info on excursions like the *Ruta del Vino* (wine route) and the *Ruta de Goya*. Students of the Romanesque should inquire about visits to the **Cinco Villas** (five villages).

MONASTERIO DE PIEDRA

Aragón Tours buses, C. Almagro, 18 (☎976 21 93 20), leave from Zaragoza and return the same evening (2hr.; July-Oct. 15 9am, return 5pm; round-trip 2350ptas/€14).

Waterfalls drop onto the dry plains surrounding the Monasterio de Piedra, about 110km southwest of Zaragoza. Founded in 1195 by an order of Cistercian monks from Tarragona, but abandoned under government orders in 1835, the monastery is now a three-star hotel. Tour guides lead visitors through the monastery, describing the customs and way of life of the monks, while pointing out various architectural styles and significant sites, among them the first monastery kitchen in Europe to serve hot chocolate. The 12th-century **Torre del Homenaje,** the only part of the existing building that hasn't since been restored, towers over the valley. (☎976 84 90 11; www.monasteriopiedra.com. Open daily 9am-8pm.) The main attraction is the surrounding park and the **Río Piedra,** which tumbles through the valley. (Park open daily 9am-nightfall. 1000ptas/€6 for monastery and park.)

DAROCA

Buses depart from Mesón Felix, C. Mayor, near Puerta Baja to: ***Daroca*** *(1½hr., 2-3 per day 7:15am-6:30pm, 730ptas/€4.40);* ***Teruel*** *(M-Sa 4 per day, 8:15am-7:40pm);* ***Zaragoza*** *(1½hr., 4:30pm, 730ptas/€4.38). Buses arriving in Daroca, the last stop on the Agreda Automóvil line, halt near Puerta Baja.*

Burros and wagons still wander the streets of Daroca (pop. 2400), a town wedged into a dramatic gorge, with burnt-sienna roofs to match the surrounding cliffs. The main sight in town is the icon-filled museum of the **Colegiata de Santa María,** a 16th-century church. To get there, take C. Juan de la Huerta from C. Mayor. (Open June-Aug. Tu-Su 11am-1pm and 5-7pm, Sept.-May Tu-Su noon-1pm and 5:30-7pm. Museum 300ptas/€1.80. The tourist office arranges guided tours.) Little Daroca hosts some lively partying during its week-long **Fiesta de Corpus Christi** (the week of May 30 in 2002). Daroca also hosts the annual **International Program for Ancient Music** during the first two weeks of August, when musicians from the world over gather to teach, learn, and give free concerts.

The town's main artery, **C. Mayor,** runs uphill from the **Puerta Baja** to the **Puerta Alta.** Daroca's walls, 4 km in circumference, were started in the 9th century and were at one time topped by 114 towers. Dirt paths along the walls reward hikers with a sentry's-eye view of the town and surrounding valleys. **La Ruta de Castillo** reveals a spectacular view of Daroca and neighboring towns (45min.). **La Ruta de las Murallas** does the whole tour in two hours. Both routes start outside Puerta Alta. The **tourist office,** Pl. España, 7, opposite the Colegiata de Santa María, provides maps of walking routes. From Puerta Alta, walk 4-5 blocks down C. Mayor and hang a right onto C. San Juan de la Huerta. (☎976 80 01 29. Open M 10:30am-2pm, Tu-Su 10:30am-2pm and 5-7:30pm.) The first floor **restaurant** at **Pensión El Ruejo** serves a satisfying 1100pta/€6.60 *menú*. Picnickers stock up at **%Día,** the supermarket on C. Mayor (open M-Sa 9:30am-2pm and 5-8pm).

TARAZONA

Therpasa buses (☎976 64 11 00) run from the station on Av. Narvarra to: ***Soria*** *(1hr., 4-7 per day, 630ptas/€3.80) and* ***Zaragoza*** *(1hr., 805ptas/€4.84). Conda buses leave from Parque de Estación, on the street to the right of the tourist office, to* ***Tudela*** *(1hr., M-Sa 7:15am-6:30pm 5-6 per day, 230ptas/€1.40). Buy tickets on board.*

Tarazona (pop. 10,750) is known as the "*Mudéjar* City." Some even liken the winding streets of its medieval quarter to those in Toledo. The town makes a nice daytrip from Zaragoza, especially during *Las Fiestas de Cipotegato* (Aug. 27-Sept. 1) The festivities begin when the jester, clad in a psychedelic getup of red, green, and yellow, is released into the crowds at noon on the 27th. After he is pelted with tomatoes, makes his way through the city with the help of his friends. Not until he has successfully completed his route is the jester's identity triumphantly released to the people. The next 6 days are ablaze with activities including *encierros*, bullfights, concerts, and dances in honor of San Atilano, Tarazona's patron saint.

Tarazona's 13th- and 15th-century **cathedral** is undergoing painstaking restorations. The towers, belfry, lantern, and plasterwork in the inner cloister are fine examples of *Mudéjar* work. From the cathedral, follow signs for Soria/Zaragoza down C. Laureles, then take your first right and pass through the arch to the octagonal **Pl. de Toros Vieja.** Built in the 18th century, the plaza included private residences with built-in balconies for the express purpose of watching corridas. Tarazona was also the seasonal residence of Aragonese kings until the 15th century. Their Alcázar has since served as the **Palacio Episcopal.** Though now the Bishop's home and closed to visitors, the exterior is still worth a peek. From the Pl. Toros Vieja, walk left 1 block, then up the stairs of the Recodos and Rúa Baja. Opposite the Palacio Episcopal, in the heart of **El Cinto** (the medieval quarter), rises the **Iglesia de Santa Magdalena** and its *Mudéjar* tower. To enter, take a left up Cuesta del Palacio from the Palacio Episcopal and then another left.

The **tourist office,** Pl. San Francisco, 1, is on the right side of the building in front of the church. (☎976 64 00 74. Open M-F 9am-1:30pm and 4:30-7:30pm, Sa and Su 10am-2pm and 4:30-7:30pm. July-Aug office open until 8pm Sa-Su.) **Banco Central Hispano,** in Pl. San Francisco (open M-F 8:30am-2:30pm, Oct.-May Sa 8:30am-1pm as well), offers no commission and a **24hr. ATM.** Local services include: **luggage storage,** at the Therpasa Bus Station (open daily 6:30am-1pm and 2-10pm; free); **emergency** ☎091; **municipal police,** Pl. San Francisco (☎976 64 16 91). The **post office,** Pl. Seo, is downhill from the cathedral. (☎976 64 13 17. Open M-F 8:30am-2:30pm, Sa 9:30am-1pm). **Postal code**: 50500.

NEAR TARAZONA: MONASTERIO DE VERUELA

Travelers with cars can visit the walled monastery of Veruela, which slumbers in the Sierra de Moncayo, 15km south of Tarazona. Its golden stone walls guard a Romanesque-Gothic church and a [illegible] Gustavo Adolfo Becquer wrote his *Cartas desde mi celda* (Letters from My Cell) within these walls. (☎976 64 90 25. Open Apr.-Sept. Tu-Su 10am-2pm and 4-7pm; Oct.-Mar. Tu-Su 10am-1pm and 3-6pm. 300ptas/€1.80.) Buses run to Vera de Moncaya, about 400m from the monastery; ask the tourist office for more information on bus schedules and possible lodging.

TERUEL

The small capital of southern Aragón, Teruel (pop. 29,300) invites visitors to step into a world of love, heartbreak, and cultural exchange. Lively and welcoming, this little town's narrow streets and old plazas belie its cosmopolitan history. From the 12th to the 15th centuries, Muslims, Jews, and Christians lived here in cultural collusion. The resulting *Mudéjar* architecture blends Arab patterns with Gothic and Romanesque touches. An easy stopover between Valencia and Zaragoza, Teruel doesn't really reach its prime until July, when citizens celebrate the resilience of their *torico* (iron bull) in an 168-hour liquor fest.

STAR-CROSSED LOVERS The tombs of Diego de Marcilla and Isabel de Segura in the **Mausoleo de los Amantes,** next to Torre San Pedro, are the source of Teruel's nickname: *Ciudad de los Amantes* (City of Lovers). The story began when Diego left Teruel to make his fortune and prove his worth to Isabel's affluent family. Five years later, he returned a rich man, just in time to watch Isabel marry his childhood rival. Diego begged for one last kiss but was refused; he immediately died of grief. At the funeral, Isabel kissed the corpse and, overcome with sorrow, died herself. The lovers are commemorated with life-size statues of the lovers, reaching out to touch hands but not quite making it. For a peek at the lovers' remains, duck down near their heads. (From Pl. Torico, take the alleyway to the left of the purple *modernista* house. Stairs lead directly to the mausoleum. Open M-Sa 10am-2pm and 5-7:30pm, Su 10:30am-2pm and 5-7:30pm. 50ptas/€0.30.)

TRANSPORTATION. Trains depart from Camino de la Estación, 1 (☎902 24 02 02), down the stairs from Pl. Ovalo to: **Valencia** (2¾hr., 3 per day 7:55am-6:33pm, 1145ptas/€6.90) and **Zaragoza** (2½hr., 3 per day 6:55am-5:59pm, 1430ptas/€8.60). **Buses** depart from the new **station** (☎978 61 07 89), Ronda de Ambeles, only a few blocks from the *casco viejo*. **La Rápida** (☎978 60 20 04) goes to **Barcelona** (5½-6½hr., M-Sa 12:30pm, 3330ptas/€20) and **Cuenca** (3hr., M-Sa 11:45am, 1220ptas/€7.30). **Samar** (☎978 60 34 50) goes to **Madrid** (4½-5hr., 3 per day M-F 7:30am-5pm, 2520ptas/€15.20) and **Valencia** (2-2½hr.; 5 per day M-Sa 7:15am-7pm, Su 8am-7pm; 1220ptas/€7.30). **Jiménez** goes to **Zaragoza** (4 per day 7am-7pm, 1195ptas/€7.20). To rent a car, call **BMW** (☎978 60 65 36. 10,000ptas/€60.00 per day plus IVA.).

ORIENTATION AND PRACTICAL INFORMATION. A small valley spanned by connecting bridges separates the *casco viejo* from its younger, modern mate. The center of the *casco* is **Pl. de Carlos Castell,** affectionately known as **Pl. del Torico.** To reach the plaza from the train station, take the staircase from the park and follow signs to the *centro.* To Pl. Torico from the new bus station, turn right out of the station and take your first left into Pl. Judería, then take zig-zagging C. Hartzenbusch into Pl. del Torico. The **tourist office** is at C. Tomás Nogues, 1. From Pl. Torico, follow C. Ramón y Cajal and take the first left; the office is one block away on the right, at the corner. (☎978 60 22 79. Open M-Sa 10am-2pm and 5-8pm, Su 10am-2pm.) Services include: the **Banco Central Hispano,** Pl. Torico, 15. (☎978 60 11 35. Open M-F 8:30am-2:30pm; Oct.-May also Sa 8:30am-1pm.), **luggage storage,** at the train station (lockers 500ptas/€3.00) or bus station (100ptas/€0.60 per piece per day; both open daily 6:30am-10:30pm); **emergency** ☎112; and the **post office,** C. Yagüe de Salas, 19. (☎978 60 11 90 or 60 11 92. Open M-F 8:30am-8:30pm, Sa 9:30am-2pm). **Postal code:** 44001.

ACCOMMODATIONS AND FOOD. Lodgings are scarce during August and *Semana Santa* and impossible to find during the *fiestas* of early July. Smack between the cathedral and the main plaza, **Hostal Aragón,** C. Santa María, 4, features simple rooms, some with TV. From Pl. Torico, head away from the Torico and take the first left as you exit the plaza. (☎978 60 13 87. Singles 2500ptas/€15, with bath 3700ptas/€22; doubles 3700ptas/€22, with bath 5500ptas/€33; triples with bath 7400ptas/€45.) Thought to be the oldest hostel in all of Spain, **Fonda el Tozal,** C. Rincón, 5, features typical *mudéjar* design, including stunning and spacious tiled bathrooms. (☎978 60 10 22. Doubles 4500ptas/€27; triples 6300/€38.)

Teruel is famous for its flavorful cured ham, *jamón de Teruel*, featured in the *tapas* bars of Pl. Torico. The streets leading away from Pl. Torico are home to most of the town's restaurants, most of which serve nearly identical fare. **Restaurante La Parrilla,** C. Estebán, 2, two blocks uphill from the tourist office, has a magnificent *menú* (1600pta/€9.60) with succulent meats grilled in a stone fireplace. (☎978 60 59 17. Open M-Sa 1-4:30pm and 8-11pm, Su noon-4:30pm. MC/V.)

SIGHTS. The mother of all Teruel's *Mudéjar* monuments is the 13th-century **Catedral de Santa María de Mediavilla.** The vast difference between the chapels is noteworthy—the gilding of the *Capilla de la Inmaculada*, dating from the 19th century are brilliant in comparison to the more subdued carvings of the 16th-century *El Retablo Mayor*. The cathedral itself has three naves, the most recent of which wasn't finished until the late 1800s. (All roads left of Pl. Torico lead one block away to Pl. Catedral. Open daily 11am-2pm and 4:30-8pm. 300ptas/€1.80 with mandatory guide.) Muslim artisans built the brick-and-glazed-tile **Torres Mudéjares** (Mudéjar Towers) between the 12th and 15th centuries, after a Christian church adapted the Almohad minarets to their own purposes. The most intricately designed of the towers is the 13th-century **Torre de San Salvador,** on C. Salvador, it is the only tower open to visitors. Climb 123 steps through several chambers to the panoramic bell tower. (Open July-Sept. daily 11am-2pm and 5-8pm; Oct.-June Sa 11am-2pm and 5-7pm, Su 11am-2pm. 250ptas/€1.50.) Teruel's Romeo and Juliet love story is kept alive at the **Mausoleo de los Amantes,** where the 1217 tragedy is immortalized (see **Star-crossed Lovers,** above. Open daily 10am-2pm and 5-8pm, 50ptas/€0.30). Behind the cathedral, the **Museo Provincial,** devoted mainly to archaeological and ethnographic pursuits, rests in the 16th-century **Casa de la Comunidad,** a leading example of the "Aragonese Renaissance" style. Don't miss the reproduction of an 18th-century chemist's shop. Rotating temporary exhibits complement the permanent collection. (Pl. Fray Anselmo Polanco. ☎978 60 01 50. Open Tu-F 10am-2pm and 4-7pm, Sa-Su 10am-2pm. Free.)

DAYTRIPS FROM TERUEL

Protected by ancient walls, medieval townships in Teruel's countryside stand amid acres of wilderness. Getting to these mystical hamlets is less of an ordeal than it once was, but unless you have a car—and there is only one rental agency in Teruel—you'll have to spend the night. The *Guía de servicios turísticos*, available at any tourist office, offers information on accommodations in the area.

ALBARRACÍN

Autotransportes Teruel (☎978 60 26 80) runs one bus from Teruel to Albarracín (30min.; departs daily 3:30pm, returns at 8:45am the next day; 400ptas/€2.40).

Just west of Teruel, the former Moorish city of Albarracín (pop. under 1000) has a surprising history of autonomy: from 1009-1113 it was a small, independent Islamic state known as Ibn Razin, and from 1170-1285 it was an independent Christian kingdom. Today, the small medina-like center bustles amidst the fading grandeur of its stone houses, small churches, and occasional towers. The **tourist office,** Pl. Mayor, 1, will direct visitors to the *pinturas rupestres*, post-Paleolithic cave paintings dating from 5000 BC, and also provides a list of [illegible] 71 00 51. [illegible] pm, Su 10am-2pm.)

RUBIELOS DE MORA

Trains (☎902 24 02 02) come from Teruel (50min., 7:55am, 440ptas/€2.64). Furio buses (☎964 60 01 00) also come from Teruel (1½hr., 2:30pm, return 6:45am).

Connoisseurs insist that the most exquisite of the medieval towns surrounding Teruel is Rubielos de Mora (pop. 600), 15km east of Mora de Rubielos. Residents live in an architectural set-piece unchanged since medieval days, complete with city gates and a 16th-century town hall featuring the requisite courtyard and dungeon. The **tourist office** is in the Ayuntamiento, Pl. Hispano América, 1. (☎978 80 40 96. Open July-Aug. daily 10am-2pm and 5-7pm; Sept.-June M-F 10am-2pm.)

MORA DE RUBIELOS

Furio (☎964 60 01 00) buses run to Mora de Rubielos (1hr., 2:30pm) from Teruel. Trains also come from Teruel (45min., 3 per day 7:55am-6:33pm, 440ptas/€2.65), but the closest train station to Mora de Rubielos is 14km away.

Forty-two km east of Teruel, Mora de Rubielos has the area's largest and best-preserved 15th-century castle. For centuries the castle and town were passed from one noble family to another until finally becoming part of Aragón in 1365. In the summer, a tourist office (☎978 80 61 32) sets up shop on C. Diputación.

ARAGONESE PYRENEES

Historians look at the Aragonese Pyrenees, note the infrequency with which northern enemies have invaded Spain, and say it all makes sense. Everyone else looks at the jagged cliff faces, deep gorges, icy rivers, and alpine meadows and can't say a word. The most popular entry point for the Aragonese Pyrenees is **Jaca,** from which most walkers head to the spectacular **Parque Nacional de Ordesa.** In the east, **Benasque** draws hard-core mountaineers with its access to the highest peaks in the Pyrenees, while the western valleys of **Ansó** and **Hecho** are ideal for less strenuous mountain rambling. The Aragonese mountains are less developed than those of Cataluña, but there are still a number of resorts awaiting skiers, including Astún, Panticosa, Cerler, and Candanchú. For details on winter in Aragón, get the free tourist office pamphlets *Ski Aragón* or *El Turismo de Nieve en España.*

JACA ☎974

For centuries, pilgrims bound for Santiago would cross the Pyrenees into Spain, stop in Jaca (pop. 14,000) for the night, and be off by sunrise. They had the right idea. Although Jaca served a brief stint as capital of Aragón (1035-1095), there is little to do here but enjoy the hustle and bustle of the city and its commodities while organizing excursions into the Pyrenees and nearby ski resorts.

TRANSPORTATION. **RENFE** trains (☎974 36 13 32; www.renfe.es; ticket booth open 10am-noon and 5-7pm) to: **Madrid** (7hr.; M-F, Su 2pm; 4400ptas/€24); **Zaragoza** (3hr.; daily 7:36am and 6:11pm; 1400ptas/€8.41). **La Oscense** buses (☎974 35 50 60) to: **Pamplona** (2hr., 1 per day, 900ptas/€5.41); **Sabiñánigo** (20min., daily 4-6 per day, 180ptas/€1.10); and **Zaragoza** (2hr., daily 3-4 per day, 1540ptas/€9.30). From Sabiñánigo, **Empresa Hudebus** (☎974 21 32 77) connects to **Torla**, near Ordesa and Aínsa. **Josefa Escartín** (☎974 36 05 08) buses go to **Ansó** (1½hr., M-Sa 6:30pm, 500ptas/€3) via **Hecho** (55min., 400ptas/€2.40) and **Siresa** (1hr., 425ptas/€2.55). **Taxis** (☎974 36 28 48) at the intersection of C. Mayor, Ave. and Regimiento Galicia.

ORIENTATION AND PRACTICAL INFORMATION. Buses drop passengers on Av. Jacetania, at the edge of the city center. From the station, walk through the plaza to C. Zocotín and continue straight ahead for 2 blocks to **C. Mayor.** A city bus runs from the **train station** (bus stop to the right of the school) to the center of town. From the train station to the center of town, take Av. Juan XXIII to its end, turn left onto Av. de Francia, continue straight as it becomes C. Primer Viernes de Mayo, and then make a left onto C. Mayor.

The staff at the **tourist office,** Av. Regimiento de Galicia, 2, off C. Mayor, speaks English. (☎974 36 00 98. Open July-Aug. M-F 9am-2pm and 4:30-8pm, Sa 9am-1:30pm and 5-8pm, Su 10am-1:30pm; Sept.-June M-F 9am-1:30pm and 4:30-7pm, Sa 10am-1pm and 5-7pm.) **Alcorce,** Av. Regimiento Galicia, 1, organizes hiking, rock climbing, spelunking, and rafting trips. (☎974 35 67 81; www.alcorceaventura.com. Guided hiking trips from 3000ptas/€18 per person per day; rafting from 5500ptas/€33; ski and snowboard rentals 2500ptas/€15 per day. Open June-Sept M-Sa 9:30am-1:30pm and 5:30-9pm; Oct.-May M-Sa 9:30am-1:30pm. MC/V.) For ski conditions, call **Teléfono Blanco** (☎976 20 11 12). Local services include: **Banco Central Hispano,** C. Primer Viernes de Mayo (open Apr.-Sept. M-F 8:30am-2:30 pm; Oct.-Mar. M-F 8:30am-2:30 pm, Sa 8:30am-1pm); **police,** C. Mayor, 24 (☎091 or 092); **Centro de Salud,** Po. Constitución, 6 (☎974 36 07 95); and the **post office,** C. Correos, 13. (☎974 35 58 86. Open M-F 8:30am-2:30pm, Sa 9:30am-1pm.) **Postal code:** 22700.

For **internet access,** try **Ciber Santi**, C. Mayor, 42-44, inside La Tienda Mayor to the right. (☎974 35 68 69. Open M-Th 11am-2pm and 4:30-11pm, Fri-Sa 11am-2pm and 4:30pm-1am, Su 5:30-11pm. 300ptas/€1.80 per 30min, 475ptas/€2.85 per hr.)

ACCOMMODATIONS AND FOOD. Jaca's hostels and *pensiones* cluster around C. Mayor and the cathedral. Lodgings are scarce only during the bi-annual *Festival Folklórico* in late July and early August. For Santiago-bound pilgrims, the **Albergue de Peregrinos** is on C. Hospital (☎974 35 51 16. Towels 200ptas/€1.20. Reception open daily 5-11pm. 700ptas/€4.21 per person.) To reach **Hostal Paris,** San Pedro, 5, from the bus station, cross the park and head to your right, circling around the church to the next plaza; look for the hostal's sign straight ahead. (☎974 36 10 20. *Semana Santa*, July 15-Sept. 15 singles 2675ptas/€16; doubles 4280ptas/€26; triples 5775ptas/€35. Low season singles 2460ptas/€15; doubles 3850ptas/€23; triples 5350ptas/€32.) The *casa rural* **El Arco**, C. San Nicolas is a pleasant alternative. Coming from the bus station, cross the park and head toward the church; the *casa* is located to the left of the photo shop. (☎974 36 44 48. Breakfast 350-600ptas/€2.10-3.60. 2000ptas/€12 per person.) **Albergue Juvenil de Escuelas Pias** (HI), Av. Perimetral, 6, offers rows of bungalows. From C. Mayor, turn left onto C. Regimiento de Galicia, then left again onto Av. Perimetral; turn off onto the unmarked driveway immediately before the skating rink. (☎974 36 05 36. Breakfast included. Doubles 1600ptas/€9.62 per person, over 25 1800ptas/€10.82, without HI 2000ptas/€12; quads 1300ptas/€7.81 per person, over 25 1500ptas/€9; without HI 1800ptas/€10.82.)

For *menús* and *tapas*, follow your nose along C. Mayor. *Bocadillos* fill the menus on Av. Primer Viernes de Mayo. **Restaurante Vegetariano El Arco,** C. San Nicolás, 4, in the bus station plaza, serves an all-veggie *menú del día*. (Entrées 1000ptas/€6. Open M-Sa 1-3pm and 8:30-11:30pm.) **Supermercado ALDI,** C. Correos, 9, next to the post office. (Open M-Sa 9:30am-2pm and 5-8pm, V.)

ARAGÓN

DAYTRIPS FROM JACA

MONASTERIO DE SAN JUAN DE LA PEÑA

Taxis (☎974 36 28 48) will make the journey for about 5150ptas/€30, with a 1hr. wait. If you are driving, park at the lot above the monastery; a shuttle picks up visitors every 30min. The adventurous can catch a bus from Jaca to Pamplona and ask to be dropped off at Santa Cruz de La Seró (C.N. 240, 295 km.). From there it is a 9km hike to the Monastery.

The spectacular **Monasterio de San Juan de la Peña** is difficult to reach—it was designed that way. Determined hermits hid the original monastery in a canyon 22km from Jaca and maintained such extreme privacy that invading Moors never discovered it or the Holy Grail supposedly [illegible] century underground church carved directly into the rock and the 12th-century cloister wedged under a massive boulder. The carved capitals of the cloister's arcade are not to be missed. Don't confuse the monastery with the uninteresting 17th-century *monasterio nuevo*, 1km up the hill in the open field. (☎974 35 51 19 or 35 51 45; www.monasteriosanjuan.com. Open Oct. 16-Mar. 15 Tu-Su 11am-2pm and 4-5:30pm; Mar. 16-May and Sept-Oct15 daily 10am-2pm and 4-7pm; June-Aug. daily 10am-2:30pm and 3:30-8pm. 500ptas/€3 includes entrance to church in Santa Cruz de la Seró, 700ptas/€4.21 includes shuttle from the parking lot.)

CASTILLO DE LOARRE

Reaching the castle requires a little ingenuity. ***La Oscense*** *(☎974 35 50 60) sends 1 bus from Jaca to Loarre, 5km from the castle (1hr., M-F 7:15am, 780ptas/€4.70); the return bus at (5pm, 655ptas/€3.91) stops only in Ayerbe, 7km away from Loarre. Trains run only to Ayerbe (1½ hr; departs Jaca daily at 7:36am and 6:11pm, returns at 8:58am and 5:18pm; 525ptas/€3.16). From there, you can request a taxi or trek the 2hr. to the town of Loarre.*

The power and magnificence of **El Castillo de Loarre** is visible for kilometers in each direction. A maze of history sits above the fields, every inch of which is open to exploration. No tours or guides shuffle people through the castle; visitors are free to investigate on their own. In the 11th century, King Sancho Ramírez built the castle in an effort to protect the Western Pyrenees from a Moorish invasion. He succeeded—sharp cliffs at its rear and 400m of thick walls to the east make it nearly impenetrable. The building's outer walls follow the rock so closely that a nighttime attacker might have seen only the silhouette of a single stone monolith. A crypt, which opens to the right of the steep entrance staircase, holds the remains of Demetrius, the French saint who died in Loarre. You can go up to the battlements of both towers, but be careful when climbing the wobbly steel rungs to the roof or descending into the dark basement. (Open Oct.-Mar W-Su 11am-2:30pm; Mar-June and Sept Tu-Su 10am-1:30 4-7pm; July-Aug. daily 10am-8pm; Free.)

VALLE DE HECHO

The craggy Valle de Hecho and its picturesque hamlets, 40km west of Jaca, are the closest hiking to the city. Under the humid influence of the Atlantic, these western slopes and their dense forests encourage a wide range of ecological diversity and are favored by hikers in search of moderate climbs. In years past, area villages have hosted the **Simposio Internacional de Escultura y Pintura Moderna.** Artists came from far and wide, turning the surrounding hills into a huge open-air museum. Remnants (46 to be precise) of this artistic era are scattered throughout Hecho. The valley is best visited during the summer, as it is extremely quiet during the rest of the year. A **Josefa Escartín** bus (☎974 36 05 08) leaves Jaca M-Sa at 6:30pm, stopping at **Hecho** (7:25pm) and **Siresa** (7:40pm) before continuing to **Ansó** (8:10pm). Every morning except Su the bus returns from Ansó (6am) via Siresa (6:30am) and Hecho (6:45am) on its way to Jaca (7:40am).

ARAGÓN

HECHO (ECHO)

Hecho (pop. 670) is the valley's geographical and administrative center, a serious title that doesn't seem to suit the small and inviting town. The Ayuntamiento houses a small **tourist office** in the summer months. (☎974 37 53 29. Open July-Sept. 15 M-Sa 10am-2pm and 5-7pm, Su 10am-2pm.) Someone upstairs in the office (M-F 8am-3pm) or downstairs in the library (M-F 5-7pm) will happily answer questions during the rest of the year. The hiking experts of **Compañía de Guías Valle de Echo** lead trips and rent cross-country skis. (☎974 37 53 87. Call ahead.) A **bank** with **24-hour ATM**, is on Pl. Alta, off of C. Mayor. (Open Nov.-May M, Tu, W, F 8:15am-2:30pm, Th 8:15am-1:45pm, 5:15-7:30pm. Apr.-Oct. M-F 8:15am-2:30pm; MC/V); **Supermercado Aldi,** is on C. Mayor (Open July-Sept. M-Sa 9:30am-2pm and 5-8pm, Su 10am-2pm; Oct.-June M-Sa 10am-2pm and 5-8pm) The **Post office**, Pl. Alta, is also off C. Mayor (Open M-F 8:30am-2:30pm, Sa 9:30am-1pm). For somewhere to stay, follow signs toward the *centro de salud* to the tall white **Casa Blasquico,** Pl. Fuente 1. (☎974 37 50 07. Breakfast 600ptas/€3.61. *Menú* 1700ptas/€10.22. Doubles 7000ptas/€42, with living room 8000ptas/€48. IVA not included. MC/V.) At half the price, the small rooms of central **Casa Marina,** C. Medio, 12, are located on the right, just up the cobblestone street from the center and across from Bar Archer. (☎974 37 50 77, Doubles 3500ptas/€21.) At the entrance to Hecho from Jaca, the well-kept sites and *albergue* bunks of **Camping Valle de Hecho** are just a short walk from town. (☎/fax 974 37 53 61. 557ptas/€3.40 per person, per tent, per car. Bunks 1100ptas/€6.61. 7% IVA not included. MC/V.)

VALLE DE ANSÓ

Farther down the road from Jaca, the little town of Ansó is set in one of the most appealing valleys in the Pyrenees, a lush growth of oak and pine trees. Like Hecho, this valley lives for July and August, when the bulk of its visitors pour in over the mountain ridges. Visitors stop in cobblestoned Ansó before heading farther up the valley to Zuriza, the departure point of the valley's best hikes.

ANSÓ

Tiny Ansó's (pop. 530) cobblestone streets and matching houses are peacefully removed from the rest of the world. At the **Museo de Etnología** inside the **Iglesia de San Pedro,** antique chorus books are displayed beside mannequins modeling traditional dress. (☎974 37 00 22. Open July-Sept. 15. M-F 10:30am-1pm and 4-7pm; during the rest of the year, the priest living in the stone house across from church can open it for you. 250ptas/€1.50.) The **tourist office** is in Pl. Domingo Miral. (☎974 37 02 25. Open July-Aug. daily 10am-2pm and 5-8pm) Next door is the **post office.** (☎ 974 37 02 25. Open M-Sa 9am-2pm.) There is a popular hike beginning from Ansó. Walk 2km south to the Hecho-Huesca fork in the road. Just above the tunnel toward Hecho rises the striking, weather-sculpted rock formation called El Fraile y la Monja (The Monk and the Nun).

Posada Magoria, C. Chapitel, 8, the corner house just below the church, offers rooms and vegetarian meals. (☎974 37 00 49. Breakfast 900ptas/€5.41, dinner 1900ptas/€11.42. Singles 5000ptas/€30; doubles with one bed 6900ptas/€42, with two beds 7900ptas/€48. MC/V.) Around the corner is **Posada Veral,** C. Cocorro, 6. (☎974 37 01 19. Breakfast 400ptas/€2.40. Lunch and dinner *menú* 1500ptas/€9 for guests only. Singles 2000ptas/€12; doubles 4000ptas/€24.) **Hostal Aisa**, located just beside the post office, offers rooms with private baths. (☎974 37 00 09. 2500ptas/€15 per person plus IVA. MC/V.) Those up for a hike will find the most affordable lodging 3km out of town at *refugio*-style **Borda Changalé**, along the road to Zuriza. (☎974 37 02 46. Ctra. Ansó. Breakfast included. *Menú del día* at the restaurant downstairs 1350ptas/€8.11. July-Aug. 6-8 bunk rooms 6000ptas/€36 for 4, each additional person 1000ptas/€6. Off-season 1500ptas/€9.02 per person.)

ZURIZA AND ENVIRONS

Around Zuriza, in the northern part of the Valle de Ansó, the terrain alternates between the shallow **Hona La Solana** (Hole of Solana) and the steep summit of **Ezcaurri.** Many hikers use the area as a base for the arduous trek to **Sima de San Martín**, a gorgeous trail along the French border. To get there, drive from Zuriza to the Isaba-Belagua crossroads and take the Belagua direction, heading north. **Camping Zuriza,** 15km north of Ansó, lies along the banks of a stream running between Ezcaurri and Hondonada. It is great spot for fishing, hiking, and kayaking (April-May). The site also provides a **supermarket, hostel,** and **pub/restaurant** where you can find information and maps (700ptas/€4.21) of nearby trails. (☎974 37 01 96 or 37 00 77. Breakfast 400ptas/€2.40. Hot showers included. Campsite 500ptas/€3 per person, per tent and per car; IVA not included. Hostel doubles 4500ptas/€27, with bath 6000ptas/€36. Year-round bunks 1100ptas/€6. MC/V.) From the campground, it's a mild day hike (5hr.) to the **Mesa de los Tres Reyes,** a series of peaks close to the borders of France, Navarra, and Aragón (hence "los tres reyes").

PARQUE NACIONAL DE ORDESA

The beauty of Ordesa tends to reduce even seasoned travelers to stupefied monosyllables. Extremely well-maintained trails cut across forest, rock face, snow-covered peak, and river, all in one day. Located just south of the French border, Ordesa includes the canyons and valleys of Ordesa, Añisclo, Escuaín, and Pineta. The park offers trails for hikers of all levels of experience, and thus attracts huge crowds in July and August. It is easiest to enter Ordesa through the village of **Torla.**

TRANSPORTATION. All **trains** along the Zaragoza-Huesca-Jaca line stop in Sabiñánigo. **La Oscense** (☎974 35 50 60) also runs a **bus** between Sabiñánigo and **Jaca** (20 min.; 2-3 per day 8am-5:15, 180ptas/€1.08.) From there, **Compañía Hudebus** (☎974 21 32 77) runs to **Torla** (55min.; Sept.-June daily 11am, July-Aug. daily 11am and 6pm; 400ptas/€2.40.) During the high season, a bus shuttles between Torla and **Ordesa** (15min.; June 30-Aug 6am-7pm, Sept. 6am-6pm; 275ptas/€1.65). When the shuttle is running, from late May-Sept., cars are prohibited from entering the park. Parking is available in Torla for 75ptas/€0.45 per hr. from 9am-8pm or

660ptas/€3.95 per day; overnight parking is free. In the off-season those without a car will have to either hike the 8km to the park entrance or catch a **taxi** (☎974 48 61 53 or 48 62 43. About 2000ptas/€12). To exit the park area, catch the bus as it passes through Torla at 3:30pm on its way back to Sabiñánigo.

PRACTICAL INFORMATION. The **visitors center** is on the left beyond the park entrance. (Open Apr. daily 9am-1:30pm and 3-6pm; May-Oct. daily 9am-2pm and 4:30-7pm). The **park info center** in Torla, across the street from the bus stop, takes over in low season. (Open M-F 8am-3pm; Jul-Sept M-F 8am-3pm, Sa-Su 9am-2pm and 4:30-7pm.) The indispensable *Editorial Alpina* guide (775ptas/€4.66) is available in town. Across from the pharmacy on C. a Ruata, **Compañía Guías de Torla** organizes rafting, canyoning, and year-round mountaineering expeditions. (☎974 48 64 22; www.guiasdetorla.com. Open daily May-June 15, Oct.-Nov. 5-9pm, late June-Sept. 8:30am-1:30pm and 5-10pm, Dec.-April available by phone. MC/V.) Local Services include: **Guardia Civil** (☎974 48 61 60), and the **post office**, on C. a Ruata at Pl. de la Constitutión (open M-Sa 9-11am). **Postal code:** 22376.

ACCOMMODATIONS. The town of **Torla** offers the greatest range of accommodations, but it tends to fill up fast in July and August—reserve ahead. The **Refugio L'Atalaya,** C. a Ruata 45, and its open kitchen are hippy-hiker heaven. Ascend C. a Ruata, following the sign across the street to the left of the bus stop pointing to "Centro Población," then continue 1 block uphill. (☎974 48 60 22. Open *Semana Santa*-Oct. 11. *Menú* 1400ptas/€8.60. Loft mats 1000ptas/€6 per person. MC/V.) Across the street is the slightly more conservative **Refugio L'Briet.** (☎974 48 62 21. *Menú* 1495ptas/€9. Sheets 500ptas/€3. Bunks 1000ptas/€6. Private rooms available. MC/V.) **Camping Río Ara** is located along the river just outside of Torla and offers a supermarket and bar. (☎974 48 62 48. Open *Semana Santa*-Oct.; 500ptas/€3 per person, per tent, and per car. IVA not included.) Closer to the park, **Camping San Antón** rents 4-person bungalows. (☎974 48 60 63. Open *Semana Santa*-Sept. 525ptas/€3.16 per person, per tent, per car. Bungalows 12,000ptas/€72.) Midway between these two, the pool, tennis courts, and bar of **Camping Ordesa** sit in the shadow of the enormous Hotel Ordesa. (☎974 48 61 25. Open *Semana Santa*-Oct. 15. *Semana Santa* 603ptas/€3.63 per person, 631ptas/€3.87 per tent and per car; 30% off in low season. AmEx/MC/ V.)

FOOD. **Supermercado Torla,** on C. a Ruata, is a few buildings down from Refugio L'Atalaya on the opposite side of the street. (☎974 48 61 63. Open May-Oct. daily 9am-2pm and 5-8pm. Nov.-April closed Su. MC/V.) Up C. a Ruata, **Restaurante Bar El Rebeco,** offers a pricey *menú* (1800ptas/€10.82); more reasonable entrées range from 800-2000ptas/€4.81-12. (☎974 48 60 68. Open May-Oct. daily 1-3:30pm and 8-10:30pm. MC/V.) **Bar Restaurante Taillon,** C. a Ruata, has sandwiches (500ptas/€3) and an impressive view of Mt. Mondaruego. The *menú* is 1600ptas/ €9.62. (☎974 48 63 04. Open May-Oct. daily 7:30am-1am.)

HIKING. If you have only a day to spend in Ordesa, the **Soaso Circle** is the most practical hike, especially for inexperienced mountaineers. Frequent signposts along the wide trail clearly mark the 5hr. (one-way) journey up to **Refugio Góriz.** The trail traverses forests, cliffs, and plateaus, passing the **Gradas de Soaso** waterfall along the way. Check weather forecasts (☎906 36 53 22 or 36 53 80) before starting out; heavy snow can make the trail impassable during winter and spring, and paths becomes dangerous in the rain. Less intrepid travelers may want to reduce the hike to 2hr. (one-way), by turning around at the **gradas**. The views to be had from **Cascada del Cueva** (Cave Falls) and especially from **Cascada del Estrecho** (Wide Falls) make this hike well worth it. Try to arrive early, especially July-Aug., as the park is often flooded with visitors by noon.

AÍNSA (L'AINSA)

An irresistibly romantic village about 1hr. away from Ordesa, Aínsa offers an adventure in time-travel. From the friendly shops along its main intersection,

FAR TREK On your way to Berlin? A *Gran Recorrido* (Great Hike) trail will get you there—eventually. One of the most beautiful and rugged stretches of the pan-European *Gran Recorrido* network treks east to west just below the French-Spanish border. Strung together by old mountain roads, animal tracks, and forest paths, the Aragonese portion of **GR-3** passes by clear mountain lakes and under, over, and through snow-covered peaks (the highest being Mt. Aneto, at 3404m). Though some parts of GR-3 are pretty gentle, the full trek across Aragon requires hiking experience, especially when snow cover is extensive. The border-to-border route takes 8 to 10 days. For detailed info on this and other GR trails, consult tourist offices in the area and the **Federación Aragonesa de Montañismo** at C. Albareda, 7 (☎976 22 79 71) in Zaragoza, and ask for the detailed and trail-specific *Topoguía* guide. The extremely useful *Editorial Alpina* also provides a good map of the route.

Aínsa leads the visitor up a winding cobblestone staircase to its perfectly preserved medieval quarter. A thousand years ago Aínsa was the capital of the Kingdom of Sobrarbe (incorporated into Aragón in the 11th century), and the ruins of its 11th-century **castle** on Pl. Mayor remind visitors of its history. In 1181, priests consecrated the **Iglesia de Santa María,** across the plaza from the castle, whose spiraling tower steps can be climbed for 100ptas/€0.60. An incredible view of the Parque Nacional de Ordesa's peaks awaits at its top.

Casa Rural El Hospital, C. Sta. Cruz, 3 is a converted stone house in the medieval quarter. (☎974 50 07 50. June 16-Sept. doubles with bath, TV, and A/C 5000ptas/€30, Oct.-June 15 4000ptas/€24. MC/V.) Other budget options surround the bus stop in the new part of town. Outside of the center is **Camping Aínsa,** Ctra. Aínsa-Campo, km 1.8. (☎974 50 02 60. 610ptas/€3.70 per person, per car, per large tent; 585ptas/€3.50 per small tent. Open *Semana Santa*-Oct. 15. MC/V.) Essential groceries as well as a few delicacies can be picked up at **Alimentación M. Cheliz,** Av. Ordesa. (☎974 50 00 62. Open July-Sept. daily 8:30am-9pm; Oct.-June M-Sa 8:30am-2:30pm and 4-8:30pm, Su 8:30am-2:30pm. MC/V.) The **Restaurante Brasería,** located near the *castillo* end of Pl. Mayor, offers a range of *menús* for 1900-2400ptas/€11.42-15. (☎974 50 09 81. Open June-Oct. daily 10am-midnight. MC/V.)

Compañía Hudebus (☎974 21 32 77) runs daily buses from **Sabiñánigo** to Aínsa, stopping in **Torla** along the way (2hr.; 11am, returning at 2:30pm; 780ptas/€4.68). **Compañía Cortés** (☎974 31 15 52) runs from Aínsa to **Barbastro** (1hr., M-Sa 7am, 660ptas/€3.95), where buses make the connection to **Benasque.** The **tourist office,** Av. Pirenáica, 1, is at the highway crossroads. (☎974 50 07 67. Open July-Aug. daily 9am-9pm; Sept, May, and June M-Sa 10am-2pm and 4-8pm, Su 10-2; Oct.-April Tu-Sa 10am-2pm and 4-8pm.) The **post office** is located on Av. Ordesa, to the right of the tourist office. (☎974 50 00 71. Open M-F 9-2 and Sa 9-12:30.) **Internet** is available at **Casa Cheliz,** Av. Ordesa, 14. (☎974 40 06 11. Open July-Sept. daily 10am-2pm and [illegible] 8:00. 1000ptas/€6 per hour, 300ptas/€1.80 min.) Although Aínsa is not as well situated for hiking as are Torla or Benasque, companies in town can arrange countless outdoor activities.

VALLE DE BENASQUE: BENASQUE

The Valle de Benasque is a haven for no-nonsense hikers, climbers, and skiers. Countless trails wind through the mountains, and the area teems with *refugios*, allowing for longer expeditions. With its many excursion companies and nearby trailheads, the mellow town of **Benasque** (pop. 1100) offers an excellent base for outdoor activities. Casual hikers are often scared off by the valley's reputation for serious mountaineering—the Pyrenees' highest peaks, including the awe-inspiring Mt. Aneto (3404m), reside in the area—but there is something here for even the most easygoing of adventurers.

ARAGÓN

TRANSPORTATION AND PRACTICAL INFORMATION. La Alta Aragonesa (☎974 21 07 00) runs buses to **Huesca** (3hr.; M-Sa 6:45am and 3pm, Su 3pm; 1410ptas/€8.50). July-Aug., the shuttle bus **Pirineos 3000** makes frequent runs from the town to the trailhead parking lots Senarta and La Besurta. To get to the **tourist office**, face the Hotel Aragüells at the main bus stop and walk 1 block down the alley between the BBVA and the building bearing the *barrabés* sign. (☎/fax 974 55 12 89. Open daily 10am-2pm and 5-9pm.) For the **Guardia Civil** call 974 55 10 08. The **post office** is in the Ayuntamiento building across from the church. (☎974 55 20 71. Open M-F 9am-noon, Sa 10:30am-noon.) **Postal code:** 22440.

ACCOMMODATIONS AND FOOD. The cheapest option is **Fonda Barrabés,** C. Mayor, 5. With your back facing the bridge, take a left onto the main road into town, passing Hotel Araguells; Barrabés is 200m ahead on the left. (☎974 55 16 54. Bunks 1200ptas/€7.21; singles 2000ptas/€12; doubles 3900ptas/€23; triples 5300ptas/€32. MC/V.) About 3km uphill from the town center, **Camping Aneto** offers a convenient starting point for a day's hike. (☎974 55 11 41. Open year-round. 500ptas/€3 per person, per tent, and per car; bunks 1500ptas/€9 with kitchen access. IVA not included. MC/V.) **Restaurante-Crêperie Les Arkades** is a piece of town history, occupying an old stone building that was constructed in 1647. (☎974 55 12 02. *Menú* 1600ptas/€9.60. Restaurant open June 22-Oct. 12 daily 1-4:00pm and 8-11pm. Bar open daily 5:30pm-3:30am.) For fresh fruits and vegetables, **Fruta Albá,** C. San Pedro, is hidden in an unmarked warehouse down the alleyway just to the left of the tourist office (open July-Aug. daily 8:30am-1pm and 5-9pm, closed Sun. throughout the rest of the year).

HIKING. If you start out early from Benasque, you can hike 8km up the valley road, past the first parking area, then climb up, up, and away, following the falls of the Río Cregueña. Four arduous hours later, you'll reach Lago de Cregueña (2657m), the largest and highest lake in the surrounding area. Those wishing to scale **Mount Aneto** (3404m), the highest of the Pyrenees, can pick up some gear and head out at 5am with the experts from the **Refugio de la Renclusa.** To reach the *refugio*, take the main road north 14km until the paved road ends; from there it's a 45min. hike. (☎974 55 21 06. Open June 22-Sept. 24. Bunk and kitchen access 600ptas/€3.61.) Many companies in Benasque organize trips. For less strenuous nature wandering, head in the opposite direction, down the main road and follow the signs to Forau de Aigualluts, a lovely pond at the base of a waterfall (40min.).

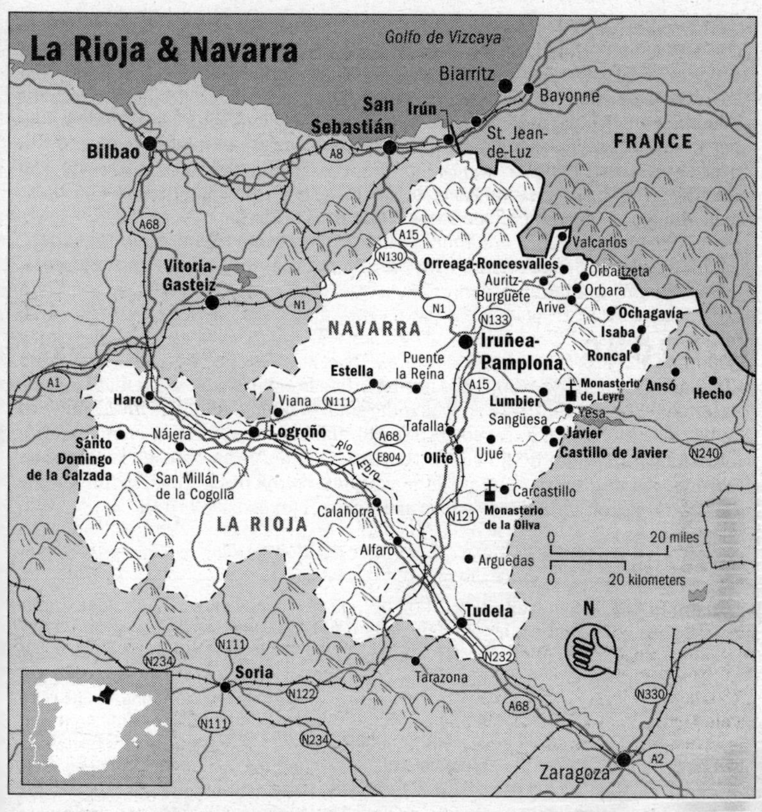

LA RIOJA AND NAVARRA

The spirit of Navarra emanates from the rustic Pyrenean *pueblos* on the French border, flows south through bustling Pamplona, to the dusty villages in the south. Bordered by the Basque Country to the west and Aragón to the east, La Rioja and Navarra's ensconced villages greet tourists with open arms and a toast of wine.

Navarra has long experienced the difficulties of Spain's on-again, off-again regionalism. It gained regional autonomy in 1512, only to see it revoked in 1833. To avoid another devastating loss, Navarrans sided with the "winners" in the 20th century, allying themselves with Franco's Nationalist forces in the Spanish Civil War. Unfortunately, they found themselves under a regime with no tolerance for regional differences. Navarra has continued to support regionalist causes, especially the re-establishment of provincial autonomy in 1983. Many of the region's northern inhabitants identify themselves as Basque and some are concerned with their separation from the País Vasco and the Basque independence movement.

Just south of Navarra, La Rioja is famous for one thing: great wine. "Rioja" is an internationally acclaimed wine classification with an 800-year tradition; both the 1994 and 1995 grapes received the highest ratings possible. The name derives from the Ebro tributary Río Oja, whose waters trickle through the vineyards. When ordering wine, asking for *"vino"* will get you the wine of the year, ordering *"crianza"* delivers higher-quality wine at least three years old, while a request for *"gran reserva"* brings the *crème de la crème* (and you'll pay for it). The best *bodegas* (wine cellars) draw from the lands in western Rioja Alta, around Haro. The *Camino de Santiago* (see **These Boots Were Made for Walking** p. 461) passes through much of La Rioja, and tourist offices can provide useful info on the route. The mountainous Sierra region, with tranquil fields at the feet of towering peaks, lines La Rioja's southern border.

LOGROÑO ☎941

With characteristic hyperbole, the tourist office brochure proclaims that Logroño (pop. 135,000) feeds both the body and the soul. In reality, although the Camino de Santiago makes a stop here, your soul will find little but bustling commerce for nourishment. The body, however, will have something to write home about. Logroño, the best entry point into the vineyard towns of La Rioja, is full of bars serving the region's renowned wines and savory, inexpensive *tapas*.

TRANSPORTATION

Trains: RENFE Pl. Europa, (☎902 24 02 02), off Av. España on the south side of town. Info open daily 7am-11pm. To: **Barcelona** (7hr., 12:36pm, 4400ptas/€27); **Bilbao** (4hr., 3:46pm, 2100ptas/€13); **Burgos** (2hr., 6:56pm, 2200ptas/€14); **Haro** (45min., 3 per day 10:05am-6:46pm, 1300ptas/€7.81); **Madrid** (5½hr., 3:20pm, 4200ptas/€26); **Zaragoza** (2-2½hr., 5 per day 12:36pm-8:03pm, 2200ptas/€14).

Buses: Av. España, (☎941 23 59 83) on the corner of C. General Vara and Av. Pío XII. Check info boards for the appropriate counter. Info open M-Sa 6am-11pm, Su 7am-11pm. To: **Barcelona** (6hr.; daily 1:30 and 5pm, plus F 9:35am; 4030ptas/€25); **Bilbao** (2hr.; 5 per day M-Sa 8:30am-7:30pm, Su 11am, 5:30, and 9pm; 1575ptas/€9.47); **Burgos** (2hr.; 4-7 per day, M-Sa 8:30am-7:30pm, Su 11am-9:45pm; 915ptas/€5.50); **Haro** (1hr.; 3-6 per day M-F 7:30am-8pm, Sa 10:15am-7:15pm, Su 10:15am-8:30pm; 365ptas/€2.20); **Madrid** (4hr.; 5-6 per day M-Th & Sa 6:45am-7pm, F 6:45am-8pm, Su 9:30am-8pm; 2650ptas/€16); **Pamplona** (2hr.; 5 per day M-Sa 7am-7pm, Su 10am, 4:30 and 7pm; 990ptas/€6); **Santo Domingo de la Calzada** (1hr., 3-9 per day, 380ptas/€2.28); **Soria** (1½hr., 5-6 per day 6:45am-7pm, 845ptas/€5.10); **Vitoria-Gasteiz** (2hr., 4-6 per day 7am-8pm, 1135ptas/€7); **Zaragoza** (2hr., 4-7 per day 7am-6:30pm, 1375ptas/€8.26).

Public Transportation: All buses run to Gran Vía, 1 block from Parque Espolón; lines #1 and 3 pass the bus station. All rides 85ptas/€0.51.

Taxis: Stands at the bus station and Parque Espolón. **Radio Taxi** (☎941 50 50 50).

Car Rental: Europcar, C. de Chile (☎941 28 60 73), on the corner of Gran Vía. Open M-F 9am-1pm and 4-7:30pm, Sa 9:30am-1pm. Min. age 25. AmEx/MC/V.

ORIENTATION AND PRACTICAL INFORMATION

Both the old and new towns radiate from the **Parque del Espolón,** a tree-lined set of gravel paths with a fountain at the center. The **casco antiguo** stretches between the park and the Río Ebro, on the far north side of the city. To reach the park from the **train station,** cross the major traffic artery of **Avenida de Lobete** and angle left on Av. España. At the **bus station** (the next major intersection), turn right onto C. General Vara de Rey, which leads north to the park (8min.) and the *casco antiguo.*

Tourist Office: Po. Espolón (☎941 29 12 60; fax 29 16 40; www.larioja.com/turismo), in Parque Espolón facing C. General Vara de Rey, in the large rotunda. English, French, and German spoken. Open June 15.-Oct. M-F 10am-2pm and 5-8pm, Sa 10am-2pm and 5-8pm, Su 10am-2pm; Nov.-May M-Sa 10am-2pm and 4:30-7pm, Su 10am-2pm.

Currency Exchange: Banco Central Hispano, on C. General Vara at the corner of Parque Espolón. **ATM**. Open M-F 8:30am-2:30pm; Oct.-Mar also Sa 8:30am-1pm.

Luggage Storage: At the **bus station** (200ptas/€1.20 per locker; large bags can be left in one of the shops; ask info desk). Open M-Sa 6am-11pm, Su 7am-11pm. At the **train station** (400ptas/€2.40). Open daily 7am-11pm.

Emergency: ☎112. **Police:** ☎091 or 092, C. Ruavieja (near Iglesia de Palacio).

Medical Services: Hospital San Millán, Av. de la Autonomía de la Rioja (☎941 29 45 00). Follow Av. de La Paz away from the Old City; take a right onto Av. de la Autonomía.

Internet Access: Centro MAIL, Av. Dr. Mújica, 6 (☎941 20 78 33). English-speaking. video game store with a dozen computers in the back. 125ptas/€0.75 for 15min. Open M-Sa 10am-2pm and 5-9pm, Su noon-2pm and 5-9pm.

Post Office: Pl. San Agustín (☎941 22 00 66), between C. San Augustín and C. Portales. Open M-F 8:30am-8:30pm, Sa 9:30am-2pm. **Postal Code:** 26070.

ACCOMMODATIONS AND CAMPING

The *casco antiguo* brims with budget *pensiones* and hostels. Try C. San Juan, the second left past Parque Espolón from the stations, and C. San Agustín and C. Laurel. Reservations are crucial for the *fiesta* week around September 21.

Residencia Universitaria (HI), C. Caballero de la Rosa, 38 (☎941 29 11 45 or 26 14 22). From the train and bus stations, go right off C. General Vara onto Mura de Cervantes, which becomes Av. Paz. After 7 long blocks, make a left on C. Caballero de la Rosa and go down 3½ blocks.Public phone, laundry (100ptas/€0.60, sign up at the desk), and 2 common rooms with TV. University dorms during the school year, also used by athletic teams in summer. Doubles with bunks and nice private bath; rooms are usually not shared. No curfew. Breakfast 200ptas/€1.20. HI card not required. Bunks 1000ptas/€6, with sheets 1350ptas/€8.11. Open July-Sept 20. Closed Sept 21-30, keep just two rooms open Oct.-June.

Fonda Bilbaína, C. Capitán Eduardo Gallarza, 10, 2nd fl. (☎941 25 42 26). Take C. Sagasta into the *casco antiguo,* turn left on C. Hermanos Moray and then right on C. Capitán Eduardo. Bright rooms with high ceilings, shiny floors, good beds, and sinks. Rooms 3000ptas/€18, with shower 3500ptas/€21, with bath 4000ptas/€24.

Hostal Sebastián, C. San Juan, 21 (☎941 24 28 00). From C. de Sagasta, off Parque Espolón, turn right onto C. Hermanos Moroy, then continue onto C. San Juan. Good beds and small sinks. Single 3000ptas/€18, doubles 4000[illegible]

Camping La Playa, Av. Playa, 6 (☎941 25 22 53), off the main highway, across the river from the casco antiguo. Free pool next door, open June 15-Sept. 15. Laundromat. 600ptas/€3.61 per person, per tent, per car. Electricity 475ptas/€2.85. Open *Semana Santa* and June-Sept. Bungalows (can fit up to five) and rooms with private baths available year-round. Sept-June singles 3500ptas/€21; doubles 5500ptas/€33; triples 7000ptas/€42. July-Aug. and *Semana Santa* singles 5000ptas/€30; doubles 7000ptas/€42; triples 8000ptas/€48. MC/V.

FOOD

Logroñeses take their grapes seriously: wine is the beverage of choice with everything. C. Laurel and C. San Juan brim with bars and cafés. The market, **Mercado de San Blas,** is in a concrete building on C. Capitán Eduardo Gallarza. Take a right off C. Mura de la Francisco de la Mata, along the park (open M-Sa 7:30am-1:30pm and 4-7:30pm). For **groceries,** head to **Champión,** Av. La Rioja, a left off C. Miguel Villanueva past the tourist office. (☎941 22 99 00. Open M-Sa 9:15am-9:15pm.)

LA RIOJA AND NAVARRA

Bar Soriano, Travesía de Laurel, 2 (☎941 22 88 07), where C. Laurel turns. No indoor seating. The specialty is *champiñones con gambas* (mushrooms with shrimp; 100ptas/€0.60), washed down with a shot of vino (75ptas/€0.45). Open daily 11am-3am.

La Taberna de Portales, C. Portales, 39 (☎941 25 40 55), across from the cathedral. Stuffs just about anything between 2 slices of hot bread, from bacon and cheese to spicy grilled beef (400-450ptas/€2.40-2.80). Open Su-F 9am-midnight, Sa 9am-4am.

SIGHTS AND ENTERTAINMENT

Housed in a Baroque palace, the **Museo de la Rioja** has a collection spanning the last 8 centuries of art. The collection originates from the 1835 state seizure of regional monasteries' and convents' artwork and wealth. (Pl. San Agustín, 23, along C. Portales and next to the post office. ☎941 29 12 59. Open Tu-Sa 10am-2pm and 4-9pm, Su 11:30am-2pm. Free.) The ornate towers of the **Catedral de Santa María de la Redonda** dominate the Pl. Mercado in the *casco antiguo*. (From C. General Vara turn left on C. Portales; the cathedral is 2 blocks away on the right. Open M-Sa 7:45am-1:15pm and 6:30-10pm, Su 8:15am-1:15pm and 6:30-9pm. Free.) The grassy knolls along the **Río Ebro** make for a nice walk; a pedestrian path runs by the bridges **Puente de Hierro** and **Puente de Piedra.**

Logroño **nightlife** begins in the *casco antiguo* along C. Laural and after midnight moves to C. Mayor along Pl. Mercado, C. Sagasta, and C. Carnicerías. The **Fiestas de San Bernabé** (June 11) bring revelry and fireworks to Logroño. The biggest party in town takes place the week of Sept. 21 for the **Fiesta de San Mateo.** That same week, locals celebrate the grape harvest with the **Fiestas de la Vendimia,** in which they make a ceremonial offering of crushed grapes to the Virgin of Valvanera. In the Parque de Espolón participants crush the grapes with their own bare feet.

DAYTRIPS FROM LOGROÑO

HARO

RENFE ***trains*** *(☎941 31 15 97) connect Logroño to Haro (35min., 3 per day, 1300ptas/€8).* ***Buses*** *from Logroño (1hr.; 3-6 per day M-F 7:30am-8pm, Sa-Su 10:15am; 365ptas/€2.20) arrive at the Haro station (☎941 31 15 43).*

The main attractions in Haro (pop. 10,000) are wine, wine, and more wine. With seventeen *bodegas*, the small town serves as the heart of La Rioja's wine industry. Most *bodegas* offer free tours of their facilities in English and Spanish between 9am and 2pm, although reservations are almost always required. **Bodegas Muga,** across the river and under the train tracks, can be visited during the week without calling ahead. (☎941 31 04 98. Tours M-F June 4-July, 11am, and 12:30pm; Aug. 20-June 3 11am and 4pm. 500ptas/€3.) **Bodegas Bilbaínas,** located across the river but before the train tracks, can be visited unscheduled on the weekends. (☎941 31 01 47. Tours Sa & Su 10am and 12pm. Free.) If you're interested in buying some of Haro's wine, try the **wine shops** on C. Santo Tomás. Most charge 200-500ptas/€1.20-3 per bottle, but locals insist that any bottle less than 450ptas/€2.70 should not be drunk. In the Estación Etnológica, the **Museo del Vino** has sleek exhibits in Spanish on everything you could ever want to know about wine. (☎941 31 05 47. Open M-Sa 10am-2pm and 4-8pm, Su 10am-2pm. 300ptas. W free.) Join the locals and *ir de vinos* ("go for wines") in the evening in **La Herradura,** the area around C. Santo Tomás, off Pl. Paz. Ask for *vino* and you'll get the vintage of the year (50-75ptas); for higher quality, order *crianza*, wine that is more than three years old (150ptas). Haro breaks out in festivities on June 24-29, culminating in the **Batalla del Vino** (June 29), when participants spray wine at innocent bystanders.

To reach **Pl. Paz** from the train station, take the road downhill, turn right and then left across the river, and follow C. Navarra uphill to the plaza (15min.). From the bus stop, follow signs to *centro ciudad* along C. Ventilla, continuing 2 blocks past the Consum supermarket. Head diagonally left across Pl. Cruz onto C. Arraball,

THAT'S A WHOLE LOT OF EGGS A visit to one of the many *bodegas* in Haro will make any visitor appreciate the art of wine-making. After the grape juice has been gathered and put into 18,000-liter barrels, workers must ensure that all the grape leftovers are removed from the juice. Every morning, one man breaks between 1000 and 2000 eggs, separating the whites from the yolks. These egg yolks are then poured into the barrel (about 540 eggs per barrel), creating a thick film on the top. This film slowly begins to sink, and after 35 days it has removed any grape debris. The yolks are then donated to neighborhood bakeries to be used in cakes.

which leads straight into Pl. Paz. The **tourist office,** Pl. Monseñor Florentino Rodríguez, has a bilingual staff. Take C. Vega from the corner of Pl. Paz; the office is in the plaza to the left around the bend. (☎941 30 33 66. Open July-Sept M-Sa 10am-2pm and 4-7pm, Su 10am-2pm; Oct.-June Su-F 10am-2pm, Sa 10am-2pm and 4-7pm.) **Banco Central Hispano,** C. Vega, 20, offers **currency exchange** with no commission and a **24hr. ATM.** (☎941 31 11 84. Open Apr.-Sept. M-F 8:30am-2pm; Oct.-Mar. M-F 8:30am-2pm and Sa 8:30am-1pm.)

SANTO DOMINGO DE LA CALZADA

Buses connect Santo Domingo to Haro (20-30min., M-F 1-4 per day 8am-7:30pm, Sa 9:15am-7:30pm, Su 4:30pm, 180ptas/€1.10) and Logroño (1hr.; 5-11 per day, M-F 8am-8:45pm, Sa 8:45am-8:45pm, Su 3pm-8:45pm; 380ptas/€2.30).

An important stop along the Camino de Santiago, Santo Domingo de la Calzada (pop. 5500) was founded with the sole purpose of aiding pilgrims. In the 11th century Saint Dominic retired to the woods southwest of Logroño in search of solitude. After witnessing the trials of pilgrims attempting to cross the river, he decided to do something to help. He built a bridge for them, created a road (*calzada*, or causeway) through the woods, and converted his hermitage into a hospice. Soon, Santo Domingo became an important stop along the Camino.

King Alfonso VI noticed the work of the hermit and donated resources for the construction of the grand **Catedral de Santo Domingo,** even setting the first stone himself. When the lavish *retablo* (altarpiece) was removed for restoration in 1994, fabulous Romanesque pillars were discovered behind it. Today the retablo sits to one side so that both the new and the old altars can be seen within the church. (☎941 34 00 33. Open M-Sa 10am-6:30pm. 300ptas/€1.80, over 65 and pilgrims 200ptas/€1.20, under 16 100ptas/€0.60.) Not far from the cathedral, but over 100 steps up, awaits an outstanding view of the city from the **Tower of the Cathedral.** The present tower, finished in 1766, is actually the third to stand in its place: the first was destroyed by lightning, the second was considered unsafe. The present one (73m high) is supported by a base of limestone and cattle horns. (Recently, the tower has been closed for [illegible]

To reach the cathedral from the bus stop at Pl. Beato Hermosilla, cross Av. Juan Carlos I and follow C. Alcalde Rodolfo Varona. Take the next left for 1 block, then turn right on C. Hilario Pérez, which ends at Pl. Santo, bordered by the cathedral and pilgrim hospice-turned-parador. The town's **tourist office** sits in Casa de Trastámara, C. Mayor, 70 off Pl. Santo. (☎941 34 12 30; fax 34 12 31. Open daily 10am-2pm and 4-7pm.) **Restaurants** cluster near the cathedral on C. Mayor and adjoining plazas, luring hungry pilgrims with generous *menús*. **Mesón Los Arcos,** C.Mayor, 68. specializes in *pimientos rellenos* (meat-stuffed peppers in tomato sauce) for 800ptas/€4.81. (☎941 34 28 90. Open daily 1-4pm and 8:30-11pm. MC/V.)

PAMPLONA (IRUÑA) ☎948

Long, long ago, Pamplona's fiesta in honor of its patron saint San Fermín was just another religious holiday. These days, from July 6-14, *San Fermines* is Europe's premier festival. Ever since Ernest Hemingway brought the city international attention with *The Sun Also Rises*, hordes of visitors from around the world have come to witness and experience the legendary running of the bulls. At the bullring, a statue of Hemingway welcomes fans to the eight-day extravaganza of dancing, dashing, and of course, drinking—no sleeping allowed.

Although the *San Fermines* may be the city's most irresistible attraction, Pamplona (pop. 180,000) is a pleasant place to visit the other 356 days of the year as well. Lush parks, a Gothic cathedral, a massive citadel, and the winding streets of the *casco antiguo* entertain those who show up in the off season. Despite being the capital of Navarra, Pamplona's roots are truly Basque. They had settled the area before the Roman "founders," who named the city after Pompey the Great.

TRANSPORTATION

Flights: Aeropuerto de Noaín (☎948 16 87 00), 6km from the center. Accessible only by taxi (about 1200ptas/€7.21). **Iberia** (☎902 40 05 00) to: Barcelona (2-4 per day); Madrid (4-6 per day).

Trains: Estación RENFE, Av. San Jorge (☎902 24 02 02). Take bus #9 from Po. Sarasate (20min., 110ptas/€0.66). Info open daily 6am-10pm. Town office, C. Estella, 8 (☎948 22 72 82; open M-F 9am-1:30pm and 4:30-7:30pm, Sa 9:30am-1pm), is located near the bus station. Pamplona doesn't have the most reliable rail connections. To: **Barcelona** (6-8hr.; 12:55am, 12:20, 5:10pm; 4400ptas/€27); **Madrid** (5hr., 7:05am and 6:10pm, 4400ptas/€27); **Olite** (40min.; M-Sa 4 per day 7:25am-8:05pm, Su 1:25pm and 8:05pm; 390ptas/€2.30); **Tudela** (1½hr., Su-F 6:50pm, 980ptas/€6); **Vitoria-Gasteiz** (1¼hr.; M-Sa 8:40am, 4:39, 7:35pm, Su 4:39 and 7:35pm; 665ptas/€4); **Zaragoza** (2hr., 6:50pm, 2200ptas/€13).

Buses: Estación de Autobuses, at the corner of C. Conde Oliveto and C. Yanguas y Miranda. **La Tafallesa** (☎948 22 28 86) to: **Olite** (50min.; M-F 7 per day 8:15am-8:30pm, Sa 6 per day 9:30am-8:30pm; 375ptas/€2.25); **Roncal** (2hr., M-F 5pm, 1080ptas/€6.50). **La Roncalesa** (☎948 22 20 79) runs buses to: **Jaca** (1¾hr.; M-Sa 8:30am, F and Su 3:30pm; 900ptas/€5.41); **San Sebastián** (1hr.; M-Sa 9 per day 7am-9pm, Su 7 per day 8:15am-9pm; 845ptas/€5.10). **Conda** (☎948 22 10 26) to: **Tudela** (1½hr., 5-8 per day 7:15am-8:45pm, 875-965ptas/€5.26-5.80); **Madrid** (5hr., 4-7 per day 7am-6:30pm, 3430ptas/€21); **Zaragoza** (2-3hr., 6-8 per day 7:15am-8:30pm, 1600-1760ptas/€9.62-10.60). **La Burundesa (ALSA)** (☎948 22 17 66) to: **Bilbao** (2hr.; M-Sa 5-7 per day 7am-7pm, Su 10:30am, 4pm, and 7pm; 1685ptas/€10.13); **Vitoria-Gasteiz** (1½hr.; M-Sa 8-11 per day 7am-8:30pm, Su 5 per day 9am-7pm; 915ptas/€5.50). **Bilman** (☎948 22 09 97) to: **Barcelona** (5½hr.; 8:30am, 4:30pm, and 1am; 2855ptas/€18). **La Estellesa** (☎948 22 22 23) to: **Logroño** (1hr., 4-5 per day 7:30am-7pm, 990ptas/€5.95).

Public Transportation: (☎948 42 32 42). Bus #9 runs from Po. Sarasate to the train station (20min., every 15min. 6:30am-10:15pm, 110ptas/€0.75). During *San Fermines* buses run 24hr. (150ptas/€0.90).

Taxis: (☎948 23 23 23 or 23 23 00), cluster at Pl. Castillo and Taconera.

Car Rental: Europcar, Hotel Blanca Navarra, Av. Pío XII, 43 (☎948 17 60 02). Take bus #15, 41 or 42 from Po. Sarasate and get off after the traffic circle on the way out of town. 21+. Open M-F 9am-1pm and 4-7:30pm, Sa 9am-1pm.

ORIENTATION AND PRACTICAL INFORMATION

The **casco antiguo,** in the northeast quarter of the city, houses almost everything of interest in Pamplona. **Pl. del Castillo** is Pamplona's center. To reach it from the **bus station,** turn left onto Av. Conde Oliveto; at the traffic circle on Pl. Príncipe de Viana, take the second left onto Av. San Ignacio, follow it to the end of the pedestrian thoroughfare Po. Sarasate, and bear right. From the **train station,** take bus #9 (110ptas/€0.75) to the last stop; cut across Po. Sarasate, and walk diagonally left to Pl. Castillo. North of Pl. Castillo, the Baroque **Casa Consistorial (Ayuntamiento)** is a marker in the swirl of medieval streets.

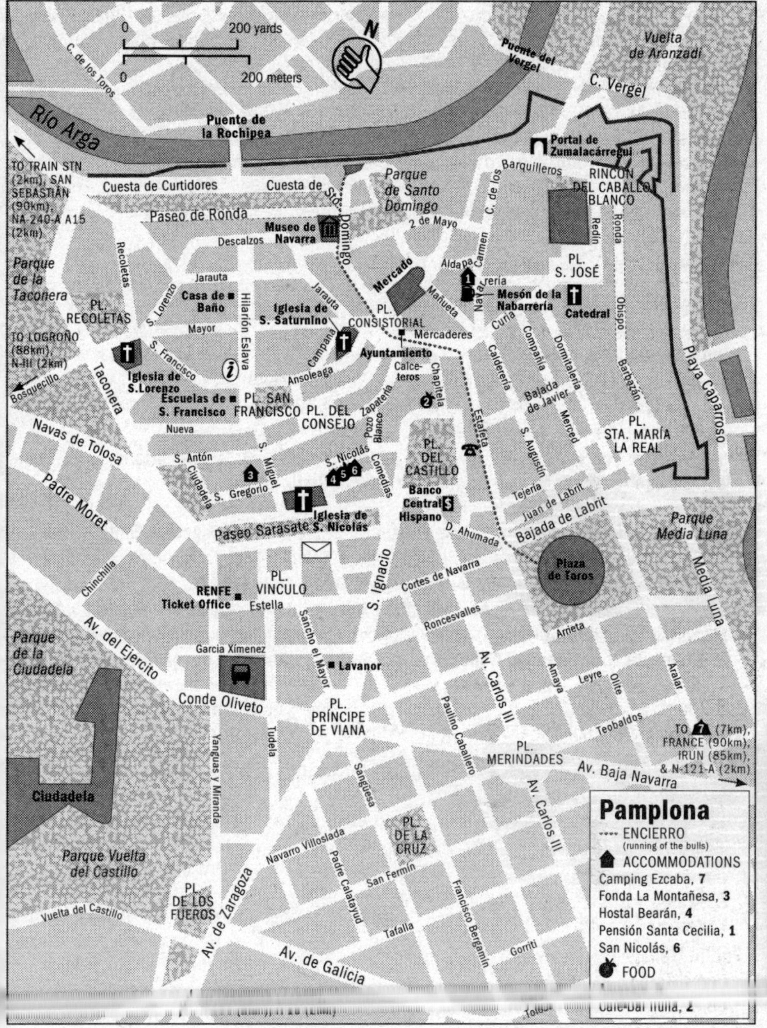

Tourist Office: C. Hilarión Eslava, 1 (☎948 20 65 40; fax 20 70 34; www.pamplona.net). From Pl. Castillo, take C. San Nicolás, turn right on C. San Miguel, and walk straight through Pl. San Francisco. Minute-by-minute guides to the festivities. Open during *San Fermines* daily 9am-8pm; July-Aug. M-Sa 10am-2pm and 4-7pm, Su 10am-2pm; Sept.-June M-F 10am-2pm and 4-7pm, Sa 10am-2pm.

Currency Exchange: Banco Central Hispano, Pl. Castillo, 21 (☎948 20 86 00), has an **ATM.** Open May-Sept. M-F 8:30am-2:30pm; Oct.-Apr. M-F 8:30am-2:30pm, Sa 8:30am-1pm; *San Fermines* 9am-1pm.

Luggage Storage: At the **bus station.** Bags 300ptas/€1.80 per day, large packs 500ptas/€3 per day. Open M-Sa 6:15am-9:30pm, Su 6:30am-1:30pm and 2-9:30pm. Closes for *San Fermines*, when the **Escuelas de San Francisco,** the big stone building at one end of Pl. San Francisco opens instead. Lines are long, and you must have a passport or ID. 300ptas/€1.80 each time you check on your luggage. Open 24hr.

Laundromats: Casa de Bao, C. Hilarión Eslava, 2 (☎948 22 17 38), at the corner of C. Jarauta. No full service during *San Fermines.* 4½ kilo wash 590ptas/€3.55, dry 565ptas/€3.40. Open Tu-Sa 8:30am-8pm, Su 8:30am-12pm.

Public Toilets and Baths: Squat **toilet booths** are set up for *San Fermines,* but the permanent bathrooms in the **Jardines de Taconera** (beyond Hotel Tres Reyes) are more comfortable. Freshen up at **Casa de Baño,** C. Hilarión Eslava, 2 (☎948 22 17 38), on the corner of C. Jarauta. Showers 125ptas, towel 45ptas, soap 45ptas. Open Tu-Sa 8:30am-8pm, Su 8am-12pm. Open daily during *San Fermines* 8am-9pm.

Emergency: ☎112. **Municipal Police:** C. Monasterio de Irache, 2 ☎092.

Late-Night Pharmacy: Changes daily. All pharmacies post the phone number and address of that evening's late-night location. Call ☎948 22 21 11 for location.

Medical Services: Hospital de Navarra (☎948 42 21 00), C. Irunlarrea. The **Red Cross** also sets up stands at the bus station and the *corrida* during *San Fermines.*

Internet Access: Kuria.Net, C. Curia, 15 (☎948 22 30 77). Convenient *casco antiguo* location. From C. Chapitela, take a right onto C. Mercaderes, following it as it becomes C. Curia and heads toward the cathedral; it's on the left. 500ptas/€3 per hr. Open M-Sa 10am-10pm, Su 4:30-9:30pm.

Post Office: Po. Sarasate, 9 (☎948 21 26 00). Open M-F 8:30am-8:30pm, Sa 9:30am-2pm; *San Fermines* M-Sa 8:30am-2pm. **Postal Code:** 31001.

While Pamplona is usually a very safe city, crime skyrockets during *San Fermines,* when assaults and muggings do occur. Apparently, some characters come with shadier intentions, more interested in tourist cash than *fiesta* excitement. Do not roam alone at night, and be extremely cautious in the parks and dark streets of the *casco antiguo.* Revelers in parks and along riverbanks can say good-bye to their wallets and money belts if they are not careful.

ACCOMMODATIONS AND CAMPING

If you are planning on finding a hotel room during *San Fermines*, good luck. If there was a lucky convergence of stars on the day of your birth and you have truckloads of cash, you *may* find a room during the first few days of the festival. Die-hard partiers book their rooms a year in advance, but most hostels and pensions don't start taking reservations until January. Expect to pay rates up to four times those normally listed (anywhere from 6000-9000ptas/€36-54 per person in most budget hotels). Early in the week, people accost visitors at the train and bus stations, offering couches and floor space in their homes. Be wary—accommodations and prices vary tremendously, and you might find yourself blowing your money for a blink of sleep on an unclean floor in a bad part of town. Check the newspaper *Diario de Navarra* for *casas particulares* and inquire at the tourist office for listings. Many who can't find rooms sleep outside on the lawns of the Ciudadela, Pl. Fueros, Pl. and Castillo, or along the banks of the river. Those who you choose this risky option should store their luggage. Parking is free on most streets during *San Fermines*, and many with cars just snooze in the back seat.

During the rest of the year, finding a room in Pamplona is no problem. Budget accommodations line C. San Nicolás and C. San Gregorio off Pl. Castillo. Most hostels follow separate price schedules for *temporada alta (San Fermines)*, *temporada media* (summer), and *temporada baja* (the rest of the year).

Pensión Santa Cecilia, C. Navarrería, 17 (☎948 22 22 30). From C. Chapitela (off Pl. Castillo), take the 1st right onto C. Mercaderes, then left onto C. Navarrería (to the left of Valles Joyería & Relojería). 18th-century mansion. Comfortable rooms with winter heating. July-Aug. singles 3000ptas/€18; doubles 5000ptas/€30; triples 6000ptas/€36. *San Fermines* 7000ptas/€42 per person. Rest of the year singles 2500ptas/€15; doubles 4000ptas/€24; triples 5000ptas/€30. MC/V.

San Nicolás, C. San Nicolás, 13 (☎948 22 13 19), next to the restaurant of the same name. Small but pleasant rooms with shared baths and decent beds. *San Fermines* dorms 5000ptas/€30. Rest of the year 2000-2500ptas/€12-18. AmEx/MC/V.

Fonda La Aragonesa, C. San Nicolás, 22 (☎948 22 34 28). The reception desk is across in Hostal Bearán. *San Fermines* doubles 12,000ptas/€75. Rest of the year singles 3745ptas/€22.25; doubles 4815ptas/€29. AmEx/MC/V.

Hostal Bearán, C. San Nicolás, 25 (☎948 22 34 28). Squeaky-clean rooms with phone, TV, bath, safebox, and a whopping pricetag. *San Fermines* doubles 15,000ptas/€90. July-Sept. doubles 6500ptas/€39. Oct.-June doubles 5500ptas/€33. AmEx/MC/V.

Camping Ezcaba (☎948 33 03 15), in Eusa, 7km down the road to Irún. City bus line 4-1 runs to the campground from Pl. de las Merindades (4 per day; 110ptas/€0.65). Hop off at the final gas station stop. Fills fast during *San Fermines.* No reservations. *San Fermines* 1370ptas/€8.25 per person, per tent, per car. Rest of the year 575ptas/€3.50 per person, 565/€3.40 per tent, per car. Amex/MC/V.

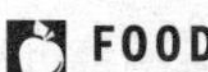

FOOD

The tiny neighborhood cafés advertise hearty *menús:* try the side streets near Pensión Santa Cecilia, C. Jarauta and C. Descalzos, near Po. Ronda, and the area above Pl. San Francisco. C. Navarrería and Po. Sarasate are lined with numerous *bocadillo* bars. The *barracas políticas* (bars organized by political interest groups that don't expect any interest in their platforms), next to the amusement park in the Ciudadela, offer cheap drinks and equally cheap ideology. Many cafés and restaurants close for one to two weeks after *San Fermines* to recover. The **market,** C. Mercado, is to the right of Casa Consistorial's façade and down the stairs (open M-Sa 8am-2:30pm). **Vendi Supermarket** is at the corner of C. Hilarión Eslava and C. Mayor. (Open M-F 9am-2pm and 5:30-7:30pm, Sa 9am-2pm; *San Fermines* M-Sa 9am-2pm. MC/V.)

Restaurante Sarasate, C. San Nicolás, 19 (☎948 22 57 27), above the seafood store. Delicious organic vegetarian dishes. Lunchtime *menú* 1350ptas/€8. Open M-Th 1:15-4pm and 8:15-11pm, F-Sa 1:15-4pm and 9-11pm.

Café-Bar Iruña, Pl. Castillo. Hemingway's favorite haunt and the backdrop for much of *The Sun Also Rises,* Café-Bar Iruña draws a crowd for its delicious *menú* (1500ptas/€9). Open M-Th 8am-11pm, F 8am-2am, Sa 9am-2am, Su 9am-11pm. MC/V.

Hong Kong, C. San Gregorio, 38 (☎948 22 66 35). Look for the red balcony. Come with friends and split a 2-, 3-, 4-, or 5-person *menú* (2800-7000ptas/€16.80-42) or try the 3-course *menú* (1000ptas/€6). Open daily noon-4pm and 8pm-midnight. MC/V.

SIGHTS

CATHEDRAL AND CHURCHES. Pamplona has rich architectural legacy. The recently restored 14th-century **Gothic cathedral** houses an ornate alabaster mausoleum where Carlos III and his wife Queen Leonor are entombed. Off the cloister is a five-chimneyed kitchen, one of four of its kind in all of Europe. *(At the end of C. Navarrería. ☎948 21 08 27. Open M-F 10am-1:30pm and 4-7pm, Sa 10am-1:30pm. Guided tours 550ptas/€3.30.)* Church lovers will also enjoy the 13th-century **Iglesia de San Saturnino,** near the Ayuntamiento, and **Iglesia de San Nicolás,** in Pl. San Nicolás. *(Both open daily 9am-12:30pm and 6-8:30pm. Free.)* For a peek at San Fermín himself, head to **Iglesia de San Lorenzo.** *(C. Mayor, 74. Open daily 8am-12:30pm and 6:30-8pm.)*

CIUDADELA. The pentagonal Ciudadela was built by Felipe II in an effort to secure the city's safety. Today it is part of a grassy park that hosts free exhibits and concerts in the summer. Its impressive walls even scared off Napoleon, who refused to launch a frontal attack and staged a trick snowball fight instead; when Spanish sentries joined in, the French entered the city through its gates. To get to the intimidating **walls** from the old quarter, pick up C. Redín at the far end of the cathedral plaza.

A left turn follows the walls past the **Portal de Zumalacárregui** and along the Río Arga. Bear left through the gardens of **Parque de la Taconera**—where some random deer, swans, and peacocks hang out—until reaching the Ciudadela. *(Av. Ejército. ☎948 22 82 37. Open daily 7:30am-10pm; closed during San Fermines. Free.)*

MUSEO DE NAVARRA. The Museo de Navarra shelters beautifully preserved 4th- and 5th-century Roman mosaics, murals from all over the region, and a nice collection of 14th- to 20th-century paintings, including Goya's portrait of the Marqués de San Adrián. *(In the* casco antiguo*, up C. Santo Domingo from Casa Consistorial. ☎948 42 64 92. Open Tu-Sa 9:30am-2pm and 5-7pm, Su 11am-2pm; San Fermines Tu-Su 11am-2pm. 300ptas/€1.80, students 150ptas/€0.90; Sa afternoons and Su mornings free.)*

ENTERTAINMENT

Plaza de Castillo is the social heart of Pamplona. The young and the restless whoop it up at bars in the *casco antiguo*. C. San Nicolás and C. San Gregorio are night-time favorites, as are C. Calderería, C. San Agustín, and C. Jaruata. A great spot to chat with friends over drinks, **Mesón de la Navarrería,** C. Navarrería draws crowds day and might. (☎948 21 31 63. Open Su-Th 10:30am-12pm and F-Sa 11am-2:30pm.) Claustrophobes escape the cramped streets of the *casco antiguo* to the bars of Barrio San Juan on Av. Bayona. **Alakarga,** Pl. Monasterio Azuelo draws a hip late-night crowd. (☎948 26 60 05. Beers 500ptas/€3; mixed drinks 800ptas/€4.80. Open Th-Sa 12am-7am; Su-W 10:30pm-6am; ring the bell to enter.)

LOS SAN FERMINES (JULY 6-14)

Visitors from the world over crowd Pamplona for the *Fiestas de San Fermín*—known to most as "The Running of the Bulls"—in search of Europe's greatest party. Pamplona delivers, with an eight-day frenzy of parades, bullfights, parties, dancing, fireworks, concerts, and wine. Pamplonese, uniformly clad in white with red sashes and bandanas, literally throw themselves into the merry-making, displaying obscene levels of physical stamina and alcohol tolerance.

Around 11am on July 6, the whole city crowds around the Ayuntamiento. The mass sings and chants *"San Fermín!"* with *pañuelos* flying until the mayor appears at noon. He fires the first rocket *(chupinazo)*, from the Ayuntamiento's balcony, and a howl explodes from the sea of expectant *sanferministas* in the plaza below. Champagne rains (be wary of flying corks) along with eggs, ketchup, wine, and flour. Within minutes the streets of the *casco antiguo* flood with improvised singing and dancing troupes. The *peñas*, societies more concerned with beer than bullfighting, lead the hysteria. At 5pm on the 6th and at 9 or 9:30am every other day, they are joined by the *Comparsa de Gigantes y Cabezudos*, a troupe of *gigantes* (giant wooden monarchs) and *zaldikos* (courtiers on horseback). *Kilikis* (swollen-headed buffoons) run around chasing little kids and hitting them with play clubs. These misfits, together with church and town officials, escort San Fermín on his triumphant procession through the *casco antiguo*. The saint's 15th-century statue is brought from the Iglesia de San Lorenzo at 10am on July 7, the actual day of *San Fermín*. (Note: virtually everything closes on the 7th; hours listed for the festival refer only to the 6th and the 8th through 14th.)

THE RUNNING OF THE BULLS

The running of the bulls, called the *encierro*, is the focal point of *San Fermines*. The ritual dates back to the 14th century, when it served the practical function of getting the bulls from their corrals to the bullring. These days, the first *encierro* of the festival takes place at 8am on July 7 and is repeated every day for the following seven days. Hundreds of bleary-eyed, hung-over, hyper-adrenalized runners flee from large bulls as bystanders cheer from barricades, windows, and balconies

A rocket marks the release of the bulls onto the 825m course. One to three animals are released from their pens as runners scurry away. If you want to participate in the bullring excitement, you can line up by the Pl. Toros well before 7:30am

RUNNING SCARED So, you're going to run with the bulls. No one wants to see you end up on evening news programs around the world, so here are a few words of *San Fermines* wisdom:

- Research the *encierro* before you run. The tourist office dispenses a pamphlet that outlines the exact route of the three-minute run and offers tips for inexperienced runners. You should also watch it once on TV to get a glimpse of what you're in for, and once in person to experience the crush and hysteria first-hand. Check out the tourist office for exhibitions on the event's tradition and history.
- Do not stay up all night carousing. Not surprisingly, hung-over foreigners have the highest rate of injury. Experienced runners get a good night's sleep before and arrive at the course no later than 7am. Many locals arrive at 6am. The course closes at 7:30am.
- Wear proper clothing (nothing loose or baggy) and appropriate shoes. Do not carry anything with you (especially a backpack or video camera).
- Give up on getting near the bulls and concentrate on getting to the bullring in one piece. Although some whack the bull with rolled newspapers, runners should never distract or touch the animals; anyone who does is likely to anger the bull and locals alike.
- Try not to cower in a doorway; people have been trapped and killed this way.
- Be particularly wary of isolated bulls—they seek company in the crowds.
- If you fall, **stay down.** Curl up into a fetal position, lock your hands behind your head, and **do not get up** until the clatter of hooves has passed.

and run in *before* the bulls are even in sight (though such a "cowardly" act will bring booing from the locals). Three to six steers accompany the six to nine bulls—watch out, they have horns, too. Both the bulls and the mob are dangerous. Runners, all convinced the bull is right behind them, flee for dear life and act without concern for those around them. Experienced runners, many of whom view the event as an athletic art form, try to get as close to the bull as possible. The course has three sharp turns which the bulls have difficulty cornering; when their legs slide out from under them, they falter, creating a pile of bull. Runners should be especially careful at the Mercaderes-Estafeta corner. After the bulls have been safely rounded into their pens inside the Pl. Toros, younger, less dangerous bulls with covered horns are then released to "play" with a mass of 350 people.

After cascading through a perilously narrow opening (where a large proportion of the injuries occur), the run pours into the bullring, amid shouts and cries from appreciative spectators. Hemingway had the right idea: don't run—watch the *encierro* from the bullring instead. Music, waves, chanting, and dancing pump up the spectators until the headline entertainment arrives. Bullring spectators should arrive around 6:45am. Tickets for the *Grada* section of the ring are available at 7am (M-F 600ptas/€3.61, Sa-Su 700ptas/€4.21). You can watch for free, but the free section is overcrowded, and it can be hard to see and breathe.

To watch one of the actual bullfights, you must wait in the line that forms at the bullring around 8pm every evening; earlier is always better (Tickets range from 2500ptas-13,500ptas/€15-69). As one bullfight ends, tickets go on sale for the next day. Though the *sol* section can get darn hot, it is cheaper and generally more fun.

THE REST OF THE DAY

Once the running is over, the insanity spills into the streets, gathering steam until nightfall when it explodes with singing in the bars, dancing in the alleyways, spontaneous parades, and a no-holds-barred party in Pl. Castillo, which quickly becomes Europe's biggest open-air dance floor. The right attire for this dance-a-thon includes sturdy shoes (there's glass everywhere), a white t-shirt (that will soon be soaked with wine), a red *pañuelo* (bandana), and a cheap bottle of champagne (to spray, of course). English speakers often congregate where C. Estafeta hits Pl. Toros, an outdoor consortium of local *discotecas*. A word to the wise: avoid the fountain-jumping (you'll know it when you see it). It is *not* a traditional part of the festivities—it was inaugurated by Americans, Aussies, and

Kiwis—and several people have died in recent years. The truly inspired partying takes place the first few days of *San Fermines.* After that, the crowds thin, and the atmosphere goes from dangerously crazed to mildly insane. The party begins (or ends) each day at 6am, when bands march down the streets, waking everyone for the running. In between, the city eases the transition with concerts, outdoor dances, and a host of other performances. The end of the festivities culminates at midnight of July 14 with the singing of *Pobre de mí* ("Poor Me"): *"Pobre de mí, pobre de mí, que se han acabado las Fiestas de San Fermín."*

Nearby towns sponsor *encierros* as well: **Tudela** holds its festival the week July 24, **Tafalla** during the week of Aug. 15, and **Sangüesa** during the week of Sept. 11. Many Pamplonese opt to take part in a festival less touristed than their own.

DAYTRIPS FROM PAMPLONA

Though the following daytrips are actually closer to small towns in the Pyrenees, especially Sangüesa, their only public transportation runs from Pamplona.

LUMBIER GORGES

Río Irati buses (☎948 30 35 70) run to Lumbier from Pamplona (1hr.; M-F 1, 6, 7pm, Sa 1:30pm and 6pm; returning to Pamplona M-F 8am and 2:30pm, Sa 2:30pm; 405-455ptas/€2.40-3.10). From Lumbier to Iso you have to walk, drive, or take a taxi.

Two fantastic gorges cut into the mountains near Pamplona. Outside the little town of Lumbier, the **Foz de Lumbier** (Lumbier Gorge) drops 50m down to the Río Irati, and a path alongside leads through old railway tunnels. 12km down the road, just before the town of Iso, the even more impressive **Foz de Arbayún,** cuts a chasm to the river below. A lookout above affords glimpses of swooping griffin vultures, while a small footpath below follows the Río Salazar toward its source.

CASTILLO DE JAVIER

La Tafallesa (☎948 22 28 86) runs a bus from Pamplona to Javier (1hr.; M-F 5pm, Sa 1pm; 525ptas/€3.20). Buses return M-S at 8am. You can also take a taxi from Sangüesa for about 1000ptas round-trip plus the wait.

Near the entrance to the small village of Javier lies the majestic **Castillo de Javier,** the birthplace of San Francisco Xavier (Javier). On the border between Navarra and Aragón, this picture-perfect castle has changed hands numerous times over the last millennium, landing finally in the Jesuits' possession. Its **Chapel of the Holy Christ** houses a 14th-century effigy that is said to have suffered a spontaneous blood-sweating fit at the moment of San Francisco Xavier's death. (Open daily 9am-1pm and 4-7pm; last entrances at 12:40 and 6:40pm. Free, but donations requested. Occasional tours in Spanish.)

MONASTERIO DE LEYRE

The La Tafallesa (☎948 22 28 86) bus that runs from Pamplona to Javier (1hr.; M-F 5pm, Sa 1:30pm; 500ptas/€3) continues to nearby Yesa for 10ptas/€0.06 more. Buses return M-Sa 8am. From Yesa, it's a 5km uphill walk to the monastery.

Windswept and austere, the Monasterio de Leyre silently surveys the foothills of the Pyrenees and a large man-made lake, Lago de Yesa. In the 12th century, Navarrese kings took up residence in the **monasterio medieval.** Because monks still live at Leyre, you can enter neither this part nor the 20th-century **monasterio nuevo,** but the dank, subterranean **cripta** eagerly welcomes visitors. The architectural highlight of the monastic complex itself is the ghoulish 12th-century **Portal de la Iglesia,** but perhaps more intriguing is the **Fuente de San Virila,** a fountain in the precise place where, according to legend, the abbot of San Virila fell into a 300-year trance induced by the singing of a nightingale. (☎948 88 41 50. Open Mar.-Oct. M-F 10:15am-2pm and 3:30-7pm, Sa-Su 10:15am-2pm and 4-7pm; Nov.-Feb. M-Fr 10:15am-2pm and 3:30-6pm, Sa-Su 10:15am-2pm and 4-6pm. 275ptas/€1.65, children 50ptas/€0.30. Gregorian mass M-Sa 9am and Su at noon.)

Connected to the monastery, the **Hospedería de Leyre** offers rooms with cozy beds and private bathrooms (☎948 88 41 00; fax 88 41 37. Breakfast 800ptas/€4.85. July-Aug. and *Semana Santa* singles 4900ptas/€30; doubles 9500ptas/€57. Rest of the year singles 4500ptas/€27; doubles 8000ptas/€48, AmEx/MC/V).

OLITE ☎948

Former home of the Navarran kings, medieval Olite's **Palacio Real** was the 15th century home of Carlos III and his court. Though the town's 1937 restoration was far from subtle, the palace's towers and spiral staircases are great fun to explore, entertaining many a childhood fairy tale. (☎948 74 00 35. Open daily July-Aug. 10am-2pm and 4-8pm; Sept.-June 10am-2pm and 4-7pm. 400ptas/€2.40; seniors and children 250ptas/€1.50; under 3 free. Guided tours in Spanish every hr. on weekends.) Between the Palacio Real and the **Palacio Viejo**, at the base of Plaza de Carlos III, is the **Iglesia de Santa María,** noted for its 14th-century façade and belfry.

TRANSPORTATION AND PRACTICAL INFORMATION. RENFE trains (☎948 70 06 28) run to: **Pamplona** (40min., 2-3 per day, 600ptas/€3.60), Tudela, and other points on the Vitoria-Gasteiz-Zaragoza line. To get from the **station** to Pl. Carlos III, take C. Estación to Bar Orly, walk through the archway, and follow Rua San Francisco past **Pl. Teobaldos,** through another arch to **Pl. Carlos III.** Buses are cheaper and more convenient. **Conda** (☎948 22 10 26) and **La Tafallesa** (☎948 22 28 86) run buses to **Pamplona** (35min.; M-F 6:45am-6:45pm, Sa 7:55am-6:45pm, Su 8:45am-8pm; 400ptas/€2.40). Conda also goes to **Tudela** (5-7 per day, 7:15am-9:20pm, 500ptas/€3). La Tafallesa arrives at Bar Orly; to reach Pl. Carlos III, follow the directions from the train station. Conda arrives at the *Carretera;* to reach Pl. Carlos III, follow C. El Portillo for a block. To find the **tourist office,** take Rua Mayor off P. Carlos III. (☎/fax 948 74 17 03. Open Apr.-Sept. M-F 10am-2pm and 4-7pm, Sa-Su 10am-2pm; Oct.-Mar. daily 10am-4pm.) Local services include: **emergency** ☎112; **banks** in Pl. Carlos III; and the **post office,** across the plaza from the palace. (☎948 74 05 82. Open M-Sa 9-11:30am.) **Postal code:** 31390

ACCOMMODATIONS AND FOOD. Olite's courtly airs are preserved in menu and accommodation prices everywhere. The 4 rooms of **Fonda Gambarte,** Rua Seco 15, 2nd fl., off Pl. Carlos III, share clean common baths. The in-house restaurant also serves its 2-course *menú* for 1400ptas/€8.40. (☎948 74 01 39. Singles 2000ptas/€12; doubles 3500ptas/€21. Restaurant open July-Sept. M-F 1-3:30pm, 8:30-11:30pm. Oct.-June daily 1-3:30pm, F-Su 8:30-11:30pm. MC/V). The pricier rooms of **Carlos III El Noble,** Rúa de Medíos, 1, off Pl. Carlos III all have TVs, fans, and private bath. (☎948 74 06 44; fax 71 24 67. Singles 5000ptas/€30; doubles July-Aug. 8500ptas/€51, Sept.-June 7500ptas/€45.) The extraordinary medieval dining room offers a M-F *menú* for 1800ptas/€10.80 (Open daily 1-4pm and 9-11:30pm. IVA not included. MC/V.) [illegible] 71 10 14), is 2km outside of town on Ctra. N-115 heading towards Peralta. (450ptas/€2.7 per person and per car, 425-500ptas/€3 per tent. 5-person bungalows 8500ptas/€51. MC/V.) **Supermarkets** line C. Mayor, off Pl. Carlos III, and a W market springs up on C. Sta. Brígada near the sports center and swimming pools (9am-1:30pm).

TUDELA

A major Muslim center until King Sancho the Strong out-muscled the Moors in 1114, Tudela (pop. 26,000) also hosted an eminent Jewish population throughout the Middle Ages. Though not worth a grand detour, the city definitely makes a pleasant stop en route to Pamplona or Zaragoza. Featuring a Romanesque **cloister,** Gothic *retablos* (altarpieces), and a chilling Last Judgment tympanum over its west portal, the Gothic **cathedral** rises over Pl. Vieja and the ancient site of the city mosque in the *casco antiguo,* across from the tourist office. (☎948 40 21 61. Open Tu-Sa 9am-1pm and 4-7pm, Su 9am-1pm. Free. M-Sa mass at 9:30, 11am, and noon. Cloister and museum featuring the cathedral's art collection, 500ptas/€3. Open Tu-Sa 10am-1:30pm and 4-7pm, Su 10am-1:30pm.)

TRANSPORTATION. RENFE trains (☎948 82 06 46) run to **Madrid** (2-3 per day, 3800ptas/€23); **Pamplona** (1-2 per day, 850ptas/€5.11); **Vitoria-Gasteiz** (3:27pm, 1480/€9); **Zaragoza** (5-6 per day M-F 6:40am-9:27pm, Sa-Su first train 8:40; 525-605ptas/€3.20-3.65). Conda **Buses** run to **Madrid** (3-4 per day M-Sa 7:30am-7pm, Su 10:30am-7pm, 2665ptas/€16); **Olite** (1hr., 5 per day 8am-6pm, 500ptas/€3); **Pamplona** (1½hr., 6-9 per day 8am-9:30pm, 945ptas/€5.80); **San Sebastián** (3-4 per day, 8am-6pm, 1800ptas/€10.90); **Soria** (daily 10:30am, 4pm, 7pm; 850ptas/€5.25);**Tarazona** (1hr., M-Sa 5 per day 10:15am-7:30pm,; 230ptas/€1.50); **Zaragoza** (M-Sa 5 per day; 7:30am-8:40pm; 800ptas/€4.80).

ORIENTATION AND PRACTICAL INFORMATION. Old town and new meet in the **Pl. de los Fueros.** To get to Pl. Fueros from the combined bus and train station, cross the plaza up Cuesta de la Estación, make the second right onto Av. Zaragoza, continue straight for 5 blocks, then turn left onto C. Gaztambide-Carrera, which leads to the plaza. The **Casa del Reloj,** with its ornate clock tower, presides over the city's west end. North of the plaza is the *casco antiguo*, overlooked by the hilltop **Castillo de Sancho el Fuerte** and **Monumento al Corazón de Jesús,** at the edge of town. The **tourist office,** on Pl. Vieja, is next to the cathedral. Facing the clock tower in Pl. Fueros, head sharply right and cross Pl. San Jaime to the street in the far corner; follow it around the corner. (☎948 84 80 58. Open May-Sept. M-F 9am-3pm and 4-7pm, Sa-Su 10am-2pm; Oct.-Apr. M-F 9am-3pm, Sa-Su 10am-2pm.)

ACCOMMODATIONS. Hotel-quality accommodations can be found at **Hostal Remigio,** C. Gaztambide, 4, on the way from the train station to Pl. Fueros. (☎948 82 08 50. Singles 2000ptas/€12, with bath 3100ptas/€19; doubles 4000ptas/€24, with bath 5300ptas/€32. Higher rates in July, Aug., and *Semana Santa.* AmEx/MC/V.) **Bar/Casa de Huéspedes Estrella,** C. Carnicerías, 14, is off C. Yanguesa y Miranda from Pl. Fueros. Ask in Gilligan's bar about rooms. (☎948 41 04 42. Reception 9am-3pm and 6pm-midnight. Closed M, but you can ring the bell next door. Doubles with shared baths, 3200ptas/€20.) Backpackers head straight to **Albergue Municipal de Juventud (HI)** on C. Camino Caritat, 17. From the train station, take a left on C. Ribaforada, when you reach the park, take a left; the hostel is two buildings down on the left. (☎948 82 63 67; fax 84 81 16. Breakfast 250ptas/€1.50. Curfew midnight. Dorms 1500ptas/€9, over 25 2000ptas/€12.) The **Internet** has reached **Cyber Centro,** Pl. Sancho el Fuerto, 12. (First 30min. 300ptas/€1.80 per min., 100ptas/€0.60 per min thereafter. Open July-Sept. M-F 10:30am-1:30pm and 5-10pm, Sa 6pm-midnight; Oct.-June M-F 10:30am-1:30pm and 4:30-10pm, Sa 4:30-midnight, Su 5-10pm.)

NEAR TUDELA: BARDENAS REALES

The awesome desert of **Bardenas Reales,** whose hills and cliffs have been wrought by erosion, covers over 400 sq. km near the beginning of the Tudela-Pamplona road. To rent a car, try **Europcar** in Tudela, C. Plaza Estación, just across the plaza from the station (☎948 84 77 08; fax 84 76 71. Open M-F 9am-1pm and 4-7pm, Sa 9:30am-1pm.) To rent a bike, take the Tudela to Pamplona bus and ask to be let off in **Arguedas** (20min., 150ptas/€0.90). There, **Ciclos Marton,** C. Real, 31, has bikes for rent. (☎948 83 15 77. 2000ptas/€12 for first day, 1000ptas/€6 each additional day. Open M-F 9am-1:30pm and 3:30-8:30pm, Sa 9am-2:30pm, Su closed but call for a rental.) Cyclists should remain on the official roads, and call ahead about weather conditions (☎906 36 53 31), as the heat can sometimes be prohibitive.

ESTELLA ☎948

Hiding between the cities of Logroño and Pamplona, charming Estella (pop. 13,000) rests in a bend of the Río Ega. What it lacks in size and glamor, it makes up for in hospitality toward the faithful. With tell-tale walking sticks in hand, pilgrims traversing the Camino de Santiago have been descending on Estella since the town's founding in 1090. With an appealing plaza, mellow cafes, and a pastry shop on every corner, the town makes a perfect place to stay if you can't find Pamplona accommodations for *San Fermines.*

ORIENTATION AND PRACTICAL INFORMATION. Two streets intersect at the heart of town. **C. San Andrés/C. Baja Navarra** runs north-south from the bus station on Pl. Coronación to the **Pl. de los Fueros,** while **Po. de la Inmaculada Concepción** runs east-west from C. Dr. Huarte to **C. Mayor** and the **Puente del Azucarero,** which leads to the old town, where most sights and the tourist office await. To get to the bridge from the bus station, go right and follow the river road to the left.

La Estellesa buses (☎948 55 01 27) leave from the station on Pl. Coronación to: **Logroño** (50min.; 8-9 per day 8:30am-8:30pm; 495ptas/€3); **Pamplona** (1hr., 4-11 per day M-Sa 6:50am-8pm, 430-510ptas/€2.50-3); **San Sebastián** (1½-2hr., 6 per day 8:45am-7:45pm, 1210ptas/€7.20); and **Zaragoza** (2½hr., M-Sa 8:30am, 1640ptas/€10). Check the second page of the local newspaper, "Noticias," for daily schedules and destinations. The **tourist office,** C. San Nicolás, 1, is straight across the bridge through Pl. San Martín. (☎/fax 948 55 63 01. Open July-Aug. 10am-8pm; Nov.-*Semana Santa* 10am-5pm; low season 10am-2pm and 4-7pm.) The local **library,** Ruiz de Alda 34-36, provides free **internet** connection to patient patrons; drop by to sign up for a 30-min. slot. (☎948 55 64 19. Open Oct.-June M-F 9am-9pm, July-Sept. 8:30am-2:30pm.) Local services include: **emergency** ☎112; **police,** Po. Inmaculada, 1 (☎092), inside the Ayuntamiento; and the **post office,** Po. Inmaculada, 5. (☎948 55 17 92. M-F 8:30am-2:30pm, Sa 9:30am-1pm.) **Postal code:** 31200.

ACCOMMODATIONS. With its proximity to Pamplona, Estella is a good place to catch some shut-eye during San Fermines. Reservations are advisable during its own August encierro (running of the bulls). From the bus station, follow C. San Andrés to C. Mayor and turn left to **Pensión San Andrés,** C. Mayor, 1. Some rooms have TVs and refrigerators. Balconies overlooking the peaceful plaza below become exhilarating lookout points during the running of the bulls in August (☎948 55 41 58. July-Aug. and *Semana Santa* singles 1900ptas/€11.50, with bath 3500ptas/€21; doubles 3500ptas/€21, with bath 5000ptas/€30. Sept.-June singles 1800ptas/€10.85, with bath 3500ptas/€21; doubles 3200ptas/€20, with bath 4500ptas/€27. MC/V.) The spacious wood-floored rooms **Hostal Cristina,** C. Baja Navarro on the corner of Pl. de los Fueros, come complete with large windows, private bathrooms and TV. (☎948 55 04 50. July-Aug. and *Semana Santa* singles 4500ptas/€27; doubles 7000ptas/€42. Sept.-June 6000ptas/€36. IVA not included.) **Fonda Izarra,** C. Calderería, 20, off Pl. Fueros, down the street to the right of Florida Bar), offers simpler rooms with light blue walls, lace curtains and fluffy bedding. (☎948 55 06 78. Breakfast 250ptas/€1.50. June-Aug. doubles 4000ptas/€24; Oct.-May 3500ptas/€21. Usually closed Sept. MC/V. From the left of the tourist office, its a 20min. walk (1km) down-river and past the factory to **Camping Lizarra**, C. Ordoiz. Let the Pamplona bus driver know and he'll save for 10 15min. with a [illegible] ket, pool, 18-bed hostel, and small restaurant-bar, are divided into four-and two-spot (*parcela* and half-*parcela*) plots; a tent and a car each count as one spot. (☎948 55 17 33; fax 55 47 55; lizarrakanpina@navarra.net. 740ptas/€4.45 per half-*parcela*, with tent, car, plus 530ptas/€3.20 per person; hostel bunks 950ptas/€5.75. Open year-round. MC/V.)

FOOD. Estella is known throughout the region for its *gorrín asado* (roast piglet, also called *gorrín de Estella*). Self-caterers head to **Autoservicio Larramendi**, C. Mayor, 58 on the right as you follow C. Mayor toward the river. (Open M-Sa 9am-1:30pm and 5-8pm. MC/V.) Save fresh fruit and vegetable shopping for streetside **Frutas Argandoña**, a few doors down (open 8:30am-1:30pm and 5-8pm). The overwhelming portions served upstairs at **Restaurante Casanova,** C. Fray Wenceslao de Oñate, 7, are sure to slow any pilgrim's progress. Upon entering Pl. Fueros, take a left and look for the wooden sign. (☎948 55 28 09. *Menú* M-F 1300ptas/€7.81. Fish and meat entrées 1200-2000ptas/€7.20-12. Open daily in summer 1-3:30pm and 8:30-11pm; low season M 1-3:30pm, Tu-Su 1-3:30pm and 8:30-11pm. MC/V.)

LA RIOJA AND NAVARRA

SIGHTS AND ENTERTAINMENT. The 12th-century **Iglesia de San Miguel** commands a view of Estella from the hilltop Pl. San Miguel. Its ornately carved stone portal depicts St. Michael fighting dragons, weighing souls, and taking care of celestial business. Up the stairs and opposite the tourist office, the late-Romanesque/early Gothic **Iglesia de San Pedro de la Rúa** with its unusual half-destroyed cloister, towers above main **Calle de la Rúa.** Officially, Estella's churches can only be visited by guided tour (offered in Spanish, English and French). Although—churches do open one hour before mass, making it possible to sneak a discreet peek. Tours of all sites (550ptas/€3.30) can be arranged through **Cultura 5,** C. San Nicolás, 3 (☎948 55 00 70), inside the tourist office, to the right. Across from San Pedro and next to the tourist office, the world's oldest representation of Roland jousts with Farragut the Moor on the columns of the 12th-century **Palacio de los Reyes de Navarra,** now the **Museo Gustavo.** Inside are the impressive works of painter Gustavo de Maesta, who spent his last years in Estella. Rotating temporary exhibits are displayed on the first floor. (☎948 54 60 37; fax 55 32 57. Open Tu-Sa 11am-1pm and 5-7pm, Su 11am-1:30pm. Free.) The week-long **Fiestas de la Virgen del Puy y San Andrés** kick off the Friday before the first Sunday in August, featuring a baby bull *encierro* (less ferocious than Pamplona's), kiddie entertainment, a fair, Navarrese dancing, and *gaitas* (bagpipes without the bags).

NAVARRAN PYRENEES

Navarra includes the most topographically diverse range of the Pyrenees. Forbidding peaks dominate the eastern Valle de Roncal, while the mountain slopes to the west allow easy access to the area's streams, waterfalls, and green meadows. Mist and fog obscure visibility at high altitudes to create a dreamy atmosphere—or nerve-racking driving conditions—depending on your point of view.

While most inhabitants log or raise cattle, tourism becoming the next booming business. The French route of **El Camino de Santiago** (see **Pilgrim's Progress,** p. 459) crosses the border at Roncesvalles and winds down through Pamplona on its way to Santiago de Compostela in Galicia. Many free and cheap *refugios* cater to certified modern-day pilgrims along the way, and Navarra's *casa rurales* (rural lodging houses) are also particularly beautiful. Picking up a free copy of the *Guía de alojamientos de turismo rurales* in any of Navarra's tourist offices. As a rule, these homes are welcoming places to stay and great budget options; doubles usually run between 3500-4800ptas/€21-29. For reservations, call the multilingual tourist office at ☎948 20 65 40. **Pamplona** is a sensible base for those dependent upon public transportation; you can head east toward **Valle de Roncal,** or north toward **Roncesvalles.** Buses are one-a-day affairs throughout most of the area.

RONCESVALLES AND AURITZ-BURGUETE

The first stop in Spain on the French Camino de Santiago path, **Roncesvalles'** mist-enshrouded 10-odd buildings rest amid miles of thickly wooded mountains. This itty-bitty town (pop. 31), 48km from Pamplona, 20km from France, and eons from reality, lives off legends and the tourists who love them. Charlemagne's favorite soldier Roland was supposedly slain just up the hill in AD 778, at the hands of the ambushing Basque-Navarrese, who were furious that Charlemagne had razed the walls of Pamplona. **Puerto Ibañeta** (1057m), less than 2km up the main road from the monastery, supposedly marks the spot where Roland breathed his final breath. The heavily restored **Capilla de Sancti Spiritus** stands over the remains of the bone heap (courtesy of dead soldiers and pilgrims), where his tomb is thought to be. The tiny 12th-century **Capilla de Santiago** is next door to the left. (The chapels can only be visited by guided tours; see below.)

Inside the **Colegiata**, up the driveway from the *capilla*, the tombs of King Sancho El Fuerte (the Strong) and his bride rest in solitary splendor, lit by the huge stained-glass windows of the **Capilla de San Agustín.** (☎948 79 04 80).

Chapel and cloister open Tu-F 10:30am-1:30pm, Sa-Su 10am-2pm and 4-7pm. 300ptas/€2; students, seniors, and pilgrims 225ptas/€1.40). In the decisive battle of the Navas de Tolosa, Sancho reputedly broke the chains protecting the Arab king Miramomolin with his own hands, then promptly decapitated him. The heavy iron chains hanging from the walls of the chamber are represented in Navarra's flag. The monastery's lovely French Gothic **church,** endowed by Sancho and consecrated in 1219, is its main attraction. (Call ☎948 76 00 00 for more info. Open daily 8am-8pm. Free. Guided visits including all monuments and the Roncesvalles museum, 500ptas/€3.)

PRACTICAL INFORMATION. La Montañesa buses (☎948 22 15 84) run to and from **Pamplona** to Roncesvalles (1¼hr.; M-F 6pm, Sa 4pm; 630ptas/€3.80. Return bus leaves Roncevalles M-Sa 6:50am). The bus stops in **Burguete** each way. A **tourist office** in the mill behind Casa Sabina Hostería offers maps and guides to the sites of Roncevalles and Camino de Santiago. (☎948 76 03 01. Open M-Sa 10am-2pm and 3-6pm, Su 10am-2pm.) For the **Banco Central Hispano** (open Apr.-Sept. M-F 8:30am-2:30pm; Oct.-Mar. M-F 8:30am-2:30pm, Sa 8:30am-1pm), **supermarkets,** and **restaurants,** head to nearby Burguete (2km south). The *menú* at Roncesvalles lone **Casa Sabina Hostería** is 1300ptas M-F and 1500ptas Sa-Su).

ACCOMMODATIONS AND FOOD. The **monastery** in Roncesvalles has free lodging for official pilgrims—enter the door to the right as you face the monastery. The attached **Oficina de Peregrinos** (☎948 76 00 00) provides credentials. Behind the monastery is **Albergue Juvenil Roncesvalles (HI),** a large, somber building that served a pilgrims' hospital in the 18th century. (☎/fax 948 76 03 02. Fantastic rec rooms in the basement. (☎/fax 948 76 03 02. Meals are only available for large groups. Members only. HI cards for sale. 4- to 11-bed dorms 1000ptas per person, with meals 2700ptas; over 26 1500ptas/€9, with meals 3200ptas/€20. Call ahead for reservations June-Aug.) Accommodations, including several *casas rurales,* are plentiful in nearby **Burguete.** Those following the **Camino de Hemingway** can check out the **Hostal Burguete,** est. 1880, San Nikolas, 71. With its high, springy beds and old-fashioned rooms, not much has changed since the big guy made a stop here himself; Ernest did some resting and writing here on his way back to Paris from *San Fermines.* (☎948 76 00 05. Breakfast 450ptas/€2.75. *Menú* 1800ptas/€11. Singles 4600ptas/€28, Aug. 5600ptas/€33.75; doubles 5900ptas/€35.50, Aug. 6900ptas/€40.25. All rooms with private bath. Open Semana Santa-Dec. 10. AmEx/MC/V.).)

VALLE DE SALAZAR: OCHAGAVÍA

On the banks of the Río Andena, **Ochagavía** (pop. 600) is the picturesque mountain village of urbanite dreams. Forty kilometers from [illegible] of a cheerful, gurgling river. Ochagavía's whitewashed houses and cobbled streets lead to forested mountains great for hiking, trout fishing, and cross-country skiing. The charming 12th-century **Hermito de Muskilda,** spiritual and cultural nexus of the town, is a 45min. hike away; follow the path from behind the church, or take the road toward the town of Izalzu and look for the stone cross. Local dances featuring elaborate costumes are performed at the sanctuary on September 8, the first day of Ochagavía's annual **festival.** (☎948 89 00 38. Open May-June M-F 4-7pm; Sa-Su 11am-2pm, 4-8pm; July-Aug. daily 11am-2pm and 4-8pm; other months Sa-Su 11am-2pm, 4-7pm.) **Hikers** will find the climb up the **Pico de Orhy** (2021m) a breeze. The one-hour trail leaving the parking lot at **Puerto de Larrau,** 9km north of Ochagavía along the highway to France, leads to panoramic views of the valley. A second quality hike (20km; 6hr. one-way) follows the Río Irati through the **Selva de Irati** to **Orbaitzeta;** hikers leave their cars at the **Ermita de las Nieves,** 24km from Ochagavía. **Cross country skiers** can also enjoy two circuit trails originating a bit farther down the same highway.

TRANSPORTATION AND PRACTICAL INFORMATION. **Río Irati** (☎948 22 14 70) runs buses to **Pamplona** (1½hr. M-Sa 7am, 900ptas/€5.50. To Ochagavía from Pamplona M-F 6:00pm, Sa 1:30pm). The **tourist office,** on the main road, is in the same building as a nature center and offers the free lodging guide, *Guía de Alojamientos Turísticos*. (☎/fax 948 89 06 41. Office open *Semana Santa* to Oct. M-Sa 10am-2pm and 4:30-7:30pm, Su 10am-2pm; Nov. to *Semana Santa* M-F & Su 10am-2pm and Sa 10am-2pm and 4-7pm. Several **ATMs** are located on the main road. In an **emergency** call ☎112. The **pharmacy** can be found at C. Urrutia, 31 (☎948 89 05 06. Open M-F 10am-2pm and 5-7:30pm, Sa 10am-2pm), and the **post office** is on C. Labaria, near the Ayuntamiento. (☎948 89 04 52. Open M-Sa 8:30-9:30am.)

ACCOMMODATIONS. Up the street from the bank and to the left, the warm and welcoming owners of **Casa Ñavarro,** rent large, immaculate rooms with balconies and couches. (☎948 89 03 35. Breakfast 400ptas/€ Reservations recommended. Singles without bath 2500ptas/€15; doubles 3800ptas/€22.50, with bath 4500ptas/€27). Across the river from the main road on the edge of town, **Hostal Orialde** has attractive, spacious rooms. (☎948 89 00 27. Breakfast 485ptas/€2.90, *Menú* 1820ptas/€11. Singles 3640ptas/€22; doubles 4600ptas/€27.75, with bath 5675ptas/€34.) Ask at the tourist office or look for the "CR" signs advertising one of the town's 25 *casas rurales*. **Camping Osate,** at the entrance to town, provides a modern campsite on the river with supermarket, bar, and **mountain bike** rentals. (☎948 89 01 84. Bikes 3000ptas/€18, 2000ptas/€12 per half day. *Menú* 1400ptas/€8.50. Rooms with bunks and private bath range 4000-8100ptas/€24-28.50. per day. Camping 500ptas/€3 per person and per car, 450ptas/€2.75 per tent. MC/V.)

VALLE DE RONCAL

Carved by the Río Esca, Valle de Roncal is a handsome valley stretching south from the French border. With its darling towns, inviting *casas rurales*, and prime hiking, Valle de Roncal is the Navarran Pyrenees at its best.

RONCAL ☎948

Smack in the center of the Valle de Roncal, the diminutive town of **Roncal** (pop. 300) puffs up with pride over two things: its famed *queso Roncal*, a sharp, sheep's milk cheese, and its world-renowned tenor, Julián Gayarre (1844-1889). **Casa Museo Julián Gayarre,** on C. Arana, occupies the singer's birthplace, showcasing his belongings and assorted memorabilia. (☎948 47 51 80. Open Apr.-Sept. Tu-Su 11:30am-1:30pm and 5-7pm; Oct.-Mar. Sa-Su 11:30am-1:30pm and 4-6pm. 200ptas/€1.20, seniors free). **La Tafallesa buses** (☎948 22 28 86) run to **Pamplona** (2hr., M-F 7am, 880ptas/€5.30). The **tourist office** on Roncal's main road, Po. de Juliana Gayarre has info on hiking and *casas rurales*. (☎948 47 52 56; fax 47 53 16. Open *Semana Santa*-Oct. 12 M-Sa 10am-2pm and 4:30-7:30pm, Su 10am-2pm; low-season M-F 10am-2pm and Sa 4:30-7:30pm.) Services include: **emergency** ☎112; **Guardia Civil** ☎948 47 50 05; and a **pharmacy,** next door to the tourist office (open July-Sept. M-F 10am-2pm and 5-8pm, Sa 10am-2pm; Low-season M-F 10am-2pm and 5-7:30pm). **Casa Villa Pepita,** Po. Julián Gayarre, 4, is across from a small playground just before the bridge. (☎948 47 51 33. Breakfast 400ptas/€2.40. Meals 1500ptas/€9. Singles 1900ptas/€11.42; doubles 3800ptas/€23, with bath 5200ptas/€31.)

ISABA AND ENVIRONS

North of Roncal, **Isaba** (pop. 550) draws hikers and skiers eager to explore the surrounding mountains. A stunning hike climbs from Isaba to **Zuriza** in the Valle de Hecho (5-6hr.). Shorter, but steeper, are the ascents from Collado Argibiela to **Punta Abizondo** (1676m) and **Peña Ezkaurre** (2050m). For more routes, ask at the tourist office. Ski trails run north of Isaba, at the **Estación de Ski Larra-Belagna,** (☎948 39 40 02). A village **festival,** featuring stone-throwing contests and a local variation of polo, runs July 25-28 in honor of San Santiago, and Isaba comes to life with dancing and general merriment on Sept. 16, in honor of San Cipriano.

Isaba's **tourist office** is located on the right as you enter town, just before the boardwalk (☎948 89 32 51. Open *Semana Santa*-Oct. 12 M-Sa 10am-2pm and 4:30-7:30pm, Su 10am-2pm; low-season M-F 10am-2pm, Sa 4:30-7:30pm.). **Telephones** and **ATMs** can be found just uphill from the tourist office. **Albergue Oxanea,** C. Bormapea, 47, offers wooden bunks and a TV lounge. (☎948 89 31 53. Breakfast 350ptas/€2.10. Meals 1200ptas/€7.20. Dorm 1000ptas/€6, with sheets 1300ptas/€7.80. Open Oct.-Dec. 15 and Apr.-June Sa-Su nights only.) **Camping Asolaze,** 6km toward France, offers a restaurant, store, and bunkbeds in addition to campsites. (☎948 89 30 34. Closed for Nov. Sheets 350ptas/€2.10. Dorm 1300ptas/€7.80. Camping 600ptas/€3.60 per person, per tent, per car. MC/V.) The mountains open into the **Valle de Belagua,** 8km north of Isaba, where **Refugio Angel Olorón** offers bunks year-round. The refuge is at km 19 on the highway toward France. (☎/fax 948 39 40 02. Breakfast 300ptas/€1.80; meals 1500ptas/€9. Dorms 1100ptas/€6.60; *Federación de Montaña* and *Carnet Jovens* members 600ptas/€3.61.)

PAÍS VASCO (EUSKADI)

PAÍS VASCO

As the Basque saying goes, "Before God was God and the rocks were rocks, the Basques were Basque." The País Vasco is officially composed of the provinces Guipuzcoa, Alava, and Vizcaya, but those who identify themselves as Basque are not restricted by boundaries. The Basque country is often thought to expand into Navarra and southwestern France. The varied landscape of the País Vasco resembles a nation complete unto itself, with cosmopolitan cities, verdant hills, industrial wastelands, and quaint fishing villages. The people are bound by their deep attachment to the land and immense cultural and national pride.

Many believe that the Basques are the native people of Iberia, as their culture and language are untraceable to any known source. Today's nationalistic sentiment stems from the 18th-century abolition of the Basque *fueros* (ancient rights of self-government), the Basques' military defeat in the late 19th-century Carlist wars, and Franco's heavy repression of Basque identity. The organization Euskadi ta

Askatasuna ("Basque Country and Freedom"; ETA) began an anti-Spanish terrorist movement that has lasted over 30 years, despite the fact that many Basque Nationalists are critical of the group and its political party, Euskal Herritarrok. The Spanish government and ETA agreed upon a truce in September 1998, but the cease-fire was broken after only 14 months and the violence continues anew.

Most Basques share a strong desire to preserve their cultural identity. Although Castilian Spanish is the predominant language, Basque *(euskera)* has enjoyed a resurgence of popularity since Franco's death. Other regional traditions like *cesta punta* or *pelota vasca* (known outside of Spain as *jai-alai*) continue to thrive. Basque cuisine is some of Iberia's finest, including *bacalao a la vizcaína* (salted cod in a tomato sauce), dishes *a la vasca* (in a delicate parsley-steeped white wine sauce), and *chipirones en su tinta* (baby squids in their own ink). *Tapas* in the País Vasco, considered regional specialties, are called *pintxos* (PEEN-chos); locals wash them down with *sidra* (cider) and the local white wine, *txakoli*.

SAN SEBASTIÁN (DONOSTIA) ☎943

Glittering on the shores of the Cantabrian Sea is San Sebastián (pop. 180,000). At the start of the 19th century it stood as one of Spain's great ports, but much of it was destroyed by Anglo-Portuguese troops during the Peninsular War (1813). The ruined walls were finally torn down in 1863 and construction of a new city began, one that gained international fame when Queen Isabel II made it her summer residence. The city's popularity has been increasing ever since, particularly among land-locked Spaniards desperate to escape central Spain. Vacationers come for its world-famous beaches and bars, as well as its strong sense of regional culture.

TRANSPORTATION

Flights: Airport in Hondarribia (☎943 66 85 00), 20km east of the city. **Interurbanos buses** to Hondarribia pass by the airport (45min.; every 15-20min, 200ptas/€1.25). A **taxi** costs 4000ptas/€24. Flights to **Madrid** (1¼hr., 3-6 per day) and **Barcelona** (1¼hr., 1-4 per day). **Iberia** (☎902 40 05 00), has an office at the airport.

Trains: San Sebastián has two train stations, Estación del Norte and Estación de Amara. **RENFE, Estación del Norte,** Po. Francia(☎902 24 02 02),on the east side of Puente María Cristina. Info open daily 7am-11pm. To: **Barcelona** (9hr., daily 10:30am, 5000ptas/€30); **Burgos** (3½hr.; 6 per day; Su-F 8:32am-10:37pm, Sa 9:02am-10:37pm; 2800-3700ptas/€17-22); **Madrid** (8hr., Su-F 10:37pm, 4900-6300ptas/€30-38); **Pamplona** (2hr., daily 10:30am, 1800ptas/€11); **Paris** (8-11hr., daily 8:05pm, 12,000-13,500ptas/€72-81); **Vitoria-Gasteiz** (1¾hr.; 8-9 per day 6:57am-10:37pm, Su 8:32am-10:37pm; 1205-2500ptas/€7-21); **Zaragoza** (4hr., daily 10:30am, 3100ptas/€19).

[illegible], to: **Bilbao** (1¼hr., every 30min. M-F 6:30am-10:30pm, Sa 7:30am-10:30pm, Su 8:30am-10:30pm; 1200ptas/€7.50); **Vitoria-Gasteiz** (2hr.; M-F 9 trips 6:15am-8:45pm, Sa 5 trips 8:15am-8:45pm, Su 2 trips 6pm and 8:45pm; 1100ptas/€6.50). **Continental Auto,** Av. Sancho el Sabio, 31 (☎943 46 90 74), to: **Burgos** (3-3½hr., 8 per day 7:15am-12:30pm, 2000ptas/€12); **Madrid** (6hr., 7-9 per day 7:15am-12:30am, 3990ptas/€24). **La Roncalesa,** Po. Vizcaya, 16 (☎943 46 10 64), to: **Pamplona** (1hr.; 9 per day 7am-9pm, Su 9am-9pm; 845ptas/€5.50). **Vibasa,** Po. Vizcaya, 16 (☎943 45 75 00), to: **Barcelona** (7hr.; 3 per day 7:30am, 3:30pm, and 11:20pm; 3430ptas/€21). **Turytrans,** Po. Vizcaya, 16 (☎943 46 23 60), to: **Paris** (11hr., 8:30pm, 8200ptas/€50). **Interurbanos** (☎943 64 13 02) to: **Hondarribia** (45min., 8:45am-10pm every 15min., 210ptas/€1.25); **Irún** (35min., every 15-30min., 175ptas/€1).

Public Transportation: (☎943 28 71 00). Each trip 115ptas/€0.60. Bus #16 goes from Alameda del Boulevard to the campground and beaches.

Taxis: Santa Clara (☎943 31 01 11), **Vallina** (☎943 40 40 40), or **Donostia** (☎943 46 46 46). Taxis to **Pamplona** take about 45min., and cost around 13,000ptas/€78.

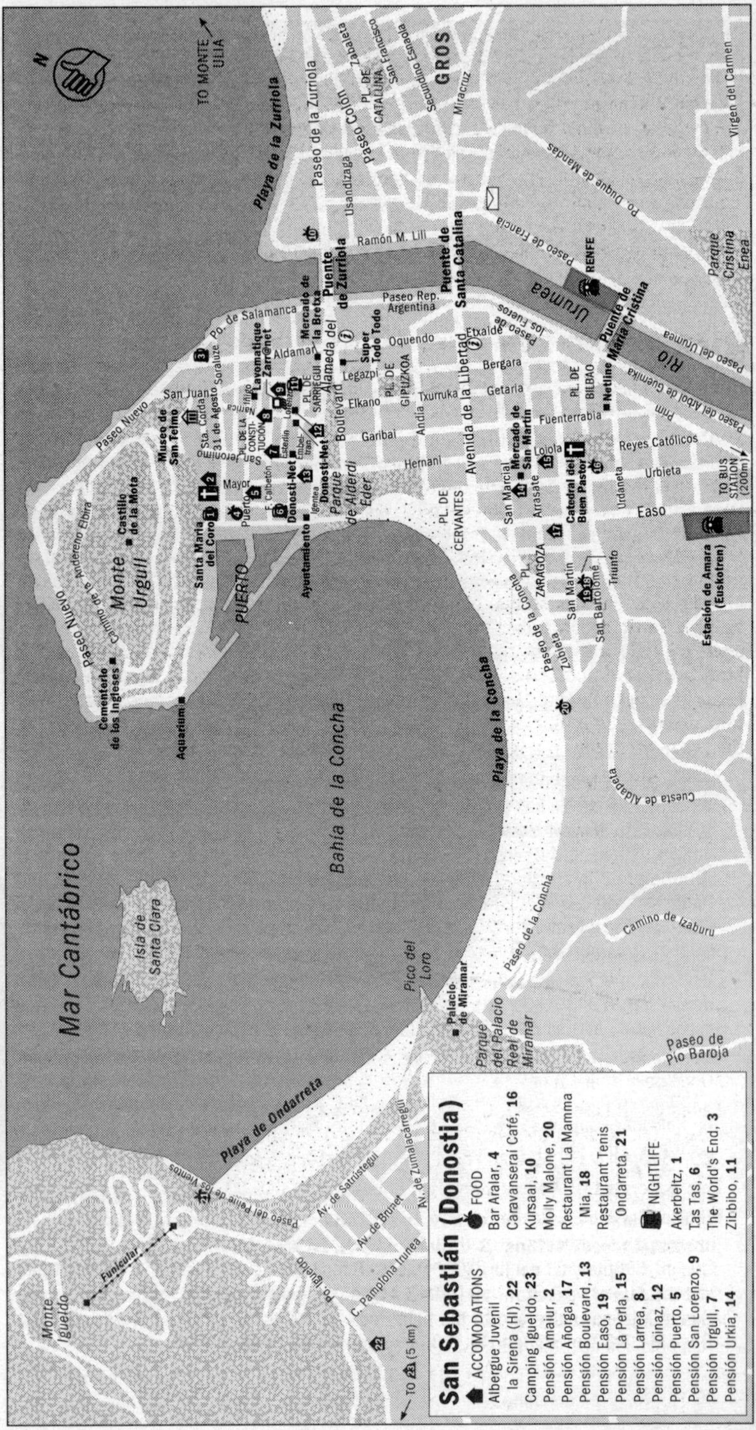

San Sebastián (Donostia)

ACCOMODATIONS

Albergue Juvenil la Sirena (HI), **22**
Camping Igueldo, **23**
Pensión Amaiur, **2**
Pensión Añorga, **17**
Pensión Boulevard, **13**
Pensión Easo, **19**
Pensión La Perla, **15**
Pensión Larrea, **8**
Pensión Loinaz, **12**
Pensión Puerto, **5**
Pensión San Lorenzo, **9**
Pensión Urgull, **7**
Pensión Urkia, **14**

FOOD

Bar Aralar, **4**
Caravanseraí Café, **16**
Kursaal, **10**
Molly Malone, **20**
Restaurant La Mamma Mia, **18**
Restaurant Tenis Ondarreta, **21**

NIGHTLIFE

Akerbeltz, **1**
Tas Tas, **6**
The World's End, **3**
Zibbibo, **11**

Mar Cantábrico
Bahía de la Concha
Isla de Santa Clara
Monte Igueldo
Funicular
Monte Urgull
Castillo de la Mota
Cementerio de los Ingleses
Aquarium
Museo de San Telmo
Santa María del Coro
PUERTO
Ayuntamiento
Donosti-Net
Lavomatique Zarr@net
Mercado de la Bretxa
Super Todo Todo
Parque de Alderdi Eder
Alameda del Boulevard
Puente de Zurriola
Puente de Santa Catalina
Puente de María Cristina
Mercado de San Martín
Catedral del Buen Pastor
Netline
RENFE
Estación de Amara (Euskotren)
TO BUS STATION (200m)
Playa de Ondarreta
Playa de la Concha
Playa de la Zurriola
Pico del Loro
Palacio de Miramar
Parque del Palacio Real de Miramar
Parque Cristina Enea
GROS
TO MONTE ULIA
TO 23 (5 km)
Río Urumea

WHAT ARE YOU SAYING? Linguists still cannot pinpoint the origin of *euskera*. Its commonalities with Caucasian and African dialects suggest that prehistoric Basques may have migrated from the Caucasus mountains through Africa. Referred to by other Spaniards as *la lengua del diablo* (the devil's tongue), *euskera* has come to symbolize cultural self-determination. Only half a million natives speak the language, chiefly in País Vasco and northern Navarra. During his regime, Franco banned *euskera* and forbade parents to give their children Basque names (like Iñaki or Estibaliz). Since his death, there has been a resurgence of everything from *euskera* TV shows to *ikastolas* (Basque schools), and the language is frequently used for street signs and menus in the País Vasco.

ORIENTATION AND PRACTICAL INFORMATION

Street and plaza signs are usually in both *castellano* and *euskera*. The street guide on the tourist office map gives both versions in its index, so don't despair when your encounter the ubiquitous "kalea" and "tx." The **Río Urumea** splits San Sebastián. The city center, most monuments, and the two most popular beaches, **Playa de la Concha** and **Playa de Ondaretta**, line the peninsula on the west side of the river. The tip of the peninsula is called **Monte Urgull.** On the east side of the river, **Playa de la Zurriola,** attracts a younger surfing and beach crowd. Inland lies the **parte vieja** (old city), San Sebastián's restaurant, nightlife, and budget accommodation nexus. South of the *parte vieja*, at the base of the peninsula, is the commercial district. The **bus station** is south of the city on Pl. Pío XII, while the **RENFE station, Barrio de Gros,** and **Playa de la Zurriola** are east of the city. The river is spanned by four bridges: Puentes Zurriola, Santa Catalina, María Cristina, and de Mundaiz (listed north to south). To get to the *parte vieja* from the train station, head straight to Puente María Cristina, cross the bridge, and turn right at the fountain. Continue four blocks north to Av. Libertad, then left and follow it to the port; the *parte vieja* fans out to the right, and Playa de la Concha to the left.

Tourist Office: Municipa, Centro de Atracción y Turismo, C. Reina Regente, 3 (☎943 48 11 66; fax 48 11 72), next to the theater and in front of the bridge Zurriola. From the train station, turn right immediately after crossing Puente María Cristina, and continue until reaching Puente Zurriola; the office is on the left. From the bus station, start down Av. Sancho el Sabio. At Pl. Centenario, bear right onto C. Prim and follow the river, until the third bridge, Puente Zurriola, look to the plaza at your left. Open June-Sept. M-Sa 8am-8pm, Su 10am-2pm; Oct.-May M-Sa 9am-1:30pm, 3:30-7pm, Su 10am-2pm.

Hiking Information: Club Vasco de Camping, San Marcial, 19 (☎/fax 943 42 84 79), 1 block south of Av. Libertad. Organizes excursions. Open M-F 6-8:30pm. **Izadi,** C. Usandizaga, 18 (☎943 29 35 20). Sells hiking guides and maps, some in English. Open M [illegible] pm, Sa [illegible]

Luggage Storage: Train station. 500ptas/€3 per day; buy tokens at the ticket counter. Open daily 7am-11pm.

Laundromat: Lavomatique, C. Iñigo, 13 (☎943 42 38 71), off C. San Juan in the Parte Vieja. 600ptas/€3.65 wash (cold water only), 450ptas/€2.75 dry. Soap 75ptas/€0.45. Open M-F 9:30-2pm and 4-7pm, Sa-Su 10am-2pm.

Emergency: ☎112. **Police: Municipal** C. Easo (☎943 45 00 00).

Medical Services: Casa de Socorro, Bengoetxea, 4 (☎943 44 06 33).

Internet Access: Netline, C. Urdaneta, 8 (☎943 44 50 76). 250ptas/€1.50 per 30min., 500ptas/€3 per hr., 3000ptas/€18 for 10hr. ticket. Open M-Sa 10am-10pm.

Post Office: Po. De Francia, 13 (☎943 44 68 26), near the RENFE station, just over the Santa Catalina bridge and to the right; look for the yellow trim on left side of street. Open M-F 8:30am-8:30pm, Sa 9:30am-2pm. **Postal Code:** 20006.

ACCOMMODATIONS AND CAMPING

Desperate backpackers will have to scrounge for rooms in July and August—particularly during *San Fermines* (July 6-14) and *Semana Grande* (starts Su the week of Aug. 15); September's film festival is not much better. To make matters worse, many pensions don't take reservations in summer. Budget options center in the *parte vieja* and the cathedral—look for signs in doorways. Solo travelers should be prepared to pay for a double, as single rooms are virtually impossible to come by. Late-night arrivals will have even less luck. The tourist office has lists of accommodations, and most hostel owners know of *casas particulares*. Owners of these *casas* often solicit guests at the RENFE station—be wary, this is illegal.

PARTE VIEJA

A bit of a hike from the bus and train stations, the *parte vieja* is brimming with reasonably priced *pensiones*. Its proximity to Playa de la Concha and the port makes this area a prime nightspot; scores of places offer a night's sleep above loud *pintxos (tapas)* bars. Call in advance for reservations.

Pensión Amaiur, C. 31 de Agosto, 44, 2nd fl. (☎943 42 96 54). From Alameda del Boulevard, follow C. San Jerónimo to its end, turn left, and look for the lower-obscured front. Nine rooms and 5 common bathrooms. *Semana Santa*-Oct. 2500-3500ptas/€15-21 per person; Nov.-*Semana Santa* 1900-2500ptas/€11.50-15 per person. MC/V.

Pensión San Lorenzo, C. San Lorenzo, 2 (☎943 42 55 16), off C. San Juan. Doubles with TV, radio, and small refrigerator. Immaculate baths. July-Sept. doubles 8000ptas/€48; June doubles 5000-7000ptas/€30-42; Oct.-May doubles 4000ptas/€24.

Pensión Larrea, C. Narrica, 21, 2nd fl. (☎943 42 26 94). July-Aug. singles 3500ptas/€21; doubles 5000ptas/€30; triples 6500ptas/€39. Sept.-June singles 2500ptas/€15; doubles 4000ptas/€24; triples 5000ptas/€30.

Pensión Loinaz, C. San Lorenzo, 17 (☎943 42 67 14), off C. San Juan. English-speaking owners. Common bathrooms. July-Aug. doubles 6500ptas/€39. Apr.-June doubles 5000ptas/€30. Sept.-March doubles 4000ptas/€24. Singles sometimes available.

Pensión Urgull, Esterlines, 10 (☎943 43 00 47). Follow the winding staircase to the 3rd floor. Rooms with balconies and sinks. Common bathrooms. Prices are not set in stone. July-Aug. doubles 6000-7000ptas/€36-42; June and Sept. doubles 4000-4500ptas/€24-27; Oct.-May singles 2500ptas/€15; doubles 3500-4000ptas/€21-24.

Pensión Boulevard, Alameda del Boulevard, 24 (☎943 42 94 05). Spacious rooms, all with radios, some with balconies. 2 large shared baths for 8 rooms. July-Aug. doubles 8000/€48; June and Sept 6000-7000ptas/€36-42; Oct.-May doubles 4000/€24.

Pensión Puerto, C. Puerto, 19, 2nd fl. (☎943 43 21 40), off C. Mayor. Spotless rooms with wood floors, closets, and comfy beds. Jul.-Aug. 4000-5000ptas/€24-30 per person; June and Sept 3000ptas/€36; low-season 2500ptas/€15 per person.

OUTSIDE THE PARTE VIEJA

Most of these places tend to be quieter than those elsewhere yet are still close to the port, beach, bus and train stations, and no more than 5min. from the old city. This area is also home to the city's most elegant boulevards and buildings.

Albergue Juvenil la Sirena (HI), Po. Igueldo, 25 (☎943 31 02 68; fax 21 40 90), a large light-pink building 3min. from the beach at the far west end of the city. Bus #24 and #27 run from the train and bus stations to Av. Zumalacárregui (the stop in front of the San Sebastián Hotel). From C. Almeda de Boulevard, bus #16 drops you off at the front door. From Av. Zumalacárregui, take the street angling toward the mountain (Av. Brunet) and turn left at its end. Clean rooms and multilingual staff. HI members and ISIC-carriers only. Laundry facilities, and kitchen available 8am-10pm. Sept.-May Su-Th midnight, F-Sa 2am. Jul.-Aug. 2070ptas/€12, over 25 2335ptas/€14 (3-night max stay if full); May-Jun. and Sept. 1885ptas/€11.35, over 25 2205ptas/€13; low-season 1700ptas/€10.20, over 25 2070ptas/€12. MC/V.

Pensión La Perla, C. Loiola, 10, 2nd fl. (☎943 42 81 23), on the street directly ahead of the cathedral. English spoken. Private baths. TVs. July-Sept. singles 4000ptas/€24; doubles 6000ptas/€36. Oct.-June singles 3500ptas/€21; doubles 4500ptas/€27.

Pensión Easo, C. San Bartolomé, 24 (☎943 45 39 12; fax 45 39 71). Head toward the beach on C. San Martín, turn left on C. Easo, and right on C. San Bartolomé. July-Sept. 15 singles 5200ptas/€31, with bath 7600ptas/€46; doubles 6600ptas/€40, with bath 9600ptas/€58. Jun. and Sept. singles 4500ptas/€27, with bath 6500ptas/€40; doubles 5500ptas/€33, with bath 7500ptas/€45. Oct.-May singles 3500ptas/€21, with bath 5500/€33; doubles 4500ptas/€27, with bath 6500ptas/€40. AmEx/MC/V.

Pensión Urkia, C. Urbieta, 12, 3rd fl. (☎943 42 44 36), located on C. Urbieta between C. Marcial and C. Arrasate and borders the Mercado de San Martín. Rooms with full bathrooms and TVs. July-Sept. doubles 6500ptas/€39; triples 9000ptas/€54. Oct.-June singles 3500-4000ptas/€21-24; doubles 4500ptas/€27; triples 6000ptas/€36.

Pensión Añorga, C. Easo, 12 (☎943 46 79 45), at C. San Martín. Shares entryway with 2 other *pensiones*. Spacious rooms have shiny wood floors and comfy beds. July-Aug. singles 4000ptas/€24; doubles 5000ptas/€30, with bath 6500ptas/€39. Sept.-June singles 3000ptas/€18; doubles 4000ptas/€24, with bath 5000ptas/€30.

Camping Igueldo (☎943 21 45 02), 5km west of town. The 268 spots fill in the blink of an eye. Beautiful views of the ocean make the drive worth it. Bus #16 ("Barrio de Igueldo-Camping") runs between the site and Alameda del Boulevard (every 30min., 125ptas/€0.75). *Parcelas* June-Aug. and *Semana Santa* 1725ptas/€10.50, extra person 525ptas/€3.20; Sept.-May 1475ptas/€9, extra person 425ptas/€3. MC/V.

FOOD

Pintxos (tapas), chased down with the fizzy regional white wine, *txakoli*, are a religion here; bars in the old city spread an array of enticing tidbits on toothpicks or bread. In the harbor, many places serve tangy sardines with slightly bitter *sidra* (cider), another regional specialty. Custom demands pouring it with arm extended so the force of the stream hitting the glass releases the *sidra's* full flavor. It is also customary to pour just enough for one or two sips at a time. From January through April, San Sebastián's gourmands turn their attention to **sidrerías,** all of which are open to the public and provide the same, standard meal (cod, beef chop, and cheese) as an accompaniment to the *sidra*.

Restaurants and bars clamor for attention on C. Fermín Calbetón, in the old quarter. The majority of restaurants offer their best deals on lunchtime *menús*. The underground shopping center located between Alameda del Boulevard and C. San Juan houses the very clean and modern **Mercado de la Bretxa** selling everything from fruits and vegetables to pintxos (open M-Sa 9am-9pm, although most vendors take lunch from 3pm-5pm). The local marketplace, **Mercado de San Martín,** on C. San Marcial between C. Loiola and C. Urbieta, sells fresh local meats, fish, and [illegible] [illegible]pm, Su [illegible]am-2pm). For **groceries,** stop by **Super Todo Todo,** Alameda del Boulevard, 3, across the street from the Mercado de la Bretxa (☎943 42 82 59. Open M-Sa 8:30am-9pm, Su 10am-2pm. MC/V.)

PARTE VIEJA

Kursaal, Zurriola, 1 (☎943 00 31 62). In an ultra-modern building across the river from the Old City. Treat yourself to an elegant lunch on their breezy patio. The chef, who also runs the very expensive restaurant upstairs, is a legend among locals. Menú M-F 1-3:30pm 1650ptas/€10, Sa-Su 2300ptas/€14, plus IVA. MC/V.

Bar Aralar, C. Puerto Kalea (☎943 42 63 78). Fresh and tasty *pintxos* (150-200ptas). An excellent place to try local cuisine. Sandwiches 200-350ptas/€0.90-2.10. Open Su-Th 11am-12am, Fr-Sa 11am-2:30am. Closed 3 weeks in Nov. and May. MC/V.

La Cueva, Pl. Trinidad, off 31 de Agosto (☎943 42 54 37). A cavernous restaurant with a patio, serving traditional seafood cuisine prepared by a talented all-female staff. M-F *Menú* 2000ptas/€12. Grilled tuna, hake, cod and squid entrées 900-2000ptas/€5.50-12. Open T-Su 1-3:30pm and 7:30-11pm. AmEx/MC/V.

NO CAMP DAVID IN SIGHT One of Europe's longest-running guerrilla rebellions—that of Basque terrorists against the Spanish government—shows no sign of ending anytime soon. Since 1968, the Basque separatist group ETA (Eskadi ta Askatasuna) has been blamed for more than 800 deaths, most of them among members of the Spanish government. A cease-fire was agreed upon in September 1998 (to negotiate bringing Basque prisoners closer to home), but ETA broke the truce in December 1999 and in the following eight months alone was pinned with nine terrorist murders. Most Spaniards are fed up with the violence. Vigils have been held nationwide, and more than half a million people marched in Madrid to protest ETA violence. Prime Minister José María Aznar has declared that he simply will not deal with terrorism. "They will not see us blink," he said at the funeral of former Basque governor Juan María Jauregui, a recent victim who had repeatedly pressed for peace talks. On the other side, Arnaldo Otegi, spokesman for Euskal Herritarok, the radical nationalists seen as ETA's political wing, has said that violence will not end until the Basques have an independent state. But by no means does the entire País Vasco support this stance. Surveys show that only about 30% of Basques hope for complete sovereignty, and fear is spreading tangibly in the region; a recent poll by a regional university showed that 70% of Basques are afraid to participate openly in politics, up 20% from three years ago. The future of Basque terrorism is uncertain at best. Jonan Fernández, coordinator of Elkarri, a nonprofit pro-separatist peace group, laments the lack of international help. "Why," he implored, "is there no Camp David for us?"

PARTE NUEVA

Real Club de Tenis Ondarreta (☎943 31 11 50 or 31 41 18), on Po. Peine de los Vientos, along the *Playa de Ondarreta.* Escape the crowded streets of the *parte vieja* to mingle with San Sebastián's preppies. *Menú* M-Sa 1550ptas/€9.35, Su 2350ptas/€14. Entrées 1700-2300ptas/€10.25-14. Open M-Sa 1-4pm and 9-11pm, Su 1-4pm. Call ahead for reservations. AmEx/MC/V.

La Mamma Mia, C. San Bartolomé, 18 (☎943 46 52 93). Freshly made pastas, including tortellini, fettucine, and lasagna dishes (945-1050ptas/€5.75-6.30). M-F luncheon *Menú* 1200ptas/€7. Open daily 1:30-4pm and 8:30pm-12:30am. MC/V.

Caravanserai Café, C. San Bartolomé, 1 (☎943 47 54 78), along the right side of the cathedral when facing its front doors. Trendy, chic, and artsy, without the pretentious prices. Fabulous vegetarian options. Entrées 750-1150ptas/€5-7 Open M-Th 8am-midnight, F-Sa 8am-1am, Su 10:30am-midnight. MC/V.

SIGHTS

San Sebastián's best sight is the city itself—parks, grandiose buildings, and attractive hillsides crowd San Sebastián's bay and the pleasant island of Santa Clara.

MONTE IGUELDO. Though the views from both of San Sebastián's mountains are quite spectacular, those from Monte Igueldo are superior. By day, the countryside meets the ocean in a line of white and blue; by night, lit by floodlights, Isla Santa Clara seems to float in a halo of light. The sidewalk toward the mountain ends just before the base of Monte Igueldo with Eduardo Chillida's sculpture *El peine de los vientos* (Wind's Comb). The walk up is not too strenuous, but the funicular is great for warmer afternoons. A small amusement park at the top aims to please with bumper cars, water rides, and trampolines, but the magnificent view is the real entertainment. *(☎943 21 02 11. Open daily June-Sept. 10am-10pm. Oct.-Feb. Sa 12-6pm; Su 11am-7pm. Mar-Jun. Sa 11am-8pm; Su 11am-9pm. Funicular runs every 15min; 125ptas/€0.75 one-way, 240ptas/€1.40 round-trip.)*

MONTE URGULL. Across the bay from Monte Igueldo, the gravel paths on Monte Urgull wind through shady woods, monuments, love-struck teenagers, and stunning vistas. The overgrown **Castillo de Santa Cruz de la Mota** tops the summit with 12 cannons, a chapel, and the statue of the *Sagrado Corazón de Jesús* blessing the city. *(Open daily June-Aug. 8am-8pm; Sept.-May 8am-6pm.)*

PASAJES DE SAN JUAN. Thirty minutes from the town center, on a hillside overlooking a small bay filled with colorful *chalupas* boats, lies the town of Pasajes de San Juan. The charming fishing village's wood-balconied homes create an enchanting time warp. The house in which Victor Hugo once lived is just to the right when exiting the ferry. *(A Herribus goes to Pasajes de San Juan every 20-30min. for 130ptas/€0.80 from Pl. Gipúzkoa).*

MUSEO DE SAN TELMO. The Museo de San Telmo resides in a Dominican monastery. The serene, overgrown cloister is strewn with Basque funerary relics, and the main museum beyond the cloister displays a fascinating array of pre-historic Basque artifacts, a few dinosaur skeletons, and a piece of contemporary art. *(Po. Nuevo. ☎943 42 49 70. Open Tu-Sa 10:30am-1:30pm and 4-8pm, Su 10:30am-2pm. Free.)*

PALACES. As soon as Queen Isabel II started vacationing here in the mid-19th century, fancy buildings began to spring up like wildflowers. **El Palacio de Mirama** has passed through the hands of the Spanish court, Napoleon III, and Bismarck; today anyone can stroll through the "cottage-style" grounds and contemplate the picturesque views of the bay. *(Between Playa de la Concha and Playa de Ondarreta. Open daily June-Aug. 9am-9pm; Sept.-May 10am-5pm.)* The other royal residence, **Palacio de Ayete,** is closed to the public, but the surrounding trails are not. *(Head up Cuesta de Aldapeta or take Bus #19. Grounds open June-Aug. 10am-8:30pm; Sept.-May 10am-5pm.)*

BEACHES AND WATER SPORTS

The gorgeous **Playa de la Concha** curves from the port to the **Pico del Loro,** the beak-shaped promontory home to the Palacio de Miramar. The virtually flat beach disappears during high tide, and each year erosion narrows the sand space a little more. Sunbathing crowds jam onto the smaller and steeper **Playa de Ondarreta,** beyond Miramar, and surfers flock to **Playa de la Zurrida,** across the river from Mt. Urguel. Picnickers head for the alluring **Isla de Sta. Clara** in the center of the bay, either by rented rowboat or public motorboat ferry (5min., June-Sept. every 30min., round-trip 325ptas/€1.95). Check at the portside kiosk for more info.

Several sports-related groups offer a variety of activities and lessons. For **windsurfing** and **kayaking,** call the Real Club Náutico, C. Igentea, 9 (☎943 42 35 75. 10-day courses 5000-8000ptas/€30-48.) For **parachuting,** try Urruti Sport, C. José María Soroa, 20 (☎943 27 81 96). **Surfers** can check out the Pukas Surf Club, C. Mayor, 5, for info on lessons and a huge variety of gear. (☎943 42 72 28; Open M-Sa 10am-1pm and 4-8pm. AmEx/MC/V.) For general information on all sports, pick up a copy of the *UDA-Actividades deportivas* brochure at the tourist office.

NIGHTLIFE

The *parte vieja* pulls out all the stops in July and August, particularly on C. Fermín Calbetón, three blocks in from Alameda del Boulevard. During the year, when students outnumber backpackers, nightlife tends to move beyond the *parte vieja*. Keep an eye out for discount coupons on the street.

The World's End, Po. de Salamanca, 14 (☎/fax 943 42 09 63). 1 block outside of the *parte vieja* in the direction of the beach. Rapidly becoming a fixture on the backpacker circuit. Great pub ambience, frequent live music, and tasty snacks (500-700ptas/€3-4.25). Open Su-Th 2pm-2:30am, F-Sa 2pm-3:30am.

Zibbibo, Pl. Sarriegi 8 (☎943 425 334). The backpacker stop en route from World's End to Tas-Tas. Plays a blend of big-hit and techno tunes. Popular "grande" *sangría* 600ptas/€3.75. Happy hour Su-Th 10:30-11:30pm. Open daily 2pm-4am. MC/V.

Bar Tas-Tas, C. Fermín Calbetón, 35 (☎943 43 06 12). A notorious hotspot for international backpackers, particularly of the blond-hair, blue-eyed variety. Drink to the tune of

A STEP ABOVE SQUASH The Basque sport known as *cesta punta*, or *jai alai*, is the world's fastest ball game. In this unique form of handball, burly players fling balls at a walled court (called a *frontón*) at speeds up to 200km per hour. The traditional game is played with bare hands, but the faster version incorporates *txisteras*, hand-held baskets of sorts. Local teams often play in public *frontones;* watch for the trademark white uniforms with red or blue sashes. Spreading beyond its homeland, *jai alai* now exists in more than 20 variants, 14 of them at the world championship level. The sport has even caught on in such far-flung places as Cancún, Cuba, and Connecticut, but sorry ladies: so far only men have played.

American pop hits during happy hour, Su-Th 8-11:30pm. An assortment of music ranging from Salsa to disco. *Sangría grande* 700ptas/€4.25. Open daily June-Sept 3pm-4am; winter 3pm-3am. AmEx/MC/V.

Akerbeltz, C. Koruko Andra Mari, 10. Face the Iglesia de Santa María on the C. 31 de Agosto, take a left; it's in the corner at road's end, just before the port. A tiny, sleek, cavernous bar. Open M-Th 4pm-2:30am; F-Sa 4pm-3:30am.

Molly Malone, C. San Marín, 55 (☎943 46 98 22), right off the Po. de la Concha, outside of the *parte vieja.* An Irish pub with descriptions of the brew selections and a mellow upstairs loft. Beer 400-600ptas/€2.40-3.60. Open Jul.-Aug. Su-Th 3pm-3am.

NEAR SAN SEBASTIÁN

HONDARRIBIA ☎943

Less than 1hr. east of San Sebastián by bus, Hondarribia (pop. 15,000) is a European beach town designed the way European beach towns should be. Stretching along the Txingudi Bay, the charming town hosts a golden sand beach and enough of flower-laden balconies to make everyone ready to just go home. Compared to chic San Sebastián, Hondarribia is refreshingly small and simple. In the peak days of summer though, the beach can become ridiculously crowded with vacationers from Madrid and Barcelona, but it's usually pleasantly calm through June.

PRACTICAL INFORMATION. Interurbanos buses (☎943 64 13 02) to **San Sebastián's** Pl. Guipuzcoa pick up in front of the post office; pay onboard (45min.; every 20min. M-Sa 7:45am-10:45pm, Su 7:45am-9:45pm, Jul.-Aug. 10:45pm; 215ptas/€1.50). **AUIF buses** (☎943 63 31 45) go to: **Irún** (10min., 10am-8pm, 135ptas/€0.81). The **airport**, C. Gabarrari Kalea, (☎943 66 85 00), is within walking distance of the town center. The **tourist office, Bidasoa Turismo,** C. Javier Ugarte, 6, is right off Pl. San Cristóbal; from the bus stop walk around to the other side of the building. English is spoken. (☎943 64 54 58. Open July-Sept M-Sa 10am-8pm. Oct.-June M-F 9am-1:30pm and 4-6:30pm, Sa 10am-2pm). Local services include: **emergency**☎112; **police,** C. Mayor, 10, (☎943 64 43 00); and the **post office,** Pl. San Cristóbal, 1. (☎943 64 12 04. Open M-F 8:30am-2:30pm and Sa 9:30am-1pm.) **Postal code:** 20280.

ACCOMMODATIONS. Reservations are key in the summer, so call ahead. The **Albergue Juan Sebastián Elcano (HI),** Ctra. Faro, sits on a hillside with a view of the beach and mountains. From the last bus stop, head to the beach on C. Itsasargi, bearing left at the coast, and continuing straight for several long blocks. At the traffic circle, turn left and follow signs up the steep hill to the hostel. A TV room and tennis and basketball courts are there for when you get tired of laying on the sand. (☎943 64 15 50; fax 64 00 28. Breakfast included. 3-night max. stay when full. Reception daily 9am-noon and 4-7pm. Sometimes closed in Dec. and Jan. so call ahead. Curfew midnight, but doors open at 1 and 2am. Members only; HI cards 1000-1500ptas/€6-9. Sheets 125ptas/€0.75. Dorms 1385ptas/€8.35, over 30 2075ptas/€13. MC/V.) **Casa Hostal Txoko Goxoa,** C. Murrua, 22, lies in the other direction from Pl. San Cristóbal. Head up C. Javier Ugarte from the tourist office, take the second right onto C. Juan Laborda, and follow the street hill until it ends. Look for the stairs on your left and hike up to the old city walls; the hostel is on your right. (☎/fax 943 64 46 58. Private baths outside the room. Breakfast 500ptas/€3. July-Sept. doubles 6500ptas/€39. Oct.-June singles 4500ptas/€27; doubles 5750ptas/€35. IVA not included. MC/V.) **Camping Jaizkibel** (☎943 64 16 79; fax 64 26 53) lies 2km from town, on Ctra. Guadelupe toward Monte Jaizkibel, and can only be reached by car or foot. The bungalows come complete with full bath and small kitchenette, and the site has hot water showers, cafeteria, restaurant, and self-service laundry. (Reception daily 9am-11pm. 600ptas/€3.61 per person, per tent, and per car. Bungalows for 1-2 people 7500-10,000ptas/€45-60, for 3-4 10,000-13,000ptas/€60-78. Bunks 1300ptas/€7.81. Open year-round.)

FOOD. Several **markets** spill onto C. San Pedro, 3 blocks inland from the port. Stock up on staples at **Charter,** C. Santiago 19. (☎943 64 15 40. Open M-F 8:30am-1:30pm and 5-8pm, Sa 8:30am-1:30pm. Sept. 16-June M-F open until 7:30pm. MC/V.) The lunch *menú* (M-F 1000ptas/€6) at **Xaia Jatetxea,** Bernat Etxepare, 4, is super-cheap. The *bolas picante de bacaloa* (fried balls of spicy cod; 200ptas/€1.20) are stirring. (☎943 64 52 57. Open M-Sa 12:30-3pm and 8-10pm. MC/V.)

SIGHTS AND EXCURSIONS. The gorgeous stone-and-timber **casco antiguo,** centered around Carlos V's imposing palace in Pl. Armas (now a *parador*—peek inside to catch a glimpse of the renovations), provides a welcome relief from Coppertone fumes. The **Parroquia de Nuestra Señora de la Asunción,** also in Pl. Armas, is a lovely 15th-century church where Louis XIV of France married, by proxy, the Spanish Habsburg María Teresa. (Open only for Mass daily at 7pm and tours; check at the front desk. 500ptas/€3.) There are several possible excursions from Hondarribia. **Monte Jaizkibel,** 6km up Av. Monte Jaizkibel, guards the **Santuario de Guadalupe.** Hiking the mountain—the highest on the Costa Cantábrica—affords incredible views of the coast; on a clear day you can see as far as Bayonne, France. **Jolaski Boats** (☎943 61 64 47) shuttle travelers 5km to **Hendaye,** a French town with a bigger beach. They leave from the pier at the end of C. Domingo Egia, off La Marina (every 15min. in summer, every 20min. in winter; 200ptas/€1.20).

IRÚN ☎943

Visitors to Irún (pop 50,000) are usually in a hurry to get somewhere else, and with good reason—the city is little more than a transportation hub with services to Madrid, San Sebastián, and the French border. **RENFE trains**, C. Estación (☎902 24 02 02) fan out to all of Spain and connect frequently to **San Sebastián** (25min., every 40min. 5:22am-10:22pm, 170ptas/€1). The train station has **currency exchange** and **luggage storage** (500ptas/€3, ask for a token at the bar; open daily 6am-10:20pm). You can check your **email** at **Tulocutorio.es**, C. Estación, 8, just 3min. [illegible] per 15min., 300ptas/€1.80 per 30min., 525ptas/€3.16 per hour. Open daily 10am-10pm.) The **Ayuntamiento (SAC office),** C. Juan de la Cruz, 2, on Pl. Zabaltza off Po. Colón, swerves as the tourist office. (☎943 64 92 00. Open M-F 8:30am-2pm and 4:30-7:30pm, Sa 9:30am-1pm. Closed afternoons in Aug.) Local services include: **emergency** ☎112; and **police,** in Pl. Ensanche (☎092). Affordable hostels line C. Estación in front of the station. A popular option is **Hostal Residencia Lizaso,** C. Aduana, 5. Follow C. Estación, bear right on Po. Colón, and take the first right. Rooms all have TV. (☎943 61 16 00. Doubles with sink 4300ptas/€26, shower 5500ptas/€33, with bath 6000-6250ptas/€36-38. IVA not included.) **Pensión Bidasoa**, C. Estación, 14, up on the left from the RENFE station, just past the church. The rooms share common baths, some have balconies. (☎943 61 99 13. Jul.-Aug. singles 3000ptas/€18, with bath 4000ptas/€24; doubles 4000ptas/€24, with bath 5500/€33. Sept-June singles 2000ptas/€12, with bath 3000ptas/€18; doubles 3000ptas/€18, with bath 4000ptas/€24. MC/V.) **Bar Restaurant Las Ruedas,** C. Estación, 20, up the street from the RENFE station in the small plaza beyond the church, serves a hearty *menú for* 1100ptas/€6.61. (☎943 61 54 26. Open daily 6am-1am.)

BILBAO (BILBO) ☎944

The economic engine of the Basque country, Bilbao (pop. 370,000), known affectionately as "Botxo" to its Basque inhabitants, has been making people wealthy since the 16th century, when its shipbuilding industries and coastal location made it a key trade link between Castile and Flanders. Today, thanks to decades of careful investment, the city is finally overcoming its reputation as a bourgeois, business-minded industrial center. Economic booms in the 19th-century funded wide boulevards lined by grandiose buildings, and 20th-century success has showered the city with a new subway system, an overhauled international airport, a stunning new bridge, and a stylish riverwalk project, all designed by renowned international architects. It is the shining, curving Guggenheim Museum, however, that has most powerfully fueled Bilbao's rise to international prominence.

TRANSPORTATION

Flights: Airport (☎944 86 93 00), 8km from Bilbao. To reach the airport take the **Bizkai Bus** (☎944 48 40 80) marked **Aeropuerto** from P. Moyua, in front of the building Hacienda (40min., M-F every 30 min. 6am-10pm, 145ptas/€0.87; Sa-Su every hr. 6am-10pm, 150ptas/€0.90). Buses return from the airport to Pl. Moyua (M-F 6:45am-10:45pm, Sa-Su 6:30am-10:30pm). **Taxis** about 2500ptas/€15. **Iberia**, C. Ercilla, 20 (info ☎902 400 500). Open daily M-F 9:30am-1:30pm and 3-6pm.

Trains: Bilbao has 3 train stations.

RENFE: Estación de Abando del Norte, Pl. Circular, 2 (☎944 23 86 23). From Pl. Circular, head right around the station and cross the Puente del Arenal to reach Pl. Arriage, the entrance to the casco *viejo*. Info open 7am-9pm. To: **Barcelona** (9½-11hr., 10am and 10:45pm, 5000-5200ptas/€30-31); **Madrid** (5¾-9hr.; Su-F 4:30pm and 11:05pm, Sa 9:50am; 4600-5800ptas/€28-35); **Salamanca** (5½-6½hr., 9:25am and 2:05pm, 3700ptas/€22).

FEVE: Estación de Santander, C. Bailén, 2 (☎944 23 22 66). From Pl. Circular, walk down C. Navarra toward the river and take a right before the bridge; it's the gilded building on the water. Info open M-F Jun.-Sept. 15 9am-2pm and 4-7pm; Sept16-May 7am-10pm. To: **Santander** (2½hr.; 9:35am, 1:35pm, and 6:35pm; 950ptas/€5.71).

Ferrocarriles Vascongados/Eusko Trenbideak (FV/ET): Atxuri Station, Cl. Atxuri, 8 (☎902 54 32 10). Follow the river south from Pl. Arriaga. To: **Guernica** (1hr.; every 30min. M-F 6:18am-10:18pm, Sa-Su 7:48am-10:18pm, 325ptas/€1.95). The train's ultimate destination is **San Sebastián** but it takes forever (2hr. 40min. versus 1 hr. in bus, 900ptas/€5.41).

Buses: The following companies are based at the **Termibús terminal,** C. Gurtubay, 1, (☎944 39 52 05; M: San Mamés) on the west side of town. To get to Pl. Arriaga from the Termibús station, take the metro to Casco Viejo, exiting at Pl. Unamuno. Take a right on C. Sombrería and the first right onto C. Correo.

ANSA (GETSA, Viacarsa): (☎944 27 42 00). To: **Burgos** (2hr., 4 per day 8:30am-7pm, 1540ptas/€9.25): **Madrid** (4-5hr.; M-F 10-17 per day 7am-1:30am, Sa-Su 8am-1:30am; 3480ptas/€21).

ENATCAR: (☎944 39 50 48). To: León (7hr., M-Sa 8:45am, 3015ptas/€18); **Salamanca** (5hr.; M-Sa 3 per day 8:30-9:15am, Su 5:30pm; 3270ptas/€20).

PESA: (☎944 24 88 99; info 902 10 12 10). To: **San Sebastián** (1¼hr.; M-F every hr. 6am-10:30pm, Sa every hr. 9am-8pm, 8:30 and 10:30pm, Su every hr. 9am-1pm, 3pm-8pm, and 8:30-10:30pm; 1200ptas/€7.21).

La Unión: (☎944 39 50 77). To: **Haro** (1hr., 3-5 per day 8:30am-7:30pm, 1120ptas/€6.73); **Logroño** (1¾hr., 3-5 per day 8:30am-7:30pm, 1575ptas/€9.47); **Pamplona** (2hr., July-Aug. 4-6 per day, M-Sa 7:30am-8pm, Su 10am-8pm; Sept.-June M-Th and Sa 7:30am-7pm, F 7:30am-8pm, Su 10am-8pm; 1580ptas/€9.50); **Vitoria-Gasteiz** (1hr.; 11-22 per day M-Th 6:45-9pm, F 6:45am-10pm, Sa 7:30am-10pm, Su 8:30am-9:30pm; 675ptas/€4.06).

ALSA Grupo: T (info ☎902 42 22 42). To: Barcelona (7¼hr.; June 30-Sept. 17 4 per day 6:30am-11pm;Sept. 18-June 29 3-4 per day M-F 6:30am-11pm, Sa-Su 10:30am-11pm; 5375ptas/€33); **La Coruña** (5½hr., 10am and 1:45am, 5975ptas/€36); **Santander** (1¼hr, 27 per day 6:15am-11pm, 900ptas/€5.41); **Zaragoza** (4hr., 4-9 per day M-Th and Sa 6:30am-8:15pm, F 6:30am-9pm, Su 6:30am-9pm; 2630ptas/€16).

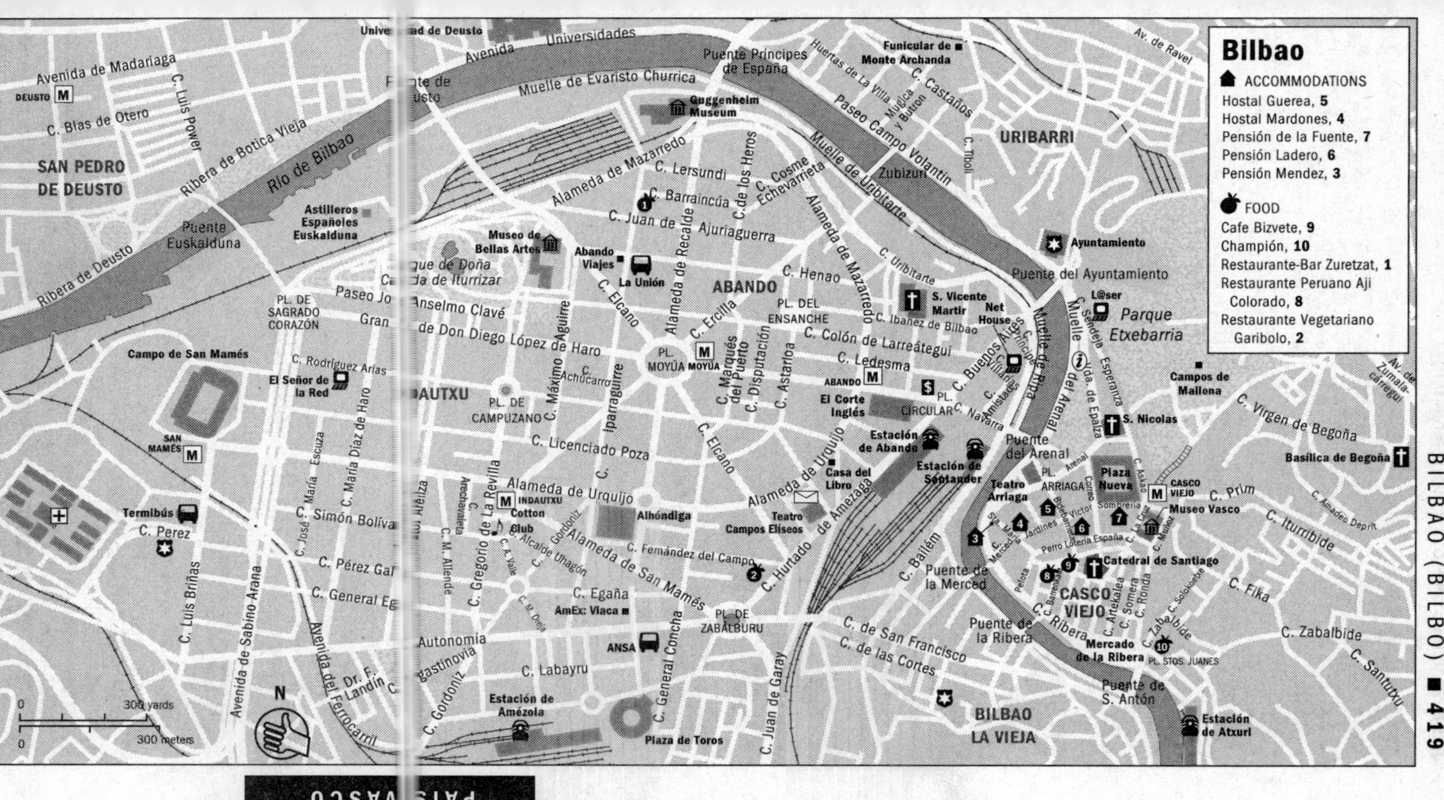
Bilbao
ACCOMMODATIONS
Hostal Guerea, 5
Hostal Mardones, 4
Pensión de la Fuente, 7
Pensión Ladero, 6
Pensión Mendez, 3
FOOD
Cafe Bizvete, 9
Champión, 10
Restaurante-Bar Zuretzat, 1
Restaurante Peruano Aji Colorado, 8
Restaurante Vegetariano Garibolo, 2
CASCO VIEJO
ABANDO
URIBARRI
BILBAO LA VIEJA
SAN PEDRO DE DEUSTO
Guggenheim Museum
Museo de Bellas Artes
Ayuntamiento
Catedral de Santiago
Museo Vasco
Mercado de la Ribera
Estación de Abando
Estación de Santander
Estación de Atxuri
Estación de Amézola
Teatro Arriaga
Teatro Campos Elíseos
Plaza de Toros
Campo de San Mamés
Basílica de Begoña
Funicular de Monte Archanda
Parque Etxebarria
Plaza Nueva
El Corte Inglés
Casa del Libro
Alhóndiga
Termibús
Puente de Deusto
Puente Euskalduna
Ría de Bilbao
Alameda de Mazarredo
Alameda de Recalde
Alameda de Urquijo
Alameda de San Mamés
Gran Vía de Don Diego López de Haro
Avenida de Sabino Arana
Avenida del Ferrocarril
Muelle de Ripa
Muelle del Arenal
Paseo Campo Volantín
Puente del Ayuntamiento
Puente de la Merced
Puente de San Antón
Puente de la Ribera
Puente de San Francisco
C. de San Francisco
C. de las Cortes
C. Hurtado de Amézaga
C. Juan de Garay
C. General Concha
C. Elcano
C. Ercilla
C. Colón de Larreátegui
C. Ledesma
C. Henao
C. Iturribide
C. Zabalbide
C. Santutxu
C. Virgen de Begoña
Avenida de Madariaga
C. Luis Power
C. Luis Briñas
N
300 yards
300 meters

Public Transportation: Bilbao recently opened a **metro** (☎944 25 40 25; www.metrobilbao.net) that has 1 line. Look for 3 interlocking red circles to find entrances, and hang onto your ticket after entering–you'll need it again to exit. Travel within 1 zone 150ptas/€0.90, 2 zones 175ptas/€1.05, 3 zones 200ptas/€1.20. 10-trip ticket within 1 zone 900ptas/€5.41, 2 zones 1050ptas/€6.31, 3 zones 1250ptas/€7.51. Trains run Su-Th 6am-11pm, Jul.-Aug. F-Sa 6am-11pm and every 30min. 11pm-6am. **Bilbobús** (☎944 48 40 80) runs 23 lines across the city (6am-11:30pm; M-F 135ptas/€0.81, Sa-Su 150ptas/€0.90). **Bizkai Bus** (☎944 54 05 44) connects Bilbao to suburbs and the airport. You can also buy a **transport uni-pass** in 1000ptas/€6, 1500ptas/€9, and 2000ptas/€12 denominations that can be used in Bilbobus, Bizkaibus, the metro, and the funicular. Using the card you get 20% off (except Bilbobus) rides that are less than an hour. Available at metro ticket machines, ONCE booths, and most kiosks.

Taxis: Teletaxi (☎944 10 21 21). **Radio Taxi Bilbao** (☎944 44 88 88).

Car Rental: Europcar, C. Licenciado Poza, 56 (☎944 42 22 26). Min. age 21 with passport and valid driver's license. Open M-F 8am-1pm and 4-7:30pm, Sa 9am-1pm. They also have an **airport location** (☎944 71 01 33). Open daily 7am-11:30pm.

ORIENTATION AND PRACTICAL INFORMATION

It's wise to get a map, as Bilbao's sights are all over the place. The city's main artery, **Gran Vía,** leads east from the oval Pl. Federico Moyúa to **Pl. Circular** (also known as Pl. Espana), the axis for many important stops and stations. Past Pl. Circular, you will cross Ría de Bilbao on Puente del Arenal, which deposits you on **Pl. de Arriaga,** the entrance to the *casco viejo* to the right of the tourist office.

Tourist Office: Oficina de Turismo de Bilbao, Pl. Arenal (☎944 79 57 60; fax 79 57 61; www.bilbao.net). Look for the big yellow "i" along the river. English spoken. Open M-F 9am-2pm and 4-7:30pm, Sa 9am-2pm, Su 10am-2pm.

Currency Exchange: Banco Central Hispano, Pl. Circular. 24hr. **ATM.** Open May-Sept M-F 8:30am-2pm, Oct.-April M-F 8:30am-2pm, Sa 8:30am-1pm.

Luggage Storage: At **Estación de Abando,** lockers 500ptas/€3. In **Termibús,** 100ptas/€0.60 per day. Both open daily 7:30am-11pm.

El Corte Inglés: Gran Vía, 7-9 (☎944 24 22 11), on the east side of Pl. Circular. Supermarket, haircuts, guidebooks, and **currency exchange.** Open M-Sa 10am-9pm.

English Bookstores: Casa del Libro, C. Urkijo, 9 (☎94 415 32 00). A terrific selection of books in English. Open M-Sa 9:30am-9pm. AmEx/MC/V.

Emergency: ☎112. **Police: Municipal,** C. Luis Briñas, 14 (☎944 20 50 00).

Medical Services: Hospital Civil de Basurto, Av. Montevideo, 18 (☎944 00 60 00).

Internet Access: El Señor de la Red, C. Rodríguez Arias, 69 (☎944 277 773). Take Gran Vía from the *casco viejo,* turn left on C. María Díaz de Haro and take your 1st right. 200ptas/€1.20 per 30min., 350ptas/€2.10 per hr. Open every day 10am-10pm. **L@Ser**, C. Sendaja, 5. If you are standing with your back to the tourist office take a left, located about a block up on the right. English-speaking owner. 150ptas/€0.90 per 15min., 250ptas/€1.50 per 30min., and 400ptas/€2.40 per hour. Also sells **phone cards**, 2000ptas/€12 per 160min. to U.S. (☎944 45 35 09. Open Su-Th 10:30am-11pm and F-Sa 10:30am-12:30am.)

Post Office: Main office, Alameda Urquijo, 19 (☎94 444 10 04; fax 443 00 24). Walk 1 block down Gran Vía from Pl. España and turn left after El Corte Inglés. Open M-F 8am-8:30pm, Sa 8am-2pm. **Postal Code:** 48008.

ACCOMMODATIONS

At any time other than during the August festivals (when rates can be higher than those listed below), it shouldn't be hard to find a reasonably priced room if you arrive before noon. **Pl. Arriaga** and **C. Arenal** have budget accommodations galore.

Albergue Bilbao Aterpetxez (HI), Ctra. Basurto-Kastrexana Errep., 70. (☎944 27 00 54; fax 27 54 79) Take bus #58 route from Pl. Circular. July-Sept. singles 2600ptas/€16, over 25 2800ptas/€17; bed in a double or triple 2400ptas/€15, over 25 2600ptas/€16. Oct.-June 200ptas/€1.20 cheaper. MC/V.

Pensión Méndez, C. Santa María, 13, 4th fl. (☎944 16 03 64). From the bridge Arenal, take C. Bidebbarrieta, after 2 blocks go right onto C. Perro; When you reach C. Santa María, turn right. Many rooms have sinks and balconies. Common baths. Singles 3000-4000ptas/€18-24, doubles 5000ptas/€30, triples 7500ptas/€45.

Pensión Ladero, C. Lotería, 1, 4th fl. (☎94 415 09 32). From the bridge Arenal, take C. Correo, take a right after 3 blocks onto C. Lotería. Modern common baths, and rooms with TVs and winter heating. Singles 3000ptas/€18; doubles 4500ptas/€27.

Hostal Mardones, C. Jardines, 4, 3rd fl. (☎94 415 31 05). From the bridge, take C. Bidebarrieta, then take the first right onto C. Jardines, hostel is on left towards the end. Some rooms with balconies, all with marble sinks. Singles 4000ptas/€24, with bath 5000ptas/€30; double with one bed 5000ptas/€30, two beds 6500ptas/€39, with bath 6000-7500ptas/€36-45; triples with bath 10,000ptas/€60.

Pensión de la Fuente, C. Sombrería, 2 (☎94 416 99 89). From the bridge Arenal, turn right on C. Correo, follow it 2 blocks past Pl. Nueva, and then turn left. Heating and TV 500ptas/€3. Singles 2500ptas/€15; doubles 4000-4500ptas/€24-27, with bath 5500ptas/€33.

Hostal Gurea, C. Bidebarrieta, 14 (☎94 416 32 99), from the bridge Arenal take the street to the right of Café Boulevard into the old city, 2 blocks down on right. Several rooms have sinks, some with balconies. Upstairs rooms can get stifling hot in the summer. TV lounge. Strict 1am curfew on weeknights. Singles 3300ptas/€20, with bath 3600-4000ptas/€22-24; doubles 4300ptas/€26, with bath 5000ptas/€30. MC/V.

FOOD

Restaurants and bars in the *casco viejo* offer a wide selection of local dishes, as well as *pintxos* and *bocadillos* aplenty. The new city has more variety but less ambiance. **Mercado de la Ribera,** on the bank of the river, is the biggest indoor **market** in Spain; it's worth a trip even if you're not eating (open M-Th and Sa 8am-2:30pm and Fr 8am-2:30pm and 4:30-7:30). Pick up **groceries** at **Champión,** Pl. Santos Juanes, just past the Mercado de la Ribera. (Open M-Sa 9:15am-9:15pm. MC/V.)

Restaurante Vegetariano Garibolo, C. Fernández del Campo, 7, (☎944 22 32 55). Right off C. Hurtado de Amézaga, about 5 blocks from the Estación de Abando. Delicious and creative *menú* (1300ptas/€7.81). Open M-Sa 1-4pm. MC/ V.

Restaurante Peruano Ají Colorado, C. Barrencalle, 5 (☎944 15 22 09), in the *casco viejo.* Specializes in *ceviche* (marinated raw fish salad; 1400-1730ptas [illegible] [illegible], bread, wine, and dessert (2000ptas/€12). Open Tu-Sa 1:30-3:30pm and 9-11:30pm, Su 1:30-3:30pm. MC/V.

Restaurante Bar Zuretzat, C. Iparraguirre, 7 (☎94 424 85 05), near the Guggenheim. High-quality seafood. Don't miss the incredibly sweet cinnamon rice pudding (500ptas/€3). Open daily 1-5pm. MC/V.

Café BiZVETE, Pl. Santiago, 6 (☎94 416 29 45). In the peaceful courtyard of the Catedral de Santiago. Sandwiches 325-600ptas/€1.95-3.60, entrées 590-925/€3.55-556. 10% extra for outside dining but well worth it. Open M-Sa 8am-9pm.

SIGHTS

THE GUGGENHEIM. Frank O. Gehry's Guggenheim Museum Bilbao can only be described as breathtaking. Lauded in the international press with every superlative imaginable, it has catapulted Bilbao straight into cultural stardom. Visitors are greeted by Jeff Koons' "Puppy," a dog composed of 60,000 plants and

PAÍS VASCO

standing almost as tall as the museum. The main attraction are the undulating segments of the building, sheathed in titanium, limestone, and glass. The US$100 million building is said to resemble an iridescent scaly fish or a blossoming flower. The amazingly light, dramatically spacious interior features a towering atrium and a series of non-traditional exhibition spaces, including a colossal 130m by 30m hall. Don't be surprised if you are asked to take your shoes off, lie on the floor, walk through mazes or even sing throughout your visit to the various eccentric exhibits. The museum currently hosts rotating exhibits drawn from the Guggenheim Foundation's collection. Sleek black-and-red suited staff slap bracelets on the streams of visitors filing through the door—may you enjoy your stay. *(Av. Abandoibarra, 2. ☎944 35 90 00; www.guggenheim.bilbao.es. Open daily July-Aug. 9am-9pm; Sept.-June Tu-Su 10am-8pm. Students 1200ptas/€7.21 and seniors 600ptas/€3.61, under 12 free. Handicap accessible. Audio tour 600ptas/€3.61. Guided tours in English Tu-F 11am, 12:30, 4:30, and 6:30pm, Sa-Su 1 and 4pm tours are sometimes canceled so you may want to call ahead to confirm. Sign up 30min. before tour at the info desk.)*

MUSEO DE BELLAS ARTES. Often overshadowed by its popular big sister, the Museo de Bellas Artes hoards aesthetic riches behind an unassuming façade. An impressive collection of 12th- to 20th-century art features excellent 15th- to 17th-century Flemish paintings, works by El Greco, Zurbarán, Goya, Gauguin, Francis Bacon, Velázquez, Picasso, and Mary Cassatt, as well as canvases by Basque painters. *(Pl. Museo, 2. Take C. Elcano to Pl. Museo, or take bus #10 from Puente del Arenal. ☎94 439 60 60. Guided visits ☎944 59 61 41. Open Tu-Sa 10am-8pm, Su 10am-2pm. 600ptas/€3.61, seniors and students 300ptas/€1.80, under 10 free. Free entrance on Wed.)*

MUSEO VASCO. Dip into Basque culture and history at the Museo Vasco, in the old city. Housed in a 17th-century building with a beautiful cloister, its exhibits cover a variety of topics, including weaving, blacksmiths, pastoral life, and the sea. *(Pl. Miguel de Unamuno, 4. From the bridge Arenal take C. Correo, to the left of Café Boulevard, for 2 blocks, turn left onto C. Sombrería, following it to the end; museum is on the right side of the plaza. ☎944 15 54 23. Open Tu-Su 11am-5pm and often in the evening from 5-8pm. 400ptas/€2.40, students 200ptas/€1.20, seniors and under 12 free. Th free.)*

OTHER SIGHTS. The best view of Bilbao's surrounding landscape and the perfect place for a picnic is at the top of **Monte Archanda,** north of the old town and equidistant from both the *casco viejo* and the Guggenheim. *(Funicular to the top every 15min.; M-F 7:15am-10pm, Sa-Su 8:15am-10pm, Jul.-Aug. until 11pm on the weekends; 125ptas/€0.75. Handicap accessible. Turn left from Pl. Arenal with your back to the new town and follow the riverside road past the Ayuntamiento. On Po. Campo de Volantín, turn right on C. Mugica Y Butrón and continue until Pl. Funicular.)* A short Metro ride to the north leads to various **beaches**, including **Plencia (Plentzia)**, **Getxo**, and **Sopelana** along the way. Along with Sopelana, Getxo attracts a surfer crowd and lies just a little nearer to the Bay of Biscay; its illuminated **Puente Colgante** (a suspension bridge constructed over 100 years ago) fords the river, leading to a plethora of all-night bars.

ENTERTAINMENT AND NIGHTLIFE

Bilbao has a thriving bar scene. In the *casco viejo* revelers spill out into the streets to sip their *txikitos* (chee-KEE-tos; small glasses of wine), especially on C. Barrencalle (Barrenkale), one of the original "seven streets" from which the city of Bilbao has grown. Teenagers and 20-somethings jam into C. Licenciado Poza on the west side of town. The **Cotton Club**, C. Gregorio de la Revilla, 25 (entrance on C. Simón Bolívar), decorated with over 30,000 beer caps, draws a huge crowd on Friday and Saturday nights while the rest of the week is a little more low-key. DJ W & Th (11pm) and F & Sa (1pm). Over 100 choices of whiskey (800ptas/€4.81). Beers 325-450ptas/€1.95-2.70. (☎94 410 49 51; Open M-Th 4:30pm- 3am, F 4:30pm-6am, Sa 6:30pm-6am, and Su 6:30pm-3am. Cash only.) For a mellower scene, munch on *pintxos* (150-200ptas/€0.90-1.20) and people-watch at Bilbao's oldest coffee shop (est. 1871), **Café Boulevard,** C. Arenal, 3. Or put on your dancing shoes and get ready to tango (Fridays at 11pm). This art-deco café was once an important site for literary meetings and one of Miguel de Unamuno's favorite haunts. (☎94 415 31 28. Open M-Th 7:30am-11:30pm, F-Sa 8am-3am, Su 11am-11:30pm. MC/V.)

The massive blow-out fiesta in honor of *Nuestra Señora de Begoña* takes place during **Semana Grande,** a nine-day party beginning the Saturday after August 15 with fireworks, concerts, theater—you name it. Ask the tourist office for a schedule of events (☎944 79 57 60). Documentary filmmakers from the world over gather for a week in October or November for the **Festival Internacional de Cine Documental de Bilbao.** During the summer, there are free **concerts** every Sunday morning at the bandstand in the Parque Arenal. For current goings-on, pick up a *Bilbao Guide* from the tourist office.

GUERNICA (GERNIKA) ☎946

On April 26, 1937, the Nazi "Condor Legion" released an estimated 29,000kg of explosives on Guernica (pop. 15,600), obliterating 70% of the city in three hours. The tragedy marked the first mass civilian aerial bombing attack, and the nearly 2000 people who were killed have been immortalized in Pablo Picasso's stark masterpiece *Guernica,* which now hangs in Madrid's Reina Sofía gallery (see **The Tragedy of Guernica,** p. 424). The small, reconstructed city is not much of an attraction in itself, but for those interested in learning more about Basque history and the infamous event that occurred here, Guernica is a rewarding daytrip.

PRACTICAL INFORMATION. **Trains** (☎902 543 210; www.euskotren.es) connect Guernica to **Bilbao** (45min., every 30min. M-F 6:15am-10:15pm (except 9:45pm); Sa-Su every 30 min. 8:15am-10:15pm (except 8:45am), 325ptas/€1.95). **Bizkai Bus** (☎902 222 265) sends more convenient, and more frequent, **buses** between Guernica and **Bilbao's Estación Abando** (55min., M-F every 30min. 6:15am-9:45pm, 315ptas/€1.90). To reach Guernica's English and French-speaking **tourist office,** C. Artekalea, 8, from the train station, walk three blocks up C. Adolfo Urioste and turn right on C. Artekalea. At the first crosswalk on the road, take a right into the alleyway and the office will be on your right. (☎946 25 58 92; fax 25 32 12; www.gernika-lumo.net. Open July-Sept. M-Sa 9:30am-7:30pm, Su 10:am-2:30pm; Oct.-June M-F 10am-1:30pm and 4-7pm, Sa 11am-1:30pm) The **post office,** C. Iparragirre, 26, is immediately to the left as you exit the train station. (☎946 25 03 87. Open M-F 8:30am-2:30pm, Sa 9:30am-1pm.). The **postal code** is 48300.

ACCOMMODATIONS AND FOOD. Although Guernica's main attractions can be seen in a daytrip from Bilbao, **Akelarre Ostatua Pensión,** C. Barrenkale, 5, offers a delightful place to stay. From the train station walk 2 blocks up C. Adolfo Urioste and take a right onto C. Barrenkale. (☎946 27 01 79; fax 27 06 75; akelarre@akelarre.euskalnet.net. Semana Santa and July-Aug. [illegible] ptas/€[illegible], doubles with bath 6500ptas/€39. Aug. 21-Sept. and weekends year round singles 3500ptas/€21; doubles 4500ptas/€27; doubles with bath 5500ptas/€33. Weekdays year round singles 3000ptas/€18; doubles 4000ptas/€24; doubles with bath 5000ptas/€30. Prices go down by 500ptas/€3 with a stay of two nights or more. MC/V). To reach **Madariaga Ostatua**, C. Industria Kalea, 10, from the train station, walk up C. Urioste and take the first left onto C. Pablo Picasso which becomes C. Undustria. (☎946 25 60 35 or 95 625 60 39. Singles run 3000ptas/€18, doubles 6000ptas/€36. If you want a restaurant with a family feel, head to **Restaurante Zallo Barri,** C. Juan Calzada, 79. After exiting the train station, walk up C. Urioste and take the second left; look for a cream-colored awning and and marble front several blocks down on the left. This place dishes out a tasty M-F luncheon *menú* (1200ptas/€7.21) with several fish, meat, and dessert choices. (☎946 25 18 00. Open daily 8:30am-11pm; *menú* offered 1-3:30pm only. AmEx/MC/V.) Another excellent dining choice is **Restaurante Boliña**, conveniently located on C. Barrenkale, 3, on the left just before Akelarre Ostatua Pensión. This classy bar/restaurant with dark woods and mellow yellow walls draws in a large local crowd.

THE TRAGEDY OF GUERNICA Founded on April 28, 1366, Guernica was virtually erased from the map on April 26, 1937. It was a Monday market day when the church bell rang three times to warn the small town of an aerial invasion. The German Condor Legion began to bomb the small town at 4:30pm and didn't stop until 7:45pm. Heavy bombs and hand grenades were first dropped from small planes in order to create a panic and a stampede. Next, low-flying planes machine-gunned those running on foot or hiding in the fields. These planes forced the townspeople into buildings, which were then wrecked and burned by 12 bombers. The entire main city was effectively demolished. Strangely, the Casa de Juntos and the oak tree were untouched, as was Franco's war-material factory a few kilometers down the road. Guernica was far behind the lines; the destruction was fueled solely by a desire to rob the anti-fascist Basque people of their desire to fight.

Many pictures, sketches, and paintings have attempted to capture this day. In a painting now at the Gernika Museoa, Sofía Gandarias depicted clocks stopped at 4:30, women holding dead children, and the words "*y del cielo lloría sangre*" (and the sky cried blood). But it was Pablo Picasso who brought the town's tragedy to international fame. The still-republican Spanish government had commissioned the artist to paint a mural for the Universal Exhibition in Paris in 1937, and he used the bombing for inspiration. In ten days he had 25 sketches; he finished the painting—his largest work—in only one month. When asked about the symbolism, Picasso answered, "The bull represents brutality and the horse represents the people." However, in regard to the painting as a whole, Picasso replied, "Let them interpret as they wish." Picasso was even approached by a German ambassador who asked of the painting, "Did you do this?" Picasso answered, "No, you did."

Friendly waitstaff and large portions of delicious foods make for a delightful lunch menú (☎946 25 03 00. Lunch *menú* M-F 1-3:30pm 1300ptas/€7.81. Wide assortment of pintxos 175-200ptas/€1.05-1.20. Open daily 8am-1:30am. MC/V.

SIGHTS. The emotional focus of Guernica is **El Arbol.** Encased in stone columns, the 300-year-old "Old Tree" (an oak) marks the old political center of the País Vasco, the place where medieval Basques gathered to debate community issues and Castilian monarchs ritually swore their respect for the autonomy of the local government. Next to the oldest tree grows an oak that was planted in 1860, and next to that, a "sapling" only 30 years old. The **Casa de Juntos,** next to the trees, is the meeting place of the Vizkaya (Basque) General Assembly. (☎946 25 11 38. Open daily June-Sept. 10am-2pm and 4-7pm; Oct.-May 10am-2pm and 4-6pm.-Free.) There are two sights worth seeing in Guernica's **Parque de los Pueblos de Europa.** Edu ardo Chillida's dramatic sculpture **Gure aitaren etxea** (Our Father's House), a peace monument, was commissioned for the 50th anniversary of the city's bombing, and it stands alongside Henry Moore's voluptuous 1986 **Large Figure in a Shelter,** which suggests a female form and symbolizes rebirth. To get to the park from the bus station, follow C. Adolfo Urioste as far as it goes. At the top follow the arrow to the right and enter the park on the corner. (Open daily June-Aug. 10am-9pm; Sept.-May 10am-7pm. Free.) The modest **Museo de la Paz de Gernika,** Foru Plaza, 1, just across the main street, C. Artekalea, from the tourist office, has an informative exhibition chronicling the bombardment in several languages. (☎946 27 02 13. Guided tours in English. Open daily June16-Aug. M-Sa 10am-7pm, Su 10am-2pm; Sept.-June15 M-Sa 10am-2pm and 4-7pm, Su 10am-2pm. While the Gernika Museum is undergoing renovations admission is free and only the basement exhibit is open, reopening is expected in Jan 2002.) Paintings and artifacts on display inside the **Museo de Euskal Herria,** C. Allende Salazar, 5, document Basque history. (☎946 25 54 51. Guided tours in English. Tu-Sa 10am-2pm and 4-7pm, Su 10am-1:30pm. Free.) The city also holds a **fiesta** on the first Saturday of every summer month (Jun.-Oct.). The tourist office offers a **historic tour** of the city's principal attractions; July-Sept M-Sa at 11am (500ptas/€3); during the rest of the year call ahead and the office will gladly arrange one (minimum of two people).

VITORIA-GASTEIZ ☎945

Vitoria-Gasteiz (pop. 220,000) is an attractive, up-and-coming city. Packed with avenues and parks, it has the highest ratio of greenery to people in all of Spain, as well as a charm that belies its status as a sleek cosmopolitan center. The city's hyphenated name testifies to its regional loyalty: renamed Villa de Nueva Vitoria by the King of Navarra in 1181, the Basques re-incorporated the city's original name upon recovering regional autonomy in 1979. Vitoria-Gasteiz should not be a priority destination, but with plenty of hiking and biking in the area, it is definitely a worthwhile place to visit for those spending some time in the País Vasco.

TRANSPORTATION

Flights: Aeropuerto Vitoria-Foronda (☎945 16 35 00), 9km out of town. Accessible only by car or taxi (about 2000ptas/€12). Info open M-F 8am-2:15pm. **Iberia** (☎945 16 37 38). Info open 6am-12am.

Trains: RENFE Pl. Estación, (☎902 24 02 02). From the center of the city follow C. Eduardo Dato, off C. Postas, to the very end, walking away from the old city. Info open 7:30am-10:30pm. To: **Barcelona** (8-14½hr., 4 per day 10:40am-12:33am, 4700ptas/€29); **Burgos** (1½hr., 2-4 per day M-Sa 7:30am-6:05pm, Su 1:40pm & 6:05pm, 1180ptas/€7.10);**Madrid** (4½-7hr., 8-9 per day M-F 7:30am-12:33am, Su 10:08am-12:33am, 4300ptas/€26);**Pamplona** (1hr., 2-3 per day M-Sa 7:50am, 3:25, 7pm, Su 3:25 and 7pm, 605ptas/€3.64); **San Sebastián** (2hr., 3 per day 9:28am, 2:17, 6:50pm, 1205ptas/€7.24); and **Zaragoza** (3hr., change in Pamplona, 2-3 per day 7:50am, 3:25pm and 7pm, Su 3:25pm and 7pm, 2385ptas/€14.33).

Buses: C. Herrán, 50, on a traffic island east of the old city. General info (☎945 25 84 00) open M-F 8am-8pm, Sa-Su 9am-7pm. **ALSA** (☎945 25 55 09; www.alsa.es; MC/V.) goes to **Barcelona** (6 1/2-7hr. 2-3 per day M-Th 7:30am & 3:45pm, F-Su 7:30m, 3:45pm & 11:15pm, 4830ptas/€29) and **Pamplona** (1½hr.; 6-11 per day M-Sa 7am-8:30pm, Su 9am-9pm; 960ptas/€5.77). **La Unión** (☎945 26 46 26) goes to **Bilbao** (1hr.; 12-21 per day M-Th 6:30am-9pm, F 6:30am-10pm, Sa 7:30am-10pm, Su 8:30am-9:30pm; 725ptas/€4.36). **Continental Auto** (☎945 28 64 66) to: **Burgos** (1½hr.; 7-9 per day M-Sa 6:45am-10:15pm and 2:05am, Su 10:45am-10pm and 2:02am; 965-1575ptas/€5.80-9.47); **Madrid** (4½-5hr.; 9-10 per day M-Sa 6:45am-8:30pm & 2:05am, Su 8:45am-10pm & 2:05pm; 3010-4440ptas/€18-27); and **San Sebastián** (1½hr., 8-10 per day 5am-11:30pm, F & Su at 1:30am as well, 1050ptas/€6.31). **Turytrans** (☎902 42 22 42) to **Zaragoza** (3hr. 5-7 per day M-Th & Sa 7:30am-9:15pm, F & Su 7:30am-10pm; 2150ptas/€27).

[illegible] Tuvisa Buses (☎945 [illegible]) cover the metropolitan area and suburbs (7am-10pm, 100ptas/€0.60); the main bus stops are on C. Monseñor Cadenay Eleta (in front of the new cathedral) and C. La Paz (in front of El Corte Inglés). Bus #2 goes from the bus station to C. Florida but it is probably easier to walk.

Taxis: Radio-Taxi (☎945 27 35 00). 24hr. service to Vitoria and surrounding areas.

Car Rental: Europcar, Adriano VI, 29 (☎945 20 04 33). Minimum age 21. Open 9am-1pm and 4-7:30pm, Sa 9am-1pm. There is also an airport office open M-F 1:30-2:45pm.

PAÍS VASCO

ORIENTATION AND PRACTICAL INFORMATION

The medieval **casco viejo** (old city) is the almond-shaped center of Vitoria-Gasteiz. At its base, **Plaza de la Virgen Blanca** marks the center of town. From the **train station,** follow C. Eduardo Dato to its end, turn left on C. Postas, and head straight to the plaza. Buses run from a glass building on C. Herrán, between C. Prudencio María Verástegui and C. Arana. To get to the center of town from the bus station, turn left on C. Herrán (with your back to the station), then make an immediate

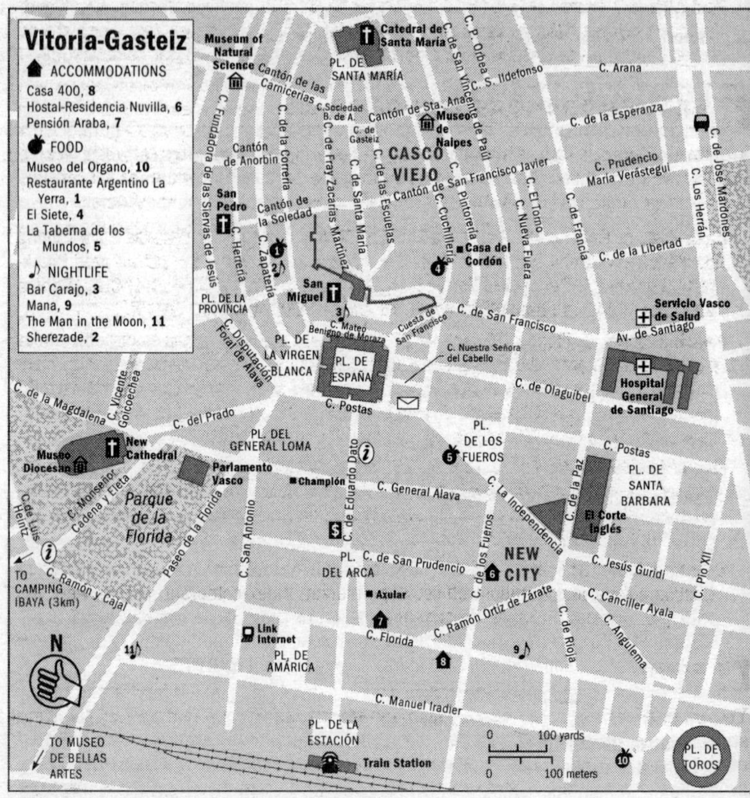

right onto C. Verástegui. Follow C. Verástegui to its end and turn left on C. Francia. Follow C. Francia for four blocks as it becomes C. Paz and turn right onto C. Postas, which leads straight to Pl. Virgen Blanca.

Tourist Office: Regional Tourist Office: Parque de la Florida (☎945 13 13 21; fax 13 02 93), on the corner with C. Monseñor Cadena. From the train station, follow C. Eduardo Dato and take the 2nd left onto C. Florida. From the bus station, head toward Pl. Virgen Blanca, but follow C. Paz 2 blocks past C. Postas to C. Ortiz de Zárate on the right, which leads to C. Florida. Open daily 9am-1pm and 3-7pm.

Currency Exchange: Banco Central Hispano, C. Eduardo Dato, 26, at the intersection with C. San Prudencio. Open M-F 8:30am-2pm, Oct.-Apr. also Sa 8:30am-1pm.

Luggage storage: At the **train station** (500ptas/€3 for a locker). Buy tokens from the ticket counter 6am-1am. At the **bus station.** 105ptas/€0.63 per piece the 1st day, 87ptas/€0.52 each additional day. Open M-Sa 8am-8pm, Su 9am-7pm.

El Corte Inglés: on the corner of C. Paz and C. Independencia (☎ 945 26 63 33), 1 block past C. Postas coming from bus station. Supermarket. Open M-Sa 10am-10pm.

Emergency: ☎112. **Police:** ☎091 or 092. C. Aguirrelande, 8.

Medical Services: Hospital General de Santiago C. Olaguíbel, 29. (☎945 00 76 00). From the bus station, go left 1 block after C. Francia becomes C. Paz. **Osakidetza Servico Vasco de Salud**, Av. Santiago, 7 (☎945 24 44 44), off C. Paz. Open M-F 5pm-12am, Sa 2pm-12am and Su 9am-12am. Medical attention is free; passport required.

Internet Access: Link Internet, C. San Antonio, 31 (☎945 13 04 84). Head down C. Florida toward the park and turn left on C. San Antonio. English-speaking staff. 110ptas/€0.66 for 24min., 275ptas/€1.65 per hr.

Post Office: C. Postas, 9 (☎945 15 46 92; fax 23 37 80), on the pedestrian street leading to Pl. Virgen Blanca. Open M-F 8:30am-8:30pm, Sa 9:30am-2pm. For Lista de Correos, walk to the C. Señora del Cabello side of the building. **Postal Code:** 01008.

ACCOMMODATIONS AND CAMPING

Vitoria-Gasteiz has only a handful of cheap hostels, although slightly more deluxe hostels abound. If you plan to drop in during the Jazz fest (third week of July) or the *Fiestas de la Virgen Blanca* (Aug. 4-9), make reservations in advance.

Casa 400, C. Florida, 46, 3rd fl. (☎945 23 38 87), right off C. Eduardo Dato coming from the train station. Much of it is used as college dorms during the school year. Breakfast 500ptas/€3. Reception 7am-11pm. No curfew. Singles 3000ptas/€18; doubles 4000ptas/€24, with bath 6000ptas/€36; triples 7000ptas/€42. MC/V.

Pensión Araba, C. Florida, 25 (☎945 23 25 88). On the road to the tourist office from the bus station; from the train station, turn right onto C. Florida. Attractive rooms have sinks and TV (some with VCRs). Elevator and parking garage (parking 1000ptas/€6 per night). Singles 3500ptas/€21, with bath 4500ptas/€27; doubles 4500ptas/€27, with bath 5500ptas/€33; triples 6600ptas/€40, with bath 7100ptas/€43.

Hostal-Residencia Nuvilla, C. Fueros, 29, 3rd fl. (☎945 25 91 51). From the bus station, on C. Herrán, follow directions to Pl. Virgen Blanca (see **Orientation,** p. 425) but take the 1st left off C. Postas. Common baths. All have balconies and marble sinks. Singles 3150-3500ptas/€19-21; doubles 4400ptas/€27; triples 6000ptas/€36.

Camping Ibaya (☎945 14 76 20), 3km from town toward Madrid. Follow Portal de Castilla west from the tourist office. Supermarket, cafe/restaurant, hot showers and laundry. 550ptas/€3.31 per person, per tent, and per car. Open year-round; MC/V.

FOOD

You can't go wrong in the *casco viejo* and the surrounding streets. From the train station, take C. Eduardo Dato, turn right on C. Postas, then turn left past the post office and go uphill, where C. Cuchillería radiates from C. San Francisco. There are *pintxos* galore in the streets around Pl. España. Fresh foods fill the **Mercado de Abastos,** on Pl. Santa Bárbara off C. Paz (open M-Th 9am-2pm and 5-8pm, F 9am-2pm and 5-8:30pm, Sa 8am-3pm). Buy groceries at **Champión,** C. General Alava, 10, between C. Eduardo Dato and C. San Antonio (open M-Sa 9:15am-9:15pm).

Museo del Organo, C. Manuel Iradier, 80 (☎945 26 40 48). Located on the right corner, just before the Pl. de Toros, on C. Maunel Iradier which runs parallel to C. Florida. A favorite among locals, with remarkably fresh, filling vegetarian cuisine at outstanding prices. M-F 4-course *menú* 1300ptas, Sa 1800ptas. Open M-Sa 1-3:30pm. MC/V.

[illegible] old quarter. Good beef entrées (1450-2850ptas/€9-18), and enticing pasta dishes (850-1100ptas/€5-7). M-F luncheon menú (1300ptas/€8). Open Su and Tu-W 1:30-4pm; Th-Sa 1:30-4pm and 9:30pm-midnight. MC/V.

La Taberna de Los Mundos, C. Independencia, 14. Serves excellent and affordable sandwiches (475-650ptas/€3-4). Entrées 1100-1500ptas/€7-9. Open M-W 9am-12am, Th 9am-1am, F 9am-2am, Sa 10:30am-2pm, and Su 12pm-12am.

El Siete, C. Cuchillería, 3 (☎945 27 22 98). Popular with locals in search of a traditional food and a lots of it. *Menú* 1250ptas/€8 (M-F 1-4pm). 20 varieties of sandwiches (400-600ptas/€2.40-3.60). Open Su-Th 10am-12:30am, F-Sa 10am-3am.

SIGHTS

The tree-lined pedestrian walkways of the new city and steep narrow streets of the *casco viejo* make for pleasant wanderings. **Plaza de la Virgen Blanca** is the focal point of the *casco viejo* and site of Vitoria-Gasteiz's *fiestas*. Beside Pl. Virgen

Blanca is the broad, arcaded **Plaza de España,** marking the division of the old town from the new. **Los Arquillos,** a series of arches that rise above Pl. España, were designed by architect Justo Antonio de Olaguíbel from 1787 to 1802 to connect the *casco viejo* with the rapidly growing new town below.

PALACIOS. Many of the old quarter's Renaissance *palacios* are open to the public as museums. The gorgeous **Palacio Augustín** houses the **Museo de Bellas Artes,** with a sculpture garden and works by Miró, El Greco, and Picasso. *(Po. Fray Francisco de Vitoria. Open Tu-F 10am-2pm and 4-6:30pm, Sa 10am-2pm, Su 11am-2pm. Free.)* The 15th-century **Casa del Cordón**—named after the stone *cordón* (rope) that runs its central arch—hosts changing exhibitions, many featuring student art. *(C. Cuchillería, 24. ☎ 945 25 96 73. Open M-Sa 6:30-9pm, Su noon-2pm and 6:30-9pm. Free.)*

CATHEDRALS. Construction of the Gothic **Catedral de Santa María** (also known as the Catedral Vieja, or Old Cathedral), at the top of the *casco viejo*, began in the 12th century; today it flaunts two especially expressive doors. *(Although it is closed for restoration, English tours of the restoration process and archaeological studies are offered Mar-Sept; ☎ 945 25 51 35 or check with the tourist office; 300ptas/€1.80 per person.)* The 20th-century neo-Gothic **New Cathedral** is in the new town. The apse hosts the **Diocesan Museum of Sacred Art,** a collection from Basque churches, including a canvas by El Greco. *(C. Monseñor Cadena y Eleta. Cathedral open M-Sa 11am-2pm. Free. Museum ☎ 945 15 06 31. Open Tu-F 10am-2pm and 4-6:30pm, Sa 10am-2pm, Su 11am-2pm.)*

ENTERTAINMENT AND NIGHTLIFE

For info on **theater** and special events, pick up the weekly *Kalea* (200ptas/€1.20) from tobacco stands or newsstands. World-class jazz grooves into Vitoria-Gasteiz in the second or third week of July for the week-long **Festival de Jazz de Vitoria-Gasteiz.** Tickets for big name performers cost 1500-4300ptas/€9-26, but there are plenty of free performances on the street. Call or visit the **Asociación Festival de Jazz de Vitoria,** C. Florida, 19, for specific concerts (☎ 945 14 19 19; www.jazzvitoria.com). On July 24-25, *Los Blusas* or "the blouses" hold their own festival with wine, music, and games. The blue (or sometimes black) shirts represent the old shepherds that used to live in Vitoria. Rockets launch the **Fiesta de la Virgen Blanca** (Aug.4-9) at 6pm on the 4th in, Pl. Virgen Blanca.

After nightfall, the *casco viejo* is the place to be. Bars line C. Cuchillería ("La Cuchi"), C. Herrería ("La Herre"), C. Zapatería ("La Zapa"), and C. San Francisco; check out **Bar Carajo,** C. Mateo Moraza, 11, for a no holds barred, all-out fiesta. Try a *marchacado* (slammer, 200ptas/€1.20). Beer 225ptas/€1.35. Open Jul.-Sept. Th-Sa 7pm-2am; during the winter it closes half hour earlier. Dancing types can head to **Mana,** C. Florida, 39. Music starts thumping at 1am, and it's packed with 20-somethings until 6am (cover 1000ptas/€6, includes 1 drink, Fridays and Saturdays only). For a pint of English Real Ale brewed on sight (500ptas/€3) try **The Man in the Moon**, C. Manual Iradier, 7, just in front of Iglesia Carmen. Catch the Thursday night jam session (starts around 10pm) or test your knowledge on Wednesdays at their weekly trivia quiz conducted in English. Not much Spanish spoken here (in fact, the locals come to practice their English) but it is a fun way to mingle with locals and travelers alike. (☎ 945 13 43 27. Open daily 8am-3am.) For more intimate socializing, **Sherezade,** C. Correría, 42, has created an atmospheric Moroccan tea room with small tables and embroidered cushions. Sip on a kiwi shake (300ptas/€1.80) or hot tea with fresh herbs blended to order (225ptas/€1.35) and let your creative juices flow—crayons and paper are provided. (☎ 945 25 58 68. Open Su-Th 3:30pm-11pm, F 3:30pm-midnight, Sa 3:30pm-1am (Jul.-Aug. opens daily at 6pm).

NORTHWESTERN SPAIN

ASTURIAS AND CANTABRIA

Jagged cliffs and precipitous ravines lend an epic scope to the tiny lands of Asturias and Cantabria, tucked between the País Vasco and Galicia. Though connected by location and landscape, Asturias and have distinct provincial personalities. With its world-class resort towns of Santander and Comillas, Cantabria appeals to Spain's vacationing elite. Inland Asturias instead draws hearty mountaineers looking to conquer the peaks of its national parks, including the Picos de Europa and the Parque Natural de Oyambre.

. Agricolar Moors had little use for the region's rough terrain, enabling the Christians to make the land their northern stronghold. The *Reconquista* officially began in the small Picos town of Covadonga, the only region never to fall to the Moors thanks to the impassable peaks of the Cordillera Cantábrica. Today, Spain's heir to the throne is titled the Príncipe de Asturias, in honor of the region's preservation of the 'true' Spain during Moorish invasions. During the Civil War this legendary spirit of defiance found outlet in the blue-collar resistance to the Fascists. Mountainous terrain has still limited the number of rail lines through the region, leaving lone roads to wind along its steep mountain sides and scalloped shores.

Asturias is famous for its apples, cheeses, wholesome fresh milk, and *arroz con leche* (rice pudding). *Sidra* (cider) and *fabada asturiana*, a hearty bean-and-sausage stew, grace menus everywhere. True Asturians can be recognized by the way they take their cider, poured from several feet above the glass and downed immediately. Cantabrian cuisine draws from the mountains and the sea, adding anchovies, tuna, and sardines to the mix. Local favorites include *cocido montanés* (bean stew) and *marmita* (tuna, potato, and green pepper stew).

ASTURIAS

Impenetrable peaks and dense alpine forests define the Asturian landscape as well as its history. Thanks to the foreboding mountains of the Picos de Europa, Asturias never fell to the bands of marauding Moors in the 8th century. The mountains have, however, finally [illegible] outdoor activities in the Picos de Europa National Park. Although it is better known for its peaks, Asturias also has a popular coastline. Not the swaths of sand and raging waves of Cantabria, Asturian beaches are more often quiet, rocky coves where tropical and alpine vegetation commingle with mountaineers.

OVIEDO ☎958

Oviedo's name comes from the Latin word for city *(ovetum)*, and for a few centuries, at least, it really was *the* city in Spain: as one of the few places able to ward off Moorish attacks, it became the epicenter of the *Reconquista*. Oviedo (pop. 200,000) was made the capital of the Kingdom of Asturias as early as 810, but the city has since faded into the background of Spanish life. The city center is pleasant enough, with an immense park, lively street musicians, beloved *churrerías*, and the promise of mountains on the horizon. Yet beyond its provincial art museum and miles of pedestrian shopping streets, there's not much to see or do in Oviedo. It is, however, the only way to access the western gates of the Picos de Europa.

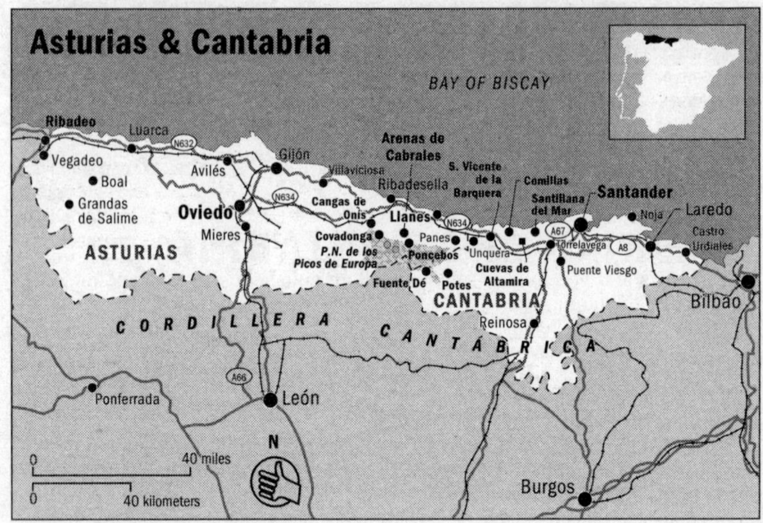

TRANSPORTATION

Flights: Aeropuerto de Ranón/Aeropuerto Nacional de Asturias (☎985 12 75 00), in Avilés, 28km northwest of Oviedo. **Prabus,** C. Marqués de Pidal, 20 (☎985 25 47 51), runs frequent buses from the ALSA station to the airport. **Aviaco** (☎985 12 76 03) and **Iberia** (☎985 12 76 07) fly to Madrid, Barcelona, and London.

Trains: Both RENFE and FEVE serve Oviedo from **Estación del Norte,** Av. Fundación Príncipe de Asturias, s/n, uphill on C. Uría from the center of town.

RENFE (☎985 24 33 64 or 25 24 02), on the first floor of the train station. Pay attention to the type of train; a slow local train through the mountains can double your travel time. Info open daily 7:45am-11:15pm. To: **Barcelona** (12-13½hr., 10:57am and 7:48pm, 6100-8000ptas/€37-48) via **Burgos** (5-6hr.,4550ptas/€28); **Gijón** (30min., every 30min. 5:18am-11:04pm, 325-375ptas/€1.95-2.25); **León** (2-2½hr.; M-F 7 per day 7:30am-11pm, Sa-Su 6 per day 1-11pm; 945-2300ptas/€5.68-14); **Madrid** (6-9hr.; 9:50am, 4:25, and 11pm; 6150ptas/€37) via **Valladolid** (4hr., 3875ptas/€24).

FEVE (☎985 29 76 56) on the third floor of the train station. Info open daily 9am-10pm or until last train. To: **Bilbao** (7hr., 9:08am, 2640ptas/€16); **Ferrol** (6½hr., 7:47am and 2:47pm, 2485ptas/€15); **Llanes** (2hr., 9:08am and 3:48pm, 900ptas/€5.40); **Ribadeo** (4hr., 7:47am and 2:47pm, 1295ptas/€7.78); **Santander** (4½hr., 9:08am and 3:48pm,1700ptas/€10.22).

Buses: There are 2 major bus lines: **Alsa** (national) and **Económicos/Ensa** (regional).

ALSA, Pl. General Primo de Rivera, 1 (☎985 96 96 96 or 902 42 22 42), unmarked, on the lower level of the white shopping building between C. Fray Ceferino and Av. General Elorza. Ticket office at C. Uría across the street from El Corte Inglés. Open M-F 9:30am-2pm and 4-8pm, Sa 9:30am-2pm. To: **Barcelona** (12hr., 7:30am and 8pm, 4825ptas/€29); **Burgos** (4¼hr., 7:30am and 8pm, 1650ptas/€9.92); **La Coruña** (4½-6¾hr., 5 per day 7am-7pm, 3275ptas/€20); **León** (1½hr., 8 per day 7:30am-10:30pm, 1140ptas/€6.85); **Madrid** (5hr.; M-F 12 per day, Sa 10 per day, Su 14 per day, 6:30am-12:30am; 3825-6000ptas/€23-36); **Santander** (3-4hr., 8-10 per day 7am-8:30pm, 1710-2800ptas/€10.28-16.83); **Santiago** (5½-7hr.; 4 per day 7am-4:30pm, Su until 7pm; 3850ptas/€23); **Vigo** (7-9hr., 7am and 3pm, 4580ptas/€28); **Valladolid** (4hr., 5 per day 7:30pm-12:30am, 3010ptas/€18).

Económicos (EASA), C. Jerónimo Ibrán, 1 (☎985 29 00 39). To: **Arenas de Cabrales** (2hr.; M-F 4 per day 9:30am-6pm, Sa-Su 9:30am and 6pm; 1060ptas/€6.37); **Cangas de Onís** (1-1½hr.; M-F 9 per day 9:30am-9:30pm, Sa-Su 7 per day 8am-9:30pm; 750ptas/€4.51); **Covadonga** (1¾hr.; M-F 4 per day 6:45am-5:30pm, Sa-Su 9:30am, 12:30, 3:30pm; 855ptas/€5.14); **Llanes** (1½-2hr., 7 per day 7am-8:30pm, 1000ptas/€6.01).

Public Transportation: TUA (☎985 22 24 22) runs **buses** 8am-10pm (12ptas/€0.72). All stops have an elaborate route of bus maps. #4 runs from the bus, FEVE, and RENFE stations up C. Uría, turning off just before Campo San Francisco. #2 runs from all of the stations to the youth hostel and hospital. #2, 3, 5, and 7 run from the RENFE station along C. Uría to the old city.

Taxis: Radio Taxi (☎985 25 00 00 or 25 25 00). 24hr. service.

Car Rental: Avis, C. Ventura Rodríguez, 12 (☎985 24 13 83). From Campo San Francisco, walk up C. Uría toward the train station, turn left on C. Gil de Jaz and right onto C. Ventura Rodríguez. Another branch is in the train station, but with irregular hours. From 9600ptas/€58 per day. Weekend specials. Min. age 25 years old and with credit card in driver's name. Open M-F 9am-1pm and 4pm, Sa 9am-1pm.

ORIENTATION AND PRACTICAL INFORMATION

At Oviedo's city center is the **Campo San Francisco,** a massive park on the slope of a hill. At its downhill base is **Calle Uría,** the city's main thoroughfare, running from the train station past the Campo. The **cathedral** lies down C. San Francisco from C. Uría. From the **train station,** exit onto Av. de Santander and C. Uría will be directly in front of you. The bus station and ENSA bus stop lie a little farther out off **Pl. General Primo Rivera,** but **C. Fray Ceferino** connects them to C. Uría. From the **ENSA bus stop** on C. Jerónimo Ibrán, walk to Pl. General Primo Rivera and follow the rotary to the right; C. Fray Ceferino will be the second street on the right. From the ALSA station, follow the rotary to the left; C. Fray Ceferino will be the second street. Walk uphill on C. Fray Ceferino, and take the third left onto C. Uría.

Tourist Office: Pl. de Alfonso II El Casto, 6 (☎985 21 33 85). Next to the cathedral. From C. Uría, walk up C. San Francisco just after Pl. La Escandalera, to Pl. de Alfonso II. English spoken. Open M-F 9:30am-1:30pm, 4:30-6:30pm; Sa 9am-2pm. **Municipal Office,** Marqués de Santa Cruz, 1 (☎/fax 985 22 75 86), corner of C. Uría, in front of the Campo San Francisco. Open M-F 10:30am-2pm, 4:30-7:30pm; Sa-Su 11am-2pm.

Currency Exchange: Banco Central Hispano, Pl. La Escandalera, s/n (☎902 24 24 24), across from the Campo San Francisco. Open Apr.-Sept. M-F 8:30am-2:30pm; Oct.-Mar. M-F 8:30am-2:30pm, Sa 8:30am-1pm.

Luggage Storage: Lockers (300ptas/€1.80; open daily 7am-11pm) at the **RENFE station.** Lockers (300ptas/€1.80; open daily 7am-11pm) at **ALSA bus station.**

English Bookstore: Librería Cervantes, C. Doctor Casal, 9 (☎985 20 77 61). A left off C. Uría when walking toward the park from the train station. Huge selection ranging from Shakespeare to Bryson. Open M-F 9am-1:30pm and 4-8pm, Sa 9am-2pm.

Emergency: ☎1006. **Police: Policía Municipal** (☎092 or 985 11 56 57), **Guardia Civil** (☎062 or 985 28 02 04). Both [illegible] s/n.

24-hour pharmacy: Farmacia Nestares, C. Uría, 36. Across the street from El Corte Inglés.

Medical Services: Hospital Central de Asturias, C. J. Clavería, s/n (☎985 10 61 00), near the Plaza de Toros. **Ambulance:** ☎985 10 89 00.

Internet Access: Laser Internet Center, C. San Francisco, 9 (☎985 20 00 66). 10am-10pm 300ptas/€1.80 per hr.; 10pm-10am 150ptas/€0.90 per hr.

Post Office: C. Alonso Quintanilla, 1 (☎985 21 41 86 or 902 19 71 97). From C. Uría, turn left onto C. Argüelles, then left onto C. Alfonso. Open M-F 8:30am-8:30pm, Sa 9:30am-2pm. **Postal Code:** 33060.

ACCOMMODATIONS

Pensiones pack the new city on C. Uría, C. Campoamor (with the RENFE station behind you, walk 1 block to the left), C. Nueve de Mayo (2 blocks off C. Manuel Pedregal), and C. Jovellanos (near the cathedral).

RESURRECTING THE TOWER OF BABLE Galicians have Gallego, Catalans have Catalan, and Asturians have...Bable? It's not an official language, but the dialect has returned full-force with the sweeping post-Franco reassertion of regional tradition, and it's now taught to children in school. The codification of a hodgepodge of more than 10 distinct traditional dialects originating in different corners of Asturias, Bable's grammar borrows from many but belongs to no one. As a result, almost no one is fluent in the tongue (you probably won't hear it on the street) and grandmothers tend to express bewilderment at their grandchildren's *bable*-ing.

Residencia Juvenil Ramón Menéndez Pidal, C. Julián Clavería, 14 (☎985 23 20 54), just off Pl. Toros. Walk down C. Uría from the RENFE station, take a right on Conde de Toreno, walk through 2 plazas past the Plaza de Toros, and turn left on C. J. Clavería (25min.). Or take bus #2 (dir.: Hospital) from Pl. Primo de Rivera or C. Uría. TV room, library, and dining room. Rooms vary in size from 4-12 bunks, but all have sinks. Only a few available in winter. Curfew 1am. Dorms 780ptas/€4.69, with breakfast 941ptas/€5.66; over 26 1066ptas/€6.41, with breakfast 1325ptas/€7.96. AmEx/MC/V.

Pensión Martínez, C. Jovellanos, 5 (☎985 21 53 44). A modern apartment building with clean, spartan rooms with sinks. Pristine communal bathrooms. Singles 1800ptas/€11; doubles 3200ptas/€19; triples 4200ptas/€25.

Pensión Riesgo, C. Nueve de Mayo, 16, 1st fl. (☎985 21 89 45). From the bus stations, walk up C. Fray Ceferino, and take the first left onto C. Nueve de Mayo; from the train station, walk up C. Uría and turn right onto C. Fray Ceferino, taking the second right onto C. Nueve de Mayo. A pleasant pension on a pedestrian street in the center. Singles 2500ptas/€15; doubles 4500ptas/€27, with shower 5000ptas/€30.

Pensión Pomar, C. Jovellanos, 7 (☎985 22 27 91). From the bus and train stations, a left off C. Uría at Pl. La Escaladera and the Teatro Campoamor. Spacious old building has 20 rooms with large windows. Communal bathrooms are somewhat dingy. Singles 2000ptas/€12; doubles 3000-4000ptas/€18-24; triples 4000-5000ptas/€24-30.

FOOD

If you have only the *pesetas* for a single drink in Oviedo, be sure to try *sidra* (cider) by the bottle (usually 250-600ptas/€1.50-3.60)—it goes fast, and much of it ends up on the floor due to the unconventional pouring method. For the best *sidra* experience, head to the wooden-beamed, ham-hung **sidrerías,** where waiters pour from above their heads and expect you swallow it all in one huge gulp. Cheap restaurants line C. Fray Ceferino, between the bus and train stations. The indoor **market** on Pl. El Fontán, is at the very end of C. Uría after Campo San Francisco. (Open M-Sa 8am-3pm.) For groceries, try **Hipercor,** C. General Elorza, 75, opposite the ALSA station in the shopping mall. (Open M-Sa 10am-9pm.)

Mesón Luferca, a.k.a. **La Casa Real del Jamón,** C. Covadonga, 20 (☎985 21 78 02). From Campo San Francisco, walk across Pl. La Escandalera, down C. Argüelles, veering left at Alcalde Manuel García Conde; C. Covadonga will be on the left. You may think you've seen a lot of hanging hams. Feed the big bad wolf inside you—huffing and puffing optional. *Tapas* 790-3500ptas/€4.75-21. Don't miss the local favorite *chorizo a la sidra* (300ptas/€1.80). Open M-Sa 8:30am-midnight. MC/V.

La Galera, C. Argüelles, 3. *Menú asturiano* 2000ptas/€12.02; lunch *menú* 1250ptas/€7.50. Restaurant open M-Sa 1-4pm and 8pm-midnight; café open M-F 8:30am-12:30pm, Sa 10am-1pm; bar open M-Sa 10am-midnight. MC/V.

Alberobella Pasta Fresca, C. Independencia, 22 (☎985 27 57 15). Walking down C. Uría toward the train station, turn left onto C. Independencia just after El Corte Inglés. Despite the fast food appearance, Alberobella makes delicious and authentic Italian concoctions, perfect for the *tapas*-weary traveler. Huge pasta dishes (700-1050ptas/€4.20-6.31). Open M-F 11am-4pm and 6:30-11:30pm, Sa-Su 6:30-11:30pm. MC/V.

La Mallorquina, C. Milicies Nacionales, s/n. Just off C. Uría across from Campo San Francisco. Sunny pastry café also offers light, vegetarian-friendly fare. Salads 1000-1900ptas/€6.01-11.42. *Menú* 1200ptas/€7.21. Open daily 10am-midnight.

SIGHTS

CATHEDRAL. Recent renovation restored Oveido's cathedral to its original beauty. Two chapels are roofed with a brilliant blue ceiling above the altar. The **Capilla de Santa María del Rey Casto,** which houses the royal pantheon (the tombs of important members of the Asturian monarchy), was chosen by Alfonso II El Casto in 802 to house the remains of Asturian monarchs and Christian relics rescued from the Moors. An intense metal relief sculpture in the unusual **Capilla de San Pedro** depicts Simon Magnus dropped from the sky by hideous demons. The cathedral complex also includes an 80m **tower** with great views of the city's rooftops, a *cámara santa* (holy chamber), a **cloister,** and a church **museum.** *(Pl. Alfonso II. Standing on C. Uría in front of Campo San Francisco, cross Pl. La Escaladera and walk up C. San Francisco to the cathedral. ☎985 22 10 33. Cathedral open daily 10am-8pm. Free. Cámara Santa 200ptas/€1.20. Museum ☎985 20 31 17. Museum, chamber, and cloister open M-Sa 10am-8pm. 400ptas/€2.40, seniors 300ptas/€1.80, children 150ptas/€0.90. Th free.)*

MUSEO DE BELLAS ARTES. The two buildings of the **Museo de Bellas Artes** in the **Palacio de Velarde** display a wide range of Asturian art and a small collection of 16th- to 20th-century Spanish works. While the upper floors display devotional art on loan from Madrid's Prado, the ground floor has a permanent collection of astonishing modern works by local artists. In addition to the Klimt-esque work of Herme Anglada Camaresa, the highlight is undoubtedly José Ramón Zaragoza's triptych of the myth of Prometheus. *(C. Santa Ana, 1, and C. Rúa, 8, just up C. Santa Ana from Pl. Alfonso II. ☎985 21 20 57. Open Tu-Sa 11am-2:30pm, 5-9pml; Su 11am-2:30pm. Free.)*

OTHER SIGHTS. Behind the cathedral is the **Museo Arqueológico-Antiguo Monasterio de San Vicente** and the **Iglesia de San Vicente,** the original urban center of medieval Oviedo. *(C. San Vicente, 3. Standing in front of the Campo San Francisco on C. Uría, cross Pl. La Escandalera and walk up C. Argüelles, follow it as it becomes C. Jovellanes, then turn right onto C. San Vicente. Museum ☎985 21 54 05. Open Tu-Sa 10am-1pm, 4-6pm; Su 11am-1pm. Church ☎985 21 18 70. Open Tu-Sa 10am-1pm, 4-6pm; Su 11am-1pm. Both free.)* The **Centro de Arte Moderno** hosts temporary exhibits of regional and national cutting edge artists. *(C. Alonso Quintanilla, 2, opposite the post office. Walk up C. Argüelles from C. Uría, and take the first left onto C. Pelayo; C. Alfonso Quintanilla is the first right. Open M-F 5-9pm, Sa 11:30am-2:30pm and 5-9pm; Su 11:30am-2:30pm. Free.)* Asturian Pre-Romanesque was the first European attempt to blend architecture, sculpture (including human representations), and mural painting since the fall of the Roman Empire. The style was developed under Alfonso II (780-840) [illegible], for [illegible] style is named. Two beautiful examples, **Santa María del Naranco** and **San Miguel de Lillo,** lie 4km outside Oviedo on **Monte Naranco.** *(☎985 25 72 08. Both open May-Sept. M-Sa 9:30am-1pm and 3-7pm, Su 9:30am-1pm; Oct.-Apr. Su-M 9:30am-1pm, Tu-Sa 9:30am-1pm and 3-7pm. 250ptas/€1.50, children 125ptas/€0.75 M free.)*

HIKING

Though not the best base for hiking in the Picos de Europa National Park (see p. 439), Oviedo is definitely the place to stock up on gear and supplies, as shops within the park and in its gateway towns can be prohibitively expensive.

Federación Asturiana de Montaña (☎985 25 23 62), C. de Julián Clavería, near the bull ring, a 30min. walk from the city center. Or take bus #2 (dir: Hospital) from C. Uría. If you walk, you'll need the full-sized map of the city from the tourist office. Organizes excursions, provides mountain guides, info on weather conditions, and advice on the best hiking routes. Instructors for paragliding to kayaking. Open M-F 6-8pm.

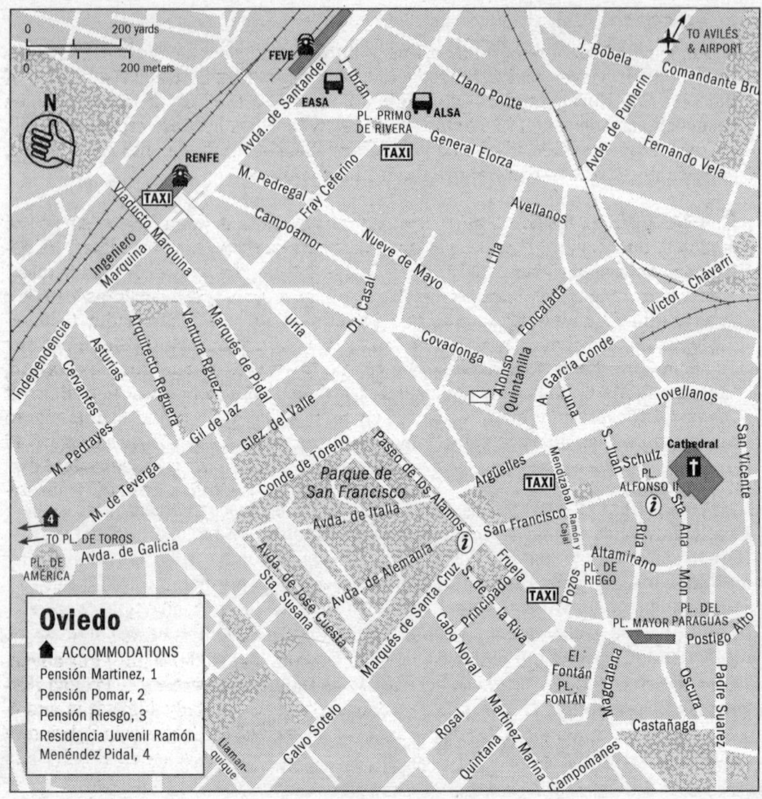

Oficina Parque Nacional de los Picos de Europa, C. Arquitecto Reguera, 13, 2nd fl. (☎985 24 14 12). Heading toward the train station on C. Uría, turn left onto C. Gil de Jaz then right onto C. Arquitecto Reguera. Excursions, camping, trail info. Open M-F 8am-3pm and 5-7pm. The office in **Cangas de Onís,** Av. Covadonga, 35 (☎985 84 91 54), is the best place to get detailed (free) information on the Picos.

Deportes Tuñon, C. Campoamor, 7. From C. Uría heading toward the train station, turn right onto C. Doctor Casal, then left onto C. Campoamor. Extensive selection of camping and rock-climbing gear, long underwear, and a few maps. Open M-F 10am-1:30pm and 4:30-8:30pm, Sa 10am-1:30pm. AmEx/MC/V.

ENTERTAINMENT

The streets south of the cathedral, around Pl. Riego, Pl. El Fontán, and Pl. El Paraguas, teem with noisy *sidrerías* and clubs. Stylish **Bar Riego,** on Pl. Riego, serves tasty *batidos* (milkshakes; 300-600ptas/€1.80-3.60) on a breezy *terraza.* (Open M-Sa noon-4pm and 8pm-2am.) Wine connoisseurs follow **la ruta de los vinos** from *bodega* to *bodega* along C. El Rosal; walk up C. Uría away from the train station to its end, and C. El Rosal will be on the right. (*Copas* 300-600ptas/€1.80-3.60.) On C. La Luna, between Alcalde García Conde and C. Jovellanos, **Danny's Jazz Café,** C. La Luna, 11, hosts all variety of acts. (☎985 21 14 83. Beers 300ptas/€1.80. Mixed drinks 600ptas/€3.60. Open daily 8pm-4am.) Oviedo celebrates its **patronal fiesta** in honor of San Mateo (Sept. 19-21).

LLANES

When tourist brochures proclaim that Asturias is a *"paraíso natural,"* Llanes must be their heaven on earth. Wedged on a narrow ledge between the heights of the Picos de Europa and the cliffs plummeting into the Bay of Biscay, Llanes seems like an apparition. While the small, rocky beaches here are crowded, this is no resort town; rather, it's a small Asturian village—complete with cows, ruins, and winding streets—rising above the frothing teal sea.

TRANSPORTATION. ALSA-Turytrans runs **buses** from C. La Bolera, s/n (☎985 40 23 22; info open M-F 8:30am-7:30pm, Sa-Su 8:30am-2pm and 3:15-8pm) to: **Bilbao/San Sebastián** (5-7hr.; 10:30am, 1:15, and 4:30pm; 2525ptas/€16); **La Coruña/Pontevedra/Santiago de Compostela/Vigo** (6-11hr., 4:55am, 3025-6000ptas/€19-36); **Madrid** (8hr., 1:45pm, 4290ptas/€26); **Oviedo** (1-1½hr.; M-F 10 per day 6:30am-10:30pm, Sa-Su 7-8 per day 8:45am-7:15pm; 1000/€6); **Santander** (2¼hr., 5 per day 10:30am-9pm, 1200ptas/€7.20). To reach the town center from the bus station, take a left onto C. La Bolera, and veer to the right as it becomes C. Cueto Bajo; at the post office, turn left onto C. Les Barqueras, which leads to the Ayuntamiento and tourist office. **Trains** chug from the FEVE station, C. Alonso Vega, s/n (☎985 40 01 24) to: **Oviedo** (2½hr., 5 per day 8:05am-8pm, 885ptas/€5.32) and **Santander** (2hr., 11:27am and 6:13pm, 810ptas/€4.87). To get to the tourist office from the train station, walk up C. Román Romano, turn left onto C. Manuel Romano, and then right onto C. Nemesio Sobrino. For a **taxi** call 24hr. ☎985 40 11 77.

PRACTICAL INFORMATION. The **tourist office** is in a 13th-century tower on C. Alfonso IX, directly behind the yellow Ayuntamiento on C. Castillo Meraderes. (☎985 40 01 64. Open July-Aug. M-Sa 10am-2pm and 5-9pm, Su 10am-3pm; Sept.-June M-F 10am-2pm and 4-6:30pm, Sa 10am-1:30pm and 4:30-6:30pm.) For adventure activities, stop by **Centro de Información de Turismo de Aventura,** C. Posada Herrera, s/n, next to the tourist office. (☎985 40 05 41. Open daily 10am-2pm and 4-10pm.) Services include: **emergency** ☎1006; **municipal police,** C. Nemesio Sobrino, s/n (☎985 40 18 87); **Farmacia Mariano Ruiz,** Pl. Parres Sobrino, 1 (open M-F 9:30am-1:30pm, 4:30-8pm; Sa 10:30am-1pm; **late-night pharmacy** location is posted in the window, though it may be a few towns over); **health center,** Av. de San Pedro, s/n (☎985 40 36 15); **CyberDream Internet Café,** C. La Calzada, 1-A. (☎985 40 06 72. 600ptas/€3.60 per hr. open M-F noon-2pm, 5-9pm; Sa-Su 5-9pm); **post office,** C. Pidal, s/n (☎985 40 11 14. M-F 8:30am-2:30pm, Sa 9:30am-1pm.) **Postal code:** 33500.

ACCOMMODATIONS AND FOOD. Rooms fill early in summer, making reservations a necessity. **Casa del Río,** Av. San Pedro, 3, a restored mansion near the beach, has wonderful with large windows rooms, some with balconies. Facing the Ayuntamiento, walk left on C. Nemesio Sobrino, and turn right onto C. San Pedro. ([illegible]. Reception 24hr. Singles 2500-3500ptas/€15-21; doubles 4500-6000ptas/€27-36, with bath and TV 5500-8000ptas/€33-48; triples 6000-7000ptas/€36-43.) The spacious and bright rooms of **Pensión La Guía,** Pl. Parres Sobrino, 1, are right in the center of town. (☎985 40 25 77. Check-out 2pm. Reservations accepted. Doubles with bath 5000-8000ptas/€30-48. MC/V.) **Albergue de la Estación,** C. Alonso Vega, s/n, at the FEVE station, is Llanes' only hostel, frequented by Spanish teens enjoying their beach weekend. The owners arrange outdoor excursions in the Picos. (☎985 40 14 58 or 610 52 81 11. Lockout 1:30-5pm. 4- to 8-bed dorms 1900ptas/€12. MC/V.) On a small bluff between the beaches, **Camping Entreplayas,** off Av. de Toro between Playas de Puerto Chico and Toro, is wildly popular, if not for its scenic views then for the neighboring bar where campers laze away their days with bikinis and beer. (☎985 40 08 88. 400ptas/€2.40 per person, per tent, and per car; electricity 300ptas/€1.80. IVA not included.)

Cafés and sidrerías line C. Las Barqueras, C. Castillo de Marqueres, and C. Nemsio Sobrino; near the beaches, reasonable local eateries are on Av. de Toro and C. Marqués de Argüelles. But the most interesting fare in town is undoubtedly served at **Sabor Latino,** C. Venezuela, 1. From the Ayuntamiento, walk up C. Nemesio Sobrino, turn right on Av. San Pedro, and then left onto C. Genaro, which becomes Av. de Méjico and brings you to the C. Venezuela. This tropical cantina serves all the Mexican favorites, including guacamole, enchiladas, and fajitas. (Bar open 10am-2am daily; restaurant 8pm-2am. Entrées 500-1800ptas/€3-10.82). For groceries, go to **El Arból,** C. Manuel Romano, 3, at the intersection with C. Román Romano near the train station. (Open M-Sa 9am-9pm.)

BEACHES. Though some of the most popular beaches in Asturias, these are not the wide swaths of sand that jump to one's mind. Rather, Llanes' beaches are tucked into coves and inlets along the coast, made all the more idyllic by the occasional rocky outcropping in the water. As these are protected waters, the sea is calm (and rather seaweedy). The compact **Playa de Sablón,** in the center of town, is the most popular—and the most crowded. From the Ayuntamiento, turn right onto C. Alonso IX, which runs straight to the beach. **Playa de Toro** is by far Llanes' prettiest and most swimmable beach, though it's still fairly crowded. It's also the only beach with any semblance of waves. From the Ayuntamiento, walk up C. Castillo Mercaderes across the river, and turn left onto Av. de la Guía at the post office, which turns into Av. de Toro. **Playa de Puerto Chico** will please those looking for total seclusion, but only if they can stand the mountains of seaweed and their accompanying stink. Follow the directions to Playa del Sablón, above, and take the steps up the hill to the **Paseo de San Pedro,** a grassy strip running along the edge of the cliffs above the sea. Plenty of benches, shade trees, and chameleons share the wide open and breezy sea views.

CANGAS DE ONÍS

During the summer months, when the streets are packed with mountaineers and vacationing families, it can seem like Cangas' (pop. 6285) telos is to help travelers spelunk and hanglide. While it's true that most visitors come to Cangas only to get closer to the Picos de Europa National Park (see p. 439), Cangas itself is, if not thrilling, a relaxing, history-rich town. Founded in 722 by the army that defeated the Moors at Covadonga, Cangas prides itself on being the first capital of the Asturian monarchy and a launch pad for the *Reconquista.* Its few sights highlight the town's Paleolithic and Celtic legacies, but the rest of this busy mountain town is devoted to the outdoors. Cangas is not the most central base for exploring the Picos, but it does have plenty of less hard-core outdoor opportunities.

TRANSPORTATION. ALSA, Av. Covadonga, 18 (☎985 84 81 33), in the Pícaro Inmobiliario building and across from the tourist office, runs **buses** to: **Arenas de Cabrales** (30min.; M-F 4 per day 11am-7:30pm, Sa-Su 11am; 310ptas/€1.86); **Llanes** (40min., 9:10am, 500ptas/€3); **Oviedo** (1½-2hr.; M-F 9 per day 6:15am-8:15pm, Sa-Su 6 per day 9:15am-8pm; 750ptas/€4.51); **Madrid** (7hr., 2:35pm, 3920ptas/€24), via **Valladolid** (5hr., 2350ptas/€15); and **Covadonga** (30min.; M-F 10 per day 8:30am-7:40pm, Sa-Su 8 per day 9:15am-7:40pm; 175ptas/€1.05; returns to Cangas 10:30am-8pm). For a taxi call **Radio Taxi** (24hr. ☎985 84 87 97 or 84 83 73) or wait in front of the Ayuntamiento, Av. Convadonga, 21.

PRACTICAL INFORMATION. The main street in Cangas de Onís is **Avenida Covadonga.** The **tourist office,** Jardines del Ayuntamiento, 2, is just off Av. Covadonga across from the bus stop. (☎985 84 80 05. Open May-Sept. daily 10am-10pm; Oct.-Apr. daily 10am-2pm and 4-7pm.) Park information is available at the **Picos de Europa National Park Visitors' Center,** Av. Covadonga, 43, in the **Casa Dago.** The office has a list of mountain *refugios,* maps, hike suggestions, and a fantastic, three-dimensional model of the park. From the bus stop, walk up Av. Covadonga toward the large church. (☎/fax 985 84 86 14. Open daily 10am-2pm and 4-6:30pm.) Services include: **Banco Central Hispano,** Av. Covadonga, 6 (☎985 84 87 84; open Apr.-Sept. M-F 8:30am-2:30pm, Oct.-Mar. also Sa 8:30am-1pm.); **emergency** ☎112;

municipal police in the Ayuntamiento on Av. Covadonga (☎985 84 85 58); **pharmacy,** Av. Castilla, 24, just off Av. Covadonga near the Puente Romano (open 9am-2pm and 4:30-7:30pm); the **health center,** C. de la Cárcel, s/n (☎985 84 85 71), down C. Emilio Laria from Av. Covadonga; **internet access** at **Ingapublic,** C. El Censo, 15 Bajo, (☎985 84 94 27; 500ptas/€3 per hr.; MC/V.); and the **post office,** Av. Constantino González, s/n, is a right off Av. Covadonga when heading toward the Puente (☎985 84 81 86; open M-F 8:30am-2:30pm, Sa 9:30am-1pm). **Postal code:** 33550.

ACCOMMODATIONS AND FOOD. A few clean *pensiones* along Av. Covadonga will gladly accept your *pesetas.* **Hospedaje Principado,** Av. Covadonga, 16, 3rd fl., is a tiny, immaculate *pensión* with TV in every room. Walking down Av. Covadonga toward the Puente Romano, Av. Castilla is the last street on the left before the bridge. (☎985 84 83 50; fax 84 83 15. Singles 2500-3000ptas/€15-18; doubles 3400-4400ptas/€20-27, with bath 5500-6500ptas/33-39.) **El Chofer,** C. Emilio Laria, 10, has clean rooms, firm beds, Oriental rugs, and hall baths. C. Emilio Laria is the street directly in front of the tourist office across Av. Covadonga. (☎985 84 83 05. Winter heating. Reception in El Chofer restaurant around the corner. Singles 2700-3200ptas/€16-19; doubles 3200-4700ptas/€19-28.) **Camping Covadonga**, in Soto de Cangas, 4km up the road toward Arenas de Cabrales (5-7 buses per day), has a cafeteria, bar, supermarket, and showers. (☎985 94 00 97. 625ptas/€3.76 per adult, 525ptas/€3.16 per child; 550-700ptas/€3-4 per tent; 875-1070ptas/€5-6.43 per car. Open *Semana Santa* and June-Sept. 20.) Most restaurants on Av. Covadonga serve *menús* slightly over 1000ptas/€6. For a do-it-yourself-meal try **Alimerka Supermercado,** Av. Covadonga, 15. (Open Su-M 9am-2pm, Tu-Sa 9am-9pm.)

SIGHTS AND EXCURSIONS. At the far end of Av. Covadonga is the **Puente Romano,** a medieval bridge with an ornate golden cross hanging from the middle. From the bridge, following Av. Covadonga into town, turning left onto C. Constantino González and crossing the river brings you to the **Capilla de Santa Cruz.** This Romanesque chapel, built in 737AD, sits atop the town's oldest monument, a Celtic *dolmen* (monolith) dating from 3000BC, which can be seen from the chapel's cave. Alas, there are no scheduled visiting hours, so check at the tourist office for info on entering. Also of interest is **Cueva del Buxu** (BOO-shoo), whose walls are adorned by 15,000-year-old paintings by Cangas' paleolithic residents. To reach the cave, follow the main road to Covadonga for 3km until the signs for the *cueva* and Cardes, the closest town, directs you left. From here, it's a gradual 1km climb past pastures to the easily missed sign to the caves, by Bar Cueva El Buxu. **Buses** to Covadonga, Llanes, and Arenas (see **Transportation,** above) run near the cave; ask to be dropped off at the **Cruce de Susierra.** Come early, as only 25 people are allowed in each day. (☎608 17 54 67. Open June-Sept. W-Su 9:30am until full; Oct.-May W-Su 9am-1pm and 3pm-5:30pm unless the limit is reached earlier. 1000ptas/€6. W free.) Those with [illegible] This route winds through Santillan, Sames, and finally to the **Desfiladero de los Beyos,** a 11km gorge filled with wet rocks and blossoming beech trees.

ADVENTURE TOURISM. Cangas de Onís is the perfect place to arrange outdoor activies, but it is imperative to reserve ahead of time, especially during the summer. **Aventura,** Av. Covadonga, 23 (☎985 84 92 61; fax 84 85 61), sets up various expeditions, including hiking (only in the low season), white-water rafting, spelunking *(espeología), barranquismo* (canyoning, swimming, and spelunking), canoeing, horseback riding, 4-wheeling, and bungee jumping. Prices range 3000-5000ptas/€18-30 per person depending on the activity, time of day, and size of the group. Prices include equipment, a guide, transportation to and from Cangas, and sometimes a bagged lunch. Discounts are offered for large groups and/or multiple activities. Call for departure times and destinations. Reservations are recommended, especially June-Aug. **Los Cauces,** Av. de Covadonga, 23, offers most of the same activities for similar prices. (☎985 94 73 18 or 84 01 38. 3000-5500ptas/€18-33 per person. Open daily 9:30am-9:30pm.) The tourist office lists other agencies.

ARENAS DE CABRALES

Some say the small town of Arenas de Cabrales (pop. 800) sits "as close to the sky as to the ground," and they are not all so far from the truth. This one-street hamlet rests on the several craggy peaks. The fog, wandering mountain goats, and breathtaking vistas make Arenas seem almost like a mountain mirage, drawing outdoor enthusiasts eager to take advantage of the excellent hiking and climbing just 6km away in the Picos de Europa National Park (see p. 439). Beyond that, there's not much to do in Arenas other than marvel.

TRANSPORTATION. **ALSA buses** (☎902 42 22 42) head to **Oviedo** (2½hr.; M-F 4 per day 7:25am-5:50pm, Sa-Su 8:35am and 5:50pm; 1060ptas/€6.37) via **Cangas de Onís** (50min.; 310ptas/€1.86) and to **Poncebos** (20min.; M-F 6 per day 10:15am-7:15pm, Sa-Su 7:15am; 125ptas/€0.75). Buses to Poncebos depart from in front of the tourist hut; the others from across the street in front of the small park (look for the ALSA sign). For a **taxi**, call Joaquín (☎985 84 64 87 or 689 38 06 03), who claims "un cliente, un amigo" and will go just about anywhere in the Asturian Picos.

PRACTICAL INFORMATION. The **tourist office,** in a hut on the main road just before the bridge, is small but helpful. (☎985 84 64 84. Theoretically open July-Sept. 20 Tu-Su 10am-2pm and 4-8pm, but in reality has no set hours.) Services include: **emergency** ☎112; **Guardia Civil,** on the main road toward Cangas near the post office (☎985 84 50 04); **Consultorio Médico** (☎985 84 55 04), uphill on the main road across the street from the **ATM** and the pharmacy; the **pharmacy** (☎985 84 50 16), next to Cajastur; and the **post office,** near the bus stop but towards Cangas (open M-Sa 9-11am). **Postal code:** 33554.

ACCOMMODATIONS AND FOOD. Since many of Arenas's visitors opt for camping, the town has few reasonably priced hotels. **El Castañeu,** down C. Pedro Niembro directly across from the tourist office, offers decent doubles and triples with breathtaking views of the Picos. (☎985 84 65 73. Reserve 2 months ahead. Winter heating. Doubles 3000-4000ptas/€18-24, with bath 3700-5000ptas/€22-30.) Family-style **Pensión Covadonga,** next door to El Castañeu, offers similarly spotless rooms with incredible mountain views. (☎985 84 65 66. Reserve 2 months early. 3000-4000ptas/€18-24, with bath 3500-5000ptas/€21-30.) **Naranjo de Bulnes Camping,** 1km east on Crta. AS-14, has campsites and cabins, as well as a cozy TV room, cafeteria, bar, and shower facilities. (☎/fax 985 84 65 78. Camping 696ptas/€4.18 per person, 642-856ptas/€3.86-5.14 per tent, 615ptas/€3.70 per car. Cabins 1-2 people 5500ptas/€33; each additional person 1000ptas/€6.)

Of the few eateries in Arenas, **Restaurant La Panera** is by far the best. Atop a small hill to the left of Banco Bilbao Vizcaya and behind La Jueya Restaurant, this restaurant has the look and the feel of an intimate alpine lodge, complete with a romantic balcony and outdoor terrace with astounding views of the surrounding peaks. From the tourist office, walk uphill on the main road; after the curve, look to the left for the restaurant's sign. (*Menú* 1500ptas/€9, main dishes 1800-2800ptas/€11-17. Open daily noon-4pm and 8pm-midnight. AmEx/MC/V.) The **Alimentación** store is opposite the tourist office. (Open daily 6:30am-7pm.)

ASTURIANS CUT THE CHEESE It's an odd selling point, but somehow Cabrales has become famous by emphasizing the unbridled moldy funkiness of its blue cheese. To produce the cheese, locals arduously empty cow, goat, and ewe udders into large tin bins. After allowing the mix to "mature," cheese-makers drain extra liquid, add a pinch of cow afterbirth and a twist of lamb fetus, store the mush inside cabbage leaves and let them stew in mountain caves in humid darkness. Half a year later the speckled brown wheels rolls out onto the sidestreets of every tourist destination in Asturias. Brave tasters rave about the pungent flavor, the creamy texture, and the "knock you to the floor and have you begging for yo' *madre*" kick.

ADVENTURE TOURISM. Novedades Cendón, across the street from the tourist office, sells basic gear and maps. (☎985 84 64 74. Open daily 10am-1pm and 3-7pm.) **PicoSport,** next door to El Castañeu, also sells gear and arranges expeditions. (☎667 64 68 60. Activities 3000-7000ptas/€18-42.) **Pico Urrielly** (☎985 85 67 70), outside of town toward Panes on AS-114, arranges hiking expeditions, spelunking, canoeing, and horseback-riding; prices range from 2000 to 8000ptas/€12-48, depending on the activity, the length of the trip, the size of the group, and the day of the week. For an incredibly knowledgeable **English-speaking guide,** call Emilio Fernández Gavela (☎985 33 12 37). Spelunkers should ask about trips to **Cueva Jou de Alda,** a fascinating nearby cave.

PICOS DE EUROPA

Three hundred million years ago, Mother Nature's mere flapping of her limestone bedsheet erected the Picos de Europa, a mountain range of curious variation and chaotic beauty. This accident of nature created a formidable border between the Asturias and Cantabria region and the rest of the Spain. In fact, this jagged barrier is one of the main reasons that Asturias never fell to the Moors, instead finding protection and divine inspiration in this otherwise impenetrable range. Although the mountains and towns here often feel as isolated and impenetrable as they were centuries ago, they are now actually part of the very civilized Picos de Europa National Park. Founded in 1918 as the National Park of Covadonga and Spain's first foray into the national park scene, Covadonga eventually grew into today's version, spanning three massifs and three provinces (Asturias, Cantabria, and Castilla y León); it is the largest national park in Europe.

The Picos are still managing to provide protection and solace, although not from marauding Moors. Instead, the ancient crags and summits shelter some of Europe's most elusive and endangered species, including wild horses, boars, bears, and *chamois* (a goat-type animal), as well as long-eared owls, Egyptian vultures, songbirds, and eagles. The scrub-spotted peaks lure thousands of outdoor enthusiasts annually, who come to explore the myriad caves and caverns carved out by centuries of glacial abuse. Along the way, discoveries are made, like the gorges and rivers that criss-cross the floor of the park and the silent alpine meadows seeming floating high above. Other European mountain ranges may stand higher than the Picos (2600m), but few are as seductive a playpen for rock-climbers, spelunkers, trekkers, and nature-lovers.

ORIENTATION

Part of the larger Cordillera Cantábrica range, the Picos de Europa consist of three mountainous massifs: the **Occidental** (Cornión), the **Central** (Urrieles), and the **Oriental** (Ándara), with the highest peak **Torrecerredo** (2646m) rising out of the Central massif. Several rivers wind [illegible] gorges are the [illegible], Dobra, and Cares. The **Garganta del Cares** (Cares Gorge), which cuts dramatic border between the Central and Oriental massifs, holds the park's most popular trails and most famous peaks: the life-claiming Peña Vieja (2613m) and Pico Tesorero (2570m), the stark Llambrión (2642m), and the mythic **Naranjo de Bulnes** (Picu Urriellu; 2519m). Serious hikers interested in multi-day treks use **Arenas de Cabrales** (see p. 438) as their base; those interested more in day hikes and guided adventure tourism start in **Cangas de Onís** (see p. 436) and **Potes** (see p. 452). Although independent adventures are definitely possible, most visitors opt for guided hikes and expeditions instead of setting out on their own.

TRANSPORTATION

Getting to the Picos is relatively easy—it's the getting around once there that's difficult. **ALSA buses** link **Cangas de Onís** (see p. 436) and **Arenas de Cabrales** (see p. 438), the gateways in the west and the north, with the towns lying just inside the park's borders, the most important of which are Covadonga and Poncebo;

La Palomera buses link **Potes,** the gateway in the east, with Fuente Dé. It is, however, much more efficient to travel by car as buses run infrequently on weekdays and service is severely limited on weekends. Route **AS-114** runs along the north edge of the Picos from **Cangas de Onís** (10km north of **Covadonga**) through **Arenas de Cabrales,** and on to **Panes,** where it intersects Route N-621. N-621 runs 50km south and west to **Potes,** where a branch leads to **Fuente Dé.**

PRACTICAL INFORMATION

Although hiking is possible May through September, the best time to visit is July and August, despite the crowds. In early summer, it is cold and stormy, with snow still a real possibility; September's weather can be equally unpredictable. If visiting during July and August, it is absolutely necessary to make reservations in the gateway cities to the park (Cangas de Onis, Arenas de Cabrales, and Potes) a month in advance.

The key to hiking in the Picos is planning ahead. Water sources and campsites are hard to come by, and few of the towns in the park have supermarkets or ATMs.

Emergency: ☎112, but the only phones are in town and at *refugios.*

Park Information: In **Asturias,** the park office is in Cangas de Onís at Av. de Covadonga, 43 (see p. 436); in **Cantabria:** Fuente De in the Ctra. Potes (☎942 73 32 01); and in **Castilla y León:** Posada de Valdeón at Ctra. Cordinanes, s/n (☎987 74 05 49; fax 74 05 79). The **Administrative Office** is in Oviedo (see p. 429). On the web: www.mma.es and http://195.61.22.30:8088/ODMMA/PH/redpn/picos.htm.

Guidebooks: In English, Robin Walker's *Picos de Europa* is the best. In Spanish, the many guides of Miguel Angel Andrados are the way to go.

Length: Most hikes in the Picos are day hikes. Much can be done two or three days based out of a single town.

Refugios and Rangers: Before embarking on any hikes in the park, be sure to pick up a list from any of the park offices of *refugios* throughout the park, which, in addition to providing shelter in the mountains, also double as ranger stations.

Gear: Basic amenities and hiking gear are available in all of the gateway towns, but **gear** is cheapest in Oviedo (see p. 429). Inside the park, **food and water** are scarce, even in the towns of Poncebos, Covadonga, and Fuente De, none of which have supermarkets. Only in Oviedo are **water purification** packets available. The free **maps** of the park provided by tourist offices are insufficient for hiking. Extensive trail maps can be purchased in just about every store in Cangas de Onís, Arenas de Cabrales, and Potes.

Tours and Guided Hikes: For information on **adventure tourism** outings see Cangas de Onís and Potes. There are no outfitters in Arenas de Cabrales. The park service offers **free guided hikes** daily, all departing between 9:30 and 10:30am from Los Lagos, Covadonga, Poncebos, and Fuente Dé, in addition to other towns throughout the park. For a complete list of hikes and departure locales, visit one of the park offices.

ACCOMMODATIONS

The easiest accommodations are in Cangas de Onís, Arenas de Cabrales, and Potes; however, these limit one to day hiking. For multi-day hikes, the 15 **refugios** (usually cabins with bunks but not blankets) scattered throughout the park are the best option. There are only five **campgrounds** in the park and all are in towns (Buferrera, Cain, Santa Marina, Caldevilla, and Fuente Dé). Other lodging options include **albergues** (hostels, usually in ancient, unheated buildings with bunks and cold water) and **casas** (buildings with bunks, hot water, and wood stoves); these, however, are also only in or near towns. In all cases you should bring a sleeping bag. The accommodations listed below are the most convenient to the hikes and excursions described. All of the park offices have a complete list of the Picos's 15 *refugios*. Prices range 500-1000ptas/€3-6 per person, and reservations are usually not accepted—though it's wise to call ahead to see if space is available before you set out. All of the towns within the park also have *pensiones* and rooms in private residences; look for *camas* and *habitaciones* signs.

HIKING AND EXCURSIONS

For multi-day routes, consult with one of the Picos de Europa park offices. In addition to the following suggested day hikes, there are numerous free guided hikes arranged through the park offices. The following hikes are listed according to the nearest trailhead or town. Before embarking on any hike, secure a good map that has all trails clearly marked. The following are merely suggestions; be sure to gather more information before departing.

COVADONGA

Covadonga is accessible only from Cangas de Onís and Oviedo. ALSA ***buses*** *(☎ 902 42 22 42) from Cangas (30min.; M-F 6 per day 8:30am-6:45pm, Sa-Su 4 per day 10am-4:40pm; 150ptas/€0.90) and Oviedo (1¾hr.; 9:30am; 805ptas/€4.84) grace Covadonga with two stops: one at the Hospedería and one uphill at the basilica.*

[illegible] mountain you see will be the salvation of Spain," prophesied Don Pelayo, the first king of Asturias, to his Christian army in 718, gesturing to the rocky promontory above what is now Covadonga. The mountain soon became the site of the first successful rebellion against the Moors, although legend claims that it was not geography but the intervention of the Virgin Mary that made victory possible. Don Pelayo became the first king of Asturias, and out of this battle grew the Reconquista. Covadonga was also the center of the first national park in Spain, the precursor to the Picos de Europa established in 1918. Visitors come to Covadonga to see the cliffside basilica, and the cave where the Virgin is said to have appeared to Don Pelayo. Nearly 1300 years ago he prayed to the Virgin for help in defeating the Moors from atop a waterfall in the **Santa Cueva.** Today, pilgrims and tourists crowd the quiet, candlelit sanctuary where the Virgin appeared to him. (Open daily 9am-9pm; in winter 9am-7pm. Free.) The **Santuario de Covadonga,** a neo-Gothic basilica built in 1901, towers above the town. (Open daily 9am-9pm; in winter 9am-7pm. Free.) The **Museo del Tesoro,** across from the basilica, displays the *Corona de la Virgen*, a gold-and-silver crown studded with 1109 diamonds and 2000 sapphires;

PARTY IN THE SKY While the mountaineers in the Picos tend to shy away from Spain's usual party life, they do indulge every once in a while. The biggest Picos party is the **Fiesta del Pastor** (July 25th) in Vega del Enol, near the glacial lakes of Ercina and Enol. Called the *Romería cerca del cielo* ("feast near the sky") for its mountainous location, the party starts at 8am, when most of the town starts the trek up to the lakes. Competitions like the Escalada a la Porre de Enol (a type of local alpinism race), the bareback horse race, and the town tug-of-war are serious affairs; the winners of the last 12 years are listed in local newspapers.

below it lies a sparkling crown crafted to honor Jesus. (Open daily 11am-2pm and 4-7:30pm. 200ptas/€1.20, children 100ptas/€0.60.) On Wednesdays, the park service offers a moderately difficult **hike** through the mountains around Covadonga (3hr.; departs at 10am from Escolania).

Covadonga's **info office,** on the main road near the Hospedería, has details on local accommodations and sights. (☎985 84 60 35. Open daily May-Oct. 10am-2pm and 3-7pm; Nov.-Apr. 11am-2pm and 3-5pm.) Cangas offers cheaper accommodations, but it's hard to resist the friendly atmosphere and stunning views of the mountains at the **Hospedería del Peregrino,** on the main highway. (☎985 84 60 47; fax 84 60 51. 1235-7350ptas/€7.42-44.17, depending on room and season. AmEx/MC/V.) The only **groceries** in town arrive for Hospedería guests twice a week (W and Sa) by truck—buy them from the driver at the hostel.

LOS LAGOS DE ENOL Y ERCINA

*These tarns, or mountain lakes, are accessible from Cangas de Onis and Covadonga (see above). ALSA **buses** (☎902 42 22 42) run from Cangas past Covadonga, continuing to the lakes (45min.; July-Aug. M-F 6 per day 8:30am-6:45pm, Sa-Su 4 per day 10am-4:40pm; Sept.-June 2 per day; 270ptas/€1.62). In Covadonga, buses leave from the basilica to follow a frightening but spectacular road lined with cliffs and precipitous pastures; the right side of the bus has the best en route views. It's not worth the trip on cloudy days.*

Perhaps the most impressive site in the park, the ice-cold **Lagos de Enol y Ercina** sparkle silently among limestone slopes and open valleys. Free guided hikes around the lakes depart from the Buferrera parking lot (M-F 3hr., 10:30am). Slightly more difficult hikes are offered W at 9:30am (5hr.) and F at 10am (4hr.). Two especially good hikes from the lakes take travelers east to the **Vega de Ario,** which offers a panoramic view of the Urrieles mountains (8-9hr.), or south to the **Mirador de Ordiales,** a vantage point overlooking the Pico de las Vidriosas, Río Pomperi, and a frightening gorge (6-7hr.). Alternatively, head west (2km) to the **Mirador de Rey** lookout point, then wander among the beeches of the **Bosque de Pome** (4-5hr.). Both lookouts are accessible by car driving from Covadonga to Los Lagos. Free guided hikes are offered at los Lagos from the Buferrera parking lot. The **Refugio de Vega de Ario** (1630m) sits just off the trails leading from the lakes, 300m past the intersection and behind the **free Buferrera campgrounds.** The refuge has 40 spots year-round and provides meals and guides. To get there by car, follow highway C-6312 (the Cangas de Onís-Panes highway), take the *desvío* (exit) for Covadongas y Lagos, go right at Lago Enol, and continue straight to the refugio. (☎639 81 20 69. Meals 650-1400ptas/€3.91-8.41. No reservations accepted. 500ptas per person/€3.)

PONCEBOS

*Poncebos is only accessible from Arenas de Cabrales. **ALSA** buses run from **Arenas de Cabrales** (20min.; M-F 6 per day 10:15am-7:15pm, Sa-Su 7:15am; 125ptas/€0.75). By car, take AS-114 to Las Arenas, then turn across the river onto AS-264 to town.*

Arenas' hiking trails actually begin 6km away from town in **Poncebos.** The walk to the trailhead threads through the feet of surrounding mountains; tight, winding roads make some corners dangerous. For those interested in spending the night, **Hostal Poncebos** (☎985 84 64 47) and **Hostal-Restaurante-Bar Garganta del Cares**

(☎985 84 64 63), have comfortable rooms. (Singles in both 3000-4000ptas/€18-24; doubles 6000ptas/€36.) Check with the tourist office about **refugio** options.

Poncebos marks the start of one of the Picos' most famous trail, the 12km **Ruta del Cares.** Chiseled out of the mountains, the gorges' vertical walls drop 200m down to the Río Cares below. The **Poncebos-Bulnes** route leads along the Río Tejo to Bulnes, a small village that is seemingly frozen in time. If this seduces you, consider tucking in at the **Albergue de Bulnes,** which has 20 beds in three rooms, a bar, library, games, showers, guides, and meals. (☎985 84 59 43. Reservations suggested. 1500ptas/€9 per person, with breakfast 2000ptas/€12.) The park service offers free guided hikes to Bulnes on Tuesday and Saturday (4hr.; departs at 10am from the small information hut on Poncebos' main highway). The **Poncebos-Invernales de Cabao-Naranjo de Bulnes** route, a killer 17km hike (10-12hr.), crawls first to Invernales de Cabao and then inches 9km farther to the Picos' most famous mountain, **Naranjo de Bulnes,** named for its unmistakable sunburnt orange face. From here you can see the major *picos* in the area and the dancing blue waves of the Bay of Biscay in the distance. Most climbers actually start the hike in Sortes and continue from there (9-10hr.). There are two *refugios* in the Naranjo de Bulnes area: **Refugio Vega de Urriellu** (☎985 94 50 24. 96 beds; 500ptas/€3 per person) and **Refugio Jou de Los Cabrones** (☎985 36 69 32. 24beds; 500ptas/€3). If the trail is open, it's worth going beyond the **Poncebos-Camareña** path, up a rocky slope that requires use of all four limbs, to the **Puertos de Ondón,** where the view is incomparable.

FUENTE DÉ

Fuente Dé is accessible only from Potes on ***ALSA buses*** *(☎902 42 22 42. 45min.; M-F 8:15am, 1, 8pm, Sa-Su 1pm; 650ptas/€3.91). Buses stop right at the cable car base.*

Only 23km from Potes, the **Teleférico de Fuente Dé** is well worth an excursion. The mind-blowing, goosebump-racing teleférico, the third largest cable car in the world, jets 750m to the mountain top (1834m) in less than 4min. (☎942 31 89 50. Open daily July-Aug. 9am-8pm; Sept.-June 10am-6pm. 1000ptas/€6, round-trip 1500ptas/€9; under 10 500ptas/€3, round-trip 750ptas/€4.51.) A zig-zagging trail ascends just left of the cable (3hr.). At the top, there are many safe routes along four-wheel-drive tracks. If you're feeling ambitious, take the northern trail to **Sortes.** Another good, less demanding Fuente Dé trek starts and ends at the cable car's lower station (11½km; 4½hr.). The **Somo Waterfall Route** swings through the Berrugas cattle sheds, the soft Bustantivo meadows, and on to the Somo waterfall.

From the top of the teleférico, it's a 4km walk to **Refugio de Aliva** (1666m), the most expensive and luxurious 'refuge' in the park. All rooms come with complete baths and heat in winter; there is also a café on site. (☎/fax 942 73 09 99. Doubles 7500ptas/€45. MC/V.) To return to road-level, retrace your steps to the teleférico or walk (3hr.) to **Espinama,** where **Habitaciones Sebrango** offers respite from the Picos. (☎942 73 66 15. Singles 4000ptas/€24; doubles 5000ptas/€30.)

CANTABRIA

Thundering surf, powdery sands, and expansive beaches define the Cantabrian shore. From the spectacle of Santander's *El Sardinero* beaches to the pristine provincial park of Oyambre, it's the shore that Cantabria is famous for. Though they have yet to see the resort build-up of Spain's more famous southern coasts, the region's beach towns are by no means untouched or secluded, While this beach scene, particularly in Santander, is what lures visitors, Cantabria has plenty of other draws, from surfing some of the world's cleanest waters and hiking in the Picos de Europa to exploring the region's Paleolithic cave drawings and marveling at renowned architecture such as Gaudí's *El Capricho.*

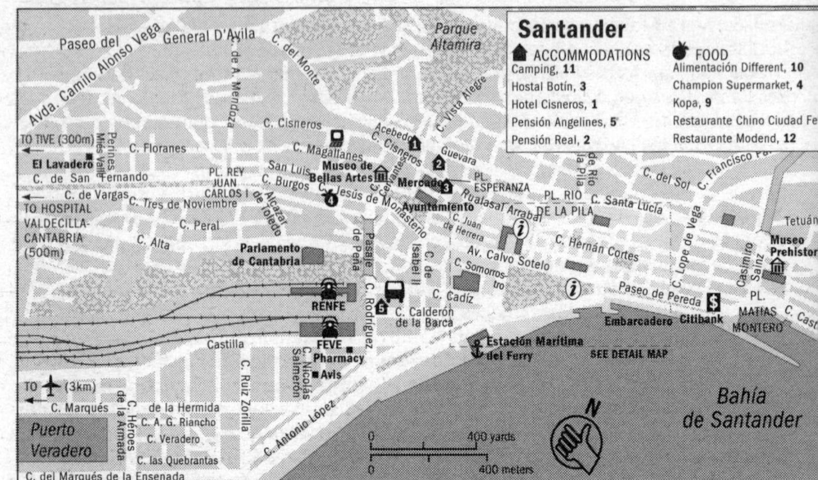

SANTANDER ☎942

Welcome to Vacationland, Spanish-style. Here in Santander (pop. 185,000), palm trees rub shoulders with pines, pasty Brits bake on the beach next to well-bronzed Spaniards, and the grime of the city center is easily forgotten on walk down *El Sardinero's* bougainvillea-filled boardwalks. Santander has been destroyed three times by natural and not-so-natural disasters—Queen Isabel nearly wiped out the population in when she contracted the clap, an explosion on a dynamite ship in 1893 leveled the city, and in 1941 another fire gutted the peninsular town. The most recent recreation of Santander has fashioned it as the "ideal city," complete with surf, sand, and sometimes sun. Those looking to get away from it all should avoid Santander, as this is "all" and then some. Those willing to share their beach space with a thousand other sun-starved bodies will, however, reap great rewards. The mountainous horizon with cliff top lighthouses is the Bay of Biscay at its best.

TRANSPORTATION

Flights: Aeropuerto de Santander, Ave. de Parayas, (☎942 20 21 00), in nearby Camargo 4km away. Daily flights to Madrid and Barcelona. Accessible by taxi only (1500ptas/€9.02). **Iberia,** Po. Pereda, 18 (☎942 22 97 00), is the only airline to service it. Open M-F 9am-1:30pm and 4-7pm.

Trains: Both the FEVE and RENFE stations are at Pl. de las Estaciones, s/n. **RENFE** (☎942 28 02 02) serves only a few destinations as Santander is the terminus of a rail line; to head elsewhere, you'll need to take a slower FEVE train to larger cities east or west of Santander. Info open 7:30am-11pm. To: **Madrid** (7hr., M-Th 8:10am, 3:45 and 11pm; F-Sa 8:10am and 3:45pm; Su 8:10am, 3:45, 5:15, and 11pm; 4500-5900ptas/€30-35); **Palencia** (2¼hr., 5 per day 8:10am-11pm, 1745-3400ptas/€11-20); **Valladolid** (5hr., 5 per day 8:10am-11pm, 2175-3900ptas/€13-24). **RENFE ticket office,** Po. Pereda, 25 (☎942 21 23 87). Open M-F 9am-2pm and 5-7pm, Sa 9am-1:30pm.

Buses: Navas de Tolosa, s/n (☎942 21 19 95), across C. Rodríguez from the train station. Info open M-F 8am-10pm, Sa 8am-1pm. To: **Barcelona** (10hr., 9am and 9:30pm daily, 6225ptas/€37.41); **Bilbao** (1½hr., 25 per day 6am-9pm, 965ptas/€5.80); **Burgos** (4hr.; 10:30am, 4:30, and 8pm daily; 3005ptas/€18); **León** (3½hr., M-Sa 9am and 4pm, 2940ptas/€18); **Oviedo** (3½hr.; M-F and Su 9 per day, Sa 7 per day, 6:30am-7:30pm; 1715ptas/€10.31); **Madrid** (6hr., 4 per day 10:30am-7pm, 3500-4750ptas/€21-27); **Salamanca** (6hr.; 9am, 4, and 8pm; 4700ptas/€29).

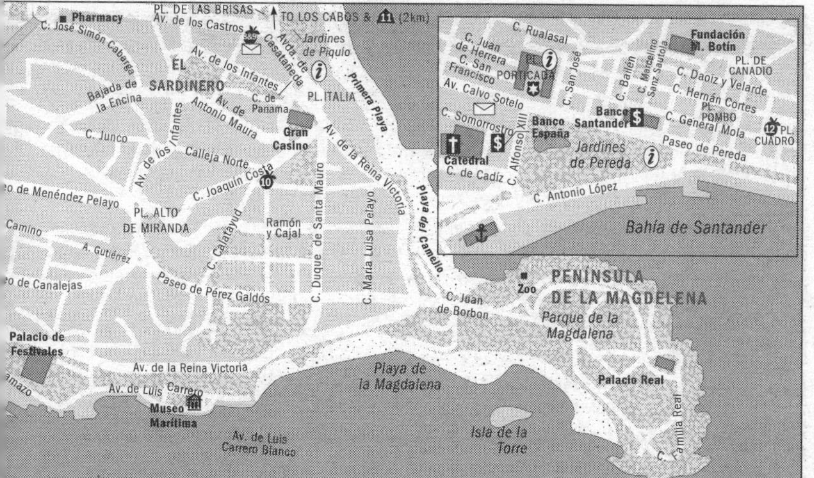

Ferries: Brittany Ferries, Estación Marítima, s/n (☎942 36 06 11; www.brittany-ferries.com), near the Jardines de Pereda. To **Plymouth, England** (2 per week, 13,400-36,400ptas/€81-219, plus 900ptas/€5.41 for seat reservation). Info M-F 9am-3:30pm and 4:30-7:30pm. In summer reserve 2 weeks ahead. **Los Reginas**, Embarcadero, s/n (☎942 21 66 19 or 21 67 53), by the Jardines de Pereda. Tours of the bay (45min., June 6-Sept. 1 3-6 per day, 425ptas/€2.55) and service to the beaches across the bay (10min., every 15min. 10am-8pm, 360ptas/€2.16).

Public Transportation: Municipal buses (info ☎942 20 07 71) run frequently throughout the city (every 15min.; July-Aug. 6am-midnight, Sept.-June 6am-10:30pm; night buses run hourly midnight-6am; 125ptas/€0.75). Buses #1, 3, 4, 5, 7, and 9 run from the Ayuntamiento stop (buses heading east stop in front of the plaza; buses heading west stop in front of Foot Locker) to El Sardinero along Paseo de Pereda and Avenida de la Reina Victoria, stopping at Pl. Italia and Jardines de Piquío. Stops are usually not marked with route numbers, but the tourist office offers bus route maps.

Taxis: Radio Taxi (☎942 33 33 33). 24hr. and service to greater Santander. Taxis wait outside the train stations, on C. Vargas and near the Ayuntamiento.

Car Rental: Avis, C. Nicolás Salmerón, 3 (☎942 22 70 25). Min. age 25, must have had driver's license for at least 1 year and a credit card in the renter's name. From 9000ptas/€54 per day. Open M-F 8am-1pm and 4-7:30pm, Sa 9am-1pm.

ORIENTATION AND PRACTICAL INFORMATION

Santander sits on a peninsula in the Bay of Biscay; its southern shores form the Bay of Santander. There are two main sections to the city: **the center,** around the train and bus stations and the Jardines de Pereda in the east, and **El Sardinero** in the west. The main thoroughfare starts at the Ayuntamiento in the center as **Avenida Calvo Sotelo,** and runs along the shore to the Jardines de Piqui in El Sardinero, changing its name to **Paseo de Pereda** and **Avenida de la Reina Victoria** along the way. At the western tip of Santander is **La Peninsula de la Magdalena,** the city's famed park. Santander is surprisingly large; the best way to get around is by city bus.

Tourist Office: Jardines de Pereda (☎942 20 30 00). From any of the stations, walk up C. Calderón de la Barca into the park; the office is off Po. de Pereda on the left just before the rotary. Bus and city maps. Open July-Sept. daily 9am-9pm; Oct.-June M-F 9am-1:30pm and 4:30-7:30pm, Sa 9am-1:30pm. **Branches** in the ferry station, Pl. Porticada, and El Sardinero across from Pl. Italia; all open July-Sept. daily 10am-9pm.

Budget Travel: TIVE, C. Canarias, 2 (☎942 33 22 15). Take eastbound bus #5 from the Ayuntamiento 6 stops to C. Camilo Alonso Vega, 22. ISIC 700ptas/€4.21. HI card 1800ptas/€10.80. Open M-F 9am-2pm.

Currency Exchange: Banco Central Hispano, Av. Calvo Sotelo, near the post office. Open May-Sept. M-F 8:30am-2:30pm; Oct.-Apr. M-F 8:30am-2:30pm, Sa 8:30am-1pm.

Luggage Storage: Lockers at the **RENFE train station,** by the ticket window (500ptas/€3 per day). Open daily 7am-11pm. Lockers at the **bus station** on the bottom level near *pasaje* 16 (500ptas/€3 per day). Open daily 7:30am-10:30pm.

Laundromat: El Lavadero, C. Mies Valle, 1 (☎942 23 06 07). From the Ayuntamiento, walk up Av. Burgos through its name change to Av. San Fernando; after Pl. Rey J. Carlos I, C. Mies Valle will be the sixth street on your right. Or, take any bus three stops past Ayuntamiento to C. Perines. Wash 375ptas/€2.25 per 6kg load, dry 225ptas/€1.35. Soap 50ptas/€0.30. Open M-F 9:30am-1:30pm, Sa 5-8pm.

Emergency: ☎112. **Police:** Pl. Porticada, s/n, and Av. del Deporte, (☎942 20 07 44).

Hospital: Hospital Universitario Marques de Valdecilla, Av. de Valdecilla, s/n (☎942 20 25 20). **Ambulances:** (☎942 31 30 00, 27 30 58, or 32 06 05).

Pharmacy: Lda. Isabel Ochoa, C. Castilla, 15. Around the corner from the train station. Open M-F 10am-2pm and 4-9pm, Sa 10am-3pm. In El Sardinero, **Rosio Castanedo Pfeiffer,** Av. de los Castros, 75. Open M-F 10am-2pm and 4-8pm, Sa 10am-2pm. For **late-night pharmacies,** call ☎942 22 02 66 to find out the pharmacist on-call. Every pharmacy also posts that week's schedule of on-call pharmacies.

Internet: Divernet Informática, C. Cisneros, 25 (☎942 24 14 25). 350ptas/€2.10 per hr. Open M-Th 9am-2pm and 4-10pm, Sa 9am-2pm and 4pm-1am, Su 4-10pm.

Post Office: Av. Alfonso XIII, s/n (☎942 21 26 73). Open M-F 8:30am-8:30pm, Sa 9:30am-2pm. **Branch** in El Sardinero on Av. Las Cruces, s/n. Open M-F 8:30am-2pm. **Lista de Correos, fax** only at Av. Alfonso XIII branch. **Postal Code:** 39080.

ACCOMMODATIONS AND CAMPING

During the summer—and particularly on weekends—all rooms are booked over a week in advance; showing up in town without a reservation will most definitely leave you homeless. The train and bus stations are loaded with *pensión* hawkers, but be wary: this is illegal, and the rooms are often far from the beaches. The highest hotel densities are near the market on Pl. Esperanza, across from the train station on C. Rodríguez, and along elegant Av. Castros in El Sardinero.

EL SARDINERO

Everyone wants to stay in El Sardinero, and for good reason: lined with beaches and promenades, El Sardinero is why people come to Santander. Unfortunately, its popularity means rooms are more expensive and hard to come by. From the Ayuntamiento stop in the city center, take bus #1, 3, 4, 5, 7, or 9 to Piquío (Hotel Colón); Av. de los Castros is directly to your left.

Pensión-Residencia Luisito, Av. Castros, 11 (☎942 27 19 71). The garrulous owner will tend to your every need, making the immense and comfortable rooms in this restored town home feel more like a grandmother's house than a *pension.* Airy rooms sport flowered sheets, terraces, sinks, and sloping ceilings. TV room on first floor. Breakfast 215ptas/€1.29. Doubles 4925ptas/€30. Open July-Sept.

Camping: Two sites lie on the scenic bluff of Cabo Mayor, 2km from Primero and Segundo Playas. From the Ayuntamiento, take bus #8 or 9 to Av. del Faro, 7 stops after Piquío. From the bus stop, turn left onto Av. del Faro and follow it into the Cabos; the campgrounds are a ten-minute walk. Alternatively, head north along coastal Ave. de Castañeda, bear right at the roundabout with the Park on your left, and then turn left onto G. Marañon; Ave. del Faro is on the right.

Camping Municipal Bellavista, Av. del Faro, s/n (☎942 39 15 30) is a 1st-class site just a few minutes from Playa de Matalenas. Reception daily 8am-midnight. 100ptas/€0.60 per person and per car.

Camping Cabo Mayor, Av. del Faro, s/n (☎942 39 15 42). Pool and tennis courts. Slightly pricier option than Bellavista. Reception daily 8am-11pm. 1500ptas/€9.02 per person and per car, 1000ptas/€6 per tent. Open July 15-Sept. 30.

Pensión Soledad, Av. Castros, 17 (☎942 27 09 36), next door to Luisito. 16 large rooms with sinks and good views. Breakfast 225ptas/€1.35. Singles 3000ptas/€18; doubles 5000ptas/€30 (IVA not included). Open July-Sept.

CITY CENTER

Although the area is loaded with cheap accommodations, only out of desperation should one stay near the stations. By day, the area is grimy, noisy, and far from the beach; by night, it's unsettling. The area north of the Ayuntamiento and Av. de Calvo Sotelo is a far more pleasant area in the center. While the beaches are a bus-ride away, restaurants, shops, and bars pack this neighborhood.

Hostal Cisneros, C. Cisneros, 8, 1st fl. (☎942 21 16 13). From the Ayuntamiento plaza, walk 3 blocks up C. Cervantes, the first street after the market. A comfortable and clean option in the center. All rooms have TV, beautiful wooden headboards, sunny terraces, and bathrooms. Reservations with 1st night's payment. Doubles 6350ptas/€39. Open June-Sept. Cash only.

Pensión Angelines, C. Rodríguez, 9, 2nd (☎942 31 25 84). Immaculate rooms with huge windows and winter heating. Strong shower. TV lounge. July-Aug. singles 3000ptas/€18; doubles 4400ptas/€27. Sept.-June singles 2000ptas/€12; doubles 3400ptas/€21.

Pensión Real, Pl. Esperanza, 1, 3rd fl. (☎942 22 57 87), in the peach building at the end of C. Isabel II. Communal baths, but all rooms have sinks. No reservations. June-Sept. doubles 5000-6000ptas/€30-36; Oct.-May 3000ptas/€18.

Hostal Botín, C. Isabel II, 1, 1st fl. (☎942 21 00 94 or 630 49 26 06). Crazy 80s comforters keep guests warm. Balconies overlook the bustling market. 25% discount on the public parking lot (100m away). Reservations accepted with pre-pay. Singles 2200ptas/€13; doubles 3500-6100ptas/21-37; triples 4600-8000ptas/€28-48; quads 6350-10500ptas/€37-63.

FOOD

CITY CENTER

Seafood restaurants crowd the **Puerto Pesquero** (fishing port), grilling up the day's catch at the end of C. Marqués de la Ensenada. From the main entrance of the train station turn right onto C. Rodríguez and right again onto C. Castilla; walk eight blocks down and turn left on C. Héroes de la Armada; cross the tracks and turn right after about 100m (20min.). Across the street from the Ayuntamiento, **Champion,** C. Jesus de Monasterio, s/n, has groceries. (Open M-Sa 9:15am-9pm.)

[illegible], C. Eduardo Benot, 6 (☎942 31 33 71). Walking away from the tourist office and the post office on Po. de Pereda, C. Eduardo Benot is on the left. Delectable Italian standards, from lasagna to *tortellini al quattro formaggio,* served in a sleek, dining room. Not particularly budget (no *menú del día,* and pasta dishes run 900-1500ptas/€5.41-9.02), but the filling, vegetarian-friendly fare and *tiramisú* are worth the extra pesetas. Open M-Sa 8pm-midnight. MC/V.

Bar Restaurante La Gaviota, C. Marqués de la Ensenada, s/n (☎942 22 11 32 or 22 10 06), at the corner of C. Mocejón in the *barrio pesquero* (fishermen's neighborhood). An elegant dining room hidden behind a rough exterior. Fresh grilled sardines (12 for 600ptas/€3.60) and *paella mixta* (600ptas/€3.60 for a *ración*). *Menú* 1200ptas/€7.21. Open daily 11:30am-4:15pm and 7:30pm-midnight. MC/V.

EL SARDINERO

The best grocery option is **Alimentación Different,** C. Joaquín de la Costa, 18, in the Hotel Sartena shopping complex. (Open M-Sa 9:30am-2:45pm and 5:45-9:30pm, Su 10am-3pm. AmEx/MC/V.)

Restaurante Chino Ciudad Feliz Iruña, C. Las Brisas, s/n (☎942 27 32 30). From steamed dumplings to heaping plates of *lo mein,* this seaside restaurant serves all the Westernized Chinese staples. Alas, no fortune cookies, but plenty of other post-meal gifts to make your family a happy one. Lunch *menú* 1500ptas/€9.02. Entrées 950-1500ptas/€5.71-9.02. Open daily 1-4pm and 7pm-midnight. MC/V.

Cafetería Kopa, C. Las Brisas, s/n, in the same building as Ciudad Feliz. Though not the most exciting fare, Kopa has what most restaurants in El Sardinero lack: good food at reasonable prices. *Menú del día* 1400ptas/€8.42. Open daily 10am-2pm.

SIGHTS

While Santander is proud of its few official architectural sights and museums, skip them in favor of its beaches and parks. Unless it rains (which is very likely), in which case Santander's amusing—and free—museums are worth a perusal. The tourist office has a list of one- to two-hour walking tours, the best way to get to know the city and feel like you actually did something during the day.

PENÍNSULA DE LA MAGDALENA. Although it can feel a bit like an amusement park at times, La Magdalena is Santander's prime attraction and one of the most beautiful parts of the city. The entire peninsula is ringed by bluffs plunging into the sea, and filled with palms and pines, and slender, calm beaches. The park's centerpiece is the *palacio*, the 20th-century, neo-Gothic mansion that was Alfonso XIII's summer home. Today, the palace houses the elite Universidad Internacional Menéndez Pelayo summer sessions on oceanography. The peninsula also shelters a mini-zoo (polar bears, penguins, and sea lions only), sports several models of mermaids and ships, and offers a free trolly ride around the park. Walking, however, is the best way to explore, and the 2km path ends with nourishment: *churrerías* flank the park's entrance. *(Península de La Magdalena. ☎942 27 25 04. Park open daily June-Sept. 8am-10pm; Oct.-May 8am-8:30pm. The palace has no scheduled visiting hours.)*

LOS CABOS. Just north of the El Sardinero beaches are more peninsular parks. While Cabo Menor and Cabo Mayor lack the attractions and action of La Magdalena, their bluffs and vistas are even more scenic. Cabo Menor, the more southern of the two, houses Santander's golf course and another mini-zoo; it also has postcard-worthy views of Cabo Mayor's 19th-century lighthouse. *(From Plaza Italia, walk up Av. de Castañeda past Pl. Glorieta Doctor Fleming, and turn right onto Av. de Pontejos, which turns into Av. del Faro and takes you up onto the cabos.)*

MUSEO DE BELLAS ARTES. Devoted to the works of local artists, Santander's Museo de Bellas Artes is surprisingly impressive. Art history buffs will enjoy the collection of 20th-century pieces, many which mimic the styles and trends of the time: much of the sculpture could easily be mistaken for Giacometti, and an entire room is devoted to forays into Cubism (and apparently Juan Gris imitation). The lower two floors feature special exhibitions of more well-known Spanish artists like Picasso and Miró. *(C. Rubio, 6. ☎942 23 94 85. From the Ayuntamiento, walk up C. Jesús de Monasterio and turn right onto C. Florida; the museum is on the right. Open July 15-Sept. 15 M-F 10:30am-1pm and 5:30-8pm, Sa 10:30am-1pm; Sept.16-June14 M-F 10am-1pm and 5-8pm, Sa 10am-1pm. Special exhibitions open until 9pm. Free.)*

CATEDRAL DE SANTANDER. Built in the Middle Ages, Santander's Gothic cathedral is often called the city's first monument. The heads of martyred Roman soldiers Emeterio and Celedonio are kept inside the ruins of an oven once used to heat Roman baths; occasionally they are taken out for religious processions. After dropping into the guillotine basket in 300 AD in La Rioja, they were brought to Santander in the 8th-century for safekeeping during the Moorish invasion. *(On Pl.*

omorrostro, just behind the post office and Banco España. ☎942 22 60 24. Open M-F 10am-pm and 4-7:30pm, Sa 10am-1pm and 4:30-8:45pm, Su 8am-2pm and 4:30pm-9pm. Free. ours in Spanish at 10:30, 11:30am, 12:45, 4:30, 5:45, 6:30, and 7:30pm daily. Free.)

MUSEO MARÍTIMO DEL CANTÁBRICO. The top floors of the Museo Marítimo hart the evolution of regional fishing-boats, while the bottom floor highlights the ea's living creatures. *(C. San Martín de Bajamar, beyond the Puerto Chico. ☎942 27 49 52. Open mid-June to mid-Sept. Tu-Sa 11am-1pm and 4-7pm, Su 11am-2pm; mid-Sept. to mid-une M-Sa 10am-1pm and 4-6pm, Su and holidays 11am-2pm. Free.)*

MUSEO DE PREHISTORIA Y ARQUEOLOGÍA. Paleolithic skulls and tools from Cantabria and Castilla y León rattle around in the miniscule Museo de Prehistoria Arqueología. Artifacts and photographs of the **Cuevas de Altamira** (see p. 450) are sad substitute for the real thing. *(C. Casimiro Sáinz, 4. ☎942 20 71 05. Open June 15-ept. 15 Tu-F 10am-8pm, Sa 10am-1pm and 4-7pm, Su 11am-2pm; Sept. 16-June 14 Tu-Sa am-1pm and 4-7pm, Su and holidays 11am-2pm. Free.)*

BEACHES

n Santander, every day is a beach day: rain or shine (but most often rain), locals lock to the beach as soon as work gets out and spend the late afternoon and vening soaking up the last rays of sun. It's easy to understand why as antander's beaches, particularly those in El Sardinero, are wide swaths of pow-ery sand. The water, however, can get very rough; it's not uncommon for five-oot breakers to crash into the beach. The water is calmer and the beaches rock-er on the bay side. The best and most popular beaches are undoubtedly **Playas rimero y Segundo** in El Sardinero. Not only does the soft sand go on forever, but he waters have been named one of the eight cleanest beaches in the world. rimero and Segundo are also the hangout of Santander's surfing crowd, which omes out during and after rain. Calmer waters but no fewer bodies line the outhern shore of La Magdalena. Rock-framed **Playa de Bikinis,** on the peninsula self, is the most secluded and the haunt of Santander's guitar-playing teens; **laya de la Magdalena** and **Playa de Los Peligros,** stretching from the peninsula to elow Av. de la Reina Victoria, are virtually waveless and therefore very popular ith families. To escape all the hordes, either head across the bay to **Playas Pun-al, Somo,** and **Loredo** lining a narrow peninsula of dunes, or hoof it up to the emote beaches of Los Cabos where **Playa de Matalenas** and **Playa de Los Molinu-os** await you without hordes of bodies.

ENTERTAINMENT AND NIGHTLIFE

he August **Festival Internacional de Santander** brings hordes of people and myriad usic and dance recitals to town, culminating in the [illegible], contact the **Oficina del Festival,** Palacio de Festi-ales de Cantabria (☎942 21 05 08), on C. Gamazo. The **Baños de Ola** is a turn-of-he-century style celebration of Alfonso XIII's discovery that, lo and behold, play-g in the waves is fun. The festival takes place in the third week of July on the El ardinero promenades, with bathers clad in antique swimming suits. That same eek, the *barrio pesquero* celebrates the patron of fishermen, **Santiago.**

Perhaps too exhausted from days spent sunbathing, everyone in Santander eems to hit the sack early. In **El Sardinero,** cafés and bars line the promenade ong Playas Primero and Segundo, with street performers offering live entertain-ent to families and teenagers. The less risk-averse spend their evenings blowing *esetas* at the **Gran Casino,** Pl. Italia, s/n. Passport, proper dress (pants and shoes), d a minimum age (18 to gamble) are required. (Open 24hr.) In the city center, niversity students and the middle aged couples *tapas*-hop around Pl. Cañadío, C. aoíz y Velarde, and C. Pedrueca; facing Banco Santander from the tourist office, alk up C. Las Infantes, which runs into C. Pedrueca. Around 2 or 3am, crowds ood **C. Río de la Pila** and **C. Casimiro Sainz.**

DAYTRIPS FROM SANTANDER

CUEVAS DE ALTAMIRA

The Altamira caves area just outside of Torrelavega on the way to Santillana del Mar. ***La Cantábrica*** *(☎942 72 08 22) sends buses from Pl. Estaciones, s/n, in Santander to Torrelavega (30min.; M-F 7 per day 9am-9:30pm, Sa-Su 5 per day 10:30am-9:30pm; 275ptas/€1.65). Ask the bus driver to let you off near the caves.*

Bison roam, horses graze, and goats butt heads on the ceilings of the limestone **Cuevas de Altamira,** dubbed the "Sistine Chapel of Paleolithic Art." The large scale polychrome paintings are renowned for their scrupulous attention to natu ralistic detail and resourceful use of the caves' natural texture. Unfortunately excessive tourism has caused substantial damage, and now only 20 people per day are allowed to visit. **To see the caves yourself, you must be at least 13 years old and must write to request permission at least one year in advance.** Rumor has it there's a three-year waiting list, but if you do write, include a photocopy of your passpor and address the request to the **Centro de Investigación de Altamira,** Santillana de Mar, Cantabria, Spain 39330. (☎942 81 80 05; fax 84 01 57)

SANTILLANA DEL MAR

Santillana del Mar is on the Santander-San Vicente de la Barquera bus line. ***La Cantábrica*** *(☎942 72 08 22) sends buses from Navas de Tolosa, s/n, in Santander (45min.; M-F 7 per day 9am-9:30pm, Sa-Su 5 per day 10:30am-9:30pm; 270ptas/€1.62). In Santillana, buses halt on C. Santo Domingo in front of the Museo Diocesano; the return bus stops in front of the stairway across the street.*

French philosopher Jean-Paul Sartre proclaimed Santillana del Mar (pop. 4,000) to be the most beautiful town in Spain, and perhaps it is: atop a hill in northern Cantabria, the town is a perfectly preserved collage of tangled stone streets and architecture dating back to the Middle Ages. Alas, Santillana's beauty is no secret an the town seems entirely devoted to the hundreds of tourists who pass through daily. The town owes its name not to its flatness (*llana*) nor its seaside perch *(del mar)*, as it has neither of those; it is named for the **Colegiata de Santa Juliana,** a 12th century Romanesque church founded by Turkish monks that holds the remains of Juliana, a woman martyred for not renouncing her virginity or faith in God. The sepulchre guards her relics and the gorgeous high altarpiece is a 15th-century Spanish Flemish painting depicting the saint's martyrdom. From the bus stop in front of the steps on C. Santo Domingo, walk uphill into town, and veer to the right at the firs fork; onto C. Cantón, which turns into C. del Río and leads you directly to the church. (Open daily 10am-1:30pm and 4-7:30pm. 400ptas/€2.40, which also gets yo into the Museo Diocesano.) From in front of the Colegiata, heading back up C. de Río leads to the **Museo del la Tortura y de la Inquisición.** This small museum reveal the dark side of Christianity with an exhibit of terrifying torture methods used during the Spanish Inquisition. The most frightening is the vaginal pear, an expanding device that, when inserted, will gouge out and burst all the abdominal organs (☎942 84 02 73. Open daily 10am-9pm. 600ptas/€3.60.) The **Museo Diocesano,** across the street from the stop on C. Santo Domingo in the Monasterio Regina Coeli, has mediocre collection of religious relics and artwork. Most interesting is the collection of over three hundred miniature figurines of the crucifixion. (Open daily 10am 1:30pm and 4-7:30pm. 400ptas/€2.40, includes admission to the Colegiata.)

The **tourist office** is in **La Casa del Aguila y la Parra** on Pl. Ramón Pelayo. From the bus stop, walk uphill on C. Santo Domingo and veer to the left at the first fork; thi leads directly onto Pl. Ramon Pelayo. (☎942 81 82 51. Open daily 9am-1pm and 6pm.) The **post office** is next door to the tourist office on Pl. Ramón Pelayo. (☎94 81 80 40. Open M-F 8:30am-2:30pm, Sa 9:30am-1pm.) **Postal code:** 39330.

COMILLAS

Comillas lies on the Santander-San Vicente de la Barquera bus route. ***La Cantábrica buses*** *(☎942 72 08 22 or 72 08 22) run from* ***Santander,*** *Navas de Tolosa, s/n (M-F 7 per day 9am-9:30pm, Sa-Su 5 per day 10:30am-9:30pm; 480ptas/€2.88).*

The beaches of Comillas (pop. 2,500) are intoxicating. From desolate and calm inlets to the wind-swept swaths of sand directly on the Bay of Biscay, Comillas' beaches are its main attraction, and drawing everyone from Spanish nobles to foreign visitors for their summers. Unlike Santillana, Comillas does not feel like a giant commercial trap. Rather, everyone shuttles serenely to the beaches, amazed to simply have access to the splendor of Comillas. This small resort town's central beach, **Playa Comillas,** is a vast expanse of silky sand and raging waves; on windy days, ten-foot breakers pound the shores. Fortunately, the lifeguards are vigilant, making bodysurfing and general wave delirium a safe possibility. From the bus stop follow up C. Marqués de Comillas uphill into town. Pass through Pl. del Generalísimo and veer left onto Cuesta General Mola; after another small square, Corro San Pedro will be on the right. From this street, turn left onto C. La Moria, and then follow the footpath downhill to the beach (10min.). Heading in the opposite direction on C. Marqués de Comillas from the bus stop will bring you, 4km later, to **Playa Oyambre,** another expansive, thundering beach. It's easier to take the La Cantabria bus toward San Vicente and ask the driver to let you off at Oyambre.

While most visitors seem to come solely for the surf, Comillas itself is equally proud of its architectural attractions. Most notable—and amusing—is **El Capricho,** Gaudí's summer palace. While it's not possible to enter the building, most visitors are content to see the bright swirling turrets and gingerbread-esque windows outside. Standing at the bus stop, you can see the colorful El Capricho on the hill above; follow the footpath across the street for a close-up view. Next to El Capricho on the same hill are the neo-Gothic **Palacio de Sobrellano** and the **Capilla-Pantheon,** which contains furniture designed by Gaudí. (Hours vary; so check with the tourist office before venturing over.) Between July 15 and 18, Comillas' **fiestas** go up in a blaze of fireworks, pole-walking, goose-chasing, and dancing in the plaza.

The **tourist office** is at C. Mariá del Piélago, 2. From the bus stop follow C. Marqués de Comillas past the turn-off for the beach, through the plaza, and then uphill one block, at which point a sign directs you to the office. (☎942 72 07 68. Open May-Sept. M-Sa 10am-1pm and 5-9pm, Su 11am-1pm and 4:30-7pm.) The **post office** is at C. Antonio López, 6, on the main road uphill from the tourist office turn-off. (☎942 72 00 95. Open M-F 8:30am-2:30pm, Sa 9:30am-1pm.) **Postal code:** 39520.

SAN VICENTE DE LA BARQUERA

La Cantábrica ***buses*** *(☎942 72 08 22) run from Santander, Navas de Tolosa, s/n (1¼hr.; M-F 7 per day 9am-9:30pm, Sa-Su 5 per day 10:30am-9:30pm; 535ptas/€3.22), stopping at Santillana del Mar and Comillas on the way. The bus station, Av. de Miramar, s/n (☎942 71 09 21) is open daily 7*[illegible]

Picture a russet castle on a hill, flags flying from turrets high above a twisting, cobblestone town. In the foreground, azure waters lap at brightly colored boats and Roman bridges, and rising high in the background are the sharp peaks of the Picos de Europa, framing the castle and town. Spanish and foreign tourists alike flock from their various Cantabrian vacation spots to snap their photo of the famous San Vicente de la Barquera (pop. 5000). After a quick stop at one of the beautiful beaches, though it's best back at Santander, as San Vicente is a one-sight town. To best view this renowned vista, turn left out of the bus station onto Av. de Miramar, and then turn left again onto the Puente de la Maza, a 15th-century stone bridge with the best vantage in town. The castle itself can only be viewed from the outside, but the 12th-century church-fortress adjacent to it, **Santa María de los Angeles,** shows off a handsome Romanesque portico. (Open daily 11am-2pm and 5:30-8:30pm.) As San Vicente is part of the Parque Natural de Oyambre, it has plenty of sandy spots for showing off those bikinis and speedos. **Playas Merón, La Maza,** and **El Rosal** are all a 15min. walk across the bay. El Rosal has the calmest waters, but it and Merón deal with a pesky low-tide, that all but empties the bay; La Maza, on the Bay of Biscay, has no low-tide problems but suffers rough waters in return. From the bus station, head across the Puente de la Maza; after crossing it, there will be signs pointing to all three beaches. After *Semana Santa*, San Vicente hosts a maritime procession called **La Folia.** Every September 7-9, the ancient feast of **La Barquera y El Mozucu** features free servings of *sorropotún*, a typical Barquera tuna-based stew. From July 14-16, the town breaks out with dances and sardine cookouts during **Las Fiestas de la Virgen del Carmen.**

The **tourist office** has branches in the bus station and on Av. Generalísimo, 20. To reach the tourist office in town from the bus station, turn right onto Av. de Miramar; at its end, turn right onto Av. Generalísimo. (☎/fax 942 71 07 99. Town office open *Semana Santa* and July-Sept. M-F 9:30am-2pm and 4-8:30pm, Sa-Su 10:30am-2pm and 4:30-8pm; rest of the year W-Sa 9:30am-2pm and 4-9pm. Bus station office open *Semana Santa* and July-Sept. M-Sa 11am-1:30pm, and 5-7:30pm; rest of the year W-Sa 11am-1:30pm.) The **post office**, is on Po. de La Barquera, 1. From the tourist office, continue on Av. Generalísimo and cross the bridge. (☎942 71 16 33. Open M-F 8:30am-2:30pm, Sa 9:30am-1pm.) **Postal code:** 39540.

POTES

The Potes (pop. 2000) tourist brochure prophesies "...*Y Volverás*" (you'll return) and it's probably right; visitors tend to fall in love with this town in the shadow of the mountains. In addition to making a great base for outdoor activities in the Picos de Europa National Park (see p. 439), Potes itself can captivate for days. From the endless monasteries dotting the surrounding hills to the streets peddling cheeses, walking sticks, and Cantabrian crafts, Potes mesmerizes its visitors.

TRANSPORTATION. **Palomera buses** (☎942 88 06 11 or 50 30 80) travel to and from **Fuente Dé** (45min.; M-F 8:15am, 1pm, and 8pm, Sa-Su 1pm; 185ptas/€1.11) and **Santander** (2½hr.; M-F 7am, 9:45am, and 5:45pm, Sa-Su 10:30am and 5:45pm; 920ptas/€5.53). **ALSA buses** (☎902 42 22 42) run to **León** (3hr., M-Sa 11am, 975ptas/5.86E). There is no bus station in Potes; all buses stop at the small hut on C. Fonfría near the tourist office, across from the municipal parking lot and in front of the Supermarket. For a **taxi** call ☎942 73 04 00. They cluster in Plaza de la Serna.

PRACTICAL INFORMATION. The **tourist office,** C. Independencia, 30, in the old church, has a list of suggested trails and *refugios* with contact info. Free tours of Potes are given daily at noon and 6pm. From the bus stop, walk up C. Fonfría toward town to Pl. de la Serna, where you'll see signs on the left for the tourist office. (☎/fax 942 73 07 87. Open daily 10am-2pm and 4-8pm) Services include: **Banco Santander,** C. Doctor Encinas, s/n, at the corner of C. San Marcial (☎902 11 22 11; open M-F 8:30am-2pm); the **Guardia Civil** (☎942 73 00 07) on C. Obispo off C. Doctor Encinas; **Farmacia F. Soberón,** C. Cantabra, s/n (☎942 73 00 08; open daily 9am-9pm); the **health center** (☎942 73 03 60) on C. Eduardo García de Enterría, inside the **Cruz Roja** (Red Cross) building (☎942 73 01 02); and the **post office,** Pl. de la Serna, s/n (open M-F 8:30am-2:30pm, Sa 9:30am-1pm). **Postal code:** 39570.

ACCOMMODATIONS AND FOOD. Several hostels are scattered on C. Doctor Encinas and on side street C. Cantabria. The cheapest rooms fill early in the day, so make reservations. The palatial rooms at **Casa Cayo,** C. Cántabra, 6, a right off C. Doctor Encinas when walking into town from the bus stop, enjoy in-room TVs, phones, bathrooms, and a cozy lounge with an even bigger TV. (☎942 73 01 50. Singles 3000ptas/€18; doubles 6000ptas/€36; triples 7000ptas/€42. MC/V.) **Hostal Lombraña,** C. el Sol, 2, has small, bright rooms with beautiful views of the mountains. Walking into town from the bus stop, it's on the right just before the bridge; look for the sign. (☎942 73 05 19. Doubles 3000ptas/€18, with bath 3400ptas/€20. IVA not included.) Closer to Panes off C. Dr. Encinas, **Fogón de Cus,**

C. Capital Palacios, 2, has sunny, ample rooms. Walking from the bus stop along C. Doctor Encinas into town, the hotel is up a stairway on the right. (☎942 73 00 60. Singles 2500ptas/€15; doubles 4000ptas/€24, with bath 4200ptas/€25. AmEx/MC/V.) There are also several *casas de labranza* (farm houses for rent) in the area; ask at the tourist office for details. The closest camping site is the first-class **Camping La Viorna,** about 1km up the road to Monasterio Santo Toribio, which helps organize excursions and has a restaurant, supermarket, and pool. (☎942 73 20 21 or 73 21 01. 600ptas/€3.60 per person, car, and tent. Open *Semana Santa*-Oct. 30.)

Potes can feed plenty of hungry hikers; C. Doctor Encino, C. Cantabria, and C. San Cayetano are packed with restaurants, tapas bars, and cafeterias. **Restaurante El Fogón de Cus** serves hearty mountain fare on white tablecloths; for a livelier atmosphere, ask for a table in the back room with the TV. The restaurant is next door to the Pensión of the same name. (☎942 73 00 60. *Menú* 1750ptas/€11. AmEx/MC/V. Open daily 1:30-4pm and 8:30-11pm.) Another delicious dining option is riverside **Restaurante La Caseta II,** C. Cantabra, 8, next door to Casa Cayo, where veal, lamb, and game are the specialties. (☎/fax 942 73 07 13. Open daily 1-4pm and 8pm-midnight.) **Supermercado Ugari,** C. Doctor Encinas, 6, stocks the basics. (Open M-F 9am-2pm and 4:30-8:30pm, Sa 9am-2pm.)

ADVENTURE TOURISM AND HIKING. The streets of Potes are lined with outfitters specializing in the latest outdoor fads. The tourist office has a list of all the outfitters in town. In the summer, it is necessary to book several days in advance. **Picos Aventura,** C. Cervantes, 3, organizes expeditions, including horseback-riding, mountain-biking, paragliding, and canyoning. The office is at the base of the bridge on C. Doctor Encinas. (☎942 73 21 61; fax 985 73 21 45. Prices range 2500-8500ptas/€15-51. Open daily 10am-2pm and 4-8pm. Closed Su Nov.-May. MC/V.) **La Liebana,** C. Independencia, 4, organizes similar outings. The office is behind the gazebo on the river on C. Doctor Encinas. (☎942 73 10 21, fax 73 10 00. Prices range 3000-8000ptas/€18-48.) The best horseback riding and paragliding trips are organized through **La Cabaña,** C. La Molina, s/n. (☎942 73 00 50; fax 73 00 51. kiko@mundivia.es. Tandem paragliding 8500ptas/€51 per flight. Horseback riding 3000-4700ptas/18.03-28.24E.) For those wanting to explore on their own, **Bustamente,** C. Dr. Encinas, 10, sells maps and guidebooks.

Urdón, 15km north of Potes on the road to Panes, is the start of a challenging 6km (4hr.) hike to **Treviso,** a tiny town where chickens outnumber human inhabitants. Trail details are on posters all over Potes. Another option for outings from Potes is **Peña Sagra,** about 13km east (2hr.) of the towns of **Luriezo** or **Aniezo.** From the summit, you can survey the Picos and the sea, 51km away. On your way down, visit **Iglesia de Nuestra Señora de la Luz,** where the beautifully carved patron saint of Picos lives 364 days a year. The Virgin, known affectionately as *Santuca* (tiny saint), is removed from the church and honored on May 2.

GALICIA (GALIZA)

If, as the old Galician saying goes, "rain is art," then there is no gallery more beautiful than the misty skies of northwestern Spain. Galicia looks and feels like no other region in the country. Often veiled in a silvery drizzle, it is a province of fern-laden eucalyptus woods, slate-roofed fishing villages, and seemingly endless white beaches. Rivers wind through hills and gradually widen into estuaries that empty into the Bay of Biscay and Atlantic Ocean.

A rest stop on the Celts' journey to Ireland around 900 BC, Galicia displays enduring Celtic influences. Ancient *castros* (fortress-villages), inscriptions, and bagpipes testify to this Celtiberian past, and lingering lore of witches, fairies, and buried treasures have earned Galicia a reputation as a land of magic. The rough terrain here has historically hampered trade, but ship-building, auto manufacturing, and even renowned fashion labels are contributing to the region's gradual modernization and development, and Galicia squirms beneath its stereotype as rural and old-fashioned. Tourists have started to permeate even the smallest of towns, and Santiago de Compostela, the terminus of the Camino de Santiago, continues to be one of the most popular backpacking destinations in the world.

Galicians speak *gallego*, a linguistic missing link of sorts between Castilian and Portuguese. While newspapers and street signs alternate between languages, most conversations are conducted in Spanish. Regional cuisine features *caldo gallego* (a vegetable broth), *vieiras* (scallops, the pilgrim's trophy), *empanadas* (turnovers stuffed with assorted fillings), and *pulpo a gallego* (boiled octopus). Regionalism in Galicia doesn't cause quite the stir it does in the País Vasco or Catalunya, but you still may see graffiti calling for "*liberdade.*"

SANTIAGO DE COMPOSTELA ☎981

Santiago (pop. 130,000) is a city of song. From the impromptu orchestra concerts on Rúa Vilar to the thumping of all-night discos, from the roving bands of *gaita* players to the cathedral's morning chimes, every street and plaza is filled with musical celebration. Perhaps these are the chords of weary pilgrims, elated to have, at long last, reached the apostle's tomb. Or perhaps these are the tunes of the Apostolo, the city's extravagant 10-day fiesta in honor of its namesake. But more likely, these are just the sounds of joy at waking up to another day in Santiago, where narrow, baroque streets empty into vast plazas, where relaxers and revelers spill out of the myriad cafés and bars, and where every day in this sun-blessed (and perhaps Apostle-blessed) city is worthy of celebration.

TRANSPORTATION

Flights: Aeropuerto Lavacolla (☎981 54 75 00 or 54 75 01), 10km away on the road to Lugo. A bus goes to Santiago, stopping at the bus and train stations and C. General Pardiñas, 26 (8 per day 8am-10pm, 125ptas/€0.75). Schedule in the daily *El Correo Gallego* (125ptas/€0.75), available at newsstands. **Iberia,** C. General Pardiñas, 36 (☎981 57 20 28 or 57 20 24). Open M-F 9:30am-2pm and 4-7:15pm.

Trains: R. Horreo, s/n (☎981 52 02 02 and 24 02 02). To: **Bilbao** (10¾hr., 9:04am, 5850ptas/€35) via **León** (6½hr., 3500ptas/€21) and **Burgos** (8hr., 4600ptas/€28); **La Coruña** (1hr.; M-F 20 per day 6:30am-10:26pm, Sa-Su 14 per day 7:12am-10:26pm; 525-650ptas/€3.16-3.90); **Madrid** (8hr.; M-F 1:47 and 10:25pm, Sa 10:30pm, Su 9:52, 1:47am, 10:30pm; 5900ptas/€35); **Vigo** (2hr.; M-F 20 per day 6:30am-10:05pm, Sa-Su 14 per day 7:33am-10:05pm; 625-1210ptas/€3.76-7.28) via **Pontevedra** (1½hr.; 530-1100ptas/€3.19-6.61).

Buses: Estación Central de Autobuses, R. de Rodríguez, s/n (☎981 58 77 00), a 20min. walk from downtown. Bus #10 and bus C Circular leave from the R. Montero Ríos side of Pl. Galicia for the station (every 15-20min. 6:30am-10pm, 105ptas/€0.63). Info open daily 6am-10pm.

ALSA (☎981 58 61 33, reservations 902 42 22 42) open daily 7:30am-9:30pm. To: **Bilbao** (11¼hr., 9am and 9:30pm, 6500ptas/€39); **Madrid** (8-9hr., 4 [illegible] [illegible] hr., 8am and 4:30pm, 7275ptas/€44).

Castromil (☎981 58 90 90 or 902 10 44 44). To: **El Ferrol** (2hr.; M-F 6 per day 9:15am-9pm, Sa-Su 4 per day 9:15am-9pm; 1050ptas/€6.31); **La Coruña** (1½hr.; M-F hourly 7am-10pm, Sa hourly 9am-10pm, Su hourly 9:15am-10:30pm; 875ptas/€5.26); **Noya** (1hr.; M-F 15 per day 6:15am-8pm, Sa 10 per day 7am-8pm, Su 8 per day 8am-8:30pm; 420ptas/€2.52); **Vigo** (2hr.; M-F hourly 6am-10pm, Sa hourly 8am-9pm, Su hourly 9am-9pm; 975ptas/€5.86) via **Pontevedra** (1½hr., 675ptas/€4.06).

Arriva/Finisterre (☎981 58 85 11) to **Finisterre** (2½hr.; M-F 7 per day 8am-7:30pm, Sa 4 per day 8am-7:30pm, Su 3 per day 8am-6:15pm; 1485ptas/€8.93).

Public Transportation: (☎981 58 18 15). Bus #6 to the train station (open daily 10am-10:30pm), #9 to the campgrounds (10am-8pm), #10 to the bus station. In the city center, almost all buses stop at Pr. Galicia, where there are two stops, one on the R. do Doutour Teixeiro side and one along R. de Montero Ríos. Except for bus #6 and 9, buses run daily 6:30am-10:30pm every 20min. (105ptas/€0.63).

Taxis: Radio Taxi (☎981 58 24 90 or 59 84 88). 24hr. Taxis wait at the bus and train stations and Pl. Galicia. For late-night service, try near the clubs in Pl. Roxa.

Car Rental: Avis at the train station, (☎981 59 61 01). Must be at least 25. Open M-F 9am-1:15pm and 4-7pm, Sa 9am-12:45pm, Su 9:30am-12:30pm.

ORIENTATION AND PRACTICAL INFORMATION

The **cathedral** marks the center of the old city, which sits on a hill above the new city. The **train station** is at the far southern end of town. To reach the old city, either take bus #6 to Pr. Galicia or walk up the stairs across the parking lot from the main entrance, cross the street, and bear right onto Rúa do Horreo, which leads to Pr. Galicia. The bus station is at the far northern end of town; the walk is over 20min., so instead take bus #10 to Pr. Galicia. In the old city, three main streets lead to the cathedral: **Rúa de Franco, Rúa de Vilar,** and **Rúa Nova.**

Tourist Office: R. do Vilar, 43 (☎981 58 40 81). English spoken. Open M-F 10am-2pm and 4-7pm, Sa 11am-2pm and 5-7pm, Su and festivals 11am-2pm. Another **branch** is in a little Modernist structure (☎981 55 51 29; fax 58 48 55), in the center of Pl. Galicia. Open M-F 10am-2pm and 5-8pm.

Currency Exchange: Banco Central Hispano, R. do Horreo, 20 (☎902 24 24 24). Open May-Sept. M-F 8:30am-2:30pm; Oct.-Apr. M-F 8:30am-2:30pm, Sa 8:30am-1pm.

Religious Services: Mass in the cathedral M-Sa 9:30, noon (Misa del Peregrino), 6, and 7:30pm (vespers); Su 10:30am, 1, 5, 7pm (vespers). Most nights also offer a special **pilgrim's mass,** featuring the *botafumeiro* (a gigantic incense burner).

Emergency: ☎112 or 900 44 42 22. **Police: Local Police,** (☎981 54 23 23).

Late-night Pharmacy: Pr. de Tournal, 11 (☎981 58 59 40). Open daily 10pm-10am.

Medical Assistance: Hospital Xeral, R. das Galeras, s/n (☎061 or 981 54 00 00).

Internet Access: Nova 50, R. Nova, 50 (☎981 56 01 00). 26 fast computers. 200ptas/€1.20 per hr., 75ptas/€0.45 minimum. Open daily 9am-1am.

Post Office: Travesa de Fonseca, s/n (☎981 58 12 52; fax 56 32 88), on the corner of R. Franco. **Lista de Correos** (around the corner, R. Franco, 6) and **fax** service. Open M-F 8:30am-8:30pm, Sa 9:30am-2pm. **Postal Code:** 15701.

ACCOMMODATIONS AND CAMPING

Nearly every street in the old city houses at least one or two *pensiones*. The liveliest and most popular streets, however, are R. Vilar and R. Raíña. Call ahead in winter when university students occupy most rooms.

Hospedaje Ramos, C. Raíña, 18, 2nd fl. (☎981 58 18 59), above O Papa Una restaurant. In the center of the *ciudad vieja.* Winter heating. Check-out 11am. Reservations recommended. Singles 1900ptas/€11.40, with bath 2100ptas/€13; doubles 3450ptas/€21, with bath 3750ptas/€23.

Hospedaje Santa Cruz, R. Vilar, 42, 2nd fl. (☎981 58 28 15). Common space includes a TV, kitchen, and washer/dryer. Winter heating. Singles 1500ptas/€9, with bath 2000ptas/€12; doubles 4000ptas/€24, with bath 5000ptas/€30.

Hospedaja Fonseca, R. Fonseca, 1, 2nd fl. (☎981 57 24 79). Colorful, sunny rooms. Singles, doubles, triples, and quads all 2000ptas/€12 per person. Open July-Sept.

Hospedaje Sofía, C. Cardenal Paya, 16 (☎981 58 51 50), off Pl. Mazarelos. Don't be confused by the restaurant and *hospedaje* Zingara downstairs; Sofía is upstairs. Communal baths. Singles 2500-3000ptas/€15-18; doubles 4500-5000ptas/€27-30.

Camping As Cancelas, R. 25 de Xullo, 35 (☎981 58 02 66), 2km from the cathedral on the northern edge of town; take bus #6 or 9 from the train station or from Pr. Galicia. Laundry, supermarket, and pool. 600ptas/€3.60 per person, 650ptas/€3.90 per car and per tent, electricity 500ptas/€3 extra.

FOOD

Tapas-weary budget travelers will appreciate Santiago's selection of restaurants. Bars and cafeterias line the streets with a variety of remarkably inexpensive *menús;* most restaurants are on R. Vilar, R. Franco, R. Nova, and R. Raíña. In the new city, look near Pl. Roxa. End your meal with a *tarta de Santiago,* rich almond cake emblazoned with a sugary St. James cross. Santiago's **market,** between Pl. San Felix and Convento de San Agustín, is a sight in its own right. (Open M-Sa 7:30am-2pm.) **Supermercado Lorenzo Froiz,** Pl. Toural, is one block from Pr. Galicia. (Open M-Sa 9am-3pm and 4:30-9pm, Sa 9am-3pm and 5-9pm. MC/V.)

O Cabaliño do Demo, R. Aller Ulloa, 7 (☎981 58 81 46). Walk to Porta Do Camino, where R. Cerca meets R. San Pedro; R. Aller Ulloa is the last stretch of R. Cerca before the Porta. Enjoy a variety of global vegetarian entrées—from Middle Eastern to Ethiopian—in this chic orange-walled restaurant. *Menú* 1100ptas/€6.60. Open M-Sa daily 2-4pm and 9pm-midnight. Café downstairs open 8am-midnight.

Restaurante Le Crêpe, Pr. de Quintana, 1 (☎981 57 76 43), across from the cathedral. Santiago's hipsters dine on authentic, perfectly thin crepes in this airy, techno-filled eatery. Open daily 1-4pm and 8pm-midnight.

SIGHTS

THE CATHEDRAL

Accessible from Pr. do Obradoiro, Pr. da Inmaculada, Pr. da Quintana, and Pr. das Praterias. ☎981 58 35 48. Open daily 7am-7pm.

Santiago's cathedral has four façades, each a masterpiece from a different era, with entrances opening to four different plazas: Praterías, Quintana, Obradoiro, and Inmaculada. From the southern **Praza das Praterías** (with the spitting sea horse), enter the cathedral through the Romanesque arched double doors. The **Torro de Reloxio** (clock tower), Pórtico Real, and Porta Santa face the **Praza da Quintana,** to the west of the cathedral. To the north, a blend of Doric and Ionic columns grace the **Praza da Inmaculada,** combining Romanesque and Neoclassical styles. Consecrated in 1211, the cathedral later acquired Gothic chapels in the apse and transept, a 15th-century dome, a 16th-century cloister, and the 18th-century Baroque **Obradoiro façade** with two towers that soar above the city. This façade faces the west and **Praza do Obradoiro,** an immense plaza scattered with souvenir hawkers and *tunas* (young lute-strumming men in medieval garb).

Many consider the Maestro Mateo's **Pórtico de la Gloria,** encased in the Obradoiro façade, the crowning achievement of Spanish Romanesque sculpture. This unusual 12th-century amalgam of angels, prophets, saints, sinners, demons, and monsters form [illegible] most rigid Romanesque statues, those in the *Pórtico* seem to smile, whisper, lean, and gab. Galician author Rosalía del Castro once remarked, "It looks as if their lips are moving…might they be alive?" The **revered remains of St. James** (Santiago) lie beneath the high altar in a silver coffer, while his bejeweled bust, polished by the embrace of thousands of pilgrims, rests above the altar. The **botafumeiro,** an enormous silver censer supposedly intended to overpower the stench of dirty pilgrims, swings from the transept during high mass and major liturgical ceremonies. Much older than the towers that house them, the **bells** of Santiago were stolen by Moorish invaders and transported to Córdoba on the backs of Christian slaves. Centuries later, when Spaniards conquered Córdoba, they took back their bells right back and completed their revenge by forcing some unlucky Moors to carry them.

MUSEUM AND CLOISTERS. Inside the museum are several gorgeous, intricate 16th-century tapestries and two poignant statues of the pregnant Virgin Mary. The museum also houses manuscripts from the *Codex Calixtinus* and Romanesque remains from one of many archaeological excavations conducted in the cathedral.

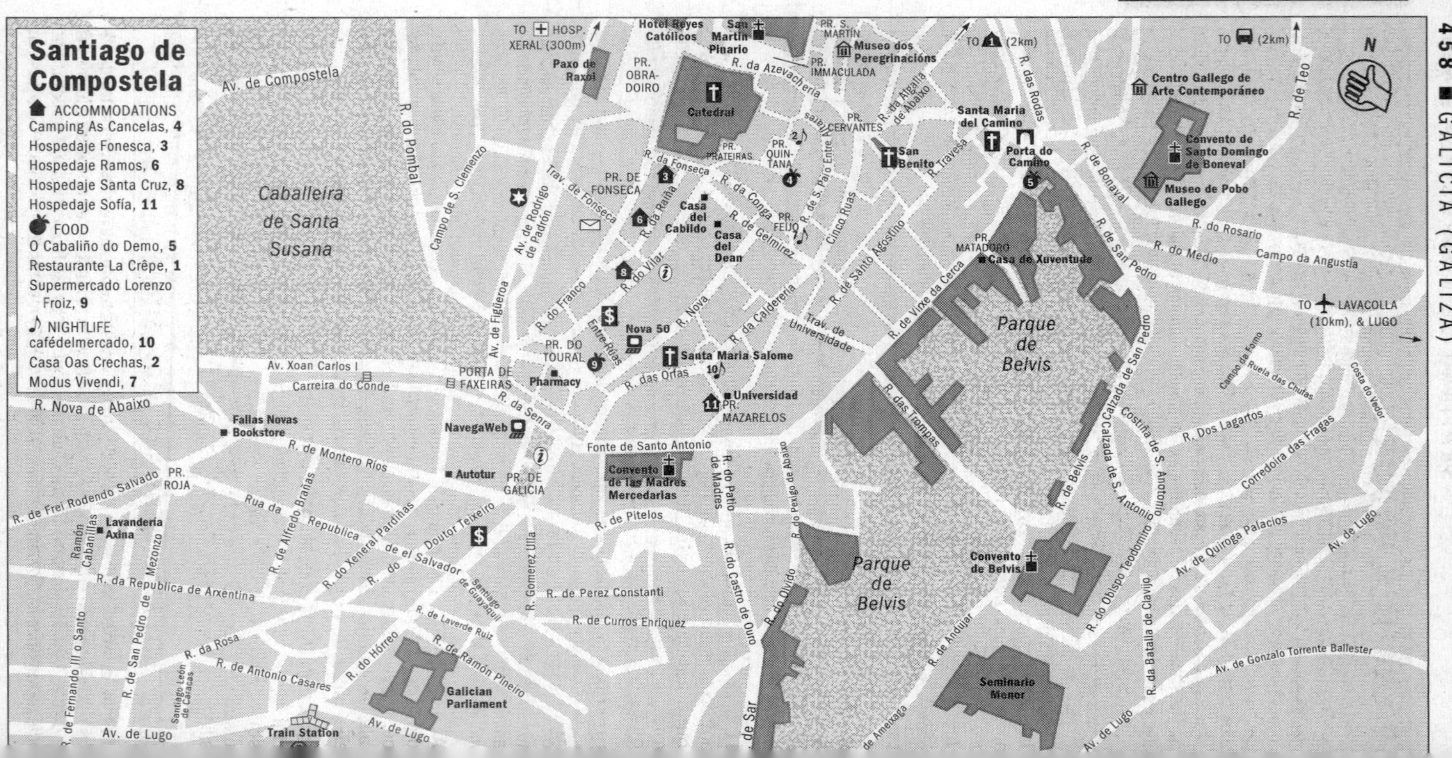
Santiago de Compostela
ACCOMMODATIONS
Camping As Cancelas, 4
Hospedaje Fonesca, 3
Hospedaje Ramos, 6
Hospedaje Santa Cruz, 8
Hospedaje Sofía, 11
FOOD
O Cabaliño do Demo, 5
Restaurante La Crêpe, 1
Supermercado Lorenzo Froiz, 9
NIGHTLIFE
cafédelmercado, 10
Casa Oas Crechas, 2
Modus Vivendi, 7
Catedral
Hotel Reyes Católicos
San Martín Pinario
Museo dos Peregrinacións
San Benito
Santa María del Camino
Porta do Camino
Casa de Xuventude
Parque de Belvis
Convento de Belvis
Seminario Menor
Centro Gallego de Arte Contemporáneo
Convento de Santo Domingo de Boneval
Museo de Pobo Gallego
Universidad
Santa María Salome
Convento de las Madres Mercedarias
Casa del Cabildo
Casa del Dean
Paxo de Raxoi
Nova 50
NavegaWeb
Autotur
Pharmacy
Fallas Novas Bookstore
Lavandería Axina
Galician Parliament
Train Station
Caballeira de Santa Susana
TO LAVACOLLA (10km), & LUGO
TO HOSP. XERAL (300m)
PR. DO OBRADOIRO
PR. DE FONSECA
PR. DO TOURAL
PR. DE GALICIA
PORTA DE FAXEIRAS
PR. ROJA
R. do Pombal
Av. de Figueroa
R. do Franco
R. do Vilar
R. Nova
Av. de Lugo
Av. Xoan Carlos I
R. Nova de Abaixo

GALICIA

PILGRIM'S PROGRESS Pilgrims are easily spotted by the crook-necked walking sticks, sunburnt faces, and shells tied onto weathered backpacks. True *peregrinos* (pilgrims) must cover 100km on foot or horse or 200km on bike to receive *La Compostela*, an official certificate of the pilgrimage issued by the cathedral. A network of *refugios* (refuges) and *albergues* (shelters) offer free lodging to pilgrims on the move and stamp the requisite "pilgrims' passports" to provide evidence of completion of the full distance. For more information and free guides to the Camino de Santiago, contact the Oficina de Acogida del Peregrino, R. Vilar, 1 (☎981 56 24 19), in the Casa del Deán. At a rate of 30km per day, walking the entire French route (from Roncesvalles in the Pyrenees to Santiago de Compostela; 750-870km), the most common pilgrimage route, takes about a month, and places you in the ranks of such illustrious pilgrims as royal couple Fernando and Isabel, St. Francis de Assisi, Pope John Paul II, and Shirley MacLaine.

'he 12th-century *Codex*, five volumes of manuscripts on the stories of the Apostle ames, includes travel information for early pilgrims. *(☎981 58 11 55. Museum open une-Sept. M-Sa 10am-1:30pm and 4-7:30pm, Su and holidays 10am-1:30pm; Oct.-Feb. M-Sa 1am-1pm and 4-6pm, Su and holidays 11am-1pm; Mar.-June M-Sa 10:30am-1:30pm and 4-:30pm, Su 10:30am-1:30pm. Museum and cloisters 500ptas/€3.)*

MUSEO DAS PEREGRINACIÓNS. This three-story Gothic building is chock-full f creatively displayed historical info about the *Camino*, including exhibits on the tes and rituals of pilgrimage, the iconography of St. James, and statues of the Virin as a baby-Jesus-toting pilgrim. *(Pl. San Miguel. ☎981 58 15 58. Open Tu-F 10am-0pm, Sa 10:30am-1:30pm and 5-8pm, Su 10:30am-1:30pm. 400ptas/€2.40, children and eniors 200ptas/€1.20, free during the Apostolo.)*

CENTRO GALLEGO DE ARTE CONTEMPORÁNEO. The expansive galleries and ooftop *terraza* of the sparkling Centro Gallego de Arte Contemporáneo (CGAC) ouse cutting edge exhibitions of boundary-bending artists from around the vorld. *(R. Ramón del Valle Inclán, s/n. Next door to the Museo de Pobo Gallego. ☎981 54 66 9; www.cgac.org. Open Tu-Su 11am-8pm. Free.)*

USEO DE POBO GALLEGO. Find out everything you have ever wanted to know bout traditional Galician living. Documentary exhibits on shipbuilding, pottery, ouse construction, and *gaitas* (the Galician bagpipe) are the highlights, but the useum also includes exhibits dedicated to Galician painting. *(Just past the Porto de amino, inside the Gothic Convento de Santo Domingo de Boneval. ☎981 58 36 20. Open ine 7-Mar. 2 M-Sa 10am-1pm and 4-7pm. Mar. 3-June 6 M-Sa 10am-2pm and 4-7pm. Free.)*

AZO DE RAXOI. The majestic façade of the former Pazo de Raxoi shines with old-accented bal[illegible] ce, it now houses the Ayuntamiento and office of the president of the Xunta de alicia (Galician government). At night, floodlights illuminate the remarkable baselief of the Battle of Clavio. *(Across Pr. do Obradoiro, facing the cathedral.)*

ONASTERIO DE SAN MARTÍN PINARIO. Once a religious center almost as powrful as the cathedral, the monastery is a mixture of Romanesque cloisters, Plateresque façades, and Baroque sculpture. This composite style is the most utstanding architecture of its type in Santiago. *(In Pr. de San Martín, across from the athedral in Pl. Inmaculada. Open Tu-Su 11:30am-1:30pm and 4:30-6:30pm. Free.)*

ENTERTAINMENT AND NIGHTLIFE

t night, crowds looking for post-pilgrimage consumption and debauchery flood celrs throughout the city. To boogie with local students, hit the bars and dance joints off r. Roxa (take R. Montero Ríos). Clubs are open roughly from midnight to 6am. The cal newspaper *El Correo Gallego* (125ptas/€0.75) and the free monthly *Compostela*

SEX-ED Although most passers-by don't notice it, Praza do Toural houses one of Santiago's most important—and infamous—sculptures: at the top of the Pazo da Bendana is a rendition of Atlas lifting up the world. University legend has that Atlas will drop the granite globe on the first female student to walk by who successfully manages to graduate a virgin. Perhaps afraid of getting crushed, Santiago's female students have yet to relieve Atlas of his burden. And they say this a holy city...

Capital list art exhibits and concert information. Consult any of three local monthlie *Santiago Días Guía Imprescindible*, *Compostelán*, or *Modus Vivendi*, for update on the live music scene. The city celebrates the **Día de Santiago** (July 25) for a full tw weeks, from July 15 to 31, in a celebration called Apostolo; on the night of the 24th, Pontifical Mass with incense is held in the cathedral during **Las Vísperas de Santiago.**

Casa oas Crechas, Vía Sacra, 3 (☎981 56 07 51), just off Pr. da Quintana. A smok stone-and-wood pub with a witchcraft theme. Renowned for its Galician folk concert Beer 250-325ptas/€1.50-1.95. Open M-F noon-2am, Sa-Su noon-4am.

cafédelmercado, R. Cardenal Playa, 3 (☎981 57 78 66). Santiago's trendiest nig spot. Pink walls, white vinyl seating, and the uber-hip strains of St-Germain and oth lounge-jazz acts attract the beautiful and the cool. Open daily 9am-2am.

Modus Vivendi, Pr. de Feijo, 1, near the cathedral. Santiago's oldest pub, it provided clubhouse for revolutionary Galician youths in the 1970s. Today, it shelters Santiago alterna-youth well into the wee hours of the night. Open daily 4pm-4am.

DAYTRIPS FROM SANTIAGO DE COMPOSTELA

The northern parts of the Rías Baixas tend to be undiscovered hamlets frequente only by pilgrims, but these small towns are an easy daytrip from Santiago.

CABO FINISTERRE

Arriva/Finisterre buses make daily trips from Santiago to Finisterre (2½hr.; M-F 7 per day 8am-7:30pm, Sa 4 per day 8am-7:30pm, Su 8am, 12:15, 6:15pm; 1485ptas/€8.95) and back (M-F 4 per day 7:50am-4:45pm, Sa 3 per day 7am-4pm, Su 1:45 and 6:45pm). The bus stop is in front of the fishing center in the harbor.

Jutting out precariously from the infamously rocky Costa de Muerte ("Coast Death"), Cabo Finisterre was once considered Europe's westernmost point, an for centuries it was a crucial port for all naval trade along the Atlantic. But Fini terre's (Fisterre, in Gallego) greater claim to fame has to do with the ancient beli that it was off these shores that the world ended, hence its name: *finis* (end *terre* (earth). Even today, it feels like the end of the earth, what with the desola town and the seemingly endless bus ride out to a lonely, wind-swept peninsula.

Those who want to get close to the water can take a **Pleasure Boat Tour** of the Ría Corcubión. (☎981 74 03 75. Leaves from the harbor; ask one of the fishermen to poi you towards the captain. 100ptas/€0.60 per person per hr.) For landlubbers, the hil from the port to the **Monte San Guillermo** is long, but the traveler will be blessed wi incredible views of the tumultuous sea and Finisterre's famous, bed-shaped **fertil rocks.** Couples having problems conceiving are advised to make a go of it on the roc under a full moon (harvest moons are even better). On the same mountain are **Pedras Santas,** two fairly large rocks which cannot be lifted by themselves, but whic slide effortlessly side-to-side if you press the right spot. Try it yourself—the conta point is well marked. Four kilometers out from town stands the **lighthouse** that h beckoned ships for years. To reach the **beach,** climb uphill from the statue at the po past C. Carrasqueira, then turn right at the first dirt road. After 50m, turn left onto t seaward path at the white house. The best beach in Finisterre, however, is on the fl and narrow isthmus that connects the peninsula with the mainland. The sands a powdery and wide and the waters calm (but frigid). Either walk the four kilomete along the road to Santiago, or take the bus and ask the driver to stop.

THESE BOOTS WERE MADE FOR WALKIN'

One night in 813, a hermit trudged through the hills on the way to his hermitage. Suddenly, miraculously, bright visions flooded his senses, revealing the long-forgotten tomb of the Apostle James. Around this *campus stellae* (field of stars) the cathedral of Santiago de Compostela was built, and around this cathedral a world-famous pilgrimage was born. Since the 9th century, thousands of pilgrims have traveled the **Camino de Santiago.** Many have made the pilgrimage in search of spiritual fulfillment, most as true believers, some to adhere to a stipulation of inheritance, a few to absolve themselves of sin, and at least one to find romance (the wife of Bath in Chaucer's *Canterbury Tales* sauntered to Santiago in **bright red stockings** to find herself a husband). Clever Benedictine monks built monasteries to host pilgrims along the *camino,* giving rise to the world's first large-scale international tourism and helping make Santiago's cathedral the **most frequented Christian shrine** in the world. In the 12th century, an enterprising French monk added a book to the *Codex Calixtinus,* a collection of stories about the apostles, that was filled with information on the quality of water at various rest stops and descriptions of villages and monuments along *La Ruta Francesa* (beginning near the French border in Roncevalles, Navarra); in essence, the **world's first travel guide.** The scallop shell was acquired by pilgrims who visited the site of Santiago's landing after visiting the cathedral; although only pilgrims on their way home used to carry the shell, it has now become a symbol of the Camino de Santiago.

For maps, brochures and tourist information, try the **Albergue de Peregrinos,** C. Real, 2, behind the bus stop/fishing building. (☎981 74 07 81. Open M-F 9:30am-1pm and 7-11pm, Sa-Su noon-2pm and 7-11pm.) If you are forced to spend the night in Cabo Finisterre, the **Hospedaje López,** C. Carrasqueira, 4, has 18 cheap, immaculate, light-filled rooms. (☎981 74 04 49. Singles 1500-2000ptas/€9-12; doubles 3000-3500ptas/€18-21; triples 4500ptas/€27.)

O CASTRO DE BAROÑA

To reach O Castro de Baroña, you'll need to make a connection in Noia. Castromil (☎981 58 90 90) runs ***buses*** *from Santiago to* ***Noia*** *(1hr.; M-F 15 per day 6:15am-8pm, Sa 10 per day 7am-8pm, Su 8 per day 8am-8:30pm; 420ptas/€2.52). From Noia, Hefsel buses stop at O Castro de Baroña (in front of Café-Bar O Castro) en route to Riveira (30min.; M-F 14 per day 6:50am-9:30pm, Sa 7 per day 8am-9pm, Su 11 per day 8am-10pm; 210ptas/€1.26). Be sure to tell the bus driver where you're going. From the bus stop,* ***follow the signs*** *to the castro. Catch the bus home across the road from* ***Café-Bar O Castro.***

Nineteen kilometers south of Noia lies one of Galicia's best preserved coastal Celtic villages, **O Castro de Baroña.** The seaside remains of a 5th-century Celtic **fortress** cover the neck of the isthmus, ascending to a rocky promontory above the sea and then descending to a crescent **beach** where clothing [illegible] shower, **Café-Bar O Castro,** Lugar Castro de Baroña, 18, in **Porto do Son** (the O Castro bus stop), offers spotless rooms upstairs. (☎981 76 74 30. Doubles 3500-4500ptas/€21-27. Open June-Aug.) The nearest town, **Baroña,** 1km north, has a supermarket, restaurant, and a bus stop. Should you get stuck in **Noia** on the way back to Santiago, several hotels are a short walk from the bus station on R. de Galicia. **Hospedaje Marico,** R. de Galicia, s/n, has plain but comfortable rooms. From the bus station, walk uphill on R. Pedra Sartaña, turn right onto R. Rosalía de Castro and then left onto R. de Galicia. (☎981 82 00 09. Singles 2000ptas/€12; doubles 2500ptas/€15, with bath 3000ptas/€18.)

MUROS

Castromil buses (☎981 58 90 90 or 902 10 44 44) run from Santiago to Muros (M-F 10 per day 6:15am-8pm, Sa 6 per day 7am-8pm, Su 4 per day 8am-8:30pm; 825ptas/€4.96). In Muros, buses stop in front of the Castromil office at Av. Calvo Sotelo, 53.

A quiet fishing village on the banks of the Ría de Muros, the town of Muros would continue its sleepy existence unnoticed were it not for its collection of traditional *gallego* architecture. While there are no specific sights to seek out, every street is lined with the region's distinctive buildings: squat, two-story limestone structures with arcaded fronts and flowering balconies above. **Curro da Praza,** Muros' main square, is perhaps the most distinguished-looking part of the city (from the bus stop, walk left on Av. Calvo Sotelo), but it's worth wandering into the uphill maze of streets behind the port for different takes on the traditional style and great views of the *mejillonerías* on the water below.

RÍAS BAJAS (RÍAS BAIXAS)

According to Galician lore, the Rías Baixas (Low Estuaries) were formed by God's tremendous handprint, with each *ría* stretching like a finger through the land. These deep navy blue bays, countless sandy coves, and calm cool waters have lured vacationing Spaniards for decades. Only recently have foreign tourists caught on to the area's unique charm, and they now arrive at the beaches in droves every summer. While not nearly as cool or rainy as their Galician neighbors (the Rías Baixas are, after all, the sunniest part of the northern Spanish coasts), the ocean wind and mildly hot summer days are still a refreshing break from the scorching heat (and hordes of tourists) of central and southern Spain.

VIGO ☎986

José María Alvarez once wrote that "Vigo does not end, it goes on into the sea." Often called Spain's door to the Atlantic, Vigo (pop. 300,000) began as a small, unobtrusive fishing port; with the arrival of the Citroen manufacturing factory, it exploded into the biggest city in Galicia. The noise and pollution can be a nuisance, but the nightlife and shopping are among the best in the region, and the city is a good base for visiting nearby daytrip villages and beaches.

TRANSPORTATION

Flights: Aeropuerto de Vigo on Av. Aeropuerto. (☎986 26 82 00), 15km from the center of Vigo. Daily flights to **Barcelona, Bilbao, Madrid,** and **Valencia.** The local R9 bus runs regularly from R. Urzáiz near R. Colón to the airport (130ptas/€0.78). **Iberia** (☎986 6 82 28) and **Air Europa** (☎986 26 83 10) have offices at the airport.

Trains: RENFE, Pr. de la Estación, s/n (☎986 43 11 14), downstairs from R. Urzaiz, is open daily 7am-11pm and runs trains to: **La Coruña** (2½hr.; M-F 14 per day 5:45am-9:30pm, Sa 9 per day 5:45am-8:55pm, Su 12 per day 5:45am-9:30pm; 1280-1505ptas/€7.69-9.05); **Madrid** (8-9hr.; Su-F 1:25 and 10:20pm, Sa 10:20pm; 5950-9150ptas/€36-55); **Pontevedra** (20min.; M-F 20 per day 5:45am-10:05pm, Sa 14 per day 5:45am-10:05pm, Su 17 per day 5:45am-10:05pm; 260-350ptas/€1.56-2.10); **Porto, Portugal** (3½hr., 8:30am and 2pm, 1990ptas/€12); **Santiago de Compostela** (2hr.; M-F 17 per day 5:45am-9:30pm, Sa 11 per day 5:45am-8:55pm, Su 14 per day 5:45am-9:30pm; 795-965ptas/€4.79-5.80).

Buses: Estación de Autobuses, Av. de Madrid, s/n (☎986 37 34 11), on the corner of R. Alcalde Gregorio Espino. **Castromil** (☎986 27 81 12) buses run to: **La Coruña** (2½hr., hourly 7am-8:30pm, 1765ptas/€10.61); **Pontevedra** (45min., every 30min. 7am-8:30pm, 310ptas/€1.86); **Santiago de Compostela** (1¼hr., every 30min. 7:30am-8:30pm, 950ptas/€5.71). For **ATSA buses** (☎986 61 02 55), buy tickets onboard. To: **Bayona** (50min.; every 30min. M-Sa 7am-10pm, Su 8am-11pm; 275ptas/€1.65); **La Guardia** (1½hr., every 30min. 7:30am-9pm, 645ptas/€3.88); **Túy** (45min.; M-F every 30min. 7:30am-9pm, Sa every hr. 8:30am-8:30pm; 355ptas/€2.13). **Auto Res, S.A.** (☎986 27 19 61) runs to **Madrid** (9hr., 6-7 per day 8:30am-11:30pm., 4300-4650ptas/€25.84-27.95).

Ferries: Estación Ría, R. As Avenidas, s/n (☎986 22 52 72), past the nautical club on the harborside walkway, runs ferries to: **Cangas** (20min.; M-F every 30min. 6:30am-10pm, Sa every hr. 6:30am-10:30pm, Su every hr. 8:30am-9:30pm; 260ptas/€1.56);

Islas Cíes (50min., 4 per day 11am-7pm, round-trip 2200ptas/€13.22); and **Moaña** (30min.; M-Sa every hr. 6:30-9:30pm, Su every hr. 8:30am-9:30pm; 215ptas/€1.29).

Car Rental: National, R. Urzáiz, 84 (☎986 41 80 76). Min. age 21. Must have had a license for at least 1yr. Open M-F 8:30am-1:30pm and 4:30-7:30pm, Sa 9am-1pm.

ORIENTATION AND PRACTICAL INFORMATION

The **Gran Vía** is Vigo's main thoroughfare, stretching south to north from Pr. América, through Pr. España, and ending at the perpendicular **Rúa Urzáiz.** A left turn (west) onto R. Urzáiz leads to Pta. do Sol and into the **casco antiguo;** most of the city's action is here in the old city and along the waterfront. As you exit the **train station** onto R. Urzáiz (up the stairs from the main entrance), go right two blocks to reach the central Gran Vía Urzáiz or left for 10min. to reach the waterfront. The city center is a 25min. trek from the **bus station.** Exit right uphill along busy Av. Madrid. Eventually, a right on Gran Vía at Pr. España leads to the intersection with R. Urzáiz. It's easier to just take the R4, 7, or 12 buses from Av. Madrid in front of the bus station to Gran Vía, R. Urzáiz, or R. Colón (130ptas/€0.78).

Tourist Office: R. Canovás de Castillo, s/n (☎986 43 05 77). From the train station, turn right on R. Urzáiz and follow it to R. Colón, where you'll veer to the right. When R. Colón reaches the water, turn left onto R. Montero Ríos. On the left as the name changes to R. Canovás de Castillo and veers left. English spoken. Open June-Sept. M-F 9:30am-2pm and 4:30-7pm, Sa-Su 10am-2pm and 5-8pm; Oct.-May M-F 9:30am-2pm and 4:30-6:30pm, Sa 10am-12:30pm.

Currency Exchange: Banco Central Hispano, R. Urzáiz, 20 (☎902 24 24 24). Open Apr.-Sept. M-F 8:30am-2:30pm; Oct.-Mar. M-F 8:30am-2:30pm, Sa 8:30am-1pm.

Luggage Storage: At the train station (500ptas/€3). Open daily 7am-9:45pm. At the bus station (400ptas/€2.40). Open M-F 9:30am-1:30pm and 3-7pm, Sa 9am-2pm.

Emergency: ☎112. **Police:** Pr. do Rei, s/n (☎986 43 22 11).

Pharmacy: C. Príncipe, 27. To the left off R. Urzáiz just before it turns into R. Colón. Open 9am-1pm and 4-7pm. All pharmacies post a rotating list of late-night pharmacies.

Medical Services: Hospital Xeral, R. Pizarro, 22 (☎986 81 60 00). **Ambulances:** ☎061, 986 41 62 26, 34 42 29, or 81 60 62.

Internet Access: CiberStation, C. Príncipe, 22, ground floor (☎986 44 76 10), a left off R. Urzáiz just before it turns into R. Colon. 300ptas/€1.80 per hr. Open 10am-3am.

Post Office: Pr. Compostela, 3 (☎986 43 81 44). A left off R. Colón. **Lista de Correos** and **fax.** M-F 8:30am-8:30pm, Sa 9:30am-2pm. **Postal code:** 36201.

ACCOMMODATIONS AND FOOD

Vigo's inexpensive rooms make the city a logical base for exploring surrounding areas. Most accommodations are clustered in the area around the train station on R. Alfonso XIII (to the right upon exiting the train station) and its side streets. **Hostal Ría de Vigo,** R. Cervantes, 14, a left off R. Alfonso XIII four blocks down from the station, has cheerful, flower-decorated rooms with private bathrooms and TVs, and balconies overlooking busy R. Cervantes. (☎986 43 72 40. Check-out 11am. Singles 2500ptas/€15.02; doubles 3500ptas/€21.03. Prices drop up to 500ptas/€3 in off-season. Cash only.) **Hostal Uruguay,** R. Cervantes, 5, just down the street from Ría de Vigo, rents clean, unadorned rooms with big windows. (☎986 22 20 28. Check-out noon. Singles 2000ptas/€12.02; doubles 3000ptas/€18.03. Cash only.) The Gran Vía and C. Venezuela, four streets uphill from R. Urzáiz off Gran Vía, are brimming with bright *cafeterías* and *terrazas*. **Restaurante Curcuma Vegetariano,** C. Brasil, 4 serves immense portions of Mediterranean veggie dishes, like *mousakka* and *couscous*. (☎986 41 11 27. Entrées 700-1200ptas/€4.21-7.21. Open M-Sa 1-4pm and 8pm-midnight.)

ENTERTAINMENT AND NIGHTLIFE

In honor of its notorious past as a haven for witches (both good and evil), Vigo hosts **Expomagia,** a celebration of all things occult, in mid-June. Watch for the magical **Fiesta de San Juan (Xuan)** on June 23rd, when neighborhoods light huge cauldrons of *aguardiente* (firewater) to make an infusion called *la queimada.* The potent potable consists of *aguardiente,* coffee, lemon, and sugar, and after careful brewing the sweet mixture is passed around in cups for all to drink and revel in traditional song and dance. A final summer festival, **Romería Vikinga,** in the seaside town of Catoira, sails into town the first week in August, when locals reenact the Viking landing, complete with period ships and costumes.

There isn't much to see or do in Vigo besides party. Starting in the late afternoon, students pack the *casco antiguo,* where cafés, bars, and discos abound just off the steep, mossy steps. **Rúa A Real,** down by the water, has a few lively spots, as does **R. Concepción Arenal.** The area around the train station—R. Cervantes, R. Lepanto, and R. Churruca, in particular—is lined with mercurial, trendsetting bars and clubs; for the latest hotspots, check the posters hanging around town advertising discos and techno music. The **El Arenal** building, R. A Real, s/n, is a complex jam-packed with discos, nightclubs, and bars playing the latest Spanish hits to trendy twentysomethings. From R. Colón, turn right on R. A Real. (Hours vary within the complex, but bars usually open 8pm-2 or 3am, clubs midnight-5 or 6am.) **Café Uf,** R. Placer, 19, is an artsy jazz/funk bar that serves specialty teas and coffees. Photographs of literati on the walls, a display of books-of-the-month, a small public library, and board games for the tongue-tied.

DAYTRIPS FROM VIGO

ISLAS CÍES

June-Sept., 4 ferries per day make the trip to and from the island, sometimes more in nice weather. Though fairly expensive, the trip is worth every peseta (50min.; to Islas Cíes 11am, 1, 5, and 7pm; returning noon, 2, 6, and 8pm; 2200ptas/€13.22 round-trip, child 700ptas/€4.21).

The Romans called them the "Islands of the Gods," and one can hardly doubt that Jupiter had at least a villa in the Islas Cíes. Guarding the mouth of the Ría de Vigo and 14km from the city, the three islands—**Illa de Monte Agudo** o del Norte, **Illa do Medio** o del Faro, and **Illa do Sur** o de San Martiño—offer irresistible beaches and cliff-side hiking trails for travelers. The islands were declared a natural park in 1980; only 2200 people are allowed in per day, ensuring wide stretches of uncrowded beach. **Playa de Figueiras** and **Playa de Rodas** gleam with fine sand and sheltered turquoise waters. For smaller, wavier, and more secluded spots, walk along the trail beyond Playa de Figueiras, which leads to a plethora of coves and rocky lookouts. A 4km hike to the left of the dock on the main "road" leads to a bird conservatory, a lighthouse, and breathtaking views. Watch out for territorial seagulls that dive-bomb hikers walking too close to the birds' spotted chicks.

CANGAS

Ferries run from the Estación Ría (☎986 22 52 72) in Vigo to Cangas (20min.; M-F every 30min. 6:30am-10am, Sa every hr. 6:30am-10:30pm, Su every hr. 8:30am-9:30pm; 260ptas/€1.56). From Cangas, an equal number return (M-F every 30min. 6am-9:30pm, Sa every hr. 6am-10pm, Su every hr. 8am-9pm).

Just across the bay from Vigo, tiny Cangas' main draw is its placid, nearly deserted beach, **Praia de Rodeira.** From the ferry terminal on Av. MonteroRíos, turn left onto Po. Marítimo, the pedestrian waterside walkway, which brings you to the beach (10min.). The cobalt waters here are virtually waveless, perfect for actual swimming. While there are no snack bars near the beach, restaurants lurk near the ferry station. The most popular is undoubtedly **Restaurante-Bar Celta,** R. Alfredo Saralegui, 28, which serves endless seafood *tapas* to the hungry hordes gathered at long tables on the street. With your back to the ferry terminal, cross the street and head up the stairs to your left; the restaurant is at the top. (*Tapas* 125-1000ptas/€0.75-6.01. Fish entrées 850-1600ptas/€9.02-9.62. Open daily 10am-midnight.) On Fridays, Cangas attracts crowds from the surrounding towns for its extravagant **market** in the harborside gardens, immediately to the left of the ferry terminal.

BAYONA (BAIONA)

Atsa buses run to and from Vigo (50min.; every 30min. M-Sa 7am-10pm, Su 8am-11pm; 275ptas/€1.65).

Twenty-one kilometers southwest of Vigo, in its own mini-estuary, Bayona (pop. 10,000) was the first European town to receive word from the New World when Columbus returned to port in March 1493. The town even boasts a reconstructed version of the famous globe-trotting ship **La Caravela Pinta** in the harbor and reenacts the landing every March. (Open W-M 8:30am-8:30pm. 125ptas/€0.75.) While this is Bayona's main historic attraction, most visitors skip the sight and head straight to its **blustery Atlantic beaches,** where brightly colored fishing boats lurk off shore and only the bravest dare to swim in the icy blue waves of the open sea. The golden sand, however, is perfect for lounging among myriad other sun worshippers. Those who get bored at the beach explore the grounds of the 16th-century **Fortress of Monte Real,** now a *parador nacional* (luxury hotel), which lurks just above the beaches. A 2km *paseo peatonal* (foot path) loops around the grounds along the shore, passing the rocks of Praia Cuncheira and Praia de los Frailes.

TÚY (TUI)

*An ATSA **bus** (☎986 61 02 55) from Vigo stops on C. Calvo Sotelo at Hostal Generosa and returns to Vigo from the other side of the street (45min., every 30min. 7:30am-9pm, 355ptas/€2.13). **Trains** (☎986 60 08 13) run from Vigo to Túy, then on to Valença and Viana do Castelo, Portugal (2 per day 9:59am and 10pm, 455ptas/€2.73). The train station in Túy, however, is far from the center of town and the border.*

While the medieval border town of Túy (pop. 16,000) offers the novel opportunity of walking into Portugal, it's more notable for its beautiful *casco antiguo* and its views of the Río Miño valley and Portugal. The centerpiece of the old city is the **cathedral;** constructed in 1120, it was the first piece of Gothic architecture in Iberia. It now houses the relics of San Telmo, patron saint of sailors, and boasts an impressive organ. One ticket gets you into the cathedral's **museum** and the **Museo Diocesano** as well. (Museo Diocesano ☎986 60 36 00. Cathedral and museums open daily July-Aug. 9am-9pm; Sept.-Dec. daily 9:30am-1:30pm and 4-8pm; Dec.-May daily 9:30am-1:30pm and 4-7pm. 400ptas/€2.40.) A 1km metal walkway over the Río Miño extends to Portugal's Valença do Minho. To get to the **tourist office** on Puente Tripe, s/n, follow Av. de Portugal from the International Bridge until you approach the little wooden cottage on your left. (☎986 60 17 89. Open July-Sept. daily 9:30am-2pm, 4:30-8pm; Oct.-June M-F 9:30am-1:30pm and 4-6pm.)

LA GUARDIA (A GUARDA)

Buses run to and from La Guardia from Vigo (1½hr., every 30min. 7:30am-9pm, 645ptas/€3.88). The bus office (open 9am-9pm) and stop in La Guardia is at the corner of C. Domínguez Fontela and C. Concepción Arenal.

Between the mouth of the Río Miño and the Atlantic Ocean, La Guardia (pop. 10,000) thrives on an active fishing industry and the 500,000 tourists who annually descend on its little beach and large mountain. The town itself is a sleepy, pastel-colored maze overlooking a bay; most visitors skip the town and head instead to its two attractions. To reach the majestic **Monte Santa Tecla** from the bus stop, turn right onto C. Domínguez Fontela and then right onto C. José Antonio. From C. José Antonio, bear right uphill onto C. Rosalía de Castro, which continues to the top (6km). Alternatively, hike 5mn. up the road and look for the steps off to the left that mark the start of a shorter, steeper pedestrian pathway through the woods (3km). The mountain's highlight are the ruins of a **Celtic castro** that lie three-quarters of the way up the mountain. The interlocking circles of the foundations of this ancient fortress village overlook frothy seas, moss-laden mountains, and the glimmer of La Guardia below. Near the peak is a **chapel** dedicated to Santa Tecla, the patron saint of headaches and heart disease. The wax body parts inside (hearts, heads, and feet) are gifts to Santa Tecla from cured worshippers. To reach La Guardia's small **beach** from the bus station, follow the signs.

PONTEVEDRA ☎986

According to legend, Pontevedra (pop. 74,000) was founded by the Greek archer Teucro as a place to convalesce after his Trojan War exploits. Today, it continues the tradition of providing a place to crash by offering reasonably priced beds for visitors flitting about the various high-priced coastal towns. Although it makes a good base, Pontevedra on the whole is not the most interesting town, and the new city is a bit of an eyesore. The old city, however—filled with palm trees, flowering balconies, stately cathedrals, and squares lined with traditional arcaded *gallego* buildings—is pleasant and inviting, making for a surprisingly enjoyable stay.

TRANSPORTATION

Trains: Alféreces Provisionales, s/n (☎902 24 02 02 or 986 85 13 13), a 20min. walk southwest of the old city. Info open daily 6am-11pm. To: **La Coruña** (3hr.; M-F 14 per day 6:17am-10:11pm, Sa 9 per day 6:17am-9:10pm, Su 12 per day 6:17am-10:11pm; 1130ptas/€6.80, express 1345ptas/€8.08); **Madrid** (11hr.; Su-F 12:35pm and 9:30pm, Sa 8:45am and 9:30pm; 6050ptas/€36); **Santiago** (1½hr.; M-F 18 per day 6:17am-10:11pm, Sa 12 per day 6:17am-9:10pm, Su 15 per day 6:17am-10:11am; 520ptas/€3.13, express 650ptas/€3.90); **Vigo** (20min.; M-F 21 per day 7:40am-11:17pm, Sa 14 per day 7:40am-11:17pm, Su 17 per day 8:54am-11:17pm; 260ptas/€1.56, express 350ptas/€2.10).

Buses: Alféreces Provisionales, s/n (☎986 85 24 08), across the street from the train station. Info open daily 9am-9:30pm. To: **Cambados** (1hr.; 12 per day M-F 7:55am-8:35pm, Sa 11:15am-8:35pm, Su 3 per day 12:30-8:35pm; 315ptas/€1.90); **El Grove/La Toja** (1hr., every 30min. 7:45am-10pm, 485ptas/€2.90); **La Coruña** (2½hr.; M-F hourly 7am-9pm, Sa hourly 8am-9pm, Su hourly 9am-8pm; 1500ptas/€9); **Madrid** (8hr., 4 per day 8:30am-10:30pm, 4300ptas/€26); **Santiago** (1hr.; M-F every hr. 7am-9pm, Sa hourly 8am-9pm, Su hourly 8am-7pm; 675ptas/€4.05); **Vigo** (1hr.; M-F hourly 6am-10pm, Sa-Su hourly 8am-8pm; 675ptas/€4.05).

Taxis: Radio Taxi (☎986 85 12 85). 24hr. 400ptas/€2.40 from the stations to town.

Car Rental: Avis, C. Peregrina, 49 (☎986 85 20 25). Rates vary with duration of rental. 1-day unlimited mileage 11,950ptas/€72. Must be 23 and have had a license for at least 1 year. Open M-F 9am-1:15pm and 4-7pm, Sa 9am-12:45pm.

ORIENTATION AND PRACTICAL INFORMATION

Six streets radiate out from **Pr. Peregrina,** the main plaza connecting the new and old cities. The main streets are R. Oliva, R. Michelena, R. Benito Corbal, and R. Peregrina. **Pr. de Galicia** is a 5min. walk from Pr. Peregrina; from Pr. Peregrina, head down R. Peregrina and veer right at the first fork onto R. A. Muruais. The **train** and **bus stations,** located across from each other, are about 1km from the old city. To get to the city center, turn left onto Av. Calvo Sotelo from the bus station entrance; from the train station, walk straight out onto Av. Calvo Sotelo after crossing the highway. Continue on Av. Calvo Sotelo for 10-15 min. as it changes to Av. de Vigo and then R. Peregrina before depositing you in Pr. Peregrina.

Tourist Office: The **main office,** R. General Mola, 3 (☎/fax 986 85 08 14). From Pr. Peregrina, walk up R. Michelena and take the 1st left onto R. General Mola. Tons of brochures and maps. English spoken. A **second office** opens in summer on Pr. de España in a small hut. Both open June-Aug. M-F 10am-2pm and 5-7:30pm, Sa-Su 10am-2pm and 5-6:30pm; Sept.-May M-F 9:30am-2pm and 4:30-6:30pm, Sa 11am-12:30pm.

Emergency: ☎112. **Police:** C. Joaquín Costa, 19 (☎091 or 986 85 38 00).

Pharmacy: R. Peregrina, 3. Open 9am-1pm and 4-8pm. Rotating list of all late-night pharmacies are posted in all pharmacy windows.

Hospital: Hospital Provincial, C. Doctor Loureiro Crespo, 2 (☎061 or 986 85 21 15).

Internet Access: Ciber Las Ruinas, R. Riestra, 21, 2nd fl. (☎986 86 63 25), just off Pr. de España. 200ptas/€1.20 per hr. Open M-F 10am-2:30pm and 5pm-2am.

Post Office: C. Oliva, 21 (☎986 84 48 64). **Lista de Correos** and **fax service** available. Open M-F 8:30am-8:30pm, Sa 9:30am-2pm. **Postal Code:** 36001.

ACCOMMODATIONS

Hotel Madrid, C. Andrés Mellado, 5 (☎/fax 986 85 10 06). Follow the directions from the stations (see above), but turn left onto R. Andrés Mellado before you reach Pr. Peregrina. Winter heating. Check-out 11am. Singles 3600-4300ptas/€22-26; doubles 6000-7500ptas/€36-45. Extra bed 2000ptas/€12. MC/V.

Casa Alicia, Av. de Santa María, 5, 1st floor (☎986 85 70 79). From Pr. Peregrina, walk up R. Michelina through Pr. de España, and turn right onto R. Mestre Mateo. Av. de Santa María will be on the right. Winter heating. Reservations recommended. Doubles 3000-3500ptas/€18-21; quads 4500ptas/€27.

Casa Maruja, Av. de Santa María, 2 (☎986 85 49 01), across the street from Casa Alicia. Small, homey rooms in this family-run pension have pleasant views of a park. Some rooms have TV and private bath. Doubles 3000ptas/€18, with bath 4000ptas/€24.

FOOD

Pontevedra prides itself on seafood. In the evenings, locals crowd tiny bars in the streets around Pr. Peregrina. C. Figueroa, Pr. da Lena, and C. San Sebastián harbor some of the most popular *marisquerías* and *tapas* bars. For groceries, there's **Supermercado Gadis,** C. Benito Corbal, 34. (Open M-Sa 9am-2pm and 5-9pm.)

Bodegón Micota, R. Peregrina, 4 (☎986 85 59 17). This basement bodega serves Spanish takes on global classics like fajitas (1100ptas/€6.60), shishkabobs (1150-1850ptas/€6.90-11.12), and fondue (1100-2000ptas/€6.60-12). The best deal at lunch is the 950pta/€5.70 *menú del día*. Open daily noon-4:30pm and 8pm-1am.

O Merlos, Av. de Santa María, 4 (☎986 84 43 43). From Pl. Peregina, take C. Michelena through Pr. de España, and turn right onto R. Mestre Mateo; Av. de Santa María will be on the right. Tasty regional platters served in a dark, wood-panelled dining room; thousands of key chains hang from the ceiling. Over 40 *tapas* (275-850ptas/€1.65-5.10). *Menú* 1200ptas/€7.20. Open Tu-Su 10am-2am. AmEx/MC/V.

SIGHTS AND ENTERTAINMENT

Pontevedra's primary sight is the [illegible] collection cover a wide range of themes, including traditional Galician cooking, sacred and contemporary art, archaeology, and glasswork. From Pr. Peregrina, walk up Po. de Antonio Odriozola, which runs between the gardens and Pr. de Ferrería; this leads to the museum on Pr. de Leña. (R. Pasantería, 10. Museum open June-Sept. Tu-Sa 10am-2:15pm and 5-8:45pm, Su 11am-2pm; Oct.-May 10am-1:30pm and 4:30-8pm. 500ptas/€3, EU members free.) In Pr. de España sit the 13th-century Gothic **Ruinas de Santo Domingo.** With moss encrusted sepulchres and the sun filtering through cracks in what remains in the structure, the ruins are an eerie time warp in the midst of the new city. (Ruins open June 1-Sept. 30 Tu-F 10am-2pm. Free.) The Basílica de **Santa María a Maior** features a golden Plateresque door, constructed in the 16th century, depicting several sculptures of Mary; at night, it's illuminated by flood-lights. From Pl. España take Av. Santa María, on the left of the Ayuntamiento. (☎986 86 61 85. Open daily 10am-1pm and 5-9pm. Under construction in summer 2001; check at the tourist office to see if it's open.)

Sunny days are sure to bring a crowd to the white-sand **beaches** of nearby Marín. A fleet of red APSA buses makes the journey from the outer corner of Pr. Galicia on Av. Augusto García Sánchez. (30min., every 15min., 120ptas/€0.72.) From the bus stop in Marin, facing the water, head left on C. Angusto Miranda around the track and up the hill. To reach **Playa Porticelo,** turn right on C. Tiro Naval Janer, continue for 15min., and bear right where the road splits. Another 10min. on foot brings you to the larger **Playa Mogor.** The festivals of **Santiago de Burgos** (July 25) and **La Peregrina** (2nd Sunday in August) bring city-wide celebration.

DAYTRIPS FROM PONTEVEDRA

The following towns are perfect daytrips from Pontevedra, as the Monbus lines run frequently, or they can be reached quickly from Santiago.

EL GROVE (O GROVE) AND LA TOJA (A TOXA)

Monbus (☎902 15 87 78) runs buses from Pontevedra to El Grove (1hr.; June-Sept. every 30min. 7:45am-10pm, less in winter; 485ptas/€2.90); an equal number return (every 30min. 6:30am-9pm). There is no bus station in El Grove; all buses stop on the waterfront at the corner of R. Beiramar and R. Pablo Iglesias. Schedules are posted at the bus stop.

Every July and August, affluent Europeans come in Land Rovers and BMWs to the fishing town of El Grove (pop. 11,000) and its swanky island partner, La Toja. Sea-saturated El Grove, on a tranquil strait west of Pontevedra, is lined with mussel farms, colorful boats, and clam-diggers. The waterfront is the main attraction, although there's no beach in town and few on-the-water activities; instead, tourists gawk at fishermen bringing their catches to the local restaurants and peruse the wares at the Friday morning market. From July to mid-October the El Grove **tourist office,** Plaza do Corgo, 1, has an office in the square near the bus stop. (☎986 73 14 15. Open July-Oct. 15 M-Sa 10am-2:30pm and 4:30-9pm, Su 11am-2:30pm.)

LA LANZADA

Some of the Monbuses (☎902 15 87 78) en route to El Grove stop at La Lanzada (1hr.; 13 per day 8:30am-10pm; 465ptas/€2.80).

Five kilometers toward Pontevedra from El Grove, La Lanzada's beach—arguably the best in Galicia—seduces topless bathers with its fine white sands and irresistible waves. This mile-long beach is protected by a dune system and occasional rocky promontories jutting into sea. While most bathers come to relax and lounge in the Atlantic, quite a few come seeking the elusive "Ninth Wave"; according to pagan legend, women who swim in exactly nine waves at moonlight will forever be cured of infertility.

SANXENXO

Monbus (☎902 15 87 78) stops in Sanxenxo on the way from Pontevedra to El Grove (1hr.; June-Sept. every 30min. 7:45am-10pm, less in winter; 270ptas/€1.65); an equal number return (every 30min. 6:55am-9:25pm). There is no bus station in Sanxenxo; all buses stop on the main highway just after the "Florida" sign. Heading downhill on any street to the left will bring you to the water and the town center.

The preferred beach resort of local Galicians, Sanxenxo is a quiet town that draws only moderate crowds, meaning its beach always has space for another body. While not as picturesque or vast as that at La Lanzada, the beach here is pleasant, with calm waters and soft golden sands. The town itself consists of only a few streets, but all are packed with cafés, *marisquerías*, upscale boutiques, and discos. Like any beach resort, beds don't come cheaply here. The best option is **Hostal Venezuela,** R. Carlos Casas, 6. The flower-themed rooms at this family-run hotel are sunny, have private baths, and some even look out onto the beach. (☎986 72 00 86. Reservations accepted. Doubles July-Aug. 6000ptas/€36; Sept.-June 5000ptas/€30.)

CAMBADOS

Plus Ultra buses run from Pontevedra to the new bus station in Cambados near Pr. Concello (1hr., 9 per day 9am-7pm, 340ptas/€2.05) and Santiago (1½hr.; M-F 8 per day 7am-7pm, Sa 8am, 3, 7pm, Su 9am and 7pm; 410ptas/€2.46).

Offering a glimpse of small-town life and a glass of good wine, harborside Cambados (pop. 14,000) makes for a quiet daytrip from Pontevedra, just 26km away. The lack of a beach has left Cambados out of the tourist loop—its taxi drivers play cards all afternoon. On a quiet hill 15min. from the center, the beautiful ruins of the **Iglesia Santa María** watch over the town's cemetery. The small park up the steps to the left of the ruins offers a lovely view of the town and the *ría*. The **Pazo de Fefiñanes,** an attractive 16th-century palace-turned-*bodega*, brims with gigantic, sweet-smelling barrels of wine; the bars and restaurants in the **Pr. de Fefiñanes** serve Cambados' prized beverage. A new **tourist office** (near the bus station) serves the town and gives good free maps. (Open M-Sa 10am-1:30pm and 4:30-7pm.)

RÍAS ALTAS

Thick fogs and misty mornings seem to have kept the Rías Altas secret from most visitors. With the exception of La Coruña, the area's busy capital, the Rías Altas seem to have been nearly forgotten, and that's the very reason to visit: isolated highways and the tiniest of coastal towns mean that the visitors who actually make it here have miles of green estuaries and secluded beaches all to themselves.

LA CORUÑA (A CORUÑA) ☎981

Unlike the rest of its Galician neighbors, La Coruña (pop. 255,000) is a *big* city, complete with high rises, expressways and sprawl. Somehow, though, La Coruña manages to preserve the feel of an old-time fishermen's port. The streets in the center are a maze of tangled, narrow alleys, teeming with raucous bars and popular *marisquerías*. The harborside walks echo with Galician legend and lore: the lighthouse was supposedly built by Hercules and the city's nickname, the Crystal City, was earned for the blinding effect of a sunset on its rows of tightly packed windows. As any proud *coruñese* will tell you, Santiago might be the northwest's most popular city, but La Coruña is the *real* Galicia.

TRANSPORTATION

Flights: Aeropuerto de Alvedro (☎981 18 72 00), 9km south. Served by **Air Europa** (☎981 18 73 08), **Iberia** (☎981 18 72 59), and **ERA** (☎981 18 72 86). Daily charters to Paris via Barcelona and London.

Trains: Estación San Cristóbal, Pr. San Cristóbal, s/n (☎902 24 02 02). Info open daily 7am-11pm. To: **Barcelona** (15-16hr., 6:50am and 5:50pm, 6500-19500ptas/€39-117); **Madrid** (8½-11hr.; Su-F 12:50 and 9:20pm, Sa 9am; 6200-17400ptas/€37-105); **Santiago** (1hr.; M-F 20 per day 5:55am-10:01pm, Sa 13 per day 5:55am-9:20pm, Su 16 per day 5:55am-10:01pm; 645-2970ptas/€3.88-18); **Vigo** (2-3hr.; M-F 13 per day 6:15am-8:40pm, Sa 8 per day 8:25am-8:40am, Su 10 per day 8:25am-8:40pm; 1265-3500ptas/€7.60-21) via **Pontevedra.**

Buses: C. de Caballeros, s/n (☎981 23 06 44 [illegible] 42). To: **Oviedo** (4½-6¾hr., 5 per day 7am-7pm, 3275ptas/€20); **Madrid** (8½hr., 5-6 per day 7:30am-10:30pm, 4955-6975ptas/€30-42); **San Sebastián** (14hr., 9am and 5:45pm, 6575ptas/€40) via **Santander** (10hr., 5020ptas/€30). **Castromil** (☎981 24 91 92 or 23 92 41) to **Santiago** (50min.-1½hr.; M-F 2 per hr. 7am-10pm, Sa-Su 8am-10pm every 1-2hr.; 875ptas/€5.26) and **Vigo** (2-2½hr., hourly 8am-8pm, 1650ptas/€9.92) via **Pontevedra** (1½-2hr., 1340ptas/€8.05). **IASA-Arriva** (☎981 23 90 01) to **Betanzos** (40min.; M-F every 30min., Sa-Su every hr., 6:30am-10:30pm; 245ptas/€1.47) and **Vivero** (3½hr.; M-Sa 6 per day, Su 4 per day 6:30am-7:30pm; 1700ptas/€10.22) with stops at **El Ferrol** and **Betanzos.**

Public Transportation: Red buses of the **Compañía de Tranvías de la Coruña** (☎981 25 01 00) run frequently (7am-11:30pm; 120ptas/€0.72). Bus stops post full itineraries; buy tickets onboard. In the city center, the main stop is the Puerto Real, just across the street from the tourist office on Av. de la Marina. Buses #1 and 1a run between the bus station and the city center; bus #14 connects the center with the museums and monuments along Paseo Marítimo.

Taxis: Radio Taxi (☎981 24 33 33). **TeleTaxi** (☎981 28 77 77). Both 24hr. With the tourist office and ocean to the right, walk along the sidewalk to the taxi stand.

Car Rental: Autos Brea, Av. Fernández Latorre, 110 (☎ 981 23 86 45 or 689 53 94 86). Min. age 21; must have had license for 1yr. From 5000ptas/€30 per day with unlimited mileage. 3-day min. rental. Open M-F 9am-1pm and 4-7pm, Sa 9am-2pm.

ORIENTATION AND PRACTICAL INFORMATION

La Coruña sits on a narrow peninsula between the Atlantic Ocean and the Ría de A Coruña. The new city stretches across the mainland; the peninsula contains the *ciudad vieja* (old city). Beaches are on the Atlantic side and the harbor is on the river. **Av. de la Marina** runs along the harbor and leads past the tourist office and the obelisk to **Puerta Real,** the entry into **Pl. de María Pita** and the *ciudad vieja.* From the bus station, take bus #1 or 1a straight to the **tourist office** at the Puerta Real stop; the stop at the bus station is on the street in front of the main entrance. To get from the train station to the *ciudad vieja,* take the city bus from the bus station. From the main entrance of the train station on Pr. San Cristóbal, cross the plaza and R. de Outeiro, then walk right on R. de Outeiro. Turn left onto R. Estaciones and then follow the pedestrian paths over the highway. The bus station and stop for bus #1 and 1a are across the street from the base of the pedestrian stairs.

Tourist Office: Dársena de la Marina, s/n (☎/fax 981 22 18 22), right off Avda. de la Marina at the Puerta Real, English spoken. Open M-F 9am-2pm and 4:30-6:30pm, Sa 10am-2pm and 4:30-7pm, Su 10am-2pm. If the Dársena tourist office is completely full, try **Turismo A Coruña,** Núñez, s/n (☎981 21 61 61), Edificio Atalaya, 1st fl., in the Jardines de Méndez Núñez. Open M-F 9am-2pm and 4-8pm.

Late-Night Pharmacy: Telefarmacia (☎981 56 09 92 or 902 13 41 34). 24hr. service.

Emergency: ☎061. **Police: Municipal,** C. Miguel Servet, s/n (☎981 18 42 25).

Medical Services: San José Health Center, C. Comandante Fontanes, 8 (☎981 22 63 35). **Ambulances,** dial ☎061.

Internet Access: Paixon E.D., C. San Nicolás, 37 (☎981 20 55 24), 1 block from C. Riego de Agua. Walking away from Pl. María Pita on C. Riego de Agua, turn right onto C. Bailén and veer to the right at the fork onto C. San Nicolás. 250ptas/€1.50 per 30min. Open daily 9am-1:30am, Sa-Su 9am-3:30am.

Post Office: C. Alcalde Manuel Casas, s/n (☎902 19 71 97), past Teatro Colón off Av. Marina, between the Puerta Real and the Jardines de Méndez Núñez. **Lista de Correos** and **fax** service. Open M-F 8:30am-8:30pm, Sa 9:30am-2pm. **Postal Code:** 15070.

ACCOMMODATIONS

There are few budget accommodations in central Coruña; the many *pensiones* near the stations are miles away from the *ciudad vieja.* The best bed hunting in the center is on C. Riego de Agua and on R. Nueva. Reservations are only necessary in August during the city's month-long festival.

Hostal Roma, Rua Nueva, 3 (☎981 22 80 75). From the Puerta Real, walk down Av. de la Marina toward the city center, and at the obelisk turn left onto R. Nueva. Common room downstairs has another TV and dining tables; no kitchen. Reception 24hr. Singles 4000-5000ptas/€24.04-30.05; doubles 6000-7500ptas/€36.06-45.08. MC/V.

Pensión la Alianza, C. Riego de Agua, 8, 1st fl. (☎981 22 81 14). Be sure to ask for a room with a window, as several have none. Spotless bathroom. Singles 2200ptas/€13; doubles 3800ptas/€22. Open May-Oct. only.

Marina Española (HI) (☎981 62 01 18; fax 22 13 36), in Sada, 20km east of La Coruña. The Empresa Calpita bus (☎981 23 90 72) runs there (30min., hourly 8:25am-10:25pm, 240ptas/€1.44) from the A Coruña bus station. Heat in winter. 3-day max. stay. HI members only. Dorms 750ptas/€4.51; over 26 1100ptas/€6.61.

FOOD

The streets around C. Estrella, C. Franja, and C. La Galera teem with cheap *marisquerías* and other restaurants. The area around C. Rubine off Playa de Raizor is fancier. The **market** is in the oval building on Pr. San Agustín, near the old town; from Pl. de María Pita, walk up C. de la Florida and then turn left on C. Trompeta, which brings you to the market. (Open M-Sa 8am-3pm.) **Supermercados Claudio** is in the basement of the market building. (Open daily 9am-3pm and 5-9pm.)

Bania Restaurante Vegetariano, C. Cordelería, 7 (☎981 22 13 01). Fresh, creative vegetarian cuisine served in a sunny environment. Immense salads (775-950ptas/€4.66-5.71). Open M-Sa 1:30-4pm and 9-11:30pm.

Café Veracruz, C. Tourinana, 58 (☎981 14 83 19). Exceptional coffees and pastries at an American-style coffee-house. Treat yourself to a cup of the exquisite Jamaican Blue Mountain (325ptas/€1.95). *Desayunos* (375ptas/€2.25) includes the South American blend of the day, fresh-squeezed orange juice, and your choice of pastry. Open daily 8am-1:30pm and 5-11pm.

SIGHTS

While La Coruña lacks many of the historic monuments of other Galician towns, it has a phenomenal series of attractions along the Po. Marítimo. To visit all of these [illegible] Marítimo, which brings you to the major museums and the Torre de Hércules.

LAS TRES CASAS CORUÑESAS

A 1200ptas/€7.21 bono ticket allows same-day admission to all three museums: the Aquarium Finisterrae, Domus, and Casa de las Ciencias and Planetarium.

AQUARIUM FINISTERRAE. Also known as **Casa de los Peces,** this new aquarium is La Coruña's magnificent homage to the sea. Inside the building, over 200 species of local marine life are displayed in vast aquariums while the downstairs room features visiting exhibitions on marine ecosystems from around the world. *(On the Po. Marítimo at the bottom of the hill from La Torre de Hércules. Also reached by bus #14 from Puerta Real. ☎981 22 72 72; www.casaciencias.org. Open daily July-Aug. 11am-11pm; Sept.-June 10am-7pm. 1000ptas/€6, children and seniors, 500ptas/€3.)*

MUSEO DOMUS. The new Domus, also called **Casa del Hombre** (House of Man), is an anthropology, natural history, and science museum all rolled into one, featuring interactive, high-tech exhibits on the human body and cultures. Watch "blood" spurt at 50kph from a model heart; hear "Hello, I love you" in over 30 languages (sadly, from a computer); and spend hours playing with microscopes, computers, and other fun gizmos. *(Santa Teresa, 1, on Po. Marítimo, between the Aquarium and Playa Orzán. ☎981 21 70 00; www.casaciencias.org. Open July-Aug. daily 11am-9pm; Sept.-June daily 10am-7pm. Children 300ptas/€1.80, seniors 100ptas/€0.60. IMAX supplement 200ptas/€1.20; check at ticket booth for schedule.)*

TORRE DE HÉRCULES. La Coruña's tourist magnet, the 2nd-century Torre de Hércules, towers over rusted ships at the peninsula's end. Legend has it that Hércules erected the tower, the world's oldest working lighthouse, upon the remains of his defeated enemy Gerión. *(On Po. Marítimo, a 20min. walk from Puerta Real. Walking from the Puerta, walk through Pl. de María Pita and from behind the Ayuntamiento, walk uphill on C. Millán Astray. Turn left onto C. de Orillamar, which turns into Av. de Navarra and brings you to the tower. Open July-Aug. Su-Th 10am-8:45pm, F-Sa 10am-11:45pm; Apr.-June and Sept. daily 10am-6:45pm; Oct.-Mar. daily 10am-5:45pm. Seniors 250ptas/€1.50, children 100ptas/€0.60.)*

MUSEO DE BELLAS ARTES. Housed in a renovated convent, this museum displays classic Spanish, French, Italian, and Flemish art as well as some local Gallego artists. Don't miss the Goya display. *(C. Zalaeta, 2. With the tourist office behind you, cross the street into the old sector and take C. Bailén until it becomes C. San Nicolás, which will run into C. Zalaeta and the museum. ☎981 22 37 23. Open Tu-F 10am-8pm, Sa 10am-2pm and 4:30-8pm. Su 10am-2pm. 400ptas/€2.40.)*

CASTILLO DE SAN ANTÓN. This fort serves as La Coruña's archaeological museum, with displays of Galician fortresses, as well as artifacts from the Roman, Bronze, and Megalithic Ages. *(Puerto Deportivo, on Po. Marítimo. From the tourist office follow Dársena de la Marina away from the port; once you reach the paseo, walk for 10min.; it's on the thin peninsula. ☎981 20 59 94. Open July-Aug. Tu-Sa 10am-9pm, Su 10am-3pm; Sept.-June Tu-Sa 10am-7pm, Su 10am-3pm. Children 100ptas/€0.60.), seniors 300ptas/€1.80.*

BEACHES

La Coruña's best beaches are the long, narrow **Playa de Riazor** and **Playa del Orzán,** which flank Paseo Marítimo on the Atlantic side of the peninsula and are separated from one another only by a small walkway. On the weekends, these calm waters are packed with bodies, but during the week they're nearly deserted. Small, secluded beaches hide farther down Po. Marítimo, including **Playas del Matadero, de Las Amorosas,** and **das Lapas,** although these tend to be rockier and seaweedier.

ENTERTAINMENT

Although it is celebrated in many parts of Europe, La Coruña greets **La Noche de San Juan** (June 23) with particular fervor since it coincides with the opening of sardine season. Locals light the traditional *aguardiente* bonfires before spending the night leaping over the flames (contrary to what you might assume, the rite is actually supposed to ensure fertility) and gorging on sardine flesh. If you drop an egg white in a glass of water on this night, it will supposedly assume the form of your future spouse's occupation; many are led to believe they'll marry a cow. The city's main festival is **Las Fiestas de María Pita,** which lasts for the entire month of August. Party-hardy Coruñeses spend the month celebrating with various concerts, parades, and a mock naval battle to honor María Pita, the woman who single-handedly rallied a defense against the invading army of Sir Francis Drake (after the town's men had fled from the port in fear).

NIGHTLIFE

In the early evening, *coruñeses* linger in Celtic pubs throughout the old city, barhopping around C. Orzán, C. del Sol, and the mess of streets near C. Franja and C. La Florida. **IriBar,** C. Panaderas, 34, is La Coruña's sleekest and most cosmopolitan lounge. (Open daily 9pm-4am.) When bars die down around 2am, **discos** pick up along the two beaches and on C. Juan Florez. **Sol. Pirámide,** C. Juan Florez, 50

THE BEAUTY OF THE BEASTS It is estimated that more than 100,000 wild horses roam the Galician hills, and records indicate that they have been there for nearly 4000 years. No longer useful as cart-pullers, few of these animals are domesticated today, but the ancient branding rituals are still celebrated every July during *La Rapa das Bestas* ("Raping of the Beasts").

"Here, we fight horses for tradition," says one rider, a sweaty, blood-speckled bandana across his hairline. The blood may not be his; for the past two hours he's straddled, head-locked, tail-pulled, herd-surfed, tackled, branded, been kicked and bitten, and most importantly, sheared numerous feisty steeds. Consistent with one of the central themes of Spanish culture–man versus beast–*La Rapa* gives a new face to the traditional noble bull-Matador dynamic. Before the festival begins, Spanish Marlboro men comb the mountains and valleys gathering wild horses. No one animal can be picked out of the writhing sea of horseflesh, but brave souls wielding scissors fight their way into the crowd, wrestle one horse at a time to submission, and send thick crops of shiny hair flying to the ground–to be collected later by children as souvenirs. By the end of the three-day festival, horses may be shaken by the unsolicited crew-cut, but unlike the unfortunate fallen bull, they will most definitely be ridden again.

(☎981 27 61 57), plays dance music loud enough to rouse the dead, while **Picasso,** C. del Sol, 21, and **Lautrec,** C. del Sol, 12, across the street, attract house-music lovers. (All open daily midnight-5am.) For a more sophisticated (and pricier) scene, *coruñeses* head to the **Swing Piano Bar,** Av. de la Marina, 32, where smoky singers and Benny Goodman tunes entertain martini drinkers. (Open daily 10pm-3am.)

THE NORTHERN COAST

The northern estuaries of Galicia are among the cleanest, loveliest, and emptiest in all of Spain. To explore the Rías Altas often means spending hours on quiet coastal roads in the misty rain; if you want to escape the beaten path, coming here may be the answer. Public transportation is reliable, but renting a car is more convenient.

Eighty-four km northeast of La Coruña, **Cedeira** has Spain's highest coastline and is home to thriving pagan cults with rituals involving worship of the hierba de enamorar (love herb). Cedeira hosts the annual **Pantín Classic** surfing competition at its famous **Playa de Pantín** and goes crazy for its annual horse-shearing festival (see **Las Rapas das Bestas,** above) every July. To reach the **tourist office,** C. Ezequiel López, 22, walk to the main street outside the bus station at Pr. Estación, s/n, and take a right. Follow the street to the small river, cross the bridge, and turn left onto C. Ezequiel López. (☎981 48 21 87. Open Apr.-Sept. M-F 10:30am-1:30pm and 5-8pm, Sa 10am-2pm, Su and holidays noon-2pm.) **IASA buses** run to **El Ferrol** (1hr., 7 per day 8am-7pm, 440ptas/€2.64), where connec- [illegible]

A tiny, beautiful old city poised between forest and sea, **Vivero** is known throughout Spain for its beaches, peaceful atmosphere, and July *fiestas*, especially **Las Rapas das Bestas.** Vivero's **tourist office,** on Av. Ramón Canosa and C. Carlos V (a cottage around the corner from the bus stop), posts info on accommodations. (☎982 56 08 79. Open daily June 15-Sept. 15 10am-2pm and 5:30-8:30pm; *Semana Santa* daily 11am-2pm and 4:30-8:30pm.) **IASA buses** connect to: **El Ferrol** (2hr., 4-6 per day 6:30am-7:30pm, 995ptas/€5.98); **Ribadeo** (1½hr., 9:15am and 3:45pm, 650ptas/€3.91); and **La Coruña** (4hr., 5 per day 6:30am-7:30pm, 1650ptas/€9.92).

The official boundary between Galicia and Asturias, **Ribadeo** lays claim to one of the most beautiful beaches in Spain, the **Praia As Catedrais.** Natural rock archways droop into the sea, and low tide reveals caverns, coves, and warm lagoons perfect for exploring and swimming. The town itself has a quiet, almost ghostly air. The **tourist office,** Pr. de España, s/n, is in the Parque de San Francisco. (☎982 12 86 89. Open M-F 10am-2:30pm and 4:40-8:30pm, Sa-Su 10am-8pm.) **IASA buses** to: **La Coruña** (2½-3½hr.; M-Sa 7:15am, 8:45am, 1:30pm, and 6:15pm; 1610ptas/€9.70); **Santiago de Compostela** (3hr., 6:30am, 1885ptas/€11.30); and **Vivero** (1½hr.; M-F 9am, 11:30am, and 6pm; Su 2:45 and 6pm; 625ptas/€3.76).

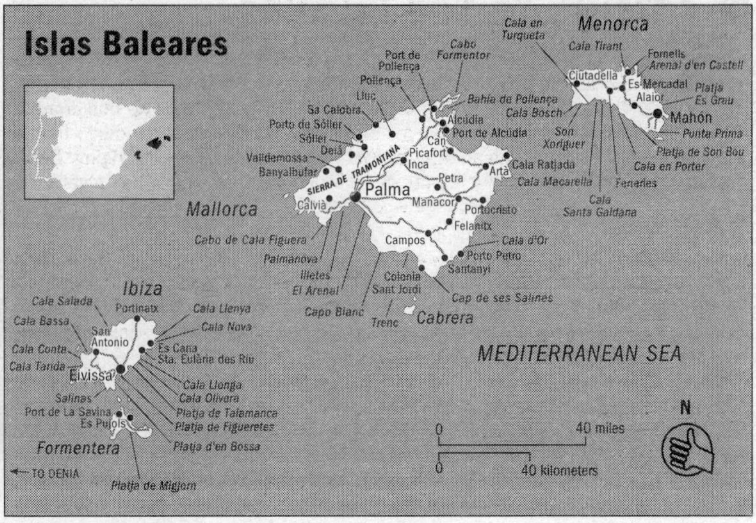

BALEARIC ISLANDS

Dreaming of the vast fortunes to be made in the 20th-century tourist industry, nearly every culture with boats and colonists to spare has tried to conquer the Balearic Islands. Spain won this race centuries ago; today, foreign invasion continues, as 2 million tourists flood the islands' discos and beaches each year.

While all four of the islands—Mallorca, Ibiza, Formentera, and Menorca—share fame for their gorgeous beaches and landscapes, each has its own characteristics. Mallorca, home to the islands' capital of Palma, absorbs the bulk of high-class, package tour invaders. With its museums and nightlife, Palma competes with Ibiza City as the Balearics' cultural hub. Mallorca also harbors natural beauty, albeit in the shadows of urbanization. Ibiza, a counter-cultural haven since the 1960s, is the style center of the islands. With its monstrous discos, and stronghold on crazy, beautiful party-goers, Ibiza affords the best nightlife in all of Europe. Formentera, Ibiza's little sister, is more peaceful with unspoiled sands and unpaved roads while Menorca, wrapped in green fields and stone walls, leads a private life of empty white beaches, hidden coves, and mysterious Bronze Age megaliths.

Summers are hot, dry, crowded, and fun; winters are chilly. Spring and autumn can be sumptuous, but the beaches remain cool; the nightlife doesn't heat up—especially on Mallorca and Menorca—until early July. Most opening hours, schedules, and prices listed are for summer months only. Off-season prices at hotels can drop by up to 50%, and hours are often cut back.

GETTING TO THE ISLANDS

Flying to the islands is cheap and faster than a ferry. Those under 26 can receive discounts from **Iberia/Aviaco Airlines** (☎902 40 05 00 in Barcelona; www.iberia.com). **SOM** (Servicios de Ocio Marítimo; ☎971 31 03 99) lines up bus companies, ferry lines, and *discotecas* for packages to Ibiza designed for disco fiends who seek transportation and an all-night party but have no use for lodging. Book tickets through a travel agency in Barcelona, Valencia, or on any of the islands.

BALEARIC ISLANDS

BY PLANE

Scheduled flights are the easiest to book and flights from Spain to any of the islands won't break the bank. Frequent flights soar from cities in Spain and throughout Europe (including Frankfurt, London, and Paris). On **Iberia** (☎902 40 05 00), many daily flights connect Palma de Mallorca and Ibiza to Madrid, Barcelona, and Valencia. Service from Alicante and Bilbao exists too, but is less frequent.

Iberia offers student fares (with an ISIC 26) on round-trip flights from Barcelona (40min., 10,000-20,000ptas/€60-120) and Madrid (1hr., 25,000-30,000ptas/€150-180). **Air Europa** (☎902 24 00 42) and **Spanair** (☎902 13 14 15; www.spanair.com) also offer inexpensive flights to the islands. Schedules and prices change, so contact a travel agent or the airlines for details. Another option is **charter flights,** which can be the cheapest and quickest means of travel. Most deals entail a stay in a hotel, but some companies (called *mayoristas*) sell unoccupied seats on package-tour flights. The leftover spots ("seat only" deals) can be found in newspaper ads or through travel agencies (check TIVE and other budget travel havens in any Spanish city). Prices during summer and *Semana Santa* are much more than in off-season (Oct.-May). Off-season, tickets are not hard to get a week or so before departure. Those traveling in July or August should reserve months in advance.

BY BOAT

Ferry service is comparable to flights in price, but longer in duration. On-board discos and small swimming pools on some boats ease the longer ride. Ferries run from Barcelona and Valencia to Palma (on Mallorca) and Eivissa (on Ibiza); ferries also run from Dénia (in Alicante) to Ibiza. Seats may be available up to an hour before departure, but it's best to reserve tickets a few days in advance.

Trasmediterránea (☎902 45 46 45; www.trasmediterranea.com) departs daily from Barcelona's Estació Marítima Moll and Valencia's Estació Marítima. Boats leave from both cities to Mallorca, Menorca, and Ibiza. Fares from the mainland to the islands is 7220ptas/€43 slowpoke, 9710ptas/€58 fast boat. Fares between the islands ranges from 3895ptas/€23 slow to 6210ptas/€37 fast.

[illegible]
Dénia (in the province of Alicante). A short trip between Dénia and Ibiza (2-4½hr., 3 per day, from 4185ptas/€25), continuing on to Palma (from 6865ptas/€41).

Pitra Car Ferries (Dénia ☎971 19 10 68), run from Denía to Formentera via Eivissa and to San Antonio de Portmany (4hr., 2 per day; 5475ptas/€33, children 2750ptas/€17, cars 15,050ptas/€90).

Buquebus (☎902 41 42 42 or 934 81 73 60) has super-fast catamaran service between Barcelona and Palma (4hr., 2 per day; 8150ptas/€49, cars 18,560/€112).

Umafisa Lines (☎902 19 10 68) has service between Barcelona and the islands 3 times per week. 7220ptas/€43, some economy tickets available for 6180ptas/€37.

INTER-ISLAND TRANSPORTATION

Flying isn't always the best way to go between islands. **Iberia** flies between Palma and Ibiza (45min., 5 per day, 8900-13,000ptas/€54-80) and between Palma and Mahón, Menorca (35min., 4 per day, from 8900ptas/€54). **Air Europa** (☎902 24 00 42) and **Spanair** (☎902 13 14 15) connect the islands at similar prices. Youth discounts are often available.

A cheaper option is to take **ferries** between islands. Ferries cost much less than planes. Prices and times are constantly changing; consult the tourist office or a travel agent for information. Ferries to and from Mahón are lengthy (6½hr.), but "fast ferries" now make the journey between the other three islands in under three hours. **Trasmediterránea** (☎902 45 46 45) sails between Palma and Mahón (6½hr., Su only, 3895ptas/€23) and between Palma and Ibiza (fast 2½hr., 1 per day at 7am from Valencia, 7:45am from Ibiza, 6210ptas/€37; slow 4½hr., 3 per week, 3895ptas/€23). There is no direct Mahón-Ibiza connection. **Trasmapi** (☎971 31 20 71) links Ibiza and Formentera (fast ferry 25min., 12 per day). **Umafisa Lines** (☎971 31 45 13) runs car ferries on the same route. **Iscomar Ferries** (☎902 119 128) runs between Menorca's Port de Ciutadella and Mallorca's Port d'Alcudia for day trips.

TRANSPORT ON THE ISLANDS

The three major islands have extensive **bus** systems, although transportation nearly comes to a halt on Sundays in most locations, so check schedules. Mallorca has two narrow-gauge **train** systems, that are more of a tourist attraction than a major mode of getting around. Intra-island travel is reasonably priced—bus fares between cities range 200-1000ptas/€1.20-6 each way. While it's possible to visit any of the islands without renting a vehicle, cars and mopeds are a great way (if you can afford it) to explore remote areas not accessible by bus service. In Mallorca and Menorca, cars are the best option, while in Ibiza, a moped is more than adequate. On Formentera, bicycles are a great way to get around, given the number of bike trails. A day's rental of a tiny standard-transmission **car** costs around 6000ptas/€36 including insurance; **mopeds** are around 3000ptas/€18; and **bicycles** a mere 1000ptas/€6. Prices drop in the off-season and for long-term rentals.

MALLORCA

Mallorca, sought after since the days of the Romans, has a long been popular, continually attracting the rich and famous. The site of the scandalous honeymoon of Polish pianist Fréderic Chopin and French novelist George Sand, Mallorca is also the choice vacation spot for Spain's royal family. Today, European package tourists have converged on the island, in some areas virtually suffocating the coastline.

There are reasons for such Mallorca lust. To the northwest, white beaches, frothy water, and olive trees adorn the jagged Sierra de Tramontana. To the east, expansive beaches sink into calm bays, while to the southeast, caves mask underground treasure. Inland, towns retain their unique culture, where windmills drawing water for almond trees power a thriving agricultural economy. Although the coastline has been sacrificed to developers, even the most jaded of travelers sigh at the expanses of sea, sand, and rock that sprawl across much of this island.

PALMA

The capital of the Balearics, Palma (pop. 323,000) does not shy away from conspicuous consumption. Restaurants cater to expensive tastes and streets bustle with shoppers buying designer clothes, leather accessories, and jewelry. Needless to say, as major cosmopolitan city, Palma offers all the amenities of a large urban center. Though flooded by *pesetas* and nearly every other currency, Palma surprises the tourist eye with its old quarter, colonial architecture, and local flavor.

TRANSPORTATION

Flights: Aeroport Son San Juan (☎971 78 90 00), 8km from downtown Palma. Bus #17 and 25 go to and from Pl. Espanya (300ptas/€1.8). **Iberia** (☎902 40 05 00),

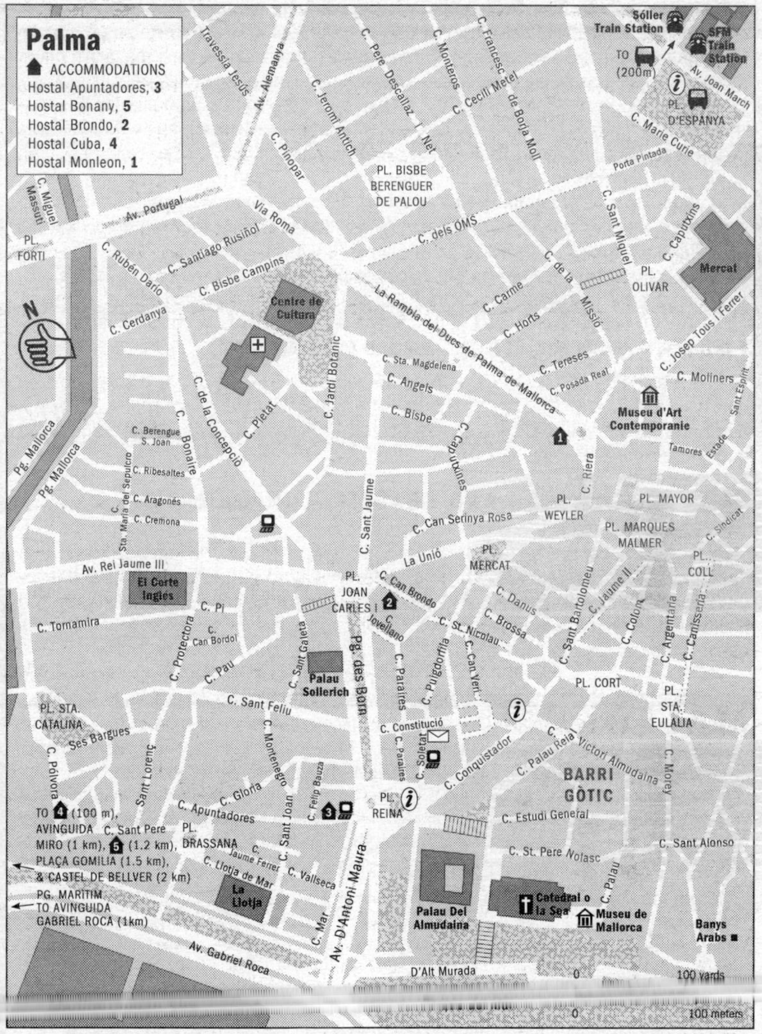

Air Europa (☎902 24 00 42), foreign carriers, and a host of charter operators all offer service to Palma. See **By Plane,** p. 475 or **Transportation,** p. 476.

Ferries: Trasmediterránea, Estació Marítim, 2 (☎902 45 46 45). Ferries dock at Moll Pelaires (south of the city). Bus #1 goes through Pg. Marítim. Tickets sold M-F 9am-1pm and 5-7pm, Sa 9am-noon. Tickets and info also available at travel agencies. Daily ferries to Barcelona, Ibiza, and Valencia. **Balearia** (☎902 16 01 80) sends ferries to Denia. See **By Boat,** p. 475, or **Transportation,** p. 476.

Trains: Ferrocarril de Sóller (☎971 75 20 51), Pl. Espanya. Runs to **Sóller** (1hr., 5 per day 8am-8:05pm, 380ptas/€2.28). Avoid the 10:40am "tourist train" when prices inflate to 735ptas/€4.40 for a 10min. stop in Mirador del Pujol d'en Banya. **Servicios Ferroviarios de Mallorca (SFM),** Pl. Espanya, 6 (☎971 75 22 45), departs to **Inca** (35min., 22 per day 5:45am-10pm, 300ptas/€1.8).

Buses: Bus travel to and from Palma is not too difficult, but travel between most other areas is inefficient and restrictive. Nearly all buses stop at the main stop on C. Eusebi Estada, several blocks down from Pl. Espanya; buy tickets on the bus. The tourist office has a detailed schedule of all buses. Some of the more popular destinations include: **Alcúdia** and **Port Alcúdia** (1hr.; M-F 16 per day 8am-9pm, Sa-Su 5 per day 9:30am-9pm; 615ptas/€3.70); **Covetes/Es Trenc** (M-F 3 per day 10am-5pm, Sa-Su 10:30am; 640ptas/€3.84); **Cuevas Drac** (M-F 4 per day 10am-1:30pm, Sa-Su 10am; 900ptas/€5.40); **Port Pollenca** (1hr.; M-F 5 per day 9am-7:15pm, Sa-Su 3 per day 10am-8:30pm); 720ptas/€4.30); **Sóller** and **Port Sóller** (45min.; M-F every hr. 7am-7pm, Sa-Su 1 and 4:30pm; 350ptas/€2.10); **Valldemossa** (30min.; M-F every 2 hr. 7:30am-7:30pm, Sa-Su 4 per day 8:30am-7:30pm; 200ptas/€1.20).

Public Transportation: Empresa Municipal de Transportes (EMT; ☎971 75 22 45). Pl. Espanya is the hub. Stops around town and as far as Palma Nova and Arenal. 175ptas/€1.05, 10 tickets 1500ptas/€9. Buy tickets onboard. Buses run approximately 6am-10pm. The airport bus, #17, runs until 1am (300ptas/€1.80). Bus #25 also goes to the airport but stops running at 10pm.

Taxis: (☎971 75 54 40). Airport fare from center of town is about 2500ptas/€15.

Car Rental: Mascaro Crespi, Av. Joan Miró, 9 (☎971 73 61 03). 4000ptas/€24 per day with insurance. Open M-Sa 8am-1pm and 3-8pm, Su 9am-1pm and 5-8pm.

ORIENTATION AND PRACTICAL INFORMATION

To get to town from the airport, take bus #17 or 25 to **Pl. Espanya** (15min., every 20min., 300ptas/€1.80). From the dock, take Pg. Marítim (a.k.a. Av. Gabriel Roca), or bus #1 to Av. D'Antoni Maura, which leads to **Pl. Reina** and **Pg. Born.** From the sea, Pg. Born leads to **Pl. Rei Joan Carles I,** the center of the old town, and **Av. Rei Jaume III,** the business artery. To the right, C. de la Unió leads (after some stairs) to **Pl. Major,** the center of Palma's pedestrian shopping district.

Tourist Offices: Palma branch, C. Sant Dominic, 11 (☎971 72 40 90). From Pl. Reina, take C. Conquistador until C. Sant Dominic; office is at bottom of stairway, below street level. Open M-F 9am-8pm, Sa 9am-1:30pm. **Info booth** in Pl. Espanya. **Island tourist office,** Pl. Reina, 2 (☎971 71 22 16) Open M-F 9am-8pm, Sa 10am-2pm.

Budget Travel: TIVE, C. Jeróni Antich, 5 (☎971 71 17 85), off Pl. Bisbe Berenguer de Palou. ISIC cards, HI cards, Interrail tickets, and mainland flights. Not for inter-island travel and charters. Open M-F 9am-2pm and 5-7:30pm.

Currency Exchange: Banco Central Hispano, Pg. Born, 17 (☎971 72 51 46). Open May-Sept. M-F 8:30am-2:30pm; Oct.-Apr. M-F 8:30am-2:30pm, Sa 8:30am-1pm.

American Express: Av. Antonio Maura, 40 (☎971 72 23 44), downtown right next to C. Apuntadores, off Pl. Reina. Open M-F 9am-1pm and 2-8pm, Sa 10am-2pm.

El Corte Inglés: Av. Rei Jaume III, 15 (☎971 77 01 77). Open M-Sa 10am-10pm.

English Bookstore: Book Inn, C. Horts, 20 (☎971 71 38 98), right off La Rambla. Open M-F 10am-1:30pm and 4:30-8pm. Hours change in Aug.

Women's Center: Centro de Derechos Mujeres, Galería, 4 (☎971 77 49 74; 24hr. hotline 900 19 10 10). Rape crisis assistance available. Open M-F 9am-2pm.

Laundromat: Lavandería Fast, Joan Miró, 5 (☎971 45 46 14). 1500ptas/€9 for 5kg washed and dried. **Coronet Lavandería,** corner of C. Annibal and C. Argentina. A block from Hostal Cuba. 1400ptas/€8.4 for 5kg. Open M-Sa 8am-1pm and 4-8pm.

Emergency: ☎112. **Police:** Av. Sant Ferrá (☎091 or 092).

Late-Night Pharmacy: Rotates daily; see listings in local paper, the *Diario de Mallorca*.

Medical Services: Clínica Juaneda, C. Son Espanyolet, 55 (☎971 73 16 47), and **Femenía,** Av. Camilo José Cela, 20 (☎971 45 23 23). **Clínica Rotger,** C. Santiago Russinyol, 9 (☎971 71 66 00), is more centrally located. All open 24hr.

Internet Access: La Red, C. Concepció, 5 (☎971 71 35 74) two blocks off of Av. Jaume III near the intersection of Pg. Born. 400ptas/€2.40 for 30min. Open daily 10am-midnight. **Cyber Central,** C. Soletat, 4 (☎971 71 29 27), in Pl. Reina. 800ptas/€4.80 per hr., students 600ptas/€3.60 per hr. Open M-Sa 9am-10pm, Su noon-8pm.

Post Office: C. Constitució, 5 (☎902 19 71 97), 1 block off Pl. Reina. Parcels upstairs. **Fax** service. Open M-F 8:30am-8:30pm, Sa 9:30am-2pm. **Postal Code:** 07080.

ACCOMMODATIONS

This resort town has few hostals or bargains. Call in advance for summer stays.

Hostal Apuntadores, C. Apuntadores, 8 (☎971 71 34 91), less than a block from Pl. Reina. Rooms are airy, bright, and in a great location. Dorms 2000ptas/€12 per person; single 3000ptas/€18; doubles 5000ptas/€30, with shower 5500ptas/€33.

Hostal Brondo, C. Can Brondo, 1 (☎971 71 90 43), off Pl. Rei Joan Carles I. Each room has character; all have beautiful wooden furniture, tasteful artwork, and clean bathrooms. Common lounge. 2 wheelchair accessible rooms. Reception M-Sa 9am-2pm and 6-8pm, Su 10am-1:30pm. Singles 3500ptas/€21; doubles 5500ptas/€33.

Hostal Cuba, C. San Magí, 1 (☎971 73 81 59), at C. Argentina, on edge of town center. From Pl. Joan Carles I, turn left and walk down Av. Jaume III, cross the river, and turn left on C. Argentina. Look for the "Restaurant Cuba" sign several blocks down. 1st floor rooms are more basic than 2nd floor. Prices may change as renovations are completed. Singles 2500-3000ptas/€15-18; doubles 5000-5500ptas/€30-33.

Alberg Platja de Palma (HI), C. Costa Brava, 13 (☎971 26 08 92), in the beach town El Arenal. Take bus #15 from Pl. Espanya (every 8min., 175ptas/€1), and get off at the corner of C. Costa Brava. Lively crowd. 4-person dorms with shower. HI card required. Breakfast included. Sheets 200ptas/€1.20. Laundry service 1000ptas/€6. Reception 8am-3am. Curfew midnight. Bed 1500ptas/€9, over 26 1700ptas/€10.20.

Hostal Monleon, La Rambla, 3 (☎971 71 53 17). Dimly lit, noisy rooms, but cheap for the area. Singles 2500ptas/€15, with shower 2800ptas/€16, with bath 3200ptas/€20; doubles 4500ptas/€27, with shower 5100ptas/€31, with bath 5600ptas/€34.

Hostal Bonany, C. Almirante Cervera, 5 (☎971 73 79 24), in a wealthy residential area 3km from the town center. Take bus #3, 20, 21, or 22 from Pl. Espanya to Av. Joan Miró and walk up C. Camilio José Cela. Take the 1st right, then the 1st left. Spacious rooms with bath and balcony. Singles 4400ptas/€26; doubles 6600ptas/€40.

FOOD

Palma's multi-ethnic restaurants are paradise for the *tapas*-sick. Pricey but popular outdoor restaurants fill **Pl. Mayor** and **Pl. Llotja,** but budget eaters head to the side streets off **Pg. Born,** to the cheap digs along **Av. Joan Miró,** or to the pizzerias along **Po. Marítimo.** Make sure to try the *ensaimadas* (pastries smothered in powdered sugar) and the *sopas mallorquinas* (a pizza-like snack of stewed vegetables over brown bread). Two **markets** vie for customers: one is in Pl. Olivar off C. [illegible]

For **groceries,** try **Servicio y Precios** on C. Felip Bauzà, near C. Apuntadores and Pl. Reina (open M-F 8:30am-8:30pm, Sa 9am-2pm), or the supermarket in **El Corte Inglés,** Av. Rei Jaume III, 15. (☎971 77 01 77. Open M-Sa 10am-10pm.)

Cellar Montenegro, C. Montenegro, 10, off of C. Apuntadores. Heaping portions of great *comida típica* in a family setting. *Menú* 1500ptas/€9. Entrées 1000-1500ptas/€6-9. Open M-F 1-4pm and 8:30pm-midnight. AmEx/MC/V.

Bon Lloc, C. San Feliu, 7, a left off C. Born, heading away from water. Ultra-hip vegetarian restaurant; *menú* features salads (950ptas/€5.70), falafel (1200ptas/€7.20), and dishes like basmati rice with chinese-style sauteed vegetables (1600ptas/€9.60). Midday *menú* 1600ptas/€9.60. Open M-Tu 1-4pm, W-Sa 1-4pm and 9-11:30pm. MC/V.

Merendero Minyones, C. Minyones, 4, a teeny booth on a small street 1 block from C. Constitució. From Pg. Born, walk up C. Constitució, take your 1st left, and then the 1st right. As cheap as they come. Takeout only. Sandwiches 175-205ptas/€1.05-1.23). Open M-F 7:30am-7:30pm, Sa 8am-2pm.

SIGHTS

Palma's architecture is a medley of Arabic, Christian, and Modernist styles: a reflection of the island's multicultural past and present. Many of its landmarks are nestled amidst the narrow streets of the Barri Gòtic (gothic quarter).

CATEDRAL O LA SEA. This Gothic giant towers over Palma and its bay. The cathedral, dedicated to Palma's patron saint San Sebastián, was begun in the 1300s, finished in 1601, and then modified by Gaudí in Modernist fashion in 1909. Now the interior and the ceiling ornamentation blend smoothly with the stately exterior. Its southern façade, perhaps the most impressive, overlooks a reflective pool and the ocean. *(C. Palau Reial, 29, off Pl. Reina. ☎971 72 31 30. Cathedral and museum open Apr.-Oct. M-F 10am-6pm, Sa 10am-2pm; Nov.-Mar. M-F 10am-3pm. 500ptas/€3.)*

PALAU DEL'ALMUDAINA. Built by the Moors, this palace was at one point a stronghold of *Los Reyes Católicos*, Fernando and Isabel. Guided tours, which pass through the museum, are given in numerous languages. *(C. Palau Reial, just off Pl. Reina. ☎971 72 71 45. Open M-F 10am-6:30pm, Sa 10am-2pm. Guided visits 650ptas/€3.91, unguided 525ptas/€3.16. Students and children 375ptas/€2.25. EU citizens free on W.)*

CASTELL DEL BELLVER. Overlooking the city and bay, Castell de Bellver was a summer residence for 14th-century royalty; it also housed Mallorca's most distinguished prisoners. The castle contains a municipal museum with paintings and archaeological displays, as well as models of archaeological digs. *(Bus #3, 21, or 22 from Pl. Espanya. ☎971 73 06 57. Castle and museum open Apr.-Sept. M-Sa 8am-8:30pm, Su 10am-5pm; Oct.-Mar. M-Sa 8am-7:15pm, Su 10am-5pm. 280ptas/€1.68.)*

MUSEU D'ART ESPANYOL CONTEMPORANI. Now part of the March Foundation, this mansion-turned-museum displays a collection of modern art, including works of the 20th century's most iconic Spanish artists, including Picasso, Dalí, Miró, Juan Gris, and Antoni Tàpies. Temporary exhibits as well. *(C. Sant Miquel, 11. ☎971 71 35 15. Open M-F 10am-6:30pm, Sa 10am-1:30pm. 500ptas/€3.)*

OTHER MUSEUMS. Palma is filled with museums. Inaugurated in December 1992, **Fundació Pilar i Joan Miró** displays the works from Miró's Palma studio at the time of his death. *(C. Saridakis, 29. From Pl. Espanya, take buses #3, 21, or 22 to C. Joan Miró. ☎971 70 14 20. Open May 16-Sept. 14 Tu-Sa 10am-7pm, Su 10am-3pm; Sept. 15-May 15 Tu-Sa 10am-6pm, Su 10am-3pm. 700ptas/€4.20.)* **Fundació "la Caixa"** hosts a collection of Modernist paintings as well as other exhibits in Domènech's Modernist Gran Hotel. *(Pl. Weyler, 3. ☎971 17 85 00. Open Tu-Sa 10am-9pm, Su 10am-2pm. Free.)* The **Casal Solleric** houses modern art. *(Pg. Born, 27. ☎971 72 20 92. Open Tu-Sa 10:30am-1:45pm, Su 10am-1:45pm. Free.)* **Centre de Cultura "Sa Nostra"** features rotating exhibits and cultural events such as lectures, concerts, and movies. *(C. Concepción, 12. ☎971 72 52 10. Open M-F 10:30am-9pm, Sa 10am-1:30pm.)* **Museu de Mallorca** is ideal for travelers interested in archaeology or medieval painting. *(C. Portella, 5. ☎971 71 75 40. Open Apr.-Sept. Tu-Sa 10am-2pm and 5-8pm; Oct.-Mar. Tu-Sa 10am-1pm and 4-8pm, Su 10am-2pm. 300ptas/€1.80.)* For those fed up with being inside, there's always **Poble Espanyol,** a small village with replications of famous Spanish architecture, replicates its namesake in Barcelona. *(C. Poble Espanyol, 39. Buses #4 and 5 pass on C. Andrea Doria. ☎971 73 70 75. Open daily 9am-8pm; Dec.-Mar. 9am-6pm. 800ptas/€4.80.)*

BEACHES. Mallorca is a huge island, and many of the best beaches are a haul from Palma. Still, several picturesque (albeit touristy) stretches of sand are accessible by city bus. The beach at **El Arenal** *(Platja de Palma, bus #15)*, 11km to the southeast (toward the airport), is the prime stomping grounds of Mallorca's most sunburned German tourists, and the waterfront area is full of German signs for restaurants, bars, and hotels. The beach is one of the longest and most crowded in the area (Germans take up a lot of space). **Aquacity** *(☎971 44 00 00)*, a water park, hoses down visitors nearby. **Palma Nova** *(bus #21)*, 15km southwest, and **Illetes** *(bus #3)*, 9km southwest, are smaller, but equally popular.

The tourist office distributes a list of over 40 nearby beaches—take your pick and remember to say *danke*.

NIGHTLIFE AND ENTERTAINMENT

Nightlife and entertainment *à la Mallorca* have a Spanish flavor often missing in the other isles, but they are still well documented for visitors. The tourist office keeps a comprehensive list of sporting activities, concerts, and exhibits. Every Friday, *El Día de Mundo* (125ptas/€0.75) publishes an entertainment supplement with listings of bars and discos, and *La Calle* offers a monthly review of hotspots.

In the past, Pl. Reina and La Llotja were the place for bar-hoppers, but a recent law requiring bars to close by 3am has shifted the action to the waterfront. While a many partiers still start their night in the *casco viejo*. **La Bodeguita del Medio,** C. Vallseca, 18, plays Cuban rhythms. (Open Th-Sa 8pm-3am, Su-W 8pm-1am.) Follow the Aussies to **Bar Latitude 39,** C. Felip Bauza, 8, a "yachtie" bar. (Beers 250ptas/€1.50. "Twofer nights"—two for the price of one—Tu, Th, and Sa 9-10pm. Open M-Sa 7pm-3am.) **Barcelona,** C. Apuntadores, 5, jams with live music from midnight to 3am. (Cover 300ptas/€1.80 for live concerts. Open daily 11pm-3am).

Palma's clubbers start the night in the *bares-musicales* on **Po. Marítimo** strip. Each mini-disco boasts different tunes, but Spanish pop dominates. Come 2am, two of the best places by the water include the salsa-happy **Made in Brasil,** Po. Marítimo, 27. (Mixed drinks 600-800ptas/€3.60-4.80; open daily 8pm-4am), and dance-crazy **Salero,** Po. Marítimo, 31 (Open daily 8pm-6am). Beaches and the nightclubs are also near **El Terreno**—several clubs and bars are centered on Pl. Gomilia and along C. Joan Miró—take caution here at night. The bars and clubs around **El Arenal** are German-owned, German-filled, and German-centric.

When the bar scene fades at 3am, partiers migrate to Palma's *discotecas*, which attract more locals than tourists. **Tito's Palace,** Po. Marítimo, is Palma's hippest disco, with two floors of house in an indoor colosseum of mirrors and lights overlooking the water. (Cover 2500-3000ptas/€15-18. Open daily 11pm-6am). **Pachá,** Av. Gabriel Roca, is a toned-down version of the Ibiza landmark, but even this little sibling has a massive dance floor, tropical terrace, and enthusiastic patrons. (Cover 2000-3000ptas/€12-18. Open daily 11pm-6:30am.)

Mallorcans use any and every occasion as an excuse to party. One of the more colorful bashes, **Día de Sant Joan** (June 24), brings singing, dancing, and drinking to Parc del Mar. The celebration begins with a fireworks display the night before.

WESTERN MALLORCA

The west coast of Mallorca is one of the most beautiful landscapes in the Mediterranean. It has inspired a range of creative minds, from lovers Chopin and George Sand to writer Robert Graves and actor Michael Douglas. Ten minutes beyond the [illegible] first cave dwellers sheltered here) and rises in tight, narrow curves. Taking the north road beyond Valldemossa, are olive groves pitching steeply toward the sea.

VALDEMOSSA

Valldemossa's storybook colonials huddle beneath the slopes of the Sierra de Tramontana. Little in this village hints at the passion that scandalized the townsfolk in the winter of 1838, when Frédéric Chopin and George Sand (her two children in tow) stayed in the monastery **Cartoixa Reial.** The Chopin memorabilia includes the piano which he had to carry up the mountain in several pieces. Short piano recitals attempt to recapture the magic in the summer. (☎971 61 21 06. Recitals every hr. on the half hr. Open M-Sa 9:30am-6pm, Su 10am-1pm. 1400ptas/€8.40. Includes entrance to the Museu Municipal and the **Palau del Rei Sancho,** where folk dances take place M and Th 11-1:30pm.) **Nord Balear buses** (☎971 49 06 80) to **Valldemossa** leave Palma at C. Arxiduc Salvador, 1 (30min., 7 per day 7:30am-7:30pm, 200ptas/€1.20). Several café-bars around

YO QUIERO BAILAR... In the words of Spanish disco-pop queen Paulina, the next phrase would run "toda la noche." But for the disco-pub owners in Palma, Mallorca, the song would more accurately end "hasta las tres"—at least in the city's *casco antiguo*, Palma's traditional bar-hopping center. For years locals and tourists alike have let loose at the numerous bars crowding the streets near C. Apuntadores, drinking and dancing 'til dawn. But with the advent of a new city law aimed at maintaining a high-class image and controlling rowdiness, establishments in Palma proper must now stop serving alcohol by 2am, and close their doors by 3am. The end result of the new regulation hasn't meant an end to Palma's nightlife, but instead a migratory shift toward the port along Po. Marítimo—great for the huge clubs and *barres-musicales* that line the water, but the end of an era for the traditional hotspots.

the main square serve simple fare—linger over your meal, because once the few stores and sights close, there's nothing else to do.

SÓLLER

Thirty kilometers up the coast from Valldemossa, Sóller basks in a fertile valley. Oranges and tomatoes are the principal crops: every plot of land is lined with citrus groves or sunburned tourists. The town, with a backdrop of spectacular mountains, is a pleasant change from Palmas' touristed beaches. In July, the Ajuntament hosts a **Festival of Folk Dancing.** The old-fashioned Palma-Sóller **train,** run by Ferrocarril de Sóller, C. Castanyer, 7, is a highlight. The brave-hearted ride between cars as they pass through orchards and tunnels. (☎971 63 03 01, Palma: 75 20 51. 5 per day 8am-8:05pm. 380ptas/€2.30.) Sóller's **tourist office,** Pl. Constitució, 1, has accommodation listings and maps. (☎971 63 02 00. Open M-F 9:30am-1:30pm and 3-6:30pm, Sa-Su 10am-1pm. Info posted in front of the church if the office is closed.) Restaurants fill Pl. Constitució, but if you don't need a full meal, try the *coca mallorquina*, a cold pizza-like snack (about 300ptas/€1.8) in local bakeries.

PUERTO DE SÓLLER

From Sóller it's a 30min. walk (or a short ride on the Nord Balear bus) to Puerto de Sóller, where a pebbly beach lines the bay. Trolleys also connect the two (every 30min. 7am-9pm, 115ptas/€0.69). The **tourist office,** C. Canonge Oliver, 10, has quality maps. (☎/fax 971 63 30 42. Open M-F 10am-1pm and 3-6:30pm, Sa 10am-1pm.) The popular restaurant downstairs serves a 1100pta/€6.60 *menú*. Two **grocery stores** are on C. Jaume Torrens, and **restaurants** line the beach. The rest of the coves are most easily explored by **boat.** On the port near the last trolley stop, **Tramontana** and **Barcos Azules** sail to **Sa Calobra,** most visitors' final destination (May-Oct. 15 3-5 per day, round-trip 2500ptas/€15). Nord Balear "tunnel express" **buses** link Puerto de Sóller to **Palma** (1hr., every hr. 7am-9pm, 350ptas/€2.10).

SA CALOBRA

Like a serpent, the road to Sa Calobra writhes back on itself over ten nail-biting km while dropping 1000m to the sea. The boat from Puerto de Sóller is easier on the nerves. (5 per day from Puerto de Sóller 10am-3pm, return 4 per day 10:45am-5pm. 1500ptas/€9.) **Torrent de Pareis,** near the bottom of the road, is a popular photo opportunity (look for a landing packed with tourists). Sa Calobra itself is a smooth pebble beach, bordered by cliffs. Like the rest of the island, its beauty is marred by an infestation of tourist restaurants, tourist gift shops, and tourists themselves.

MONESTIR DE LLUC

Tucked away in the mountains, the Monestir de Lluc is an ambiguous destination: though there is little of interest to the secular traveler, the monastery is filled with religious tourists. Twenty kilometers from the coast in Escorca, Lluc is the home of the 700-year-old *La verge de Lluc (The Virgin of Lluc)*. Behind the monastery, the **Vía Crucis** winds around a hill, over olive trees, and past jingling goats. Gaudí designed the path's Stations of the Cross. Monks, pilgrims, and a few guests stay at Lluc's **monastery.** (☎971 51 70 25. True pilgrims stay for a donation—others pay 4000ptas/€24 for doubles with bath.) The store sells groceries, and its restaurant-bar offers expensive food and drink. To reach the monastery, take **Autocares Alorda** direct from Palma (1hr.; M-Sa 10am and 4:30pm, Su 9:15am; 545ptas/€3.30); it is also possible to get there from Alcúdia, Inca, Port Pollença, or Sa Calobra.

NORTHERN MALLORCA

Known for their long beaches and fine sand, the northern gulfs of Mallorca are popular among the older, package-tour crowd, and much of the coast is swamped beyond belief. The drive can be stunning, but those searching for secluded coves for their dilly-dallying are best off exploring other parts of the island.

PUERTO DE ALCÚDIA

Puerto de Alcúdia is far from undiscovered. The beaches along the shallow bay are packed with hotels, bars, and pizzerias. The excessive number of arcades and ice cream stands testify to Puerto de Alcúdia's popularity among families with children of the little-and-screaming variety. If you're looking for more than a beach, visit Alcúdia's old town with **14th-century ramparts, Roman remains** dating from 2 BC, and town walls from a medieval series of razings and rebuildings. (15min. walk; buses depart every 15min. from C. dels Mariners.) The **Museu Pollentia** documents archaeological discoveries on Mallorca. (☎971 54 70 04. Open M-F 10am-2pm and 5-7pm, Sa-Su 10:30am-1pm. 200ptas/€1.20.) **Parc Natural de L'Albufera,** walking distance from the beach, is filled with marshes, flowers, and dunes. (Open daily 10am-7pm, in winter until 5pm. Free.) The tourist office has a brochure of 10 hiking/biking excursions. **Buses,** leaving from Pl. Espanya in Palma (☎971 54 56 96), run to Alcúdia (595ptas/€3.57) and Puerto de Alcúdia (615ptas/€3.69) from Pl. Espanya in Palma (1hr.; M-Sa 16 per day 8am-9pm, Su 5 per day 9:30am-9pm). The bus to Port Pollença and Cap de Formentor leaves from C. dels Mariners. The **tourist office** is on Pg. Marítim, in a small plaza at the far end of the beach, on your left as you face the water. (☎971 54 72 57. Open M, W-Sa 9:30am-8pm; Tu 9:30am-1:30pm and 4-8pm.) **Police:** ☎971 54 50 78.

Hostal Calma, C. Teodoro Canet, 25, is a semi-budget options, with pleasant rooms with private bath. (☎971 54 85 85. Singles 4500ptas/€27, doubles 7000ptas/€35.) **Alberg Victoria (HI),** Ctra. Cap Pinar, 4, lies 100m from a beach on the Bahía de Pollença. From the town center, signs lead 4km to Malpas, where signs point to the hostel (1hr. walk or 1100pta/€6.6 taxi ride). Reserve in advance for summer. (☎971 54 53 95. Breakfast included. Members only. 1500ptas/€9, over 26 1700ptas/€10.) For food, hit up one of the **restaurants** along the port, or head to **Supermercats** [illegible] to get groceries.

PORT POLLENÇA (PUERTO POLLENSA)

Calmer and classier than its neighboring beach towns, Port Pollença features a beautiful beach adjacent to the port. Popular among British and northern Europeans, the cafes, restaurants, and pubs cater to a more refined crowd of middle-aged tourists, although the town isn't particularly expensive. The area hosts a **music festival** July-Sept. A complete schedule of events and list of ticket vendors is available at the tourist office (tickets 1000-5000ptas/€6-30). **Hostal Corro,** C. Joan XXIII, 68, offers air-conditioned accommodations only blocks from the beach. (☎971 86 50 05. Singles 4000ptas/€24; doubles 5000ptas/€30; triples 6000ptas/€36.) **Rent March,** C. Joan XXIII, 89, rents bikes and mopeds (☎971 86 47 84. Open Mar.-Nov. M-Sa 9am-1pm and 3-8pm, Su 9am-2:30pm. Bikes 700ptas/€4.2 per day; mopeds 3000-3300ptas/€18-19.8 per day). The **tourist office,** C. Monges, is one block from the bus stop. (☎971 86 54 67. Open M-F 8am-3:30pm, Sa 9am-1pm.) In an emergency, dial ☎112 or the **police** ☎971 53 04 37. **Autocares Mallorca buses** connect

Alcúdia and Pollença (20min., every 15min. 8:30am-1:30pm and 3-8pm, 150ptas/€0.90). **Autocares Villalonga** (☎971 53 00 57) goes to Palma (1hr., 5 per day 7:15am-5:30pm, 720ptas/€4.30). Buses stop at the rotary at the end of Pg. Saralegui.

CAP DE FORMENTOR

A trek to Cap de Formentor, 15km northeast of Port Pollença, leads to seaside cliffs. Before the final kilometer, the road drops to **Platja Formentor,** where a canopy of evergreens seems to sink into the water. **Buses** drop you off at a road 6km away from the end of Cap de Formentor, where a lighthouse and a view await. **Autocares Villalonga,** San Isidro, 4 (☎971 53 00 57), sends one bus daily from Palma (10:15am, returns 3:30pm; 800ptas/€4.80). **Autocares Mallorca** buses (☎971 5456 96) also leave from Port Pollença (2 per day 9am-2:15pm, 400ptas/€2.40). A **boat** (☎971 86 40 14) goes to Platja Formentor from Port Pollença's Estació Marítima (every hr. 10am-4pm, returns every hr. 10:30am-5:30pm; round-trip 975ptas/€5.85).

SOUTHEAST MALLORCA

The signs along the highway of Mallorca's southeast coast might as well read "Welcome tourist hordes," as much of the area has been built up by developers. On the coast, east of Cap de Salinas, Mallorca's southernmost point, scalloped fringes of bays are the developers' most recent discovery. Still, the breathtaking scenery and intriguing caves remain relatively unspoiled.

CUEVAS DRACH. The Cuevas Drach, near Porto Cristo, are among the island's most dramatic natural wonders, with their red and pink stalagtites. A 30min. walk into the depths of the cave is one of the largest underground lakes in the world. The performances given by classical musicians boating across the lake are filed somewhere between absurd and bizarre; audience members can take free boat rides at concert's end. *(A bus runs from Palma to the caves, leaving from the main station by Pl. Espanya. M-Sa 4 per day 10am-1:30pm, Su 10am; 900ptas/€5.40.)*

TRENC. West of Cap de Salinas and east of Cap Blanc sprawls one of Mallorca's best beaches, Es Trenc. In most cases, a 1-2km walk is usually enough to put plenty of sand between you and the thickest crowds. *(Buses run to Es Trenc in the summer from Pl. Espanya in Palma, M-Sa 3 per day 10am-5pm, Su 10:30am; 640ptas/€3.84.)*

MENORCA

Menorca's beaches, rustic landscape, and picturesque town draw ecologists, sun worshippers, and photographers. In 1993, UNESCO declared the island a biosphere reserve; since then, administrators have put effort into preserving Menorca's natural harbors, pristine beaches, rocky northern coast, and network of farmlands. The act has also encouraged protection, excavation, and study of Menorca's stone burial chambers and homestead complexes, remnants of a mysterious Talayotic stone-age culture dating from 1400 BC. Since its incorporation into the Catalan kingdom in 1287, Menorca (pop. 69,000) has endured a succession of foreign invaders—Arab, Turkish, French, and British. After occupying the island several times during the 18th century, the Brits have returned to dominance as tourists, with children and German neighbors in tow. Quieter and more upscale than the other Balearics, Menorca attracts wealthy young families in search of a peaceful beach vacation and has less to offer budget travelers than its larger neighbors. Most families that come here tend to stay in resorts and apartments along the beaches; the towns themselves sometimes offer reasonable prices. Students make their appearance here before the real tourist season starts, usually in the spring, while everyone else arrives full-force come August. Menorca's main cities, Mahón and Ciutadella, serve as gateways to the island's real attractions.

MAHÓN (MAÓ)

Atop a steep bluff, Mahón's (pop. 25,000) whitewashed houses overlook a well-trafficked harbor. The British occupied the city for most of the 18th century, leaving Georgian doors, brass knockers, and wooden shutters in their wake. Two centuries later, the predominance of British tourists testifies to their continuing influence. Most people clear out during the day, using the town as a jumping off point for the numerous beaches nearby; public buses go to some of the more popular stretches of sand. The city comes alive in early evening when sunburnt visitors return from the beaches. Despite the presence of bars and clubs, Mahón's nightlife is more centered around lingering over dinner than all-night partying.

TRANSPORTATION

Flights: Airport (☎971 15 70 00), 7km out of town. **Iberia/Aviaco** (☎971 36 90 15); **Air Europa** (☎971 24 00 42 or 15 70 31); **SpanAir** (☎971 15 70 98). In summer advance booking is essential. See **By Plane,** p. 475, or **Transportation,** p. 476.

Ferries: Estació Marítima, on Moll Andén de Ponent (☎971 36 60 50). Open M-F 8am-1pm and 5-7pm, Sa 8am-noon, Su 8-10:30am and 3:350-5:15pm. **Trasmediterránea** (☎971 36 29 50) sends ferries daily to Barcelona, and weekly to Valencia and Palma. For fares, routes, and schedules, see **By Boat,** p. 475, or **Transportation,** p. 476.

Buses: Check the tourist office or the newspapers *Menorca Diario Insular* and *Menorca* for schedules. There is no central bus station; buses stop around Pl. s'Esplanada. **Transportes Menorca (TMSA),** C. José M. Quadrado, 7 (☎971 36 03 61), off Pl. s'Esplanada. Check schedules for Sunday service. To: **Ciutadella** via **Ferreries** and **Es Mercadal** (1hr., 6 per day 8am-7pm, 585ptas/€3.51); **Es Castell** (every 30min. 7:45am-8:45pm, 145ptas/€0.87); **Platja Punta Prima** (9 per day 8:30am-7:30pm, 170ptas/€1.02); **Son Bou** (7 per day 8:45am-7pm, 275ptas/€1.65). Some depart from Pl. s'Esplanada, some from nearby C. Quadrado; check signs at the bus stop. Tickets available when boarding the bus or at office on C. Quadrado. **Autobuses Fornells Roca Triay** (☎971 37 66 21) buses depart from C. Vassallo, off Pl. s'Esplanada. To: **Arenal d'en Castell** (7 per day 9:30am-7pm); **Es Grau** (4 per day 10am-6:15pm); **Fornells** (4 per day 11am-7pm); **Son Parc** (3 per day 1-7pm). Buy tickets on board.

Taxis: Main stop at Pl. s'Esplanada (☎971 36 12 83), or **Radio Taxi** from anywhere on the island (☎971 36 71 11). To: **airport** (1300ptas/€7.8); **Cala Mesquida** (1300ptas/€7.80); **Cala'n Porter** (1900ptas/€11.40); **Es Castell** (800ptas/€4.80).

Car Rental: Autos Menorsur, C. Luna 23 (☎971 36 56 66), off C. Hannóver. July-Aug. 5000ptas/€30 per day, 30,000ptas/€180 per week; substantial discounts in low season. English spoken. Open M-F 9am-2pm and 5-9pm, Sa-Su 9am-2pm.

Bike and Scooter Rental: Motos Menorca, Moll de Levante, 35-36 (☎971 35 47 86), Puerto de Mahón. Summer prices are [illegible] 6200-7000ptas/€37-42 per week. Scooters 3500-4500ptas/€21-27 per day, 15,500-25,000ptas/€93-150 per week. Open Apr.-Sept. daily 9:30am-1:30pm and 5-7:30pm.

ORIENTATION AND PRACTICAL INFORMATION

Take a taxi (1300ptas/€7.80) between the **airport** and Mahón. To get to the heart of the city from the **ferry station,** go left (with your back to the water) about 150m, then turn right at the steps that cut through the serpentine **Costa de ses Voltes.** The steps end between Pl. Conquesta and Pl. Espanya. To reach **Pl. de s'Esplanada,** take Portal de Mar to Costa de Sa, which becomes C. Hannóver and C. Ses Moreres, and continue to the plaça. To reach **Pl. de la Miranda,** walk through Pl. Espanya and Pl. Carme; when you reach Pl. Princep, turn left, and Pl. Miranda is 100m ahead.

Tourist Office: Sa Rovellada de Dalt, 24 (☎971 36 37 90; fax 36 74 15), from Pl. s'Esplanada, head down C. Ses Moreres one block, and take the first left. Some English spoken. Open M-F 9am-1:30pm and 5-7pm, Sa 9am-1pm. Summer office at the airport (☎971 15 71 15) provides similar materials. Open daily Mar.-Oct. 8:30am-10:30pm.

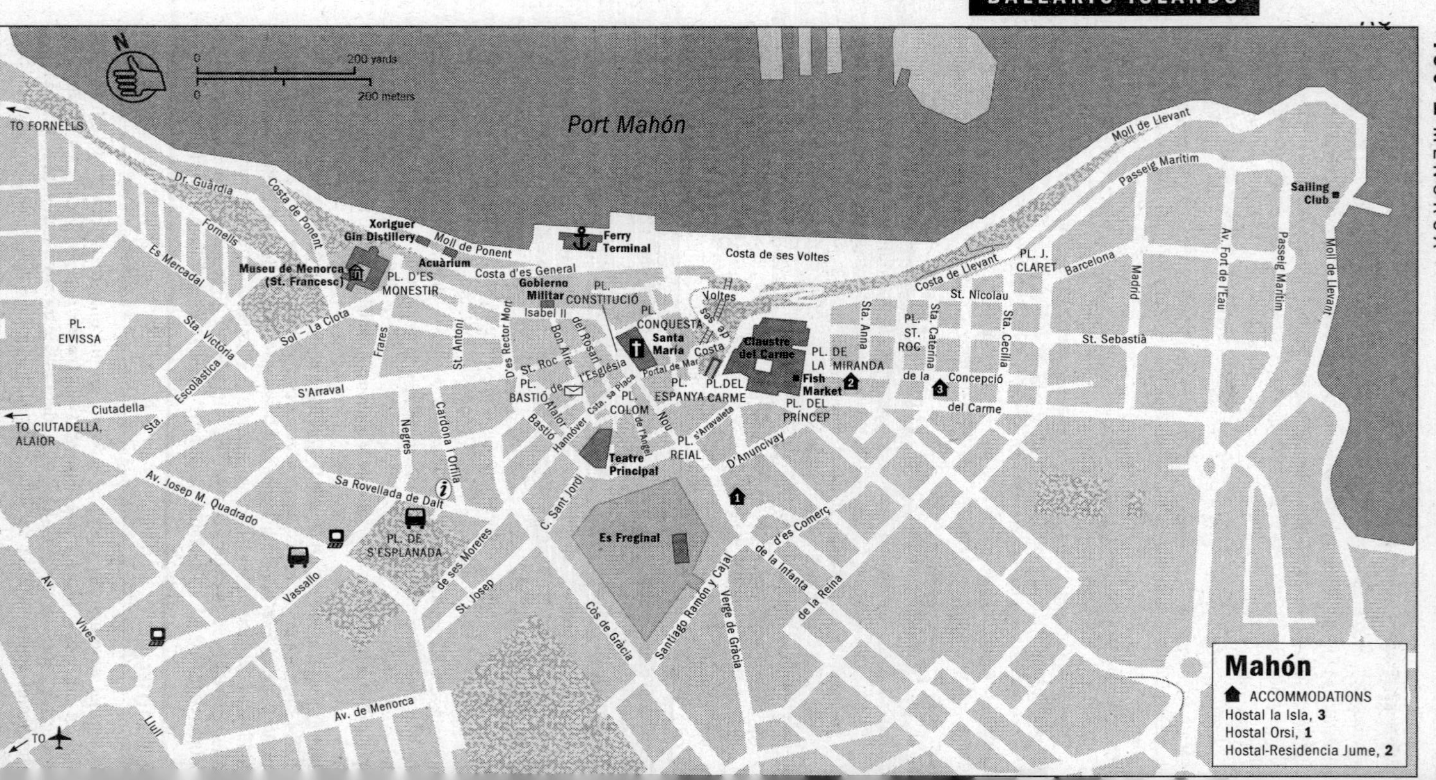
Mahón
ACCOMMODATIONS
Hostal la Isla, 3
Hostal Orsi, 1
Hostal-Residencia Jume, 2
N
0
200 yards
0
200 meters
Port Mahón
TO FORNELLS
Dr. Guàrdia
Costa de Ponent
Fornells
Es Mercadal
Xoriguer Gin Distillery
Moll de Ponent
Acuàrium
Museu de Menorca (St. Francesc)
PL. D'ES MONESTIR
Ferry Terminal
Costa de ses Voltes
Costa d'es General
Gobierno Militar
PL. CONSTITUCIÓ
Isabel II
PL. EIVISSA
Sta. Victòria
Sol – La Clota
Frares
St. Antoni
D'es Rector Mort
Bon Aire
del Rosari
PL. CONQUESTA
Santa Maria
Voltes
sas
de
Costa
Claustre del Carme
Portal de Mar
St. Roc
l'Església
PL. BASTIÓ
de
Escolàstica
S'Arraval
Ciutadella
TO CIUTADELLA, ALAIOR
Sta.
Negres
Cardona i Orfila
Atalor
Bastió
Hannover
Csta. sa Plaça
PL. COLOM
de l'Àngel
Nou
PL. ESPANYA
PL.DEL CARME
s'Arravaleta
PL. REIAL
Teatre Principal
D'Anuncivay
PL. DE LA MIRANDA
Fish Market
PL. DEL PRÍNCEP
Sta. Anna
PL. ST. ROC
Sta. Caterina
de la
Concepció
del Carme
Sta. Cecília
St. Nicolau
Costa de Llevant
PL. J. CLARET
Barcelona
Madrid
St. Sebastià
Av. Fort de l'Eau
Passeig Marítim
Moll de Llevant
Sailing Club
Av. Josep M. Quadrado
Sa Rovellada de Dalt
C. Sant Jordi
Es Freginal
d'es Comerç
de la Infanta
de la Reina
Santiago Ramón y Cajal
Verge de Gràcia
Còs de Gràcia
PL. DE S'ESPLANADA
de ses Moreres
St. Josep
Vassallo
Av. Vives
Llull
Av. de Menorca
TO

Currency Exchange: Banks with 24hr. **ATMs** line C. Hannóver and C. Nou.

Emergency: ☎112. **Police: Municipal,** Pl. Constitució (☎971 36 39 61).

Pharmacy: Check the list outside of any pharmacy for the *farmacia de guardia.*

Medical Assistance: Hospital Verge del Toro, C. Barcelona, 3 (☎971 15 77 00; emergency 36 77 26), near Pg. Marítim. English spoken. **Ambulance:** ☎061.

Internet Access: Menorca Compunet, C. Vasallo, 48, four blocks from Pl. s'Esplanada. 500ptas/€3 per hr. Open M-F 10:30am-2pm and 4:30-7:30pm, Sa 10:30am-1pm.

Pans & Pans, Pl. s'Esplanada (☎971 35 10 68), on the corner of Av. Josep Quadrado. 350ptas/€2.10 per 30min., 800ptas/€4.80 per hr.

Post Office: C. Bon Aire, 11-13 (☎971 35 66 34), at C. Esglésias. From Pl. s'Esplanada, take C. Moreres until it turns into C. Hanover, then take the first left. Open M-F 8:30am-8:30pm, Sa 9:30am-2pm. **Postal Code:** 07703.

ACCOMMODATIONS

It's easier to find a room in Menorca than on the other islands, but it's still a good idea to call ahead, especially in July and August.

Hostal La Isla, C. Santa Catalina, 4 (☎/fax 971 36 64 92). Take C. Concepció from Pl. Miranda. Immaculate, classy rooms; all have with private bath. Restaurant downstairs (see **Food,** below) has a cheap, typical *menú.* Singles 2500ptas/€15, with breakfast 2900ptas/€18; doubles 5000ptas/€30, with breakfast 5600ptas/€34. MC/V.

Hostal Orsi, C. Infanta, 19 (☎971 36 47 51). From Pl. s'Esplanada, take C. Moreres as it becomes C. Hanover. Turn right at Pl. Constitució and follow C. Nou through Pl. Reial; Orsi is on the left. Friendly, American expats keep clean rooms. Breakfast included. Owners aren't always in, so call before arriving. Laundry 1000ptas/€6. Oct.-June singles 2500ptas/€15; doubles 4300ptas/€30, with shower 4800ptas/€29. July and Sept. singles 2800ptas/€17; doubles 4900ptas/€29, with shower 5800ptas/€35. Aug. singles 3500ptas/€21; doubles 5800/€35, with shower 6800ptas/€41. MC/V.

Hostal-Residencia Jume, C. Concepció, 6 (☎971 36 32 66; fax 36 48 78), off Pl. Miranda. Bright hallways lead to rather boring rooms in tip-top shape, all with full baths. Breakfast included. June-Aug. 3000ptas/€18 per person; Sept.-May 2800ptas/€17.2 per person. Closed Dec. 15-Jan. 5.

FOOD

Bar-cafés around Pl. Constitució, Reial, and s'Esplanada serve *platos combinados* (450-850ptas/€2.70-5.10) to sidewalks of hungry customers, although the majority of tourists head to the scenic restaurants on the port, where prices match the atmosphere. Seafood is a bit hit [illegible] ad of other favorites. Regional specialties include *sobrassada* (soft sausage spread), *crespells* (biscuits), and *rubiols* (turnovers filled with fish or vegetables). *Mahónesa* (mayonnaise), which was invented on the island, is popular in many of the more exotic dishes. There is a produce **market** in the cloister of the church in Pl. Espanya (open M-Sa 9am-2pm). **Groceries** are sold at **Miny Prix,** C. J.A. Clavé and Av. Menorca (open M-Sa 8am-2pm and 5-8:30pm). **Grand General Delicatessen,** Moll de Llevant, 319 has fresh, cheap vegetarian dishes, fish and meat entrées, and Italian sandwiches. The 20min. walk from the port is well worth it. (Sandwiches 250-350ptas/€1.50-2.10, entrées 650-1000ptas/€3.90-6. Open daily noon-midnight.)

SIGHTS

The most awe-inspiring sights in Menorca lie outside of its cities, although Mahón has a few attractions. The **Museo de Menorca,** Av. Dr. Guàrdia, an old Franciscan monastery closed in 1835, displays excavated items and exhibits on Menorcan history dating back to Talayotic times. (☎971 35 09 55. Open Tu-Su

10am-2pm and 5-8pm. 300ptas/€1.80.) Founded in 1287 and rebuilt in 1772, the **Església de Santa María La Major** trembles from the 51 stops, four keyboards, and 3210 pipes of its über-organ, built by the Swiss Juan Kilburz in 1810. Mahón's **Festival de Música de Maó** in July and August showcases the immense instrument. (Pl. Constitució. Festival concerts start at 9:30pm; see tourist office for upcoming events. Seat "donation" 500ptas/€3.) The **Arc de Sant Roc,** up C. Sant Roc from Pl. Constitució, the last fragment of the medieval wall built to defend the city from marauding Catalan pirates, straddles the streets of Mahón. You can get sauced off free liquor samples at the **Xoriguer Gin Distillery** on the port. Through glass windows at the back of the store, visitors watch their drinks bubble and froth in large copper vats. (☎971 36 21 97. Open M-F 8am-7pm, Sa 9am-1pm.) Mahón is close to numerous **archeological sites,** including prehistoric caves, settlements, and monuments, but they are only accessible by car; see tourist office for information on a self-guided driving tour.

NIGHTLIFE AND ENTERTAINMENT

Mahón is not known for its nightlife. Weekdays are quiet except in August. A string of *bares-musicales* line the **Costa d'els Generals,** near the water. The colorful, lively **Tse Tse Bar,** Moll de Ponent, 14, fills nightly with a young, energetic 18-20 year-olds eager to take advantage of the ample dance floor. An upstairs *terraza* with a bar has an unbeatable view of the harbor. (Beer 400ptas/€2.40, mixed drinks 800ptas/€4.80. Open daily 10pm-4am, in winter Th-Sa same hrs.) One of the more fashionable places on the strip is **Akelarre,** a spacious, trendy bar and jazz and dance club. Dancing begins at midnight, while occasional free jazz concerts start earlier. A mixed straight and gay crowd fills the dance floors upstairs. (Open daily June-Oct. 8am-5am; Nov.-May 7:30pm-4am. Live music W-Th 11pm-2am. No cover.) Away from the port, **Discoteca Sí,** C. Virgen de Gràcia, 16, turns on the strobelight only after midnight, while **Nou Bar,** C. Nou, 1, 2nd fl., serves drinks to a calm, older crowd. (Open daily noon-3pm and 7:30pm-3am.)

From May to September, merchants sell shoes, clothes, and souvenirs in **mercadillos** held daily in various town squares (Tu and Sa Mahón; F and Sa Ciutadella; Th Alaior; Su Mercadal; Tu and F Ferrerias; M and W Es Castell). On July 16, Mahón's **Verge del Carme** celebration brings a colorfully trimmed armada into the harbor.

NEAR MAHÓN

PLATGES DE SON BOU. The longest beach on the island, Son Bou offers 4km of sand on the southern shore, covered with throngs of sunburned tourists. As the most popular of Menorca's beaches, it's also the most visitor-friendly, with frequent bus service to and from Mahón and Ciutadella, endless beach chairs and umbrellas for rent, cafes, and even *discotecas* only two blocks from the sand. *(Transportes Menorca buses leave from C. Josep Quadrado, on the corner of Pl. s'Esplanada in Mahón to the beaches; 30min., 7 per day, 8:45am-7pm, 275ptas/€1.65.)* For those that choose to stay late, **Disco/Bar Copacabana,** in the Nuevo Centro Comercial, on the left when heading away from the water, is the best place to rock your evening, all the while with a great view of the water. *(No cover. Open May-Oct. daily 11pm-3:30am.)*

ARENAL D'EN CASTELL. Breathtaking views, calm water, and packed sands make this tiny cove a popular destination for daytrippers from Mahón and the vacationing families who populate the upscale resorts and condos that dot the slope above the beach. From Arenal, a tourist train, "Arenal Na Macaret Express," makes the short trip from the bus stop in Arenal across a narrow strip of land to **Macaret,** a tiny fishing village with an even tinier beach. *(Autocares Fornells buses leave from C. Vasallo in Mahón; M-Sa 7 per day 9:30am-7pm, Su 11am and 7pm; 265ptas/€1.59.)*

CALEN PORTER. Expansive and extremely touristy, Calen Porter greets thousands of visitors each summer with its gleaming whitewashed houses, orange stucco roofs, and red sidewalks. Its small but well-used beach lies at the bottom of a steep, ouldered hillside, but pedestrian access is easy via the main road and a marked taircase. (*TMSA buses run to and from C. Josep Quadrado, on the corner of Pl. s'Esplanada, in Vahón, 7 per day 9:30am-7:30pm, 170ptas/€1.02.)*A 10min. walk away, the **Covas d'en Koroi** caves dominate cliffs high above the sea. Inhabited by a network of bars dur- ng the day, and a popular disco, sometimes home to foam parties, takes over at night. (☎971 37 72 36. Bars open Apr.-Oct. daily 10:30am-9pm, disco open nightly at 1pm; cover for bars or disco 700ptas/€3.5, includes one drink.)

ES GRAU. The center of the biosphere, Albufera Es Grau entices visitors with agoons, pine woods, and farmland, as well as diverse flora and fauna. Recre- ational activities include hiking to the coves across the bay. **Illa d'en Colom,** a tiny sland with more beaches, is just a boat ride away. (*Autocares Fornells buses leave rom C. Vasallo in Mahón; 4 per day 10am-6:15pm.)*

PUNTA PRIMA. While this popular beach may not be as secluded or expansive as some of the island's others, it draws many a crowd with its proximity to Mahón, shallow waters, and local atmosphere. A lighthouse on a narrow strip of land across from the beach overlooks the coastline. *(TMSA buses run to and from Pl. s'Esplanada in Mahón, 8 per day 9:30am-7:30pm, 170ptas/€1.02.)*

BALEARIC ISLANDS

CIUTADELLA (CIUDADELA)

Ciutadella's (pop. 15,000) narrow, cobblestoned paths weave between neighbor- hoods nearly undisturbed by tourists, while only blocks away, restaurants, shops, and postcard vendors compete for attention in the crowded plazas. There is a seductive charm to the city's ancient streets, broad *plaças*, and winding port.

TRANSPORTATION

Buses: Transportes Menorca buses leave from C. Barcelona, 8 (☎971 38 03 93), and go to Mahón (6 per day, 585ptas/€3.51). **Autocares Torres,** (☎971 38 64 61), offers daily service from in front of the ticket booth in Pl. s'Esplanada to surrounding beaches, all of which are 15-30min. away. To: **Cala Blanca** (15 per day 9am-11pm, 160ptas/€0.96); **Cala Blanes, Los Delfines,** and **Cala Forcat** (23 per day 7am-11:35pm, 160ptas/€0.96); **Cala Bosch** and **Son Xoriguer** (24 per day 7am-midnight, 160ptas/€0.96); **Sa Caleta** and **Santandria** (18 per day 7am-11pm, 160ptas/€0.96).

Ferries: Iscomar de Ferrys(☎902 11 91 28) runs between Ciutadella and **Alcúdia, Mallorca** (2½hr.; M-F 11:30am and 8pm, Sa-Su 8pm; 4800ptas/€28.8). **Cape Balear** (☎902 10 04 44) connects Ciutadella to **Cala Ratjada, Menorca** (55min., May-Oct. 9am and 9pm, 6000ptas/€36).

Taxis: (☎971 38 28 96 or 38 11 97). Pl. s'Esplanada is a prime hailing spot.

Bike and Scooter Rental: Bicicletas Tolo, C. Sant Isidor, 28-34 (☎/fax 971 38 15 76), across the street from Hostal Oasis. Bike rental 700-900ptas/€4.21-5.41 per day, 3300-4300ptas/€20-26 per week. Scooters 5800-11,000ptas/€35-66 for two days, 16,000-31,000ptas/€96-190 per week. Open M-F 9am-1pm and 4-7:30pm, Sa9am-1pm and 6:30-7:30pm, Su 9:30-11am.

Car Rental: Europcar, Av. Jaume I, 59 (☎971 38 29 98). Min. age 21. Rental from 7000ptas/€35 per day and from 35,000ptas/€210 per week. Open daily 9am-8pm.

ORIENTATION AND PRACTICAL INFORMATION

To get from the **bus station** to **Plaça de la Catedral** and the tourist office, head left alf a block, take a left on Camí de Maó, go straight through Pl. d'Alfons III, and ontinue along C. de Maó as it turns into Quadrado (Ses Voltes) after crossing Pl. Nova. To get from Pl. Catedral to **Plaça de s'Esplanada** (also called Pl. Pins), exit he plaza on C. Major d'es Born with the cathedral behind you and to the right, ross P. Born on its right side, and bear diagonally across to the left. The **port,** and its accompanying street, C. Marina, lie below the rest of the city and can be reached via a stone stairway just off the corner of Pl. Born.

Tourist Office: Pl. Catedral, 3 (☎971 38 26 93). English, German, French, and Italian spoken. Open M-F 9am-1:30pm and 5-7pm, Sa 9am-1pm.

Banks: BBVA, Pl. Born, 14 (☎971 48 40 04). Open M-F 8:30am-2pm. **ATMs** are scattered throughout town.

Emergency: ☎112. **Police:** Pl. Born (☎971 38 07 87).

Medical Emergencies: Clínica Menorca Canonge Moll, (☎971 48 05 05). Open 24hr.

Internet Access: Accesso Directo, Pl. s'Esplanada, 37 (☎971 38 42 15). 200ptas/€1.2 per 30min. Open M-Sa 9am-midnight, Su 3pm-midnight.

Post Office: Pl. Born (☎971 38 00 81). Open May-Oct. M-F 8:30am-8:30pm, Sa 9:30am-1pm; Nov.-Apr. M-F 8:30am-2:30pm, Sa 9:30am-1pm. **Postal Code:** 07760.

ACCOMMODATIONS

Hostels are packed (and pricey) during peak season (June 15 to early Sept.) Always call ahead in the summer.

Casa de Huespedes Sa Posada, C. Ibiza, 14 (☎971 38 58 96), off Pl. s'Esplanada. If you're lucky enough to score one of the seven double rooms at this tiny hostal, you'll be rewarded with some of the cheapest and comfiest accommodations Ciutadella has to offer. Smallish rooms all have private baths. Aug. doubles 4600ptas/€28, July and Sept. doubles 4000ptas/€24, Oct.-May doubles 3600ptas/€22.

Hostal Residencia Oasis, C. Sant Isidre, 33 (☎971 38 21 97). From Pl. s'Esplanada take Av. Capitá Negrete to Pl. d'Artrutx and then C. Sant Isidre. A centrally located floral paradise with its own greenhouse. Gorgeous patio and glass-enclosed dining area. Breakfast included. Doubles with bath 6600ptas/€40.

Hotel Geminis, C. Josepa Rossinyol, 4 (☎971 38 58 96; fax 38 36 83). Take C. Sud off Av. Capital Negrete coming from Pl. s'Esplanada and turn left onto C. Josepa Rossinyol. Almost perfect, maybe even worth the splurge. Beautiful rooms with phones, baths, fans, and TVs. Outdoor terrace has small pool. Mid-June-Sept. singles 5400ptas/€33; doubles 9100ptas/€55. Apr.-mid-June singles 4200ptas/€25; doubles 7200ptas/€43. Oct.-Mar. singles 3500ptas/€21; doubles 5900ptas/€35.

FOOD

Most of Ciutadella's food options are fairly touristy. Nicer restaurants surround the port area, while more generic spots near Pl. s'Esplanada and along C. Quadrado offer cheaper fare. Shop at the **market** on Pl. Llibertat or **Supermercado Diskont,** C. Purísima, 6 (☎971 38 32 68. Open M-Sa 8:30am-2pm and 4-9pm).

El Mexicano Express, Pl. s'Esplanada, 47 (☎971 48 16 46). Brightly colored decorations, outdoor tables, a huge indoor seating area, and by far the best gut-filling Mexican food around. Burritos, tacos, quesadillas, and enchiladas 375-550ptas/€3.10-3.30. Open daily in summer 10:30am-11:30pm, in winter 1-4pm and 7:30-11:30pm. V.

La Guitarra, C. Dolores, 1 (☎971 38 13 55). Take C. Major d'es Born off Pl. Born, then turn right onto Carres del Roser, which leads to C. Dolores. If you're looking for traditional island cuisine, descend down into this stone cave-turned-restaurant and sample such regional specialties as the mysterious *sopas mallorquinas,* a traditional meat and veggie soup (825ptas/€4.95). *Menú* 1495ptas/€9. Entrées 1100-3000ptas/€6.60-18. Open June-Sept. M-Sa 12:30-3:30pm and 7-11:30pm. MC/V.

SIGHTS AND ENTERTAINMENT

An interesting complement to Menorca's beaches are the remnants at Menorca's various archaeological sites. Dating from the Bronze Age, the **Naveta des Tudons**

HOLD YOUR HORSES! Every last Thursday in June, Ciutadella celebrates *La Fiesta de San Juan,* a wild festival that rivals the infamous *San Fermines* in recklessness. The party begins with the arrival of the *fabioler* (herald of the ceremony) on a white horse. Playing a drum and flute, he gallops through town for four hours with crowds of drunken Menorcans following close behind. At 6pm sharp, village men ride 250 wild horses through town on their hind legs. Successfully bipedal horses are rewarded with cheers of *"Olé!"* and the rest charge into the crowd, often knocking over bystanders. In 1999, one particularly off-balance horse came crashing down on the mayor of Menorca, ending his term for good. *Note bene* for future office-holders: some P.R. opportunities just aren't worth it.

ne of the oldest structures in Europe, sits 4km from the city. These ruins of comunity tombs are the island's best preserved. **Torretrencada** and **Torrellafuda** were ounded towers that overlooked the countryside. Both protect Stonehenge-like *ıulas,* formations that have stood for over 3000 years. Buses don't come near hese sights, so consider **hiking** (about 5km) along C. Cami Vell de Maó. The escriptive *Archeological Guide to Menorca* is available at the tourist office.

The Ciutadella community is one of early-to-bedders. **Asere,** C. de Curniola, 23, ne block off Pl. Nova, spices things up a bit with a Cuban theme and frozen rinks (open F-Sa 8pm-midnight). From the first week in July to the beginning of eptember, Ciutadella hosts the **Festival de Música d'Estiu,** featuring some of the orld's top classical musicians. Tickets (1600-3500ptas/€9.6-21) are sold at Foto orn, C. Seminari, 14 (☎971 38 17 54), and at the box office (open daily 9:30am-:30pm and 5-8pm). Concerts take place in the cloisters of the seminary. On the 2nd of June, even veteran partiers of Palma and Ibiza join locals as they burn galons of midnight oil during the **La Fiesta de San Juan,** Menorca's biggest *fiesta.* A eek before the festivities, which include jousting and equestrian displays, a man lad in a sheepskin carries a decorated lamb on his shoulders through the city.

BEACHES

he more popular Menorcan beaches, those accessible by bus from Mahón and iutadella, are located in somewhat built up, touristy areas and are overrun by esort hotels, bars, restaurants, and postcard shops. Many Menorcan beaches are ocated in small coves, thus the more accessible ones can get fairly packed during ıe day. Never fear: because Menorca is home to over 80 beaches, with a car, ıoped, or a little legwork, endless stretches of less-crowded beaches are easily ccessible. The northern beaches are rocky but less crowded. Finer sands, however, are hidden under hundreds of tourists on the southern coast. The beaches [illegible] ar, request the *Let's Go to the Beach* pamphlet (no relation) at the tourist office.

EAR CIUTADELLA

NORTH SHORE. The stretch east of Cala Morell is home to some of the most utstanding and pristine beaches on the island. **Platges d'Algaiarens** may be the ıperstar of the series, which also includes Cala en Carabó, Penyal de l'Anticrist, a Falconera, and the beautiful Cala del Pilar Ets Alocs. *(Cars can go only up to a few n from these beaches; from there you must walk.)*

ALA BOSCH. Five-star resorts provide the backdrop for this popular cove situ:ed between jagged cliffs. Because of its proximity to Ciutadella, this is one of the ıore crowded beaches, but with fruit sellers and restaurants, it's worth visiting. *ccessible by Torres bus from Ciutadella; 24 per day 7am-midnight, 160ptas/€0.96.)*

ORNELLS. A small fishing village known for its lobster farms, Fornells has only ecently begun to attract tourists. Windsurfers zip around Fornells' long, shallow port, while beach gurus make excursions to **Cala Tirant** and **Binimella,** both a only few kil meters west. Fornells also serves as a calm base from which to explore coves an jagged cliffs by car or bike, as bus service is very limited. *(Autobuses Roca Triay buses ru to Fornells from C. Vassallo in Mahón; 30min., 5 per day.)*

SON XORIGUER. Located just down the road from Cala Bosch, this beach isn quite as hectic as its neighbor, and is equally beautiful. *(Accessible by a Torres bus fro Ciutadella; 24 per day 7am-midnight, 160ptas/€0.96)*

IBIZA

Perhaps nowhere on Earth does style rule over substance more than on the islan of Ibiza (pop. 84,000). Once a 60s hippie enclave, Ibiza has long forgotten her roo in favor of a new-age decadence. Disco fiends, high-fashion gurus, movie star and party-hungry backpackers arrive in droves to debauch in the island's outr geous, sex- and substance-driven summertime culture. However, not every nig in the island has to come out of some Guy Ritchie/Madonna wet dream; much Ibiza's craziness, see-and-be-seen, and disco culture is just at a few megaclubs. A for the rest, it's all what you make of it. It's not uncommon to see people arrivin at discos in jeans or shorts, or to spend a night just chilling at a waterfront bar. thriving gay community lends credence to Ibiza's image as a center of toleranc but the island's high price tags preclude true diversity.

Amazingly enough, there is more to Ibiza than its famous nightlife; the beach and mountains are some of the most spectacular in all the Balearics. The island rich history has left its mark in the form of several ancient castles—the mo prominent in Eivissa (Ibiza City) itself. Since the Carthaginians retreated to Ibi from the mainland in 656 BC, the island's list of conquerors reads like a "Who Who of Ancient Western Civilization." Perhaps the most famous was the 1235 inv sion by the Catalans, who brought Christianity and constructed the massiv Renaissance walls that still fortify Eivissa.

EIVISSA (IBIZA CITY)

Eivissa (pop. 35,000) is the world's biggest 24-hour party. The town itself is like D Jekyll and Mr. Hyde. During the day, families meander and sightsee through th walled Dalt Vila and the city streets remain tranquil while the majority of visito are sleeping off hangovers, tanning at nearby beaches—Eivissa could easily b mistaken for any other seaside village in Spain. At night, however, there's no mi taking this town for any other. Flashy bars appear seemingly out of nowhere, fi ing street after street with neon lights, blasting music, and fast-talking cl promoters; grab a front-row seat at the outdoor tables to enjoy the prime peop watching action. Come 3am, the scene migrates to the clubs, where parties la until dawn—and often well into the next day...then it all begins again.

TRANSPORTATION

Flights: Airport (☎971 80 90 00), 7km south of the city. Buses (number #10) r between the airport and Av. Isidor Macabich, 20, in town (30min., every hr. 7:30a 10:30pm, 125ptas/€0.75). Info booth open 24hr. for tickets and reservations. **Iberi** Pg. Vara de Rey, 15 (☎902 40 05 00 or 971 30 03 00), has flights to Alicante, Barc lona, Madrid, Palma, Madrid, and Valencia. **Air Europa** and **Spanair** offer simi options. For routes and schedules, see **By Plane,** p. 475, or **Transportation,** p. 476.

Ferries: Estació Marítima, at the end of Av. Bartolomé Roselló. Directly across t street from the tourist office. To get to the city center and bus stop from the waterfro take Av. Bartolomé Roselló, which becomes Av. Isidor Macabich. **Trasmediterrán** (☎971 31 51 00) sells tickets at Estació Marítima and sends ferries to Palma, Barc lona, and Valencia. **Trasmapi-Balearia** (☎971 31 40 05) runs daily to and from Dén

PEEP THIS The local paper *Diario de Ibiza* (www.diariodeibiza.es; 125ptas/€0.75) has an *Agenda* page that lists essential information including the bus schedule for the whole island, the ferry schedule, the schedule of all domestic flights to and from Ibiza for the day, water and weather forecasts, info on the island's 24hr. pharmacies, a list of 24hr. gas stations, and important phone numbers.

near Alicante; a connection in Eivissa continues to and from Palma. **Umafisa Lines** (☎971 21 02 01) sends ferries to and from Barcelona 3-4 times per week. For rates, fares, and schedules, see **By Boat,** p. 475, or **Transportation,** p.475. For transport to the island of Formentera, see **Formentera: Getting There and Away,** p. 498.

Buses: Ibiza has a fairly extensive bus system, although some to more remote beaches and villages only run a few times per day, so plan accordingly. The main bus stop is on Av. Isidor Macabich, past Pl. Enrique Fajarines when walking away from the port. For an exact schedule, check the tourist office or *El Diario.* Intercity buses are 250ptas/€1.50 or less and run from Av. Isidor Macabich, 42 (☎971 31 21 17) to **San Antonio** (M-Sa every 15min., Su every 30min. 7am-11:30pm) and **Santa Eulária** (M-F every 30min., Sa-Su every hr. 7:30am-11:30pm). Buses (☎971 34 03 82) to the beaches cost 125ptas/€0.75 and leave from Av. Isidor Macabich, 20, or Av. Espanya to: **Cala Tarida** (5 per day 9:45am-5:45pm); **Cap Martinet** (M-Sa 11 per day 8:15am-8:15pm); **Platja d'en Bossa** (every 30min. 8:30am-11pm); **Salinas** (every hr. 9:30am-7:30pm).

Taxis: ☎971 30 70 00 or 30 66 02.

Car and Motorbike Rental: Casa Valentín, Av. B.V. Ramón, 19 (☎971 31 08 22), the street parallel to Pg. Vara de Rey. Mopeds 3000-5000ptas/€18-30 per day. Cars from 6400ptas/€39. Open daily 9am-1pm and 3:30-8:30pm.

ORIENTATION AND PRACTICAL INFORMATION

Three distinct sections make up the city. **Sa Penya,** in front of Estació Marítima, is mobbed with bars, and boutiques. Atop the hill behind Sa Penya, high walls circle **Dalt Vila,** the old city. **Sa Marina** and the commercial district occupy the gridded streets to the far right (with your back to the water) of the Estació. **Av. Espanya,** continuing from Po. Vara de Rey, heads toward the airport and local beaches.

Tourist Office: C. Antoni Riquer, 2 (☎971 30 19 00; www.ibizaonline.com), across from where the ferries come in. Open M-F 9:30am-1:30pm and 5-8pm, Sa 10:30am-1pm. Also a **booth** at the airport arrival terminal (☎971 80 91 18; fax 80 91 32). Open May-Oct. M-Sa 9am-2pm and 3-8pm, Su 9am-2pm.

Currency Exchange: Stores that change money are all over town, but stick to banks and ATMs; they offer better rates and are a safer bet. **La Caixa,** Av. Isidor Macabich. Good exchange rates for cash and traveler's checks.

Laundromat: Wash and Dry, Av. España, 53 (☎971 39 48 22). Wash and dry 700ptas/€4.20 each. **Internet** access 900ptas/€5.40 per hr. Open M-F 10am-3pm and 5-10pm, Sa 10am-5pm.

Emergency: ☎112. **Police:** C. Vicent Serra (☎971 31 58 61).

Medical Assistance: Hospital (☎971 39 70 00), Barrio Can Misses, to the west of town. **Ambulance:** ☎971 39 32 32. **Hospital Nuestra Senora** (☎971 39 70 21).

Internet Access: Centro Internet Eivissa, Av. Ignacio Wallis, 39 (☎971 31 81 61). 500ptas/€3 per hr. Open M-Sa 10am-midnight, Su 5pm-midnight. **Ciber Matic,** C. Cayetano Soler, 3 (☎971 30 33 82), off Pl. Parc. 300ptas/€1.80 per 30min., 500ptas/€3 per hr. Open M-Sa 10am-11pm.

Post Office: C. Isidor Macabich (☎971 31 43 23). From the port, follow Av. Isidor Macabich to its end. **Lista de Correos.** Open M-F 8:30am-8:30pm, Sa 9:30am-2pm. **Postal Code:** 07800.

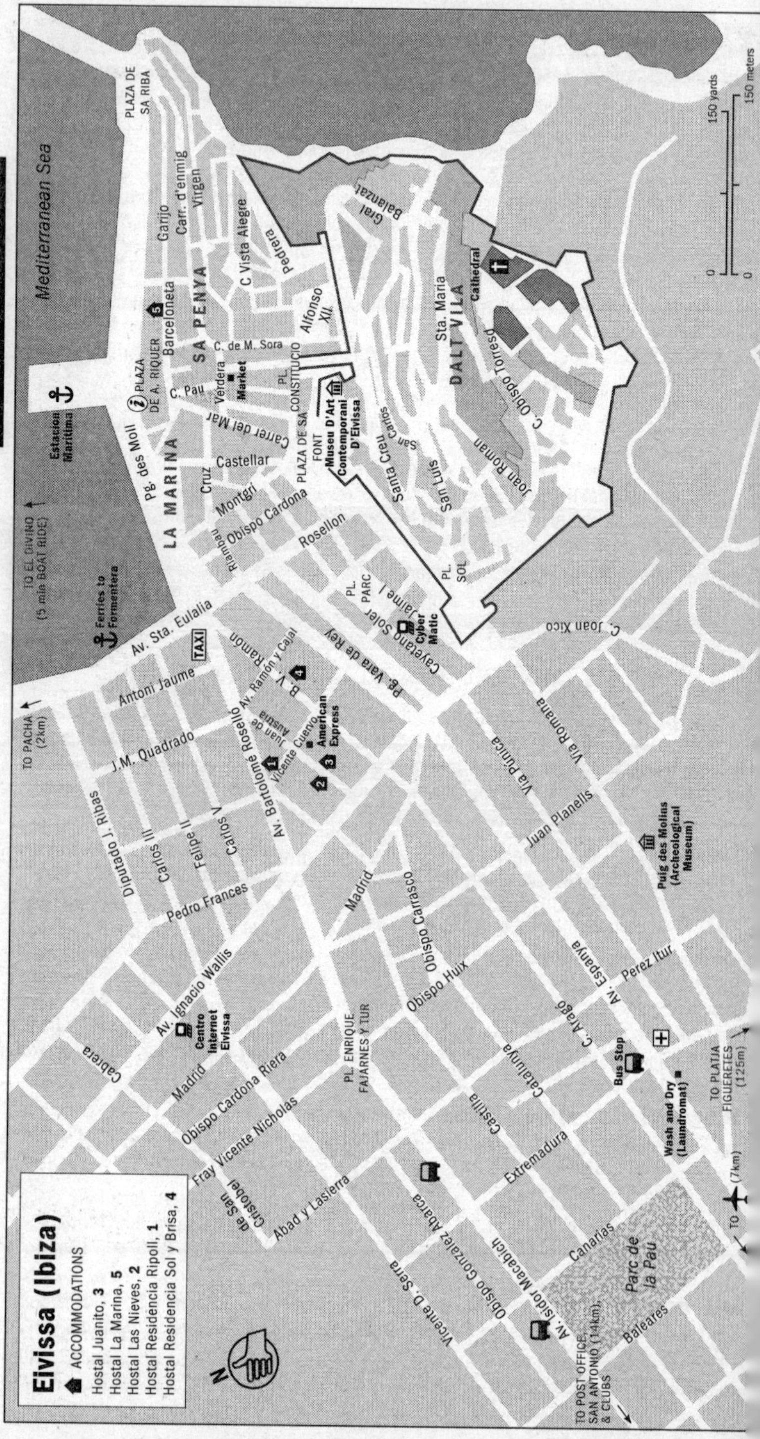

Eivissa (Ibiza)

ACCOMMODATIONS

- Hostal Juanito, 3
- Hostal La Marina, 5
- Hostal Las Nieves, 2
- Hostal Residencia Ripoll, 1
- Hostal Residencia Sol y Brisa, 4

ACCOMMODATIONS

Decent, cheap hostals in town are rare, especially in the summer—but then again, who actually *sleeps* here anyway? Call several weeks in advance for summer stays, when prices climb and hostals fill fast. The letters "CH" *(casa de huespedes)* mark many doorways, but the owner can often only be reached by the phone number on the door. Eivissa has a relatively safe and up-all-night lifestyle, and owners offer keys for 24hr. entry. All prices listed below are for high-season and can drop by as much as 2000ptas/€12 in the off-season.

Hostal Residencia Sol y Brisa, Av. B. V. Ramón, 15 (☎971 31 08 18; fax 30 30 32), parallel to Pg. Vara de Rey. Upstairs from Pizzeria da Franco (signs point the way to the pizzeria). Clean and in a perfect port-side location, but rooms are sweltering hot in summer. Very social atmosphere. Singles 3500ptas/€21; doubles 6000ptas/€36.

Hostal Residencia Ripoll, C. Vicente Cuervo, 14 (☎971 31 42 75). Fastidiously clean hallways and bathrooms and unusually large, fan-cooled rooms are by far the best in town. The singles are a bit pricey, though. July-Sept. singles 4500ptas/€27; doubles 6500ptas/€39; 3-person apartments with TV, patio, and kitchen 12,000ptas/€72.

Hostal Juanito and Hostal Las Nieves, C. Juan de Austria, 17-18 (☎971 19 03 19). Run by the same owner, both hostels offer cheap housing in a central area. Rooms are basic and bare-walled, but more than adequate for sleeping off a hangover. Singles 3000ptas/€18; doubles 6000ptas/€36, with bath 7500ptas/€45.

Hostal La Marina, Puerto de Ibiza, C. Barcelona, 7 (☎971 31 01 72; fax 31 48 94), across from Estació Marítima and right in the middle of the raucous bar scene–don't stay here if you plan on going to bed before the wee hours of the morning when things quiet down. Four separate buildings offer different levels of lodging, ranging from stark to plush. The best (and most expensive) have TV, A/C, private bath, carpeting, and balcony. Singles 4500-8000ptas/€27-48; doubles 7000-16,000ptas/€42-96.

Camping: Es Cana (☎971 33 21 17; fax 33 99 71). 500ptas/€3 per person, 600ptas/€1.80 per site, 450ptas/€2.70 for a tent. Bungalow 2250ptas/€14. Reserve via fax. **Cala Nova** (☎971 33 17 74). 500ptas/€3 per person, 475ptas per tent/€2.85. Both sites close to Sta. Eulária del Río.

FOOD

Inexpensive cuisine is hard to find; full meals rarely cost less than 1500ptas/€9 in the port and downtown areas, and its not uncommon to see budget travelers stocking up at grocery stores or chowing down at big fast food joints to save their *pesetas* for the discos. Ibizan dishes worth hunting down are *sofrit pagès*, a deep-fried lamb and chicken dish; *flao*, a lush lemon- and mint-tinged cheesecake; and [illegible] pudding made from eggs and bits of *ensaimada* (candied bread). The **market,** at C. Extremadura and C. Canarias, sells meat, fruits, and vegetables (open M-Sa 7am-1pm). For **groceries,** try **Hiper Centro,** C. Ignasi Wallis, near C. Juan de Austria. (☎971 19 20 41. Open M-Sa 9am-2pm and 5-9pm.)

Mama Pat's Curry y Más, C. Espanya, 43. Not only does Mama Pat's have some of the cheapest food around, it also has some of the most creative. Authentic Caribbean cuisine or awesome chicken, veggie, and lamb curry entrées (1000-1300ptas/€6-9). Vegetarian options. *Menú* 1000ptas/€6. Open daily 8am-3am.

Casa Alfredo, Passeig Vara de Rey, 16. Fish, meat dishes, and heavenly desserts fill the *menú* that locals call the best in town. Open M-Sa noon-3pm, 8:30pm-midnight.

SIGHTS AND BEACHES

Wrapped in 16th-century walls, the **Dalt Vila** (High Town) hosts urban bustle in the city's oldest buildings. Its twisting streets lead to the 14th-century **cathedral,** built in several phases and styles. The main portion is the Gothic contribution of 14th-

BALEARIC ISLANDS

century builders. (Open M-Sa 10:30am-1pm.) Next to the cathedral stands the **Museu Arqueològic D'Eivissa,** home to a variety of regional artifacts. (Open Tu-Sa 10am-1pm and 5-10pm, Su 10am-2pm. 300ptas/€1.80, students 150ptas/€0.90.) Amid stone walls, the small **Museu D'Art Contemporani D'Eivissa** displays a range of art exhibitions; the permanent collection features artists connected with the Pitiuses. (C. Sa Carrosa, on the left when entering through Dalt Vila's main entrance. ☎971 30 27 23. Open M-F 10am-1:30pm and 5-8pm, Sa 10am-1:30pm. 200ptas/€1.20, students free.) The archaeological museum, **Puig des Molins,** Vía Romana, displays Punic, Roman, and Iberian artifacts. Adjoining the Puig is the Punic-Roman **necropolis.** (Both open M-Sa 10am-2pm and 5-8pm. 200ptas/€1.20.)

The power of the rising sun draws thousands of topless solar zombies to nearby tanning grounds. **Platja Figueretes,** a thin stretch of sand in the shadow large hotels, is the best foot-accessible beach from Eivissa. To get there, walk down Av. Espanya for about 10min., and take a left on C. Juan Ramón Jiménez. Farther down, **Platja d'en Bossa** is the liveliest of Ibiza's beaches, home to numerous beach bars, as well as throngs of sun-seeking tourists. **Platja des Duros** is tucked in across the port bay from Sa Penya and Sa Marina, just before the lighthouse. At **Platja de Talamanca,** the water—more an enclosed bay than open sea—is accessible on foot by following the road to the new port and continuing on to the beach (20min.). **Playa de Las Salinas** is one of Ibiza's most popular and famous beaches (especially among those who like to give a glimpse of their nipples and nana to the sun), although others are actually more scenic. More private coastal stretches lie in the northern part of the island and are accessible by car or scooter.

NIGHTLIFE

The crowds return from the beaches by nightfall, an hour when even the stores dazzle with throbbing techno and flashing lights. Herds of men and women representing each club parade through the streets, advertising their disco and trying to outdo others. Meanwhile, seaport bars crawl with aggressive club promoters.

Bars in Eivissa are crowded between midnight and 3am and are everyone's first stop before hitting the discos. The scene centers around **C. Barcelona** and spins outward from there into the sidestreets. **C. Virgen** is, the center of gay nightlife and utterly outrageous fashion. Cocktails cost as much as 1800ptas/€10.20 and beer rings in at around 1000ptas/€6, so either preparty on your own, or head to the cheaper bar scene in San Antonio if you plan on drinking a lot.

The island's **discos** (virtually all have a mixed gay/straight crowd) are world-famous—veterans claim that you will never experience anything half as wild or fun. The best sources of information are disco-goers and the zillions of posters that plaster the stores and restaurants of Sa Marina and Sa Penya. There is something different each day of the week, and each club is known for its once-a-week theme party—be sure to hit up a club on a popular night, or you'll end up shelling out a lot of money for a not-so-happening party. For listings, check out *Ministry in Ibiza* or *DJ*, free at many hostels, bars, and restaurants. Drinks at Ibiza's clubs cost about 1800ptas/€10.20 and covers start at 5000ptas/€30. If you know where you're going ahead of time, buy your disco tickets from a promoter at or in front of the bars in town; you'll save anywhere from 1000-3000ptas/€6-18 off what you would pay at the door, and it's completely legit. Generally, disco-goers pub-hop in Eivissa or San Antonio and jet off to clubs via bus or taxi around 3am. The **Discobus** runs to all the major hotspots (leaves Eivissa every hr. 12:30am-6:30am, schedule for other stops available at tourist office and hotels, 250ptas/€1.50).

Privilege, on the Discobus to San Antonio or a 1500ptas/€9 taxi from city. The world's largest club, according to the Guinness Book. Packs in up to 30,000 and has everything from double-digit bars to a stage set in a pool for bizarre acrobatics. *The* place to be on M for its world-infamous "manumission" parties that feature live sex shows. Cover 5000-8000ptas/€30-48, includes 1 drink. Open June-Sept. daily midnight-7am. V.

Pachá, 20min. walk from the port, 2min. in a cab.Most famous club chain in Spain, and the most elegant of Ibiza's discos. F night's Ministry of Sound brings the biggest crowd; "Made in Italy: Gangsters" nights on M are also number one. The only club in Ibiza open year-round. Cover 5000-8000ptas/€30-42. Open daily midnight-7:30am.

Amnesia, on the road to San Antonio; take the Discobus. Converted warehouse with psychedelic lights and movie screens has two gigantic rooms; a largely gay crowd tends to congregate in the one to the left of the entrance. Legendary foam parties Su and W. Best known for cream parties on Th, when London DJs play hard house or trance. Cover 5000-8000ptas/€30-42. Open daily midnight-7am.

Space, Platja d'en Bossa. Starts hopping around 8am, peaks mid-afternoon, and doesn't wind down until past 5pm. The metallic get-up and techno music is almost as hardcore as the dancers. An outdoor dance terrace has a more low-key atmosphere. Known for its Su morning show, Sa-Tu mornings are all popular too. Cover 5000ptas/€30 and up.

Eden, C. Salvador Espíritu, across from the beach in San Antonio. Gaining in popularity, Eden pulls out all the stops for "Judgement Sunday," when DJ Judge Jules attracts huge crowds. Popular among British visitors. Retro nights on Tu feature house from the past decade. Cover 5000-8000ptas/€30-42. Open daily midnight-7am.

El Divino, Puerto Ibiza Nueva, small, but energetic, terraced club right on the water overlooking Eivissa—worth coming to just for the view, although the exotic dancers, thumping house, and lively crowd aren't too shabby either. Non-tourist crowd. El Divino fliers serve as free passes for the disco shuttle boat—otherwise, it costs 150ptas/€0.90 one-way. Cover 5000ptas/€30. Open mid-June to mid-Sept. nightly midnight-6am.

Es Paradis Terrenal, C. Salvador Espiru, 20, in San Antonio, portside. Looks are deceiving—a classy environment hosts some not-so-classy behavior at water parties on Tu and Sa. Cover 6000ptas/€36. Open midnight-6am.

SAN ANTONIO DE PORTOMANY

Every summer, masses of young Brits migrate to San Antonio. The rowdy nightlife and a down-to-earth atmosphere combine with its proximity to some of the island's best beaches to turn the town into a twenty-something enclave. With two clubs, a plenty of bars, and cheaper food and accommodations than in Eivissa, San Antonio is the perfect budget alternative to its sister city's high prices and lifestyle.

TRANSPORTATION AND PRACTICAL INFORMATION. San Antonio is connected to the rest of the island by the **buses** from Pg. Mar. To: **Cala Bassa** (8 per day 9:30am-6:30pm, 170ptas/€1.02); **Cala Conta** (7 per day 9:10am-6pm, 170ptas/€1.02); **Cala Tarida** (8 per day 9:30am-6:30pm, 170ptas/€1.02); **Eivissa** (25min.; every 30min. M-Sa 7-9:30am and 10-11:30pm, every 15min. 9:45am-9:30pm, Su every 30min. 7:30am-10:30pm; 225ptas/€1.35); and **Santa Eulária** (M-Sa 4 per day [illegible] 170ptas/€1.02). [illegible] San Antonio for **Dénia** (see **Transportation**, p. 476). Smaller companies run daily **boats** to nearby beaches. Signs posted daily along the port have schedules. For a **taxi,** call 971 34 07 79. San Antonio is very easy to get around, as major streets lie on something of a grid. For **car** and **moped rental,** try **Motos Luis,** Av. Portmany, 5. (☎971 34 05 21. Mopeds 3200ptas/€20 and up. Cars 6400ptas/€38 and up. Open M-Sa 9am-2pm and 4-8pm, Su 9am-2pm.) The **tourist office** is a stone building in the middle of the pedestrian thoroughfare by Pg. Fonts. (☎971 34 33 63. Open M-F 9:30am-2:30pm and 3-8:30pm, Sa 9am-1pm, Su 9:30am-1:30pm.) In an **emergency,** call ☎112 or the **police,** Av. Portmany, km 14 (☎971 34 08 30). There is a **Centro de Salud** on C. Alicant (☎ 971 34 51 21).

ACCOMMODATIONS AND FOOD. Hostals in San Antonio, full of Brits, are numerous and cheap. In the height of summer, call well in advance for any summer stay; in the low season prices drop. The large bedrooms, huge TV lounge, and great location make **Hostal Salada,** C. Soletat, 34, the best bargain in town. Walk up C. Bartolomé Vicente Ramon from the port and turn left on to C. Soletat. (☎971 34 11 30. Singles 2500ptas/€15; doubles 4000ptas/€24; triples 5000ptas/

€30.) **Hostal Residencia Roig,** C. Progreso, 44, has gorgeous and clean rooms, with private bath. (☎971 34 04 83. Singles 3500ptas/€21; doubles 7000ptas/€42.) Another option is the more basic **Hostal Rita,** C. Bartolomé Vicente Ramon, 17B. Doubles and triples have private baths; singles share common bathrooms. (☎971 34 63 32. Singles 3300ptas/€20; doubles 6500ptas/€39; triples 8800ptas/€53.) **Restaurants** are everywhere in San Antonio. A variety of choices are available at the outdoor cafes along Pg. Mar or on its sidestreets leading uphill. Of the more trendy beachfront establishments, **Terraza Kiwi Beach,** Av. Doctor Fleming, 2-4, stands out. The orange building right on the water serves a combination of cheap sandwiches, salads, blended fruit drinks and milkshakes, as well as wide range of alcoholic favorites. (Entrées 400-800ptas/€2.40-4. Alcoholic milkshakes 900ptas/€5.40, non-alcoholic shakes and smoothies 450-800ptas/€2.70-4. Open daily 10am-4am.)

BEACHES AND ENTERTAINMENT. The **beaches** near San Antonio are some of Ibiza's best and are fairly accessible. The town itself is situated on a long, narrow strip of sand, but better beaches are only a stone's throw away. Check out **Cala Bassa,** one of the more popular tanning spots, for a gorgeous (and sometimes nude) beach; accessible by bus. **Cala Gració,** 1½km from San Antonio, is easily reached by foot. **Santa Eulária** is more built up, but it's substantially larger than some of the other beaches nearby. Hoof it or bike to the small coves of **Es Pouet** and **Caló des Moro.** San Antonio's **nightlife** revolves largely around three main areas: waterfront bars on the far end of town (including **Café del Mar,** "the original sunset bar"), near the littered beach of Es Ganguil; the crowded streets of town, packed with low-key watering holes and drunk pre-partiers; and the clubs (**Eden** and **Es Paradis Divino**), beach bars and mini-discos in front of the town's beach. After the competitive club scene of Eivissa, the whole menu of nightlife options in San Antonio can be a much more pleasant, relaxed, and vibrant.

FORMENTERA

The tiny island of Formentera is Spain's version of island paradise. Despite the recent invasions by bourgeois, beach-hungry Germans and Italians, the island's stunning beaches maintain a sense of hypnotic calm. Join Formentera's "save our island" spirit by hiking or renting a bike—the tourist office offers a comprehensive list of "Green Tours" for hikers and cyclists, and bike paths are plentiful. The island itself is pricy, and often is visited simply as a daytrip from Eivissa.

TRANSPORTATION. Ferries at Estació Marítima, near the Burger King in Eivissa, offer transportation. **Pitra** car ferries (☎971 19 10 88), **Trasmapi-Balearia** (☎971 31 20 70), and **Umafisa** car ferries (☎971 31 45 13) all run to and from Formentera. If you're in a hurry, choose **Línea Jet's** speedy ride (25min., 16 per day 7:45am-8:30pm, 2150ptas/€13) or ride with the trucks on the cheaper, slower mother ship (1hr.; M-Sa 9 per day 6:45am-8pm, Su 5 per day 9am-8pm; 1325ptas/€7.95). For transport between Formentera and the mainland, see **By Boat,** p. 475.

PRACTICAL INFORMATION. Atop the northern side of the island is its main port, **La Savina.** The main artery runs from the port (km 0) to the eastern tip, **Punta D'Esfar** (km20). The island's "capital," **San Francisco,** off the main artery at km 3.1, has the basics but little else. **Es Pujols,** km 4, is the liveliest town on the island. **Buses** run from La Savina to **Es Pujols** (9 per day 8:30am-7:15pm); **Playa Illete** (10:30am and 5pm); **Playa Migjorn** (7 per day 9:45am-7:15pm); and **San Francisco** (12 per day 8:30am-7:15pm). For a **taxi,** call ☎971 32 80 16. **Car-scooter-bike rental booths** line the dock in La Savina. (Cars 5000-6000ptas/€30-36 per day. Scooters 3000-3500ptas/€18-21. Bikes 500-1000ptas/€3-6.) Although all rental agencies are more or less the same, **Autos Ca María** offers friendly service and advice on routes. (☎971 32 29 21. Cars 5500ptas/€33. Scooters 3000ptas/€18. Bicycles 500-1000ptas/€3-6.

Open daily 9am-9pm. MC/V.) All the main roads have lanes for scooters to putter along freely with bicycles. The **tourist office,** Edificio Servicios La Savina, is at the port. (☎971 32 20 57. Open M-F 10am-2pm and 5-7pm, Sa 10am-2pm.) For **police** dial ☎971 32 20 22 and the **medical center** dial ☎971 32 23 69. **Postal code:** 07870.

ACCOMMODATIONS AND FOOD. Formentera offers the top shelf of hostel-living—and prices certainly reflect it. There are virtually no budget options, so be prepared to either shell out or head back to Ibiza for the night. Almost all of the island's hostels are hotel-quality with attentive staff; the best of them are tucked away on their own stunning, deserted beaches. At **Hostal Costa Azul,** Playa de Migjorn, km 7, serene rooms are complemented by a quiet beach. (☎971 32 80 24. Doubles before July 15 6900ptas/€41, after July 14 9700ptas/€58.) **Hostal Mayans** is in Formentera's Es Pujols. The double rooms are spacious, with fridges, balconies, and large bathrooms, and—believe it or not—are some of the cheapest in town. (☎971 32 87 24. Breakfast included. Doubles 12,000ptas/€73.)

Gobble down *paella* (1300ptas/€7.80) at **El Mirador,** at km 14.3, overlooking both the island and the water. (☎971 32 70 37. Open daily 12:30-4pm and 7-11pm.) Check out the varied restaurants in Es Pujols for both *comida típica* and more international cuisine. **Supermarkets** line all of the major roads in Formentera.

BEACHES. To bask on Formentera's best beaches, take Av. Mediterránea from the port, turn left at the sign pointing toward Es Pujols, and take another left onto the dirt road at the sign marking Verede de Ses Salines. Paths to the right lead to Platja de Llevant, a long strip of fine sand. Farther up the peninsula, roads to the left lead to Platja de Ses Illetes, with its more popular, but rocky, swimming holes. Platja de Migjorn, the longest beach on the island, is slightly rocky but less crowded than the others. A tourist boat also runs to Ses Illetes and Espalmador from La Savina (leaves La Savina at 10:15, 11:45am, and 1:15pm; returns at 4:15, 5:30, and 6:45pm; round-trip 1500ptas/€9). For sailing, windsurfing, and canoe rental try Wet 4 Fun on Es Pujols beach. (☎971 32 18 09. Sailboats 5900ptas/€35.6 per hr. Windsurfing 2200ptas/€13 per hr. Canoes 900ptas/€5.40 per hr., 2000ptas/€12 per half-day.) For stunning dry-land sightseeing, those with mopeds should drive through the mountainous regions of La Mola to Punta de Sa Ruda or cruise by the groves of olive trees to Cap de Barbaria.

CANARY ISLANDS

From the snowy peak of Mount Teide to the fiery volcanos of Timanfaya, the Canary Islands have enchanted humanity since the beginning of time. Homer and Herodotus often referred to them as gardens of astounding beauty, and the lost civilization of Atlantis was said to have left behind these seven islands when it sank into the ocean. Since then, the Canaries have been known as the "Fortunate Isles" for it is the incomparable natural beauty—the volcanic wastelands, the wind-swept dunes, and the misty forests—that gives them their magic.

The islands were once inhabited by *Guanches*, light-skinned and blond-haired hunters and gatherers, descendants of Berbers who migrated to the islands from North Africa. European raids began when the Romans heard tales of the enchanting isles from the Mauritanians who were in contact with the Guanches. Yet in 1479 the Canaries became Spanish territory and by 1496, after nearly a century of battle with the Guanches, the Spaniards wrested control of the islands. After the conquest, the Spaniards developed a booming plantation economy based on banana, sugar, and wine production on which the islands still depend on today.

The coastal towns are an eclectic mix of craft stalls, surf shops, fruit stands, and high-priced resorts, while their inland hamlets remain largely unchanged. The spoken Spanish here resembles that of Cuba and Puerto Rico more than that of the mainland and Canarian fare is marked by a heavy influence of the Mediterranean. Yet remnants of Guanche culture—like *plátano* (banana) dishes and place names such as Tenerife—still remain as a nostalgic reminder of the islands' past.

TRANSPORTATION TO THE ISLANDS

Located off the western coast of Morocco, the Canaries make for a long haul by boat (15hr. from Spain) but a relatively quick flight (2½-3½hr.) from mainland Spain. Competitive fares and quick flights make flying the best option. Many airlines fly direct from Spain, Portugal, Morocco, the US, and northern Europe. Flights from Madrid, which are the most frequent, are also the cheapest. European tourists, primarily Germans, flock to the islands in January and February; airfares during this time are the most expensive. As long as you plan ahead, getting to the Canary Islands does not have to be prohibitively expensive. Prices are the same whether you purchase your tickets in Spain or abroad.

Iberia/Aviaco (24hr. ☎902 400 500; www.iberia.com) flies from Madrid and Barcelona to the islands of Gran Canaria, Tenerife, and Lanzarote. A standard round-trip ticket costs 70,000-80,000ptas/€420-480.

Air Europa (24hr. ☎902 24 00 42) and **Spanair** (☎ 902 13 14 15; www.spanair.com) fly to the islands at cheaper rates (round-trip 25,000-60,000ptas/€150-360).

Trasmediterránea (☎902 45 46 45; www.trasmediterranea.com) cruises from Cádiz, Spain to the islands of Gran Canaria, Tenerife, and La Palma (15hr.-2 days; departs from Cádiz Sa, returns W; round-trip with dorm bed 59,865ptas/€360).

INTER-ISLAND TRANSPORT

Traveling between the islands by boat is the cheapest alternative. There are two types of water transport: ferries and jetfoils (both carry cars). For shorter trips ferries are the best option. Jetfoils, which are faster and more comfortable, also cost almost twice as much—consider taking them on the longer voyages. Prices for both ferries and jetfoils vary with accommodation; travelers can choose between a *butaca* (a seat like those on buses) and a *camarote a compartir* (a dorm bed).

Three major lines serve the five islands. The offices at each city's ports offer timetables and fares, although it is just as easy to check times and fares online or by phone. Arrive at least an hour before departure to buy your ticket.

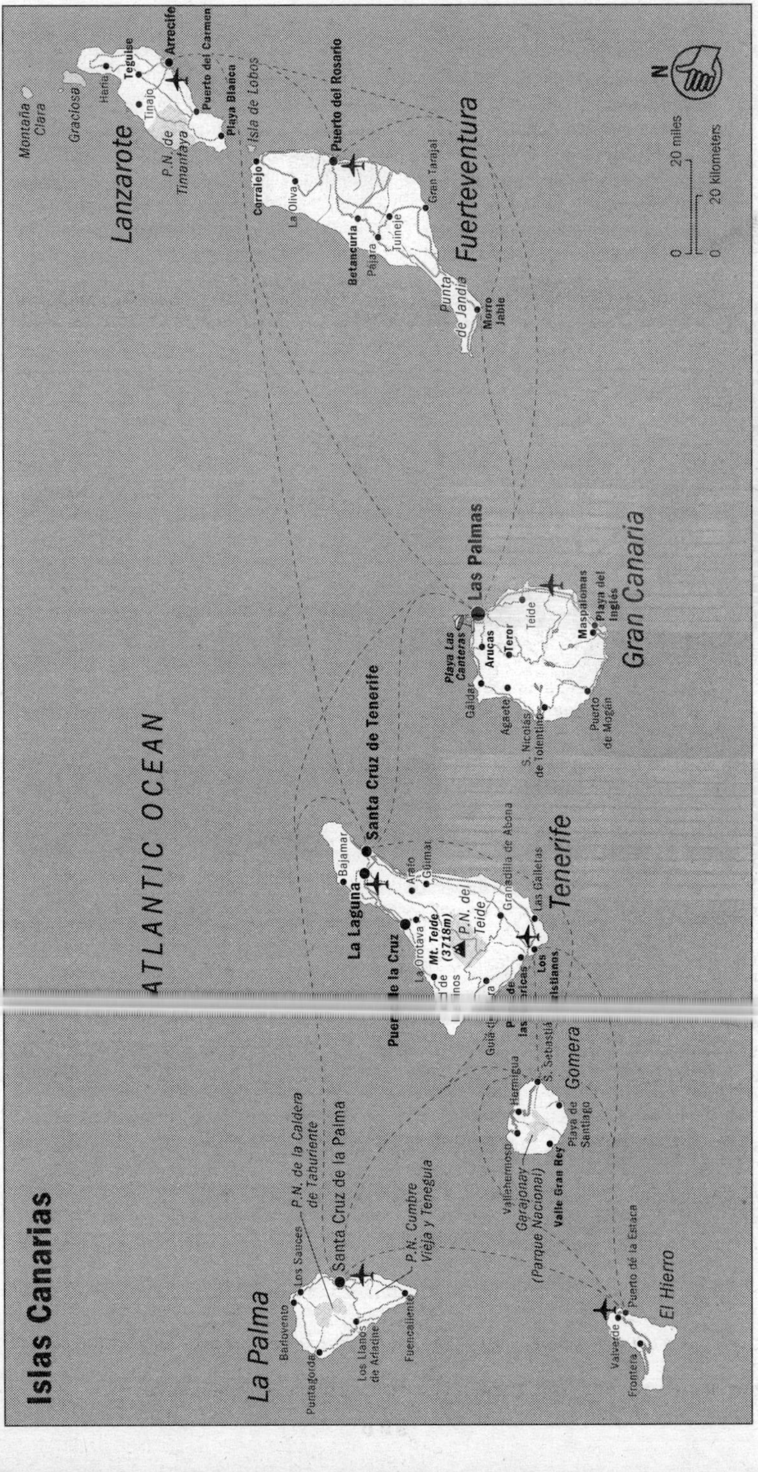

Islas Canarias

ATLANTIC OCEAN

La Palma
Barlovento
Los Sauces
P.N. de la Caldera de Taburiente
Santa Cruz de la Palma
Puntagorda
Los Llanos de Aridane
P.N. Cumbre Vieja y Teneguía
Fuencaliente

El Hierro
Puerto de la Estaca
Valverde
Frontera

Gomera
Hermigua
S. Sebastián
Playa de Santiago
Vallehermoso
Garajonay (Parque Nacional)
Valle Gran Rey

Tenerife
Santa Cruz de Tenerife
La Laguna
Bajamar
Arafo
Güímar
Granadilla de Abona
Las Galletas
Los Cristianos
La Orotava
Mt. Teide (3718m)
P.N. del Teide

Gran Canaria
Las Palmas
Playa Las Canteras
Arucas
Teror
Teide
Gáldar
Agaete
S. Nicolás de Tolentino
Puerto de Mogán
Maspalomas
Playa del Inglés

Fuerteventura
Puerto del Rosario
Corralejo
La Oliva
Betancuria
Pájara
Tuineje
Gran Tarajal
Punta de Jandía
Morro Jable

Lanzarote
Arrecife
Teguise
Haría
Tinajo
Puerto del Carmen
Playa Blanca
P.N. de Timanfaya
Isla de Lobos
Graciosa
Montaña Clara

N

0 20 miles
0 20 kilometers

Fred Olsen (☎922 62 82 00; www.fredolsen.es) runs both jetfoils and ferries. MC/V.

Trasmediterránea (24hr. ☎902 45 46 45; www.trasmediterranea.com). Runs ferries from Cádiz, Spain as well. Ticket windows open 1hr. prior to departure. MC/V.

Naviera Armas (☎928 47 45 45; fax 47 45 47; www.naviera-arms.com). Ferries between selected islands. Bring copies of student ID cards to get the discount. MC/V.

Iberia/Aviaco (☎902 40 05 00) has daily flights between the islands. All prices listed are one-way. **Gran Canaria** to: **Fuerteventura; La Gomera** (45min., 2 per day, 8000ptas/€48); **La Palma** (30min., 1 per day, 10,000ptas/€60); **Lanzarote; Tenerife** north and south airports (30min., 10 per day, 6000ptas/€36). **Spanair** (☎902 13 14 15) connects only Gran Canaria and Tenerife (5000ptas/€30).

Origin	Destination	Duration	Frequency	Time	Price
+Las Palmas	Morro Jable	4hr.	1 per day	7am	3010ptas
*Las Palmas (bus to Agate)	Santa Cruz, Tenerife	1hr.	6 per day	7:30am-8:30pm	3360ptas
+Las Palmas	Santa Cruz, Tenerife	6hr.	M-F 2 per day, Sa-Su 1 per day	7am and 3:15pm, Sa-Su 7am	
Las Palmas	Santa Cruz, Tenerife	6hr.	Th	10:30am	3005ptas
*Las Palmas	Puerto Rosario	6hr.	1 per day	5pm	3080ptas
Las Palmas	Puerto Rosario	8hr.	M,W,F,Sa	midnight	3985ptas
+Las Palmas	Puerto Rosario	8hr.	Tu, Th	11:50pm	
Las Palmas	Arrecife	8hr.	2-3 per week	2:30pm or midnight	3895ptas
+Las Palmas	Arrecife	10hr.	M, W, F	11:50pm	
Las Palmas	Santa Cruz, La Palma	9½hr.	W	10:30pm	5120ptas
*Los Cristianos	San Sebastián	40min.	7 per day	8am-8:30pm	2280-2760ptas
+Playa Blanca	Corralejo	45min.	5 per day	7am-7pm	1700ptas
*Playa Blanca	Corralejo	45min.	4-5 per day	8am-6pm	1850ptas
*Puerto del Rosario	Las Palmas	7hr.	1 per day	9am	3080ptas
Puerto del Rosario	Las Palmas	7hr.	M, W, F, Sa	M-F 1pm, Sa 3pm	3895ptas
+ Puerto del Rosario	Las Palmas	8hr.	W, F	1pm	1850ptas
*Puerto del Rosario	Arrecife	5hr.	1 per day	11:55pm	
Santa Cruz, La Palma	Los Cristianos	5hr.	M-Sa	1:45pm	2995ptas
Santa Cruz, La Palma	San Sebastián	3½hr.	M-Sa	1:45pm	2415ptas
Santa Cruz, La Palma	Valverde	9½hr.	M-Sa	1:45pm	2995ptas
San Sebastián	Los Cristianos	1½hr.	1 per day	5:15pm	2140ptas
*San Sebastián	Los Cristianos	40min.	6 per day	7:30am-6:30pm	2280-2760ptas
San Sebastián	Santa Cruz, La Palma	3½hr.	M-Sa	10:15am	2415ptas
*San Sebastián	Valverde	3hr.	1 per day	9:30am	2540ptas
San Sebastián	Valverde	3½hr.	1 per day	10:15am or 7:15pm	2615ptas
*Valverde	San Sebastián	2½hr.	1 per day	1:30pm	2540ptas
Valverde	Los Cristianos	8hr.	1 per day	11:45am or 2pm	2615ptas
Valverde	Santa Cruz, La Palma	14hr.	Sa-W	11:45pm	2995ptas

Origin	Destination	Duration	Frequency	Time	Price
+Santa Cruz, Tenerife	Arrecife	20hr.	M, W, F	7:30pm	4740ptas
Santa Cruz, Tenerife	Las Palmas	3½hr.	Sa	9am	3005ptas
*Santa Cruz, Tenerife	Las Palmas	2hr.	6 per day	7:30am-8:30pm	3360-4070ptas
+Santa Cruz, Tenerife	Las Palmas	3½hr.	M-F 2 per day, Sa-Su 1 per day	11am and 7:30pm Sa-Su 7:45pm	
+Morro Jable	Las Palmas	4hr.	1 per day	7pm	6000ptas
*Arrecife	Puerto del Rosario	3hr.	5 per day	8am-6pm	4020ptas
+Arrecife	Las Palmas	8hr.	Tu, Th, Sa	1pm	
Arrecife	Las Palmas	8hr.	T, Th	noon	3895ptas
+Corralejo	Playa Blanca	45min	5 per day	8am-8pm	1700ptas
*COrralejo	Playa Blanca	45min	4-5 per day	9am-7pm	1850ptas

Unless otherwise noted, all ferries are run by Trasmediterránea. * denotes Fred Olsen jetfoils. + denotes Naviera Armas.

GRAN CANARIA

Often called the "miniature continent," Gran Canaria sports a wide range of climates, from the snow-covered Pico de las Nieves (1950m) to the rolling dunes of Maspalomas. Although it is the least appealing of the islands, nothing stops the foreign visitors (mostly German) from packing flank to flank on Gran Canaria's eastern and southern beaches. For tanning, it doesn't get much simpler than this. The interior towns are less touristed, but why go? Gran Canaria's parched mountains pale in comparison to the peaks and national parks of Tenerife and Lanzarote.

LAS PALMAS

The urban mecca of the Canaries, Las Palmas (pop. 360,000) moves to the rhythm of jackhammers by day and disco-bass by night. Residents of varied ethnic backgrounds mix with bronzed, fun-loving Europeans who are all cruising toward one inevitable destination—the beach. The city's streets buzz with the frenzied commerce of a duty-free port where everything from cigarettes to tanning lotion is for sale. Unless you like sketchy clubs and Euro-trash on your beach towel, your stay in Las Palmas need not extend past the wait at a seaside café for a transportation link to cleaner, less commercialized parts of the islands.

TRANSPORTATION

Flights: (24hr. ☎928 57 90 00). **Buses** run from Parque San Telmo's Estación de Guaguas to the airport (#60, 45min., every hr. 6:30am-2am, 245ptas/€1.50). **Iberia** (☎928 37 08 77). **Air Europa** (☎928 57 95 84). **Spanair** (☎928 57 94 07).

Buses: Estación de Guaguas (☎928 36 83 35; info 36 86 35), on the sea side of Parque San Telmo. Office open M-F 6:30am-8:30pm. Buses here are called *guaguas*. **Líneas Global** (☎902 28 38 11 10) connects Las Palmas to the rest of the island. A blue **tarjeta insular** pass (2000ptas/€12) works on municipal and island-wide buses and is a good investment for those exploring the surroundings by bus as it gives a 30% discount on all fares. To: **Arucas** (#205, 209, 210, and 234; every 30min. 6am-11pm; 245ptas/€1.50); **Maspalomas-Playa de Inglés** (#5 and 30; 30min.; every 20min. 5:20am-9:20pm; Playa Inglés 625ptas/€3.75, Maspalomas 685ptas/€4.10); **Puerto Mogan** (#1, 20min., every 20min. 5:40am-7pm, 975ptas/€5.85); **Puerto Rico** (#91, 4 per day 6am-8:15pm, 845ptas/€5.10); **Teror** (#216 and 218, every 30min. 7am-9:30pm, 245ptas/€1.50). Yellow **Guaguas Municipales,** C. León y Castillo, 330 (☎928 44 65 00) travel within the city. Bus #1 runs 24hr. from Puerto de la Luz to Teatro Pérez Galdós, passing Parque San Catalina and Parque San Telmo. Individual ride 130ptas/€0.75; 10-ride "bono" available at tobacco shops for 800ptas/€4.80.

Ferries: Trasmediterránea (☎928 47 44 39; fax 26 30 77) runs jetfoils from Muelle Santa Catalina. **Fred Olson** (☎922 62 82 31 or 928 22 81 66) and **Naviera Armas** (☎928 26 70 00) ferries depart from Muelle León y Castillo. Fred Olson's ferry to Tenerife departs from the town of **Agate.** A free bus leaves Parque Santa Catalina 1hr. before the ferry leaves; you must have a ferry ticket to board the bus. Ferry tickets are sold at the docks or any travel agency. For more info, see **Inter-Island Transport,** p. 503.

Taxi: Radio Taxi (☎928 46 22 12 or 46 18 18). **Taxi Radio** (☎928 46 56 66).

Car Rental: Hertz, at the airport (☎928 57 95 77). Another branch in the Jetfoil office at Muelle de Sta. Catalina. Ford Fiesta 5100ptas/€31 per day, including tax, insurance, and unlimited mileage. Open M-Sa 8am-7:30pm. Cars can be taken to other islands.

ORIENTATION AND PRACTICAL INFORMATION

To get around Las Palmas, you must use the bus system. The city is loosely divided into a series of districts, connected by the **Av. del Marítima del Norte,** running north to south along the east coast, and **Av. León y Castillo,** which runs parallel through the city center. All major services can be found on this thoroughfare. **Parque Sta. Catalina,** framed by **Playa de Las Canteras** on the west and **Puerto de la Luz** on the east, is packed with accommodations, bars, discos, and sex shops—stay here for beach and bus access. Farther south through a series of residential neighborhoods lies **Triana,** a shopping district with the city's bus station. **Vequeta,** home to the city's historical district, branches south from Triana. Buses #1, 12, 13, 15, and 41 run between Parque Sta. Catalina and Vequeta. **Parque Sta. Catalina** houses the tourist office; all directions in Las Palmas are given from there.

Tourist Offices: Main office, Pl. Ramón Franco (☎/fax 928 26 46 23), in front of Parque Sta. Catalina, in a colonial-style house. Multilingual staff. Open M-F 9am-2pm. The central **town-run office,** in the old Ayuntamiento, across Pl. Sta. Ana from the cathedral. Open M-F 10am-5:30pm. **Centro de Iniciaturas y Turismo** (☎928 24 35 93), in Pueblo Canario. Open M-F 10am-1pm and 5-8pm.

Currency Exchange: Banco Central Hispano, C. Nicolás Estévanez, 5 (☎902 24 24 24). No commission. Open 8:30am-2pm. **ATMs** line Parque Sta. Catalina.

Laundromat: Lavasec, C. Joaquín Costa, 46 (☎928 27 46 17). Wash, dry, and iron (up to 7kg) 1000ptas/€6. Open M-F 9am-1pm and 4-8pm, Sa 9am-3pm.

Emergency: ☎112. **Police: Policía Municipal** in Parque Sta. Catalina (☎928 26 05 51).

Hospital: Hospital Insular, Pl. Dr. Pasteur (☎928 44 40 00). **Ambulance:** ☎928 24 50 23. **Interclinic,** C. Sagasta, 62 (☎928 27 88 26 or 26 90 98). From Parque Sta. Catalina, turn left on C. Luis Morote, then right on C. Sagasta. A 24hr. emergency clinic geared towards tourists. English spoken.

Internet: CyberFoto Star, C. Luis Morote, 14B (☎928 22 48 13). 75ptas/€0.45 per 30 min., 150ptas/€0.90 per hr. Open 9am-11pm every day.

Post Office: Main office, Av. Primero de Mayo, 62 (☎928 36 13 20). **Lista de Correos.** Open M-F 8:30am-8:30pm, Sa 9:30am-2:30pm. **Postal Code:** 35007.

ACCOMMODATIONS AND CAMPING

It's very difficult to find a place to stay without advance notice and nearly impossible during high season (Dec.-Feb., especially during *Carnaval*). If the places listed below are full, calling the **Reservations Center** (☎928 38 46 46 or 38 47 47; after hours fax 38 48 48) can save a lot of time; ask for Sr. Cabrera. Singles are limited, and solo travelers will often end up paying for a double. Las Palmas probably has the cheapest accommodations on the island, but since most of them are unimpressive, be sure to examine a room before committing to stay.

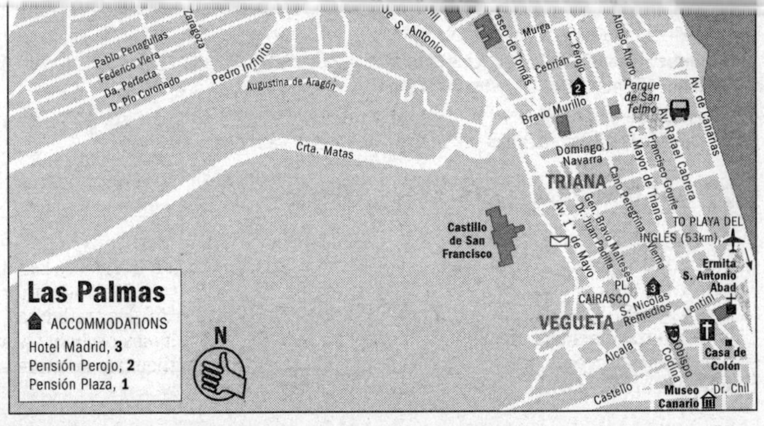

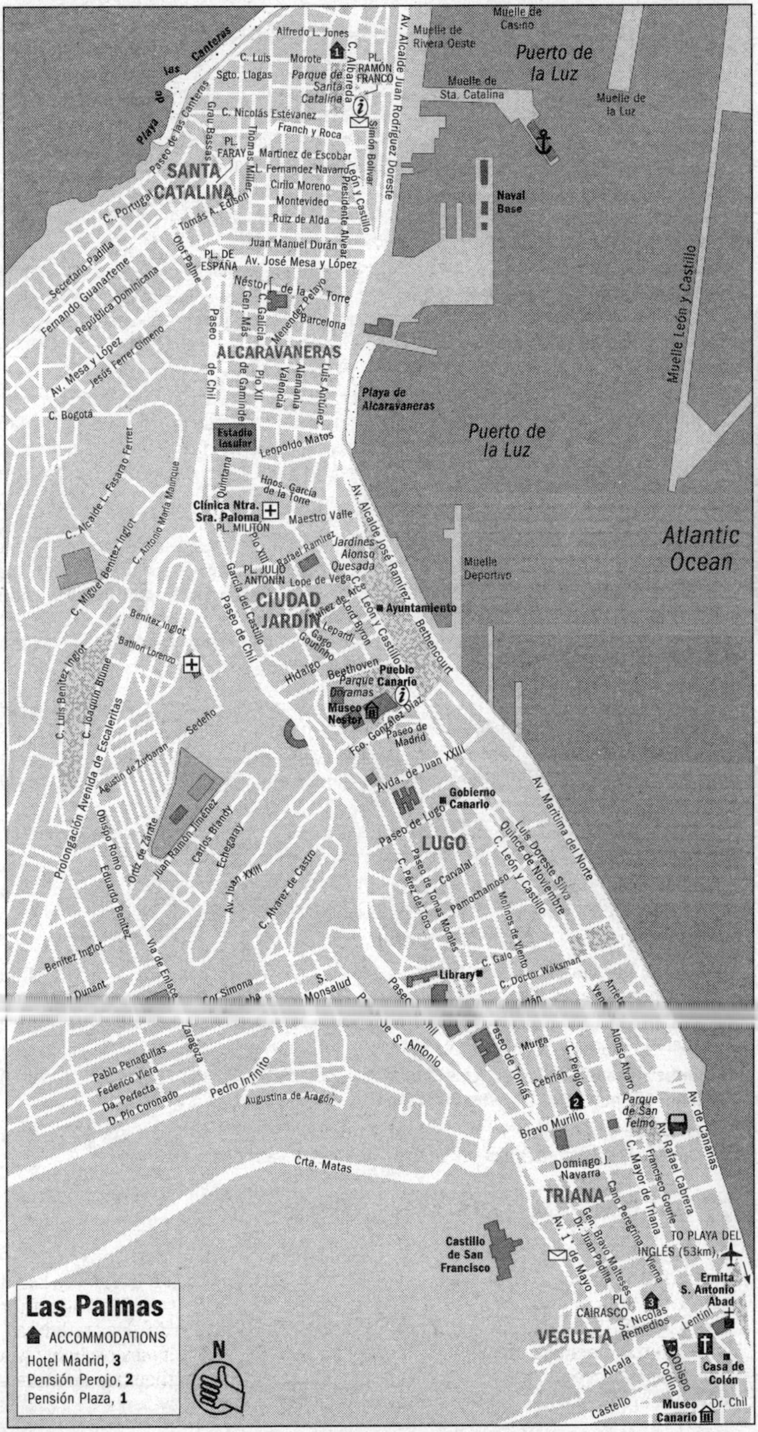

Las Palmas
ACCOMMODATIONS
Hotel Madrid, 3
Pensión Perojo, 2
Pensión Plaza, 1
N
Puerto de la Luz
Atlantic Ocean
Muelle de Casino
Muelle de Rivera Oeste
Muelle de Sta. Catalina
Muelle de la Luz
Naval Base
Muelle León y Castillo
Muelle Deportivo
Playa de las Canteras
Playa de Alcaravaneras
SANTA CATALINA
ALCARAVANERAS
CIUDAD JARDÍN
LUGO
TRIANA
VEGUETA
Parque de Santa Catalina
PL. RAMÓN FRANCO
PL. FARAY
PL. DE ESPAÑA
PL. MILITÓN
PL. JULIO ANTONIN
PL. CAIRASCO
Estadio Insular
Clínica Ntra. Sra. Paloma
Jardines Alonso Quesada
Ayuntamiento
Pueblo Canario
Parque Doramas
Museo Nestor
Gobierno Canario
Library
Parque de San Telmo
Castillo de San Francisco
Ermita S. Antonio Abad
Casa de Colón
Museo Canario
TO PLAYA DEL INGLÉS (53km)
Av. Alcalde Juan Rodríguez Doreste
Av. Alcalde José Ramírez Bethencourt
Av. Marítima del Norte
Av. de Canarias
Av. José Mesa y López
Av. Mesa y López
Paseo de Chil
Paseo de las Canteras
León y Castillo
Alfredo L. Jones
C. Luis Morote
Sgto. Llagas
C. Albareda
C. Nicolás Estévanez
Franch y Roca
Martinez de Escobar
L. Fernandez Navarro
Cirilo Moreno
Montevideo
Ruiz de Alda
Juan Manuel Durán
Tomás A. Edison
C. Portugal
Secretario Padilla
Fernando Guanarteme
República Dominicana
Olof Palme
Grau Bassas
Thomas Miller
Simón Bolívar
Presidente Alvear
Néstor de la Torre
Barcelona
Menéndez Pelayo
C. Galicia
Gen. Más de Gaminde
Pío XII
Valencia
Alemania
Luis Antúnez
Leopoldo Matos
Hnos. García de la Torre
Maestro Valle
Quintana
Rafael Ramírez
Lope de Vega
García del Castillo
Lord Byron
Lepanto
Gago Coutinho
Hidalgo
Beethoven
Fco. González Díaz
Paseo de Madrid
Avda. de Juan XXIII
Paseo de Lugo
C. Bogotá
Jesús Ferrer Gimeno
C. Alcalde L. Fasaro Ferrer
C. Antonio María Manrique
C. Miguel Benítez Inglot
Benítez Inglot
Batllori Lorenzo
C. Luis Benítez Inglot
C. Joaquín Blume
Prolongación Avenida de Escaleritas
Agustín de Zurbarán
Sedeño
Obispo Romo
Eduardo Benítez
Ortiz de Zárate
Juan Ramón Jiménez
Carlos Blandy
Echegaray
Av. Juan XXIII
C. Álvarez de Castro
Paseo de Tomás Morales
C. Pérez del Toro
Carvajal
Pamochamoso
Luis Doreste Silva
Quince de Noviembre
C. León y Castillo
Molinos de Viento
C. Galo
C. Doctor Waksman
Benítez Inglot
Dunant
Vía de Enlace
S. Monsalud
Zaragoza
Pablo Penagullas
Federico Viera
Da. Perfecta
D. Pío Coronado
Pedro Infinito
Augustina de Aragón
Crta. Matas
Murga
C. Perojo
Cebrián
Alonso Álvaro
Bravo Murillo
Av. Rafael Cabrera
Francisco Gourie
C. Mayor de Triana
Domingo J. Navarra
Cano
Peregrina
Gen. Bravo
Dr. Juan Padilla
Av. 1° de Mayo
Malteses
Viera
S. Nicolás
Remedios
Lentini
Obispo Codina
Alcalá
Castello
Dr. Chil

Hotel Madrid, Pl. Cairasco, 4 (☎928 36 06 64; fax 38 21 76), in the Triana-Vegueta district, inland from C. Lentini; enter through Café Madrid on the plaza. Excellent location. Franco stayed in room #3 the night before the Civil War began. Singles 3500ptas/€21, with bath 4500ptas/€27; doubles 4500ptas/€27, with bath 5500ptas/€33.

Pensión Plaza, C. Luis Morote, 16 (☎928 26 52 12), the red building facing Parque Sta. Catalina. Location makes up for the negligible water pressure. Self-service laundry 1200ptas/€7.20. 24hr. reception. Singles 2600ptas/€16, with bath 3100ptas/€19; doubles 3600ptas/€22, with bath 4100ptas/€25; doubles for 1 person 3100ptas/€19, with bath 3600ptas/€22. Extra beds 1000ptas/€6.

Pensión Perojo, C. Perojo, 1 (☎928 37 13 87), inland from the Estación de Guaguas off C. Bravo Murillo. Lots of street noise, but these simple, sparse rooms are a short walk from the old city. Some rooms given to quasi-permanent residents. Singles 2500ptas/€15; doubles 3500ptas/€21; triples 4500ptas/€27.

Camping Guantánamo (☎928 56 02 07), in Mogán (a port town in the south). See **Buses** for transportation info. Ranked a 3rd-class site, near a eucalyptus forest and a hunting zone. Plenty of amenities, including a snack-bar, supermarket, restaurant, and pharmacy. 376ptas/€2.26 per person and per car, 428ptas/€2.57 per large tent.

FOOD

Las Palmas' cuisine is as international as its fluctuating population. A typical night might involve eating Indian *tapas* and swinging to Moroccan pop music in an Irish pub. Most restaurants cater to tourists, serving German *paella*, hamburgers, and pizza. For **groceries, Cruz Mayor** has a branch on C. Nicolás Estévanez, 38, in the new city, and C. Pérez Galdós, 17, in the Triana district (both open M-Sa 8:30am-8:30pm). **Mercado de Vegueta,** C. Mendizábal, a sensory parade of fresh fruit, dairy, fish, and olive stands. (Open daily 6am-2pm.) **Hipócrates,** C. Colón, 4 (☎928 22 64 15), across from Casa-Museo Colón in Vegueta, offers romantic vegetarian dining with a simple *menú* for 1400ptas/€8.40. (Open daily 1-4pm and 8:30pm-midnight, closed Su evenings and M afternoons.) **Casa Montesdeoca,** toward the sea from Casa de Colón, serves delicious entrées (650-2300ptas/€4-14) in a 16th-century garden courtyard. (☎928 33 34 66. Open M-Sa 12:30-4pm, 8pm-midnight.)

SIGHTS AND NIGHTLIFE

The easiest "sight" to see is Las Palmas' **historic neighborhood;** its colonial and neoclassical architecture and open markets make for a sweet respite from the new city's commercial buildings. For history buffs, the **Museo Canario,** C. Verneau, 2, off Dr. Chil, provides a comprehensive background on Guanche society. If the second floor's collection of Cro-Magnon skulls (the largest in the world) doesn't freak you out, inspect the mummies for a sure scream. (☎928 33 68 00; fax 33 68 01. Open M-F 10am-8pm, Sa-Su 10am-2pm. Guided tours run every 45min. 10am-2pm and at 6 and 7pm. 500ptas/€3, students 200ptas/€1.20.) The 16th-century Gothic **Catedral de Sta. Ana** houses the **Diocesan Museum of Religious Art,** C. Espíritu Santo, 20. From the bus stop, go left up C. Cavo Sotello and left on C. Obispo Cobina. José Luján Pérez, the Canaries' favorite sculptor, designed the Neoclassical façade. (☎928 31 49 89. Open M-F 9am-1:30pm and 4-6:30pm, Sa 9am-2pm. 400ptas/€2.40.) Columbus purportedly stayed several times in the old-style **Casa de Colón,** C. Colón, 1, as a last stop before the New World. The museum contains various artifacts of early transatlantic voyages and investigations of pre-columbian cultures. (Follow C. Espíritu Santo from Pl. Santa Ana. ☎928 31 23 73 or 31 23 84. Open Tu-F 9am-7pm, Sa-Su 9am-3pm. Free.) In the white-washed **Pueblo Canario** (Canarian Village), dedicated to the dissemination of Canarian culture, resides the **Museo Néstor,** a stunning collection of painter Néstor Martín-Fernández de la Torre's beautiful, pudgy figures. As per Néstor's request, Su mornings fill Pueblo Canario with traditional Canarian folk dance and music from 11:30am-1pm. (In Dorames Park to the left when facing the hotel. Take bus #1, 15, or 41.

☎928 24 51 35. Open Tu-F 10am-8pm, Su 10:30am-2:30pm. 150ptas/€0.90, students free.) The city's new pride and joy, the **Museo Elder de la Ciencia y la Tecnología,** on the port side of Parque Sta. Catalina, is a state-of-the-art exploration of state-of-the-art subjects, from energy and transport to a space station and a science workshop. (☎828 01 18 18; www.museoelder.org. Open Tu-Su 10am-8pm. 500ptas/€3.)

The **Playa de Las Canteras,** one of Europe's most famous beaches, is the only reason to stay in Las Palmas. The café-lined shore is packed with beach-goers who enjoy tanning, scuba diving, surfing, and windsurfing. The reef-sheltered lagoon is known as "the world's largest swimming pool." From Parque de Sta. Catalina, take a left on C. Luis Morote, and follow it to the end. **Medusa Sub,** Bernardo de La Torre, 33, specializes in diving, instructional courses, and equipment rental and sales. (☎928 26 27 86. Open M-F 11am-2pm and 5-9pm, Sa 11am-1pm and 6-8pm).

Nightlife in Las Palmas is nothing remarkable, with overpriced drinks (around 600ptas/€3.60), flashing lights, and thumping bass. Most popular spots (including karaoke bars) are located around Parque Sta. Catalina. Take advantage of year-round outdoor terraces on Pl. España and along Po. Canteras. **Palacio Latino,** C. Luis Morote, 51, is your standard *discoteca,* while **Pequeña Habana,** C. Fernando Guanarteme, 45, sizzles with salsa until 4am on weekend nights. Solo women travelers should be careful lest they find themselves with an unwanted friend.

CANARY ISLANDS

DAYTRIPS FROM LAS PALMAS

Las Palmas itself is no reason to come to the Isla de Gran Canaria. Use the cheap accommodations as a base for visiting more appealing parts of the islands, especially the sunny southern beaches and quaint interior villages.

MASPALOMAS

Buses run to and from the airport (#4, 5, 30, 61, 90; 40min.; every 30min. 6:30am-9pm; 350ptas/€2.10); Las Palmas (#4, 5, 30, 61; 1hr.; every 15min. 6:30am-9:30pm; 645ptas/€3.90); Puerto Mogan (#32 and 61; 30min.; every 20min. 7am-8:30pm; 435ptas/€2.60); and Puerto Rico (#32, 39, 61; 30min.; every 20min. 7am-8:30pm; 305ptas/€1.80).

Located on the southern tip of Gran Canaria, the 17km of Maspalomas' shoreline are the best beaches in the Canary Islands. The famed **Playa del Inglés** offers parasailing, surfing (the current world-champion lives 5min. away), jet-skiing, scuba diving, and deep-sea fishing. The secret has long been out, and planeloads of European tourists swarm the coast every year. The crowds are worth putting up with, though, to see the awesome, wind-swept **Dunas de Maspalomas** beyond the beach, a subtle reminder that the Canaries share their latitude with the Sahara. (To get to the dunes from the beach, face the water and walk right, down Playa del Inglés or walk to the bottom of Av. Tirajana.)

Other good beaches include the flawless, quieter **Playa de Maspalomas** and the [illegible] pleasant afternoon than Playa del Inglés. **Water Sport Center,** in the Kabash shopping center, rents jetskis (☎928 76 66 83. 5000-6000ptas/€30-36 for 20min.) and **Tortuga** (☎928 77 02 18), Edificio Habitat, offers diving trips. For exploring the dunes and surrounding areas, **Happy Biking,** in Jumbo Center, rents bikes, equipment, guides, and picnic supplies. (☎928 76 82 98. 1500-4000ptas/€9-24 per day.)

The town of Playa del Inglés itself is little more than a cement wasteland of tourist-oriented infrastructure. If you must stay here, **Residencia San Fernando,** C. La Palma, 16, which goes by several other names, including "Casa de Huéspedes" and "Hotel," is the only budget accommodation in town. Follow Av. Tirajana uphill away from the beach; La Palma is the second right after the highway. Rooms are bare and clean, although bathrooms leave a little to be desired. (☎928 76 39 06. Singles 2000ptas/€12; doubles 3000ptas/€18) The **tourist office** is on C. San Bartolomé de Tirajana, next to the Centro Comercial Yumbo. (☎928 77 15 50. Open in summer M-F 9am-2pm and 3-8pm, Sa 9am-1pm; in winter M-F 9am-9pm.)

ARUCAS

Buses #205, 206, 209, 210, and 234 travel from the Las Palmas station to Arucas (every 30min. 6am-11pm, 245ptas/€1.50).

Arucas, a delightful mountain town set on a dormant volcano, has a stunning neo-Gothic church and a genuine, relaxed atmosphere—as an essential daytrip from Las Palmas, it is worth tearing yourself away from the beach to take in the town's splendor. Once the center of sugar and rum production on the island, the town now prides itself of its stunning good looks. Overlooking a set of gardens, the **Church of San Juan Bautista** is a magnificent structure almost wholly constructed by local stonemasons and artisans between 1909 and 1977. (Open daily 9am-1pm and 4-7pm. Free.) A short walk up out of town leads to the **Montaña de Arucas,** which features breathtaking panoramic views of the island. To get to the **tourist office** from the bus station, walk uphill to **Parque de La Paz,** and head right on C. León y Castillo to Pl. Constitución. (☎928 60 58 16. Open M-F 9am-2pm and 5-8pm, Sa 9am-1pm). There is one (and only one) place to stay in Arucas: a little *albergue* called **La Granja Escuela Anatol,** C. Ruz de Pineda, 5, which provides a home for scholars—and for you, too, if you reserve in advance. (☎/fax 928 60 55 44. 3200ptas/€19 per person.) At **Café El Parque,** Pl. San Juan, 2, a quiet seat with a view of the church, a *torija* (cinnamon pastry), and a *café con leche* can be yours for only 300ptas/€1.80. (☎928 60 25 90. Open M-Su 10am-1am: closed W.)

CANARY ISLANDS

TEROR

Ultinsa buses #216 and 218 run from Las Palmas to Teror (every 30min. 7am-9:30pm, 245ptas/€1.50.) Bus #215 connects Arucas and Teror (every hr. 6am-9:55pm, 145ptas/€0.85).

Gran Canaria's patron saint, **La Virgen del Pino,** once resides in **Teror,** a picture-perfect village tucked away in the mountains. The town's church was built on the spot where 17th-century conquistador Don Juan de Frías saw a vision of the Virgin. On Sept. 8 the entire island pays its respects to their founding saint in rousing celebration. In the plaza facing the church is a small museum, **Casa de los Patrones de la Virgen,** the preserved 17th-century summer home of Manrique de Lara.

TENERIFE

Tenerife was aptly named from the Guanche words *tener*, meaning "sky," and *ife*, meaning "fire." In fact, the volcanic peak of Tenerife, El Teide (3718m), is the tallest mountain in Spain. During the Spanish conquest, the island was divided up into nine distinct *menceyatos*, and each developed its own architecture and culture. Although the island is now united, its broken landscape is indicative of its diverse flora; the northern half of the island is a verdant and hilly garden, laced with undiscovered beaches, while the south is an arid and endless black-sand beach, crowded with development. Tenerife's interior offers the Canaries' greatest hiking, a welcome escape from sun-scorched beaches, and sauerkraut *paella*. For those who long for still more seclusion, Santa Cruz and Los Cristianos provide transportation to the westernmost islands of El Hierro, La Palma, and La Gomera, not yet sacrificed to the lesser god of Tourism.

SANTA CRUZ DE TENERIFE

Before the Spanish Civil War, the government sent troublesome officers to out-of-the-way provinces. As a result, Franco became the General-in-Chief of the Canaries, scarring the port city of Santa Cruz (pop. 250,000) with the first shots of the Civil War. A somber cross commemorating the war-victims presides over the Plaza de España, but the city focuses on the future. With an ever-expanding tourist industry, the port is a steel sea of ferries, jetfoils, and freighters, and the horizon is filled with cranes. Fortunately, although Santa Cruz rivals Las Palmas in commercialism, the city is comparatively more scenic, pleasant, and upbeat.

TRANSPORTATION

Flights: See both **Transportation** sections, p. 500, for info on flights to, from, and around the islands. There are 2 airports on Tenerife. The majority of national flights head to the northern airport, **Los Rodeos** (☎922 63 58 00; www2.aena.es/ae/tfn/index.html) Los Rodeos is a few kilometers west of Santa Cruz. From Los Rodeos, buses #102, 107, and 108 run to town (20min., every 20min. 6am-midnight, 150ptas/€0.90). International flights dominate the south's larger **Reina Sofía** airport (☎922 75 92 00 or 75 90 00; www2.aena.es/ae/tfs/hometfs.htm). From Reina Sofía, bus #341 heads to town (every hr. 5:30am-12:10am, 230ptas/€1.37). **Iberia** (☎922 75 92 85), **Spanair** (☎922 75 91 50), and **Air Europa** (☎922 75 92 44) all fly to the island.

Buses: TITSA (☎922 21 56 99 or 24hr. 53 13 00; www.titsa.com) serves all towns from **Estación de Guaguas,** Av. Tres de Mayo, 57, down C. José Antonio Rivera from Pl. España. Some lines do not run during the summer, so call ahead for information. To **Los Cristianos/Playa de América** (#110 and 111; 1hr., every 30min. 5:30am-11pm; 950ptas/€5.70) and **Puerto de la Cruz** (#102 has stops, #103 runs direct; 1hr., every 30min. 6:15am-9:40pm, then 11pm, 12:45, 3:15, 4:45am; 550ptas/€3.30). Those planning to explore the island by bus should invest in the **bonobus** ticket (2000ptas/€12). The amount deducted from the card is 30% less than the cost of individual tickets on short rides and 50% for distances greater than 20km.

Ferries: Trasmediterránea (☎922 24 30 11). **Fred Olsen** (☎922 62 82 00) runs a **free bus** from the main station to Los Cristianos for departures to La Gomera and El Hierro 90min. prior to departure. See **Inter-Island Transport,** p. 503.

Car Rental: There are agencies throughout the city; many cluster around Pl. España. **Autos ADA,** C. Emilio Calzadilla, 10 (☎922 27 49 53; fax 242 756). Cheapest car 4400ptas/€26.40 per day, including insurance, unlimited mileage and taxes. You must be 23 or have 3yrs. of driving experience. Open M-F 7:30am-8pm, Sa 8am-1pm and 4-7pm, Su 9am-noon. **Avis** (☎922 25 87 13), in the northern airport.

PIGEON SOUP The most important workers at Tenerife's airports wear their wings permanently: 21 intensively trained hawks patrol the skies above Los Rodeos and Reina Sofía, killing and scaring off seagulls and pigeons. The wayward gulls have caused near-wrecks in the past as they are sucked into plane engine turbines, and with an attractive landfill nearby, they flock in by the thousands. Fortunately, the hawks—especially the females—have carried out quite an effective anti-gull campaign. The best part? The search-and-destroy superstars only require wages of 120ptas/€0.70 a day in food. Handlers report that the hawks would never attack humans. Hitchcock would beg to differ.

ORIENTATION AND PRACTICAL INFORMATION

Despite its extensive bus system, Santa Cruz is easily navigable on foot. The port city radiates from the **Plaza de España.** C. Castillo runs perpendicular to the water into the commercial district. Av. José Antonio Primo de Rivera and Av. Anaga originate in Pl. España and run along the waterfront, separating the port and the city. To get to Pl. España from the **ferry terminals,** turn left onto Av. Anaga, sometimes identified as Av. Francisco la Roche, and follow it to the plaza (10min.). From the **bus station,** head right down Av. Tres de Mayo towards the water, then take a left on Av. José Antonio Primo de Rivera, continuing on to the plaza (15min.).

Tourist Office: Pl. España, s/n (☎922 23 95 92), on the corner of Av. José Antonio Primo de Rivera and the plaza. Facing the monument, it's in the far right corner. Open July-Sept. M-F 8am-5pm and Sa 9am-noon; Oct.-June M-F 8am-6pm, Sa 9am-1pm.

Police: Av. Tres de Mayo, 72 (☎922 60 60 92). Follow Av. Tres de Mayo past the intersection with Av. de La Salle, the station is on the right.

Pharmacy: Many are located along C. Castillo and its extensions. To reach a large one in **Pl. San Francisco** (☎922 24 72 11), take a right onto C. San Francisco from C. Castillo. Open M-F 9am-1pm, 5pm-7pm, Sa 9am-1pm. MC/V.

Hospital: In an **emergency** dial ☎112. In La Laguna, north of Santa Cruz, **Hospital Universitario de Canarias**, Urb. Ofra s/n (☎922 67 80 00 or 67 82 83) offers comprehensive attention. Buses #014, 015 make frequent stops at the main station (☎922 25 94 12). The **Red Cross** is available for immediate attention, C. San Lucas, 60 (☎922 28 29 24). From C. Castillo, turn right onto C. San Lucas; it's across from the church.

Internet Access: El Navegante, C. Combate, 12 (☎922 24 15 00). From Pl. España, follow C. Béthencourt Alfonso and its continuation, C. Pérez Galdós. Turn right onto C. Combate; look on the right. A bar-cum-email kiosk. *Tapas* washed down with email from 300ptas/€1.80 per 30min. Open M-Th 9am-10:30pm, F-Sa 10:30am-11pm.

Post Office: Av. Benito Pérez Armas, 2. (☎922 24 20 02). From the center, follow Av. de San Sebastián past the stadium. Take your first left onto C. Heliodoro Rodríguez López. Follow onto it's continuation, C. Tome Cano Heliodoro, and a right onto C. Fragata Danmark. Open M-F 8:30am-8:30pm, Sa 9:30am-2pm. **Postal code:** 38007.

ACCOMMODATIONS

Unfortunately for budget travelers, hostels and *pensiones* in Santa Cruz are few and far between. What does exist fills up quickly, so reserve in advance. C. Castillo and C. Béthencourt Alfonso are scattered with one- and two-star hotels which are both luxurious and pricey. The tourist office has lists of accommodations, and their map marks hotels; make use of free 2min. phone calls to reserve a room.

Hotel Horizonte, C. Sta. Rosa de Lima, 11 (☎922 27 19 36; fax 24 36 79). From Pl. España take C. La Marina, turn left onto C. Emilio Calzadilla, then right onto C. Sta. Rosa de Lima. A reception stuffed with fresh flowers welcomes visitors for a stay of supreme service and spotless rooms. The spacious, flower-filled rooms all have private baths. An ample breakfast is served in, you guessed it, a flowered lounge (500ptas/€3). Singles 3000ptas/€18; doubles 6000ptas/€36; triples 7000ptas/€42.

Pensión Casablanca, C. Viera y Clavijo, 15 (☎922 27 85 99). Take C. Béthencourt Alfonso which becomes C. Pérez Galdós and then C. de Viera y Clavijo. Creative cabins come in pink, blue or green varieties. Common baths. Reservations are highly recommended as the rooms are few. Singles 2500ptas/€15; doubles 3000ptas/€18.

Hotel Anago, C. Imeldo Serís, 19 (☎922 24 50 90; fax 24 56 44). From the plaza, go left on C. General Gutiérrez and right on C. Imeldo Seris. Spacious and spartan rooms; many with balconies. Singles with shower 3843ptas/€23, with bath 4850ptas/€29; doubles with shower 6295ptas/€38, with bath 8033ptas/€48. AmEx/MC/V.

FOOD

Santa Cruz's restaurants are the unfortunate result of the city's burgeoning international tourist industry; *casas de china*, waikiki bars, cookie-cutter Italian Bistros, and German *paella* spots line the streets. Cafés, restaurants, and bars crowd Pl. España, but **Av. Anaga** has better deals (*menús* for 950ptas/€5.70) and chic *terrazas*. Local eats can be found along **C. Imeldo Serís.** The **Mercado de Nuestra Señora de Africa,** across the river and one block inland from the Museo de la Naturaleza y el Hombre (see **Sights,** next page), sells meat and produce most mornings. **La Hierbita,** C. Clavel, 19. From Pl. España, take C. General Gutiérrez, a right onto C. Imeldo Serís, and another right onto C. Cruz Verde. Take your first left and sample Canarian specialties. (☎922 24 46 17. Open M-Sa 11am-4pm, 7pm-11pm.)

SIGHTS AND ENTERTAINMENT

Santa Cruz's museums and sights are seen by most tourists as little more than air-conditioned beach breaks, which is too bad because an exploration of the city can be one of the most fruitful in the Canaries. At the **Museo de la Naturaleza y el Hombre,** C. Fuente Morales, s/n, off C. San Sebastián, elaborate audio-visual exhibitions transport you to the Canaries' archaeological past, detailing everything from pre-historic marine biology to Guanche burial practices in Lanzarote and La Palma. On the lighter side, have a go at sculpting your own ceramic pots in the museum's classroom. (☎922 20 93 20. Open Tu-Su, 10am-7pm. 400ptas/€2.40, students 200ptas/€1.20. 50% discount with *bonobus* pass. Su free.) The intricate woodwork of the 16th-century **Iglesia de la Concepción** is worth the architectural pilgrimage. To reach the Pl. de la Iglesia, turn left onto C. Bravo Murillo from the tourist office. (Mass M-Sa 7pm, Su 10am, noon, and 1pm. Open M-F 8am-7:30pm.) A different variety of splendor can be found in the breathtaking frescoes of the 17th-century **Iglesia de San Francisco** in Pl. San Francisco. From Pl. España, turn right onto C. Cruz Verde, follow it for two blocks to Pl. San Francisco. (Mass M-Sa 8am, Su 8, 10am, 8pm. Open M-Sa 8am-7pm.) The **Parque García Sanabria** doubles as an impressive garden and an open-air sculpture museum with avant-garde works by Pablo Serrano, Rafael Soto, and Gustavo Torner.

BEACHES AND NIGHTLIFE

As on Gran Canaria, the **beaches** are Tenerife's true attraction. The black sand of **Almáciga** (bus #246), **Benijo** (bus #246), and **Las Gaviotas** (bus #245), and the golden sand of **Las Teresitas** (bus #910), an artificial beach, lie near Santa Cruz; all are accessible by frequent buses departing from the central bus station.

In Tenerife, warm summer **nights** bring out latin lovers of both sexes. Exploding from Av. Anaga's bar-discos at 4am, the drunken parade of stilettos marches on to the sizzling **terrazas del verano** running down Av. José Antonio Primo de Rivera's waterfront. One of the three adjoining outdoor clubs, a night at **El Primero** (open 11pm until dawn) goes by in a blur of booze promotions, seductive platform dancers, and bursting sequined halters until dawn. The young'uns of Santa Cruz take a pause to down cheap vodka-colas in the plaza beforehand since drinks in the clubs run 800ptas/€4.80. Entrance is free. **Camel Bar,** Av. Anaga, 41, is a virtual shrine to the phallic-nosed mascot of the tobacco giant, sporting old posters and advertisements urging readers to smoke. Trendy music and a long bar keep the local crowd dancing (open daily 9pm-5am.) The party at disco-bar **Noctua Anaga,** Av. Anaga, 35, spills out to its streetside tables until dawn.-(☎922 29 04 61. Open 10am-5am)

LOS CRISTIANOS AND PLAYA DE LAS AMÉRICAS

The white sand on man-made Playa de las Américas is the first clue of what awaits a visitor to Tenerife's main southern attractions: just about everything has a whiff of the fake, from the frat-boy nightlife to the fast food chains. The sand here was brought in from the Sahara desert to complement the nearby gray-sand Los Cristianos beach. Developed into full-fledged resorts in the 1960s and 70s, these two adjacent towns probably have more sub-par five-star hotels than local residents. Their beaches are hardly the equals of Fuerteventura's, but Las Américas and Los Cristianos can serve as a base for exploring other shores in the south, including **Playa del Médano,** one of Tenerife's best and a windsurfing hot-spot. Most importantly, ferries to La Gomera depart from Los Cristianos.

TRANSPORTATION. Although Playa de las Américas and Los Cristianos are actually two separate towns and municipalities (accounting for the high taxi fare between the two, about 600ptas/€3.60), they are considered one by tourists and tourist offices alike. The pedestrian **Paseo Marítima** connects Los Cristianos to its northern neighbor, Playa de las Américas. **Ferries** leave from the port in Los Cristianos, connecting Tenerife to the western islands. **Fred Olson** (☎922 79 05 56) and **Trasmediterránea** (☎902 45 46 45) run ferries to **Santa Cruz** (on La Palma), **San Sebastián** (on Gomera), and **Valverde** (on El Hierro). For more info, see **Inter-Island Transport,** p. 503. **Buses** run from the stops along Av. Juan Carlos in Los Cristianos to **Puerto de la Cruz** (#343, 4 per day 9am-5:45pm, 1395ptas/€8.40), the **Reina Sofía airport** (#487, every hr. 7:20am-9:20pm, 300ptas/€1.80), and **Santa Cruz** (#110, 111; every 30min. 6am-10pm, then 11:15pm, 12:30, and 4:30am; 900ptas/€5.40). For Playa de las Américas, the bus stops all along Av. Puig Lluvina. Buses #342, 487, 467, 470, 442, 487, and 441 all link Playa de las Américas and Los Cristianos, stopping frequently along the shore. Buses from Santa Cruz run directly from Los Cristianos along the outer highway to Costa Adeje's bus station. Get off at Los Cristianos and connect with one of the above buses to get to Pl. Américas.

PRACTICAL INFORMATION. To reach the **tourist office** from Los Cristianos' bus stop, walk downhill on Av. Juan Carlos and take a right onto Av. de Amsterdam; it's on your left in the Centro Cultural (☎922 75 71 37. Open M-F 9am-4pm.) Services include: **banks,** centered around Pl. Carmen and Av. General Franco in Los Cristianos (most open M-F 9am-1pm, 4pm-7pm.); **police,** on Av. Valle Menéndez, in Los Cristianos (☎922 79 78 50); **internet access** at **Atlantis Net,** C. General Franco, 36. (☎922 75 37 17. 600ptas/€3.60 for 30min., 1000ptas/€6 per hr.); and the **post office** on C. Sabandenos, just follow yellow *correos* signs from Pl. Carmen. (☎922 79 10 56. Open M-F 8:30am-2:30pm, Sa 9:30am-1pm.) **Postal code:** 38650.

ACCOMMODATIONS AND FOOD. Pl. Américas is full of resort hotels, so unless you're planning to splurge, stick to C. General Franco or C. Paloma in Los Cristianos. Although there are quite a few *pensiones*, they are almost always full, so be sure to call ahead. An option is **Pensión La Playa,** C. Paloma, 9. From Av. General Franco, turn uphill onto C. Estocolmo; C. Paloma is your first left. The basic rooms with aqua decor and lively plant life can be a squeeze. (☎922 79 22 64. Communal bathrooms. Singles 3000ptas/€18; doubles 4000ptas/€24.) **Pensión Corisa,** C. Amalia Alayón, 18. From Pl. Carmen, bear right onto Amalia Alayón, parallel to C. General Franco; across from the gas station. The neat furniture forges comfort out of small rooms yet common baths are spotless and the price is right. (☎922 79 07 92. Singles 2500ptas/€15; doubles 4000ptas/€24.) **Food** in both towns caters to international taste buds and big budgets but is marginally better in Los Cristianos, away from the beachfront pizzerias. For groceries, go to **Supermercado Carolina,** C. General Franco, 8. (☎922 79 30 69. Open M-Sa 8am-8:30pm. V.)

BEACHES AND NIGHTLIFE. Playa de las Américas makes the most postcard appearances, but **Playa Vistas** in Los Cristianos is less crowded. Either way, you will tan. Lining each beach are kiosks and parked info-vans, full of fliers for **water sports** and **scuba diving.** For **fishing,** booths on the far end of Los Cristianos beach offer daily excursions for 2000ptas/€12. **Water Sports & Charters** (☎922 71 40 34; booking office open 10am-4:30pm) has a monopoly over water sports centers on several beaches around Playa de las Américas; parasailing is 3500ptas/€21 for 10min. If the tourists on the beach aren't enough for you, **Odyssey 3** leaves Los Cristianos for multilingual whale-watching. (☎922 75 24 16. Cruises leave 10:30am, 12:30, and 2:45pm; 1800ptas/€10.85.) Nightlife centers on Playa Américas, where a collage of fluorescent lights, bikini contests, and beer averaging 400ptas/€2.40 awaits—plenty of two-story discos illuminated by flashing neon signs hawk 2-for-1 drink promotions to thirsty foreigners. The **Verónicas** complex offers an imitation Ministry of Sound and your standard Shamrock Pub. Down C. Rafael Puig Lluvina to the Hotel Conquistador you can find **Metrópolis**, a classier local crowd grooving Spanish pop hits spiced with early-morning salsa spells.

PUERTO DE LA CRUZ

Filled with a wholesome energy in its colorful streets, this port town (pop. 25,000) is one of the most enjoyable urban spots in the islands. Once a capital of the wine trade and an important 17th-century connection to the New World, Puerto de la Cruz draws an assorted mix of sailors and visitors: the steep streets are filled with African vendors, Spanish fishermen, tanned Europeans, and some unusually large lizards. Puerto de la Cruz serves as a base for exploring the Orotava region and Teide National Park, as frequent buses depart from this western destination.

ORIENTATION AND PRACTICAL INFORMATION. Buses, C. Pozo, 1 (☎922 38 18 07), leave for: **El Teide** (#348; 1½hr., 9:15am; 625ptas/€3.75); **La Orotava** (#350, 352, 345, 101, 353; 20-30min.; every 30min. 6:30am-8:30pm, every hr. 9:30pm-1:10am; 150ptas/€0.90); **Playa de las Américas** (#343; 1hr., 4 per day 9am-5:35pm, 1550ptas/€9.30); and **Santa Cruz** (#101, 102, and 103; 1hr.-2hr.; every 30min. 6:15am-9:40pm, then 11pm, 12:45, 3:15, and 4:45am; 550ptas/€3.30). Puerto de la Cruz expands from Playa San Telmo past **Pl. del Charco,** ultimately reaching the sands of Playa Jardín. To get to Pl. Charco from the bus station, turn right on C. Pozo as you exit, continue onto C. Dr. Ingram, and turn left on C. Blanco (10min.). The **tourist office** sits on Pl. Europa. From Pl. Charco, head toward the port on C. Blanco, and turn right on C. Santo Domingo; the office is on the left at the far end of the plaza. (☎922 38 60 00. Open July-Sept. M-F 9am-7pm, Sa 9am-noon; Oct.-June M-F 9am-8pm, Sa 9am-1pm.) Services include: **emergency** ☎112; **police,** on Pl. Europa (☎922 37 84 48); and a **post office,** C. Pozo, 14, across from the bus station. (☎922 38 58 02. Open M-F 8:30am-2:30pm, Sa 9:30am-1pm.) **Postal code:** 38400.

ACCOMMODATIONS AND FOOD. *Pensiones* are comfortable and plush in Puerto de la Cruz—reserve in advance if you don't want to pay hotel prices. The tourist office has an extensive list of accommodations. An excellent option is **Pensión los Geranios,** C. Lomo, 14. From Pl. Charco, turn left on C. Felipe, right on C. Pérez Zamora, and left on C. Lomo. (☎922 38 28 10. Doubles, 3800ptas/€22.85.) Plenty of cafés line the Pl. del Charco. For something a little more refined, try **La Rosa de Bari,** C. Lomo, 23, featuring fresh pastas and other Italian fare. (☎922 36 85 23. Entrées 600-1500ptas/€3.60-9. Open Tu-Su 12:30-3pm and 6:30-11pm.)

SIGHTS AND ENTERTAINMENT. The parade of flowers, tourists, bathing suits and palm trees makes Puerta de la Cruz a sight in itself. The small **Museo Arqueológico,** C. Lomo, 9, features exhibits on the processes and ceremonies used [illegible] (☎922 37 14 65. Open Tu-Sa 10am-1pm and 5-9pm, Su 10am-1pm. 150ptas/€0.90, students 75ptas/€0.45.) Far more interesting are the city's **botanical gardens,** C. Retama, 2. To reach them, climb from Playa San Telmo on C. de la Hoya and continue onto C. Calzada Martiánez until you reach Av. del Marqués Villanueva del Prado. Follow the road past the Canary Centre; the gardens are on your left. Buses to Orotava and Santa Cruz pass by as well. (☎/fax 922 38 35 72. Open M-Su Apr.-Sept. 9am-7pm, Oct.-Mar. 9am-6pm. Free.) Although great beaches are lacking, the amusing **Lago Martiánez,** a nature-based water park, fills the tanning and swimming voids. Nearby, **Playa Jardín** is preferable to the smaller **Playa Martiánez.**

Party-primed locals and tourists mix in Puerto's nightlife. **Color Café,** building Rincón del Puerto 1st floor, Plaza del Charco, is a Cuban-themed bar overlooking the plaza featuring cool jazz. (☎629 70 90 81. Open M-Su 7:30 until late. Drinks 400-600ptas/€2.40-3.60.) Although high-season covers the winter months, tourists are also drawn to the **Fiestas de Julio,** two weeks of live performances and festive meals centered around July 16th's **Fiesta de la Virgen del Carmen,** in which an image of the fisherman's saint is paraded through town and out into the ocean.

DAYTRIP FROM PUERTO DE LA CRUZ

LA OROTAVA

Buses #350, 101, and 353 run from Puerto de la Cruz (30min.; at least every 30min. 6:30am-8:30pm, every hr. 9pm-1:10am; 145ptas/€0.85).

Named after the lush valley that spreads out below its balconies, the small town of La Orotava warrants a daytrip from Puerto de la Cruz. Nobility resided here in the 17th and 18th centuries, leaving a number of elegant squares, streets, and churches renowned for their façades. If you intend to visit the sights, plan a weekday for the jaunt—most establishments here are closed on weekends.

The tourist office map cites over 15 sights; though it would take forever to see them all, the following walking-tour should take two hours. From the tourist office, turn left down C. Tomás Zerolo to find **Iglesia de Santo Domingo,** whose chapel houses several notable paintings and a museum examining handicrafts of Spain and Latin America. (Church open during mass. Free. Iberoamerican Museum, C. Tomás Zerolo, 34. ☎922 32 17 46. Open M-F 9:30am-6pm, Sa 9am-2pm. 350ptas/€2.10.) Next up, **Iglesia de la Concepción,** off C. Cologón, is a National Artistic Monument and perhaps the Canaries' most graceful Baroque building. Rebuilt in the late 18th century after earthquakes ravaged it, the church has a marble dome over the altar and its myriad works. Especially delicate is Angelo Olivari's rendition of the Concepción. Check out the church's collection of jewels brought over from the Americas. (Open M-Sa 9am-1pm and 4-8pm. Free.) From the church, go uphill on C. Tomás Pérez and right on C. Carrera to see the neo-classical **Palacio Municipal** and the **Pl. del Ayuntamiento.** The cobblestones in the plaza are the result of regal egotism—Alfonso XIII ordered the streets paved before he visited. (Open 9am-2pm. Free.) Just up C. Tomás Perez, the sensory explosion of **Hijuela del Botánico,** behind iron gates, offers celestial walkways through manicured displays of tropical flora. (Open M-F 8am-2pm. Free.) From the bus station, head downhill on C. Tejar and take a left onto C. Calvario to the **tourist office,** C. Carrera del Escultor Estévez, 2. (☎922 32 30 41. Open M-F 10am-6pm).

EL TEIDE NATIONAL PARK

Towering 3718m over Tenerife, Spain's highest peak presides over a vast, unspoiled wilderness. El Teide itself forms the northern ridge of a much larger volcano that erupted millions of years ago; the remaining 17km-wide crater, the **Caldera,** only hints at the size of the explosion. Once gracing the Spanish 1000ptas note, the Spanish park service likes to say that the peak allows us to ponder "our miserly insignificance." El Teide shadows peaceful fields of the most vibrant wildflower fields on earth. Though dormant, the area's volcanic activity has not yet ceased. In 1798, during the last major eruption, lava seeped down the slopes of **Pico Viejo** (3102m), creating a stunning, 800m crater. **Las Cañadas,** comprised of collapsed craters, is another extra-terrestrial product of the sinking process. Among the 400 species that inhabit the diverse terrain, watch out for the large **Lagarto Tizón,** a stone-camouflaged lizard, lurking in the park.

The park is accessible by **bus** from Puerto de La Cruz. Only one bus a day, #348, departs from the station at 9:15am and leaves El Teide at 4pm (1½hr., 1800ptas/€10.80). Renting a **car** provides flexibility and allows exploration of the wildly different but equally beautiful views of the eastern (from Puerto de la Cruz) and western (from Los Cristianos) access roads. Bus #348 stops first at the **visitors center.** (☎922 29 01 29. Open 9am-4:15pm daily.) The bus then continues to the **cable car,** which climbs the final 1000m, ending next to Teide's peak. (Daily 9am-5pm; 3000ptas/€18, children 1800ptas/€10.80). It stops last at the **Parador,** which has free brochures, maps, and a restaurant but is less helpful than the visitors center.

By calling the national park information service in Santa Cruz (☎922 29 01 29 or 29 01 83. Open M-F 9am-2pm) you can reserve a spot on one of the **free guided hikes** that depart daily or inquire about the most scenic routes for the day. Nine **unguided hikes** allow for independent pacing and meandering. The Parador occupies an idyllic setting next to the emblematic **Roques de García** (2140m), rock chimneys and remnants of volcanic eruptions that face their creators, Mt. Teide and Pico Viejo. An enjoyable three-hour hike circles the huge formations of **Guajara's** peak and leaves plenty of time to spare for bus-riders. Hikes to the Teide's peak require strong legs and an ample start to complete in a day, though it is possible. Alternatively, walkers spend the night at **Refugio Altavista,** past the Montaña Blanca, and hike the last hour up to mountain to catch the early-morning sunrise. To reserve a spot contact the office in Santa Cruz. (☎922 23 98 11. Open M-F 9am-2pm, 2000ptas/€12 per person.) The summit is difficult to reach in the winter, especially as the refuge is only open from March to October.

FUERTEVENTURA

Named Fuerteventura after the "strong winds" that whip along the western coast, the second largest island in the archipelago is not a major budget destination in the Canaries. Conqueror Jean de Béthencourt established a permanent base here in the 15th century, but Fuerteventura has had a relatively quiet history, save the occasional pirate raid. Today Europeans fly in here by the jumbo-jet so those in search of touristless peace will have to escape to small towns in the mountains.

PUERTO DEL ROSARIO

Until 1957, Fuerteventura's whitewashed capital was known as Puerto de Cabras (Goats' Harbor) for the abundance of, you guessed it, billy-goats-gruff. Although goats may still outnumber citizens in the island's inner *pueblos*, Puerto del Rosario (pop. 17,000) has continued to grow as an important port and fishing center since its founding in the 18th century. Lined with cement houses, the modest neighborhoods border on bleak, and most visitors do little more than pass through the city on their way to fairer sands—it makes an excellent base for daytripping.

TRANSPORTATION. Trasmediterránea (☎928 85 00 95) and **Naviera Armas** (☎928 85 15 42) run ferries to and from Las Palmas; for more information, see **Inter-Island Transport,** p. 500. **Tiadhe buses** (☎928 85 21 66) run to: **airport** (#3, 10; 20min.; 13 per day 7am-8pm; 140ptas/€0.85); **Bentacuria** (#2, 1hr., M-Sa 11am and 2:30pm, 430ptas/€2.60); (#6, 45min., every 30min. 7am-10pm, 370ptas/€2.20); and **Morro Jable** (#1, 10; 2hr.; M-Sa 8 per day 7am-7pm, Su 4 per day; 1100ptas/€6.60). For a **taxi,** dial ☎928 85 00 59. For **car rental, Orlando** has offices at the airport (☎928 86 90 [illegible] in Corralejo (☎928 53 50 34). Cars begin at 4400ptas/€27 per day, including insurance. You must be 21 to rent.

ORIENTATION AND PRACTICAL INFORMATION. Everything in Puerto del Rosario is within easy walking distance. **C. León y Castillo** is the main thoroughfare, running downhill to the port and ferry station. **Av. Primero de Mayo,** which runs perpendicular to C. León y Castillo and parallel to the water, is the town's commercial drag. The **tourist office,** Av. Constitución, 5, down the street from the bus station and 2 blocks from Av. Primero de Mayo, has a handy map of Fuerteventura's major towns. (☎928 53 08 44. Open M-F 8am-2pm.) **Banks** are centered on Av. Primero de Mayo. In an **emergency,** dial ☎112 or the **police,** C. 23 de Mayo, 16 (☎928 85 05 03). Fuerteventura's main **hospital** is on Ctra. Aeropuerto (☎928 86 20 00). A **pharmacy** is on Av. Primero de Mayo, 43. (☎928 53 17 21. Open M-F 9am-1pm and 5-7pm.) A back room of the S.O.S. market has 2 brand new computers offering **Internet** access (200ptas/€1.20 per 30min.). The office is off Av. Primero de Mayo on C. el Rosario. The **post office** can be found at C. Primero de Mayo, 58. (☎928 85 04 12. Open M-F 8:30am-8:30pm, Sa 9:30am-1pm.) **Postal code:** 35600.

ACCOMMODATIONS AND FOOD. Unprepared budget travelers may find themselves stuck in Puerto del Rosario for a night or two until accommodations in other, more scenic towns open up. Singles everywhere are in short, short supply. The majority of the budget accommodations are at the end of C. León y Castillo and its continuation past the port, C. Almirante Lallermand. **Hostal Tamasite,** C. León y Castillo, 9, has clean, pretty rooms right on the waterfront. Though few have a view, they come complete with TVs and phones. (☎928 85 02 80. Singles 3300ptas/€20; doubles 5600ptas/€34.) At the foot of C. León y Castillo, near the water, **Hostal Roquemar** has spotless, comfortable rooms with TVs, private baths and telephones. (Av. Marítima, ☎928 85 03 59. Singles 5000ptas/€30, with balcony 5500ptas/€33; doubles 6000ptas/€36.) For spartan rooms with communal bathrooms, try **Pensión Macario,** C. Almirante Fontán Lobe, 12 a left off C. Almirante Lallermand before C. Juan XXIII. (☎928 85 11 97. Reserve well in advance. Singles 3500ptas/€21; doubles 4000ptas/€24.) Food in Puerto del Rosario is equally basic; *cafeterías* are scattered along Av. Primero de Mayo and C. León y Castillo. *Tapas* recommendations from the friendly owners at **Getaría Taberna,** C. Guise, 3, are a standout in the generic *cafetería* scene. It's a bit hard to find on a small alley next to Hostal Tamasite. (Open M-Sa 10am-4pm and 7pm-1am.)

SIGHTS AND ENTERTAINMENT. Although Puerto del Rosario is an island capital and important port, it offers few diversions. Locals will even tell you that the beaches are sandboxes compared to Corralejo's. The town's only museum, **Casa Museo de Unamuno,** C. Rosario 11, displays various furnishings and books used by the exiled philosopher Miguel de Unamuno in re-created rooms from his home. (Open M-F 9am-1pm, Sa 10am-1:30pm. Free.) Although the town houses the barracks of the Spanish Foreign Legion, the nightlife is limited to little more than a beer at an average bar. For discos and dancing, head to Corralejo.

CORRALEJO

Corralejo's center is a zoo of German and English families, car rental shops, and restaurants (replete with owners hustling amblers toward their tables). To the south, however, those in search of water sports will appreciate the protected sand dunes unfolding into a crystal ocean where wind and sea are the only sounds. Daily ferries to Playa Blanca, Lanzarote, make Corralejo a necessary stop.

TRANSPORTATION. **Fred Olsen** and **Naviera Armas** run daily **ferries** to **Playa Blanca, Lanzarote** (see **Inter-Island Transport,** p. 500). To reach the center from the **port**, take C. Bral García Escamez and turn left onto C. la Milagrosa, then turn left to reach the end of **Av. General Franco** (20min.). **Tiadhe** runs **buses** from the **station** on Av. Juan Carlos Primero (☎928 85 21 66), off C. Lepanto, to **Puerto del Rosario** (#6, 45min., every 30min. 7am-10pm, 370ptas/€2.20). From the bus station next to the post office, follow the length of C. Lepanto towards the water to the **car rental** shops on Av. General Franco. Support local establishments by renting from **Autos Hernández**, Av. General Franco, 7. (☎928 53 56 60; fax 86 70 45. Open 9am-2pm, 5pm-7pm. Min. age 21. Unlimited mileage. Prices start at 4500ptas/€27.) For a **taxi,** call ☎928 86 61 08 or hail one next to Los Corales Supermercado.

ORIENTATION AND PRACTICAL INFORMATION. All activity extends from **Avenida General Franco,** where tourists walk from the sand dunes in the south to their apartments in the north by the port. The **tourist office** is in Pl. Pública, off the end of Av. General Franco nearest the port. (☎928 86 62 35. Open in summer M-F 9am-1pm and 5-7pm; winter M-F 9am-1pm and 4-7pm, Sa 9am-noon). For a little beach reading, there is **Corralejo Book Swap Shop,** C. Crucero Balear, off Av. General Franco (open M-Sa 9am-1pm and 6-9pm, Su & holidays 9am-1pm). Services include: **emergency,** ☎112; **police,** Po. Atlántico (☎928 86 61 07), near the intersection with Av. General Franco; **hospital,** at Av. General Franco, 13 (☎928 53 64 32;

open M-Sa 9am-8:30pm, Su 10am-1pm.; **pharmacy,** at Av. General Franco, 46. (☎928 86 60 20; open M-F 9am-1:30pm, 5-9pm.); **internet access** at **Internet Saloon,** C. Juan Sebastián Elcano, 22, left off C. Lepanto (☎928 53 59 56. 400ptas/€2.40 per 30min. Open M-Sa 9am-1pm and 5-8pm.); and the **post office,** C. Isaac Peral (☎928 53 50 55; open M-F 8:30am-2:30pm, Sa 9:30am-1pm.). **Postal code:** 35660.

ACCOMMODATIONS AND FOOD. Apartments and hotels line the beach, but budget accommodations are rare. Unless you reserve ahead, you might find yourself back in Puerto del Rosario for the night. With a convenient beachfront location and plenty of quiet, **Hotel Corralejo**, C. la Marina, 1, is the choice for simple rooms with ocean views. (☎/fax 928 53 52 46. Singles 4180ptas/€25; doubles 5225ptas/€31; triples 6270ptas/€38.) The English-speaking crew at **Hostal Manhattan,** C. Gravina, 24, a left off Av. General Franco when heading toward the port, offers plain, cool rooms, all with bath. (☎928 86 66 43. Singles 3500ptas/€21; doubles 6000ptas/€36. MC/V.) Unfortunately, **food** in Corralejo is not much better than anywhere else on the islands. Restaurants line Av. General Franco and breakfast deals abound. Food spots on the waterfront are the cheapest; keep an eye out for *menús del día*. A retreat from Av. General Franco's boundless *cafeterías* will land you with reasonably priced *pescado* (1200ptas/€7.20) and large portions of two-person specials at **Avenida,** C. Pizarro. (☎928 86 71 45. Open M-Sa 10:30am-11pm). For standard supplies, try **Los Corales Supermarket,** Av. General Franco, 40 (☎928 86 70 43; open M-Sa 9am-9:30pm, Su 2-9pm).

CANARY ISLANDS

ENTERTAINMENT AND BEACHES. The Fiestas del Carmen, beginning every July 16 and lasting for two weeks, makes for a particularly lively visit. During the festival such decidedly un-holy events as volleyball competitions and outdoor dances help celebrate the town's patron saint before she is led on a watery parade through the port. Nightlife in Corralejo is a parade of tipsy tourists and leering locals. Bars tend toward the cliché with surf or pub themes; most of them can be found along Av. General Franco and in the connecting shopping centers. The Venue, in the Caleta Dorada Complex, has live music, while the Irish Pub rings only with the husky laughter of a crowd red-faced with cheap beer (300ptas/€1.80).

Like nearby Morro Jable, Corralejo offers little beyond the beach. The **Parque Natural de Corralejo y Lobos** contains protected and rugged sand dunes for soaking up the sun's rays. Although nudists flop all over the place, the more buttoned-up are still welcome. Adventure companies compete for business along Av. General Franco, catering to all athletic tastes and abilities. **Dive Centre,** C. Nuestra Señora del Pino, 36, (☎928 53 59 06) offers dive trips, lessons, and equipment rental. **Celia Cruz** rigs daily trips on glass-bottomed catamarans. (☎610 86 48 91. 1300-5000ptas/€7.50-9 per person.) **Ventura Surf,** in the Apartamentos Hoplaco complex on Av. General Franco, rents windsurfing equipment (3900ptas/€23 per day) and offers a [illegible] those wanting extra assistance. (☎928 86 62 95. Open daily 10am-6pm.)

BETANCURIA

An escape from the touristed coast line, Fuerteventura's amber interior reveals rocky villages, fallen windmills, and small farms with owners as tough as their goats. Betancuria, named by the self-effacing Jean de Béthencourt, has been carved out of the side of a dormant volcano; shady palms and pockets of lush vegetation rise out of the dry, rocky mountains like a Jericho of sorts. From the bus stop it's an easy walk to the central **Iglesia de Santa María.** Betancuria's tranquil state offers a restful night's stay (especially if you miss the only bus back to Puerto Rosario). **Vicente Ruiz Méndez,** Roberto Trondán, 2, on the opposite side from the Museo Arquelógico, is a sometimes-pension that might be able to put you up if you're stranded in town. It's run by a charming civil war veteran whose wife was supposedly the first female mayor of any town in Spain (☎928 97 80 95; 2000ptas/€12). Only two **buses** (#2, 45min., 11am and 2:30pm, 410ptas/€2.45) run M-Sa from Puerto del Rosario, and **only one bus runs back** (12:30pm) so plan your trip wisely.

MORRO JABLE

Although rumored to be the site of buried German treasure, the only foreign gold in Morro Jable (pop. 6500) dangles from the wrists of the peninsula's many tourists; heavenly white sand and turquoise water have turned this former fishing village into a choice destination for pasty-fleshed Europeans in search of vitamin D.

TRANSPORTATION. Though there is no designated bus station in town, **Tiadhe** buses (☎928 85 21 66) stop at the Centro Commercial de Jandía before terminating on C. Gambuesas (across from the post office) in pueblo Morro Jable. **Buses** run to **Costa Calma** (#5, 1hr., 11 per day 8:30am-9pm, 400-500ptas/€2.40-3) and **Puerto del Rosario** (#1, 2hr., 8 per day 6am-7pm, 1100ptas/€6.60). **Taxis** (☎928 54 12 57) stand at the port in Morro Jable. A ride to Jandía costs 350ptas/€2.10. **Orlando,** in Apartamentos El Matorral, rents cars; as the peninsula's rough dunes are best navigable with four-wheel-drive vehicles, it is worth spending those extra *pesetas.* (☎928 54 04 09. Min. age 21. Rates start at 5197ptas/€31 per day. AmEx/V.)

ORIENTATION AND PRACTICAL INFORMATION. Morro Jable spreads along the beach, with local life to one side and resorts to the other, all the way to Jandía. **Av. Jandía,** which becomes **Av. del Saladar,** connects the two sides. Most hotels and restaurants line these two streets. Most of the town's roads inevitably lead to the beach. The **tourist office**, Av. Saladar, is on the Centro de Comercial de Jandía. (☎928 54 07 76. Open M-F 9am-3:30pm.) Services include: **emergency,** ☎112; the **police,** C. Hibisco, 1 (☎928 54 10 22); **pharmacy,** C. Senador Cabrera, 23 (☎928 54 10 12. Open M-F 9am-1pm, 5-7pm. Sa until 1pm.); the **Centro Médico Jandía,** at the Centro Comercial de Jandía. (☎928 54 15 43. Open 24hr.); internet access at **Internet Café Jandía,** Centro Comercial Jandía, location 14a (Open M, T, Th, F 10am-12pm, 2pm-9pm. W, Sa, Su 6pm-9pm. 500ptas/€3.00 per 30min.); and the **post office** on the corner of C. Buenavista and C. Gambuesa. (☎928 54 03 73. Open M-F 8:30am-2:30pm, Sa 9:30am-1pm.) **Postal code**: 35625.

ACCOMMODATIONS AND FOOD. Budget accommodations are to be found in Morro Jable, clustering around C. Maxorata and C. Senador Velázquez Cabrera; Jandía's aliens are from a different universe than the budget traveler, and their visits are more of an out-of-pocket experience. It is imperative that you call ahead for reservations; many unprepared travelers find themselves catching a bus to Puerto del Rosario for the night. **Hostal Maxorata,** C. Maxorata, 31, has fresh and airy double rooms, some with views of the beach. (☎928 54 10 87. 3000ptas/€18; with bath 4000ptas/€24.) Jandía's **restaurants** are fit with the roller-suitcase crowd—Italian bistros, dime-a-dozen seafood joints, and German *konfiterias* line the beach. For a calm seaside escape, try Morro Jable's best near the port. **Av. del Mar,** Av. del Mar, 1, at the end of the string of restaurants, offers fresh fish (900-1500ptas/€5.40-9) and a fabulous patio. (☎928 84 43 35. Open daily 10:30-11pm.)

ENTERTAINMENT AND BEACHES. With neither museums nor cultural centers, Morro Jable's only distraction from the beach is the **Centro Comercial de Jandía,** located on Av. Saladar; it is here that the town's sparse **nightlife** takes place, concentrated in a few raucous bars selling imported beers (500ptas/€3) to soothe the sunburn. Morro Jable's **beaches** are lined with bodies in various states of undress from early morning to late night. Blessed with some of the islands' calmest waters and lushest sea life, Morro Jable also offers excellent opportunities to practice **water sports.** The stiff breeze off the peninsula's southern tip justify the innumerable **windsurfing** schools who set up camp on the beach (the coast hosted last year's world freestyle competition in July). **Barakuda Club,** Av. Saladar, offers **scuba diving** and equipment rental (☎928 54 14 18. Dives Su-F at 9:30am and 2:30pm. 5000ptas/€30 per dive; 4000ptas/€24 with your own equipment.)

LANZAROTE

Having avoided constructions of the high-rises and resorts that mar its western neighbors, Lanzarote is only beginning to blemish a landscape that has changed little over the last few decades. The Spanish called this isle the *"isla tranquila"* because of its peaceful nature, and even today the name still fits. Ferry companies make it rather difficult to access the island, but Lanzarote definitely merits a visit.

ARRECIFE

Meaning "rocky reef," Arrecife, Lanzarote's hamlet capital (pop. 30,000), resides on the island's eastern coast, fringed with blackened lava and yellow sands. Home to the archipelago's largest fishing fleet, the harbor is packed with peeling boats. Tourism remains relatively subdued here and the city has little to offer beyond an art museum and providing an excellent base for exploration of Lanzarote.

TRANSPORTATION. Lanzarote Airport serves the other islands and mainland Spain. Bus #4 runs from the airport to Arrecife (20min., every 30min. 8:20am-7:20pm, 125ptas/€0.75), stopping at the end of Av. Fred Olsen; follow it along the water to Av. Gen. Franco. The **bus station** (☎928 81 15 22), C. Vía Medular, is open daily 8am-10pm. To get from there to the center of town, turn left on C. Vía Medular and right on C. León y Castillo. A more accessible stop is in front of Playa Reducto on Av. Fred Olsen, a continuation of Av. Gen. Franco. Buses run to: **Costa Teguise** (#1, every 20min. 6:40am-11:40pm, 145ptas/€0.85); **Maguez** (#7, 4 per day 11:45am-8pm, 330ptas/€1.97); **Playa Blanca** (#6, 6 per day 6am-8:15pm, 435ptas/€2.60); **Puerto del Carmen** (#2, 40min., every 20min. 6:20am-11:20pm, 130ptas/€0.77); and **Teguise** (#7, 9, and 10; 6 per day 7:40am-8pm; 130ptas/€0.77). **Naviera Armas** (☎928 82 49 30) and **Trasmediterránea** (☎928 81 10 19) run frequent **ferries** to **Las Palmas** (on Gran Canaria) and less-frequent service to **Santa Cruz de Tenerife.** Trips to **Corralejo** or **Puerto Rosario** (on Fuerteventura) depart from **Playa Blanca**; **Fred Olsen** runs a free bus there from Puerto del Carmen at 9am and 5pm. For more info, see **Transportation,** p. 500. For **car rental,** try **Auto Timanfaya,** C. Luis Morote, 28. (☎928 81 30 23. Cars begin from 3500ptas/€21 per day. Minimum age of 21 years old or at least 3 years of driving experience. Open M-F 9am-2pm and 5-8pm, Sa 9:30am-2pm.) **Taxis** (☎928 80 31 04**)** can be found at each end of Av. León Castillo.

CANARY ISLANDS

ORIENTATION AND PRACTICAL INFORMATION. Arrecife is easy to navigate on foot. **Av. Generalísimo Franco** hugs the coast while and its numerous continuations spread from the **port** to the west and the Playa Reducto to the east. The **tourist office** (☎/fax 928 81 18 60. Open M-F 8am-2pm, Sa 9am-2pm.) is on the avenue, near its intersection with **Av. de León Castillo,** the main pedestrian thoroughfare, which runs perpendicular to the ocean. **Banks** lining Av. de León Castillo will **exchange currency** and are home to many 24hr. **ATMs.** In an **emergency,** call ☎112 or dial the **police,** Av. Coll, 5 (☎928 80 16 36), along the water towards the Castillo de San José. In case of an emergency dial **medical emergencies** ☎061 or contact the **Red Cross** (☎928 81 22 22). There is a **pharmacy** on Av. de León Castillo, 41. (☎928 81 10 72. Open M-F 9am-1pm, 5pm-8pm.) Check your email at **CyberMouse Servi Computer**, C. Coronel Bens, 14; take a left off Av. Generalísimo Franco, coming from Ave. de León Castillo. (☎928 80 50 36. 300ptas/€1.80 per hr. in the morning 450ptas/€2.70 per hr. after noon. Open M-Su 10am-2pm, 4:30pm-10pm.) Send letters home at the **post office** on Av. Generalísimo Franco, 8. (☎928 80 06 73. Open M-F 8:30am-8:30pm, Sa 9:30am-1pm.) **Postal code:** 35500.

ACCOMMODATIONS AND FOOD. While the other towns in Lanzarote often have only one *pensión*, Arrecife has a few more options. A number of accommodations occupy the area at the pedestrian end of Ave. de León Castillo nearest the bus station. The tourist office has a list of accommodations with phone numbers and addresses (but no prices). **Residencia Cardona** C. 18 de Julio, 11, has a lounge flanked by monstrous rooms with pay-TV, telephones, and gleaming bathrooms. From the tourist office, turn left on Av. Generalísimo Franco and right on C. 18 de Julio. Reserve well in advance. (☎/fax 928 81 10 08. Singles 4000ptas/€24; doubles 5000ptas/€30; triples 6000ptas/€36.) **Hostal San Gines,** C. Molina, 9, has clean, ample rooms complete with private baths and pink bedspreads. From the tourist office, walk down Av. de León Castillo; when it curves right, take the first left. (☎928 81 23 51. Singles 2600ptas/€26, with bath 2450ptas/€15; doubles 4800ptas/€26.) The new supermarket, **Hiperdino,** is halfway down the pedestrian section of Av. de León Castillo (open M-F 9am-1:30pm and 5-9pm, Sa 9am-1:30pm). **Castillo de San José Restaurante and Bar,** Pto. de Naos, beneath the modern art museum outside of town, is perhaps the loveliest restaurant in the Canaries. Blended into the castle, wrapped in glass, and overlooking the harbor, the dining room has a view well worth the price. (☎928 81 23 21. *Tapas* 600-1900ptas/€3.60-11.40. Open daily 1-4pm and 8-11:30pm; bar open 11am-1am.)

SIGHTS AND ENTERTAINMENT. Arrecife is graced with the Canaries' best museum, the **Museo Internacional de Arte Contemporáneo,** to the west of town, off Av. Naos. The original building, an 18th-century fortress built by Carlos III, was intended to defend the island from pirate attacks. It was originally known as the "Fortress of Hunger," as its construction added to the famine plaguing Lanzarote. Two centuries later, its simple stonework epitomizes **César Manrique's** revitalization of the island's history and architecture. Exhibits rotate frequently, but geometric and abstract works (including those by Manrique himself) form part of the permanent collection, affixed to the fort and hanging into the restaurant below. (☎928 81 23 21. A 40min. walk; taxis from town cost 400ptas/€2.40, and are safer after dark.Open daily 11am-9pm. Free.) On Av. Generalísimo Franco, next to the tourist office, the **Castillo de San Gabriel** houses the **Museo Arqueológico.** Pottery shards and a few Guanche skeletons occupy the erstwhile fort. The castle's terrace has excellent views. (Open T-F 10am-1pm, 4-7pm, Sa 10am-1pm. 300ptas/€1.80.) **C. José Antonio** fills Arrecife's **nightlife** quota with small, rambunctious bars, restaurants, and few dance spots. On weekends, this street is a sea of bar-hopping. There's nary a nun in the packed **El Convento,** C. José Antonio Ribera, 76. The **Go Goa Bar**, C. José Antonio, 61, oozes orientalism. Next door, the same owners have tried a different theme with **Sunami,** C. José Antonio, 59.

PUERTO DEL CARMEN

Puerto del Carmen, Lanzarote's largest tourist resort, lacks both the beaches and the character of Lanzarote's small towns. Primarily British tourists flock to the hotels, packaged and lobster-tied by one of many tour companies. **Avenida de las Playas** squeezes in endless restaurants, bars, and bazaars, for sunburned ambling tourists. Aside from the strip, the yellow sands of **Playa Blanca** supply the only entertainment. Offshore reefs, however, offer some of the islands best **scuba diving.** For more information try the **Delfín Club,** Av. Playas, 38, in the Centro Aquarium, which runs four dives a day from 10am-3:30pm. (☎928 51 42 90. 5500ptas/€33 for a beginner's course; 4200ptas/€25 for certified dives needing equipment; 3100ptas/€19 if you have your own. Open M-Sa 9am-6pm.)

Bus #2 runs between Arrecife and Puerto del Carmen and stops along Av. Playas (40min., every 20min. 6:20am-11:20pm, 200ptas/€1.20). **Fred Olsen** (☎922 62 82 31) and **Naviera Armas** (☎928 51 79 12) also run buses to Playa Blanca to meet their ferry departures. The **tourist office** is at Av. las Playas near the beach. (☎928 51 33 51; fax 51 56 15. Open M-F 10am-5pm). To explore the island to its fullest, rent a car—there are good deals along Av. Playas. **Lanzauto,** Av. Playas, 19, rents from 4000ptas/€24 per day, insurance and unlimited mileage included. (☎928 51 06 18. Min. age 21. Open M-F 8:30am-1pm and 4-8pm, Sa-Su 8:30am-1pm and 6-8pm.)

CANARY ISLANDS

PARQUE NACIONAL DE TIMANFAYA

Known as **Montañas de Fuegos** (Fire Mountains), the barren landscape of Lanzarote's national park erupts with evidence of the six-year explosion that began in 1730. Resembling the surface of the moon, copper *hornitos* (mud-volcanos) and blackened folds of solidified lava carve their way into the loose soil; only lichen seems to survive in the scorching ground. The only way to view the volcanic route is by tour bus. The mandatory 30-minute tour is restrictive but extremely informative. (☎928 84 00 56. Park open daily 10am-6pm. 1000ptas/€6. Tour leaves from the entrance booth.) The magic tricks of **Islote de Hilario's** geothermal heat are the tour's highlight. Legend has it that the hermit Hilario, who lived here with his lone camel, planted a fig tree whose fruit was consumed by the underground fires. Similar spectacles are performed by park employees to demonstrate the effects of the 400°C temperatures below—a piece of brush put into the earth bursts into a ball of flames, and water poured into a metal pipe turns into fountains of steam.

The **El Diablo** restaurant that now occupies the *islote* was designed by César Manrique and constructed using only stone, metal, and glass (due to the high temperatures). Volcanic heat seeping from the earth powers the kitchen's grill. The panoramic view from the dining room is the best on the island, extending from the arid mountains to the azure sea. (☎928 84 00 57. Open daily noon-3:30pm.) Unfortunately, no buses run to the park; you'll need to rent a car.

TEGUISE

Brushing the side of the Guanapays mountains (452m), Teguise is hands-down Lanzarote's prettiest village, perfect for wandering walks. Frequent buses run daily from Arrecife to Teguise (#7, 9, and 10; 6 per day 7:40am-8pm; 120ptas/€0.70), stopping in front of the Ayuntamiento. To get to the **Plaza de la Constitución,** the center of town, face the Ayuntamiento, turn right on C. Santo Domingo, right on C. Morales Lemes, then right into the plaza, the site of the **Sunday market.** Teguise is famous for its authentic Canary Islands cuisine, and food stands flood the town on market day. **Iglesia de la Virgen de Guadalupe** resides in the corner of the plaza. The pleasant and simple exterior belies its modern interior, which is only saved from complete banality by a number of dignified icons.

Across from the church's entrance lies the 18th-century **Casa Museo Palacio Spinola,** named after a wealthy local merchant. César Manrique oversaw renovations to restore the island's official museum. Old photos of festivals and Canarian customs fill the simple rooms. (☎928 84 51 81. Open M-F 10am-5pm and Sa-Su 10am-4pm. 500ptas/€3.) The 16th-century **Castillo Santa Bárbara** offers one of the island's best views. Built by Sancho de Herrera on the side of the Guanay volcano, a series of pirate sieges led King Felipe II to order extensive renovations. Today it houses the **Museo del Emigrante Canario,** whose centerpiece is a provoking ethnographic chronicle of the island's first 12 families to emigrate. The collection, however, barely rivals the castle itself, with its views of the town and lava landscape. (About a 30min. up-hill walk. Exit Pl. Constitución on C. Herrera y Rojos, following the main highway, enter at the Castillo Santa Bárbara sign, up the mountain to the castle. (☎928 84 50 01. Open Tu-F 10am-4pm, Sa-Su 11am-3pm. 500ptas/€3.)

GOMERA

Many believe the verdant island of Gomera, with its terraced gorges and steep mountain passes, to be the most blessed of all the Canaries. Disco babies look elsewhere; La Gomera's relative isolation and small, stony beaches keep the droves of tourists at bay. Surrounded by bananas and avocado plantations, and freshened by a constant breeze, the island's main town, San Sebastián, is refreshingly provincial, unscarred by day-trippers from Tenerife. Gomera's crown jewel, however, is the spectacular Garajonay National Park, the last refuge for a species of forest that died out elsewhere millions of years ago.

SAN SEBASTIÁN DE GOMERA

Heading off to find the mythical Middle Passage to India, Christopher Columbus dropped anchor here for a few days. He gathered water from the well, prayed at the church, and fell in love with a girl before "discovering" the Americas. May your stay be as storied. These days most explorers breeze through this charming town on their way to the sandy beaches in the south. Still, as a transportation hub filled with affordable accommodations, good restaurants, and wholesome local feel, San Sebastián makes an excellent base for discovering the rest of La Gomera.

TRANSPORTATION

Buses: The main bus stop is by the ferry station on the port. Three lines start in the port and branch out across the island (675ptas/€4.05). Not all buses actually stop at the **bus station**, Vía de Ronda, on the corner of Av. Colón, (☎922 14 11 01), so the port is your best bet. Line 1 to **Valle Gran Rey** with stops in the **Parque de Garajonay** (M-Sa 10:30am, 2, 5:30, 9:30pm; Su 10:30am, 5:30pm). Line 2 to **Vallehermoso** with stops in **Agulo** and **Hermigua** (M-Sa 10:30am, 2, 5:30, 9:30pm; Su 10:30am, 5:30pm). Line 3 to **Playa Santiago** and **Alajero** (M-Sa 10:30am, 2, 5:30, 9:30pm; Su 10:30am, 5:30pm). Line 5 to the **airport** (M-Sa 8:15am, 2:45pm).

Ferries: Trasmediterránea (☎920 87 13 24) and **Fred Olson** (☎922 87 10 07) run daily ferries to **Los Cristianos** and **El Hierro.** See **Transportation,** p. 503, for details.

Car Rental: In the port terminal, **Hertz** (☎922 87 00 28). Opel Corsa with insurance 4705ptas/€28.30 per day; cheaper weekly. Min. age 21. Open M-F 9am-1pm and 4-7pm, Sa 9am-1pm. AmEx/MC/V.

ORIENTATION AND PRACTICAL INFORMATION

Navigating San Sebastián is a breeze. From the port, **Av. Fred Olsen** becomes **Av. de los Descubridores** and runs along the entire coast, intersected midway by **Calle del Medio,** the town's main drag, at Pl. Américas. To get to the plaza from the **port,** walk down the wharf and turn left on Av. Fred Olsen; the plaza is on the right (5min.). If you arrive after dark, consider taking a quick taxi into town (300ptas/€1.80), as the streets aren't clearly named and are difficult to maneuver in the dark. **Buses** stop at the port, meeting most ferries (though they're quick to leave once the ferry has arrived). If you've rented a **car,** turn right on C. Vía de Ronda and left on C. Sur to head out of town toward Valle de Gran Rey. Use extreme caution driving the island; blind corners on narrow mountain passes and wide-turning buses can be treacherous—honk that horn. **Beep.**

Tourist Office: C. Real, 4 (☎922 14 15 12; fax 14 01 51; www.gomera-island.com), behind Pl. Américas on the corner of C. Medio. Open M-Sa 9am-1pm and 4-6pm, Su 10am-1pm. The **Park Service,** C. Sur, 6 (☎922 87 01 05). Take a left onto Av. Colón from C. Medio, and follow it across the highway and the bridge, following signs to Valle Gran Rey; the office is on the right at the second bend. Open M-F 8am-3pm.

Currency Exchange: Banks line Pl. Américas. Open M-F 8:30am-2pm, Sa 8:30am-1pm. **BBVA** is on C. Medio. Open M-F 9am-1:30pm.

Laundromat: Lavandería HECU, C. Medio, 76 (☎922 14 11 80). Open M-F 8:30am-1:30pm, 5-8pm, Sa 8:30am-1:30pm. 700ptas/€4.20 wash, 700ptas/€4.20 dry.

Emergency: ☎112.

Pharmacy: Pl. Constitución, 14 (☎922 14 16 05). Next to the tourist office in Pl. Américas. Open M-F 9am-1:30pm, 5-8pm, Sa 9-1:30pm.

Hospital: Nuestra Sra. de Guadalupe (☎920 14 02 02). From Pl. Américas, go away from the port, turn right on C. Vía Ronda, left across the bridge, and take the 1st right.

Internet Access: Pedalán Informática, C. Medio, 79 (☎922 87 20 17). 750ptas/€4.50 per hr. Open M-F 9:30am-1pm and 4:30-8pm, Sa 10am-2pm.

Post Office: C. Medio, 60 (☎922 87 10 81). Open M-F 8:30am-2:30pm, Sa 9:30am-1pm. **Postal code:** 38800.

ACCOMMODATIONS

San Sebastián's budget accommodations are more budget than anywhere in the Canaries. *Pensiones* offer double rooms in old Canary-style homes; most have communal baths. For longer stays, *apartamentos* can be a bargain. *Pensión* signs hang out of windows on C. Medio. Pricier hotels reside on C. Ruiz de Padrón.

Pensión Victor-Leralita, C. Medio, 23 (☎670 51 75 65 or 81 32 01). A 250-year-old house with flower beds and vines along the outdoor patio. High wood-beamed ceilings and common baths. Ask for the room with the terrace. Noisy restaurant downstairs has tasty sandwiches (200ptas/€1.20). Singles 2500ptas/€15; doubles 3000ptas/€18.

Apartamentos San Sebastián, C. Medio, 20 (☎922 14 14 75 or 653 96 21 66; fax 922 87 13 54). Breezy and newly furnished apartments with 2 twin beds, a kitchen, TV, and living room. Reception is in the money exchange office to the right when facing the entrance. Open 8:30am-1pm and 4-8pm. Multi-day stays for 2 people 5500ptas/€33; 1 person 5000ptas/€30. One-night stays 6000ptas/€36.

Pensión Colón, C. Medio, 59 (☎/fax 922 87 02 35). Tiled floors and austere rooms surround a quiet courtyard, though the windowless rooms can get stuffy. Singles 2500ptas/€15, negotiate 2000ptas/€12 for multi-day stays; doubles 3500ptas/€21.

FOOD

San Sebastián is filled with authentic Canarian restaurants and cheap *tapas* joints. Nicer options surround Pl. Constitución, and typical bars and *mesones* line C. Ruiz de Padrón and C. Medio. For a meal on the run, try **Super Mercado Brito,** Pl. Constitución, 14. (☎922 14 18 18. Open M-Sa 8am-2pm and 4pm-10:45pm, Su 8am-1:30pm. MC/V.) Wednesdays and Saturdays a **fruit and vegetable market** fills the plaza with great deals on fresh produce. **Bar-Restaurant Cubino,** C. Virgen de Guadalupe, 2, off Pl. Constitución, serves delicious seafood and meat dishes in healthy portions to a local crowd. (☎922 86 03 83. Entrées 600-1500ptas/€3.60-9. Open W-M 9am-4pm and 7pm-midnight.) In **Gomera Garden,** C. Medio, 12, carefully prepared local fare graces candlelit tables in a romantic interior garden. (☎922 14 12 63. Entrées 700-1400ptas/€4.20-8.40. Open daily noon-4pm, 6:30-11pm.)

SIGHTS

The few sights in San Sebastián are centered on a foreigner: Columbus. C. Medio's only church (down the street from the Columbus Casino) is the **Iglesia de la Asunción,** where Columbus prayed before he left. The carved woodwork adorning the simple church is typical of Canarian architecture. Nearby, the **Casa de Colón,** C. Medio, 56, hosts a small and unimpressive exhibit on the explorer's life. Don't miss the religious icon made out of pure sugar. (Open M-F 4-7pm. Free.) The **Torre del Conde,** a small 15th-century fort, looms over the beach. In 1488, the wife of the murdered governor Hernán Peraza bolted herself inside as she watched the citizens take control of the port. Now it displays Gomeran cartography. (Open Tu-F 10am-1pm.) The tourist office is located inside **La Casa de la Aguada,** which features the well from which Columbus drew water to "baptize the Americas."

No Canarian city would be complete without a **beach.** Although there is a small patch of black sand in front of Pl. Américas, **Playa de la Cueva** has more sand, calmer waters, caved cliffs, and a view of Tenerife, if more wind. From Pl. Américas, follow Av. Fred Olsen toward the port and curve away from the wharf.

GARAJONAY NATIONAL PARK

Blanketed in thick mist and fog that produces a "horizontal rain," the Garajonay National Park sustains the last **laurisilva forest** on earth. Once ubiquitous in the Mediterranean basin, these moss-filled forests fell victim to the Ice Age millions of years ago. Hikers in Garajonay wade through lush ferns, myriad streams, and dripping plants to reach a stunning mountaintop view of the other islands. The park maintains numerous trails and **three self-guided paths,** most originating from **Contadero.** Take the bus (line #1) to Valle Gran Rey and get off at *Pajarito;* if you bear right, the trailhead is 1km up the road. Remnants of volcanic activity, **Los Roques,** line the roadside. A **car** greatly facilitates exploration of the park, but several of the best trails are reachable via bus. Strangely, the **visitors center** (☎922 80 09 93) is in **Agulo,** 9km outside of the park (open daily 9:30am-4:30pm). To get to the visitors center take bus #3 from San Sebastián (45min., 4 per day 10:30am-9:30pm) and get off at the Las Rosas stop. The **Park Service,** Cta. General de Sur, 20, in San Sebastián, has the same info. (☎922 87 01 05. Open M-F 8am-2:30pm). Either office can make the reservations required for the free guided tours (Sa 10am, meet in La Laguna Grande; tour in Spanish only), and both carry the booklet whose descriptions corresponds to the numbered wooden signs on the park trails.

VALLE GRAN REY

Green terrace farms slosh back from sandy beaches into the deep gorge of the "Valley of the Great King." The mellow shores keep a tourist population content with sunbathing, cliff-exploring, and water sports, while farmers work the peaceful valley above. Because of its beaches, Valle Gran Rey is probably the nicest place to base a stay in La Gomera, but it can be slightly expensive.

The most popular beaches are **Playa de Aruga** and **Playa las Américas,** a short walk left (when facing the beach) of Vueltas. The sandy **Playa de Calera** and **Playa de Puntilla,** which stretch left from La Playa, have calm waters. **Playa del Inglés** features more waves, nearby cliffs, and naked bodies, a 10min. walk from La Playa. With your back to the tourist office turn right, take your first right, and follow the road as it becomes dirt, to the beach. **Bus #1** runs from San Sebastián to the Valle Gran Rey's three small villages: **La Calera, La Playa,** and **Vueltas,** in that order. (2hr.; M-F 5 per day 5am-6:30pm, Su 8:30am and 3pm; 675ptas/€4.) La Caleras sits up higher in the valley, while La Playa and Vueltas cover the shores below. The sides of the triangle they form are less than a kilometer long. Street signs are nonexistent, but the area is easy to navigate—for help, stop at the **tourist office** in La Playa on C. Noria. From the La Playa bus stop, face the beach, head right on the main road and turn left on C. Noria. (☎/fax 922 80 54 58. Open in winter M-Sa 9am-1:30pm and 4-6:30pm, Su 10am-1pm; in summer M-Sa 9am-1pm and 4-6pm, Su 10am-1pm.)

Unfortunately, Valle Gran Rey's charm and scenery come at a price—expensive accommodations. The few *pensiones* only offer doubles. There are many *apartamentos* to be had if you ask around—one place to inquire is the **San José** restaurant just to the right of the tourist office in La Playa. (☎922 80 53 31. Single apartment

2500ptas/€15; double apartment 4000ptas/€24.) **Casa Bella Cabellos** on C. La Alameda in La Calera offers great views from modern, balconied apartments, as well as simple wooden doubles in an antique home. From the bus stop, head back up the valley and take the first left (almost an uphill U turn), follow the road past the San Sebastián bar, then bear right at the "do not enter sign," and follow the road up the hill until it flattens out. It's on the left. (☎922 80 51 82. 3 night minimum. Double with fridge 3500ptas/€21; 4-person with kitchen 6500ptas/€39. House rooms 2500ptas/€15.) Also in La Calera, **Pensión Parada** offers simple doubles (a bath for every 2 rooms) right next to the bus stop and a 10min. walk from the beach. (☎922 80 50 52; fax 28 13 10. 3000ptas/€18.)

EL HIERRO

The smallest of the Canary Islands, El Hierro was thought by Ptolemy to be the edge of the world. Even now, few come here to its scattered villages and jagged coastline. But those who do will be dutifully rewarded. With a horizon free of high-rise resorts but full of jagged juniper trees, El Hierro offers visitors an opportunity to explore traditional interior towns and small fishing ports.

The port town and tourist center **La Restinga** is renowned for its scuba diving. Farther north is **El Pinar,** a series of small villages encircled by pine forests. To the east emerges **Malpaso** peak (1501m), El Hierro's zenith. Unfortunately, beaches are scarce and inferior to the golden stretches on Gran Canaria and Fuerteventura. On the western coast, the sun-addicted can get their fix at **Playas del Verodal** and **Arenas Blancas.** To the northeast, the capital city of **Valverde** serves as little more than a bridge to the ferry stations and airport (see **Inter-Island Transport,** p. 500). The main **tourist office,** C. Licenciado Bueno, 1 (☎922 55 03 02), is located here. El Hierro is most accessible by ferry from Los Cristianos. **Trasmediterránea** comes from San Sebastián de Gomera (3½hr., 10:15am and 7:15pm, 3247ptas/€19.55); **Fred Olsen** sails from Los Cristianos on Tenerife (3hr., 8am, 2850ptas/€17.30).

LA PALMA

Painted green and lush by heavy rainfalls, it's easy to see the origins of La Palma's nickname, "*isla bonita.*" Although the island was an important transatlantic port during colonial days, today relatively few visitors sail into the capital of **Santa Cruz.** With colonial houses and carved balconies lining the streets, the port city retains the old world charm of its glory days. Sharp coastlines and cliffs trace the island and dissuade sunbathers, but hikers will discover a mountainous paradise, as La Palma is the world's steepest island. A volcanic crater almost 10km wide, **La Caldera de Taburiente,** commands the center. Thick Canarian pines cover the rest of the national park, and a world-renowned observatory caps the **Roque de los Muchachos.** Although the northern town of **Los Llanos de Ariadne** has a stunning **botanical garden** in the **Pueblo Parque La Palma,** the volcanos to the south offer more opportunities for hiking. The views from **Volcán Teneguía** and **San Antonio** stretch to the neighboring eastern islands. Contact the **tourist office** (☎922 41 21 06) for details on exploring the island. Ferry companies make it difficult to access La Palma, so be sure to plan ahead; see **Inter-Island Transport,** p. 500 for more details. **Trasmediterránea** offers the most options, with ferries from **San Sebastián** (3½hr., M-Sa 10:15am, 2415ptas/€14.50) and **Valverde** (14hr., Sa-W 11:45pm, 2995ptas/€18).

JUST GIVE A WHISTLE No, it's not the moped alarm and probably not that sleazy guy across the street; that piercing noise you just heard is a demonstration of **El Silbo,** the Guanche whistle language. This is not just your average whistle; "speakers" make full use of both hands to manipulate the sound. The language, which has a complete alphabet, developed in order to communicate over long distances across the island's rough terrain. During the Spanish conquest, El Silbo dwindled, and today it is only used to garner a few *pesetas* from amazed tourists.

PORTUGAL

ESCUDOS

US $1= 235.3$	100$=US $0.42
CDN $1= 154.1$	100$=CDN $0.65
EUR 1= 200.5$	100$=EUR 0.50
UK £1= 332.1$	100$=UK £0.30
IR £1= 254.6$	100$=IR £0.39
AUS $1= 121.9$	100$=AUS $0.82
NZ $1= 97.2$	100$=NZ $1.03
SAR 1= 29.1$	100$=SAR 3.44
MOR 1DH= 19.8$	100$=MOR 5.07DH
SP 1PTA= 1.2$	100$= SP 82.99PTAS

Country Code: 351. **International dialing prefix:** 00.

LIFE AND TIMES

During the 14th and 15th centuries, Portugal was one of the most powerful nations in the world, ruling a wealthy empire that stretched from America to Asia. Although the country's international prestige declined by 1580, Portuguese pride did not. During the following centuries, Portugal struggled to assert its national identity (and its uniqueness from Spain). Modern Portugal, with its stable democracy and fast-growing economy, has proved the strength of its national character.

HISTORY AND POLITICS

EARLY HISTORY. The settlement of Portugal began around 5500 BC when neolithic cultures entered from Andalucía. Other than some banging of stones, their impact was negligible, leaving the real work of settling Portugal to be done hundreds of years later. Several tribes inhabited the Iberian Peninsula during the first millennium BC, including the **Celts,** who began to settle in northern Portugal and Spanish Galicia in the 9th and 8th centuries BC, and the **Phoenicians,** who founded several fishing villages along the Algarve and ventured as far north as modern-day Lisbon. The **Greeks** and **Carthaginians** soon followed, settling the southern and western coasts. After their victory over Carthage in the Second Punic War (218-201 BC) and their defeat of the Celts in 140 BC, the **Romans** gained control of Portugal, integrating the region into their Iberian province of Lusitania. Six centuries of Roman rule, which introduced the *Pax Romana* and "latinized" Portugal's language and customs, also paved the way for Christianity.

VISIGOTHS AND ARABIAN KNIGHTS (469-1139). When the Roman Empire declined in the 3rd and 4th centuries AD, the Iberian Peninsula felt the effects. By AD 469, the **Visigoths,** a tribe of migrating Germanic people, had crossed the Pyrenees, and for the next two centuries they dominated the peninsula. In AD 711, however, the Muslims (also known as the **Moors**) invaded Iberia, toppling the Visigoth monarchy. Although these invaders centered their new kingdom of *al-Andalus* in Córdoba, smaller Muslim communities settled along Portugal's southern coast, an area they called the *al-Gharb* (now the Algarve), and after nearly four centuries of rule, the Muslims left a significant legacy of agricultural advances, architectural landmarks, and linguistic and cultural customs.

Portugal
N
Valença do Minho
Vila Nova de Cerveira
Parque Nacional da Peneda-Gerês
Rio Minho
Caminha
MINHO
Viana do Castelo
Serra do Gerês
Caldas de Gerês
Parque Natural de Montesinho
Bragança
Rio Cávado
Braga
Barcelos
TRÁS-OS-MONTES
Guimarães
COSTA VERDE
Serra do Marão
Amarante
Vila Real
Porto
DOURO LITORAL
DOURO ALTO
Espinho
Rio Douro
ATLANTIC OCEAN
Ovar
BEIRA ALTA
Aveiro
BEIRA LITORALL
Viseu
Rio Mondego
Luso
Buçaco
Guarda
Serra da Estrela
Coimbra
COSTA DA PRATA
Figueira da Foz
Conimbriga
Rio Zêzere
Serra da Gardunha
Leiria
BEIRA BAIXA
Nazaré
Batalha
Castelo Branco
São Martinho do Porto
Fátima
Alcobaça
Tomar
Ilhas Berlengas
Caldas da Rainha
Serra de Aire
Cabo Carvoeiro
Óbidos
Rio Tejo
Serra de São Mamede
Castelo de Vide
Peniche
Marvão
ESTREMADURA
Vila Franca de Xira
Santarém
Crato
Portalegre
SPAIN
Ericeira
Mafra
RIBATEJO
Sintra
Queluz
Lisbon
Cascais
Estoril
ALTO ALENTEJO
Estremoz
Elvas
Parque Nacional de Arrabida
Setúbal
Évora Monte
Évora
Cabo Espichel
Tróia Peninsula
Serra de Ossa
Sesimbra
COSTA AZUL
Sines
Santiago do Cacém
Beja
BAIXO ALENTEJO
Rio Guadiana
Rio Mira
COSTA DOURADA
Mértola
Serra de Monchique
Lagos
Silves
ALGARVE
Portimão
Albufeira
Tavira
Cabo de São Vicente
Sagres
Faro
Olhão
Vila Real de Santo António
Golfo de Cádiz

PORTUGAL

THE CHRISTIAN RECONQUISTA AND THE BIRTH OF PORTUGAL (1139-1415). Though the *Reconquista* officially began in 718, it didn't pick up steam until the 11th century, when Fernando I united Castilla and León and provided a strong base from which to reclaim territory. In 1139, **Afonso Henriques** (Afonso I), a noble from the frontier territory of Portucale (a region centered around Porto), declared independence from Castilla and León. Soon thereafter he named himself the first King of Portugal, though the papacy did not officially recognize the title until 1179.

With the help of Christian military groups like the Knights Templar, the new monarchy battled Muslim forces, capturing Lisbon in 1147. By 1249, the *Reconquista* defeated the last remnants of Muslim power with successful campaigns in the Alentejo and the Algarve. The Christian kings, headlined by **Dinis I** (Dom Dinis; 1279-1325), promoted use of the Portuguese language (instead of Spanish) and with the **Treaty of Alcañices** (1297) settled border disputes with neighboring Castilla and asserted Portugal's identity as the first unified, independent nation in Europe.

THE AGE OF DISCOVERY (1415-1580). The reign of **João I** (1385-1433), the first king of the House of Aviz, ushered in unity and prosperity never before seen in Portugal. João increased the power of the crown and in so doing established a strong base for future Portuguese expansion and economic success. The Anglo-Portuguese alliance which he secured with the **Treaty of Windsor** (1386) would come to influence Portugal's foreign policy well into the 19th century.

The 15th century was one of the greatest periods in the history of maritime travel and naval advances. Under the leadership of João's son, **Prince Henry the Navigator,** Portugal established itself as a world leader in maritime science and exploration. Portuguese adventurers captured the Moroccan city of Ceuta in 1415, discovered the Madeiras Islands in 1419, happened upon the uninhabited Azores in 1427, and began to exploit the African coast for slaves and riches a few years later.

Bartolomeu Dias changed the world forever when he rounded Africa's Cape of Good Hope in 1488. Dias opened the route to the East and paved the way for Portuguese entrance into the spice trade. The Portuguese monarchs may have turned down **Christopher Columbus,** but they funded a number of momentous voyages. In 1497, they supported **Vasco da Gama,** who led the first European naval expedition to India; successive expeditions added numerous East African and Indian colonies to Portugal's empire. Three years after da Gama's voyage, **Pedro Álvares Cabral** claimed Brazil for Portugal, and Portugal established a far-flung empire.

Portugal's monarchy reached its peak with **Manuel I The Fortunate** (1495-1521) on the throne. Known to foreigners as "the King of Gold," Manuel controlled a spectacular commercial empire. However, before the House of Aviz lost power in 1580, signs of future decline were already becoming evident, and it was not long before competition from other commercial powers took its toll.

IF GILLIGAN HAD BEEN SO LUCKY Paradise on earth? Start with water, water, everywhere. Add some volcanic eruptions, for solidity's sake. Mix in hearty, friendly, and pleasingly relaxed inhabitants. Pepper it with astounding beauty, alluring beaches, and filter out pollution, persecution, and stress. Voilà!—you have Portugal's Atlantic islands, the Azores and Madeiras, considered by many to be the world's most beautiful and most serene. While beyond the average *Let's Go* budget, these isles are integral to the national landscape.

The **Madeiras**—Madeira, Porto Santo, and Desertas—rise abruptly from the ocean off Africa's northwestern coast. Once an important stop-over for budding explorers, today their climate, colorful fauna, tropical fruits, and luxurious hotels make them a strong contender for the ideal resort spot. Immortalized in *Moby Dick,* the nine islands of the **Azores** boast rolling hills, lush fauna, cavernous lakes, glimmering seas, and friendly inhabitants. Tranquil and tempting, the Azores will leave the particularly melodramatic to muse (as one brochure claims) "Is this the home of God?"

THE HOUSES OF HABSBURG AND BRAGANÇA (1580-1807). In 1580, Habsburg King of Spain **Felipe II** asserted his claim to the Portuguese throne, and the Iberian Peninsula was briefly ruled by one monarch. For 60 years the Habsburg family dragged Portugal into several ill-fated wars, including the Spanish-Portuguese Armada's crushing loss to England in 1588. Inattentive King Felipe did not even visit Portugal until 1619—his priorities were elsewhere—and by the end of Habsburg rule, Portugal had lost much of its once vast empire.

In 1640, during a rebellion against King Felipe IV, the **House of Bragança** engineered a nationalist rebellion. After a brief struggle they assumed control, once again asserting Portuguese independence from Spain. To secure its independence, the Bragança dynasty went to great lengths to reestablish ties with England. Nearly half a century later, **João V** (1706-1750) had restored a measure of prosperity, using newly discovered Brazilian gold and diamonds to finance massive building projects, including the construction of extravagant palaces.

The momentous **Earthquake of 1755** devastated Lisbon and southern Portugal, killing over 15,000 people. Despite the damage, dictatorial minister **Marquês de Pombal** was able to rebuild Lisbon while instituting national economic reform.

NAPOLEON'S CONQUEST AND ITS AFTERMATH (1807-1910). Napoleon took control of France in 1801 and set his sights on the rest of Europe. When he reached Portugal, his army encountered little resistance. Rather than risk death, the Portuguese royal family fled to Brazil. **Dom João VI** returned to Lisbon in 1821, only to face an extremely unstable political climate. Amidst turmoil within the royal family, João's son **Pedro** declared independence for Brazil the following year, becoming the country's first ruler. More problems developed when João died in 1826. The **Constitution of 1822,** drawn up during the royal family's absence, had severely limited the power of the monarchy, and after 1826, the **War of the Two Brothers** (1826-1834) between constitutionalists (supporting Pedro, the new king of Brazil) and monarchists (supporting Miguel, Pedro's brother) reverberated through Portugal. Eight gory years later, with Miguel in exile, Pedro's daughter **Maria II** (1834-1854) ascended to the throne at a mere 15 years old. The next 75 years brought continued tensions between liberals and monarchists.

FROM THE "FIRST REPUBLIC" TO SALAZAR (1910-1974). Portugal spent the first few years of the 20th century trying to recover from the political discord of the previous century. On October 5, 1910, 20-year-old King **Manuel II** fled to England. The new government, known as the **First Republic,** earned worldwide disapproval for its expulsion of the Jesuits and other religious orders, and the conflict between the government and labor movements heightened tensions at home. Portugal's decision to enter **World War I** (even though on the side of the victorious Allies) proved economically fatal and internally divisive. The weak republic wobbled and eventually fell in a 1926 military coup. General **António Carmona** took over as leader of the provisional military government, and in the face of financial crisis, he appointed **António de Oliveira Salazar,** a prominent economics professor, his minister of finance. In 1932 Salazar became prime minister, but he soon evolved into a dictator. His *Estado Novo* (New State) granted suffrage to women, but did little else to end the country's authoritarian tradition. While Portugal's international economic standing improved, the regime laid the cost of progress squarely on the shoulders of the working class, the peasantry, and colonial subjects in Africa. A terrifying secret police (PIDE) crushed all opposition to Salazar's rule, and African rebellions were quelled in bloody battles that drained the nation's economy.

REVOLUTION AND REFORM (1974-2000). The slightly more liberal **Marcelo Caetano** dragged on the increasingly unpopular African wars after Salazar's death in 1970. By the early 70s, international disapproval of Portuguese imperialism and the army's dissatisfaction with colonial entanglements had led General António de Spinola to call for decolonization. On April 25, 1974, a left-wing military coalition calling itself the Armed Forces Movement overthrew Caetano in a quick coup. The **Revolution of the Carnations** sent Portuguese dancing into the streets; today every town in Portugal has its own Rua 25 de Abril. The Marxist-dominated armed forces established a variety of civil and political liberties and withdrew Portuguese claims on African colonies by 1975.

The socialist government nationalized several industries and appropriated large estates in the face of substantial opposition. The country's first elections in 1976 put the charismatic socialist Prime Minister **Mario Soares** into power. When a severe economic crisis exploded and foreign debt, inflation, and unemployment skyrocketed, Soares instituted "100 measures in 100 days" to shock Portugal into economic shape. Through austere reforms, he helped stimulate industrial growth. The landmark year 1986 brought Portugal into the European Community (now the European Union), ending its age-old isolation from more affluent northern Europe. Despite challenges by the newly formed Social Democratic Party (PSD), Soares won the elections in 1986, becoming the nation's first civilian president in 60 years. Forced to step down because of constitutional limitations, Soares was replaced by the Socialist former mayor of Lisbon, **Jorge Sampaio,** in 1995. During the 1990s, the Portuguese government instituted a series of programs to prepare the country for economic integration with the rest of Europe.

CURRENT EVENTS. The European Union declared that Portugal qualified for inclusion in the EU Economic and Monetary Union (EMU) in 1998, and the nation continues in its quest to catch up economically with the rest of Western Europe. The EU summit on employment and economic reform was held in Lisbon in March 2000 and identified as target goals for Portugal improvements in budget imbalances, venture capital development, and the educational system.

On the international political front, Portugal and Indonesia have agreed to cooperate over the reconstruction of East Timor, an ex-Portuguese colony which Indonesia invaded 25 years ago. Prime Minister Guterres is eager to position Portugal as an interface between the European Union and Indonesia in their mutual efforts to promote stability and democracy in East Timor.

THE ARTS

PAINTING AND SCULPTURE

The Age of Discovery (1415-1580) was an era of vast cultural exchange with Renaissance Europe and beyond. Flemish masters such as **Jan van Eyck** brought their talent to Portugal, and many Portuguese artists polished their skills in Antwerp. King Manuel's favorite, High Renaissance artist **Jorge Afonso,** created realistic portrayals of human anatomy. Afonso's best works hang at the Convento de Cristo in Tomar and Convento da Madre de Deus in Lisbon. In the late 15th century, the talented **Nuno Gonçalves** led a revival of the primitivist school.

Portuguese Baroque art featured even more diverse styles and themes. Woodcarving became extremely popular in Portugal during the Baroque period. **Joachim Machado** carved elaborate crèches in the early 1700s. On canvas, portraiture was head and shoulders above other genres. The prolific 19th-century artist **Domingos António de Sequeira** depicted historical, religious, and allegorical subjects using a technique that would later inspire French Impressionists. Porto's **António Soares dos Reis** brought Romantic sensibility to 19th-century Portuguese sculpture.

In the 20th century, Cubism, Expressionism, and Futurism trickled into Portugal despite Salazar-inspired censorship. More recently, **Maria Helena Vieira da Silva** has won international recognition for her abstract works, and the master **Carlos Botelho** has become world-renowned for his wonderful vignettes of Lisbon life.

ARCHITECTURE

Portugal's signature **Manueline** style celebrates the prosperity and imperial expansion of King Manuel I's reign (see **The Age of Discovery,** p. 528). Manueline works routinely merge Christian images and maritime motifs. Their rich and lavish ornaments reflect a hybrid of Northern Gothic, Spanish Plateresque, and Moorish influences. The Manueline style found its most elaborate expression in the church and tower at **Belém,** built to honor Vasco da Gama. Close seconds are the **Mosteiro dos Jerónimos** in Belém and the **Abadia de Santa Maria de Vitória** in Batalha.

Though few actual Moorish structures survived the Christian *Reconquista*, their style influenced later Portuguese architecture. One of Portugal's most beautiful traditions is the colorfully painted ceramic tiles which grace many walls, ceilings, and thresholds. Carved in relief by the Moors, these ornate tiles later took on flat, glazed Italian and northern European designs. Despite the fact that many of these tiles are blue, their name does not come from *azul*, the Portuguese word for blue, but rather from the Arabic word *azulayj*, meaning little stone. Numerous museums showcase collections of *azulejos*, including Lisbon's Museu do Azulejo and Coimbra's Museu Machada do Castro.

LITERATURE

ORIGINS OF PORTUGUESE LITERATURE. Portugal's literary achievements, mostly lyric poetry and realist fiction, can be traced back to the 12th century, when the lyrical aspects of Portuguese were solidified by poet-king **Dinis I.** Dinis made Portuguese the region's official language (one of the first "official" non-Latin Romance vernaculars). **Gil Vicente** (1465-1537), court poet to Manuel I, is considered Portugal's equivalent to Shakespeare in style and importance. Vicente wrote dramas (tempered with comic relief) about peasants, nature, and religion. The witty realism of his *Barcas* trilogy (1517-1519) influenced contemporaries Shakespeare and Cervantes and earned him a distinguished place in literary ranks.

PORTUGUESE LITERARY RENAISSANCE. Portuguese literature blossomed during the Renaissance, most notably in the letters of **Francisco de Sá de Miranda** (1481-1558) and the lyrics of **António Ferreira** (1528-1569). During the Age of Discovery, conquest abroad inspired both historians and poets. An explorer himself, the humanist **João de Barros** (1496-1570) penned *Décadas da Ásia*, a history of Portuguese conquest in Goa. Influenced by the *Décadas*, the writer **Luís de Camões** (1524-1580) celebrated Vasco de Gama's sea voyages to India in Portugal's greatest epic, *Os Lusíadas* (*The Lusiads*, 1572), modeled on the Latin classic, the *Aeneid* (see **Ladies' Man,** p. 557).

NINETEENTH CENTURY LITERARY MOVEMENTS. Spanish hegemony, intermittent warfare, and imperial decline conspired to make the literature of the 17th and 18th centuries somewhat less triumphant than that of past eras. The 19th century, however, saw a dramatic rebirth of Portuguese literature. Poet **João Baptista de Almeida Garrett** (1799-1854) and historian **Alexandre Herculano** (1810-1877), who were both exiled because of their liberal political views, integrated Portuguese literature with the Romantic school of fiction they encountered while in exile. A lyric poet, dramatist, politician, revolutionary, frequent exile, and legendary lover, Garrett is credited with reviving drama in Portugal. His most famous play is *Frei Luís de Sousa* (*Brother Luís de Sousa*, 1843).

Portuguese literature shifted from romantic to realist when political thinkers dominated the rise of the literary intelligentsia, the **Generation of 1870.** The most visible figure to influence this shift in the late 19th century was novelist and life-long diplomat (residing almost always outside Iberia) **José Maria Eça de Queiroz.** He conceived of a distinctly Portuguese social realism, and he documented 19th-century Portuguese society, sometimes critical of its bourgeois elements. His best works were *O Crime do Padre Amaro (The Sin of Father Amaro)* and *Os Maias (The Mayas)*.

CONTEMPORARY LITERATURE. **Fernando Pessoa** (1888-1935) was Portugal's most famed and creative writer of the late 19th and early 20th centuries. Pessoa wrote in English and Portuguese and developed four distinct styles under four different names: Pessoa, Alberto Caeiro, Ricardo Reis, and Alvaro de Campos. His semi-autobiography, *Livro do Desassossego (The Book of Disgust)* is his only prose work, posthumously compiled and today seen as a modernist classic. Other influential writers of the 20th century include **Aquilino Ribeiro,** author of *O Homem que Matou o Diabo (The Man Who Killed the Devil)*, and **José Maria Ferreira de Castro,** widely known for his realist fiction, especially his novel *A Selva (The Jungle)*.

Contemporary writers, like **Miguel Torga,** have gained international fame for their wonderfully satirical novels. **José Saramago,** winner of the 1998 Nobel Prize for literature, is perhaps Portugal's most important living writer. His work, written in the realist style and laced with irony, has achieved new acclaim in the post-Salazar era. He is best known for *Baltasar and Blimunda*, the story of lovers who escape the Inquisition in a time machine, and *The Stone Raft*, a satire about Iberia's isolation from the rest of Europe.

The end of Salazar's reign brought literary liberation. Female writers, long discouraged or censored, have come out of the woodwork with a vengeance. In **Novas Cartas Portuguesas** *(New Portuguese Letters)*, the "Three Marias" (the authors) expose the mistreatment of women in a male-dominated society. Other acclaimed post-Salazar authors include **António Lobo Antunes** and **José Cardoso Pires.** Antunes has achieved the status of Saramago but with a dramatically different style, one known for its scattered form and psychoanalytic themes. Pires' works often comment on the repression of the Salazar regime, and his novel *Balada da Praia dos Cães (Ballad of Dog's Beach)* exposes the terror of Salazar's secret police.

MUSIC

PORTUGAL

The **fado** is said to cause the chords of the Portuguese soul to vibrate melancholically or passionately. Named after fate, *fado* is a musical tradition unique to Portugal, identified with a sense of *saudade* (yearning or longing) and characterized by tragic, romantic lyrics and mournful melodies. These solo ballads, accompanied by the acoustic *guitarra* (a flat-backed guitar, like a mandolin), appeal to the romantic side of Portuguese culture. **Amalia Rodrigues** (1920-1999) is often spoken of in association with the tradition; she has become, in her lifetime, an internationally known star as a singer of fado and Portuguese folk music. For more information on fado, see **Achy Breaky Heart,** p. 563.

Apart from its folk tradition, the music of Portugal has yet to achieve international fame. Portuguese opera peaked with **António José da Silva** (1705-1739), a victim of the 1739 Inquisition. The Renaissance in Portugal led to the development of pieces geared for solo instrumentalists and vocals. Italian **Domenico Scarlatti** (1685-1757), brought to Lisbon by João V, composed brilliant keyboard pieces. His preeminent Portuguese contemporary, Coimbra's **Carlos Seixas,** thrilled 18th-century Lisbon with his genius and contributed to the development of the sonata form. **Domingos Bomtempo** (1775-1842) introduced symphonic innovations from abroad and helped establish the first Portuguese Sociedade Filarmónica, modeled after the London Philharmonic, in Lisbon in 1822.

Although the French invasion, Civil War, and decreased patronage somewhat stifled Portuguese music, folk music and dancing are still quite popular in rural areas. In the latter half of this century, Joly Braga Santo has led a modern revival of Portuguese classical music. The Calouste Gulbenkian Foundation in Lisbon has also kept Portuguese music alive, sponsoring a symphony orchestra since 1962, and hosting popular local folk singers (including Fausto and Sérgio Godinho), ballets, operas, and jazz festivals. The Teatro Nacional de São Carlos, which has its own orchestra and ballet company, has further benefitted Portuguese music. The Teatro has spawned a group of talented young composers, including Filipe Pires, A. Vitorino de Almeida, and Jorge Peixinho, all of whom have begun to make their mark in international competitions.

LANGUAGE

Thanks to the Romans who colonized Iberia in the late third century BC, practiced Romance speakers will find Portuguese an easy conquest (though pronunciation may be difficult). Although this softer sister of Spanish is closely related to the other Romance languages, modern Portuguese is an amalgam of diverse influences. A close listener will catch echoes of Italian, French, Spanish, Arabic, and even English and Slavic. Portugal's global escapades also spurred the spread of its language. Today, Portuguese (the world's fifth-most-spoken language) binds over 200 million people worldwide, most of them in Portugal, Brazil, Mozambique, and Angola. Prospective students of the language should note the differences between Brazilian and continental Portuguese, mainly in pronunciation and usage.

Some may be heartened to know that English, Spanish, and French are widely spoken throughout Portugal, especially in tourist-oriented locales. Look to the *Let's Go* glossary in the back of this book for terms (or their Castilian cousins) that are used in this guide (see **Glossary,** p. 736).

FOOD AND DRINK

TYPICAL FARE

The Portuguese season their dishes with olive oil, garlic, herbs, and sea salt but use relatively few spices, despite their historic role in bringing Eastern flavorings to Europe. The geography of Portugal means miles of coastlines; seafood forms the core of Portuguese cuisine and is usually prepared as simply as possible to emphasize freshness. Seafood lovers will enjoy *chocos grelhados* (grilled cuttlefish), *linguado grelhado* (grilled sole), and *peixe espada* (swordfish), to name a few. The more adventurous should try the *polvo* (boiled or grilled octopus), *mexilhões* (mussels), and *lulas grelhadas* (grilled squid). Meat is treated in the opposite manner from seafood; the taste is extensively embellished and even masked by heavy sauces in Portuguese cooking. Pork, chicken, and beef appear on most menus and are often combined as *cozida à portuguesa* (boiled beef, pork, sausage, and vegetables). True connoisseurs add a drop of *piri-piri* (mega-hot) sauce on the side. An expensive delicacy is freshly roasted *cabrito* (baby goat). No matter what you order, leave room for *batatas* (potatoes), prepared countless ways—including *batatas fritas* (french fries)—which accompany each meal.

The widespread availability of excellent produce means that **sopas** (soups) are usually made from local vegetables. As they can serve as a cheap alternative to a full meal, they are tasty and can often be substantial in consistency. Common soups are *caldo de ovos* (bean soup with hard-boiled eggs), *caldo de verdura* (vegetable soup), and the tasty *caldo verde* (a potato and kale mixture with a slice of sausage and olive oil). **Sandes** (sandwiches) such as the *bifana* or *prego no pão* (meat sandwich) may be no more than a hunk of meat on a roll. Cows, goats, and ewes please the palate by providing raw material for Portugal's renowned **queijos** (cheeses). Vegetarians should accustom themselves to the cheese sandwich and Portugal's delectable bread.

Portugal's favorite **dessert** is *pudim*, or *flan*, a rich, caramel custard similar to *crême bruleé*. For the sweet tooth in all of us, the almond groves of the Algarve produce their own version of marzipan. For something different, try *pêras* (pears) drenched in sweet port wine and served with raisins and hazelnuts on top. Most common are countless varieties of inexpensive, high-quality **sorvete** (ice cream)—look for vendors posting the colorful, ubiquitous "Olá" sign. *Pastelarías* (bakeries) are in most towns, and tasty **pastries** make for a cheap (80-180$) breakfast.

EATING OUT

Portuguese eat their hearty midday meal—*almoço* (lunch)—between noon and 2pm and *jantar* (dinner) between 9pm and midnight. Both meals entail at least three courses. There are no greasy lumberjack breakfasts to be found in Portugal—a pastry (80-180$) from a *pastelaría* (bakery) and coffee from a café suffices for *pequeno almoço* (breakfast). If you get the munchies between 4 and 7pm, snack bars sell **sandes** (sandwiches) and sweet cakes. It is advisable to make reservations when dining in some of the more upscale city restaurants.

A full meal costs 1000-2000$, depending on the restaurant's location and quality. **Meia dose** (half portions) cost more than half-price but are often more than adequate—a full portion may satisfy two. The ubiquitous **prato do dia** (special of the day) and **ementa** ("*menú*" in Portuguese) of appetizer, bread, entree, and dessert will stifle the loudest stomach growls. The **ementa turística** (tourist *menú*) is usually not a good deal—restaurants with menus translated into multiple languages are more likely to charge exorbitant prices. Standard pre-meal bread, butter, cheese, and pâté may be dished without your asking, but these pre-meal munchies are not free (300-500$ per person). You may appreciate them, however, since chefs only start cooking after your order; be prepared to wait. In restaurants (but not cafés), a service charge of 10% is usually included in the bill. When service is not included, it is customary to leave about 5 to 10% as a tip. Vegetarians may find themselves somewhat in the cold in Portugal, but given the availability and high quality of fresh fruits and vegetables, making special requests to chefs may prove fruitful. Smoking is still generally accepted in most establishments although there has been a recent move in Parliament to institute no smoking zones in some areas.

DRINKS

The exact date marking the birth of Portuguese wine is unknown, though 5000 B.C. is often used as an estimate. Though it does not quite rival the international renown of French and German wines, the quality and low cost of Portuguese *vinho* (wine) is truly astounding; the reds are perhaps the best known. The pinnacle, **vinho do porto** (port), pressed (by feet) from the red grapes of the Douro Valley and fermented with a touch of brandy, is a dessert in itself. Chilled, white port can be a snappy aperitif, while ruby or tawny port makes a classic after-dinner drink. A six-month-long heating process gives **Madeira** wines their unique "cooked" flavor. Try the dry Sercial and Verdelho before the main course, and the sweeter Bual and Malmsey after. Sparkling *vinho verde* is picked and drunk young; it comes in red and white versions. The red may be a bit strong but the white is brash and delicious by any standard; the latter is exported rather than consumed, and classifies as a semi-sparkling wine. The Adega Cooperatives of Ponte de Lima, Monção, and Amarante produce the best of this type. Excellent local table wines include Colares, Dão, Borba, Bairrada, Bucelas, and Periquita. If you can't decide, experiment with the **vinho de casa** (house wine); either the *tinto* (red) or the *branco* (white) is a reliable standby. Tangy **sangría** comes filled with fresh orange slices and makes even a budget meal festive at a minimal expense (usually around 500$ for a half-pitcher). Essential to your Portuguese drinking vocabulary should be the following terms: *adega*: a cellar or winery, *branco*: white wine, *claro*: new wine, *doce*: sweet wine, *espumante*: sparkling wine, *garrafa*: a bottle, *rosado*: a rosé wine, *seco*: dry wine, *vinho de mesa*: table wine, and *vinho verde:* a young wine.

Bottled Sagres and Super Bock are excellent beers. If you don't ask for it *fresco* (cool), it may come *natural* (room temperature). A tall, slim glass of draft beer is a **fino** or an **imperial,** while a larger stein is a **caneca.** To sober up and wake up, order a **bica** (cup of black espresso), a **galão** (coffee with milk, served in a glass), or a **café com leite** (coffee with milk, served in a cup).

MEDIA

Portugal's most widely read daily newspapers are *Público* (www.publico.pt), *Diário de Notícas* (www.dn.pt), and *Jornal de Notícas.* If you haven't yet mastered Portuguese, check out *The News*, Portugal's only online English language newspaper, at www.the-news.net. Those interested in international news stories can also pick up day-old foreign papers at larger newsstands.

Portuguese TV offers four main channels: the state-run Canal 1 and TV2 and the private SIC (Sociedade Independente de Communicação) and TVI (TV Independente). Couch potatoes can also enjoy numerous cable channels, most of which air Brazilian and Portuguese soap operas and subtitled foreign sitcoms.

SPORTS

Futebol (soccer to Americans) is the sport of choice for just about everyone. The country has shown signs of making it big—at the 1996 European Championships, the national team ousted Denmark en route to the semifinals—but has fallen short at crucial moments, such as the World Cup '98 qualification matches. Games create a crazed fervor throughout Portugal. Lisbon's club, **Benfica,** possesses some of the best players in the world. Native Portuguese have also made names for themselves in long-d istance running, where marathon-queen **Rosa Mota** dominated her event for a number of years. For recreation other than jogging and pick-up soccer, native Portuguese often turn to the sea. **Windsurfers, body-surfers,** and **surfers** make waves along the north coast; **snorklers** and **scuba divers** set out on mini-explorations in the south and west.

RECOMMENDED READING

FICTION: PORTUGUESE AND FOREIGN. For the scoop on Portuguese classics in most every genre, check out **Literature** (p. 531). The more famous works have been translated into English; for additional options, consult your librarian. *Selected Letters and Journals*, by Lord Byron, narrates the days Byron spent in Portugal. The Portuguese classic *The Lusiads*, by Luís de Camões, chronicles Portuguese exploration during the Age of Discovery. *The Last Kabbalist of Lisbon*, by Richard Zimler, is a fantastic murder mystery exploring the world of Portugal's 16th-century Jewish mystics. To see why José Saramago won the 1998 Nobel Prize in Literature, read *Baltasar and Blimunda* or *The Stone Raft*.

HISTORY AND CULTURE. David Birmingham's *A Concise History of Portugal* (1991) packs it all in one handy volume. Elanea Brown's *Roads to Today's Portugal: Essays on Contemporary Portuguese Literature, Art, and Culture* (1983) provides a good introduction to 20th-century Portuguese culture. Though somewhat outdated, A.H. de Oliveira Marques's *History of Portugal* is among the most comprehensive Portuguese history texts available. *Modern Portugal* (1998), edited by António Costa Pinto, covers 20th-century Portuguese history from the rise of Salazar to the evolution of the nation's resilient democracy. *Europe's Best-Kept Secret: An Insider's View of Portugal* (1997), by Costa Matos, is a witty account of Portuguese culture and history, including amusing anecdotes about peculiar Portuguese personalities.

ESSENTIALS

The information in this section is mostly designed to help travelers get their bearings once they are in Portugal. For information about general **travel preparations** (including passports and permits, money, health, packing, international transportation, and more), consult the **Essentials** section at the beginning of this book (p. 8). That chapter also has important information about alternatives to tourism (**work** and **study** programs in Portugal, p. 49) and for those with specific concerns: **women travelers** (p. 45); **older travelers** (p. 46); **bisexual, gay, and lesbian travelers** (p. 47); **travelers with disabilities** (p. 47); **minority travelers** (p. 48); **travelers with children** (p. 48); and travelers with **dietary needs** (p. 49).

GETTING THERE AND AROUND

Portugal is easily accessible by plane from the US and Europe. Long-distance trains run from **Madrid** (p. 82) to Lisbon, and buses run from **Sevilla** (p. 193) to Lagos. Closer to the border, trains run from **Huelva** (easily accessible from Sevilla, p. 195) and **Cáceres** (p. 180) to Portugal. Trains and buses run from **Badajoz** (p.

190), only 6km from the border, to Elvas and elsewhere. **Ciudad Rodrigo** (p. 160) lies only 21km from the border. In the north, trains run from **Vigo** (p. 462) to Porto; from **Túy** (p. 465), you can walk across the Portuguese border to Valença do Minho.

BY PLANE

Most major international airlines serve Lisbon; some serve Porto, Faro, and the Madeiras. **TAP Air Portugal** (in US and Canada ☎800-221-7370; in UK 207 630 07 46; in Lisbon 21 843 11 00; www.tap.pt) is Portugal's national airline, serving all domestic locations and many major international cities. **Portugália** (www.pga.pt) is a smaller Portuguese airline that flies between Porto, Faro, Lisbon, all major Spanish cities, and other Western European destinations. Its offices include Lisbon (☎21 842 55 00) and Manchester, UK (☎161 489 50 40).

BY TRAIN

Caminhos de Ferro Portugueses is Portugal's national railway, but for long-distance travel outside of the Braga-Porto-Coimbra-Lisbon line, the bus is much better. The exception is around Lisbon, where local trains and commuter rails are fast and efficient. Most trains have first- and second-class cabins, except for local and suburban routes. When you arrive in town, go to the station ticket booth to check the departure schedule; trains often run at irregular hours, and posted schedules *(horarios)* are not always accurate. Unless you own a Eurailpass, the return on **round-trip tickets** must be used before 3am the following day. Anyone riding without a ticket is fined over 3500$. Children under four travel free; ages four to 11 pay half-price. **Youth discounts** are only available to Portuguese citizens. Though there is a Portugal Flexipass, it is not worth purchasing.

BY BUS

Buses are cheap, frequent, and connect just about every town in Portugal. **Rodoviária** (national info ☎21 354 57 75), the national bus company, has recently been privatized. Each company name corresponds to a particular region of the country, such as Rodoviária Alentejo or Minho e Douro, with notable exceptions such as EVA in the Algarve. Private regional companies also operate, among them **Cabanelas, AVIC,** and **Mafrense.** Be wary of non-express buses in small regions like Estremadura and Alentejo, which stop every few minutes. Express coach service *(expressos)* between major cities is especially good; inexpensive city buses often run to nearby villages. Schedules *(horarios)* are usually printed and posted, but double-check with the ticket vendor to make sure they are accurate.

BY CAR AND THUMB

Portugal has the highest rate of automobile accidents, per capita, in Western Europe. The new highway system (IP) is quite good, but off the main arteries, the narrow, twisting roads prove difficult to negotiate. The locals' testy reputation is well deserved. Speed limits are effectively ignored, recklessness common, and lighting and road surfaces often inadequate. Buses and trucks are safer options. Moreover, parking space in cities borders on nonexistent. **Gas** comes in super (97 octane), normal (92 octane), and unleaded. Gas prices may be high by North American standards—130-200*escudos* (or US$0.58-0.88) per liter.

Portugal's national automobile association, the **Automóvel Clube de Portugal (ACP),** R. Rosa Araújo, 42, 1250 **Lisbon** (☎12 318 01 00), provides **breakdown** and **towing service** (M-F 9am-5pm) and **first aid** (24hr.).

In Portugal, **hitchers** are rare. Beach-bound locals occasionally hitch in summer but otherwise stick to the inexpensive bus system. Rides are easiest to come by between smaller towns. Best results are reputedly at gas stations near highways and rest stops. *Let's Go* does not recommend hitchhiking (see p. 45).

MONEY

Official **banking hours** are Monday through Friday 8:30am to 3pm, but play it safe by giving yourself some extra time. For more information on money, see p. 13. **Taxes** are included in all prices in Portugal and are not redeemable like those in Spain and Morocco, even for EU citizens. **Tips** are customary only in fancy restaurants or hotels. Some cheaper restaurants include a 10% service charge; if they don't and you'd like to leave a tip, round up and leave the change. Taxi drivers do not expect a tip unless the trip was especially long. **Bargaining** is not customary in shops, but you can give it a shot at the local *mercado* (market) or when looking for a *quarto*.

SAFETY AND HEALTH

EMERGENCY ☎	Dial 112 for police, medical, or fire.

In Portugal, the highest rates of crime have been in the Lisbon area, especially on buses, trams, in train stations, and in airports. Exercise the most caution in the Alfama district, the Santa Apolonia and Rossio train stations, Castelo de São Jorge, and in Belém. The towns around Lisbon with the most reported crimes in recent years are Cascais, Sintra, and Fátima. Thieves sometimes try and distract people by staging loud arguments, passing a soccer ball back and forth on a crowded street, asking for directions, pretending to dance with their victim, or spilling something on their victim's clothing. Motorists should be wary of "Good Samaritans" who have been known to help ailing motorists by the side of the road and then steal their cars.

Like Spain, Portugal poses no particular health risks to travelers. For general **health** information, see p. 19. The public health system in Portugal is quite good, and many doctors speak English. A private clinic might be worth the money for convenience and quick service; most travel insurance will pick up the tab. For small medical concerns, Portuguese *farmacías* offer basic drugs and medical advice and are easy to find in most towns.

ACCOMMODATIONS

YOUTH HOSTELS

Movijovem, Av. Duque de Ávila, 137, 1069 Lisbon (☎21 359 60 00; fax 359 60 01; www.pousadasjuventude.pt), the Portuguese Hostelling International affiliate, oversees the country's HI hostels. All bookings can be made through them. A bed in a *pousada da juventude* (not to be confused with plush *pousadas*) costs 2000-3000$ per night and slightly less in the off-season (breakfast and sheets included). Lunch or dinner usually costs 900$, snacks around 250$. Rates may be higher for guests 26 and older. Though often the cheapest option, hostels may lie far from the town center. Check-in hours are 9am to noon and 6pm to midnight. Some have lockouts 10:30am to 6pm, and curfews might cramp club-hoppers' style. The maximum stay is eight nights unless you get special permission.

To stay in an HI hostel an **HI card** (3000$) is usually mandatory. Although they are sold at Movijovem's Lisbon office, it is more convenient to get an HI membership before leaving home. To reserve a bed in the high season, obtain an **International Booking Voucher** from Movijovem (or your country's HI affiliate) and send it from home to the desired hostel four to eight weeks in advance. In the off-season (Oct.-Apr.), double-check to see if the hostel is open. Large groups should reserve through Movijovem at least 30 days in advance. For more info, see **Hostels,** p. 25.

PENSÕES AND HOTELS

Pensões, also called **residencias,** are a budget traveler's mainstay. They're far cheaper than hotels and only slightly more expensive (and much more common) than crowded youth hostels. Like hostels, *pensões* generally provide sheets and towels and have commons rooms. All are rated on a five-star scale and are required to visibly post their category and legal price limits. (If you don't see this information, ask for it.) During the high season, many *pensões* do not take reservations, but for those that do, booking a week ahead is advisable.

Hotels in Portugal tend to be pricey. Room prices typically include showers and breakfast, and most rooms without bath or shower have a sink. However, many force you out by noon. When business is weak, try bargaining down in advance—the "official price" is just the maximum allowed.

ALTERNATIVE ACCOMMODATIONS

Quartos are rooms in private residences, similar to *casas particulares* in Spain. These rooms may be your only option in less touristed, smaller towns, or the cheapest one in bigger cities. The tourist office can usually help you find a *quarto.* When all else fails, ask at bars and restaurants for names and addresses, but you should try to verify the quality of the rooms. Prices are often flexible, and can drop as much as 500-1000$ with bargaining.

Pousadas, like Spanish *paradores,* outperform standard hotel expectations (and, unfortunately, rates). They are castles, palaces, or monasteries converted into luxurious, government-run hotels. "Historical" *pousadas* play up local crafts, customs, and cuisine and may cost as much as expensive hotels. Most require reservations. Priced less extravagantly are *regional pousadas,* situated in national parks and reserves. For info, contact ENATUR, Av. Santa Joana Princesa, 10, 1749 Lisbon (☎ (21) 844 20 00; www.pousadas.pt).

CAMPING

In Portugal, over 150 **official campgrounds** *(parques de campismo)* feature tons of amenities and comforts. Most have a supermarket and cafés, and many are beach-accessible or near rivers or pools. Given the facilities' quality and popularity, happy campers are those who arrive early; urban and coastal parks may require reservations. Police have been cracking down on illegal camping, so don't try it. Tourist offices stock *Portugal: Camping and Caravan Sites,* a free guide to official campgrounds. Otherwise, write the **Federação Portuguesa de Campismo e Caravanismo,** Av. Coronal Eduardo Gallardo, 24D, 1170 Lisbon (☎21 812 68 90).

KEEPING IN TOUCH

Most useful communication information (including **international access codes, calling card numbers, country codes, operator** and **directory assistance,** and **emergency numbers**) is listed on the **inside back cover.**

PHONES. Portugal's national telephone company is **Portugal Telecom.** Phone offices exist in most cities, but there is little need to use them as all services are available in phone booths, located on the street and in post offices. Pay phones are either coin-operated or require a phone card; both are common. The country uses both the **Credifone** and **Portugal Telecom** systems. For both systems, the basic unit for all calls (and the price for local ones) is 18$. The Telecom phone cards, using "patch" (not strip) cards, are most common in Lisbon and Porto and increasingly elsewhere. Credifone cards, with magnetic strips, are sold at drugstores, post offices, and locations posted on phone booths, and are most useful outside these two big cities. Private calls from bars and cafés cost whatever the proprietor decides, typically 30-40$; a posted sign usually indicates the rates. City codes all have a two before them, and local calls do not require dialing the city code.

As of October 31, 1999, all of the city codes in Portugal changed. There is now a 2 before every old city code. (For example, Lisbon's code is now 21 as opposed to 01.) All numbers listed in *Let's Go* are updated to include the change.

Calling cards probably remain the best method of making international calls (see p. 29 for more details). The numbers to access major calling card services (including AT&T, MCI, Canada Direct, BT Direct, Ireland Direct, Telstra Australia, Optus Australia, Telecom New Zealand, and Telkom South Africa) are listed on the inside back cover. To **call home with a calling card,** contact the operator for your service provider in Portugal by dialing the appropriate toll-free access number (see p. 29).

MAIL. Mail in Portugal is somewhat inefficient—**Air mail** *(via aerea)* can take from one to two weeks (or longer) to reach the US or Canada. It is slightly quicker for destinations in Europe and longer for Australia, New Zealand, and South Africa. **Surface mail** *(superficie)*, for packages only, takes up to two months. **Registered** or **blue mail** takes five to eight business days (for roughly 3 times the price of air mail). **EMS** or **Express Mail** will probably get there in three to four days for more than double the blue mail price. **Stamps** are available at post offices *(correios)* and automatic stamp machines are outside post offices and in central locations around cities. Also at post offices, **fax** machines are available for public use.

EMAIL. Email is both faster and more reliable than the standard mail system. Cybercafés are common in cities and most smaller towns, and are listed in the Practical Information section and in the index under Internet access. When in doubt, try the library; they often have at least one computer equipped for Internet access. For information on how to obtain a free email account, see p. 31.

PORTUGAL

EMBASSIES AND CONSULATES

Embassies and consulates are usually open Monday through Friday, mornings and late afternoons, with *siestas* in between—call for specific hours.

Australian Embassy: Refer to the Australian Embassy in Paris: 4, rue Jean Rey, 15th arrondisement Paris 75724 France (☎01 40 59 33 00; fax 01 40 59 35 38). An embassy in Lisbon is scheduled to open soon, but the embassy in Paris will still offer information and can redirect calls.

British Embassy: R. São Bernardo, 33, 1249 **Lisbon** (☎21 392 40 00; fax 392 41 83; information.section@lisbon.mail.fco.gov.uk). **Consulates:** Av. Boavista, 3072, 4100 **Porto** (☎22 618 47 89; fax 610 04 38); Largo Francisco A. Mauricio, 7-10, 8500 **Portimão** (☎28)241 78 04; fax 241 78 06).

Canadian Embassy: Av. Liberdade, 144/56, 4th fl., 1269 **Lisbon** (☎21 316 46 00; fax 316 46 91). **Consulate:** R. Frei Laurenço do Santa Maria, 1, 1st fl., 8000 **Faro** (☎89 80 37 57; fax 88 08 88).

Irish Embassy: R. Imprensa à Estrela, 4th fl., Ste. 1, 1200 **Lisbon** (☎21 392 94 40; fax 397 73 63).

New Zealand Embassy: Refer to New Zealand Embassy in Italy: Via Zara, 28, **Rome** 00198 (☎ 396 441 71 71; fax 396 440 29 84; nzemb.rom@agora.stm.it). **Consulate:** Av. Antonio Agusto Aguiar, 122, 9th fl., 1050 **Lisbon** (☎21 350 96 90; fax 347 20 04).

South African Embassy: Av. Luis Bivar, 10, 1097 **Lisbon** (☎21 353 50 41; fax 353 57 13; email SAfrican.Embassy@individual.EUnet.pt).

US Embassy: Av. das Forças Armadas, 1600 **Lisbon** (☎21 726 91 09; fax 727 91 09). **Consulate:** same address and ☎; fax 21 727 23 54.

HOLIDAYS

As in Spain, festivals form a large part of local culture. Portugal hosts plenty of lively fairs and religious celebrations, some of which span weeks or months. The list below includes major Portuguese festivals for 2002. For more information on regional events consult the local tourist office.

DATE	FESTIVAL	LOCATION
January 1	New Year's Day	National
January 6	Epiphany	National
February 12	Carnival	National
March 24-31	Holy Week	National
March 28	*Senhor Ecce Homo* (Maundy Thursday)	National
March 29	Good Friday	National
March 31	Easter	National
April 25	Liberation Day	National
May 1	Labor Day	National
early May	*Queima das Fitas* (Burning of the Ribbons)	Coimbra (p. 619)
May 30	Corpus Christi	National
June	*Feira Internacional de Lisboa*	Lisbon (p. 541)
first week of June	*Feira Nacional de Agricultura (Feira do Ribatejo)*	Santarém (p. 600)
June 10	*Portugal Day*	National
mid-June	*Festa de Santo António*	Lisbon (p. 541)
first week of July	*Festas da Rainha Santa*	Coimbra (p. 619)
second week of July	*Feira Popular*	Coimbra (p. 619)
late July	*Festa do Sardinha*	Peniche (p. 604)
August 15	Feast of the Assumption	National
October 5	Republic Day	National
November 1	All Saints' Day	National
December 9	Feast of the Immaculate Conception	National
December 25	Christmas	National
December 31	New Year's Eve	National

LISBON (LISBOA)

Many ancient civilizations claim to have settled Lisbon, with one legend even crediting Odysseus as its founder. Officially, Lisbon is thought to have been inhabited over 3000 years ago by Phoenicians, Greeks, and Carthaginians in turn, until the Romans arrived in 205 BC. Under Julius Caesar's reign, Lisbon became the most important city in Lusitania; in 1255, it was made the capital of the kingdom of Portugal. City and empire reached their apex at the end of the 15th century when Portuguese navigators pioneered explorations of Asia, Africa, and South America. A huge earthquake on November 1, 1755, touched off the nation's fall from glory—close to one-fifth of the population died in the catastrophe and two-thirds of Lisbon crumbled down. Under the authoritarian leadership of Prime Minister Marquês de Pombal, the city recovered with the construction of magnificent new squares, palaces, and churches in the style and architecture of the Enlightenment.

Lisbon has seen more than its share of changes over the course of the 20th century. During World War II, Lisbon's neutrality and Atlantic connections made the city a rendezvous for spies on both sides. In 1974, when Mozambique and Angola won independence, hundreds of thousands of refugees converged upon the Portuguese capital. Today, Portuguese of African, Asian, and European origin coexist in the capital city. In 1998, the World Expo descended upon Lisbon, providing the impetus for massive construction projects and a citywide face-lift while helping to renew Lisbon's seat at the forefront of European culture. Since then, the revival has continued, as more tourist hotspots and sites of cultural interest emerge.

INTERCITY TRANSPORTATION

BY PLANE

All flights land at **Aeroporto de Lisboa** (☎21 841 37 00), on the city's north edge. Walk out of the terminal, turn right, and follow the road around the curve to the bus stop. From here take **bus** #44 or 45 (15-20min., every 12-15min., 175$) to Pr. Restauradores (#44 runs to Pr. Restauradores weekdays only); the bus stops in front of the tourist office. Or take the express **AeroBus** to the same location (bus #91; 15min., every 20min. 7am-9pm, 460$/€2.30); the bus, which leaves from the airport exit, is a better option during rush hour. A **taxi** from downtown costs about 2000$/€10, plus a 300$/€1.50 luggage fee. Ask at the tourist office located inside the airport about the **voucher** program, which allows visitors to buy pre-paid vouchers for a cab rides from the airport, avoiding potential problems with fare dishonesty. Major airlines have offices at Pr. Marquês de Pombal and along Av. Liberdade. Call for the current rates, as prices almost always fluctuate.

TAP Air Portugal, Aeroporto de Lisboa, Ed. 19 R/C, ground level (☎21 841 50 00; www.tap.pt). Open M-F 9am-6pm.

Iberia, R. Barata Salgueiro, 28, 6th floor (☎21 355 81 19; www.iberia.com).

Portugália Airlines, Aeroporto de Lisboa, Ed. 70, Rua C (☎21 842 55 00; www.pga.pt).

BY TRAIN

Train service in Lisbon is potentially confusing, as there are three stations in Lisbon and one in Barreiro, each serving different destinations. Be aware that Portuguese trains are usually quite slow. For further info about Portugal's national railway system call **Caminhos de Ferro Portuguêses** (☎800 200 904; www.cp.pt).

Estação Rossio, (☎21 346 50 22), between Pr. Restauradores and Pr. Dom Pedro IV (Rossio), up the stairs. M: Rossio or Restauradores. Services points west. **Info office** on ground level open daily 10am-1pm and 2-7pm, for domestic window 7am-3:30pm, for international window 9:15am-noon and 1-5:30pm. English spoken. To **Sintra** (45min., every 15-30min. 6am-2am, 210$/€1.), via **Queluz** (140$/€0.70).

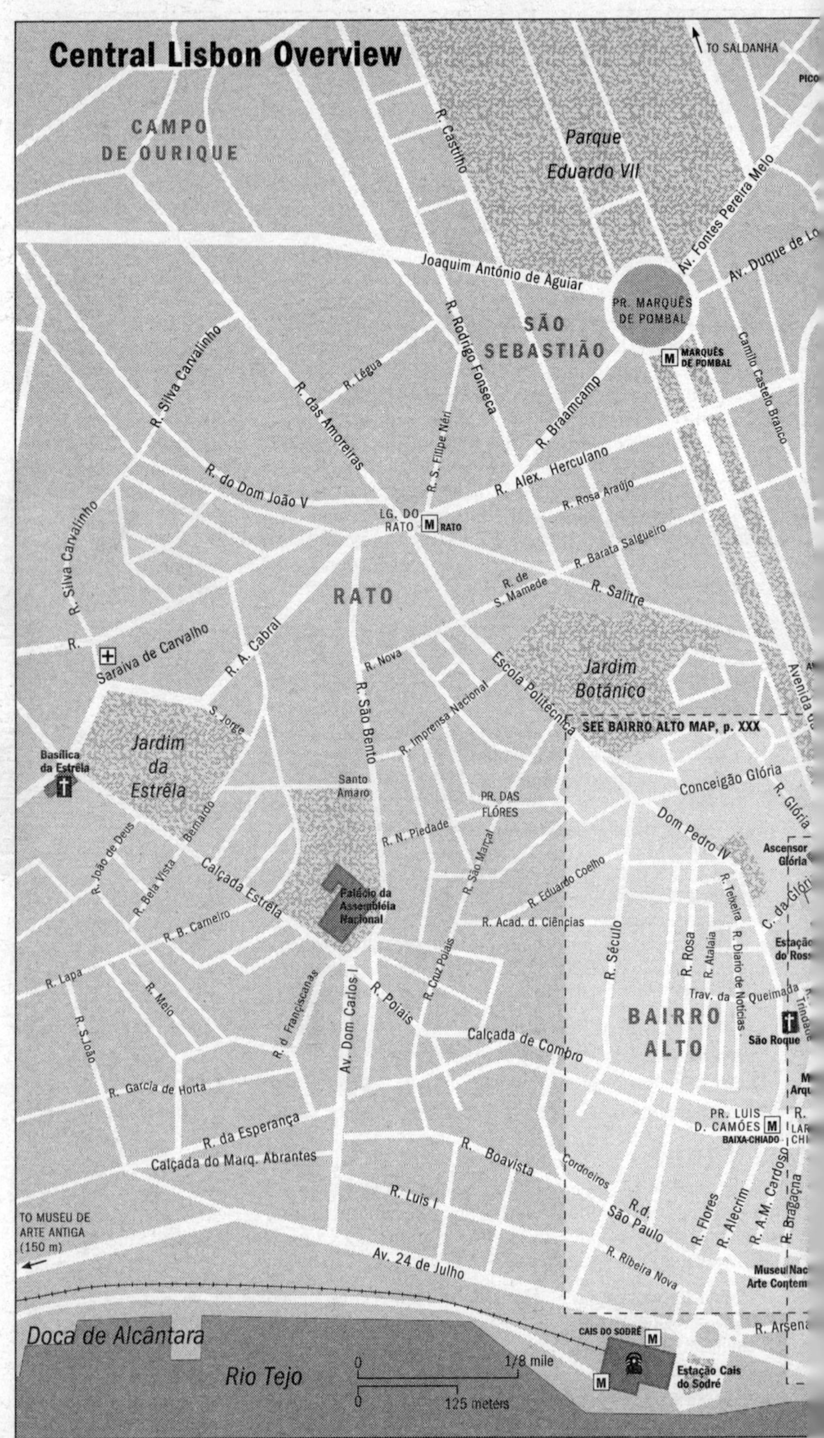
Central Lisbon Overview
TO SALDANHA
CAMPO DE OURIQUE
R. Castilho
Parque Eduardo VII
Av. Fontes Pereira Melo
Joaquim António de Aguiar
Av. Duque de Loulé
PR. MARQUÊS DE POMBAL
SÃO SEBASTIÃO
MARQUÊS DE POMBAL
R. Rodrigo Fonseca
Camilo Castelo Branco
R. Silva Carvalinho
R. Légua
R. das Amoreiras
R. S. Filipe Néri
R. Braamcamp
R. do Dom João V
R. Alex. Herculano
R. Rosa Araújo
LG. DO RATO
RATO
R. Silva Carvalinho
R. Barata Salgueiro
R. de S. Mamede
R. Salitre
RATO
R. Saraiva de Carvalho
R. A. Cabral
R. Nova
Escola Politécnica
Jardim Botânico
Avenida
S. Jorge
R. São Bento
R. Imprensa Nacional
SEE BAIRRO ALTO MAP, p. XXX
Basílica da Estrêla
Jardim da Estrêla
Santo Amaro
PR. DAS FLÓRES
Conceição Glória
R. Glória
Bernardo
R. N. Piedade
Dom Pedro IV
R. João de Deus
R. São Marçal
Ascensor Glória
Calçada Estrêla
R. Bela Vista
Palácio da Assembléia Nacional
R. Eduardo Coelho
R. Teixeira
C. da Glória
R. B. Carneiro
R. Acad. d. Ciências
R. Século
R. Rosa
R. Atalaia
R. Diario de Notícias
R. Lapa
R. Meio
R. d. Franciscanas
Av. Dom Carlos I
R. Cruz Polais
R. Poiais
Trav. da Queimada
R. Trindade
BAIRRO ALTO
São Roque
R. S.João
Calçada de Combro
R. Garcia de Horta
PR. LUIS D. CAMÕES
BAIXA-CHIADO
R. da Esperança
Calçada do Marq. Abrantes
R. Boavista
Cordoeiros
R. Luis I
R.d. São Paulo
R. Flores
R. Alecrim
R. A.M. Cardoso
R. Bragança
TO MUSEU DE ARTE ANTIGA (150 m)
Av. 24 de Julho
R. Ribeira Nova
Museu Nac Arte Contem
R. Arsenal
Doca de Alcântara
CAIS DO SODRÉ
Rio Tejo
0
1/8 mile
0
125 meters
Estação Cais do Sodré

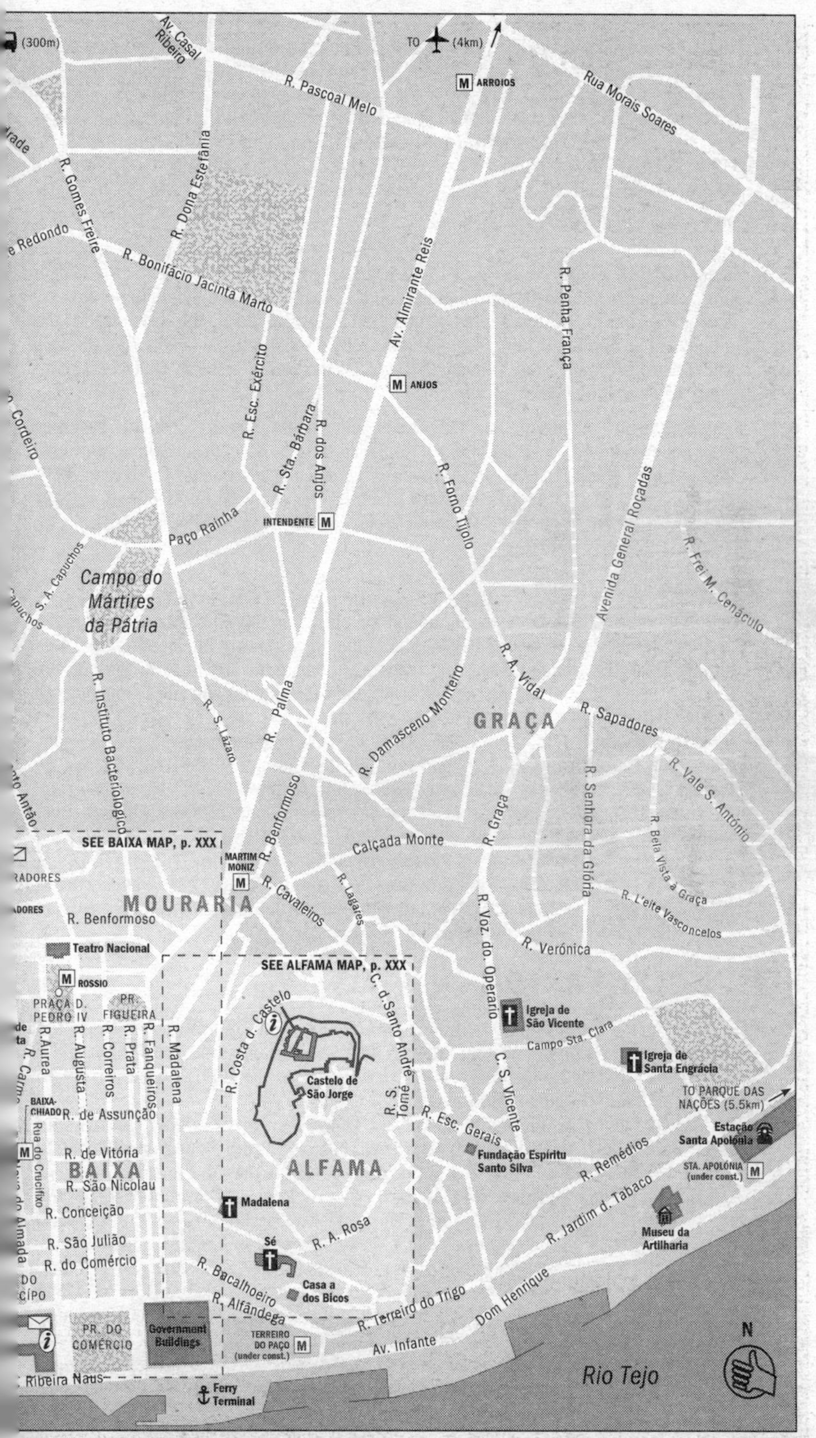
(300m)
Av. Casal Ribeiro
TO (4km)
M ARROIOS
R. Pascoal Melo
Rua Morais Soares
R. Gomes Freire
R. Dona Estefânia
Redondo
R. Bonifácio Jacinta Marto
Av. Almirante Reis
R. Penha França
M ANJOS
R. Esc. Exército
R. Sta. Bárbara
R. dos Anjos
R. Forno Tijolo
Cordeiro
Avenida General Roçadas
INTENDENTE M
Paço Rainha
R. Frei M. Cenáculo
S. A. Capuchos
Capuchos
Campo do Mártires da Pátria
R. A. Vidal
R. Sapadores
GRAÇA
R. Instituto Bacteriológico
R. S. Lázaro
R. Palma
R. Damasceno Monteiro
R. Vale S. António
R. Senhora da Glória
R. Bela Vista à Graça
R. Graça
R. Benformoso
SEE BAIXA MAP, p. XXX
Calçada Monte
MARTIM MONIZ M
R. Cavaleiros
R. Lagares
R. L'eite Vasconcelos
MOURARIA
R. Benformoso
R. Voz. do. Operario
R. Verónica
Teatro Nacional
SEE ALFAMA MAP, p. XXX
M ROSSIO
PRAÇA D. PEDRO IV
PR. FIGUEIRA
R. Costa d. Castelo
C. d. Santo André
Igreja de São Vicente
Campo Sta. Clara
R. Aurea
R. Augusta
R. Correiros
R. Prata
R. Fanqueiros
R. Madalena
Castelo de São Jorge
C. S. Vicente
Igreja de Santa Engrácia
R. S. Tomé
TO PARQUE DAS NAÇÕES (5.5km)
BAIXA-CHIADO
R. de Assunção
R. Esc. Gerais
Estação Santa Apolónia
Rua do Crucifixo
R. de Vitória
BAIXA
ALFAMA
Fundação Espírito Santo Silva
R. Remédios
STA. APOLÓNIA (under const.) M
R. São Nicolau
Madalena
R. Jardim d. Tabaco
R. Conceição
R. A. Rosa
Museu da Artilharia
R. São Julião
Sé
R. do Comércio
R. Bacalhoeiro
Casa a dos Bicos
R. Alfândega
R. Terreiro do Trigo
Dom Henrique
PR. DO COMÉRCIO
Government Buildings
TERREIRO DO PAÇO (under const.) M
Av. Infante
N
Ribeira Naus
Ferry Terminal
Rio Tejo

Estação Santa Apolónia, (☎21 888 40 25), Av. Infante Dom Henrique, east of the Alfama on the banks of the Rio Tejo, runs the international, northern, and eastern lines. All trains to Santa Apolónia also stop at the **Estação Oriente** (M: Oriente) by the Expo grounds. The international terminal has **currency exchange** and an **info desk** (English spoken). To reach downtown from the station, take bus #9, 39, 46, or 90 to Pr. Restauradores and Estação Rossio. To: **Aveiro** (3-3½hr., 4 per day 9:05am-8:05pm, 3240$/€16); **Braga** (5hr., 2 per day 7:55am-5:55pm, 2800$/€14); **Coimbra** (2½hr., 7 per day 8:05am-8:05pm, 1510-2700$/€7.55-13); **Madrid** (10hr., 1 per day 10:05pm, 8200$/€41); **Porto** (4½hr., 12 per day 7:55am-8:05pm, 2080-3700$/€10-19).

Estação Cais do Sodré, (☎21 347 01 81), just beyond the end of R. Alecrim, to the right of Pr. Comércio when walking from Baixa. M: Cais do Sodré. Take the metro or bus #1, 44, or 45 from Pr. Restauradores or bus #28 from Estação Santa Apolónia. To: the monastery in **Belém** (10min., every 15min. 5:30am-2:50am, 140$/€0.70); **Cascais** and **Estoril** (30min., every 20min., 210$/€1); the youth hostel in **Oeiras** (20min., every 15min., 170$/€0.85).

Estação Barreiro, across the Rio Tejo, serves points south. Station accessible by ferries from the Terreiro do Paço dock off Pr. Comércio. Ferries leave every 30min. and take 30min.; ferry ticket included in the price of connecting train ticket (otherwise 85$/€0.42, 200$/€1 round-trip). To: **Évora** (2½hr., 7 per day 6:50am-11:50pm, 1200$/€€); **Lagos** (5½hr., 5 per day 7:35am-7:45pm, 2800$/€14); **Setúbal** (1½hr., every hr. 7:55am-6:50pm, 210$/€1).

BY BUS

Arco do Cego, Av. João Crisóstomo, around the block from M: Saldanha. Exit the metro onto Av. República and walk 1 block up from the *praça* (toward the McDonald's), then turn right onto Av. Duque d'Ávila, and take a right before the McDonald's. The bus station is a beige building on the corner of Av. João Crisóstomo and Av. Defensores de Chaves. All "Saldanha" buses (#36, 44, 45) stop in the *praça* (175$/€0.87). Fast **Rede Expressos** (☎21 354 54 39 or 310 31 11; www.rede-expressos.pt) goes to many destinations. To: **Braga** (5hr., 6 per day 7am-12:15am, 2500$/€13); **Caldas da Rainha** (1¼hr., 10 per day 7am-11pm, 1000$/€5); **Coimbra** (2½hr., 16 per day 7am-12:15am, 1500$/€7); **Évora** (2hr., 13 per day 7am-9:30pm, 1500$/€7); **Faro** (5hr., 2600$/€13); **Lagos** (5hr., 9 per day 5am-1am, 2500$/€13); **Peniche** (2hr., 11 per day 7am-7:30pm, 1050$/€5); **Portalegre** (4½hr., 8 per day 7:30am-9:55pm, 1700$/€8.50); **Porto** (4hr., 7per day 7am-12:15am, 2300$/€12), via Leiria; **Tavira** (5hr., 5 per day 5am-1am, 2500$/€13); **Vila Real St. Antonio** (6hr., 7 per day 5am-1am, 2600$/€13), via **Setúbal** (45min., 600$/€3).

ORIENTATION

Lisbon and its surrounding areas have an efficient system of public transportation of subways, buses, trams, and funiculars. The city center is made up of three *bairros* (neighborhoods): the Baixa, (low district, resting in the valley), the Bairro Alto (high district), and the hilly Alfama.

The **Baixa,** Lisbon's old business center, is the center of town, sandwiched between Bairro Alto and Alfama. Its grid begins at the **Praça Dom Pedro IV** (better known as the **Rossio**) and ends at the **Praça do Comércio** on the **Rio Tejo**. Once the site of the royal palace, Praça do Comércio was nicknamed **Terreiro do Paço** (the palace terrace) after it was destroyed in the 1755 earthquake. For tourists, Rossio is the center of the city. Adjacent to Rossio are **Praça dos Restauradores,** where buses from the airport stop and the tourist office is located, and **Praça da Figueira.** Pr. Restauradores lies just above the Baixa, and from it the sprawling **Av. da Liberdade** runs uphill to the new business district centered around **Praça do Marquês de Pombal,** while Praça da Figueira extends towards the Alfama.

The **Bairro Alto** is a mix of narrow streets, parks, and Baroque churches. Bairro Alto is one of Lisbon's party districts; the streets are crowded until well past midnight. Nightlife areas include the **Avenida 24 de Julho** and the touristy **Docas de Santo Amaro,** as well as the developments across from the **Santa Apolónia** station.

On the other side of the Baixa (to the right with your back to the river), is the **Alfama,** Lisbon's famous medieval Moorish neighborhood. Alfama, the lone survivor of the 1755 earthquake, is the city's oldest district. Alfama is made up of a labyrinth of narrow alleys and stairways beneath the **Castelo de São Jorge.** Expect to get lost. Without a detailed map expect to get twice as lost. The twisting streets either change names every three steps or include several different streets under the same name. Streets are labeled either *travessas* (side streets), *ruas* (streets), *calçadinhas* (walkways), or *escadinhas* (stairways). A street-indexed *GeoBloco* **Planta Turística de Lisboa** or the *Poseidon* **Planta de Lisboa** (with Sintra, Cascais, and Estoril on the back) are good maps and well worth the money (both sold in Estação Rossio and at most newsstands for 1500$/€7).

Stretching along the river from the Baixa's waterfront are some of the fastest growing parts of Lisbon. The former Expo '98 grounds, now called the **Parque das Nações** (Park of Nations), welcomes visitors both day and night, while the **Alcântara** and the Docas do Santo Amaro show off Lisbon's most happening nightlife.

LOCAL TRANSPORTATION

Lisbon has a efficient buses, subways, trams, funiculars, and trains. Use them to full advantage—no suburb takes longer than 90min. to reach. If you don't speak Portuguese, taxi drivers may rip you off by charging an exorbitant fare or not returning your change. Make sure you know in advance what the fare should be.

Buses: CARRIS (☎21 361 30 00; www.carris.pt) runs the buses, trams, and funiculars in Lisbon. Fare 175$/€0.88 within the city; pay on the bus. If you plan to stay for any length of time, consider a *passe turístico* (tourist pass), good for unlimited travel on all CARRIS transports. 1-, 3-, 4-, and 7-day passes available (460$/€2.30, 1100$/€5.50, 1810$/€9, 2560$/€13). Passes sold in CARRIS booths located in most network train stations and the busier metro stations (e.g. Restauradores). Open daily 8am-8pm. You must show a passport to buy a tourist pass.

Subway: Metro (☎21 355 84 57; www.metrolisboa.pt) covers downtown and the modern business district in 4. A red "M" marks Metro stops. Tickets 100$/€0.50. Buy them at window or from vending machines. Book of 10 tickets 900$/€4.50. Trains run daily 6:30am-1am, though some stations close earlier.

Trams (CARRIS): Everywhere 175$/€0.88. Many date from before WWI. Line #28 is great for sight-seeing in the Alfama and Mouraria (stop in Pr. Comércio). Line #15 heads from Pr. Comércio or Pr. Figueira to Belém.

Funiculars (CARRIS): Everywhere 175$/€0.88. Funiculars link the lower city with the residential area. One goes up Ascensor Glória from Pr. Restauradores to Bairro Alto.

Taxis: Rádio Táxis de Lisboa (☎21 811 90 00), **Autocoope** (☎21 793 27 56), and **Teletáxis** (☎21 811 11 00). Along Av. Liberdade and Rossio. Luggage 300$/€1.50.

Car Rental: Pick up cars at the airport or in one of several locations downtown. Contact the agencies for pickup locations. **Budget,** R. Castilho, 167B (☎21 386 05 16; fax 383 09 78); **Hertz,** R. Castilho, 72A (☎21 381 24 30; fax 387 41 64); **Avis,** R. Castilho (☎21 356 11 76; fax 356 11 70); **Mundirent,** R. Conde Redondo, 38A (☎21 313 93 60; fax 313 93 69); **Solcar,** R. São Sebastião da Pedreira, 51D (☎21 313 90 70; fax 356 05 04); **Alô Car,** R. Quirino da Fonseca, 22B/C (☎21 843 88 50; fax 846 00 64). See **By Car,** p. 42 for toll-free numbers to get rates and other info from home. If you're just planning on visiting Lisbon, a car is unnecessary.

PRACTICAL INFORMATION

TOURIST AND FINANCIAL SERVICES

Tourist Office: Palácio da Foz, Pr. Restauradores (☎213 46 33 14, fax 352 57 89), M: Restauradores. Open daily 9am-8pm. The **Welcome Center,** Pr. Comércio (☎21 031 28 10, fax 031 28 19) is the main office for the city. Sells tickets for sightseeing buses and the "Lisboa Card" which includes transportation and entrance to most sights for a flat fee ($2200/€11 for 24hr., 3600$/€18 for 48hr., 4600$/€23 for 72hr.; children 880$/€4.40, 1240$/€6, 1750$/€9). English spoken. Open daily 9am-8pm. An office at the **Aeroporto de Lisboa** (☎21 845 06 06), just outside the baggage claim area. English spoken. Open daily 6am-2am. Look for kiosks that read "Ask me about Lisboa" at Santa Apolónia, Belém, and other locations around the city.

Budget Travel: Movijovem, Av. Duque d'Ávila, 137 (☎213 59 60 00), at the bus stop, in the alley, on the right. M: São Sebastião. Open daily 9am-7pm. V.

Embassies: see **Embassies and Consulates,** p. 539.

Currency Exchange: Banks are open M-F 8:30-3pm. **Cota Câmbio,** R. Áurea, 283 (☎213 42 52 32 or 347 00 73), 1 block off Pr. Dom Pedro IV in the Baixa. Open M-Sa 9am-8pm. The main post office, most banks, and travel agencies also change money. Ask about fees first–they can be exorbitant (1000$/€10 or more).

American Express: Top Tours, Av. Duque de Loulé, 108 (☎213 19 42 90). M: Marquês de Pombal. Exit the metro stop and walk up Av. Liberdade toward the Marquês de Pombal statue, then turn right; the office is 2 blocks up on the left side of the street. Handles all AmEx functions. English spoken. Open M-F 9:30am-1pm and 2:30-6:30pm.

LOCAL SERVICES

Luggage Storage: Estação Rossio. Lockers 550$/€2.75 for 48hr. Open daily 8:30am-11:30pm. Also available at Estação Sta. Apolónia.

English Bookstore: Livraria Británica, R. Luís Fernandes, 14-16 (☎21 342 84 72), in the Bairro Alto. Walk up R. São Pedro de Alcântara and keep going straight as it becomes R. Dom Pedro V and then R. Escola Politécnica. Turn left on R. São Marcal, then right after 2 blocks onto R. Luís Fernandes. Open M-F 9:30am-7pm. AmEx/MC/V.

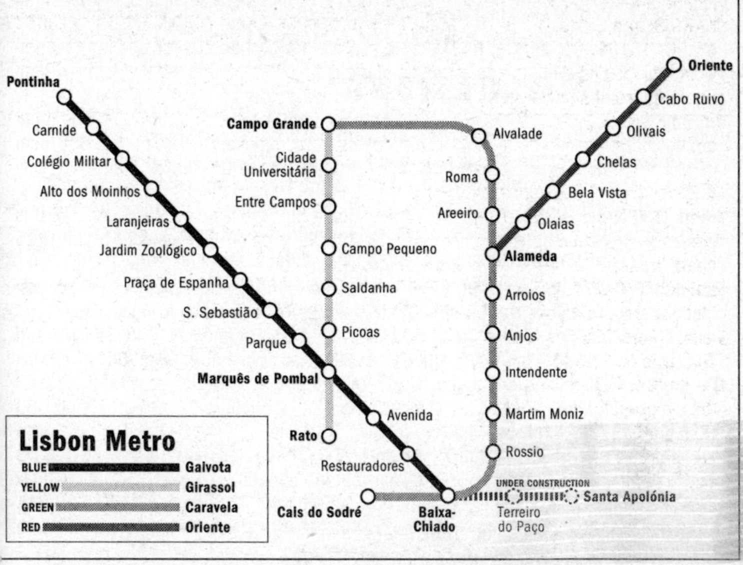

LISBON

Library: Biblioteca Municipal Central (☎ 21 797 38 62), Palácio Galveias. M: Campo Pequeno. Open M-Tu 10am-8pm, W-F 10am-7pm, Sa 10am-5pm.

Shopping Center: Amoreiras Shopping Center de Lisboa (☎21 381 02 00 or 381 02 40), on Av. Duarte Pacheco, near R. Carlos Alberto da Mota Pinto. Take bus #11 from Restauradores. 383 shops including a huge **Pão de Açúcar** supermarket, English bookstores, and a 10-screen **cinema.** Open daily 10am-midnight. **Colombo,** Av. Lusiada (☎21 711 36 36), in front of Benefica stadium. M: Colégio Militar-Luz. The largest shopping mall in Portugal, with over 500 shops and a 10-screen cinema. **Centro Vasco de Gama,** Av. Dom João II (☎21 893 06 01). M: Oriente. Open daily 10am-midnight.

Laundromat: Lavatax, R. Francisco Sanches, 65A (☎21 812 33 92). Wash, dry, and fold 1100$/€5.50 per 5kg load. Open M-F 8:30am-1pm and 3-7pm, Sa 8:30am-1pm.

EMERGENCY AND COMMUNICATIONS

Emergency: ☎112. **Police:** R. Capelo, 13 (☎21 346 61 41). English spoken.

Late-Night Pharmacy: ☎118 (directory assistance). Posted on the door of every pharmacy is the address of the next night's neighborhood pharmacy to provide this service.

Medical Services: British Hospital, R. Saraiva de Carvalho, 49 (☎21 395 50 67). **Cruz Vermelha Portuguesa,** R. Duarte Galvão, 54 (**ambulance** 21 942 11 11).

Telephones: Portugal Telecom, Pr. Dom Pedro IV, 68 (☎808 21 11 56). M: Rossio. Has pay phones and booths for international calls. Pay the cashier after your call or use a phone card. **Phone cards** come in 50 units (650$/€3.25), 100 units (1300$€6.50), or 150 units (1900$/9.50). Buy them here or at neighborhood bookstores and stationers. Local calls consume at least 1 unit. Office open daily 8am-11pm. V.

Internet Access: Web C@fe, R. Diário de Notícias, 126 (☎21 342 11 81). 300$/€1.50 per 15min., 500$/€2.50 per 30min., 700$/€4.50 per 45min., 800$/€4 per hr. Open daily 4pm-2am. **Ciber Chiado,** Largo Picadeiro, 10 (☎21 322 57 64), Largo Chiado down R. Raiva de Andrade. Upstairs in the National Cultural Center building. Ring the bell to enter. 250$/€1.25 per 15min., 400$/€2 per 30min., 550$/€2.75 per 1hr., 800$/€4 per 2hr. Open M-F 4pm-midnight, Sa 8pm-midnight. **Cyber.bica,** R. Duques Bragança, 7 (☎21 342 11 00), further down the street from Ciber Chiado. 150$ per 15min/€0.75. Open M-F 9am-midnight, Sa 7pm-midnight.

Post Office: Marked by red *Correios* signs. **Main office** (☎21 323 89 71; fax 323 89 76), Pr. Restauradores. International express mail (EMS). Open M-F 8am-10pm, Sa-Su 9am-6pm. Another large office (☎21 322 09 21; fax 322 09 27) at Pr. Comércio. Open M-F 8:30am-6:30pm. Credit cards not accepted. **Postal Code:** 1100 for central Lisbon.

ACCOMMODATIONS

A price ceiling supposedly restricts the amount hostels can charge for particular types of rooms, so if the fee seems padded request the printed price list. During low--season, prices generally drop—try bargaining. Many establishments have rooms with only double beds and charge per person. Expect to pay 3000-5000$/€15-25 for a single and 5000-9000$/€25-45 for a double, depending on amenities.

Most hotels are in the center of town on Av. Liberdade, while many convenient budget hostels are in the Baixa along the Rossio and on R. Prata, R. Correiros, and R. Ouro. Lodgings near the Castelo de São Jorge or in the Bairro Alto are quieter and closer to the sights. If central accommodations are full, head east to the hostels along Av. Almirante Reis. At night, be careful in the Baixa, the Bairro Alto, and especially the Alfama; many streets are isolated and poorly lit.

YOUTH HOSTELS

Pousada da Juventude de Lisboa (HI), R. Andrade Corvo, 46 (☎21 353 26 96; fax 21 353 75 41). M: Picoas. Exit the metro station, turn right, and walk 1 block; the hostel is on your left. HI card required. June-Sept. dorms 2900$/€15; doubles with bath 6500$/€33. Oct.-May dorms 2000$/€10; doubles 5000$/€25. MC/V.

Pousada da Juventude de Parque das Nações (HI), R. de Moscavide, lote 4-71-01 (☎21 892 08 90; fax 21 892 08 91). M: Oriente. Exit the station and go left on Av. Dom João II, walking past the Park of Nations until the street intersects with R. de Moscavide. The striped building on the corner. A long way from downtown. Internet 100$/€0.50 for 15min., 150$/€0.75 for 30min. HI card required. June-Sept. dorms 2100$/€11, doubles 5100$/€26. Oct.-May dorms 1700$/€8.50, doubles 4300$/€22.

Pousada da Juventude de Catalazete (HI), Estrada Marginal (☎21 443 06 38), in the coastal town of Oeiras. Take a train from Estação Cais do Sodré to Oeiras (20min., every 15min. 5:30am-2:30am, 170$/€0.88). Exit through the train station underpass, go right and cross the street. Go straight (following the signs to Lisbon) as the street curves under a bridge and through a residential district. Keep going as the street becomes R. São Pedro de Ariero and then R. Cidade do Mendelo. It will become a miniature highway; turn left under the bridge at the INATEL sign. Follow the signs into the INATEL complex, past the guard, past the apartments' reception building, continuing straight on the only road in the complex. Turn left at the sign for apartments 84-142; the hostel is the big yellow building. June-Sept. dorms 2000$/€10, doubles with bath 5100$/€25. Oct.-May 1700$/€8.50, doubles 4300$/€22.

BAIXA

Dozens of hostels surround the three connected *praças* that form the heart of downtown Lisbon. Staying in this area is quite convenient as it makes a good base for visiting sights in and around the city. Most hostels, though, are on the top floors of buildings, often overlooking noisy streets; none are especially memorable; it makes sense to just go for the lowest price. It's best to reserve at least a week ahead in summer, but it's usually possible to find a room somewhere.

Hospedagem Estrela da Serra, R. dos Fanqueiros, 122, 4th fl. (☎21 887 42 51), at the end of R. São Nicolau, on the edge of the Baixa toward the Alfama. Bare-bulb lamps and balconies. Singles 2000-2500$/€10-13; doubles 3000-4000$/€15-20.

Residencial Duas Nações, R. Vitória, 41 (☎21 346 07 10), on the corner of R. Augusta, 3 blocks from M: Baixa-Chiado. Breakfast included. May-Sept. singles 3500$/€18, with bath 6500$/€33; doubles 4500$/€23, with bath 8500$/€43; triples with bath

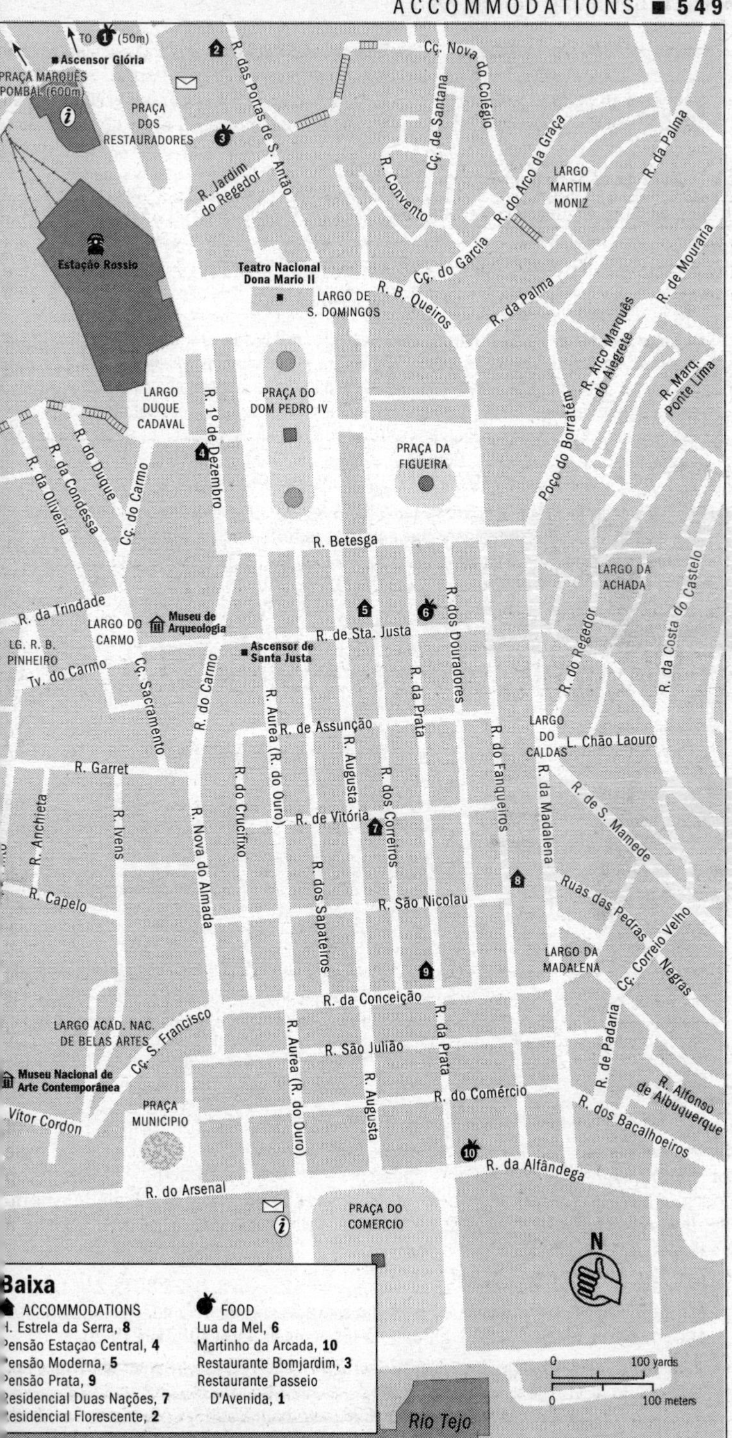

TO 1 (50m)
Ascensor Glória
PRAÇA MARQUÊS POMBAL (600m)
PRAÇA DOS RESTAURADORES
R. das Portas de S. Antão
R. Jardim do Regedor
Estação Rossio
Teatro Nacional Dona Mario II
LARGO DE S. DOMINGOS
Cç. Nova do Colégio
Cç. de Santana
R. Convento
R. do Arco da Graça
LARGO MARTIM MONIZ
R. da Palma
Cç. do Garcia
R. B. Queiros
R. da Palma
R. de Mouraria
R. Arco Marquês do Alegrete
R. Marq. Ponte Lima
Poço do Borratém
LARGO DUQUE CADAVAL
R. 1º de Dezembro
PRAÇA DO DOM PEDRO IV
PRAÇA DA FIGUEIRA
R. do Duque
R. da Condessa
R. da Oliveira
Cç. do Carmo
R. Betesga
LARGO DA ACHADA
R. da Costa do Castelo
R. da Trindade
LARGO DO CARMO
Museu de Arqueologia
R. de Sta. Justa
Ascensor de Santa Justa
R. dos Douradores
LG. R. B. PINHEIRO
Tv. do Carmo
Cç. Sacramento
R. do Carmo
R. Aurea (R. do Ouro)
R. de Assunção
R. da Prata
R. do Regedor
LARGO DO CALDAS
L. Chão Laouro
R. Garret
R. do Crucifixo
R. Augusta
R. dos Correiros
R. do Fanqueiros
R. da Madalena
R. de S. Mamede
R. Anchieta
R. Ivens
R. Nova do Almada
R. de Vitória
R. dos Sapateiros
Ruas das Pedras Negras
R. Capelo
R. São Nicolau
Cç. Correio Velho
LARGO DA MADALENA
R. da Conceição
LARGO ACAD. NAC. DE BELAS ARTES
Cç. S. Francisco
R. São Julião
R. de Padaria
R. Alfonso de Albuquerque
Museu Nacional de Arte Contemporânea
R. do Comércio
R. dos Bacalhoeiros
Vitor Cordon
PRAÇA MUNICIPIO
R. da Alfândega
R. do Arsenal
PRAÇA DO COMERCIO
N
0 100 yards
0 100 meters
Rio Tejo
Baixa
ACCOMMODATIONS
H. Estrela da Serra, 8
Pensão Estaçao Central, 4
Pensão Moderna, 5
Pensão Prata, 9
Residencial Duas Nações, 7
Residencial Florescente, 2
FOOD
Lua da Mel, 6
Martinho da Arcada, 10
Restaurante Bomjardim, 3
Restaurante Passeio D'Avenida, 1

10,500\$/€53. Oct.-Apr. singles 3000\$/€15, with bath 6000\$/€30; doubles 4000\$/€20, with bath 7500\$/€38; triples with bath 8500\$/€43. AmEx/MC/V.

Residencial Florescente, R. Portas de Santo Antão, 99 (☎21 342 66 09), 1 block from Pr. Restauradores. M: Restauradores. All rooms with phone and TV. June-Sept. singles 5000\$/€25, with bath 8000\$/€40; doubles 6000\$/€30, with bath 9000\$/€45; triples 9000\$/€45, with bath 12,000\$/€60. Oct.-May 1000\$/€5 less. AmEx/MC/V.

Pensão Estação Central, Calçada da Carmo, 17, 2nd-3rd fl. (☎21 342 33 08), a block from the central station, across the Largo Duque Cadaval. M: Rossio. Rather small and plain rooms, but inexpensive and central. Also a lounge with TV. Rooms without full bath have shower. June-Sept. singles 3000\$/€15, with bath 4000\$/€20; doubles 5500\$/€28, with bath 6500\$/€33. Oct.-May 500\$/€5 less.

Pensão Moderna, R. Correeiros, 205, 4th fl. (☎21 346 08 18), 1 block from Pr. Figueira, toward the river. M: Rossio. Be aware of the sketchy neighborhood this place finds itself in. Dine, the 74-year old Mozambican owner, enjoys chatting with guests for hours in front of the TV. Long communal balcony that connects most of the rooms. June-Oct. singles 3500\$/€18, doubles 5000\$/€25, triples 9000\$/€45, quads 12,000\$/€60, quints 15000\$/€75; Nov.-Feb. singles 2500\$/€13, doubles 4000\$/€20, triples 7500\$/€38, quads 10,000\$/€50, quints 15,000\$/€75.

Pensão Prata, R. Prata, 71, 3rd fl. (☎21 346 89 08), 2 blocks from Pr. Comércio near the corner of R. da Conceição; the entrance is to the right of the Pastelaria Flor da Prata. M: Rossio. Some small baths. July-Sept. singles 5000\$/€25, with bath 6000\$/€30; doubles 6000\$/€30, with bath 7000\$/€35; triple 7000\$/€35. Oct.-June singles 3500-4000\$/€18-20, with bath 4000-5000\$/€20-25; doubles 4000\$/€20 with bath 5000\$/€25; triple 6000\$/€30. Must pay in advance.

IN AND AROUND THE BAIRRO ALTO

The Bairro Alto is harder to reach and has fewer budget accommodations than the Baixa, but it can be a good place to stay for views of the city and proximity to nightlife. If you have luggage, you may want to reach the Bairro by way of the Ascensor Glória from Pr. Restauradores.

Casa de Hóspedes Globo, R. Teixeira, 37 (☎/fax 21 346 22 79), on a small street across from the Parque São Pedro de Alcântara at the top of the funicular. From the park entrance, cross the street and go one block on Trav. da Cara, then turn right onto R. Teixeira. All rooms with phones, most with TV, and all but two with bath. Laundry 2000\$/€10 per load. June-Sept. singles 3000-4000\$/€15-20, with bath 5000\$/€25; double with bath 6000\$/€30; triple with bath 8000\$/€40.

Residencial Camões, Tr. Poço da Cidade, 38, 1st fl. (☎21 347 75 10), off R. Misericórdia. From the top of Ascensor Glória, turn left onto R. São Pedro, which becomes R. Misericórdia; Tr. Poço da Cidade is the 5th right. In the heart of the party district—it may get noisy at night. TV lounge. English spoken. Breakfast included. Singles 2500-3000\$/€13-15; doubles 5500-7500\$/€28-38, with bath 6500-8000\$/€33-40; triples with bath 8000-10,000\$/€40-50.

Pensão Londres, R. Dom Pedro V, 53, 2nd-4th fl. (☎21 346 22 03). From the top of the Ascensor Glória, turn right onto R. São Pedro de Alcantara and continue past the park as the road curves left and becomes R. Dom Pedro IV; the pensão is on the corner of R. da Rosa, above Pastelaria S. Roque. Rooms with phones, some with TVs and panoramic views of the city. Breakfast included. Singles 5500-9000\$/€28-45; doubles 7700-12,200\$/€39-61; triples 15,200\$/€76; quads 17,200\$/€86. MC/V.

ALFAMA

The Alfama has fewer options for accommodation and less competition for prices but staying there can be a nice change of pace (especially after the Baixa grid).

Pensão Ninho das Águias, R. Costa do Castelo, 74 (☎21 885 40 70), right behind the Castelo. From Pr. Figueira take R. Madalena to Largo Adelino Costa, then head uphill to R. Costa do Castelo; climb the spiral staircase, then ring the bell and wait to be let in

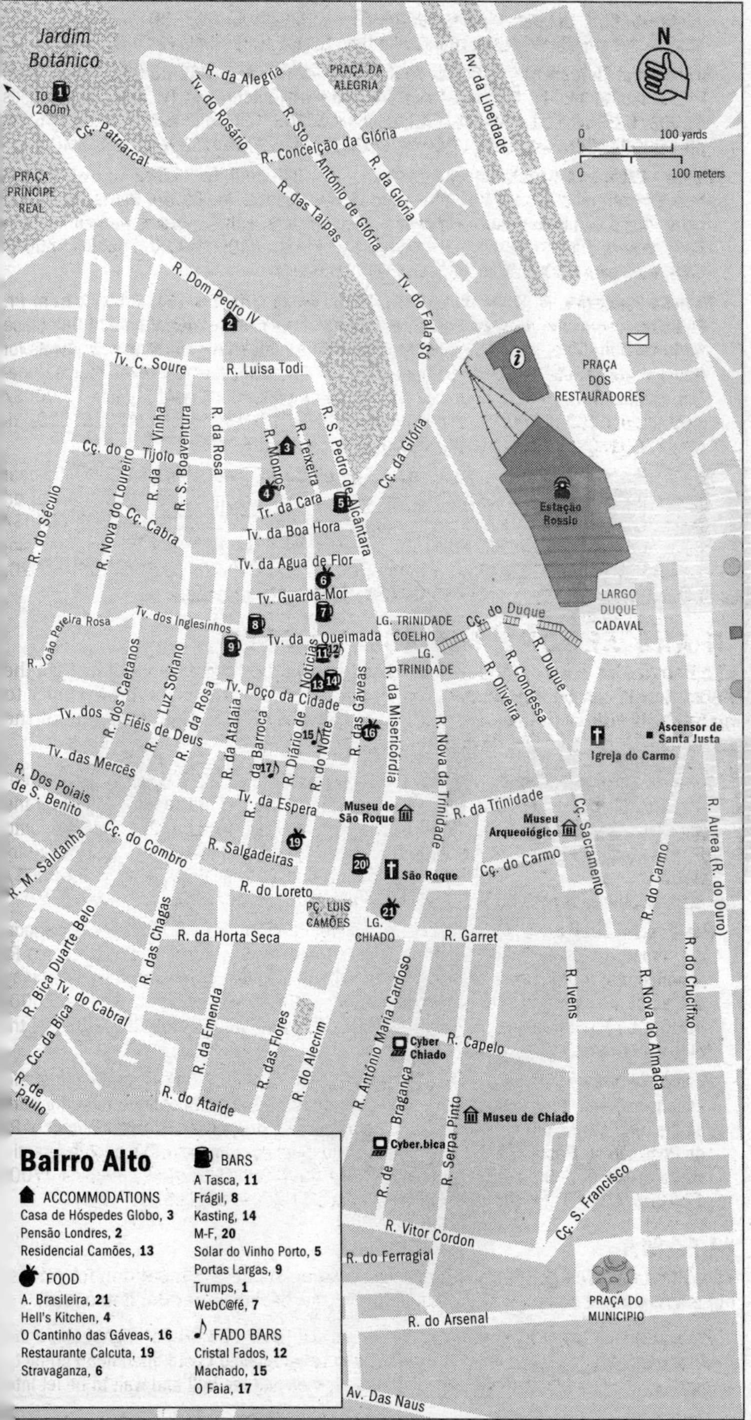
Bairro Alto
ACCOMMODATIONS
Casa de Hóspedes Globo, 3
Pensão Londres, 2
Residencial Camões, 13
FOOD
A. Brasileira, 21
Hell's Kitchen, 4
O Cantinho das Gáveas, 16
Restaurante Calcuta, 19
Stravaganza, 6
BARS
A Tasca, 11
Frágil, 8
Kasting, 14
M-F, 20
Solar do Vinho Porto, 5
Portas Largas, 9
Trumps, 1
WebC@fé, 7
FADO BARS
Cristal Fados, 12
Machado, 15
O Faia, 17
N
0
100 yards
100 meters
Jardim Botánico
TO 1 (200m)
PRAÇA PRÍNCIPE REAL
PRAÇA DA ALEGRIA
PRAÇA DOS RESTAURADORES
Estação Rossio
LARGO DUQUE CADAVAL
LG. TRINIDADE COELHO
LG. TRINIDADE
Ascensor de Santa Justa
Igreja do Carmo
Museu de São Roque
Museu Arqueológico
São Roque
PÇ. LUIS CAMÕES
LG. CHIADO
Cyber Chiado
Museu de Chiado
Cyber.bica
PRAÇA DO MUNICIPIO
R. da Alegria
Tv. do Rosário
R. Sto. António de Glória
R. Conceição da Glória
R. da Glória
R. das Taipas
Av. da Liberdade
Cç. Patriarcal
R. Dom Pedro IV
Tv. do Fala Só
Tv. C. Soure
R. Luisa Todi
R. S. Pedro de Alcântara
Cç. da Glória
R. Teixeira
R. Monros
Cç. do Tijolo
R. da Vinha
R. S. Boaventura
R. da Rosa
Tr. da Cara
Tv. da Boa Hora
Tv. da Agua de Flor
Tv. Guarda-Mor
R. do Século
R. Nova do Loureiro
Cç. Cabra
Tv. dos Inglesinhos
R. João Pereira Rosa
Tv. da Queimada
R. dos Caetanos
R. Luz Soriano
Tv. Poço da Cidade
Tv. dos Fiéis de Deus
R. da Atalaia
R. da Barroca
R. Diário de Notícias
R. do Norte
R. das Gáveas
R. da Misericórdia
R. Nova da Trinidade
R. Oliveira
R. Condessa
R. Duque
Cç. do Duque
Tv. das Mercês
R. Dos Poiais de S. Benito
Tv. da Espera
R. da Trinidade
Cç. Sacramento
Cç. do Combro
R. Salgadeiras
Cç. do Carmo
R. M. Saldanha
R. do Loreto
R. do Carmo
R. Aurea (R. do Ouro)
R. Bica Duarte Belo
R. das Chagas
R. da Horta Seca
R. Garret
R. Ivens
R. Nova do Almada
R. do Crucifixo
Tv. do Cabral
Cç. da Bica
R. de Paulo
R. da Emenda
R. das Flores
R. do Alecrim
R. António Maria Cardoso
R. Capelo
R. do Ataide
R. de Bragança
R. Serpa Pinto
Cç. S. Francisco
R. Vitor Cordon
R. do Ferragial
R. do Arsenal
Av. Das Naus
LISBON

the garden. Spectacular views of Lisbon from the garden and from the tower at the very top of the staircase. Best views from #5, 6, 12, 13 or 14. Mostly double beds, so it's a far better deal for couples. All rooms with phones. English spoken. May-Aug. singles 5000$/€; double bed 7500$/€38, with bath 8000$/€40; one double 7500$/€38; one triple 10,000$/€50. Sept.-Apr. singles 5000$/€25; double bed 6000$/€30, with bath 6500$/€33; double 6000$/€30; triple 7500$/€38.

Pensão Estrela, R. dos Bacalhoeiros, 8 (☎21 886 95 06). An under-discovered option in the lower part of Alfama. Bargain for lower prices in winter. Checkout 11am. June-Sept. singles 4000$/€20; doubles 6000$/€30; one triple 9000$/€45. Oct.-May singles 2500-3000$/€13-15; doubles 4000-5000$/€20-25; triple 7500$/€38. The similar **Pensão Verandas** (☎21 887 05 19) a floor up has comparable rooms and prices.

Pensão Beira Mar, Largo do Terreiro do Trigo, 16 (☎21 887 15 28). The large "Recommended by *Let's Go*" sign at the front door is from many years back. Probably the cheapest option in the Alfama for solo travelers. Some rooms with a view of the river

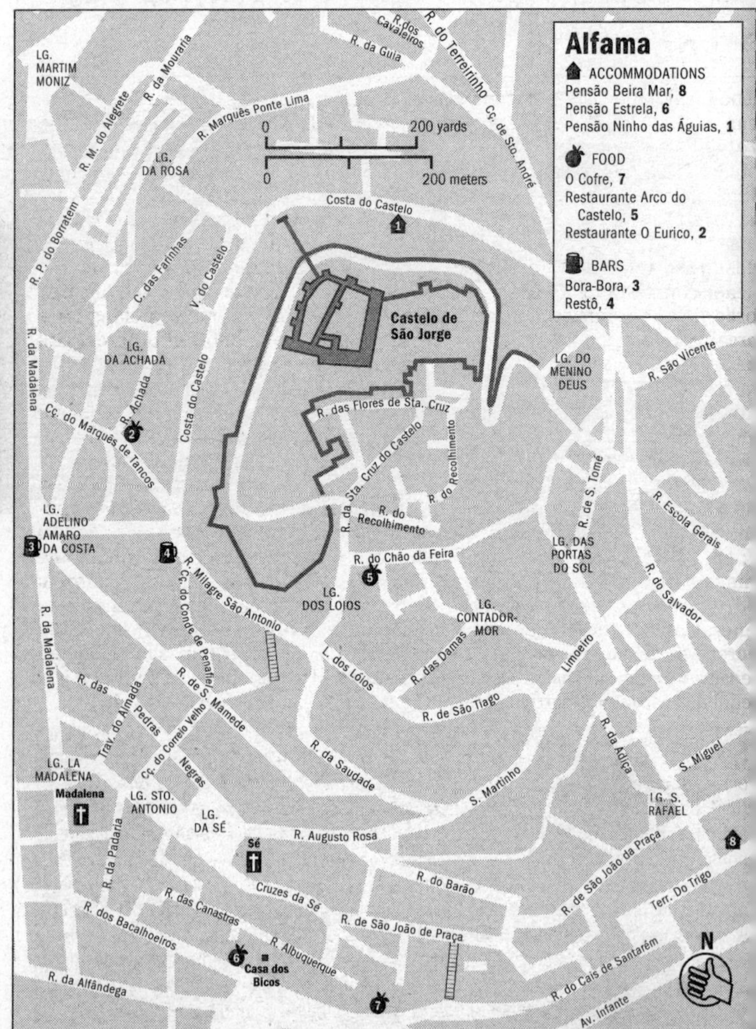

cost a bit more. June-Aug. singles 3000$/€15; doubles 6000-8000$/€30-40; quads 12,000$/€60. Oct.-May singles 2000$/€10; doubles 4000$/€20; quads 8000$/€40. Bargain for lower prices, especially in winter.

AMPING

lthough camping is popular in Portugal, campers are often prime targets for ieves. Info on campgrounds is available from the tourist office in the free bookt *Portugal: Camping and Caravan Sites*. There are 30 campgrounds within a 5-minute radius of the capital; listed below is the only one in Lisbon proper.

Parque de Campismo Municipal de Lisboa (☎21 760 96 20; fax 760 96 33), on the road to Benfica. Take bus #43 to the Parque Florestal Monsanto. Pool and supermarket. Reception daily 9am-9pm. July-Aug. 800$/€4 per person and per tent, 500$/€2.50 per car. June and Sept. 720$/€3.60 per person and per tent, 450$/€2.25 per car. Oct.-May 560$/€2.80 per person and per tent, 350$/€1.75 per car.

FOOD

isbon has some of the least expensive restaurants and best wine of any Euroean capital. A full dinner costs about 1800-2200$/€9-11 per person and the *rato do dia* (special of the day) is often a great deal. One full meal will probbly be enough to keep you full all day. Until then, just snack on surprisingly lling, incredibly cheap, and sinfully delicious Portuguese pastries; *pastelars* (pastry shops) are everywhere. The sign of a good restaurant is a clientele ade up of as many locals as tourists; the odd toddler running among tables dds to the authenticity. In Lisbon, the closer to the industrial waterfront, the eaper the restaurant. The south end of the Baixa, near the port, and the area ordering the Alfama are particularly inexpensive. If you are searching for a argain, avoid restaurants with menus translated into a Babel of different lanuages, as well as restaurants that advertise themselves as being *típico* or *adicional*—for truly typical and traditional meals, go to one of the places ith a menu scribbled in blue and red marker on a paper table liner posted outde the door. Lisbon abounds with seafood specialties such as *amêjoas à bulão pato* (steamed clams), *creme de mariscos* (seafood chowder with matoes), and a local classic, *bacalhau cozido com grão e batatas* (cod with ick peas and boiled potatoes, doused in olive oil). Belém offers worldmous pastries. **Antiga Confeitaria de Belém,** R. de Belém 84-92 (☎21 363 80 ; fax 363 74 23). Ever since a monk from the nearby monastery brought the ique recipe of the world-famous *pastéis de Belém* to this pastry shop in 37, the secret has been passed along with extreme care from generation to neration. Of the 100 people who currently work here, only 3 know the cret—these chosen few have signed notarized contracts, vowing to keep the easured recipe in the shop where it belongs. The president of Portugal is a equent customer. Pastries (140-250$/€0.70-1.25) and coffee 90$/€0.45..

SUPER COCK A few days in Portugal and you'll start to notice something of a national obsession with roosters. A very special rooster, that is–*o galo de Barcelos* (the cock of Barcelos). This particular animal, with flowers and hearts on its wings and tail, may seem like a psychedelic symbol of sorts, but it actually serves an altogether nobler cause. Once upon a time in the sleepy town of Barcelos, an innocent man was condemned to die for a crime he didn't commit. As his last wish he asked to have dinner with the judge so that he could try one last time to prove his innocence. The judge, who was having roast chicken for dinner that night, obliged. When the man saw the chicken at dinner, he blurted out that the cock would crow to prove his innocence. And sure enough the *galo* did–or so the story goes–forever securing itself a special place in Portuguese folklore as a symbol of truth, justice and faith. A superhero of sorts.

SUPERMARKETS

Mercado Ribeira (☎21 346 29 66), a vast market complex inside a warehouse on Av. 24 de Julho, just outside the Estação Cais do Sodré. Accessible by bus #40 or tram #15. Go early for the freshest selection. Open M-Sa 6am-2pm.

Supermercado Pão de Açúcar (☎21 382 66 80), Amoreiras Shopping Center de Lisboa, Av. Duarte Pacheco. Take bus #11 from Pr. Restauradores or Pr. Figueira. Open M-Sa 10am-8pm, Su 10am-6pm.

BAIXA

Although the Baixa is home to Lisbon's most tourist-oriented restaurants, it also has decent food at reasonable prices. Look for *pastelarias*—more than just pastry shops, they are less tourist-oriented and often have very good deals for lunch. On R. Portas de Santo Antão, seafood restaurants stack the day's catch in their windows; however, but these places are almost entirely for tourists and the prices are somewhat inflated. A few blocks toward the Alfama is where many of the cheaper and less aggressive eateries can be found, especially along Calçada de Santa Ana.

Martinho da Arcada, Pr. do Comércio, 3 (☎21 887 92 59), at the back left corner of the plaza when facing the river. Founded in 1782, this is the oldest restaurant in Lisbon. The restaurant is a bit expensive but the **café** next door offers the best lunch deal in the Baixa from noon-3pm. Open M-Sa 7am-10pm.

Pastelaria Anunciada, Largo da Anunciada, 1-2 (☎21 342 44 17), on the corner of R. de S. José. Specialties include *bacalhau à minhota* (codfish 1250$/€6.25). Open daily 6:30am-10pm, serves meals noon-10pm.

Lua da Mel, R. Prata, 242 (☎21 887 91 51), on the corner of R. Santa Justa. Caramelized everything draws crowds to this diner-style pastry shop. Pastries 110-200$/€0.55-1. Try the house specialty *Lua da Mel*. Open M-F 7:30am-9pm, Sa 7:30am-7pm.

Restaurante Bonjardim, Trav. Santo Antão, 11 (☎21 342 43 89), off Pr. Restauradores. The self-proclaimed *rei dos frangos* (king of chicken) legitimately rules the roost with its great roast chicken. Open daily noon-11:30pm. AmEx/MC/V.

Churrascaria Gaúcha, R. Bacalhoeiros, 26C-D (☎21 887 06 09), 1 block from the river towards the Alfama, near Pr. Comércio. South American-style *churrasco* (roasted meat) dishes. The place to go if you're craving a steak at midnight. Most entrées 1000-2000$/€5-10. Open M-Sa 9am-2am. AmEx/MC/V.

Restaurante Passeio D'Avenida (☎21 342 37 55), Av. Liberdade, just up from Pr. Restauradores. This café occupies the little park in the middle of the busy avenue. Outdoor seating for coffee (100-340$/€0.50-1.70) and sandwiches (350-600$/€1.75-3). Also a restaurant, entrées 1100-2500$/€5.50-13. Open daily 9am-2am. AmEx/MC/V.

A Lanterna, Calçada de Santa Ana, 99 (☎21 886 42 04), up the hill from R. Portas de Santo Antão, toward the Alfama. One of the many similar restaurants along this street. This is a pleasant escape from the tourist traps on the streets below. Entrées 700-900$/€3.50-4.50. Open M-Sa 9am-midnight, meals noon-3pm and 7-10pm.

Pastelaria Suíça, Pr. D. Pedro IV, 96-101 (☎21 321 40 90). Super-modernized and super-touristy, this is the largest and best-known *pastelaria* in the Baixa. Nevertheless, try a *pastel de nata* (180$/€0.90 at the bar) or one of their many other pastries (140-210$/€0.70-1). Open daily 7am-9pm.

BAIRRO ALTO

The narrow streets of the Bairro Alto are lined with bars and restaurants; the prices range from modest to inflated, and the patrons follow accordingly.

Restaurante Calcuta, R. do Norte, 17 (☎21 342 82 95), near Lg. Camões. Indian restaurant with wide selection of vegetarian options. Vegetarian entrées 900-1000$/€4.50-5. Meat entrées 1200-1700$/€6-8.50. Fixed price *menú* 2400$/€12. Try the *bebinka* for dessert. Open M-F noon-3pm and 6:30-11pm, Sa-Su 6:30-11pm.

LISBON

Hell's Kitchen, R. Atalaia, 176 (☎21 342 28 22). From the top of C. Glória (the steep hill from Pr. Restauradores), walk a few blocks up Trav. da Boa Hora and turn right on R. Atalaia; look for a small, black building. Entrées (1100-1600$/€5.50-8), including vegetarian options. Falafel with salad 1100$/€5.50. Open Tu-Su 8pm-12:30am.

Stravaganza, R. Grémio Lusitano, 18-26 (☎21 346 88 68), 1 block from the top of C. Glória, at R. Diário de Notícias. Italian food in an art-deco setting. Entrées 1600-3400$/€8-17, pizzas 1300-2100$/€6.50-11. Sa-Su 7pm-2am. AmEx/MC/V.

A Brasileira, R. Garrett, 120-122 (☎21 346 95 41). Considered by many to be "the best café in Portugal;" it has the best after-dinner scene. A group of intellectuals tends to gather at the first two tables. Mixed drinks 1000$/€5. A restaurant downstairs; specialty is *bife à brasileira* (2200$/€11). Open daily 8am-2am.

O Cantinho das Gáveas, R. das Gáveas, 82-84 (☎21 342 04 60), at the corner of Trav. Poço Cidade. Young, mixed crowd of customers. Entrées 990-1890$/€5-9.50. Specialties include *arroz de polvo caldoso* (octopus rice, 1290$/€6.45). Fish grilled outside in June. Open daily noon-3pm and 7pm-midnight. AmEx/MC/V.

ALFAMA

The winding streets of the Alfama conceal a number of tiny, unpretentious restaurants, often packed with the neighbors and friends of the owners. Lively chatter echoes through the damp, narrow alleys. Watch the clock—the labyrinthine Alfama grows dangerously dark after nightfall.

Churrasqueira O Cofre, R. dos Bacalhoeiros, 2C-D (☎21 886 89 35), at the foot of the Alfama near Pensão Estrela. A display case at the entrance shows everything available for grilling. Entrées 1300-2200$/€6.50-11. Open daily 9am-midnight, meals noon-4pm and 7-11:30pm. AmEx/MC/V.

O Eurico, Largo de S. Cristóvão, 3-4 (☎21 886 18 15), on C. do Marques de Tancos. Run by owner Eurico Ferreira for the past 32 years, this simple restaurant serves generous portions and is packed with workers at lunchtime. Entrées 800-1600$/€4-8. Open M-Sa 9am-10pm, meals noon-4pm and 7-10pm.

Costa do Castelo, Calçada Marquês de Tancos, 1-1B (☎21 888 46 36), just behind the Castelo in Alfama. The bar/café has a romantic view of the city from its outdoor patio. *Tapas* 400-500$/€2-2.50. Drinks 300-700$/€1.50-2.50. Open Tu-Su 12:30pm-2am.

SIGHTS

BAIXA

Although the Baixa features few historic sights, a lively atmosphere surrounding the neighborhood's three main *praças* make it a monument in its own right.

AROUND THE ROSSIO. Begin your tour of Lisbon's 18th-century history in its heart—the **Rossio.** The **Praça Dom Pedro IV,** the city's main square, was once a cattle market, a stage for public executions, a bullring, and a carnival ground. The *praça* is now the domain of drink-sipping tourists and ruthless local motorists circling the central statue of Dom Pedro IV. A statue of Gil Vicente—Portugal's first great dramatist (see **Literature,** p. 531)—peers down from the top of the **Teatro Nacional de Dona Maria II** (easily recognized by its large columns) at one end of the *praça.* Adjoining the Rossio is the elegant **Pr. Figueira,** which lies on the border of the hilly streets of the Alfama district.

AROUND PRAÇA DOS RESTAURADORES. An obelisk and a bronze sculpture of the "Spirit of Independence" in the **Pr. dos Restauradores,** just past the train station when walking from the Rossio, commemorate Portugal's independence from Spain (1640). The tourist office and numerous shops line the *praça* and C. Glória—the hill that leads to Bairro Alto. Pr. Restauradores is also the start of **Av.**

da Liberdade, one of the Lisbon's most elegant promenades. Modeled after the boulevards of 19th-century Paris, this mile-long thoroughfare ends at **Pr. do Marquês de Pombal;** from there an 18th-century statue of the Marquês overlooks the city.

AROUND PRAÇA DO COMÉRCIO. The grid of pedestrian streets on the other side of the Rossio from Pr. Restauradores caters to ice-cream eaters and window shoppers. After the earthquake of 1755, the Marquês de Pombal designed the streets to serve as a conduit for goods from the ports on the Rio Tejo to the city center. Built at the height of Enlightenment urban planning, each street was designated for a specific trade; *sapateiros* (shoemakers), *correeiros* (couriers), and *bacalhoeiros* (cod merchants) each had their own avenue. Two centuries later, the streets of the Baixa retain their commercial nature. Pedestrians wander the wide mosaic sidewalks, cars race down the stately avenues, and visitors swarm upscale shops along the side streets. From the streets of the Baixa, all roads lead to **Pr. do Comércio** on the banks of the Tejo. Also known as **Terreiro do Paço** (the palace terrace) ever since the royal palace which stood there was destroyed in the Earthquake of 1755, Pr. Comércio lies before the towering **statue of Dom João I,** cast in 1755 from 940 lbs. of bronze. The *praça* now serves as the headquarters of several Portuguese government ministries. Its center has been relegated to less dignified use as a fairgrounds for concerts and other events.

BAIRRO ALTO

In the Bairro (the hip name for Chiado), pretentious intellectuals mix with insecure teens and idealistic university students. It's the only place in Lisbon that never sleeps; there is as much to do here at night as there is to see during the day. At the center of the neighborhood is **Pr. Camões,** which adjoins **Largo Chiado** at the top of R. Garrett, a good place to rest and orient yourself while sightseeing. *To reach Rua Garret and the heart of the chic Chiado neighborhood, turn left when exiting the elevator and walk 1 block; Rua Garret is on the right.*

LISBON

AROUND THE ASCENSOR DE SANTA JUSTA. The **Ascensor de Santa Justa,** a historic elevator built in 1902 inside a Gothic wrought-iron tower, once served as transportation up to the Bairro Alto but now just takes tourists up to see the view and then back down again. *(Elevator runs M-F 7am-11pm, Sa-Su 9am-11pm.)*

MUSEU NACIONAL DE ARTE ANTIGA. This museum hosts an interesting survey of European painting dating back as far as the 12th century and ranging from Gothic primitives to 18th-century French masterpieces. *(R. das Janelas Verdes, Jardim 9 Abril. 30min. down Av. Infante Santo from the Ascensor de Santa Justa. Buses #40 and 6 stop to the right of the museum exit and head back to the Baixa. ☎21 391 28 00. Open Tu 2-6pm, W-Su 10am-6pm. 600$/€3, students 300$/€1.50. Free Su before 2pm.)*

MUSEU DO CHIADO. An educational experience awaits in this museum, courtesy of Portugal's most famous post-1850 artists. Though the permanent collection is somewhat small, the Museu do Chiado is known for hosting important exhibits. *(R. Serpa Pinto, 4. From Pr. Camões, go through Largo Chiado and down R. Garrett, turn right onto R. Serpa Pinto, and walk 2 blocks downhill. ☎21 343 21 48. Open Tu 2-6pm, W-Su 10am-6pm. 600$/€3, ages 14–25, seniors, and teachers 360$/€1.80. Free Su before 2pm.)*

IGREJA DE SÃO ROQUE. This church is dedicated to the saint who saved the Bairro Alto from the devastation of the great earthquake. Inside the church, the **Capela de São João Baptista** (4th from the left) is ablaze with gems and precious metals. The chapel caused a stir upon its installation in 1747 because it took three ships to bring it from Rome, where it was built. *(Largo Trinidade Coelho. From Carmo head uphill on R. Garret until R. Misericórdia. ☎21 323 53 83.)* Next door, the **Museu de São Roque,** with its own share of gold and silver, features European religious art from the 16th to 18th centuries. *(☎21 323 53 82. Open Tu-Su 10am-5pm. 200$/€1, students and seniors free. Sunday free.)*

LADIES' MAN Pr. Camões, in the heart of the Bairro Alto off R. Garrett, is marked by a monument to Luís de Camões. Camões, whose 16th-century *Os Lusíadas* chronicled his nation's discoveries in lyric verse, is considered Portugal's greatest poet. Most likely born in Lisbon in 1524 (accounts of his life vary slightly), this swashbuckling stud had so many affairs with ladies of the court that he fled to North Africa to escape their vengeful husbands (official sources say his politics got him banished). Camões led an adventurous life for a poet, enlisting as a common soldier in the army in 1547. His service took him all over the globe, including the Arab and Indian coasts and numerous stops in Portugal's expanding empire; all the while he was working on his verses. By the time he made his way back to Lisbon in 1570, Camões had lost an eye in battle, been jailed and injured in a sword duel, and survived a shipwreck off the coast of Cambodia (clutching his precious poetry the whole time, of course). Two years later (1572) he published *Os Lusíadas;* despite its success he died in poverty somewhere in Asia in 1580. Portugal was never able to recover his body, but Camões is remembered with an honorary tomb just outside Lisbon in Belém's Mosteiro dos Jerónimos and on streets across the country which bear his name.

PARKS. For a perfect picnic, head to the **Parque de São Pedro de Alcântara.** The Castelo de São Jorge in the Alfama stares back from the cliff opposite the park; the city of Lisbon twinkles below. A mosaic points out the landmarks included in this vista. *(On the right off R. São Pedro de Alcântara—the continuation of R. Misericórdia. It's a 5-min. walk up R. Misericórdia from Pr. Camões; the park is right next to C. Glória.)* More greenery awaits uphill along R. Dom Pedro V at the **Parque Príncipe Real,** which connects to Lisbon's extensive **Jardim Botánico.** Across from the church on Largo Estrela, the wide asphalt paths of the **Jardim da Estrêla** wind through flocks of pigeons and lush flora. (Open 8am-9pm.) Park walkways are popular for Sunday strolls, and the benches fill with smoochers. Behind the park tropical plants and cypress trees, odd gravestones mark the **Cemitério dos Inglêses** (English Cemetery).

LISBON

CHURCHES. For more neighborhood flavor, walk uphill through Pr. Camões and take R. Loreto, which turns into Calçada do Combro. Walk over the hill and down to where it levels out; from here turn right onto Tr. Convento de Jesús. Flowered balconies and hanging laundry frame the **Igreja das Mercês,** a handsome 18th-century Travertine building on a small *praça*. Back on Calçada do Combro, a few hundred meters ahead, is Largo António Sousa de Maced and a fork in the road. Follow the right fork onto R. Poiais de São Bento, which becomes Calçada da Estrêla and leads to more churches, including the ornate **Basílica da Estrêla.** Built in 1796, the basilica's dome, poised behind a pair of tall belfries, steals the sky. Half-mad Maria I, desiring a male heir, made fervent religious vows promising God anything and everything if she were granted a son. When a baby boy was finally born, she built this church. Ask the sacristan to show you the gigantic 10th-century manger scene. *(On Pr. Estrela. Accessible by tram #28 from Pr. Comércio. ☎21 396 09 15. Open daily 8am-12:30pm and 3-7:30pm. Free.)*

ALFAMA

The Alfama, Lisbon's medieval quarter, was the lone neighborhood to survive the famous 1755 earthquake. The area descends in tiers from the **Castelo de São Jorge** facing the Rio Tejo. Between the Alfama and the Baixa is the quarter known as the **Mouraria** (Moorish quarter), ironically established after Dom Afonso Henriques and the Crusaders expelled the Moors in 1147. Here, Portuguese grandmothers gossip and school boys play soccer amidst camera-toting tourists, all enjoying the enchanting ambiance of Alfama's streets. Watch out for muggers, especially at night; visit by day without handbags or other snatchables. Though the constant hike that defines Alfama sightseeing is half the fun, the tired and lazy will want to hop on the scenic tram #28 from Pr. Comércio (175$/€0.88), which winds up through the neighborhood past most of its sights.

THE LOWER ALFAMA. While any of the small uphill streets east of the Baixa lead to the Alfama's maze of streets, the least confusing way to see the neighborhood is by climbing up R. Madalena, which begins 2 blocks away from Pr. Comércio (take R. Alfandega from the *praça*). Veer right when you see the **Igreja da Madalena** in the Largo Madalena on the right. Take R. Santo António da Sé and follow the tram tracks to the cleverly designed **Igreja de Santo António da Sé,** built in 1812 over the saint's alleged birthplace. The construction was funded with money collected by the city's children, who fashioned miniature altars bearing images of the saint to place on doorsteps—a custom reenacted annually on June 13, the saint's feast day and Lisbon's largest holiday. *(☎21 886 91 45. Open daily 8am-7pm. Mass daily 11am, 5 and 7pm.)* In the square beyond the church is the solid 12th-century **Sé de Lisboa.** Although the interior of the cathedral is unremarkable, its sheer antiquity and relic-filled treasury make it an intriguing visit. *(☎21 887 72 44. Open M 10am-5pm, Tu-Su 10am-6pm. Treasury open 10am-5pm. 400$/€2.)*

CASTELO DE SÃO JORGE. Near the top of the Alfama lies the **Castelo de São Jorge,** which offers spectacular views of Lisbon and the ocean. Built in the 5th century by the Visigoths and enlarged in the 9th century by the Moors, this castle was a playground for the royal family between the 14th and 16th centuries. Anyone can wander around the ruins, soak in the views, explore the ponds, or gawk at the exotic birds in the gardens. *(From the cathedral, follow the yellow signs for the castle on a winding uphill walk. Castle open daily Apr.-Sept. 9am-9pm; Oct.-Mar. 9am-67pm. Free.)*

MUSEU DAS ARTES DECORATIVAS. The furnishings and ornamentation in this museum convey a good sense of 18th-century palatial luxury. The bookstore has monographs in English on Portuguese art. *(Largo Portas do Sol, 2. To reach the museum, head up to the castle and turn right onto Largo Portas do Sol. ☎21 881 46 00. Open Tu-Su 10am-5pm. 500$/€2.50, seniors and children under 12 250$/€1.25.)*

ALONG TR. SÃO VICENTE. On the far side of the castle, follow the tram tracks along Tr. São Tomé (which becomes R. São Vicente) to Largo São Vicente and the **Igreja de São Vicente de Fora.** Built between 1582 and 1629, it is dedicated to Lisbon's patron saint. Ask to see the *sacristia* with inlaid walls of Sintra marble. *(From the bottom of R. Correeiros in the Baixa, take bus #12 or tram #28 (165$/€0.83). Open Tu-Sa 9am-6pm, Su 9am-12:30pm and 3-5pm. Free. Chapel next door with scenic view 600$/€3.)* At the **Feira da Ladra** (flea market) in the church's backyard, the din of a lively social scene drowns out the cries of merchants hawking used goods. *(Tu and Sa 7am-3pm.)* The **Igreja de Santa Engrácia (National Pantheon)** is farther down toward the coast. The church and its dome took almost 300 years to complete (1682-1966). *(Walk along R. São Vicente and keep left as the road branches. Open Tu-Su 10am-5pm.)*

CONVENTO DA MADRE DE DEUS. A 16th-century convent houses the **Museu Nacional do Azulejo,** devoted to the art of the *azulejo* tile, first introduced by the Moors (see **Architecture,** p. 530). On display are Portuguese, Spanish, and Dutch tiles from the last 500 years. Through a Manueline doorway, the Baroque interior of the church is an explosion of oil paintings, *azulejos*, and gilded wood. The rapturous excess continues in the choir and the **Capela de Santo António.** *(R. Madre de Deus, 4. Follow Av. Infante Dom Henrique, which runs parallel to the Rio Tejo. The avenue leads to the Estação Santa Apolónia; from outside the station, take bus #13. ☎21 814 77 47. Open Tu 2-6pm, W-Su 10am-6pm. 400$/€2, students 200$/€1.)*

SALDANHA

Though most of Saldanha is dedicated to Lisbon's business affairs, this modern district has two excellent museums, both owned by the Fundação Gulbenkian.

MUSEU CALOUSTE GULBENKIAN. When oil tycoon Calouste Gubenkian died in 1955, he left his extensive art collection (some of it purchased from the Hermitage in St. Petersburg, Russia) to his beloved Portugal. Though the philanthropist was of Armenian descent and a British citizen, it was Portugal he chose to call home. (The Portuguese also gave him a substantial tax break in return.) The collection is divided into sections of ancient art—Egyptian, Greek, Roman, Islamic, and Oriental—and European pieces from the 15th to 20th centuries. Highlights include the Egyptian room, Rembrandts, Monets, Renoirs, and a Rodin. *(Av. Berna, 45. M: Palhavã or São Sebastião. Bus # 16, 31, 46. ☎21 782 30 00. Open Tu-Su 10am-5pm. 500$/€2.50, free Su mornings for students and seniors.)*

MUSEU DO CENTRO DE ARTE MODERNA. Though not as famous as its neighbor, this museum is home to an extensive collection of modern art. Most of the works are by Portuguese artists, but the museum also houses pieces by other notable 20th-century artists. Make sure to spend some time in the sculpture gardens. *(R. Dr. Nicolau Bettencourt. M: São Sebastião. Bus #16, 31, 46. ☎21 795 02 41. Open Tu-Su 10am-5pm. 500$/€2.50, free Su mornings for students and seniors.)*

BELÉM

Belém is more of an outlying suburb than a neighborhood of Lisbon, but its high concentration of monuments and museums makes it a crucial stop in any comprehensive tour of the capital. Belém is imperial glory at the service of culture; here, a number of museums and historical sites showcase the opulence and extravagance of the Portuguese empire. To visit Belém is to understand *saudade*, the "nostalgic yearning" expressed musically in *fado* (see **Achy Breaky Heart**, p. 563). *To get to Belém, take tram #15 from Pr. Comércio (15min.), bus #28 or 43 from Pr. Figueira (15min.), or the train from Estação Cais do Sodré (10min., every 15min., 140$/€0.70). From the train station, cross the tracks, then cross the street and go left. The Padrão dos Descobrimentos is by the water, across the highway on your left (use the underpass), while the Mosteiro dos Jerónimos is to the right, through the public gardens. From the bus station, follow the avenue straight ahead. All museums free Su before 2pm.*

MOSTEIRO DOS JERÓNIMOS. Established in 1502 to give thanks for the success of Vasco da Gama's expedition to India, the Mosteiro dos Jerónimos was granted UN World Heritage status in the 1980s. The country's most refined celebration of the Age of Discovery, it showcases Portugal's native Manueline style combining Gothic forms with early Renaissance details. The main door of the church, to the right of the monastery entrance, is a sculpted anachronism; Prince Henry the Navigator mingles with the Twelve Apostles on both sides of the central column. The symbolic tombs of Luís de Camões (see **Ladie's Man,** p. 557) and navigator Vasco da Gama lie in two opposing transepts. Inside the monastery, the octagonal cloisters of the courtyard drip with stone carvings, a contrast to the simplicity of the rose gardens in the center. *(☎21 362 00 34. Open Tu-Su 10am-5pm. 600$/€3, students 300$/€1.50. Free Su 10am-2pm. Cloisters open Tu-Su 10am-5pm. Free.)*

TORRE DE BELÉM. One of two well-known towers on Belém's waterfront, the Torre de Belém rises from the north bank of the Tejo and is surrounded by the ocean on three sides. Built under Manuel I from 1515-1520 as a harbor fortress, it originally sat directly on the shoreline; today, due to the receding beach, it is only accessible by a small bridge. Nevertheless, this symbol of Portuguese grandeur and member of the UN's World Heritage list offers spectacular panoramic views of Belém, the Tejo, and the Atlantic beyond. *(A 10min. walk along the water from the monastery. Take the underpass by the gardens to cross the highway. ☎21 362 00 34. Open Tu-Su 10am-6pm. 600$/€3, students and seniors 300$/€1.50.)*

MONASTERY MUSEUMS. The intriguing **Museu da Marinha** displays the Portuguese prowess in the shipping business. Globes from the mid-18th century show the assumed boundaries of the continents with incredible accuracy. *(At the far end of the monastery complex. ☎21 362 00 19. Open Tu-Su June-Aug. 10am-6pm; Sept.-May 10am-5pm. 500$/€2.50, students 200$/€1. Free Su 10am-2pm.)* The **Museu Nacional de Arqueologia** uses artifacts of various media to depict Portugal's history. *(From the monastery, go right; once inside the monastery complex, the entrance is around the corner. Open Tu 2-6pm, W-Su 10am-6pm. 400$/€2, students 200$/€1. Free Su before 2pm.)*

CENTRO CULTURAL DE BELÉM. Contemporary art buffs will bask in the glow of the gigantic, luminous **Centro Cultural de Belém.** With four pavilions holding regular world-class exhibitions, several art galleries, and a huge auditorium for concerts and performances, the center provides slick entertainment amid a slew of imperial landmarks. *(Across the street from the monastery museums. ☎21 361 24 00; www.ccb.pt. Open daily 9am-10pm. Exhibitions 11am-7:15pm; prices vary.)*

PADRÃO DOS DESCOBRIMENTOS. Along the river is the Padrão dos Descobrimentos, built in 1960 to honor Prince Henry the Navigator. The view here is similar to that from the torre, but here an elevator (rather than stairs) transports visitors 50m up to a small terrace. Hold onto your hat; it can get windy at the top. The Padrão also hosts temporary exhibits. *(Across the highway from the monastery. ☎21 303 19 50. Open Tu-Su 9am-5pm. 350$, students 175$/€0.88.)*

PALÁCIO NACIONAL DE AJUDA. Back toward the hub of Belém is the Palácio Nacional da Ajuda on Largo Ajuda, a short bus ride from the emerald hills overlooking Belém. Constructed in 1802, the 54 chambers are a telling display of decadence. *(Take tram #18 (Ajuda) to the palace back door, or walk up Calçada de Ajuda (20min). ☎21 363 70 95. Open Th-Tu 10am-4:30pm. 600$/€3, students free. Free Su 10am-2pm.)*

PARQUE DAS NAÇÕES

The easiest way to reach the park from Lisbon is to take the metro to the end of the red line (Linha Oriente, 100$/€0.50). The Oriente stop has escalators rising up to the park's main entrance at the Centro Vasco de Gama. Alternatively, city buses #5, 10, 19, 21, 25, 28, 44, 50, 68 and 114 all stop at the Oriente station (175$/€0.88).

LISBON

The **Parque das Nações** (Park of Nations; ☎21 891 93 33; www.parquedasnacoes.pt) inhabits the former Expo '98 grounds 6km from downtown,. In the mid-1990s, the area was a muddy wasteland along the banks of the Tejo; in just a few years the city transformed the land, preparing the grounds for the millennium's last World Exposition. After Expo '98, the government took a risk, pumping millions of dollars into the land and converting it into the Parque das Nações. Fortunately, the gamble has paid off. Today, the park is packed—day and night—with people enjoying its futuristic yet graceful setting. If the proposed construction goes according to plan, the park will soon become a small city. The entrance to the park leads through the Centro Vasco de Gama **shopping mall** (☎21 893 06 01; open daily 10am-midnight) to the center of the grounds, where several information kiosks provide maps and offer free luggage storage (open 9:30am-8pm). For those who don't want to walk between attractions, a **teleférico** (gondola) connects one end of the park to the other (8min.; M-F 11am-8pm, Sa-Su 10am-9pm; 500$/€2.50, under 18 or over 65 250$/€1.25).

The biggest attraction is the **Pavilhão dos Oceanos,** the largest oceanarium in Europe. The enormous new aquarium has interactive sections showcasing the four major oceans (down to the sounds, smells, and climates). All of these connect to the main tank, which houses fish, sharks, and other sea creatures. Worth the trip just to see the adorable sea otters playing in the water. *(Open daily Apr.-Sept. 10am-7pm, Oct.-Mar. 10am-6pm. 1700$/€8.50, under 18 or over 65 900$/€4.50.)* Another solid draw is the **Pavilhão do Conhecimento** (Knowledge Pavilion), an interactive science museum. *(☎21 891 71 12. Open Tu-F 10am-5pm, Sa-Su 11am-6pm. 800$/€4, under 18 or over 65 400$/€2.)* Other **pavilions** scattered throughout the park, including the **International Fairgrounds,** accommodate rotating exhibits during the year. The **Atlantic Pavilion** (host to many of Lisbon's big concerts) and the 145m **Torre Vasco de Gama** (the city's tallest building) grab visitors' attention with their striking, 21st-century architecture. An elevator ascends 300 ft. to the observation tower, which offers spectacular views of the city. *(Open daily 10am-8pm. 500$/€2.50, under 18 or over 65 250$/€1.25.)*

ENTERTAINMENT

Agenda Cultural and *Follow Me Lisboa*, free at kiosks in the Rossio, on R. Portas de Santo Antão, and at the tourist office, have information on concerts, movies, plays, and bullfights. They also have lists of museums, gardens, and libraries.

BARS AND CLUBS

The Bairro Alto is the first place to go for nightlife. In particular, **R. Norte, R. Diário de Notícias,** and **R. Atalaia** have many small bars and clubs packed into three short blocks, making club-hopping as easy as crossing the street. Most gay and lesbian places are between Pr. Camões and Trav. da Queimada, as well as in the **Rato** area near the edge of Bairro Alto past the Pr. Príncipe Real. There are plenty of options outside the Bairro as well: the **Docas de Santo Amaro** host a strip of touristy waterfront bars, clubs, and restaurants while the **Av. 24 de Julho** and the **R. das Janelas Verdes** in the **Santos** area above have some of the most popular bars and clubs. Newer expansions include the area along the river across from the **Sta. Apolónia** train station, where the glitzy new club Lux is located.

At clubs, pants and dark shoes are expected—some places have uptight fashion police at the door. Inside, beer ranges from 400-600$/€2-3. Some clubs charge a cover (generally 1000-2000$/€5-10). As for timing, there's no reason to show up at a club before midnight; crowds flow in around 2am.

DOCAS DE SANTO AMARO

Cosmos, Doca de Santo Amaro, Armazem 243 (☎21 397 27 47). Restaurant (open daily 11am-midnight) gives way to a Eurotrash techno scene. Torches welcome the crowd of trendy 20-somethings out on the patio. Cover 2000$/€10, includes 4 beers or 2 mixed drinks. Disco open midnight-6am.

Salsa Latina, Gare Marítima de Alcântara (☎21 395 05 55), in its own building just across the parking lot from the cluster at Doca de Santo Amaro. Sophisticated crowds come for the live salsa (on the weekends after midnight). Minimum consumption 2000$/€10. Open M-Th 8-11pm, F-Sa 8pm-1:30am.

AVENIDA 24 DE JULHO AND SANTOS

Litro e Meio (1,5 LT.), R. das Janelas Verdes, 27 (☎21 395 05 26), in the Santos area above the clubs on Av. 24 de Julho. This friendly new bar attracts a mostly young crowd and plays house and latin music. Steps lined with torches lead to a large, pleasant patio in back, and there's a narrow upper level inside too. Most popular between 1 and 2:30am before clubbing on the street below. Minimum consumption usually 1000$/€5. Beer 300$/€1.50, mixed drinks 700$/€3.50. Open M-Sa 10pm-4am.

Kapital, Av. 24 de Julho, 68 (☎21 324 25 90). The classiest club in Lisbon, with a ruthless door policy that makes admission a competitive sport. Don't expect to get in; for the best chance, go with Portuguese regulars and keep your mouth shut. Three floors, with a nice terrace at the top and a dance floor on the bottom. If you're still there at the 6am closing time, take the back tunnel directly into neighboring Kremlin to continue partying. Open M-Sa 11pm-6am.

Kremlin, Escandinhas da Praia, 5 (☎21 395 71 01), off Av. 24 de Julho next to Kapital. Run by the same management, but a more mixed crowd including Kapital rejects and the post-Kapital migration. Now has metal detectors due to a shooting incident last year. Door policy is harsh but not impossible. Set in an old convent, Kremlin has giant fake statues and three rooms with throbbing house and dance music. Cover usually 1000$/€5 for women and 2000$/€10 for men, includes one drink. Open F-Sa midnight-9:30am, Th midnight-8am, Tu-W midnight-6am.

Indústria, R. do Instituto Industrial, 6 (☎21 396 48 41), just off Av. 24 de Julho across the avenue from the Outback Steakhouse. A happy alternative to the classy K's further up the street, Indústria is an old factory where the crowd is young enough to smile. Older clubbers may feel ancient here. The door policy may act tough but isn't really too harsh; usually free for women and 2000$/€10 minimum consumption for men. Open F-Sa (and eves of holidays) midnight-6:30am.

SANTA APOLÓNIA

Lux/Frágil, Av. Infante D. Henrique, A (☎21 882 08 90). In a class and location of its own, Lux is the newest big thing in Lisbon; take a taxi to the area across from the Sta. Apolónia train station to get to this imaginative mix of lights and boxes. Minimum consumption 2000$/€10. Open Tu-Sa 6pm-6am; arrive after 2am if you want company.

BAIRRO ALTO

Trumps, R. Imprensa Nacional, 104B (☎21 397 10 59), down R. Dom Pedro IV from the Bairro Alto, on the fifth street on the left after the Pr. Príncipe Real. Lisbon's biggest gay club. Minimum consumption 1000$/€5. Starts going after 1:30am. Phenomenally gay live shows (W and Su at 2:30am) feature men in tight underwear. Open F-Sa 11:30pm-6:30am, Tu-Th and Su 11:30pm-4:30am.

Kasting, R. do Norte, 122, between Trav. da Queimada and Trav. Poço Cidade. One of the hippest new places in the Bairro, Kasting plays house music for a young crowd. Minimum consumption start at 1000$/€5 for women and 2000$/€10 for men. Most popular 1-3am. Open Tu-Sa 10:30pm-4am.

Portas Largas, R. Atalaia, 105 (☎21 346 63 79), at the end of Trav. da Queimada. The original rendezvous point for the Bairro's gay community, but also a popular bar for others (about 90% gay in summer, 50% gay in winter). Portuguese music before midnight and techno afterwards. Open July-Sept. 7pm-3:30am, Oct.-June 8pm-3:30am.

M-F (Mistura Fina), R. das Gáveas, 15 (☎21 342 08 49), just off Pr. Camões. This chill new bar attracts an artsy gay and straight crowd. A big metal leg sculpture straddles the corner of the bar. Fills up after 12:30am. Open daily 4pm-2am.

A Tasca Tequila Bar, Trav. da Queimada, 13-15 (☎21 343 34 31). This classy Mexican bar is an ideal place for some after-dinner cocktails and shmoozing before heading off to the louder bars and discos. Cocktails 1000$/€5, "Quickies" (including Blow Job, Orgasmo, and Multi-Orgasmo) 500$/€2.50. Open daily 6pm-2am.

Solar do Vinho do Porto, R. São Pedro de Alcântara, 45 (☎21 347 57 07), at the top of the steps through the large doorway. Product of a government institute created in 1933 for the purpose of certifying and promoting Port wine, the *Solar* is a mature setting ideal for sipping the stuff, with plush red chairs and an appropriately snooty air. Enjoy a glass before moving on to more active nightlife. Open M-Sa 2pm-midnight.

Frágil, R. Atalaia, 126 (☎21 346 95 78), across the street from Portas Largas. Once the best club in Lisbon, and still decent despite being well past its peak. Plays house music for a mostly gay crowd (60-70%); different DJs nightly. Minimum consumption 3000$/€15, or more at whim. Open M-Sa 11:30pm-4am.

ALFAMA

Restô, R. Costa do Castelo, 7. Known as Chapitô, as identified by the large white sign at the entrance, this bar is located at a circus school. The huge outdoor patio has one of the best views of the city to be found anywhere. Filled with a young crowd, especially 10pm-midnight. Live Portuguese guitar F-Su. *Caipirinha* 800$/€4. Beer 250$/€1.25. Open M-F 7:30pm-2am, Sa-Su 11pm-2am.

Bora-Bora, R. da Madalena, 201 (☎21 887 20 43). A Polynesian bar with a dark wood interior. Exotic cocktails served in extremely exotic cups. All cocktails 1050$/€5.25; most popular is the *pinho frio*. Open F-Sa 8:30pm-3am.

FADO

Lisbon's trademark is the heart-wringing *fado*, an expressive art that combines elements of singing and narrative poetry (see **Music,** p. 532). *Fadistas*, cloaked in black dresses and shawls, perform emotional tales of lost loves and faded glory. Their melancholy wailing is expressive of *saudade*, an emotion of nostalgia and yearning; listeners are supposed to feel the "knife turning in their hearts." On weekends, book in advance by calling the venues. The Bairro Alto has many *fado* joints off R. Misericórdia and on side streets radiating from the Museu de São

ACHY BREAK HEART If your heart is broken at the moment, then *fado* will not only captivate it but nurse you back to health. The melodies and lyrics of *fado* drip with the wrenching pain of unrequited passion. Although *fado* may have been rooted in African slave songs, the legendary *fadista* (*fado* singer) **Maria Severa** (1810-1836) made *fado* quintessentially Portuguese. Severa achieved mythical status because of her moving lyrics, through which she expressed her own real-life dramas. Modern *fadistas*, including **Amália Rodrigues** and **Argentina Santos**, have helped secure *fado* as a cultural fixture in all of Portugal. *Fado* houses, including **Machado** in Lisbon (p. 562), are the best places to enjoy an intimate *fado* moment with that significant other before they break your heart.

Roque; it is the best place in the city for top-quality *fado*. All of the popular houses have high "minimum consumption" requirements and inflated prices. To avoid these, try exploring nearby streets; various bars and other small venues often offer free performances. Otherwise, treat the minimum consumption as a cover charge and pick one of the places to go for coffee and dessert (which should cost enough to rack up the minimum). These places are quite touristy but do feature Portugal's top names in fado. All have acts every 20 minutes or so.

Machado, R. Norte, 91 (☎21 322 46 40). Founded in 1937, Machado is one of the larger fado restaurants (capacity 180 people) and features some of the best known fadistas and guitarists. Eating dinner here, however, will cost at least your daily budget. Entrées 3950-13500$/€20-68. Min. consumption 3100$/€15. Open Tu-Su 8pm-3am; *fados* start at 9:15pm. AmEx/MC/V.

O Faia, R. Baroca, 56 (☎21 342 67 42), between R. Atalaia and R. Diário de Notícias. Elegant and expensive. Some of Portugal's better known *fadistas* perform nightly. Minimum consumption 3500$/€18, includes 2 drinks. Entrées 3500$/€18 and up; fixed price *menú* 7000$/€35. Open M-Sa 8pm-2am; fado starts at 9:45pm. AmEx/MC/V.

O Forcado, R. da Rosa, 221 (☎21 346 85 79). A traditional restaurant that features fado from Coimbra and Lisbon as well as folk music and dance. Decorated with bullfighting pictures and azulejos. Minimum consumption 3000$/€15. Entrées 3500-4000$/€18-20. Open Th-Tu 8pm-1:30am; fado starts at 9:15pm. AmEx/MC/V.

Cristal Fados, Trav. da Queimada, 9 (☎21 342 67 87), on the corner of R. do Norte. A notch below the others, but this means you can actually have dinner without blowing your daily budget. Minimum consumption 1500$/€8. Entrées 1500-2500$/€8-13. Open 8:30pm-1am; fado Th-Su only. AmEx/MC/V.

FESTIVALS

Those who love to mingle with the public will want to visit Lisbon in June. Open-air *feiras* (fairs)—smorgasbords of eating, drinking, live music, and dancing—fill the streets. After savoring *farturas* (Portuguese doughnuts) and Sagres beer, join in traditional Portuguese dancing. On the night of June 12, the streets become a haven for those who like to dance because of the huge **Festa de Santo António**: banners are strung between streetlights and confetti falls like snow during a parade along Av. Liberdade; young crowds absolutely pack the streets of the Alfama, and grilled sardines and *ginginha* are sold everywhere. Commercial *feiras* combine shopping and cultural involvement. Bookworms burrow for three glorious weeks in the **Feira do Livro** (in the Parque Eduardo VII behind Pr. Marques Pombal from late May to early June). The **Feira Internacional de Lisboa,** which has moved to the Park of Nations, occurs every few months, while in July and August the **Feira de Mar de Cascais** and the **Feira de Artesania de Estoril** take place near the casino. Year-round *feiras* include the **Feira de Oeiras** (Antiques) on the fourth Sunday of every month, and the **Feira de Carcanelos** for clothes (Th 8am-2pm). Packrats should catch the **Feira da Ladra** (flea market), held behind the Igreja de São Vicente de Fora in the Alfama neighborhood (Tu and Sa 7am-3pm). Take bus #12 or tram #28.

OTHER FUN THINGS TO DO

BULLFIGHTING

Portuguese bullfights (differing from the Spanish variety in that the bull is not killed) take place most Thursdays from the end of June to the end of September at **Praça de Touros de Lisboa**, Campo Pequeno (☎21 793 21 43. Open 10pm-2am). The Praça de Touros is due to re-open in May after a series of renovations, but you'll want to call ahead or check at the tourist office to confirm that it's open before trekking out. Take the Metro to "Campo Grande" or bus #1, 44, 45, or 83.

BOAT CRUISES

Boats leave from the **Estação Fluvial do Terreiro do Paço** off Pr. Comércio, stopping at the Parque das Nações (45min.) and Belém (2hr.). (☎21 882 03 48; fax 21 882 03 65. Boats run Apr.-Sept. 11am and 3pm, Oct.-Mar. 3pm only. Children 6-12, $3000/€15; students 26 and under 1500$/€8.)

FUTEBOL

If sports are your thing, catch a *futebol* (soccer) match. Lisbon has two professional teams featuring some of the world's finest players: **Benfica** at the Stadium of Light (☎21 726 61 29. M: Colégio Militar Luz), and **Sporting** at Alvalade Stadium (☎21 756 79 14. M: Campo Grande). Check the ABEP kiosk in Pr. Restauradores or the sports newspaper *A Bola*.

THEATER

The **Teatro Nacional de Dona Maria II,** Pr. Dom Pedro IV stages performances of classical Portuguese and foreign plays (☎21 347 22 26. 700-2000$/€3.50-10, 50% student discount). At Lisbon's largest theater, the **Teatro Nacional de São Carlos,** R. Serpa Pinto, 9, near the Museu do Chiado in the Bairro Alto, opera reigns from late September through mid-June. (☎ 21 346 59 14. Open daily 1-7pm).

MOVIES

São Jorge theater (☎21 242 25 23), at the corner of Av. Liberdade and Av. Condes, directly across the square from the Pr. Restauradores tourist office. Huge 10-screen cinemas are also located in the **Amoreiras** (near **M: Marques Pombal**) and **Colombo (M: Colegio Militar Luz)** shopping centers and on the top floor of the **Centro Vasco de Gama (M: Oriente).** American movies are shown with Portuguese subtitles (Tu-Su 900$/€0.75, M 600-900$/€0.30-0.45).

DAYTRIPS FROM LISBON

The following coastal towns, many of them with beautiful beaches or sights, can be refreshing diversions from the city. Pay close attention to transportation links as you plan daytrips from Lisbon; many of these places lie en route to other destinations (including Sintra and Setúbal, see **Near Lisbon,** p. 568).

ESTORIL

***Trains** from Lisbon's Estação Cais do Sodré (☎213 42 48 93; M: Cais do Sodré) run to Estoril (30min., approximately every 20min. 5:30am-2:30am, 210$/€1) continuing to Cascais (also a pleasant 20-min. walk along the beach from Estoril). Stagecoach **bus** #418 to Sintra departs Av. Marginal, down the street from the train station (35 min., every hr. 6:10am-11:40pm, 460$/€2.3).*

Even though Estoril is home to Europe's largest casino, its best asset is its beaches, all of which are lined with bars and restaurants along the seacoast. One of the city's five beaches, **Praia Estoril Tamariz,** greets visitors upon arrival, and the palm-lined **Parque de Estoril** lies just across the street. To exit the train station, use the underpass; take a left to get to the beach or a right to go to the casino and the rest of the town. The **Casino Estoril** in Praça José Teodoro dos Santos is well worth a visit even for non-gamblers, as it offers free shows and concerts as well as a newly-renovated game room and over 1000 slot machines. A nightly laser show lights up the garden starting at 9:30pm, and shows in the casino's theater start at 11pm. Every Wednesday in the Wonder-Bar, the *fado* concert features some of Portugal's most acclaimed singers. Be sure to reserve at least 2 days in advance. (☎214 66 77 00. Dress code: no sneakers, jeans, shorts, swimwear, or hats allowed anywhere in the casino; jackets required for the game room, but can be borrowed at the entrance if you leave an ID. Slots and game room 18+. Game room entrance 1000$/€5 per day or 1500$/€7.5 per week. Passport required. Open daily 3pm-3am.)

The **tourist office,** on Arcadas do Parque, is across the street from the train station and to the left of the park. (☎21 466 38 13; fax 21 467 22 80. Wheelchair accessible. Open M-Sa 9am-7pm, Su 10am-6pm.) If you need a place to stay after the casino closes, the most convenient is **Residencial São Cristóvão,** Av. Marginal, 7079. Facing the park, from the train platform, turn right, passing the gas station and continue up Av. Marginal for about 2 blocks. This residencial has bright, clean rooms and a large kitchen. Enjoy the continental breakfast included. (☎/fax 214 68 09 13. 24hr reception. Checkout noon. Reserve a month ahead in summer if you will be staying for 3 or more days. Ask for lower rates in winter. Doubles 10,000$/€50, with bath 12,500$/€60; triple 15,000$/€75.) Those willing to spend a bit more of their casino winnings a bit farther away from the beach will be rewarded by the lovely **Pensão Pica Pau,** R. D. Afonso Henriques, 48. From the train station, take a left and walk past the tourist office, then take a right at the church onto R. Fausto Figueiredo. Walk up to the junction and take a right; you'll see the white building with the lawn in front. Azulejo tiles line all the hallways of this pension, which seems more like a posh beach resort hotel with bar and pool in the back. (☎214 66 71 40; fax 67 06 64. July-Sept. singles 10,000$/€50; doubles 12,000$/€60; triples 15,600$/€75. Apr.-Oct. singles 8,000$/€40; doubles 10,000$/€50; triples 13,000$/€65. Nov.-Mar singles 6,000$/€30; doubles 8,000$/€40; triples 10,500$/€52.)

CASCAIS

To get to Cascais from neighboring Estoril, take a right onto the walkway at Praia Estoril Tamariz and walk along the coast about 20min. ***Trains*** *from Lisbon's Estação Cais do Sodré (☎21 342 48 93; M: Cais do Sodré) head to Cascais via Estoril (30min., approximately every 20min. 5:30am-2:30am, 210$/€1). Stagecoach* ***bus*** *#417 leaves from outside the train station for Sintra (40min., every hr. 6:35am-7:08pm, 460$/€2.3). To visit* ***Praia de Guincho****, a popular windsurfing beach considered by many to be best of the coast, take the circular route bus #405/415 to the Guincho stop (22 min., every 1-2 hr. 7:39am-5:34pm, 320$/€1.6). The last bus to Cascais is at 8:01pm.*

Although the town is pleasantly serene during the off-season, the summer crowds seem to define the flavor of Cascais rather than spoil it. The beaches, especially the **Praia da Rainha** and the **Praia da Ribeira,** are filled in balmy weather with tanners in various states of undress; anyone with the desire to go topless is welcome here. To reach the Praia de Ribeira, simply take a right upon leaving the tourist office and walk down Av. Dos Combatantes de Grande Guerra until you see the water. Those in search of shade should head to the expansive **Parque Municipal da Gandarinha** (open daily 10am-6pm). About 1 km farther outside of Cascais, another 20 min. walk up Av. Rei Humberto de Itália, lies the **Boca de Inferno** (Mouth of Hell), so named because of the cleft carved in the rock by the Atlantic surf. As the sun sets, the pubbing picks up on **R. Frederico Arouca,** the main pedestrian street.

To get to the **tourist office**, Av. Dos Combatantes de Grande Guerra, 25, from the train station, cross the Largo da Estaçaõ square and take a right at the McDonald's onto Av. Valbom; the office is at the end of this shop-lined street. (☎214 86 82 04. Open July-Sept. 15 M-Sa 9am-8pm, Su 10am-6pm; Sept. 16-June M-Sa 9am-7pm, Su 10am-6pm.) To spend the night, you might want to consider **Residencial Parsi,** R. Afonso Sanches, 8, facing the Praia da Ribeira in the Largo 5 do Outubro, behind the big statue of D. Pedro. All rooms have baths and TVs and a room with a view of the ocean is worth asking for. (☎214 84 57 44; fax 21 481 82 22. June-Sept. 15 singles 5000$/€25; double 6000$/€30, with bath 7000-9000$/€35-45. Sept. 16-May singles 5000$/€25; double 7000$/€35, with bath 9000-12,000$/€45-60. AmEx/MC/V.)

QUELUZ

The best way to get to Queluz is by train. Take the Sintra line from Lisbon's Estação Rossio (M: Rossio) or Estação Sete Rios (M: Jardim Zoológico) and hop off at the Queluz-Belas (not Queluz-Massomá) stop (25min., every 15min., 140$/€0.7). To get to the palace, exit the train station through the ticket office and head left on Av. Antonio Ennes, continuing straight as the street becomes Av. República. Follow the signs until you see the expansive pink palace; the entrance is to the left of the statue of Dona Maria I.

Queluz itself is nothing too remarkable, but the **Palácio Nacional de Queluz** makes it a worthwhile stop along the way to Sintra. In the mid-18th century, Dom Pedro III turned an old hunting lodge into this summer residence with the help of Portuguese architect Mateus Vicente de Oliveira and French sculptor Jean-Baptiste Robillon. The well-ordered garden makes the palace feel like a miniature Versailles; however the *azulejo*-lined canal is purely Portuguese. Highlights inside include the **Sala dos Embaixadores,** with its gilded thrones, marble floors, and Chinese vases and the **Quarto Piquenique's** gilded beehive-style ceiling. Of historical interest is the curiously named **Quarto Don Quijote** where Dom Pedro I, the first emperor of Brazil, drew his last breaths. (Open W-M 10am-5pm. Palace 600$/€3, garden 100$/€0.50. Seniors and students 300$/€1.50.)

MAFRA

Green-and-white Mafrense buses run from Lisbon's Campo Grande (M: Campo Grande) and stop in the square across the street from the palace; Mafrense buses serve Lisbon (1-1½hr., every hr. 5:30am-9pm, 550$/€2.7) and Ericeira (20min., every hr. 7:30am-midnight, 240$/€1.20). Don't take the train from Lisbon's Estação Santa Apolónia unless you're up for the 7km walk to Mafra; the station is out in country where cabs are rare.

An attractive stop on the way to Ericeira from Lisbon, Mafra is home to one of Portugal's most impressive sights and one of Europe's largest historical buildings, the **Palácio Nacional de Mafra.** Built by Dom João V in honor of the birth of his first child, the massive building took 50,000 workers to build and includes a monastery, palace, library, and a large church. For the tour, enter through the door to the left of the main steps of the palace. The monastery has its own hospital and infirmary, as well as a **Sala de Penitencia** where the Franciscan monks punished themselves—note the whip on the wall and the skull above the bed. The palace on the third floor features two towers 230 meters apart, one for the queen and one for the king. You can look down the hall from one to the other when there are no tour groups blocking the view. The **Throne Room,** where the king gave his speeches, is covered with murals representing his eight ideal virtues. Also look for the **Music Room,** decorated with King Carlos's watercolors, and the **Game Room,** which contains billiard and lion-pocketed snooker tables. The **biblioteca** contains 38,000 volumes from the 16th, 17th, and 18th centuries, many of which were bound by the monks. Note the drawer-steps at the bottom of each Brazilian bookcase that allowed the monks to reach the top shelf. From the balcony of the **Sala de Bênção** (Blessing Room), king João V blessed the people of Mafra; the windows on the opposite wall look down into the church, allowing the royal family to view mass from their quarters. The **Baroque church** below is renowned for its bell towers and its unique collection of 6 organs. (☎261 81 75 50. Open W-M 10am-5pm. Daily 45min. tours in English 11am and 2:30pm. Students $600/€3, seniors 300$/€1.5, under 14 free.)

To reach the **tourist office** on Av. 25 de Abril take a right off the main steps of the palace onto Terreiro D. João and bear left, passing the post office on your left; the office will be on the right down the road, behind the fountain. (☎261 81 20 23. Open M-F 9am-7pm, Sa-Su 9:30am-1pm, 2:30-6pm.) If you get hungry after visiting the palace, try **Restaurante O Brasão,** Tr. Manuel Esteves, 7, across the street from the Palácio Nacional. (☎261 81 56 87. Open daily 9am-midnight.)

ERICEIRA

Mafrense buses run from Lisbon's Campo Grande (M: Campo Grande) to Ericeira (1¼-1½hr., every hr. 6:30am-11:20pm, 740$/€4.45). Ask the bus driver to drop you off at the stop nearest the center, or just get off at the bus station. Buses run to: Mafra (25min., every hr. 5:15am-9:05pm, 240$/€1.44); Sintra (50min., every hr. 6:30am-8:30pm, 420$/€2.52); and Lisbon (1¼hr., hourly 5:15am-9:05pm, 740$/€4.45).

Ericeira is a pleasant fishing village whose beaches have been discovered by surfers. Despite its rising popularity, the town seems to have handled the attention responsibly, more or less holding onto its traditional flow of life while visitors come to play in the waves and animate the **Praça da República.** Beachgoers find their way along the coast to the nearby **Praia do Norte**, a long beach to the right of the port, and the **Praia do Sul** on the other side. Surfers head beyond the Praia do Norte to the more pristine **Praia de São Sebastião** or 3km farther to the **Praia da Ribeira d'Ilhas,** where the World Surfing Championships were held in 1994. The surf-shop **Utilmar,** near the town center on R. 5 de Outubro, 25A, rents out surfboards and bodyboards. (☎261 86 23 71. Surfboard or bodyboard 3000$/€15 per day, 5000$/€25 with wetsuit. AmEx/MC/V.)

To get to the **tourist office,** R. Eduardo Burnay, 46, from the bus station, cross the road (EN 247-2), turn left, and walk uphill. Then turn right onto Calçada do Rego and take a right at the fork onto R. Paróquia. After 3 blocks take a left onto R. 5 de Outubro, which runs to the small pedestrian square Pr. República. The tourist office is the white building with blue trim on the opposite end of the square. The office also rents out bikes during the summer. (☎261 86 31 22. Apr.-Sept. half-day 9:30am-2:30pm or 2:30pm-8pm, 500$/€2.50; full day 9:30am-8pm, 900$/€4.50. Open Su-Th 9:30am-8pm, F-Sa 9:30am-midnight, with longer summer hours.) **Restaurante O Jogo da Bola,** Travessa do Jogo da Bola, 3, just across the street to the left of the tourist office, is a popular nightstop where you can sample traditional local dishes anytime from noon until after midnight. (☎261 88 46 46. Entrées 800-2200$/€4-11; Beer 120-170$/€0.60-0.85. Open Th-Tu noon-2am.) Many more seafood restaurants can be found along **R. Eduardo Burnay,** which runs from the Praça de República to the right of the tourist office. In the evening, head over to **Neptuno Pub,** R. Mendes Leal, 12. After facing the tourist office from the Praça da República, walk one block to the right and take a left onto R. Mendes Leal. A friendly Irish pub that often has someone playing traditional Portuguese guitar and *fado* music. Their motto is, "A pleasant atmosphere, where one drink is not enough." (☎261 86 20 17. Open daily 7pm-2am. It sometimes opens at noon during the summer.) If you choose to stay or if you miss the last bus back to Lisbon (9:05pm), you might have trouble finding a cheap room in summer. One of the most suitable places to stay is **Residencial Fortunato**, R. Dr. Eduardo Burnay, 7, a few blocks past the tourist office on the right side of the street. All rooms come with bath and TV. (☎261 862 829. June-Sept. Complicated pricing scheme, but never too expensive. Aug. 8-Aug. 31 singles 8500$/€43; doubles 9500$/€48. July 16-Aug. 7 singles 8000$/€40; doubles 9000$/€45. July 1-15 singles 7500$/€38; doubles 8500$/€43. June singles 6500$/€33; doubles 7500$/€38. Oct.-May singles 5500$/€28; doubles 6500$/€33.)

SESIMBRA

The best way to get to Sesimbra is to take a Transtejo ***ferry*** *from Lisbon to Cacilhas (10min., every 15min. 5:50am-9:30pm, 100$/€0.50) from the dock at Pr. Comércio and then catch a TST bus to Sesimbra (45min.-1hr, 15 per day 6:40am-12:40am, 480$/€2.40). Alternatively, Covas e Filhos and TST buses go directly to Sesimbra (1hr., 7 per day, 8am-7:30pm, 580$/€2.90) from Lisbon's Pr. de Espanha (M: Palhavã), but the traffic is murder. Covas e Filhos and TST* ***buses*** *leave from Sesimbra's main bus station on Av. Liberdade to: Cacilhas (45min.-1hr., 12 per day, 5:40am-11pm, 480$/€2.40); Lisbon*

(1hr., 8 per day 6:30am-6:10pm, 580$/€2.90); Setúbal (45min., 9 per day 6:20am-6:50pm, 450$/€2.20).

The agenda in Sesimbra is refreshingly simple: go to the beach, gape at the **Moorish castle,** eat seafood, and relax. Come for a day and you'll feel welcome; spend the night and you'll feel like a local. For those who pride themselves on being outdoorsy, a steep hour-long hike above town to the Moorish castle rewards with a luminous view of the ocean and surrounding mountains. To reach the castle from the beach, follow the yellow and green signs and take R. Gen. Humberto Delgado to the marked path. (Castle open June-Sept. 7am-8pm, Oct.-May 7am-7pm. Free.)

To get to the **tourist office,** Largo da Marinha, 26-27, from the bus station take a left onto Av. Liberdade and walk downhill to the end, then take a right; the office is across the street from the beach. (☎212 23 57 43. Open daily June-Sept. 9am-8pm; Oct.-May 9am-12:30pm and 2-5:30pm.) Restaurants cluster in the plaza above the tourist office along Largo da Marinha. **Casa Isaías,** R. Coronel Barreto, 2 (☎914 57 43 73), up the street from Lg. do Município, at the end of the block on the right. As local a restaurant as you will ever find, Isaías grills fish in an outdoor brick oven. Inexpensive rooms are difficult to find, especially in the summer.

NEAR LISBON

SINTRA ☎219

Called paradise by some, Sintra is indeed a lovely place to visit. Many a Portuguese king chose to vacation here and with good reason. Set on emerald hills dotted with ancient villas, the town charms with its peaceful streets lined with geraniums and bougainvillea. If you are hoping to get away from the frantic pace of Lisbon city life, a walk through this town will calm even the most weary of travelers.

TRANSPORTATION

Trains: To **Sintra:** Trains depart from **Lisbon's** Estação Rossio and Estação Sete Rios (45min., every 15min. 6am-2am, 210$/€1). From **Sintra:** Estação de Caminhos de Ferro, Av. Dr. Miguel Bombarda (☎219 23 26 05). To **Lisbon's** Estação Rossio and Estação Sete Rios (45min., every 15min. 6:07am-2:07am, 200$/€1).

Buses: To **Sintra:** Lisbon's **Stagecoach** buses come from **Cascais** (#417, 40min., every hr. 6:35am-7:08pm, 520$/€2.60; or #403, 1¼hr., every 1-1½hr. 6:40am-7:45pm, 740$/€3.70) and **Estoril** (#418; 36min; every hr. M-F 6:10am-11:40pm, Sa-Su 6:10am-9:40pm; 460$/€2.30). **Mafrense** buses come from **Ericeira** (50min., every hr. 6:25am-7:25pm, 410$/€2). Bus #434 does a circuit in Sintra connecting its three major sights. A day rover ticket (1250$/€6.30) covers all Stagecoach routes in the area. From **Sintra: Stagecoach** (☎214 83 20 55; fax 86 81 68), on Av. Dr. Miguel Bombarda just outside the train station. To: **Cascais** (#417, 40min., every hr. 7:20am-8:30pm, 520$/€2.60; or #403, 1hr., every 1-1½hr. 6:30am-7:55pm, 740$/€3.70); **Estoril** (#418, 40min., every hr. 6:50am-midnight, 440$/€2.20); **Mafrense** buses, just down the street from the Stagecoach buses. To **Ericeira** (50min., every hr. 7:25am-8:25pm, 410$/€2) with connections to points north.

ORIENTATION AND PRACTICAL INFORMATION

Situated 30km northwest of Lisbon and 10km north of Estoril, Sintra is split into three parts: the modern **Estefânia** around the train station, where most budget accommodations and banks are located; **Sintra-Vila,** where the historic sights settle on the mountainside; and **Portela de Sintra**, where shops and municipal offices cluster. To get to the old town from the train station (a 15 min. walk), take a left out of the train station's ticket office, and turn right down the small hill at the next intersection. One block down the hill, turn left again at the fountain in front of the

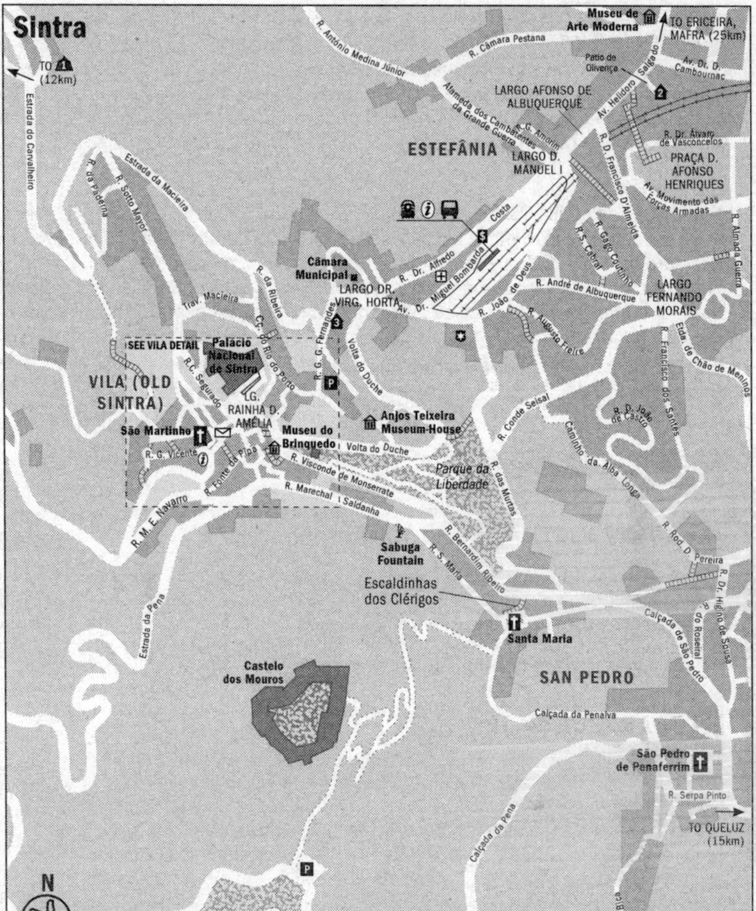

Sintra

TO 1 (12km)
Estrada do Carvalheiro
R. António Medina Júnior
R. Câmara Pestana
Museu de Arte Moderna
TO ERICEIRA, MAFRA (25km)
Patio de Olivença
Av. Dr. D. Cambournac
Salgado
2
LARGO AFONSO DE ALBUQUERQUE
Alameda dos Combatentes da Grande Guerra
R. G. Amorim
Av. Heliodoro
R. Dr. Álvaro de Vasconcelos
PRAÇA D. AFONSO HENRIQUES
ESTEFÂNIA
LARGO D. MANUEL I
R. D. Francisco D'Almeida
Av. Movimento das Forças Armadas
R. da Padeira
Estrada da Maceira
R. Sotto Mayor
Costa
R. Almada Guerra
R. S. Cabral
R. Gago Coutinho
Câmara Municipal
R. Dr. Alfredo
Av. Dr. Miguel Bombarda
R. André de Albuquerque
LARGO FERNANDO MORAIS
R. da Ribeira
Trav. Macieira
LARGO DR. VIRG. HORTA
R. João de Deus
R. G. G. Fernandes
3
R. Augusto Freire
Cc. do Rio do Porto
SEE VILA DETAIL
Palácio Nacional de Sintra
Etda. de Chão de Meninos
R. C. Segurado
Volta do Duche
R. Francisco dos Santos
VILA (OLD SINTRA)
P
LG. RAINHA D. AMÉLIA
R. Conde Seisal
R. D. João de Castro
Anjos Teixeira Museum-House
São Martinho
Museu do Brinquedo
Volta do Duche
R. G. Vicente
R. Fonte da Pipa
R. Visconde de Monserrate
Parque da Liberdade
R. das Murtas
Caminho da Alba Longa
R. Marechal Saldanha
R. M. E. Navarro
R. Bernardim Ribeiro
R. Rod. D. Pereira
Sabuga Fountain
R. S. Maria
R. Dr. Higino de Sousa
Escaldinhas dos Clérigos
R. do Roseiral
Calçada de São Pedro
Estrada da Pena
Santa Maria
Castelo dos Mouros
SAN PEDRO
Calçada da Penalva
São Pedro de Penaferrim
R. Serpa Pinto
TO QUELUZ (15km)
Calçada da Pena
P
N
0 200 yards
0 200 meters
Palácio da Pena
TO 4 (250m)
SANTA EUFÉMIA
R. do Rio da Bica
R. do Capitão

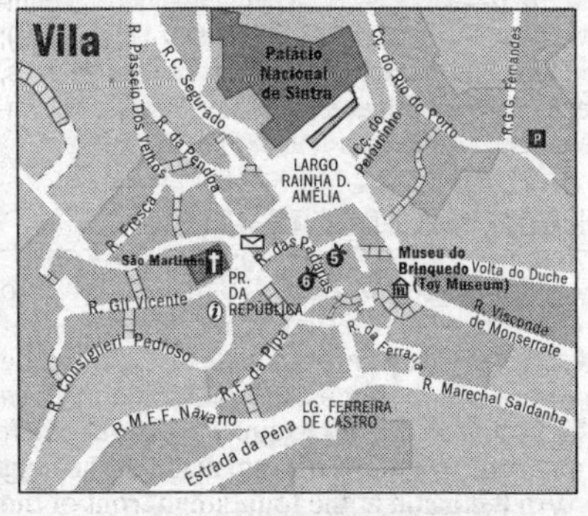

ACCOMMODATIONS

Camping, **1**
Casa Adelaide, **3**
Pensão Económica, **2**
Pousada da Juventude, **4**

FOOD

Alcobaça, **5**
Casa Piriquita, **6**

castle-like **Câmara Municipal,** following the road as it curves past the **Parque da Liberdade.** From there, head up the hill to the **Pr. da República;** the Palácio Nacional de Sintra is the large white building on the right.

Tourist Office: Sintra-Vila, Pr. República, 23 (☎219 23 11 57; fax 23 51 76) is in the historic center. From the Pr. República, with the palace at your right, walk straight ahead 1 block; the tourist office is beyond the palace in a columned marble building. Open June-Sept. daily 9am-8pm; Oct.-May 9am-7pm.

Currency Exchange: Banco Totta e Açores, Sintra-Vila, R. Padarias, 4 (☎219 10 68 70; fax 10 68 71). On the popular uphill side street off the main *praça*. Open M-F 8:30am-noon, 1pm-3pm. **ATMs** also line Av. Heliodoro Salgado in modern Sintra.

Emergency: ☎112. **Police:** R. João de Deus, 6 (☎21 923 09 35), behind the end of the train tracks as you walk toward Sintra-Vila. **Local emergency service:** ☎219 10 69 00.

Medical Services: Centro de Saúde, R. Alfredo do Costa, 34, 1st fl. (☎219 23 21 22). **Hospital Fernando Fonseca (Amadora-Sintra)** in nearby Amadora (☎214 34 82 00).

Internet Access: At **Loja do Arco,** R. Arco do Teixeira, 2 (☎21 910 61 51; fax 21 910 61 49; www.rigra.pt). First 30min. for 500$/€2.5, 250$/€1.25 for each add'l 15min.

Post Office: Av. Movimento das Forças Armadas, 1 (☎219 23 91 51; fax 23 91 56). Internet access. Open M-F 8:30am-6pm. **Postal Code:** 2710.

ACCOMMODATIONS AND CAMPING

Accommodations can be affordable, and Sintra makes a good base for daytrips to surrounding historical sights and coastal towns. Just be sure to make reservations, as some places can fill up months ahead in advance.

Pousada da Juventude de Sintra (HI), Santa Eufémia at S. Pedro de Sintra, (☎219 24 12 10; fax 219 23 31 76). Hike 2km uphill to São Pedro or hail a taxi in front of the train station (weekdays 1800$/€9; weekends 2000$/€10). Alternatively, take bus #434 from the train station or from the bus stop in the old town (exit the tourist office and take a left turn in the *praça;* the stop is on the left across from a fountain) to the Palácio de Pena (600$/€0.30 all-day pass). Walk through the palace garden to the hostel. Dining room, sitting room, TV with VCR, stereo, and winter heating. Breakfast included. HI membership required. June 16-Sept. 15 dorms 1900$/€9.50 per person; doubles 4200$/€21, with bath 4600$/€23. Sept. 16-June 15 dorms 1500$/€7.50 per person; doubles 3500$/€17; with bath 3800$/€19. MC/V.

Casa Adelaide, R. Guilherme G. Fernandes, 11 (☎219 23 68 73). From the train station, head downhill toward Sintra-Vila, walk past the Câmara Municipal at Largo Dr. Virg Horten and turn left onto R. Guilherme Fernandes; enter through the back patio half a block downhill on the left. Singles 4000$/€20; doubles 5000$/€25; triples 6000$/€30. Ask for lower rates in winter; you can probably bargain down to 3000$/€15.

Pensão Economica, Pátio de Olivença, 6 (☎219 23 02 29). Take a right out of the train station, and walk up Av. Dr. Miguel Bombarda as it turns into Av. Heliodoro Salgado. Watch for a dead-end street to intersect Av. Salgrado on the right side; the *pensão* is at end of this alley, just down the hill. Well-kept rooms with small low beds and decorative ceramics. One double and one triple available. Common bathroom. Singles 4000$/€20, with TV 5000$/€25; double 5000$/€25; triple 2000$/€10 per person.

Camping: Parque de Campismo da Praia Grande, Praia Grande, Av. Maestro Frederico de Freitas, 28 (☎219 29 05 81; fax 29 18 34; wondertur@ip.pt), on the Atlantic coast 12km from Sintra. Reception daily until 7pm. 570$/€2.84 per person.

FOOD

Pastelarias (pastry shops) and restaurants crowd **R. João de Deus** (the street parallel to the train station across the tracks) and **Av. Helidoro Salgado** in modern Sintra. In the old town **R. das Padárias** (near the Palácio Nacional) is lined with

QUEIJADAS DE SINTRA There's a lot of history packed into those little cheese pastries you'll see being proudly sold in the *pastelarias* of Sintra. *Queijadas* date back to the 13th century and were once used as a form of currency to pay landlords. The queijada's ascent to fame began in 1756, when a woman named Maria started making queijadas to sell to the public at the entrance of the town. After the railroad tracks linking Sintra to Lisbon were completed in 1887, famous writers began to pass through the town, and they were so impressed by the little sweet that it soon made its way into many classic works of Portuguese literature. Maria's descendants still run the oldest pastry shop in Sintra, and they have joined with the three other prestigious names of the queijada tradition—Preto, Gregorio, and Piriquita—to form an association for the protection of the authenticity and integrity of *queijadas de Sintra*. All the shops use the same ingredients to prepare the pastries: cheese, wheat flour, sugar, egg yolk, and cinnamon, in a shell made of just flour and water. However, according to Francisco Barreto das Neves, the current grandfather of the Sapa tradition and self-proclaimed head of quality control, there are countless variables in the process of production that make the queijadas different in every shop.

eateries. On the 2nd and 4th Sundays of every month, take bus #435 from the train station to the nearby São Pedro (15min., 220$/€1.10) for a spectacular **market.**

Pastry shops: Fábrica das Verdadeiras Queijadas da Sapa, Volta do Duche, 12 (☎219 23 04 93). From the train station, head down Av. Dr. Miguel Lombarda past Restaurante Apeadeiro, and bear left onto Volta do Duche; the shop will be on the right. The oldest pastry shop in Sintra. Founded in 1756 and at its current location since 1890, Sapa is still run by the same family. Try a *queijada* (120$/€0.6) pastry or buy a *pacote* (package) for the road (600$/€3). Open Tu-F 9am-6pm, Sa-Su 9am-7pm. **Casa Piriquita,** R. Padarias, 1 (☎219 23 06 26), up a small side street off Pr. República. One of the four classic pastry shops of Sintra, Piriquita has the advantage of being right in tourist central. Bright yellow tiles cover the façade, and *fado* music floats into the narrow street. The counter is flanked by a marble-floored coffee and tea room. Try one of their *queijadas* (110$/€0.60) Open W-M 9am-10pm.

Alcobaça, R. Padarias, 9 (☎219 23 16 51), up R. Padarias from Pr. República, and just beyond Casa Piriquita. A frame on the wall showcases paper currency of many nations, representative of the range of tourists who come here. Shellfish lovers will enjoy the *arroz de marisco* (1600$/€8). Open noon-11pm daily. Closed Dec. 12-26.

SIGHTS

CASTELO DOS MOUROS. You're not likely to forget a walk along the walls of this 8th century Moorish castle—or the views; from the walls and turrets, a panorama of sandy coast and mountains runs for miles. The view-struck are usually sun-struck; a bottle of water is recommended. (*Bus #434 runs to the top from outside the tourist office. 600$/€3 for all-day pass. If you want to walk (1-1½hr.), start at the Museu do Brinquedo off Pr. República and follow R. Visconde de Monserrate up the hill; continue straight as it becomes R. Bernardim Ribeiro, then take a right up the Escadinhas dos Clerigos and walk to the fork at the end. Turn left onto the Calçada da Santa Maria (toward the church), then right when you see a sign for Casa do Adro. Take another right at the first side street and follow it up the mountain to the Castelo. Open June-Sept. 9am-8pm, Oct.-May 9am-7pm. Free.)*

PALÁCIO NACIONAL DE SINTRA. Also known as the Paço Real or Palácio da Vila, the palace presides over Pr. República. Once the summer residence of Moorish sultans and their harems, the Paço Real and its gardens were built in two stages. Dom João I built the main structure in the 15th century; a century later, Dom Manuel I created the best collection of *azulejos* in the world. He added various wings to create a unique mix of Moorish, Gothic, and Manueline styles. The palace has more than 20 rooms, including the *azulejo*-covered **Sala dos Árabes** and the majestic **Sala dos Brasões.** You may notice a bird theme: doves symbolizing the Holy Spirit line the walls of the **Capela,** while magpies cover the ceiling of the **Sala das Pegas;** and swans grace the ceiling of the **Sala dos Cisnes.** *(At Largo da Rainha Dona Amélia. ☎219 10 68 40. Open Th-Tu 10am-5:30pm. Closed bank holidays. Buy tickets by 5pm. 600$/€3, with student ID 300$/€1.50)*

PALÁCIO DA PENA. Built in the 1840s by Prince Ferdinand of Bavaria, the husband of Queen Maria II, this otherworldly Palácio looks like it belongs in Disney World. Nostalgic for his country, the prince rebuilt and embellished the ruined monastery with the assistance of a Prussian engineer, combining the artistic heritages of both Germany and Portugal. The result is a Bavarian castle decorated with Arabic minarets, Gothic turrets, Manueline windows, and a Renaissance dome. Interior highlights include the chapel, a fully furnished kitchen, incredible views from the Queen's terrace, and **Her Majesty's Toilet**—crafted entirely in *azulejos. (About 1km farther uphill from the Castelo dos Mouros. July-Sept. Tu-Su 10am-6:30pm; Oct.-June Tu-Su 10am-5pm. 600$/€3, students 400$; Oct.-Apr. 200$./€1)*

MUSEU DO BRINQUEDO (TOY MUSEUM). The toy museum, which grew out of the private collection of João Arbue's Moreira, displays a fascinating three-floor assortment of over **20,000 toys** in Sintra's old fire station. According to Moreira, the unifying theme of his museum is to show the history of humanity by way of toys; this philosophy is what connects the pieces of this eclectic collection of cars, trains, LEGOs, dolls, lead soldiers, and many other items. The collection includes trinkets from all over the world as well as traditional Portuguese playthings. Especially intriguing is the second floor, which presents the entire history of war, from Adam and Eve to World War II. *(R. Visconde de Monserrate, 28. ☎219 10 60 16. Open Tu-Su 10am-6pm. 600$/€3, children under 3 and students 300$/€1.50.)*

SINTRA MUSEU DE ARTE MODERNA. This musuem houses contemporary works by Andy Warhol and Gerhard Richter amongst others in a 19th-century building. *(Past the train station in modern Sintra, on Av. Heliodoro Salgado. ☎219 24 81 70. Open Tu-Su 10am-6pm. 600$, students 300$, children under 10 free; seniors and under 18 free on W.)*

SETÚBAL

☎265

An important urban and economic center in Roman times, today Setúbal is now a major fishing port and one of Portugal's major industrial cities. The daily catch, auctioned off at the municipal fish market, shapes the restaurant menus. The city's fine castle, some of Portugal's brightest *azulejo*-covered alleys, and the waters of the largely rural Costa Azul warrant at least a day's visit from Lisbon.

TRANSPORTATION

Trains: leave from either the central **Praça de Quebedo** or **Estação de Setúbal** (☎265 23 88 02), in Pr. Brasil for **Faro** (4hr., 3 per day 9:20am-8:25pm, 2000$/€10) and **Lisbon's** Estaçao Barreiro (1½hr., every hr. 5am-midnight, 210$/€1.1).

Buses: Setublanse, Av. 5 de Outubro, 44 (☎265 52 50 51). From the city tourist office, walk up R. Santa Maria to Av. 5 de Outubro and turn left; the station is about 2 blocks down on the right, in the building with the word "Rodoviaria" in big letters written vertically down the front. To: **Évora** (daily express bus 1¾hr, 10:20am, 1400$/€7; other buses 2¼hrs.-2½hrs, 7 per day 6:30am-6:45pm, 980$/€4.90) and **Lisbon's** Praça de Espanha (45min., every 30min. 6am-10pm, 580$/€2.90). **Covas & Filhos,** Av. Alexandre Herculano (☎21 223 31 03), a right 2 blocks past the Setublanse station, goes to **Sesimbra** (45min., 9 per day 7:20am-8pm, 425$/€2.10).

Ferries: Transado, Doca do Comércio (☎265 23 51 01), off Av. Todi at the east end of the waterfront. Trips run back and forth from Setúbal to **Tróia** (15min., every 15-45min. around the clock, 180$/€0.90. Children 5-10 90$/€0.45, under 5 free.

Taxis: (☎265 23 33 34), along Av. Todi and by the bus station.

ORIENTATION AND PRACTICAL INFORMATION

Setúbal's spine is **Av. Luisa Todi,** a long boulevard parallel to the Rio Sado. Inland from the river and Av. Todi lies a dense district of shops and restaurants centered around **Pr. de Bocage.** Pr. Bocage leads to another major thoroughfare, **Av. 5 de Outubro.** Perpendicular to Av. 5 de Outubro, **Av. da Portela** runs past the train station.

Tourist Office: Posto de Turismo da Costa Azul, Trav. Frei Gaspar (☎265 53 91 20), just off Av. Luisa Todi near Lg. Misericordia. Wheelchair accessible. Open May-Sept. Su 9:30am-12:30pm; Sa and M 9:30am-12:30pm, 3-7pm; Tu-F 9:30am-7pm; Oct.-Apr. Sa and M 9:30am-12:30pm, 2-6pm; Tu-F 9:30am-6pm.

Currency exchange: Av. Todi is lined with **banks.** All open M-F 8:30am-3pm. **Caixa Geral de Depositos**, Av. Todi (☎265 53 05 00).

Emergency: ☎112. **Police:** Av. Todi (☎265 52 20 22), at Av. 22 de Dezembro.

Medical Services: Hospital on R. Camilo Castelo Branco (☎265 52 30 24).

Internet Access: Ciber Centro, Av. Bento Gonçalves, 21A (☎265 23 48 00). 6 computers. 500$/€2.50 per 30min., 450$/€2.24 with student ID. Open M-F 9am-11pm.

Post office: Av. Mariano de Carvalho (☎265 52 86 20), at Av. 22 de Dezembro. **Posta Restante.** Open M-F 8:30am-6:30pm. **Postal code:** 2900.

ACCOMMODATIONS AND CAMPING

There are a few good, cheap pensions along **Av. Todi** and near the **Pr. de Bocage.** Alternatively, ask at the tourist office for a list of quartos in private houses.

Pensão Bom Amigo, R. Concelho, 7 (☎265 52 62 90), off Pr. Bocage and next to the Câmara Municipal, has rooms some with Praça views. July-Sept. singles 3500$/€18, with bath 4000$/€20; doubles 4000$/€20, with bath 6000$/€30. Oct.-June singles 3000$/€15, with bath 3500$/€18; doubles 3500$/€18, with bath 5000$/€25.

Pensão O Cantinho, Beco do Carmo, 1-9 (☎265 52 38 99), off Av. Todi behind Lg. do Carmo. The rooms above the restaurant are startlingly cheap. Reserve a month ahead in summer. Single 2000$/€10, with bath 3000$/€15; double with bath 4500$/€23.

Camping: Get-away-from-it-all types will want to escape to **Parque Natural da Arrábida** or one of the smaller locations near Setúbal in Azeitão or Sesimbra. Closer to the center of town is **Toca do Pai Lopes,** on the riverbank of R. Praia da Saúde (☎265 53 18 20), past Doca dos Pescadores on the road to Outão. June-Aug. 310$/€1.50 per person, 270-485$/€1.30-€2.40 per tent, 270$/€1.30 per car. Sept.-May 220$/€1.10 per person, 185-340$/€0.90-1.70 per tent, 185$/€0.90 per car.

FOOD

Setúbal is full of restaurants offering the town specialties (including grilled fish and fried calamari) at very affordable prices; there's no reason to pay more than 1500$/€8 for a memorable meal. A row of seafood places line the end of **Av. Todi** just up the street from Doca do Comercío; you can watch as they cut and fry your fish on grills set up along the sidewalk. Pick up **groceries** and fresh baked goods at **Pingo Doce,** Av. Todi, 149. (☎265 52 61 05. Open 8am-10pm daily).

O Cantinho, Beco do Carmo, 1-9 (☎265 52 38 99), off Av. Todi behind Lg. do Carmo. You basically pick what you want and they throw it on the outdoor grill for you. Excellent grilled fish (800-1500/€4-7.50) and try the orgasmic *doce são marcos* dessert (250$/€1.30). Open F-W 9am-11pm; meals served noon-3pm, 7-11pm.

Casa de Santiago, Av. Todi, 92 (☎265 22 16 88), right next to the Avis office. Known by locals as *choco frito,* their most popular dish, this is one of the better seafood places in town. Try the house specialty, *choco frito* ($950/€4.70). Meals served noon-3pm; 6:30-10pm. Open M-Sa 9:30am-3pm, 6:30pm-10pm.

Jardim de Inverno, R. Álvaro Luz, 48-50 (☎265 23 93 73). From Pr. Bocage, walk 2 blocks past the post office on R. Álavro Castelões and turn left onto this side street; the *jardim* is at the end on the right. A nice escape, especially if grilled fish doesn't agree with you. Try *bife na frigideira* (950$/€4.70). Open M-F 8:30am-7pm.

SIGHTS AND ENTERTAINMENT

The most impressive sight in town is not really in town. The 16th-century **Fortaleza de São Filipe** sits on top of a hill just outside the city. Designed by the Italian military engineer Filipe Terzi, the castle was built from 1582 to 1600 to complement the Fortaleza de Santiago at Outão. Today, part of it houses a national inn. A phenomenal view of the Sado River rewards visitors. To reach the castle, take Av. Todi to its end (towards the beaches), turn right onto Escadinhas do Castelo, then ascend R. Estrada do Castelo about 15min. It's approximately a 40min. walk from the town center. During the last week of July and first week of August, the **Fiera de Santiago** brings an amusement park, bullfighting, and folk music to Setúbal.

DAYTRIPS FROM SETÚBAL

Outside of town are the beaches of peninsular **Tróia,** a 15min. ferry ride away from Doca do Comércio (15min., every 15-45min. 180$/€0.90, children 5-10 90$/€0.45, under 5 free.) To the west of Setúbal is **Parque Natural da Arrábida,** a large nature preserve that includes a variety of nature trails and the pristine **Praia da Figueirinha,** 9km from Setúbal. Also near Setúbal is the **Reservado Natural do Estuário do Sado**. Outdoor adventurers can contact **Mil Andanças,** Av. Todi, 121 (☎265 53 29 96), for somewhat pricy mountain biking, hiking, canoeing, and other nature trips. Before setting off on your own, check with **PNA**, Pr. da República for nature tourism information. (☎265 54 11 40. Open 9am-12:30pm and 2-5:30pm daily.)

ALGARVE

Behold the Algarve: a desert on the sea, a vacationland where happy campers from the world over bask in the sun. Nearly 3000 hours of annual sunshine have transformed this former fishermen's backwater into one of Europe's favorite vacation spots. In July and August, tourists mob the Algarve's resorts, packing bars and discos from sunset at 10pm until long after sunrise. Still, not all is excess in the Algarve. The region between Faro and the Spanish border remains untouched, and to the west of Lagos, towering cliffs shelter immaculate beaches. During the off-season, the resorts empty and wildlife of a different sort arrives, as roughly one-third of Europe's flamingos migrate to the wetlands surrounding Olhão.

Few vacationers in search of wild parties and perfect tans pause to appreciate local culture, but the Algarve does have a long and varied history, dating back millenia. From 4000 BC, sacrifices were offered at desolate and mist-shrouded Sagres, long considered to be the end of the world. The Romans established prosperous trading communities in the Algarve, but their influence was far eclipsed by the Moors, who arrived in the early 8th century and gave the region its name, Al-Garb, which comes from the Arabic verb "garaba" or "to sink down with the sun." Within 200 years of the Christian reconquest in the 13th century, the Algarve became Portugal's principal center of exploration. Prince Henry the Navigator built his famed navigational school in Sagres and caravels launched from Lagos reached distant ports in Africa, Asia, and America.

With nearly a hundred miles of coastline, the Algarve has perfected the art of delicious seafood; local favorites include *sardinhas assadas* (grilled sardines), and *caldeirada* (seafood chowder). Almonds and figs also make their way into most regional cooking, especially the divine desserts like *figos cheios* (figs filled with a thick paste made of ground almonds, cacao, cinnamon, and lemon peel).

ALGARVE

LAGOS ☎282

In the 17th century, travelers ventured here for the indigo and sugar markets; today they come for the meat market that is Lagos by night. As the town's countless expats will attest, Lagos (pop. 22,000) is a black hole: come for two days and you'll be tempted to stay a month. The Algarve's capital for almost 200 years, Lagos launched many of the caravels that brought Portugal power and fortune in 15th and 16th centuries. A massive earthquake in 1755 destroyed most traces of Lagos's golden age, but no one's complaining; visitors swarm the town each summer in search not of history but of legendary beaches and backpacker hedonism.

TRANSPORTATION

If you are trying to get to Lagos from northern Portugal, you must go through Lisbon; those coming from the east must transfer in Faro.

Trains: (☎282 76 29 87 or 79 23 61), across the river (over the pedestrian suspension bridge) from the main part of town. To: **Beja** (4hr., 2 per day 8:50am and 5pm, 1330$/€6.70) via Faro; **Évora** (6hr., 2 per day 8:50am and 5pm, 1930$/€9.70) via Faro; **Faro** (1¾hr., 9 per day 5:55am-10:30pm, 750$/€3.74); **Lisbon** (4-4½hr., 6 per day 6:55am-10:30pm, 2110-2280$/€10.50-11.40); **Silves** (40min., 7 per day 6:55am-10:30pm, 260$/€1.30); **Vila Real de Santo António** (4hr., 6 per day 6:55am-10:30pm, 1010$/€5.05).

Buses: The **EVA** bus station, off Av. Descobrimentos (☎282 76 29 44), is just before R. Porta de Portugal (when walking into town) and across the channel from the train station and marina. To: **Albufeira** (1¼hr., 7 per day 7am-6pm, 730$/€3.65); **Faro** (2½hr., 6 per day 7am-5:15pm, 850$/€4.25); **Huelva, Spain** (4¾hr., 2 per day 7:30am and

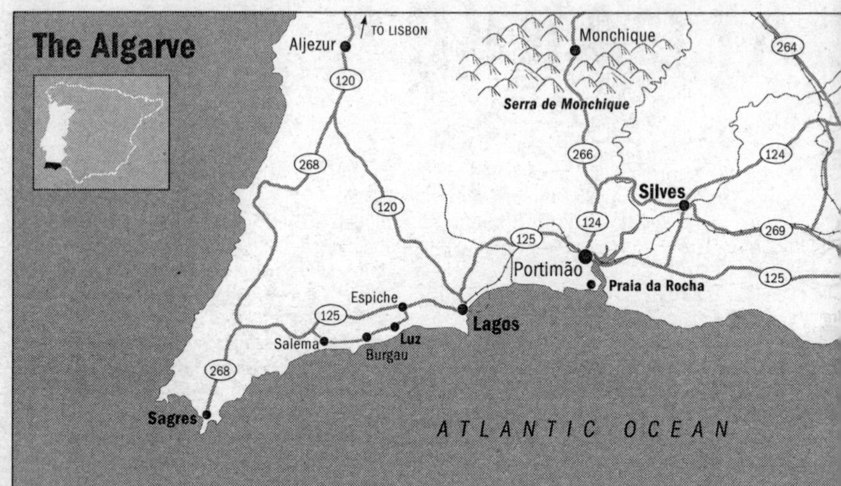

2pm, 3000$/€15); **Lisbon** (5hr., 12 per day 7:40am-1:30am, 2500-2600$/€12.50-13); **Portimão** (40min., 14 per day 7:15am-7:15pm, 370$/€1.85); **Sagres** (1hr., 17 per day 7:15am-8:30pm, 480$/€2.40).

Taxis: Lagos Central Taxi (☎282 76 24 69) 24hr. service to Lagos and environs.

Car Rental: Minimum age 21 for vehicles, 16 for motorbikes.

Marina Rent A Car, Av. Descobrimentos, 43 (☎282 76 47 89). June-Sept. cars start at 8700$/€43.40 per day; May-June and Oct. 7500$/€37.41; Nov.-Apr. 6500$/€32.42; tax and insurance included. AmEx/MC/V.

Motoride, R. José Afonso lote 23-C (☎282 76 17 20), rents bikes (1000$/€5 per day) and scooters (4000-4800$/€20-24 per day; min. age 16; must have license). Open daily 9am-7pm.

Hertz-Portuguesa, Rossio de S. João Ed. Panorama, 3 (☎282 76 98 09), behind the bus station off Av. Descobrimentos. Cars start at 10,000$/€50 per day, tax and insurance included.

ALGARVE

ORIENTATION AND PRACTICAL INFORMATION

Running the length of the channel, **Avenida dos Descubrimentos** is the main road that carries traffic to and from Lagos. From the **train station,** walk through the pastel pink marina and cross the channel over the pedestrian suspension bridge; turn left onto Av. Descubrimentos. Exiting the **bus station,** walk straight until you hit Av. Descubrimentos and turn right. After 15m, take another right on to R. Porta de Portugal to reach **Praça Gil Eanes,** the center of the old town. A cornucopia of restaurants and accommodations surrounds the goofy statue of Dom Sebastião that presides over the square. From Praça Gil Eanes, bars and hostels line **R. Afonso Dalmeida, R. 25 de Abril,** and **R. Silva Lópes.** Follow R. Silva Lopes to R. General Alberto Silveira to reach the grotto-lined beach of **Praia Doña Ana.**

Tourist Office: R. Vasco de Gama (☎282 76 30 31), an inconvenient 25min. walk from the bus station. Follow R. Vasco da Gama until it crosses Av. da República, from there it's another 150m on the right. Open daily 9:30am-12:30pm and 2-5:30pm.

Currency Exchange: Cota Cambios, Pr. Gil Eanes, 11 (☎282 76 44 52), to the left of the Dom Sebastião statue. 500$/€1.50 commission on currency. Open June-Sept. M-F 9am-10pm, Sa-Su 10am-8pm; Oct.-May M-F 9am-7pm, Sa-Su 10am-7pm.

English Bookstore: Loja do Livro, R. Dr. Joaquim Telo, 3 (☎282 76 73 47). Best selection in Lagos of best-sellers, pulp romances, and travel guides. Open June-Aug. M-F 10am-1pm and 3-11pm, Sa 10am-1pm; Sept.-May M-F 10am-1pm and 3-7pm.

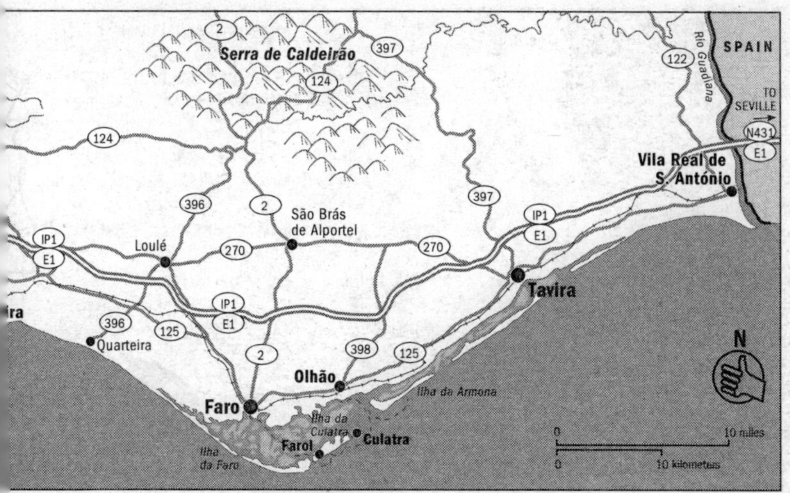

Laundromat: Lavandaria Miele, Av. Descubrimentos, 27 (☎282 76 39 69). Wash and dry 1250$/€6.23 per 5kg. Open M-F 9am-1pm and 3-7pm, Sa 9am-1pm.

Scuba Diving: Blue Ocean Diving Center (☎/fax 282 78 27 18). About a 30min. walk out of the old city, at Motel Ancora, on the road to Porto de Mós. Medical license required for difficult dives. Lessons in English, French, German, and Portuguese. Half-day (in swimming pool) 4800$/€24; full-day (in swimming pool and sea) 9000$/€45.

Parasailing: Marina de Lagos (☎916 00 44 40). Diagonally to the left of the pastel pink building when facing the channel. Portuguese and English spoken. Group and family discounts. Parasailing 7000$/€35; observing on the boat 2500$/€13.

Grotto Boat Tours: Companies offering tours of the coastal cliffs and grottoes set up shop on Av Descobrimentos. Most tours 45min. and start at 4000$/€20 for 2 people. Smaller boats are preferable, as they can maneuver into rock caves and formations.

Emergency: ☎112. **Police:** on R. General Alberto Silva, (☎282 76 29 30).

Pharmacy: Farmácia Silva, R. 25 de Abril, 9 (☎282 76 28 59).

Medical Services: Hospital, R. Castelo dos Governadores (☎282 76 30 34).

Internet Access: The Em@il Box (Ciaxa de Correieo), R. Cândido dos Reis, 112 (☎282 76 89 50), has 4 computers. 200$/€1 per 10min., 400$/€2 per 20min., 1000$/€5 per hr. Open June-Sept. M-F 9:30am-8pm, Sa 4-8pm; Oct.-May. M-F 9:30am-5:30pm.

Post Office: R. Portas de Portugal (☎282 77 02 50), between Pr. Gil Eanes and the river. Open M-F 9am-6pm. **Postal Code:** 8600.

ALGARVE

ACCOMMODATIONS

ı the summertime, *pensãoes* (and the youth hostel) fill up quickly; reserve rooms ıore than a week in advance. If full, the youth hostel will happily refer you to a *ıarto* near the hostel (close to the nightlife) for about the same price. A mob of ıcals trying to rent rooms in their homes will probably be waiting to greet you at ıe bus or train station. Though these rooms are often inconveniently located, they an be the best deals in town at 2000-3000$/€10-15 per person in summer. Try hag-ing with owners before you decide, as room quality varies greatly.

Pousada da Juventude de Lagos (HI), R. Lançarote de Freitas, 50 (☎282 76 19 70; fax 76 96 84). From the train and bus stations, head into town on Av. Descubrimentos, turn right at Pr. Infante Don Henrique, pass the slave market and follow Tr. Do Mar to R. Lançarote de Freitas. Friendly staff and lodgers congregate in the courtyard. Breakfast

included. In summer, book through the central **Movijovem** office (☎21 359 60 00). July-Sept. dorms 2500$/€13; doubles with bath 4300$/€22. Oct.-June dorms 1700$/€8.50; doubles with bath 3800$/€19. AmEx/MC/V.

Residencial Rubi Mar, R. Barroca, 70 (☎282 76 31 65; fax 76 77 49), off Pr. Gil Eanes toward Pr. Infante Dom Henrique. Centrally located. 8 great rooms. Breakfast included. July-Oct. doubles 7000$/€35, with bath 8500$/€43; quads 15,000$/€75. Nov.-June doubles 5500$/€28, with bath 6500$/€33; quads 10,000$/€50.

Residencial Gil Vicente, R. Gil Vicente, 26, 2nd fl. (☎/fax 282 76 29 82), behind the youth hostel. Business card advertises it as a "gay guest house," but it's open to anyone. Friendly owner has a wealth of information about the local and Lisbon gay scenes. Medium-sized rooms are somewhat stuffy but have high ceilings, TVs, and private baths. Reserve a month ahead in the summer. Apr.-Oct. singles 5000$/€25; doubles 6000-7000$/€30-35. Nov.-Mar. singles 3000$/€15; doubles 5000$/€25. AmEx/MC/V.

Residencial Caravela, R. 25 de Abril, 8 (☎282 76 33 61), just up the street from Pr. Gil Eanes. 16 small but well-located rooms off a courtyard, some with balconies. Singles 4300$/€22; doubles 6000$/€30, with bath 6500$/€32; triples 9000$/€45.

Camping: The way most Europeans experience the Algarve; sites are crowded and expensive. **Camping Trindade** (☎282 76 38 93), just outside of town. Follow Av. Descobrimentos toward Sagres. 580$/€2.90 per person, 630-735$/€3.15-3.67 per tent, 620$/€3.10 per car. **Camping Valverde** (☎282 78 92 11), on a beach 5km outside Lagos and 1.5km west of Praia da Luz. Free showers. 790$/€3.94 per person, 650-790$/€3.24-3.94 per tent, 680$/€3.40 per car.

FOOD

Tourists can peruse multilingual menus around Pr. Gil Eanes and R. 25 de Abril, but the cheapest dining option in Lagos is the local produce **market,** on Av. Descobrimentos five min. from the town center, or **Supermercado São Toque,** R. Portas de Portugal, 61. (☎282 76 28 55. Open July-Sept. M-F 9am-8pm, Sa 9am-7pm; Oct.-June M-F 9am-7:30pm, Sa 9am-7pm.) Traditional Portuguese restaurants do exist in Lagos. The most expensive are on R. Silva Lopes and R. 25 de Abril. Cheaper seafood entrées (1200-1600$/€6-8) can be found near **Pr. Luis Camoes.**

Casa Rosa, R. Ferrador, 22 (cell ☎936 511 10 52). A backpacker's culinary Mecca, this Lagos mainstay serves whopping portions for next-to-nothing. Gorge on a wide range of entrées with many vegetarian options (700-1400$/€3.50-7). Monday is all-you-can-eat spaghetti and garlic bread day (999$/€5). Due to the crowds, service can be (unusually) slow. Happy hour-and-a-half 10:30pm-midnight. Late breakfast served M-F noon-2:30pm. Open daily 7pm-2am.

Snack-Bar Caravela, R. 25 de Abril, 14 (☎282 76 26 83), just off Pr. Gil Eanes. Well-touristed, but for good reason–it's a great place to people watch and their pizza is the best in town. Outdoor seating on a pedestrian street. Pizzas 850-1350$/€4.24-6.73. Pasta 900-1175$/€4.50-5.86. Open daily 9am-2am. AmEx/MC/V.

A Vaca, R. Silva Lopes, 27 (☎282 76 44 31), on the left side of the street, heading towards Igreja de Santo António. Mostly German patrons savor delicious crepes and traditional home-style Swiss dishes. Crêpes 800-1100$/€4-5.50. Entrées 950-1950$/€4.74-9.73. Open daily Apr.-Oct. noon-2am; Nov.-Mar. M-F noon-2am. MC/V.

SIGHTS AND BEACHES

Although sunbathing and non-stop debauchery have long erased memories of Lagos's rugged, sea-faring past, most of the city is still surrounded by a nearly intact 16th-century wall. The **Fortaleza da Ponta da Bandeira,** a 17th-century fortress holding maritime exhibitions, overlooks the Marina. (☎282 76 14 10. Open Tu-Sa 10am-1pm and 2-6pm, Su 10am-1pm. 330$/€1.64, students 170$/€0.85, children 13 and under free.) Also on the waterfront is the old **Mercado de Escravos** (slave market). Legend has it that the first sale of African slaves in Portugal took place here in 1441. Today the waterfront and marina offer jet-ski rentals, scuba diving lessons, sailboat trips, and motorboat tours of the coastal rocks and grottoes (see Local Services, p. 577). Lagos' **beaches** are seductive any way you look at them. Flat, smooth, sunbathing sands (crowded during the summer, pristine in the off-season) line the 4km long **Meia Praia,** across the river from town. Hop on the 30-second ferry near Pr. República (70$/€0.35 each way). For cliffs that plunge into the sea hiding smaller, less-crowded beaches and caves, keep the ocean on your left and follow Av. Descobrimentos toward Sagres to **Praia de Pinhão** (20min.). Five minutes farther down the coast lies **Praia Dona Ana,** with sculpted cliffs and grottoes that appear on at least half of all Algarve postcards.

NIGHTLIFE

You're tan, you're glam, now go find yourself a (wo)man. The streets of Lagos pick up as soon as the sun dips down, and by midnight the city's walls are shaking. The area between **Pr. Gil Eanes** and **Pr. Luis de Camões** is filled with cafés. R. Cândido dos Reis, R. do Ferrador, and the intersection of R. 25 de Abril, R. Silva Lopes, and R. Soeiro da Costa are packed with bars and clubs that rarely close until well past 5am. Staggered happy hours make drinking easy, even on the tightest of budgets.

The Red Eye, R. Candido Dos Reis, 63, near Monty's Bar. The hottest new place in town. 20-something Brits and Aussies flood in around midnight for classic rock and cheap liquor. Some dancing, but mostly a bar pick-up scene. Fraternity posters and occasional streakers. Mixed drinks 500-700$/€2.50-3.50. Open daily 3pm-2am.

Taverna Velha (The Old Tavern), R. Lançarote de Freitas, 34 (☎282 76 92 31), down the street from Pousada da Juventude. Backpackers and expats mingle with the friendliest staff around. Nightly showings of American movies at 5:30pm, followed by the Simpsons. Happy "hour" with 2-for-1 beers or cocktails 9pm-midnight. Beer 250-500$/€1.25-2.50. Mixed drinks 500-700$/€2.50-3.50. Open M-Sa 4pm-2am, Su 8pm-2am.

Whyte's Bar, R. Ferrador, 7. A Lagos institution for over ten years. Live DJ keeps it packed all night long. Additional dancing on the basement level during crowded summer months. Nightly happy hour. Beer 500$/€2.50. Mixed drinks 500-700$/€2.50-3.50. Open daily Oct.-June 8pm-2am; July-Sept. 7pm-2am.

Lançarote Bar, R. Lançarote da Freitas, near Pousada da Juventude. A sound system and large dance floor make this one of the best places to get your groove on between 12:30-2am. Make sure to sample Paulo's white sangría (200$/€1). Open daily until 2am.

Monty's Bar, R. Candido dos Reis, 119, just up the street from R. Lançarote da Freitas. Those in the know converge here between 2-3:30am, when other bars have closed and the Phoenix is still empty. Beer 350$/€1.75. 2-for-1 mixed drinks with shots.

Phoenix Club, R. São Gonçalo, 29 (☎282 76 05 03), near the Old Tavern. Rises from the early morning ashes for after-hours dancing. Pop and techno. No stringent dress code, but tight black outfits abound. Beer 600$/€3. Cover 1000$/€5, includes 2 beers or 1 mixed drink. Open nightly 1-6am, but the crowds don't arrive until 3:30am.

Joe's Garage, R. 1 de Maio, 78, one block from Whyte's Bar. With its sawdust-covered floor and dread-locked clientele, the rowdiest, and possibly raunchiest, bar in Lagos. Beer 350$/€1.75. 2-for-1 beers or drinks 10pm-midnight. Open daily 10pm-2am.

DAYTRIPS FROM LAGOS

PRAIA DA ROCHA

To reach Praia da Rocha from Lagos, first take a bus to Portimão from the main bus station (40min., 14 per day 7:15am-8:15pm, 360-450$/€1.80-2.24), then switch to the Praia da Rocha bus, which stops in front of the nearby Portimão Honda dealership (10min., every 30min. 7:30am-8:30pm, 230$/€1.15).

A short jaunt from Lagos, this grand beach is perhaps the very best the Algarve has to offer. With vast expanses of sand, surfable waves, rocky red cliffs, and plenty of secluded coves, Praia da Rocha has a well-deserved reputation (and the crowds to match). The **tourist office,** at the end of R. Tomás Cabreina, offers maps and lists of accommodations and restaurants. (☎282 41 91 32. Open daily May-Sept. 9:30am-7pm; Oct.-Apr. M-F 9:30am-12:30pm and 2-5:30pm, Sa-Su 9:30am-12:30pm.)

LUZ, BURGAU, AND SALEMA (40MIN.)

These towns are all accessible by the bus running from Lagos to Sagres (12 per day 7:15am-8:30pm). To reach Luz, get off at Espiche, 10min. away (170$/€0.85); to Burgau, ride 20min. (340$/€1.70); and to Salema 40min. (310$/€1.55). Scootering oneself is a more windblown option (see Car Rental, p. 576). Be sure to return bus schedules.

These three small towns on the way to Sagres make perfect daytrips from Lagos. Less "discovered" than their larger neighbor and a bit more charming than windswept Sagres, they offer a quiet alternative to crowded Lagos. All three towns feature lovely beaches (although Salema is less developed.) Try asking around for a *quarto* if you find yourself stranded at night. Fresh fruits, cheeses, and olives are sold by local farmers each morning at the main square in Salema, and decent bars and restaurants line the beachfront in all three towns.

SAGRES ☎282

Marooned atop a plateau at the most southwestern point in Europe, Sagres was for centuries considered the end of the world. Battered by ceaseless winds, the surrounding cliffs plunge hundreds of feet into the Atlantic. It was at Sagres that Prince Henry founded his school of navigation and organized voyages of exploration to the far reaches of the globe. Large tour groups and upscale vacationers are discouraged by the desolate location and relative lack of recreation, making Sagres a perfect destination for travelers in search of uncharted beauty.

TRANSPORTATION AND PRACTICAL INFORMATION **EVA buses** (☎282 76 29 44) run from **Lagos** (1hr., 17 per day 7:15am-8:30pm, 480$/€2.40); check the schedule at the Lagos bus station before leaving to avoid getting stranded. The friendly, English-speaking staff at the **tourist office** on R. Comandante Matoso, up the street from the bus stop, dispenses maps and information on Sagres's illustrious history. (☎282 62 48 73. Open Tu-Sa 9:30am-12:30pm and 2-5:30pm.) Walking away from the tourist office, toward the fort, are Pr. República and privately-run **Turinfo.** The energetic, English-speaking staff recommends accommodations, offers internet access (600$/€3 for 30min.), rents **bikes** (1900$/€9.50 per day, 1200$/€6 per half-day), gives info on **jeep tours** of a nearby nature preserve (7200$/€36, including lunch), and provides **scuba** advice. They'll even do your **laundry** (1300$/€6.50 per load) and offer commission-free **currency exchange.** (☎282 62 00 03. Open daily 10am-1pm, 2-6:30pm 7pm.)

ACCOMMODATIONS AND FOOD Finding a bed in Sagres is not hard; windows everywhere display multilingual signs for rooms, many in boarding houses with guest kitchens. Prices range 3000-5000$/€15-25 for singles and doubles, 4000-7000$/€20-35 for triples. Follow R. Comandante Matoso towards the tourist office and take a left on R. Patrão António Faustino to reach **Atalaia Apartamentos;** the beautiful, fully-furnished rooms and apartments are great deals. (☎282 62 44 87. Apartments for July 2-Oct. 8000$/€40; Nov.-Mar. 5000$/€25; Apr.-June 6000$/€30.) Open-air **camping** is strictly forbidden, so head to the **guarded ground** just off E.N. 268. (☎282 62 43 51; fax 62 44 45. June-Sept. 600-700$/€3-3.50 per person, 500-850$/€2.50-4.24 per tent, 350-450$/€1.75-2.24 per car; Oct.-May 500$/€2.50 per person, 400-600$/€2-3 per tent, 250$/€1.25 per car. Reception open daily June-Sept. 8am-11pm; Oct.-May 9am-7pm.) For groceries, try the **market,** on R. Mercado, which intersects R. Comandante Matoso not far from the tourist office (open M-Sa 8am-9pm), or **Supermarket Alisuper,** on R. Comandente Matoso (☎282 62 44 87; open daily 9am-8pm). **O Dromedário Bistro,** on R. Comandante Matoso, whips up innovative pizzas (740-1180$/€3.70-5.90) and vegetarian dishes (890-1310$/€4.44-6.53). The bar is a Sagres hotspot by night. (☎282 62 42 19. Open daily 10am-midnight; bar open until 2am. Closed Jan.-Feb.)

SIGHTS AND ENTERTAINMENT Near town lurks the must-see **Fortaleza de Sagres,** the outpost where Prince Henry stroked his beard and founded his famous **school of navigation.** The pentagonal 15th-century fortress and surrounding paths yield vertigo-inducing views of the cliffs and sea. (Fortress open May-Sept. 10am-8:30pm; Oct.-Apr. 10am-6:30pm. 600$/€3.) Six kilometers farther west lies the desolate **Cabo de São Vicente,** which features the second most powerful lighthouse in Europe, a towering structure that overlooks the southwest tip of the continent and shines over 100km out to sea. On weekdays, you can take the bus from the bus station on R. Comandante Matos near the tourist office (10min.; 11:15am, 12:30, 4:15pm; 180$). On weekends, you're on your own—it's an hour on foot, but is also accessible by bike (see **Turinfo**, above).

Several **beaches** fringe the peninsula, most notably **Mareta,** located at the bottom of the road from the town center. Rock formations jut into the ocean on both sides of this sandy crescent. Though not as picturesque or intimate as the coves of nearby **Salema** and **Luz,** Mareta is popular for its length and isolation. Just west of town, **Praia de Martinhal** and **Praia da Baleeira** have great **windsurfing.**

Although Sagres may seem dead upon arrival, it definitely develops a pulse at sundown; in the summertime around 10pm. At night, the young crowd fills the lively bar **Rosa dos Ventos** in Pr. República. (☎282 62 44 80. Beer 150$. Mixed drinks 300$. Open daily 10am-2am.) Another hotspot is **Água Salgada,** on R. Comandante Matoso, 75m beyond the tourist office, going away from the fortress. Next door is **O Dromedário** (see **Accommodations and Food,** above), where trendy young locals let loose and a request-taking DJ keeps the party raving (☎282 62 42 97. Beer 200$/€1. Mixed drinks 650-900$/€3.24-4.50. Open daily 10am-2am.)

SILVES ☎282

Sleepy Silves was once the Moorish capital of the Algarve; from the mid-11th to mid-13th centuries it was larger than Lisbon with a population of 30,000 and a bustling port. In 1189, however, English crusaders en route to the Holy Land sacked the city. Tortured and stripped of their possessions, the Moorish inhabitants managed briefly to regain control, but in 1249, Christian rule was reestablished permenently. River silting, earthquakes, and epidemics have done little to rejuvenate Silves over the past 700 years, although cork production brought an economic boom in the 1800s. Today, travelers venture to Silves to escape overcrowded beach towns and experience quirky local attractions, like the annual Beer Festival.

TRANSPORTATION. The train station, **Estação Cams Ferro** (☎282 44 23 10), is 1km out of town, so the best way to get to Silves is by **bus.** If you do take a train, catch the "Estação" bus from the train station to town (10min., 6 per day 7:15am-7:40pm, 85$/€0.42). **Trains** run to: **Faro** (1hr., 8 per day 6:30am-11pm, 520$/€2.60); **Lagos** (40min., 6 per day 8:09am-5:56pm, 260$/€1.30); **Lisbon** (4-5hr., 2 per day 9:25am and 11:03pm, 1900-2280$/€9.50-12) usually via **Funcheira; Portimão** (20min., 6 per day 8:09am-5:56pm, 170$/€0.85). **Buses** depart the bus stop next to the municipal market on route EN 124 for **Portimão** (30min., 11 per day 7:15am-6:10pm) and the bus stop on the other side of the road, farther away from the castle for **Albufeira** (40min., 7 per day 6:40am-6:50pm, 510$/€2.55) and **Lisbon** (4hr., 4 per day 8:20am-6:20pm, 2500$/€13).

PRACTICAL INFORMATION. The **EVA bus office,** on R. Francisco Pablos, is just next to the municipal food market (☎282 44 23 38. Open M-F 8am-noon and 2-6pm). To get to the **tourist office,** R. 25 de Abril, 26-28, from Lg. António Enes, follow R. Francisco Pablos to its intersection with R. 25 de Abril and continue up the steps; the office lies ahead. (☎282 44 22 55. May-Sept. open daily 9:30am-1pm and 2-5:30pm; Oct.-Apr. M-F 9:30am-1pm and 2-5:30pm.) Just uphill from the tourist office is **Rua da Sé,** with its old cathedral and municipal museum, and **Rua do Castelo,** which curves past the castle. The **Centro de Saúde** (health center), is located just outside of town on R. Cruz de Portugal (☎282 44 00 20).

ACCOMMODATIONS AND FOOD. Inexpensive lodging is hard to come by in Silves. Ask at the tourist office or in any restaurant or bar for help in finding a private *quarto* (2000-5000$). **Residencial Sousa,** R. Samora Barros, 17, just down the steps from the tourist office, offers small, simple rooms. There is no reception desk; ask one of the café workers next door for assistance if the owner isn't around. (☎282 44 25 02. July-Aug. singles 3000$/€15; doubles 6000$/€30; triples 7500$/€38. Sept.-June singles 2000$/€10; doubles 4000$/€20; triples 5000$/€25.) Camping is available in the neighboring town of Armação de Pera, accessible by bus (20-30min., 6 per day 7:50am-7:15pm, 340$/€1.70). The **Armação de Pera campsite** is close to the beach (June-Sept. 650$/€3.24 per person, 600-750$/€3-3.74 per tent, 550$/€2.74 per car; 50% discount Oct.-May), while **Caliço** is 2km inland (600$/€3 per person, 600-700$/€3-3.50 per tent, 500$/€2.50 per car; 50% discount Oct.-May). For fresh fruits, vegetables, and fish, try the **mercado** municipal on Lg. António Enes (open M-Sa 8:30am-2pm). For spectacular views of the town and tasty brick oven pizza, try **Café Inglês,** Rua do Castelo, 11, between the cathedral and the castle walls. During summer months, check out the roof-top bar. (☎289 5[illegible] 51 32. Vegetarian calzone 1400$/€7. Pizza 1050-1500$/€5.24-7.50. Open daily 9:30am-6pm, June-Sept. 10pm-12am. AmEx/MC/V.)

SIGHTS AND ENTERTAINMENT. Silves is home to the 13th-century Gothic Sé Velha (old cathedral), as well as a massive red sandstone-lined *castelo*. Start your sight-seeing at the **Museu Municipal de Arqueologia,** R. das Portas de Loulé, 10, built around a 12th-century Moorish well (open daily 9am-6pm, 300$). From there head up R. da Sé to the **Sé Velha.** The cathedral, thought to have been built in the 13th century on the site of a mosque, has undergone a series of renovations, most of them after the 1755 earthquake. (Open daily 8:30am-8:30pm. Mass M-F 9am, Su 8:30am, 10:15am and noon. Free.) Just up the hill from the cathedral lies the **castelo.** As you walk the ramparts, imagine yourself a Moorish archer fending off advancing crusaders from the surrounding hills. Don't miss the "idealized" 14ft. statue of Portuguese warrior Sancho I in the courtyard. (☎282 44 56 24. July-Aug. open daily 9am-8pm; Apr.-June and Sept. 9am-7pm; Oct.-March 9am-5pm. 250$/€1.25 for castle walls and garden. 650$/€3.24 with art exhibit.) From the castle, turn left onto R. do Castelo and then right down R. Gregório Mascarenhas to get to the **Museu da Cortiça** (Cork Museum). Silves once served as the center of Portugal's cork industry, and this museum provides a fascinating look at both tra tion and industrialization in Portugal, with photographs, machines, and plenty of ›rk in various processing stages. (☎282 44 04 80. Open daily June-Aug. 9:30am-:45pm and 2-9:45pm; Sept.-May 9:30am-12:45pm and 2-7pm. 250$/€1.25. Children 12 125$/€0.62, under 6 free.) In the same complex as the cork museum (known as e Fábrica do Inglês), subdued Silves comes to life for 10 days in mid-June with e **Festival da Cerveja** (Beer Festival) when locals crowd the old mill to swig beers every kind and color. (☎282 44 04 40. Starts the 3rd week in June, and is usually en 6pm-1am. Tickets 1300$/€6.50, includes 2 mugs of beer.)

LBUFEIRA ☎289

hen the clubs die down in the morning, the drilling begins. Dynamite and con-ete have transformed the once pristine cliffs of Albufeira into an uncontainable :panse of high-rise hotels and condominiums. Sun, surf, and beer keep hordes of iddle-aged northern Europeans coming on package tour; nary a Portuguese ams the cobblestone streets. It may appear that there is little "authentic" Portu-:ese culture here, but a stroll through the old town or along the east edge of the ach hints at Albufeira's humble fishing origins. For those too jaded to care, the aches are packed all day and the nightlife jumps from dusk till dawn.

TRANSPORTATION. EVA buses connect the **train station** (☎289 57 16 16) to the wn center (every hr. 7:05am-8:20pm, 200$/€1). To: **Faro** (45min., 6 per day i9am-5:15pm, 340$/€1.70); **Lagos** (1hr., 10 per day 7:45am-11:30pm, 520$/€2.60); **bon** (4-5½hr., 5 per day 7:45am-7:10pm, 2030$/€10); **Olhão** (1½hr., 6 per day 5am-11:55pm, 370$/€1.85); **Tavira** (2hr., 6 per day 5:15am-11:55pm, 620$/€3.10); d **Vila Real de Santo António** (2¼hr., 6 per day 5:15am-11:55pm, 770$/€3.85). The 'A **bus station** (☎289 58 97 55), in nearby Caliços is somewhat more conveniently :ated, although a local bus transfer is still necessary to reach the center of town. **ses** head to: **Faro** (1hr., 15 per day 7:05am-7:30pm, 600$/€3); **Lagos** (1½hr., 7 per y 8:40am-8:10pm, 645-850$/€3.22-4.25); **Lisbon** (3½-4hr., 8 per day 6:35am-2:30am,)0-2800$/€13-14); **Tavira** (1½hr., 4 per day 8:45am-11:15pm, 780$/€3.90).

ORIENTATION AND PRACTICAL INFORMATION. The old bus station ıs recently demolished to make room for condo developments. From the w "bus station," a parking lot in a field outside of the city, it is at least a min. trek to the town center. The EVA bus from the train station also dumps ssengers here. Take city bus "A" from the new bus station to Av. da Liber-de (every 20min., 9am-9pm, 100$/€0.50). To reach the **tourist office,** R. 5 de ıtubro, 8, follow Av. da Liberdade downhill until reaching Tr. 5 de Outubro d take a right. Turn left when this small street intersects R. 5 Outubro and go aight for 50m. The English-speaking staff at the tourist office offers maps, a t of rooms, and brochures on water sports, including fishing and scuba div-;. (☎289 58 52 79. June-Sept. open daily 9:30am-7pm; Oct.-May 9:30am-:0pm.) For a **taxi** to locations in Albufeira and surrounding environs, call dio Taxis (☎289 58 32 30.) **Banks** surround the touristy Largo Eng. Duarte checo. There is a **laundromat** at Bellavista Comercial (☎289 58 89 56). In an **ergency** dial ☎112; **police** are on Av. 25 de Abril (☎289 51 32 03). For a **phar-cy,** head to Farmácia Piedade on R. Joáo de Deus (☎289 58 75 50). Located nearby Caliços is the Centro de Saúde or **hospital** (☎289 58 75 50). The **post ice** is next to the tourist office on R. 5 de Outubro. (☎289 58 08 70; fax 58 32 Open M-F 9am-12:30pm, 2:30-6pm.) **Postal code:** 8200.

ACCOMMODATIONS AND FOOD. Most lodgings in Albufeira are oked solid by package tours from late June through mid-September. Fear t—with some luck, reasonably priced accommodations can be found. Ask : *quartos* at the tourist office or at any restaurant or bar. You will most ely be accosted by room renters at the bus and train stations as well. Don't afraid to barter, but be sure to see the room before agreeing to pay. Most of

ALGARVE

these places are located at least 10min. from the beach. A single should co around 3000$/€15, a double, 4000$/€20; expect prices to rise in June and Jul There are a few pensions closer to the center of town. **Residencial Capri,** Av. D Liberdade, 83, features spacious rooms, many with verandas on to the stre below, all with TVs and hotel-quality bathrooms replete with wrapped soa Ask the owner for information on the hottest local clubs. (☎289 51 26 91. Sep June singles 5000$/€25; doubles 7000$/€35; quad 9000$/€45. August singl 6000$/€30; doubles 8000$/€40; quad 11,000$/€55.) Down the road is **Residenci Limas,** R. Liberdade, 25-27, which offers comfortable medium-sized doubles c a pedestrian street near Largo Eng. Duarte Pacheco. (☎289 51 40 25; fax 58 5 02. Doubles 5000-6000$/€25-30, with bath 6000-8000$/€30-40; discounts durir the winter.) Open-air camping is illegal, but weary travelers can pay for the ri and glitz of **Parque de Campismo de Albufeira,** a few kilometers outside town the road to Ferreiras. It's more like a shopping mall than a campground, wi four swimming pools, three restaurants, tennis courts, and a supermarke (☎289 58 76 29; fax 58 76 33. June-Sept. 850$/€4.25 per person and per ca 795$/€4 per tent; Oct.-May 50% discount.) For fresh fruits and vegetable check out the **mercado municipal** (open daily 8am-1:30pm; Th offers the mo variety). To get there, follow R. Da Figueria from the main bus station and ta a right on Es. Vale Pedras. Locals recommend **Tasca do Viegas,** R. Cais Herc ano, 2, near the fisherman's beach. (☎289 51 40 87. Fish entrées 1200-2100$/€ 10.50. Meat entrées 1000-2600$/€5-13. Open daily noon-11pm).

SIGHTS AND BEACHES Once the last Moorish outpost in southern Port gal, Albufeira preserves its graceful architectural heritage in its **old quarter,** off Miguel Bombarda and Pr. Miguel Bombarda. From the main square, take Tr. 5 Outubro across R. 5 de Outubro and walk up R. Igreja Nova toward the beach. Ti minarets pierce the small Byzantine dome of the **Santana** chapel and an exquis filigree doorway heralds the **São Sebastião** church. (Open evenings in summ Free.) An ancient Gothic portal fronts the **Misericórdia** (near Pr. República and t beach; closed to the public), and a barrel-vaulted interior receives worshippe into the **Matiz.** (Open W-Sa 2-6pm, Su 10am-1pm. Free.)

Albufeira's spectacular slate of **beaches** ranges from the popular **Galé** and **S Rafael** (4-8km toward Lagos) to the chic **Falésia** (10km toward Faro). To get to t centrally-located beach **Inatel** from the main square (Lg. Eng. Duarte Pacheco), f low Av. 25 de Abril to its end and continue down R. Gago Coutinho until you the sand. The beautiful but packed **Praia de Albufeira** awaits through the gate to t tourist office. It pays to explore beyond these popular options, as many small a relatively uncrowded beaches await discovery.

ENTERTAINMENT Bars and restaurants line all the streets of Albufei clubs blast everything from salsa to techno to *fado* as soon as the sun sets and continue until it rises. One prime spot is **Fastnet Bar,** R. Cândido dos Re 5, which is generally packed with northern Europeans. (☎289 58 91 16. Be 300-500$/€1.50-2.50. Mixed drinks 750-950$/€3.25-4.74. Open daily noon-4a Down the street is **Classic Bar,** R. Cândido dos Reis, 10, with its Grecian dec and a gaggle of tourists grooving to everything from pop and rock to disco a house. (☎289 51 20 75. Beer 300-400$/€1.50-2. Mixed drinks 950$/€4.74. Op daily June-Sept. noon-4am; Oct.-May noon-midnight.) At **Café Latino,** on R. L ino Coelho in the old town, salsa tunes complement a phenomenal seasi view. (☎289 58 51 32. Beer 200-300$/€1-1.50. Coffee 100-150$/€0.50-0.75. Op daily 10am-2am.) The only thing strange about nearby **Bar Bizzaro,** R. Dr. Fru oso Silva, 30, is that you might actually get a glimpse of locals. This down- earth café-bar hosts live Brazilian music Tuesdays at 9pm. (☎289 51 28 2 Beer 250-400$/€1.25-2. Open daily 9am-2am.) Many of the hottest new clubs a just outside of Albufeira (600-1200$/€3-6 by taxi), including **Locomia, IRS Dis** or **Kiss Disco** (all open daily 2am-6am).

FARO ☎289

Although many northern Europeans begin their holidays in Faro (pop. 55,000), the Algarve's capital and largest city, few bother to stay long enough to absorb its charm and local color. The city is divided into two parts, each with its own personality: a modern, commercial shopping district with a slick marina, and a quiet historical neighborhood, contained within the walls of the perfectly preserved old town. The calm beaches of the estuary's islands satiate those seeking the sun.

TRANSPORTATION

Flights: The international **Aeroporto de Faro** (☎289 80 08 00; flight info ☎289 80 08 01), 5km west of the city, has a police station, bank, post office, car rental companies, and tourist info booth. Open daily 10am-midnight. Buses #14 and 16 run from the street opposite the bus station to the airport (20min., every hr. 7:10am-8:40pm, 170$/€0.85). From May 15-Oct. the **aerobus** runs from the big EVA Hotel on the main *praça* to the airport (15min., every hr. 8:15am-8:15pm, free with plane ticket). Taxis to and from the airport cost 1400-1600/€7-8.

Trains: (☎289 80 17 26), Largo Estação, conveniently located near the center of town, next to the bus station. To: **Albufeira** (45min., 14 per day 7:20am-11pm, 300$/€1.50); **Beja** (3hr., 2 per day 9:05am and 5:30pm, 1330$/€6.63); **Évora** (5hr., 2 per day 9:05am and 5:30pm, 1650$/€8.23); **Lagos** (2hr., 7 per day 7:20am-8:45pm, 750$/€3.74); **Lisbon** (5-6hr., 6 per day 7:20am-11pm, 2400$/€12); **Vila Real de Santo António** (1½hr., 13 per day 6:10am-12:30am, 520$/€2.25).

Buses: EVA Av. República (☎289 89 97 00). To: **Albufeira** (1hr., 8-17 per day 6:30am-8pm, 600$/€3); **Beja** (3-3½hr., 7 per day 7:45am-4pm, 1550$/€7.73); **Lagos** (2hr., 8 per day 7:30am-5:30pm, 750$/€3.74); **Olhão** (20min., every 20-40min. 7:35am-7:30pm, 230$/€1.15); **Tavira** (1hr., 11 per day 7:15am-7:30pm, 435$/€2.17); and **Vila Real de Santo António** (1½hr., 9 per day 7:15am-6:20pm, 625$/€3.12). **Renex** (☎289 81 29 80), across the street, provides express long-distance service to: **Braga** (8½hr., 8 per day 5:15am-1:15am, 3600$/€18) via Lisbon; **Lisbon** (4hr., 7 per day 5:15am-1:15am, 2700$/€13.50); **Porto** (7½hr., 8 per day 5:15am-1:15am, 3500$/€17.50) via Lisbon. **Intersul** (☎289 89 97 70) runs to **Sevilla, Spain** (3000$/€15) with connecting buses to France and Germany.

Taxis: Táxis Rotáxi (☎289 89 57 95). **Táxis Auto Faro** (☎289 89 22 75). Taxis gather near Jardim Manuel Bívar (by the tourist office) and at the bus and train stations.

ORIENTATION AND PRACTICAL INFORMATION

Faro's ritzy center hugs the **Doca de Recreio,** a marina lined with luxuriously apportioned ships and bordered by the Jardim Manuel Bívar. If you prefer to arrive by train or bus, follow Av. da República towards the harbor. Emptying into a delta of smaller pedestrian streets at **Praça Dr. Francisco Gomes,** the city's main thoroughfare. Enter the old city through the **Avio da Vila,** a stone arch next to the tourist office, on the far side of the garden which borders Praça Dr. Francisco Gomes.

Tourist Office: R. Misericórdia, 8 (☎289 80 36 04), at the entrance to the old town. From the bus or train station, turn right down Av. República along the harbor, then turn left past the garden. From the main square, go past the garden; the office is to the left of the arch with the clock and bell tower. English spoken. Open June-Aug. M-Su 9:30am-7pm; Sept.-May M-Su 9:30am-5:30pm. The **regional tourism office** is on Av. 5 de Outubro, 18-20 (☎289 80 04 77) From the main square, follow R. Dr. Francisco Gomes as it becomes R. de Santo António and then Av. 5 de Outubro; the office is on the right. Open June-Aug. M-F 9am-7pm; Sept.-May M-F 9am-5:30pm.

Currency Exchange: Cota Cambios, R. Dr. Francisco Gomes, 26 (☎289 82 57 35), off Pr. Gomes. No commission on currency exchange. Open June M-F 8:30am-9pm, Sa 10am-7pm, Su 10am-4pm; July-Sept. M-F 8:30am-9pm, Sa 10am-8pm, Su 10am-7pm; Oct.-May M-F 8:30am-7pm, Sa 10am-2pm.

Laundromat: Sólimpa, R. Batista Lopes, 30 (☎289 82 29 81), up R. 1 de Maio. Wash and dry 350$/€1.75 per kg. Open M-F 9am-1pm and 3-7pm, Sa 9am-1pm.

Emergency: ☎112. **Police:** R. Polícia da Segurança Pública (☎289 82 20 22).

Hospital: R. Leão Pinedo, (☎289 89 11 00), just north of town.

Internet Access: Free at the **Instituto Português de Juventude,** next to the youth hostel (open M-F 9am-7pm; 30min. limit). Also at the **Ciencia Viva** (Science Alive museum), near the old city on R. Comandante Francisco Manuel (☎289 89 09 20). From Pr. Gomes, walk through the gardens and turn right, heading toward the docks. Unlimited use 400$/€2, students 200$/€1. Wed. 50% off. Open July-Sept. 15 Tu-Su 4-11pm; Sept. 16-June Tu-F 10am-5pm, Sa-Su 3-7pm.

Post Office: Largo Carmo (☎289 899 899), across from the Igreja de Nossa Senhora do Carmo. Open M-F 8:30am-6:30pm, Sa 9am-12:30pm. **Postal Code:** 8000.

ACCOMMODATIONS

Lodgings surround the bus and train stations. Most of the low-end budget *pensões* are plain but adequate. For something cheap and cheerful, try to scrape up a *quarto* from the tourist office's top-20 list of possibilities.

Pousada da Juventude (HI), R. Polícia de Segurança Pública (☎/fax 289 82 65 21), opposite the police station. Sleep easy at the cheapest place in town, under the vigilant eye of the nearby Faro police department. Rooms feature bunk beds. Neo-Baroque TV atrium. Singles 1900$/€9.50; doubles 4200$/€21, with bath 4600$/€23.

Pensão-Residencial Central, Largo Terreiro Do Bispo, 12 (☎289 80 72 91), near the pedestrian area up R. 1 de Maio. Clean, bright, comfortable rooms, all with bath and TV, some with terraces. June-Sept. singles 5000$/€25; doubles 7000-7500$/€35-37.50. Oct.-May singles 5000$/€25; doubles 6500-7000$/€32.50-35.

Residencial Madalena, R. Conselheiro Bivar, 109 (☎289 80 58 06; fax 80 58 07), close to the train and bus stations, follow R. Gil Eanes to R. Infante Dom Henrique and take a right. 22 warmly decorated rooms with dark wooden molding. All have baths, phone, and TV. Breakfast included. Singles 5650$/€28; doubles 8300$/€42.

Pensão São Filipe, R. Infante Dom Henrique, 55, 2nd fl. (☎/fax 289 82 41 82). From the train station go up R. Ventura Coelho 3 blocks and turn right onto R. Infante Dom Henrique. Close to the center of town and only a 5min. walk from the train and bus stations, this place offers 10 quiet rooms. Oct.-June singles 5000$/€25; doubles 6500$/€32; July-Sept. singles 7000$/€35; doubles 8500$/€43.

Pensão-Residencial Oceano, R. Ivens, 21, 2nd fl. (☎289 82 33 49). From Pr. Gomes, head up R. 1 de Maio; it's 1 block up on the right. White rooms with framed prints, all with bath, phone, and TV. July-Sept. singles 7000$/€35; doubles 8000$/€40; triples 10,500$/€53. 500-1000$/€2.50-5 discount Apr.-June and Oct. Nov.-Mar. singles 5500$/€28; doubles 6500$/€33; triples 8000$/€40. AmEx/MC/V.

ALGARVE

FOOD

Almonds and figs are native to the Algarve; local bakeries take good advantage of this and transform them into delicious marzipan and fig desserts. Faro has some of the Algarve's best cafés, many along **R. Conselheiro Bívar,** off Pr. Gomes. At the **market,** away from the center in Largo Dr. Francisco Sá Carneiro, locals barter fresh seafood (open daily 8am-1:30pm). Stroll to R. Santo António, a pedestrian district where costly *marisqueiras* and credit cards reign, or shop at **Supermercado Minipreço,** Largo Terreiro do Bispo, 8-10. (☎289 80 77 34. Open M-Sa 9am-8pm.)

Creperia, Pr. Ferreira d'Almeida, 27 (☎918 21 03 34), at the end of R. 1 de Maio. The crepe may not be indigenous to the Algarve, but this is one of the least expensive restaurants in Faro. Delight in a variety of gourmet options, from asparagus and cream to hot chocolate, kiwi, banana and apple. (300-700/€1.50-3.50). M-Sa 10am-12am.

Pastelaria Chantilly, R. Vasco da Gama, 63A (☎289 82 07 80), near Creperia and Pr. Ferreira d'Almeida. Indulge in marzipan sweets (110-280$/€0.55-1.40). Coffee 80-170$/€0.40-0.85. Open daily June-Aug. 8am-midnight; Sept.-May M-Sa 8am-7pm.

SIGHTS AND ENTERTAINMENT

ᶠaro's old town is a jewel—untouristed and traditional, it is a medley of ornate churches, museums, and shops selling local handicrafts. From Pr. Gomes, walk through the gardens to get to the entrance of the old town. Next to the tourist office, the early 19th-century **Arco da Vila** pierces the old city wall.

CAPELA DOS OSSOS. Step into **Igreja de Nossa Senhora do Carmo** to inspect the Capela dos Ossos (Chapel of Bones), a wall-to-wall macabre bonanza of crusty bones and fleshless skulls "borrowed" from the adjacent cemetery. Though not as spectacular as Évora's bone chapel, it's still worth a look. *(Lg. Carmo. ☎289 82 44 90. Open M-F 10am-1pm and 3-5pm, Sa 10am-1pm. Church free, chapel 120$/€0.60.)*

MUSEU DA MARINHA. The Museu da Marinha displays three notable boat models: the boat that took Vasco da Gama on his journey to India in 1497; a boat used on a Portuguese expedition up the Congo River in 1482; and a boat that out-gunned several Turkish galleons in 1717. *(☎289 80 36 01. Open M-F 2-4:45pm. 100$/€0.50.)*

CATHEDRAL (SÉ). A narrow road leads through an Arab portico to the Renaissance cathedral, which stands in a deserted square. The **Capela do Rosário,** decorated with 17th-century *azulejos* and a red chinoiserie organ, interrupt the cathedral's understated Renaissance interior. Under the cathedral—a site once sacred to Romans, Visigoths, and Moors—lie traces of Neolithic civilization. The striking **cloister** is an ideal spot to relax with a book from the municipal library, housed in the same building. *(Open M-Sa 10am-6pm. 250$/€1.25.)*

OTHER SIGHTS. The city's **Museu Regional do Algarve de Etnografia,** Pr. Liberdade, , introduces visitors to the folk life of the Algarve, with photos of the once-tranquil fishing villages of Lagos, Albufeira, and Faro. *(☎289 82 76 10. Open M-F 9am-12:30pm and 2-5pm. 500$/€2.50.)* Behind the church, **Museu Municipal de Arqueológico e Lapidar** flashes assorted royal memorabilia from diamond-studded hairpins to swords. *(☎289 87 08 70. Open M-F 10am-6:30pm. 110$/€0.55.)*

ENTERTAINMENT. Sidewalk **cafés** crowd the pedestrian walkways off the garden in the center of town, and several **bars** populated by a young crowd liven R. Conselheiro Bívar and its side streets. One notable spot is **Upa Upa Café & Bar,** R. Conselheiro Bívar, 51, where the mixed crowd of locals and tourists spills out into the large patio. *(☎289 80 78 32. Beer 300-500$/€1.50-2.50. Mixed drinks 600-700$/€3-3.50. Open daily 9pm-4am.)* Faro's rock-free **beach** hides on an islet off the coast. Take bus 16 from the bus station or the stop in front of the tourist office, just across the garden from Pr. Gomes (5-10min., every hr. 7:10am-8:40pm, 170$/€0.85).

OLHÃO ☎289

Olhão (ol-yahn), 8km east of Faro, prefers fish to tourists. For hundreds of years, the few inhabitants of the area were fishermen, and modern locals have continued the tradition, helping to create one of Portugal's most productive fishing industries. The bustling fish market on Av. 5 de Outubro supplies seafood to restaurants throughout the Algarve. Still, there is more to Olhão than tuna and cuttlefish. Beyond this no-frills town lie gorgeous beaches and the **Parque Natural da Ria Formosa,** with its numerous species of exotic birds (including flamingos).

TRANSPORTATION. The **train station** is on Av. Combatentes da Grande Guerra one block from Av. República. (☎289 70 53 78. Open daily 6:20-11am, 11:40am-:30pm, 8:10-10:45pm.) **Trains** run to: **Faro** (10min., 17 per day 6:55am-0:45pm, 150$/€0.75); **Tavira** (30min., 6 per day 6:20am-12:45am, 240$/€1.20); and

Vila Real de Santo António (1¼hr., 6 per day 6:20am-12:45am, 400$/€2). The **bus sta tion** is on R. General Humberto Delgado, one block from Av. República. (☎289 7(21 57. Open daily 7am-8pm.) **Eva buses** run to: **Faro** (20min., 11 per day 6:40am 7:50pm, 210$/€1.05); **Tavira** (40min., 11 per day 7:35am-7:50pm, 330$/€1.65); **Vila Real de Santo António** (1½hr., 9 per day 7:35am-6:40pm, 600$/€3).

ORIENTATION AND PRACTICAL INFORMATION. To reach the **port,** first locate tree-lined **Av. República.** From the train station, turn left on Av. Combatentes da Grande Guerra and take a right on Av. República, after passing the Palace of Justice. From the bus station, turn right on R. General Humberto Delgado and then take another right onto Av. República. Once on Av. República, go straight until reaching Olhão's main church. Veer left on R. do Comércial and continue as far as possible. From the end of R. do Comércial, turn left on R. Olhanense and follow the street until it reaches Av. 5 de Outubro and the sea. The **tourist office** is on Lg Sebastião Martins Mestre, a small road that intersects with the end of R. Comércio. Its English-speaking staff has maps, ferry schedules, and sometimes free **luggage storage** during the day—ask nicely. (☎289 71 39 36. May-Sept. open Tu-Th 9:30am-7pm, F-M 9:30am-noon and 1-5:30pm; Oct.-Apr. open M-F 9:30am-noon and 1-5:30pm.) In an **emergency,** call ☎112. The **post office** is at Av. República, 17 (☎289 70 06 03; open M-F 8:30am-6pm). **Postal code:** 8700.

ACCOMMODATIONS AND FOOD. **Pensão Bela Vista,** R. Teófilo Braga, 65-67, is off a dusty side street around the corner from the tourist office. Carpet lined hallways link sitting rooms with plush sofas. Nine cheerful rooms have TVs and some come with baths. Exit the tourist office, follow Traversa da Lagoa to R. Teófilo Braga and turn right. (☎289 70 25 38. Singles 4000$/€20; doubles 6000$/€30. **Pensão Boémia,** R. Cerca, 20, from the train or bus station, take Av. República and turn right on R. 18 de Junho. After four blocks, turn left again. Away from the shore and the center of town, but with all the modern amenities. Bright, clean rooms, all with bath, TV, and air conditioning. (☎/fax 289 71 45 13. Breakfast included. Singles 5000-7000$/€25-35; doubles 8000$/€40. Discount in the winter AmEx/MC/V.) Olhão's highly recommended year-round campground is the **Parque de Campismo dos Bancários do Sul e Ilhas.** It's off the highway outside of town and can be accessed by "Camara Municipal de Olhão" buses (9 per day 7:45am-7:15pm) which leave from in front of the gardens on R. 5 de Outubro. (☎289 70 0: 00; fax 70 03 90. Showers included. July-Aug. 640$/€3.20 per person, 450-1080$/€2.24-5.40 per tent, 540$/€2.70 per car; June and Sept. 540$/€2.70 per person, 390-410$/€1.95-2.05 per tent, 450$/€2.24 per car; Oct.-May 320$/€1.60 per person, 240-540$/€1.20-2.70 per tent, 270$/€1.35 per car.)

Supermercado São Nicolau, R. General Humberto Delgado, 62, lies up the block from the bus station (open M-Sa 8am-8pm). The **market,** housed in two red brick buildings, is adjacent to the city gardens along the river, near Pr. Patrão J. Lopes (open M-Sa 8am-1:30pm). Many eateries on Av. 5 de Outubro grill the day's catch. At **Casa de Pasto O Bote,** Av. 5 de Outubro, 122, pick your slippery, silvery meal from the trays of fresh fish and watch it get charcoal-grilled right before your eyes (☎289 72 11 83. Entrées 850-1400$/€4.24-7. Open M-Sa 11am-3pm and 7-11pm).

A SLUG IN THE FACE Escargot? Well, not exactly. One of Portugal's favorite snack foods is the lowly *caracol* (snail). Unlike their classier French counterparts, *caracóis* are eaten in massive portions, boiled in shells with just a pinch of salt and a sprig of fresh oregano. No forks here–pile a heap of the gooey guys on to your plate and skewer them with a toothpick. True connoisseurs use a needle-like spine carved out of palm leaves. If the dainty method doesn't suit you, crack the shell between your teeth. On a rainy day you might see folks prodding along the roadside in search of a snack; feel free to join in the fun. Alternatively, save your energy (the little fellas are surprisingly quick)–*caracóis* are served at restaurants across the country.

DAYTRIPS FROM OLHÃO

ARMONA, CULATRA, AND FARO

*Ferries go to **Armona** from Olhão's dock, ; buy tickets from the stand (15min.; June M-F 9 per day 7:40am-7:30pm, Sa-Su 11 per day 8am-7:30pm; July-Aug. 13 per day 7:30am-8pm; Sept.-May 8:30am, noon,5pm; last return trip in June 8pm, July-Aug. 8:30pm, 180$/€0.90). Another fleet serves **Culatra** (30min.; June-Aug. every 2hr. 7am-7:30pm; Sept.-May 4 per day 7am-6:30pm; 190$/€0.95; last return trip June-Aug. 8pm) and **Farol** (45min.; June-Aug. every 2hr. 7am-7:30pm; Sept.-May 4 per day 7am-6:30pm; last return trip in June-Aug. 8:20pm, 240$/€1.20).*

Long expanses of uncrowded, sandy beach and sparkling sapphire sea surround **Ilhas Armona, Culatra,** and **Faro,** the three major islands off the coast of Olhão. Armona is the closest, followed by Culatra, and then Faro; all three are easy day-trips from Olhão. The farther away you go, the quieter the beaches become, although all of them have barely a fraction of the human traffic in more touristed parts of the Algarve. The islands and sandbars just offshore fence off the Atlantic, creating an important wetland habitat **(Parque Nacional da Ria Formosa)** for birds, fish, and other creatures. During the winter, roughly one-third of Europe's flamingo population can be found here. If you miss the last ride back from Armona, accommodations are available at Orbitur's **campsite** on the central path, five minutes from the dock, but at 9300$/€47 per night from July to August, it's best not to find yourself stranded here. (☎289 71 41 73. Open May-Oct.)

TAVIRA ☎281

Farmers tease police by riding their mopeds over the Roman pedestrian bridge, but that's about as crazy as Tavira gets. For most visitors to this easy-going fishing port, that's just fine. White houses and palm trees fringe the river banks, and colorful Baroque churches dot the hills above. Tavira has recently become a haven for travelers in search of tranquil beaches, but the town has kept its calm.

Most of Tavira's sights are scattered throughout the side streets off Pr. República. Exit straight from the bus station, follow R. dos Pelames to the footbridge and take a right. A few meters on the right, stone steps lead past the **tourist office** to the **Igreja da Misericórdia,** a 16th-century church with an interior lined by wax-like religious statues, many of which are over 200 years old. (Open daily 9:30am-noon and 2:30-5:30pm. Free.) At the end of Trav. da Fonte, a narrow street to the left of the church, lie the crumbling walls of the city's **Castelo Mouro** (Moorish Castle). Nestled between several stone towers is the serene garden of **Santa Maria do Castelo,** a church originally built on the site of an ancient mosque but largely reconstructed after the earthquake of 1755. (Castle and church open daily 9am-5pm. Free.) The seven-arched pedestrian **Ponte Romana** footbridge leads to Pr. 5 de Outubro and many of Tavira's best restaurants. Local beaches, including **Araial do Barril,** are accessible year-round by the bus to Pedras Del Rei (10min., 8 per day 8:25am-6:10pm, 170$/€0.82). To reach the golden shores of **Ilha da Tavira,** an island 2km away, follow the directions to the island's campsite (below).

Trains (☎281 32 23 54) leave Tavira for: **Faro** (40min., 6 per day 6:24am-10:14pm, 300$/€1.44); **Olhão** (30min., 6 per day 6:24am-10:14pm, 250$/€1.20); and **Vila Real de Santo António** (30min., 14 per day 6:55am-1:10am, 260$/€1.10). **EVA buses** (☎281 32 25 46) leave from the station upriver from Pr. República for **Faro** (1hr., 11 per day 6:50am-7:10pm, 435$/€2.09); **Olhão** (45min., 11 per day 6:50am-7:10pm, 330$/€1.58); and **Vila Real de Santo António** (40min., 10 per day 6:55am-7:20pm, 405$/€1.94). From the **train station** you can catch the local TUT bus to the town center (10min., every 30min. 8am-8pm, 150$/€0.72) or call a taxi (☎281 32 15 44; about 650$/€3.24). The **tourist office** on R. Galeria, 9 is staffed by English speakers. (☎281 32 25 11. Open daily summer F-M 9:30am-12:30pm and 2pm-6pm, Tu-Th 9:30am-7pm; winter M-Su 9:30am-1pm and 2pm-5:30pm.) Rent **bikes** and **scooters** from **Loris Rent,** on R.

Galeria next to the tourist office. (☎281 32 52 03. Mountain bikes 800-1000$/€3.84-5 per day. Scooters 3000-4800$/€14-23 per day.) In an **emergency** dial ☎112; for **police** call ☎281 32 20 22; the **Centro de Saúde** can be reached at ☎281 32 90 00. **Internet access** is available at **Snack-Bar Bela Fria** (see **Accommodations and Food,** below), but don't be fooled by the "free Internet" signs; you have to pay 200$/€0.80 per 15min., 600$/€2.88 for an hour. The **post office,** is on R. Liberdade, 64, one block uphill from Pr. República (open M-F 9am-6pm). **Postal code:** is 8800.

There is no shortage of accommodations in Tavira. To find **Pensão Residencial Lagôas Bica,** R. Almirante Cândido dos Reis, 24, cross the pedestrian bridge from the side of town with the bus station and continue straight down R. A. Cabreira; turn right and go down one block. This *pensão* has well-furnished rooms, an outdoor patio, a lounge, washing facilities, and a fridge for guest use. (☎281 32 22 52. July-Sept. singles 3500$/€16.80; doubles 5000$/€24, with bath 7000$/€33.60. 500$/€2.40 cheaper in winter.) Back on the other side of the river, recently renovated **Pensão Residencial Castelo,** R. Liberdade, 22, has bright, spacious rooms and apartments, all with bath, phones, and TV. (☎281 32 07 90; fax 32 07 99. Handicap accesible. Breakfast included. Singles 4000$/€20; doubles 6000$/€24; apartments 8000$-12,000$/€38-57, 4-person max.) The privately run **Ilha de Tavira campground,** with its entourage of snack bars and restaurants, sprawls on the beach of an island 2km from Pr. República. (☎281 32 44 55; fax 32 17 16. Reception 8am-11pm. Showers 200$/€0.96. 1370$/€6.58 for one person in a tent, 1900$/€9.12 for two people in a tent. Open May-Oct. 15.) To get there, take the ferry from the "Quatro Águas" dock at the end of Estrada das 4 Aguas, a 2km walk downstream along the river, or catch the summer ferry from Lg. Dr. José Pires Padinha, just up R. Cais from Pr. República. (Sept. 16-June ferry 200$/€0.96 round-trip. July-Sept. 15 ferry every 15min. 8:30am-midnight, 250$/€1.20 round-trip.) Cafés and restaurants line Pr. República and opposite the garden on R. José Pires Padinha. One local favorite is **Restaurante Bica**, R. Almirante Candido dos Reis, offering hearty portions of freshly caught seafood, as well as salads and meat dishes. Try the four-course *menú toristico* for 1500$/€7.20 (☎281 32 38 43. Entrées 800-1800$/€3.84-8.64). Directly across from the bus station, **Snack-Bar Bela Fria,** R. Pelames, 1, offers lighter meals and Internet access. (☎281 32 53 75. Sandwiches 230-550$/€1.15-2.74. Desserts 120-550$/€0.60-2.74. Coffee 90-150$/€0.45-0.75.) MC/V.

VILA REAL DE SANTO ANTÓNIO ☎281

Located at the east end of the Algarve and at the mouth of the Rio Guadiana, Vila Real de Santo António is a common transfer point for travelers going to Spain. Chartered and planned in 1773, the city is an excellent example of 18th-century urban design. Marooned travelers frequently spent the night here before the construction of a highway bridge between Spain and Portugal in 1992; now most people simply pass through. **Trains** (☎281 51 37 77) run to **Faro** (1hr., 6 per day 6am-9:45pm, 520$/€0.45) and **Lagos** (3hr., 3 per day 6:35am-9:45pm, 1010$/€5). To get to Spain, you can take the **ferry** to **Ayamonte, Spain** (every 30min. 8am-8pm, 180$/€0.90 per person, 480$/€2.40 per car) and from the main square catch a direct **bus** to **Huelva, Spain** (2hr., every hr., 540ptas/€2.70). **Eva buses** (☎281 51 18 07) from Vila Real to the rest of the Algarve are more expensive, reliable, and faster than trains. They service **Faro** (1½hr., 9 per day 7:05am-6:30pm, 625$/€3.11) and **Tavira** (40min., 9 per day 7:05-6:30pm, 405$/€2). **Rede Expressos** buses go to **Lisbon** (6hr., 5 per day 6:30am-11:15pm, 2600$/€13), leaving from the esplanade near the train station and the river. Buses to **Sevilla, Spain** (3hr., 2 per day 9:10am and 5:15pm, 1800$/€9) eliminate the hassle of train-ferry-bus transfers. If stranded for a night, try the **Pousada da Juventude (HI),** R. D. Sousa Martins, 40, a white building on the fifth street from the river, two blocks to the left of R. Teófilo Braga. A living room, bar, kitchen, and washing facilities complement spotless quarters. (☎/fax 281 54 45 65. June-Aug. dorms 1700$/€8.50; doubles 3800$/€19. Sept.-May dorms 1400$/€7; doubles with bath 3200$/€16.)

CENTRAL PORTUGAL

ALENTEJO

The Alentejo province covers almost one-third of Portugal, but with a population barely over half a million it remains the country's least populated and least touristed region. Its arid plains stretch to the horizon, punctuated only by olive trees. The region is known for its wine and its cork—more than two-thirds of the world's cork comes from here. Évora, Elvas, and other medieval towns preserve their relatively pristine state in the Alentejo Alto (upper), while Beja remains the only major town on the seemingly endless Alentejo Baixo (lower) plain. The Alentejo is-best in the spring; if you come in summer, be prepared for fiery temperatures.

ÉVORA ☎266

Designated a World Heritage site by UNESCO, Évora (pop. 35,000) is the capital and the largest city of the Alentejo region. The historic center is home to medieval palaces while Évora's cathedral stands near the central plaza with the remains of a Roman temple. The students of the University of Évora (UÉ) liven up the town, especially during the end of class celebration of *Queima das Fitas* (last week of May) when their festivities culminate with the burning of their graduation ribbons to mark which faculty they belong to.

TRANSPORTATION

Trains: Av. dos Combatentes de Grande Guerra (☎/fax 266 70 21 25). To: **Beja** (2hr., 4 per day 7:35am-7:15pm, 770-1050$/€3.80-5.20); **Faro** (5hr., 4 per day 7:35am-7:15pm, 1650$/€8.20); **Lisbon** (3hr., 5 per day 5:15am-12:40am, 1380$/€6.90) **Porto** via Lisbon (6½hr., 3 per day 5:15am-2:15pm, 2650$/€13.20).

Buses: Av. Sebastião (☎266 76 94 10), about 300m outside the town wall. Much more convenient than trains. To: **Beja** (1-1½hr., 6-8 per day 8:45-12:45am, 1200$/€6); **Elvas** (1½-2hr., 3-5 per day 8am-9:05pm, 1300$/€6.50); **Faro** (5hr., 4 per day 8:45am-6pm, 1900$/€9.50); **Lisbon** (2-2½hr., every 1-1½hr. 6am-8pm, 1550$/€7.70); **Portalegre** (1¾-2hr., 3-5 per day 10:15am-5:40pm, 950-1350$/€4.70-6.70); **Porto** (6-8½hr., 4-6 per day 6am-8pm, 2700$/€13.50) via **Braga** (7¾-9¾hr., 4-6 per day 6am-8pm, 3000$/€15); **Setúbal** (1¾hr., 4 per day 8:30am-8pm, 1300$/€6.50).

Taxis: (☎266 73 47 34 or 73 47 35). Taxis hang out 24hr. in **Pr. Giraldo.**

ORIENTATION AND PRACTICAL INFORMATION

Évora is accessible by train from most major cities, including Lisbon, but buses are more convenient. No direct bus connects the **train station** to the center of town; to walk, go up Av. Dr. Baronha and continue straight as it turns into R. República at the city wall, until you reach the **Pr. do Giraldo.** To avoid the hike, hail a taxi (600$/€3) or flag down bus #6 (140$/€0.70), which halts a short way down the tracks. To get to Pr. Giraldo from the **bus station,** turn right up Av São Sebastião, and continue straight when it turns into R. Serpa Pinto at the city wall.

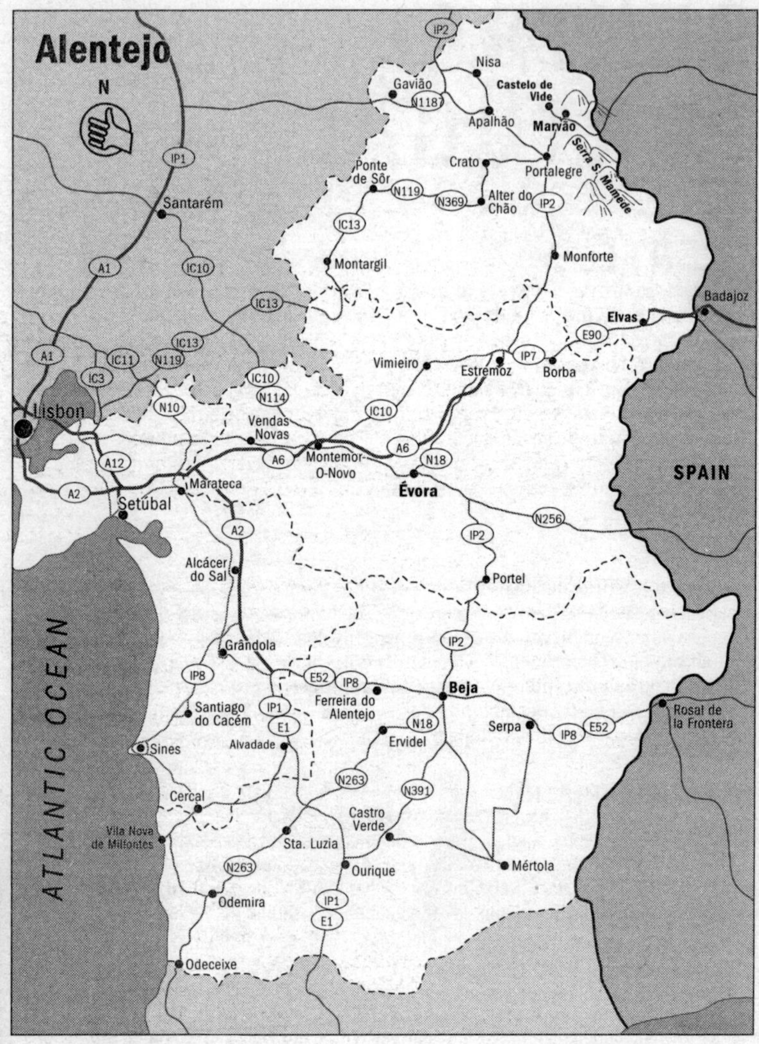

Tourist Office: Pr. Giraldo, 73 (☎266 70 26 71), in the plaza at the corner of R. Raimundo. Luggage storage. Wheelchair accessible. Open Apr.-Sept. M-F 9am-7pm, Sa-Su 9am-12:30pm and 2-5:30pm; Oct.-Mar. 9am-12:30pm and 2-5:30pm.

Currency Exchange: 24hr. ATM outside the tourist office. Several banks line **Pr. Giraldo,** all open M-F 8:30am-3pm. **Crédito Predial Português**, Pr. Giraldo, 67 (☎266 74 50 40) is right next to the tourist office.

Emergency: ☎112. **Police:** R. Francisco Soares Lusitano (☎266 70 20 22).

Hospital: Hospital do Espirito Santo (☎266 74 01 00), Lg. Senhor da Pobreza, near the city wall and the intersection with R. Dr. Augusto Eduardo Nunes.

Internet Access: Oficin@, R. Moeda, 27 (☎266 70 73 12), off Pr. Giraldo. 100$/€0.5 per 10min. 500$/€2.5 per hr. Open Apr.-Sept. Tu-F 8pm-3am daily, Sa 9pm-3am. Oct.-Mar. Tu-F 8pm-2am, Sa 9pm-2am.

Post Office: (☎266 74 54 82; fax 74 54 86), R. Olivença. From Pr. Giraldo, walk up R. João de Deus, take your first right onto R. Nova, the first left uphill, then right at Pr. de Sertória. **Posta Restante** and **fax.** Open M-F 8:30am-6:30pm. **Postal Code:** 7000.

ACCOMMODATIONS AND CAMPING

Most hostels cluster on side streets off **Pr. Giraldo**; they are crowded in the summer, especially during the Feira de São João in late June, so reserve ahead. Prices sometimes drop 500-1000$/€2.50-5 in winter. Private *quartos*, 4000-5000$/€20-25 per double, are pleasant summer alternatives to crowded *pensões*.

Pousada da Juventude (HI), R. Miguel Bombarda, 40 (☎266 74 48 48; fax 266 74 48 43). From the tourist office, cross Pr. Giraldo and take a right on R. República, then bear left on R. Miguel Bombarda; the hostel is on the right. Lounge with pool table, kitchen, and laundry room. Luggage storage available. Breakfast included. Lockout 11am-3pm. Without HI card is 400$/€2 more per night. In summer, reserve through **Movijem** (☎21 359 60 00). June 16-Sept. 15 dorms 2500$/€12.5; doubles with bath 6000$/€30. Sept. 16-June 15 dorms 2000$/€10; doubles 5000$/€25. **Closed for renovation Jan.-Apr. 2002.** Internet access will be included in renovations.

Casa dos Teles, R. Romão Ramalho, 27-31 (☎266 70 24 53). Take a right out of the tourist office and then another onto R. Romão Ramalho; it's two blocks down on the left. June-Sept. one person 4000-5000$/€20-25, with bath 5000-6000$/€25-30; double 6000-7000$/€30-35, with bath 7000-8000$/€35-40; three people 7000-8000$/€35-40. Oct.-May 1000-2000$/€5-10 less.

Casa Palma, R. Bernardo Matos, 29-A (☎266 70 35 60). Take a right out of the tourist office and then the first right onto R. Bernardo Matos; the house is three blocks down on the left. Over 100 years old, this well-kept house has a pleasant homey atmosphere. Apr.-Oct singles 5000$/€25, with bath 7000-7500$/€35-38; doubles 7000-7500$/€35-38, with bath 8500-9000$/€43-45. Nov.-May about 1000$/€5 less.

Pensão Giraldo, R. Mercadores, 27 (☎266 70 58 33). From the tourist office, turn left and walk 2 blocks, then turn left out of Pr. Giraldo onto R. Mercadores. All rooms have TVs. Reserve a week ahead. If you reserve a room, you must tell them when you'll be coming and show up within 15min. of that time. 10% discount for two or more nights. July-Sept. singles 5000$/€25, with bath 6500-7000$/€32.4-35; doubles 6500-7000$/€33-35, with bath 9800$/€49; room with two queen-size beds 11,000$/€55 for 3, 12,500$/€63 for 4-5 people. Mar.-June singles 4500$/€23, with bath 6000$/€30; doubles 6000$/€30, with bath 7500$/€38; 8500-9000$/€43 for 3, 9000$/€45 for 4. Oct.-Feb. singles 4000$/€20, with bath 5500$/€28; doubles 5500$/€28, with bath 6500-6900$/€33-35; 7500$/€38 for 3, 8000$/€40 for 4. AmEx/MC/V.

Orbitur's Parque de Campismo de Évora (☎266 70 51 90; fax 70 98 30), a 3-star park on Estrada das Alcáçovas, which branches off at the bottom of R. Raimundo. A 30min. walk to town, but two buses run to the nearby Vila Lusitano stop from Pr. Giraldo: (#5; 10-20min., M-F 10 per day 7:45am-7:15pm, Sa 3 buses 8:25am-12:35pm; #8; 15min., M-F 6 per day 9:40am-5:45pm, Sa 9:25am, Su 2:50pm and 7:05pm.) A taxi is 600$/€3. Washing machine and a market. Reception 8am-10pm. Five sets of seasonal prices. 400-680$/€2-3.40 per person, 200-340$/€1-1.70 per child, 310-960$/€1.50-4.80 per tent, 340-600$/€1.70-3 per car. AmEx/MC/V.

FOOD

Restaurants are scattered near **Pr. Giraldo,** especially along **R. Mercadores,** but many are tourist-oriented; to find Portuguese food for Portuguese people, it helps to wander a bit away from the center. The **market,** which sells crafts and other regional goods as well as cheese and produce, is just past the corner of R. Rebública and R. Cicioso when walking from Pr. Giraldo (open Tu-Su 8am-1pm).

Pastelaria Bijou, R. da República, 15, just off Pr. Giraldo. A variety of excellent pastries displayed beneath the long marble countertop. Ask for a *briza*, a pastry with sweet potato, almond, and cinnamon, and see why flakiness can be a beautiful thing. Pastries 120-280$/€0.60-1.40. Coffee 80-120$/€0.40-0.60. Open daily 7am-7:30pm.

Adega do Neto, R. Mercadores, 46 (☎963 94 73 19), off Pr. Giraldo, across from Pensão Giraldo. Locals flock for typical Alentejan dishes for under 1200$/€6. Entrées 700-1000$/€3.50-5. Open M-Sa noon-3:30pm, 7-10pm.

Pane & Vino, Páteo do Salema (☎266 74 69 60). From Pr. Giraldo, go up R. 5 de Outubro and take a right onto R. Diogo Cão. Pretend you're in Rome. The only 100% Italian restaurant in Évora and popular among students, who gather in the spacious dining room. *Pizza pane & vino* for two (2800$/€14). Open Tu-Su noon-3pm, 6:30-11pm.

SIGHTS

CAPELA DOS OSSOS. The Capela dos Ossos (Chapel of Bones) warmly welcomes visitors: "*Nós ossos que aqui estamos, pelos vossos esperamos*" ("We bones that are here are waiting for yours"). In order to clear many local cemeteries and create needed space in town, three Franciscan monks used the remains of over 5000 people to build this chapel. Femurs, skulls, tibias, and pelvic bones line the wall and ceiling, while the bones of the three founders lie unexposed in stone sarcophagi to the right of the altar. *(Pr. 1 de Mayo. Follow R. República from Pr. Giraldo, then take a right into the Pr. 1 de Mayo; enter the chapel through the door of the Convento de São Francisco to the right of the church steps. ☎266 70 46 21. Open Apr. and June-Sept. M-Sa 9am-1pm, 2:30-6pm, Su 10am-1pm; May and Oct.-Mar. M-Sa 9am-1pm, 2:30pm-5:30pm, Su 10am-1pm. Entrance 100$/€0.50. Photography permit 50$/€0.25.)*

CHURCH AND PALACE. Immediately facing the temple is the Igreja de São João Evangelista (1485). The church and the ducal palace next door are owned by the Cadaval family, descendants of the dukes. The interior of the church is covered with dazzling *azulejos*. *(Largo Conde do Vila Flor. Open Tu-Su 10am-12:30pm and 2-6pm. 500$/€2.50 for church, 850$/€4.20 for church and exhibition hall in neighboring palace.)*

CATHEDRAL. The 12 Apostles adorning the doorway of this colossal 12th-century cathedral are masterpieces of medieval Portuguese sculpture. The **cloister** was designed in the 14th-century Romanesque style, with staircases spiraling to the terrace. The **Museu de Arte Sacra,** in a gallery above the nave, houses the cathedral's treasury and a 13th-century ivory *Virgem do paraíso*. *(From the center of Pr. Giraldo, head up R. 5 de Outubro to the end. Cathedral open daily 9am-12:30pm and 2-5pm. Free. Cloisters open daily 9am-noon and 2-4:30pm. Museum open Tu-Su 9am-noon and 2-4:30pm. Cloisters and museum, 500$/€2.50. July-Sept. 15 ticket includes visit to the tower from the museum. For just the cloister on M, 300$/€1.50.)*

NIGHTLIFE AND ENTERTAINMENT

Évora's nightlife is fueled largely by the students from the university, who fill the bars after midnight and then move on to the clubs.

Jonas, R. Serpa Pinta, 67 (☎964 82 16 47), down the street from Pr. Firaldo. Orange textured walls give this bar a warm cavernous feel, while the blue-lit room upstairs is made for chilling. Age 20-40 crowds after midnight. Popular Brazilian *caipirinhas* 500$/€2.50. Open M-Sa 10:30pm-3am.

Bar UÉ, R. Diogo Cão, 19 (☎266 74 39 24). From Pr. Giraldo go up R. 5 de Outubro and take a right onto R. Diogo Cão, then follow the road around to the left; UÉ is on left. Only students are allowed into this university bar. *The* place to meet people before deciding to head out elsewhere. Open Tu-Su noon-2am; serves food 1-3pm, 7:30-9:30pm.

Inox, R. do Muro, 3. Past Tasca do Comendinha, farther down along the aqueduct and to the right. Named for the building material that gives this disco its industrial look, Inox is the dominant new player of the Évora clubbing scene. Twentysomething crowd gets going at 1am. Transitions from bar to disco at 3am. No cover during the week 500$/€2.50 minimum consumption on weekends. Open Tu-Sa 10:30pm-5am.

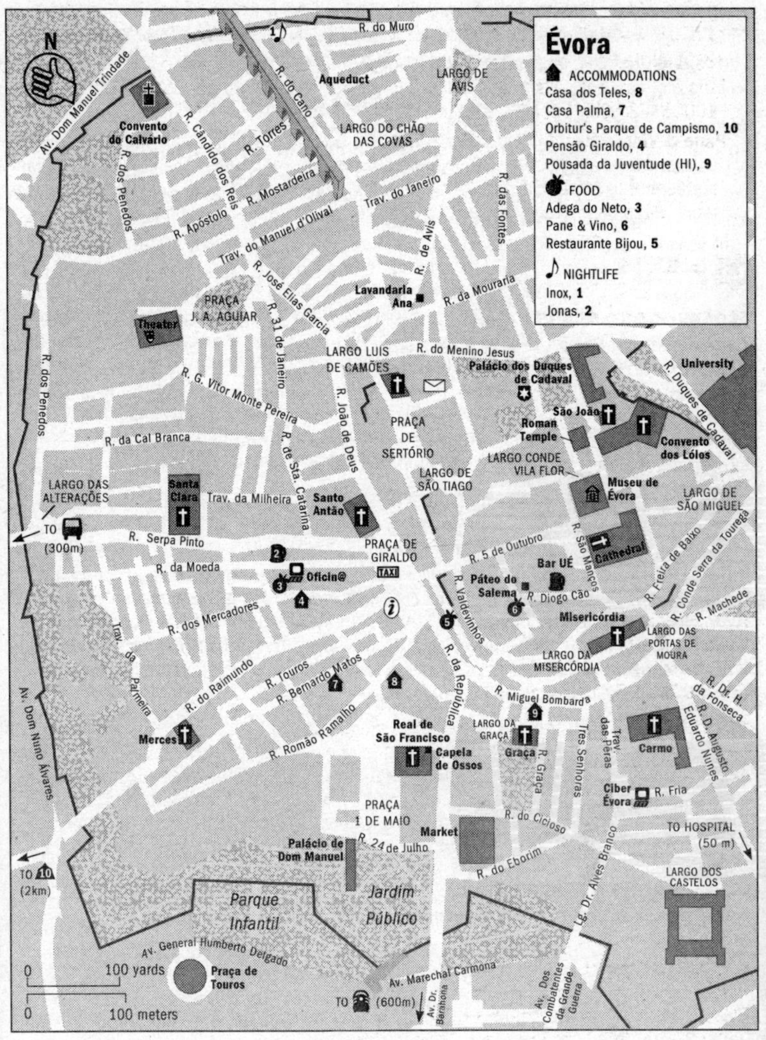

ELVAS ☎268

Even if you're just stopping over in Elvas on your way elsewhere, a day here is not a wasted one. 12km from the Spanish border, the quiet hill town has a pleasant main square and steep streets that lead down to the fortified city walls. Its proximity to Spain made Elvas an especially important military stronghold.

TRANSPORTATION. The nearest **train station** (☎268 62 28 16) is 3km away in the town of Fontainhas and has service to **Badajoz, Spain** (17min., 12:12pm, 170$/€0.80). **Buses** are the best transportation option from Évora, with a convenient **station** (☎268 62 28 75) and go to: **Albufeira** (5½hr., 6:40am, 2200$/€11); **Beja** (3½hr., 6:40am, 1700$/€8.50); **Caia,** on the border (30min., 6:40am and 2pm, 240$/€1.20); **Évora** (1½hr., 3-4 per day 6:40am-4:25pm, 900$/€4.50 morning, 1300$/€6.50 afternoon); **Faro** (6½hr., 6:40am, 2400$/€12); **Lisbon** (2¾-4hr, 5-7 per day 5am-6:30pm, 1800$/€9); **Portalegre** (1½hr., M-F 7am, 750$/€3.70). A **taxi** (☎268 62 22 87) is the only transport from the train station to town (about 1000$/€5).

ORIENTATION AND PRACTICAL INFORMATION. Buses stop near the edge of town. To get to the **tourist office** from the bus station, take a right and go through the Largo da Misericordia; then continue up to R. Cadeia, and take a left into Pr. República—the *turismo* will be on the right. Trains arrive 3km away in Fontainhas; if you arrive at the train station and are prepared to do the 3km trek to the center on foot, take a right onto Estrada das Fontainhas and then take a left onto Estrada de Campo Maior at the traffic circle; continue straight and then take a right, passing under the giant Portas de Olivença, and go up R. Olivença until it reaches Pr. República. (☎268 62 22 36. Open Apr.-Sept. M-F 9am-6pm, Sa-Su 10am-12:30pm and 2-5:30pm; Oct.-Mar. 9am-5:30pm daily.) Services include: **emergency** ☎112; **police,** R. André Gonçalves (☎268 62 26 13); and the **hospital** (☎268 62 22 25). For **internet access,** check out **O Livreiro de Elvas,** R de Olivença, 4-A, a little bookstore with 2 computers in back. Watch your head as you enter the back room! (☎268 62 08 82. 170$/€0.80 for 15min., 290$/€1.40 for 30min. Open M-F 9:30am-1pm and 3:15-7:15pm, Sa 9:30am-1pm.) The **post office** is one block behind the tourist office. (☎268 62 26 96. Open M-F 9am-6pm.) **Postal code:** 7350.

ACCOMMODATIONS AND FOOD **António Mocisso e Garcia Coelho,** R. Aires Varela, 15. From the tourist office, take a right out of the *praça* and then your first left (to the right of Banco Espirito Santo); go left at the end of the street and the reception will be on the right. Comfortable rooms with TVs, private baths, and pinewood ceilings. Reservations recommended during the summer. (☎268 62 21 26. Breakfast 500$/€2.50. Singles 3500$/€18; doubles 5500$/€28; quads 10,000$/€50 or 7500$/€38 for 3) Campers may try **Camping Torre Des Arcas,** in an orchard 4km from Elvas accessible via the bus to Varche and a 10min. walk from the orchard. (☎268 62 60 30. 500$/€2.50 per person, 250$/€1.75 per child under 12, 600-800$/€3-4 per car and tent. Owner also apartment rooms, including the "Bishop's Bedroom." Minimum rental 7500$/€38 for 2, 8000$/€40 for 3; plus Bishop's bedroom 3500$/€17.5 for 2, 4000$/€20 for 3.) For fresh fish, fruits, and vegetables, try the **mercado municipal** on Av. São Domingos (open M-Sa 8am-1pm). Fans of roast meat will love **Canal 7,** R. Sapateiros, 16. Exit Pr. República on R. Sapateiros to the left of Banco Espirito Santo, and follow the curving road to the left toward the oven. Known around town for its excellent *frango assado* (roast chicken 700$/€3.5 for half); also does whole roasted pig (2500$ per kilo). Entrées 750-1200$. (☎268 62 35 93. Open 11am-3pm, 6-10pm; Su take-out only.)

SIGHTS Elvas's main sight, the **Aqueduto da Amoreira,** emerges from a hill at the entrance to the city. Begun in 1529 and finished almost a century later (1622), the colossal structure is Europe's largest aqueduct (its 843 arches span almost 8000m). The **castelo,** above Pr. República, has a great view of the aqueduct and the infinite rows of olive trees on the horizon; a stairwell to the right of the entrance leads up to the castle walls. (Castle open 9:30am-5:30pm. 250$/€1.25; age 14-25 and seniors 125$/€0.6, under 14 free.) The **Igreja de Nossa Senhora da Assunção** in Pr. República has *azulejos* and a beautifully ribbed ceiling. (Open M-F noon-1pm, 3-6:30pm. Mass Su 6pm.) Behind the cathedral and uphill to the right is the **Igreja de Nossa Senhora da Consolação dos Aflitos,** also known as **Freiras.** Its octagonal interior has beautiful geometric tiles. (Open Tu-Su 9:30am-12:30pm and 2:30-5:30pm.) In the three-sided *praça* stands the 16th-century **pelourinho,** an octagonal pillory (originally a medieval whipping post) culminating in a pyramid.

CASTELO DE VIDE

Situated 600m above sea level on the edge of the Serra de São Mamede, Castelo de Vide (pop. 4500) is a charming town of whitewashed houses and cobblestone streets. The **castelo,** completed in 1280, overlooks the historic center and offers stunning views of surrounding mountains. (Open daily July-Sept. 9am-6pm; Oct.-

June 9am-5pm. Free.) The **medieval quarter** is Castelo de Vide's unique attraction. Located just below its castle, the old town consists of steep and narrow cobblestone alleys overflowing with potted plants, roses, and sunflowers. The town center surrounds the two 19th-century plazas, evidence of Castelo's popularity as a spa resort over 100 years ago. On weekends, the only way to get to **Marvão** is by taxi (about 2000$/€10). During the week, **buses** run from behind the tourist office to **Marvão** (25min., M-F 5:30pm, 170$/€0.80) and **Portalegre** (30min.; M-F 4 per day 8:05am-4:50pm, Sa-Su 8:05am and 4:50pm; 310-1000/€1.50-5), which offers frequent connections to larger cities. The **train station,** which lies 4km out of town, is accessible only by taxi (☎245 90 12 71; 750$/€3.74). Trains run to **Lisbon** (5hr., 2 per day 6:15am and 5:55pm, 2500$/€13) and **Madrid.** The **tourist office,** R. Bartolomeu Alferes da Santa, 81, offers maps, helps find accommodations, and provides short-term **luggage storage.** (☎245 90 13 61. Open daily July-Sept. 9am-7pm; Oct.-June 9am-12:30pm and 2-5:30pm.) Services include: **emergency** ☎112; **police** on Av. Anamenha (☎ 245 90 13 14); the **health center** (☎245 90 11 05) behind the tourist office.

MARVÃO

The ancient walled town of Marvão (pop. 190) sits on a mountaintop, surrounded by the hillsides and meadows of the **Parque Natural de São Mamede.** Almost all of the whitewashed houses of this ageless town still lie within the 17th-century walls. Marvão's 13th-century **castelo,** atop the ridge at the west end of town, guard this town that hasn't been seized in 700 years. Prior to the castle's construction, however, Marvão passed through several different owners, among them the Romans, the Visigoths, and the Moors. Remnants of these early days are on display at the **Museu Municipal,** near the castle in the **Igreja de Santa Maria.** (Open daily 9am-12:30pm and 2-5:30pm. 200$/€1, students with ID 150$/€0.75. **Buses** run to **Castelo de Vide** (25min., M-F 7:15am and 1:05pm, 170$/€0.80) and **Portalegre** (50min., M-F 7:15am and 1:05pm, 330$/€1.60). Ask at the tourist office about express buses to **Lisbon** (5½hr., 7:30am, 2100$/€11); you must buy tickets one day in advance. To get to the **train station** (☎245 99 22 88), 9km north of town in Beirã, where service to Lisbon and Madrid is available, you'll have to take a taxi (☎245 99 32 72). Taxis are also a valid option for getting to **Castelo de Vide** (about 2000$/€10). If you arrive by bus, you will be dropped off just outside the town wall. Enter through one of the gates and proceed up R. Cima until you see the pillory (ancient stone whipping-post) in Pr. Pelourinho.From Pr. Pelourinho, R. Espíritu Santo leads toward the castelo and the **tourist office.** (☎245 99 38 86. Open July-Sept. M-F 9am-6:30pm, Sa-Su 10am-12:30pm and 2-6:30pm; Oct.-June daily 9am-12:30pm and 2-5:30pm.) Services include: **emergency** ☎112 and **police** ☎245 99 36 17.

BEJA ☎284

Standing out amid the vast, monotonous wheat fields of the southern Alentejo, Beja is a relaxed, friendly town that is proud of its varied history and architecture. Its current name, is a corruption of its original name, Pax Julia, given to Beja by the Romans in 48 BC to commemorate the peace with the Lusitanians. The city was then conquered by the Moors in 715, and proceeded to change ownership 13 times before becoming a Christian possession in 1232 under Dom Sancho II. The city maintains a medieval feel and tranquility that most tourists come to cherish.

TRANSPORTATION. Trains run from the station (☎284 32 50 56), about 1km outside of town to: **Évora** (1½hr., 5 per day 7:45-8:40pm, 780-1110$/€3.90-5.54); **Faro** (3½hr., 9:30am and 9:13pm, 1730$/€8.63) via **Funcheira; Lisbon** (2½-3hr., 4 per day 5am-7:20pm, 1350-1590$/€6.73-8). The **bus station** (☎284 31 36 20) is on R. Cidade de São Paulo, near the corner of Av. Brasil. Buses go to: **Évora** (1hr., 5 per day 7:10am-7:15pm, 1300$/€6.50); **Faro** (3½hr., 3 per day 10:10am-7:20am, 1800$/€9); **Porto** (8½-10hr., 4 per day 9am-2:30pm, 3300$/€17) via **Lisbon; Lisbon** (3¼hr., 6 per day 7:10am-3pm, 1750$/€8.73); **Picalho,** a border town with connections to Spain (2hr., 5 per day 10:50am- 9:15pm, 580-1200$/€6).

UNREQUITED LOVE The city is known for a tale of passion: when the French troops came to Portugal during the war of Restoration in 1666, the young nun Mariana Alcoforado fell hopelessly in love with the knight Chimilly, whom she saw passing by from her now-famous window overlooking the Porta de Mértola. The nun wrote five passionate letters to her love, and these were soon published in Paris under the title *Five Love Letters of a Portuguese Nun*. Mariana died at the age of 83, but her letters remained to tell her story of unrealized passion and to inspire future artists and lovers. It has never been known whether the hun ever spoke to the object of her desire.

PRACTICAL INFORMATION. The **tourist office,** R. Capitão J. F. de Sousa, 25, provides luggage storage (☎/fax 284 31 19 13. Open May-Sept. M-F 9am-8pm, Sa 10am-1pm, 2-6pm; Oct.-Apr. M-Sa 10am-1pm and 2-6pm.) **Banks** are open M-F 8am-3pm. Exchanging travelers' checks can be extremely difficult in Beja, so be sure to have an alternate source of cash. **Luggage storage** is also available at the bus station on weekdays (350$/€1.75 per day). Services include: **emergency** ☎ 112; the **police** on R. D. Nuno Álvares Pereira, ☎ 284 32 20 22, one block downhill from the tourist office. To get to the **post office,** on Largo do Correio, take a left out of the tourist office, then a right on R. Infantaria 17; it's on the right. (☎ 284 31 12 70. **Poste Restante** and **fax service** (440$/€2.20 per page). Open M-F 9am-6pm. **Postal code:** 7800.

ACCOMMODATIONS. Beja is a very pleasant place to stay for the night, and there are several truly excellent options for accommodations. Most are located within a few blocks of the tourist office. **Pousada de Juventude de Beja (HI),** R. Professor Janeiro Acabado (☎ 284 32 54 58, fax 32 54 68). From the front of the bus station, walk away from the center (and the Pr. Tavares traffic circle) on R. Cidade de São Paulo, then take a right on R. Professor Janeiro Acbado; the hostel is on the left. This hostel offers a living room with TV and games, laundry room, and a kitchen. June 16-Sept. 15 dorms 1900$/€10, doubles 4200$/€21, with bath 4600$/€23; Sept. 16-June 15 dorms 1500$/€8, doubles 3500$/€18, with bath 3800$/€19. Open 8am-noon and 6pm-midnight. **Residencial Rosa do Campo,** R. Liberdade, 12 (☎ 284 32 35 78). Take a right out of the tourist office and walk a short three blocks down; the house will be on the right after the park on the left. The extremely kind owners offer spacious, air-conditioned rooms in their newly-renovated private home. All rooms come with TV and private bath. Singles 4000-5000$/€20-25; doubles 7000$/€35; room with 4 beds 3000$/€15 per person. A secluded annex just around the block has one huge (70 square meter) room with five beds, a bath, and a refrigerator, and rivals youth hostel prices. Stay there alone and you practically have a studio apartment for the night. For one person 3000$/€15, 2 for 5000$/€25, 3 for 6000$/€30, 4 for 8000$/€40, 5 for 10,000$/€50. **Residencial Bejense,** R. Capitão J. F. de Sousa, 57 (☎ 284 31 15 70; fax 284 31 15 79). Take a left out of the tourist office and walk just a little bit down the street. This 3-star lodging house, with azulejo-lined hallways, has large rooms with tiled floors, TVs, phones, and A/C. Singles 5500$/€28; doubles 8000$/€40, with 3rd bed 9500$/€48. AmEx/MC/V.

FOOD AND NIGHTLIFE. Beja is one of the best places to taste authentic (and affordable) Portuguese cuisine. The municipal **market** sets up in a building on Lg. de Mercado, one block up and one block to the right from the bus station (open M-Sa 6am-1:30pm). **Restaurante Saiote,** R. Biscainha, 6, off R. Capitão J. F. de Sousa, to the right before the intersection of R. Portas de Mertola. Basic and dependable, Saiote is a popular working-class place that gets loud and busy at lunchtime. (☎ 284 32 02 59. *Bife com cogumelos e natas* (950$/€4.74). Open M-Sa noon-3:30pm, 7-10:30pm.) At night, the locals head out to **Ritual,** R. Moeda, 9, down the street from Pr. República. One of the slightly classier bars, it's popular for pre-clubbing and gets a peak crowd at 1am. (☎ 968 02 33 68. Beer 200-250$, hard drinks 500$. Open M-Sa 10pm-4am.)

SIGHTS. Beja's historical sites are scattered, but the outstanding **Museu Rainha Dona Leonor** makes an excellent starting point. Take a right from the tourist office and walk into the Pr. Diogo Fernandes de Beja. Go right on R. Dr. Brito Camacho, and through Lg. de São João to Lg. da Conceiçao; the museum is on your right. Built on the site where Sister Mariana Alcoforado fell in love with the French officer, the museum features a replica of the cell window through which the nun watched the object of her passion. Inside, the gilded church's 18th-century *azulejo* panels depict the lives of Mary and St. John the Baptist. Nearby are *intaglio* marble altars and panels of *talha dourada* (gilded carvings). The *azulejos* and Persian-style ceiling make the chapter house look like a mini-mosque. (Largo de Conceição. ☎ 284 32 33 51. Open Tu-Su 9:45am-12:30pm and 2-5:30pm, last entry 12:15pm and 5:15pm. 100$/€0.50. Su free. Ticket also good for the Museu Visigótico behind the castle, which displays artifacts. Same hours.)

One block downhill from the Museu Rainha Dona Leonor is the 13th-century, **Igreja de Santa María da Feira,** transformed into a mosque during the Moorish invasion and back into a church when the city reverted to Portuguese control—the result is a notable mix of architectural styles. A miniature bull on its corner column symbolizes the city's spirit. (Largo de Santa María. Church open daily 10am-1pm and 3-7pm. Free. Mass daily 6:00-6:30pm, also Su noon.) From here, R. Aresta Branco leads past handsome old houses to the **Castelo de Beja**, built around 1300 on the remnants of a Roman fortress. (Open May-Sept. Tu-Su 10am-1pm and 2-6pm; Oct.-Apr. 9am-noon and 1-4pm. Free.) The castle still has an enormous marble keep, vaulted chambers, stones covered with cryptic symbols, and walls covered with ivy. The castle's **Torre de Menagem** provides an impressive view of the vast Alentejan plains (100$ to go up the tower). Between the police station and the center of town lies the **Convento de São Francisco**, R. Dr. Nuno Alvares Pereira (☎ 284 32 84 41). The convent has been turned into a state-run luxury pousada; however, you can still go in and see the lobby and cloister of the convent.

RIBATEJO AND ESTREMADURA

Serrated cliffs and whitewashed fishing villages line Estremadura's Costa de Prata (Silver Coast), whose beaches rival even those of the Algarve. Throngs of tourists and summer residents populate seafront Nazaré and Peniche. Smaller, less touristed towns with sparkling beaches line the coast, and the rugged and beautiful Ilhas Berlingas lie just offshore. Nearby, the fertile region of the Ribatejo ("banks of the Tejo") is perhaps the gentlest and greenest in Portugal. Known as the "Heart of Portugal," it is famous for its pastures that border the arid Alentejan plain and Estremaduran wetlands. It is home to some of the country's finest sights, from the ornate monasteries in Alcobaça and Batalha, the mysterious medieval town of Óbidos. In this region just north of Lisbon, sights and history are packed into towns still untouched by commercial tourism.

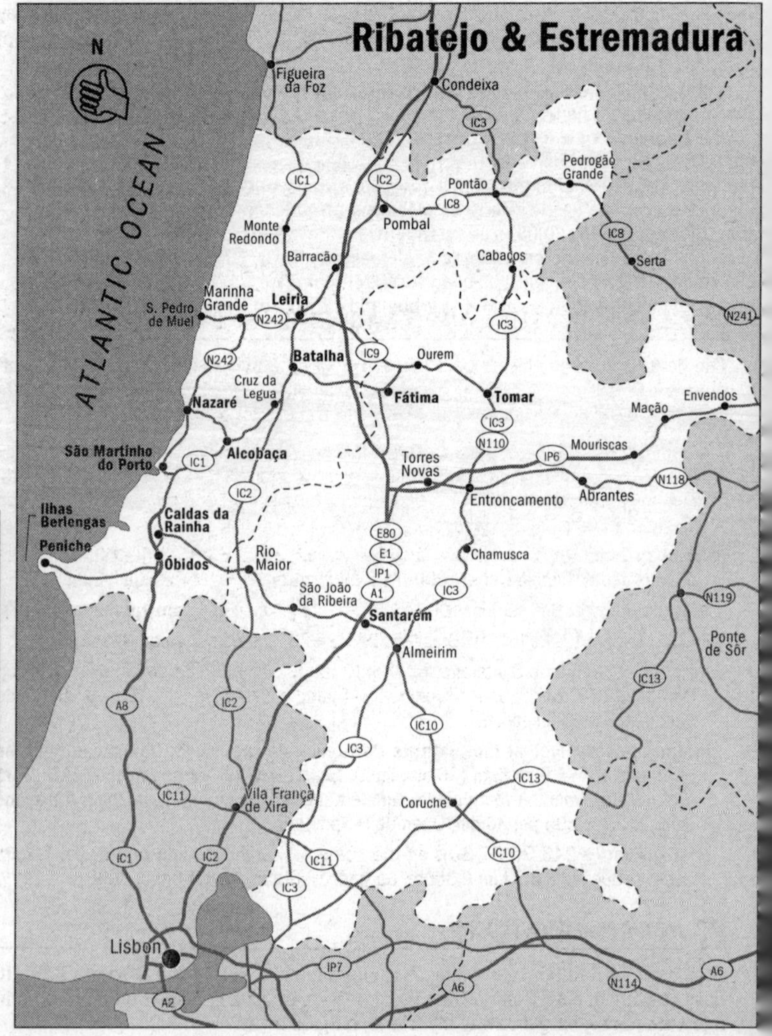

SANTARÉM ☎243

Perhaps the most charming of Ribatejo's cities, Santarém (pop. 50,000) presides from atop a rocky mound over the calm Rio Tejo and the tranquil green pastures. Once a ruling city in the ancient Roman province of Lusitania, and later a flourishing medieval center, Santarém has a long history of prosperity. It was also the capital of Portuguese Gothic style; its many appealing churches today display a mind-boggling range of architectural trends.

TRANSPORTATION

Trains: Station (☎243 32 11 99), on Estrada da Estação, 2km outside town. **Bus** service to and from the station (10min., every 30min.-1hr., 210$/€1.04). To: **Coimbra** (2hr., 11 per day 6:25am-1:10am, 1020-1400$/€5.09-7); **Faro** via Lisbon (4hr., 6 per day, 1700$/€8.50); **Lisbon** (1hr., 37 per day 4:40am-3:55am, 670-1050$/€3.34-5.24); **Portalegre** (3hr., 4 per day 8:50am-9pm, 1120$/€5.60); **Porto** (4hr., 4 per day 9:55am-8:55pm, 1720-2100$/€8.58-12); **Tomar** (1hr., every hr. 6:20am-1:25am, 520$/€2.60).

Buses: Rodoviária do Tejo (☎243 33 32 00), on Av. Brasil, not far from the main *praça*. To: **Braga** (5hr., 10:45am and 6:45pm, 2200$/€11); **Caldas da Rainha** (1½hr., 3-5 per day 7:20am-6:20pm, 730$/€3.64); **Coimbra** (2hr., 10:45am and 6:45pm, 1450$/€7.23); **Faro** (7hr., 4 per day 10:30am-4:30pm, 2600$/€13); **Leiria** (1½hr., 5 per day 8:15am-6:45pm, 920-1550$/€4.60-7.73); **Lisbon** (1¼hr., 10 per day 7am-7:15pm, 1000$/€5); **Nazaré** (1¼hr., 8:15am and 5:30pm, 880$/€4.40); **Porto** (4hr., 10:45am and 6:45pm, 2100$/€10.50).

Taxis: Scaltaxis (☎243 33 29 19) has a stand across from the bus station.

ORIENTATION AND PRACTICAL INFORMATION

The densely packed streets between **Praça Sá da Bandeira** (the main square) and the park **Portas do Sol** (above the Tejo) form the core of Santarém. **Rua Capelo Ivêns,** which begins at the *praça*, is home to the tourist office and many hostels.

Tourist Office: R. Capelo Ivêns, 63 (☎243 30 44 37), down from the main *praça*. Maps and info on festivals, accommodations, and transportation. Friendly and helpful English-speaking staff. Open Tu-F 9am-7pm, Sa-Su 10am-12:30pm and 2:30-5:30pm, M 9am-12:30pm and 2-5:30pm.

Currency Exchange: Banco Nacional Ultramarino (☎243 33 30 07), at R. Dr. Texeira Guedes and R. Capelo Ivêns. 1000$/€5 commission. Open M-F 8:30am-3pm.

Luggage Storage: Bus station. 100$/€0.50 per bag. Open M-F 9am-1pm, 2pm-7pm.

Emergency: ☎112. **Police:** Av. Brasil, (☎243 32 20 22), near the bus station.

Hospital: Av. Bernardo Santareno, (☎243 30 02 00). From Pr. Sá da Bandeira, walk up R. Cidade da Covilhã, as it becomes R. Alexandre Herculano and then Av. Bernardo Santareno. English spoken.

Internet Access: Free at the **Instituto Português da Juventude,** downstairs from the youth hostel, M-F 9am-8pm (30min. limit). **e-planet,** Av. Madre Andaluz, 16B (☎91 495 47 80). From the youth hostel, turn left and walk 5min. down the road; it's on the right. 210$/€1.05 per 30min. Open daily 2pm-2am.

Post Office: (☎243 30 97 30), on the corner of Largo Cândido and R. Dr. Texeira Guedes. Open M-F 8:30am-6:30pm, Sa 9am-12:30pm. **Postal Code:** 2000.

ACCOMMODATIONS

Prices are fairly high year-round, but may increase during the Ribatejo Fair (10 days starting in early June). The tourist office can usually help you find a room in a private house; bargain away my friend, bargain away!

Pousada da Juventude de Santarém (HI), Av. Grp. Forcados Amadores de Santarém, 1 (☎/fax 243 39 19 14), near the bullring. From the bus station, turn right onto Av. Brasil, walk 4 blocks, then turn right onto Lg. Cândido dos Reis, follow it as it becomes Av. Dom Afonso Henriques and then curves past the bullring; the hostel is on the left, upstairs from the Instituto Português da Juventude. Rooms are clean and comfortable. Breakfast included, 8:30-10am. Reception 8am-noon and 6pm-midnight. Check-in after 6pm and check out before 11am. Lockout 11am-6pm. June 16-Sept. 15 dorms 1900$/€9.50; doubles with bath 4600$/€23. Sept. 16-June 15 dorms 1500$/€7.50; doubles with bath 3800$/€19.

Residencial Abidis, R. Guilherme de Azevedo, 4 (☎243 32 20 17 or 32 20 18), around the corner from the tourist office. Centrally located, with 27 nice rooms and living rooms on each floor. Breakfast included. Singles 3500-4000$/€17.43-20, with bath 5500$/€27.43; doubles 4500-5000$/€22.45-25, with bath 7000$/€35.

Residencial Muralha, R. Pedro Canavarro, 12 (☎243 32 23 99; fax 32 94 77), next to the medieval wall. Rooms, all with TV and most with private bath. Reserve a week ahead in summer. Singles 3500$/€17.46, with bath 5000-6500$/€25-32.42; doubles with bath 6500-9700$/€32.42-48.38.

Pensão José Rodrigues, Trav. do Froes, 14 (☎243 32 30 88). Inexpensive rooms in a central location. Singles 2500$/€12.50; doubles 5000$/€25.

FOOD

Eateries cluster around the parallel R. Capelo Ivêns and R. Serpa Pinto. The **municipal market,** in the pagoda on Lg. Infante Santo near the Jardim da República, sells fresh produce (open M-Sa 8am-2pm). **Supermercado Minipreço,** R. Pedro Canavarro, 31, is along the street leading from the bus station to R. Capelo Ivêns (open M-Sa 9am-8pm). If you're in the mood for home-style cooking, **Casa d'Avó,** R. Serpa Pinto, 62, serves Portuguese dishes (950$/€4.74) as well as sandwiches (200-350$/€1-1.75) and sweets (110-350$/€0.55-1.75) on petite tables surrounded by cast-iron garden chairs. (☎243 32 69 16. Open M-F 9am-7pm, Sa 9am-2pm. Closed Aug.)

SIGHTS

GARDENS. **Portas do Sol,** a paradise of flowers and fountains surrounded by Moorish walls, is best visited on a clear day, when the walls offer a lovely view of the plains and the Tejo flowing by on its way to Lisbon. *(Take R. Serpa Pinto from Pr. Sá da Bandeira to Pr. Visconde de Serra Pilar, then continue on R. Cons. Figueiredo Leal, which becomes Av. 5 de Outubro and head straight into the Portas do Sol. Open daily 8am-11pm. Free.)*

PRAÇA VISCONDE DE SERRA PILAR. Centuries ago, Christians, Moors, and Jews gathered for social and business affairs in this *praça*. *(Take R. Serpa Pinto from Pr. Sá da Bandeira.)* The 12th-century **Igreja de Marvilha,** off the *praça*, has a 17th-century *azulejo* interior. *(Open Tu-Su 9:30am-12:30pm and 2-5:30pm. Free.)* The early Gothic purity of nearby **Igreja da Graça** contrasts sharply with Marvilha's overflowing exuberance. Within Graça's chapel lies Pedro Alvares Cabral, the explorer who "discovered" Brazil and one of the few to live long enough to return to his homeland. *(Church and chapel open Tu-Su 9:30am-12:30pm and 2-5:30pm. Free.)*

IGREJA DO SEMINÁRIO DOS JESUÍTAS. The austere façade of the Igreja do Seminário dos Jesuítas dominates Pr. Sá da Bandeira, Santarém's main square. Stone friezes carved as ropes separate the three stories and Latin biblical mottos embellish every lintel and doorway. *(Open Tu-Su 9:30am-12:30pm and 2-5:30pm. Free. If it is closed, enter through the door to the right of the entrance and ask Sr. Domingos to unlock it.)*

TORRE DAS CABAÇAS. The medieval Torre das Cabaças (Tower of the Gourds) was named after the eight earthen bowls installed in the 16th century to amplify the bell's ring. Inside the tower is the Museu de Tempo (Time Museum), with clocks, clocks, and more clocks. *(Take R. São Martinho from Pr. Visconde de Serra Pilar. Open Tu-Su 9:30am-12:30pm and 2-5:30pm. 200$/€1 for each, 250$/€1.75 for both.)*

ENTERTAINMENT

Around the corner and two blocks down from the bus station, **Cervejão,** Av. António Maria Baptista, 10, is the place to drink baby. The name means "big beer" and lots of it can be found here indeed. (☎243 26 43 33. Cocktails 500$/€2.50. Open M-Sa 4pm-midnight) For unrestrained daytime partying, the **Feira Nacional de Agricultura** (also known as the Feira do Ribatejo), a national agricultural exhibition, is a good pick. Tens of thousands of people come for the 6- to 10-day bullfighting and horse-racing orgy, which starts in early June. During the **Festival e Seminário Nacional de Gastronomia** (the last half of October), each region of Portugal has one day to prepare a typical local feast, complete with entertainment.

ÓBIDOS

Óbidos has a medieval heart: the 12th-century village defended by formidable walls remains the center of any visit. An approach through the stone gate evokes the melancholy of the town's varied history. The **castelo** on the coast, a Moorish fortress rebuilt in the 12th century, gradually lost its strategic importance as the ocean receded. Although the castle itself, now a luxury *pousada*, opens only to guests, everyone is free to walk the 1.5km of its **walls.** The 17th-century *azulejo-*

"G" RATED. The story of Santarém's founding could have been a Disney movie. All the elements are there: beautiful girl, frustrated love, bitter jealousy, a little bit of magic, and no sex whatsoever. The daughter of two 7th-century nobles, Iria was sent to a convent at an early age to live a life of purity and utter devotion to God. Soon Iria blossomed into an attractive young woman and fell in love with a noble named Britaldo. The two contented themselves with innocent hand-holding (her being a nun-in-training and all) and tried to live happily ever after. Enter Remígio, a former teacher of Iria's, now madly in love with her as well. Cue the jealous rage. Remígio decides if he can't have Iria, no one can, and slips a potion into her soup that makes her look pregnant. Needless to say, sex is a convent no-no, and so the townspeople cast Iria into the river. Her nun friends (where is good ol' Britaldo now?) form a search party and eventually find her body washed up on the shore. Before anyone can give her a proper burial, the river rises, giving the girl a watery grave. Santarém was founded on this tragic site, "Santarém" being derived from "Santa Iria." Today a statue of her by the river just marks the spot where Iria is said to lie still.

filled **Igreja de Santa Maria,** to the right of the post office in the central *praça*, displays Josefa de Óbidos's vivid canvases off the main altar. It was also the site of the 1441 wedding of 10-year-old King Afonso V to his 8-year-old cousin, Isabel. Let's Go does not recommend booty at such a young age. (Open daily Apr.-Sept. 9:30am-12:30pm and 2:30-7pm; Oct.-March 9:30am-12:30pm and 2:30-5pm. Free.)

The **tourist office** is a small green cottage just up the steps from the bus stop, across from Porta da Vila. (☎262 95 92 31, fax 95 50 14. Open May-Sept. M-F 9:30am-7pm, Sa-Su 10am-7pm; Oct.-Apr. M-F 9:30am-6pm, Sa-Su 10am-6pm.) There are many private rooms for rent in Óbidos, as advertised by the signs on and around R. Direita, but it may be difficult to find a good price. **ÓbidoSol,** R. Direita, 40, a charming 17th century home that has 3 rooms with window seats, an azulejo-covered common bath, and a large living room. Reservations recommended, especially during the summer. (☎262 95 91 88. June-Sept. double bed 5000$/€25, doubles 6000$/€30; Oct.-May double bed 4000$/€20, doubles 5000$/€25. Ask for a 1000$/€5 discount if you are alone.) "Typical" **restaurants** (most with typical tourist prices) and several **markets** cluster on and around R. Direita. Eat light and save your *escudos* for Óbidos's signature *ginja* (wild cherry liqueur); stores on R. Direita sell small bottles for about 350$/€1.75.

Buses, which stop just outside the town gate, are more convenient. Connections to: **Caldas da Rainha** (20min., 24 per day 7:35am-8:35pm, 170$/€0.85); **Lisbon** (1¼hr., M-F 4 per day 7:05am-4:10pm, 860$/€4.30); and **Peniche** (40min.; M-F 10 per day 8:10am-7:40pm, Sa 7 per day 8:10am-7:40pm, Su 5 per day 9:40am-7:40pm; 385$/€1.92). On weekends you must stop in Caldas da Rainha to go to Lisbon (1½hr., 5-7 per day 7am-9pm, 1000$/€5). Buses stop a few stairs down from the main gate. No bus schedules are posted here, so ask at the tourist office.

PENICHE ☎262

Many travelers overlook Peniche, a seaport town 22km west of Óbidos en route to the Ilhas Berlengas. What they miss is a lively city close to good beaches and hiking. Home to Portugal's second largest fishing fleet, Peniche is so enthralled with seafood that it used to dedicate an entire festival to the sardine; only recently it expanded the revelry to fishing and seafood in general.

TRANSPORTATION

Buses: R. Dr. Ernesto Moureira, (☎262 78 21 33), on an isthmus outside the town walls. To: **Alcobaça,** via Caldas da Rainha (1¾hr., 3 per day 10:45am-5:10pm, 1150$/€5.73); **Caldas da Rainha** (1hr., 8 per day 8am-7:30pm, 435-850$/€2.17-4.24); **Leiria,** via Caldas da Rainha (2hr., 3 per day 10:45am-5:10pm, 1400$/€7); **Lisbon** (2hr., 12 per day 6am-8:45pm, 1050$/€5.24); **Nazaré** (1½hr., 4 per day

10:45am-6pm, 730-1100$/€3.64-5.50); **Porto** (6½hr., 3 per day 7am-6pm, 2100$/€11); **Santarém,** via Caldas da Rainha (1½hr., 3 per day 7am-5:10pm, 850$/€4.24). Peniche is only accessible by bus.

Taxis: (☎262 78 44 24 or 78 29 10), in Pr. Jacob Pereira and Lg. Bispo Mariana.

ORIENTATION AND PRACTICAL INFORMATION

Most of Peniche's points of interest are situated in or around the grid of streets between **Largo Bispo Mariana** and the **fortaleza** on the coast. **Praça Jacob Rodrigues Pereira** marks the center of town, near the tourist office and the start of **Avenida do Mar,** which runs along the river to the docks and fishing port.

Tourist Office: (☎/fax 262 78 95 71), R. Alexandre Herculano. From the bus station, take a left and cross the river over Ponte Velha to the right. Turning left on R. Alexandre Herculano, walk alongside the public garden, and follow signs to the office. Open July-Sept. daily 9am-8pm; Oct.-May 10am-1pm and 2-5pm; June 9am-7pm.

Bank: Caixa Geral de Depósitos, on R. Alexandre Herculano, down the street from the tourist office. Open M-F 8:30am-3pm.

Emergency: ☎112. **Police:** R. Herois Ultramar (☎262 78 95 55).

Hospital: (☎262 78 09 00), on R. Gen. Humberto Delgado. From the tourist office, turn right onto R. Alexandre Herculano and take the first left onto R. Arquitecto Paulino Montez; walk all the way up the street, passing the post office, then take a right onto R. Gen. Humberto Delgado, and the hospital is down the road on the left.

Internet Access: On Line Cyber Café, R. António Cervantes, 5 (☎96 685 77 49), near the fortaleza, has 4 computers. 120$/€0.60 per 15min., 100$/€0.50 per 15min. after the first hr. Coffee 80-120$/€0.40-0.60. Beer 150$/€0.75. Mixed drinks 500$/€2.50. Open daily 10:30am-2am.

Post Office: (☎262 78 00 60), R. Arquitecto Paulino Montez. From the tourist office, turn right on R. Alexandre Herculano, left on R. Arquitecto Paulino Montez, and walk 3 blocks. **Posta Restante** and **fax.** Open M-F 9am-6pm. **Postal Code:** 2520.

ACCOMMODATIONS AND CAMPING

Peniche's budget accommodations are located above restaurants of the same name; look for signs to find a *residencial* on or behind Av. do Mar. Hostels do fill quickly, especially from June to August; try to arrive early in the day. Persistent elderly matrons renting rooms in their private houses gather in Pr. Jacob Rodrigues Pereira, usually around the benches in front of Sapateria Tina. Rooms in private houses may be good budget options, but insist on seeing them first and inquire about hot water and amenities.

Residencial Mira Mar, Av. Mar, 40-44 (☎262 78 16 66), near the docks and above the seafood restaurant of the same name. Large rooms with padded doors, all with TV and bath. Reserve two weeks ahead in summer. July-Sept. singles 4000$/€20, doubles 7000$/€35; Oct.-June singles 3000$/€15, doubles 6000$/€30. AmEx/MC/V.

Residencial Marítimo, R. António Cervantes, 14 (☎262 08 34 07), off the *praça* in front of the fortress. Newly decorated rooms, all with TV and private bath. Breakfast included. Singles 3000-3500$/€15-21; doubles 5000-7500$/€30-45.

Residencial Cristal, R. M. G. Freitas de Andrade, 14-16 (☎262 78 27 24). From Pr. Jacob Pereira, 3 blocks up R. Latino Coelho, and take a right onto R. de Andrade; it's on the left one block down. Reception 8am-midnight. Breakfast included. July-Sept. only, 8:30-10am. July-Sept. singles 3500$/€17.50, doubles 6000$/€30, triples 7500$/€37.40; Oct.-June singles 2500$/€12.50, doubles 5000$/€25, triples 6000$/€30.

Municipal Campground (☎262 78 95 29; fax 78 96 96), 2km outside of town, at least a 30min. walk from downtown. From the bus station, turn left onto Av. Porto de Pesca to reach EN 114, following it through the traffic circle and past the waterpark; the campsite is on the left. Or take a taxi (about 500$/€2.50 from downtown). Open year-round. 390$/€1.94 per person. 220$/€1.10 per child age 6-12, under 6 free. 320-800$/€1.60-4 per tent. 320$/€1.60 per car. Free hot showers.

FOOD

The restaurants that line **Av. do Mar** serve excellent fresh grilled seafood—see the raw choices on display in the cases along the sidewalk. Despite the multilingual menus, the prices are reasonable and there are plenty of locals mixed in among foreign visitors. Peniche's *sardinhas* (sardines) are exceptional, as are the seafood *espetadas* (skewers). The outdoor cafés on **Pr. Jacob Rodrigues Pereira** are lively, particularly on Sundays, when the rest of town is quiet. The **market,** on R. António da Conceição Bento, stocks fresh produce (open Tu-Su 7am-1pm).

Restaurante Mira Mar, Av. do Mar, 42 (☎262 78 16 66). One of the best of the string of restaurants along Av. do Mar. An energetic staff of young girls races around the tables; the place gets loud and happily busy at dinner time (especially 9-10pm). Entrées 900-1400$/€4.50-7. Excellent *crème de marisco* (shellfish soup, 400$/€2). Open 10am-11:30pm; meals noon-3pm and 8-10:30pm. AmEx/MC/V.

Ristorante Il Boccone, Av. do Mar, 4 (☎262 78 24 12), at the beginning of the row of restaurants along Av. do Mar. Recently opened by an Italian owner. Excellent pizza (850-1550$/€4.24-7.73) and pasta dishes (800-1450$/€4-14.50). Open Tu-Su 10am-2am; meals noon-4pm, 8pm-midnight.

Café Oceano, Pr. Jacob Pereira, 12-13 (☎262 78 23 15), just up from the tourist office. Popular café in the main square; perfect for people watching. Sandwiches 180-400$/€0.90-2. Coffee 80-170$/€0.40-0.85. Gourmet ice cream 160-800$/€0.80-4. Specialty *pasteis de Peniche* (almond pastries, 140$/€0.70). Open daily 8am-midnight.

SIGHTS

FORTALEZA. António Salazar, Portugal's longtime dictator, chose Peniche's formidable 16th-century fortress for one of his four high-security political prisons. Its high walls and bastions later became a camp for Angolan refugees. It now houses the **Museu de Peniche,** highlighted by a small but fascinating anti-Fascist exhibition. Photos and text trace the dictatorship and underground resistance from the seizure of power in 1926 to the coup that toppled the regime on April 25, 1974. *(Campo da República, near the dock where boats leave for the Ilhas Berlengas. Fortaleza open Tu-Su 10:30am-noon and 2-5:30pm. Free. Museum ☎262 78 01 16. Open Tu-Su 10:30am-noon and 2-5:30pm. 200$/€1, under 16 free.)*

BEACHES. For sun and surf, head to any of the town's three beaches. The beautiful but windy **Praia de Peniche de Cima,** along the north crescent, has the warmest water. It merges with another beach at **Baleal,** a small fishing village popular with tourists. The southern **Praia do Molho Leste,** known to many as "super-tubos" because of its big surf, is a bit cooler. Beyond it is the crowded **Praia da Consolação.** The strange humidity at this beach supposedly cures bone diseases. Unfortunately, on windless days, it also traps the less than tantalizing aroma of nearby sewers. *(Buses 7am-7pm, 180$/€0.90. Check with the tourist office for changes.)*

ENTERTAINMENT AND NIGHTLIFE

Peniche's nightlife can be a rewarding experience if you know how to do it right. The town caters to every kind of taste, from booty-shaking intellectuals to martini-popping beautiful people to happy-go-lucky twenty-somethings. Bring it baby. Peniche's biggest festival takes place on the first Sunday of August, when boats—bedecked in wreaths of flags and flowers—file into the harbor in the procession that launches the two-day **Festa de Nossa Senhora da Boa Viagem,** celebrating the protector of sailors and fishermen. The town lets loose with carnival rides, live entertainment, wine, and seafood. Mid-September brings the **Sabores do Mar** festival, focused on fishing, *fado*, and folklore.

Café Cartaxo, Trav. dos Proletários, 3 (☎96 436 66 80), behind the Igreja São Pedro. A pleasant little Celtic bar in action for over 100 years. Popular among chess players; boards are available on the shelf near the entrance. Port wine (300-900$/€1.50-4.50). Open daily 1:30pm-2am.

Bar No. 1, R. Afonso Albuquerque, 14 (☎262 78 45 41), close to the intersection with R. José Estevão. Popular with both tourists and locals; its friendly owner works the DJ booth. The bar hosts 10 small art exhibits per year. Beer and shots 150-300$/€0.75-1.50. Mixed drinks 600$/€3. Open daily noon-2am.

Karas, Estrada Marginal Norte (EN-114), complex #1 (☎262 78 55 79), a 10-15 minute walk from Pr. Jacob Pereira along the coast. The most popular disco within walking distance gets moving at 3-5am. Minimum consumption 1000$/€5. Beer 400$/€2. Mixed drinks 700$/€3.50. In August, open Tu-Su midnight-6am; during the rest of year, open only Saturdays, same hours.

EXCURSIONS

To truly enjoy the ocean air, hike around the peninsula (8km). Start at **Papôa,** just north of Peniche. From Pr. Jacob Pereira, take R. Alexandre Herculano and then Av. 25 de Abril and follow the signs along the coast. Then stroll out to the tip, where orange cliffs rise from a swirling blue sea. Nearby lie the sparse ruins of an old fortress, **Forte da Luz.** The endpoint of the peninsula, **Cabo Carvoeiro,** is the most popular and dramatic of Peniche's natural sights. The fortress's **farol** (lighthouse) punctuates the extreme west end of the peninsula. The **Nau dos Corvos** (Crow's Ship), an odd rock formation, promises a seagull's-eye perspective.

DAYTRIPS FROM PENICHE

ILHAS BERLENGAS (1HR.)

*Several companies operate boats from Peniche's public dock. Largest is the **Viamar ferry** (☎262 78 56 46; fax 78 38 47. Ticket booth open 8:30am-5:30pm), which offers crossings 3 times a day (40min.; July-Aug. 3 per day 9:30, 11:30am, and 5:30pm, return trips at 10:30am, 4:30, and 6:30pm; May 15-June and Sept. 1-15, 10am, returns 4:30pm). Reserve 3-4 days in advance. Arrive 1 hr. in advance, 2½ hr. in August. A same-day round-trip ticket (3000$/€15, children age 5-12 $2000/€10, under 5 free). 9:30am departure, 4:30pm return; 11:30am departure, 6:30pm return. To stay overnight, buy a 2000$/€10 one-way ticket each way. The crossing from Peniche to the island is rough: many experience bouts of seasickness. (To get through the ordeal, try inhaling as the boat goes up and exhaling as it goes down.) Trips by **Berlenga Turpesca** (☎262 78 99 60) include visits to the Berlenga caves and **Berlenga Praia** (☎917 60 11 14) also offers crossing.*

The rugged, Ilhas Berlengas (Berlenga Islands) rise out of the Atlantic Ocean, 12km northwest of Peniche. The main island of Berlenga and archipelago of several smaller islands (the Farilhões, Estelas, and Forcados), that's home to thousands of screeching seagulls. The **Reserva Natural da Berlenga,** home to wild black rabbits, lizards, and a very small fishing community. Deep gorges, natural tunnels, and rocky caves carve through the main island. Although it is fringed with several protected beaches, the only one accessible by foot lies in a small cove by the landing dock. For beach-goers willing to brave the cold, dips in the calm water bring instant respite from the heat. Hikers can trek to the island's highest point for a gorgeous view of the 17th-century **Forte de São João Batista,** now a hostel run by the Associação Amigos da Berlenga (AAB).

NAZARÉ ☎262

It's hard to tell where authenticity stops and tourism starts in Nazaré. Fishermen clad in traditional garb stroll barefoot and women typically don seven petticoats, thick shawls, and gold earrings. The day's catch dries in the hot sun, locals string their nets along the shoreline esplanade, and streetside entrepreneurs sell everything from fishing nets to seashell necklaces. "Traditional" lifestyle has become the basis of Nazaré's most thriving business: tourism. But if Nazaré is part theater, at least it puts on a good show. August is not the time to drop anchor here, though; prices usually double and sunbathers jostle for tiny spots on the sand.

TRANSPORTATION

Buses: Av. Vieira Guimarães, (☎262 55 11 72), perpendicular to Av. República. More convenient than taking the train (6km away). To: **Alcobaça** (30min., 14 per day 7:10am-8pm, 230$/€1.15); **Batalha** (50min., 5 per day 7:10am-6:45pm, 470$/€2.34); **Caldas da Rainha** (1¼hr., 11 per day 6:30am-7:15pm, 435$/€2.17); **Coimbra** (2hr., 5 per day 6:25am-7:25pm, 1400$/€7); **Fátima** (1½hr., 3 per day 7:10am-5pm, 570$/€2.84); **Leiria** (1¼hr., 10 per day 6:45am-7:10pm, 470-570$/€2.34-2.84); **Lisbon** (2hr., 8 per day 6:50am-8pm, 1250$/€6.24); **Peniche** (1½hr., 6 per day 8:35am-6pm, 740$/€3.70); **Porto** (3½hr., 5 per day 6:25am-7:25pm, 1800$/€9); **São Martinho do Porto** (20min., 11 per day 6:50am-8pm, 250$/€1.25); **Tomar** (1½hr., 3 per day 7:10am-5pm, 850$/€4.24).

Taxis: ☎262 55 31 25.

ORIENTATION AND PRACTICAL INFORMATION

All of the action in Nazaré—beaches, nightlife, and most restaurants—takes place in the **new town** along the beach. Its two main squares, **Praça Sousa Oliveira** and **Praça Dr. Manuel de Arriaga,** are near the cliffside away from the fishing port. Either the cliffside funicular or a winding road leads up to the **Sítio,** the old town, which preserves a sense of calm and tradition less prevalent in the crowded resort below. To get to the tourist office from the bus station, take a right toward the beach and then a right onto Av. República; the office is a 5min. walk along the shore, between the two major *praças.*

Tourist Office: beachside on Av. República, (☎262 56 11 94). English-speaking staff provides maps as well as entertainment and transportation info. Open daily July-Aug. 10am-10pm; Sept. 10am-8pm; Oct.-March 9:30am-1pm and 2:30-6pm; Apr.-June 15 10am-1pm and 3-7pm; June 15-30 10am-1pm and 3-8pm.

Banks: Several major banks on and around Av. República. Open M-F 8:30am-3pm.

Emergency: ☎112. **Police:** (☎262 55 12 68), 1 block from the bus station at Av. Vieira Guimarães and R. Sub-Vila.

Hospital: Hospital da Confraria da Nossa Senhora de Nazaré (☎262 56 11 16), in the Sítio district on the cliffs above the town center. **Centro de Saúde** (☎262 55 11 82), in the new part of town.

Internet Access: At **municipal library,** Av. Manuel Remigio (the continuation of Av. República in the direction of the port), computers for public use. Open M-F 9:30am-1pm and 2-7pm.

Post Office: Av. Independência Nacional, 2 (☎262 56 16 04). From Pr. Souza Oliveira, walk up R. Mouzinho de Albuquerque. It's 1 block past Pensão Central. **Fax** and **Posta Restante.** Open M-F 9:30am-12:30pm and 2:30-6pm. **Postal Code:** 2450.

ACCOMMODATIONS AND CAMPING

Nazaré is home to the most aggressive room-renters in Portugal; insistent old ladies swarm arriving buses at the station and line Av. República, waving colored signs and relentlessly proffering rooms in their houses. Be sure to check that the owners are authorized by the tourist office (in the form of an authorization card from the city or the tourist bureau) and insist on seeing the room (and feeling the hot water) before settling the deal. Bargaining is fair practice. For lodging, look above the restaurants on Pr. Dr. Manuel de Arriaga and Pr. Sousa Oliveira.

Vila Turística Conde Fidalgo, Av. da Independência Nacional, 21-A (☎/fax 262 55 23 61), 3 blocks uphill from Pr. Sousa Oliveira. Prices skyrocket in July-Aug., but it's a great deal the rest of the year, especially in June. Reception 9am-1am. Reservations recommended in the summer and require 50% pre-payment if far in advance. Sept.-June singles 3000$/€15; doubles 4000$/€20, with kitchen 5000$/€25. July singles 6000$/€30; doubles 7000$/€35, with kitchen 12,000$/€60; August singles 8000$/€40; doubles 9000$/€45, with kitchen 12,000$/€60.

Hospedaria Ideal, R. Adrião Batalha, 98 (☎262 55 13 79), between the two main *praças*. Reception 10am-10pm in the restaurant downstairs. If traveling with a friend, check out if they are offering the "Pensão Completa" package, which includes a double room and all three meals for two people for only 14,000$/€70. Sept. 16-June singles 3000$/€15; doubles 5000-6000$/€25-30. July-Sept. 15 singles 6000$/€30; doubles 8000-9000$/€40-45.

Camping: Vale Paraíso, Estrada Nacional 242 (☎262 56 18 00; fax 56 19 00), 2½km out of town. Take the bus to Alcobaça or Leiria (15min., 8 per day 7am-7pm). Also rents bungalows and apartments. Swimming pools, a restaurant-bar, a supermarket, and occasional Internet access. Laundry. Pool open June-Sept. 350$/€1.75. Apr.-May and Oct. free; Nov.-Mar. closed. June-Sept. 650$/€3.25 per person, 540-770$/€2.70-3.84 per tent, 540$/€2.70 per car; Apr.-May and Oct. 540$/€2.70 per person, 460-635$/€2.30-3.17 per tent, 455$/€2.27 per car; Nov.-Mar. 400$/€2 per person, 355-485$/€1.77-2.42 per tent, 350$/€1.75 per car. Free showers. AmEx/MC/V.

FOOD

For groceries, check out the **market** across from the bus station (open daily July-Sept. 8am-1pm; Oct.-June Tu-Su 8am-1pm). **Supermarkets** line R. Sub-Vila, parallel to Av. República (open daily June-Aug. 9am-10pm; Sept.-May 9am-8pm).

A Tasquinha, R. Adrião Batalha, 54 (☎262 55 19 45), 1 block left of Pr. Dr. Manuel de Arriaga. Perhaps the only restaurant in Nazaré with a Portuguese-only menu; locals and tourists jostle for seats at this popular restaurant, which is packed at 1-2pm and 8-9pm. Carlos, the friendly English-speaking owner is happy to help with ordering. Most entrées 800-1350$/€4-6.50. Open Tu-Su noon-3pm and 7-11pm. AmEx/MC/V.

Pastelaria Batel, R. Mouzinho de Albuquerque, 2 (☎262 55 11 47), at the corner of Pr. Sousa Oliveira. The best known pastry shop in Nazar, with a 32-year history, Batel is the place to try the sweet local specialties. All pastries 120$/€0.60. Try the *tamáres* (little boats with egg filling capped with chocolate), *sardinhas* (flaky pastry, not fish), and *Nazarenos* (almond pastry). Open June-Aug. daily 8am-2am; Sept.-May Th-Tu 8am-2am

ENTERTAINMENT

The main attraction of Nazaré is certainly not hard to find: the expansive **beach** runs alongside the main road. After catching the sun's rays, you can take the **funicular** (3min., every 15min. 7:15am-9:30pm, every 30min. 9:30pm-midnight, 115$/€0.58 one-way, or 280$/€1.40 for 6 trips) which runs from R. Elevador off Av. República to the **Sítio,** a clifftop area of Nazaré. With its uneven cobbled streets, weathered buildings, and staggering views of the town and ocean, Sítio makes for a perfect picnic and a quick shag. Around 6pm, fishing boats return to the **port** beyond the far left end of the beach; eavesdrop as local restaurateurs spiritedly bid for the most promising catches at the **fish auction** (M-F 6-10pm).

Cafés in Pr. Sousa Oliveira teem with people past midnight. The intimate bar **Ta Bar Es,** R. de Rio Maior, 20-22, just off R. Mouzinho Albuquerque near Pr. Dr. Manuel de Arriaga is a mellow haven from the sun by day but livens up at night, with live Brazilian and Portuguese music most summer evenings after 11pm. (☎262 08 21 73. Coffee 100$/€0.50. Before 7pm, beer 150-400$/€0.75-2, mixed drinks 500$/€2.50. After 7pm, beer 200-500$/€1-2.50, mixed drinks 700$/€3.50. Open daily 2pm-4am. Closed first 2 weeks of Nov.)

On Saturday afternoons in May and June, locals dress in traditional outfits and haul the fishing nets out of the water, enacting the old-fashioned technique in an event known as **Arte Xávega**. During the summer, look out for late-night **folk music** gatherings on the beach. **Bullfights** are also popular; Nazaré is on the schedule that brings *corridas* to a different city in the province each summer weekend (usually Sa 10pm; tickets start at 2500$/€24.50).

DAYTRIPS FROM NAZARÉ

ALCOBAÇA

With the nearest train station 5km away in Valado dos Frades, buses are the best way to reach Alcobaça. The bus station on Av. Manuel da Silva Carolino (☎262 58 22 21) offers service to: Batalha (30min., 8 per day 7:30am-7:10 pm, 385$/€1.92); Coimbra (2hr., 7:30am and 4:25pm, 1325$/€6.61); Leiria (1hr., 7 per day 7:30am-7:10pm, 470$/€2.34); Lisbon (2hr.; M-F 5 per day, Sa-Su 3 per day 6:30am–6pm; 1300$/€6.50); Nazaré (25min., 12-15 per day 7:30am-8:20pm, 230$/€1.15); Porto (3½hr., 4:25pm, 1650$/€8.23).

A sleepy town in the hills not too far from the coast, Alcobaça welcomes thousands of visitors each year for one reason: its impressive **Mosteiro de Santa Maria de Alcobaça,** the oldest church in Portugal. The town was founded in 1153, following King Afonso Henriques's expulsion of the Moors, as a grant from the king to Cistercian monks. Afonso was attempting to secure Christianity in the region, and the monks responded with the construction of their new monastery which began in 1178. Additions continued over the course of several centuries. Today it is the largest building of the Cistercian order in all of Europe and was recently granted UN World Heritage status. In the smaller naves adjacent to the towering central one, the **tombs** of King Pedro I and his wife Inês de Castro display sophisticated carvings and immortalize one of Portugal's great love stories (see **Eat your heart out, Don Juan,** p. 631). Surrounding the monastery's cloisters are numerous Gothic rooms, most notably the immense **kitchen** and **refectory** (the monks could roast more than 6 oxen at a time), the **Sala dos Monges** (Monk's Hall), and the **Sala dos Reis** (Hall of Kings). (☎262 50 51 20. Monastery open daily Apr.-Sept. 9am-7pm; Oct.-Mar. 9am-5pm. Cloisters open daily Apr.-Sept. 9am-6:30pm; Oct.-Mar. 9am-4:30pm. 600$/€3, age 14-25 300$/€1.50, under 14 free. Su before 2pm free.)

The **Museu da Vinha e do Vinho** (Museum of Wine and Winemaking), 5min. from the bus station on R. Leiria (which branches off R. dos Combatentes on the way out of town), has an interesting exhibition about the history and methods of Portugal's wine industry. (☎262 58 22 22. Open May-Sept. Tu-F 9am-12:30pm and 2-5:30pm, Sa-Su 10am-12:30pm and 2-6pm; Oct.-Apr. M-F 9am-12:30pm and 2-5:30pm. 300$/€1.50, students 150$/€0.75)

The **tourist office** sits on the corner of Pr. 25 de Abril. The English-speaking staff hands out accommodation lists and town maps that fold into wallet-size cards. (☎262 58 23 77. Open daily May-Sept. 10am-1pm and 3-7pm; Oct.-Apr. 10am-1pm and 2-6pm.) Should you decide to spend the night in Alcobaça, **Pensão Corações Unidos,** R. Frei António Brandão, 39, off Pr. 25 de Abril, has 20 rooms. (☎/fax 262 58 21 42. Reception 8am-midnight. July-Sept. singles 3000$/€15, with bath 3500$/€17.50; doubles 6000$/€30, with bath 7000$/€35. Oct.-June singles 2500$/€12.50, with bath 3000$/€15; doubles 5000$/€25, with bath 6000$/€30. AmEx/MC/V.)

SÃO MARTINHO DO PORTO

***Trains** run from the station (☎262 98 94 85) to Leiria (1½hr., 5 per day 9:50am-8:10pm, 400$/€2) and other points north and south. **Buses,** faster and more convenient, run to Nazaré (20min., 7 per day 9:30am-7:30pm, 225$/€1.12) and other towns. Both train and bus schedules are posted in the tourist office. The bus stops on the main road leading into town.*

Countless ages of smashing surf hollowed out surrounding coastal cliffs to create the bay of São Martinho do Porto. Nearly enclosed on all sides, the town lies at the base of the inlet, while its windless, swimmer-friendly **beach** sweeps 3km along and around the bay, forming an almost perfect circle. With its red-roofed houses crowding down a palm-studded hillside to a small and colorful fishing harbor, São

Martinho do Porto has an almost Mediterranean charm. An ideal escape from crowded Peniche and Nazaré. Vacationers crash the peace in July and August.

The **tourist office,** on Lg. Frederico Ulrich at the end of Av. 25 de Abril, provides a list of private rooms (☎262 98 91 10. Open June-Sept. Tu-Su 10am-1pm and 3-7pm; Oct.-May Tu-Su 10am-1pm and 2-6pm.). A congenial place to stay is **Casa Luz,** R. José Bento da Silva, 3, at the top of R. D. Pedro V; it's the white house to the left of the stairs. (☎262 98 91 39. Open May-Sept. only. Reserve at least a month ahead for August. May-July and Sept. singles 4000$/€20; doubles 5000$/€25. Aug. singles 5000$/€25; doubles 6000$/€30.)

LEIRIA ☎244

Capital of the surrounding district and an important transport hub, prosperous and industrial Leiria fans out from a fertile valley, 22km from the coast. An impressive ancient castle peers over the city, gazing down upon countless shops, a shady park and—at the moment—a lot of construction. Chosen to host the Euro 2002 soccer finals, Leiria is busy preparing itself for the crowds that will soon flood the city. Leiria makes a practical base for exploring the nearby region, with buses to Alcobaça, Batalha, and Fátima, as well as the beaches of the Costa da Prata.

TRANSPORTATION

Trains: Station (☎244 88 20 27), 3km outside town. Buses run between the station and the tourist office (15min., every hr. 7:05am-7:20pm, 150$/€0.75). To: **Coimbra** (1½hr., 10 per day 2am-10:15pm, 1150$/€5.75); **Figueira da Foz** (1hr., 3 per day 10:30am-5:45pm, 1150$/€5.75); **Lisbon** (1¾hr., 9 per day 3am-11pm, 1400$/€7).

Buses: (☎244 81 15 07), just off Pr. Paulo VI, next to the main park and near the tourist office in an exhaust-filled building; the ticket office is down the steps in back. Buses are the most convenient transport out of Leiria. Express buses are twice the price of regional buses. To: **Alcobaça** (50min., 6 per day 7:15am-7:10pm, 470-950$/€2.40-4.75); **Batalha** (20min., 9 per day 7:15am-7:10pm, 210$/€1.05); **Coimbra** (1hr., 11 per day 7:15am-2am, 1150$/€5.75); **Fátima** (1hr., 6 per day 7:15am-7:05pm, 380-800$/€1.90-4); **Figueira da Foz** (1½hr., M-F 8 per day 7:55am-6:35pm, 670-1150$/€3.34-5.75); **Lisbon** (2hr., 11 per day 7:15am-11pm, 1400$/€7); **Nazaré** (1hr., 6-9 per day 7:50am-7:10pm, 490-1100$/€2.44-5.50); **Porto** (3½hr., 10 per day 7:15am-2am, 1800$/€9); **Santarém** (2hr., 5 per day 7:15am-7:05pm, 900-1550$/€4.50-7.75); **Tomar** (1½hr.; M-F 7:15am and 5:45pm, Sa 6:15pm; 570-1200$/€2.85-6).

Taxis: ☎244 81 59 00 or 244 88 15 50. Taxis gather at the Jardim Luís de Camões.

ORIENTATION AND PRACTICAL INFORMATION

At the practical and commercial center of Leiria is the **Jardim Luís de Camões**. The castle up on the hill is a 20-minute climb from the town below.

Tourist Office: (☎244 82 37 73; fax 83 35 33), in the Jardim Luís de Camões, across the park from the bus station. English speaking staff presents visitors with maps, accommodations lists, and a precise model of Batalhás monastery–made entirely of sugar. Obtaining hard information, however, may prove a struggle. Free short-term **luggage storage.** Open daily May-Sept. 10am-1pm, 3-7pm; Oct.-Apr. 10am-1pm, 2-6pm.

Emergencies: ☎112. **Police:** Largo Artilharia, 4 (☎244 81 37 99).

Hospital: (☎244 81 70 00), on R. Olhalvas, along the road to Fátima.

Internet Access: The **library,** Largo Cândido dos Reis, 6 (☎244 82 08 50), a few doors down from the HI hostel, offers free access (1hr., twice a week); sign up in advance. Open M 1-5:45pm, Tu-F 10am-12:30pm, 1-5:45pm; Oct.-May also Sa 3-6:30pm. Both post offices charge 360$ per hour.

Post Office: Downtown office (☎244 82 04 60), in Largo Santana on Av. Combatentes da Grande Guerra, between the tourist office and the youth hostel. Label **Posta Res-**

tante mail "Estação Santana." Open M-F 8:30am-6pm. **Main office,** Av. Herois de Angola, 99 (☎244 84 94 10), a bit farther away, past the bus station toward the mall. Open M-F 8:30am-6:30pm, Sa 9am-12:30pm. **Postal Code:** 2400.

ACCOMMODATIONS

Pousada da Juventude de Leiria (HI), Largo Cândido dos Reis, 9 (☎/fax 244 83 18 68). From the bus station, walk to the cathedral and exit Lg. da Sé (next to Lg. Cónego Maia) onto R. Barão de Viamonte. Lg. Cândido dos Reis is 6 blocks ahead; the hostel is on the left. Kitchen, TV room, and game room with pool table (400$/€2 per hr.). Breakfast included, 8:30-10am. Reception daily June 16-Sept. 15 8am-midnight; Sept. 16-June 15 8am-noon and 6pm-midnight. Lockout noon-6pm (bag drop-off still available). June 16-Sept. 15 dorms 1900$/€9.50; doubles 4200$/€21. Sept. 16-June 15 dorms 1500$/€7.50; doubles 3500$/€17.50. AmEx/MC/V.

Residencial Dom Dinis, Tr. Tomar, 2 (☎244 81 53 42; fax 82 35 52). Turn left after exiting the tourist office, cross the bridge over Rio Lis, walk 2 blocks, then turn left again; the hostel is on the right. 24 bright, comfortable rooms with bath, telephone, and cable TV. Breakfast included, 8-10:30am. Singles 4500$/€22.50; doubles 6500$/€32.50; triples 7500-8500$. AmEx/MC/V.

Pensão Alcôa, R. Rodrigues Cordeiro, 24 (☎244 83 26 90), off Pr. Rodrigues Lobo, and next to the restaurant of the same name. All 16 rooms come with bath and cable TV. Doubles Breakfast included, 8:30-10:30am. Oct.-June 15 solo 4000$/€20; double/triple 3000$/€15 per person. June 16-Sept. solo 4500$/€22.50; double/triple 3000$/€15 per person. Ask for a 500$/€2.50 discount.

FOOD

On the far side of the castle from the bus station, The **market** stands on Av. Cidade de Maringá sell fresh produce (open M-F 8am-4pm, Sa 8am-1pm). Groceries and fresh baked bread can be purchased at **Supermercado Ulmar,** Av. Heróis de Angola, 56, just past the bus station. (☎244 83 30 42. Open M-Sa 8am-9pm, Su 10am-1pm and 3-8pm.) Budget eateries line the side streets between the park and the castle; other quality finds are near Pr. Lobo and the youth hostel.

Os Novos, Av. Combatentes da Grande Guerra, 77 (☎244 82 58 90), near the youth hostel. Inexpensive café/restaurant offers combination plates (entreés with fries, rice, and salad; 750-800$/€3.75-4). Daily specials 850-900$/€4.24-4.50. Open 10am-11pm; meals served noon-3pm and 7-11pm.

Self-Service Frazão, R. da Vitória, 27 (☎244 81 36 20), just off Lg. da Sé. A cheap place popular with local workers at lunchtime; good for take-out. Entrées 800-1200$/€4-6. Two daily specials (750$/€3.75). Open noon-3pm and 7-9pm.

NIGHTLIFE

The outdoor tables in **Pr. Rodrigues Lobo** are filled with chattering folk on summer evenings. Lined with popular student bars, **Largo Cândido dos Reis** runs through the old part of town, known by locals as the **Terreiro.** Larger, less student-oriented bars and clubs are located in the commercial center and on the other side of the Jardim Luís de Camões. Nightlife is liveliest Sept.-May, when the students are in town.

Anubis, Lg. Cândido dos Reis, 19 (☎933 00 23 00), across from the youth hostel. You won't go wrong if you spend the entire night on this street. Proud to be #1 in Portugal for mini-beers (20cL, 150$/€0.75), this friendly student-filled bar has neither bouncer nor drink minimum. Beer 150$/€0.75. Open M-Sa 8:30pm-2am.

Xannax Dance Club, R. C. Mouzinho de Albuquerque, 168 (☎244 83 37 14), just under the Seat sign, next to the car dealership. Latin bar transitions to house music disco after 3am, when white walls dance with lights from the disco ball. Tu ladies' night feature male strippers and 500$/€2.50 open bar for women. W-Th student nights. F "flower power" night features 80's-90's music until 4am. Beer 200-400$/€1-2. Mixed drinks 700-900$/€3.50-4.50. Open M-Sa 10pm-6am. Closed July-Aug. 16.

SIGHTS AND ENTERTAINMENT

From the main square, follow the signs past the austere **sé** (cathedral) to the city's most significant monument, the **Castelo de Leiria.** Built by Dom Afonso Henriques after he snatched the town from the Moors, this granite fort presides atop the crest of a volcanic hill on the north edge of town. Left to crumble for hundreds of years, the castle retains only the **torre de menagem** (homage tower) and the **sala dos namorados** (lovers' hall). The terrace opens onto a panoramic view of the town and river. *(☎244 81 39 82. Castle open Apr.-Sept. M-F 9am-6:30pm, Sa-Su 10am-6:30pm. Oct.-Mar M-F 9am-5:30pm, Sa-Su 10am-5:30pm. 155$/€0.80.)* The **Teatro José Lúcio da Silva,** on the corner of Av. Heróis de Angola behind the bus station, shows features films. *(☎244 82 36 00. Ticket office open daily 7-10pm. 600-700$/€3-3.50. The tourist office has schedules of current features.)*

BEACHES

Several nearby beaches are easily accessible via bus. July-Sept. 14, buses run from the station to: **Praia de Viera** (45min., 9 per day 7am-6:35pm, 150$/€0.75; last return 7:25pm); **Praia Pedrógão** (1hr., 6 per day 8:25am-6:35pm, 170$/€0.85; last return 6:15pm); and **São Pedro de Muel** (45min.; M-F 8 per day 7:55am-6:30pm, Sa 7 per day 6:55am-5:30pm, Su 7 per day 7:55am-5:30pm; 150$/€0.75; last return 7:15pm). Check at the bus station or the tourist office for up-to-date schedules.

BATALHA ☎244

The only reason to visit Batalha (pop. 7500) is the gigantic **Mosteiro de Santa Maria da Vitória,** rivaling Belém's Mosteiro dos Jerónimos in its monastic splendor. Built by Dom João I in 1385 to commemorate his victory over the Spanish, its complex of cloisters and chapels remains one of Portugal's greatest monuments.

TRANSPORTATION. Buses stop in Lg. 14 de Agosto de 1385 across the street from the monastery. Inquire at the tourist office for info or call the bus station in Leiria (☎244 81 15 07). Buses from Batalha to: **Leiria** (20min., 10 per day 7:50am-8:25pm, 210$/€1.05); **Lisbon** (2hr., 6 per day 7:25am-6:55pm, 1200$/€6); **Nazaré** (1hr., 13 per day 7:35am-6:50pm, 520$/€2.60), via **Alcobaça** (45min., 385$/€1.92); **Tomar** (1½hr.; 8:05am, 12pm, 6pm; 520$/€2.60), via **Fátima** (40min., 290$/€1.45).

ORIENTATION AND PRACTICAL INFORMATION. The **tourist office** is on Pr. Mouzinho de Albuquerque along R. Nossa Senhora do Caminho, just across from the monastery. The most visited tourist office in the region, with its friendly English-speaking staff offers maps and bus information as well as accommodation lists and **luggage storage.** (☎244 76 51 80. Open daily May-Sept. 10am-1pm and 3-7pm; Oct.-Apr. 10am-1pm and 2-6pm.) In case of **emergency** call ☎112 or the **police** at ☎244 76 51 34, on R. Mouzinho de Albuquerque, across the street from the bus stop. The **health center** is on Estrada da Freiria, next to a school (☎244 76 52 46; fax 76 72 53). **Internet** access is available free at the Instituto Português da Juventude, the Edificio dos Antigos Paços do Concelho; it's across Pr. Mouzinho de Albuquerque from the tourist office, with the entrance in back. (☎244 76 63 21. One computer; flexible 15-minute time limit. Open M-F 1:30-5:30pm.) The **post office,** in Lg. Papa Paulo VI, near the freeway entrance, has **fax** services (440$/€2.20 per page) and **Posta Restante.** (☎244 76 51 11; fax 76 91 06. Open M-F 9:30am-1pm and 2:30-6:30pm.) **Postal code:** is 2440.

ACCOMMODATIONS AND FOOD. Pensão Residencial Gladius, Pr. Mouzinho de Albuquerque, 7, has seven comfortable rooms, all with TV, nifty globe lamps, and bath. Two rooms have a view of the plaza. (☎244 76 57 60. Reception 9am-11:30pm. June-Sept. singles 4000$/€20; one double 6000$/€30; triples 8000$/

€40. Oct.-May singles 4000$/€20; double 5000$/€25; triples 7000$/€35. **Pensão Vitória,** on Lg. da Misericórdia next to the bus stop, has three rooms, each with one double bed; solo travelers can ask for a discount. (☎244 76 56 78. Reception 9am-midnight. Rooms 3500$/€17.50.) The restaurant below offers daily specials for 900-1300$/€4.50-6.5 and *frango assado na brasa* (half-chicken, 900$/€4.50). Meals served daily noon-3pm and 7-11pm. Several inexpensive *churrasqueiras* (barbecue houses) and **cafés** line the squares flanking the monastery.

SIGHTS. Batalha's **monastery complex** has been granted UN World Heritage status. Its flamboyant façade soars upward in Gothic and Manueline style, opulently decorated and topped off by dozens of spires. Napoleon's troops sacrilegiously turned the nave into a brothel. The **Capela do Fundador,** immediately to the right of the church, shelters the elaborate sarcophagi of Dom João I, his English-born queen Philippa of Lancaster, and their son Prince Henry the Navigator. The rest of the complex is accessible via a door in the nave of the church; enter through the broad Gothic arches of the **Claustro de Dom João I,** the delicate columns which initiated the Manueline style. Adjacent to the cloister lies the **Tomb of the Unknown Soldier,** always guarded by two motionless men in uniform. Through the **Claustro de Dom Afonso V,** out the door and to the right are the impressive **Capelas Imperfeitas** (Unfinished Chapels), with massive buttresses designed to support a large dome that was never actually constructed; the project was dropped when Manuel I ordered his workers to build the monastery in Belém instead. (Open daily Apr.-Sept. 9am-6pm; Oct.-Mar. 9am-5pm. 600$/€3, under 25 with student ID 360$/€1.80, seniors 300$/€1.50, under 14 free. Su before 2pm, free. Church free.)

Twenty minutes out of town, nature is at its most psychedelic in the spectacular series of underground *grutas* (caves) in Estremadura's natural park between Batalha and Fátima. The **Grutas de Mira de Aire** are the deepest; though **Grutas de Santo António** and **Alvados** are equally impressive. From Batalha, take a bus to Torres Novas (20min., 6 per day 7:35am-7:40pm, 350$/€1.75; last bus back to Batalha 6:30pm). Ask the driver to stop at the grutas. (Caves open daily Oct.-Mar. 9:30am-5:30pm. Apr.-May 9:30am-6pm. June and Sept. 9:30am-7pm. July-Aug. 9:30am-8:30pm. 700$/€3.50, students and seniors 500$/€2.50.)

FÁTIMA ☎249

Fátima used to be a sheep pasture; now the once-quiet town has become a religious center defined by its total immersion in holy fervor. A sign at the entrance of the town's holy Santuário complex states, "Fátima is a place for adoration; enter as a pilgrim." Only Lourdes rivals this site in popularity with Christian pilgrims, as the miracles believed to have occurred here attract an endless international procession of religious groups. The plaza in front of the church, larger than St. Peter's Square in the Vatican, floods with pilgrims on the 12th and 13th of each month.

TRANSPORTATION

Trains: The **Caxarias** station (☎249 57 43 50), 10km out of town, is more (though still not quite) convenient than the Fátima station (☎249 56 61 22), 22km away. From Caxarias to: **Coimbra** (1hr., 14 per day 5:25am-1:55am, 680$/€3.34); **Lisbon** (2½hr., 9 per day 6:50am-11:30pm, 1040$/€5.20); **Porto** (4hr., 12 per day 5:25am-1:55am, 1330$/€6.63); **Santarém** (1½hr., 10 per day 6:50am-9:35pm, 620$/€3.10). **Buses** run between Caxarias train station and the bus station (30min., 7 per day 7:50am-7:50pm, 360$/€1.80) as well as the Fátima train and bus stations (45min., 5 per day 6:10am-6:35pm, 405$/€2.02).

Buses: Av. Dr. José Alves Correia da Silva (☎249 53 16 11). To: **Batalha** (30min., 3 per day 9am-6:35pm, 290$/€1.45); **Coimbra** (1½hr., 9-13 per day 7:45am-7:40pm, 1500$/€7.50); **Leiria** (1hr., 13 per day 7:45am-8pm, 490-800$/€2.44-4); **Lisbon** (1½-2½hr., 11-17 per day 7am-5pm, 1400$/€7); **Nazaré** (1½hr.; 9am, 1:55pm,

6:25pm; 600$/€3); **Porto** (3-3½hr.; 11 per day 7:45am-9:30pm, Sa last bus 5:30pm; 1900$/€9.50); **Santarém** (1hr., 7 per day 7:30am-5:45pm, 1150$/€5.74); **Tomar** (1¼hr.; 8:30am, 12:30pm, 6:35pm; 480$/€2.40).

Taxis: ☎249 53 21 92, gather next to the bus station.

ORIENTATION AND PRACTICAL INFORMATION

ctivity in Fátima centers around the basilica complex. The Santuário de Fátima the huge, open praça that fills with visitors on special occasions and the 12th nd 13th of each month. The bus station and tourist office are on Avenida D. José lves Correia da Silva, which runs just south of the Santuário. The **tourist office** n Av. D. José Alves Correia da Silva, is in a lovely stone building with a wooden oof. From the bus station, take a right and walk ten minutes; the office is on the ght, a short way past the Santuário. (☎249 53 11 39. Open daily June-Sept. 0am-1pm and 3-7pm. Oct.-May 10am-1pm and 2-6pm.) The Plaza of the Santuário has its own office, on the left side when facing the basilica. English-speaking staff provides info about the Santuário. (☎249 53 96 23. Open M-Sa 9am-6pm, u 9am-5pm.) Several major **banks** have branches the commercial center; open 30am-3pm. Services include: **emergency:** ☎112; **police:** Av. D. José Alves Correia da ilva (☎249 53 97 30), **Centro de Saúde**, on R. Jacinta Marto (☎249 53 18 36); and **internet access** is available at **X-Medi@,** R. S. João de Deus, 13 (☎249 53 22 60), in the Edificio arandas de Fátima, a few blocks behind and to the right of the basilica. The **post office** on R. Cónego Formigão. (☎249 53 18 10. Open M-F 8:30am-6pm.) **Postal Code:** 2495.

ACCOMMODATIONS AND FOOD

cores of hostels surround the basilica complex; prices vary little. During the and pilgrimages of the 12th and 13th of every month, the population and prices se. It's always best to reserve one week ahead, and at least a month prior on summer weekends and holidays. The plain but comfortable rooms of **Residencial São ancisco,** R. Francisco Marto, 100, just off the Santuário, all come with TV, phone nd private baths, some with private balconies. (☎249 53 30 17; fax 53 20 28. eception 7:30am-midnight. Breakfast included. Singles 3000$/€15; doubles 5000$/ 25; triples 7000$/€35.) **Residência S. Jorge,** R. Santa Cruz, 4, off R. Jacinta Marto ear the Wax Museum, has hotel-like rooms with TV, private bath, and greenriped bedspreads. During the day, enter through the souvenir shop next door on e left. (☎/fax 249 53 14 64. Reception 8am-midnight. Lockout midnight. Singles 00$/€20; doubles 6000$/€30; triples 9000$/€45. AmEx/MC/V.) **Restaurants** and ack bars cluster in the commercial centers along R. Francisco Marto, R. Santa abela, and R. Jacinta Marto.

SIGHTS

ll leafy trees shade the sanctuary from the commercial area, where insistent ndors pawn off overpriced pseudo-religious memorabilia.

SANTUÁRIO DE FATIMA. The modern holy sanctuary is a visually overwhelming site, whether eerily vacant or packed with worshippers. Many of the devout avel the length of the plaza on their knees, all the way from the cross to the pelinha, praying for divine assistance or giving thanks to the Virgin Mary. At the d of the plaza rises the **Basílica do Rosário** (erected in 1928), featuring a crystal uciform beacon atop the tower's seven-ton bronze crown. Inside are the tombs the blessed children who witnessed the apparitions; Francisco lies in the right ve, while Jacinta is in the left nave. (*Open daily 7:30am-10:30pm. Mass F-W at 7:30, 9, am, 3, 4:30, and 6:30pm.)* To the left, in front of the Basílica do Rosario, is the **apelinha das Aparições,** where the miracles allegedly took place. Sheltered neath a metal and glass canopy, the Little Chapel of the Apparitions was built in 19 at the site of the apparitions. Religious groups from all over the world make pilgrimages to the site and perform mass at the chapel; an international mass i many languages is held there every Thursday at 9am. A candlelight procession i held every evening at 9:30pm from April to October.

MUSEUMS. The **Museu de Arte Sacra e Etnologia** exhibits Catholic icons from var ous centuries. *(R. Francisco Marto, 5. Three blocks from the basilica. ☎249 53 94 7(Open Tu-Su Apr.-Oct. 10am-7pm. Nov.-Mar. noon-5pm. 400$/€2, seniors and students 200$ €1.)* To the left of the basilica, through the park, and in the complex beneath th Hotel Fátima, the **Museu Fátima 1917 Aparições** uses light, sound, and speci effects to re-create the apparition. This is as close to kitsch as Catholicism gets i Portugal. *(R. Jacinta Marto. ☎249 53 28 58. Open daily Apr.-Oct. 9am-7pm. Nov.-Mar. 9ar 6pm. 400$/€2, children under 12, 200$/€1).*

TOMAR ☎24

The arcane Knights Templar—part monks, part warriors—plotted crusades fro Tomar (pop. 22,000) for centuries. A celebrated convent-fortress sitting hig above the old town served as the Knights' powerful and mysterious headquarter Known as the Convento de Cristo, the complex ingeniously combines archite tural styles from the 12th to 17th centuries. Today, Tomar rests peacefully in th shade of the eucalyptus and sycamore trees lining the banks of the Rio Nabão.

TRANSPORTATION

Trains: Av. Combatentes da Grande Guerra (☎249 31 28 15), at the southern edge town. As Tomar is the northern end of a minor line, most destinations require a transf at Entroncamento; be sure to check your ticket. **Ticket office** open M-F 5am-8:30p and 9:30-10:30pm; Sa 5:30-8:30am, 9:30am-6:30pm, and 7:30-10:30pm; S 6:30am-10:30pm. To: **Coimbra** (2½hr., 6 per day 6:05am-6:05pm, 960-1200$ €4.80-6); **Lisbon** (2hr., 18 per day 5:05am-10:05pm, 1010-2040$/€5.04-10); **Por** (4½hr., 7 per day 8:05am-8:05pm, 1510-2210$/€7.55-11); **Santarém** (1hr., 12p day 5:05am-10:05pm, 520-840$/€2.60-4.20).

Buses: Rodoviária Tejo Av. Combatentes Grande Guerra (☎249 31 27 38), next to t train station. Express buses are twice the price of regular buses; check with the tick office to confirm schedules and fares. To: **Coimbra** (2½hr., 7am, 1650$/€8.25 **Fátima** (30min., 3 per day 7:50am-5:20pm, 490-1000$/€2.45-5); **Figueira da F** (4½hr., 7am, 1650$/€8.25); **Lagos** (9hr.; M-Sa 9:15am via Santarém and Évor 10:15am via Lisbon, Su 10:15am via Lisbon; 3200$/€16); **Leiria** (1hr.; M-F 2 per d 7:15am and 5:45pm, Sa 7am; 590-1200$/€3-6); **Lisbon** (2hr., 4 per day 9:15ar 6pm, 1200$/€6); **Nazaré** (1½hr., 3 per day 7:50am-5:20pm, 880-1780$/€4.4 8.90); **Porto** (4hr., 7am, 2100$/€11); **Santarém** (1hr.; 9:15am, 6pm; 1200$/€6).

Taxis: (☎249 31 37 16 or 31 23 73). Cabs cluster near the bus and train stations, well as on R. Santa Iria, across the river.

ORIENTATION AND PRACTICAL INFORMATION

The **Rio Nabão** divides Tomar. Almost everything travelers need—the train and b stations, accommodations, and sights—lies on the west bank. The lush **Parq Mouchão** straddles the two banks, while the ancient **Ponte Velha** (old bridge) co nects the two. From the **Ponte Nova** (new bridge), **Av. Dr. Cãndido Madureira** leads **Pr. Infante Dom Henrique**, behind which lie the trails of the **Parque da Mata Nacion dos Sete Montes** (Park open daily 10am-6pm. Free.) The **bus** and **train stations** sit ne to each other on **Av. Combatentes da Grande Guerra,** near the outskirts of town. T pedestrian-only **Rua Serpa Pinto** cuts across the town from the river to the cast and connects the Ponte Velha to the main square, **Praça da República.**

Tourist Office: Casa Vieira Guimarães, R. Serpa Pinto (☎/fax 249 32 24 27 or 32 14), on the corner of Av. do Marquês de Tomar, across the street from the regional to ist office and the Ponte Velha. From the bus or train station, take a right onto Av. Co batentes de Grande Guerra and then a left onto Av. Torres Pinheiro and continue straight past the traffic circle on R. Everaro; the office is on the left just past the bridge. Short-term **luggage storage.** Open daily July-Sept. 10am-8pm, Oct.-June 10am-6pm.

Emergency: ☎112. **Police:** R. Dr. Sousa (☎249 31 34 44).

Hospital: Av. Cândido Madureira (☎249 32 11 00), down from the tourist office.

Internet Access: INCA, R. João do Santos Simões, 60 (☎249 32 16 06), over the bridge, off R. Marqués Pombal. 375$/€1.85 per 30min. Open M-F 9:30am-1pm and 3-7pm, Sa 10am-1pm. Available free at nightspot **Casablanca,** R. São João, 83 (☎249 31 47 57), between the tourist office and Pr. República. Open M-Sa 10pm-4am.

Post Office: Av. Marquês de Tomar (☎249 31 04 00; fax 31 04 06), across from Parque Mouchão. **Fax** and **Posta Restante** available. Open M-F 8:30am-6pm, Sa 9am-12:30pm. **Postal Code:** 2300.

ACCOMMODATIONS AND CAMPING

Finding accommodations is only a problem during the **Festival dos Tabuleiros,** which takes place once every four years (next in 2003). **R. Serpa Pinto,** is lined with quality lodging, while cheaper options lie closer to the bus and train stations.

Residencial União, R. Serpa Pinto, 94 (☎249 32 31 61; 32 12 99), halfway between Pr. República and the bridge. The nicest budget accommodation in Tomar, in a central location. The 28 bright, plush rooms all have TV, phone, and private bath. A well-stocked bar welcomes weary travelers. Breakfast included. Reception 8am-midnight. Reservations recommended for July and Aug. Apr.-Sept. singles 4500$/€23; doubles 7000$/€35; 3rd person 1000$/€5 more. Oct.-Mar. singles 4000$/€20; doubles 6500$/€33; 3rd person 500$/€2.50 more.

Residencial Luz, R. Serpa Pinto, 144 (☎/fax 249 31 23 17; www.residencialluz.com), down the street from Residencial União. 14 clean and comfy rooms, most with private bath, TV, and phone. TV room with leather couches. May 16-Sept. singles 3500$/€18, with bath 3700$/€19; doubles 6000$/€30, with bath 6500$/€33; one large quad with bath 9000-12,000$/€45-60. Mar.-May 15 and Oct. singles 3000-3500$/€15-18, with bath 3500-3700$/€18-19; doubles 5000$/€25, with bath 6000$/€30; quad 8000-9000$/€40-45. Nov.-Feb. singles 3000$/€15, with bath 3500$/€18; doubles 4500$/€23, with bath 5000$/€25; quad 6500-7000$/€33-35.

Casa de Dormidas D. Gualdim, R. de D. Aurora de Macedo, 46 (☎249 31 19 03 or 32 28 78 or 914 76 51 01). Run over to the Casa Costa shop on Av. Dr. Cândido Madureira, 18, at the corner of R. dos Moinhos near the traffic circle, and speak with owner José Fernandes Costa. Singles 2500$/€13; doubles 5000$/€25. For the absolute rock bottom deal in town, ask about his rooms without bath at **Casa de Dormidas Convento,** Av. Combatentes de Grande Guerra, 7 (Singles 2000$/€10; doubles 3000$/€15).

Camping: Parque Municipal de Campismo (☎249 32 98 24; fax 32 26 08), on the river, across Ponte Velha and to the left, near the stadium and swimming pool. Thickly forested campground with pool. Free showers. Reception daily 8am-1pm and 3-5pm. June-Sept. 450$/€2.25 per person, 380$/€1.90 per tent, 410$/€2.10 per car, 260$/€1.35 for electricity; Oct.-May 50% less.

FOOD

Tomar has a couple of excellent "ethnic" restaurants as well as traditional Portuguese options. The lush **Parque Mouchão** is the perfect place for a picnic. The open **market,** across the river on the corner of Av. Norton de Matos and R. Santa Iria, provides all but the red checkered clanket (open Tu, Th-F 8am-2pm; the larger F market has a flea market portion as well). Several inexpensive **mini-markets** line the side streets between the tourist office and Pr. República.

Ristorante/Pizzeria Bella Italia, R. Everard, 91 (☎249 32 29 96), near the river, between the 2 main bridges. Friendly family serves delicious pastas (800-1400$/€4-7) and pizzas (800-1800$/€4-9), as well as meat entrées (1150-2750$/€5.75-13.75).

A SYNAGOGUE'S CONVERSION The 15th century synagogue of Tomar remained active for less than 40 years after construction was completed: in December of 1496, King Dom Manuel obeyed the wishes of his Castillian queen (Dona Isabel) and forced Portuguese Jews to either convert to Christianity or leave the country by October of the following year. Those who converted were called the New Christians. Some Jews, called the *Morranos,* continued to practice their religion in private despite outward conversion until the synagogue was vacated and twenty years later was converted into a prison (curiously, King Manuel granted a charter mandating that New Christians could not be imprisoned). After the prison was transferred to the town hall in the mid-16th century, the old synagogue came to be used as a Christian chapel, and likely served this role until the early 19th century. Historical records show that the space was then used as a hay loft, and later as a cellar and grocery warehouse. Finally, in 1921, the building was named a national monument. It now houses a museum that tells the story of the ancient Portuguese Jews, as well as the international history of the Jewish people.

Specialties include *pasta mista* (2400$/€12, serves 2). The *tiramisú* (500$/€2.50) is the most popular dessert. Open daily noon-3pm and 7-11pm. MC/V.

Salsinha Verde, Pr. da República, 19 (☎249 32 32 29), at the corner of the main plaza, to the left when facing the town hall. Local students pop *petingas* (small fish, 30$/€0.15) at the bar. Entrées served in the dining room 700-1350$/€3.50-6.73. Cheaper *pratos do dia* (daily specials, 600$/€3). *Bifinhos com cogumelos* (pork, 900$/€4.50; less on M when one of the specials). Open M-Sa 8am-midnight.

SIGHTS

CONVENTO DE CRISTO. The mysterious grounds of the Convento de Cristo display an intriguing range of architecture and landscaping. The first structure was built by the Knights Templar in 1160, but successive centuries have added an eclectic collection of various cloisters, convents, and buildings. An ornate octagonal canopy protects the high altar of the **Templo dos Templares,** modeled after the Holy Sepulchre in Jerusalem. Below stands the **Janela do Capítulo** (chapter window), an exuberant tribute to the Age of Discovery. One of Europe's masterpieces of Renaissance architecture, the **Claustro dos Felipes** honors King Felipe II of Castile, who was crowned here as Felipe I of Portugal during Iberia's unification (1580-1640). Stairs spiral upward to the sweeping views of the **Terraço da Cera.** Tucked behind the Palladian main cloister and the nave is the **Claustro da Santa Bárbara,** where grotesque gargoyle rain-spouts writhe in pain as they cough up a fountain. On the northeast side of the church is the Gothic **Claustro do Cemitério.** *(Walk out of the tourist office and take the 2nd right; bear left at the fork. Pedestrians can take the steeper dirt path a bit after the fork on the left or follow the cars up the paved road. From Pr. República, walk behind the praça and pick up the path. ☎249 31 34 81. Open daily June-Sept. 9am-6pm; Oct.-May 9am-5pm. 600$/€3, under 25 300$/€1.50; under 14 free.)*

MUSEU LUSO-HEBRAICO ABRAÁO ZACUTO (SINAGOGA). Portugal's most significant reminder of its once vibrant Jewish community, this synagogue has served numerous functions since its construction between 1430 and 1460 (see **A Synagogue's Conversion,** p. 618). The space is now a museum of international Jewish history, housing a collection of tombstones, inscriptions, and donated pieces from around the world. *(R. Dr. Joaquim Jaquinto, 73. Open daily 10am-1pm and 2-6pm. Free.)*

ENTERTAINMENT

For a week near the end of June, handicrafts, folklore, *fado,* and theater storm the city during the **Feira Nacional de Artesanato,** but the biggest party in Tomar is the **Festa dos Tabuleiros,** which takes place only once every four years (the next will occur in 2003). Tomar also hosts four summer **bullfights;** look for large, brightly colored posters advertising the *corridas.*

THE THREE BEIRAS

The Three Beiras region offers a sampling of the best of Portugal: the pristine beaches of the coast, the rich greenery of the interior and the ragged peaks of the Serra de Estrela. The Beira Litoral (Coastal Region) encompasses the unspoiled Costa da Prata (Silver Coast) beginning at the resort town of Figueira da Foz and passing through up-and-coming Aveiro on the way to Porto. The soil in this region yields some of Portugal's best farmland, and the countryside is dotted with red-roofed farmhouses surrounded by endless expanses of corn, sunflower, and wheat fields. A vibrant university city, Coimbra overlooks the region from its perch above the Rio Mondego. Unlike more progressive towns to the west, the mountainous extremes of Beira Alta and lowland Beira Baixa have retained their wealth in tradition, not yet swept away by the prosperity of economic boom.

COIMBRA ☎239

The country's only university city from the mid-16th to the early 20th century, Coimbra is still a mecca for youth and backpackers alike. A slew of cheap cafés and bars coupled with an energetic student body keep Coimbra swinging from September through May. Beautifully situated on the Rio Mondego, the city has long since forgotten its infamous roles as center of the Portuguese Inquisition and educator of one-time economics professor Antònio Salazar, the former dictator of Portugal. Today, Coimbra's atmosphere keeps visitors coming year-round.

TRANSPORTATION

Trains: (info ☎239 83 49 98). **Estação Coimbra-A (Nova)** is 2 blocks from the lower town center. **Estação Coimbra-B (Velha)** is 3km northwest of town. Regional trains stop first in Coimbra-B, then continue to Coimbra-A, departing in reverse order. Long-distance trains arriving from/departing for cities outside the region stop in Coimbra-B only. If your train stops only at Coimbra-B, it is easiest to take a connecting train to Coimbra-A (4min., immediately after trains arrive, 140$/€0.70 or free if transfer). Trains to: **Aveiro** (30min.-1hr., 22 per day 5:10am-3:10am, 540-1300$/€2.70-6.50); **Braga** (3hr., 9:55am and 7:55pm, 1230-1650$/€6.10-8.20); **Figueira da Foz** (1¼hr., 24 per day 5:20am-12:20am, 290$/€1.40); **Lisbon** (3hr., 23 per day 5:35am-2:20am, 1550-2700$/€7.70-13.50; **Ovar** (1½hr., 21 per day 5:10am-3:10am, 780-1200$/€4-6); **Porto** (2hr., 21 per day 5:10am-3:10am, 1050-1900$/€5.20-9.50).

Buses: RBL station (☎239 82 70 81), near the end of Av. Fernão Magalhães, on the university side of the river 10min. out of town, and past Coimbra-A. Buses to: **Évora** (4hr., 9:30am and 4:15pm, 2000$/€10); **Faro** (8hr., 3 per day 9:25am-2:10am, 3000$/€15); **Figueira da Foz** (1½hr., 9 per day 7:20am-6:35pm, 570$/€2.80); **Lisbon** (2½hr., 17 per day 7:30am-2:15am 1550$/€7.70); **Luso** and **Buçaco** (45min.; M-F 7 per day 7:35am-7:20pm, Sa 9am, 12:45pm, Su 10:15am, 5:30pm; 480$/€2.40); **Porto** (1½hr., 10 per day 8:30am-9:30pm, 1400$/€7). The **AVIC station,** R. João de Ruão, 18 (☎239 82 01 41), between R. Sofia and Av. Fernão Magalhães, next door to Viagem Mondego. To: **Condeixa** (25min., 14 per day 7:35am-7:35pm 250$/€1.25) and **Conímbriga** (30min.; 9:35am, return bus 6pm; 280$/€1.40).

Public Transportation: SMTUC buses and street cars. Round-trip ticket 170$/€0.80 at kiosks and vending machines or 230$/€1.20 on the bus. Book of 10 800$/€4 or 3 day tourist pass 1230$/€6.10 sold at vending machines at Lg. Portagem, Pr República, and throughout the city.

Taxis: Politaxis (☎239 48 40 45). Outside Coimbra-A and the bus station.

Car Rental: Avis (☎/fax 239 83 47 86; reservations toll-free 800 20 10 02), in Coimbra-A. Min. age 21. Open M-F 8:30am-12:30pm and 3-7pm. Cars start at 15,000$/€75 per day.

ORIENTATION AND PRACTICAL INFORMATION

Coimbra's steep streets rise in tiers above the **Rio Mondego.** Of the three major parts of town, the most central is the **Baixa** (lower town), site of the **tourist office** and the Coimbra-A **train station,** and set within the triangle formed by the river **Largo da Portagem,** and **Pr. 8 de Maio.** Coimbra's ancient **university district** is atop the steep hill overlooking the lower town. On the other side of the university, the area around **Pr. da República** is home to cafés, a shopping district, and the youth hostel.

Tourist Office: (☎239 85 59 30; fax 82 55 76), off Lg. Portagem, in a yellow building 2 blocks up the river from Coimbra-A. From the bus station, turn right and follow the avenue to Coimbra-A, then continue to Lg. Portagem (15min.). Open June-Sept. M-F 9am-7pm, Sa-Su 10am-1pm and 2:30-5:30pm; Oct.-May M-F 9am-6pm, Sa-Su 10am-1pm and 2:30-5:30pm. English-speaking staff provides maps and accommodation lists as well as transportation and regional info. **University branch office** (☎239 83 25 91), in Lg. Dom Dinis. Open M-F 9am-6pm, Sa-Su 9am-12:30pm and 2-5:30pm. Another **branch office** (☎239 83 32 02) is in Pr. República. Open M-F 10am-6:30pm.

Budget Travel: Tagus (☎239 83 49 99; fax 83 49 16), R. Padre António Vieira. Handles student and youth budget travel. Open M-F 9:30am-6pm.

Currency Exchange: Montepio Geral Lg. Portagem (☎239 85 17 00), near tourist office. 1000$/€5 commission. above 10,000$/€50. Open M-F 8:30am-3pm.

Luggage Storage: Café Cristal, Lg. Anreias, 5, off Av. Fernão Magalhães (☎239 82 39 44), across the street and to the left of Coimbra-A. 250$/€1.25 per bag for 4hr. drop off. Open daily 5:30am-10pm.

Laundromat: Lavandaria Lucira, Av. Sá da Bandeira, 86 (☎239 82 57 01). Wash and dry 1100$/€5.50 per load. Open M-F 9am-1pm and 3-7pm, Sa 9am-1pm.

Emergency: ☎112. **Police:** ☎239 82 95 65. Special division for foreigners *(Serviço de Estrangeiros)*, R. Venâncio Rodrigues, 25 (☎239 82 37 67).

Hospital: Hospital da Universidade de Coimbra (☎239 40 04 00 or 40 05 00; fax 82 39 07), Lg. Professor Mota Pinto and Av. Dr. Bissaya Barreto. Take the #7 or #29 bus to the Hospital stop.

Internet Access: Post Net, R. Antero de Quental, 73 (☎239 84 10 25), between Pr. República and the youth hostel. 150$/€0.75 per 15min.; 500$/€2.50 per hr. Open M-F 10am-midnight, Sa 2pm-midnight, Su 7pm-midnight. **@ caffé,** Lg. da Sé Velha, 4-8 (☎239 83 81 64), across from the old cathedral charges 300$/€1.50 per 1hr. (See **Nightlife** p. 625.)

Post Office: Central office (☎239 85 07 70; toll-free 800 20 68 68), in the pink building on Av. Fernão de Magalhães. Open M-F 8:30am-6:30pm. **Telephones** and **fax** service available. **Branch office** (☎239 85 18 20; fax 85 18 26), Pr. República, between the youth hostel and the university. Label **Posta Restante** "Estação Santa Cruz." Open M-F 9am-6pm. **Postal Code:** 3000 for central Coimbra.

ACCOMMODATIONS

Pensão Santa Cruz, Pr. 8 de Maio, 21, 3rd fl. (☎/fax 239 82 61 97; www.pensaosantacruz.com), directly across from the Igreja da Santa Cruz. From Lg. Portagem, follow R. Ferreira Borges as it becomes R. Visconde da Luz and leads to the plaza. A friendly family pension with comfortable rooms, most with cable TV and some with bath. 2 rooms share a balcony overlooking the plaza, ideal for viewing free summer concerts. July-Sept. single or double 4000$/€20, with bath 5500$/€28; triples 5000$/€25, with bath 6000$/€30. Oct.-June single or double 3000$/€15, 4000$/€20; triples 4000$/€20, 4500-5000$/€23-25. Discounts for extended stays.

Pousada da Juventude de Coimbra (HI), R. Henrique Seco, 14 (☎239 82 29 55; fax 82 17 30). From either Coimbra-A or Lg. Portagem, walk 20min. uphill along R. Olímpio Nicolau Rui Fernandes to Pr. República, then up R. Lourenço Azevedo (to the left of the park). Take the 2nd right; the hostel is on the right. Kitchen, TV room, and heavenly showers. Laundry 1000$/€5 per load. Reception daily 8am-noon and 6pm-midnight. Lockout noon-6pm. Bag drop-off available (except M-F 1-2pm and Sa-Su noon-6pm). June 16-Sept. 15 dorms 1900$/€9.50; doubles with bath 4600$/€23. Sept. 16-June 15 dorms 1700$/€8.50; 3 doubles with bath 4300$/€22.

Residencial Vitória, R. da Sota, 11-19 (☎239 82 40 49 or 84 28 96; fax 84 28 97), across from Coimbra-A. Rooms and prices to suit any budget. Newly renovated rooms each have bath, phone, TV, and A/C. 24hr. reception. New rooms: singles 5000$/€25; doubles 7000$/€35; triples 9000$/€45. Older rooms: singles 2500$/€13, with shower 3000$/€15; doubles 4000$/€20, 5000$/€25. MC/V.

Residência Solar Navarro, Av. Emídio Navarro, 60-A, 2nd floor (☎239 82 79 99), past the tourist office and across from the park; look for the green Delta sign. All rooms with bath and TV, some with balconies and views of the park across the street. 24hr. reception. Singles 2500$/€13; 1 double 5000$/€25; 1 triple 7500$/€38; 1 enormous room with 5 beds 12,500$/€62.

Residencial Domus, R. Adelino Veiga, 62 (☎239 82 85 84; fax 83 88 18), between Coimbra-A and Pr. do Comércio. A 3-star *residencial* with a more economical annex across the street in the Residencial Moderna building. Central location and kind staff. Main rooms all have bath, phone, and cable TV; annex rooms are without bath, 24hr. reception. July-Sept. main rooms: singles 5500$/€28, doubles 7500$/€38, 1 triple 8500$/€43. Annex: singles 4000$/€20; doubles 5000$/€25. Oct.-June main rooms: singles 4000$/€20; doubles 6000$/€30; triples 7000$/€35; Annex: singles 3500$/€18, doubles 4000$/€20. Discounts for extended stays.

Residência Lusa Atenas, Av. Fernão Magalhães, 68, upstairs (☎239 82 64 12; fax 82 01 33), between Coimbra-A and the bus station, next to Pensão Avis, under a neon sign. Rooms with bath, phone, A/C, and cable TV. Slanting top floor ceilings. TV room with cushy brown couches. Reception 8am-midnight. July-Aug. singles 4000-5000$/

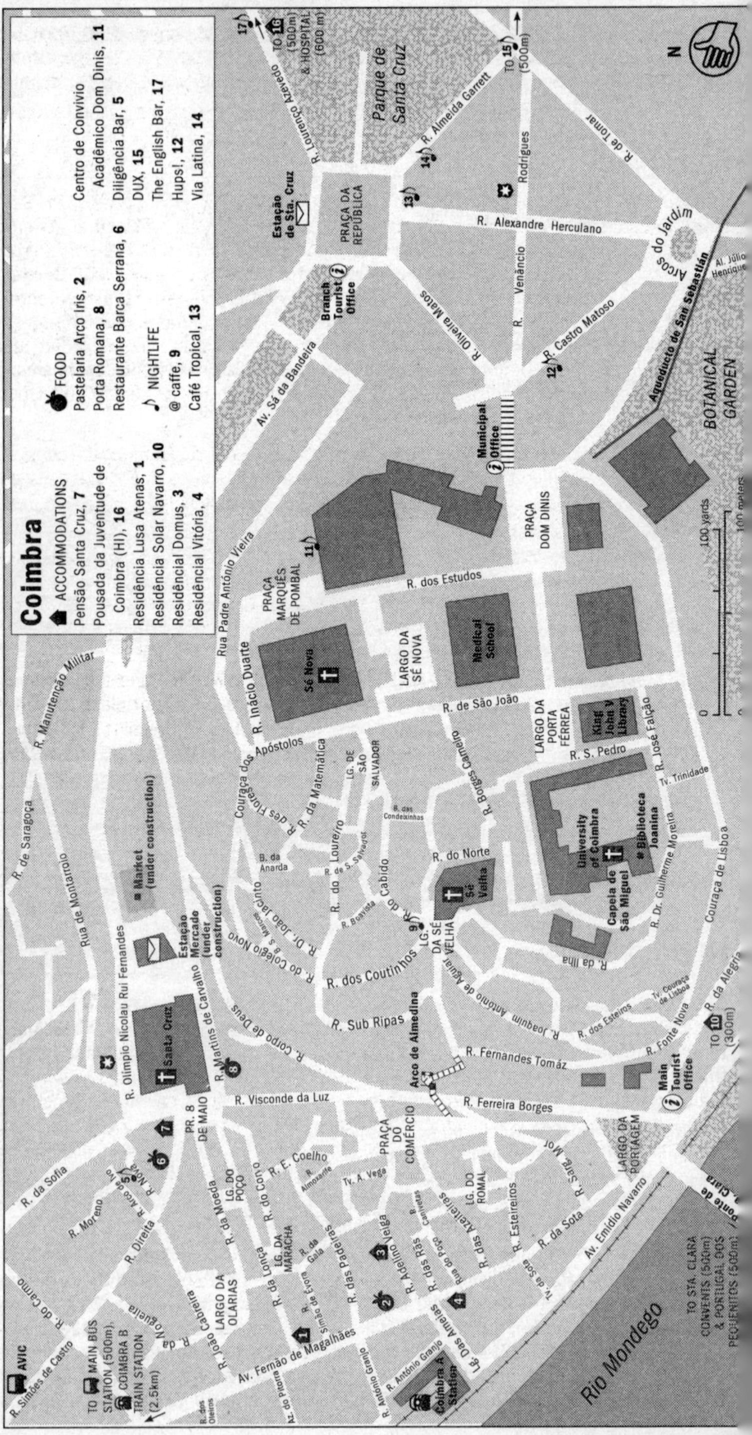

Coimbra

ACCOMMODATIONS
- Pensão Santa Cruz, 7
- Pousada da Juventude de Coimbra (HI), 16
- Residência Lusa Atenas, 1
- Residência Solar Navarro, 10
- Residêncial Domus, 3
- Residêncial Vitória, 4

FOOD
- Pastelaria Arco Iris, 2
- Porta Romana, 8
- Restaurante Barca Serrana, 6

NIGHTLIFE
- @ caffe, 9
- Café Tropical, 13
- Centro de Convivio Acadêmico Dom Dinis, 11
- Diligência Bar, 5
- DUX, 15
- The English Bar, 17
- Hups!, 12
- Via Latina, 14

€20-25; doubles 6000-7000$/€30-35; triples 9000$/€45; quads 10,000$/€50. May-June singles 3500-4000$/€18-20; doubles 5000-6000$/€25-30; triples 7500$/€38; quads 8000$/€40. Sept.-Apr. singles 3000-3500$/€15-18; doubles 5000$/€25; triples 6000$/€30; quads 8000$/€40.

FOOD

The culinary masters of Coimbra serve the areas around R. Direita off of Pr. 8 de Maio, the side streets between the river and Largo Portagem, and university-side Pr. República. Restaurants serve up steamy portions of *arroz de lampreia* (rice cooked with lamprey meat). The cheapest meals around are found at **UC Cantina,** the university's student cafeteria, on the right side of R. Oliveiro Matos. An international student ID is (theoretically) mandatory. Get your apples and bananas at the enormous green warehouse **mercado,** on the right just past the post office and uphill on R. Olímpio Nicolau Rui Fernandes (open M-Sa 8am-1pm). **Supermercado Minipreço,** R. António Granjo 6C, is in the lower town center. (☎239 82 77 57. Open M-Sa 8:30am-8pm, Su 9am-1pm and 3-7pm.)

Porta Romana, R. Martins de Carvalho, 10 (☎239 82 84 58), just up from the Igreja da Santa Cruz in Pr. 8 de Maio. Amiable staff serves surprisingly affordable Italian dishes. Pizzas 700-1200$/€3.50-6. Pastas 950-1200$/€4.70-6. Open July-Aug. M-Sa 7am-midnight, Su 6pm-midnight; Sept.-June M-F 7am-midnight.

Restaurante Barca Serrana, R. Direita, 46 (☎239 82 06 16), a short way down R. Direita from Pr. 8 de Maio. A popular and inexpensive lunch spot. Enjoy an entrée (750-1400$/€3.70-7) in the dining room or back, or sit snug up to the wide counter. 2 specials per day 700$/€3.50. Open M-F 9am-11pm, Sa 9am-4pm; meals served M-F 11:30am-3pm and 8-11pm, Sa 8-11pm only.

Café Santa Cruz, Pr. 8 de Maio, 5 (☎239 83 36 17), right next to the church. Formerly part of the cathedral, this is the city's most famous café—a popular place for coffee (100-200$/€0.50-1) and people-watching. Features a vaulted ceiling and stained glass windows. Best on summer nights during the free concerts in the square. Sandwiches 250-420$/€1.25-2.1. Open May-Sept. M-Sa 7am-2am, Oct.-Apr. M-Sa 7am-midnight. Scheduled to close for renovations from late-Sept. until Dec. 2001.

Pastelaria Arco Iris, Av. Fernão de Magalhães, 22 (☎239 83 33 04), across from the Coimbra-A station. True to its name (rainbow), the glass-faced cases of Arco Iris display a colorful variety of pastries (110-170$/€0.50-0.80. Coffee 90-180$/€0.45-0.90. Open M-Sa 7:15am-8:30pm, Su 8am-8:30pm.

SIGHTS

OLD TOWN. Take in Coimbra's old town sights by making the arduous climb from the river up to the university. Begin the ascent at the ancient **Arco de Almedina,** a remnant of the Moorish town wall, one block uphill from Largo Portagem, next to the Banco Pinto e Sotto Mayor. The gate leads to a street aptly named R. Quebra-Costas (Back-Breaker Street). Up a narrow stone stairway looms the 12th-century Romanesque **Sé Velha** (Old Cathedral). Don't miss the peaceful cloister upstairs from the main nave. *(Open M-Th 10am-noon and 2-7:30pm, F-Su 10am-1pm. Cathedral free. Cloisters 150$/€0.75, students 100$/€0.50)* Follow the signs to the nearby 16th century **Sé Nova** (New Cathedral), whose exterior was completed by architects for the resident Jesuit community. *(Open Tu-Sa 9am-noon and 2-6:30pm. Free.)*

THE UNIVERSITY. Though many buildings have since been built of the 1950's functional concrete, the original law school still retains its spot on the architectural Dean's List. Enter the center of the old university through the **Porta Férrea** (Iron Gate), off R. São Pedro. *(Uphill from the new cathedral. Open daily May-Sept. 9am-7:30pm, Oct.-Apr. 9:30am-12:30pm and 2-5:30pm.)* The staircase at right leads up to the **Sala dos Capelos** (Graduates' Hall), where portraits of Portugal's kings (6 of whom were born in Coimbra) hang below a 17th-century ceiling. *(Open daily 9:30am-*

12:30pm and 2-5pm. 500$/€2.50) The **university chapel** and mind-boggling, gilded 18th-century **Biblioteca Joanina** (the university library) lie past the Baroque clock tower. *(☎239 85 98 41. Open daily May-Sept. 9am-7:30pm, Oct.-Apr. 9:30am-noon and 2-5:30pm. 500$/€2.50, teachers and students free. A booklet of tickets for all university sights can be purchased for 800$/€4 from the office in the main quad.)*

ACROSS THE RIVER. Cross the bridge in front of Largo Portagem to discover the 14th-century **Convento de Santa Clara-a-Velha.** Far-seeing contractors laid the convent's foundation on solid swampland soil, causing it to sink with each passing year. Today more than half of its structure is submerged in the morass. Abandoned in 1687, the convent was recently renovated to reveal an ancient church founded in 1330 by Queen Isabel, wife of Dom Dinis. The Queen's Gothic tomb has been relocated uphill at the **Convento de Santa Clara-a-Nova.** *(☎164 916 77. Open daily 8:30am-6pm. Church free. Cloisters 100$/€0.50)*

OTHER SIGHTS. Downhill from the university, alongside the Aqueducto de São Sebastião, are to the sculpture and fountains of the **Jardim Botânico** public gardens. *(☎239 82 28 97. Open daily June-Sept. 9am-7pm; Oct.-May 9am-5:30pm. Gardens free. Greenhouses 250$/€1.25, students and over 65 150$/€0.75.)* Down the large staircase and past Pr. República is the lush **Santa Cruz Park,** also known as the Jardim da Sereia (Mermaid's Garden), and its beautiful moss-covered fountain. *(☎239 82 29 41. Church open M-Sa 9am-noon and 2-5:45pm. Cloisters and sacristy 200$/€1.)*

NIGHTLIFE

After dinner, outdoor cafés surrounding Pr. República buzz with animated conversation from midnight to 2am, after which crowds move on to the bars and dance clubs further afield. Nights are best Sept.-May, when the students are in town. Bars and clubs are listed in chronological order by peak hour.

Café Tropical, Pr. República, 35 (☎239 82 48 57). On your mark–the place to start the night. Tables outside, inside, and upstairs fill with students after midnight. Beer 130-250$/€0.60-1.25. Mixed drinks 600$/€3. Open M-Sa 9am-2am.

Diligência Bar, R. Nova, 30 (☎239 82 76 67), off R. Sofia. Shamelessly touristy, yet still preserves an intimate and pleasant atmosphere. Excellent *fado* performed nightly after 10pm. *Sangría* 1850$/€9.20 per liter. Open M-Sa 6pm-2am, Su 7pm-2am.

The English Bar, R. Lourenço de Almeida Azevedo, 24 (☎919 50 94 39). Bottom floor restaurant serves traditional English pub grub, while a top floor DJ spins 70's and 80's music to an age 20-40 bar-side crowd. Huge backyard patio. Beer 250-350$/€1.25-1.75. Mixed drinks 500-600$/€2.50-3. Best F-Sa at midnight. Open M-Sa 10pm-4am.

Centro de Convívio Acadêmico Dom Dinis, Lg. D. Dinis (☎239 83 85 38), near Sé Nova. A study hall by day, the University owned *centro* wakes nightly with a DJ M-Th and live music performed by student groups F-Sa 1-3am. Entrance only with an ISIC or college ID. Beer 170$/€0.80. 100$/€0.50 minimum. Best Sept.-May after 1am, especially Th. Open Sept.-July M-Sa 10pm-3am.

@ caffé, Lg. da Sé Velha, 4-8 (☎239 83 81 64). Much more than an Internet spot, this is one of the newest dance clubs in Coimbra. Walls made of stone, wood, and metal, reverberate with house to Brazilian to African to pop. Minimum 500$/€2.50 after 11pm. Beer 250$/€1.25. Mixed drinks 500$/€2.50. Open June-Sept. 15 M-Sa 11am-4am; Sept. 16-May M-Sa 9pm-4am.

Hups!, R. Castro Matoso, 11 (☎932 22 21 02). One of the few parties continuing until Sunday night, this new dance club attracts a mostly age 25-40 crowd. African music night on W. Minimum 1000$/€5 for men, 500$/€2.50 for women. Beer 300$/€1.50. Mixed drinks 800-1000$/€4-5. Open Tu-Su 10pm-5am.

Via Latina, R. Almeida Garrett, 1 (☎239 82 02 93). Large dance club popular with students during the week and older Coimbra residents F-Sa. Latin music Sa-Th, F house. Two 1100-liter tanks of bar-side Super Bock fuel the whole operation. Minimum M-Th

A GUIDE TO DRINKING IN PORTUGAL Have you ever arrived at a seemingly promising bar or club, only to find that you're the only one keeping the bartender company? Portuguese people may act laid-back, but when it comes to nightlife, they know exactly where to show up and when. After dinner, at around 11pm to midnight, people begin to congregate at cafés; later, between 1am and 3am, crowds fill up smaller bars and the energy starts to build up in the streets. At around 3-4am, it's safe to starting heading off to the larger dance clubs and discos, which close anywhere from 6am to 10am. On a larger scale, inland towns and university towns have the best nightlife starting in October, while beach towns (unsurprisingly) peak in July and August; nightclub staff often travel between the inland and the beach for the different seasons. As for drinking, here is some essential vocabulary: for a draft beer, ask for an *Imperial* or a *fino*; if you want a bottle, ask for a *garafa*. Lovers of dark beer should ask for a *cerveja preta*. Drinks such as vodka, rum, and gin are known as *bebidas brancas* ("white drinks").

500$/€2.50 for men and 300$/€1.50 for women, F-Sa 1000$/€5 for men and 750$/€3.50 for women. Tu ladies' night (3 drinks with entrance). Beer 300$/€1.50. Mixed drinks 700-800$/€3.50-4. Open M-Sa 11pm-7am.

DUX, Av. Afonso Henriques, 43 (☎239 40 40 47), near the youth hostel. Owned in part by the well-known Portuguese magician Luis de Matos, this modernist maze is a weekend playground for the elite crowd. Stern "greeters" guard its bright white entrance. Best 3-4am. Minimum 1200$/€6 for men, 600$/€3 for women. Beer 400$/€2. Mixed drinks 800$/€4. Best 3-4am. Open F-Sa 11pm-6am.

ENTERTAINMENT

Students run wild during Coimbra's infamous week-long festival, the **Queima das Fitas** (Burning of the Ribbons), in the first or second week of May. The festivities begin when graduating seniors set fire to their narrow freshman ribbons and receive wide, ornamental replacements. Live choral music echoes in the streets during the **Festas da Rainha Santa,** held the first week of July. During even-numbered years, two processions of the statue of Rainha Santa (one at the beginning, one at the end) more visibly reflect the festival's religious roots, from whence all of this rollicking came. The firework-punctuated **Feira Popular** in the second week of July offers carnival rides and games across the river, as well as traditional Portuguese dancing exhibitions.

FIGUEIRA DA FOZ

Figueira da Foz may work best as a night-trip—if you're up to it. The ambitious arrive in the evening, only to return to Coimbra on a morning train, bleary-eyed but content after a night of wild partying. Figueira is at its peak during July and August. The town's daytime highlight is a 3 sq. km beach of Sahara-like sand, where bronzed couples roam the shoreline hand-in-hand, perfecting their already perfect tans. At night, rowdy youths crowd the numerous bars and discos, trying their luck at Figueira's infamous casino.

TRANSPORTATION. Trains are the best transport from Coimbra to Figueira da Foz (1½hr; M-Sa 20-24 per day 5:20am-12:20am, Su 17 per day 6:19am-12:20am; 290$/€1.45). From Figueira station, it's an easy stroll to the tourist office and the beach (25min). With the river on your left, follow Av. Saraiva de Carvalho as it becomes R. 5 de Outubro at the fountain and then curves into Av. 25 de Abril.

ORIENTATION AND PRACTICAL INFORMATION. Packed with hotels, beachfront **Avenida 25 de Abril** runs the length of Figueira, turning into **Rua 5 de Outubro** after the fortress, before becoming **Avenida de Saraiva de Carvalho,** as it leads toward the train station. Four blocks inland and parallel to Av. 25 de Abril, **Rua Bernardo Lopes** is lined with semi-affordable hostels and restaurants, as well as the casino-cinema-disco heart of the city's nightlife. The **tourist office,** Av. 25 de Abril, 19, is under the Esplanada Silva Guimarães, next to the Aparthotel Atlântico facing the beach. (☎233 40 28 27; fax 40 28 28. No maps or luggage storage. Open June-Aug. daily 9am-midnight; Sept. 9am-11pm; Oct.-May M-F 9am-5:30pm, Sa-Su 10am-12:30pm and 2:30-6:30pm.) The **police** are on R. Joaquim Carvalho (☎233 42 88 81), by the bus station. Take the "Gala" or "Hospital" bus (from in front of the market on R. 5 de Outubro; 120$/€0.60) or catch a cab (about 1000$/€5) to the **hospital** (☎233 40 20 00), across the river in the Gala district. Above the Bompreço supermarket is the **Crackport Ciber Café,** R. Rancho das Cantarinhas, 68. (☎233 41 32 48. 125$/€0.60 for 15min. Open daily 2:30pm-1am.)

ACCOMMODATIONS AND FOOD. A spattering of reasonable hostels line R. Bernardo Lopes and R. Miguel Bombarda. Just two blocks from the tourist office and above an Indian restaurant of the same name, the rooms of **Pensão Residencial Bela Figueira,** R. Miguel Bombarda, 13, are clean and close to the beach. (☎233 42 27 28; fax 42 99 60. Singles 2900-4500$/€14.50-22.40, with bath 3800-6500$/€18.90-32.40; doubles 3800-6800$/€19-34, with bath 4800-8500$/€24-42.40; triples 4500-7500$/€22.40-37.40, with bath 5800-9500$/€29-47.40. AmEx/MC/V.) To reach the **Parque Municipal de Campismo da Figueira da Foz Municipal** on Estrada Buarcos, walk up Av. 25 de Abril with the beach on your left, turn right at the roundabout on R. Alexandre Herculano, then left at Parque Santa Catering. A taxi from the bus or train station runs (600$/€3). Swank grounds have an Olympic-size pool (350$/€1.75 per day), tennis courts, market, and currency exchange. (☎233 40 28 10. 2-person min. per party. Reception daily June-Sept. 8am-8pm; Oct.-May 8am-7pm. Quiet hours midnight-7am. Showers 110$/€0.55 for 7min. Sites 400$/€2 per person, 300-400$/€1.50-2 per tent, 300$/€1.50 per car.

Several restaurants and snack bars are scattered along **R. Bernardo Lopes** and the beach. A local **market** sets up beside the municipal garden on R. 5 de Outubro (open daily June-Sept. 15 7am-7pm; Sept. 16-May M-Sa 7am-4pm). Fill your beach basket at **Supermercado Ovo,** on the corner of R. Francisco António Dinis and R. Bernardo Lopes. (☎233 42 00 52. Open M-Sa 8am-8pm, Su 9am-2pm.) Directly across from the casino, popular **Caçarola Dois,** R. Bernardo Lopes, 85-87, specializes in seafood. Inexpensive sandwiches (300-500$/€1.5-2.5) and combination plates (950-1100$/€4.3-5.5) are easier on the budget. Open late for the gambling and clubbing crowds. (☎233 42 69 30. Open June-Sept. daily and Oct.-May Tu-Su 9am-5am; serves food after noon. AmEx/MC/V.)

SIGHTS AND ENTERTAINMENT. Just up from the public gardens on R. 5 de Outubro, the **Museu Municipal Dr. Santos Rocha,** in Parque Abadias, displays ancient coins and the fashions of Portuguese nobility. (R. Caloust Gulbenkian. ☎233 40 28 40. Open Tu-Su 9:30am-5:15pm. Free.) Figueira's partying lifestyle shifts from high gear to warp speed during the month-long **Festa de São João,** usually starting in mid-June and continuing through the first week of July. On the night of June 23, the eve of the **Dia de São João,** crowds of party goers dance in the streets and on the beach, gleefully bonking each other on the head with plastic noisemakers. After a spectacular fireworks display at 1am, crowds continue the in-town party or congregate around bonfires along the beach until the 5am *banho santo* (holy bath), when the brave take a dip in the ocean. The popular **casino complex,** on R. Dr. Calado, at the corner of R. Bernardo Lopes, houses a nightclub, cinema, and arcade (☎233 40 84 00. Entrance 18+ with ID. Casino open daily 3pm-3am. Slot machines and bingo free. Game room open July-Aug. 4pm-3am, Sept.-June M-F 5pm-3am and Sa-Su 4pm-3am. Day pass 700$/€3.50. Cinema Tu-Su 650$/€3.30, M 500$/€2.50. No shorts or sneakers.) On R. Joaquim Sotto Mayor, the continuation of R. da Liberdade running parallel to the beach, the modest exterior of **Palácio Sotto Mayor** conceals the shameless extravagance within; lavish green marble columns line the main hallway and gold leafing covers the ceiling. (☎233 42 20 41. Open Sept.-May Sa-Su 2-6pm, June-Aug. Tu-Su 2-6pm. 200$/€1.)

NIGHTLIFE. The summer nightlife in Figueira de Foz limbers between 10pm and 2am and runs on until dawn. Many bars and clubs with nightly summer hours are only open F-Sa during the rest of the year. On winter weekdays, nightlife remains back in Coimbra. Crowds fill several nearby bars before hitting the club scene. Grab a Bacardi (600$/€3) at Cuban bar **Havana,** R. Cândido dos Reis, 86, for the intimate area upstairs near the DJ booth. Thursdays feature live Latin music. Best around 11pm. (☎233 43 48 99. Beer 150$/€0.75. Open Tu-Su 8pm-4am.) The versatile new **Art Café,** Esplanada Silva Guimarães, 3, on the terrace above the tourist office, features a downstairs dance floor populated by clubbers ages 18-25, and a chill bar and art gallery upstairs, frequented by a somewhat older crowd. (Enter through the door to the left of the downstairs bar). *Fado* is featured on W after 11pm. (☎233 42 08 82. Minimum downstairs 500$/€2.50. Beer 200$/€1. Mixed drinks 700$/€3.5. Downstairs open June 15-Sept. 15 daily noon-4am, Sept. 16-June 14 M-W noon-midnight, Th-Sa noon-4am. Upstairs year-round M-Sa 8pm-4am.) Pubbers of all ages tread the inlaid Johnnie Walker mosaic of Irish-type **Rolls Bar,** on R. Poeta Acácio Antunes, 1E. (1 drink minimum. Beer 200-400$. Mixed drinks 500-800$/€2.50-4. Open July-Aug. daily, Sept.-June M-Sa, 5pm-6am.) Under the regal ceilings of a casino hall, club **Katigo** spins commercial music until 4am, then house music until dawn. Peaks at 3am. (Minimum 1000$/€5. Beer 350$/€1.75. Mixed drinks 700$/€3.50. Open July-Aug. daily, Sept.-June Th-Sa, midnight-6am.) End the night and bring on the morning at the **Discoteca Bergantim,** R. Dr. Lopes Guimarães, a block up from the beach. Crowds groove to pop and rock between 5-7am; don't bother coming before 4am. (☎233 42 71 29. Minimum 800$/€4 for women, 1000$/€5 for men. Beer 300$/€1.50. Mixed drinks 800$/€4. Open July-Aug. daily, Sept.-June F-Sa, 2-8am)

DAYTRIPS FROM COIMBRA

CONÍMBRIGA

AVIC ***buses*** *(☎239 82 37 69) run each morning from Coimbra to the ruins (30min., M-F 9:05 and 9:35am, Sa-Su 9:35am only, 290$/€1.45) and return in the afternoon (M-Sa 1pm and 6pm, Su 6pm only); inquire at the Coimbra tourist office for up-to-date schedules. Buses from Coimbra run more frequently to sleepy Condeixa, 2km away from Conímbriga. If you're ready to head back to Coimbra early, walk the 30min. through the olives groves or take a taxi (☎239 94 12 43) to Condeixa to catch another bus back to Coimbra (25min.; 6-30 per day M-F 6:35am-10pm, Sa-Su 7:05am-6:05pm; 260$/€1.30).*

Sixteen kilometers south of Coimbra, Conímbriga is home to the **Ruínas de Conímbriga,** Portugal's largest Roman settlement. Highlights include a 3rd-century town wall, an ancient but luxurious villa, and baths complete with sauna and furnace room. Stunningly well-preserved mosaics are visible under the shelter of a glass canopy. (Open daily Mar. 16-Sept. 15 9am-8pm; Sept. 16-Mar. 15 9am-6pm. Ticket office closes 30min. before the ruins. 600$/€30, under 25 and seniors 300$/€1.50, under 14 free.) The ticket price for the ruins includes nearby **Museu Monográfico de Conímbriga** and its displays of regional artifacts. (☎239 94 11 77. Same hours as the ruins, but closed M.) The **tourist office** is inside the museum. (☎239 94 47 64; fax 94 14 74. Open daily 9am-12:30pm and 2-5:30pm.)

BUÇACO FOREST AND LUSO

Buses *run from Coimbra to Buçaco (45min.; M-F 7 per day 7:35am-7:20pm, Sa 9am and 12:45pm, Su 10:15am and 7:20pm; 500$/€2.50), before continuing on to Viseu. Buçaco station is on Av. Fernão de Magalhães, near the palace and a 15min. walk from downtown (last return bus to Coimbra daily at 6:25pm). Buses back to Coimbra depart a few blocks from the Luso tourist office, across from the natural springs (35min.; M-F 5 per day 7:35am-6:35pm, Sa 10:35am and 6:35pm, Su 4:35pm; 470$/€2.30).*

Home to Portugal's most revered forest, Buçaco (also spelled Bussaco) has drawn wanderers in their escape from the city for centuries. Benedictine monks settled the Buçaco area in the 6th century, established a monastery, and remained in control until the 1834 disestablishment of all religious orders. The forest owes its fame, however, to the Carmelites, who arrived here nearly 400 years ago. Selecting the forest for their *desertos* (isolated dwellings for penitence), they Carmelites planted over 700 types of trees and plants brought from around the world by missionaries. In the center of the forest, adjoining the old Carmelite convent, is Dom Carlos's exuberant **Palácio de Buçaco.** Now a luxury hotel, the building is a flamboyant display of neo-Manueline architecture. The *azulejos* on the outer walls depict scenes from *Os Lusíadas*, the great Portuguese epic about the Age of Discovery (see **Literature,** p. 531). In the forest itself, landmarks include the lovely **Fonte Fria** (Cold Fountain), the **Vale dos Fetos** (Fern Valley), and the **Porta de Rainha** (Queen's Gate). A one-hour hike along the Via Sacra leads past 17th-century chapels to a sweeping panorama of the countryside from the **Cruz Alta** viewpoint.

A 3km walk downhill from Buçaco leads to the quiet, small town of **Luso**, Portugal's greatest source of bottled water. The town has a spa, fountains, baths, swimming pools, and a **bottling plant** (guided tours Tu and Th 3pm; reserve in advance at the *casino* down the street from the tourist office). Locals visit the crisp, cold spring **Fonte de São João** at all hours to refill their water bottles. The **tourist office,** R. Emídio Navarro, 136, in the center of town, has a friendly English-speaking staff who provides maps and short-term **luggage storage.** (☎/fax 231 93 91. Open July-Sept. M-F 9:30am-1pm and 2-7pm, Sa-Su 10am-1pm and 3-5pm; Oct.-June M-F 9:30am-12:30pm and 2:30-6pm; Sa 10am-1pm; occasional longer hours.)

AVEIRO ☎234

Through the old center of Aveiro wind a network of canals, along which traditional *moliceiros* (seaweed-coated fishing boats reminiscent of Venice's gondolas) drift out to sea. This storied maritime town has inspired an amalgam of historical anecdotes. Here stands the convent where the canonized princess Santa Joana once lived (see p. 630). But Aveiro is perhaps best known for its numerous beaches, all of which are easily accessible by buses and ferries from town.

TRANSPORTATION

Trains: Lg. Estação (☎234 38 16 32), at the end of Av. Dr. Lourenço Peixinho. Trains to: **Braga** (2hr., 10:35am and 8:35pm, 990$/€4.90); **Coimbra** (1hr., every hr. 6:10am-1:10am, 540-1300$/€2.75-6.50); **Lisbon** (5hr., 14 per day 6:45am-8:50pm, 1780-3250$/€8.90-16.20); **Ovar** (20min., 21 per day 4:35am-1:10am, 260$/€1.30); **Porto** (45min., 21 per day 4:35am-1:10am, 330$/€1.60).

Ferries: TransRia (☎234 33 10 95) ferries depart for the beach at **São Jacinto** from the Vera Cruz docks, the site of the old fish auction (M-F 9 per day 7:05am-12:45am, Sa-Su 8 per day 8:20am-12:45am, last return ferry at midnight; 250$/€1.25). From the tourist office follow R. João Mendonça as it winds around the park, turn left on R. João Afonso, and then right on R. B. Machado; the ferry dock is on a continuation of this street.

Taxis: (☎234 42 29 43 or 42 37 66). Taxis gather about the train station on Av. Lourenço Peixinho and along the canal in Pr. Humberto Delgado.

ORIENTATION AND PRACTICAL INFORMATION

Aveiro is split by its central canal and parallel street, **Avenida Dr. Lourenço Peixinho,** which runs from the train station to **Pr. Humberto Delgado.** The fishermen's quarter, **Beira Mar,** lies north of the central canal (the side with the train station). The residential district and Aveiro's historical monuments lie in the south end of the city. To reach the **tourist office** from the train station, walk straight up Av. Dr. Lourenço Peixinho until you reach the bridge (about 15min.); the office is on the next block.

Tourist Office: R. João Mendonça, 8 (☎234 42 36 80; fax 42 83 26), off Pr. Humberto Delgado, on the street to the right of the canal facing the lagoon. Open daily July-Sept. 9am-8pm; Oct.-June M-F 9am-7pm, Sa 9:30am-1pm and 2-5:30pm.

Currency Exchange: Banks lining Av. Dr. Lourenço Peixinh are generally open M-F 8:30am-3pm. **ATMs** can be found on Av. Dr. Lourenço Peixinho, as well as Pr. Humberto Delgado and Pr. Marquês de Pombal.

Emergency: ☎112. **Police:** Pr. Marquês de Pombal, ☎234 42 20 22.

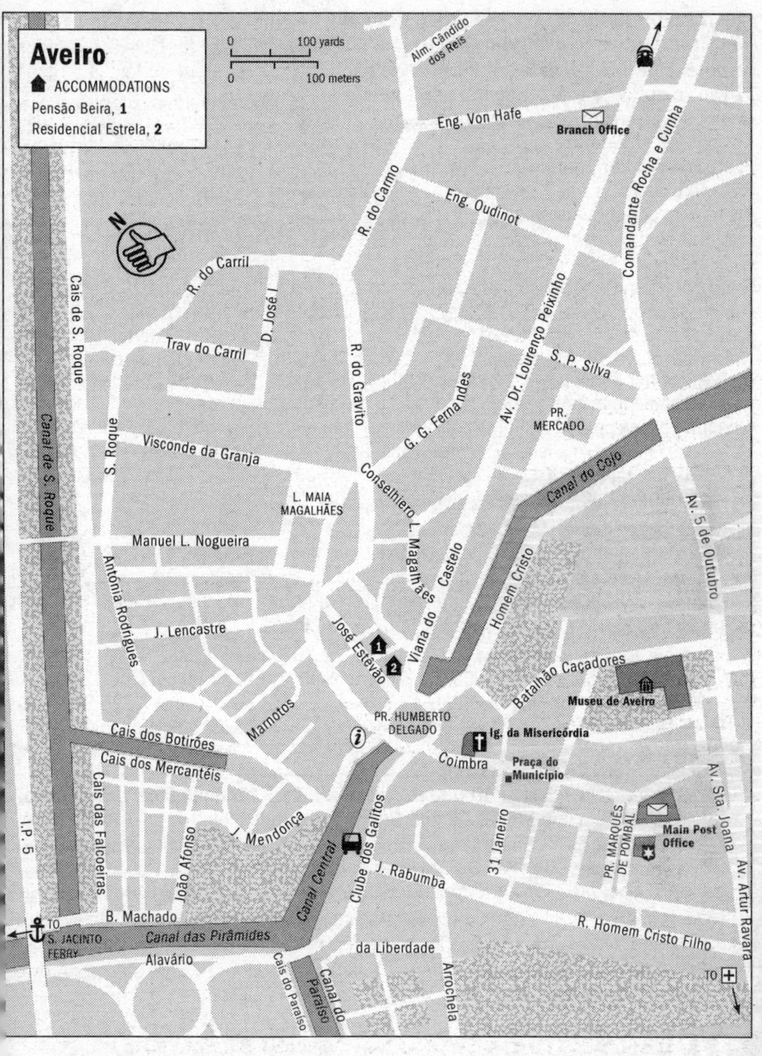

Hospital: ☎234 37 83 00, Av. Dr. Artur Ravara, near the park across the canal.

Internet Access: Cidade Digital, in Pr. da República across from the statue of José Estevão. Free internet. There is usually a short wait; sign up on the waiting list and hang around until your name is called. Time limit 30min. Open M-Sa 10am-8:30pm.

Post Office: Main office (☎234 38 08 40), Pr. Marquês de Pombal, across the canal and up R. Coimbra. Open M-F 8:30am-6:30pm, Sa 9am-12:30pm. **Branch office,** Av. Dr. Lourenço Peixinho, 169B (☎234 38 04 90), 2 blocks from the train station. Open M-F 8:30am-6:30pm. **Postal Code:** 3800 for north of the canal, 3810 for south.

ACCOMMODATIONS AND CAMPING

Inexpensive hostels line the streets of the old town, north of Pr. Humberto Delgado, and on the side of the canal with the tourist office; look for signs advertising *quartos* or *dormidas*. Hostel prices generally fall during the winter. Those lining **Av. Dr. Lourenço Peixinho** and the streets around **Pr. Marquês de Pombal** are somewhat expensive, but serve as good backups.

Residencial Estrela, R. José Estêvão, 4 (☎234 42 38 18), off Pr. Humberto Delgado, on the right 1 block before the tourist office. All but 2 rooms have baths, TVs, and decorated ceilings. June-Aug. singles 3500$/€18, with bath 5000$/€25; doubles 6000$/€30, with bath 6500$/€32.40; triples with bath 8000$/€40; one quad 10,000$/€50. Sept.-May singles 3000$/€15, with bath 3500$/€17.50; doubles 4000$/€20, with bath 5000$/€25; triples with bath 7000$/€35; quad 8000$/€40.

Pensão Beira, R. José Estêvão, 18 (☎234 42 42 97), off Pr. Humberto Delgado just past Residencial Estrela. Large rooms, all with TVs and all but one with private bath. Apr.-Sept. singles 4000-5000$/€20-25; doubles 6000-8000$/€30-40; triples 7500-9000$/€38-45; quads 10,000-12,000$/€50-60. Oct.-Mar. singles 3500$/€18; doubles 5000$/€25; triples 6000$/€30; quads 8000$/€40.

Residencial Palmeira, R. de Palmeira, 7-11 (☎234 42 25 21 or 81 56 58). Take a left out of the tourist office, then left again on the first street; it's up the street, across from the post office. Standard rooms, all with TV and all but one with bath. 24hr reception. Reserve 2 weeks ahead in summer. June-Sept. singles 4000$/€20; doubles 6000$/€30; one triple 7500$/€38. Oct.-May singles 3500$/€17.5; doubles 5000$/€25; triple 6000$/€30. One single without bath, 500$/€2.50 less.

Hospedagem Rossio, R. Dr. Barbosa de Magalhães, 24 (☎234 42 98 57), past the tourist office, and across from the park. These are the cheapest beds in town. Adequate rooms, some with curious windows overlooking the reception desk. Payment required in advance. Singles 2500$/€12.50, with bath 3000$/€15; doubles 4000$/€20, with bath 5000$/€25; one triple 4000-5000$/€20-25.

Camping Municipal de Aveiro (☎/fax 234 33 12 20), in São Jacinto. Owned by the city hall. Reception 8am-7pm. 360$/€1.80 per person, 165$/€0.80 per tent, 120-320$/€0.60-1.80 per car. Open Jan.-Nov.

FOOD

Seafood restaurants cluster around the fish market off Pr. do Peixe ("fish square"), in the old town, a few blocks behind the tourist office. Aveiro's specialty-pastry, called *ovos moles* (sweetened egg yolks), can be sampled at most of the *pastelarias* (pastry shops) along-Av. Dr. Loureço Peixinho and R. J. Mendonça. **Supermercado Pingo Doce,** R. Batalhão Caçadores, 10, is across the canal from the tourist office. (☎234 38 60 42. Open daily 9am-10pm.)

Restaurante Zico, R. José Estêvão, 52 (☎234 42 96 49), off Pr. Humberto Delgado. Filled with local workers at lunchtime. Entrées 800-2000$/€4-20. Open M-Sa 8am-2am; serving noon-4pm and 7-11:30pm.

Casa Necas, R. Tenente Resende, 51-53 (☎234 42 37 81), just off Pr. do Peixe. A small and solid Portuguese menu. Friendly staff and friendly prices. Entrées 650-800$/€3.20-4 for large half-portions and 1200-1400$/€6-7 for full portions. Fixed price menu 1400$/€7. A house specialties is *vitela assada* (veal, 700$/€3.50 half-portion) Open M-Sa noon-2:30pm and 7-9:30pm.

SIGHTS

Simple but strikingly blue *azulejos* cover the walls of the **Igreja da Misericórdia,** in Pr. República, across the canal and a block uphill from the tourist office. (☎234 42 67 32. Open M-F 10am-12:30pm and 2:30-5pm.) In the same square, the regal **Câmara Municipal** (city hall) displays its French design and bell tower. The old town's main attraction is the **Museu de Aveiro,** R. Sta. Joana Princesa. It was here that King Afonso and his daughter Infanta Joana, who wished to become a nun despite her father's objections, fought it out in 1472. Luckily for the poor and sick of Aveiro, she won. Beneath *azulejo* panels depicting the story of her life is one of

EAT YOUR HEART OUT, DON JUAN There's love, and then there's *love*. Dom Pedro I was in the latter. While a prince, he fell head-overheels for Inês de Castro, the daughter of a Spanish nobleman and lady-in-waiting to his first wife. Pedro's father, Afonso IV, objected to the romance, fearing that such an alliance would open the Portuguese throne to Spanish domination. Despite his father's opposition to the marriage, Pedro fled with Inês to Bragança, where the couple secretly wed. Soon thereafter, the disgruntled Afonso had Inês killed. Upon rising to the throne two years later, Pedro personally ripped out the hearts of the men who had slit his young wife's throat and proceeded to eat them. Henceforth, the hardy king became known as Pedro the Cruel. In a macabre ceremony, he had Inês's body exhumed, dressed her meticulously in royal robes, set her on the throne, and officially deemed her his queen; he even, according to legend, made his court kiss her rotting hand. She was eventually reinterred in an exquisitely carved tomb in the king's favorite monastery, the Mosteiro de Santa Maria de Alcobaça. The king later joined her. The inscription on their tombs reads, *"Até ao fim do mundo"* (until the end of the world).

the most famous works of art in Portugal, Santa Joana's Renaissance tomb supported by the heads of four angels. (☎234 42 32 97. Open Tu-Su 10am-5:30pm. 300$/€2.50, students and seniors 150$/€0.75, under 14 free. Su before 2pm free.)

BEACHES AND ENTERTAINMENT

Some of the beach towns near Aveiro boast beautiful sand dunes well worth a daytrip from Aveiro. Like the natural reserve at the **Dunas de São Jacinto** (10km away), most of them are easily accessible by ferry (see **Ferries,** p. 628). Closer to Aveiro, the beaches **Barra** and **Costa Nova** can be reached by bus from the *canal central* or train station stops (15min.; July-Aug. 17 per day 7:10am-8:45pm; Sept.-June M-F 14 per day 7:10am-8:10pm, Sa-Su 11-12 per day 8:20am-8:10pm; 250$/€1.75).

At night, the bars around **Pr. do Peixe** fill to overflowing. Other popular places line R. Canal de São Roque. Check out **Salpoente,** on Cais de São Roque, or neighboring **Estrondo Bar** and **Urgência,** on R. São Roque.

DAYTRIP FROM AVEIRO

OVAR

Buses *stop in front of the train station, as well as near the tourist office and to the right of the garden (M-F 21 per day 7:10am-8:10pm, Sa 11 per day 7:10am-7:10pm, Su 5 per day 9:30am-8:10pm; last return bus M-F 7:20pm, Sa-Su 6pm; 140$/€0.70). The* ***train*** *station (☎256 58 59 76), on Lg. Serpa Pinto, off R. António Coentro Pinho, has service to Aveiro (20min., 19 per day 5:45am-12:45am, 260$/€1.3).*

This *azulejo*-filled town, bounded on two sides by pine forest and on the other side by an isolated beach, is a relaxing stopover on the way to Porto. While there's not much to do here except hang out at the beach, **Praia do Furadouro,** no one seems to mind. The **tourist office,** on R. Elias Garcia, has maps as well as info about accommodations and transport. From the train station, head straight up the street, through the traffic circle on Pr. São Cristóvão, and take Av. Bom Reitor (the 2nd left; not the sharp left, but the one across the rotary), following it as it becomes R. Elias Garcia. (☎256 57 22 15; fax 58 31 92. Open July-Aug. M-F 9am-7pm, Sa-Su 10am-1pm and 3-6pm; Sept.-June M-Sa 9:30am-12:30pm and 2-5:30pm.) For food, shop at the **mercado municipal** (open Th and Sa 8am-15pm) on R. Gomes Freire. is **Pousada da Juventude de Ovar (HI),** on Av. Dom Manuel I (EN 327), is difficult to reach from the center of town, but within convenient walking distance from the Furadouro beach. Take the bus toward the beach and get off at the Carregal stop, just before the traffic circle, then turn right onto Av. Dom Manuel I (follow the signs to Porto), and walk for about 10min. (☎/fax 256 59 18 32. Reception 8am-midnight. Reservations recommended 3 days ahead in summer. June 16-Sept. 15 dorms 1900$/€9.50; doubles with bath 4600$/€23. Sept. 16-June 15 dorms 1500$/€7.5; doubles with bath 3800$/€19.)

NORTHERN PORTUGAL

DOURO AND MINHO

Although their landscapes and Celtic history invite comparison with the northwest of Spain, the Douro and Minho regions of northern Portugal are more populated, developed, and wealthier than Spanish Galicia. Thanks to the area's mineral wealth, these regions have had a prosperous history. The evidence is everywhere from the abundance of luxurious villas to the traditional female dress, which customarily feature layers of gold necklaces encrusted with charms. This affluence has a legacy as old as Portugal's landscape. The Kingdom of Portugal originated here in 1143 when Afonso Henriques defeated the Moors in Guimarães.

Ultimately, though, wealth and history take a backseat to the region's spectacular greenery. Douro and Minho are a haven for nature lovers: hundreds of trellised vineyards burgeoning with grapes for *porto* and *vinho verde* wines beckon connoisseurs, and houses tiled in brilliant *azulejos* draw visitors to peaceful streets. The region's mild coastal climate is too cool to attract the beach crowd until July, and only a few ambitious travelers ever make it past Porto and the Douro Valley to the greens and blues of the Alto Minho, which hugs the Spanish border. The cities of Vila Nova de Cerveira, Braga, Viana do Castelo, and Guimarães will reward the intrepid traveler with their unspoiled charm.

PORTO (OPORTO) ☎22

Porto is one of Portugal's most sophisticated and modern cities. Although it is a center for all sorts of arts and commerce, the source of its greatest fame (and its name) is its sugary-sweet port wine. Founded by English merchants in the early 18th century, the port industry is at the root of the city's successful economy and

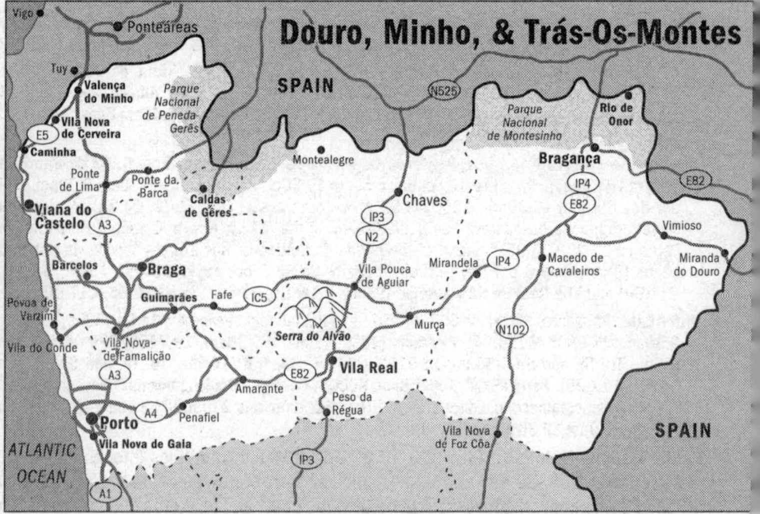

provides good enough reason in itself to come visit. But there's more to Porto than just port. Magnificently situated on a gorge cut by the Douro River, just 6km from the sea, Portugal's second-largest city is characterized by an elegance reminiscent of Paris or Prague, and it often seems more vibrant than Lisbon. Granite church towers pierce the sky, orange-tiled houses huddle close along the river, and three graceful bridges span the gorge above. All this has recently earned Porto the honor of being named a Cultural Capital of Europe 2001 and a place on the UNESCO World Heritage list. This level of recognition has not only initiated a massive "urban regeneration" project but has also focused attention on the city's culture.

TRANSPORTATION

Flights: Aeroporto Francisco de Sá Carneiro (☎22 941 32 60), 20km from downtown Porto. City bus (#56) goes to the airport from R. Carmo (in front of Hospital São António) but can be very slow due to traffic. The **aerobus,** which leaves from Av. dos Aliados near Pr. Liberdade, is more efficient (40min., every 30min. 7am-6:30pm, 500$/€2.50). Buy tickets on board, at an **STCP** window, or at a participating hotel. Even quicker is a **taxi** (20-30min., about 2500-3000$/€12.50-15). **TAP Air Portugal,** Pr. Mouzinho de Albuquerque, 105 (☎22 608 02 31), flies to major European cities.

Trains: Estação Campanhã (☎22 536 41 41), on R. da Estação. Most trains pass through this main station, east of the center. Trains run from Campanhã to: **Aveiro** (1¼hr., 30 per day 5:05am-11:15pm, 330$/€1.65); **Braga** (1½-1¾hr., 21 per day 5:20am-11:20pm, 330-530$/€1.65-2.64); **Coimbra** (2hr., 17 per day 5:05am-12:05am, 1050$/€5.24); **Faro** (9hr.; Tu, Th and Su 10:10pm; 3090$/€14.45); **Lisbon** (3½-4½hr., 14 per day 6am-8:05pm, 2150-3700$/€10.72-18.46); **Madrid** (13-14hr., 6:10pm, 9030-9655$/€45.03-48.13), with transfer at Entroncamento; **Viana do Castelo** (1½-2hr., 12 per day 5:35am-12:35am, 780-800$/€3.89-3.99); **Vigo, Spain** (2½hr., 7:40am and 6:55pm, 2225$/€11.10). **Estação São Bento** (☎22 200 27 22), Pr. Almeida Garrett, centrally located 1 block off Pr. Liberdade, is the terminus for trains with mostly local and regional routes. If your train stops at Estação de Campanhã, it is usually best to take a connecting train to São Bento. Frequent connections to **Estação São Bento** (5-10min., every 20-30min. 5:55am-11:10pm, 150$/€0.75). Buses #34 and 35 also connect Campanhã to downtown (every 30min., 180$/€0.88).

Buses: There is no central bus station; over 20 different companies operate out of garages all over the downtown area.

Rede Expresso (☎22 205 24 59), R. Alexandre Herculano, 366, in the Garagem Atlântico, has buses to: **Braga** (1¼hr., 8 per day 9:25am-12:15am, 870$/€4.35); **Bragança** (5hr., 7 per day 7:15am-8:15pm, 1500$/€7.50); **Coimbra** (1½hr., 11 per day 7:15am-12:45am, 1410$/€7.00); **Lisbon** (4hr., 12 per day 7:15am-12:45am, 2300$/€11.47); **Viana do Castelo** (1¾hr., 10:55am and 6:40pm, 1500$/€7.48). **REDM** (☎22 200 31 52), R. Dr. Alfredo Magalhães, 94, 2 blocks from Pr. República, has buses to **Braga** (1hr.; M-F 26 per day 6:45am-8pm, Sa-Su 9-12 per day 7:15am-8pm; 680$/€3.40).

Rodonorte (☎22 200 43 98), R. Ateneu Comercial do Porto, 1 block from R. Sá da Bandeira, goes to **Vila Real** (1¾hr.; M-F 16 per day 6:50am-10:30pm, Sa 7 per day 6:50am-9:20pm, Su 7 per day 6:50am-10:30pm; 1050$/€5.24) via **Amarante** (1hr.; 850$/€4.24). A nice little secret: Rodonorte buses have free bottled water for the asking. **Renex,** Campo dos Martires da Patria (☎22 200 33 95), in front of the Jardim de Cordoaria, has express service via Lisbon to **Lagos** (8½hr., M-F 6 per day 5:30am-1:15am, Sa-Su 5 per day 7:30am-1:15am, 3600$/€17.96) and **Vila Real de São António** (9½hr., 5 per day 9am-1:15am, 3600$/€17.96).

Internorte, Pr. Galiza, 96 (☎22 605 24 20) has international service to: **Berlin** (39hr., Tu and F 9:30am, 25,930$/€129.34); **Brussels** (28hr., Tu and F 9:30am, 19,745$/€99.08); **Geneva** (30hr.; Tu, Th, and Sa 9:30am; 16,930$/€84.45); **Madrid** (10½hr.; Tu, Th, and Sa-Su 9am; 5470$/€27.25); **Paris** (27hr., Tu-Sa 8am, 9000$/€44.89). Booking tickets 3 days in advance is strongly re- commended. Office open M-F 9am-12:30pm and 2-6:30pm, Sa 9am-12:30pm and 2-4pm, Su 9am-12:30pm and 2-5:30pm.

Public Transportation: STCP (☎808 20 01 66) operates **tram** lines throughout the city (single ticket 85$/€0.42) and farther reaching **buses.** Buy bus tickets ahead of time (95$/€0.40) from small kiosks around the city, or at the **STCP** office, Pr. Almeida Garrett, 27, half a block downhill and across the street from Estação São Bento. Tickets purchased on the bus cost twice as much. One-day unlimited tickets (500$/€2.49) are also a good deal (buy onboard). STCP office open M-F 8am-7:30pm, Sa 8am-1pm.

Taxis: Radiotáxis, R. Alegria, 1802 (☎22 507 39 00). Taxis hang out on Av. dos Aliados and along the river in the Ribeira district.

ORIENTATION AND PRACTICAL INFORMATION

Porto's heavy traffic and chaotic maze of one-way streets fluster even the most well-oriented of travelers. The city center is a bit easier to navigate where hillside **Praça da Liberdade** is joined to **Praça General Humberto Delgado** by **Avenida dos Aliados.** One of Porto's two train stations, **Estação São Bento,** lies just off Pr. Liberdade. The other, **Estação de Campanhã,** is 2km from the city center along the river. Between the Rio Douro and the city center lies the **Ribeira** district, where much of Porto's sights and nightlife are located on steep and narrow sidestreets. Directly across from the Ribeira, the two-level **Ponte Dom Luís I** spans the river to **Vila Nova de Gaia,** where the port wine-lodges are located. Back on the other side of the river, is the **Foz** district, where beaches and nightclubs are the main attraction.

Tourist Office: Main office, R. Clube dos Fenianos, 25 (☎22 339 34 72; fax 332 33 03), off Pr. Liberdade. From the train station, take a right and cross the street to get to Pr. Liberdade; the tourist office is on the left side of the avenue further up, at the end of the square. Open July-Sept. daily 9am-7pm; Oct.-June M-F 9am-5:30pm, Sa-Su 9:30am-4:30pm. Smaller **Ribeira branch,** R. Infante Dom Henrique, 63 (☎22 200 97 70), open during the same hours, offers the same services. **ICEP (national tourism) office,** Pr. Dom João I, 43 (☎22 205 75 14; fax 205 32 12), 1 block from Av. dos Aliados between Pr. Gen. Humberto Delgado and Pr. Liberdade. Open July-Aug. daily 9am-7:30pm; Apr.-June and Sept.-Oct. M-F 9am-7:30pm, Sa-Su 9:30am-3:30pm; Nov.-Mar. M-F 9am-7pm, Sa-Su 9:30am-3:30pm. **ICEP airport branch** (☎22 941 25 34; fax 941 25 43) open daily 8am-11:30pm. There are also 24hr. multilingual **computer info stands** in the main shopping centers and the larger squares; one sits in front of the McDonald's in Pr. Liberdade.

Budget Travel: Tagus, R. Campo Alegre, 261 (☎22 609 41 46). English-speaking staff; advice and student rates. Open M-F 9am-6pm, Sa 10am-1pm.

Currency Exchange: Portocâmbios, R. Rodrigues Sampaio, 193 (☎22 200 02 38), off Pr. Gen. Humberto Delgado, just across from the tourist office. Open M-F 9am-6pm, Sa 9am-noon. An **automatic exchange machine** is halfway up Av. dos Aliados.

American Express: Top Tours, R. Alferes Malheiro, 96 (☎22 207 40 20). Facing the town hall at the top of Pr. Liberdade, take Av. dos Aliados 1 block past the tourist office (stay on the left side of the street) and turn left onto R. Alferes Malheiro. Handles all AmEx functions. Open M-F 9:30am-1:30pm and 2:30-6:30pm.

Luggage Storage: Free in the **tourist office** during the day. At **Estação São Bento** (2100$/€10.50 per 48hr.). Open daily 5:15am-midnight.

Laundromat: Lavanderia Tropical, R. Bragas, 329 (☎22 205 13 97), off R. Mártires da Liberdade. Wash and dry 500$/€2.50 per kg. Open M-F 8:30am-12:30pm and 2-7pm, Sa 9:30am-1pm.

Emergency: ☎112. **Police:** R. Clube dos Fenianos, 11 (☎22 208 18 33), right next to the main tourist office off Pr. Liberdade.

Late-Night Pharmacy: Rotation list posted on the door of every pharmacy (and printed in many newspapers) gives the address and phone number of pharmacy of 24hr. duty.

Hospital: Hospital de Santo António (☎22 207 75 00), R. Alberto Aires Gouveia, downtown between the Estação São Bento and the Palácio de Cristal.

Internet Access: Portweb, Pr. Gen. Humberto Delgado, 291 (☎22 200 59 22), a few doors down from the main tourist office, has a bar and a room full of computers. Before 4pm, 100$/€0.50 per hr. After 4pm, 240$/€1.20 per hr. Coffee 80$/€0.40. Open M-Sa 10am-2am, Su 3pm-2am.

Post Office: (☎22 340 02 00), Pr. Gen. Humberto Delgado. Fax, phones, Posta Restante. Most services closed after 6pm. Open M-F 8:30am-9pm, Sa-Su 9am-6pm. **Postal Code**: 4000 for central Porto.

ACCOMMODATIONS AND CAMPING

Hostels in Porto are rarely charming and are often overpriced; the best plan is just to find someplace cheap and central. For the best deals, look west of Av. dos Aliados, or on R. Fernandes Tomás and R. Formosa, perpendicular to Av. dos Aliados. Prices usually dip in the off season.

Pousada da Juventude do Porto (HI), R. Paulo da Gama, 551 (☎22 617 72 57; fax 22 617 72 47), 3km from town center in the Foz district. Bus #35 from Estação Campanha or #36 from Boavista stop in front of the hostel; #37 from Pr. Liberdade stops a block away on R. Diogo Botelho. In a somewhat dodgy neighborhood; women should be cautious walking about at night. Reception daily 8am-midnight. Checkout 11am. June-Sept. dorms 2500$/€12.50; doubles with bath 6000$/€30. Oct.-May dorms 2000$/€10; doubles with bath 5000$/€25. MC/V.

Pensão Duas Nações, Pr. Guilherme Gomes Fernandes, 59 (☎22 208 96 21 or ☎/fax 22 208 16 16). From the train station, cross the street and turn right into Pr. Liberdade and then left onto R. Dr. Artur de Magalhães Basto, which turns into R. Fábrica and then R. Sta. Teresa; it's across the square at the top. Already quite popular among British and other foreign travelers. Room #18 on the roof is especially cool. Breakfast M-Sa 8-11am in the restaurant below (200-580$/€1.00-3.00). Laundry 1500$/€7.50 per load. Internet 100$/€0.50 per 15min. Reserve ahead. Singles 2200-2500$/€11.00-12.50, with bath 3800$/€19; doubles 3800$/€19, with bath 5000-6000$/€25-30; triples 6000$/€30, with bath 7000$/€35; quads 7500$/€37.50, with bath 8500$/€42.50; one room with 6 beds and bath 2200$/€11 per person.

Pensão Portuguesa, Tr. Coronel Pacheco, 11 (☎22 200 41 74), off R. Mártires da Liberdade, up the street from Pr. Carlos Alberto. Cheap and adequate rooms a few blocks away from the noise of the city center. July-Aug. singles 2500$/€12.50, with bath 3000$/€15; doubles 3000$/€15, with bath 4000$/€20; Sept.-June singles 2000$/€10, with bath 2500$/€13; doubles 2500$/€13, with bath 3500/€18.

Casa de Hóspedes Europa, R. do Almada, 398 (☎22 200 69 71), near the corner of R. Dr. Ricardo Jorge, up the street from the main tourist office. Above a restaurant of the same name, in a central location with friendly owners and inexpensive rooms. May 16-Sept. 15 singles 2500$/€13, with bath 3500$/€18; doubles 4000/€20, with bath 5000$/€25. Sept. 16-May 15 singles 2000$/€10, with bath 3000$/€15; doubles 3500$/€18, with bath 4000$/€20. AmEx/MC/V.

Camping: Prelada (☎22 831 26 16), on R. Monte dos Burgos, in Quinta da Prelada, 3km from the town center and 5km from the beach. Take bus #6, 50, 54, or 87 from Pr. Liberdade (only #50 and 54 run at night) Reception 8am-1am. 620$/€3.10 per person, 520-590$/€2.60-3.00 per tent, 520$/€2.60 per car. **Salgueiros** (☎22 781 05 00; fax 781 01 36), on R. do Campismo near Praia Salgueiros in Vila Nova de Gaia, is less accessible and less equipped campsite, but it is also less expensive and closer to the beach. To get there, catch the green Espírito Santo bus from Pr. da Batalha in front of the Teatro Nacional de São João (180$/€0.87). 300$/€1.50 per person, 300-400$/€150-2.00 per tent, 150$/€0.75 per car.

FOOD

The city center is full of mediocre snack bars, but there are also plenty of good deals for lunch and afternoon munchies at restaurants and cafés. Budget meals can be found near Pr. Batalha on R. Cimo de Vila and R. Cativo. Places selling *bifanas* (small pork sandwiches) line R. Bomjardim. More cheap eateries are located around the Hospital de Santo António and Pr. Gomes Teixeira, a few blocks west of Pr. Liberdade. At dinnertime, the Ribeira district along the river is

NORTHERN PORTUGAL

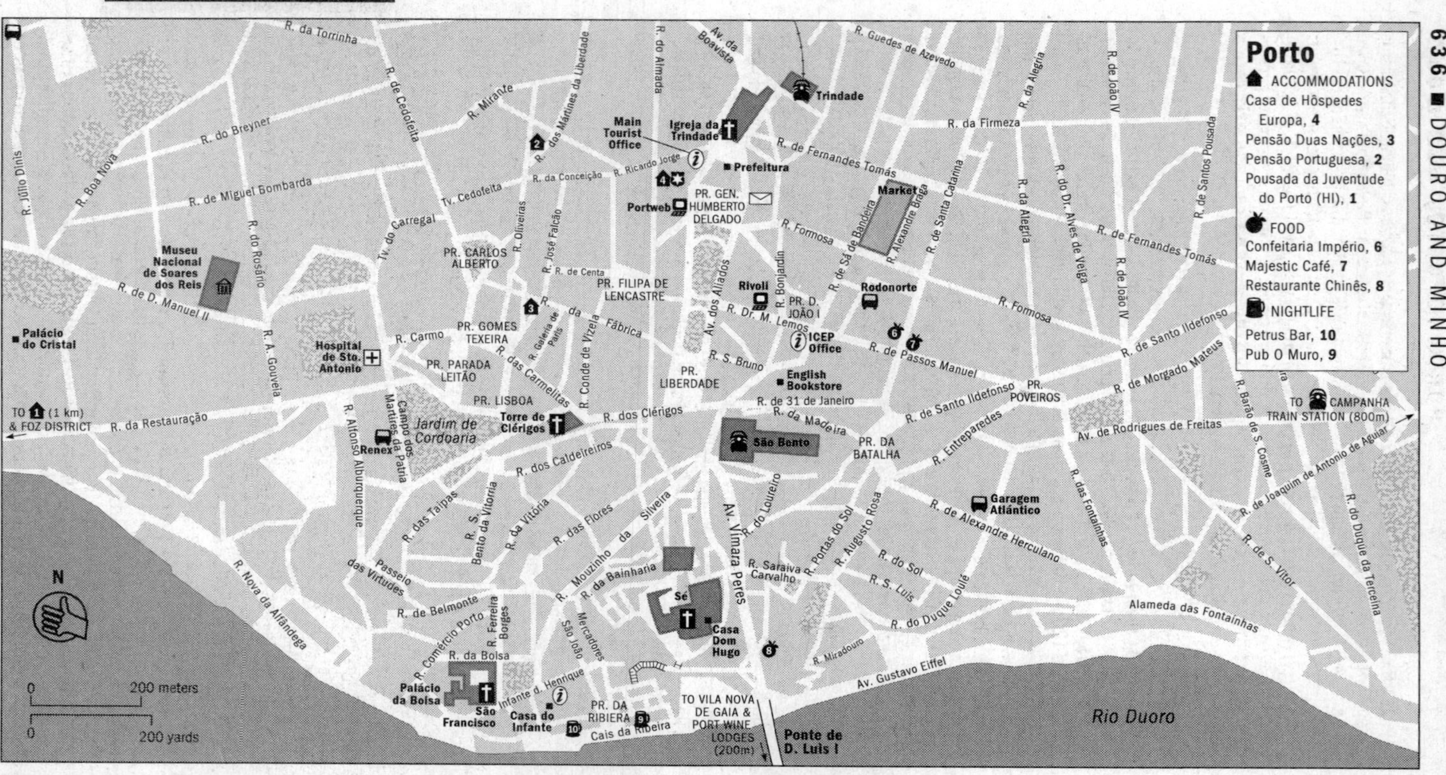

the place to look for quality and affordable restaurants, particularly on C. Ribeira, R. Reboleira, and R. Cima do Muro. Adventurous eaters can try the city's specialty, *tripas à moda do Porto* (tripe and beans). The **Mercado de Bolhão,** on the corner of R. Formosa and R. Sá de Bandeira, has fresh bread, cheese, meats, and excellent olives, as well as fresh produce on its upper level (open M-F 8:30am-5pm, Sa 8:30am-1pm). If you are in the mood to spend, the more expensive (touristy) restaurants border the river, in the Ribeira district, particularly on C. Ribeira, R. Reboleira, and R. Cima do Muro.

Majestic Café, R. de Santa Catarina, 112 (☎22 200 38 87). Founded in 1921, this is the oldest and most famous café in Porto, with a fancy classical decor of chandeliers and patina-covered mirrors. Tourists settle into fine chairs and rest their coffee cups on marble-topped wooden tables while classical music floats through the air. Sandwiches 400-1750$/€2.00-8.75. Fancy-shmancy pastries 200-650$/€1-3.25. A selection of fine cigars 1200-4500$/€6-23. Open M-Sa 9:30am-midnight. AmEx/MC/V.

Confeitaria Império, R. de Santa Catarina, 149-151 (☎22 200 55 95), across the street from the Majestic Café. Founded in 1941, this *pastelaría* has excellent pastries (95-170$/€0.50-€0.90), as well as inexpensive lunch specials (600$/€3) served in the back dining room. Try the *especialidade Império* pastry (120$/€0.60). The *lanche especial* (ham-filled pastry bread, 230$/€1.15) is a popular snack. Open M-Sa 7:30am-8:30pm. A newly opened branch at R. Fernandes Tomás, 755, is the largest self-service café in the city and sells a variety of meals and snacks.

A Grade, R. de S. Nicolau, 9 (☎22 332 11 30), in the Ribeira district. Up from Largo de Terreiro, just past Adega S. Nicolau. A friendly restaurant furnished with old-fashioned wooden tables and benches. The tasty lunch menu is a great deal (1000$/€5). Entrées are 1000-2000$/€5-10, while specialties like *polvo assado no forno* (octopus) and *cabrito assado no forno* (goat) run about 1750$/€8.85. Open daily M-F 8am-midnight; meals served noon-3:30pm and 7:30-11pm.

Restaurante Chinês, Av. Vímara Peres, 38 (☎22 200 89 15), on the left just before you cross the top level of the main bridge (Ponte Dom Luís I). Some of the best Chinese food in Porto. Rice and noodles 280-950$/€1.40-4.75. Entrées 880-1150$/€4.40-5.75. Open daily noon-3pm and 7-11pm. AmEx/MC/V.

SIGHTS

Your first brush with Porto's rich stock of fine artwork may be in, of all places, the **São Bento train station,** home to a celebrated collection of *azulejos*. Outside the station and at the top of adjacent **Pr. da Liberdade,** the formidable **Prefeitura** (City Hall) is a monument to Porto's late 19th-century greatness.

CATHEDRAL. Fortified on the hilltop slightly south of the train station is Porto's pride and joy, the Romanesque *sé*. Built in the 12th and 13th centuries, the Gothic, *azulejo*-covered cloister was added later in the 14th century. The **Capela do Santíssimo Sacramento,** to the left of the high altar, shines with solid silver and plated gold. During the Napoleonic invasion, crafty townspeople whitewashed the altar to protect it from vandalism. Climb the staircase to the **Renaissance chapter house** for a splendid view of the old quarter. *(Terreiro da Sé. ☎22 205 90 28. From Pr. Liberdade, walk past Estação São Bento and uphill on Av. Afonso Henriques; the cathedral is on the right. Open M-Sa 9am-12:30pm and 2:30-6pm, Su 2:30-6pm. Cloister 250$/€1.25.)*

PALÁCIO DA BOLSA. The elegant Palácio da Bolsa (Stock Exchange) was built from 1842 to 1910 over the ruins of the Convento de São Fransisco, after the convent was destroyed by fire in 1832. At the entrance is the **Pátio das Nações** (Hall of Nations), which was once a courtyard and served as the trading floor of the stock exchange. The domed ceiling is decorated with the coats of arms of 20 countries friendly with Portugal. Leading up to the top floor is the **Escadaria Nobre** (Noble Staircase), decorated with carved granite, and topped with two giant bronze chandeliers. Among the exquisitely decorated rooms is the **Sala dos Retratos** (Portrait Room), which features a wooden table that took an artisan 3 painstaking years to carve (and earned him a top prize at an exhibition in Paris). The most striking room of the Palácio is the opulent **Sala Árabe** (Arabic Hall), which took 18 years to complete in the Moorish style. The green crests on the ceiling proclaim "Allah above all," and its gold and silver walls are covered with the oddly juxtaposed inscriptions "Glory to Allah" and "Glory to Queen Maria II." Note that the door to the hall is set slightly off-center—an intentional alteration to symbolize that only Allah is perfect. The various rooms of the Palácio are now used for occasional ceremonies and official receptions. *(R. Ferreira Borges. ☎ 22 339 90 00. From the town center, walk past Estação São Bento and downhill on R. Mouzinho da Silveira to the square; signs lead the way. Open daily 9am-7pm. Multilingual tours every 30min. 800$/€4)*

MUSEU DE ARTE CONTEMPORÂNEA. Part of the Serralves Foundation, this museum rotates temporary exhibits of contemporary Portuguese art and architectural design. The building crowns an impressive 44 acres of sculpted gardens, fountains, and old farmland tumbling down toward the Douro River. *(R. D. João de Castro, 210. ☎ 22 615 65 00. Several kilometers out of town, on the way to the beach. Bus #78 leaves from Av. dos Aliados; ask the driver to stop at the museum (30min., return buses run until midnight). Museum open Tu-W, Th 10am-10pm, Sa-Su 10am-8pm. Park closes at sundown. 800$/€4. Free Su before 2pm.)*

IGREJA E TORRE DOS CLÉRIGOS. The 18th century **Igreja dos Clérigos,** decorated with Baroque and Rococo carvings, is most notable for its tall granite bell tower: the **Torre dos Clérigos** is the city's tallest landmark, reaching a height of 75.6 meters. Atop the 200 steps await spectacular views of Porto and the Rio Douro Valley. *(R. dos Clérigos. ☎ 22 200 17 29. Church open M-Th 10am-noon and 2-5pm, Sa 10am-noon and 2-8pm, Su 10am-1pm. Tower open daily June-July 10am-7pm, Aug. 10am-10pm, Sept.-May 10am-noon and 2-5pm. Church free; tower 200$/€1.)*

MUSEU NACIONAL DE SOARES DOS REIS. A former royal residence, this 18th-century museum houses an exhaustive collection of 19th-century Portuguese painting and sculpture, much of it by Soares dos Reis, often called Portugal's Michelangelo. *(R. Dom Manuel II, 44. ☎ 22 339 37 70. From the town center, walk down R. Clérigos and R. Restauração, then take R. Dom Manuel II past the churches and forested park (10min.). Open Tu 2-6pm, W-Su 10am-6pm. 600$/€3, seniors and students 300$/€1.50)*

IGREJA DE SÃO FRANCISCO. The Gothic and Baroque Igreja de São Francisco glitters with one of the most elaborately gilded wooden interiors in Portugal. Under the floor, thousands of human bones are stored in preparation for Judgment Day. *(R. Infante Dom Henrique. ☎ 22 206 21 00. From Pr. Liberade, follow the directions to Palácio da Bolsa. Open daily 9am-6pm. 500$/€2.50, students 250$/€1.25.)*

JARDINS DO PALÁCIO DE CRISTAL. These beautiful gardens lie outside the Palácio de Cristal (Glass Palace), near the hospital. Geese, swans, ducks, peacocks, fountains, and the best-kept garden in Portugal welcome those in search of a good reading spot. The new Biblioteca Municipal Almeida Garrett (municipal library) is now located at the gardens. *(R. D. Manuel II. ☎ 22 605 70 80. Exit Pr. Liberdade on R. Clérigos and follow the road around the hospital (right on R. Alberto Gouveia) before taking a left on R. Dom Manuel II. The park and palace are on the left, after the Museu Nacional de Soares dos Reis (10-15min.). Park open daily until dark. Library open M-Sa 10am-6pm.)*

BEACH AND ESPLANADE. Porto's rocky beach, in the ritzy **Foz** district in the west end of the city, is a popular destination despite the pollution. Beyond the Foz district, on the city's western coastline are the beaches of **Matosinhos.** *(Bus #1 from the São Bento train station heads to both Foz and Matosinhos.)* Between Foz and downtown, at the bottom of the hill on R. Alfândega, past a marvelous dock filled with shops and restaurants, runs the esplanade in **Ribeira.** *(Bus #1 from the São Bento train station or tram #1 from the Igreja de São Francisco.)*

THE STUFF THAT PORT IS MADE OF Port wine is unusually sweet not just because of the grapes it is made from, but because 170-proof brandy is added to the fermenting juice only 2 days after harvesting (in a ratio of 80% grape juice to 20% brandy). The hard alcohol stops the fermentation process, leaving nearly half the natural grape sugar in the wine. Equally important to the making of good port, however, is the immense amount of human labor it requires. Because of the harsh, unpredictable weather in the area, the harvest must be timed precisely (usually mid-Sept. to mid-Oct.) and finished quickly. Mountain villagers flood in and work 12-hour days until the crop is completed. Until 20 years ago, the men spent their evenings crushing grapes by foot in huge concrete troughs, arms linked, and legs purple to their thighs; only recently was this intense labor of love replaced by machines.

PORT LODGES

Now for the reason you came to Porto. All of the port wine lodges are located across the river in the nearby suburb, **Vila Nova da Gaia.** To get there, walk down to the Ribeira district and cross the lower level of the large **Ponte Dom Luís I.** Most of the lodges offer free tasting tours, on which you can note the differences between British and Portuguese lodges. Be measured in your tasting; it's easy to get carried away with all the free port. You still need to cross the bridge to get back to the city.

Taylor's, R. do Choupelo, 250 (☎22 371 99 99), in the center on town. From Av. Diogo Leite (the main street), take a left on R. de França, which turns into R. do Choupelo. Follow it uphill as it curves; Taylor's is on the right. Ask for your wine on their terrace, which has an amazing view of the Rio Douro. Free tours (every 20-30min.) and tasting. Open Aug. M-Sa 10am-6pm, Sept.-July M-F 10am-6pm; last visit starts 5pm.

Sandeman, Lg. Miguel Bombarda, 3 (☎22 374 05 33), just off Av. Diogo Leite. The big-shot of Vila Nova da Gaia, with costumed guides and a souvenir shop. As Entrance exhibit in a room off to the right details the history of Sandeman. Tours (every 15min.) last about 30min. 500$/€2.50 entrance, under 16 free. Tickets are good for a 500$/€2.50 discount at the gift shop. Open Apr.-Sept. daily 10am-12:30pm and 2-6pm; Oct.-Mar. M-F 9:30am-12:30pm and 2-5pm. AmEx/MC/V.

Ferreira, R. Carvalhosa, 19 (☎22 374 61 00), one block up from the end of Av. Ramos Pinto. Sip your port in the tasting room among heavy wooden tables and untapped casks filled with more burgundy *liquor.* Tours 500$/€2.50, credited toward purchase of a bottle of port. Open Apr.-Oct. every 20min. M-F 10:15am-12:30pm and 2-5:45pm, Sa 10:30am-12:30pm; Nov.-Mar. every hr., M-F 9am-noon and 2-5pm. AmEx/MC/V.

Quinta do Noval, Av. Diogo Leite, 256 (☎22 377 02 82), on the main street. No tours, but plenty of free tasting. The portly tables and chairs resembling wine casks have a view of the river. Open daily June-Sept. 10am-8pm; Oct.-May M-F 8am-5pm.

NIGHTLIFE

The place to party on weekend nights is the tirelessly fun **Ribeira,** where bars vibrate with the rhythms of Brazilian and Latin tunes. Pr. Ribeira, M. Bacalhoeiros, and R. Alfândega harbor most of the bars and pubs. Be cautious, as Pr. Ribeira and Cais do Ribeira can be unsafe at night. Most clubs are located along the river in the **Foz** district and in the new industrial zones; nightlife in Porto is hard to follow without a car. Bus #1 runs all night from Pr. Liberdade to the beach at Matosinhos, passing Foz along the way. A taxi to Foz from downtown costs about 700$/€3.50.

Solar do Vinho do Porto, R. Entre Quintas, 220 (☎22 609 47 49), off R. Dom Manuel II, by the Palácio de Cristal. Take the 1st left after the palace park, continue downhill to the fork, turn left at the park, then right at the fountain and down some stairs. Sister of the *Solar* in Lisbon, this is a good choice if you're still not tired of tasting port. Once a manor house, its upscale lounge has a terrace with a gorgeous river view. Port starts at 200$/€1.50, and climbs to over 3000$/€15. Open M-Sa 2pm-midnight. MC/V.

Petrus Bar/Wine Caffé, R. Fonte Taurina, 97 (☎91 986 77 80), with one entrance through the patio on Cais do Ribeira and another on the narrow street leading from Largo de Terreiro. The patio is a perfect spot to enjoy the view of the wine lodges across the river. During the day, Petrus is a cool escape from the sun. At night, lounge music cools to jazz, soul, and blues. Live music on the patio (Sa 3-7pm), inside W 10pm-2pm. Beer 300-500$/€1.50-2.50. Mixed drinks 700$/€3.50. Open daily 10:30am-5am.

Pub O Muro, Muro dos Bacalhoeiros, 87-88 (☎22 208 34 26), on a pedestrian street in the Ribeira district. A restaurant at dinnertime, but also a good place to start the night with a few drinks overlooking the river. Beer 200$/€1. Open Tu-Su noon-2am.

Discoteca Swing, Praceta Engenheiro Amaro Costa, 766 (☎22 609 00 19), near R. Júlio Dinis. Swinging action for a mixed gay-straight crowd grooving to alt-rock, new wave, and pop. Cover 1000$/€5.00. Open daily 11pm-4am, but the fun starts around 1am.

ENTERTAINMENT

For two weeks in February, Porto hosts the **Fantasporto Film Festival,** screening international fantasy, sci-fi, and horror flicks for crowds of film enthusiasts. Early June brings the **Festival Internacional de Teatro de Expressão Ibérica,** which showcases free performances of Portuguese and Spanish theater, including pieces from the nations' former colonies. Porto's biggest party, however, is a lot less cerebral. On the nights of June 23-24, the city lets loose with the **Festa de São João,** when locals storm the streets for free concerts, folklore, *fado*, and (of course) wine. The tourist office doles out info detailing Porto's upcoming events to celebrate its status as a Cultural Capital of Europe.

DAYTRIP FROM PORTO

AMARANTE

Rodonorte buses stop at the station (☎255 42 21 94) in Largo Conselheiro António Cândido, across the river from the sights and tourist office. ***Buses*** *go to: Bragança (2¾hr.; 8 per day Su-F 6-8 per day 7:50am-10:20pm, Sa 4 per day 7:50am-7:15pm; 1550$/€7.75); Guimarães (1¼hr., M-F 10:40am and 6pm, 520-850$/€2.60-4.25); Porto (1hr.; M-F 10 per day 7:05am-9pm, Sa 5 per day 8:40am-7:40pm, Su 7 per day 8:40am-11:10pm; 850$/€4.25); Vila Real (45min.; M-F 16 per day, Su 7 per day 7:50am-11:30pm, Sa 7 per day 7:50am-10:20pm; 850$/€4.25).*

From a distance, the quiet, religious town of Amarante (pop. 5600) appears a sprinkling of whitewashed houses over an emerald green valley. Amarante's historic and modern neighborhoods are divided by the lazy Rio Tâmega and its shaded weeping willow banks. Once a Portuguese stronghold against Napoleonic troops, the historic **Ponte de São Gonçalo** leads over the river and into **Praça da República,** home to the one-time Convento de São Gonçalo, and now divided into a church, museum, and town hall. The Romanesque **Igreja de São Gonçalo** is the resting place of the town's patron saint, whose tomb lies in the gilded chapel beside the altar. (Open daily 8am-7pm. Free). Next door, the **Museu Municipal Amadeo Souza Cardoso** displays contemporary paintings and sculpture. (Open Tu-Su 10am-12:30pm and 2-5:30pm. Last entry 5pm. 200$/€1.00, students and seniors 100$/€0.50, under 15 free). A short trek up R. 5 de Outubro offers a view of the ghostly remains of the **Solar dos Magalhães,** a burned-out manor which serves as a sordid but hauntingly beautiful reminder of Napoleon's pyromaniacal legacy.

To get to the **tourist office,** from the bus station, cross the street, turn right, and follow R. 31 de Janeiro until the bridge. Cross the bridge into Pr. República and onto Alameda Teixeira de Pascoães; the office is inside the museum entrance on the right. (☎255 43 22 59; fax 42 02 03. Open July-Aug. M-F 9am-7pm, Sa-Su 10am-7pm; Sept.-June M-F 9am-12:30pm and 2-5:30pm, Sa-Su 10am-12:30pm and 2-5:30pm.) Amarante specializes in sweet pastries, a tradition begun by the nuns of the Convento de Santa Clara. Culinary talent and divine inspiration shape *ovos* *moles* (sweet egg) and *ameêndoa* (almond) into heavenly confections. The **Festa de São Gonçalo,** on the first weekend in June, features these and other sweet tooth regional recipes. The best year-round shop to sample remains the **Confeitaria da Ponte,** R. 31 de Janeiro, 17, on the right just before the Ponte de São Gonçalo on the modern side of town. (☎255 43 20 34. Regional pastries 130$/€1.15; other pastries 100$/€0.50. Open daily 8am-11pm.) Just across the street from the confeitaria, the popular **Tasquinha da Ponte** serves two tasty daily specials, one meat and one fish dish. (☎255 43 37 15. Entrées 1200-1800$/€6-9. Open daily 9am-midnight.)

Budget accommodations are hard to come by in Amarante; it's best to return to Porto or spend the night eastward in Vila Real. Those set on staying can try **Casa de Hóspedes,** R. Cândido dos Reis, 288, upstairs and to the left. Take R. 5 de Outubro out of Pr. da República and continue uphill; the *casa* is on the right. Owned by Isaura de Jesus Pinheiro, the ten rooms of this private house each come with clean common baths and some with balconies. Genuine hospitality makes guests reluctant to leave; several have delayed departure for over a decade! (☎255 42 33 27 or 965 43 43 50. Kitchen use 500$/€2.50. Laundry 600$/€3 per load. Reserve ahead. Singles 3000$€15; doubles 5000$/€25; triples 6000-7000$/€30-35.)

BRAGA ☎253

Braga (pop. 160,000) originally served as the capital of a district founded by Celtic tribes in 300 BC. In 27 BC it became "Bracara Augusta," a Roman administrative center. Today's residents still consider their city's beautiful gardens, plazas, mu- seums, and markets worthy of the nickname "Portuguese Rome." The city is widely considered to be the most politically conservative in all of Portugal. Not surprisingly, the 1926 coup that paved Salazar's path to power was launched from here (see History, p. 529). During Holy Week, religious processions cross flower-carpeted streets and somber devotion explodes at night into fireworks and dancing. Those who come to Braga expecting just to pass through often end up staying for several days, as the city makes a convenient base for several worthwhile daytrips and itself is quite pleasant, when it's not raining.

TRANSPORTATION

Trains: (☎253 26 21 66), on Largo Estação. Less convenient than the bus. Trains to: **Coimbra** (4hr., 7:50am and 6:50pm, 1150$/€5.75); **Lisbon** via Porto (2 per day 7:50am and 6:50pm, 2800$/€14); **Porto** (1½hr., 11 per day 5:20am-10:05pm, 330$/€1.15). To get to **Valença, Viana do Castelo,** and **Vila Nova de Cerveira,** make a connection at **Nine** (20min., 14 per day 5:20am-10:05pm, 170$/€0.90).

Buses: (☎253 61 60 80 or 253 68 31 33), Central de Camionagem, a few blocks north of the city center. **Rodoviária** to: **Coimbra** (3hr., 6-9 per day 6am-11:30pm, 1600$/€8); **Faro** (12-15hr., 9 per day 6am-11:30pm, 3400$/€17); **Guimarães** (1hr., every 30min. 7am-8pm, 385$/€1.90); **Lisbon** (5¼hr., 8-9 per day 9:30am-11:30pm, 2300$/€12); **Porto** (1½hr., every 45min. 6:45am-8pm, 680$/€3.40). **Hoteleira do Gerês** to: **Caldas de Gerês** (1½hr., 17-18 per day 6am-11:30pm, 1500$/€7.50).

Taxis: ☎253 61 40 19.

ORIENTATION AND PRACTICAL INFORMATION

Braga's focal point is the **Praça da República,** a spirited square bordered by gardens and filled with cafés and fountains. The **Avenida Liberdade** stems out from the square. Pedestrian thoroughfare **Rue do Souto,** begins at the tourist office corner of Pr. República, eventually becoming R. Dom Diogo de Sousa and then R. Andrade de Corvo, before leading straight to the **train station.** To get to Pr. República from the **bus station,** take a left with your back to the entrance, and turn right up the commercial street. Continue straight under the concrete building onto Pr. Alexandre Herculana, then take R. dos Cháos straight ahead into the square.

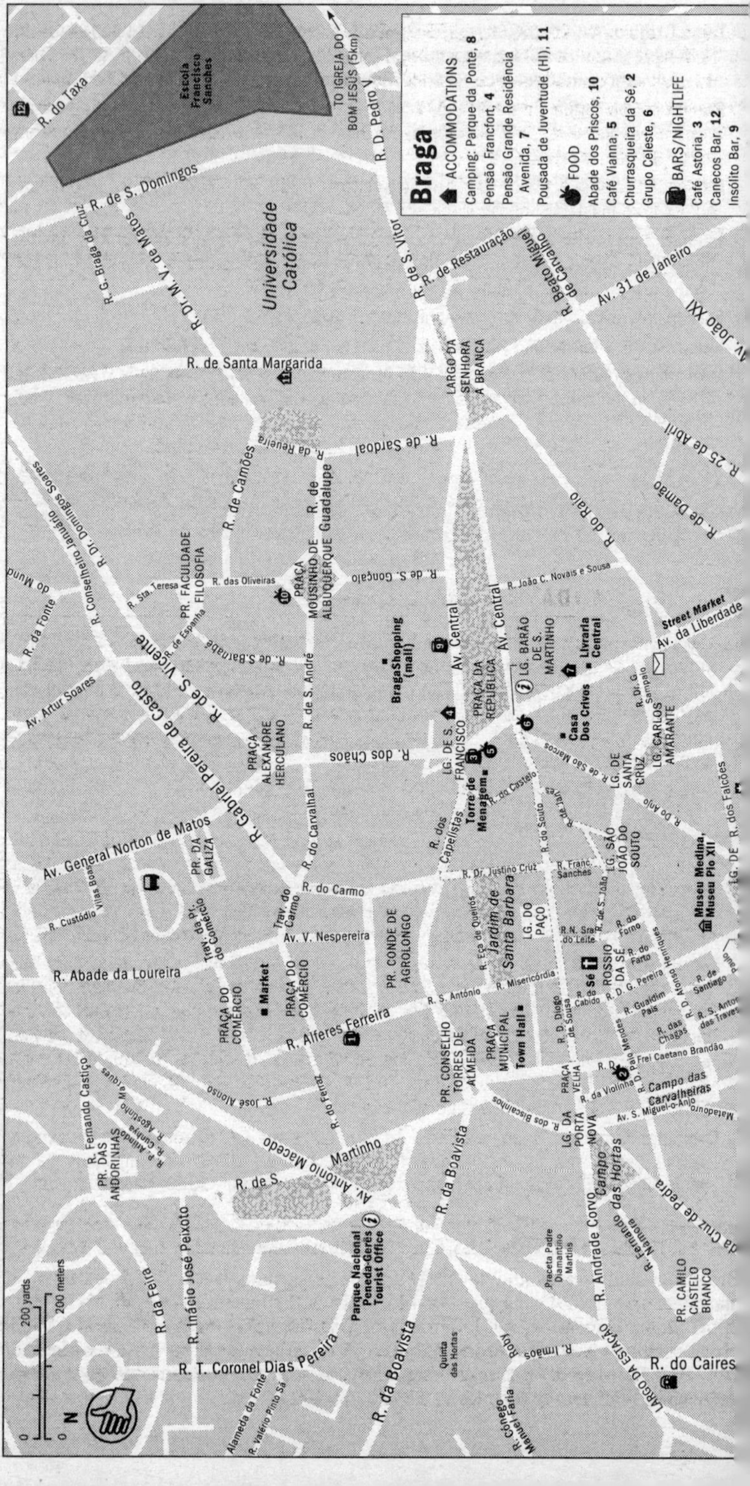

Braga

ACCOMMODATIONS
Camping: Parque da Ponte, **8**
Pensão Francfort, **4**
Pensão Grande Residência Avenida, **7**
Pousada de Juventude (HI), **11**

FOOD
Abade dos Priscos, **10**
Café Vianna, **5**
Churrasqueira da Sé, **2**
Grupo Celeste, **6**

BARS/NIGHTLIFE
Café Astoria, **3**
Canecos Bar, **12**
Insólito Bar, **9**

Tourist Office: Av. Central, 1 (☎253 26 25 50), on the corner of Av. Liberdade in Pr. República. Short-term **luggage storage.** Open July-Sept. M-F 9am-7pm, Sa-Su 9am-12:30pm and 2-5:30pm; Oct.-June M-F 9am-7pm, Sa 9am-12:30pm and 2-5:30pm.

Budget Travel: Tagus, Pr. Município, 7 (☎253 21 51 44). Student flights and other services. Open June-Sept. M-F 9am-6pm, Sa 9am-12:30pm; Oct.-May M-F 9am-12:30pm and 2:30-6pm. AmEx/MC/V.

Currency Exchange: Caixa Geral de Depósitos (☎253 60 01 00), on Pr. República, across from the tourist office. Open M-F 8:30am-3pm.

English Bookstore: Livraria Central, Av. Liberdade, 728 (☎253 26 23 83), next to Residência Avenida. A small selection of books and travel guides in English. Open M-F 9am-12:30pm and 2:30-7pm, Sa 9am-1pm. AmEx/MC/V.

Emergency: ☎112. **Police:** R. dos Falcões, 12 (☎253 20 04 20).

Hospital: Hospital de São Marcos, Lg. Carlos Amarante (☎253 61 38 00).

Internet Access: Instituto Português da Juventude, R. de Santa Margarida, 6 (☎253 20 42 50), in the same building as the youth hostel, with the entrance around back. Free. Open M-F 9am-7:30pm. **Videoteca Municipal,** R. do Raio, 2 (☎253 26 77 93), has 10 computers. Free 1hr. limit. Open M-Sa 10am-12:30pm and 2-6:30pm.

Post Office: (☎253 20 03 64) Av. Liberdade, 2 blocks downhill from the tourist office, in the grand building on the right side of the street. For **Posta Restante,** indicate "Estação Avenida" in the address. **Telephones, fax,** and other services. Open M-F 8:30am-6pm. **Postal Code:** 4700.

ACCOMMODATIONS AND CAMPING

Pousada da Juventude de Braga (HI), R. Santa Margarida, 6 (☎/fax 253 61 61 63). From the tourist office entrance, take a right and follow Av. Combatentes before turning. left at the intersection with R. Santa Margarida; the hostel is up the hill on the left, behind with the yellow gate. A taxi from the train station costs 800$/€4. Crowded dorm rooms, with 8-10 beds each, are offset by a friendly atmosphere and a convenient location. Fills with school groups Apr.-May and tourists June-Aug. Reception 8am-midnight. June 16-Sept. 15 dorms 1700$/€8.50; double with bath 4100$/€20. Sept. 15-June 15 dorms 1500$/€7.50, double with bath 3800$/€19. MC/V.

Pensão Grande Residência Avenida, Av. Liberdade, 738, 2nd fl. (☎253 60 90 20; fax 60 90 28), around the corner from the tourist office. Rooms with phones, TV, and fans. June-Sept. singles 3000-4000$/€15-20, with bath 4500$/€23; doubles 5000$/€25, with bath 6000$/€30; triples 6500$/€33. Oct.-May singles 3000$/€15, with bath 4000$/€20; doubles 4500$/€23, with bath 5500$/€28; triples 6000$/€30. MC/V.

Pensão Residencial Francfort, Av. Central, 7 (☎253 26 26 48), in Pr. República. This place has seen more glamorous days; if you look closely, you can see the marks on the red-tiled façade where the white letters of "Hotel" once were. Some rooms overlook the fountain in Pr. República. Reception 8am-midnight. Midnight curfew. May-Sept. singles 3000$/€15, with bath 5000$/€25; doubles 4000$/€20, with bath 6000$/€30. Oct.-Apr. singles 2500$/€13, with bath 4000$/€20; doubles 3500$/€18, with bath 5000$/€25. 30% more for 3rd person on a cot.

Camping: Parque da Ponte (☎253 27 33 55), 2km down Av. Liberdade from the center, next to the stadium and the municipal pool. Buses every 20min. 6:30am-11pm. Laundry facilities. 360$/€1.80 per person, 280$/€1.40 per tent, 300$/€1.50 per car.

FOOD

Braga has many cafés and several superb restaurants, but little in between. A **market** sets up in Pr. Comércio, two blocks from the bus station (open M-Sa 7am-3pm). **Grupo Celeste,** on Av. Liberdade across from the tourist office, is a local chain serving cheap fast food (☎253 21 54 95. Open June-Sept. 7am-midnight, Oct.-May 7am-10pm.) For more fast eats and a movie theater head to the **BragaShopping** mall, facing the plaza (☎253 20 80 10).

Churrasqueira da Sé, R. D. Paio Mendes, 25 (☎253 26 33 87), on the street running from the front entrance of the cathedral. An efficient and popular restaurant, serving generous half-portions to lunchtime crowds. The *prato do dia* (650-950$/€3.25-4.80) is always a good deal. Open Th-Tu 9:30am-3pm and 6:30-9:30pm.

Café Vianna, Pr. República, 87 (☎253 26 23 36), behind the fountain. Packed at midnight in summer. *Prato do dia* (850$/€4.25). Open May-Sept. daily, Oct.-Apr. M-Sa, 8am-2am. AmEx/MC/V.

Abade de Priscos, Pr. Mouzinho de Albuquerque, 7, 2nd floor (☎253 27 66 50). Named after a priest widely considered to be Portugal's best chef, this restaurant proudly serves traditional Portuguese cuisine. The menu is small, and all the entrées are prepared with great care (1200-2000$/€6-10). Open Tu-Sa noon-12:30pm and 7:30-9:30pm, M 7:30-9:30pm. Closed for the last 3 weeks of July.

SIGHTS

CATHEDRAL. Braga's *sé*, Portugal's oldest cathedral, has undergone a series of renovations since its construction in the 11th and 12th centuries. Guided tours (in Portuguese) of its treasury, choir, and chapels run frequently during visiting hours. The treasury showcases the archdiocese's most precious paintings and relics. On display is the *Cruz do Brasil*, a plain iron cross from the ship Pedro Álvares Cabral commanded when he discovered Brazil on April 22, 1500. Perhaps most curious are the cathedral's collection of *cofres cranianos* (brain boxes), one of which contains the 6th-century cortex of São Martinho Dume, Braga's first bishop. Near a Renaissance cloister lie the cathedral's two historic chapels. The more notable, **Capela dos Reis,** guards the 12th-century stone sarcophagi of Dom Afonso Henriques's parents as well as the mummified remains of a 14th-century archbishop. Also of interest is the choir—its organ has 2424 fully functional pipes elaborately decorated in gold. *(☎253 26 33 17. Cathedral and treasury open daily June-Aug. 8:30am-6pm; Sept.-May 8:30am-5pm. Cathedral free. Treasury and chapels 400$/€2)*

IGREJA DO BOM JESÚS. Braga's most famous landmark, Igreja do Bom Jesús, is actually on a hillside 5km outside of town. Built in an effort to re-create Jerusalem in Braga, this 18th-century church was to provide Iberian Christians with a pilgrimage sight closer to home. To visit Bom Jesús, take either the 285m ride on the antique funicular (8am-8pm, 200$/€1.00) or a 25-30min. walk up the granite-paved pathway. On the way up, check out the 365-step zig-zagging **staircase** depicting, among other things, the five senses (the "smell" fountain spouts water through a boy's nose), the virtues, and the prophets. The church, Braga's most elite resorts, a few small cafés, and stunning sunset views await at the top. *(Buses labeled "#02 Bom Jesús" depart at 10min. and 40min. past the hour from Av. Liberdade in front of Farmácia Cristal. Buses stop at the bottom of the stairway; the last bus is around 8:30pm. 200$/€1.)*

ENTERTAINMENT

Braga's biggest festival of the year is the **Festa de São João,** a week-long celebration that reaches its peak on the night of June 23rd. The biggest bash is supposedly in Porto, but the *bracarenses* don't fall too far behind; traditional folk music, good food, concerts and general revelry take over Av. da Liberdade and Lg. São João da Ponte. Don't be surprised to see locals running around beating each other on the head with toy hammers; few seem to remember the origin of this bizarre ritual, but the older folk will tell you that it's a tribute to Sao João, Protector of the Head.

NIGHTLIFE

The cafés in **Pr. República** fill with students after midnight. Other nightspots include **R. do Taxa** and **Pr. Conde de Agrolongo** (a.k.a. Campo da Vinha). The area around Pr. do Comércio between Trav. do Carmo and R. Alferes Ferreira is known to be quite dangerous at night; be cautious when walking here after dark.

Café Astória, Pr. República, 5 (☎966 08 36 97), next door to Café Vianna. The two-floor bar upstairs is a popular student hangout post-midnight. Wide-eyed angels hang from the ceiling. Beer 150$/€0.75. Open M-Sa 8am-4am, Su 10am-2am.

Insólito Bar, Av. Central, 47 (☎968 01 62 40), on the main avenue, between Pr. República and the youth hostel. Owned by the city academic association, the live music in the large yard out back attracts a university crowd of students and professors. Minimum consumption M-Th 200$/€1, F-Sa 500$/€2.50. Beer 200$/€1. Mixed drinks 500$/€2.50. Open M-Sa 10pm-4am. Closed Aug.

Canecos Bar, R. Dr. Alberto Cruz, 142 (☎253 26 09 84), off R. do Taxa. From the youth hostel, take a left, go up the street to the plaza, and take a right onto R. Bento Miguel; then bear right onto R. do Taxa and take a left onto R. Alberto Cruz, and it's on the left. Watch your vowels when you order your beer: a *caneco* (140$/€0.70) is a half-pint and a *caneca* (250$/€1.25) is a pint. For something stronger, try the *tic-tic*, guaranteed to make your head swim (rum, absinthe, and coffee liqueur, lit on fire and shaken; 600$/€3.). Open daily 7pm-2am. Closed Aug. 16-31.

Populum, Pr. Conde Agrolongo, 115 (☎253 61 09 66), off R. Alferes Ferreira. Popular among the young non-student crowd. All you can drink 2000$/€10.00 for men, 1000$/€5 for women. Thursday is ladies' night; women free. Open Th-Sa 10pm-5am.

DAYTRIPS FROM BRAGA

MOSTEIRO DE TIBÃES

A city bus labeled "Sarrido" heads 6km from Braga to the monastery. Buses leave from Pr. Conde de Agrolongo, 1 block up R. Capelistas from Pr. República. (25min., every 2hr. at 5 and 35 past the hour, 8:05am-7:35pm).

Surrounded by unspoiled forest, this peaceful 11th-century Benedictine monastery has suffered from centuries of neglect. Stone tombs rattle eerily underfoot in the weathered cloister. (The monastery is currently undergoing much-needed restoration; check with the tourist office or the monastery office to find out what areas are open for visits.) Adjoining the cloister, is an exceptionally preserved church. (☎253 62 26 70. Open Tu-Su 10am-noon and 1-6:30pm. 800$/€4.00, age 14-25 400$/€2, under 14 free.)

GUIMARÃES

REDM buses (☎253 51 62 29) come from Braga to Guimarães (40 min., M-F 19 per day 7:15am-8:35pm, Sa-Su 13-15 per day 8am-8:35pm; 400$/€2.), and return (40min; M-F 19 per day 6:30am-8:30pm, Sa-Su 13-15 per day 6:55am-8:30pm; 400$/€2.).

Ask any Portugal native about the city of Guimarães (pop. 60,000), and they will tell you that it was the birthplace of the nation. Ask any native of Guimarães, and they will add with a rivalrous glint in their eye, that their city is also better than Braga. It is here that one of Portugal's most gorgeous palatial estates resides. The **Paço dos Duques de Bragança** (Ducal Palace) is modeled after the manor houses of northern Europe. A museum inside includes furniture, silverware, tapestries, and weapons once used at the palace. In the banquet hall, tables that once seated 15th-century nobles now serve presidents of Portugal. At dinnertime, at least a quarter of the 39 fireplaces burn in an attempt to heat the building. Don't miss the elaborate Pastrana tapestries in the **Sala dos Pasos Perdidos** (Hall of Lost Footsteps) or the interesting display of archaic weaponry in the **Sala das Armas** (Arms Room). Up a few steep steps from the courtyard, is the **Capela.** (Chapel open daily 9:30am-12:30pm and 2-5:30pm. 600$/€3, seniors and students 300$/€1.50. Su mornings free.) Overlooking the city is the **Monte da Pena,** home to an excellent campsite as well as picnic areas, mini-golf, and cafés. To get there, take the **teleférico** (skyride) which runs in summer from Lg. das Portas to the mountaintop (☎253 51 50 85. June-July and Sept. M-F 11am-7pm, Sa-Su 10am-8pm, Aug. daily 10am-8pm. 300$/€1.50, or 500$/€2.50 roundtrip.)

The main **tourist office** is on Alameda de São Dámaso, 83, facing Pr. Toural. From the bus station, take Av. Conde Margaride to the right, walk uphill, and turn right at the fork onto R. Paio Galvão; the tourist office is on the far corner of Pr. Toural. The English-speaking staff distributes maps and brochures, and offers short-term **luggage storage.** An electronic sign outside across the street displays opening hours for all sights. (☎253 41 24 50. Open June-Sept. M-Sa 9:30am-7pm, Oct.-May M-Sa 9:30am-6pm) The **train station,** is a 10min. walk down Av. Afonso Henriques from the tourist office. The **bus station** (☎253 51 65 29), is in the **GuimarãeShopping** complex, on Alameda Mariano Felgueiras. To get there, follow Av. Conde Margaride downhill. Services include: **emergency:** ☎112; **police** on Alameda Alfredo Pimenta, ☎253 51 33 34; **hospital** on R. dos Cutileiros (☎253 51 26 12). Follow the crowds for lunch at **Restaurante O Pinguim,** Trav. do Picoto, off R. Picoto. From Lg. Navarros de Andrade, go up Av. Humberto Delgado (across the square from the post office) and take a left onto R. Picoto up the hill, then another left off the street as it curves to the right. Or, from the Casa de Retiros, take a right and then a left onto Trav. do Picoto. Their specialty is *bacalhau à pinguim* (2500$/€12.25 serves 2); other entrées run 950-1800$/€4.75-9. (☎253 41 81 82. Open Tu-Su 8am-10:30pm; serves meals 11:30am-3:30pm and 7-10:30pm. AmEx.)

BARCELOS

Getting from Braga to Barcelos and back is easy; it makes for an ideal morning visit. REDM buses (☎253 80 83 00) leave from Av. Sidónio Pais, 245, across from Campo da República, and run to Braga frequently (40-50min., M-Sa 6:30am-7:20pm, Su 7:30am-7:20pm, 320$/€1.60).

Barcelos is known throughout Portugal for its cock (see **Super Cock,** p. 553). But the town also hosts one of the largest weekly markets in all of Europe: vendors from the entire region come every Thursday to sell everything from fruits and vegetables to local ceramics. This market, the **Feira de Barcelos,** was inaugurated in 1412 by Dom João I at the request of his son, Dom Afonso. Vendors begin to arrive at the huge, central **Campo da República** late Wednesday night, and by 8am Thursday morning the market is going at full force. Old ladies carry live roosters by the feet, artisans display inexpensive traditional ceramics, and aggressive pastry sellers work from trucks on the edge of the square along Av. da Liberdade. Even if you miss market day, it's still worth the trip to visit Barcelos. The **Templo do Bom Jesus** in main Lg. da Porta Nova, built in 1704, is an octagonal Baroque church with golden altar. In Lg. do Município is the 17th-century **Igreja Matriz,** a Gothic church built by Count Alfonso. Behind the church is the 14th century **Paço Condal,** site of the famous monument to the Barcelos cock. The Paço has also hosted the **Museu Arqueológico** since 1920. (All sights open daily 9am-noon and 1-5pm. Free.)

The **tourist office,** in Lg. da Porta Nova, is in the Torre da Porta Nova, part of the town's original 15th century wall and the only remaining of three towers that once formed the entrance to the ancient city. The office doubles as a large artisan craft shop and provides short-term **luggage storage.** (☎253 81 18 82. Open Mar.-Oct. M-10am-6pm, Sa 10am-12:30pm and 2:30-5:30pm, Su 2:30-5:30pm; Nov.-Feb. M-9:30am-5:30pm, Sa 10am-12:30pm and 2:30-5pm.) Services include: **emergency** ☎112 and the **police** on Av. Dr. Sidónio Pais, (☎253 80 25 70).

PARQUE NACIONAL DE PENEDA-GERÊS

A crescent-shaped natural reserve along the Spanish border, the Parque Nacional de Peneda-Gerês became Portugal's first protected area in 1971. This park consists of the northern **Serra da Peneda** and the southern **Serra do Gerês;** its base is **Caldas de Gerês**, a spa town in the south. The park is certainly not undiscovered, as it is one of the most popular destinations for Portuguese vacationers July and August; however, those who leave the hub can find areas to relax at any time of year.

The main **park information office** is located in Braga, on Av. António Macedo (☎253 20 34 80; fax 61 31 69. Open M-F 9am-12:30pm and 2:30-5:30pm.) The **Gerês branch office** (☎253 39 01 10), on Av. Manuel Francisco da Costa uphill from the municipal tourist office has an English-speaking staff that can assist with hike planning. More casual hikers tend to stay south, where the few roads provide scenic and manageable journeys, while more dedicated visitors usually head to the trails of the north. In both areas, numerous hamlets and villages offer accommodations, campsites, and food. Hikers can attempt the 10 to 12-hr. trek along an ancient Roman road beginning in Braga; the route runs along the **Vilarinho das Furnas** reservoir, an optimal place for swimming and camping. In the height of summer, one might be able to catch a view of the village that was submerged when the reservoir was dammed. Another possible hike follows the road toward **Portela do Homem,** a small town on the Portuguese-Spanish border with a river pool at the bottom of the **Minas dos Carris** valley. Southeast of Gerês is **Miradouro do Gerês,** a popular site overlooking the **Caniçada** reservoir—beware the *en masse* migration of weekend picnickers. The village of **Rio Caldo,** at the base of the Caniçada reservoir just 8km south of Gerês, offers windsurfing and waterskiing.

The main attraction of Gerês is the **Spa Caldas de Gerês,** open from May to October. The spa complex includes a pool, tennis, horseback riding, hiking services, canoeing, and nautical sports along with its famed waters. Next-door **Parque dase Termas** has flourine mineral waters. (☎253 39 11 13. 170$/€0.85, children under 12 80$/€0.40. Pool open Apr.-July and Sept. 10am-6pm, Aug. 10am-8pm. M-F 700$/€3.50, Sa-Su 1100$; under 7 M-F 400$/€2.00, Sa-Su 650$/€3.25.)

To get to the **tourist office** from the bus stop, walk uphill along Av. Manuel Francisco da Costa; the office is surrounded by a semicircle of shops. The English-speaking staff provides info on the national park and short-term **luggage storage.** (☎253 39 11 33. Open M-Sa 9am-12:30pm and 2:30-6pm.) The **police** (☎253 39 11 37) are just off Av. Manuel Francisco da Costa. The **post office** is located off the rotary that leads uphill into the center. (☎253 39 00 10; fax 39 00 16. Open M-F 9am-12:30pm and 2-5:30pm.) There are plenty of *pensões* in Gerês. One option is **Casa de Ponte,** on Av. D. João V. From the bus stop, head downhill until you see the hostel on the left corner where the road splits, next to the Escola Primaria. The rooms have baths, and TVs; most have porches overlooking the garden. English-speaking owner. (☎253 39 11 25. Midnight curfew. Aug.-Oct. singles 5000$/€25; doubles 8000$/€40; triples 9000$/€45. May-July singles 4000$/€20; doubles 6000$/€30; triples 7000$/€35. Nov.-Apr. singles 3000$/€15; doubles 4000$/€20; triples 7000$/35) For camping, try **Camping Vidoeiro,** by the river and 1km outside of town. Facing the tourist office, take the uphill road to the left to get to the site. (☎253 39 12 89. Open May 15-Oct. 15. Reception 8am-7pm. 400$/€2.00 per person, 350-450$/€1.75-2.25 per tent, 450$/€2.25 per car.) Meals in Caldas de Gerês are available at the *pensões* throughout town. Restaurants and cafés lie along Av. Manuel Francisco da Costa, up around the corner from the bus stop. **Empresa Hoteleira do Gerês** (☎253 61 58 96) runs **buses** from Gerês to **Braga** (1½hr.; M-Sa 10-17 per day 6:30am-7:30pm, Su 7 per day, 6:30am-9pm; 575$/€2.90).

VIANA DO CASTELO ☎258

In the northwestern corner of the country, Viana do Castelo (pop. 20,000), is one of the loveliest coastal cities in all of Portugal. The church on the hill above the city watches over Viana's lively history center, the **Praça da República,** and its wide main avenue running to the sea. Even those intending only on passing through on their way to Galicia soon discover the town's charm: excellent food, and beaches, and intriguing architecture, including a bridge designed by Gustave Eiffel.

TRANSPORTATION

Trains: (☎258 82 13 15), at the top of Av. Combatentes da Grande Guerra, under the Santa Luzia hill. From the bus station, go left on Av. Capitão Gaspar de Castro through a pedestrian underpass (15min.), or take the bus (110$/€0.60). Trains to: **Porto** (2hr., 13-14 per day 5am-9:27pm, 800$/€4.00); **Vigo, Spain** (2½hr., 2 per day 9:18am and 8:30pm, 1565$/€7.80); **Vila Nova de Cerveira** via **Caminha** (1hr., 8 per day 7:44am-8:30pm, 310$/€1.55).

Buses: Rodoviária (☎258 82 50 47) departs from **Central de Camionagem,** on the eastern edge of town, to **Braga** (1½hr.; M-Sa 6-8 per day 7am-6:35pm, Su 4 per day 8:15am-6:35pm; 700$/€3.50). **AVIC** (☎258 82 97 05) and **Auto-Viação do Minho** (☎258 80 03 41) go to **Porto** (2hr.; M-F 9 per day 6:45am-6:30pm, Sa-Su 4-6 per day 8:20am-6:30pm; 750-1050$/€3.50-5.25); **Lisbon** (5½hr.; Su-F 3 per day 8am-11:45pm, Sa 7am and 12:30pm; 2500$/€18).

Taxi: Táxis Vianenses ☎258 82 66 41 or 82 23 22. Taxis can be found along Av. Combatentes da Grande Guerra.

ORIENTATION AND PRACTICAL INFORMATION

Wide, main **Ave. dos Combatentes da Grande Guerra** runs from the **train station** to the port. Most accommodations and restaurants are located on or just off the Avenida. The **historic center** stretches east of the Avenida around **Praça da República,** while the fortress and sea lie to the west.

Tourist Office: (☎258 82 26 20 or 258 82 49 71; fax 82 78 73), R. do Hospital Velho at the corner of Pr. Erva. From the train station, take the 4th left at the sharp corner onto R. da Picota and then a quick right into Pr. Erva. Open May-July and Sept. M-Sa 9am-1pm and 2:30-6pm, Su 9:30am-1pm; Aug. daily 9am-7pm; Oct.-Apr. M-Sa 9am-12:30pm and 2:30-5:30pm.

Currency Exchange: Montepio Geral, Av. Combatentes, 332 (☎258 82 88 97), near the train station. Open M-F 8:30am-3pm. On-site 24hr. **ATM.**

Emergency: ☎112. **Police:** R. de Aveiro, ☎258 82 20 22.

Hospital: Hospital de Santa Luzia, (☎258 82 90 81), Estrada de Santa Luzia, off Av. 25 de Abril.

Internet Access: Available free at the **Biblioteca Municipal** (public library) on R. Cândido dos Reis, up from Pr. República. (☎258 80 93 02. 5 computers. ID required. Strict 30min. limit and often a 1hr. wait. Open M-F 9:30am-12:30pm and 2-7pm, Sa 9:30am-12:30pm).

Post Office: (☎258 80 00 80), Av. Combatentes da Grande Guerra, across from the train station. **Posta Restante** and **fax.** Open M-F 8:30am-6pm. **Postal Code:** 4900.

ACCOMMODATIONS AND CAMPING

Accommodations in Viana do Castelo are easy to find, although they are not particularly cheap. *Quartos particulares* (private rooms) are the best option in the center of town. Check the tourist office's list of accommodations or look on side streets off Av. Combatentes da Grande Guerra.

Pousada de Juventude de Viana do Castelo (HI), R. da Argaçosa (Azenhas D. Prior) (☎258 80 02 60; fax 82 08 70), right on the marina, off Pr. de Galiza.Rooms with balconies and great views of the marina. Lounge with a pool table (600$/€3 per hour) and free ping-pong. Bar, common kitchen, and dining hall (lunch 12:30-1:30pm, dinner 7:30-8:30pm; 950$/€4.75. Laundry 1000$/€5 per load. Internet access 300$/€1.50 per 30min., 500$/€2.50 per 1hr. Reception 8am-midnight. Checkout 10am. Reservations recommended. Sept. 16-June 15 dorms 2000$/€10; doubles with bath 5000$/€25. June 16-Sept. 15 dorms 2500$/€18; doubles with bath 6000$/€30.

Pensão Guerreiro, R. Grande, 14 (☎258 82 20 99; fax 82 04 02), at the corner of Av. Combatentes da Grande Guerra. TV is free with a deposit. June-Sept. 15, Dec. 16-31, Apr. singles 3500$/€18; doubles 5500$/€28; triples 6000$/€30; quads 6500$/€33. Jan.-Mar., May, Sept. 16-Dec.15 1500$/€8 discount.

Pensão Dolce Vita, R. Poço, 44 (☎258 82 48 60), across from the tourist office. Rooms with baths surround a common TV lounge. June-Sept. singles 4000$/€20, doubles 6000$/€30; Oct.-May singles 2000$/€10, doubles 4000$/€20. AmEx/MC/V.

Pensão Vianense, Av. Conde da Carreira, 79 (☎258 82 31 18), across from the train station on a side street off the top of Av. Combatentes da Grande Guerra. 9 rooms, all without bath. June-Sept. singles 3000$/€15.00, doubles 6000$/€30.00; Oct.-May singles 2500$/€12.50, doubles 5000$/€25.00. AmEx/MC/V.

Residencial Viana Mar, Av. Combatentes da Grande Guerra, 215 (☎/fax 258 82 89 62). July-Aug. singles with shower 4500$/€22.50, with bath 5500$/€27.50, doubles 5000$/€25.00, with shower 6500$/€32.00, with bath 8500$/€42.50; Sept.-June singles with shower 3000$/€15.00, with bath 4000$/€20.00, doubles 4500$/ €22.50, with shower 5000$/€25.00, with bath 6000$/€30.00. AmEx/MC/V.

Camping: Orbitur (☎258 32 21 67; fax 32 19 46), at Praia do Cabedelo. Catch a TransCunha "Cabedelo" bus (6 per day, 7:35am-6:45pm, 150$/€0.75) from the bus station or from Lg. 5 de Outubro. A well-equipped campsite with free showers. Apr.-Sept. 600-680$/€3.00-3.40 per person, 470-960$/€2.34-4.80 per tent, 520-600$/€2.60-3 per car; Oct.-Nov. and Jan.-Mar. 400$/€2 per person, 310-550$/€1.60-2.75 per tent, 340$/€1.65 per car. Open Jan. 16-Nov. 30.

FOOD

People eat well in Viana do Castelo. The local specialties are *arroz de sarabulho* (rice cooked in blood and served with sausages and potatoes) and *bacalhau à Gil Eanes* (cod cooked with milk, potato, onion and garlic, and oil). Most budget restaurants lie on the small streets off Av. Combatentes da Grande Guerra. The **municipal market** is on R. Martim Velho, in front of Pr. Dona Maria II. (☎258 82 26 57. Open M-Sa 8am-3pm.) A **weekly market,** which attracts many of the same vendors as the market in Barcelos, is held on Fridays in Campo do Castelo, in front of the castle. For groceries, go to the **Pingo Doce** on R. de Aveiro (Open daily 9am-10pm).

Confeitaria Natário, R. Manuel Espregueira, 37 (☎258 82 23 76), just off Av. Combatentes da Grande Guerra. People line up at 10:30am to catch the meat and fish pastries hot out of the oven (120-200$/€0.60-1). Their delicious specialty are *bolas de berlim* (140$/€0.75), a sweet pastry made with fresh egg cream. Open W-M 9am-10pm.

Arcada, R. Grande, 34-36 (☎258 82 36 43). Take a right out of the tourist office and then the second right; it's on the left. This classic *casa de pasto* is the oldest in the historic center (founded in 1950). Entrées 1000-1700$/€5.00-8.50. Freshest fish Tu-Th. Open May-Sept. daily; Oct.-Apr. M-F, noon-3pm and 7-11pm. V.

Maria de Perre, R. de Viana, 118 (☎258 82 24 10), on the last side street to the left off Av. Combatentes heading toward the water. Live piano upstairs on weekends. Entrées 900-2100$/€4.50-10.50. Open Tu-Sa 10am-3pm and 7-11pm, Su 10am-3pm. AmEx/MC/V.

Restaurante Dolce Vita, R. Poço, 44 (☎258 82 48 60), at the corner of Pr. Erva, across the square from the tourist office. Excellent oval-shaped brick-oven pizzas (850-1050$/ €4.25-5.25). Portuguese dishes 1200-2000$/€6-10. Open daily noon-3pm and 7:30-10:30pm. AmEx/MC/V.

Ruela Bar, Av. Campo do Castelo, 11 (☎258 81 10 72), on the avenue below the castle, across from the large square. Popular with students at lunchtime for its *prato do dia* (600$/€3), burgers and sandwiches (160-480$/€0.80-2.40), combination plates (600-680$/€3-3.40). Open M-Sa 11:30am-3pm, 6pm-midnight.

SIGHTS

All roads in Viana do Castelo do not lead to the beach. Some run parallel. Even in a country famed for its impressive squares, Viana do Castelo's **Pr. da República** is remarkable. Its centerpiece is a 16th-century fountain encrusted with sculptures and crowned with a sphere bearing a cross of the Order of Christ. The small **Paço do Conselho** (1502), formerly the town hall, seals off the square to the east. Diagonally across the plaza, granite columns support the playful and flowery façade of the **Igreja da Misericórdia** (1598, rebuilt in 1714). Known for its *azulejo* interior, the **Monte de Santa Luzia,** overlooking the city, is crowned by magnificent Celtic ruins and the **Templo de Santa Luzia,** an early 20th-century neo-Byzantine church. Though the tempting funicular no longer runs, you can always reach the hilltop by walking up the long stairway beginning behind the train station. The view of Viana from the hill is fantastic, especially from the top of the church; take the elevator (130$/€0.65) up the tower, or climb the narrow stairway that leading to the **Zimbório** at the very top. For more great views of the harbor and ocean, visit the **Castelo de São Tiago da Barra,** built in 1589 (around a 14th century tower) by Felipe I of Spain. To reach the castle from the train station, take the 2nd right off Av. Combatentes onto R. General Luís do Rego and walk 5 blocks.

BEACHES

Viana do Castelo and the surrounding coast features excellent beaches that satisfy everyone from sunbathers to windsurfers. **Praia Norte,** at the end of Av. do Atlântico at the west end of town, is easy to reach and has swimming pools. **Praia da Argaçosa,** a small beach on Rio Lima next to the youth hostel and marina, fills with sunbathers in summer. Getting to the beaches on the other side of the river requires taking the TransCunha bus from Lg. 5 de Outubro across the bridge (6 per day, 7:35am-6:45pm, 150$/€0.75) to the **Praia do Cabedelo,** a great beach for windsurfing. A short train ride north of Viana leads to the **Praia do Bico** in Afife, frequented by surfers (10min.), and the large **Praia de Âncora** (15min.). Farther north are the beaches of **Moledo** and **Caminha.**

ENTERTAINMENT AND NIGHTLIFE

The cafés and bars around Pr. República fill with people in the evening. The most popular place in Viana is **Bar Glamour,** R. da Bandeira, 183, down the street from the plaza and away from the main avenue. The interior dance floor and garden feature live music on Thursdays, and Karaoke on Tuesdays. On weekends, the crowd is age 16-20 before 1am and mostly 25+ later. (☎258 82 29 63. Minimum consumption Su-Th 1 drink, Cover F-Sa 500$/2.50. Open daily 10pm-4am.) Viana's biggest festival of the year is the **Festa de Nossa Senhora da Agonia,** in August.

DAYTRIPS FROM VIANA DO CASTELO

CAMINHA

Trains come from Viana do Castelo to Caminha station (☎258 92 29 25), on Av. Saraiva de Carvalho, (30min., 8 per day 7:44am-8:30pm, 240$/€1.20). From Caminha to Vila Nova de Cerveira (10min., 8 per day 8:50am-8:39pm, 260$/€1.30).

While everyone else keeps going, slip off the train into Caminha (pop. 20,000) to enjoy the entrancing green hills, wide beaches, and peaceful medieval square. The village is slightly larger than its cousin, Vila Nova de Cerveria, five stops down the line. The latter may have a youth hostel, but Caminha has a **beach.** Put on your bathing suit, turn left on the riverside road, and keep going along the river about 1.5km to bask in the sun or be whipped by the wind (on brisk days). The **tourist office** is on R. Ricardo Joaquim Sousa; from the **train station**, walk straight ahead on Av. Manuel Xavier to the traffic circle, go down Tr. São João (diagonally to the left), and take the first left. (☎258 92 19 52. Open M-Sa 9:30am-12:30pm and 2:30-6pm.) Services include: **emergency** ☎112; the **police** (☎258 92 11 51); and the **health center** at Av. S. João de Deus, 20 (☎258 71 93 00).

VILA NOVA DE CERVEIRA

Trains come from Viana do Castelo (1hr., 8per day 7:44am-8:30pm, 310$/€1.55), via Caminha, and return from the Vila Nova station (☎251 79 62 65), on R. da Estação (40min.; M-Sa 8 per day 5:29am-8:27pm, Su 9 per day 5:29am-9:35pm; 310$/€1.55). Trains also go from Vila Nova to: Valença do Minho (20min., 8 per day 8:42am-8:49pm, 200$/€1) and Porto (2hr.; 7 per day 5:29am-8:27pm, Su 8 per day 5:29am-9:35pm; 1110$/€5.50). Three bus companies take the same route as the train—upstream to Valença and down the coast to Porto. Frequent Courense, AVIC, and A.V. Minho buses depart from the round Centralo de Camionagem building between the center of town and the train station on R. da Estação (☎251 79 43 14).

Just across the Rio Minho from Spain, Vila Nova de Cerveira (pop. 11,000) is a sleepy town with lush mountain scenery and a pleasant historic center. A walk along the walls of the 14th-century **castelo** (now the luxurious Pousada Dom Dinis) offers great views of the countryside. The town was named in honor of the deer that once populated the land. According to local legend, the deer community dwindled until only the Rei Veado (king deer) remained, who was eventually killed in a duel with a knight. You can hike up the winding road, to the **deer statue** (4km); from the main road just to the east of town, turn right and start climbing at the "Lovelhe Igreja" sign. A large **weekly market** is held every Saturday in Pr. da Galiza. Hordes of Spaniards come here from across the border to buy the inexpensive food and clothing. The **tourist office,** in Pr. Município, has maps and information about festivals, as well as short-term **luggage storage.** From the train station, turn left and go up R. da Estação past the right side of the round bus station; the office is in a yellow building at the end of the street, across the intersection. (☎251 70 80 23; fax 70 80 24. Open M-Sa 9:30am-12:30pm and 2-6pm, Su 9:30am-12:30pm.) Services include: **emergency** ☎112; the **police** on R. do Forte (☎251 79 51 13); and the **health center** at Lg. das Oliveiras (☎251 79 52 89). If you decide to stay, head to **Pousada de Juventude de Vila Nova de Cerveira (HI),** Largo 16 de Fevereiro, 21. (☎/fax 251 79 61 13. June 16-Sept. 15 dorms 1700$/€8.50; doubles 3800$/€19, with bath 4100$/€21; Sept. 16-June 15 dorms 1400$/€7; doubles 3200$/€16, with bath 3500$/€18.) Have lunch at **Restaurante A Forja,** R. 25 de Abril, 63. It serves affordable and generous half-portions. (☎251 79 53 11. Open Tu-Su 8am-midnight.)

VALENÇA DO MINHO

Valença do Minho is a stop on the Porto-Vigo train line; the station (☎251 82 41 55) is at Lg. da Estação. Service to: Vila Nova de Cerveira (20min., 9 per day 5:30am-9:10pm, 200$/€1); Viana do Castelo (1hr., 9 per day 5:30am-9:10pm, 410$/€2.05); Porto (4hr., 7 per day 8:25am-9:10pm, 1050$/€5.25); Vigo, Spain via Redondela, Spain (1hr., 2 per day 9:59am and 9pm, 1365$/€7).

Valença do Minho is more a stop-over than a daytrip; its preeminent monument, the 17th-century **fortaleza** (fortress), can be glimpsed while crossing the border into Spain. Crowds of Spanish tourists overrun the main commercial center and aptly titled Av. de Espanha. Away from the bustle, excellent views of the Rio Minho and the surrounding landscape can be had from the fortress as well as from the **Monte do Faro,** 4km up the road, overlooking the coastline and the Galician mountains. A **weekly market,** held every Wednesday, attracts plenty of shoppers.

To find the central **tourist office** from the train station, walk through the rotary and turn right on the main avenue, continuing until you reach the grassy hill of the fortress and Ave. de Espanha. The office gives out maps and brochures. (☎251 82 33 74. Open daily 9:30am-12:30pm and 2:30-6pm; Sept.-May 9:30am-12:30pm and 2-5:30pm). **Emergency** ☎ 112. **Police** (☎251 82 21 25) at Acesso à Fortaleza. A **health center** (☎251 82 43 15) is on R. Val Flores.

TRÁS-OS-MONTES

The country's roughest and most isolated region, Trás-Os-Montes ("behind the mountains") is a land of extremes. The frigid winters and the sweltering summers lead transmontanos to describe their seasons as "nine months of winter and three months of hell." The landscapes of Trás-Os-Montes are some of the most incredible in all of Iberia. The region's economy is based on agriculture and commerce, as there are practically no industries; consequently, the region is one of the poorest and least expensive of Portugal. Meanwhile, the trasmontanos themselves, though known for their toughness, are quite possibly the friendliest people in Portugal.

Trás-Os-Montes has long been home to Portugal's political and religious exiles. Dom Sancho I practically had to beg people to settle here after he incorporated it into Portugal in the 12th century. And it was here that the Jews chose to hide during the Inquisition. Today, it is the region's isolation, combined with its beauty and tranquility, that is its biggest appeal. With its conical stacks of hand-cut hay, old stone houses, and centuries-old festivals, it is one of the last outposts of traditional Portugal. The gastronomic specialities, served in generous portions, hint at the region's rustic character: *cozido à portuguesa* is made from sausages, pig parts, carrots, and turnips, and it takes some serious hikes to burn off the hearty *feijoada à trasmontana* (bean stew). But the most prized dish is probably *posta a mirandesa*, locally bred beef which locals claim is the most tender in the world.

BRAGANÇA ☎273

Wedged in a narrow valley between two steep slopes, Bragança (pop. 40,000), is a proud and steadfast wilderness outpost. While most visitors come for the clean air, blue skies, and olive-covered hillsides—or perhaps the massive 12th-century castle—it is the people of Bragança that really make it unique; its substantial distance from the rest of Portugal seems to have preserved in local residents an almost archaic sense of hospitality and festivity. Bragança is also the perfect base for exploring the **Parque Natural de Montesinho,** which extends north into Spain.

TRANSPORTATION

Trains: No train service. Nearest station is 1 hr. away **Mirandela,** (accessible by bus).

Buses: The bus station (commonly known as the old train station) is at the top of Av. João da Cruz. **Rodonorte** (☎273 30 01 83) buses go to: **Porto** via **Mirandela** and **Vila Real** (5hr., 4-6 per day 6am-5pm, 1540$/€77); **Lisbon** (8hr., 3 per day 6-11am, 2780$/€14). **Rede Expressos** (☎273 33 18 26) buses go to: **Coimbra** (6hr.; M-F 6 per day, Sa 5 per day 6am-9:30pm; 1900$/€9); **Lisbon** (8hr.; M-F 8 per day, Sa-Su 6 per day 6am-9:30pm; 2700$/€14); **Porto** (5hr.; M-F 8 per day, Sa-Su 6 per day 6am-11pm; 1600$/€8); **Vila Real** (2hr.; M-F 6 per day, Sa-Su 3 per day 2-7pm; 1350$/€6.75). **Internorte** runs to **Braga** (5hr., 2 per day 4:15pm and 1:15am, 1700$/€8.50); **Zamora, Spain** (2½hr.; M-Sa 2pm, Su 5:45pm; 2150$/€11).

Taxis: (☎273 32 21 38). Cabs congregate near the post office and old train station.

ORIENTATION AND PRACTICAL INFORMATION

The bus station is at the top of **Avenida João da Cruz;** from the bottom of this avenue, downward-sloping R. Almirante Reis leads to budget pensões and the **Praça da Sé** at the heart of the old town. **Avenida Sá Carneiro**, wide and commercial, leads to the local Instituto Polite'cnico. To reach the **fortress,** situated on a hill west of Pr. Sé, take **Rua Combatentes da Grande Guerra** from Pr. Sé, walk uphill, and enter through the opening in the stone walls.

Tourist Office: (☎273 38 12 73; fax 30 42 98), Av. Cidade de Zamora. With your back to the bus station's front entrance, cross Av. João da Cruz and take a right, then take the next left onto R. S. Anto'nio. Follow this street, keeping the cemetery on your right, then take a right at the traffic circle and continue down R. D. Abi'lio das Neves; the office will be on the corner on the right. Short-term **luggage storage.** Open May-Sept. M-F 9am-7pm, Sa 9am-12:30pm and 2-5pm, Su 9am-1pm; Oct.-Apr. M-F 9am-12:30pm and 2pm-5pm, Sa 10am-12:30pm.

Currency Exchange: Banco Nacional Ultramarino, Av. João da Cruz, 2-6 (☎273 33 12 65), next to the post office has **ATMs.** Open M-F 8:30am-3pm, **San Vitur,** run by Rede Expressos with a branch at the bus station and a main office on Av. Joã da Cruz, also does exchange (☎273 33 18 26).

English Bookstore: Livraría Ma'rio Péricles, R. Combatentes da Grande Guerra, 180 (☎273 32 25 49) A few doors down from Restaurante Poças. Open M-F 9:30am-12pm and 2-7pm, Sa 9:30am-1pm. AmEx/MC/V.

Emergency: ☎112. **Police:** R. Dr. Manuel Bento (☎273 30 34 00), by the town hall.

Hospital: Hospital Distrital de Bragança ☎273 31 08 00, Av. Abade de Baçal, before the stadium on the road to Vinhais.

Post Office: (☎273 31 00 71), at the corner of R. Almirante Reis and R. 5 de Outubro, at the end of Av. João da Cruz. Open M-F 9am-5pm. **Postal Code:** 5300.

ACCOMMODATIONS AND CAMPING

Accommodations in Braganc;a are so cheap that the youth hostel is more for HI groupies than for budget travelers. Plenty of cheap pensões and residenciales line Pr. da Sé and R. Almirante Reis.

Pousada de Juventude—Bragança, Forte de São João de Deus (☎273 30 46 00; fax 32 61 36), off Av. 22 de Maio. Somewhat removed from the center of town. 24 dorms with 4 beds each. Kitchen, playroom, and sitting room. Laundry facilities. Check-in after 6pm. Sept. 16-June 15 dorms 2000$/€10; doubles with bath 5000$/€25. June 16-Sept. 15 dorms 2500$/€13; doubles with bath 6000$/€30. MC/V.

Pensão Poças, R. Combatentes da Grande Guerra, 200 (☎273 33 14 28 or 273 33 12 16). From the bus station, walk down Av. João da Cruz and pass to the left of the "Correios" building onto R. Almirante Reis, then continue down the street and through the plaza and bear right; it's just ahead on the left, with the reception in the restaurant. Clean common baths with good showers. Includes breakfast, 8:30-11am. Singles with or without bath 2000$/€10; doubles 4000$/€20; triples 6000$/€30. AmEx/MC/V.

Camping: Parque de Campismo Municipal do Sabor (☎273 33 15 35), 6km from town on the edge of the Parque Natural de Montesinho, on the road to Portelo (N103-7)park. The #7 STUB bus (yellow and blue) toward Meixedo goes by the campground, leaving from the Caixa Geral de Depósitos on Av. João da Cruz, (10min., M-F 12:44pm and 6pm, also 2:10pm from Sept.-June; Sa 1:35pm; 130$/€0.65). If you choose to hike, be careful—roads are narrow and curvy. Reception 8am-midnight. Open May-Oct. Electricity 200$/€1. 300$/€1.50 per person and per car, 300-450$/€1.50-2.25 per tent.

Parque de Campismo Cêpo Verde (☎273 99 93 71), in Gondesende, 8km out on the road to Vinhais (N103). Swimming pool 250$/€1.25. Electricity 275$/€1.40. 500$/€2.50 per person, 300-500$/€1.50-2.50 per tent, 300$/€1.50 per car.

FOOD

The region is celebrated for its *presunto* (cured ham) and *salsichão* (sausages), as well as the local delicacy, *alheiradas*, sausages made with bread and various meats (see **That Can't be Kosher,** p. 657). You can find these at **Supermercado Bem Servir,** R. Abílio Beça, 120, below Pr. da Sé (open M-F 8:30am-7pm, Sa 8:30am-1pm). Restaurants in Bragança tend to serve generous quantities of food; half-portions are almost always enough for one person. Be prepared for lots of meat.

Restaurante Poças, R. Combateantes da Grande Guerra, 200 (☎273 33 14 28), off Pr. da Sé. One of the best places to try the local specialties. Entrées 1000-1800$/€5-9. Open 8am-midnight; serves meals noon-3pm and 7-10:30pm. AmEx/MC/V.

Restaurante Dom Fernando, R. Rainha D. Maria II, 197 (☎273 32 62 73), in the Cidadela (inside the castle walls), upstairs above the bar. Given its location, this restaurant should be more touristy, more expensive, and less good. Fortunately, it's not. Entrées 900-1500$/€4.50-7.50. *Menú* (1800$/€6). Open June-Sept. daily, Oct.-May F-W, 9am-10pm. Sometimes stays open later in summer.

O Bicas, Lg. de Tombeirinho, 13 (☎963 08 82 01), up from Pr. da Se'. Ask Toni to make you a meaty *francesinha* (900$/€4.50) A good place to go for some petiscos (small plates, 350-900$/€1.75-4.50). Popular during afternoon snacktime (5-7pm) but serves food all day. Open M-Sa 8am-2am.

SIGHTS

Uphill from Prac;a da Se' is the old town and its 12th century brooding **castelo;** the castle's tower is from the 15th century. The castle is encircled by massive restored walls that provide phenomenal views of Bragança and Spain. Inside the walls, the castle's **Museu Militar** has a wide range of odd military paraphernalia, from medieval swords to a World War I machine gun to African art collected by Portuguese soldiers. (Open F-W 9-11:45am and 2-4:45pm. 250$/€1.25. Free Su mornings.) The venerable **pelourinho** (pillory) in the square behind the castle bears a coat of arms at the base of the whipping post is a granite pig, a vestige of pagan ideology and the place where sinners and criminals were bound during the Middle Ages. The **Domus Municipalis,** behind the church across the square from the castle, once served as the city's municipal meeting house. Today, it is the only existing example of Roman civil architecture on the Iberian Peninsula.

ENTERTAINMENT AND NIGHTLIFE

The most important festival in Braganc;a is the **Festa de Nossa Senhora das Grac;as,** celebrated annually in mid-August. The biggest day is August 22nd; the holiday is marked with fireworks on the night of the 21st. During the **Festa do Estudante,** the town's *tunas* (student music groups) gather to play for the entire town. Braganc;a may be isolated and little-touristed, but locals and students from the polytechnic institute ensure good nightlife in the city. A popular student hangout, especially after 1am on weekends, is **Zona+,** Av. Sa' Carneiro, 2A, downstairs, below Confeitaria Veneza with the door to the right. (☎933 37 63 95. Open M-Sa 10pm-3am.) A classier place is **Central Pub,** R. do Poço, 18, above Pr. da Se', on a cross street between R. Almirante Reis and R. 5 de Outubro. The red glow from the sign at the entrance leads to two distinct spaces: an elegant upstairs pub that plays 60's music and rotates art exhibitions every 3 weeks, and a disco/bar downstairs: a sign on the wall declares "Beer is my friend." (☎273 33 13 09. Open daily 1pm-3pm.)

DAYTRIP FROM BRAGANÇA

PARQUE NATURAL DE MONTESINHO

For directions, maps, brochures and advice on visiting the natural park, inquire at the ***information office*** *in Bragança, R. Co'nego Albano Falcão, 5 (in Bairro Salvador Nunes Teixeira). Walk downhill from the tourist office on Av. Cidade de Zamora, take the first left on a paved street and the first left again; it's at the end of the street on the right. Park trails are unmarked, but the office has maps and can help plan hikes. (☎273 38 14 44; fax 38 11 79. Open M-F 9am-12:30pm and 2-5:30pm.) There is no camping allowed in the park, but the info office rents* ***Casas Abrigos*** *(traditional houses, also called Casas de Naturaeza) for reasonable prices. (☎273 38 12 34 or 38 14 44). Doubles 5000-7500$/€25-38; quads 10,000$/€50.) Getting to the park can be complicated, as bus service is quite limited; indeed, the schedules almost seem to have been designed in such a way as to thwart day-trippers.* ***Buses*** *to the border village of Rio de Onor leave from Braganc;a on Av. João da Cruz, in front of Banco Nacional Ultramarino near Pr. da Se' (Sept.-June daily, and the 3rd, 12th, and 21st of summer months, at 2:09pm; return bus runs all year Su-F at 6:50pm). Hitching a ride, though not recommended by Let's Go, is not difficult and is often the only way to visit the park.*

One of the largest protected areas in Portugal, the **Parque Natural de Montesinho** covers 290 square miles between Bragança and the Spanish border. The park consists of 88 traditional *aldeias* (villages) inhabited by 8800 mostly elderly residents; the population is diminishing as young people move out, but a program aims to keep people there and maintain the traditional life of the area. Rich with tradition, these villages preserve age-old communal customs and enact ancient rituals, from the carving of pigs, to lively festivals such as the Festa dos Rapazes (see **Gotcha, Girl!** p. 655). Some of the villages can be reached in a day's hike or bike ride, but visitors with more time often design multi-day hikes between villages.

The old mountain paths linking the park's villages lead through rolling woodlands of (oak, chestnut, pine, and cherry trees. Pombais Pombales, (pigeon lofts) dot the landscape, and the land is home to many rare and endangered species including the) Iberian wolf, royal eagle, and black stork, among others). The area's rivers are also replete with fish; trout fishing is one of the main local livelihoods and is nearly as popular among park visitors as are hiking and horseback riding. The riverbanks are ideal spots for picnics. If you have only one day to visit the park, the most worthwhile trip is to **Rio de Onor,** a village near the northeast corner, on the border with Spain. Here the Portuguese and Spanish have lived together for centuries, intermarrying and even speaking their own hybrid dialect, rionorés. A subtle stone post, with a "P" for "Portugal" carved into one side and an "E" for "España" on the other, marks the border. Villagers cross into Spain for groceries and back into Portugal for coffee at **Cervejaria Preto,** a bar that's not hard to find, as it's the only one in town. You can eat on the stone tables overlooking the river.

GOTCHA, GIRL! The Festa dos Rapazes, an ancient ritual enacted in the villages of the Parque Natural de Montesinho, is certainly not lacking for erotic innuendo. The festival, which coincides with the winter solstice, has regional variations but the general idea is the same everywhere. On December 26th or January 6th, the single young men of the villages dress up as *caretos*, wearing shaggy colored suits and diabolic painted masks, and proceed to prowl around in groups in search of lone females. Upon finding a *rapariga*, they surround her and one of the caretos grabs and shakes her, knocking the bells attached to his belt against her hips (the verb is *chocalhar*). According to traditional rules, the girl, once grabbed, is not permitted to escape; the only way for her to get away is to let it happen. The *festa* continues to this day, as shy young men take advantage of the event to meet and flirt with local girls.

VILA REAL ☎259

Vila Real (pop. 25,000) presides over the edge of the gorges of the Corgo and Cabril Rivers in the foothills of the Serra do Marão. The wonderfully untouristed town center is surrounded by new neighborhoods reaching into the hills, a lively main street, and a few cafés. As the principal commercial center for the southern farms and villages of Trás-Os-Montes, Vila Real is a good point of departure for excursions into the fields and slopes of the Serra do Alvão and Serra do Marão.

TRANSPORTATION

Trains: (☎259 32 21 93), Av. 5 de Outubro. To get to Vila Real's center, walk up Av. 5 de Outubro over the iron bridge onto R. Miguel Bombarda and turn left on R. Roque da Silveira. Continue to bear left until Av. 1 de Maio. Trains take longer than buses and require transfers at Régua. To **Porto** (4½hr., 5 per day 7:20am-7:45pm, 1080$/€5).

Buses: Rodonorte (☎259 34 07 10), R. D. Pedro de Castro, on the square directly uphill from the tourist office. To: **Amarante** (45min.; M-F 13 per day 6:25am-8:20pm, Sa 8 per day 8am-7pm, Su 8 per day 8am-10:30pm; 850$/€4.25); **Bragança** (2hr.; 5-9 per day, 8:45am-11pm; 1450$/€7.25); **Guimarães** (1.5hr., M-W 4 per day 6:25am-5:20pm, Th-F 5 per day 6:25am-7pm, Sa 10am, Su 3 per day 4:30-7pm, 1100$/

€5.50); **Lisbon** (6.5hr.; M-F 3 per day 8am, 1:10pm, 5:20pm; Sa 3 per day 9:30am, 1:10pm, 5:20pm; Su 5 per day 9:30am-10:40pm; 2600$/€13); **Porto** (1.75hr.; 8-13 per day, M-F 6:25am-8:20pm, Sa 8am-7pm, Su 8am-10:30pm; 1050$/€5.25). **Ruicar,** R. Gonçalo Cristóvão, 16 (☎259 32 47 61), up the street across from Rodonorte, sells tickets for Rede Expressos, which stop in front of Rodonorte. Less service and extremely complicated schedules. Most useful for late-night weekend buses.

Taxis: Radiotáxis (☎259 37 31 38). Cabs cluster along Av. Carvalho Araújo.

ORIENTATION AND PRACTICAL INFORMATION

Vila Real's old neighborhood is centered around **Avenida Carvalho Araújo,** a broad tree-lined avenue that runs downhill from the bus station to the Câmara Municipal. Most of the town's cafés, shops and hostels are here. The bus stops at Rodonorte Station on **Rua Don Pedro de Castro;** go right upon exiting to get to the main avenue.

Tourist Office: Av. Carvalho Araújo, 94 (☎259 32 28 19; fax 32 17 12), to the right and downhill from the bus station, across the street. English-speaking staff. Also short-term **luggage storage.** Open June-Sept. M-F 9:30am-7pm, Sa-Su 9:30am-12:30pm and 2-6pm; Apr.-May M-F 9:30am-12:30pm and 2-7pm, Sa 10am-12:30pm and 2-5pm; Oct.-Mar. M-F 9:30am-12:30pm and 2-5pm, Sa 10am-12:30pm and 2-4:30pm.

Currency Exchange: Realvitur, Largo Pioledo, 2 (☎259 34 08 00), 4 blocks uphill from the tourist office and to the right. Open M-F 9am-7pm, Sa 9am-1pm. **ATMs,** Av. Carvalho Araújo, 84, at Banco Pinto and Sotto Mayor, next to the tourist office.

Emergency: ☎112. **Police:** Lg. Condes de Amarante (☎259 33 02 40), 1 block over from Av. Carvalho Araújo.

Medical Services: Hospital: Distrital de Vila Real (☎259 30 05 00), north of town in Lordelo. More convenient is the **Centro de Saúde** (☎259 32 40 95), on R. Dr. Manuel Cardona, by the youth hostel.

Post Office: (☎259 33 03 00), Av. Carvalho Araújo, across the street and to the right of the tourist office. Open M-F 8:30am-6pm, Sa 9am-12:30pm. **Postal Code:** 5000.

ACCOMMODATIONS AND CAMPING

Rooms in Vila Real are cheap and plentiful, making the town a convenient place to stay either as a stop-over or as a base for exploring the region. Several cafés along Av. Carvalho Araújo advertise rooms.

Pousada da Juventude da Vila Real, R. Dr. Manuel Cardona (☎259 37 31 93; fax 37 33 93; vilareal@movijovem.pt), just across the river from the town center. From the bus station, cross the street and follow the street to the right 2 blocks to Lg. Pioledo. Take a right onto Rampa do Calvario and then a left on Av. Almeida Lucena, which becomes R. Dr. Manuel Cardona after the intersection with the large avenue. The youth hostel is on the left; head down the driveway, around to the back, and up the stairs. All rooms have terraces. TV room, patio, and kitchen. Breakfast included. Reception 8am-noon and 6pm-midnight. June 16-Sept. 14 dorms 1900$/€9.50; 4 doubles with bath 4600$/€23. Sept. 16-June 15 dorms 1500$/€7.50; doubles with bath 3800$/€19.

Residencial São Domingos, Trav. de São Domingos, 33 (☎259 32 20 39), the last of three hostels on a side street off Av. Carvalho Araújo, to the right next to the cathedral. Old rooms, but all (except one) with private bath, TV, and phone. Large TV room with couches. June-Sept. singles 2500$/€13, doubles 4500$/€23, triples 6000$/€30. Oct.-May singles 2000$/€10, doubles 4000$/€20, triples 5000$/€25. **Residencial Mondego,** Trav. de São Domingos, 11 (☎259 32 30 97), just up the street, has the same owners and prices, and uses the reception desk at São Domingos.

Camping: Parque de Campismo Municipal de Vila Real (☎259 32 47 24), R. Dr. Manuel Cardona, across the river and past the youth hostel, at the end of the street on the right. 550$/€2.75 per person, 350$/€1.75 per tent and per car. Free showers. Reception daily June-Aug. 8am-11pm; Sept.-May 8:30am-5pm. Open Jan. 16-Dec. 15.

FOOD

Eating well in Vila Real is easy and inexpensive. There are plenty of options, with lots of good restaurants and cafés located along the central streets. The main avenue (Av. Carvalho Araújo), and the parallel R. Anto'nio de Azevedo are good places to look; restaurants on R. Teixeira de Sousa tend to be more touristy, but there are some cheaper ones there as well. The cafés along Av. Carvalho Araújo and in the square at the bottom of the avenue fill with people at night. The **Mercado da Praça,** R. D. Maria das Chaves, 75, hosts a large regional market twice a week (Tu and F 8am-noon) and a regular market more frequently (M-Sa 8am-7pm).

Churrasqueira Real, R. Teixeira Sousa, 14 (☎259 32 20 78), midway up the street. Basic decor; the focus here is on grilled meat, and they do it right. Entrées 500-1700$/€2.50-8.50, served with rice, fries, and salad. Open Tu-Su 9am-11pm; serves meals noon-2pm and 7-9:30pm. Another branch is located at R. D. Pedro Castro, 15.

Pizzaria Topolino, Pr. Luis de Camões, 2 (☎259 32 77 01), down R. Anto'nio de Azevedo behind the tourist office. Excellent pizzas (800-1500$/€7.50) and pastas (1100-1500$/€5.50-7.50). Open daily noon-3pm and 7-11pm. AmEx/MC/V.

Restaurante Museu dos Presuntos, Av. Cidade de Orense, 43 (☎259 32 60 17), at R. D. Afonso III and R. Morgado de Mateus. From the tourist office, cross Av. Carvalho Arau'jo, take a right, and continue up R. D. Pedro de Castro; after passing the Rodonorte station, bear right at the fork onto R. D. Pedro de Menezes and then take a right onto R. D. Afonso III, and it will be at the end of the street across the intersection. This "ham museum" is a bit of a hike from the town center, but it's worth it for the *presunto* combinations. Open W-Th and Sa-M 12:30-2:30pm and 7-9:30pm, F 7-9:30pm only.

THAT CAN'T BE KOSHER The *alheira* sausage, a specialty of the Tra's-Os-Montes region, was invented by escaping Jews as part of an ingenious plan to save themselves from the Spanish Inquisition. At the time, all Portuguese households had pork sausages hanging from the kitchen ceiling. To blend in without using pork, Jews began to make look-alike sausages filled with chicken, turkey, duck, and pigeon. Officers of the Spanish Inquisition who saw the sausages concluded that the residents could not possibly be Jews, and continued on their way. Today, *alheiras* have been adopted by Christians and are made with pork, among other ingredients.

SIGHTS AND EXCURSIONS

Vila Real makes a good base for seeing the nearby natural parks, but the churches in town are worth visiting before you go (and serve as a fine escape from the sun as well). The 15th-century **sé** (cathedral), with its simple interior divided by thick, arched columns, looms at the lower end of Av. Carvalho Araújo. (Opens only for mass M-F 7:30am and 6:30pm, Sa-Su 9am, noon, and 6pm) Two blocks east of the cathedral, at the end of R. Central, the **Capela Nova** (New Chapel) blushes behind a floral façade. (Open daily 8:30am-6pm. Free.) One block up R. 31 de Janeiro, in Largo São Pedro, the **Igreja de São Pedro** is resplendent with 17th-century azulejos. (Open daily 9am-5pm. Free.) At the corner of R. Teixeira de Sousa and Av. 1 de Maio is the 16th century **Igreja da Miserico'rdia**, recently reopened after years of renovations. (Open daily 9am-5pm. Free.) The **Parque Natural do Alvão** is, a protected area reaching to the edge of the mountainous Serra country 15km north of Vila Real. For maps and hiking info, visit the **park information office,** Lg. dos Freitas, at the bottom of Av. Carvalho Arau'jo behind the Cámara Municipal. (☎259 30 28 30; fax 30 28 31. Open M-F 9am-12:30pm and 2-5:30pm.)

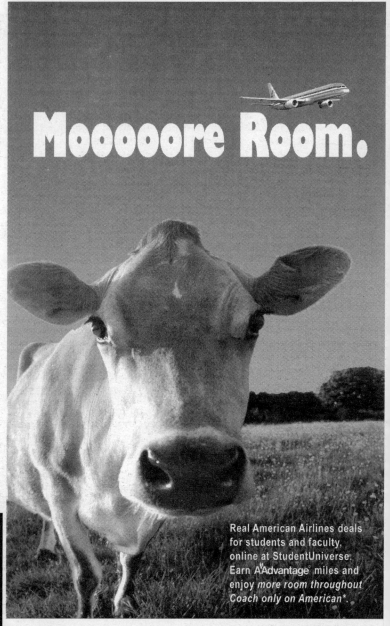

Mooooore Room.

Real American Airlines deals for students and faculty, online at StudentUniverse. Earn AAdvantage miles and enjoy *more room throughout Coach only on American**.

StudentUniverse.com

featuring AmericanAirlines

800.272.9676

RESTRICTIONS: A portion of or all travel may be on American Eagle, American's regional airline affiliate. American Airlines, American Eagle and AAdvantage are marks of American Airlines, Inc. American Airlines reserves the right to change AAdvantage program rules, regulations, travel awards and special offers at any time without notice, and to end the AAdvantage program with six months notice. American Airlines is not responsible for products or services by other participating companies. *Only American has removed rows of seats throughout Coach to provide more room for more Coach passengers than any other airline. Now available on all two-class aircraft; three-class aircraft reconfiguration in progress; not available on American Eagle.

NORTHERN PORTUGAL

MOROCCO المغرب

DIRHAMS

US $1= 10.9DH	1DH=US $0.09
CDN $1= 7.4DH	1DH=CDN $0.14
EUR 1= 9.6DH	1DH=EUR 0.1
UK £1= 15.8DH	1DH=UK £0.06
IR £1= 12.2DH	1DH=IR £0.08
AUS $1= 6.3DH	1DH=AUS $0.16
NZ $1= 4.6DH	1DH=NZ $0.22
SAR 1= 1.6DH	1DH=SAR 0.64
SP 1PTA= 0.06DH	1DH=SP 17.3PTAS
POR 1$= 0.05DH	1DH= POR 20.8$

Country Code: 212. **International dialing prefix:** 00.

A MOROCCAN INTRODUCTION

When the weather is clear, it is quite easy to see across the Straight of Gibraltar from the hills of southernmost Andalucía. Even more alluring, the faint ridges of the Atlas Mountains are visible along the horizon. From this perspective, Morocco easily fulfills its story-tale role as the gateway to the Orient. On the ground, things are a little bit different—Morocco has much more to offer than stories of smoking hash with Paul Bowles and smoking yet more hash with Jimi Hendrix. After even a short stay in Andalucía, or much else of the Iberia, the heavy influence of North Africa pekes the curiosity of most budget travelers; the close proximity of the two continents has served for centuries as trading route for language, religion, graceful Arab archwork, and the occasional imperial dynasty. Many visitors to Spain wish to see something of the other half of this exchange. Fortunately, the ease of getting to Morocco makes this curiosity worth cashing in on.

Morocco is not included in this guide with the same type of comprehensive coverage as the Iberian countries receive, but rather to provide a guide for a brief visit to the country during more extensive travel in Spain and Portugal. Covering main cities, this section will guide you through the most accessible of sights and towns. So, as the draw of Morocco pulls you south through Andalucía, give in to Morocco and skim across the Straight (see **Ferries and Hydrofoils** p. 668).

LIFE AND TIMES

Morocco has carved its identity out of a host of influences: African, European, and the Middle Eastern. It combines Arab culture and religion, African history and landscape, European influences and ties, and languages of all three. At the same time, the country teeters between the past and present as both a civilization descended from nomads and a modern nation that has struggled against imperial powers for its sovereignty.

HISTORY AND POLITICS

PRE-ISLAMIC. Archaeological evidence along Morocco's Atlantic coast suggests that regions of the country have been settled for anywhere in the spectrum 100,000 to 1,000,000 years. The **Berber** people arrived between 4000 and 2000 BC; evidence

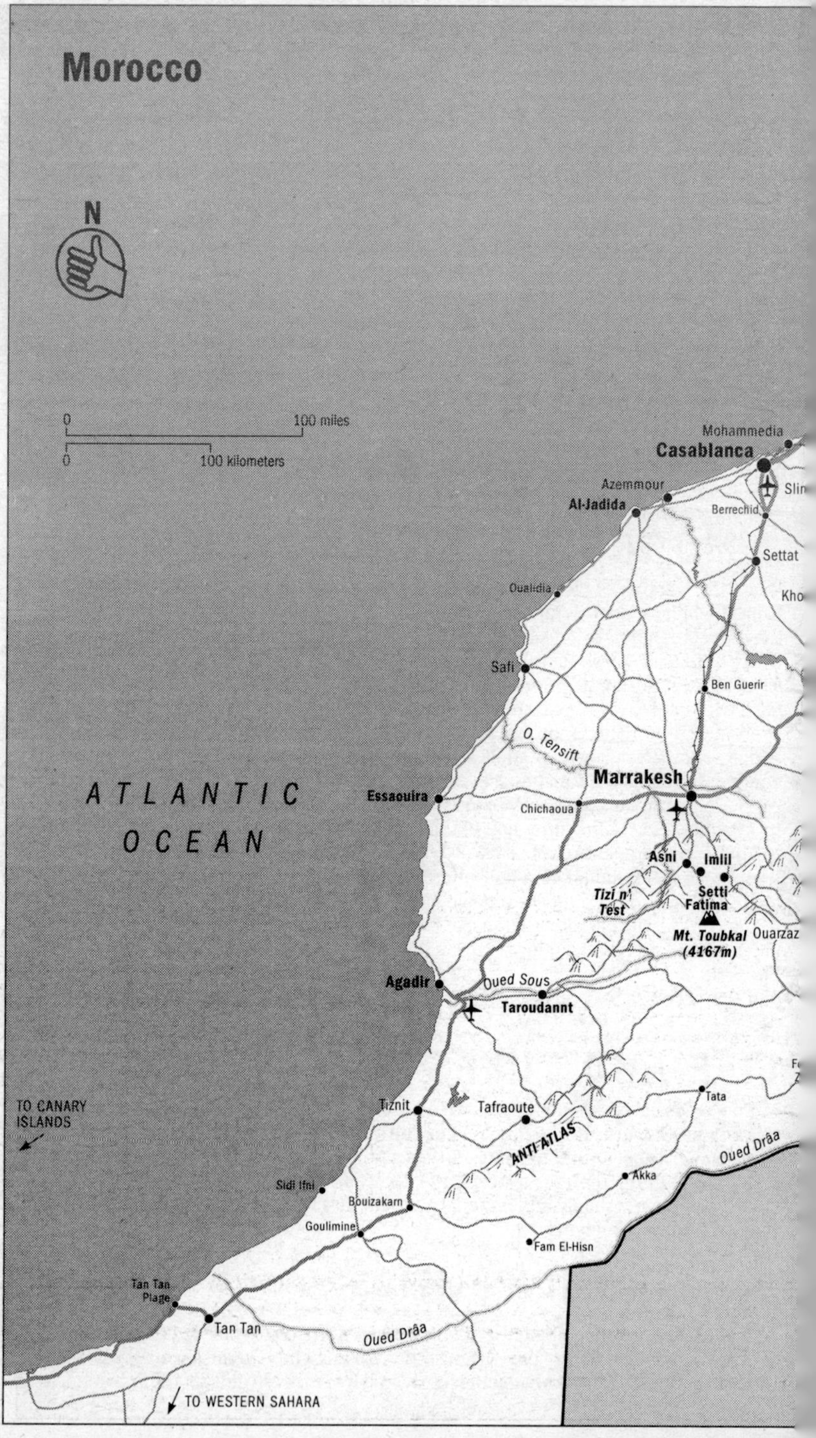

Morocco

N

0 100 miles
0 100 kilometers

Mohammedia
Casablanca
Azemmour
Al-Jadida
Berrechid
Slin
Settat
Kho
Oualidia
Safi
Ben Guerir
O. Tensift
Marrakesh
ATLANTIC OCEAN
Essaouira
Chichaoua
Asni
Imlil
Tizi n' Test
Setti Fatima
Mt. Toubkal (4167m)
Ouarzaz
Agadir
Oued Sous
Taroudannt
F
Z
Tata
TO CANARY ISLANDS
Tiznit
Tafraoute
ANTI-ATLAS
Oued Drâa
Akka
Sidi Ifni
Bouizakarn
Goulimine
Fam El-Hisn
Tan Tan Plage
Tan Tan
Oued Drâa
TO WESTERN SAHARA

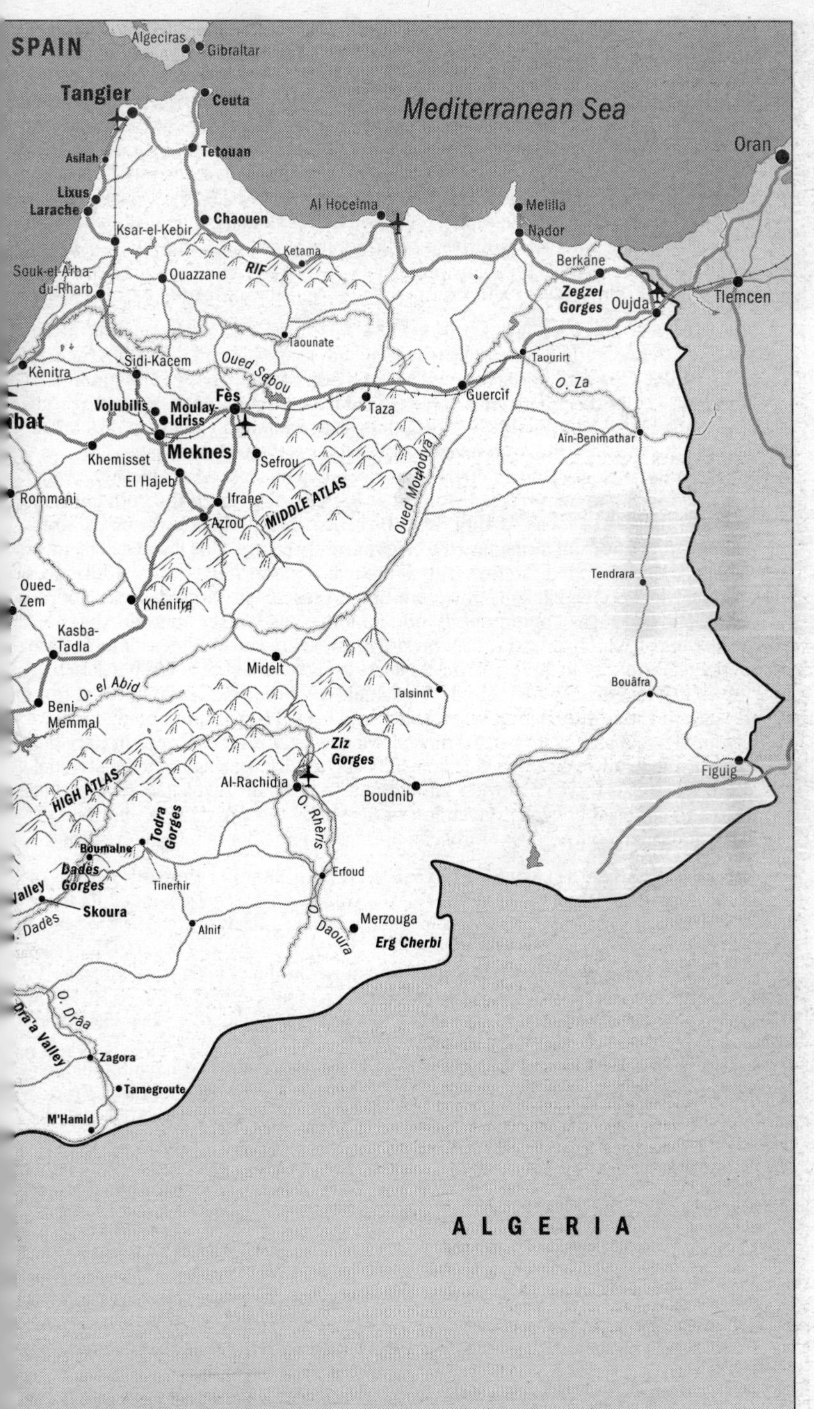
SPAIN
Algeciras
Gibraltar
Tangier
Ceuta
Mediterranean Sea
Oran
Asilah
Tetouan
Lixus
Larache
Al Hoceima
Melilla
Chaouen
Nador
Ksar-el-Kebir
Ketama
Berkane
Souk-el-Arba-du-Rharb
Ouazzane
RIF
Zegzel Gorges
Oujda
Tlemcen
Taounate
Taourirt
Kènitra
Sidi-Kacem
Oued Sebou
O. Za
Guercif
Fès
Taza
Volubilis
Moulay-Idriss
Aïn-Benimathar
Meknes
Sefrou
Khemisset
El Hajeb
MIDDLE ATLAS
Oued Moulouya
Rommani
Ifrane
Azrou
Tendrara
Oued-Zem
Khénifra
Kasba-Tadla
Midelt
Bouâfra
O. el Abid
Talsinnt
Beni-Memmal
Ziz Gorges
Figuig
HIGH ATLAS
Al-Rachidia
Boudnib
O. Rhèris
Todra Gorges
Boumalne
Dadès Gorges
Tinerhir
Erfoud
Skoura
O. Dadès
Merzouga
Alnif
O. Daoura
Erg Cherbi
O. Drâa
Drâ'a Valley
Zagora
Tamegroute
M'Hamid
ALGERIA

of the use of early Berber tools can still be found in rock carvings scattered throughout the High Atlas Mountains. Though the **Phoenicians** began to explore the area in the 12th century BC and developed colonies along the coast, they exerted little control or influence over the area. The **Romans** sacked Carthage, near modern Tunis in Tunisia, and in 146 BC brought about a major change in the history of Morocco. Rome became dependent on North Africa's agricultural supply and the Romans created the province of Mauritania Tingitana in what is now Morocco. When the *Pax Romana* deteriorated in the 4th century AD, the Romans abandoned Morocco. By 420 the country was ruled by the Vandals, followed by a period of brief **Byzantine** rule. Each of these civilizations faced similar problems—it was impossible to exert any control over the land without a reliable overland route. As a result, the majority of the country remained unexplored for centuries.

THE RISE AND FALL OF ISLAM (669-1554 AD). Morocco achieved stability in the late 7th and early 8th century when Muslim armies invaded North Africa. In 669 AD, **Uqba bin Nafi al-Fihri** spread the religion of the prophet Muhammad to Morocco. The Berbers could not hold off the Muslim troops, so instead of fighting they made peace with the leader Musa ibn Nusayr and many converted to Islam. This set the stage for the Arab invasion of Spain less than 50 years later.

Arab rule was short-lived in Morocco, ending in 740 AD. Although Arabs remained in the Maghreb, they would not regain power until the 20th century. Instead, a series of local Muslim dynasties rose up to take control of the area, claiming descent from Muhammad to legitimize their rule. **Idris ibn Abdullah,** after fleeing Arabia, founded the first truly Moroccan state in 789 AD. When Idris was poisoned in 791 AD, his son's kingdom did not last. Over the next few hundred years, Morocco was conquered by one minor dynasty after another, the most important of which was the **Almoravid Dynasty** from the Western Sahara, that founded Marrakesh in 1062, and the **Almohad Dynasty,** that conquered it in 1160.

A golden age during the reign of the **Marinid** (a Berber dynasty that ruled from the 13th to 15th centuries) and then **Wattasid** rule (1244-1554) promoted a cultural and intellectual boom and tied Morocco to Spain. As Muslim influence in Christian Iberia waned, however, the Spanish became aggressive. During the Spanish Inquisition in 1492, a wave of Jewish immigrants from Spain fled to Morocco when forced to choose between conversion or death. By the early 1500s, the Iberians had established control over Moroccan ports and a number of inland territories.

THE EUROPEAN CONTENDERS (1415-1912). The **Saadis** reunited Morocco. Under **Ahmed al-Mansour**—a.k.a. Ahmed the Gilded—Morocco expanded its trade in Timbuktu and parts of the Sudan. When the **Alawite dynasty** overthrew the Saadis in 1659, they took over Marrakesh and Fez. The Alawite dynasty rules to this day.

Morocco was one of the first African countries to be colonized by Europe. In 1415, Portugal seized Sebta (Ceuta) and began erecting forts along the coast. Spain took possession of Melilla in 1497; it is still a Spanish enclave. The Saadians were able to push the Iberians back for several centuries, ruling the rest of the country from Marrakesh and remaining in power until the 17th century. England took possession of Tangier in 1662 and Spain controlled the northern coast. France invaded after winning the battle of Isly in 1844; but their major stroke of luck did not come until the death of Sultan Hassan in 1893 and the ascension of his 13-year-old son Abd al-Aziz to the throne. Under the **Treaty of Fez,** March 30th, 1912, Morocco became a protectorate of France. The northernmost part of the country fell to the Spanish, while Tangier was governed by a European council.

STRUGGLE FOR INDEPENDENCE (1921-1977). In 1921, **Abd al-Krim,** now considered the founder of modern Morocco, organized a rebel army that fought Spain over control of the Rif Country. Rifian tribes managed to get as far as Fez before a combined French and Spanish army drove them out in 1927.

Morocco's nationalist movement began in 1944 with the founding of the Independence Party, **Istiqlal;** by 1947 it had gained the support of the Moroccan Sultan, **Moulay Muhammad V.** The French deported nationalist leaders and exiled Muhammad in 1953. The ensuing popular unrest, combined with revolt in Algeria, forced the French to concede. Muhammad was returned to the throne on November 18, 1955 and signed a treaty of independence for French Morocco on March 2, 1956. The independence of most of Spanish Morocco followed one month later.

Muhammad V's successor, **King Hassan II,** came to the throne in 1961 and introduced a constitution favoring monarchists. This was heavily protested by the opposition party UNFP; in 1963, ten of UNFP's leaders, including **Ben Barka,** were implicated in a plot to overthrow the monarchy and sentenced to death. In 1965, King Hassan declared a national **state of emergency,** snagging direct control of executive and legislative powers. Hassan's 1970 constitution ended the emergency and restored limited parliamentary government, but two military coups and governmental divisions delayed democratic parliamentary elections until 1977.

Perhaps the most significant of Hassan's political triumphs was the **Green March** in 1975. The Spanish, who had long since controlled the Spanish Sahara, were confronted with a Saharan rebel group—the **Polisario Front**—precisely as General Franco (see p. 55) lay dying. Hassan capitalized on Spanish weakness, marching his troops into the Sahara. Because the Polisario Front was disorganized and the Spanish were preoccupied, Hassan was successful. Unfortunately, peace did not come easily or immediately. The Polisario Front gained support from the Algerians, but they were at war in the Sahara until the UN declared a cease-fire in 1989.

MODERN MOROCCO (1977-1999). Today Morocco is nominally a **constitutional monarchy:** though assisted by a parliament and Chamber of Representatives, the king can dissolve parliament. Under Hassan, censorship ruled out opposition from such groups as trade union activists and university radicals. A drought further sapped monarchist support, but after sluggish industrial growth, riots, and the drain of war in the Western Sahara, Morocco began to recover in the 90s. Islamist movements throughout North Africa have kept Morocco cautious, though King Hassan's regime was stable in comparison to those in neighboring countries. Morocco's relations with neighbors are strained, particularly with Algeria, where illegal arms shuttling resulted in the closing of the Morocco-Algeria border in 1994. Southern Europe, also aligned against Islamist infiltration, has been taking a greater interest in Morocco, and has advocated tighter border controls.

In June 1999, President Mubarak of Egypt and King Hassan II met and established a trade agreement between Morocco and Egypt. They signed nine accords, one of which established a joint company for international trade. The leaders also discussed issues relating to the Middle East. Both countries agreed that it is essential that Israel carry out all agreements it has made toward the peace process, and noted that the United States and Europe need to continue to contribute as well. Morocco remains in opposition to Israeli occupation of Jerusalem and what they consider to be Palestine. Despite all the advances the country has made, Morocco remains a nation where almost half of the population lives below the poverty line, sometimes on less than a dollar a day. The country faces a 55% illiteracy rate.

CURRENT EVENTS. This past year has been one of readjustment and drastic change for Morocco. In July 1999, King Hassan, who had ruled the country as an autocratic leader since 1968, died of a heart attack, leaving his then 36-year-old son to govern. Over the past year, King Muhammad VI, the new king who is widely respected both by his people and the international community, has taken steps to reverse many of his father's restrictive policies in efforts to liberalize the political situation and to improve Morocco's human rights record. One of the most important reforms Muhammad has instituted has been the removal of restrictions on the practice of Islam. During the previous decade, other countries in the region had seen a massive revival of Islam, but Morocco, due to strict limitations imposed by the government, was resistant to it. Under Mohammed, however, new mosques have been sprouting up across the country. He released Islamic fundamentalist leader Sheikh Abd al-Salam Yassine, who had been under house arrest for 10 years by the government, and launched the Hassan II Foundation to combat poverty.

Among the more pressing issues currently facing Morocco is what to do with the **Western Sahara.** In the summer of 1999 the UN named a special representative to oversee the referendum on independence for Western Sahara, which was annexed by Morocco in 1975 (see above). The date of the referendum has been pushed back again and again for a decade. The UN will eventually help determine if Western Sahara should be a part of Morocco or if it will be granted independence. The decision is a contentious issue, tearing families and neighbors apart. To complicate matters, hundreds of thousands of Moroccans have recently been lured to the Western Sahara through tax breaks, subsidies, and public works projects.

LANGUAGE

Morocco is a paradise for polyglots. Although Classical Arabic (*al-Fusha*) is the official language of Morocco, it is rarely spoken and has become an almost exclusively written language. Most Moroccans speak the modern dialect called *Darija*, a compacted **Arabic** peppered with **Spanish** and **French,** as well as French proper. Whether Arabic, French, or Spanish, each language absorbed into the Morocco has been sprinkled and spiced. In this book, **city names** appear first in English, then in Arabic. (Fez is here written neither as Fès, the French spelling, nor Faas, the Arabic spelling.) Also, a massive naming shift from European to Arabic is underway on **street signs**, so some of the streets mentioned in this book may go by a different title (here they are listed in both French and Arabic when necessary). *Rues* and *calles* (streets and roads) may become *zanqats*, *derbs*, or *sharias*.

RELIGION

The religion of Islam was founded by the Arab prophet Muhammad in 622 AD. Informed of his prophetic calling by the angel Gabriel, Muhammad is believed by Muslims to be the end of a long chain of visionaries that includes Abraham, Moses, Elijah, and Jesus. Muhammad led his followers until his death in 632, during which time his words and deeds were recorded in *hadiths* (sayings) that comprise the *Sunna*, or examples of Muhammad. Following his death, the issue of who would rule divided Muslims into two branches, the Sunni and the Shi'a. The Sunni wanted Muhammad's successor chosen from a community of men; they believe strongly in God's will and predestination, while the Shi'ites believe in free will and insist on his successor being a blood relative of their prophet. More than 99% of Moroccans are Sunni Muslim, though Morocco also has a small Jewish minority and an even smaller Christian one. Islam is the official state religion.

At the heart of the Islamic faith is the Arabic word *islam*, meaning submission. The believer, or *Muslim*, accepts complete submission to the will of God *(Allah)* as embodied in the Qu'ran (book of recitation). This Arabic text is considered by Muslims to be a miracle—perfect, immutable, and untranslatable; it replaces all earlier revealed books and is the final definitive form of God's word. Unlike the Christian conception of Jesus, the Islamic view considers Muhammad a human messenger of God. All practicing Muslims must adhere to the five pillars of Islam: the formal profession of faith, prayer toward Mecca five times daily, alms-giving, fasting during the month of Ramadan, and, if possible, a pilgrimage to Mecca.

Moroccan Islam is somewhat unique. While there is the inevitable difference between popular and orthodox Islam in Morocco, there is less of a gap between the religious intellectuals and the general public than in other Arab countries. An additional Muslim category is Sufism, a mystical twist to Islam that is based on the belief that Muslims will find the truth of God's love and knowledge through a personal experience with God. Sufis were once quite politically influential; they are still a large presence, but their influence in politics has faded. Morocco has had its share of Islamic fundamentalist movements, but they have been substantially weaker than those in other North African countries, due to the popular belief that the king is a religious as well as political leader.

UNDERSTANDING RAMADAN It is believed that Muhammad received the Qur'an during the month of **Ramadan.** Fasting during this holy month is the fourth pillar of Islam. Between dawn and sunset, Muslims are not permitted to smoke, have sexual intercourse, or let any food or water pass their lips; exceptions are made for pregnant or menstruating women, the sick, and travelers (though all must make up the fast at a later date). Fasting is meant to teach Muslims to resist temptation and thereby control all their unchaste urges. Ideally, Muslims read the Qur'an during the daylight hours. By experiencing hunger they are meant to better understand the plight of the poor and to be more thankful for the food which God has provided them. It is insensitive to eat in public during Ramadan. Ramadan inspires a sense of community. As soon as the sun sets, the fast is broken and a night of feasting, and visiting of friends and relatives begins. The revelry lasts until dawn, when the fast begins again.

THE ARTS

ART AND ARCHITECTURE

Diverse architectural forms define Moroccan landscapes and cityscapes. An intense climate, combined with Berber austerity and Islamic privacy give **Berber architecture** an enclosed and stark nature. Kasbahs, the monumental houses of the Berbers, feature central courtyards, narrow passageways, animal shelters, simple high towers, thick walls, and plain façades. *Qsour* (plural of *qsar*; or fortified Berber villages) house densely packed "apartments." Built of *pisé* (packed earth). many are gradually turning to ruins, unable to withstand wind and sand storms.

In the 10th century, Fez residents built the first Moroccan **mosques** (sometimes called *djemmas* or *masajid*), al-Andalus and the Qairaouine. The *qibla* (wall) contains the *mihrab* (prayer niche), which faces Mecca. There are two basic designs for mosques: Arab-style, based on Muhammad's house with a pillared cloister around a courtyard, and Persian-style with a vaulted arch on each side. Attached to most mosques, Qur'anic schools *(madrasas)* have classrooms, libraries, and a prayer hall around a central courtyard and fountain.

In order to avoid idolatry, Muslim artists are forbidden from portraying figures of people, animals, or even plants. The result is a style of incredibly ingenious geometric and calligraphic decorations. Colorful patterns swirl across tiles, woodwork, stone, and ceramic. In less doctrinaire times, Almoravid artists slipped in designs that vaguely resemble leaves and flowers. **Calligraphy,** particularly elegant renderings and illuminations of the Qur'an, became another outlet for creativity as well as religious devotion. Sultans reserved their most dazzling designs for **imperial palaces,** with long, symmetrical reception and dwelling rooms studded with decorative gates, hidden gardens, and tiny pools and fountains.

Non-Muslims are usually prohibited from entering Moroccan mosques, though visitors may glimpse the splendor of interior courtyards from doorways. Out of respect, non-Muslin guests should keep a distance during services (five times daily; Fridays at midday).

CRAFTS

Turquoise genies and **carpet** connoisseurs will differentiate between rugs and *kilims*. While rugs are knotted and bordered by a shag ruffle, *kilims* are woven and ruffleless. The most valuable carpets will be older, with detailed embroidery, and colored with vegetable pigments instead of chemical dyes. A sniff test will differentiate currant crimson from red#5. Higher quality rugs will also be woven of wool or linen, not cotton. Berber patterned carpets from the Rif or Middle and High Atlas mountains are filled with and a wide variety of colorful markings. Those from Rabat and other coastal cities are modeled on the famed Turkish carpets.

Fez has been the center of a renowned **leather** industry since the 15th century. High-quality Moroccan leather can be purchased where it's made for a fraction of its international price. Fez is also the center for Moroccan **pottery** and is famous for its classic blue-and-white designs. Saharan and Berber **terra-cotta** ware are also common, and the South is known for its distinctive **silver jewelry,** often inlaid with colorful stones or glass. Moroccan woodwork is amazing; craftsmen seem to effortlessly transform blocks of cedar into delicate and intricate pieces.

All of the above are to be found in Moroccan **souqs** (markets). Those in more touristed areas target foreign travelers for the sale of craftwork; the wise will make for local *souqs* to do their real purchasing. Bargaining in Morocco is serious business, as much an everyday engagement as a cultural art form. Approach with vigor: a reasonable final price should be about 50% of your seller's original quote. To avoid unnecessary market hassle, declare that you've finished your shopping already or claim (penniless) student status. If your heart is set on a certain pair of slippers and their price refuses to drop, try walking out the door and down the block: the owner is quite likely to chase after you with a better offer. Even if he doesn't, you'll find the same item two stores down. (See also **Bargaining 101** p. 686)

FOOD AND DRINK

Moroccan chefs lavish aromatic and colorful spices on their dishes—pepper, ginger, cumin, saffron, honey, and sugar are culinary staples. The distinctive Moroccan flavor comes from a unique blend of spices, known as *ras al-hanut*. However, no matter how delicious everything may seem, be prepared to get sick at least once, as Morocco is full of things to which tourists are not immune. Taking extra precautions may help. Bottled mineral water is the way to go, as is peeling all fruits and vegetables. The truly cautious may avoid salads as well, or at least be sure they are washed in purified water. Most food sold on the street, especially meat, can be quite dangerous. In general, beware of anything sold on the street.

TYPICAL FARE

Moroccan cuisine consists mainly of couscous, *tajine*, and soups. **Tajine** is a stew steamed in an oven in a cone-shaped clay dish. It usually consists of some kind of meat, chicken, lamb, or pigeon along with an assortment of vegetables, olives, and prunes. Vegetarian forms of *tajine* are common as well. **Couscous** is a seminola-grain pasta about the size of sesame seeds, and is also served with meat or vegetables. The most popular of the Moroccan soups is **harira,** a salty chick-pea soup, sometimes containing meat (it is served every day during Ramadan). **Baguettes** and **honey-soaked pastries** are everywhere, as are delicious Moroccan breads.

Other common dishes include **poulet** (chicken), which can be prepared either *rôti* (roasted on a spit with olives) or *limon* (with lemon). Pricier and harder-to-find specialties include **mechoui,** whole lamb spitted over an open fire, and **pastilla,** a combination of pigeon or chicken, onions, almonds, eggs, butter, cinnamon, and sugar under a pastry shell. For a lighter treat, slurp sweet natural yogurt with mounds of peaches, nectarines, or strawberries, or try an oily Moroccan salad with finely chopped tomatoes, cucumbers, and onions. Snackers munch briny olives (1dh per scoop), roasted almonds, dried chick-peas, and cactus buds (1dh per bud). Oranges abound as the cheapest, sweetest, safest fruit in the country.

EATING OUT

The restaurant scene in Morocco depends on whether you're in a big city or small town. As eating out isn't common practice for locals, eateries in large, modern cities cater mainly to foreign tourists, featuring comprehensive menus of typical French or Moroccan cuisine. Seeking out **authentic** regional cuisine in larger cities often requires an adventurous expedition into the maze of the

CULT FICTION Paul Bowles has become somewhat of a cult figure in Morocco and is considered one of America's best expatriate writers. He initially gained fame through his involvement in radical politics, but Bowles turned from politics to travel after marrying Jane Auer in 1938, and he ultimately settled in Morocco on the advice of Gertrude Stein. It was there that he began to use Moroccan drugs to enhance his creativity (don't get any ideas) and started writing fiction. His first and most famous novel, *The Sheltering Sky* (1949), details the lives of an American couple and their struggle with Moroccan culture and themselves. Many reviewers likened the novel to the works of Poe (who happened to be Bowles's childhood idol) and Hemingway. From that point on, most of Bowles's fiction was set in Morocco, though his only other piece to gain much fame was *The Spider's House* (1955). When Jane died in 1973, Bowles's work showed signs of a loss of hope. His career, however, received a boost in the early 1990s when Bernardo Berotolucci made a movie of *The Sheltering Sky*, starring Deborah Winger and John Malkovich. He died in Tangier in November 1999.

medina. Tiny, often indistinguishable restaurants hide the most tantalizing dishes. A complete meal includes a choice of entree (*tajine*, couscous, or perhaps a third option), salad or *harira*, a side of vegetables, and yogurt or an orange for **dessert.** Less expensive *tajine* is made with *kefta* (a ground beef cooked in an array of herbs and spices) and often served on a baguette, as is *merguez (*a spicy beef or lamb sausage). Almost every Moroccan main course includes meat; *cous aux légumes* (couscous with vegetables) will usually be the closest **vegetarian** option. The best bet for strict vegetarians is to cook with produce from the market, or to request an omelette at restaurants. Lunchtime runs from noon to 2pm, dinner 7 to 9pm. If a service charge isn't automatically included, a 10% **tip** will suffice.

DRINKING

Although tap water is drinkable in most parts of the country, bottled, purified water is a safer bet. If you get a bottle that isn't completely sealed, return it—chances are the bottle has been filled with tap water. Orange juice and other fruit drinks are popular, but make sure that they are diluted with purified water.

Despite Islam's prohibition of alcohol, Morocco is a wine-lover's paradise. The local wines are excellent. While the two best wines are the Cabernet Medallion and Beauvillion (about 80dh a piece), the less expensive Vabernet du President, Amazir, and Guerraine Rouge are also quite good (all about 35dh). Moroccan, French, and Spanish **wines** are available in supermarkets and some restaurants (but not in the medina). Watery local **beer,** usually Stork or Flag Speciale, is not particularly good. Moroccan **bars** are entirely male and focus on heavy drinking; otherwise, they are pricey, tourist-oriented, and tend to attract sleazy types. More pleasant are the many Moroccan coffee houses where you can get inexpensive Moroccan **coffee** and **tea.** Espresso is widespread and popular, as is coffee, which is almost always sweetened with sugar and milk. Green tea is sipped with fresh mint leaves and lots of sugar, and is a staple of the Moroccan diet.

SPORTS

Moroccans are deeply passionate about soccer, and there are intense rivalries between competing clubs. Their national team was undefeated in qualifying matches for the 1998 World Cup, and only narrowly missed advancing to the second round. Basketball runs a distant second to soccer, but is still popular. Team sports remain fairly limited to men, although other participatory sports abound. Skiing is common in the High Atlas Mountains (late December to early March) and is possible in the Middle Atlas Mountains as well, hiking is available everywhere, water sports are popular on the Atlantic coast, and biking takes place nationwide.

RECOMMENDED READING

LITERATURE ABOUT MOROCCO

In Morocco, by Edith Wharton. Episodic descriptions of Rabat, Salé, Fez, and Meknes.

Morocco That Was, by Walter Harris. A turn-of-the-century journalist's diary, featuring a wry account of a Brit's kidnapping by the international bandit Raissouli.

The Voices of Marrakech, by Bulgarian Nobel Prize recipient Elias Canetti. Eloquently records a European Jew's encounter with Moroccan Jews.

The House of Si Abd Allah, edited by noted scholar Henry Munson. An oral history of a Moroccan family which provides insight into the country's social history.

The Sheltering Sky, The Spider's House, Days: Tangier Journal, by Paul Bowles. Numbingly gorgeous introductions to the country and to Bowles (see **Cult Fiction,** above).

MOROCCAN LITERATURE IN ENGLISH

Love With a Few Hairs, The Lemon, and **M'hashis,** by Muhammad Mrabet. Bits of contemporary Moroccan life, translated by Paul Bowles.

The Battle of Three Kings, by Youssef Necrouf. An entertaining account of medieval violence and intrigue under the Saadian dynasty.

Dreams of Trespass (Tales of a Moroccan Girlhood), by Fatima Mernissa. The author's story of growing up in Fez in the 1950s.

ESSENTIALS

The information in this section is designed to help travelers get their bearings once they are in Morocco. For info about general **travel preparations** (including passports and permits, money, health, packing, international transportation, and more), consult the **Essentials** section at the beginning of this guide. Essentials also contains important information about alternatives to tourism and offers tips for travelers with specific concerns: **women travelers** (p. 45); **older travelers** (p. 46); **bisexual, gay, and lesbian travelers** (p. 47); **travelers with disabilities** (p. 47); **minority travelers** (p. 48); **travelers with children** (p. 48); and travelers with **dietary concerns** (p. 49).

TRANSPORTATION

BY PLANE

Royal Air Maroc (in Casablanca ☎022 31 41 41 or airport 022 33 90 00; in US 800-344-6726; in UK 171 439 43 61), Morocco's national airline, flies to and from most major cities in Europe, including Madrid and Lisbon. Domestically, a network of flights radiates from the Mohammed V Airport outside Casablanca. Planes fly daily to Marrakesh, Agadir, Tangier, and Fez and occasionally to Ouarzazate as well.

If you hope to see a lot of Morocco in a short time, flying can be both a convenient and affordable option; you don't have to commit to a flight until the day before, and the price of the ticket always remains the same, whenever you buy it. Royal Air Maroc (RAM) and its competitor, **Regional Airlines,** fly to all major domestic cities. RAM offers the best deals for students and the under-26 crowd, though Regional Airlines often flies more frequently within the country.

BY FERRY AND HYDROFOIL

For travel from Spain to Morocco, the most budget-minded mode is by sea. Spanish-based **Trasmediterranea** (☎34 902 45 46 45, www.trasmediterranea.es/homei.htm) runs ferries on a shuttle schedule from **Algeciras** (☎34 956 65 62 44, Recinto del Puerto, s/n.) to **Cuenta** (☎34 956 50 94 11; Muelle Cañonero Dato, 6) and **Tangier**. Trasmediterranea is represented in Tangier by **Limadet** (☎212 39/93 50 76; 3, Rue IBN Rochd., Tangier). "Fast" Ferries run from Algeciras to Ceuta (45 min., every hr., 8am-10pm; 3000-4000ptas/€18-24). Algeciras to Tangier (2½hrs., every hr., 8am-10pm, 5000ptas/€30). **Comarit** (☎956 66 84 62, www.comarit.com; Avda. Virgen della Carmen, 3-1°Cial.) runs from Algeciras to Tangier, and offers **vehicle transport.** (3-4 per day; Class "B" 3740ptas, compact car 11,540ptas). Jump on line for Comarit's unpredictable weekly schedule, .

BY TRAIN

Where possible, trains are the best way to travel. They are faster than buses, more comfortable, and fairly reliable and prompt. Second-class train tickets are slightly more expensive than corresponding CTM bus fares; first-class tickets cost around 20% more than those second-class.

The main line runs from Tangier via Rabat and Casablanca to Marrakesh. A spur connects Fez, Meknes, and points east. There is one *couchette* train between Fez and Marrakesh. Tickets bought on board cost at least 10% more and may cause trouble with the conductor. No student fares are available. Be wary of old schedules that show times for the Atlantic coast, south of Casablanca—this route has been out of service for a few years now. InterRail (see p. 38) *is* valid in Morocco, but Eurail is not. Fares are so low, however, that InterRail is not worth it.

BY BUS

In Morocco, bus travel is less frequent and less reliable than in Spain or Portugal. Plan well ahead if you are thinking of using buses as your method of transport. They're not all that fast and they're not very comfortable, but they're extremely cheap and travel to nearly every corner of the country. **Compagnie de Transports du Maroc (CTM),** the state-owned line, has the fastest, most luxurious, most reliable, and generally most expensive buses (though "expensive" here means just a few more dirhams). In many cities, CTM has a station separate from other lines; reservations are usually not necessary. *Let's Go* lists CTM stations in each city. Several dozen other private companies operate as well. Though they may offer more frequent departures, the comfort level is so low, you'll probably wish you had waited for the next CTM. Other private companies, called **cars publiques** (a.k.a. *souq* buses), have far more departures and are generally slower, less comfortable, and cheaper. In the bus stations, each bus company has its own info window; window-hop for information on destinations and schedules.

The **baggage check** at CTM bus depots is usually safe. Your bags, however, may not be accepted for storage if you don't have padlocks on the zippers. Private bus companies also have baggage checkrooms; they're generally very trustworthy.

BY TAXI

Two separate hordes of taxis prowl Moroccan streets: intra-urban *petit taxis* and inter-urban *grand taxis*, both dirt cheap by European standards. *Petit taxis*, small Renaults or Fiats that can each hold a strict maximum of three passengers, are all painted in one color depending on the municipality (red in Fez, blue in Meknes, etc.) and can't leave the city or take you to the airport. Make sure the driver turns the meter on; they are required to do so by law. If the driver won't turn it on, agree on the price before you go (around 50% of what the driver asks is fair). There is a 50% surcharge after 8pm. Don't be surprised if the driver stops for other passengers or picks you up with other passengers in the car, but if you are picked up after the meter has been started, note the initial price.

Grand taxis, typically beige or dark-blue Mercedes sedans, are the most expensive way to travel, but do go just about everywhere. Unlike their *petit* cousins, they don't usually cruise for passengers, congregating instead at a central area in town. They hold up to six passengers (four in the back, two in the front), but if you plan on taking a long ride, you might buy two spaces to allow for extra room. A taxi won't go until it is filled with passengers going in the same direction. Ask other passengers what they are paying to avoid being ripped off.

BY CAR AND BY THUMB

There are two reasons to rent a car in Morocco: large group travel, or travel to areas not reached by Morocco's public transportation system. Otherwise, car rental is unnecessary. Moroccan roads can be very dangerous; reckless passing maneuvers, excessive speed, shoddy maintenance, and poorly equipped vehicles are all par for the course.

Hertz, Avis, and **Europcar** all rent cars; expect to pay about 400dh per day for an economy car, including taxes and insurance. Large local firms such as **Afric Car, Moroloc,** and **Locoto** offer cars for considerably less money but are also less reliable. Both international and local firms are easy to find in all major cities. Before you leave the lot, make sure that you have a full spare and a complete toolkit.

Once in your car, you face a myriad of complications, the most serious being **security checks.** Virtually any trip you take will bring you to at least one checkpoint. Expect to be pulled over and asked to produce your passport and proof of rental. One tactic if pulled over is to immediately ask for directions, either in French or Arabic. You also may be stopped for **traffic violations,** real or not. The fine is payable on the spot in dirhams and may be negotiable; asking for a receipt could be construed as provocative. Whatever you do, **do not travel with drugs in your car.**

Routes goudronées (principal roads), marked "P," are paved and connect cities. **Pistes** (secondary roads), designated "S," are very rough. If traveling in the **desert,** be sure to bring at least 10L of bottled water for each person and for the radiator. Move rapidly over sand; if you start to bog down, put the car in low gear and step on the gas. If you come to a stop in soft sand, push. **Gas** costs about 10dh per liter.

Driving in Morocco without the **Michelin map** of Morocco all but ensures that you will get lost. Fortunately, it is available both abroad and in Morocco. Even with the map, you still should inquire about road conditions. One place to make such inquiries is the automobile association, **Touring Club du Maroc,** 3 av. F.A.R., Casablanca (☎022 20 30 64).

Almost no one in Morocco **hitches,** although flagging down buses and trains can feel like hitchhiking. Transportation is dirt cheap by European and North American standards. If Moroccans do pick up a foreigner, they will most likely expect payment for the ride. Hitching is more frequent in the south and in the mountains, where transportation is irregular. *Let's Go* does not recommend hitchhiking.

MONEY

In Morocco, **banking hours** are Monday through Friday 8:30 to 11:30am and 2:30 to 4:30pm, during Ramadan from 9:30am to 2pm. In the summer, certain banks close at 1pm and do not re-open in the afternoon. Do not try the **black market** for currency exchange—you'll be swindled. As in Europe, **ATMs** are the best way to change money. Also know that it is very difficult to change back upon departure.

Taxes are generally included in the price of purchases, though in malls and *grandes surfaces* (supermarkets and larger superstores) you will find a 7% Value-Added Tax on food and a 22% tax on luxury goods.

Tipping a small amount after restaurant meals, while certainly not necessary, is a nice gesture given the extreme degree of poverty of many Moroccan citizens.

Bargaining is definitely a legitimate part of the Moroccan shopping experience—it is most commonly accepted in outdoor markets. There are some guidelines to consider when bargaining. Tailor your bargaining to the situation—offering 40% of the asking price may be too much or too little, depending on where the seller has started. Decide what the item is actually worth to you, and use that as a benchmark. Do not appear overly eager, point out imperfections in the item or mention that you saw the item elsewhere at a lower price, naming that price. Begin to walk away when the seller has quoted a "minimum" price. Do not try to bargain in supermarkets or established stores.

SAFETY AND SECURITY

EMERGENCY ☎ | **Police:** ☎19. **Highway services:** ☎177.

Morocco has received a bad rap among travelers. While the **crime rate** is higher than in Spain or Portugal, there is more to Morocco than just hustlers and drugs. Visitors should be suspicious of people offering free food or drinks, as they have been known to be drugged. Large cities like Tangier and Fez are filled with fake guides offering a tour of the city for a small price; they should be avoided; there is a reason these people aren't employed by hotels and tour agencies.

Debates between the Moroccan government and the Algerian-based Polisario Front over possession of the Western Sahara resulted in a guerrilla war until the late 1980s. The UN called a cease-fire in 1991, but there are still unexploded **landmines** in the area. Travel to Western Sahara is difficult and not recommended; those interested can obtain clearance information from the Moroccan embassy.

Women travelers will probably have extra difficulties traveling through Morocco without a male companion. At the very least, they should never travel alone. Visitors will feel safer and more comfortable (and will avoid offending local sensibilities) by not wearing short skirts, sleeveless tops, and shorts; moreover, females should always wear bras. Regardless, non-Moroccan women may be gawked at, commented upon, approached by hustlers, followed in a crowd, or even groped on the street. Moroccan woman may "hiss" at indecently clad female travelers. The best response to male harassers may be silence, but yelling "*shuma*" (meaning shame) may well embarrass them, especially in the presence of onlookers. If an uncomfortable situation persists, look out for a policeman.

HEALTH

All travelers in Morocco face a different set of health issues than in Spain and Portugal; food and waterborne diseases in particular are a common cause of illness. The CDC recommends that travelers drink only bottled or boiled water, avoiding tap water, fountain drinks, and ice cubes. It is also advisable to only eat fruit and vegetables that are cooked and that you have peeled yourself. Stay away from food sold by street vendors, and check to make sure that dairy products have been pasteurized. There is only a slight malaria risk in Morocco, but it would still be wise to take extra precaution against insect bites and consider getting a vaccine before leaving. For further information, see **Health** on p. 23.

While there is a public health system in Morocco, travelers should seek out a private clinic, as these offer the best, most dependent, and affordable care. There are few English speaking doctors, though French is widespread; try to learn a few basic words of medical vocabulary in French in case of an emergency. Private clinics are to be found in large cities and university towns with medical schools, such as Casablanca and Rabat. Travelers with significant medical problems that might need sudden and immediate attention are advised to stay in the larger cities for reasons of accessibility. Abortion is not legal in Morocco, and is not available in public clinics, though one can find private clinics that will perform them.

ACCOMMODATIONS

YOUTH HOSTELS

The **Federation Royale des Auberges de Jeunesse (FRMAJ)** is the Moroccan Hosteling International (HI) affiliate. Beds cost 20-40dh per night, and there is a surcharge for non-members everywhere but in Casablanca. Some hostels sell HI memberships on the spot. Call ahead for reservations as beds can be popular. To reserve beds in high season, get an International Booking Voucher from FRMAJ (or your nearby HI affiliate) and send it to the hostel 4 to 8 weeks in advance. You'll probably need to bring your own sleepsack and towel, and there are usually curfew and lock-out times. For hostel addresses, write to FRMAJ, Parc de la Ligue Arabe, B.P. 15998, Casa Principale, Casablanca 21000 (☎ 022 47 09 52; fax 22 76 77). For more info on national youth hostel associations, see **Accommodations,** p. 25.

HOTELS

Although there is an official star system for rating hotels in Morocco, the number of stars reflects little more than price. Hotels that are not part of the system are not necessarily worse—their standards vary greatly—but are usually cheaper. Rooms can vary widely even within a particular hotel, so ask to see another room if you don't like the first, or find another hotel, often next door. Cheap hotels in Morocco are really cheap—as little as 40dh per night. Listings are generally divided between medina and *ville nouvelle* establishments. Medina hotels are usually cheaper than their *ville nouvelle* counterparts, but less comfortable and with fewer amenities. Hot showers, when available, may cost extra (usually less than 10dh). Cold showers are usually free. Many hotels offer laundry service.

CAMPING

Camping is popular and cheap (about 10dh per person), especially in the desert, mountains, and beaches. Like hotels, conditions vary widely. You can usually expect to find restrooms, but electricity is not as readily available. Use caution if camping unofficially, especially on the beaches, as theft is a problem.

KEEPING IN TOUCH

Most useful communication information (including international access codes, calling card numbers, country codes, operator and directory assistance, and emergency numbers) is listed on the inside back cover of this book.

TELEPHONES

Morocco has recently invested hundreds of millions of dollars into modernizing its telephone system, resulting in markedly improved services. Pay phones accept either coins or Moroccan phone cards. Available at post offices, phone cards are usually in denominations too large to be practical. Entrepreneurial Moroccans hang around phone banks and let you use their phone cards. You pay for the units used—typically 2dh per unit, a rate not much worse than doing it yourself. To use the card, insert and dial 00. Once the dial tone turns into a tune, dial the number.

Phone offices *(téléboutiques)* are located in most cities. If you can't find one, head to the post office—they always have at least one phone for international calls. To make a collect call, ask the desk attendant at the local telephone office to place a call *en P.C.V.* ("ahn PAY-SAY-VAY"). Write down your name and the country, state, city, and telephone number you want to call. Collect calls can also be made from payphones; simply dial 12 and ask to call *en P.C.V.* Remember that the initial zero (0) in **city codes** is dialed only when calling from another area within Morocco; from outside of Morocco the number is omitted. Local calls do not require dialing any portion of the city code.

The best way to make international calls is with a **calling card** (see **By Telephone,** p. 29). To **call home with a calling card,** contact the operator for your service provider in Morocco by dialing the appropriate toll-free access number (see page 29).

MAIL

Sending something **Air mail** *(par avion)* can take a week to a month to reach the US or Canada (about 10dh for a slim letter, postcards 4-7dh). Less reliable **surface mail** *(par terre)* takes up to 2 months. **Express mail** (*recommandé* or *exprès postaux*), is slightly faster than regular air mail and more reliable. Post offices and some *tabacs* sell **stamps.** For very fast service (2 days to the US), your best bet is DHL (www.dhl.com), which has drop-off locations in most major cities.

EMAIL

Yes, email has reached Morocco. Cyber-cafés are common in major cities and the more touristed towns. *Let's Go* lists internet access and rates where applicable.

EMBASSIES AND CONSULATES

In Morocco, most embassies and consulates are open Monday through Friday from around 8am to noon; some reopen after lunch until 6pm.

Algerian Embassy: 46-48 rue Tarek Ibr Ziad, B.P. 448, **Rabat** (☎037 76 55 91; fax 037 76 22 37).

British Embassy: 17 bd. de la Tour Hassan, B.P. 45, **Rabat** (☎037 73 14 03 or 72 09 06; fax 70 45 31). **Consulates:** 43 bd. d'Anfa, B.P. 13, #762, **Casablanca** (☎022 20 33 16 or 22 33 19 or 22 33 76; fax 20 74 34; 41); bd. Mohammed V, B.P. 2122, **Tangiers** (☎039 94 15 57; fax 94 22 84).

Canadian Embassy: 13 Bis, Jaafar Assadik, B.P. 709, Agdal, **Rabat** (☎037 67 28 80; fax 67 21 78).

Irish Embassy: Refer to the Irish Embassy in Lisbon (p. 539). In case of emergency, contact any Commonwealth embassy.

Australian Embassy: Refer to the Canadian Embassy in Rabat (above). In case of emergency, contact any Commonwealth embassy.

New Zealand Embassy: Refer to the New Zealand Embassy in Spain (p. 75). In case of emergency, contact any Commonwealth embassy.

South African Embassy: 34 r. de Saadiens, **Rabat** (☎037 70 67 60; fax 70 67 56; sugas@mail.sis.ne.ma), opposite the mausoleum.

US Embassy: 2 av. de Mohamed El Fassi, **Rabat** (☎037 76 22 65, after-hours line 76 96 39; fax 76 56 61). **Consulate:** 8 bd. Moulay Youssef, **Casablanca** (☎022 26 45 50; fax 20 41 27).

HOLIDAYS

Moroccans celebrate several secular and Islamic holidays. The dates of all Muslim holidays, which begin at sundown before the day listed, are based on the lunar calendar and are valid for 2002 only. Be aware that many establishments are closed during most holidays, particularly the religious ones (and if the holidays fall near a weekend, places are likely to remain closed for an extended period.)

DATE	FESTIVAL	LOCATION
January 1	New Year's Day	National
January 11	Independence Manifesto	National
March 3	National Day	National
March 6	'Eid al-Adha	National
March 26	Islamic New Year	National
May 1	Labor Day	National
May 23	National Day	National
July 30	Ras al-Sana	National
August 14	Reunification Day	National
August 20	Anniversary of the King's and People's Revolution	National
August 21	Young People's Day	National
November 6	Anniversary of the Green March	National
November 18	Independence Day	National
Nov. 6 to Dec. 1	Ramadan	National
December 16	'Eid al-Fitr	National

EXPLORING MOROCCO

For many travelers weary of another visit to a Spanish cathedral, a short excursion across the Strait of Gibraltar into Morocco becomes unexpectedly the highlight of their trip. Passersby don't pass you by—everyone wants to know your name. Fruits and vegetables are sold right off the street—next to stinking fish. And old men squat on the side of the road, wrapped in hooded garments. Excitement and adventure need not be planned for or paid for lavishly: just step outside your hotel door and wander down an ancient medina street. While Morocco offers a manageable, if at times stressful, introduction to both the Islamic and African world, it's the proud and hospitable nation's own unique blend of languages, landscapes, and people which defy any preconceptions and exceed all expectations. The country, still largely inhabited by an ancient race of people known as Berbers, has a fascinating history as the crossroads between two rich continents. Physically, the nation contains unparalleled raw beauty in the form of lush valleys, enormous desert dunes, ancient imperial cities, and North Africa's highest mountains. And finally, there is Morocco in its modern mutation, a nation that struggles to balance a youthful and striving face with its traditional ways. Whichever Morocco visitors choose to focus on, the country never fails to reward the traveller.

THE MEDITERRANEAN COAST

Northern Morocco comprises Mediterranean ports and beaches and the jagged Rif Mountains. The most accessible region from Spain, the Mediterranean coast is a common point of entry into the country; precisely because of its proximity to Europe and the prevalence of European influence throughout its history, the area, where French, Spanish, and Arabic architecture, lifestyles, and language overlap, is rarely considered "real Morocco." The Mediterranean cities provide a taste of the country, but they may not leave visitors with the most favorable impression. Those interested in observing true Moroccan culture should keep pushing south.

TANGIER طنجة ☎039

For travelers venturing out of Europe for the first time, disembarking in Tangier (pop. 500,000) can be a stressful experience. Many traveler's stories make the city out to be a living nightmare, but, despite the very real difficulties of traveling through the city, it remains the best way to enter from Spain. While there is little to see in Tangier and most choose to skip it altogether, Tangier interests visitors with its complex history and edgy urban pace. For centuries the region bounced from one imperial power to the next (Phoenicians, Romans, Portuguese, British, and Spaniards, to name a few), culminating in 1923 with the declaration of Tangier as an "international zone" loosely governed by the US and eight European powers. Law enforcement dwindled, and the city began to attract rich heiresses, drug users, spies, and Beat Generation poets. When Morocco declared its independence in 1956, the new government tried to change Tangier's image, closing down most of the brothels and increasing police presence. But the city's days as an international zone have left behind a mottled legacy. The Café de Paris—*the* café of WWII spies—still bustles, the Anglican church still conducts mass, and a gay community remains surprisingly visible. On the underside, a black market still thrives, hashish still flows from the Rif, and hotels still rent by the hour. Nevertheless, rising tourism (thanks to expanded ferry service) has propelled Tangier forward.

TRANSPORTATION

Flights: Royal Air Maroc (☎039 37 95 08), pl. France. To Barcelona, Casablanca, Madrid, Marrakesh, London and New York. **British Airways,** 83 rue de la Liberté (☎039 93 52 11), off of pl. France, flies to London (M and Th noon). Open M-F 8am-noon and 3-6:45pm. A taxi to the **airport,** 16km from Tangier, costs 80-100dh for up to 6 people.

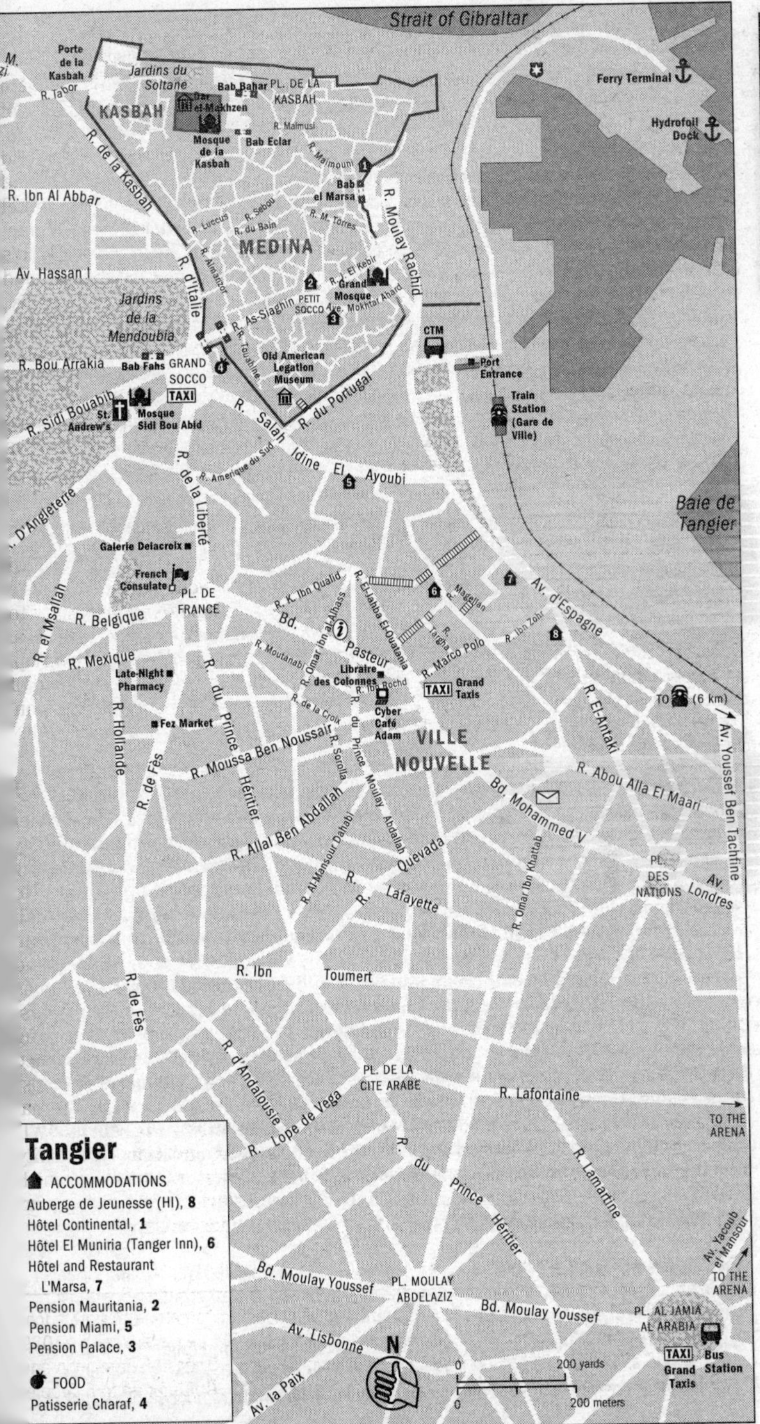

Tangier
ACCOMMODATIONS
Auberge de Jeunesse (HI), 8
Hôtel Continental, 1
Hôtel El Muniria (Tanger Inn), 6
Hôtel and Restaurant L'Marsa, 7
Pension Mauritania, 2
Pension Miami, 5
Pension Palace, 3
FOOD
Patisserie Charaf, 4
Strait of Gibraltar
Ferry Terminal
Hydrofoil Dock
Porte de la Kasbah
Jardins du Soltane
R. Tabor
KASBAH
Dar el-Makhzen
Bab Bahar
PL. DE LA KASBAH
R. Malmusi
Mosque de la Kasbah
Bab Eclar
R. Maimouni
Bab el Marsa
R. de la Kasbah
R. Ibn Al Abbar
R. Luccus
R. Sebou
R. du Bain
R. M. Torres
MEDINA
R. Moulay Rachid
Av. Hassan I
R. Almanzor
R. d'Italie
R. J. El Kebir
Grand Mosque
Ave. Mokhtar Ahardan
R. As-Siaghin
PETIT SOCCO
Jardins de la Mendoubia
CTM
Port Entrance
R. Bou Arrakia
Bab Fahs
GRAND SOCCO
R. Touahine
Old American Legation Museum
Train Station (Gare de Ville)
TAXI
R. Sidi Bouabib
St. Andrew's
Mosque Sidi Bou Abid
R. Salah Idine El Ayoubi
R. du Portugal
R. de la Liberté
R. Amerique du Sud
D'Angleterre
Baie de Tangier
Galerie Delacroix
French Consulate
PL. DE FRANCE
R. el Msallah
R. Belgique
R. K. Ibn Oualid
R. Omar Ibn al Alhass
Bd. Pasteur
R. El-Jabha El-Ouatania
Magellan
Av. d'Espagne
R. Targha
R. Ibn Zohr
R. Marco Polo
R. Mexique
Late-Night Pharmacy
R. Moutanabi
Libraire des Colonnes
R. Ibn Rochd
Grand Taxis
R. de la Croix
Cyber Café Adam
TO (6 km)
R. Hollande
Fez Market
R. du Prince Héritier
R. Moussa Ben Noussair
R. Sorolla
R. du Prince Moulay Abdallah
VILLE NOUVELLE
R. El-Antaki
Av. Youssef Ben Tachfine
R. Abou Alla El Maari
R. de Fès
Bd. Mohammed V
R. Allal Ben Abdallah
R. Al-Mansour Dahabi
Quevada
R. Omar Ibn Khattab
PL. DES NATIONS
Av. Londres
R. Lafayette
R. Ibn Toumert
R. d'Andalousie
PL. DE LA CITE ARABE
R. Lafontaine
TO THE ARENA
R. Lope de Vega
R. du Prince Héritier
R. Lamartine
Av. Yacoub el Mansour
Bd. Moulay Youssef
PL. MOULAY ABDELAZIZ
PL. AL JAMIA AL ARABIA
Av. Lisbonne
Av. la Paix
N
0
200 yards
200 meters
Grand Taxis
Bus Station

Trains: Trains leave from **Mghagha Station** (☎039 95 25 55), 6km from the port (not the old station on av. d'Espagne). A *petit taxi* to the station costs around 15dh. 2nd class to: **Asilah** (1hr., 3 per day 7am-10:30pm, 13dh); **Casablanca** (6hr., 3 per day 7am-10:30pm, 114dh); **Fez** (5½hr., 4 per day 7am-10:30pm, 93dh); **Meknes** (5hr., 4 per day 7am-10:30pm, 77dh); and **Rabat** (5½hr., 3 per day 7am-10:15pm, 87dh).

Buses: Non-CTM buses leave from av. Yacoub al-Mansour at pl. Jamia al-Arabia, 2km from the port entrance. Ask blue-coated personnel or check the boards for ticket info. The standard price for luggage is 5dh. A *petit taxi* from the port to the terminal costs 8dh. To: **Casablanca** (6hr., 15 per day 5am-11:15pm, 69dh); **Ceuta** (40min., 7 per day 6:15am-2:45pm, 10dh); **Fez** (6hr., 10 per day 8:40am-9:30pm, 63dh); **Marrakesh** (10hr., 5 per day 6:45am-8:30pm, 115dh); **Meknes** (5hr., 10 per day 6am-2:15pm, 57dh); **Rabat** (5hr., 15 per day 5am-11:15pm, 57dh); and **Tetouan** (1hr., 10 per day 7am-10pm, 14dh). The **CTM Station** (☎039 93 11 72) near the port entrance offers pricier and posher bus service to the same destinations.

Ferries: The cheapest and most convenient option is to buy a ticket at the port agent, 46 ave. d'Espagne. (☎039 94 26 12), though ticket agencies are located throughout the city. You'll need a boarding pass (available at any ticket desk) and a customs form (ask uniformed agents). Near the terminal, pushy men with ID cards will try to arrange your ticket and fill out your customs card for 10dh; just do it yourself. To: **Algeciras** (2½hr., every hr. 7am-9pm, 2960ptas or 210dh) and **Tarifa** (35min.; 3-5 per day; 200dh).

Taxis: *Grand taxis* to nearby locations (Tetouan, Ceuta, Asilah). Prices subject to bargaining, but a fair price is 20dh per person when taxis are full (6 passengers). They can be found everywhere, but they congregate by the main bus stop, the Grand Socco, and the intersection of bd. Pasteur and bd. Mohammed V.

Car Rental: Avis, 54 bd. Pasteur. Open daily 8am-noon and 2-7pm. **Hertz,** 36 av. Mohammed V (☎039 93 30 31). Open M-Sa 8:30am-noon and 2-6:30pm, Su 9am-noon. Both agencies, working together, charge about 500dh per day with a 20% tax for a Fiat Palio. Min. age 25 for all cars. A special international license is not required.

ORIENTATION

Tangier is made easy to navigate by the **av. d'Espagne,** a large boulevard that runs from the port along the waterfront to the train station 6km away. Many of the ville nouvelle hotels are located about 1.5km down av. d'Espagne away from the ferry terminal (a *petit taxi* should cost 5dh, but if you don't have a lot of baggage and you have your wits about you, it's better to walk). Hustlers tend to prey on fresh meat here, but confidence will send them away. Adjacent to the ferry terminal area on av. d'Espagne is the **CTM station.** Rue du Portugal heads uphill from near the CTM station and represents the border between the ville nouvelle and the medina. You can enter the medina and easily find some of its accommodations by turning right above the CTM station, continuing uphill on rue de la Plage. Soon you will reach the large, busy rotary known as **Grand Socco,** the center of activity directly above the medina. From the Grand Socco, you can head down into the medina via rue al-Siaghin, which leads to the **petit socco** or walk down the bustling rue d'Italie (to the right of the Grand Socco) which skirts the medina's western wall.

The ville nouvelle's main commercial road is the **boulevard Pasteur** which connects the main square, **pl. de France,** with another main commercial street, bd. Mohammed V. This strip includes many banks, the post office, and cafés.

PRACTICAL INFORMATION

Tourist Office: 29 bd. Pasteur (☎039 94 80 50). Some English, French, and Spanish spoken. Glossy brochures and basic map, but nothing to get all excited about. List of accommodations available. Open M-F 8:30am-7:30pm.

Currency Exchange: There is a branch of **BMCE** on most ferries and one in the port complex, although these only change cash. BMCE's **main office** in Tangier is located at 21 bd. Pasteur (☎039 93 11 25). No commission here, but other Moroccan banks charge fees for exchanging traveler's checks. Open M-F 8:15am-2:15pm. There is an **ATM** on bd. Pasteur. Travel agencies near the port are required to change money at official rates. Major banks line bd. Pasteur and bd. Mohammed V.

Luggage Storage: At the **train station** for 5dh per bag. Open 24hr. Also at the **bus station** for 4dh per bag. Open daily 5:30am-12:30am.

English Bookstore: Librairie des Colonnes, 54 bd. Pasteur (☎039 93 69 55), near pl. France. English classics, French and Spanish fiction, and literature on Moroccan culture. Open M-F 9:30am-12:30pm and 4-7pm, Sa 9:30am-1pm.

Police: ☎19, at the port and main train station.

Late-Night Pharmacy: 22 rue de Fez (☎039 94 21 85), 2 blocks from bd. Pasteur at pl. France across from Cinema Le Paris (really, it's there). Medicine dispensed through tiny windows in the green wall left of the entrance. Open M-Th 9am-1pm and 4-8pm, F 9am-12:30pm and 4-8:30pm, Sa 9am-1pm, Su 9am-8pm. Call in an emergency.

Medical Services: Red Cross, 6 rue al-Monoui Dahbi (☎039 94 25 17), runs a 24hr. English-speaking medical service. **Ambulance:** ☎039 31 27 27.

Internet Access: Cyber Café Adam, 2 rue Ibn Roched, off the intersection of bd. Pasteur and bd. Mohammed V. 10dh per hour. Open daily 8:30am-2am.

Post Office: 33 bd. Mohammed V (☎039 93 25 18), the downhill continuation of bd. Pasteur. **Poste Restante.** Open M-Th 8:30am-6:30pm, Sa 8:30am-12:15pm.

ACCOMMODATIONS

Whether you stay in the *ville nouvelle* or the medina, you are bound to meet some hustlers "welcoming" you to Morocco. It's best to make a reservation ahead, have your guard up when you arrive, and have a sense of where you're going when you hit town. Expect to pay around 50-60dh for a single and 80-100dh for a double, though rates may decrease in winter. Reservations are usually required in August.

MEDINA

The most convenient hostels are near **rue Mokhtar Ahardan** (formerly rue des Postes), off the Petit Socco. From the Grand Socco, take the first right down rue al-Siaghin to the Petit Socco. Rue Mokhtar Ahardan begins at the end of the Petit Socco closest to the port. At night the smaller streets off the medina can be unsafe.

Pension Mauritania (☎039 93 46 77), rue des Almohades at the Petit Socco. A backpacker's mecca. Shared toilets, free cold showers, and clean rooms. Great views of the medina and port from some rooms. 45dh per person.

Pension Palace, 2 rue Mokhtar Ahardan (☎039 93 61 28). Downhill, on the alley exiting the Petit Socco to the right. Stark rooms inhabited by students. The courtyard starred in Bertolucci's adaptation of *The Sheltering Sky*. Singles 40dh; doubles 80dh, with bath 120dh; triples 120dh, with bath 150dh; quads 120dh, with bath 200dh.

Hôtel Continental, 36 Dar Baroud (☎039 93 10 24; fax 039 93 11 43), overlooking the port. From the ferry terminal, bear right around the CTM station, then follow the hotel's many signs. A grand hotel furnished with a mix of Moroccan ornament and art deco. Home to newbie visitors and aging hippies. Breakfast included. Showers hot only in the mornings. Reservations recommended. Singles 284dh; doubles 365dh; triples 435dh.

VILLE NOUVELLE

Hotels line av. d'Espagne as it heads away from the port. The best values lie a few blocks uphill toward bd. Pasteur and bd. Mohammed V.

Hôtel El Muniria (Tanger Inn) (☎039 93 53 37), rue Magellan. Take 1st right after Hôtel Biarritz on av. d'Espagne, walking away from the medina, and follow as it winds uphill. William Burroughs wrote *Naked Lunch* in room #9 (unfortunately now the owner's room). Ask for room #4, where Jack Kerouac and Allen Ginsberg stayed. A great deal for Tangier, with spacious rooms, hot showers, and towels. Singles 100dh; doubles 130dh.

Auberge de Jeunesse (HI), 8 rue al-Antaki (☎039 94 61 27), down av. d'Espagne away from the port and half a block up the road to the right, after Hôtel Marco Polo. A backpacker hotspot. New, firm dormitory beds. Hot showers 5dh. Office open M-Sa 8-10am, noon-3pm, and 6-11pm, Su 8-10am and 6pm-midnight. Closes at 10:30pm in winter, though there is some flexibility. HI members 27dh; non-members 29.50dh.

Pension Miami, 126 rue Salah Eddine al-Ayoubi (☎039 93 29 00), off av. d'Espagne. 45 rooms, carved high ceilings, and a balcony on each floor. Basic communal bathroom. Hot showers 10dh. Singles 50dh; doubles 80dh; triples 120dh; quads 160dh.

Hôtel L'Marsa, 92 av. d'Espagne (☎039 93 23 39), away from the port on the main drag; you can't miss its restaurant (see **Food,** below), which juts out onto the sidewalk. Clean rooms with closets and mirrors. A good deal for the location. Hot showers 7dh. Laundry 5dh per piece. Singles 50dh; doubles 100dh; quads 200dh. MC/V.

FOOD

MEDINA

The medina dining experience begins at the **Grand Socco,** where you can stall-hop for all types of delights. Head from the Grand Socco toward the Petit Socco and you will find a slew of inexpensive local eateries. On the corner near the pl. France sprawls a huge **market.** The best pastries in town can be found at **Café Patisserie Charaf,** 28 rue Smarine, just below the Grand Socco in the medina.

Restaurant Hammadi, 2 rue de la Kasbah (☎039 93 45 14), the continuation of rue d'Italie just outside the medina walls. Specialties are *tajine* (40dh) and couscous (45dh). Beer and wine served. Entrées 40-60dh. A 10% tax is added to each meal. Open daily 11am-3pm and 7pm-midnight. MC/V.

VILLE NOUVELLE

The restaurants along av. d'Espagne tout unspectacular and overpriced *menus touristiques* for 50dh and up. Beachfront restaurants run by the high-end hotels are just what you'd expect—expensive and boring. You're better off scouting around **pl. France.** For a snack, hot sandwiches can be found all along bd. Pasteur.

L'Marsa, 92 av. d'Espagne (☎039 93 19 28). This popular restaurant and café has outdoor dining and a mixed Italian and Moroccan menu. Praiseworthy pizzas (23-35dh) pasta, and Italian ice cream (12-25dh). Women traveling alone should avoid the rooftop terrace, a choice pick-up spot for Moroccan men. Entrées 25-70dh. Open daily June-Aug. 5am-3am; Sept.-May 5am-midnight. MC/V.

Restaurant Africa, 83 rue Salah Eddine al-Ayoubi (☎039 93 54 36), just off av d'Espagne near Pension Miami, opposite old train station. A quiet, dimly-lit place for Moroccan standards. Omelettes (15dh) and tajine (30dh). Beer served. Big 4-course *menu du jour* 50dh. Entrées 25-80dh. Open daily 9am-12:30am.

Brahim Abdelmalek, 14 rue de Mexique (☎039 93 17 96), under dirty white awning King Hassan II grabbed lunch here and you can too for less than 15dh. Owner claims to have invented Moroccan-style sandwich craze in 1960. Open daily 10:30am-midnight.

SIGHTS

IN AND NEAR THE MEDINA

OLD AMERICAN LEGATION. In contrast to the frenzy of Tangier's medina goings-on, the Old American Legation is austere and refined. In 1821 this became the first foreign property acquired by the United States. The museum contains documents relating to Tangier's international past, including correspondence between George Washington and his "great and magnanimous friend" Sultan Moulay ben Abdallah. Morocco was the first nation to recognize merica's independence, thus commencing a long history of friendly relations etween these two countries. There is also a room dedicated to famous expat riter Paul Bowles featuring photographs from Tangier's storied "interzone" ays. The friendly curators will give excellent tours on request, but calling first s recommended. *(8 rue d'America. Enter the medina via the steps on rue du Portugal nd look for the yellow archway emblazoned with the US seal. ☎039 93 53 17. Open M-10am-1pm and 3-5pm. Donation suggested.)*

AR AL-MAKHZEN. An opulent palace, currently under renovation, with hand-oven tapestries, inlaid ceilings, and foliated archways, the Dar al-Makhzen was nce home to the ruling pasha of Tangier and is now the Museum of Moroccan Art. he collection includes intriguing exhibits of ceramics, carpets, silver jewelry, eapons, and musical instruments, with plaques in French and English. *(Currently ndergoing renovations; call to see if it has reopened. The easiest way to reach the museum and e pl. de la Kasbah grounds is to enter the medina from the porte de la Kasbah gate and stick to e rampart wall until you reach the wide open space of pl. de la Kasbah. The museum is to the ght. ☎039 93 20 97. Open W-M 9am-12:30pm and 3-5:30pm. 10dh.)*

ARKETS. The medina's commercial center is the **Grand Socco.** This busy square nd traffic circle is cluttered with fruit vendors, parsley stands, and *kebab* and fish alls. Off of rue de Fez is the small but colorful **Fez Market** where local merchants ater to Tangier's European community. *(Uphill on rue de la Liberté, across pl. France, nd 2 blocks down rue de Fez on the right.)* Berbers from the Rif come to the **Dradeb dis-ict** (west of the Grand Socco along rue Bou Arrakia and rue de la Montagne) very Thursday and Sunday to vend pottery, olives, mint, and fresh fruit. Unless angier is your only stop, it is best to wait until elsewhere to buy crafts.

THER SIGHTS. Rue Riad Sultan runs alongside the **Jardins du Soltane,** where arti-ans weave carpets, and continues to **place de la Kasbah,** a sunny courtyard with a romontory offering views of Spain and the Atlantic Ocean. With your back to the ater, walk toward the far right corner of the plaza; just around the corner to the ght the **Mosque de la Kasbah** rears its octagonal minaret. Outside of the medina, 7th- and 18th-century bronze cannons hide in the **Jardins de la Mendoubia,** a peace-l park that seems far away from the excitement of the Soccos. *(Opposite rue de la berté, where rue Bou Arrakia joins the Grand Socco, through the white gate marked #50.)*

ENTERTAINMENT

he most popular evening activity in Tangier is sipping mint tea in front of a café n pl. de France or bd. Pasteur. The **Café de Paris,** 1 pl. de France, hosted countless ndezvous between spies during WWII. Coming from the Grand Socco, look to e left. (☎039 93 84 44. Tea and coffee 5-6dh. Open daily 7am-11:30pm.) Inside the edina, **Café Central,** was a favorite of William S. Burroughs (off the Petit Socco; me hours and prices). Cafés tend to attract a male crowd, but female tourists ould not be afraid to grab a table and an orange juice—it's perfectly acceptable.

The best place for a beer with little hassle is the **Tanger Inn,** rue Magellan (open m-late). Those in search of a quiet drink can try **Negresco,** 20 rue Mexique, off e pl. France. The city's longest-running bar, it attracts expats and backpackers. 039 93 80 97. Beer 15-18dh. Mixed drinks 30-35dh. Open daily 10am-midnight.)

EUTA (SEBTA) سبتة ☎039

hose travelers hoping to avoid the mess of Tangier altogether may opt to ferry to e Spanish enclave Ceuta (pop. 70,000; called *Sebta* within Morocco) and from ere cross the Moroccan border, only 5km away. Most visitors don't stay in euta, moving on immediately to Tetouan (35 min. away) or Chefchaouen (allow 4 .) for their first night. If you're trapped in Ceuta, there is a helpful **tourist booth** 956 50 6275) in the ferry terminal that has a map. There are plenty of accommo-tion options available in Ceuta itself should you need to spend the night.

BORDER CROSSING. To reach the Moroccan border from Ceuta, grab a taxi from the town center (800ptas/€4.80) or take **bus #7** (80ptas/€0.47); to reach the bus stand from the ferry (5-min. away), exit the terminal and take a left, at the end of the street (at the water) take a right up the hill, and then right again to the stand. Taxis and buses stop short of the border; you must cross on foot and have your passport stamped. Expect to be immediately accosted by guides wanting to escort you to their favorite cousin's rug emporium, but just head straight to the parking lot where **grand taxis** await (see p. 669). **Cash** exchange is also available at the border; do it here rather than in Ceuta. From the border, *grand taxis* to Tetouan (when full) are 15-20dh per person. From there you can connect to the more mellow Chefchaouen, by catching a bus or taxi. If you are heading to Algeciras (see p. 236) from Ceuta, there are sixteen **fast-ferry** departures (35min., 7:30am-10:30pm, 3400ptas/€21).

TETOUAN تطوان ☎03

For a small city, Tetouan (pronounced *tet-ta-wan)* maintains a remarkable pace th[at] can be intimidating for new arrivals in Morocco. Of Spanish origins, the city contai[ns] its share of hustlers and the down-and-out, both of whom a tourist will inevitab[ly] encounter. Its two pleasant plazas, pl. Moulay al-Mehdi and place Hassan II, connect[ed] by Calle Mohammed V, offer some respite. To reach **pl. Moulay al-Mehdi,** the heart [of] the *ville nouvelle*, from the **bus station,** follow av. Mohammed V four blocks uphi[ll]. The medina, the palace, and the spacious pl. Hassan II are halfway between the static[n] and the plaza, while the plaza itself is home to Pension Iberia, the **BCME bank,** the **po[st] office** (open M-F 8:30am-12:15pm and 2:30-6:30pm, Sa 8:30-11:30am) and **telephone[s]**. **Internet** can be found just down the street to the left of the BMCE. **CTM buses** (☎039 [...] 20 61) provide a receipt for luggage (5dh). Buses to **Casablanca** (7hr., 120dh); **Chefch[a]ouen** (1½hr., 25dh); **Fez** (5hr., 60dh); **Rabat** (6hr., 100dh); and **Tangier** (1½hr., 15dh) a[re] relatively frequent as several companies run out of Tetouan. **Grand taxis** (15-20dh) [to] Ceuta also leave from near the bus station. Taxis to Chefchaouen (25dh when full) ru[n] from a stand 10min. away; walk from pl. Moulay al-Mehdi away from the bus static[n] along rue Achra Mai and bear left onto rue al-Jazair. The **tourist office** is a half bloc[k] down av. Mohammed V toward the medina, and has a map and info on guides. (Ope[n] M-F 8:30am-noon and 2:30-6:30pm.) Reach **police** at ☎19.

For accommodations, by far the best option is **Pension Iberia,** pl. Moulay a[l-]Mehdi, on the third floor above BMCE. Clean, breezy rooms make up for the lo[ng] walk upstairs. (☎039 96 36 79. Hot showers 5dh. Singles 40dh; doubles 70dh; t[ri]ples 105dh.) **Hotel Príncipe,** 20 rue Youssef, has archaically furnished rooms, a[ll] with bath and toilet. (☎039 96 27 95. Singles 70dh; doubles 100dh.) The pocke[t-]sized *pastillas* (lamb-filled pastries, 6dh) at **Café-Patisserie Smir,** 17 Calle Moha[m]med V towards the palace, make a perfect lunch-on-the-go, though there is also [a] balcony on which to enjoy the pastries (1-5dh). A popular place among Morocca[n] families, the café is also comfortable for women. (Open daily 6am-9pm.)

CHEFCHAOUEN (CHAOUEN) شفشاون ☎03

High in the Rif Mountains lies the mellow, whitewashed Chefchaouen (po[p.] 30,000). While no longer the complete escape from hustlers it once was, Chaouen['s] relaxed atmosphere and cool mountain air still refresh even the weariest of trav[el]ers. Tourists are attracted by both its manageable, Mediterranean medina and t[he] proximity to *kif* (hashish) farms, which have dominated the hills for centurie[s]. Chaouen is perfect for your first or last couple days in Morocco.

TRANSPORTATION. The **bus station** (☎039 98 95 73) is far downhill fro[m] town. **Buses** heading south fill up, so get tickets early. **CTM** and **other buses** goes [to] **Fez** (5hr., 1:15 and 3pm, 45-55dh); **Ouazzene,** the best bet for connections (1h[r.,]

7am, 1:15pm, and 3:30pm; 18dh); **Tangier** (via Tetouan, 28-33dh); and **Tetouan** (1½hr., 7 per day 6:45am-6pm, 16-18dh). To get to **Ceuta,** you must go through Tetouan. Private companies also have daily buses to Fez and Meknes. **Grand taxis** are the easiest way to get to **Tetouan** (24dh) and **Ceuta,** although they often take a while to fill. **Taxis** leave a block downhill from pl. Mohammed V.

PRACTICAL INFORMATION. From the **bus station,** head up the steep hill and turn right after several blocks onto the large road, which leads to the tree-filled, circular pl. Mohammed V; it's about a 20min. walk to the center of town (or a few dirhams for a cab). Cross the plaza and continue east on **av. Hassan II,** the *ville nouvelle's* main road. Here you'll find currency exchange at the **BMCE** (open M-F 8:15am-2:15pm), the **post office** with **telephones** (open M-F 8:30am-12:15pm and 2:30-6:30pm), and **internet** at **IRIC,** 10 av. Hassan II, for 10dh per hr. (☎039 98 97 15; open daily 9am-midnight). Chaouen has no tourist office. Av. Hassan II ends at the Bab al-Ain, the main gate into the **medina.** From Bab al-Ain, the main street, twists uphill to **place Uta al-Hammam,** the plaza at the heart of the medina. **Hospital Mohammed V** is a block west from pl. Mohammed V, and police can be reached at ☎19.

ACCOMMODATIONS AND FOOD. Chefchaouen has a slew of colorful budget hotels. Inside the medina, head uphill from Bab al-Ain; hotels are clustered all along this street and around pl. Uta al-Hammam. The best of the lot is **Hotel Andalus,** 1 rue Sidi Salem, directly behind Credit Agricola on pl. Uta al-Hammam, in the medina. The friendly owner Ahmed takes great pride in this clean, comfortable, and relaxing pension. With cheap rates, a gorgeous terrace, and large common room, it's one of Morocco's best deals. (☎039 98 60 34. Singles 30dh; doubles 60dh; triples 90dh; quads 120dh; lovely terrace 20dh. Prices include hot shower.) Tucked in the corner of whitewashed walls and next to a *hammam,* **Pension la Castellana,** 4 Sidi Ahmad Bouhali, caters almost exclusively to backpackers and encourages long stays. Walk to the end of pl. Uta al-Hammam to get there. (☎039 98 62 95. Communal kitchen and common room with stereo. Free hot showers. Singles 30dh; doubles 60dh; triples 90dh; quads 120dh.) A final option inside the medina is **Pension Znika,** 4 rue Znika, which has well-kept rooms though not as much atmosphere. (☎039 98 66 24. Singles 30dh, doubles 60dh, triples 90dh.) The best choice outside the medina is **Hotel Rif,** just outside the medina walls on rue Hassan II, has clean rooms, great views, a TV lounge, and terraces decorated in an odd combination 16th-century Moroccan and 1970s Americana motifs; they also can help with **mountain hikes** (just ask for affable owner Younes). Follow rue Hassan II to the right around the medina; it's on the left after a few blocks. (☎/fax 039 98 69 82. Singles 50dh, with shower 90dh; doubles 80dh, with shower 120dh; triples 120dh, with shower 160dh. MC/V.) For a quick bite, **Chez Aziz,** just outside Bab al-Ain, the medina's gate, has cheap, tasty snacks. (Shrimp 15dh. Sandwiches 10-30dh. Open daily noon-midnight.) Inside the medina, outdoor seating is available in pl. Uta al-Hammam at various restaurants; **Paloma** is one of the best. (Chicken tajine 25dh. Open daily 8am-11pm.) More upscale choices are along av. Hassan II.

SIGHTS. Chefchaouen's steep **medina** is one of Morocco's best. It's uncrowded and more relaxed than those of larger cities. Enter through Bab al-Ain and walk uphill toward pl. Uta al-Hammam, the center of the medina. In the *place* are several outdoor cafés, the 16th-century **Grand Mosque** with its red-and-gold minaret, and a 17th-century kasbah built by Moulay Ismail, Morocco's famous rogue. Inside the kasbah stands the 15th-century **Tower of Homage.** (Open daily 9am-1pm and 3-6:30pm. 10dh.) Chefchaouen's **souq** operates Mondays and Thursdays outside the medina and below both av. Hassan II and av. Allal ben Abdalallah.

HIKING. Chefchaouen is a good place to hike. For trailhead or map info, see Ahmed at Hotel Andalus or Younes at Hotel Rif. To obtain a friendly guide, contact Mouden Abdeslam (mobile ☎062 11 39 17). Follow the **Ras al-Ma River** (still known as Hippie River from the days Chaouen attracted many) upstream into the hills for just a few kilometers for spectacular results. For a quick view of the city, hike to the Hotel Asmaq (follow signs for the *ville nouvelle*). Behind the hotel, there's a path that winds up the peak to the left, and then runs down into the valley. You might try reaching the "Spanish mosque" about halfway up the peak to the right of the medina or the spectacular rocky arch known as the **Pont de Dieu.** Most of the hikes are quick one-hour round-trip affairs, though it takes a full day to reach the Pont de Dieu. Finally, with much planning or a guide, an **overnight hike** to villages in the mountains where Berbers will host you, can be extremely memorable.

THE MIDDLE ATLAS الاطلس المتوسط

Lacking the international influences which mold the coast or the remoteness of points farther south, the Middle Atlas is Morocco's heartland—the place where traditional culture and political dynasties were formed. Home to the Roman ruins of Volubilis and the imperial cities of Meknes and Fez, the region is full of historical points of interest. The area is not wallowing in the past, though. Modernization creates stunning contrasts, as represented by the thousands of satellite dishes facing skyward from Fez's medieval medina homes.

MEKNES ☎055

After uniting Morocco under his brutal rule, the rouge-Sultan Moulay Ismail chose Meknes as his seat of power in 1672 and tried to turn this relative backwater into a capital to rival Versailles. Though less arresting than Morocco's other imperial cities, Meknes remains a pleasant and manageable city where visitors can take leisurely enjoyment of a few impressive monuments left by Moulay Ismail as well as the world-renowned ruins of Volubilis nearby. Named for the Berber tribe Meknassa, this provincial capital, lying amid a agricultural checkerboard 1 hr. west of Fez and 3 hr. east of Rabat, has the largest Berber population in Morocco.

TRANSPORTATION

Trains: Meknes has 2 stations. Use the **Meknes al-Amir Abdelkader Station** (☎055 51 61 35), on rue d'Alger, 2 blocks from av. Mohammed V. The misnamed **Meknes Main Station** is farther from the center of town. The two have nearly identical service. To: **Casablanca** (3¾hr., 8 per day 7:50am-3:30am, 81dh); **Fez** (50min., 9 per day 9:55am-2am, 16.50dh); **Marrakesh** (8hr., 5 per day 7:50am-8:45pm, 153dh); **Rabat** (2½hr., 8 per day 7:50am-3:30am, 55.50dh); **Tangier** (4hr., 4 per day 8am-2:15am, 60dh).

Buses: CTM (☎055 51 47 59), on av. des F.A.R., a shiny, new station about 5 blocks from av. Mohammed V (take a left when exiting the station; ave. Mohammed V will be to the right). To: **al-Rachidia** (6hr., 10pm, 80dh) via Fez; **Casablanca** (4hr., 10 per day 4am-11pm, 63dh); **Fez** (1hr., 8 per day 11am-4am, 18dh); **Marrakesh** (8hr., 7pm, 132dh); **Rabat** (3hr., 10 per day 4am-11pm, 38dh); **Tangier** (5hr., 3 per day 2-7pm, 70dh). **Private companies** depart from a station on av. Mellah just outside Bab al-Khemis, on the far side of the medina away from the *ville nouvelle*. A *petit taxi* is necessary.

Taxis: *Grand Taxis* cluster, among other places, on av. des F.A.R., across from Hotel Continental, next to the private bus station, and outside the al-Amir Abdelkader train station. To **Fez** (17dh), **Moulay Idriss** (8dh), and **Rabat** (40dh).

ORIENTATION AND PRACTICAL INFORMATION

The river **Oued Boufrekane** divides Meknes into three "boroughs:" the **medina**, the neighboring **imperial city**, and the modern **ville nouvelle**. The train and CTM buses deposit passengers in the *ville nouvelle*. Tree-lined **avenue Mohammed V,** the new city's main drag, intersects with av. Hassan II. From the intersection, follow av. Hassan II, which turns into av. Moulay Ismail, to approach the medina via Bab Bou

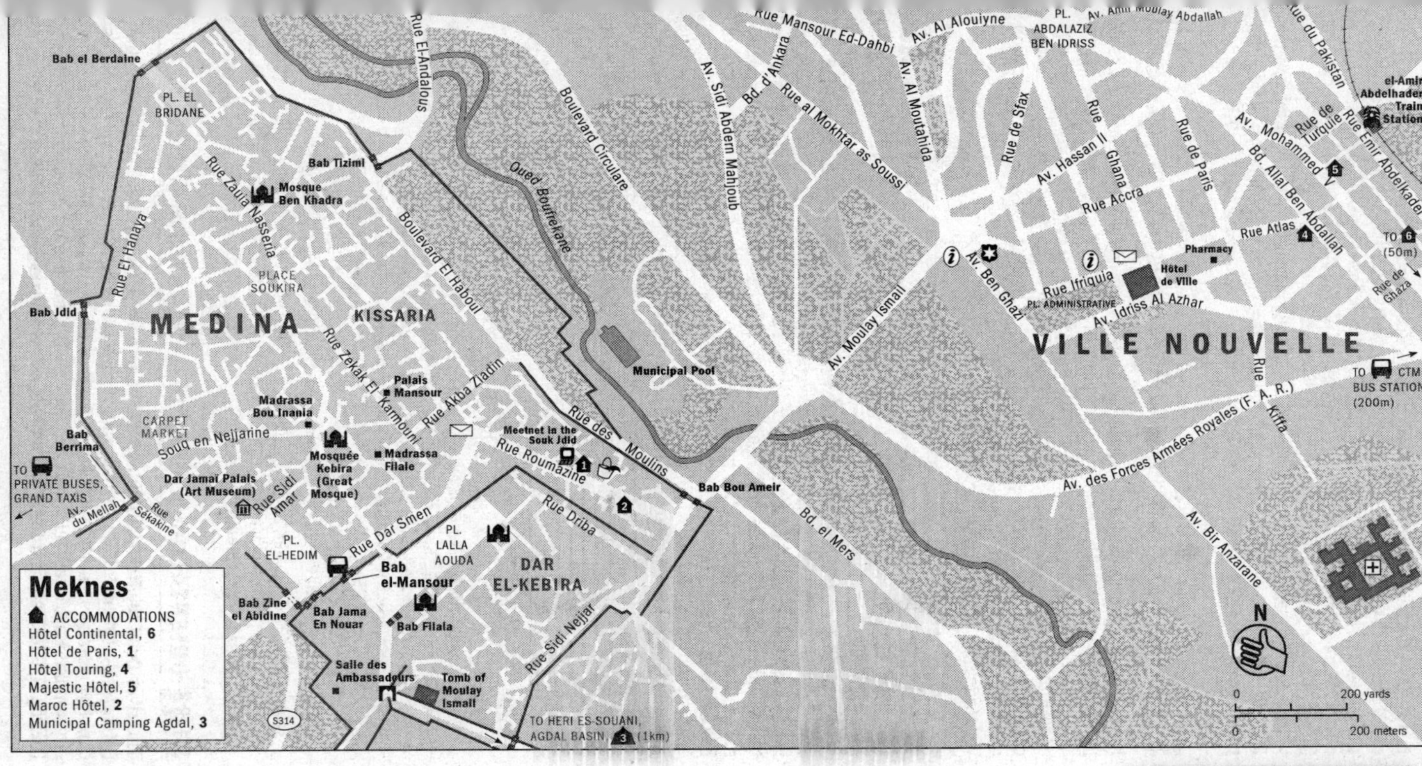
Meknes
ACCOMMODATIONS
Hôtel Continental, 6
Hôtel de Paris, 1
Hôtel Touring, 4
Majestic Hôtel, 5
Maroc Hôtel, 2
Municipal Camping Agdal, 3
VILLE NOUVELLE
MEDINA
KISSARIA
DAR EL-KEBIRA
Av. Mohammed V
Bd. Allal Ben Abdallah
Rue Emir Abdelkader
Rue de Turquie
Rue du Pakistan
Rue de Paris
Rue Ghana
Rue Accra
Rue Atlas
Av. Hassan II
Rue de Sfax
Av. Ben Ghazi
Av. Idriss Al Azhar
Rue Ifriquia
PL. ADMINISTRATIVE
Hôtel de Ville
Pharmacy
Rue Kiffa
Av. des Forces Armées Royales (F. A. R.)
Av. Bir Anzarane
TO CTM BUS STATION (200m)
TO 6 (50m)
Rue de Ghaza
el-Amir Abdelhader Train Station
PL. ABDALAZIZ BEN IDRISS
Av. Al Moutahida
Av. Al Alouiyne
Rue Mansour Ed-Dahbi
Rue al Mokhtar as Soussi
Bd. d'Ankara
Av. Sidi Abdern Mahjoub
Av. Moulay Ismail
Bd. el Mers
Boulevard Circulare
Oued Boufrekane
Rue El-Andalous
Boulevard El Haboul
Municipal Pool
Bab Bou Ameir
Rue des Moulins
Rue Roumazine
Meetnet in the Souk Jdid
Rue Driba
Rue Sidi Nejjar
Rue Akba Ziadin
Palais Mansour
Madrassa Filale
Rue Zekak El Karmouni
Mosquée Kebira (Great Mosque)
Madrassa Bou Inania
Bab Tizimi
Mosque Ben Khadra
Rue Zaouia Nasseria
PLACE SOUKIRA
PL. EL BRIDANE
CARPET MARKET
Souq en Nejjarine
Dar Jamaï Palais (Art Museum)
Rue Sidi Amar
Rue Dar Smen
PL. EL-HEDIM
PL. LALLA AOUDA
Bab el-Mansour
Bab Filala
Bab Jama En Nouar
Salle des Ambassadeurs
Tomb of Moulay Ismail
Bab Zine el Abidine
Rue El Hanaya
Rue Sekakine
Bab el Berdaine
Bab Jdid
Bab Berrima
TO PRIVATE BUSES, GRAND TAXIS
Av. du Mellah
TO HERI ES-SOUANI, AGDAL BASIN (1km)
S314
N
200 yards
200 meters

Amir. To reach the colossal **Bab al-Mansour** (the entrance to the imperial complex) and **Plaza al-Khedim** (the medina's main square), head up the hill from Bab Bou-Amir, take a right on rue Roumazine and then a left on rue Dar Smen. Local buses #5, 7, and 9 (1.50-2.30dh) shuttle between the CTM bus station and Bab al-Mansour (a 20min. walk); a *petit taxi* should cost 8dh, a *grand taxi* 2dh.

Tourist Office: 27 pl. Administrative (☎055 52 44 26; fax 51 60 46). From the Abdelkader train station, go straight 2 blocks, turn left on av. Mohammed V, and make an immediate right. Cross rue Allal ben Abdallah, continue toward the Hôtel de Ville, and veer right. The tourist office is on the right just after the post office. Some English spoken. Brochure with basic map of city. Official but unnecessary local guides: half-day 120dh, full-day 150dh. Open July-Sept. M-F 8am-6:30pm; Oct.-June M-F 8:30am-noon and 2:30-6:30pm. **Syndicat d'Initiative** (☎055 52 01 91), on Esplanade de la Foire, off av. Moulay Ismail and inside the yellow gate. Open M-F 8:30am-noon and 3-6pm.

Currency Exchange: BMCE, 98 av. des F.A.R. (☎055 52 03 52). **ATM**. Exchange window open daily 10am-2pm and 4-8pm. **Hôtel Rif,** on Zenkat Accra, cashes traveler's checks for a fee. **Banks** line both Mohammed V and Hassan II.

Late-Night Pharmacy: Red Cross Emergency Pharmacy (☎055 52 33 75), in pl. Administrative. Open daily 8:30am-8:30pm.

Hospitals: Hôpital Moulay Ismail (☎055 52 28 05 or 52 28 06), on av. des F.A.R.

Internet Access: In the *ville nouvelle,* there are many choices, including **Safarynet,** av Hassan II, by the local bus stop. 7dh per hr. Open daily 9am-7pm. **Meetnet in the Souk Jdid,** 38 rue Roumazine, in the Medina. 6dh per hr. Open Sa-Th 10:30am-11:45pm, F 10:30am-12:20pm and 3-11:45pm.

Post Office: pl. Administrative. **Poste Restante** at the side entrance. Open M-Sa 8am-3:30pm. **Branch office** on rue Dar Smen, near the medina.

ACCOMMODATIONS

MEDINA

Rue Roumazine and rue Dar Smen house most of the medina's budget hotels, although even backpackers opt for plusher accommodations in the *ville nouvelle.*

Maroc Hôtel, 7 rue Roumazine (☎055 53 00 75), off rue Roumazine. Clean, small rooms situated around a leafy courtyard. Cold showers and squat toilets. Breakfast 20dh. Hot showers 10dh. 60dh per person.

Hôtel de Paris, 58 rue Roumazine, opposite a dentist's office. Look for the sign that says "Hôtel." Basic and clean. Shower and hammam available next door, both 6dh. Singles 35-40dh; doubles 70dh; triples 90dh; nice terrace 20dh but beds are rough.

Municipal Camping Agdal (☎055 55 53 96), on the ramparts of the medina behind Agdal Basin. Follow the signs from Bab Mansour (15 min. walk) or Bab Bou Amir. Outdoes any option in the hotel scene. Set in a beautiful, wooded park with amenities such as hot showers (7dh) and a kitchen. Restaurant's 3-course *menu* 55dh. Reception daily 8am-1pm and 4-8pm. 17dh per adult, 12dh per child, 10dh per tent, 17dh per car.

VILLE NOUVELLE

The *ville nouvelle* offers greater comfort, easier access to banks, CTM buses, and trains, but prices are higher than in the medina. Most of the cheapest hotels lie around av. Mohammed V and rue Allal ben Abdallah.

Majestic Hôtel, 19 av. Mohammed V (☎055 52 20 35; fax 055 52 74 27), near the train station. Comfortable rooms, a newly renovated courtyard, cozy lounge, modern bathrooms, and free hot showers. Breakfast 24dh. Backpacker dorm on terrace 60dh, includes breakfast. Singles 112-189dh; doubles 150-225dh; triples 217-292dh. Prices depend on bathroom options. Off-season 10% discount.

Hôtel Continental, 92 av. des F.A.R. (☎055 52 54 71), at the intersection with Mohammed V. Look for neon blue sign. A perfectly adequate choice. Spacious rooms with red drapes; lounge and café area on second floor; and friendly reception. Singles with shower 109dh, with shower and toilet 137dh; doubles 141dh/162dh.

Hôtel Touring, 34 rue Allal ben Abdallah (☎055 52 23 51), on the street parallel to Mohammed V away from the train station, near the intersection with rue Atlas. One of the cheapest places in the *ville nouvelle,* this hotel is dark but clean and spacious. Singles 74dh, with shower 106dh; doubles 95dh, with shower 134dh.

FOOD

MEDINA

Vendors in the **place al-Khedim** hawk *merguez* (spicy moroccan sausage) sandwiches, freshly made potato chips, corn on the cob and fresh OJ. Other inexpensive fare sizzles in the one-man *brochetteries* on **rue Dar Smen.** Few places have menus, let alone copies in English or French—most have their options on display. The daily **vegetable market** sprouts beside Bab Mansour.

Restaurant Economique, 123 rue Dar Smen, opposite Bab Mansour, under the hand-painted sign. Friendly manager serves tasty staples at reasonable prices. Try the excellent chicken with veggies (25dh). Couscous or *tajine* 25dh. Open daily 7am-10pm.

VILLE NOUVELLE

Like the very concept of the *ville nouvelle* itself, most of the best options are imported from abroad. This time, however, they're worth checking out.

New Mex Snack Grille, 20 rue de Paris; tucked away off rue de Paris; look for the sign. Sick of *tajine?* Afraid of it? Come here for shockingly good Tex-Mex fare (34-45dh) complemented by a very refreshing, A/C-fueled atmosphere. Friendly manager also serves pizzas and sandwiches (30-45dh). Open daily 11:30am-11pm.

Pizzeria le Four, av. Zenkat Atlas (☎055 52 08 57), off av. Mohammed V near the train station. Flavorful Italian cuisine, attentive waitstaff, and romantic, candle-lit ambiance are perfect for your first Moroccan date. Also good for women travellers. A/C and liquor license. Pasta and pizza 40-50dh. 14% tax. Open daily noon-3pm and 7pm-midnight.

Restaurant Marhaba, 23 av. Mohammed V (☎055 52 16 32). A couple of doors from Hôtel Majestic. Serves up a great bargain—bread, eggs, corn fritters, and *harira* for 3.60dh. No vegetarian options. Entrées 18-30dh. Open daily 11am-11pm.

SIGHTS

Meknes's best sights cluster around the magnificent **Bab al-Mansour,** which has become a national symbol. Through the gate lie the remainders of Meknes's imperial past, and in front of it thrives the medina and the lively pl. al-Khedim.

IMPERIAL MEKNES

Weakened by war, weather, and the Great Earthquake of 1755, the ramparts of the **Dar al-Kebira** (Imperial City) testify to Meknes's former glory. Sultan Moulay Ismail, who, along with Hassan II, is perhaps Morocco's most revered visionary, personally supervised the building of over 25km of protective **walls** for his city within a city. Strolling about the site with a pick-ax and whip in hand, the sultan criticized and occasionally decapitated workers who displeased him. Gathering materials from sights all over Morocco, including Roman marble from the ruins at Volubilis, Moulay Ismail created a radiant city. Ismail razed part of the medina to create **place al-Khedim** (Plaza of Destruction), an approach to **Bab al-Mansour,** Morocco's finest gate. Today, only the walls and several large monuments remain.

TOMB OF MOULAY ISMAIL. The tomb, along with its accompanying **mosque,** is one of only two Moroccan religious buildings open to non-Muslims and well worth a visit. After several bright yellow antechambers lies a larger courtyard. At the far left end is an ornately designed room from which you can view the tomb itself. The tomb is flanked by two functioning grandfather clocks, a consolation prize from

BARGAINING 101 You'll have to do it for everything from carpets to camel treks, so you might as well do it right. First off, you never have to buy anything just because you look in the shop; feel free to say nothing interests you in a shop and move on. Once you've found something you want, let the shopkeeper be the first to offer a price. You'll then be expected to make a counter-offer; don't be intimidated by the shopkeeper's enthusiasm or claim that he's "making you a good price." Decide what you want to ultimately pay (anywhere from one-tenth to half of the initial price) then offer one-third to half of *that*. The shopkeeper may respond by laughing or calling you a Berber (the true skinflints), at which point you may choose to politely but firmly walk out. (Generally, you should leave at least once when haggling over a big purchase.) Invariably, you will be dragged back in. You can gauge the seller's willingness to negotiate by how quickly (and by how much) he drops his price. If you're traveling with a friend, it can be useful to play good-cop/bad-cop with the storekeeper, one of you always saying the item is too expensive or that you need to move on.

If you're at a impasse, you can try any of the following: 1) You've seen the same thing elsewhere for X (lower) price. 2) You like it but it is flawed; point out inconsistencies, blemishes, etc. 3) You are a student/budget traveler (sellers scale their prices to what you look like you can pay). 4) Tell them you have made your final offer.

In larger souks, the same goods are often available at several stores, so don't be afraid to try a couple of negotiations until you find a price you like. By the fourth haggle of your day you will be much more comfortable. Be wary of shopkeepers trying to sell you something that is somehow "unique;" there are no special years, months or weeks on the calendar of Berber carpet makers, so don't pay as if there were. On the other hand, remember that each new shopkeeper is a whole new ballgame.

Louis XIV after he refused Moulay Ismail's proposal to his daughter (don't feel sad for ol' Moulay; he already had over 300 lovers). Photographs are allowed. *(Through the 2 blue arches, and then immediately to the left. Open Sa-Th 9am-noon and 3-6pm, F 3-6pm. Free, but donations requested at the room of the tomb.)*

SALLE DES AMBASSADEURS. Standing by itself in an open court is the green-tiled roof of the recently restored Salle des Ambassadeurs, where Ismail conducted affairs of state. Ask the guard to unlock the doors to the so-called **"Christian Dungeon,"** a 6 sq. km. underground storehouse and granary for the Sultan, his entourage, and their horses. This storehouse is said to have once housed some 50 to 100,000 Christian prisoners. Since the "dungeon" remains a cool 15°C even in summer, it is the perfect place to avoid the midday sun. *(From pl. al-Khedim, go through Bab al-Mansour or one of the nearby smaller gates, walk straight, and follow the wall on the right around the bend. Open daily 9am-noon and 3-6pm. 10dh.)*

OTHER IMPERIAL CITY SIGHTS. A short trek from Moulay Ismail's tomb is the **Heri al-Souani** (storehouse), a cool granary with immense cisterns designed to withstand prolonged sieges. Trees and birds have invaded, giving it a jungle-like feel. *(Open daily 9am-noon and 3-6pm. 10dh.)* Below lies the **Agdal Basin,** once Moulay Ismail's private country club and his reservoir in case of siege. His wives (more than 300 of them) and their 800 kids were said to swim there to escape the stifling summer heat. Today, it is a good place for an evening stroll. *(To get to the Heri al-Souani and Agdal Basin from Bab al-Mansour, take a petit taxi for 7dh. Free.)*

MEDINA

Meknes's medina is more pleasant, tranquil, and compact than those of the other imperial cities. Facing the Dar Jamaï Museum of Moroccan Art, take the alley to the left of the entrance. Push straight ahead to **Souq al-Nejjarine,** a major street. Heading left here brings you first to the **textile souq,** the **carpenters' souq,** and the **carpet market.** The rest of the medina is best explored like any other: wander until you get lost, then try to find your way out.

GREAT MOSQUE AND MADRASA BOU. While everything except the green-glazed minaret of the Great Mosque *(al-masjid al-kebira)* is off-limits to non-Muslims, the breathtaking 14th-century Madrasa Bou Inania, across from it, is not. A college of theology and Muslim law, this *madrasa* typifies traditional Merenid architecture—the courtyard combines cedar, stucco, and mosaics with characteristic flair. Upstairs are a number of cells, each of which snugly hosted at least two students. The roof, which you may have to unlock yourself, offers a splendid view of the minaret of the Great Mosque and the rooftops of Meknes. *(Face Dar Jamaï in pl. al-Khedim, turn right onto rue Sidi Amar, and enter the medina. Follow the alley as it turns left, then fork right. Madrasa open daily 9am-noon and 3-6pm. 10dh.)*

DAR JAMAÏ PALACE. For over a year, Dar Jamaï Palace has been closed for renovations. It is aiming to reopen in March of 2002. Built in the 19th century by one of Sultan Moulay Hassan I's powerful government ministers, the Dar Jamaï Palace houses the **Museum of Moroccan Art**. Most pieces are contextualized in restored versions of the rooms in which they were originally displayed. *(At the far end of pl. al-Khedim. ☎055 53 08 63. Closed for renovations until at least 2002; call for updates. 10dh.)*

DAYTRIPS FROM MEKNES

VOLUBILIS تجولوبيلى

*There are no direct buses to Volubilis: a **taxi** is the most reliable and convenient method of transport. While you can hire a grand taxi near the private bus station in Meknes, you need a 6-person party to get the cheapest fare and taxis rarely fill up; alone it will cost 100dh. The surest way is to take a grand taxi to Moulay Idriss (30 minutes; 8dh per place) and then from Moulay Idriss, either walk if it's not too hot (4km; 40 minutes; straight from junction with Moulay Idriss and then left at the sign for Oualili) or save your energy and take another taxi from Moulay Idriss (10dh total). Alternatively, you can also try grabbing a **bus** from Meknes to Ouezzane (every hr. 7am-7pm, 10dh) and asking the driver to drop you off near the ruins. To get back to Meknes, hop on a tour bus or wait by the parking lot for a taxi; they are infrequent but not rare. Don't leave the return for too late as rides dry up as it gets later. In general, leave yourself at least 1.5 hr. to enjoy the ruins.*

Thirty-three kilometers from Meknes lie the dramatic ruins of Volubilis, the best-preserved Roman site in Morocco and perhaps all of North Africa. Surrounded by beautiful country-side and containing an extensive collection of **Roman mosaics,** Volubilis has deservedly earned must-see status. Once a major center for the olive oil trade, the city flourished under Roman rule, reaching its zenith in the 2nd and 3rd centuries AD when it became the capital of the kingdom of Mauritania. The Romans, who viewed their North African possessions as a bread basket for their European citizens, ordered the deforestation of the area to make room for grain crops; from that point on local resources dwindled and the city began to decline. When Moulay Idriss took control of the city in the 18th century, he siphoned off much of the residential population to Fez and Meknes, and claimed many of the city's pillars and stones for his own palace. The Lisbon Earthquake of 1755, which wreaked devastation all along the Atlantic seaboard, finally sealed the city's fate.

When US General George C. Patton visited the ruins, he declined an offer of a guided tour—he believed he had been stationed here as a Roman centurion in his previous life and thus knew his way around. If you've been equally lucky, stop reading here. Otherwise, head past the ticket office and over a bridge, take a left and climb the steps to the top, where among the ruins of a housing and industrial area are several **olive presses.** In this area, you'll also find the **House of Orpheus** which includes a few well-preserved mosaics including one which depicts the Orpheus myth. Nearby is a small building containing a restored olive press and then further on are the towering columns of the **capitol** (dating from 218 AD) and arches of the **basilica.** The basilica, despite its name, served as the courthouse during Roman times. Follow the path to the **House of the Athlete** on the left, named for its mosaic depicting the victor of a *desultor* race (which involved mounting a moving horse). In the middle of town looms the **Triumphal Arch,** built in AD 217 to celebrate Emperor Caracalla and his scheming mother Julia Domna. Julia assured her son's power by helping him murder his rival Gota in AD 212. The gate marks the beginning of the town's main street, **Decumanus Maximus.** The houses along the street, including the **House of the Ephebus** and the **House of the Knight,** have impressive mosaics of Dionysus, Hercules, Orpheus, and other mythical figures. From the top of the hill is an amazing panoramic view of Volubilis. The **Tangier Gate,** with the **Gordien Palace** just before it, is atop the hill. Walk down the hill and head toward the only tree in front. Under it is the **Cortege of Venus,** which holds several mosaics including *Chariot Race*, *Bacchus Surrounded by the Four Seasons*, *Diana Bathing*, and the *Abduction of Hylas by Nymphs*, all dating as far back as the late 2nd or early 3rd century AD. Cross the stream back to the ticket gate to see the ruins of a **Temple** dedicated to Jupiter, Juno, and Minerva.

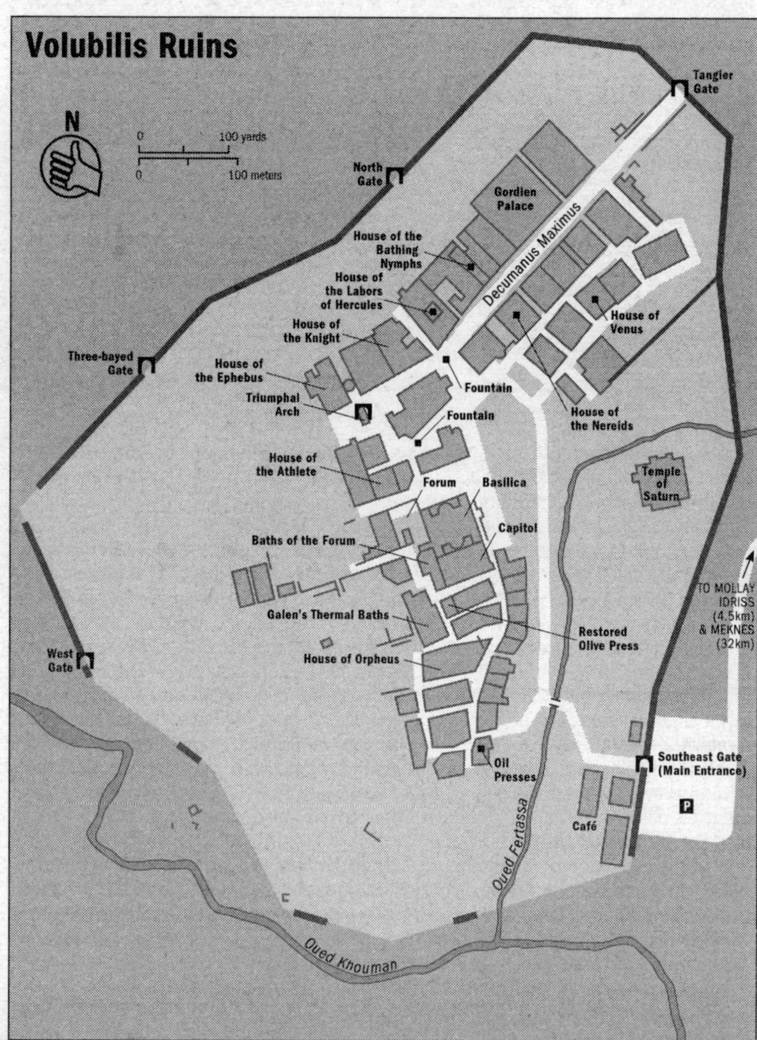

The ruins are open daily sunrise to sunset (admission 20dh). They are more peaceful and scenic in the early morning or late afternoon. Be sure to bring a hat, sunscreen, water, and sunglasses (if possible) if you are visiting in the afternoon as the sun can be simply ferocious. You might also prepare a picnic snack or lunch in Meknes to bring and enjoy on the grounds at Volubilis. There is, however, a small and overpriced café at the sight. Volubilis is one place where you might seriously consider hiring a guide (through the ticket office for roughly 20-30dh per person) if you are interested in historical detail. While placards labeling sights have been recently added, they are very brief.

MOULAY IDRISS

Take a grand taxi (8dh) from the private bus station in Meknes.

Four kilometers before Volubilis, the road from Meknes passes through Moulay Idriss, a pilgrimage site named after the man who spread Islam through Morocco. A third-generation descendant of Mohammed, Idriss united the Berber tribes and founded the country's first dynasty. Non-Muslims cannot spend the night or visit the mosques or shrines; but Moulay Idriss is an easy stop on the way to Volubilis and is refreshingly tourist-free. From the taxi parking lot, walk up the hill to the left and you will reach the main square of the town. Cafés and food stalls are located here. To reach the mausoleum of Moulay Idriss, head straight from the main square through the arch; the mausoleum is straight ahead to the left beyond the three-arched gateway. For views of the city, ascend to the medina by heading under the arch to your right at the mausoleum viewing area. From the medina's *petit* and *grand* terraces, there are wonderful views of the city. Young and eager locals (don't worry, they'll find you) can lead you there for a few dirhams and point out the only **cylindrical minaret** in Morocco.

FEZ فاس ☎055

Fez's bustling, colorful medina epitomizes Morocco—no visit to the country is complete without seeing it. Artisans bang out sheets of brass, donkeys strain under crates of Coca-Cola, children balance trays of dough on their heads, and tourists groups struggle to stay together. Along narrow streets, the scent of *brochettes* on open grills combine with whiffs of hash, the sweet aroma of cedar shavings, and the stench of fresh fish brought at daybreak from the coast. Since UNESCO designated Fez a World Heritage Site in 1981, the city's walls have been largely restored, and fresh plaster and cobblestones make this medieval city even more fantastic. Founded in the 8th century by Moulay Idriss I, Fez rose to prominence with the construction of the Qairaouine, a university-mosque complex, which was one of the world's first universities. With such a wealth of resources, Fez emerged as the most prominent city in the Maghreb, nurturing (or destroying) political dynasties and handing down legal rulings to the rest of the region. Today, post-independence Fez has been somewhat eclipsed by Rabat (the political capital), Casablanca (the economic capital), and Marrakesh (the tourist capital). While modern Fez is an expansive city containing a conspicuously middle-class *ville nouvelle*, it remains at the artistic, intellectual and spiritual helm of the nation and is central to many Moroccans' sense of national pride.

TRANSPORTATION

Flights: Aérodrome de Fès-Saïs (☎055 62 47 12), 12km out of town on the road to Immouzzèr. Bus #16 leaves from pl. Mohammed V (3dh). *Grand taxis* (120dh) also run there. **Royal Air Maroc** (☎055 62 55 16), 54 av. Hassan II, flies daily to **Casablanca.** Also services Tangier, Marrakesh, Marseilles, and Paris.

Trains: (☎055 93 03 33), av. Almohades, at rue Chenguit; a five-minute taxi ride to the Ville Nouvelle (5dh) or about ten minutes to the medina's Bab Boujeloud (10dh). 2nd-class trains are comfier than buses, and only cost a few dirhams more. To: **Casablanca**

(4.5hr., 8 per day 7:15am-2:40am, 97dh); **Marrakesh** (9hr., 5 per day 7:15am-2:40am, 130dh); **Meknes** (1hr., 9 per day 7:15am-2:40am, 16.50dh); **Rabat** (3½hr., 8 per day 7:15am-2:40am, 72dh); **Tangier** (5hr., 4 per day 7:15am-1:20am, 72dh).

Buses: CTM (☎055 73 29 92) stops near pl. d'Atlas, at the far end of the *ville nouvelle*. From pl. Florence, walk down bd. Mohammed V for fifteen minutes and turn left onto av. Youssef ben Tachfine. At pl. d'Atlas, take the 1st right. To: **Casablanca** (5hr., 9 per day 7am-1am, 85dh); **Chefchaouen** (4hr., 3 per day 8am-11:45pm, 50dh); **Marrakesh** (8hr., 2 per day, 130dh); **Meknes** (1hr., 6 per day 9:30am-1am, 18dh); **Rabat** (3hr., 9 per day 7am-1am, 55dh); **Tangier** (6hr., 3 per day 11am-1am, 85dh).

Public Transportation: Pl. Mohammed V and pl. Résistance are the major hubs for city buses. Important routes include: bus #9 and 11 from the Syndicat d'Initiative to **Bab Boujeloud** and **Dar Batha;** #3 from the train station and pl. Mohammed V to **Bab Ftouh;** #4 from pl. Résistance to **Bab Smarine** in Fez al-Jdid. They cost 2.2dh; fares increase 20% July-Sept. 15 after 8:30pm, Sept. 16-June after 8pm.

Car Rental: Avis, 50 bd. Chefchaouni (☎055 62 67 46). **Hertz,** 1 Kissauiat de la Foire (☎055 62 28 12). Fiat Palios 500dh per day excluding tax.

Taxis: Some prices are fixed such as *grand taxis* to: Meknes (400dh), Rabat (800dh), Volubilis/Moulay Idriss (800 round-trip). A loop of Fez and around the medina costs 200dh. See the tourist office if you have questions. Stands at the post office, Syndicat d'Initiative, Bab Boujeloud, and Bab Guissa. *Petit taxis* should always use a meter. Fares increase 50% July-Sept. 15 after 8:30pm, Sept. 16-June after 8pm.

ORIENTATION AND PRACTICAL INFORMATION

Fez is large and spread out but still manageable. Essentially three cities in one: the fashionable, French-built **ville nouvelle,** 1.5km from the medina; the Arab **Fez al-Jdid** ("New Fez"), containing the Jewish cemetery and the palace of Hassan II, next to the medina; and the enormous medina of **Fez al-Bali** ("Old Fez") housing nearly 500,000 residents. The *ville nouvelle* is most convenient for services and has the quietest accommodations; its two central streets are **av. Hassan II** and **bd. Mohammed V,** which intersect at **pl. Florence,** the center of activity. Walking down av. Moulay Youssef from the *ville nouvelle* brings you to pl. Alaouites in Fez al-Jdid, directly in front of the king's palace, **Dar al-Makhzen.** After passing through Bab Smarine on the left, rue Fez al-Jdid takes you the length of the palace. At the end, a right through Bab Dakakeen leads to Fez al-Bali and its main gate **Bab Boujeloud.** The two main streets of Fez al-Bali are **Tala'a Kebira** and **Tala'a Seghira,** although they are barely wide enough for its shops, a donkey, and your backpack.

Tourist Office: Syndicat d'Initiative (☎055 62 34 60), pl. Mohammed V. Helpful *Fassi* (citizens of Fez) answer almost any question. Limited English spoken. Same meager maps by the Moroccan National Tourism Office. Hire official local guides here for 120dh for half-day or 150dh for full-day; national guides for 150dh for half-day, 250dh for full day. Open M-F 8:30am-noon and 2:30-6:30pm, Sa 8:30am-noon.

Currency Exchange: BMCE, pl. Mohammed V, opposite the Syndicat d'Initiative, to the right of the main bank entrance. Handles MC/V and traveler's checks transactions and has **ATMs.** Open M-F 8:15-2:15pm. **Sheraton Fez Hôtel,** at the end of av. Hassan II, 4 blocks from the post office, has after-hours exchange.

Luggage Storage: At the train station. 2.5dh per bag per day. Open 24hr. Also at the CTM station. 5dh per bag per day. Open 24hr.

Police: ☎19.

Late-Night Pharmacy: Municipalité de Fès (☎055 62 33 80), av. Moulay Youssef off Pl. Résistance, 5min. uphill from the royal palace. Open daily 8pm-8am.

Hospital: Ghastani (☎055 62 27 76), at the end of av. Hassan II away from the medina.

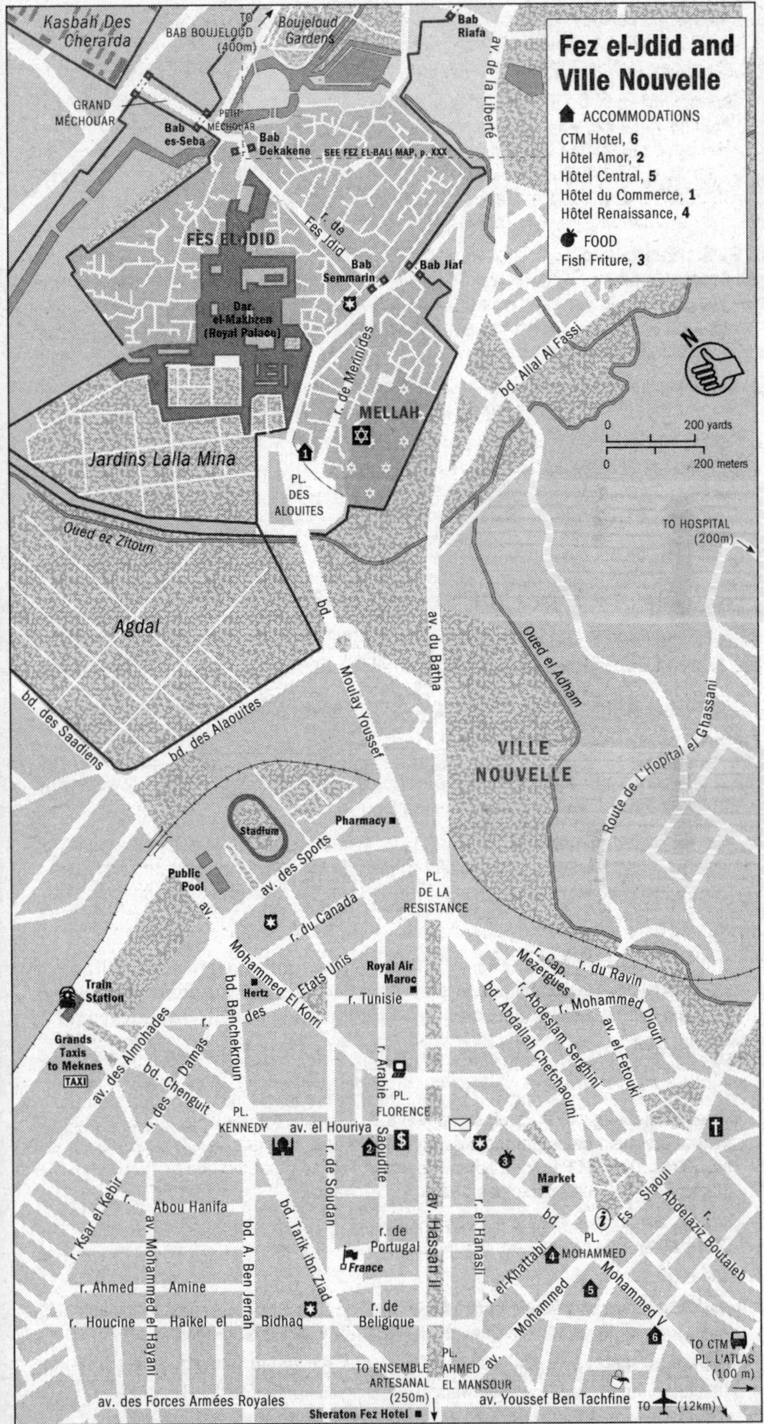
Fez el-Jdid and Ville Nouvelle
ACCOMMODATIONS
CTM Hotel, 6
Hôtel Amor, 2
Hôtel Central, 5
Hôtel du Commerce, 1
Hôtel Renaissance, 4
FOOD
Fish Friture, 3
Kasbah Des Cherarda
TO BAB BOUJELOUD (400m)
Boujeloud Gardens
Bab Riafa
av. de la Liberté
GRAND MÉCHOUAR
PETIT MÉCHOUAR
Bab es-Seba
Bab Dekakene
SEE FEZ EL-BALI MAP, p. XXX
r. de Fès Jdid
FÈS EL-JDID
Bab Semmarin
Bab Jiaf
Dar el-Makhzen (Royal Palace)
r. de Merinides
MELLAH
bd. Allal Al Fassi
200 yards
200 meters
Jardins Lalla Mina
PL. DES ALOUITES
Oued ez Zitoun
TO HOSPITAL (200m)
Agdal
bd. Moulay Youssef
av. du Batha
Oued el Adham
bd. des Saadiens
bd. des Alaouites
VILLE NOUVELLE
Route de L'Hopital el Ghassani
Stadium
Pharmacy
Public Pool
av. des Sports
PL. DE LA RESISTANCE
r. du Canada
av. Mohammed El Korri
r. Cap. Mezergues
r. du Ravin
r. des Etats Unis
Royal Air Maroc
Train Station
Hertz
r. Tunisie
r. Abdesiam Serghini
r. Mohammed Diouri
bd. Benchekroun
bd. Abdallah Chefchaouni
av. el Fetouki
Grands Taxis to Meknes
TAXI
av. des Almohades
r. des Damas
bd. Chenguit
r. Arabie Saoudite
PL. FLORENCE
PL. KENNEDY
av. el Houriya
r. de Soudan
Market
r. Abou Hanifa
av. Mohammed el Hayani
r. Ksar el Kebir
bd. A. Ben Jerrah
bd. Tarik ibn Ziad
av. Hassan II
r. el Hanasli
bd. Es Slaoui
Abdelaziz Boutaleb
r. de Portugal
France
PL. MOHAMMED
r. el-Khattabi
av. Mohammed V
r. Ahmed Amine
r. Houcine Haikel el Bidhaq
r. de Beligique
TO CTM PL. L'ATLAS (100 m)
TO ENSEMBLE ARTESANAL (250m)
PL. AHMED EL MANSOUR
av. des Forces Armées Royales
av. Youssef Ben Tachfine
Sheraton Fez Hotel
TO (12km)

Internet Access: Soprocon, off pl. Florence, upstairs from a teleboutique. 10dh per hr. Open daily 9am-11pm.

Post Office: At the corner of av. Hassan II and bd. Mohammed V in the *ville nouvelle*. **Branch offices** at pl. d'Atlas and in the medina at pl. Batha. All open July-Sept. 15 M-F 8:30am-2:30pm; Sept. 16-June M-F 8:30am-12:15pm and 2:30-6:30pm.

ACCOMMODATIONS

VILLE NOUVELLE

Rooms here are convenient to local services and more comfortable than those in the medina, which is only a quick cab ride away. The cheapest lodgings clump on or just off bd. Mohammed V, between av. Mohammed al-Slaoui near the bus station and av. Hassan II near the post office.

Hôtel Central, 50 rue Brahim Roudani (☎055 62 23 33), off pl. Mohammed V. The best deal in the *ville nouvelle*. Clean rooms with better than average furnishings. Singles 59dh, with shower 89dh; doubles 89dh/119dh; triples 150dh/180dh.

Hôtel Amor, 31 rue Arabie Saoudite (☎055 62 27 24), off pl. Florence. A good choice for those with a little more to spend. All rooms are clean, nicely furnished, and have private bath. Singles 164dh; doubles 198dh.

Hotel CTM, off bd. Mohammed V, (☎055 62 28 11) between pl. Mohammed V and the CTM bus station. Basic rooms with rock hard beds, but clean and cheap. Singles 50dh, with shower 65dh; doubles 65dh, with shower 85dh.

Hôtel Renaissance, 29 rue Abd al-Krim al-Khattabi (☎055 62 21 93), just before pl. Mohammed V coming from pl. Florence. If all you want is a place to put your bags and rest your head, then the cheapest of the *ville nouvelle* hotels is passable. Squat toilets. Hot showers 6dh. Singles 50dh; doubles 90dh; triples 120dh; quads 140dh.

FEZ AL-JDID

Fez al-Jdid has only one hotel of note, but the location is perfect—close to the medina without the annoyance of hustlers.

Hôtel du Commerce (☎055 62 22 31), pl. Alaouites, by the Royal Palace. That this place is always packed is a testament to the friendly owners, comfortable rooms, and affordable prices. Views of palace grounds. Cold showers. Singles 50dh; doubles 90dh.

FEZ AL-BALI

Around the Bab Boujeloud area is the place to go for budget rooms. Although they're less pleasant than those in the *ville nouvelle*, and hustlers may seem to have tourist-radar, they're still and perfect for that 24 hr. medina experience.

Hôtel Cascade, 26 Serrajine Boujeloud (☎055 63 84 42), just inside Bab Boujeloud and to the right. Friendly, Berber manager Said offers many perks such as free hot showers, free luggage storage, a modern toilet, a tap for hand-washing clothes, and a laundry service (30dh for 15-20 pieces). As a result of all this, Cascade is a popular place with backpackers and families. Adequate rooms. The terrace provides a bird's-eye view of the medina. 40dh per person; terrace 20dh.

Hôtel Lamrani (☎055 63 44 11), Tala'a Seghira. Enter Bab Boujeloud; take the 1st right, then a left and through the arch. Unusually clean, with in-room sinks. Backpackers head here when the Cascade is full. Nearby *hammam* 6dh. Singles 50-60dh; doubles 80-120dh; triples 150-180dh.

Hotel Erraha (☎055 63 32 26). Follow the alley on the right of the café to the right just before Bab Boujeloud. Basic rooms. Singles 40dh; doubles 70dh; triples 100dh.

Hotel Mauritania, 20 Serrajine Boujeloud, (☎055 63 35 18), to the right after the Bab Boujeloud. Small rooms. Hot showers 10dh. Singles 40dh; doubles 100dh.

FOOD

VILLE NOUVELLE

Cheap sandwich dives, cafés, and juice shops line both sides of bd. Mohammed V. The *ville nouvelle* is stricken with more than its fair share of western-style fast food joints that offer a time-out for those overwhelmed by real Moroccan fare. Back in search of local eats, poke through stalls of fresh food at the **central market** on bd. Mohammed V, two blocks up from pl. Mohammed V. (Open daily 7am-1pm.)

Restaurant Fish Friture, 138 bd. Mohammed V. (☎055 94 06 99), tucked away off bd. Mohammed V, near pl. de Florence. A small and relaxing maritime-themed restaurant with friendly service. Good for lunch or dinner with excellent fish brochettes (60dh) and other Moroccan standards (entrées 35-50dh; set *menus* up to 130dh). Open daily 10am-3pm and 6pm-midnight. MC/V.

SEE FEZ EL-JDID AND VILLE NOUVELLE MAP, p. XXX

Fez el-Bali

ACCOMMODATIONS
Hôtel Cascade, **3**
Hôtel Erraha, **6**
Hôtel Lamrani, **2**
Hôtel Mauritania, **5**

FOOD
Restaurant Dar Jamai, **1**
Restaurant des Jeunes, **4**

FEZ AL-BALI

Food stalls line Tala'a Kebira and Tala'a Seghira, near the Bab Boujeloud entrance to Fez al-Bali and a couple minutes further down. A feast of *harira* (spicy lentil soup), roasted peppers and eggplant, potato fritters, and bread will only set you back 10dh at the stalls inside, while a good *kefta* (ground meat) sandwich goes for 15dh. Directly across from Hotel Cascade and Restaurant des Jeunes by Bab Boujeloud, **La Kasbah** has a pleasant rooftop terrace perfect for a quiet meal. For some of the cheapest eateries in Morocco, go left from Tala'a Kebira at Madrasa al-Atarrine (see p. 696), and head into the medina toward pl. Achabine. Also, consider splurging on an inexpensive Moroccan specialty restaurants listed below.

Restaurant des Jeunes, 16 rue Serrajine (☎055 63 49 75), next to Hotel Cascade by Bab Boujeloud. A tourist favorite. Friendly staff serves regional favorites. Entrées 20-30dh. Set *menu* 35dh. Open daily 6am-midnight.

Restaurant Asmae, 4 Derb Jeniara (☎055 741 210), located near the Qairouine Mosque. A traditional Moroccan restaurant where you'll leave filled to the gills. Choose among ten four-course meals (100-130dh). Open daily noon-midnight.

Restaurant Dar Jamai, 14 Foundouk Lihoudi (☎055 63 56 85), 100 meters from the Palais Jamai. Traditional feasting at affordable prices in this pillow-filled hideaway. 3- or 4-course *menu* 80-120dh. Open daily noon-11pm.

SIGHTS

FEZ AL-BALI

Fez's medina is the handicraft capital of the country and exports goods around the world. With over 9000 streets and nearly 500,000 residents, the crowded medina is also possibly the most difficult to navigate in all Morocco. But it is also the most rewarding as its narrow streets contain fabulous mosques, *madrassas*, *souqs*, and unparalleled frenzy. Tucked away off narrow alleys are craftsmen working at trades completely uninfluenced by modern industry and machinery. The medina is quieter and less crowded between noon and 3pm.

WITH A GUIDE. The first approach is simple and recommended in spite of the cost: hire an official guide. **Official guides** are available at the Syndicat d'Initiative. They'll save you time, discourage hustlers, and provide detailed explanations. (Don't assume they'll help you bargain for goods however.) You have the option between a "local" or "national" guide for either a half-day (3 hrs.) or full-day (5hrs.+) tour. Both types are adequate though national guides have earned a higher qualification (and therefore can provide tours of the whole country). Local guides cost 120/150dh and national guides 150/200dh. Based in Fez, national guide Abdemajid-Alaoui (or simply "Majid") is highly recommended (mobile ☎067 08 51 09). He offers friendly and informative tours of Fez in English, Spanish, or French. You might also try Ahmed (mobile ☎062 04 28 23). Though much cheaper, **unofficial guides** are illegal, often lack historical knowledge, and usually take travelers only to shops from which they will get a 25% commission. Whether you hire an official guide or an unofficial guide, nail down an itinerary and price beforehand and establish your aversion to shopping.

WITHOUT A GUIDE. To keep hustlers and merchants at bay, ignore calls or hisses and simply say "Non, merci" or "la shukran" to those who approach you directly. Remember: walking downhill will take you farther into the medina, while trekking uphill will lead you out (to Bab Boujeloud). Without a guide, there are two classic approaches to exploring the medina. The first way is to head to the main gateway Bab Boujeloud and wander down **Tala'a Kebira** from there. Virtually all of the sights in Fez's medina lie along the Tala'a Kebira (a.k.a. the Grand Tala'a), old Fez's main street and an essential reference point for anyone attempting to navigate the medina. The Tala'a Kebira heads downhill from Bab Boujeloud to the Qairaouine Mosque area. The **Bab Boujeloud** is the main entrance to the medina; faux guides tend to gather here. Once

SEEING RED One may see the hands, feet, and hair of Moroccan women decorated with the original temporary tattoo, *henna*. Stemming from the Arabic words meaning "tenderness" and "good luck," henna is made from the leaf of the *tafilat* plant, ground into a powder and mixed with warm water or tea to make a paste. The dye comes in different colors, including red, black, and green, and it has three main uses: as a medicine; for pregnant women in their seventh month; and for marriage ceremonies and the "Festival of the Girls" on the 27th day of Ramadan. The application of the design to the skin, which can take hours, is both an art and a ceremony unto itself. The intricate motifs are painted on freehand or using a pattern and are left to sit anywhere from a couple of hours to an entire day or overnight before being rubbed off. The resulting decorations may last on the skin for weeks.

you pass the gate, however, they will tend to leave you alone. Built in 1912 by the Frenchman Maréchal Lauyote to gain the confidence of the locals, the *bab* is tiled in blue on one side (the color of Fez) and green on the other (the favorite color of Mohammed and consequently the color most identified with Islam). The square just inside the *bab* is where the Moroccan revolution against the French occupation began. Down to the right is the **Tala'a Seghira,** Fez's other main street, lined mostly by shops catering to locals (i.e., the famed underwear *souq*). The second classic approach is to taxi inside the medina to the more centrally located **Place Rsif** nearby the Qaraouine Mosque. This choice puts you right near the center of the sights described below. The final option, though you'll be vulnerable to hustlers, is simply to get lost in the magnificent atmosphere that is Fez's medina. When you're done, ask merchants or women how to get to Tala'a Kebira and follow it back uphill to Bab Boujeloud.

BOU INANIA MADRASA. At the head of the main thoroughfare Tala'a Kebira is the spectacular Bou Inania Madrasa and mosque, a school built in 1326 for teaching the Qur'an and Islamic sciences. The intricacy of the cedar and stucco work make this arguably the best *madrasa* in Morocco and perhaps even the world—not bad for a college dorm. Classes were held in the courtyard and the adjacent salons, and the students lived three or four to a two-by-two-meter cell on the upper floor. It's no surprise that this building came at a ridiculous cost. When the Merenid Sultan Abou Inan was presented with the totals for the construction, he simply threw them into the canal separating the mosque from the *madrasa*, exclaiming that no price tag could be placed on beauty. *(Closed for renovations in 2001; reopening date uncertain. Open daily 9am-5:30pm. 10dh.)*

FUNDUQS. Plunging ahead down Tala'a Kebira, you'll notice a series of *funduqs* (old inns now used as factories) on the left side. First is the drum *funduq*, where skins are stretched over hoops to produce the right tone. Next is the *funduq* for honey, olive oil, and butter, which was formerly a mental hospital. Lastly, you'll sniff the products of the **sheepskin funduq,** just after the parking lot on the left.

NEJJARINE MUSEUM OF ART. To get to the **place Nejjarine,** with its tiled fountain, step off the Tala'a Kebira, head into the spice souq (described below) and turn right at the sign for the Henna souq. Go down the ramp, turn right and then left; the museum is off a small courtyard. The displays are of any types of Moroccan woodwork—tools, instruments, decorated doors, etc. Today, its rooftop **salon de thé** (tea room) offers a tranquil escape from the rushing traffic of peddlers and tourists, as do its bathrooms, Morocco's finest. *(Open daily 10am-5pm. 10dh.)*

SPICE SOUQ AND OTHER MARKETS. Back on the Tala'a Kebira, the **Attarine ("Spice") Souq,** perhaps the most exotic market, awaits. When spices were a more prestigious commodity, its vendors got the privileged spot near the mosque. Off to the right at the beginning of the spice *souq* is the **Henna Souq,** which sells the plant used to temporarily tattoo women at weddings (see **Seeing Red,** above). At the far end is the **Maristan Sidi Frej,** which was built in 1286 and was the model for Western psychiatric hospitals. Toward the end of the Attarine Souq are several turn-offs into a **cloth market,** selling slippers and *djellabas* (robes), and a **dried fruit market.**

ZAOUIA MOULAY IDRISS II. Walking through the fruit market leads to the Zaouia Moulay Idriss II, the tomb of the Islamic saint credited with founding Fez. A pilgrimage site to this day, many Moroccans come to pray, light a devotional candle, or receive a blessing. Pilgrims touch the tomb through a slot in a brass star and you can make a wish by placing your hand on the star and offering a donation. Three head-high wooden barriers on the streets surrounding the tomb delineate a sacred zone and were built to prevent donkeys from entering holy ground. As usual, non-Muslims are not allowed to enter but can peer through the doors.

MADRASA AL-ATTARINE. The Tala'a Kebira ends at Madrasa al-Attarine, which dates from 1324. Though often overlooked by visitors, this could be the most peaceful place in the old city. Built by Abou Siad, a Merenid, it is one of the smallest *madrasas* in Morocco, but is notable for its details and mosaics. The intricacies of the carvings are spectacular—they rival the Bou Inania's both in beauty and in style. *(Open daily June-Aug. 9am-6pm; Sept.-May 9am-5pm. 10dh.)*

QAIRAOUINE MOSQUE. Exiting the *madrasa*, turn left, and then left again; a few meters down is a little opening into the Qairaouine mosque. It contains 14 gates, 6 fountains (three for men and three for women), and can hold up to 20,000 worshippers (second only to Hassan II in Casablanca). Founded in 857 by Fatima al-Fihri, a woman, the mosque is also one of the oldest universities in the world. It trained students in logic, math, rhetoric, and the Qur'an while Europe stumbled through the Dark Ages. You can thank (or curse) the mosque for educating Pope Sylvester II, who introduced algebra and the modern number system. Non-Muslims can take pictures through the portals but may not enter. Its library, off-limits to tourists, holds what some think is the oldest manuscript of the Qur'an in North Africa.

METAL SOUQ AND TANNERIES. Keeping the mosque on the right, you'll eventually come to pl. Seffarine, known for its fascinating **metal souq,** which deafens travelers with incessant cauldron-pounding. There are several potential routes from here. To reach the **tanneries,** turn sharply left and continue to bear left (follow the worn, six-sided cobblestones). Once the smell becomes intense, head right down a microscopic alley (a tannery "*guardien*" has probably grabbed you by now; 10dh is the basic fee). From a balcony above, you may view skins being soaked in green liquid, rinsed in a washing machine/cement-mixer hybrid, dunked in diluted pigeon excrement or waterlogged wheat husks (for suppleness), and saturated in dye. The dyeing process takes one week (except for the expensive yellow color of saffron that is dyed by hand and takes two days). The entire tanning process takes up to two weeks for one piece. Beware—the pervasive odor of the tanneries is not for the faint of stomach and can be overpowering on the hottest days. To exit the medina or reach **Bab al-Rcif,** a major bus and cab hub, follow the street heading away from the mosque to its end, turn left, and then right.

THE DAR BATHA MUSEUM. The beautiful Dar Batha Museum, located by Hotel Batha, with its well-kept garden, makes an excellent diversion for those tired of the endless, winding medina streets. The building itself, a 19th-century palace, may be the highlight of the museum. The spacious Andalucian mansion headquartered Sultan Hassan I and his playboy son, Moulay Abd al-Aziz, during the last years of decadence before the French occupation. The museum, which hosts Moroccan music concerts in September, chronicles Fez's artistic history. The keynote is the display of ceramics with the signature "Fez blue" (derived from cobalt) on a white enamel background. *(Start at Bab Boujeloud, head straight down the Tala'a Seghira, take the 1st right past the movie theater, then turn right again at pl. l'Istiqlal, home to the museum. Open W-Th and Sa-M 8:30am-noon and 2:30-6pm, F 8:30-11:30am and 3-6pm. 10dh.)*

ANDALOUS QUARTER. The Andalous Quarter is across the Oued Fez (Fez River) from the heart of Fez al-Bali and best accessed via Place Rcif. Many of the Moors who fled from Muslim Spain to Morocco during the 15th-century *Reconquista* settled around the grand Almohad house of worship in Fez, the **Andalous Mosque.** Its main attraction is the grandiose 13th-century doorway. *(To find the mosque, cross pl. Rcif, go through a small arched gate, turn right, and follow the wall on the right. From Fez al-Bali, cross the river at Port Bein al-Mudun near the tanneries and head straight down rue Seffrah.)*

FEZ AL-JDID

Christians, Jews, and Muslims once coexisted in Fez al-Jdid, which was built by the Merenids in the 13th century. The gaudy **Dar al-Makhzen,** the former palace of Hassan II, shunned by King Mohammed VI's for its excess, borders pl. Alaouites. Tourists may enter the grounds but not the guarded palace of course. Near to the palace is the *mellah* or Jewish ghetto. Today, there are few Jews left in Fez, as the majority left for Israel in 1948. The placement of the ghetto near to the palace is not arbitrary as here the Jews could be easily protected and, more importantly, easily taxed. Diagonally off the plaza, grande rue des Merinides runs up to Bab Smarine and its seven bronze gates installed by King Hassan II in 1968. Just before the beginning of the main street is a peaceful, 17th-century **Jewish cemetery,** which provides the resting place for over 12,000 people. On the site is also a small synagogue. (Cemetery open daily dawn-dusk; free though a donation may be requested). Off this boulevard, the meter-wide streets open into miniature underground tailors' shops, half-timbered houses, and covert alleyways. The **jewelers' souq** glitters at the top of grande rue des Merinides. Cackling chickens, salty fish, and dried okra vie for attention in the **covered market,** inside Bab Smarine at the entrance to Fez al-Jdid proper.

Bear left at the end of rue des Fez al-Jdid into the **Petit Méchouar;** on the left is **Bab Dakakeen,** the back entrance to the Dar al-Makhzen. **Bab al-Seba,** an imperial gate, opens onto the **Grand Méchouar,** a roomy plaza lined with street lamps. From here it's an easy walk to Bab Boujeloud—turn through the opening to the right of Bab al-Seba, continue straight for 250m, veer to the right, and pass through a large arch at the end of the road. The entrance to the refreshing **Boujeloud Gardens,** a refuge from the midday sun, is on the right. (Open Tu-Su. Free.) The deteriorating gardens were a gift from Hassan I to the people of the medina as an act of goodwill. Inside is the delightful **Café Restaurant Noria,** known as Lovers' Café, a pleasant place for female travelers (as well as male) to relax under the grape-leaf arbor. (Coffee 5dh. Couscous 35dh.) **Bab Boujeloud** lies another 300m down the street.

OUTSIDE THE MEDINA

For fantastic views of Fez, head to the hills on either side of the city. The ramparts of Borj Nord (Arms Museum), the Merenid Tombs and the Palais des Merenides provide good vantage points. All 3 are located on the same hill overlooking Fez. Be careful after dark as aggressive hustlers are known to frequent the area.

BORJ NORD AND THE MERENID TOMBS. To reach Borj Nord and the nearby tombs (they can be spotted from the ground), grab a *petit taxi* from the medina (5dh) or exit the medina through a small gate to the right on pl. Baghdadi when walking from Bab Boujeloud toward Fez al-Jdid. Turn right on the main road, walk past the bus station 200m, then take a small path that winds its way up the hillside; the tombs are to the right and Borj Nord is to the left. The **Palais des Merenides,** a 5-star hotel, overlooks the tombs from one of the most picturesque hillsides in the Maghreb. From here, the medina reveals itself with the delicate beauty that inspired Paul Bowles and countless other Orientalist writers. The panorama is particularly impressive in the half-light of dawn or dusk; during calls to prayer, when over a hundred *muezzin* summon the faithful, the experience is almost mystical.

SHOPPING AND CRAFTS

The medina of Fez is the handicraft capital of Morocco. The city is particularly famous for its twice-baked blue pottery and tannery, but you can find all sorts of Moroccan goods here. To get the most out of the experience and the least out of your wallet, you'll need time, patience, and a good poker face. There is no sure-fire strategy when bargaining for goods. In general, try to get an idea of prices before heading into a shop and don't be afraid to walk away once inside. Quality of products—from *djelabahs* (the hooded garment) to rugs—can vary widely. Don't pay top dollar for something that's a dirham a dozen (for more bargaining strategy, see **Bargaining 101** p. 686). The following is a list of quality shops located in the medina (with the exception of the pottery shop). They are as interesting for their managers and buildings as they are for their products.

Société Fakhkhari, 16 Quartier des Potiers, Route Sidi Harazem (☎055 64 93 22), outside the medina in the hills by Borj Sud. Guides take groups to this outstanding craftshop. Take a tour (ask for Moustafa or Ahmed) of fascinating work areas and then buy a piece fresh of pottery from the 450-degree oven. A *petit taxi* here 7-10dh.

Berber House, 51 Derb Sidi Moussa (☎055 74 12 68). From Zaouia Moulay Idriss II, turn left after wooden bar and straight for 50 meters. Specializes in Berber tribe blankets and *kilims* and sells cheaper blankets made on location. Open daily 9am-9pm.

El Haj Ali Baba, 10 Hay Lablida (☎055 63 66 25). This shop offers wonderful views of the enormous tannery and dye wells below and sells a vast array of goods.

Dar Zaouia, 4 Derb Jeniara Blida (☎055 63 55 12). A 15th-century house now filled with modern rugs and Berber *kilims* instead of harems. Open daily 8:30am-7:30pm.

Herboriste Ibn Sina, 6 Fondouk Lihoudi Zaouia (☎055 63 74 17). Spiritual medicine recipes kept in the family and dispensed in little bottles. Open daily 8am-9pm.

L'Art Islamique, 36 Derb Touil (☎055 74 12 04). Berber jewelry, Judaica, and antiques. Open daily 8am-7:30pm

THE ATLANTIC COAST

The towns along Morocco's Atlantic coast are undoubtedly more liberal, laid-back, and open than their conservative cousins in the interior. Men and women alike go to the beach regularly to sunbathe, swim, surf, and windsurf, usually among European tourists. The west coast contains Morocco's industrial boom towns—Casablanca, the country's commercial center, and Rabat, its most westernized city—which, while very much part of the modern country, are avoided by those with limited time in their itinerary. If you're headed to the coast, your best bets are the peaceful and tranquil smaller cities like Essaouira and Asilah.

ASILAH اصيلة ☎039

Just a short trip from Tangier, Asilah offers sandy shores, a laid-back atmosphere, and a brilliant white medina. Over the last 1000 years, every European power from the Vikings to the French have sent flotillas, armies, and even a crusade to wrench tiny Asilah from Moroccan hands. Rarely did Europeans last more than a generation or two before being sent packing from this fabled port city. Except for the first two weeks in August when an international art festival is held, Asilah remains a peaceful spot for kicking back and soaking up the sun on Atlantic beaches.

TRANSPORTATION. The **train station** (☎039 41 73 27) is a 25 min. walk from town on the Tangier highway, past a strip of campgrounds. To get to town from the station, simply follow the road by the beach, keeping the sea to the right. A taxi to town costs about 10dh. **Trains** run to: **Casablanca** (6hr., 3 per day 7:45am-11pm, 101dh); **Fez** (5-6hr., 3 per day 7:45am-11pm, 81dh); **Marrakesh** (9hr., 11pm, 132-173dh); **Meknes** (4-5hr., 3 per day 7:45am-11pm, 61dh); **Rabat** (5hr., 3 per day 7:45am-11pm, 77dh); and **Tangier** (40min., 4 per day 5:15am-9:20pm, 14dh). **CTM** and **private bus companies** share the bus station (☎039 41 80 91). From pl. Mohammed V, head away from the medina and after one block, take a right on av. de la Liberté. The station is a block up on the left. **Buses** to: **Casablanca** (4½-5½hr., 4 per day 5:45am-10:15pm, 60dh); **Fez** (3½hr., 3 per day 10:45am-11pm, 55dh); **Larache** (45min., 14 per day 11:45am-5:15pm, 10dh); **Marrakesh** (9hr., 7:30am and 5pm, 130dh); **Meknes** (4hr., 5 per day 10am-11pm, 40dh); **Rabat** (4hr., 4 per day 5:45am-11:15pm, 50dh); and **Tangier** (1hr., every 30min. 7:45am-5:15pm, 10dh). Many buses arrive full, so get to the station early. **Grand taxis** cluster in pl. Mohammed V, by the bus station, and head to Tangier (12dh) and Larache (12dh).

ORIENTATION AND PRACTICAL INFORMATION. The main street heading into town is bd. Mohammed V, which ends at the town's center, **pl. Mohammed V** (a traffic circle). Here you'll find a **BMCE bank.** The main strip of restaurants, accommodations, and cafés are located on rue Zallakah, which radiates from pl. Mohammed V and the adjoining av. Hassan II which borders the medina. There is a small **liquor shop** on rue Zallakah, two doors down from Hotel Marhaba (closes at 9pm). The town **market** takes place on av. Hassan II and its continuation along the medina. **Internet** can be found across from the medina on av. Hassan II. (8dh per hour. Open daily 9am-late.) To get to the **post office** from pl. Mohammed V, take bd. Mohammed V and turn right onto pl. Nations Unies. The post office is 20m up on the left. (☎039 41 72 00. Open M-F 8am-noon and 2:30-6:30pm.)

ACCOMMODATIONS AND FOOD. Most hotels cluster around pl. Mohammed V and off av. Hassan II. In the months of July and August, they brim with French and Spanish beachgoers; call at least a day in advance to reserve a room. If you want to splurge on a slightly nicer bed, **Hotel Patio de la Luna,** 12 Plaza Zelaka, is a good place to do it. The airy rooms, all with shower and toilet, are spotlessly clean. (☎039 41 60 74. Singles 200dh; doubles 320dh.) Back to normal budget fare, **Hôtel Sahara,** 9 rue Tarfaya, a block inland from av. Mohammed V and two blocks before pl. Mohammed V, has immaculate rooms maintained by a Spanish-speaking staff. However, it is a 10 min. walk from the action in and around the medina. (☎039 41 71 85. Hot showers 5dh. Singles 98dh; doubles 126dh; triples 186dh; quads 252dh.) A sign on av. Hassan II points you to **Hôtel Belle Vue** where rooms with dressers, couches, and murals of sunbathers on the walls await. (☎/fax 039 41 77 47. June-Aug. singles 100dh; doubles 200dh; triples 300dh; quads 400dh. Sept.-May singles 50dh; doubles 120dh; triples 180dh; quads 250dh.) To be right by the beach, try **Camping As-Saada,** 700m toward town from the train station. As-Saada is tidier and cheaper than its neighbor Camping Echrigui. (☎039 41 73 17. 12dh per person; 10dh per tent and per car. Showers 10dh. Bungalows 100dh.)

The restaurants and cafés along Hassan II all have similar prices and fare. Those facing the ramparts just before heading up av. Hassan II specialize in seafood and serve good meals for 40dh and up. **Al Kasaba,** rue Zallakah, toward the ocean and past Hôtel Marhaba, is the best restaurant in town. Patrons dine on delicious seafood and pasta on a terrace overlooking the port. (☎039 41 70 12. Entrées 30-100dh. Open daily 9am-4pm and 7pm-midnight. Closes earlier in winter. MC/V.)

SIGHTS AND BEACHES. Asilah's stunning **medina** is bounded by heavily fortified 15th-century Portuguese walls. The Bab Kasaba, the gate off rue Zallakah, leads past the **Grand Mosque.** Right across from the mosque is the modern and spacious **Centre Hassan II des Rencontres Internationales** which houses a collection of excellent art created during the great **International Festival.** Outfitted with tables and chairs, it is also a good place to read and relax. (☎039 41 70 65. Open 9am-12:30pm and 3:30-7:30pm. Free.) During the festival (held during the first two weeks of August) artists from all over the Arab and African world flock to Asilah, but the city glows with artistic flair year-round; walls are covered with murals, music fills the air, and locals seem to be constantly dancing on the beaches. There are two popular beaches. The closest is toward the train station along the Tangier-Asilah highway (15 min. from the medina). The nicest however, in the opposite direction, is the enclosed **Paradise Beach,** an hour's walk from the medina. Those with extra cash can take a horse-drawn wagon for around 150-200dh round-trip or try to persuade a taxi to make the bumpy trip. Some men might jeer at the sight of foreign women swimming; if you feel uncomfortable, walk to a less-crowded area.

LARACHE الاعرايش ☎039

A sleepy city by day, Larache only comes alive at night. Without a touristy veneer, the city makes it an appealing stop for those with an extra day to spend on the Atlantic Coast. While there isn't too much to do in Larache itself, this former Spanish colony (with the Spanish-style architecture to prove it) does provide a perfect base for a trip to the nearby Roman ruins at Lixus.

TRANSPORTATION. CTM buses go to and from: **Asilah** (50min., 4 per day 11:15am-10:45pm, 13dh); **Casablanca** (4hr., 3 per day 8:15am-6pm, 82dh); **Fez** (5hr., 3 per day 4:30-10:15pm, 61dh); **Rabat** (3hr., 3 per day 8:15am-6pm, 56dh); **Marrakesh** (9hr., 6pm, 143dh); **Meknes** (4hr., 3 per day 4:30-10:15pm, 46dh); and **Tangier** (1½ hr., 4 per day 11:15am-10:30pm, 29dh). **Private buses** leave from the same station and send packed buses to the same locations at cheaper prices. **Taxis** park outside the bus station. **Local buses** (2.5dh) depart Kasbah de la Cigogne off av. Mohammed V, traveling to **Lixus** (buses #4 and 5) and the **beaches** (bus #4).

ORIENTATION AND PRACTICAL INFORMATION. Buses to Larache drop off passengers five blocks from the spacious **place de la Libération,** the center of activity. From the station, exit from where the buses enter, turn right, and head down **av. Mohammed ben Abdallah,** which runs into pl. Libération (about 8min.). Branching off pl. Libération to the right is the main artery, **bd. Mohammed V.** Also off pl. Libération, **Bab al-Khemis** (also called Bab Medina) leads to the **medina** and the **Zoco de la Alcaicería** (a.k.a. Zoko Chico). Larache's **beach,** beyond the medina and across the Loukkos estuary, is accessible by bus (2.50dh) or boat (2dh over, 4dh back; yes, in Morocco getting there is only half the battle, or price). There is no tourist office in Larache. **Banks,** across from the post office on bd. Mohammed V heading away from pl. Libération, exchange money and have **ATMs.** Contact the **police** at ☎19. **Pharmacie Centrale** is located just off pl. Liberation at 1 av. Mohammed ben Abdallah. (Open daily 9am-1pm and 4-8pm.) **Internet** at **M@rnet,** 4 rue Mouatamid ben Abbad (☎039 91 68 84. 10dh per hr. Open Sa-Th 10am-midnight, F 10am-3:30pm.) **Telephones** are located in the **post office.** (Open M-F 8:30am-noon and 2:30-6:30pm. Phones inside available M-Sa 8:30am-noon and 2:30-6:30pm.)

ACCOMMODATIONS AND FOOD. While there are extremely basic hotels in the medina, many nicer budget options can be found on av. Mohammed ben Abdallah and off pl. Libération. The best bargain is the **Pensión Amal,** 10 av. Abdallah ben Yassine. From the bus station entrance, turn right and head straight for five blocks until you see the sign. (☎039 91 27 88. Hot showers 6dh; cold showers 2dh. Singles 50dh; doubles 70-80dh; triples 90dh; quads 115dh.) **Hôtel España,** 2 Hassan II, off pl. Libération, is part of the family of once-grand hotels that are worth the extra cash; the large rooms have TVs and bathrooms are modern. (☎039 91 31 95. Singles 120dh, with bath 204dh; doubles 162dh, with bath 243dh; triples 200dh, with bath 313dh; quads with bath and TV 350dh). Cheap and redundant **restaurants** line pl. Libération and the Zoko. **Restaurant Eskala** (☎039 91 41 80), immediately to the left after passing through the main medina gate off pl. Liberation, serves outstanding couscous for 40dh.

SIGHTS. Though most tourists come to Larache to visit the Roman ruins of Lixus, Larache itself can make for pleasant wandering. The main area of sights is two blocks down bd. Mohammed V away from pl. Libération. Here you'll find the old city walls and a ruined **kasbah** built by the Portuguese in the 16th century. Around the corner next to the citadel sits the tiny **archaeological museum,** which contains a limited assortment of Roman and Phoenician artifacts. (☎039 91 20 91. Open M-Sa 9am-noon and 3-6pm. 10dh.) The **Kasbah de la Cigogne,** located near the minaret of the mosque, is Larache's only intact 17th-century fortification. Unfortunately it's not open to visitors. From pl. Libération head into the Moorish area (Bab al-Khemis) of the medina and turn right into **Zoco de la Alcaicería,** a Spanish-built, 17th-century courtyard, now a bustling *souq*. Down the walkway, where couples and families stroll at sunset, is the **beach** across the **Loukkos estuary.** Entrepreneurial boatmen ferry passengers over for 2dh (4dh back) from dawn to dusk. Make sure not to miss the last boat (usually around 7pm).

DAYTRIP FROM LARACHE

LIXUS

Lixus is located 5km north on the highway to Tangier. Let's Go does not recommend hitchhiking but some report that it is the best way to get to and from Lixus (give the driver a few dh). Alternatively, take ***bus*** *#4 or 5 from the stop near Kasbah de la Cigogne in Larache*

(2.5dh) and tell the ticket collector you want to go to Lixus (pronounced "lix-OOS") or take a petit taxi for 25-30dh. You can't take a bus back as they don't stop at Lixus. Instead, walk along the highway (45min.), flag down one of the rare taxis, or hitchhike.

Though not as impressive as Volubilis (see p. 687), the Roman ruins of Lixus is one of the Atlantic Coast's most interesting sights. It figured prominently in Greco-Roman mythology as the place where Hercules completed his 11th labor: collecting the golden apples from Mount Atlas. In real life, it was settled by an ancient sun-worshipping cult and became a highly successful **Phoenician settlement** around 1000 BC. As with all things Phoenician, the area fell to the Romans around 140 BC, and within a few years it had become a rich trading city occupying an important place in the Roman Empire. Unfortunately, the city lost prominence with the Empire's fall, and by the 5th century it was totally abandoned.

Today, the ruins remain largely abandoned, not to mention unrestored, unguarded, and unmarked (besides a sign at their base on the highway). Exploration is thus unlimited, relaxing, but unguided unless you employ one of the locals who may approach you. To explore Lixus on your own, begin along the highway where you'll find the silo and **factory** where *garum*, Lixus's famous fish-intestine paste, was made and stored for shipment. Walking past the factory, along the highway away from Larache, take a path to the left up the hill toward the ruins of a Greco-Roman **theater** featuring what was once one of the ancient world's largest orchestra pits; it was later converted to an **amphitheater** and, during Spanish occupation, a bullring. Located near the theater are the famous **Mosaic of the Sea God** and the **Roman baths.** Follow the fork uphill and head left to temples, villas, churches, and a views of the entire site as well as a Larache and the estuary.

RABAT الرباط ☎037

Rabat is like an ex-con come clean. Actually, it's more like an ex-con who has become president. Back in its florid past, Rabat was home to merciless pirates who plundered ships throughout the Mediterranean and Atlantic. The Alawites subdued these buccaneers around 1700, and with the rogues and their treasure gone, Rabat sunk into obscurity until 1912 when the French selected it as the seat of government. Today, as a political and business capital, Rabat's streets are overrun by ranks of uniformed, public employees. The city also hosts a swelling upper-middle class, not to mention the guarded residence of King Mohammed VI himself. Admittedly, Rabat lacks the tradition of Fez, the color of Marrakesh, and the European flair of Casablanca. However, surrounding the rather sedate city center lies an outstanding array of sights which can be enjoyed at a leisurely pace. Rabat's cosmopolitan comforts and moderation can provide a manageable introduction to Morocco or be the perfect antidote for the weary traveler.

TRANSPORTATION

Flights: Rabat is served by its own minor airport, as well as the larger Mohammed V in Casablanca. **Royal Air Maroc** (☎037 70 97 66), on av. Mohammed V across from the train station. Open M-Sa 8:30am-12:15pm and 2:30-7pm. **Air France,** 281 av. Mohammed V (☎037 70 77 28). Open M-F 8:30am-12:15pm and 2:30-7pm, Sa 9am-noon.

Trains: By far the most convenient method of arrival and departure is via the **Rabat Ville Station,** (☎037 73 60 60) av. Mohammed V at av. Moulay Youssef. To: **Casablanca Port** (1hr., 19 per day 6:45am-8pm, 29dh); **Casablanca Voyageurs** (1 hr., 17 per day 3:30am-11:30pm, 29dh); **Fez** (4hr., 8 per day 7:15am-11:45pm, 72dh); **Marrakesh** (5hr., 8 per day 3:30am-11:30pm, 101dh); **Meknes** (3hr., 8 per day 7:10am-11:40pm, 55.50dh); **Tangier** (5½hr., 4 per day 7:40am-1:20am, 89dh).

Buses: All companies operate from an enormous station (☎037 28 02 62), on the road to Casablanca, at pl. Mohammed Zerktouni. It's several kilometers from the town center, so take a *petit taxi* (12dh) or bus #30 from av. Hassan, near rue Mohammed V (2.50dh). **CTM** tickets at window #15; other windows are private companies. CTM to:

Casablanca (1hr., 10 per day 3:20am-10:30pm, 30dh); **Fez** (3½hr., 8 per day 8:30am-7:30pm, 58dh); **Meknes** (2½hr., 7 per day 8:30am-7:30pm, 41dh); **Tangier** (5hr., 5 per day 7:30am-1am, 90dh); **Tetouan** (6hr., 6pm and midnight, 92dh).

Taxis: Stands can be found at the train station, in front of the bus station, and at the entrance to the medina by the corner of av. Hassan II and av. Mohammed V. Expect to pay about 18dh from the bus station to the center of town.

Car Rental: Budget (☎062 38 80 38), in the train station. Fiat Uno starting at 474dh per day, plus 2.5dh per km. Open M-F 8am-noon and 2:30-7pm, Sa 9am-noon and 3-6pm, Su 9am-noon. Min. age 21 for most cars. **Hertz,** 467 av. Mohammed V (☎/fax 037 70 92 27), across from the train station.

ORIENTATION AND PRACTICAL INFORMATION

Rabat could not be easier to navigate. Rabat's main street, **av. Mohammed V,** runs uphill from the **medina** past the post office and train station, to the **Great Mosque (al-Sounna).** Exiting the train station (the Rabat Ville stop), turn left up av. Mohammed V to reach most budget hotels and **bd. Hassan II,** which runs perpendicular to av. Mohammed V along the medina's walls. The waterfront area along the Bou Regreg River contains many of Rabat's important sights including the **Kasbah, Hassan Tower,** and **Mausoleum of Mohammed V,** not to mention, Rabat's sister city **Salé** (see p. 706) across the river itself.

Tourist Office: The tourist office situation in Rabat is bleak as there is nothing within the city itself. The **main office** is located in the posh suburb of Agdal. ☎037 68 15 31. Open M-Th 8:30am-noon and 2-6:30pm, F 8:30am-11:30pm and 3-6:30pm.

Currency Exchange: Banks and **ATMs** are located on av. Mohammed V and av. Allal ben Abdallah. **BMCE** is located at 260 av. Mohammed V (24hr. ATM outside) and at the train station. Open M-F 8:15am-2:15pm.

Luggage Storage: At the train station (15dh per bag per day, must be locked, locks for sale (7dh) in station). Open daily 7am-10:30pm. At the bus station (3dh per day).

English Bookstores: English Bookshop, 7 rue Alyamama (☎037 70 65 93). Behind the train station; heading from the medina, take av. Moulay Youssef off av. Mohammed V just after the station and bear right on to rue Alyamama. Open M-F 9am-12:30pm and 3:30-7pm. **American Bookstore,** 4 rue Tanger (☎037 76 87 17). Take av. Mohammed V past the Grand Mosque to the right and turn left 3 blocks later; the shop is at the end of the road in the American Language Institute. Open M-F 9:30am-12:30pm and 2:30-7:30pm, Sa 10am-12:30pm and 1:30-5:30pm.

Emergency: ☎19. **Police:** rue Soekarno, off av. Mohammed V.

Late-Night Pharmacy: Pharmacie de Préfecture (☎037 70 70 72), av. Moulay Rachid. From post office, cross av. Mohammed V and veer right onto rue al-Qahira. On your right a few blocks down and across from Theatre Mohammed V. Open nightly 8:30pm-8am.

Hospital: Hôpital Avicenne (☎037 67 28 71), av. Ibn Sina, at the end of bd. d'Argonne away from the medina. US citizens can also go to the **US Embassy** (see p. 673) for medical assistance.

Internet Access: Cyber-Espace Menara, in the Maroc Telecom building across from the post office on ave. Mohammed V, has the fastest connections in Morocco. No need to bring a book here. 12dh per hour. Open daily 9am-9pm.

Post Office: (☎037 72 36 46), av. Mohammed V at rue Soekarno, to the left when leaving the train station. Open M-Sa 8:30am-6:30pm and Su 8:30-11:30am.

ACCOMMODATIONS

The medina has several good options for bargain hunters. The cushier hotels are off **av. Mohammed V** and **av. Allal ben Abdallah.** From the train station, turn left onto av. Mohammed V and walk toward the medina; av. Allal ben Abdallah runs parallel, one block to the right. None of the accommodations are far from the modern conveniences of the *ville nouvelle.*

VILLE NOUVELLE

Hôtel de la Paix, 2 rue Ghazza (☎037 73 20 31 or 037 72 29 26), on the corner of av. Allal ben Abdallah and rue Ghazza, about 10min. from the train station and 2 blocks before the medina. Rooms with full baths, some with phones. Ask for a balcony. Singles 157dh; doubles 183dh. There are also more spartan rooms (70-90dh).

Auberge de Jeunesse (HI), 43 rue Marassa (☎/fax 037 72 57 69), 2 blocks along the medina walls on the road perpendicular to av. Hassan II. Modern toilets; almost a tie with Hôtel de la Paix. Breakfast 14dh. Reception open June-Aug. 9am-midnight, Sept.-May 8-10am, noon-3pm, and 6:30-10:30pm. Dorms 35dh, members 30dh.

Hôtel Central, 2 rue al-Basra (☎037 70 73 56; fax 037 72 83 10). From the train station, cross av. Mohammed V, walk 2 blocks toward the medina, and turn right; it's on the corner of rue al-Basra and rue Dimach. Big rooms with high ceilings, sinks, and firm beds. Hot showers 10dh. Singles 80dh, with shower 100dh; doubles 110dh, with shower 136dh; triples 140dh, with shower 172dh; quads 170dh, with shower 208dh.

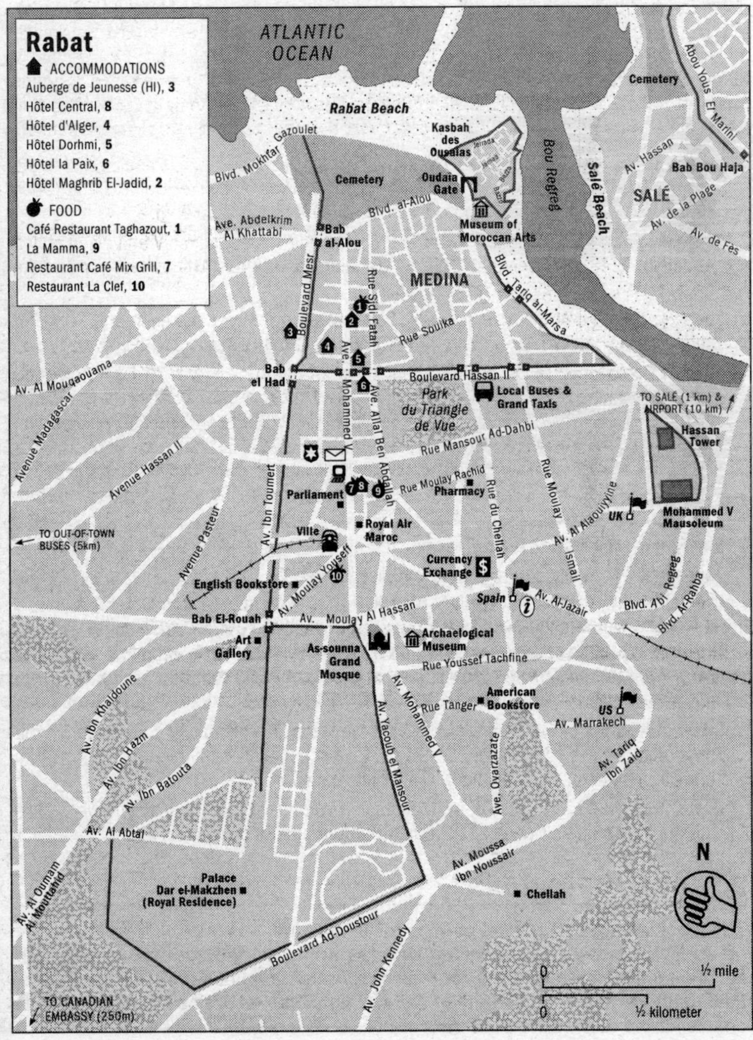

MEDINA

Hôtel Dohrmi, 313 av. Mohammed V (☎037 72 38 98), 1½ blocks inside the medina walls, on the right. Female management makes women feel at home. Some rooms with toilets. Hot showers 7dh. Singles 80dh; doubles 110dh; triples 160dh; quads 200dh.

Hotel D'Alger, 34 rue Souk Semmarine, (☎037 72 48 28). For the best bargain or a nice modern bathroom, come here. Clean rooms at very reasonable rates. No reservations. Singles 35dh, with shower and toilet 70dh; doubles 70dh, with shower and toilet 100dh.

Hôtel Maghrib El-Jadid, 2 rue Sebbahi (☎037 73 22 07), at av. Mohammed V, a few blocks past Hôtel Dohrmi on the right. Spotless rooms with small beds complemented by a rooftop terrace. English spoken. Cold showers 4dh; hot showers 7.50dh. Singles 50dh; doubles 90dh; triples 135dh; quads 160dh. Additional bed 45dh.

FOOD

Along with scores of traditional restaurants, Rabat is filled with mediocre international food options. Some might enjoy **Hong Kong,** a Chinese/Vietnamese restaurant on av. Mohammed V one block towards the train station from av. Hassan II (open noon-2pm and 7-midnight), or **Taki Fried Chicken** (☎037 20 28 83), Rabat's original fast food, in a small arcade across from the Parliament. A **food market** sits at the entrance to the **medina** at av. Mohammed V, and there are *brochetteries* and sandwich shops within the medina walls.

Restaurant Café Mix Grill, av. Mohammed V (☎037 20 83 27), one block from the post office toward the train station. Crepes (12dh), excellent shawarma (25dh), and pizza (26-50dh) available at this modern and clean spot. Open daily 7:30am-midnight.

Restaurant La Clef, av. Moulay Youssef (☎037 70 19 72). Comfortable restaurant with Moroccan standards from 50dh. Facing the train station, take the street on the left. The restaurant is upstairs from the café on the left. Open daily noon-3pm and 7-10:30pm.

La Mamma, 6 rue Tanda (☎037 70 73 29), behind the Hotel Balima complex on av. Mohammed V. The relaxed, candle-lit ambiance at night compensates for the rather bland pizzas (60dh). Also grilled food. Open daily noon-3pm and 7pm-1am.

Café Restaurant Taghazout (☎037 72 40 61), across from Hotel Maghrib El-Jadid. Generally considered one of the best and cheapest restaurants in the medina. Entrées 23-36dh. Open daily 7:30am-11pm.

SIGHTS

THE HASSAN TOWER. Across town, along av. Abi Regreg (near the Moulay Hassan bridge to Salé), towers the famous minaret of the **Hassan Mosque,** a testament to the ambition of Sultan Yacoub al-Mansour. The mosque was to be al-Mansour's greatest achievement, to be built in the same style as the Giralda of Sevilla and the Koutoubia of Marrakesh. The courtyard was once the prayer hall of what was to be the largest mosque in the Muslim world, begun in 1195 to commemorate a victory in Spain but abandoned shortly thereafter upon the sultan's death. All that remains are the 44m minaret (meant to reach a staggering 60m) and stubby reconstructions of the support pillars (which were originally destroyed by an 18th-century earthquake). Several have benches—great places for a picnic or to read a book. Also on the same site, directly in front of the minaret, is the Tomb of the Unknown Soldier, marked by the blank tombstone. *(Follow bd. Hassan II to the right when facing the medina; after a 15min. walk, the tower will be on the right. Open daily sunrise to sunset. Free.)*

MOHAMMED V MAUSOLEUM. The Mausoleum of King Mohammed V faces the Hassan Mosque across the plaza. A tribute to the king who led Morocco's independence movement and lent his name to seemingly every third street in the country, the gorgeous mausoleum is open to non-Muslims. Ascend the stairs and pass by the spectacularly clad guards who keep company with Mohammed V and his marble sarcophagus. Make sure to look up—not just down at the tomb—as the ceiling above is equally beautiful. *(Open daily sunrise to sunset. Free.)*

KASBAH DES OUDAIAS. Compared to Fez or Marrakesh, there is little of interest to travelers in Rabat's medina. The **Kasbah des Oudaias,** however, just outside the medina, is striking. It used to be a pirate stronghold until Moulay Idriss sent Saharan mercenaries to oversee the buccaneers' tributes of gold and slaves. Exiting the kasbah via Bab Oudaia and heading through the keyhole-shaped gate down the stairs leads to the sublime **Andalucian gardens,** of medieval Islamic-Spanish design and French construction. *(On your right after you enter the gate.)* The **Museum of Moroccan Arts,** next to the gardens, was the 17th-century hideaway of the infamous Moulay Ismail. The excellent ethnographic collection shows off the sultan's private apartment, signature Rabat-style carpets, traditional local costumes, and musical instruments. A charming café lies on the opposite side of the garden. *(Follow av. Mohammed V. through the medina and take a right on bd. al-Alou to its end, a 15min. walk. The kasbah is just to the left and gardens and museum just to the right. Museum and gardens open 8am-noon and 2-7:30pm. Museum entrance 10dh.)*

THE CHELLAH. Beyond the city walls at the end of av. Yacoub al-Mansour loom the deteriorating but none the less remarkable ruins of the Chellah, a former Roman city. In the 14th century the ruling Merenids encircled the city with walls and converted it into a royal necropolis. Because of its tranquil aura and spectacular views, the Chellah is often called one of the most romantic sites in Morocco. Others might argue that Chellah is for the birds. Storks have completely taken over the site, building their enormous nests throughout the ruins and lush gardens. Still, the Chellah makes for pleasant wandering. From the gate, descend through the overgrown gardens to reach the necropolis and its ruined mosque. Step inside to see the 13th-century tombs of Sultan Abu Yacoub Youssef and the adjacent stork-filled minaret. On the way back, a path to the right circles the Roman ruins, once the sight of a military camp and the first occupied territory in the region, and now a popular local picnic spot. *(Follow av. Mohammed V to the al-Sounna Mosque (see below) and keep going, keeping the palace wall on the right. At the end of the road (15min.), the Chellah is diagonally across the square to the left. Open daily, sunrise to sunset. 10dh.)*

ARCHAEOLOGICAL MUSEUM. Near the al-Sounna Mosque, the Archaeological Museum may be the best of Morocco's lackluster museums. The museum traces pre-historic and pre-Islamic history and contains wonderful collections from the ruins of Volubilis and Lixus, including an assortment of Hellenistic bronze works, all cast before 25 BC. For those travelers with Volubilis or Lixus on their itineraries, this is a very rewarding stop. *(Walk down av. Mohammed V away from the medina and bear left at the Grand Mosque onto Abd al-Aziz; the museum is on the next street off Abd al-Aziz to the left, near the Hôtel Chellah. ☎037 70 19 19. Open daily 9am-5:30pm. 10dh.)*

OTHER SIGHTS. Rabat's principal place of worship, the splendid **al-Sounna Mosque** towers above the *ville nouvelle.* Although non-Muslims cannot enter, they may peek in. The salmon-pink **Bab al-Rouah** (Gate of Winds) is a massive four-arched gate, one of the most decorated and impressive in all of Morocco. The nearby **art gallery** houses an often-changing collection of paintings and sculpture. *(Facing the Grand Mosque with the train station at your back, follow av. Moulay Hassan to the right for 10min. Open daily 8:30am-noon and 2:30-8pm. Free.)* For a refreshing swim, Rabat's best beach is **Tamara Plage,** about 2km from town (bus #33 runs directly there), or the city beach in front of the kasbah is also pleasant, though crowded.

ENTERTAINMENT

The **Royal Movie Theater,** on av. Allal ben Abdallah, a few blocks off the medina shows popular films dubbed into French (1 screen, 4 shows per day, 20dh). Rabat has a few nightclubs, though most are at least a few kilometers away from the center. One of the best, however, is near the medina; **Amnesia,** 18 rue Monastir near the Royal Movie Theater, has a dress code (☎037 70 18 60; W-Sa midnight-4am).

DAYTRIP FROM RABAT

SALÉ سلا

To get to Salé, you can take a **grand taxi** *(3dh),* **local bus** *#6 or 12 (2.5dh), or simply walk (30min. from av. Mohammed V). Taxis and buses leave from bd. Hassan II in Rabat and drop passengers off at Bab Mrisa of the Salé medina. If you decide to take the bus, make sure to let the driver know where you want to get off. If you choose to walk from Rabat, head toward the Hassan Tower on av. Hassan II and cross the bridge to Salé; if you want, take a boat ride back (3dh per person). Catch the boat at the base of the bridge. Salé's petit taxis are not allowed to make the trip to Rabat.*

Across the Bou Regreg River from Rabat sits Salé, an ancient trading city that has recently come to be considered a suburb of the ever-expanding Rabat. This virtually tourist-free "White City" may need a good scrubbing, but it makes for an intriguing half-day trip from Rabat. The medina in Salé has three main attractions: the **souqs** along the rue Grande Mosquée, those along **rue Kechachine,** and the **Grand Mosque** and its accompanying 14th-century *madrasa* (college of theology, literature, and law). The best way to see these sights is to enter the medina through **Bab Bou Haja** (along the medina wall parallel to the river) which provides passage to the main plaza, **Place Bab Khebaz.** Nearby are Salé's traditional souqs. The **Grand Mosque** and **Madrasa** are located just before the cemetery. To reach them can be complicated but friendly shopkeepers can point the way (from Bab Bou Haja, take a left and head straight; you'll know you're close when the path and the walls suddenly become shiny white and clean).

CASABLANCA الدار البيضاء ☎022

Casablanca (known as "Casa"), sprawls under the Maghreb sun. Already the largest city in Morocco, with nearly 4 million inhabitants (up from a mere 20,000 in 1900), Casablanca continues to attract rural Moroccans seeking urban prosperity. Here in the country's economic capital and Africa's largest port, Western dress predominates, and women participate actively in city life. With its early 19th-century French boulevards and parks and decaying Art Deco buildings, Casablanca can feel more like a European city whose sun has set. That is until one visits the spectacular modern wonder, the Hassan II Mosque, the third largest mosque in the world. Backpackers generally view Casa as little more than a transport hub—and not without reason. Unfortunately there is no Rick's Café Américain in the kasbah and no one looking at you, kid, except the hustlers who prowl the port and medina. The movie *Casablanca* was based more on Tangier anyway.

TRANSPORTATION

Casa is Morocco's transportation hub for planes, trains, and buses. The **Casa Port train station** is near the youth hostel and the city center; the **Casa Voyageurs train station** is near nothing, a 50-minute walk from Casa Port or a 30dh *petit taxi* ride. To get from Casa Port to the **CTM bus station,** conveniently located downtown, cross the street, follow bd. Houphëit-Boigny to the head of pl. Nations Unies. At the rotary, take a sharp left onto the wide av. Armée Royale, and watch for Hôtel Safir on the right; the station is behind and to the right of the hotel. Expect to be offered "help" when disembarking in Casablanca and be weary of *petit taxi* drivers offering highly inflated rates; if you can, demand that drivers turn on the meter. Accommodations are almost all within walking distance but be careful at night.

Flights: Aéroport Mohammed V (☎022 53 90 40) handles international and domestic flights. Trains run between the airport terminal and the Casa Port train station (45min., 9 per day 5:15am-8:45pm, 30dh), stopping at Casa Voyageurs en route. Make sure to get on a train that runs to Casa Port. **Royal Air Maroc** (☎022 31 41 41), at the airport and 44 av. des F.A.R., sells tickets for international and domestic (Agadir, Marrakesh) flights. Open M-F 8:30am-12:15pm and 2:30-7pm, Sa 8:30am-noon and 3-5pm. For more information see **Transportation,** p. 668.

Trains: There are two main train stations: **Casa Port** (☎022 27 18 37), located on the waterfront close to the heart of the city, and **Casa Voyageurs** (☎022 24 38 18), located 4km outside the city center on bd. Ba Hammed. Casa Port has northbound service to **Rabat** (1hr., 17 per day 6:45am-8:45pm, 27dh). For southbound service, you must go to Casa Voyageurs. Service to: **Fez** via Meknes (5¼hr., 7 per day, 117dh); **Marrakesh** (3½hr., 8 per day, 75dh); **Meknes** (4½hr., 7 per day, 81dh); **Tangier** (6hr., 3 per day, 116dh; possible transfer at Sidi Kacem).

Buses: CTM, 23 rue Léon L'Africain (☎022 45 80 00), off rue Chaouia. To: **Agadir** (10hr., 6 per day 5:30am-5pm, 145dh); **al-Jadida** (1½hr., 6 per day 5:30am-3pm, 25dh); **Essaouira** (5½hr., 2 per day 5:30am and 7pm, 115dh/100dh); **Fez** (6hr., 8 per day 7am-10pm, 90dh); **Marrakesh** (4hr., 6 per day 7:30am-midnight, 70dh); **Meknes** (5hr., 9 per day 7am-2am, 70dh); **Rabat** (1½hr., 18 per day 6am-11:30pm, 30dh); **Tangier** (6½hr., 6 per day 6am-11:30pm, 120dh).

Car Rental: Casa has dozens of companies. For rates and more detailed info about renting a car in Morocco, see **By Car**, p. 670. **Budget,** 15 av. des F.A.R. (☎022 31 31 24), has good rates. Min age 21. Open M-F 8:30am-noon and 2:30-7pm, Sa 9am-noon and 3-6pm, Su 9am-noon. **Avis,** 19 av. des F.A.R. (☎022 31 24 24). Min. age 25. Open M-F 8am-7pm, Sa 8am-noon and 2-5pm, Su 8am-noon.

ORIENTATION AND PRACTICAL INFORMATION

The city has two main squares, **pl. Nations Unies,** below the landmark clock tower and a 5 min. walk from Casa Port, and **pl. Mohammed V.** Pl. Nations Unies spreads out in front of the Hyatt Regency at the intersection of bd. Mohammed V, av. Hassan II, and av. Forces Armées Royales (F.A.R.). Pl. Mohammed V lies six blocks away from the port along av. Hassan II. Budget accommodations lie around rue Allal ben Abdallah, parallel and in between bd. Mohammed V and av. des F.A.R.

Tourist Office: Syndicat d'Initiative et de Tourisme, 98 bd. Mohammed V (☎/fax 022 22 15 24), at rue Chaouia, about 4 blocks down from pl. Nations Unies. English spoken. Open M-F 8:30am-noon and 2:30-6:30pm, Sa 9am-1pm, Su 8:30am-noon and 3-5:30pm. The **Office de Tourisme,** 55 rue Omar Slaoui (☎022 27 95 33 or 27 11 77; fax 022 20 59 29), has similar services. From pl. Mohammed V, take av. Hassan II, turn left on rue Reitzer, and then right. Open M-F 8:30am-noon and 2:30-6:30pm.

Currency Exchange: When the many **banks** in the city are closed, try the airport and larger hotels, which change money at Morocco's official, uniform rates. The **Hyatt Regency, Hôtel Suisse,** and **Hôtel Safir** near the bus station and the other big hotels near pl. Nations Unies are all safe bets. 24 hr. **ATMs** are everywhere.

American Express: Voyages Schwartz, 112 av. du Prince Moulay Abdallah (☎022 22 29 47). They offer standard services but won't receive wired money. Open M-F 8:30am-noon and 2:30-6:30pm, Sa 8:30am-noon.

English Bookstore: American Language Center Bookstore (☎022 27 95 59), bd. Moulay Youssef at pl. Unité Africaine. Vast array of novels and reference books. Open M-F 9:30am-12:30pm and 3:30-6:30pm, Sa 9:30am-noon.

Emergency: ☎19. **Police** on bd. Brahim Roudani.

Late-Night Pharmacy: Pharmacie de Nuit (☎022 26 94 91), pl. Nations Unies. Open nightly 8pm-8am. Other pharmacies are found on almost any city block.

Medical Assistance: Croix-Rouge Marocaine, 19 bd. al-Massira al-Khadra (☎022 25 25 21). **S.O.S. Medicins,** 81 av. F.A.R. (☎ 022 44 44 44).

Internet Access: EuroNet, 51 rue Tata. 15dh/hr. Open daily 8am-11pm.

Post Office: Bd. Paris, at av. Hassan II. **Poste Restante** and telephones. M-Th 8:30am-noon and 2:30-6:30pm, F 8:30-11:30am and 3-6:30pm.

In Casablanca, ***petit taxi*** drivers are particularly flagrant in failing to turn on the meter or taking scenic routes. Be sure to double check the meter and have a sense of the route.

ACCOMMODATIONS

For budget deals look along **rue Chaouia** and **rue Allah Ben Abdallah;** avoid the overpriced medina. It's worth the effort to scout out the room first or visit a couple hotels before choosing as even within hotels the quality of rooms and beds can vary significantly. Casa is very noisy so try to obtain a room away from the street. As street names in Casa are changing rapidly from French to Arabic, some listings below note particularly recent or confusing changes.

Auberge de Jeunesse (HI), 6 pl. Ahmed Bidaoui (☎022 22 05 51). 10 min. from Casa Port; head right along bd. Almohades which runs outside the medina wall, and go left up a small ramp-like street. Blue signs point the way. Pleasant lounge and modern bathrooms. Breakfast included (8-9:30am). Reception open daily 8-9:30am and noon-11pm. Lock-out 9:30am-noon. Dorms 45dh; doubles 120dh; triples 180dh.

Hotel Colbert, 38 rue Chaouia (ex-rue Colbert) (☎022 31 42 41), across from the flower shops. Friendly management maintains spotless rooms and better rates, making Colbert a cut above its area competitors. Usually booked so arrive early. Singles 63dh, with shower 84dh; doubles 78dh/100dh; each additional person 36dh.

Hotel des Negociants, 116 Allah Ben Abdallah (☎022 31 40 23). A new addition to the block and it shows: rooms and bathrooms sparkle. A few basic singles 80dh each. Regular singles 100dh, with shower 180dh; doubles 140dh/220dh.

Hotel Lausanne, 24 rue Tata (ex-rue Poincare) (☎022 26 86 90). Rooms all with hot showers and TVs. Singles 229dh; doubles 273dh; triples 350dh; quads 427dh.

Hotel Touring, 87 av. Allah Ben Abdallah (☎022 31 02 16). Big, comfortable beds, tables, and electrical outlets are a bonus in the rooms of this otherwise no-frills hotel. Hot showers 5dh. Singles 64dh; doubles 78dh.

Hôtel de Foucauld, 52 rue Arabi Jilali (ex-rue Foucauld) (☎22 26 66). From bd. Felix Houphëit-Boigny, take a left on av. des F.A.R., then the 1st right; it's adjacent to Hôtel Perigord. No frills, no amenities, but basic rooms. Singles 75dh, with bath 120dh; doubles 120dh/150dh; triples with bath 180dh.

Hôtel Excelsior, 2 rue al-Amraoui Brahim (☎022 20 02 63; fax 022 26 22 81). Just opposite the clock tower and across pl. des Nations Unies. A doorman a nice hotel does not make. Modern bathrooms. Tries to maintain some semblance of its former glory but only the doubles and triples provide truly decent value. Optional overpriced breakfast included in prices (33dh per person). Singles 284dh; doubles 365dh; triples 489dh.

FOOD

While it's true that cosmopolitan Casablanca offers everything from French *haute cuisine* to Korean food to McDonald's, most restaurants are geared towards the city's wealthy business clientele. A safe bet is to sit down at one of the casual and inexpensive rotisserie chicken restaurants which line the bottom of **rue Chaouia** in the *ville nouvelle* around the corner from rue Allah Ben Abdallah. Good values are also available near pl. Nations Unies and in the medina, though prices there are a bit higher. For fresh meats and produce, try haggling at the **central market,** 7 rue Chaouia (open daily 8am-1pm). And two blocks away from the center at 132 Hassan II is **L'Oliveri,** perhaps the best ice cream shop around.

Restaurant Snack Bar California, 19 rue Tata (☎022 29 49 44), midway down the street. A welcoming atmosphere for women and its spectacular vegetarian couscous (40dh) is a rarity in Casa. Check out funny photo-menu of entrées with uncooked meat and add your comments to the tourist diary. A darling of the travel guides, locals probably wouldn't be caught dead here. Oh well. Entrées 20-50dh. Open daily 10am-1am.

Taverne au Dauphin, 115 bd. Felix Houphëit-Boigny (☎022 22 12 00), up the road from the port. Tuxedoed waiters serve sizzling seafood to Casablancan professionals in lively

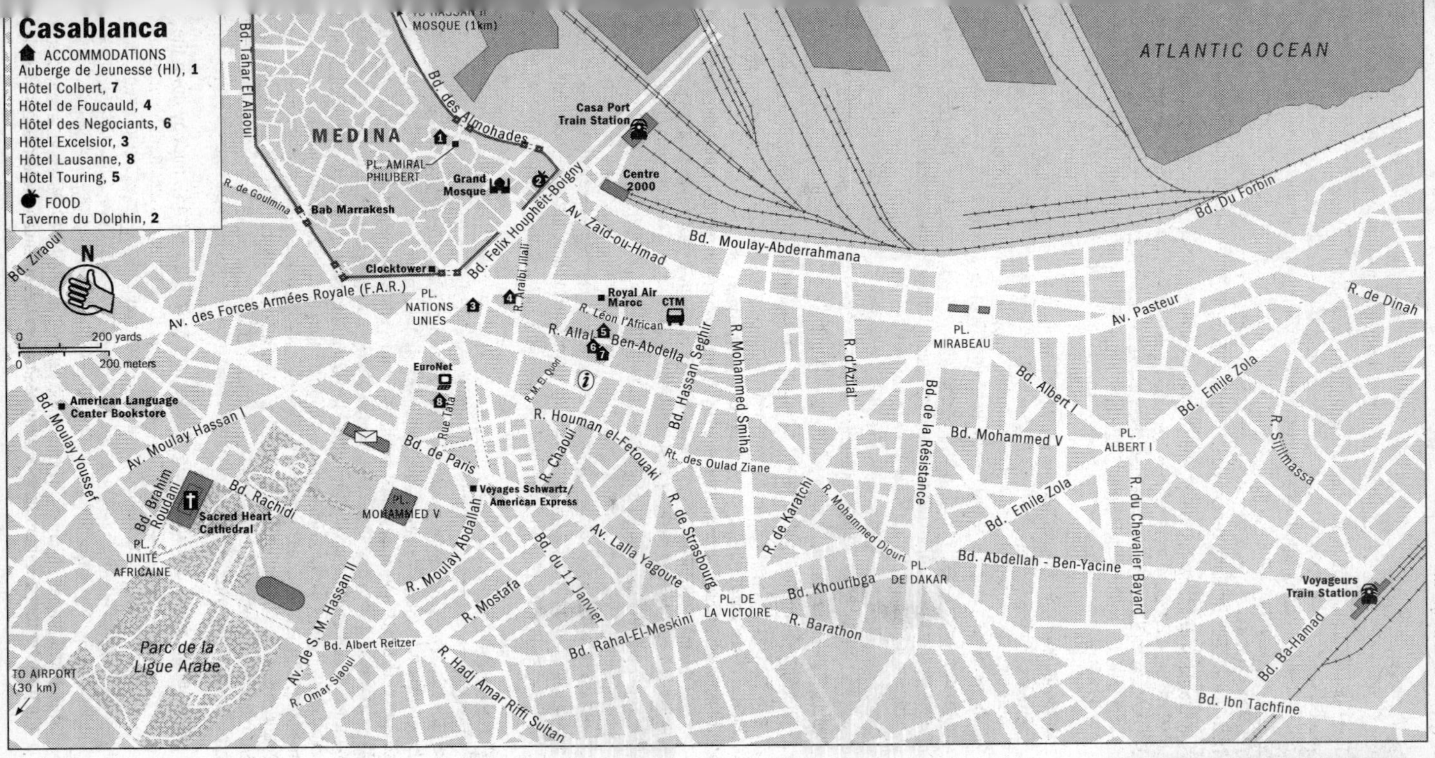
Casablanca
ACCOMMODATIONS
Auberge de Jeunesse (HI), 1
Hôtel Colbert, 7
Hôtel de Foucauld, 4
Hôtel des Negociants, 6
Hôtel Excelsior, 3
Hôtel Lausanne, 8
Hôtel Touring, 5
FOOD
Taverne du Dolphin, 2
N
0 200 yards
0 200 meters
ATLANTIC OCEAN
MOSQUE (1km)
MEDINA
Casa Port Train Station
Centre 2000
Grand Mosque
PL. AMIRAL PHILIBERT
Bab Marrakesh
Clocktower
PL. NATIONS UNIES
Royal Air Maroc
CTM
EuroNet
American Language Center Bookstore
Voyages Schwartz/ American Express
PL. MOHAMMED V
Sacred Heart Cathedral
PL. UNITÉ AFRICAINE
Parc de la Ligue Arabe
TO AIRPORT (30 km)
PL. MIRABEAU
PL. ALBERT I
PL. DE DAKAR
PL. DE LA VICTOIRE
Voyageurs Train Station
Bd. Tahar El Alaoui
Bd. des Almohades
R. de Goulmina
Bd. Ziraoui
Bd. Felix Houphët-Boigny
Av. Zaïd-ou-Hmad
Bd. Moulay-Abderrahmana
Bd. Du Forbin
R. de Dinah
Av. Pasteur
Av. des Forces Armées Royale (F.A.R.)
R. Araibi Jilali
R. Léon l'Africain
R. Allal Ben-Abdella
Bd. Hassan Seghir
R. Mohammed Smiha
R. d'Azilal
Bd. de la Résistance
Bd. Albert I
Bd. Emile Zola
R. Sijilmassa
Bd. Mohammed V
R. M. El Quodi
Rue Tata
R. Houman el-Fetouaki
Rt. des Oulad Ziane
Bd. Moulay Youssef
Av. Moulay Hassan I
Bd. de Paris
R. Chaoui
R. de Strasbourg
R. de Karatchi
R. Mohammed Diouri
Bd. Emile Zola
R. du Chevalier Bayard
Bd. Brahim Roudani
Bd. Rachidi
R. Moulay Abdallah
Bd. du 11 Janvier
Av. Lalla Yagoute
Bd. Khouribga
Bd. Abdellah - Ben-Yacine
R. Mostafa
Av. de S. M. Hassan II
Bd. Albert Reitzer
Bd. Rahal-El-Meskini
R. Barathon
Bd. Ba-Hamad
R. Omar Slaoui
R. Hadj Amar Riffi Sultan
Bd. Ibn Tachfine

atmosphere. House specialties include *crevettes grillées* (grilled shrimp, 55dh) and *filet de lotte* (filet o' fish, 70dh). Limited selection of non-seafood options. Entrées 45-100dh. Beer 15dh. Open M-Sa noon-3pm and 7-11pm. V.

Point Central, 89 rue Allah ben Abdallah, next door to Hotel Touring. Moroccan standards (18-28dh). Open M-F noon-2pm and 8-9:30pm, Sa 8-9:30pm.

SIGHTS

HASSAN II MOSQUE. The biggest sight in Casa, literally, is the glorious Hassan II Mosque, the third-largest mosque in the world. If you're within striking distance of Casa, it warrants a special trip or detour. Built on the orders of former king of Morocco Hassan II, it's very easy to find: from anywhere in Casa, look toward the sea and spot the minaret (200m high, the tallest minaret in the world). Begun in 1980 and inaugurated in 1994, this massive structure carried a price tag of over US$800 million (much of it collected from the Moroccan people through "universal voluntary conscription"). Designed by a Frenchman, the mosque was constructed by 3300 master Moroccan craftsmen who worked day and night to complete the project. The prayer hall, much larger than St. Peter's in Rome, combines glass, marble, and precious wood in a space that holds over 25,000 worshippers under the glow of 56 chandeliers. The plaza accommodates another 80,000. Here, technology galvanizes religious devotion; at one end of the prayer hall, silver electric gates weighing over 34 tons open only once a year—during the birthday celebration for the prophets—for a grand entrance by his living descendant, the King himself; the hall also boasts a retractable roof, the floor is heated, and a 20 mi. long laser beam shoots from the minaret toward Mecca. Hassan II graciously wanted his Mosque to be accessible to non-Muslims (unlike every other one in the country); take advantage of the tour which offers access to otherwise restricted areas in order to truly appreciate the Moroccan craftsmanship and awe-inspiring beauty of this national and religious monument. *(Walk past the medina along the coastal road for about 15min., or take a petit taxi (no more than 10-15dh though drivers will often ask for an unmetered 20dh). Tours take 1 hr. and are given Sa-Th 9, 10, 11am, and 2pm. Tours in English, French, and Arabic. 100dh, students 50dh. Elevator up the side of the minaret 10dh.)*

OTHER SIGHTS AND ENTERTAINMENT. There's a reason Hassan II chose Casa as the site for his mosque—there just isn't much else here. Casa is too preoccupied with commerce to maintain a romantic veneer. A small and decaying **medina** disappoints veterans of Fez and Marrakesh, and the portside **Centre 2000,** meant to be a tourist draw, is just a collection of unexciting western cafés and restaurants. Casa is known for its twentieth century civic architecture. Government buildings, Art Deco relics of the French occupation, surround the green **place Mohammed V.** Two blocks farther south along av. Hassan II sprawls the **Parc de la Ligue Arabe,** the grandest of Casa's parks. In the northwest corner you can enjoy a nice **picnic** in the shadows of the old **Sacred Heart Cathedral,** built in 1930. Casa may not be the best city to try out Moroccan nightlife though there are many cabarets, bars and discos scattered about town. These establishments are entirely male (besides the prostitutes), focus on heavy drinking, and are quite expensive. The best bet for nighttime activities are the big hotel bars such as **Hôtel Safir** on av. des F.A.R.

AL-JADIDA الجديدة ☎023

Al-Jadida (pop. 150,000), a 2 hr. bus ride from Casablanca, is one of Morocco's largest Atlantic beach towns. With its quiet Cité Portugaise, palmy boulevards, and some of the country's most pleasant beaches, al-Jadida serves as a prime destination for foreign and domestic tourists alike. The city's European feel comes courtesy of the Portuguese—al-Jadida (formerly known as Mazagan) was their first and last Moroccan outpost. Once Morocco won independence, the city was renamed al-Jadida ("The New One") and became a retreat for Marrakesh's affluent families. Al-Jadida remains a summer getaway site largely for Moroccans, especially in July and August when crowds pack the town in the name of sand and surf.

TRANSPORTATION

From al-Jadida, **CTM,** on bd. Mohammed V., sends **buses** to **Casablanca** (2hr., 6 per day 8:30am-4:30pm, 24dh) and **Essaouira** (3hr., 7:15am, 54dh). The CTM bus to Essaouira begins in Casablanca and often has few seats left by the time it arrives in al-Jadida; purchase a ticket in advance. Slightly cheaper and less reliable **non-CTM buses** run from the same station to: **Casablanca** (almost every hour 4:15am-7:30pm, 21dh), **Essaouira** (5 per day), **Rabat** (10 per day 4:15am-5:30pm), and **Marrakesh** (10 per day 5am-4:30pm, 35dh).

ORIENTATION AND PRACTICAL INFORMATION

From the **bus station,** exit left on bd. Mohammed V and continue up to the city center (10min.). First you'll reach **pl. Mohammed V,** the center of town, which joins bd. Mohammed V at the post office. Most services, including the tourist office and post office, are located nearby. Straight ahead from pl. Mohammed V is **pl. al-Hansali** (a pedestrian square), which is packed at night, and finally **pl. Mohammed ben Abdallah,** which connects bd. Suez to the conspicuous, walled **Portuguese city**.

Tourist Office: Syndicat, in pl. Mohammed V, next to Bata Shoes. Extremely friendly service. Some English spoken. Open Th-Tu 9am-12:30pm and 3-7pm.

Currency Exchange: There are many banks located in and around pl. Mohammed V. **Wafabank,** on pl. Mohammed V, has a 24hr. **ATM**. Bank open M-F 8:15am-3pm.

Police: ☎ 19. Stations at the bus station, by the city beach, and on av. al-Jamia al-Arabi.

Late-Night Pharmacy: Pharmacie de Nuit (☎ 023 35 52 52). From pl. Mohammed V, face the post office; take av. Jamai al-Arabia to the left of the post office; walk past photo shops and take second left into small arcade area. Open nightly 9pm-8am.

Medical Assistance: Hospital (☎ 023 34 20 04 or 023 34 20 05), rue Roux, near rue Boucharette in the south of town. **Ambulance:** ☎ 023 34 37 30. Preferable to the hospital is **Clinique Ennakil,** on av. Jamai Ababia.

Internet Access: There are cybercafés scattered about town. Most charge 10 dh/hr.

Post Office: Pl. Mohammed V. **Poste Restante** at first window to right. Open M-F 8:30am-noon and 2:30-6:30pm.

ACCOMMODATIONS AND CAMPING

Al-Jadida has a decent number of budget hotels. As usual, ask to see a room before you commit; rooms vary in quality even within a hotel. Reservations are a good idea in July and August, when the town fills up and prices rise.

Hôtel Bourdeaux, 47 rue Moulay Ahmed Tahiri (☎ 023 37 39 21). A few narrow streets away from pl. al-Hansali; follow signs at the end of the pl. al-Hansali toward the medina (about 100m). The best of the budget hotels with bright, clean, and modern rooms. Rooftop lounge. Hot shower 5dh. Singles 41dh; doubles 57dh; triples 78dh.

Hôtel de Provence, 42 rue Fquih Mohammed Errafil (☎ 023 34 23 47; fax 023 35 21 15). From the bus station, turn left off av. Mohammed V (away from the beach) at the post office. The "in" hotel for English speakers, with all the amenities (toilet paper, towels, nice sheets, and currency exchange). Continental breakfast (33dh) at the adjacent French/Moroccan restaurant. The spotless rooms include shower and toilet. Singles 186dh; doubles 229dh; triples 427dh. MC/V.

Hôtel Maghreb/Hôtel de France, 16 rue Lescould (☎ 023 34 21 81), just off pl. al-Hansali, toward the water. Two adjoining hotels that have seen better days provide absurdly large rooms with high ceilings. Most come with sinks and bidets, and some with excellent views of the sea. Hot showers 5dh. Singles 41dh; doubles 57dh. Extra bed 21dh.

Camping Caravaning International, 1 av. des Nations Unies (☎ 023 34 27 55). From pl. Mohammed V, take av. Jamia al-Arabi to the left of the post office. Take the 6th right. Better yet, grab a *petit taxi* for 8dh. Electricity, showers, and bungalows (231dh for 2). 14dh per adult, 16dh per tent, 8.5dh per car plus 4dh *emplacement* and 10% VAT.

FOOD

Cheap eateries serve *brochettes* along **pl. Mohammed V.** Most restaurants cluster in and around **pl. al-Hansali** and numerous cafés dot the waterfront. On Sundays, a weekly **souq** that sells everything from fruit to cow lungs is held by the lighthouse around rue Zerktouni.

Snack Ramissis, around the corner form Hotel Magreb and Hotel France, toward the waterfront. Plates of fresh fried fish and shrimp run 20-30dh. Open noon-4am.

La Broche, 8 pl. al-Hansali (☎023 37 26 49), next to Paris Cinema. Reliable Moroccan standards, pasta, and veggie options (20-60dh). Open M-Sa noon-3pm and 7-11pm.

Snack Le Dauphin, 18 av. Fquih Med Raf II, off Bd. Mohammed V by pl. Mohammed V. A cheery spot with tasty Lebanese-style shawarma (15dh). Open daily 11am-2:30am.

SIGHTS

Al-Jadida's main attractions are its **Cité Portugaise,** at the end of av. Mohammed V, and its nearby **beaches.** During the first week of August, there is a festival which includes a fantasia ceremony and Moroccan dance.

CITÉ PORTUGAISE. The heart of al-Jadida is its lovely ramparted **Cité Portugaise,** completed in 1502 by Portuguese traders. In 1769, Moroccan forces finally sent them packing, but not before the retreating Portuguese blasted the old town walls to bits. After a sultan renovated the ramparts in the 19th century, the city was rebuilt as a Jewish settlement *(mellah)* mostly populated by merchants. *(Enter through the first fortified gate off pl. Mohammed ben Abdallah at the top of bd. Suez.)*

Up rue Mohammed Hachemi Bahbai on the left, a yellow plaque marks the entrance to the famed **Portuguese Cistern,** a Gothic structure lucky enough to have survived the Portuguese bombardment. It was designed in 1514 as an arsenal and later converted into a cistern. The water, illuminated by a shaft of light from the roof, reflects the cistern's columns and arches. The riot scene in Orson Welles's *Othello* was filmed here. *(Open Oct.-Apr. 9am-1pm and 3-6pm; May-Sept. 9am-1pm and 3-7:30pm. Guided tour available but unnecessary)* To join the locals promenading along the city's **ramparts,** either continue along and up a ramp or head back toward the gate (and then down the street to the left), where there's a rickety staircase. Guards—when around—let you in and out for a tip of a few dirhams.

BEACHES. Everyone is headed there. The town beach is popular among football-playing and sun-bathing locals and stretches a good distance to the south, ideal for long walks. The beach is excellent, but it's crowded. For less populated beaches, head south of town beyond the Cité Portugaise. The favorite **Sidi Bouzid,** 5km to the south, is sprawling and chic with wide beaches and good swimming. Take a *grand taxi* (5dh per person) or the #2 bus (2.50dh) from near the Cité Portugaise. The bus, which stops ten minutes short of the beach itself (follow the crowd), makes frequent return trips. A taxi may be preferable as the bus makes many stops and can be crowded. If you are looking for Morocco's best beach, a good candidate is the splendid **Oualidia,** about 78km south of al-Jadida (20dh per person in a *grand taxi* or get one of the buses headed to Safi or Essaouira to drop you off). Accommodations are available there though they can be pricey.

ESSAOUIRA الصويرة ☎044

Essaouira is one of Morocco's most enchanting communities. Piracy boosted this port in the 18th century, when Sultan Muhammad ben Abdallah leveled the Portuguese city of Mogador and constructed the town fortifications to protect his merry band of pirates. In the late 1960s, the arrival of Jimi Hendrix and Cat Stevens triggered a mass hippie migration, and over the next decade, Essaouira achieved international fame as an expat enclave. Though most of the hash smoke has cleared, Essaouira remains one of Morocco's most laid-back cities. The miles of beautiful beaches are often too windy for sunbathing, but the fortified medina and plendid scenery provide ample diversion. In early June, acclaimed musicians lescend on the town for the Festival of Essaouira, a celebration of local and interational jazz. Essaouira is very popular with European tourists, and the high per:entage of foreigners means that women travelers might feel more comfortable.

TRANSPORTATION

Buses: Supratours buses leave from the Bab Marrakesh, across the square at **Agence Supratours** (☎044 47 53 17), where tickets are sold. To: **Agadir** (2½hr., 33 per day 5:30am-3:30pm, 40dh); **al-Jadida** (3hr., 5 per day 8:30am-12:30am, 56dh); **Casablanca** (5hr., 26 per day 5am-12:30am, 77dh; midnight express 100dh); **Marrakesh** (2½hr., 10 per day 4am-5pm, 43dh). The fastest and most luxurious bus to **Marrakesh** (2½hr., 5pm, 40dh) is run by **ONCF,** the train company. **CTM** runs from regular bus station outside the medina, a fifteen minute walk from Place Moulay Hassan. To: **Agadir** (2½hr., 12:30pm, 43dh); **Al-Jadida** (3½ hr., 11:15am, 64dh); **Casablanca** (6½hr., 11:15am and midnight, 88dh/105dh); **Marrakesh** (2½hr., 5pm, 45dh). Private bus companies make daily runs to **Meknes, Rabat, Taroudannt,** and **Casablanca.**

ORIENTATION AND PRACTICAL INFORMATION

;uses arrive at the **bus station,** about 1km from the medina along bd. Industrie. :xit the rear of the station (where the buses park) and walk to the right, passing wo *souqs* (or deserted wastelands, depending on the hour), to reach the medina ate, **Bab Doukkala** (10min.). The gate opens onto **av. Mohammed Zerktouni,** one of wo main arteries; the other is the parallel street of **rue Mohammed ben Abdallah.** To each the city center from Bab Doukkala, continue on av. Mohammed Zerktouni as , becomes av. l'Istiqlal (at an intersection surrounded by *souqs*). Walk until you ee a clock tower and gate on the right. Go through the gate, pass through the quare, and follow the road as it winds to **pl. Moulay Hassan,** the heart of Essaouira.

Tourist Office: Syndicat d'Initiative du Tourism, rue de Caine (☎044 47 50 80). From the top of pl. Hassan (away from the port), take a right and follow the road as it zig-zags 1 block beyond a gate. Some English spoken. Open M-F 9am-noon and 2:30-6:30pm.

Currency Exchange: Banks cluster around pl. Moulay Hassan. **Bank Credit du Maroc,** pl. Moulay Hassan (☎044 47 58 19), cashes traveler's checks and has an **ATM.** Open M-F 8:30-2:15pm. Higher rates at **Hôtel Beau Rivage.** Open 24hr.

Luggage Storage: Available 24hr. at the bus station (5dh per bag).

Police: ☎19, in the *ville nouvelle* near the tourist office.

Hospital: av. al-Moquamah (☎044 47 27 16), next to the post office.

Curious Bookshop: Galerie Aida, 2 rue de la Skala (☎044 47 62 90), off pl. Moulay Hassan. An interesting collection of crafts, books, and art. Open daily 10am-8pm.

Internet Access: Several teleboutiques offer internet access, but the cheapest is at **Mogador Informatique,** av. Oqba ben Nafil (☎044 47 50 65), 2 blocks away from the post, on the left (3rd fl.). 10dh per hr. Vague hours; usually daily 9am-midnight.

Post Office: av. al-Moqamah at Lalla Aicha, the first left after Hôtel les Isles when walking away from the medina by the shore. Near the radio tower. **Poste Restante** and **telephones.** Open 8:30am-noon and 2:30-6:30pm.

ACCOMMODATIONS

'hough once Morocco's best kept secret, Essaouira has lost its anonymity; reserations may be necessary in summer. There are a number of nice, cheap hotels.

Hôtel Smara, 26 rue Skala (☎044 47 56 55). From the top of pl. Moulay Hassan, head toward the ramparts and take a right at their base (3min.). The hotel isn't spotless but you can't beat the dramatic views. Arrive early—this is the most popular hotel among backpackers. Breakfast 10dh. Laundry around 2dh per piece. Some English spoken. Singles 62dh; doubles 84dh, with ocean view 124dh; triples 126dh; quads 158dh.

Hôtel Souiri, 37 rue Attarine (☎044 47 53 39), off rue Sidi Mohammed Ben Abdallah. Centrally located, the extra dirhams may be worth the comfort. Singles 95dh, with shower 220dh; doubles 150dh/310dh; triples 225dh/375dh.

Hôtel Tafraout, 7 rue Marrakesh (☎044 47 62 76). From the top of pl. Hassan, take a right and then a quick left onto the busy rue Sidi Mohammed ben Abdallah. Look for the sign a few blocks up. Newly renovated rooms; a good mid-range option. Hot shower 6dh. Singles 100dh, with shower 150dh; doubles 150dh/250dh. Extra bed 50dh.

Hôtel Majestic, 40 rue Derb Laalouj (☎044 47 49 09). From pl. Moulay Hassan, head away from the port down the street to the right; take a quick left and then another. A good value. Free hot showers. Singles 70dh; doubles 130; triples 160dh.

Hôtel Beau Rivage (☎/fax 044 47 59 25), in pl. Moulay Hassan. Large, old hotel located above the main square's cafés. Shows its age but it's still well-maintained. Some rooms with balconies, and a pleasant terrace. Singles 75dh; doubles 130dh, with shower 230dh; triples 180dh/280dh; quads with shower 240dh. Extra bed 50dh.

FOOD

Informal dining, mostly geared toward tourists, is common near the port and pl. **Moulay Hassan.** At the **port fish grilles,** fried sardines (with fish, bread, and tomatoes; 20dh) and grilled shrimp (25dh) are sure bets. The so-called **Berber cafés,** near Porte Portugaise and off av. l'Istiqlal, have low tables, straw mats, and fresh fish *tajine* and couscous (20dh). Establish prices before biting in.

Restaurant Laayoune (☎044 47 46 43). From the top of pl. Hassan (away from the port), take a right and continue past rue Sidi ben Mohammed Abdallah. Follow the road as it turns right and then left; the restaurant is ahead on the left. Outstanding Moroccan food at reasonable prices, served in a beautiful, well-decorated setting. Also crêpes (14dh). Four set *menus* from 45-72dh. Open daily noon-4pm and 7-11pm.

Chez Sam (☎044 47 65 13), past the food stalls, at the very end of the port, right on the water. Pricey and touristy; walls plastered with Hollywood movie stars, but has a nice ocean view and the town's only liquor license. Steaming heap of mussels 25dh. Fish dishes 40-70dh. *Menu* 75dh. Open daily noon-3pm and 7:30-10:30pm. AmEx/MC/V.

Dar Baba Restaurant, 2 rue Marrakesh (☎044 47 68 09), near the Hôtel Tafraout. Elegant home of the city's only Italian cuisine. Entrées 35-45dh. Open Tu-Su 6:30-9:30pm.

SIGHTS

While many flock to Essaouira to simply sit back, relax, and do nothing at all, the ramparts, shops, museums, and the beaches can distract one for hours on end.

RAMPARTS AND PORT. The view of the medina from the coastal walls provides the backdrop for one of the nicest walks in Morocco. Two *skalas* (forts) scowl atop the fortifications. Buttressed by formidable ramparts, dramatic, sea-sprayed **Skala de la Ville,** up the street from Hôtel Smara, is the nicer of the two (it's also free). Visitors can go up the large turret and artillery-lined wall to where the cannons, gifts to the sultan from European merchants, face the sea and the medina. The other fort, **Skala de Port,** offers a view of the port and the medina. *(10dh).*

MEDINA SHOPS AND MUSEUMS. Follow the sound of pounding hammers and the scent of *thuya* wood to the **carpenters' district,** comprised of cell-like niches set in the **Skala Stata de la Ville.** The craftsmen here inlay cedar and *thuya* wood with lemonwood and ebony to create some of the best woodwork in Morocco. On sale are unique masks and statues, as well as the more typical boxes, chess sets, dice, and desk tools. For a quality overview of Essaouira's goods and prices, go to the cooperative **Afalkai Art,** 9 pl. Moulay Hassan (open daily 9am-8pm) and browse the many shops lining **rue Abd al-Aziz al-Fechtaly** (off rue Sidi ben Abdallah). The prices are best and the marketing the least aggressive at the carpenters' workshops themselves. For silver jewelry, head to the *souq,* located just outside the medina walls on Av. Oqba ben Nafil. Look for the sign that says "bijoux" above the entrance o

PURPLE ISLES HAZE While certain stimulants are still available (especially for foreigners), Essaouira's heyday of "good times" was in the early 1970s when Jimi Hendrix and fellow hippies took over the isles. The fort on the beach, **Borj al-Berad,** and the inland ruins supposedly served as inspiration for Hendrix's song *Castles Made of Sand.* When he tried to buy the Berber village-turned-hippie-colony of **Diabat,** the Moroccan government decided that it had enough of Hendrix and his long-haired expat friends and expelled most non-Moroccans. Today, the village residents have almost forgotten their raucous past; the Purple (Isles) Haze has burned away.

the right, about a block from rue de Caire on the right. **Museum Mohammed ben Abdallah,** near the Hôtel Majestic on rue Derb Laalouj, is in the former residence of a *pasha.* It features antique woodwork and important manuscripts, including a 13th-century Qur'an. *(☎044 47 53 00. Open W-M 9am-noon and 3-6:30pm. 10dh.)* Galleries dot the medina—the best one, **Galerie of Frederic Damgaard,** near the clock tower, displays modern art crafted by local artists. *(Open 9am-1pm and 3-7pm. Free.)*

BEACHES. Though infamous for its winds, the wide beach of Essaouira is still one of Morocco's finest. With courts for basketball and volleyball along its pedestrian walkway, it's also one of the most lively and crowded. To get to the sand, head to the port and veer left; you can't miss it. Windsurfing clubs cluster on the beach and rent boards by the hour. Try **Fanatic Fun Center** for good deals on rentals. *(☎044 34 70 13. Windsurfing boards with harness and wet-suit 100dh per hr. or 300dh for a half day; body boards 20dh per hr. or 150dh per day; jet-skis 60dh per 15min.)* **Sidi Kaoki** (below) is *the* place for true windsurfing enthusiasts, but the wind is a little much for beginners.

PURPLE ISLES. Just off-shore from Essaouira are the famed Purple Isles where rare birds still hang out and get high. Dominated by the **Isle of Mogador,** the Isles are now a nature reserve for the rare Eleanora's falcons. A Berber king from Mauritania, Juba II, set up dye factories on the islands around 100 BC, producing the purple dye used to color Julius Caesar's cape, among other things, and giving the Isles their name. In 1506, the Portuguese, under King Manuel, contributed a fortress and Moulay Hassan added a prison. Visiting the Isles is possible, but extremely difficult, requiring permission from the town council.

THE HIGH ATLAS الاطلس الاعلى

Hollywood has anointed southern Morocco one of the most beautiful regions in the world, as evidenced by the numerous movies which have been filmed here over the last fifty years. The terrain in the mountains and their foothills is the most varied in the country, exercising the full palette of colors and forms that Morocco has to offer. Whether providing as a lookout, or a backdrop, the High Atlas are a thing of beauty. At their feet, with its unique architecture and exotic bazaar, Marrakesh vies with the natural scenery for a traveler's attention.

Falling southeast from the Atlas ranges and stretching through Ouarzazate to the sand-dune seas of the Sahara is Morocco's desert. Mountainous and desolate, its deep reds and oranges are softened only by the rare green veins of oases that creep through the valley floors. Set into this landscape are fantastic Berber towns and kasbahs, where *pizid* (mud and straw) castles tower over the road. Even though excursions are possible by local transportation, a rental car is useful for exploring this southeasternmost part of Morocco.

MARRAKESH مراكش ☎044

As it has for centuries, Marrakesh exerts an unshakable grip on the traveler. Tourists are still a minority at the Djema'a al-Fna, the medina's main square, where lively crowds of snake charmers, musicians, boxers, acrobats, mystics, dentists, scribes, and storytellers practice their crafts. Marrakesh's souqs and craftwork are some of Morocco's best and, in general, the bustling city is more tourist-friendly (and tourist-ridden) than the rest of Morocco. The Almoravid dynasty founded the city in 1062, elevating an infamous highwaymen's outpost to the status of cultural capital and infusing it with the Andalucian influences from their Spanish empire. Yet for all of the excitement and history embodied here, travelers should make sure to break its hold and push southward into the tranquillity and beauty of the Atlas Mountains and deserts that lie on and just beyond Marrakesh's horizon.

TRANSPORTATION

Flights: Aéroport de Marrakesh Menara (☎044 44 79 10 or 44 78 65), 5km south of town. Taxi from town 10dh per person. Bus #11 from the Koutoubia Mosque to the airport (about 7am-10pm, 3dh). Domestic and international flights on **Royal Air Maroc** (☎044 42 55 00), 197 av. Mohammed V. Open M-F 8:30am-12:15pm and 2:30-7pm.

Trains: (☎044 44 65 69), av. Hassan II. Going away from the medina on av. Mohammed V, turn left on av. Hassan II (40min.). A taxi to or from pl. Djema'a al-Fna costs 10dh. To: **Casablanca** (4hr., 8 per day 1:30am-9pm, 76dh); **Fez** (8hr., 4 per day 7:15am-2:15pm, 171dh); **Meknes** (7hr., 6 per day 7:15am-7pm, 153dh); **Rabat** (5hr., 8 per day 1:30am-9pm, 154dh); **Tangier** (8hr., 3 per day 7:15am-9pm, 188dh). There is an **overnight train** for Tangier that leaves at 9pm with stops in Casablanca and Rabat. For a *couchette* (200dh including train fare) book one day in advance.

Buses: (☎044 43 39 33), outside the medina walls by Bab Doukkala. To get there, walk out of the medina on av. Mohammed V, pass through Bab Larissa, and then turn right continuing along the walls to Bab Doukkala. The station is to the left. Arrive 30min.-1hr early, as seats fill quickly. **CTM** is window #10. To: **Agadir** (4hr., 3 per day 4:45am-6:30pm, 64dh); **Casablanca** (4hr., 10 per day 4am-8pm, 43dh); **Essaouira** (3hr., 7:30pm, 33dh); **Fez** (10hr., 5 per day 6:30am-9pm, 130dh); **Meknes** (8-9hr., 5 per day 6:30am-9pm, 115dh); **Ouarzazate** (4½hr., 5pm, 67dh); **Rabat** (5hr., 10 per day 5am-9pm, 55dh); **Taroudannt** via Agadir (6hr., 4:30 and 6pm, 83dh); **Zagora** (4-5hr., 4 per day 10am-10pm, 79dh). **Private companies** run frequently to destinations throughout Morocco including **Agadir** (10 per day), **al-Jadida** (11 per day), **Asni** (every 30min., 10 dh), **Casablanca** (every hour), **Essaouira** (7 per day), **Rabat** (14 per day), **Setti Fatma** (every 30min., 13dh); and **Zagora** (3 per day).

Grand Taxis: It's best to start from Bab al-Rob, where you can share a taxi to Asni or Setti Fatma. 15dh per person for 6 passengers; slightly more for smaller groups.

Car Rental: Hertz, 154 bd. Mohammed V (☎044 43 99 84). Fiat Palios for 300dh per day plus 2.5dh per km or 500dh per day for unlimited mileage. Min. age 21 for small cars, 25 for all others. Open M-F 8am-noon and 3-6:30pm, Sa 9am-noon and 3-6pm, Su 9am-noon. **National,** 1 rue de la Liberté (☎044 4306 83), off av. Mohammed V. Min. age 21. Many hotels (like Hôtel Ali) arrange rentals too. Don't hesitate to bargain.

ORIENTATION AND PRACTICAL INFORMATION

Marrakesh and its medina are more spacious than Morocco's other imperial cities but just as crowded and noisy. Most of the excitement, as well as budget food and accommodations, centers on the **Djema'a al-Fna** and the **medina** streets directly off of it. The **bus** and **train stations,** administrative buildings, and luxury hotels are in **Guéliz** *(ville nouvelle)* down av. Mohammed V; from the Djema'a al-Fna, walk to the towering Koutoubia Minaret and turn right. Also in the Guéliz are most of the car rentals, newsstands, banks, and travel agencies. Bus #1 runs between the minaret and the heart of the Guéliz (1.50dh). Or take one of the many *petits taxis* or horse-drawn carriages (15dh, sometimes more at night).

In Marrakesh, ***petit taxi*** drivers are particularly notorious about failing to turn on the meter or taking scenic routes. Be sure to double check the meter to make sure it's on—don't be afraid to insist—and have a clear sense of the route.

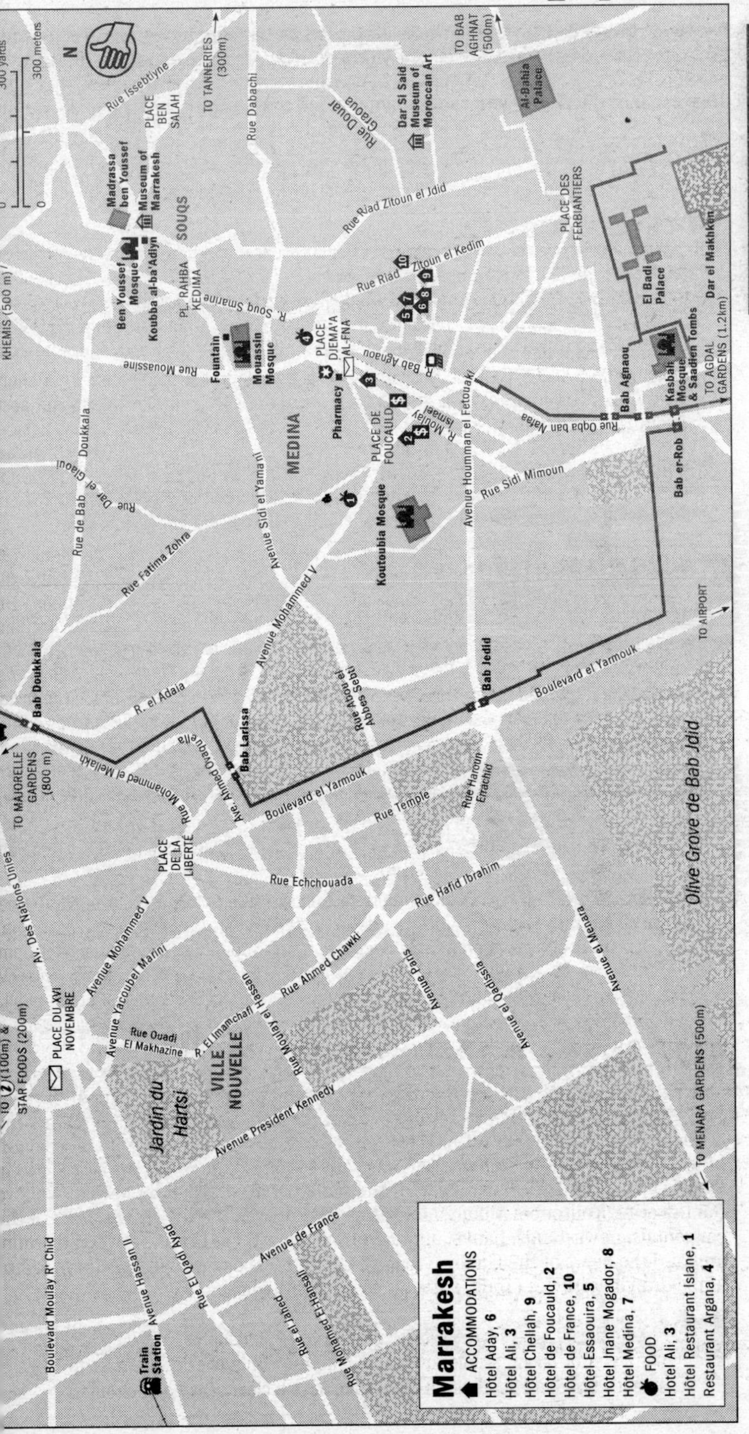

Marrakesh

ACCOMMODATIONS
- Hôtel Aday, 6
- Hôtel Ali, 3
- Hôtel Chellah, 9
- Hôtel de Foucauld, 2
- Hôtel de France, 10
- Hôtel Essaouira, 5
- Hôtel Jnane Mogador, 8
- Hôtel Medina, 7

FOOD
- Hôtel Ali, 3
- Hôtel Restaurant Islane, 1
- Restaurant Argana, 4

MEDINA
VILLE NOUVELLE
SOUQS
PLACE DJEMA'A AL-FNA
PLACE DE FOUCAULD
PLACE DE LA LIBERTE
PLACE DU XVI NOVEMBRE
PLACE BEN SALAH
PL. RAHBA KEDIMA
PLACE DES FERBLANTIERS
Koutoubia Mosque
Mouassin Mosque
Ben Youssef Mosque
Madrassa ben Youssef
Museum of Marrakesh
Koubba al-ba'Adiyn
Fountain
Pharmacy
Dar Si Said Museum of Moroccan Art
Al-Bahia Palace
El Badi Palace
Kasbah Mosque & Saadien Tombs
Dar el Makhzen
Bab Doukkala
Bab Larissa
Bab Jedid
Bab er-Rob
Bab Agnaou
Jardin du Hartsi
Olive Grove de Bab Jdid
Train Station
TO TANNERIES (300m)
TO BAB AGHMAT (500m)
TO AGDAL GARDENS (1.2km)
TO AIRPORT
TO MENARA GARDENS (500m)
TO MAJORELLE GARDENS (800 m)
TO 2 (100m) & STAR FOODS (200m)
Avenue Mohammed V
Boulevard el Yarmouk
Avenue Houmman el Fetouaki
Rue Sidi Mimoun
Avenue Sidi el Yamani
Rue Fatima Zohra
Rue de Bab Doukkala
Rue Dar el Glaoui
Rue Mouassine
R. Soug Smarine
Rue Riad Zitoun el Kedim
Rue Riad Zitoun el Jdid
Rue Dabachi
Rue Douar Graoua
Rue Issebtiyne
R. Bab Agnaou
R. Moulay Ismael
Rue Oqba ban Nafaa
R. el Adaia
Rue Mohammed el Mellakh
Ave. Ahmed Oueqelia
Rue Temple
Rue Haroun Errachid
Rue Abou el Abbes Sebti
Rue Echchouada
Rue Hafid Ibrahim
Rue Ahmed Chawki
Avenue Paris
Avenue el Qadissia
Avenue el Menara
Av. Des Nations Unies
Avenue Yacoubel Marini
Rue Ouadi El Makhazine
R. El Imamchafi
Rue Moulay el Hassan
Avenue President Kennedy
Avenue de France
Avenue Hassan II
Rue El Qadi Ayad
Boulevard Moulay R' Chid
Rue el Jahed
Rue Mohamed El Hansali
300 yards
300 meters

Tourist Office: Office National Marocain du Tourisme (ONMT), av. Mohammed V (☎044 43 61 79), at pl. Abdel Moumen ben Ali; 35min. walk from Djema'a al-Fna. Mediocre map and list of **official guides** (half-day 120dh, full day 150dh). Open daily 8:30am-noon and 2:30-6:30pm; summer 7:30am-3pm; Ramadan daily 9am-3pm.

Currency Exchange: Banks with 24hr. **ATMs** line av. Mohammed V and av. Hassan II in the Guéliz and cluster in the medina around the post office. Most touristy hotels will change money 24hr. Try Hôtel Ali (where else?) or Hôtel Essaouira.

Police: (☎19), off Djema'a al-Fna.

Late-Night Pharmacy: (☎044 44 54 26), off Djema'a al-Fna, on the way to av. Mohammed V, on the right. Open Tu-Su 9pm-6am.

Medical Emergency: Doctor on call until 10pm at the late-night pharmacy. It's best to avoid the government-run *polyclinique;* ask your consulate to recommend a private physician. See **Embassies and Consulates,** p. 673.

Internet Access: Ice-cold and cheap at **Cyber Bab Agnaou,** on rue Bab Agnaou, the pedestrian mall off Djema'a al-Fna. 10dh per hr. Open daily 8am-11pm. Also **Hôtel Ali.** 20dh per hr. Open daily 8am-10pm.

Post Office: Pl. 16 Novembre (☎044 43 09 77), off av. Mohammed V. It's a madhouse. Unreliable **Poste Restante.** Open M-F 7:30am-3pm. **Branch office** (☎044 44 09 77) in the Djema'a al-Fna. Open M-F 7:30am-3pm.

ACCOMMODATIONS

In abundant supply, all of Marrakesh's cheap accommodations are within a stone's throw of the Djema'a al-Fna. It's always worthwhile to see your room before you take it. Many places allow you to sleep on the rooftop terrace for about 20dh.

Hôtel Essaouira, 3 Derb Sidi Bouloukat (☎044 44 38 05). From Djema'a al-Fna, facing the post office, head down the road in the left corner, through an archway. Take the first right after the Hôtel de France and look for the signs. A colorful and stylish hostel with the best terrace in town, a café, and laundry basins. Hot showers 5dh. Luggage storage 5dh per day. 40dh per person, but there are few singles; doubles 80dh; terrace 20dh.

Hôtel Medina, 1 Derb Sidi Bouloukat (☎044 44 29 97), beside the Hôtel Essaouira (and run by its manager's cousin). Laid-back atmosphere, spotless beds, and a colorful courtyard adorned with traditional mosaic patterns. Laundry basins and a terrace café. Breakfast 9dh. Hot showers 5dh. 40dh per person, students 35dh; terrace 20dh.

Hôtel Ali, rue Moulay Ismail (☎044 44 49 79; fax 44 05 22), past the post office off the Djema'a al-Fna. The self-contained tourist compound known as Hôtel Ali has good suites with soap, towels, usually A/C, and toilet paper. English spoken. Also has a restaurant, an internet café, and arranges expeditions into the High Atlas. If it's full, don't agree to go to Hôtel Farouk. Dorms or terrace 40dh, includes breakfast. Singles with fan and shower 100dh; doubles with A/C and shower 150dh; triples with A/C 200dh.

Jnane Mogador Hotel, 116 Riad Zitoun Qedim (☎044 42 63 23), off Deb Sidi Bouloukat by Hotel Medina; look for the big wooden door. A new hotel done right. Rooms have fancy modern bathrooms, stained glass windows, and large, comfortable beds. Terrace café. Singles 180dh; doubles 260dh; triples 360dh; quads 440dh.

Hôtel de Foucauld, off pl. de Foucauld (☎044 44 54 99). If you're desperate for A/C, Foucauld is the best bet and most affordable. Singles 150dh; doubles 270dh.

Hôtel Chellah, 14 riad Zitoun Qedim (☎044 44 29 77). From Djema'a al-Fna, walk down the same street as to Hôtel Essaouira, but take the next right. Clean and pleasant. Hot showers 10dh, cold showers 2.5dh. Breakfast 10-15dh. Rooms 50dh per person.

Hôtel de France, 197 Riad Zitoun Qedim (☎044 44 30 67). Not the shiniest of rooms but beds are larger than most. Singles 40dh; doubles 80dh; triples 120dh.

Hôtel Aday, 11 Derb Sidi Bouloukat (☎044 44 19 20), across from Hôtel Medina. Small terrace and basic rooms. Singles 50dh; doubles 80dh; terrace 20dh includes shower.

FOOD

For delicious dinner bargains, have no fear and head for the **food stalls** in pl. Djema'a al-Fna. Food vendors contribute to the square's madness—dozens of stalls deal from early evening until after midnight. Follow the crowds to the best *harira* (spicy bean soup; 2dh), *kebab* (skewered meat; 2dh each), and fresh-squeezed orange juice (2.5dh). Prime numbered stalls are usually safe bets. On the other end of the price spectrum, Marrakesh also contains many **"palace restaurants"** where music, outrageous portions and liquor combine for a memorable if expensive evening (usually 300-600dh per person). **Restaurant Yacout** is expensive (500-600dh per person) but superb. (☎044 38 2900. Reservations required.) For lunch, the restaurants off Bab Agnaou are popular with tourists. For pastries try the neon-blazing **Patisserie des Princes** on Bab Agnaou or the understated **Mik Mak,** next to Hôtel Ali. Two **markets** peddle fresh produce along the fortifications surrounding the city, far from pl. Djema'a al-Fna. A daily vegetable and fruit market lies just outside Bab Aghmat. Bab al-Kemis has a lively Thursday market.

Hôtel Ali, (see **Accommodations,** above). An all-you-can-eat Moroccan buffet dinner situated 4 floors above the bustle of the pl. Djema'a al-Fna on the rooftop of the Hôtel Ali. A good place for women traveling alone. 50dh for Ali guests, 60dh for all others. Served daily 7-10pm. A hearty **breakfast** is served on the first floor as well.

Hotel Restaurant Islane, rue Mohammed V (☎044 44 00 81), on the roof of the Hôtel Islane across the street from the Koutoubia Mosque. Brick oven pizza and pasta (40-60dh) and a nice view of Koutoubia mosque. A refreshing escape from typical Moroccan fare. Good for women traveling alone. Open daily noon-3pm and 7-11pm. MC, V.

Star Foods, off pl. Abdel Boumem Ben Ali, in Gueliz, across from Hotel Café Renaissance. This diner makes a double cheeseburger that would make any American proud (28dh). Open daily 8:30am-11pm. Afterwards head across the street to **Café Renaissance** for a beer (15-20dh) to wash it down. Open 6:30am-11pm.

Restaurant Argana, off pl. Djema'a al-Fna. It's more about the views than the food here though pastas and Moroccan fare is fine (40-60dh). Open 5am-11:30pm.

SIGHTS

DJEMA'A AL-FNA. Welcome to the Djema'a al-Fna (Assembly of the Dead), one of the world's most frantically exotic squares, where sultans once beheaded criminals and displayed the remains (hence the name). Crowds of thousands participate in the bizarre bazaar that picks up in the afternoon and peters out after midnight. While snake-charmers and water-sellers pose to entice tourists, the vast majority of the audience are townspeople and Berbers from outlying villages. Solitary figures consult with potion dealers and fortune tellers; crowds congregate around the preachers, storytellers, and musicians; women have their children blessed by mystics; and promoters encourage bets on boxing matches between young boys (and girls). People come back night after night for the wonderful food and the chance to watch something spectacular.

MEDINA AND SOUQS. Second only to Fez, Marrakesh's medina contains a fantastic array of crafts and artisans. A worthwhile survey of the medina (primetime is 5-8pm) begins at the *souqs*. Although dazzling and overcrowded, the maze of noisy streets doesn't necessitate a guide. If you do get lost, ask a merchant for directions, or a child will lead you out for a few dirhams. From the Djema'a al-Fna, enter the medina directly across from the Café-Restaurant-Hôtel de France. This path runs to the medina's main thoroughfare; turn toward the enormous **souq smarine** (textiles) by taking a left at the **pottery souq.** Berber blankets and yarn pile the alleyways of the **fabric souq.** Head through the first major orange gateway and make a quick right to the Zahba Qedima, a small plaza containing the **spice souq,** complete with massive sacks of saffron, cumin, ginger, and orange flower, as well as the apothecaries' more unusual wares—goat hoof for hair treatment, ground-up ferrets for depression, and live chameleons for sexual frustration. Nearby is **La Criée Berbère** (the Berber Auction), once a slave-trading center. Nowadays it hosts aggressive carpet merchants. Farther on are the bubbling vats of the **dye souq.** Fragrant whiffs of cedar signal the nearby **carpentry souq,** where workers carve chess pieces with astounding speed. Go left through these stalls to see the 16th-century **Mouassin Fountain** bathe its colorful, but grime-covered, carvings. On the road going right where the **souq attarine** (perfume) forks, an endless selection of colorful leather footwear glows at the **babouche souq** (untinted yellow is traditional for men; women wear the fancier models). The right fork at the end of the street leads to the **cherratine souq,** which connects the *babouche souq* to the **souq al-kebir,** the leather *souq.* Those with strong stomachs can visit the **tanneries;** continue through the *souqs* and take a right after the Madrasa ben Youssef; head straight for 10 minutes through a run down stretch of the medina; the tanneries are on your right.

AL-BAHIA PALACE. The ruthless late-19th-century vizier Si Ahmad Ibn Musa, also known as Ba Ahmed, constructed this palace, naming it al-Bahia (The Brilliance). Serving as the de facto seat of government for the man who ruled in the sultan's stead, al-Bahia was built in an effort to assert Morocco's historical and cultural significance and thus stave off European domination. Today, it's impressive ceilings are beautifully preserved, although little artwork or furniture adorn its halls. Occasionally it serves as a gallery for modern art. *(From the Djema'a al-Fna, walk down rue Riad Zitoun al-Kedim to its end at pl. Ferbiantiers, then turn left and follow road as it curves to a red archway which opens onto a long, tree-lined avenue that leads to the palace door. Open Sa-Th 8:30-11:45am and 2:30-5:45pm, F 8:30-11:30am and 3-5:45pm. 10dh.)*

MUSEUM OF MARRAKESH. Featuring both thematic exhibits on Moroccan culture and private collections, the Museum of Marrakesh is one of Morocco's best museums. The building itself, a 19th-century palace, is lavishly decorated and contains a traditional hamman for visitors to explore. There is also a pleasant café and shop on the site. The exhibits change a few times every year. *(Off the open plaza at the end of rue Souq Smarine in the back of the medina. Around the corner from the Madrasa and Koubb al-Ba-Adiyn. ☎044 39 09 11. Open daily 9am-6pm. 30dh, students 10dh.)*

KOUTOUBIA MOSQUE. Almost every tour of Marrakesh begins at the 12th-century Koutoubia Mosque, whose magnificent **minaret** presides over the Djema'a al-Fna. Crowned by a lantern of three golden spheres, the minaret is the oldest (and best) surviving example of the art of the Almohads who made Marrakesh their capital from 1130 to 1213. At their peak they ruled a region stretching from Spain to present-day Tunisia, and one of the minaret's two siblings is the Giralda in Sevilla. In 1157, Abd al-Mumin acquired one of four editions of the Qur'an authorized by the Caliph Uthman and used it as inspiration for the design of the second Koutoubia Mosque. Possession of this holy book turned Marrakesh into a center of religious study. In fact, the name Koutoubia comes from the Arabic *koutoubiyyin* ("of the books"). Art historians revere the minaret, which has influenced eight centuries of Islamic architecture. *(Entrance is forbidden to non-Muslims.)*

MADRASA BEN YOUSSEF. In 1565, Sultan Moulay Abdallah al-Ghalib raised the Madrasa ben Youssef in the center of the medina. It reigned as the largest Qur'anic school in the Maghreb until closing in 1960. One of the most beautiful buildings open to non-Muslims, the Andalucian architectural style includes the requisite calligraphy, courtyard, and intricate floral designs. Visitors can roam the students' cells and appreciate the size of their hostel rooms. *(Walk down the main souq street (rue Souq Smarine) and bear right onto rue Souq al-Kebir; follow it to its end. Open June-Aug. Tu-Su 9am-1pm and 2:30-6pm; Sept.-May Tu-Su 9am-6:30pm. 20dh, students 10dh.)*

KOUBBA AL-BA'ADIYN MONUMENT. Beside the Madrasa protrudes the unpainted cupola of 12th-century Koubba al-Ba'adiyn, the oldest monument in town, the only relic of the Almoravid dynasty and the original from which all other Moroccan buildings have borrowed their unique style. Though excavated around the middle of the 20th century, much remains hidden either underground or by other structures. If you've had enough of keyhole arches, pine cone and palm motifs, and intricate dome carvings, ask the guard to open an ancient wooden door to the subterranean cisterns. *(Walk down the main souq street (rue Souq Smarine), bear right onto rue Souq al-Kebir, and turn left at the Madrasa. Open daily 9am-5:30pm. Bang on the door if it's closed. 10dh, plus 5-10dh tip for the custodian-guide.)*

SAADIAN TOMBS. Modeled after the interior of the Alhambra in Granada, the Saadian Tombs served as the royal Saadien necropolis during the 16th and 17th centuries, until Moulay Ismail walled them off to efface the memory of his predecessors. In 1912 the burial complex was rediscovered during a French aerial survey. The first room after the entrance is home to the Sultan's mother. Next door is the most impressive **Hall of the Twelve Columns** where trapezoidal tombs rise from a pool of polished marble. One **mausoleum,** the tomb of Sultan Yacoub al-Mansour (the Victorious), brims with illuminated mosaic tilework. Both date from the late 16th century. The sultan's four wives, 23 concubines, and the most favored of his hundreds of children are buried in the third room; the unmarked tombs belong to the women. The minaret of the Mosque of the Kasbah, al-Mansour's personal mosque, towers above the complex. *(From Djema'a al-Fna, walk away from the souqs to the walkway left of Banque de Maghreb and walk for 5min. to Bab al-Rob; take a left through Bab Agnaou and follow the signs. English tours. Open daily 8:30-11:30am and 2:30-5:45pm. 10dh.)*

DAR SI SAID. This 19th-century palace was built by Si Said, brother of Grand Vizier Ba Ahmed and chamberlain of Sultan Moulay al-Hassan. Although not as architecturally intricate as al-Bahia or as interesting as the medina souqs, it houses the **Museum of Moroccan Art,** which features splendid Berber carpets, pottery, jewelry, Essaouiran ebony, and Saadian woodcarving. It is one of the best classical Moroccan art museums in the country, it is well worth a visit. *(Go toward al-Bahia, and continue on rue Zitoun al-Jadid, taking the 2nd right heading toward the Djema'a al-Fna and then the first left onto the alley where the museum resides. Open W-Th and Sa-M 9-11:45am and 2:30-5:45pm, F 9-11:30am and 3-5:45pm. 10dh.)*

GARDENS. The midday sun in Marrakesh can be cruel; since the 12th century, rulers have dealt with it by constructing massive irrigated gardens. Only the most extravagant and least Moroccan of these gardens, the **Majorelle Gardens,** allows for a true escape. Designed by French painter Jacques Majorelle in the 1920s, the gardens are owned and maintained today by fashion designer Yves Saint-Laurent (who occasionally zips around the Djema'a al-Fna on his moped). There are exquisitely engineered explosions of colorful flowers and array of fascinating trees and cacti from around the world—the gardens' large admission fee is clearly put to good use. On the same site is the small **Museum of Islamic Art.** *(From Djema'a al-Fna, walk toward Koutoubia Mosque and take a right on av. Mohammed V. After exiting the medina, take a right and follow the walls to the bus station. Bear left onto bd. Safi and turn right onto av. Yacoub al-Mansour; the gardens are on the left. Better yet, take a petit taxi (10dh). Open daily June-Aug. 8am-noon and 3-7pm; Sept.-May 8am-noon and 2-5pm. Gardens 15dh; museum 10dh.)* The luxurious **gardens at Hotel La Mamounia,** Marrakesh's most extravagant hotel (once frequented by Winston Churchill) can be visited in the morning though you must be dressed smartly and act it as well. *(The hotel is located 5 minutes from Djema'a al-Fna on av. Houman el Fetouaki just before exiting through Bab Jedid. Open to the public until 2pm, although the doormen will often turn you away even earlier.)* The two other enormous "gardens" are really just expanses of olive trees created centuries ago. The **Menara Gardens** and the **Agdal Gardens** provide little shade and little beauty though they occupy many square kilometers outside the medina.

NIGHTLIFE

Most travelers hang around the Djema'a al-Fna or in one of the terrace cafés that overlooks it for most of the night. If you'd rather take part in the more international pastime of beer sipping, try the **bars** at the **Tazi** (☎044 44 27 87) and **Foucauld** (☎044 44 54 99) hotels, where locals and tourists mix with the help of 15dh Flag *spéciales.* (Both bars open at 9pm. Cover 50dh.) To find the Tazi, head away from the Djema'a al-Fna 200m down the street to the left of the Banque du Maroc. For the Foucauld, turn right by the Tazi onto the road that becomes av. Mohammed V and walk two blocks. For a change of scene, try the **Diamant Noir,** a nightclub on Mohammed V in Guéliz or **Café Renaissance** on pl. Abdelmoumen Ben Ali.

DAYTRIPS FROM MARRAKESH

Marrakesh should never be the end of the road; travelers should make every effort to push farther south for excursions into the High Atlas Mountains (see p. 715) or east toward the Cascades D'Ouzoud. Morocco's most dramatic landscape lies beyond the High Atlas in the Kasbah-filled oases of the southern deserts (see p. 726). **Hôtel Ali** (yet again! see **Accommodations,** p. 718) organizes trips (one to four days) to the Cascades, into the mountains, and throughout the gorges and deserts of the south. Prices depend on the size of the group but average around 300-400dh per person per day (usually includes transport, room, and meals).

CASCADES D'OUZOUD

Options are rental car, grand taxi, or bus. A car is the easiest, fastest way to visit the Cascades (3hr., 167km northeast on S508). ***Bus*** *for Azilal (window #18) run from the main station in Marrakesh (3½hr., 2 per day 8:30am-2pm, 40dh). Ask to be dropped off at the turn-off for the Cascades and then join a grand taxi (10dh) for the rest of the way or, to be safe, continue to Azilal and grab a place in one of the taxis headed to the falls (40min.; 15dh). The return trip may be difficult. If you miss 1 of the 2 buses running from Azilal to Marrakesh, organize a group to share a grand taxi back to Marrakesh from either Azilal or, if you're lucky, the falls themselves (400dh). The most convenient option is to arrange a round-trip grand taxi from Djema'a al-Fna for about 550dh.*

The Cascades D'Ouzoud adorn posters in hotel rooms across Morocco for good reason: they are the stuff lazy vacations are made of. At the Cascades, you can swim in refreshing pools, search for Barbary apes in the surrounding valley trees, or kiss behind a waterfall. Once you get beyond the unnecessary guides at the top of the waterfall, you can find relative tranquillity by the river below where the waterfall crashes into a large pool. From the top of the falls, take the path to the left and descend the stairs. You are better off crossing the river and hiking down to the many more secluded pools below. Spending the night at the Cascades can be highly enjoyable as there are plenty of excellent campgrounds and cafés where you can be put to sleep by the sound of rushing water and find yourself completely free to explore the surrounding valley (no tent is necessary as thin mattresses and blankets are provided). Wimpy travelers can try the **Hotel Restaurant Café Camping Dar Essalam** (☎ 023 45 96 57) for somewhat dilapidated rooms at 50-70dh apiece.

SETTI FATMA

To get to Setti Fatma, take a bus from Marrakesh's Bab al-Rob station (1½hr., 6am-noon, 10dh); buses run back to Marrakesh at 4 or 5pm and 7:30am. Grand taxis also make frequent runs (15dh). If you have a car, go 57km south on S513; ignore the first "P" (for parking) sign in Asgaour, even if men try to tell you can't drive further. You can in fact drive right to Setti Fatma and park near the taxi stand for free.

The **Ourika Valley,** just south of Marrakesh, is a popular vacation destination for city residents; with its grassy farmlands, lush greenery, and hillside roses, it makes for a refreshing break from Marrakesh. While in the winter, the area is a renowned skiing spot, in the summer, the small town of Setti Fatma and its collection of seven small waterfalls and cool pools are a favorite. Getting to the falls from the town requires a fair amount of hiking. Start by crossing the river near the farthest cluster of hotels and cafés and clamber up to the first, most popular cascade (45min.). Climbing farther up yields a much more isolated and tranquil waterfall and pool, perfect for a lounging afternoon. All the waterfalls can be explored in just a few hours. Crowd-lovers will want to go to Setti Fatma during the **moussem** (festival) in early August, when hundreds of Moroccans descend upon the tiny town. For a look at some traditional Berber villages, continue past the line of cafés and hotels to the end of the road and then head along the river or the village mule paths into the valley. Finally, Setti Fatma marks the end of the Imlil-Setti Fatma hike through the High Atlas Mountains (see p.

724). If you want to spend the night in the area, first try the clean and adequate **Café-Restaurant Asgaour** near the bridge (singles 50dh; doubles 70dh; triples 100dh) or the hodgepodge of rooms at **Auberge Tafoukt,** a bit farther from the center of town (heading back toward Marrakesh), high above the river (singles or doubles 100dh). The restaurant at Asgaour serves decent, if unexciting, food (entrées 30-80dh).

HIGH ATLAS MOUNTAINS الاطلس الاعلى

With manageable hikes and access to isolated Berber villages, the High Atlas mountains are one of the highlights of any Moroccan itinerary. Unlike those of its European counterparts, the range's trails have yet to be fitted for tourists, and the valleys below remain green, unspoiled, and very accessible. Even travelers with limited funds, time, and skills can huff to the summit of **Djebel Toubkal,** North Africa's highest peak (4167m), in only two days—little more than a sleeping bag, food, water, and sturdy shoes is necessary. Treks of up to two weeks are also plausible, but for long trips, unless one is skilled and equipped with a full outfit of backpacking equipment (i.e., stove, tent, water purification system, compass, maps, etc.), the services of a guide and/or mule and muleteer are rather essential, as there are numerous unmarked trails. **Official guides** (ask to see their papers) or **mules** can be hired in **Imlil** for 250dh per day and 75dh per day respectively (not including tip). Alternatively, treks can be organized in Marrakesh at **Hôtel Ali** (see p. 718). From Hôtel Ali, prices are about 300dh per day per person, with everything from food-and-shelter deals to guide-and-mule setups. During the **winter,** snow covers Toubkal and the upper valleys and full alpine gear and an experienced guide are completely necessary. No matter what time of year, **altitude sickness** is a potential risk, as the altitude change from Marrakesh is drastic.

Two hikes are outlined below: the popular ascent of Toubkal, through the towns of **Asni** and **Imlil,** and a moderate three-day trek from Imlil to Setti Fatma. (*The Atlas Mountains, Morocco* by Robin G. Collomb is a renowned source).

ASNI ☎044

Grand taxis and buses from Marrakesh will go no farther than Asni, making a stop here on your way to Imlil an inevitability. There's no reason to hang around for long, although Asni is a good place to stock up on provisions; you can get everything from sardines to a can opener here. Most people move on to Imlil for their first night or to arrange for guides and/or mules. If you get stuck, there is a surprisingly good, bare-bones **youth hostel** at the far end of town (turn left before the abandoned Hôtel du Toubkal), which has free cold showers and cooking facilities (30dh per bed; camping 30dh). To get to Asni from Marrakesh, take one of the frequent **buses** (dawn to dusk, 10dh) or a *grand taxi* (about 15dh per person).

IMLIL ☎044

The tiny village of Imlil is the ideal base for trips into the High Atlas. There are plenty of places to stay, eat, and stock up on supplies, and the crisp mountain air and constant sound of running water soothe tired climbers and invigorate future ones. Martin Scorcese used this village as the setting for his film *Kundun,* which told the story of the Dalai Lama, substituting the Atlas Mountains for the Himalayas and the village mosque for a Buddhist temple. In the center of town, next to the Club Alpine Français refuge, is the **official bureau of guides** (☎/fax 044 48 56 26). Ask questions and pick a personal guide (250dh per day) from the photos on the wall, although if you're only aiming to top Toubkal, no guide is necessary (see **The Toubkal Trek,** below). To get to Imlil from Asni, hop on the first truck up, crowding in with the produce and poultry (20dh). The ride is an experience in itself; stand in the back and don't let anyone try to charge you more or take you to any shops. For those with their own wheels, parking is available in front of the Bureau (10dh).

There are a bunch of high-quality hotels that will provide meals (with a few hours notice) and store luggage as you trek. **Hôtel El'Aine,** at the start of town on the right, boasts a lovely courtyard, garden, terrace, and even a library of old French mountain books. The owners are extremely helpful with any trekking info you might need. (☎044 48 56 25. Hot showers included. 50dh per person.) The **Hôtel Café Soleil** has clean rooms with futons on the floor, although the showers are cold. (☎/fax 48 56 22. 40dh per person.) It also serves quality food (entrées 25-35dh) and rents hiking gear. At **Café Aksoual** (☎044 48 56 12), you can sleep on its nice terrace (15dh) and store luggage(10dh). The **Shopping Centre** down the street also rents boots (30dh per day) and skis (150dh per day).

THE TOUBKAL TREK

The ascent of Djebel Toubkal is the most popular hike in the High Atlas and requires no special preparation. The entire hike can be completed from Imlil in two days with an overnight stay at the Toubkal Refuge, 3-4hr. from the summit.

Beginning from Imlil, the first challenge of the hike is finding the trailhead, which is about an hour's walk from Imlil. Walk uphill on the village's only road, taking a sharp right when you see a large boulder. Then veer onto a smaller path to the left (look for the sign for the Toubkal Kasbah on a building). Follow this path up past the kasbah for about 15min. until it joins a dirt road, weaving to the left. After five or 10min. you'll see the pleasant village of Aroumd on the opposite bank of the river. Past Aroumd, you descend into a broad valley; the trailhead is on the opposite side (through a small village—look for the very small yellow sign). This path is clear the entire way up the mountain. At about the 2- to 2½-hour mark you'll reach the tiny outpost of Sidi Chamarouch, home to a fiercely guarded marabout shrine and expensive beverages. A room here costs 50dh and *tajine* is 100dh (talk about a cornered market). The village marks the spring snow line, so be prepared for icy conditions through late April.

Another 3hr. gets you to the **Toubkal** (or Neltner) **Refuge,** where hikers from all over the world trade stories at night (32dh with CAF card, 48dh with other club cards, 64dh without; breakfast 30dh and lunch 50dh; gas burner 7dh). If you don't stay at the refuge, any use of its facilities is strictly prohibited. It gets mighty cold during all parts of the year at this altitude, so most hikers choose to spend the night here and ascend to the summit (3-4hr.) early the next morning. This strategy also allows for the best view, as clouds tend to move in during the afternoon. To ascend the summit choose between the south or north routes. The south is a bit easier though both are characterized by fields of loose rock (scree) which can make both the ascent and descent rather difficult. After reaching the summit, most people descend back to Imlil on the same day. (Approx. 6hr.)

IMLIL TO SETTI FATMA TREK

This excellent, moderate 2-night, 3-day trek passes through ancient Berber villages and over stunning mountain passes. No guide and special equipment is necessary and provisions such as water and accommodation are available on the route. Regardless, some hikers choose to hire a guide or a mule in Imlil for convenience.

DAY 1: IMLIL TO OUNESCRA. In Imlil, hike up the main road for a few minutes and then veer left past a large boulder and over a bridge spanning the river; pick up the dirt road on the other side. Most of the first day's trek is along this dirt road as it winds through the valley. After 1½hr., a trail leaves the road for the steep ascent to the top of the mountain pass (although one can stick to the road to reach the same point). The views from the pass are tremendous. From the top, the rest of the day is a steady and very enjoyable downhill hike along the road. After 1hr., at the road's end, veer left across the river to Ounescra; you'll backtrack a bit past the orange schoolhouse to the wonderful **Gite de Soleil** (30dh per person; water and meals available) for your first night's stay. (Approx. 4hr.)

DAY 2: OUNESKRA TO LAUSENNE OR TIMICHI. . The hardest day of the hike, this stage often takes a full 8hr. From Ouneskra, follow the mule path as it clings to the left bank of the river and climbs steadily toward the mountain pass (which will always be in sight). After 1hr., the ascent becomes gradually steeper and more difficult until it transforms into long, but relatively mellow, switch-backs

40 KILOMETERS AND A MULE Ever wonder how wilderness guides get away with being the most expensive things you'll ever have to pay for in Morocco? Well, there are only 44 of them (licensed, that is) and they go through a hell of a lot to get where they are. Every year, the Club Alpine Français sends delegates to Casablanca to administer a three-day test. For the first two days, would-be guides are given a practical exam in Arabic and French on topics ranging from Berber history to wilderness survival. On the third day, applicants are sent to the backcountry, where they must hike 40km in under six hours. Understandably, not everyone makes the cut. Those who do are each required to take the Club Alpine representatives on a guided hike. The delegates can ask any question they can think of, from the height of the summit to the length of the hike to what to do with toilet paper in the woods. If applicants answer satisfactorily, they are granted status as certified guides and are legally required to collect 250dh per day (as opposed to the unlicensed 100dh).

for the 45min. climb over the pass. From the windy pass, the rest of the day consists of a steady downhill on rocky switchbacks that can be a bit tough on the legs. The descent passes juniper trees and becomes more relaxed as it approaches Lausenne where there's the excellent and tranquil Gite de Iabasen offering beds for 30dh. Otherwise, continue another 20min. to Timichi where there's another gite at the bottom of the hill across the river from the mosque. (Approx. 7-8hr.)

DAY 3: TO SETTI FATMA. The last day contains a few climbs but is mostly a steady downhill run. From Timichi, stick to the path for 1hr. as it follows the river through the valley until it forks. Take the lefthand route which climbs rather steeply for 20min. before becoming a well-beaten mule path. This path winds through the valley towards Setti Fatma for nearly 2hr. It ends at the riverbed where a small stand sells soda. To reach Setti Fatma proper and its stand of *grand taxis* heading for Marrakesh, walk along the river for 20min. until you reach a paved road, then continue past the cafés and hotels. For details on Setti Fatma, a pleasant place to spend an afternoon, see p. 722. (Approx. 4hr.)

TIZI-N-TEST

The direct route between Marrakesh and Taroudannt, the **Tizi-n-Test** is one of the most entertaining drives in the country. Built by the French in the 1920s and 30s, the road is still deemed so laborious and time-consuming that almost all buses prefer to take a longer, roundabout path via Agadir. You are more likely to find a bus traveling the Tizi-n-Test leaving from the smaller towns of Asni and Taliouine. However, Tizi-n-Test is best explored with a car. Along the way, **Ijoukak** can be a good base for trekking, although it is not as established as other parts of the High Atlas. Several kasbahs established by the Goundafi family can be explored. The **Tin Mal Mosque,** an excellently preserved specimen of 12th-century Almohad architecture, offers a rare chance for non-Muslims to peek at a part of life usually kept secret from visitors. The mosque is unique in that the minaret is on the eastern side and the *mihrab* does not point toward Mecca. Driving oneself through the treacherous switchbacks of the pass is not recommended. Buses don't come here so you would have to be on your own, and driving through the treacherous switchbacks of the pass is very dangerous. Be extremely careful, for road accidents here are an everyday occurrence and fatalities are frighteningly frequent.

TIZI-N-TICHKA

The route from Marrakesh to Ouarzazate, known as the Tizi-n-Tichka, will entertain passengers and drivers alike. While not as breathtaking as its western cousin Tizi-n-Test, the diverse landscape is eye-catching. As you wind south from Marrakesh, the land becomes more and more arid; geology lovers will delight in the numerous terraced plateaus. **Buses** run quite often (see the Marrakesh and Ouarzazate sections), as do *grand taxis* (500dh total). However, renting a car from Marrakesh with a drop-off later in Ouarzazate might be worth the expense.

About two hours south of Marrakesh by car is the town of **Telouet,** 21km from the main road (P31) and home to a remarkable **Glaoui Kasbah.** Inhabited by the powerful Glaoui family up until the middle of this century, the walls of this extravagant palace slowly crumble. Ask the caretaker to let you in (tip about 10dh) and he'll explain in French how the one preserved part of the kasbah was used for feasts. Of particular note are the skylights and extensive mosaics in the main quarters. Transport to Telouet is difficult and expensive, so it's better done as a short excursion on route from Marrakesh or possibly as a daytrip from Ouarzazate.

THE SOUTHERN DESERTS

From kasbah-hopping to camel caravans, the Southern Deserts are where romantic visions of Morocco are fulfilled. Though travel can be complicated (a rental car is often a good choice), the Dadés and Dra'a valleys, with their grand, palm-filled oases, charming villages, and staggering landscapes, are endlessly rewarding.

OUARZAZATE ☎044

Although once envisioned by the Moroccan government as a tourist mecca (they built a four-lane highway and erected five-star hotels), this French-built administrative center never lived up to expectations. Instead, it has found its niche as one of Morocco's most convenient little staging towns. You can arrange everything here for your journey south from picking up a rental car to buying some *bon bons* or *stylos* for the kids you're bound to meet along the way. Besides the Taourirt Kasbah and a few good shops for buying gifts, there's nothing to see or do in town, but no matter: everyone's on their way out anyway.

TRANSPORTATION. The **CTM station** (☎044 88 24 27) is located in the center of town, one block from the main street. **Buses** go to: **Agadir** via Agdz and Zagora (6hr., noon, 100dh); **Marrakesh** (4hr., 2 per day 8:30am and 9pm, 70dh); **M'Hamid** (6½hr., 4:30pm, 68dh); and **Zagora** (4:30pm, 46dh). For destinations in the **Dadés Valley** (Skoura, Boumaln du Dadés, and Tinerhir), it's necessary to catch a **private bus** company. **Grand taxis** line up by the bus station and run fairly often to destinations such as **Marrakesh** (4hr., 70dh), **Skoura** (1hr., 13dh), and **Zagora** (3hr., 45dh). If the taxis are not full (fewer than 6 people crammed in), be prepared to pay extra. There are a dozen **rental car** agencies in Ouarzazate, including Hertz, Avis, and Eurocar, all on av. Mohammed V. Larger companies charge about 500dh per day for a Fiat Uno (unlimited mileage); local companies offer fewer services but charge half that. Try **LocaSud,** 33 av. Mohammed V, for rates as low as 300dh per day with unlimited mileage. (Min. age 21. Open M-F 8:30am-noon and 2:30-8pm, Sa-Su 8:30am-noon and 2-8pm.) Check out any car—especially the spare tire and repair kit—before making any payments and don't hesitate to bargain. Hôtel Royal rents **mopeds** (150dh per half-day, 250dh per day; haggling acceptable).

ORIENTATION AND PRACTICAL INFORMATION. The main street in Ouarzazate is **av. Mohammed V,** home to most administrative buildings, budget hotels, and restaurants. The helpful **tourist office,** on av. Mohammed V where the road forks to follow the Oued Dra'a and the Oued Dadès, offers bus info and a directory of hotels in the Dra'a and Dadès Valleys. (☎044 88 24 85. Open M-Th 8:30am-noon and 2:30-6:30pm, F 8:30-11:30am and 3-6:30pm.) **Currency exchange** and **ATMs** at the banks on av. Mohammed V; four- and five-star hotels will only exchange cash. **Librairie Chaab,** 12 av. Mohammed V, has sells 30dh basic maps. (Open daily 8am-noon and 2-10pm.) **Internet** access is at **Info-Ouar,** around the corner from Café-Restaurant Essalam on rue de Marché. (☎044 88 45 60. 20dh per hr. Open daily 9am-midnight.) The **post office,** with **telephones,** is on av. Mohammed V by the tourist office. (Open M-F 8:30am-3:30pm.)

ACCOMMODATIONS AND FOOD. For inexpensive lodging, try av. Mohammed V or the parallel streets. **Hôtel Royal,** 24 av. Mohammed V next to Chez Dimitri, has welcoming, if simple rooms and can help with rental cars and expeditions. (☎044 88 22 58. Cold showers 3dh. Warm showers 10dh. Singles 36dh, with shower 80dh; doubles 72dh, with shower 92dh; triples 73dh, with shower 93dh; quads with shower 134dh.)

The **Hôtel Bab Es Sahara,** on the corner of pl. Mouhadine where buses arrive, has big, cheap rooms. It also has a restaurant, currency exchange, and accepts credit cards. (☎044 88 47 22; fax 88 44 65. Singles 50dh, with bath 80dh; doubles 80dh, with bath 130dh; triples 120dh, with shower 160dh.) The **supermarket** on av. Mohammed V across the street from Hôtel Royal, has an unrivaled selection of cured meats, canned goods, chocolate, wine, cold beer, and European goods. The best restaurant value in town is the **Café-Restaurant Essalam,** av. Prince Héritier Sidi Mohammed, just off av. Mohammed V. The *tajine* or couscous *menu* is 55dh; big parties can order a pigeon *pastilla* for a negotiable 200dh. (☎044 88 23 76. Open daily 7am-11pm.)

SIGHTS. The nearest example of desert architecture is the **Taourirt Kasbah,** once a Glaoui stronghold. The kasbah, 1½km east of town, was built in the mid-18th century and occupied until 1956. Recently restored, its interior is an entertaining maze of winding streets, stairways, and balconies. To get there, walk down av. Mohammed V, bear left at the tourist office, and head toward Club Med; it's right before the blue-awninged **Café de la Kasbah.** (Open daily 8:30-6:30pm. 10dh.)

NEAR OUARZAZATE

The area to the north of Ouarzazate is a hot and dusty palette of desert browns and greens, periodically interrupted by small Berber **kasbahs.** The plateaus of the pre-Sahara here are spectacular in their vastness; the scale of towns is difficult to determine against such a background. Perhaps the most spectacular of the kasbahs is in the village **Aït Benhaddou,** 21km on the road toward Marrakesh. Built in the 17th century and last inhabited by the Glaoui family in 1955, the kasbah has been designated a UNESCO World Heritage site but is still home to a few Berber families. A member of the family will show you around for a 10dh tip. Some rooms still have intricate stone carvings and vegetable-dyed cedar wood ceilings. The terrace has a great view of the surrounding mountains. Movie buffs may recognize the forest of tapered turrets and backdrop—they're the region's film stars, featured in *Lawrence of Arabia* and *Jesus of Nazareth.* The best way to get here is to take a *grand taxi* from Ouarzazate (about 250dh min. round-trip; the driver will wait, but don't pay him until the journey is complete). It's also a beautiful ride on a rented moped, as long as the gas tank is full. From Marrakesh, take the second signed road (the paved one) to Aït Benhaddou and drive until restaurants appear on the right (10km). Park in front, and walk toward the kasbah in the distance (5min.). You'll have to cross a riverbed to get to the entrance.

THE DRA'A VALLEY وادي درعة

South of Ouarzazate, passing through Agdz and Zagora and ending in M'Hamid, is the narrow Dra'a Valley, along which stretches a nearly continuous grove of palm trees strewn with kasbahs and *qsours* (fortified strongholds). This scenic route is best covered by rental car, although people also hop from village to village by bus, taxi, or thumb (hitchhiking, although not recommended by *Let's Go*, is common in the south). Allow at least two days to reach M'Hamid. Expeditions by camel or 4x4 vehicles are best taken from M'Hamid, but those pressed for time or money may choose to wait until Erg Chebbi for their desert excursion.

OUARZAZATE TO ZAGORA

The route south from Ouarzazate (P31) is unexciting for the first 15km, although a lunar landscape extends in all directions. Volcanic rock soon gives way to an oasis of sorts; a small road to the left leads to the **al-Mansour al-Dahbi reservoir,** formed by heavy rains in 1989. **Aït Saoun** is the first *qsour* along the way and marks the beginning of a steep ascent over the **Tizi-n-Tinififft,** which ultimately reaches an altitude of 1660m. On the way back down, the road passes by several kilometers of stratified rock until the start of the Dra'a's main oases. The first city to take advantage of the waters is **Agdz,** 67km south of Ouarzazate. Set below **Djebel Kissane,** an imposing peak of the Djebel Sharo to the east, the town mainly functions as a resting point before continuing south; buses stop for 30min. to allow passengers to grab a drink. If you have time and your own vehicle, there is a palmery to the left when approaching from Ouarzazate, with a few small kasbahs within.

Just a few kilometers south of Agdz, the real *qsours* begin. The road intersects the Dra'a River, at which point there is a remarkable series of villages: each community is divided into several clusters surrounding an oasis, with smaller homes adjoining central, fortified kasbahs. **Tamnougalt,** 6km south of Agdz, was once the area's capital. The next *qsour*, **Timiderte,** boasts another Glaoui Kasbah worth investigating only if you have not yet seen one. Next is **Tangihlit** and its explosion of palm trees; its neighbor **Tamezmoute** has another large kasbah. Just 37km north of Zagora, the larger **Tinezouline** has a kasbah and a lively Monday *souq*. At the **Azlag Pass** just before Zagora the valley opens again to a vast ocean of palms.

HUSTLERS AND HITCHERS. Many hustlers pose as hitchhikers or victims of auto breakdowns along the Ouarzazate to Zagora road. They invite anyone who picks them up back to their place in "gratitude" for the ride, and once there, try to force the driver to take a camel trek, buy jewelry, etc. Don't stop; just smile and wave as you go by.

ZAGORA اكويزة ☎044

Stiflingly hot, Zagora is the traditional jumping-off point for treks and excursions into the valley or desert. It is perhaps most famous for the half-serious sign at the lower end of town: "To Tombouktou 52 *jours*—by camel." Zagora itself is not a very appealing place, and for those who wish to take a camel trek, M'Hamid offers a more authentic experience. The only time worth spending in Zagora is during the Mouloud, when the city celebrates the **Moussem of Moulay Abdelkader Jilali.**

Numerous **trek agencies** line av. Mohammed V, with the best and cheapest deals at the hotels or campgrounds (**Hôtel des Amis** and **Camping Sindibad** are good bets). Expect to pay around 200-250dh per person per day for trips around Zagora and 300dh per person per day to trek near M'Hamid (transportation included). The more people trekking, the cheaper the price per person.

The best-priced accommodation is the **Hôtel des Amis** in the middle of av. Mohammed V, with slightly dingy but decent rooms. (☎044 84 79 24. Singles with shower 35dh; doubles 50dh, with shower 60dh; triples with shower 75dh; 20dh to sleep on the roof. MC/V.) Signs indicate the way to **Camping Sindibad,** av. Hassan II, just off av. Mohammed V. Spots are shaded by rare trees and covered with grass; there is also a pool at no extra charge. (☎044 84 75 53. Hot showers 5dh. 10dh per person, 5dh per car, 10dh per caravan.) Both accommodations have restaurants. All **buses** stop on av. Mohammed V, the road that the highway turns into, although **CTM** (☎044 84 73 27) stops on the far side of town while other private companies stop on the near side, along with **grand taxis.** CTM buses run to: **Casablanca** (12hr., 7pm, 170dh); **Marrakesh** (6hr., 7pm, 82-110dh); and **Ouarzazate** (2hr., 7pm, 36-45dh). The best way to get to M'Hamid is by *grand taxi* (25dh). Every sort of tourist and financial service is along av. Mohammed V, including **banks,** the **post office,** an **internet café,** and most hotels and restaurants.

SOUTHERN DRA'A

To cross the Dra'a at the southern edge of Zagora, travel out of town (away from Ouarzazate) for 3km and watch for a dirt road on the left (at the sign for Camping de la Montagne de Zagora). This rough track trundles its way to **Djebel Zagora,** a lone volcanic outcrop overlooking the fertile Dra'a. The best time to visit the mountain is at sunset, when the peaks shimmer in the dying light.

TAMEGROUTE. Just off the main highway is the town of Tamegroute, an oasis of date palms and *qsours*. Here, in what seems to be the middle of nowhere, is Morocco's best historical resource, Tamegroute's **library,** containing 4000 Moroccan manuscripts dating from the 11th to the 18th centuries. The collection includes a history of Fez, a copy of Bukhari's *Hadish*, poetry of al-Andalusi, countless astronomical algebraic charts, Muhammad's family tree, and a history of Egypt. The library's most treasured document is a history of Islam written on gazelle skin in 1063 by the great legal authority Iman Malik. To get to the library,

ROCK THE KASBAH Most of the ruined structures you'll pass while traveling in Morocco are **kasbahs,** four-towered fortified structures built for one family and its livestock. **Qsours,** while not necessarily larger, are fortified villages with any number of towers, designed for any number of families. Either of these (or a section of a city) may be referred to as a **mellah,** which means it was once inhabited by Jews. The structures were almost all built with **pizid,** a mixture of straw and mud that needs to be reapplied every year; that is why there are so many ruined kasbahs that date back only 40 or 50 years. The first floor of each is generally used for animals, the second for dining and the kitchen, and the third for living and sleeping. The prefixes **Ben** and **Aït** modify the family name: Ben means "son of," while Aït refers to the entire family.

ignore the painted *bibliothèque* signs (a scam) and turn left (coming from Zagora) down the only paved road. Just after the pavement ends, walk straight for a block and look for a large gate on the right; this leads to the library courtyard. (Open daily 9am-noon and 3-6pm. Free, but tip the multilingual caretaker around 5dh.)

TINFOU. Just south of Tamegroute along the main road, the **Dunes of Tinfou** rise from the valley floor in smooth golden mounds. They are rare in that they can be easily reached by foot or any kind of car from the main road. Just watch for a well-marked dirt turn-off on the left as you come from Zagora. **Hotel Repos du Sables** is located on the road to M'Hamid with the dunes of Tinfou as a dramatic backdrop. It is one of the best places to spend the night in all of Morocco. With fantastic art on the walls and a laid-back atmosphere, it's worth making the effort to stay here. (☎044 84 85 66. Singles 100dh; doubles 150dh.)

M'HAMID ☎044

M'Hamid is literally the end of the road. Forty-five kilometers from the Algerian border and 97km from Zagora, M'Hamid stands as the outpost at the edge of the great deserts. Even if you're not planning a camel trek from here, the drive to M'Hamid is exciting in itself. M'Hamid lacks all but the most basic facilities; electricity made its debut a few years back. (As did Hilary and Chelsea Clinton on their tour of Africa.) This is the best place for guided **camel treks** into the Sahara, which range from 300 to 400dh per person per day with meals included. **Four-by-four trips,** and even trips with your own car, can be arranged as well. One of the best centers from which to plan a trip is **Hôtel-Restaurant Sahara** (☎/fax 044 84 80 09; talk to Habi or M'Barek Naamani). Slightly more expensive are the tours organized by **L'Hôtel Iriqui.** (☎044 84 80 23; www.iriqui.com; booking in Ourzazate ☎044 88 57 99. MC/V.) If you start here in M'Hamid instead of in Zagora, you can reach endless seas of sand dunes and isolated oases within five- or six-days and very impressive landscapes in only a one- or two days. The best times to go are November or December, when temperatures are least extreme. Spend the night at the newly expanded **Hôtel-Restaurant Sahara,** which offers rooms with free hot showers. (Singles 40dh; doubles 75dh; triples 105dh; sleeping in a Berber tent 10dh.) The hotel also serves food, including camel meat (entrées 15-5dh). One **CTM bus** leaves each day for **Marrakesh** via Ouarzazate and Zagora (11hr., 5am, 100dh), as well as one privately-owned bus (11hr., 7am or 2pm, 90dh). **Taxis** and trucks are more frequent. There are no banks and only a tiny **post office.**

THE DADÈS VALLEY

Broader and drier than the Dra'a Valley, the Dadès Valley stretches eastward from Ouarzazate. The valley's main attractions are the **Dadès** and **Todra Gorges,** extending north into the dry escarpment of the High Atlas. The kasbahs of the **Skoura** oasis make for an interesting stop on the way to the gorges. It's possible to get from the Dadés to the Todra across the **Djebel Sharo** range, but a four-wheel-drive vehicle is required. If you are planning to go off-road and into the mountains, you are best off hiring a guide or making arrangements with an expedition company.

SKOURA ☎044

Forty-two kilometers east of Ouarzazate is the kasbah-filled oasis of Skoura, surrounded by fields of grain and roses. From Ouarzazate, turn left off the highway to reach the first kasbah, **Ben Moro.** Recently restored and converted into a hotel, it was previously owned by five generations of Moros; the first Moro built it in the 17th century. The hill and horse decorations above the doorways indicate that the Moro family was once a nomadic Berber tribe. Walking about 200m down any of the paths directly behind Ben Moro leads to the **Amridil Ksar**, located just across the river. An old Glaoui home, it gained fame with its appearance on the 50-dirham bill. Still inhabited by the Nassar family, it is usually open to visitors (knock on the front door). You can spend the night for 100dh or just tour the grounds with the caretaker. Nearby is the **mellah** Kasbah Aït Sidi Maocti, with its intricate exterior carvings. The owner of the Ben Moro Kasbah, Mohammed Sibir, is happy to show anyone around (tip 10-20dh). The town of Skoura itself has little to offer, so plan to move on once you've seen the kasbahs. **Buses** may stop on the Ouarzazate to al-Rachidia route, but a *grand taxi* from Ouarzazate should cost no more than 20dh.

BOUMALNE DU DADÈS ☎044

At a key junction between the Dadès Gorge and the Djebel Sharo, Boumalne du Dadès has succeeded where its neighbors have failed: not a single faux guide bothers visitors to this tourist-friendly, attractive town. Its vantage point from a steep cliff over the Dadès River has made sunset-watching a popular local pastime. If you can't make it up to the Dadès Gorge itself by nightfall (a much nicer place to spend the night), the best place to stay in Boumalne is the recently expanded **Hôtel Al Manadar,** five minutes up the hill from the main square. (☎044 83 01 72. Singles 100dh; doubles 130-160dh; triples 180dh.) Its **restaurant** serves good food with a minimal wait (*menu* 60dh; entrées 35dh).The highway turns into the main road (P32) and goes through town and up the cliff to reach the plateau above. **Buses** arrive on the lower part of this street. The **CTM** office is farther downtown. Buses run to **al-Rachidia** (4hr., 12:30pm, 42dh) and **Marrakesh** via Ouarzazate (7hr., 9am, 70dh). Non-CTM buses go to **Agadir** (8hr., 130dh) and **Rabat** (12hr., 160dh). **Grand taxis** leave from near the bus station for Ouarzazate and Tinerhir, while minibuses and lorries (pickup trucks) will carry you up the Dadès Gorge for around 15-20dh. The **post office,** with several **téléboutiques,** is on top of the hill (a left at the Shell gas station; a 20min. walk). There are several **internet cafés** in town as well.

DADÈS GORGE ☎044

Bizarre limestone rock formations, kasbahs, and sweeping changes in color mark the winding road through the Dadès Gorge, more tranquil and more beautiful than its neighbor, the Todra Gorge. A single paved road runs up into the gorge from Boumalne past small villages and lush palmeries for over 50km. If driving, the route is best taken slowly and with frequent stops to enjoy the landscape changes, or for hikes down into the valley. For those without transport, lorries run quite frequently to and from the gorge or taxis can be hired in Boumalne. Hitchhiking is also possible, but *Let's Go* doesn't recommend it. You can base yourself at one of the hotels listed below; an hour's walk from either reveals great scenery.

There are many places to stay and eat along the road, the best being the **Restaurant Hôtel La Gazelle du Dadès,** at 27km from Boumalne, which has a friendly atmosphere. (☎044 83 17 53. Singles 70dh; doubles 80-100dh; triples 100dh; *salon* or terrace 25dh with mattress and shower; **camping** 10dh per person with shower.) Through the hotel, hire a **guide** (300dh per person for 24hr. with meals), arrange **rafting expeditions** when the water is high (Jan.-Apr.; 200dh per person per day), and rent **bikes** (60dh per day). Its **restaurant** also serves filling meals (3-course *menu* 60dh). Another solid option in the gorge is the **Auberge des Gorges du Dadès,** at 25km from Boumalne. The hostel offers rooms around a courtyard, arranges **treks,** and has a restaurant. (☎/fax 044 83 17 10. Singles 100dh; doubles 140dh.)

TINERHIR (TINGHIR) ☎044

While it's preferable to stay the night in Todra gorge itself, Tinerhir is provides the nearest conveniences. The eastern part of town (on the right when coming from Ouarzazate) contains an old medina and *mellah* worthy of exploration.

The highway turns into av. Mohammed V as it reaches the town. **Buses** arrive just off it, in pl. Principale. Parallel to av. Mohammed V is av. Hassan II, where most of the cheaper hotels and restaurants are located. Buses go to **Marrakesh** via Ouarzazate (private lines 8am-6pm, around 80dh) and **al-Rachidia** (private lines 7:30am-6pm, 28dh). **Grand taxis** running east and west and **lorries** going up the gorge (15-20dh) leave on the other side of the garden between the two main roads. **Banks** line av. Mohammed V. The **post office** is near the taxi stand on av. Hassan II.

Hôtel Tomboktou, Av. Bir Anzarane; from Ourzazate, turn right onto the paved road before the center of town, has traditionally decorated rooms in a restored kasbah. (☎044 83 51 81; fax 83 35 05. Singles 89dh, with bath 250dh; doubles 156dh, with bath 350dh.) For a cheaper stay, budget hotels line the strip of av. Hassan II opposite the park. Next to the CTM office is the student-oriented **Résidence El Fath,** 56 av. Hassan II. The owner will arrange **bike rentals** for exploring the gorge and its **restaurant** serves good rotisserie chicken. (☎044 83 48 06. Bikes 100dh per day. Singles 40dh; doubles 80dh; triples 90dh.) Just outside of town toward Ouarzazate is **Camping Ourti,** av. Mohammed V, which has bungalow-type rooms (35dh per person) and a swimming pool which is 10dh but free for guests. (☎ 044 83 32 05. Camping 12dh per person, 10dh per tent, 8dh per car.) Camping Ourti will also arrange outings up the gorge and to palmeries.

TODRA GORGE ☎044

The road out of Tinerhir snakes up the **Todra River Valley** for 14km before reaching the mouth of the **gorge** (5dh entrance fee per car). From here, hike up between the towering walls. Todra is more developed than the Dadès; while more extensive facilities are available, privacy and the sense of wilderness are lost. Still, the hike is spectacular. Almost 1000ft. high, the sienna walls frame a blue strip of sky above and fall to a rocky riverbed below. A half-day hike is enough to appreciate the magnificence of the gorge, but a few days, or even a week, will allow you to climb well into the High Atlas. Rock climbing is popular, but there are no agencies with equipment or guides. Along the way to the gorge are a trio of beautiful campgrounds. **Auberge de l'Atlas** is slightly better than the other two facilities. Rooms are big and bright with pine furniture, and the campsites are well shaded. (☎/fax 044 89 50 46. Camping 10dh per person, 15dh per tent, 15dh per car. Doubles 90dh; triples 140dh; Berber tent 20dh; terrace 20dh). Its **restaurant** serves standard fare (menu 50-60dh). **Café-Restaurant Auberge Étoile des Gorges** has eight worn rooms; better yet, sleep on the roof below the walls of the gorge. (☎044 83 51 58. Singles 50dh; doubles 100dh; salon 20dh; roof 10dh.) Its **restaurant** serves entrées for 35-40dh and a menu for 50-60dh. You can also arrange rock climbing and guided trips here. At the end of the road is the comfortable **Hôtel Les Roches,** which is frequented by tour groups. The rooms are decent, but for a more enchanting night's rest, sleep on the rooftop terrace under the high rock walls. (☎044 83 48 14; fax 83 36 11. Singles 120dh; doubles 200dh; triples 275dh; terrace 50dh. AmEx/MC/V.) The **restaurant** serves average food (entrées 50dh for hotel guests, 70dh otherwise).

THE ZIZ VALLEY

AL-RACHIDIA الرشيدية ☎044

Although named after the first Alawite sultan, Moulay al-Rashid, al-Rachidia was founded by the French as an administrative capital and military outpost. Today, al-Rachidia's university and successful businesses have brought the town an air of prosperity and friendliness; it offers little to do or see, but the town makes a pleasant stop for travelers heading into the southern deserts and gorges.

All **buses** arrive in town at the main bus station (☎044 57 20 24) at pl. Principale, just off the town's main street, av. Moulay Ali Cherif. Buses go to **Casablanca** via **Rabat**

(16hr.; CTM 8pm, private companies 5 per day 5:30-10pm; 133-160dh); **Erfoud** and **Rissani** (1hr.; CTM 5am, private companies 5 per day 7:30am-7:30pm; 15-20dh); **Fez** (8hr., private companies 10 per day 7am-11:15pm); **Marrakesh** (11hr.; CTM 5:45am, private companies 8:30am and 7pm; 115dh); **Meknes** (7 hr.; CTM 10pm, private companies 4 per day 6am-10pm; 80dh); **Ouarzazate** (CTM 7am, private companies 5 per day 10am-7pm; 168dh). **Grand taxis** go to **Erfoud** (16dh); **Rissani** (20dh) and **Tinerhir** (about 50dh). There are several **banks** in town, although none have ATMs. Services include **police** ☎19, at the bus station, and a dingy **Red Cross,** av. Moulay Ali Cherif next to Restaurant Imilchil.

Most budget hotels are near the bus station. **Hotel El Ansar,** 34 rue Ibn Batouta, behind the bus station and to the left, has the best value, with sparkling rooms and free hot showers. (☎044 57 39 19. Singles 40dh; doubles 60dh; triples 80dh.) Most restaurants and **markets** cluster on av. Moulay Ali Cherif. For fresh produce, try the **supermarket,** across from Hotel M'Daghra. (Open Sa-Th 8am-1pm and 4-9:30pm.) **Café-Restaurant Echajara,** 38 av. Moulay Ali Cherif (☎044 57 15 10), serves a complete *menu* for 30dh. Here you can also find Larbi Lamhamdi, who will arrange sunrise/sunset **tours** to the **Merzouga dunes** (250dh).

ERFOUD ارفود ☎044

One of the last places to fall to the French (in 1932), Erfoud today has little of the spark of revolution left. Although famous for its marble fossils and its annual date festival (in October), Erfoud itself has little to entertain visitors. If you're heading for the dunes of Merzouga, you're better off avoiding Erfoud and its hustler and staying at one of the accommodations by the dunes themselves.

CTM **buses** depart from av. Mohammed V, Erfoud's main street, and go to **al-Rachidia** (8:30am, 15dh); **Rissani** (2hr., 6am, 6dh); and **Meknes** (8hr., 8:30pm, 95dh). All other destinations require transit through al-Rachidia. More frequent private buses leave from pl. des F.A.R., at the far end of av. Mohammed V. **Grand taxis** go to **al-Rachidia** (16dh) and **Rissani** (6dh), departing from the intersection of av. Mohammed V and av. Moulay Ismail. **Banks,** a **hospital,** and the **post office** are there as well.

Erfoud's hotels are all on the expensive side. **Hôtel Merzouga,** 114 av. Mohammed V, outshines the rest, offering spotless and cheery rooms with showers. (☎044 57 65 32. Singles 60dh; doubles 80dh; triples 120dh; terrace 25dh.) The hotel's **restaurant** serves traditional Moroccan cuisine (3-course *menu* 40dh).

NEAR ERFOUD: THE DUNES OF MERZOUGA الشبى

About 50km south of Erfoud is one of Morocco's most enduring images: the monstrous **al-Chebbi** dunes of Merzouga. The largest in the world—some claim they are up to 125m tall—they definitely warrant a visit. They are most enchanting at sunrise and sunset, when golden light and cooler air make for a captivating experience. Legend has it that the dunes have more than just aesthetic value—it is said that submersion in the sweltering sand will cure heart disease and rheumatism.

To explore the dunes, you can arrange excursions from Erfoud—hire a 4x4 *grand taxi* (5-6hr., 400-500dh per taxi) in pl. des F.A.R. or join the air-conditioned package tour (600dh per car) leaving from Hôtel Merzouga. Alternatively, take a *grand taxi* from Erfoud to one of the accommodations by the dunes and arrange your excursion there. Those with their own vehicles should consider enlisting a guide to help navigate through the sand-blown *piste.* One highly recommended guide is **Ali** from **Abira Transport;** save money by booking directly through him. In the town of Merzouga, several Berber families rent out their camels for treks up and over the dunes (50dh per hr., 50dh per day). Ask any driver or hotel owner to point you to one of these spots; camels will be waiting.

"Hotels" near the dunes are mostly indistinguishable concrete block buildings but allow wonderful, doorstep access to the dunes; most of these hotels arrange tours into the dunes where you can sleep on the sand under the stars instead. **Auberge-Restaurant-Camping La Caravane** has a free campground-type enclosure, as well as small rooms with Berber blankets. (☎044 35 16 54; fax 57 52 19. Singles 50dh; doubles 100dh; triples 120dh.) Austere **Hotel Er-Chebbi** is no different from its neighbors, but it does have a telephone. (☎044 35 16 26. 60dh for 1 or 2 people.)

APPENDIX

CLIMATE

In the following charts, the first two columns for each month list the average daily minimum and maximum temperatures in degrees Celsius and Fahreinheit. The rain column lists the average number of days of rain that month.

SPAIN

	JANUARY			APRIL			JULY			OCTOBER		
	°C	°F	Rain	°C	°F	Rain	°C	°F	Rain	°C	°F	Rain
Barcelona	6-13	42-55	5	11-18	52-64	9	21-28	70-82	4	15-21	42-70	9
Madrid	2-9	36-48	8	7-18	45-64	9	17-31	62-88	2	10-19	50-66	8
Málaga	8-17	46-62	7	13-21	55-70	6	21-29	70-84	0	16-23	61-73	6
Santiago de Compostela	5-10	41-50	21	8-18	46-64	7	13-24	55-75	1	11-21	52-70	10
Sevilla	6-15	42-59	8	11-24	52-75	7	20-36	68-97	0	14-26	57-61	6

PORTUGAL

	JANUARY			APRIL			JULY			OCTOBER		
	°C	°F	Rain	°C	°F	Rain	°C	°F	Rain	°C	°F	Rain
Faro	9-15	48-59	9	13-20	55-68	9	20-28	68-82	0	16-22	61-72	6
Lisbon	8-14	46-57	15	12-20	54-68	15	17-27	62-81	2	14-22	57-72	9
Porto	5-13	41-55	18	9-18	48-64	18	15-25	42-77	5	11-21	52-70	15

MOROCCO

	JANUARY			APRIL			JULY			OCTOBER		
	°C	°F	Rain	°C	°F	Rain	°C	°F	Rain	°C	°F	Rain
Fez	4-16	39-61	8	9-23	49-73	9	18-36	64-97	1	13-26	55-79	7
Marrakesh	4-18	39-64	7	11-26	52-79	6	19-38	66-100	1	14-28	57-82	4
Rabat	8-17	46-62	9	11-22	52-72	7	17-28	63-73	0	14-25	57-77	6
Tangier	8-16	46-61	10	11-18	52-64	8	18-27	64-81	0	15-22	59-72	8

TIME ZONES

Spain is 1 hour later than Greenwhich Mean Time (GMT) and 6 hours later than US EST. **Portugal** and **Morocco** are on GMT and 5 hours later than EST. Thus, when it is 3pm in New York, it is 8pm in Portugal and Morocco and 9pm in Spain. Spain and Portugal, together with the rest of Europe, switch to and from Daylight Savings Time about one week before the US does. Morocco does not switch, and is thus 4 hours later than US EST and 2 hours earlier than Spain in the summer.

ADDRESSES

Spain and Portugal: "Av.," "C.,""R.," and "Trav." are abbreviations for street, "Po." and "Pg." for promenade, "Pl." for square, and "Ctra." for highway. A building's number follows the street name. **Morocco:** "av.," "bd.," "rue," and "calle" mean street; "pl." is a plaza. The building number comes before the street name, when there is one. When hunting for an address, note that many streets are being renamed in Arabic; "rue" and "calle" may be replaced by "zankat," "derb," or "sharia."

APPENDIX

SPANISH PHRASEBOOK

Spanish pronunciation is very regular. Vowels are always pronounced the same way: *a* ("ah" in father); *e* ("eh" in essence); *i* ("ee" in eat); *o* ("oh" in oat); *u* ("oo" in boot); *y*, by itself, is pronounced like *ee*. Most consonants are the same as English. Important exceptions are: *j* ("h" in "hello"); *ll* ("y" in "yes"); *ñ* ("gn" in "cognac"); *rr* (trilled "r"); *h* is always silent; *x* retains its English sound. The stress in Spanish words falls on the last syllable, unless the word ends in a vowel, an "s", or an "n". All exceptions require a written accent on the stressed syllable. *Let's Go's* Portuguese and Moroccan Arabic phrasebooks provide pronunciation tips (see below).

ENGLISH	SPANISH	ENGLISH	SPANISH
The Bare Minimum			
Yes/No	Sí/No	**Do you speak English?**	¿Habla (usted) inglés?
Hello	Hola (Sí on the phone)	**I don't understand**	No entiendo
Good morning	Buenos días	**I don't speak Spanish**	No hablo español
Good afternoon	Buenas tardes	**What/When**	¿Qué?/¿Cuándo?
Good evening/night	Buenas noches	**Where/How**	¿Dónde?/¿Cómo?
Goodbye	Adiós/Hasta luego	**Who/Why**	¿Quién?/¿Por qué?
Please/Thank you	Por favor/Gracias	**How are you?**	¿Cómo está (usted)?
Excuse me	Perdón/Perdóname	**Good/Bad/So-so**	Bién/Mal/Así así
Help	¡Socorro!	**What time is it?**	¿Qué hora es?
No smoking/Got a lighter (cigarette)?	No fumar/¿Tiene fuego (un cigarillo)?	**How much does it cost?**	¿Cuánto cuesta?
Here/There/Left/Right/Straight	Aquí/Allí/Izquierda/Derecha/Recto	**Can you drop me off here?**	¿Usted me puede dejar aqui?
Open/Closed	Abierto/Cerrado	**My name is...**	Me llamo...
Hot/Cold	Caliente/Frío	**What is your name?**	¿Cómo se llama?
Where is a late-night pharmacy?	¿Dónde está una farmacia de guardia?	**Is there a telephone that I could use?**	¿Hay un teléfono que podría usar?
Where is the toilet?	¿Dónde está el lavabo?	**I'm sick.**	Estoy enfermo/a.
Accommodation and Transportation			
I want/I would like	Quiero/Quisiera	**How do I reach...?**	¿Cómo llego a...?
I would like a room	Quisiera un cuarto	**One ticket to...**	Un billete para...
Do you have any rooms?	¿Tiene cuartos libres?	**Bus (Train) station/Airport**	Estación de Autobús (Tren)/Aeropuerto
I would like to reserve a room, please.	Quisiera reservar una habitación, por favor.	**How much is the fare to...?**	¿Cuánto vale el billete a...?
bath/shower/water	baño/ducha/agua	**train/plane/bus**	tren/avión/autobús
key/sheets	llave/sábanas	**round-trip**	ida y vuelta
air conditioning	aire acondicionado	**How long is the trip?**	¿Cuánto dura el viaje?
Hotel/Hostel/Campgrounds/Inn	Hotel/Hostal or Albergue/Camping/Posada	**At what time does it leave/arrive?**	¿A qué hora sale/llega?
Food and Dining (also see Glossary)			
breakfast	desayuno	**the check, please**	la cuenta, por favor
lunch	almuerzo	**drink**	bebida
dinner	cena	**dessert**	postre
Can I get this without the meat?	¿Me puede preparar este plato sin carne?	**Can you please bring me...?**	¿Me puede traer... por favor?"
Days			
Sunday	domingo	**today**	hoy
Monday	lunes	**tomorrow**	mañana
Tuesday	martes	**day after tomorrow**	pasado mañana
Wednesday	miércoles	**yesterday**	ayer
Thursday	jueves	**day before yesterday**	antes de ayer/anteayer
Friday	viernes	**week**	semana
Saturday	sábado	**weekend**	fin de semana

PORTUGUESE PHRASEBOOK

ENGLISH	PORTUGUESE	PRONOUNCIATION
Yes/No	Sim/Não	seeng/now
Hello	Olá	oh-LAH
Good day, afternoon/night	Bom dia, Boa tarde/noite	bom DEEer, BOAer tard/noyt
Goodbye	Adeus	ah-DAY-oosh
Please	Por favor	pur fah-VOR
Thank you	Obrigad(o)/(a) (to male/female)	oh-bree-GAH-doo/dah
Sorry	Desculpe	dish-KOOL-peh
Excuse me, please	Desculpe	dish-KOOLP
Do you speak English?	Fala inglês?	FAH-lah een-GLAYSH?
I don't understand	Não entendo	now ayn-TAYN-do
Where is...?	Onde é que é ...?	OHN-deh eh keh eh...?
How much does this cost?	Quanto custa?	KWAHN-too KOOSH-tah?
Do you have a single/double room?	Tem um quarto individual /duple?	tem om KWAR-toe een-DE-vee-DU-ahl/DOO-play?
Help!	Socorro!	so-ko-RO!

APPENDIX

MOROCCAN PHRASEBOOK

ENGLISH	MOROCCAN ARABIC	FRENCH
Hello (polite)	assa-LAA-mu-'a-LEY-kum / 'a-LEY-kum as-sa-LAAM (response)	Bonjour (day) / Bonsoir (night)
Hello/How are you?	la-BAS?	Ça va?
Fine, thanks	la-bas, al-HAM-du-li-lah	Tres bien, merci
Yes/No	EE-yeh/LA	Oui/Non
Please	min FAD-lak (m), min FAD-lik (f)/'AF-fak (m), 'AF-fik (f)/al-LAH-yikhaleek	S'il vous plaît
Thank you	shukran/mercee	Merci
I want (I would like)...	bgheet...	Je voudrais...
I need/I don't need	khuss-NEE/ma-khuss-NEESH	J'ai besoin de/Je n'ai pas besoin de
Where is...?	feen...?	Où est...? / Où se trouve...?
When is...?	fo-QASH...?	A quelle heure est...?
Bus/Taxi/Train	ut-tu-BEES/TAK-see/al-MA-shina	Bus/Taxi/Train
Hotel/Bathroom	u-TEEL/TWA-let or ham-MAM	Hôtel/Toilette
Is there a room?	wesh kayn beet?	Est-ce qu'il y a une chambre libre?
I don't speak Arabic (French)	ma-kan-tkal-LAMSH al-'arabi (al-fransawee)	Je ne parle pas arabe (français)
Do you speak English?	wesh-kat-TKAL-lim in-GLEE-zee?	Parlez-vous anglais?
How much does it cost?	sh-HAL ta-MAN?	Combien ça coute?
Let's work on a better price.	DIR-l-na shee taman mezyan / wa-TSOW-wab m'ana (very colloquial)	Faites-moi un bon prix.
A lot/A little bit	bez-ZAF/sh-WEEY-ya	Beaucoup/Un peu
Cheap/Expensive	ri-KHEES/GHEH-lee	Pas cher/cher
I'm not interested	ma bagh-EESH	Je ne suis pas interessé
Excuse me	SMEH-li	Pardon
Help!	an-NAJ-da! an-qee-DOO-nee!	Au secours!

ARABIC NUMERALS										
0	1	2	3	4	5	6	7	8	9	10
٠	١	٢	٣	٤	٥	٦	٧	٨	٩	١٠
sifir	waahid	itnayn	talaata	arba'a	khamsa	sitta	sab'a	tamaniya	tis'a	'ashara

GLOSSARY

In the following glossary we have tried to include the most useful shortlist of common terms possible, particularly words we use in the text and those that you will encounter frequently in food menus. Non-Castilian Spanish words are specified as **C** (Catalan), **B** (Basque), or **G** (Gallego), respectively. In the Morocco glossary section, **A** stands for Moroccan Arabic and **F** refers to French.

SPAIN: TRAVELING

abadía: abbey
abierto: open
ajuntament (C): city hall
albergue: youth hostel
alcazaba: Muslim citadel
alcázar: Muslim palace
autobús: bus
avenida: avenue
avinguda (C): avenue
ayuntamiento: city hall
bahía: bay
bakalao: Spanish techno
baños: baths
barcelonés: of Barcelona
barrio viejo: old quarter
biblioteca: library
bodega: wine cellar
buceo: scuba diving
cajero automático: ATM
calle: street
cambio: currency exchange
capilla: chapel
carrer (C): street
casa particular: lodging in a private home
caseta: party tent for Sevilla's *Feria de Abril*
castell (C): castle
castillo: castle
catedral: cathedral
cerrado: closed
calabacín: zucchini
caldo gallego: white bean and potato soup
carretera: highway
churrigueresco: ornate Baroque architecture style
ciudad vieja: old city
ciutat vella (C): old city
colegio: school
consigna: luggage storage
Correos: post office
corrida: bullfight
cripta: crypt
croquetas: fried croquettes
encierro: running of the bulls
entrada: entrance
ermida (C): hermitage
ermita: hermitage
església (C): church
estación: station
estanco: tobacco shop
estanque: pond
estany (C): lake
extremeño: of Extremadura
fachada: façade
feria: outdoor market or fair
ferrocarriles: trains
fuente: fountain
gallego: of Galicia
gitano: gypsy
glorieta: rotary
iglesia: church
igrexa (G): church
IVA: value-added tax
jardín público: public garden
judería: Jewish quarter
kiosco: newsstand
librería: bookstore
lista de correos: poste restante
litera: sleeping car (in trains)
llegada: arrival
madrileño: Madrid resident
madrugada: early morning
manchego: from La Mancha
menú: full meal with bread, drink and side dish
mercado: market
mercat (C): market
mezquita: mosque
mirador: lookout point
monestir (C): monastery
monte: mountain
mosteiro (G): monastery
Mozárabe: Christian art style
Mudéjar: Muslim architectural style
muelle: wharf, pier
muralla: wall
museo: museum
museu (C): museum
nezakalturismoa (B): rural tourism
palau (C): palace
parador nacional: state-owned luxury hotel
paseo, Po.: promenade
passeig, Pg. (C): promenade
plaça, Pl. (C): square
plateresque: architectural style noted for its facades
platja (C): beach
plaza, Pl.: square
praza, Pr. (G): square
puente: bridge
rastro: flea market
real: royal
REAJ: the Spanish HI youth hostel network
Reconquista: the Christian reconquest of the Iberian peninsula from the Muslims
refugio: shelter, refuge
reina/rey: queen/king
retablo: altarpiece
ría (G): estuary
río: river
riu (C): river
rua (G): street
sacristía: part of the church where sacred objects are kept
sala: room or hall
salida: exit, departure
Semana Santa: Holy Week, leading up to Easter Sunday
serra (C): mountain range
seu (C): cathedral
sevillanas: type of flamenco
sida: AIDS
sierra: mountain ranges
sillería: choir stalls
tienda: shop or tent
tesoro: treasury
torre: tower
universidad: university
v.o.: *versión original*, a foreign-language film subtitled in Spanish
valle: valley
zarzuela: Spanish light opera

SPAIN: FOOD & DRINK

a la plancha: grilled
aceite: oil
aceituna: olive
adabo: battered
aguacate: avocado
ahumado/a: smoked
ajo: garlic
al horno: baked
albóndigas: meatballs
alioli: Catalan garlic sauce
almejas: clams
almuerzo: midday meal
alubias: kidney beans
anchoas: anchovies
anguila: eel
arroz: rice
arroz con leche: rice pudding
asado: roasted
atún: tuna
bacalao: salted cod
bistec: steak
bocadillo: sandwich
bollo: bread roll
boquerones: anchovies
brasa: chargrilled
cacahuete: peanut
café con leche: coffee w/milk
café solo: black coffee
calamares: calamari, squid
caldereta: stew
calimocho: red wine and coke
callos: tripe
camarones: shrimp
caña: small beer in a glass
canelones: cannelloni
cangrejo: crab
carne: meat
cava (C): champagne
cebolla: onion
cena: dinner
cerdo: pig, pork
cereza: cherry
cervecería: beer bar
cerveza: beer
champiñones: mushrooms
choco: cuttlefish
chorizo: spicy red sausage
chuleta: chop, cutlet
chupito: shot
churros: fried dough sticks

cocido: cooked; meat and peas stew
conejo: rabbit
coñac: brandy
copas: drinks
cortado: coffee with little milk
crudo: raw
cuchara: spoon
cuchillo: knife
cuenta: the bill
desayuno: breakfast
dorada: sea bass
empanada: meat/pastry pie
ensaladilla rusa: vegetable salad with mayonnaise
entremeses: hors d'oeuvres
escabeche: pickled fish
espagueti: spaghetti
espárragos: asparagus
espinacas: spinach
fabada asturiana: bean soup with sausage and ham
flan: crème caramel
frambuesa: raspberry
fresa: strawberry
frito/a: fried
galleta: cookie
gambas: prawns
gazpacho: cold soup with garlic and tomato
guindilla: hot chili pepper
guisantes: peas
helado: ice cream
horchata: sweet almond drink
horneado: baked
huevo: egg
jamón dulce: cooked ham
jamón serrano: cured ham
jatetxea (B): restaurant
jerez: sherry
langosta: lobster
langostino: large prawn
lechuga: lettuce
lomo: pork loin
manzana: apple
manzanilla: dry, light sherry
mejillones: mussels
melocotón: peach
menestra de verduras: vegetable mix/pottage
merienda: tea/snack
merluze: hake
migas: fried breadcrumb dish
morcilla: blood sausage (black pudding)
muy hecho: well-done (steak)
natillas: creamy milk dessert
paella: rice and seafood dish
pastas: small sweet cakes
patatas bravas: potatos in spicy tomato sauce
patatas fritas: French fries
pavo: turkey
pechuga: chicken breast
pepino: cucumber
pescaíto frito: tiny fried fish
picante: spicy
pimienta: pepper
piña: pineapple
pintxo (B): Basque for tapa
plancha: grilled
plátano: banana
plato del día: daily special
plato combinado: entrée and side order
poco hecho: rare (steak)
pollo: chicken
pulpo: octopus
queso: cheese
rabo de toro: bull's tail
ración: small dish
rebozado: battered and fried
refrescos: soft drinks
relleno/a: stuffed
salchicha: pork sausage
sangría: red wine punch
seco: dried
sesos: brains
setas: wild mushrooms
sidra: cider
solomillo: sirloin
sopa: soup
taberna: tapas bar
tapa: bite-sized snack
tenedor: fork
ternera: beef, veal
terraza: patio seating
tinto: red (wine)
tortilla española: potato omelette
tostada: toast
trucha: trout
tubo: tall glass of beer
uva: grape
vaca, carne de: beef
verduras: green vegetables
vino: wine
vino tinto: red wine
xampanyería (C): champagne bar
yema: candied egg yolk
zanahoria: carrot
zarzuela de marisco: shellfish stew
zumo: fruit juice

PORTUGAL: TRAVELING

alto/a: upper
autocarro: bus
bairro: town district
baixo/a: lower
berroes: stone pigs found in Trás-Os-Montes
bicyclete tudo terrano: mountain bike
bilhete: ticket
bilheteria: ticket office
câmara municipal: town hall
camioneta: coach
capela: chapel
casa de abrigo: shelter-house, usually in parks
castelo: castle
centro de saúde: state-run medical center
chegadas: arrivals
cidade: city
claustro: cloister
conta: bill
coro alto: choir stalls
Correios: post office
cruzeiro: cross
Dom, Dona: courtesy titles, usually for kings and queens
domingo: Sunday
entrada: entrance
esquerda: left (abbr. E, Esqa)
estação rodoviária: bus station
estrada: road
feriada: holiday
floresta: forest
fortaleza: fort
grutas: caves
horario: timetable
igreja: church
ilha: island
intercidade: inter-city train
lago: lake
largo: small square
ligação: connecting bus/train
livraria: bookstore
miradouro: lookout
mosteiro: monastery
mouraria: Moorish quarter
mudança: switch/change
obras: construction
paco: palace
paragem: stop
partidas: departures
pelourinho: stone pillory
pensão (s.), pensões (pl.): pension(s)/guesthouse(s)
ponta: bridge
porta: gate
pousada da juventude: youth hostel
pousada: state-run hotel
praça: square
praça de touros: bullring
praia: beach
PSP: Polícia de Seguranca Pública, the local police force
quarta-feira: Wednesday
quarto de casal: room with double bed
quinta-feira: Thursday
quiosque: kiosk; newsstand
res do chao: ground floor, abbr. R/C
residencial: guesthouse, more expensive than *pensões*
retablo: altarpiece
ribeiro: stream
rio: river
romaria: pilgrimage-festival
rossio: rotary
rua: street
sábado: Saturday
saída: exit
sé: cathedral
segunda-fiera: Monday
selos: stamps
sexta-feira: Friday
terça-fiera: Tuesday
termas: spa
tesouro: treasury
torre de menagem: keep
tourada: bullfight
turismo: tourist office
vila: town

PORTUGAL: FOOD AND DRINK

açorda: thick soup with bread
adega: wine cellar, bar
aguardente: firewater
alface: lettuce
alho: garlic
almoço: lunch

ameijoas: clams
Antigua: aged grape brandy
arrufada de Coimbra: raised dough cake with cinnamon
assado (no forno): baked
azeitonas: olives
bacalhau: cod
bacalhau à Gomes de Sá: cod with olives and eggs
bacalhau à transmontana: cod braised with cured pork
balcao: counter in bar or café
batata: potato
batido: milkshake
bem passado: well done
bica: espresso
bifinhos de vitela: veal filet with wine sauce
bitoque de porco: pork chops
bitoque de vaca: steak
bolachas: cookies
café com leite: coffee with milk, in a mug
caldeirada: shellfish stew
caldo: broth/soup
caldo verde: cabbage soup
camaröes: shrimp
caneca: pint-size beer mug
caracóis: snails
carioca: cafe mixed with hot water; like American coffee
carne: meat
carne de vaca: beef
cebola: onion
cerveja: beer
chourico: sausage
churrasqueira: BBQ house
cogumelos: mushrooms
conta: bill
couvert: cover charge added to bill for bread
cozido: boiled
ementa: menu
ervilhas: green peas
esacalfado: poached
espadarte: swordfish
espetadas: skewered meat served with melted butter
esturjão: sturgeon
fatia: slice
feijao: bean
frango: chicken
frito: fried
galao: coffee with hot milk
gasosa: lemonade
gelado: ice cream
grao: chick peas
grelhado: grilled
guisado: stewed
hamburger no prato: hamburger patty with fried egg
imperial: tall thin beer glass
jantar: dinner
lagosta: lobster
laranja: orange
linguica: very thin sausage
maca: apple
manteiga: butter
mariscos: shellfish
massapão: marzipan
mexilhöes: mussels
no churrasco: barbequed
no forno: baked
padaria: bakery
panado: breaded
pao: bread
pastelaria: pastry shop
pequena almoço: breakfast
peru: turkey
pimentos: peppers
polvo: octupus
porço: pork
posta: slice of fish or meat
prato do día: dish of the day
presunto: ham
quiejo: cheese
recheado: stuffed
salmão: salmon
sande: sandwich
sobremesa: dessert
sopa juliana: soup with shredded vegetables
sumo: juice
tasca: bistro/cafe
tigelada: sweet egg dessert
tomatada: rich tomato sauce
tosta: grilled cheese
tosta mista: grilled ham and cheese sandwich
toucinho do ceu: "Bacon of Heaven," an egg dessert
verdures: vegetables
vinho branco: white wine
vinho de casa: house wine
vinho verde: young wine
vitela: veal

MOROCCO

adhan (A): call to prayer
agneau (F): lamb
aguelmane (A): lake
aourir (A): small mountain
aujourd'hui (F): today
azrour (A): rock
auberge de jeunesse (F): youth hostel
azib (A): shepherd's hut
bastilla (A): pigeon pie
bab (A): gate
beurre (F): butter
bière (F): beer
billet (F): ticket
birra (A): beer
blanc (F): white
boeuf (F): beef
borj (A): tower
boulettes de viande (F): meatballs
brochettes (F): shish-kebab, usually lamb
bus (F): bus
chambre (F): room
chameau (F): camel
chaud (F): hot
compris (F): included
consigne (F): left luggage
couscous (F): semolina grain
couscous bidaoui (A): couscous with 7 vegetables
cornes de gazelles (F): pastry horns with marzipan
coûter (F): to cost
crevettes (F): shrimp
demain (F): tomorrow
djebel (A): mountain peak
douche (F): shower
droite (F): right
ejben (A): cheese
erg (A): sand dune
fassi (A): resident of Fes
fermé (F): closed
forsheta (A): fork
frites (F): French fries
froid (F): cold
fromage (F): cheese
gare (F): train station
gare routière (F): bus station
gauche (F): left
glace (F): ice cream
hadj (A): Mecca pilgrimage
hammam (A): public bath
harira (F): Moroccan lamb-based soup
hier (F): yesterday
huile (F): oil
djellaba (A): traditional Moroccan garment
djoutia (A): flea market
kasbah (A): family fortress
kefta (F): Moroccan burger
l-habra (A): steak
l'houli (A): mutton
légume (F): vegetable
lehmama (A): pigeon
litham (A): veil
louer (F): to rent
louz (A): almonds
madrassa (A): school
makhzen (A): government
malka (A): spoon
mechoui (A): roast lamb
medina (A): old Arabic city
mellah (A): Jewish quarter
mihrab (A): prayer niche
msalla (A): prayer area
moos (A): knife
mosquée(F): mosque
moussem (A): festival
musée (F): museum
nouveau/nouvelle (F): new
oignons (F): onions
ouvert (F): open
pain (F): bread
palais (F): palace
pastilla (F): chicken, almond paste, and spices in a pastry
piscine (F): pool
poisson (F): fish
poste (F): post office
poulet (F): chicken
qahwa: coffee
qniya (A): rabbit
qsar, qsour (pl.) (A): fortified village with curved, white-washed houses
rouge (F): red
rue (F): street
salle de bain (F): bathroom
shrab (A): wine
souq (A): market
tajine (F): Moroccan stew
timbre (F): stamp
tmer (A): dates
toilette (F): toilet
train (F): train
viande (F): meat
vieux/vielle (F): old
ville (F): city
vin (F): wine
voiture (F): car
zelidj (A): decorative tiles

AVERAGE TRAVEL TIMES IN SPAIN AND PORTUGAL

	Algeciras	Badajoz	Barcelona	Bilbao	Córdoba	Granada	León	Málaga	Madrid	Pamplona	Salamanca	San Sebastián	Santiago	Sevilla	Toledo	Valencia	Zaragoza
Algeciras																	
Badajoz	10hr.																
Barcelona	19½hr.	13½hr.															
Bilbao	11-13hr.	10-11½hr.	8-11hr.														
Córdoba	5-6hr.	6hr.	11hr.	9-11hr.													
Granada	5-7hr.	7½-9½hr.	12-13hr.	10-12hr.	3hr.												
León	11hr.	8½hr.	11½hr.	7hr.	7-9hr.	10hr.											
Málaga	5½hr.	7-8hr.	13hr.	11-13hr.	2½-3hr.	2hr.	9-11½hr.										
Madrid	6hr.	4½hr.	7hr.	5-7hr.	2-6hr.	5hr.	4½-5½hr.	4-6hr.									
Pamplona	11hr.	9½hr.	6-8hr.	2hr.	9hr.	10hr.	4hr.	9-11hr.	5hr.								
Salamanca	9hr.	5½hr	11½hr.	5½-6½hr.	6-8hr.	8hr.	3hr.	7-9hr.	3hr.	6-7hr.							
San Sebastián	12-14hr.	10-12hr.	7-10hr.	11hr.	10-12hr.	11-13hr.	5¼hr.	12-14hr.	6-8hr.	1-2hr.	5½-6½hr.						
Santiago de Compostela	14hr.	12-13hr.	15hr.	11hr.	11-13hr.	13hr.	5½hr.	12-14hr.	7½-8hr.	12hr.	7-8hr.	12hr.					
Sevilla	4-5hr.	4½hr.	13-16hr.	8-11hr.	1½hr.	3-5hr.	7-9hr.	2½-3hr.	2½-3½hr.	8hr.	8hr.	9-11hr.	11hr.				
Toledo	6hr.	5hr.	7hr.	6-8hr.	3-5hr.	14hr.	6hr.	5-6hr.	1½hr.	9hr.	4hr.	7-9hr.	12hr.	3hr.			
Valencia	13-15hr.	10hr.	4-6hr.	12hr.	7hr.	8hr.	10-13hr.	11hr.	5-7½hr.	10hr.	8-10½hr.	10hr.	11hr.	9hr.	5-7½hr.		
Zaragoza	9hr.	8hr.	4hr.	4hr.	6-8hr.	8hr.	5½-6hr.	7-9hr.	3hr.	2hr.	7hr.	4hr.	11-12hr.	8½hr.	4hr.	6hr.	

Braga	Coimbra	Évora	Faro	Fátima	Lisbon	Porto	
	4hr.	9-10hr.	12-15hr.	5½hr.	8½hr.	2hr.	Braga
		6hr.	12hr.	1½hr.	3hr.	3hr.	Coimbra
			6hr.	5½hr.	3hr.	7hr.	Évora
				7½hr.	5hr.	8½hr.	Faro
					2½hr.	3½hr.	Fátima
						6hr.	Lisbon
							Porto

APPENDIX

Travel Cheep.

Visit **StudentUniverse** for real deals on student and faculty airline tickets, rail passes, and hostel memberships.

StudentUniverse.com

Real Travel Deals

800.272.9676

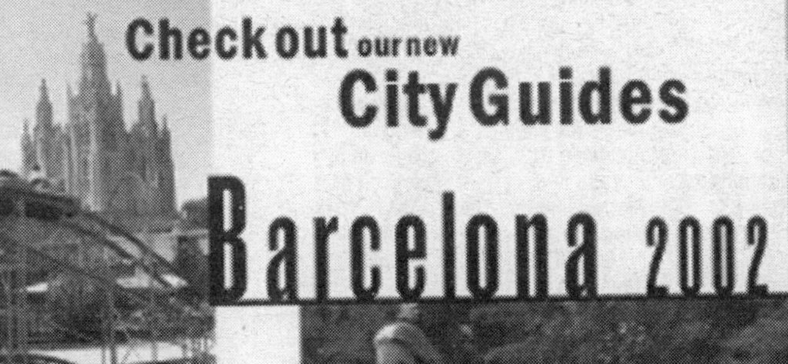

otos
lking tours
rvice directory
nusing anecdotes
tailed map coverage

msterdam 2002

u know you love
ur special Let'sGoThumbpicks

APPENDIX

INDEX

INDEX

DOWNLOAD

Let's Go: Amsterdam
Let's Go: Barcelona
Let's Go: Boston
Let's Go: London
Let's Go: New York City
Let's Go: Paris
Let's Go: Rome
Let's Go: San Francisco
Let's Go: Washington, D.C.

Let's Go

For Your PalmOS™ PDA

Pocket-sized and feature-packed, Let's Go is now available for use on PalmOS-compatible PDAs. **Full text, graphical maps,** and **advanced search capabilities** make for the most powerful and convenient Let's Go ever.

PalmOS is a registered trademark of Palm, Inc.

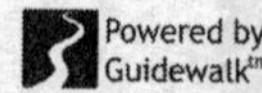

©2000 Yahoo! Inc.

Will you have enough stories to tell your grandchildren?

Yahoo! Travel

Do You Yahoo!?™

CHOOSE YOUR DESTINATION SWEEPSTAKES

No Purchase Necessary.

Explore the world with Let's Go® and StudentUniverse!
Enter for a chance to win a trip for two to a Let's Go destination!

Separate Drawings! May & October 2002.

GRAND PRIZES:

Roundtrip StudentUniverse Tickets

✓ Select one destination and mail your entry to:

- ☐ Costa Rica
- ☐ London
- ☐ Hong Kong
- ☐ San Francisco
- ☐ New York
- ☐ Amsterdam
- ☐ Prague
- ☐ Sydney

* Plus Additional Prizes!!

Choose Your Destination Sweepstakes
St. Martin's Press
Suite 1600, Department MF
175 Fifth Avenue
New York, NY 10010-7848

Restrictions apply; see offical rules for details by visiting Let'sGo.com or sending SASE (VT residents may omit return postage) to the address above.

Name: ______________________

Address: ______________________

City/State/Zip: ______________________

Phone: ______________________

Email: ______________________

Grand prizes provided by:

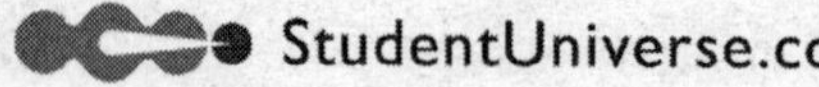

Real Travel Deals

Drawings will be held in May and October 2002. NO PURCHASE NECESSARY. These are not the full official rules, and other restrictions apply. See Official Rules for full details.
To enter without purchase, go to www.letsgo.com or mail a 3"x5" postcard with required information to the above address. Limit one entry per person and per household.

Void in Florida, Puerto Rico, Quebec and wherever else prohibited by law. Open to legal U.S. and Canadian residents (excluding residents of Florida, Puerto Rico and Quebec) 18 or older at time of entry. Round-trip tickets are economy class and depart from any major continental U.S. international airport that the winner chooses.
All mailed entries must be postmarked by September 16, 2002 and received by September 27, 2002.
All online entries must be received by 11:59 pm EDT September 16, 2002.

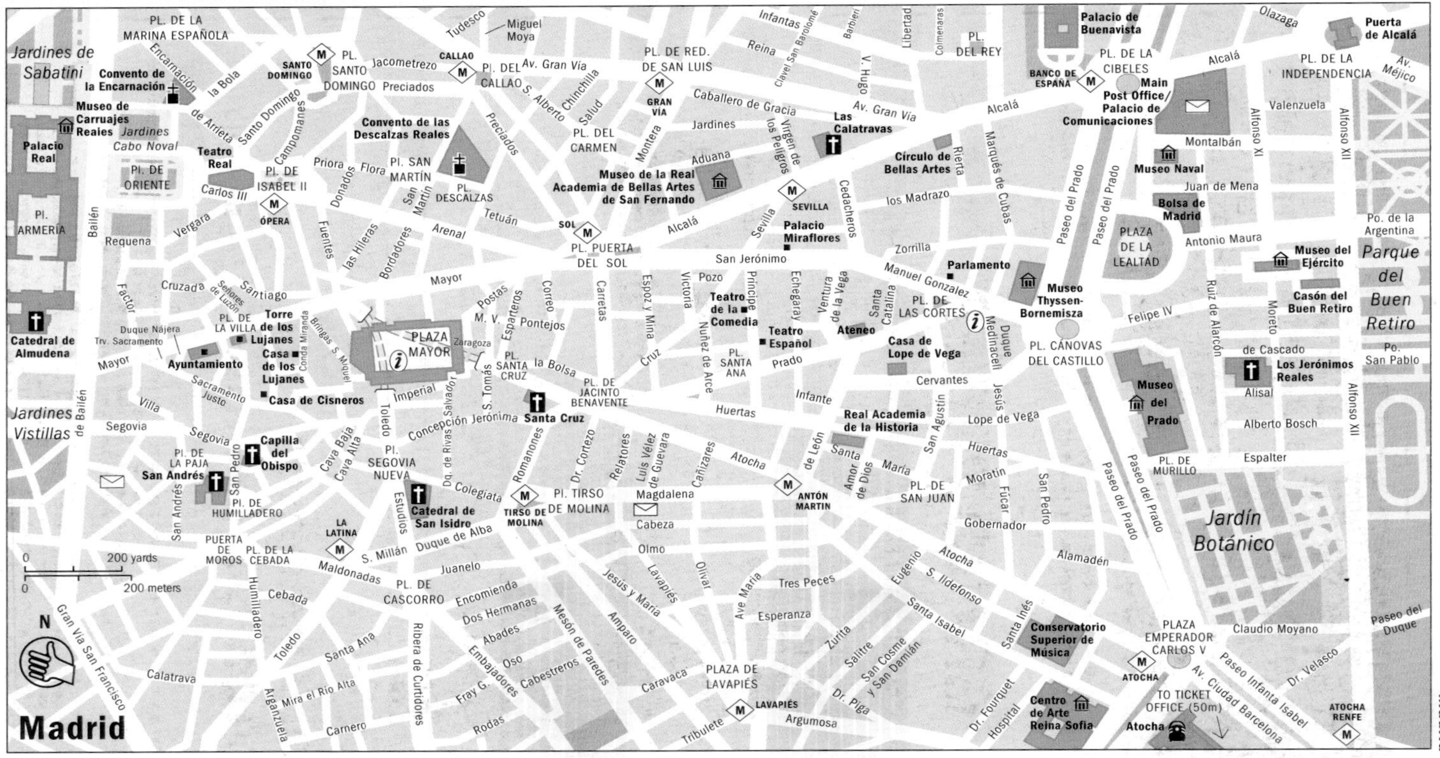
Madrid
N
0
200 yards
0
200 meters
Jardines de Sabatini
Palacio Real
Pl. Armería
Catedral de Almudena
Jardines Vistillas
de Bailén
Museo de Carruajes Reales
Convento de la Encarnación
Pl. de la Marina Española
Encarnación
Jardines Cabo Noval
Pl. de Oriente
Teatro Real
Carlos III
Pl. de Isabel II
Ópera
Santo Domingo
Pl. Santo Domingo
Campomanes
la Bola
de Arrieta
Bailén
Requena
Vergara
Factor
Cruzada
Duque Nájera
Trv. Sacramento
Mayor
Ayuntamiento
Pl. de la Villa
Torre de los Lujanes
Casa de los Lujanes
Casa de Cisneros
Conde Miranda
Bringas
S. Miguel
Sacramento
Justo
Señores de Luzón
Santiago
Villa
Segovia
Pl. de la Paja
San Andrés
Capilla del Obispo
San Pedro
Pl. de Humilladero
Puerta de Moros
Pl. de la Cebada
Humilladero
Cebada
Toledo
Arganzuela
Mira el Río Alta
Carnero
Santa Ana
Calatrava
Gran Vía San Francisco
Maldonadas
La Latina
S. Millán
Pl. de Cascorro
Ribera de Curtidores
Cava Alta
Cava Baja
Pl. Segovia Nueva
Estudios
Catedral de San Isidro
Colegiata
Duque de Alba
Juanelo
Encomienda
Dos Hermanas
Abades
Oso
Embajadores
Fray G.
Rodas
Cabestreros
Mesón de Paredes
Amparo
Jesús y María
Lavapiés
Olmo
Cabeza
Magdalena
Olivar
Caravaca
Plaza de Lavapiés
Lavapiés
Tribulete
Argumosa
Pl. Tirso de Molina
Tirso de Molina
Romanones
Dr. Cortezo
Relatores
Luis Vélez de Guevara
Cañizares
Toledo
Imperial
Plaza Mayor
Zaragoza
Dq. de Rivas
Salvador
Concepción Jerónima
S. Tomás
Pl. Santa Cruz
Santa Cruz
Pl. de Jacinto Benavente
la Bolsa
Pontejos
Esparteros
M. V.
Postas
Correo
Carretas
Espoz y Mina
Cruz
Victoria
Pozo
Nuñez de Arce
Pl. Santa Ana
Teatro de la Comedia
Teatro Español
Principe
Prado
Echegaray
Huertas
Atocha
Antón Martín
Pl. Puerta del Sol
Sol
Mayor
Arenal
Bordadores
las Hileras
Donados
Fuentes
Priora
Flora
San Martín
Pl. San Martín
Convento de las Descalzas Reales
Pl. Descalzas
Tetuán
Preciados
Jacometrezo
Callao
Pl. del Callao
Tudesco
Miguel Moya
Av. Gran Vía
S. Alberto
Chinchilla
Salud
Pl. del Carmen
Montera
Gran Vía
Pl. de Red. de San Luis
Caballero de Gracia
Jardines
Aduana
Museo de la Real Academia de Bellas Artes de San Fernando
Alcalá
San Jerónimo
Sevilla
Palacio Miraflores
Virgen de los Peligros
Reina
Infantas
Clavel
San Bartolomé
Barbieri
V. Hugo
Las Calatravas
Cedacheros
Ventura de la Vega
Ateneo
Santa Catalina
Casa de Lope de Vega
Cervantes
Infante
de León
Santa María
Amor de Dios
Real Academia de la Historia
Pl. de San Juan
San Agustín
Zorrilla
los Madrazo
Círculo de Bellas Artes
Rierta
Marqués de Cubas
Libertad
Colmenares
Pl. del Rey
Manuel Gonzalez
Pl. de las Cortes
Parlamento
Duque Medinaceli
Jesús
Lope de Vega
Moratín
Fúcar
Gobernador
San Pedro
Alamadén
Tres Peces
Esperanza
Ave María
Zurita
Santa Isabel
S. Ildefonso
Eugenio
San Cosme y San Damián
Salitre
Dr. Piga
Dr. Fourquet
Hospital
Santa Inés
Conservatorio Superior de Música
Centro de Arte Reina Sofia
Atocha
Atocha Renfe
To Ticket Office (50m)
Av. Ciudad Barcelona
Paseo Infanta Isabel
Dr. Velasco
Claudio Moyano
Plaza Emperador Carlos V
Paseo del Prado
Pl. de Murillo
Museo del Prado
Pl. Cánovas del Castillo
Museo Thyssen-Bornemisza
Felipe IV
Plaza de la Lealtad
Bolsa de Madrid
Museo Naval
Antonio Maura
Juan de Mena
Montalbán
Ruiz de Alarcón
Espalter
Alberto Bosch
Alisal
de Cascado
Moreto
Los Jerónimos Reales
Casón del Buen Retiro
Museo del Ejército
Jardín Botánico
Alfonso XII
Alfonso XI
Paseo del Duque
Po. San Pablo
Parque del Buen Retiro
Po. de la Argentina
Av. Méjico
Puerta de Alcalá
Pl. de la Independencia
Valenzuela
Olazaga
Alcalá
Pl. de la Cibeles
Palacio de Buenavista
Main Post Office/ Palacio de Comunicaciones
Banco de España

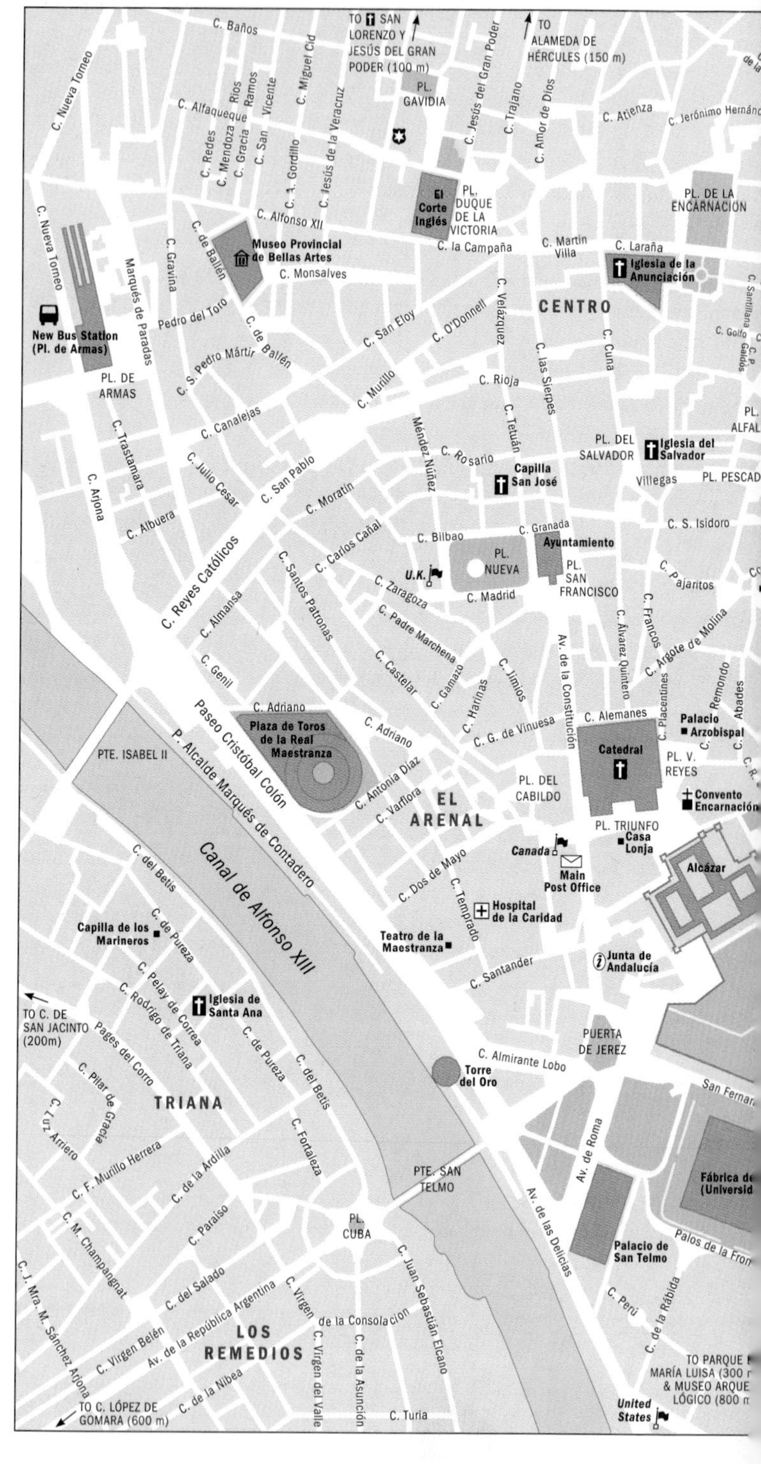

TO SAN LORENZO Y JESÚS DEL GRAN PODER (100 m)
TO ALAMEDA DE HÉRCULES (150 m)
C. Baños
C. Nueva Torneo
C. Alfaqueque
PL. GAVIDIA
El Corte Inglés
PL. DUQUE DE LA VICTORIA
PL. DE LA ENCARNACIÓN
Museo Provincial de Bellas Artes
Iglesia de la Anunciación
CENTRO
New Bus Station (Pl. de Armas)
PL. DE ARMAS
PL. DEL SALVADOR
Iglesia del Salvador
PL. PESCAD
Capilla San José
Ayuntamiento
PL. NUEVA
U.K.
PL. SAN FRANCISCO
Plaza de Toros de la Real Maestranza
PTE. ISABEL II
Paseo Cristóbal Colón
P. Alcalde Marqués de Contadero
Canal de Alfonso XIII
EL ARENAL
PL. DEL CABILDO
Catedral
Palacio Arzobispal
PL. V. REYES
Convento Encarnación
PL. TRIUNFO
Casa Lonja
Alcázar
Canada
Main Post Office
Hospital de la Caridad
Teatro de la Maestranza
Junta de Andalucía
Capilla de los Marineros
Iglesia de Santa Ana
TO C. DE SAN JACINTO (200m)
TRIANA
PUERTA DE JEREZ
Torre del Oro
PTE. SAN TELMO
Fábrica de (Universid
Palacio de San Telmo
PL. CUBA
LOS REMEDIOS
TO PARQUE MARÍA LUISA (300 m) & MUSEO ARQUEOLÓGICO (800 m)
United States
TO C. LÓPEZ DE GOMARA (600 m)
C. Turia
C. Juan Sebastián Elcano
Av. de las Delicias
Av. de Roma
Av. de la República Argentina
C. Reyes Católicos
Av. de la Constitución
C. las Sierpes
C. Tetuán
C. Velázquez
C. Cuna

ENA
C. Peñuelas
C. del Sol
PONCE
LEÓN
C. Salecianos
C. Arroyo
C. San Juan Bosco
C. Venecia
C. Dr. Delgado Riog
C. Urquiza
C. María Auxiliadora
C. Saturno
C. Arroyo
C. Pérez Hervás
C. Esperanza de la Trinidad
N
PUERTA OSARIO
C. Gonzalo Bilbao
C. Jose Laguillo
Estación de
Santa Justa
C. Azafrán
C. Santiago
C. Imperial
C. de los Navarros
C. Conde Negro
C. Recaredo
C. Vir. de Gracia y Esperanza
C. Arroyo
C. Amador de Los Ríos
C. Jupiter
C. Lope de la Vega
C. Padre Méndez Casariego
C. Guadalupe
PL. CARMEN
BENÍTEZ
C. Beata Juana Jugan
Casa de
Pilatos
PL.
PILATOS
C. Fray Alonso
C. Juan de Vera
C. Juan Antonio Cavestany
C. Campo de los Martires
C. Lictores
C. Pablo Picasso
PL. SAN
AUGUSTÍN
Av. Luis Montoto
LA CALZADA
PL. DE LAS
MERCENARIAS
C. la Florida
C. Averroes
C. San Benito
PL. DEL
SACRIFICIO
C. Céspedes
C. San Clemente
Av. Menéndez Pelayo
Ruinas
Acueducto
C. Via Cruces
S. Florencio
C. Pilar
C. Archeros
C. Cano y Cueto
SANTA
CRUZ
Jimenez Aranda
José Cámara
Fernando Tirado
Virgen Valvanera
Eduardo Rivas
Maese Farfán
María la Blanca
C. A. Fernández
C. J. María
Moreno Galván
Fuenteovejuna Trovador
C. Demetrio de los Ríos
Manuel Pérez
Jardines
de
Murillo
C. General Ríos
Pirineos
Oscar Carvallo
Av. Eduardo Dato
Menéndez Pelayo
C. Capitán Vigueras
C. Juan de Matacarriazoa
San Bernardo
Cofia
Av. de Cádiz
Gallinato
Tentudla
Portaceli Huestes
Av. De La Buhaira
PL. DE
SAN
SEBASTIAN
Av. Málaga
Estación
Prado San
Sebastián
C. Diego Riaño
C. José María Osborne
Virgen de
la Sierra
Campamento
Av. Carlos V
Infanta Luisa de Orleans
Infante Carlos de Borbón
Enramadilla
Barrau
0
200 yd
0
200 m
de Portugal
C. Ciudad Ronda
Dr. A. C. Llado
Enramadilla
Dr. Pedro
Castro
PL. DE
ESPAÑA
Sevilla

Madrid Metro

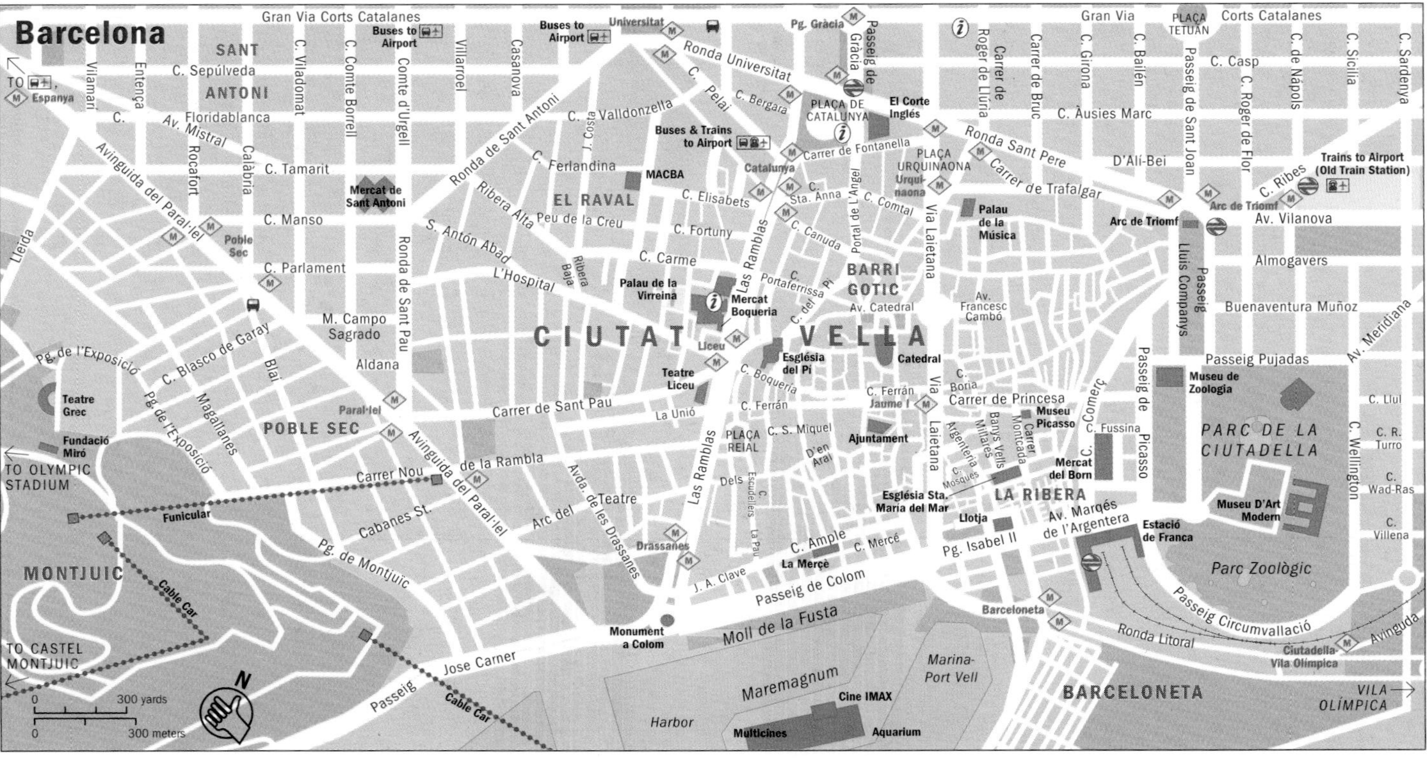
Barcelona
Gran Via Corts Catalanes
SANT ANTONI
C. Sepúlveda
Floridablanca
Av. Mistral
TO Espanya
Vilamarí
Entença
C. Viladomat
C. Comte Borrell
Comte d'Urgell
Villarroel
Casanova
Buses to Airport
Buses to Airport
Universitat
Pg. Gràcia
Passeig de Gràcia
Ronda Universitat
C. Pelai
C. Bergara
PLAÇA DE CATALUNYA
El Corte Inglés
Buses & Trains to Airport
Catalunya
Carrer de Fontanella
PLAÇA URQUINAONA
Urquinaona
Ronda Sant Pere
Carrer de Trafalgar
Carrer de Roger de Llúria
Carrer de Bruc
C. Girona
C. Bailén
C. Àusies Marc
Gran Via
PLAÇA TETUAN
Corts Catalanes
Passeig de Sant Joan
C. Casp
C. Roger de Flor
C. de Nápols
C. Sicilia
C. Sardenya
D'Alí-Bei
C. Ribes
Trains to Airport (Old Train Station)
Arc de Triomf
Arc de Triomf
Av. Vilanova
Almogavers
Buenaventura Muñoz
Passeig Lluis Companys
Av. Meridiana
Passeig Pujadas
Museu de Zoologia
PARC DE LA CIUTADELLA
C. Llul
C. R. Turro
C. Wellington
C. Wad-Ras
C. Villena
Museu D'Art Modern
Parc Zoològic
Estació de Franca
Passeig Circumvallació
Ronda Litoral
Avinguda
Ciutadella-Vila Olímpica
VILA OLÍMPICA
BARCELONETA
Barceloneta
Lleida
Avinguda del Paral·lel
Rocafort
Calàbria
C. Tamarit
Mercat de Sant Antoni
C. Manso
Poble Sec
C. Parlament
Ronda de Sant Antoni
C. Valldonzella
J. Costa
C. Ferlandina
MACBA
EL RAVAL
Ribera Alta
Peu de la Creu
S. Antón Abad
L'Hospital
Ribera Baja
C. Elisabets
C. Fortuny
C. Carme
Palau de la Virreina
Mercat Boqueria
Las Ramblas
C. Sta. Anna
C. Canuda
Portal de L'Angel
C. Comtal
Via Laietana
Palau de la Música
C. Portaferrissa
C. del Pi
BARRI GOTIC
Av. Catedral
Av. Francesc Cambó
CIUTAT VELLA
Liceu
Església del Pi
Catedral
Teatre Liceu
C. Boqueria
C. Ferrán
Jaume I
C. Boria
Carrer de Princesa
Museu Picasso
C. Comerç
C. Fussina
Passeig de Picasso
M. Campo Sagrado
Ronda de Sant Pau
Aldana
Pg. de l'Exposició
C. Blasco de Garay
Blai
Teatre Grec
Pg. de l'Exposició
Magallanes
Paral·lel
POBLE SEC
Fundació Miró
TO OLYMPIC STADIUM
Carrer de Sant Pau
La Unió
C. Ferrán
PLAÇA REIAL
C. S. Miquel
D'en Arai
Ajuntament
Argenteria
Banys Vells
Millares
Carrer Montcada
Mercat del Born
C. Mosques
LA RIBERA
Església Sta. Maria del Mar
Llotja
Av. Marqués de l'Argentera
Pg. Isabel II
Carrer Nou
de la Rambla
Avinguda del Paral·lel
Avda. de les Drassanes
Dels
C. Escudellers
La Pau
Teatre
Arc del
Cabanes St.
Funicular
Pg. de Montjuïc
Drassanes
C. Ample
C. Mercè
La Mercè
J. A. Clave
Passeig de Colom
MONTJUIC
Cable Car
Monument a Colom
Moll de la Fusta
TO CASTEL MONTJUIC
Jose Carner
Passeig
Cable Car
N
0
300 yards
0
300 meters
Harbor
Maremagnum
Cine IMAX
Multicines
Aquarium
Marina-Port Vell

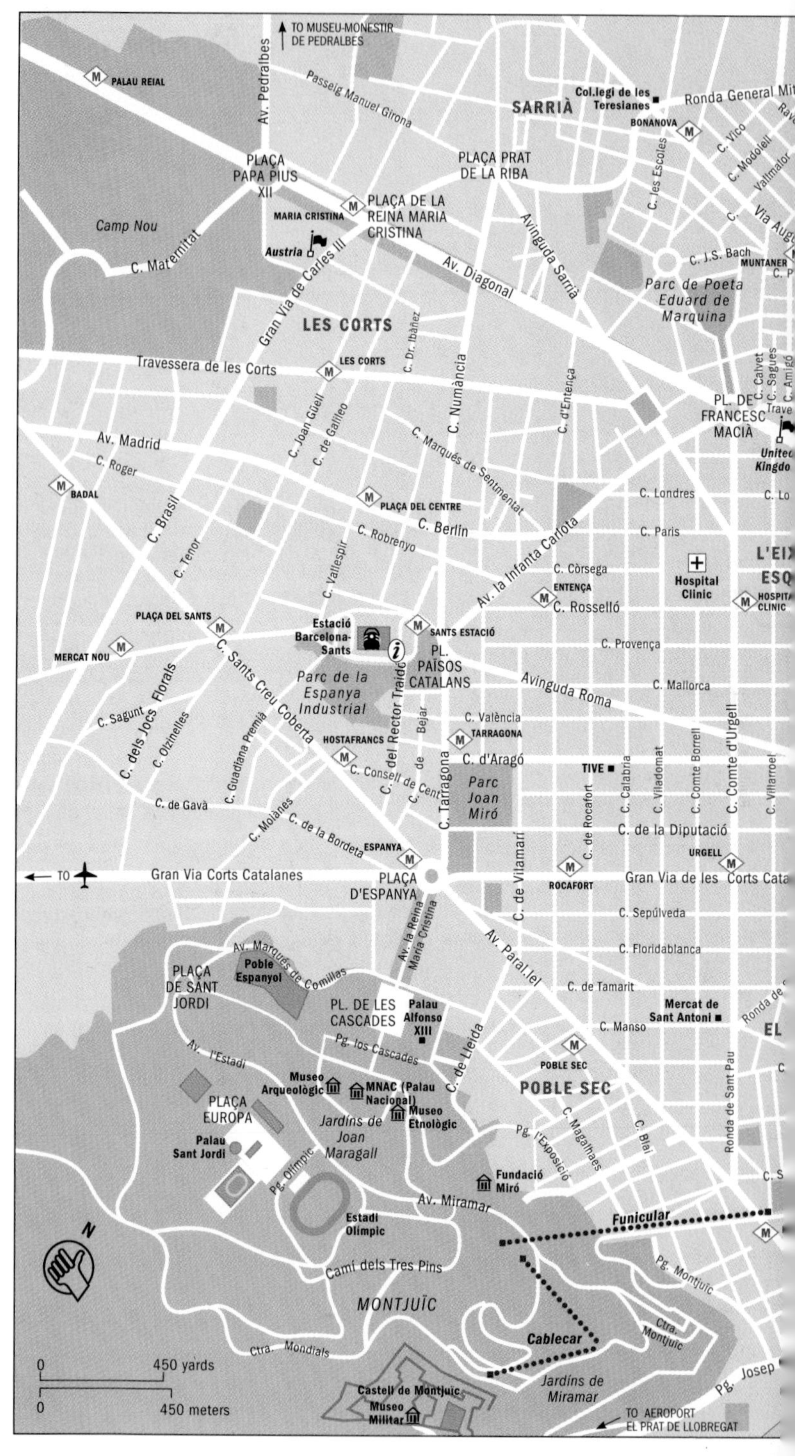
TO MUSEU-MONESTIR DE PEDRALBES
PALAU REIAL
Av. Pedralbes
Passeig Manuel Girona
SARRIÀ
Col.legi de les Teresianes
Ronda General Mit
BONANOVA
PLAÇA PAPA PIUS XII
PLAÇA PRAT DE LA RIBA
PLAÇA DE LA REINA MARIA CRISTINA
MARIA CRISTINA
Camp Nou
Austria
C. Maternitat
Gran Via de Carles III
Av. Diagonal
Avinguda Sarrià
C. J.S. Bach
MUNTANER
Parc de Poeta Eduard de Marquina
LES CORTS
Travessera de les Corts
LES CORTS
C. Dr. Ibañez
C. Numància
C. d'Entença
PL. DE FRANCESC MACIÀ
United Kingdom
Av. Madrid
C. Roger
BADAL
C. Joan Güell
C. de Galileo
C. Marqués de Sentmenat
PLAÇA DEL CENTRE
C. Londres
C. Berlin
C. Robrenyo
C. Paris
C. Brasil
C. Tenor
C. Vallespir
Av. la Infanta Carlota
C. Còrsega
Hospital Clinic
ENTENÇA
C. Rosselló
HOSPITAL CLINIC
PLAÇA DEL SANTS
Estació Barcelona-Sants
SANTS ESTACIÓ
MERCAT NOU
C. Sants Creu Coberta
PL. PAÏSOS CATALANS
C. Provença
Parc de la Espanya Industrial
C. del Rector Triadó
Avinguda Roma
C. Mallorca
C. dels Jocs Florals
C. Sagunt
C. Olzinelles
C. Guadiana Premià
C. València
HOSTAFRANCS
TARRAGONA
C. Bejar
C. d'Aragó
C. Consell de Cent
TIVE
C. Tarragona
Parc Joan Miró
C. de Rocafort
C. Calabria
C. Viladomat
C. Comte Borrell
C. Comte d'Urgell
C. Villarroel
C. de Gavà
C. Moianès
C. de la Bordeta
C. de la Diputació
ESPANYA
URGELL
TO
Gran Via Corts Catalanes
PLAÇA D'ESPANYA
ROCAFORT
Gran Via de les Corts Catalanes
C. de Vilamarí
C. Sepúlveda
Av. la Reina Maria Cristina
C. Floridablanca
Av. Paral.lel
Av. Marquès de Comillas
Poble Espanyol
PLAÇA DE SANT JORDI
C. de Tamarit
PL. DE LES CASCADES
Palau Alfonso XIII
Mercat de Sant Antoni
Ronda de
C. Manso
Pg. los Cascades
Av. l'Estadi
POBLE SEC
C. de Lleida
Museo Arqueològic
MNAC (Palau Nacional)
POBLE SEC
PLAÇA EUROPA
Museo Etnològic
Jardins de Joan Maragall
C. Magalhaes
C. Blai
Ronda de Sant Pau
Palau Sant Jordi
Pg. l'Exposició
Pg. Olímpic
Fundació Miró
Av. Miramar
Funicular
Estadi Olímpic
Camí dels Tres Pins
Pg. Montjuïc
MONTJUÏC
Cablecar
Ctra. Montjuïc
Ctra. Mondials
0 450 yards
0 450 meters
Castell de Montjuïc
Museo Militar
Jardins de Miramar
Pg. Josep
TO AEROPORT EL PRAT DE LLOBREGAT

Barcelona
PARK GÜELL
Parc Carmel
Parc de les Aigües
PLAÇA DE LESSEPS
LESSEPS
Travessera de Dalt
Av. la República Argentina
C. Verdi
C. Pàdua
C. Zaragoza
C. Vallirana
C. Sanjoanistes
C. Guillem Tell
PL. MOLINA
C. Lincoln
Casa Vicens
FONTANA
C. Gran de Gràcia
Sant Marc
GRÀCIA
GRÀCIA
C. Sant Salvador
C. de Martí
Providència
C. Robí
d'Astúries
C. de l'Or
C. Sant Lluís
C. Terol Bruniguer
C. Ramón y Cajal
Travessera de Gràcia
C. Siracusa
C. Torrent de l'Olla
Montseny
Ros de Olano
C. Torrent de les Flors
C. Sors
C. l'Escorial
C. Alegre de Dalt
C. Coloma
C. Camèlies
PLAÇA ALFONS EL SAVI
ALFONS X
Ronda Guinardó
C. Pi. i Margall
JOANIC
Via Augusta
C. Martínez
C. Sant Antoni Maria Claret
C. Indústria
L'EIXAMPLE DRETA
HOSPITAL DE SANT PAU
Diagonal
PLAÇA JOAN CARLES I
C. Bonavista
C. Còrsega
American Express
DIAGONAL
C. de Bailen
Pg. de Sant Joan
C. Roger de Flor
C. Nàpols
C. Sicília
C. Sardenya
C. Marina
Av. de Gaudí
C. Còrsega
C. Rosselló
LA SAGRADA FAMILIA
CARTAGENA
C. Provença
OVENÇA
La Pedrera
VERDAGUER
La Sagrada Familia
Rambla de Catalunya
Passeig de Gràcia
C. Pau Claris
C. Roger Llúria
C. València
PLAÇA JACINT VERDAGUER
Av. Diagonal
Fundació Tàpies
PG. DE GRÀCIA
C. d'Aragó
PLAÇA PABLO NERUDA
C. Cartagena
Manzana de la Discòrdia
C. Consell de Cent
GIRONA
C. de la Diputació
C. Bruc
TETUÁN
PLAÇA TETUAN
Gran Via de les Corts Catalanes
(Pg. Carles I)
Plaza de Toros Monumentales
MONUMENTAL
PL. DE LES GLÒRIES CATALANES
Teatre Nacional de Catalunya
GLÒRIES
Auditori Municipal
PG. DE GRÀCIA
Ronda Universitat
C. Casp
C. Girona
C. Bailen
C. d'Ausiàs Marc
CATALUNYA
PLAÇA DE CATALUNYA
Aerobus
URQUINAONA
Ronda de Sant Pere
Fontanella
C. Tànger
UTAT VELLA
Portal de l'Àngel
ARC DE TRIOMF
Estació Nord
C. de Marina
Palau de la Música Catalana
S. Pere Més Alt
MARINA
Av. Meridiana
Las Ramblas
S. Pere Més Baix
C. dels Almogàvers
PLAÇA DE PI
Palau de la Generalitat
LA RIBERA
Sta. Maria del Pi
United States
C. Comerç
C. Pamplona
C. d'Alaba
C. d'Àvila
CEU
PL. DE ST. JAUME
Pg. Pujades
BOGATELL
Ajuntament
C. Princesa
Museu Picasso
C. Llull
JAUME I
Pg. Picasso
Museu d'Art Modern
POBLE NOU
C. Ramón Turró
C. Ciutat
Via Laietana
Passeig Born
Santa Maria del Mar
GÒTIC
PARC DE LA CIUTADELLA
Carrer Wellington
Av. Marquès de l'Argentera
Av. Bogatell
Estació França
Parc Zoologic
ASSANES
Pg. Colom
Av. d'Icària
Pg. Circumval.lació
Avinguda d'Icària
Vila Olímpica
Moll de la Fusta
CIUTADELLA-VILA OLÍMPICA
Moll d'Espanya
The Towers
PORT OLÍMPIC
BARCELONETA

Barcelona Metro

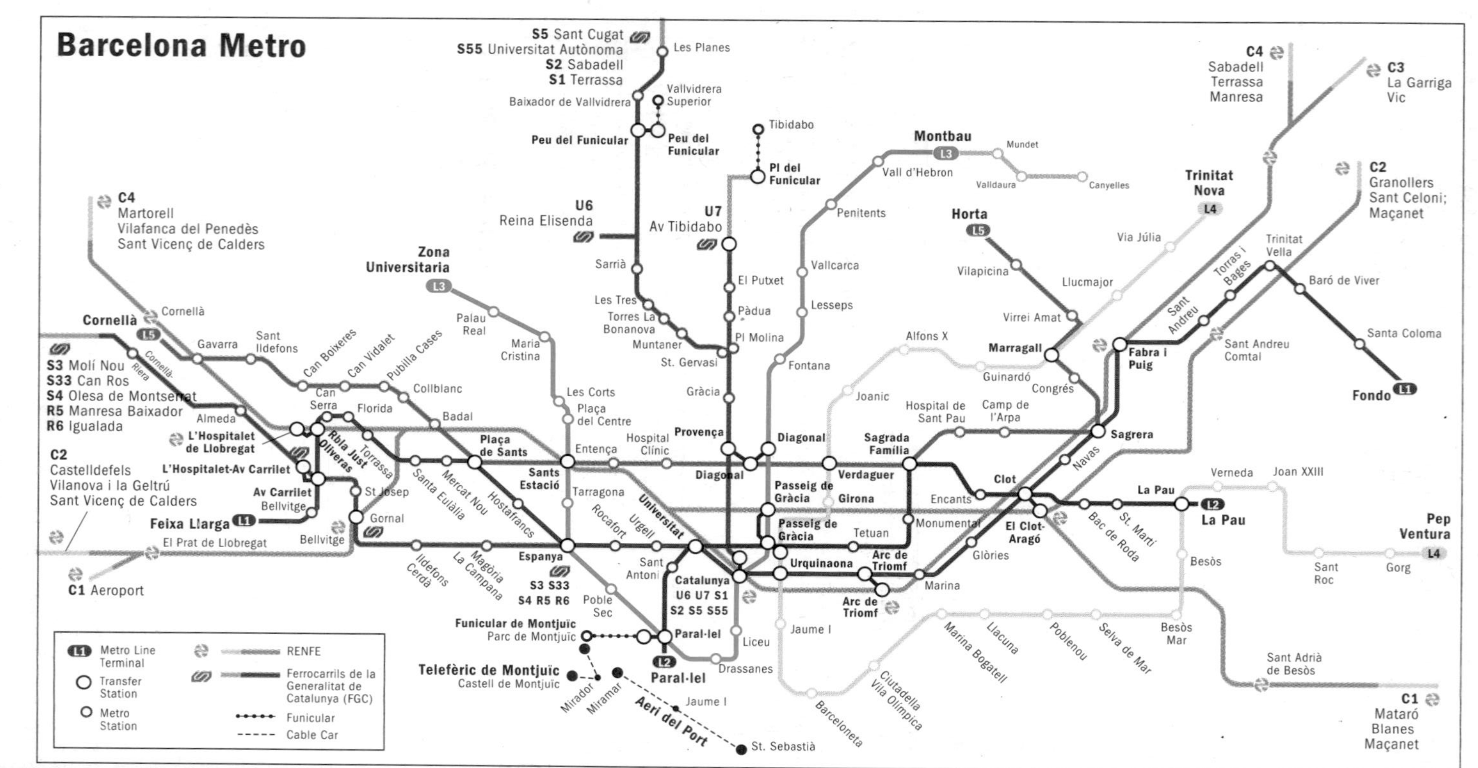